INTERNATIONAL LAW

INTERNATIONAL LAW

Fourth Edition

EDITED BY

MALCOLM D EVANS

Professor of Public International Law, University of Bristol

OXFORD

UNIVERSITY PRESS

OXFORD
UNIVERSITY PRESS

Great Clarendon Street, Oxford, OX2 6DP,
United Kingdom

Oxford University Press is a department of the University of Oxford.
It furthers the University's objective of excellence in research, scholarship,
and education by publishing worldwide. Oxford is a registered trade mark of
Oxford University Press in the UK and in certain other countries

First edition 2003
Second edition 2006
Third edition 2010

Impression: 2

Published in the United States of America by Oxford University Press
198 Madison Avenue, New York, NY 10016, United States of America

British Library Cataloguing in Publication Data
Data available

Library of Congress Control Number: 2013952621
ISBN 978-0-19-965467-3
Printed in Great Britain by
Ashford Colour Press Ltd

OUTLINE CONTENTS

PART VII THE APPLICATION OF INTERNATIONAL LAW

CONTENTS

PART I THE HISTORY AND THEORY OF INTERNATIONAL LAW

PART II THE STRUCTURE OF INTERNATIONAL
LEGAL OBLIGATION

PART III THE SUBJECTS OF THE INTERNATIONAL LEGAL ORDER

PART IV THE SCOPE OF SOVEREIGNTY

PART V RESPONSIBILITY

PART VI RESPONDING TO BREACHES OF INTERNATIONAL OBLIGATIONS

21 THE USE OF FORCE AND THE INTERNATIONAL
LEGAL ORDER   618
Christine Gray

PART VII THE APPLICATION OF INTERNATIONAL LAW

22 THE LAW OF THE SEA   651
Malcolm D Evans

PREFACE TO THE FOURTH EDITION

It hardly seems possible that four years should have already passed since the third edition of *International Law* was published, but the pace of development in many areas of international law has been such as to make that time rush by and it is now appropriate that a new edition should appear. The format, and aims, of the book remain largely as they were. The more obvious changes are new chapters by Surya Subedi on international investment law (which replaces the more general chapter on international economic law found in the previous editions) and by Sir Nigel Rodley on international human rights law. Other chapters have been significantly remodelled and updated, reflecting the changing focuses of the various subject areas and the interconnections between them as well as more detailed developments in law and practice.

With so much to choose from, it would be invidious to highlight particular changes—but it is worth mentioning the significance of developments relating to both State and personal immunities in a spate of highly significant domestic and international judicial decisions as well as the conclusion of the Articles on the Responsibility of International Organisations. These developments have had a major impact on many of the areas explored in this volume.

What seems to be the ever-increasing pace of change possibly reflects the heightened awareness of the importance of international law and the role it plays in the ordering of international affairs. It is certainly becoming increasingly visible (and audible) in domestic legal and political debate and this suggests that such pace of change is not likely to be reduced in the coming years. This also finds reflection in the ever-expanding body of international legal scholarship. The editor cannot be the only one who feels daunted—if not overwhelmed—by the ever-increasing volume, depth, and richness of the reflections and analyses which are now appearing. I am, then, so very grateful to each and every contributor to this volume, who have wrestled with all these developments and synthesized them into (relatively) short and (certainly) readable and accessible essays which provide authoritative guides to, and analyses of, the subjects which they address. I am also so very grateful to the staff at the Oxford University Press, and in particular to Carol Barber and Hannah Marsden, without whom this project would have long since sunk in the seas of my disorder. Of course, I remain immensely grateful also to all those who read and use this book, and I continue to hope that it finds favour as a means of furthering the education and understanding of students, scholars, and practitioners of international law.

Malcolm D Evans
January 2014

FROM THE EDITOR'S INTRODUCTION
TO THE FIRST EDITION

International law is a rich and varied subject, bearing upon most of the great issues facing individuals and communities. This work aims to capture something of that breadth and diversity by drawing on the knowledge and experience of a broad range of contributors who are intimately engaged in its teaching and practice. It is designed to present the essential elements of the international legal system in a clear and accessible fashion, but seeks to go further, addressing a number of key questions which challenge many of the assumptions upon which the international legal system is founded. It also seeks to provide a succinct introduction to a range of topics that are subject to increasingly detailed international regulation.

Parts I–VI consider the key building blocks of the subject whilst Part VII provides a series of introductory overviews of particular areas of contemporary interest. The structure, coverage, and level of the book are intended to reflect the requirements of undergraduate courses in public international law, although it will also be of use on general courses at the masters' levels as well as being of interest to academics and practitioners.

Although structured to form a coherent presentation of international law, each chapter can be read as a self-contained unit, balancing exposition with argument and reflecting the distinct perspective of its author(s). No attempt has been made to harmonize the views expressed or to produce a single 'voice'. Even if this had been possible, it would have been undesirable. As any teacher—as any lawyer—knows, opinions are best formed through exposure to competing argument. The chapters in this volume combine to address international law from a variety of perspectives: rather than one voice there is a range of voices and a range of opinions. It is to be hoped that this will be a source of stimulation, since the work as a whole aims to be more than just a compendium of knowledge. It aims to be a resource of value to all those interested in probing and testing the international legal enterprise.

NEW TO THIS EDITION

- New chapter on International Human Rights Law by Sir Nigel Rodley
- New chapter on International Investment Law by Surya Subedi
- Key new materials and cases covered in this fourth edition include:
  - ILC Articles on the Responsibility of International Organisations
  - ICJ decisions in *Jurisdictional Immunities of the State (Germany* v *Italy), Questions relating to the Obligation to Prosecute or Extradite (Belgium* v *Senegal)* and *Territorial and Maritime Dispute (Nicaragua* v *Colombia)*
  - ICC judgments in *Prosecutor* v *Lubanga* and *Prosecutor* v *Ngudjolo Chui*
  - ECHR judgments in *Al-Skeini and Others* v *the United Kingdom*; *Al-Jedda* v *the United Kingdom*; *Hirsi Jamaa* v *Italy*; *Nada* v *Switzerland*
  - Domestic court judgments, including *Democratic Republic of Congo and others* v *FG Hemisphere Associates LLC* (China); *Netherlands* v *Nuhanović* (the Netherlands); *Koibel* v *Royal Dutch Petroleum Co* (USA); *Yousuf* v *Samantar* (US); *Khurts Bat* v *Investigating Judge of the Federal Court of Germany* (UK); *NML Capital Ltd* v *The Republic of Argentina* (UK)

NOTES ON CONTRIBUTORS

Ademola Abass LLM, PhD, is Head of the Peace and Security Program, the United Nations University, Belgium, and formerly Professor of International Law and International Organization at Brunel University, West London. He researches in Public International Law and Peace and Security, and is the author of *Complete International Law: Text, Cases and Materials*, (1st edn 2012) (Oxford: Oxford University Press) (2nd edn forthcoming, 2014) among others. He has consulted for several international organizations and States. He is a member of the Academic Council on the United Nations Systems and a Fellow of the Cambridge Commonwealth Society.

Dapo Akande is Associate Professor of Public International Law at the University of Oxford and Yamani Fellow at St Peter's College, Oxford. He is also Co-Director of the Oxford Institute for Ethics, Law and Armed Conflict and of the Oxford Martin Programme on Human Rights for Future Generations. He has held visiting professorships at Yale Law School (where he was also Robinna Foundation International Fellow) at the University of Miami Law School. He is a member of the Editorial Board of the *American Journal of International Law* and the Scientific Advisory Board of the *European Journal of International Law*; and the Editorial Board of the *African Journal of International and Comparative Law*. He has advised States, international organizations and non-governmental organizations on matters of international law.

Alan Boyle is Professor of Public International Law at the University of Edinburgh School of Law. His publications include *International Law and the Environment* (with PW Birnie and C Redgwell) (2009) (Oxford: Oxford University Press) and *The Making of International Law* (with C Chinkin) (2007) (Oxford: Oxford University Press). He is a barrister at Essex Court Chambers in London and appears before the ICJ, ITLOS, and PCA.

Matthew Craven is Professor of Public International Law at the School of Oriental and African Studies, University of London. His publications include *The Decolonization of International Law: State Succession and the Law of Treaties* (2007) (Oxford: Oxford University Press) and *The International Covenant on Economic, Social and Cultural Rights: A Perspective on its Development* (1997) (Oxford: Oxford University Press).

James Crawford, AC, SC, FBA is Whewell Professor of International Law, University of Cambridge. He was a member of the International Law Commission from 1992–2001 and was its Special Rapporteur on State Responsibility (1997–2001). He is a member of Matrix Chambers and has an extensive practice before international courts and tribunals. His recent work includes *Brownlie's Principles of Public International Law* (8th edn 2012) (Oxford: Oxford University Press) and *State Responsibility: The General Part* (2013) (Cambridge: Cambridge University Press).

Robert Cryer is Professor of International and Criminal Law at the University of Birmingham. His teaching and research interests are in international law, criminal law, humanitarian law, and legal theory. He is the author of, *inter alia, Prosecuting International Crimes: Selectivity and the International Criminal Law Regime* (with Neil Boister) (2005) (Cambridge: Cambridge University Press), *The Tokyo International Military Tribunal: A Reappraisal* (2008) (Oxford: Oxford University Press), and *An Introduction to International Criminal Law and Procedure* (with Håkan Friman, Darryl Robinson, and Elizabeth Wilmshurst) (3rd edn 2014) (Cambridge: Cambridge University Press).

Eileen Denza was formerly Assistant Lecturer in Law, Bristol University, a Legal Counsellor to the Foreign and Commonwealth Office, Counsel to the EC Committee of the House of Lords and Visiting Professor of Law at University College London. Her publications include *Diplomatic Law* (3rd edn 2008) (Oxford: Oxford University Press) and *The Intergovernmental Pillars of the European Union* (2002) (Oxford: Oxford University Press).

Malcolm D Evans, OBE, is Professor of Public International Law at the University of Bristol and a former Dean of its Faculty of Social Sciences and Law. His areas of special interest are the law of the sea and the international protection of human rights, and in particular the freedom of religion and the prevention of torture. His principal publications include *Religion and International Law in Europe* (1997) (Cambridge: Cambridge University Press); *Preventing Torture* (1998) (Oxford: Oxford University Press); *Combating Torture in Europe* (2001) (Strasbourg: Council of Europe Press); *Manual on the Wearing of Religious Symbols* (2009); *The Optional Protocol to the UN Convention against Torture* (with Professor R Murray, *et al*) (2011) (Oxford: Oxford University Press) and numerous edited collections. He is co-General Editor of the *International and Comparative Law Quarterly*, and is currently Chair of the United Nations Subcommittee for Prevention of Torture.

Malgosia Fitzmaurice holds a chair of public international law at the Department of Law, Queen Mary, University of London. She also teaches general international law and the law on the protection of the marine environment at the IMO International Maritime Law Institute at Malta. Her main research interests include international environmental law, the law of treaties, the international water law and indigenous peoples. She has published widely on these subjects. She has participated in many international conferences and has taught in many law schools abroad, including recently at Berkeley University School of Law and the Sorbonne-Pantheon.

Hazel Fox CMG QC (Lady), Member of the Institut de Droit International, Bencher of Lincoln's Inn and Hon Fellow of Somerville College, University of Oxford; formerly Director of the British Institute of International and Comparative Law and General Editor of the *International and Comparative Quarterly*, author of the *Law of State Immunity* (3rd edn 2013 with Philippa Webb) (Oxford: Oxford University Press).

Christine Gray, MA, PhD, is Professor in International Law at the University of Cambridge. She is author of *International Law and the Use of Force* (3rd edn, 2008) (Oxford: Oxford University Press) and of *Judicial Remedies in International Law* (1990) (Oxford: Oxford University Press) as well as of many articles on the use of force.

Martti Koskenniemi, Professor of International Law, University of Helsinki, Hauser Global Visiting Professor of Law, New York University School of Law and a former member of the International Law Commission. His principal publications include *The Gentle Civilizer of Nations: The Rise and Fall of International Law 1870–1960* (2001) (Cambridge: Cambridge University Press) and *From Apology to Utopia: The Structure of International Legal Argument* (2005) (Reissue with a New Epilogue) (Cambridge: Cambridge University Press).

Robert McCorquodale is the Director of the British Institute of International and Comparative Law, and Professor of International Law and Human Rights at the University of Nottingham. He is co-author of one of the leading texts in international law, *Cases and Materials on International Law* (5th edn 2010) (Oxford: Oxford University Press), and is on the editorial board of a number of respected academic journals. He has published widely about international law, especially on international human rights law and on the impact of non-State actors on international law, as well as giving advice and training on these issues around the world.

John Merrills BCL, MA, is Professor of International Law (Emeritus) at the University of Sheffield, a former Dean of the Faculty of Law, and an Associate Member of the

Institut de Droit International. He is the author of *International Dispute Settlement* (5th edn, 2011) (Cambridge: Cambridge University Press), *Human Rights in Europe* (2001) (Manchester: Manchester University Press), *Judge Sir Gerald Fitzmaurice and the Discipline of International Law* (1998) (the Hague: Kluwer Law International) and several other books, as well as numerous articles in law reviews.

Stephen C Neff is a Reader in International Law at the University of Edinburgh, specializing in the history of international law. His publications include *Friends But No Allies: Economic Liberalism and the Law of Nations* (1990) (New York: Columbia University Press); *The Rights and Duties of Neutrals: A General History* (2000) (Manchester: Manchester University Press); and *War and the Law of Nations: A General History* (2005) (Cambridge: Cambridge University Press). He writes a regular column, 'Historic Moments', for the *International Judicial Monitor*. He is also the author of a forthcoming book on the general history of international law.

Phoebe Okowa is Reader in Public International Law at Queen Mary, University of London. She has written extensively in many areas of Public International Law. Her most recent publication is *Environmental Law and Justice in Context* (with Jonas Ebbesson) (2009) (Cambridge: Cambridge University Press). She is also the co-editor of Foundations of Public International Law (Oxford: Oxford University Press) and author of *State Responsibility for Transboundary Air Pollution in International Law* (2000) (Oxford: Oxford University Press).

Simon Olleson MA (Cantab), LLM (NYU), Dip Int Law (Cantab) is a barrister at 13 Old Square Chambers, Lincoln's Inn, London, specializing in public international law.

Catherine Redgwell, BA (Hons), LLB, MSc, is Chichele Professor of Public International Law and a Fellow of All Souls College, Oxford, and has published extensively in the international law field, particularly within the areas of environmental law, energy law, and treaty law. She is joint editor of the *British Year Book of International Law* and co-editor of the *Oxford Monographs in International Law* series.

Sir Nigel Rodley KBE is Professor of Law and Chair of the Human Rights Centre, University of Essex. A former UN Commission on Human Rights Special Rapporteur on the question of torture (1993-2001), he has been a member of the Human Rights Committee established under the International Covenant on Civil and Political Rights since 2001. He is currently serving as Chair of the Committee (2013-14). He is also President of the International Commission of Jurists. Honours include a knighthood 'for services to human rights and international law' in 1998 and the American Society of International Law 2005 Goler T Butcher Medal for his 'distinguished contribution to international human rights law'. His many scholarly publications include *The Treatment of Prisoners under International Law* (3rd edn with Matt Pollard, 2009) (Oxford: Oxford University Press).

Iain Scobbie LLB (Hons) (Edin), LLB (Cantab), GDIL (ANU), PhD (Cantab), is professor of public international law at the University of Manchester. He has written on diverse matters such as the jurisprudence and practice of the International Court, legal aspects of the Israel-Palestine question, and the law of armed conflict, as well as the theory of international law.

Dinah Shelton is the Mantt/Ahn Professor of Law (Emeritus) at The George Washington University Law School, USA. She is a member of the Board of Editors of the *American Journal of International Law* and a consultant to various international organizations. She has authored prize-winning books on international human rights law and published numerous articles in journals throughout the world. From 2010 to 2014 she served as a member of the Inter-American Commission on Human Rights and was its president in 2011. She received a doctorate honoris causa from the University of Stockholm, Sweden, and is the recipient of both the Elisabeth Haub Prize and the Wolfgang Burhenne medal for international environmental law, the Stefan Riesenfield award in international law from the University of California, Berkeley School of Law, and the Goler Butcher medal from the American Society of International Law for her work in human rights.

Christopher Staker BA LLB (Hons) (Adelaide), DPhil (Oxford) is a barrister at Thirty Nine Essex Street Chambers in London. Positions that he has previously held include Deputy (Chief) Prosecutor of the Special Court for Sierra Leone (Freetown, Sierra Leone), Principal Legal Secretary at the International Court of Justice (The Hague, Netherlands), Senior Appeals Counsel at the International Criminal Tribunal for the Former Yugoslavia (The Hague), Counsel Assisting the Solicitor-General of Australia, and Counsel in the Office of International Law of the Australian Attorney-General's Department (Canberra, Australia). He has appeared as counsel before international and national courts, including the International Court of Justice, International Tribunal for the Law of the Sea, international criminal courts, and the High Court of Australia. He has authored various publications on international law and related areas.

Surya P Subedi OBE is Professor of International Law at the University of Leeds and a practising Barrister of the Middle Temple. He also is the UN Special Rapporteur for Human Rights in Cambodia and a member of an Advisory Group on Human Rights to the British Foreign Secretary. He has published a number of books, including *International Investment Law: Reconciling Policy and Principle* (2nd edn 2012) (Oxford: Hart Publishing). His name has been designated to serve on the Panels of Arbitrators and of Conciliators of the International Centre for Settlement of Investment Disputes. He was elected to the *Institut de Droit International* in 2011. He is the founder Editor of the *Asian Journal of International Law* (published by Cambridge University Press) and a founder and Vice-President of the Asian Society of International Law. He holds a DPhil in law from the University of Oxford, an LLM with Distinction from the University of Hull and an LLB from Tribhuvan University, Nepal.

Hugh Thirlway MA, LLB, Dr. en droit, spent most of his career in the legal department of the Registry of the International Court of Justice, including many years as Principal Legal Secretary and Head of Department, but he served also as Professor of International Law at the Graduate Institute of International Studies in Geneva; having now retired from the service of the ICJ he remains Visiting Professor at a number of European universities. His long series of detailed and authoritative studies of the Court's case law in the *British Yearbook of International Law* have recently been assembled and issued in a single publication by Oxford University Press, who are also about to publish his full-length study of the sources of international law.

David Turns is Senior Lecturer in International Laws of Armed Conflict at the Defence Academy of the United Kingdom (Cranfield University). From 1994 to 2007 he was Lecturer in Law at the University of Liverpool, and he taught previously at the London School of Economics. In 2002 he was a Visiting Professor at the Institute for International Law and International Relations, University of Vienna. Since 2008 he has been the Chairman of the UK National Group of the International Society for Military Law and the Law of War, and a Member of the Society's Board of Directors. He is on the Visiting Faculty of the International Institute of Humanitarian Law (San Remo) and the NATO School (Oberammergau), has taught on military staff and legal advisers' courses in several countries and has published widely in the field of international law.

Nigel D White is Professor of Public International Law at the University of Nottingham, formerly Professor of International Law at the University of Sheffield. In addition to publishing over 60 substantial articles and essays, he is author of several books including *Keeping the Peace: The United Nations and the Maintenance of International Peace and Security* (2nd edn 1997) (Manchester: Manchester University Press), *The Law of International Organisations*

(2nd edn 2005) (Manchester: Manchester University Press), *The UN System: Toward International Justice* (2002) (Boulder, Co: Lynne Rienner), and *Democracy Goes to War: British Military Deployments under International Law* (2009) (Oxford: Oxford University Press). He has co-authored a number of books including, most recently, *Collective Security: Theory, Law and Practice* (with Nicholas Tsagourias) (2013) (Cambridge: Cambridge University Press). He is also co-editor of a number of leading collections, including *The UN, Human Rights and Post Conflict Situations* (2005) (Manchester: Manchester University Press), *International Conflict and Security Law* (2005) (Cambridge: Cambridge University Press), *European Security Law* (2007) (Oxford: Oxford University Press), *International Law and Dispute Settlement* (2010) (Oxford: Hart Publishing), *International Organizations and the Idea of Autonomy* (2011) (Abingdon: Routledge), and *Counter-Terrorism: International Law and Practice* (2013) (Oxford: Oxford University Press). He is co-editor of the *Journal of Conflict and Security Law* published by Oxford University Press.

Chanaka Wickremasinghe is a Legal Counsellor in the Foreign and Commonwealth Office. He was formerly a lecturer in law at Bristol University and a research officer at the British Institute of International and Comparative Law.

Spencer Zifcak is Allan Myers Professor of Law and Associate Dean (Research) in the Faculty of Law at the Australian Catholic University. He has been a Visiting Fellow at Wolfson College Oxford, Trinity College Dublin and in 2010 was Benjamin Meaker Visiting Professor at the Institute of Advanced Studies at the University of Bristol. His two most recent books are *Globalization and the Rule of Law* (2005) (Abingdon: Routledge) and *United Nations Reform: Heading North or South* (2009) (Abingdon: Routledge).

ABBREVIATIONS

AALCC	African Asian Legal Consultative Committee
ACHR	American Convention on Human Rights
AFP	Australian Federal Police
AIA	Advanced Informed Agreement
AJIL	*American Journal of International Law*
API	Application Program Interface
ARIO	Articles on the Responsibility of International Organizations
ARSIWA	Articles on the Responsibility of States for Internationally Wrongful Acts
ASCOBANS	Agreement on the Conservation of Small Cetaceans of the Baltic and North Seas
ASEAN	Association of Southeast Asian Nations
ATCA	Alien Tort Claims Act (US)
AU	African Union
BCN	biological, chemical, nuclear (weapon)
BITs	Bilateral Investment Treaties
BverfGE	*Die Entscheidungen des Bundesverfassungsgerichts*
BYIL	*British Yearbook of International Law*
CAFTA	Central American Free Trade Agreement
CBD	Convention on Conservation of Biological Diversity
CCAMLR	Convention on the Conservation of Antarctic Marine Living Resources
CCSBT	Commission for the Conservation of Southern Bluefin Tuna
CEDAW	Convention on the Elimination of All Forms of Discrimination Against Women
CERD	International Convention on the Elimination of All Forms of Racial Discrimination
CESCR	Committee on Economic, Social and Cultural Rights
CFC	Convention on Fisheries and Conservation of the Living Resources of the High Seas
CFCs	chlorofluorocarbons
CFI	Court of First Instance
CIS	Commonwealth of Independent States
CITES	Convention on International Trade in Endangered Species
CLC	Convention on Civil Liability for Oil Pollution Damage
CMLR	*Common Market Law Review*
COP	Conference of the Parties
CPT	Committee for the Prevention of Torture and Inhuman or Degrading Treatment or Punishment

CSC	Continental Shelf Convention
CSCE	Conference on Security and Cooperation in Europe
DEA	Drug Enforcement Administration
DRC	Democratic Republic of the Congo
DSB	Dispute Settlement Body
DSU	Dispute Settlement Understanding
EAC	East African Community
EBRD	European Bank for Reconstruction and Development
EC	European Community
ECE	(United Nations) Economic Commission for Europe
ECJ	European Court of Justice
ECOMOG	Economic Community of West African States Monitoring Group
ECOSOC	Economic and Social Council
ECOWAS	Economic Community of West African States
ECSI	European Convention on State Immunity
ECtHR	European Court of Human Rights
EEC	European Economic Community
EEZ	Exclusive Economic Zone
EFZ	Exclusive Fishing Zone
EHRR	*European Human Rights Review*
EIA	Environmental Impact Assessment
EJIL	*European Journal of International Law*
EU	European Union
EUROFIMA	European Company for the Financing of Railroad Rolling Stock
FAO	Food and Agriculture Organization
FATF	Financial Action Task Force
FCCC	Framework Convention on Climate Change
FCN	Friendship, Commerce and Navigation (Treaties)
FCO	Foreign and Commonwealth Office
FGM	Female Genital Mutilation
FRY	Federal Republic of Yugoslavia
FSIA	Foreign Sovereign Immunities Act (US)
GA	General Assembly
GAB	General Agreements to Borrow
GATS	General Agreement on Trade in Services
GATT	General Agreement on Tariffs and Trade
GEF	Global Environmental Facility
HCHR	High Commissioner for Human Rights
HIPC	Heavily Indebted Poor Countries

HLPF	High-Level Political Forum
HRC	Human Rights Committee
HRLJ	*Human Rights Law Journal*
HSC	High Seas Convention
IAC	Iraqi Airways Company
IACHR	Inter-American Commission on Human Rights
IAEA	International Atomic Energy Authority
IBRD	International Bank for Reconstruction and Development (World Bank)
ICAO	International Civil Aviation Organization
ICBP	International Council for Bird Preservation
ICC	International Criminal Court
ICCPR	International Covenant on Civil and Political Rights
ICESCR	International Covenant on Economic, Social and Cultural Rights
ICISS	International Commission on Intervention and State Sovereignty
ICJ	International Court of Justice
ICLQ	*International and Comparative Law Quarterly*
ICOMOS	International Council on Monuments and Sites
ICRC	International Committee of the Red Cross
ICSID	International Centre for the Settlement of Investment Disputes
ICTR	International Criminal Tribunal for Rwanda
IDA	International Development Agency
IFAD	International Fund for Agricultural Development
IFC	International Finance Corporation
IGAD	Intergovernmental Authority on Development
IGO	Inter-Governmental Organization
IHL	International Humanitarian Law
IHRL	International Human Rights Law
IHRR	*International Human Rights Reports*
ILA	International Law Association
ILC	International Law Commission
ILM	International Legal Materials
ILO	International Labour Organization
ILR	International Law Reports
IMF	International Monetary Fund
IMO	International Maritime Organization
IMT	International Military Tribunal
IPCC	Intergovernmental Panel on Climate Change
Iran-USCTR	Iran-US Claims Tribunal Reports
ISA	International Seabed Authority
ITC	International Tin Council

ITLOS	International Tribunal for the Law of the Sea
ITO	International Trade Organization
ITTA	International Tropical Timber Agreement
ITU	International Telecommunications Union
ITC	International Tin Council
IUCN	International Union for the Conservation of Nature
IWRB	International Waterfowl and Wetlands Research Bureau
KAC	Kuwait Airways Corporation
LMO	Living Modified Organism
LNTS	League of Nations Treaty Series
LOAC	Law of Armed Conflict
LOSC	Law of the Sea Convention
LRTAP	Long-Range Transboundary Air Pollution
MAI	Multilateral Agreement on Investment
MARPOL	International Convention for the Prevention of Pollution from Ships
MERCOSUR	Mercado Común del Sur or Mercado Común del Cono Sur
MIGA	Multilateral Investment Guarantee Agency
NAB	New Arrangements to Borrow
NAFO	North Atlantic Fisheries Organization
NAFTA	North American Free Trade Agreement
NAM	Non-Aligned Movement
NATO	North Atlantic Treaty Organization
NGOs	Non-Governmental Organizations
NLM	National Liberation Movement
NYBIL	*Netherlands Yearbook of International Law*
nyr	not yet reported
OAPEC	Organization of Arab Petroleum Exporting Countries
OAS	Organization of American States
OASTS	Organization of American States Treaty Series
OAU	Organization of African Unity
ODIL	*Ocean Development and International Law*
OECD	Organization for Economic Cooperation and Development
OECS	Organization of East Caribbean States
OEEC	Organization for European Economic Cooperation
ONUC	United Nations Operation in the Congo (Organisation des Nations Unies au Congo)
ONUCA	United Nations Observer Group in Central America
OPEC	Organization of Petroleum Exporting Countries
OPRC	Oil Pollution Preparedness and Response Convention
OSCE	Organization for Security and Cooperation in Europe

OSPAR	Convention for the Protection of the Marine Environment of the North-East Atlantic
PCIJ	Permanent Court of International Justice
PIC	Rotterdam Convention on Prior Informed Consent
PLO	Palestine Liberation Organization
PMSC	Private Military Security Company
POPs	Persistent Organic Pollutants
POW	Prisoner of War
PSI	Proliferation Security Initiative
R2P	Responsibility to Protect
Recueil des Cours	*Recueil des cours de l'Académie de droit international*
RFB	Regional Fisheries Body
RFMO	Regional Fisheries Management Organisation
RGDIP	*Revue General de Droit International Public*
RIAA	*Reports of International Arbitral Awards*
RSC	Rules of the Supreme Court (UK)
SADC	South African Development Community
SBDC	Sea-Bed Disputes Chamber
SC	Security Council
SCSL	Special Court for Sierra Leone
SDR	Special Drawing Rights
SFRY	Socialist Federal Republic of Yugoslavia
SIA	State Immunity Act 1978 (UK)
SPS	Sanitary and Phytosanitary Measures
SSA	Straddling Stocks Agreement
SSC	UN Agreement on Straddling Stocks and Highly Migratory Species
STL	Special Tribunal for Lebanon
SUA	Convention Rome Convention on the Suppression of Unlawful Acts Against the Safety of Maritime Navigation
TAC	Total Allowable Catch
TNCs	Transnational Corporations
TPRM	Trade Policy Review Mechanism
TRAFFIC	Trade Records Analysis of Flora and Fauna in Commerce
TRIMs	Trade-Related Investment Measures
TRIPS	Agreement on Trade-Related Aspects of Intellectual Property Rights
TSC	Territorial Sea and Contiguous Zone Convention
TWAIL	Third World Approaches to International Law
UAE	United Arab Emirates
UEMO	Union Economique de Monétaire Ouest-Africaine
UN	United Nations

UNAMIR	United Nations Assistance Mission for Rwanda
UNCAT	Convention against Torture and Other Cruel, Inhuman or Degrading Treatment or Punishment
UNCC	United Nations Compensation Commission
UNCITRAL	United Nations Commission on International Trade Law
UNCLOS	United Nations Conference on the Law of the Sea
UNCTAD	United Nations Conference on Trade and Development
UNDP	United Nations Development Programme
UNEF	United Nations Emergency Force
UNEP	United Nations Environment Programme
UNESCO	United Nations Educational, Scientific and Cultural Organization
UNGA	United Nations General Assembly
UNHCR	United Nations High Commissioner for Refugees
UNICEF	United Nations International Children's Economic Foundation
UNIDO	United Nations Industrial Development Organization
UNITA	União Nacional para a Independência Total de Angola
UNMIK	United Nations Mission in Kosovo
UNOSOM	United Nations Operation in Somalia
UNPROFOR	United Nations Protection Force
UNTAET	United Nations Transitional Administration in East Timor
UNTS	United Nations Treaty Series
UNYB	*United Nations Yearbook*
UPU	Universal Postal Union
VCCR	Vienna Convention on Consular Relations
VCDR	Vienna Convention on Diplomatic Relations
VCLT	Vienna Convention on the Law of Treaties
WEOG	Western Europe and Others Group (Nations)
WHC	World Heritage Convention
WHO	World Health Organization
WIPO	World Intellectual Property Organization
WMD	Weapons of mass destruction
WMO	World Meteorological Organization
WTO	World Trade Organization
WWF	World Wildlife Fund
YBIEL	*Yearbook of International Environmental Law*
YBILC	*Yearbook of the International Law Commission*
YIHL	*Yearbook of International Humanitarian Law*

TABLE OF INTERNATIONAL INSTRUMENTS AND OTHER DOCUMENTS

TABLE OF DOMESTIC
INSTRUMENTS BY COUNTRY

TABLES OF INTERNATIONAL CASES

INTERNATIONAL CRIMINAL COURT

INTERNATIONAL CRIMINAL TRIBUNAL FOR THE FORMER YUGOSLAVIA

AFRICAN COMMISSION ON HUMAN AND PEOPLES' RIGHTS

EUROPEAN COURT OF HUMAN RIGHTS

INTER-AMERICAN COURT OF HUMAN RIGHTS

UN HUMAN RIGHTS COMMITTEE

UN COMMITTEE AGAINST TORTURE

EUROPEAN COURT OF JUSTICE

TABLE OF DOMESTIC
CASES BY COUNTRY

UNITED STATES OF AMERICA

PART I

THE HISTORY AND THEORY OF INTERNATIONAL LAW

1

A SHORT HISTORY OF INTERNATIONAL LAW

Stephen C Neff

SUMMARY

This history will emphasize broad trends in international law, in both the conceptual sphere and in State practice. The discussion will move chronologically, beginning with a cursory look at the ancient world, followed by a rather fuller discussion of the great era of natural law in the European Middle Ages. The classical period (1600–1815) witnessed the emergence of a dualistic view of international law, with the law of nature and the law of nations co-existing (more or less amicably). In the nineteenth century—the least known part of international law—doctrinaire positivism was the prevailing viewpoint, though not the exclusive one. Regarding the inter-war years, developments both inside and outside the League of Nations will be considered. Since the post-1945 period will occupy most of the remainder of this book, this discussion will confine itself to a few historically-oriented comments on some of its most general features.

I. INTRODUCTION

It is pleasing to note that the scandalous neglect of the history of international law, which prevailed for so long, has, at long last, begun to be redressed in a significant fashion. A significant step was the founding of a journal dedicated to the subject in 1999. In addition, a series of important monographs have been published in Germany, beginning in 2001. In the English-speaking world too, there has been a steady growth of attention to the subject. It may be too early to proclaim the onset of a Renaissance—or, more accurately, a 'naissance'—and there are many large areas yet to be thoroughly explored. But there is no doubt that optimism is in the air and that the future looks brighter than ever.

This short history—inevitably very short history—can give only the most general flavour of the major periods of development of international law. It will accordingly not be possible to give more than the most token attention to developments outside the Western mainstream. Both ideas and State practice will be covered. The ideas chiefly concern what international law was thought to consist of in past times. State practice is concerned with what States actually did. It was the two in combination—if not always in close harmony—that made international law what it became.

II. ANCIENT WORLDS

For a vivid indication of how persons from even the most diverse cultures can relate to one another in a peaceful, predictable, and mutually beneficial fashion, it is difficult to top Herodotus's description of 'silent trading' between the Carthaginians and an unnamed North African tribe in about the sixth century BC. When the Carthaginians arrived in the tribe's area by ship, they would unload a pile of goods from their vessels, leave them on the beach and then return to their boats and send a smoke signal. The natives would then come and inspect the goods on their own, leave a pile of gold, and retire. Then the Carthaginians would return; and, if satisfied that the gold represented a fair price, they would take it and depart. If not satisfied, they would again retire to their ships; and the natives would return to leave more gold. The process would continue until both sides were content, at which the point the Carthaginians would sail away with their gold, without a word exchanged between the two groups. 'There is perfect honesty on both sides', Herodotus assures us, with no problems of theft or conflict (Herodotus, Histories, p 336).

This silent-trading arrangement may have been successful in its way, but a process of interaction so inflexibly ritualistic and so narrow in subject matter could hardly suffice for political interactions between States, even in ancient times. Most people probably have the feeling that something rather more elaborate is required to merit the grand name of 'international law'. Indeed, the ambiguity of the term 'international law' leads to various different answers to the question of when international law 'began'. If by 'international law' is meant merely the ensemble of methods or devices which give an element of predictability to international relations (as in the silent-trading illustration), then the origin may be placed virtually as far back as recorded history itself. If by 'international law' is meant a more or less comprehensive substantive code of conduct applying to nations, then the late classical period and Middle Ages was the time of its birth. If 'international law' is taken to mean a set of substantive principles applying uniquely to States as such, then the seventeenth century would be the starting time. If 'international law' is defined as the integration of the world at large into something like a single community under a rule of law, then the nineteenth century would be the earliest date (perhaps a trifle optimistically). If, finally, 'international law' is understood to mean the enactments and judicial decisions of a world government, then its birth lies (if at all) somewhere in the future—and, in all likelihood, the distant future at that.

If we take the most restricted of these definitions, then we could expect to find the best evidence for a nascent international law in the three areas of ancient Eurasia that were characterized by dense networks of small, independent States sharing a more or less common religious and cultural value system: Mesopotamia (by, say, the fourth or third millennium BC), northern India (in the Vedic period after about 1600 BC), and classical Greece. Each of these three State systems was characterized by a combination of political fragmentation and cultural unity. This enabled a number of fairly standard practices to emerge, which helped to place inter-State relations on at least a somewhat stable and predictable footing. Three particular areas provide evidence of this development: diplomatic relations, treaty-making, and the conduct of war.[1] A major additional contribution of the Greek city-States was the practice of arbitration of disputes, of which there came to be a very impressive body of practice (see Ager, 1996).

---

[1] On the Middle Eastern and Greek practice, see generally Bederman, 2001. On ancient India, see Bhatia, 1977.

It was not inordinately difficult for some of these practices to extend across deeper cultural lines as well. The earliest surviving complete treaty text is between Egypt and the Hittite Empire, from the thirteenth century BC. The agreement concerned an imperial division of spheres of influence, but it also dealt with the extradition of fugitives. The problem of good faith and binding force was ensured by enlisting the gods of both nations (two thousand strong in all) to act as guardians (Bederman, 2001, pp 147–50).

With the advent of the great universal religions, far more broadly-based systems of world order became possible. One outstanding example was the Islamic empire of the seventh century AD and afterwards. Significantly, the body of law on relations between States within the Muslim world (the Dar al-Islam, or 'House of Islam') was much richer than that regarding relations with the outside world (the Dar al-Harb, or 'House of War'). But even with infidel States and nationals, a number of pragmatic devices evolved to permit relations to occur in predictable ways—such as 'temporary' truces (in lieu of treaties) or safe-conducts issued to individuals (sometimes on a very large scale).[2]

In Western history, the supreme exemplar of the multinational empire was Rome. But the Roman Empire was, in its formative period, a somewhat tentative and ramshackle affair, without an over-arching ethical or religious basis comparable to the Islamic religion in the later Arab empire. That began to change, however, when certain philosophical concepts were imported from Greece (from about the second century BC). The most important of these was the idea of a set of universal principles of justice: the belief that, amidst the welter of varying laws of different States, certain substantive rules of conduct were present in all human societies. This idea first surfaced in the writings of Aristotle (Rhetoric, p 1370). But it was taken much further by the philosophers of the Stoic school, who envisaged the entire world as a single 'world city-State' (or *kosmopolis*) governed by the law of nature. Cicero, writing under Stoic influence, characterized this law of nature as being 'spread through the whole human community, unchanging and eternal' (Cicero, Republic, pp 68–9).

This concept of a universal and eternal natural law was later adopted by two other groups, the Roman lawyers and the Christian Church, and then bequeathed by them to medieval Europe. The lawyers in particular made a distinction that would have a very long life ahead of it: between a *jus naturale* (or natural law properly speaking) and a *jus gentium* (or law of peoples). The two were distinct, but at the same time so closely interconnected that the differences between them were often very easily ignored. Natural law was the broader concept. It was something like what we would now call a body of scientific laws, applicable not just to human beings but to the whole animal kingdom as well. The *jus gentium* was the human component, or sub-category, of it. Just as the law of nature was universal in the natural world, so was the *jus gentium* universal in the human world.

III. THE MIDDLE AGES: THE NATURAL LAW ERA

The European Middle Ages offers an intriguing picture of dizzying variety and complexity, combined—not always very coherently—with the most sweeping universality. The variety was most apparent in the de-centralized world of feudalism, with its complex and interlocking layers of rights and duties, and its diffusion of governmental powers and jurisdictions. The universality was evident in two major spheres: philosophically and jurisprudentially,

[2] On Islamic views of international law, see generally Khadduri, 1955; and Allain, 2011.

in the continued stress on natural law; and politically, in the Holy Roman Empire and in the revival of Roman law which underpinned it.

A. THE UNIVERSALIST OUTLOOK: MEDIEVAL NATURAL LAW

During the Middle Ages, natural-law conceptions, inherited from the classical world, developed under the umbrella of the Catholic Church. But it must be remembered that natural law was not Christian in its inception, but rather was a legacy of the ancient Stoic and Roman legal traditions. The dominant approach—represented outstandingly by Thomas Aquinas—was rationalist in outlook, holding the content of the natural law to be susceptible of discovery and application by means of human reason rather than of revelation.

Natural law is one of the many parts of international law that have never received the systematic study that they merit. In the present context, only a few of its most salient features can be noted.[3] Perhaps its single most outstanding feature was its all-embracing character. It encompassed and regulated the natural and social life of the universe in all its infinite variety—from the movements of the stars in their courses to the gurgling of the four humours through the veins and arteries of the human body, from the thoughts and deeds of all of the creatures of land, sea, and air, to those of human beings and the angels in the heavens. Its strictures applied universally to all cultures and civilizations, past, present, and future.

There continued to be, as in the ancient period, a distinction between the *jus naturale* and the *jus gentium*, though still without any very sharp line between the two. The *jus gentium* was much the lesser of the two. Sometimes it was seen as the detailed application of general principles to the specific conditions of everyday life. Sometimes it was seen as a sort of secondary or 'watered-down' version of natural law, applicable to a frail humanity in its current corrupt and sinful condition. As such, it dealt with such matters as the resort to force. In fact, its most conspicuous achievement was the development of the doctrine concerning just wars, which basically allowed the taking of arms, as a last resort, for the vindication of legal rights.[4]

It must be stressed that this medieval *jus gentium* did not consist entirely, or even primarily, of what would now be called rules of international law. Instead, it was a collection of laws common to all nations, dealing with all aspects of human social affairs—contract, property, crime, and the like. It was more in the nature of an ethical system of universal or trans-cultural scope. Rulers were subject to the strictures of both natural law and the *jus gentium*—but so were private individuals.

B. THE PLURALIST OUTLOOK: THE ITALIAN CITY-STATES

Even if (as the natural-law writers maintained) the whole of human society formed a single moral and ethical community, there was no denying that the world also consisted of a welter of different polities, of a bewildering variety of sorts, and of varying degrees of independence from one another—extending all the way of the great empire of Rome itself (ie of Byzantium) to the patchwork of feudal jurisdictions which carpeted Western Europe.

---

[3] For a good short account of medieval natural-law theory, see generally Gierke, 1938.

[4] For a thorough exposition of medieval just-war theory, see Russell, 1975. For a shorter account, see Neff, 2005, pp 44–68.

Nowhere was the tension between the universalistic and the pluralistic tendencies of the period more evident, in practice, than in the debates over the legal status of the various 'independent' city-states of northern Italy. These obtained substantial de facto independence from the Holy Roman Empire in the late twelfth century, when the cities of the Lombard League defeated the forces of Emperor Frederick I. There was, however, considerable debate over what this 'independence' really meant. To this matter, two of the most prominent medieval lawyers—Bartolus of Sassoferato and his student Baldus of Ubaldis, who both wrote in the fourteenth century—turned their attention. Broadly speaking, the conclusion of Bartolus (largely echoed by Baldus) was that the cities were independent in the sense of being wholly self-governing and independent of one another, but that, in their relations inter se, they continued to be subject to rules of the Empire. Here we see the first glimmer, in European society, of the concept of independence of States operating in conjunction—sometimes very uneasily—with subjection to a larger set of norms governing inter-State relations (Hinsley, 1986, pp 81-2, 88-90, 167-74). For this reason, Bartolus has been called, with some justice, the first theorist of international law (Sereni, 1943, pp 58–63).

C. DEVELOPMENTS IN STATE PRACTICE

It is from the pluralist rather than the universalist side of the great medieval conceptual divide that we must look for innovations in State practice. The reason is easily seen: it is in the day-to-day relation of different States and peoples with one another that the practical problems of law are most likely to arise.

Much of the State practice in the Middle Ages consisted of traditional ways inherited from ancient times. The area of diplomatic relations is an example, with diplomats increasingly being accorded a broad (but not absolute) degree of immunity from judicial process in host States. Beginning in about the eleventh century, European (chiefly Italian) States began to conclude bilateral treaties that spelled out various reciprocal guarantees of fair treatment. These agreements, sometimes concluded with Muslim States, granted a range of privileges to the foreign merchants based in the contracting States, such as the right to use their own law and courts when dealing with one another. The same process was at work in the sphere of maritime trading. The seafaring community made use of the laws of Oléron (which were actually a series of court decisions from the small island of that name in the Bay of Biscay), and also of a code of rules called the Consolato del Mare, compiled in about the thirteenth century for the maritime community of Barcelona. These codes governed the broad range of maritime activities, including the earliest rules on the rights of neutral traders in wartime.

Certain aspects of the conduct of war witnessed a high level of refinement in the Middle Ages—most notably the law on the ransoming of prisoners of war (a welcome step forward from the alternatives of enslavement and summary killing). The 'law of arms' (as it was known) was expounded in the fourteenth century, first by John of Legnano and later by a monk named Honoré de Bonet (or Bouvet), whose book entitled *The Tree of Battles*, of the 1380s, became very influential.[5] Accounts of medieval warfare, however, incline observers to harbour grave doubts as to whether even these practical rules exerted much real influence.

With the European explorations of Africa and, particularly, the New World from the fourteenth century onward, questions of relations with non-European societies assumed

---

[5] On medieval law on the conduct of war, see Keen, 1965.

an urgent importance—while, at the same time, posing an immense practical test for the universality of natural law. The Spanish conquest of the Indian kingdoms in the New World sparked especially vigorous legal and moral debates (if only after the fact). The Dominican scholar, Francisco de Vitoria, in a series of lectures at the University of Salamanca delivered in 1539, concluded that the Spanish conquest was justified, on the ground that the Indians had unlawfully attempted to exclude Spanish traders from their kingdoms, contrary to natural-law rules. But he also confessed that his blood froze in his veins at the thought of the terrible atrocities committed by the Spanish in the process.[6] In 1550–51, there occurred one of the major legal confrontations of history, when two prominent figures—Juan Inés de Sepúlveda and Barolomé de las Casas—debated, at length, the lawfulness and legal bases of the Spanish conquests in the New World, under the judgeship of the theologian and philosopher Domingo de Soto. The result, alas, was inconclusive, as Soto declined to render a judgment (Pagden, 2001, pp 77-9).

In short, medieval international law was a jumble of different beliefs and practices—from the rarefied conceptions of the law of nature, to the more serviceable rules by which various communities conducted their actual day-to-day business, from warfare and diplomacy, to buying and selling.

IV. THE CLASSICAL AGE (1600–1815)

In the seventeenth and eighteenth centuries, a new spirit entered into doctrinal thought on international law. This is sometimes put in terms of a secularization of natural-law thought. That, however, is a very misleading characterization, since natural-law itself was (and had always been) primarily secular in nature. What was new in the seventeenth century was something quite different: the making of a clear and sharp distinction, for the first time, between the *jus gentium* (or law of *nations*) and natural law (the law of *nature*). International law was seen as a kind of alliance or confederation between these two bodies of law, which were now seen as conceptually quite distinct from one another.

The leading figure in the making of this distinction was the Spanish Jesuit writer Francisco Suárez, in a *Treatise on Laws and God the Lawgiver*, published in 1612. The distinction was basically a simple one. The law of *nature* is universal and eternal. Its basis is reason. Humans did not make this law, but they can apply their gift of rationality to discern its content. The law of *nations*, in contrast (ie the *jus gentium*), is a purely human creation, a product of human will and initiative. As such, it is subject to alteration from time to time and can vary from place to place. In addition, it is a law that is created by, and is applicable to, relations between States. This law of nations was, in short, international law in our modern sense of that term.

It should be appreciated, though, that international relations were seen to be regulated by *both* the law of nations and the law of nature. Moreover, the two bodies of law, although conceptually distinct, were seen as operating in close alliance with one another, with natural law at the foundation of the *jus gentium*. The *jus gentium* could depart from natural law in certain respects. It could, for example, permit certain things that natural law forbade—though only in the restricted sense that it could refrain from inflicting punishments for violations of natural-law principles. Illustrations included the capture of private property

---

[6] Vitoria, 'On the American Indians', in *Political Writings*, pp 231–292; Letter to Miguel de Arcos, ibid, pp 331–333.

in wartime and the taking of reprisals. The *jus gentium* could not, however, actually alter the content of natural law.

A. GROTIUS AND HOBBES

If Suárez was the principal innovator of this new way of looking at international law, its best-known expositor was the Dutch writer Hugo Grotius, whose major work *On the Law of War and Peace* was published in Paris in 1625—a work so dense and rich that one could easily spend a lifetime studying it (as a number of scholars have).[7] Grotius's principal purpose in this work was to apply the principles of *natural* law to international affairs. But in the course of his book, he also pointed out many applications of the law of nations as well. Grotius sometimes referred to this as the 'voluntary' law, to emphasise its origin as an expression of human will.

Grotius's writing was hugely influential in European thought for many centuries. As recently as 2008, his authority was invoked by the World Court.[8] Lawyers following his lead—or actually Suárez's lead—became known as 'Grotians'. Sometimes they were called 'eclectics' to reflect the single most outstanding, or defining, feature of the Grotian approach: its dualistic outlook, ie its insistence on international law as a combination of the law of nature and the law of nations. Indeed, the expression 'law of nature and nations' was a common shorthand in the seventeenth and eighteenth centuries for what would later be called simply 'international law'.

The Grotian, or dualistic, view of international law did not go unchallenged. A rival school known as the 'naturalists' rejected the dualistic stance, insisting instead that relations between States are governed exclusively by natural law alone. The so-called law of nations was merely usage, *without* binding legal force. The leading figure in the naturalist tradition was the English writer Thomas Hobbes, whose master work *Leviathan* was written in 1651, shortly after Grotius's death. In his writing, Hobbes advanced a picture of natural law, and of the state of nature in which it prevailed, that was radically at odds with that of Grotius and his medieval forebears. Grotius and his followers regarded the pre-political condition of human society as orderly and law-governed (governed, that is, by natural law). Hobbes, in contrast, regarded the pre-political state of nature as a chaotic, even violent, world. Natural law did govern this woeful scene, but natural law was seen to consist, in effect, of a single fundamental right and a single fundamental duty. The right was the right of self-preservation (Hobbes, *Leviathan*, pp 80–84). The duty was the obligation to carry out contracts voluntary entered into. This obligation to adhere to contracts provided a means of bringing some semblance of order to the primordial chaos of the state of nature. This was the means by which political societies, with well-defined rights and duties, could be brought into being—by way of Hobbes's famous social contract.

Between independent States, however, there was no social contract and no single political society. States lived, in short, continued to live in the state of nature *vis-à-vis* one another. But the duty to adhere to contracts still held, and it could enable at least a semblance of order to be brought to bear. In areas where States had common interests, treaty relations would be feasible. But the Hobbesians, or naturalists, denied that the general

---

[7] Much of the study of Grotius has been by political scientists rather than specifically by international lawyers. Remarkably, there is no comprehensive and accessible survey of his international legal thought and influence in English. For an older work that is still of value, see Knight, 1925. For a brief overview of his legal thought, see Tuck, 1999, pp 78–108. For a more thorough study, see Haggenmacher, 1983.

[8] *Sovereignty over Pedra Branca/Pulau Batu Puteh, Middle Rocks and South Ledge (Malaysia/Singapore)*, Judgment, ICJ Reports 2008, p 12, para 53.

customary practices of States could have any such legal force. Only explicit arrangements, consciously and voluntarily assumed by States, could be legally binding.

From a modern vantage point, the divide between the Grotians and the naturalists is not so easily discerned. The reason is that most of the naturalists held of a view of natural law that was nearer to Grotius than to Hobbes. The outstanding example is the German natural-law writer Samuel Pufendorf.[9] He had the highest regard for Grotius's ideas about natural law, while firmly denying the validity of the so-called law of nations or customary law. The effect was that the Grotians and the naturalists, in combination, developed and elaborated natural-law thought to an extent far beyond anything that their medieval ancestors had dreamt of. This period became, veritably, the golden age of natural-law thought (or systematic jurisprudence, as it was sometimes termed).

The culmination of this systematic natural-law movement came in the mid-eighteenth century, at the hands of the German philosopher Christian Wolff, who fittingly had been trained as a mathematician. Wolff's massive eight-volume encyclopaedia of natural law contained detailed discussions of practically everything under the sun and even beyond (including a discourse on the characteristics of the inhabitants of other planets)—while paying virtually no heed to State practice. It holds an honourable place on the list of the world's great unread masterpieces.[10]

The most famous and influential writer in the Grotian tradition was the Swiss diplomat Emmerich de Vattel, whose famous exposition of *The Law of Nations*, published in London in 1758. As the first systematic international-law treatise of the modern kind, it would not look drastically out of place on a twenty-first century bookshelf, as the works of Grotius or Wolff certainly would. Instead of setting out a grand philosophical scheme, Vattel's intention was to provide a sort of handbook for lawyers and statesmen. Moreover, its graceful style ensured it a wider usage by lawyers, judges, and lay persons than any other international writing had previously had. It can make a good claim to being the greatest international-law textbook ever written. With it, we stand at the threshold of modern international-law writing.[11]

In a number of ways, Vattel's treatise was a popularization of Wolff's ideas, but it was written in a very different spirit. Where Wolff had been disdainful of the voluntary law, Vattel fully embraced it, cheerfully and candidly expounding it alongside the natural law whenever appropriate. He has been accused of inconsistency—of constantly being on both sides of issues—but that charge is unfair. The fact is that he had two bodies of law to expound, which sometimes provided differing solutions to practical problems. He was generally very forthright about which law he was treating at any given time. It is we who tend to misunderstand the nature of his task because the dualistic mentality of that era is so foreign to us.

The best example of the dualistic 'method' concerned war. The natural law on just wars allowed a State to resort to force in self-help to vindicate a legal right that had actually been violated (or was threatened with violation)—so that, in a given conflict, one side would be fighting justly, and the other one not. The voluntary law, however, was not concerned over which party had the stronger legal claim to use force (ie it did not deal with the *jus ad bellum*, in legal terminology). Instead, it simply treated each side as if it had lawfully resorted to war. It then contented itself with regulating the conduct of wars, fixing rules for both

---

[9] See Pufendorf, 1934.

[10] On Wolff's cosmological views, see Wolff, 1737. Only the final volume of the main work on natural law concerned international law. For an English translation, see Wolff, 1934.

[11] On Vattel, see generally Jouannet, 1998.

parties to apply, on an even-handed basis, in their contention against one another (the *jus in bello*, in the common legal parlance). In effect, then, the natural law saw war in terms of law enforcement and as a sanction for wrongdoing. The voluntary law, in contrast, saw war more in terms of a duel.

B. THE LAWS OF NATURE AND NATIONS IN ACTION

The writing of Grotius and Hobbes and their followers was not done in a vacuum. Various forces were at work in this period, which served to give this new law of nations a concrete reality. One of the most important of these trends was the emergence (gradual to be sure) of strong central governments, at least in Western Europe, which increasingly gained the upper hand over the older, diffused jurisdictions of the feudal age. Particularly important for this trend was the innovation of standing armies in place of the older temporary feudal levies. In addition, these centralising nation-States were coming to be seen as permanently existing, corporate entities in their own right, separate from the rulers who governed them at any given time—with long-term interests and political agendas of their own.

At least some of the flavour of the medieval natural law survived, however, chiefly in the form of the idea of the existence of something that has come to be called the 'community of States'. The clearest symbol of this—if that is the right word for it—was the peace settlement arrived at in Westphalia in 1648, at the conclusion of the Thirty Years War in Germany. It is curious that something called the 'Westphalian system' is sometimes spoken of as a synonym of anarchy or of radical views of absolute State sovereignty—conceptions which actually belong (as will be seen) to the nineteenth century and not to the seventeenth.[12] In reality, the Westphalian settlement was an arrangement reached *within* the framework of the Holy Roman Empire, with certain prerogatives of the imperial government carefully preserved—ie, with the older medieval idea of 'independent' States being subject, at the same time, to certain higher norms. The Peace of Westphalia did, however, provide a sort of template for later times in the way in which it marked out a division of labour (so to speak) between national and international spheres, placing religion carefully in the realm of domestic law.

The idea of a community of States—distinct from, but also analogous to, a community of individual persons—was apparent in sundry other ways in the seventeenth and eighteenth centuries. One of these was in the concept of a balance of power. This was hardly an altogether new idea, but in this period it attained a formal articulation and recognition that it had never had before (most notably in the Peace of Utrecht in 1713, at the conclusion of the War of the Spanish Succession). In conjunction with this concept, the period was one of limited—though also of frequent—warfare. At least in Western Europe, war was largely conducted with trained professional forces, and for limited ends. As a result, European diplomacy bore more resemblance to a meticulous game of chess than to a lurid Hobbesian inferno of mayhem and turmoil. Even warfare often had a ritualistic air, with its emphasis on manoeuvre and siege rather than on pitched battle.

Economic relations manifested much this same combination of cooperation and competitiveness. On the competitive side, this period marked the high tide of mercantilism, with its intense rivalry for trade advantage. But there was also a high degree of cooperation, under an ever-strengthening rule of law, chiefly in the form of a network of treaties of friendship, commerce and navigation (FCN treaties in the standard legal parlance),

---

[12] See, for example, the discussion of the 'logic of Westphalia' in Falk, 1975, pp 59–69.

which provided a range of safeguards for merchants operating in and trading with foreign countries.

V. THE NINETEENTH CENTURY (1815–1919)

The nineteenth century, extraordinarily, is the least explored area of the history of international law. Its outstanding feature was the rise, and dominance, of the legal philosophy known as positivism. This conferred onto international law a scientific gloss—or alternatively, in the opinion of some, tied it into a narrow straitjacket. But positivism did not, or not quite, have the century to itself. A new tendency known as the historical school of law made some important contributions; and natural law, against heavy odds, managed to survive, although in new and unexpected ways.

A. 'THE PUBLIC LAW AND SYSTEM OF EUROPE'

With the definitive defeat of revolutionary and imperial France in 1815, the victorious European powers (Britain, Prussia, Russia, and Austria) crafted a new kind of peace settlement, based not merely on the balance of material power between the major States but also on a set of general principles of a more substantive character. These general principles were, to be sure, of a decidedly conservative character. The goal was to craft a continent-wide set of political arrangements that would (they hoped) keep the scourge of revolution from breaking out again.

The peace settlement was to be policed by the major powers—who were, of course, self-appointed to the task—by way of military intervention where necessary. The powers even had a grand name for their enterprise: the 'public law and system of Europe'. This legal order was based on faithful adherence to treaty commitments, together with respect for established laws and legitimate governments and property rights within the States of Europe. But it also included a duty on the part of rulers to 'earn' their legitimacy by providing responsible and efficient government to their peoples and also by cooperating with movements for orderly and peaceful change.

A few of these interventions by the Concert of Europe may be noted briefly. The first ones were in the cause of 'legitimacy' in the 1820s, when there were military interventions to subdue revolutions in Naples and Sardinia (by Austria) and in Spain (by France). Also in the 1820s, the intervention of Britain, France, and Russia in the Greek independence struggle led to independence for the Kingdom of Greece. Great-power involvement similarly led to Belgian independence in the 1830s. Sometimes the powers intervened diplomatically in post-war peace settlements, if the terms imposed on the losing side looked to be too destabilizing for the continent as a whole. This occurred in 1878, when the major powers stepped in to prevent Russia from exacting too harsh a peace against Turkey after a victorious war.

On at least some of these occasions, humanitarian considerations played a part, alongside the more usual political jockeying. The most common cause for concern on this front was the relief of Christian populations that were held to be victims of oppression in the Ottoman Empire. This was certainly one of the motivations for Greek intervention in the 1820s. In 1860, the powers intervened in a communal-violence crisis in the Mount Lebanon area. The most forceful of these great-power humanitarian actions was probably the one in Crete in 1897, when the powers stepped in to stop atrocities and counter-atrocities between Greeks and Turks. In virtually none of these cases was there a pure humanitarian motive, untouched by any other consideration. But some (arguable) precedents were established for later advocates of the lawfulness of humanitarian intervention.

The Concert of Europe 'system' (if it could really be called that) was overtly hegemonic, in modern parlance. There was little sign of any principle of equality of States. Still, the Concert of Europe did at least provide an ideal—if not always the reality—of collective, orchestrated State action for the preservation of international peace. To that extent, it foreshadowed the post-1945 UN. International lawyers, however, never gave it much attention.[13] Instead, their ambitions were directed to another end: to unshackling international law from its natural-law heritage and making it something like a science in the modern sense of that term.

B. THE POSITIVIST REVOLUTION

On the conceptual front, the major feature of the nineteenth century was the dominant role of positivism. The expression 'positive law' had been in use since the Middle Ages (since at least the fourteenth century) to refer to the man-made law of particular States, in contrast to divine law (ie the commands of God) or natural law. What was new in the nineteenth century, however, was something called a 'positive philosophy', the chief propounder of which was the French social philosopher Auguste Comte. By 'positive', Comte meant something like 'scientific' or 'objective' or 'empirical', in contrast to speculative or religious modes of thought. He maintained that the human race had gone through three great historical stages: the theological, the metaphysical, and (now) the 'positive'. In the theological stage, religious ideas had been dominant. In the metaphysical stage, legalistic and jurisprudential thinking had prevailed—meaning, in essence, natural law. But the third age—the 'positive' era (as Comte called it)—was now dawning, promising the true and final liberation of the human mind from the superstitions and dogmas of the past.

In its original form, positivism envisaged the emergence of a sort of technocratic utopia, in which the world would be governed not by clerics or politicians or lawyers (as in the past benighted ages of theology and metaphysics), but rather by engineers and industrialists and financiers. This vision had first been put forward by the eccentric French nobleman, the Comte de St-Simon, in the early nineteenth century.[14] (Auguste Comte's early career, incidentally, had been spent as St-Simon's secretary.) This early vision, taken to its logical conclusion, envisaged the obsolescence of the nation-State.

This original positivism of St-Simonian and Comte was a strange amalgam of technocracy and evangelism. Indeed, positivism actually did become a religion, with the most influence, as it happened, in Brazil (whose national flag is emblazoned with the positivist motto 'Order and Progress'). Not surprisingly, lawyers turned the positive philosophy in a somewhat different direction.

1. The positive philosophy applied to international law

As noted earlier, there was nothing the least bit new in the nineteenth century about the idea of positive law. What was distinctive about positivism as a school of jurisprudential thought was the doctrinaire insistence that positive law is the only true law, ie the wholesale and principled rejection of natural law as being legally binding. Natural law could still

---

[13] For one of the few legal texts to treat this subject, see Dupuis, 1909. See also Simpson, 2004, which devotes considerable attention to the policing practices of the major powers in the nineteenth century.

[14] On St-Simonism, see Manuel, 1956.

be important as an inspiration to law-makers, but it was not accepted by positivist writers as being legally binding in its own right. Stated in terms of received categories of thought, it would be said that the law of nations was now held (by positivists) to constitute the *whole* of international law, on its own.

Positivism was not a single, monolithic school of thought. It came in three principal versions (which have never received widely known labels). One of these could be called 'empiricist' because of its belief that the content of law is to be induced from State practice, with customary law as the leading form of international law.[15] A second approach could be called the 'common-will' variant, which emphasized treaties as the primary form of international law. A third approach could be called (with caution) 'voluntarist', since it insisted on voluntary self-restraint by States as the source of international law. What is often called 'positivism' was actually a rather untidy *mélange* of these three streams of thought. In the present context, only a few of the most salient features of this *mélange* can be highlighted.

One of the most central aspects of positivism was its close attention to questions of the sources of international law—and, in particular, to the proposition that international law was, fundamentally, an outgrowth or feature of the will of the States of the world. Rules of law were created by the States themselves, by consent, whether express (in written treaties) or tacit (in the form of custom). International law was therefore now seen as the sum total, or aggregation, of agreements which the States of the world happen to have arrived at, at any given time. In a phrase that became proverbial amongst positivists, international law must now be seen as a law between States and not as a law above States. International law, in other words, was now regarded as a corpus of rules arising from, as it were, the bottom up, as the conscious creation of the States themselves, rather than as a pre-existing, eternal, all-enveloping framework, in the manner of the old natural law. As a consequence, the notion of a systematic, all-encompassing body of law—so striking a feature of natural law—was now discarded. International law was now seen as, so to speak, a world of fragments, an accumulation of specific, agreed rules, rather than as a single coherent picture. In any area where agreement between States happened to be lacking, international law was, perforce, silent.

Another important effect of positivism was to replace the older, medieval, teleological picture with what might be termed an instrumentalist outlook. That is to say, the law was no longer seen as having any innate goal of its own, or as reflecting any universal master plan. Instead, the law was now regarded, in technocratic terms, as a means for the attainment of goals which were decided on by political processes. Law, in short, was now seen as a servant and not as a master. It was to be a tool for practical workmen rather than a roadmap to eternal salvation.

Closely allied to the consent-based view of international law was the firm insistence of most positivists on the centrality of the State as the principal (or even the sole) subject of international law, ie as the exclusive bearer of rights and duties on the international plane. States were now perceived as possessing what came to called 'international personality'— and, crucially, as also possessing a set of fundamental rights that must be protected at all times. Foremost of these fundamental rights was the right of survival or self-preservation. This meant that, in emergency situations, States are entitled to take action that would otherwise be contrary to law.

The most dramatic illustration of this point in the nineteenth century occurred in 1837, when the British government, faced with an insurgency in Canada, sent troops into the USA, in pursuit of insurgents who were using that country's territory as a safe

---

[15] For a classic exposition of the empiricist variant of positivism, see Oppenheim, 1908.

haven. They succeeded in capturing the miscreants, killing several persons in the process and destroying a boat named the Caroline. The USA vigorously objected to this armed incursion into its territory. Britain justified its action as self-defence. The diplomatic correspondence between the two countries in this dispute produced the classic exposition of the principle of self-defence: action in the face of a crisis that is 'instant, overwhelming, leaving no choice of means, and no moment for Deliberation'.[16] This remains today as the canonical statement of the criteria for the exercise by States of self-defence (although it really was a statement of the general principle of necessity rather than of self-defence *per se*).

The stress on the basic rights of States also gave to positivism a strongly pluralistic cast. Each nation-State possessed its own distinctive set of national interests, which it was striving to achieve in an inherently competitive, even hostile, environment. Each State was sovereign within its territory. And each State's domestic law could reflect that country's own particular history, values, aspirations, traditions, and so forth. It was in this period that the principle of 'the sovereign equality of States' became the fundamental cornerstone—or even the central dogma—of international law, along with the concomitant rule of non-intervention of States into the internal affairs of one another.

A final point is in order concerning the technocratic outlook of positivism. This had the important effect of de-politicising international law, at least in principle. International lawyers in the nineteenth century became increasingly reluctant to trespass into areas of political controversy. In this regard, they presented a sharp contrast to their natural-law forbears, who had proudly worn the mantle of the social critic. The positivist lawyers were more inclined to themselves instead as the juridical counterparts of Comte's engineers. In particular, it came to be widely agreed that fundamental national-security interests were questions of politics and not of law—a distinction that Grotius and Vattel would have found difficult to grasp. By the same token, positivism had a strongly non-moralistic flavour. Nowhere were these features more important than on the subject of war. Positivists tended to the rights and wrongs of a State's decision to resort to war (the *jus ad bellum*) as a political rather than a legal issue. Instead, war was now seen as an inevitable and permanent feature of the inter-State system, in the way that friction was an inevitable and permanent feature of a mechanical system.

2. The professionalization of international law

The scientific and technocratic and a-political ethos of positivism brought a new sense of precision, a business-like character to the study and practice of international law. One consequence of this was an increasing sense of professionalism and, to a certain extent, of corporate solidarity. An important sign of this was the founding, in 1873, of two major professional bodies in the field, the International Law Association and the Institut de Droit International. This was also the period in which international law became a subject of university studies in its own right, separate from general jurisprudence—and, in particular, from the study of natural law. (This is also a subject which still awaits detailed treatment.)

The nineteenth century was also the period in which major systematic treatises began to be written in the various European languages. Where Vattel had led, many followed. In 1785, Georg Friedrich de Martens wrote an important treatise, which departed from earlier writing in being based primarily on State practice rather than on natural-law doctrine. In English, the most notable early exposition was by Henry Wheaton, an American

---

[16] 29 *British and Foreign State Papers*, pp 1137–1138.

diplomat and legal scholar, whose *Elements of International Law* was published in 1836. Its popularity is indicated by the fact that it was translated into French, Spanish, and Italian, with new editions produced for fully a century after the first one. Wheaton was followed in Britain by Robert Phillimore, whose treatise of 1854–61 ran to four volumes (with two further editions). The first major German-language exposition was by Auguste Wilhelm Heffter in 1844 (which ran to eight editions by 1888). The first treatise to be a conscious embodiment of the positive philosophy was by an Argentinian diplomat, Carlos Calvo, in 1868.[17] This text expanded from two to six volumes over the course of five editions to 1896. The French were slightly later in the field, with a *Précis du Droit des Gens*, by Théophile Funck-Brentano and Albert Sorel in 1877. More influential was the *Manuel de Droit International Public* by Henry Bonfils in 1894 (with eight editions by the 1920s). One of the most popular texts was that of the Swiss writer Johann Kaspar Bluntschli, whose exposition in 1868 took the form of a systematic 'code'.[18]

C. DISSIDENT PERSPECTIVES

If positivism was by far the dominant trend in nineteenth-century international law, it fell short of having a complete monopoly. For one thing, natural law—that venerable legacy of the past—showed its resilience, tenaciously surviving in the deeply inhospitable intellectual climate of positivism. Its principal adherent was the Scottish writer James Lorimer. But it also had support from Bluntschli.

In addition, several new approaches to international law were pioneered in the nineteenth century. One of these was liberalism, the essence of which was the centrality of private individuals rather than of States. States were seen as institutions whose function was to promote the rights and interests of private parties, rather than to promote the so-called 'national interest' of the State *itself*. Liberalism did not attract the explicit support of any important treatise writer, but its impact may be seen in several areas. One was the increased emphasis of freedom of trade in goods, as well as free movement of people and of capital. There also came to be, during this period, a focus on what would later be termed human rights. In the nineteenth century, this took the form of an assertion that there was an international minimum standard of treatment, in the area of civil rights, which any person was entitled to receive from any foreign State. This idea, however, met with staunch resistance from positivist writers, most notably from Calvo, whose 'Calvo Doctrine' insisted on giving the priority to the sovereign right of States to determine their *own* standards of treatment in their own territories.

A second new school of thought was the nationality school. Its distinguishing feature was the contention that the true collective unit, for purposes of international law, is not the *State*, but rather the *nation*. Nations were seen as, essentially, cultural or historical units, bound together by shared languages, literary inheritances, customs, religions or historical traditions. The best-known champion of this was the charismatic Italian idealist (and sometime revolutionary) Giuseppe Mazzini. In the international legal profession, its foremost spokesman was the Italian scholar and political figure Pasquale Mancini. So strong was the Italian connection that this was sometimes referred to as the 'Italian school' of international law. Its most important feature was the contention that there was a kind of natural-law right on the part of nations to form themselves into States.[19] The nationality

---

[17] Calvo, 1880–81. For the first edition, in Spanish, see Carlos Calvo, *Derecho internacional teórico y práctico de Europa y América* (2 vols, Paris: D'Amyot, 1868).

[18] Bluntschli, 1870.   [19] On the nationality school, see Sereni, 1943, pp 155–78.

school's approach thereby became the ancestor of the later law of self-determination of peoples.[20]

A third new approach may be labelled, for lack of widely known existing term, 'solidarism'. This is to reflect its core belief, that international law should be based on the *interdependence* of peoples rather than on the *independence* of States, as the positivists held. Solidarists thereby sought to mount a frontal challenge to positivism by displacing State sovereignty and independence from their central roles in international law. Solidarism, like liberalism, did not receive systematic doctrinal treatment in the nineteenth century. But its impact was visible in the array of international organizations that began to be assembled in this period. Its ethos is also evident in the willingness of some lawyers to countenance intervention in the internal affairs of other States, most prominently on humanitarian grounds to protect vulnerable groups from oppression (as, most notably, Christians in the Ottoman Empire).

D. THE ACHIEVEMENTS OF THE NINETEENTH CENTURY

One explanation for the remarkable lack of attention by international lawyers to the nineteenth century lies perhaps in the pervasive dominance of doctrinaire positivism over international legal writing generally. There was much, admittedly, that was unattractive about nineteenth-century positivism, particularly to modern eyes—its doctrinaire quality, its narrow horizons, its lack of high ideals, the aura of superficiality raised to the pitch of dogma, its narrowly technocratic character, its ready subservience to power. But it would be wrong to judge it on these points alone because its solid achievements were many. If it lacked the breadth and idealism of natural-law thought, it also discarded the vagueness and unreality that often characterized natural-law thought at its worst. In many ways, positivism was a breath (or even a blast) of fresh air, countering the speculative excesses of natural-law thought. Even if positivism sometimes went too far in the opposite direction, we should nonetheless appreciate the valuable services that it performed in its time.

It is clear from even a cursory survey of the nineteenth century that, when the wills of States were coordinated, impressive results could follow (see generally Lyons, 1963). In the spirit of the St-Simonians, there were various forms of what would come to be called the functional cooperation of States. Progress on this front was most notable in the areas of international communication and transportation: from the international river commissions that were set up to ensure freedom of navigation on the Rhine and Danube Rivers (which had been commercial backwaters since the Middle Ages), to special arrangements for the Suez and Panama Canals, to the founding of the International Telegraphic and Universal Postal Unions (1865 and 1874 respectively). In the spirit of the liberal economists, policies of tariff reduction gathered momentum (with conclusion of the Cobden-Chevalier Treaty in 1860 between France and Britain being the seminal event). Barriers between States were assiduously broken down in other ways as well. The late nineteenth century became an age of remarkable freedom of movement of peoples, with migration on a massive scale (passports were unnecessary for much of international travel in the nineteenth century). Capital too moved with great freedom, thanks to the linking of currencies through the gold standard. The period was, in short, a great age of globalization, with the world more closely integrated economically than it would be for many decades thereafter (and in some ways more so than today: see Neff, 1990, pp 38–71).

---

[20] See Craven, Ch 8 of this book.

The positivist era was also the period in which we first see the international community 'legislating' by way of multilateral treaties, for the most part in areas relating to armed conflict. The first major example of this was the Declaration of Paris of 1856. It restricted the capture of private property at sea, by providing that 'free ships make free goods' (ie that enemy private property could not be captured on a neutral ship). It also announced the abolition of privateering. Within five years, it attracted over 40 ratifications. In 1868, the Declaration of St Petersburg contained a ban on exploding bullets. More importantly, it denounced total-war practices, by stating that the only permissible objective of war is the defeat of the enemy's armed forces. Alongside the law of war—and in some ways in close partnership to it—was the full flowering of the law of neutrality, which, for the first time, emerged in the full light of juridical respectability as a sort of counterpart to the unrestricted right of States to resort to war on purely political grounds.[21]

There was 'legislation' in other fields too. On the humanitarian front, the period witnessed a concerted effort by the nations of the world to put an end to slave trading. The culmination of this effort occurred in 1890, when the General Act of the Brussels Conference established an International Maritime Office (at Zanzibar) to act against slave trading. In the less-than-humanitarian sphere of imperialism, the major powers established, by multilateral treaty, the 'rules of the game' for the imperial partitioning of Africa. This took place at the Berlin Conference of 1884–5. (Contrary to the belief of some, that conference did not actually allocate any territories; it established the criteria by which the powers would recognize one another's claims.)

The culmination of nineteenth-century international legislation—and the arrival of parliamentary-style diplomacy and treaty-drafting—came with the two Hague Peace Conferences of 1899 and 1907. The first Conference drafted two major conventions: one on the laws of war and one on the establishment of a Permanent Court of Arbitration (which was actually a roster of experts prepared to act as judges on an ad hoc basis, and not a standing court). The Second Hague Peace Conference, in 1907, was a much larger gathering than the earlier one (and hence less Europe-dominated). It produced 13 conventions on various topics, mostly on aspects of war and neutrality.[22]

Yet another major achievement of the nineteenth century was in the area of the peaceful settlement of disputes. Although it was widely agreed that fundamental security issues were not justiciable, the nineteenth century marked a great step forward in the practice of inter-State arbitration. The trend began with the Jay Treaty of 1794, in which the USA and Britain agreed to set up two arbitration commissions (comprising nationals of each country) to resolve a range of neutrality and property-seizure issues that had arisen in the preceding years. These were followed by a number of ad hoc inter-State arbitrations in the nineteenth century, of which the most famous, again between Britain and the USA, took place in 1871–72, for the settlement of a host of neutrality-related issues arising from the American Civil War.[23]

For all the impressiveness of these achievements, though, the state of the world was well short of utopian. Economic inequality grew steadily even as growth accelerated. The subjection of much of the world to the European imperial powers, together with the 'gunboat diplomacy' that sometimes followed in the wake of legal claims, stored up a strong reservoir of ill-will between the developed and the developing worlds. Nor did the Concert of Europe prove adequate, in the longer term, to the maintenance of international peace.

[21] For the most magisterial exposition of this subject, see Kleen, 1898–1900.
[22] For an informative and lively account of these conferences, see Tuchman, 1966, pp 265–338.
[23] For a detailed and informative account, see Crook, 1975.

The Franco-Prussian War of 1870-71 proved, all too dramatically, that war between major powers, on the continent of Europe, was far from unthinkable—and the steady advance in weapons technology and armaments stockpiles promised that future wars could be far more deadly than any in the past. In due course, the Great War of 1914-18 delivered—spectacularly—on that menacing promise.

VI. THE TWENTIETH AND TWENTY-FIRST CENTURIES (1919–)

Since much of this book will cover twentieth-century developments, no attempt will be made at comprehensive coverage here, particularly of the post-1945 period. But certain aspects of both the inter-war and the post-1945 periods which have received comparatively little attention so far will be emphasized.

A. THE INTER-WAR PERIOD

The carnage of the Great War of 1914–18 concentrated many minds, in addition to squandering many lives. Many persons now held that nothing short of a permanently existing organization dedicated to the maintenance of peace would suffice to prevent future ghastly wars. Their most prominent spokesman was American President Woodrow Wilson. The fruit of their labours was the establishment of the League of Nations, whose Covenant was set out in the Versailles Treaty of 1919. This new system of public order would be of an open, parliamentary, democratic character, in contrast to the discreet great-power dealings of the Concert of Europe. The League was, however, tainted from the outset by its close association with the Versailles peace settlement, an incubus which it never managed to shake off.

1. The League and its supplements

The League was a complex combination of conservatism and boldness. On the side of conservatism was the decision to make no fundamental change in the sovereign prerogatives of nation-States as these had developed up to that time. No attempt was made to establish the League as a world government, with sovereign powers over its member States. Nor did the Covenant of the League prohibit war. Instead, the resort to war was hedged about with procedural requirements—specifically that either a judicial or political dispute-settlement process must be exhausted before there could be war between League member States. On the side of boldness was the Covenant's provision for automatic enforcement action against any League member State resorting to war without observing the peaceful-settlement rules. This enforcement took the form of economic sanctions by all other League member States, a tactic inspired by the Allied blockade of Germany during the Great War.

In due course, two major initiatives supplemented the League's efforts to maintain peace. In 1928, the Pact of Paris was concluded, in which the States parties forswore any resort to war as a means of national policy. The practical effects of this initiative, however, were not impressive. For one thing, no sanctions were provided. It was also carefully understood by the signatories that self-defence action would be permitted—a potentially large loophole. The second initiative was the Stimson Doctrine of 1932, announced by the USA (and named for its Secretary of State at the time) in the wake of Japan's occupation of Manchuria. It held that any situation brought about by aggression would not be accorded legal recognition by the USA. Here too, the immediate material impact was not great; but it had some precedential value, since the UN General Assembly would later (in 1970) endorse it as a general principle of international relations.[24]

Only on one occasion was the sanctions provision of the Covenant invoked: against Italy for its invasion of Ethiopia in 1935–6. The sanctions failed to save Ethiopia, since the conquest was completed before they could have any serious effect. This failure led to a period of profound soul-searching amongst international lawyers as to what the role of law in the world should be (see Niemeyer, 1940). It similarly led States into desperate searches for alternative sources of security to the League Covenant. A number of countries, such as Switzerland, Belgium, and the Scandinavian States, reverted to traditional neutrality policies. But there were also a number of imaginative proposals for informal, but coordinated, action by States against aggressors (eg Cohn, 1939; Jessup, 1936). There was even a sort of return to ad hoc great-power management, in the form of a collective and coordinated non-intervention policy organized by the major powers at the outbreak of the Spanish Civil War in 1936. Unfortunately, this effort too was largely unsuccessful because of inadequate implementation and great-power rivalry (see Watters, 1970).

2. The achievements of the inter-war period

Although the League failed as a protector against aggressors, it would be far wrong to suppose that the inter-war period was a sterile time in international law generally. Precisely the opposite was the case. It was a time of ferment, experiment, and excitement unprecedented in the history of the discipline. A World Court (known formally, if optimistically, as the Permanent Court of International Justice) was established as a standing body, with its seat at The Hague in the Netherlands. It did not have compulsory jurisdiction over all disputes. But it decided several dozen cases, building up, for the first time, a substantial body of international judicial practice. These cases were supplemented by a large number of claims commissions and arbitrations, whose outpourings gave international lawyers a volume of case law far richer than anything that had ever existed before.

The codification of international law was one of the ambitious projects of the period. A conference was convened for that purpose by the League of Nations in 1930, but its fruits were decidedly modest (consisting mainly of clarifications of various issues relating to nationality). But there were further initiatives by the American States in a variety of fields. These included a convention on the rights and duties of States in 1933, which included what many lawyers regard as the canonical definition of a 'State' for legal purposes.[25] The American States also concluded conventions on maritime neutrality, civil wars, asylum, and extradition.

The inter-war period also witnessed the first multilateral initiatives on human rights. A number of bilateral conventions for the protection of minorities were concluded between various newly created States and the League of Nations. In the event, these proved not to be very effective; but they set the stage for later efforts to protect minority rights after 1945, as well as human rights generally. The principle of trusteeship of dependent territories was embodied in the mandates system, in which the ex-colonies of the defeated countries were to be administered by member States of the League. But this was to be a mission of stewardship—'a sacred trust of civilization'—under the oversight of the League. Finally, the League performed heroic labours for the relief of refugees, in the face of very great obstacles—in the process virtually creating what would become one of the most important components of the law of human rights.

---

[24] UN Declaration on Friendly Relations between States, GA Res 2625 (24 October 1970).
[25] See Craven, Ch 8 of this book.

It was a period also of innovative thinking about international law. That the doctrinaire positivism of the nineteenth century was far from dead was made apparent by the World Court in 1927, when it reaffirmed the consensual basis of international law, in the famous (or infamous) *Lotus* case.[26] But positivism also came under attack during this period, from several quarters. One set of attackers were the enthusiasts for collective security, as embodied in the League of Nations. The American scholar Quincy Wright was a notable exemplar. This group were sympathetic to the return of just-war ideas, with the Covenant's restrictions on the resort to war and the provision for collective aid to victims of unlawful war. Their single most notable contention was that neutrality must now be regarded as obsolete.

Within the positivist camp itself, a sweeping revision of nineteenth-century thought was advanced by writers of the Vienna School, led by Hans Kelsen. They discarded the State-centred, consent-based, pluralistic elements of nineteenth-century positivism, while retaining its general scientific outlook. The Vienna School then reconceived international law—and indeed the whole of law—as a grand, rationalistic, normative system.[27] The French lawyer Georges Scelle advanced a broadly similar vision, but from the solidarist (or sociological) vantage point, in contrast to the austere formalism of Kelsen.[28] Scelle in fact provided the first systematic exposition of the solidarist philosophy. In his vision of international law as a global constitutional law, he became the chief intellectual ancestor of the later constitutionalist movement. There was even something of a revival of natural-law thought, most notably in the writings of Louis Le Fur in France and of Alfred Verdross in Austria (who was something of a maverick member of the Vienna School).[29]

In short, the inter-war period did not bring an end to war or aggression. But it was the most vibrant and exciting era in the history of the discipline up to that time (and perhaps since).

B. AFTER 1945

In the immediate aftermath of the Second World War, international law entered upon a period of unprecedented confidence and prestige, for which 'euphoria' might not be too strong a word. International lawyers even found themselves in the (unaccustomed) role of heroic crusaders, with the dramatic prosecutions of German and Japanese leaders for crimes under international law at Nuremberg and Tokyo in the late 1940s (see generally Taylor, 1992; and Cryer and Boister, 2008). At the same time, great plans for the future were being laid.

1. Building a new world

The founding of the UN in 1945, to replace the defunct League of Nations, was a critical step in the creation of a new world order. With the UN came a new World Court (the International Court of Justice, or ICJ), though still without compulsory jurisdiction over States.[30] The heart of the organization was the Security Council, where (it was hoped) the victorious powers from the Second World War would continue their wartime alliance in

---

[26] '*Lotus*', Judgment No 9, 1927, PCIJ, Ser A, No 10.

[27] On the Vienna School, see Kunz, 1934. For a clear and succinct account, see Friedmann, 1967, pp 275–87. See also Nijman, 2004, pp 149–92.

[28] See Scelle, 1932–34. See also René-Jean Dupuy, 'Images de Georges Scelle,' 1 *European Journal of International Law* 235–239 (1990); and Nijman, 2004, pp 192–242.

[29] See Le Fur, 1932; and Verdross, 1927.   [30] See Thirlway, Ch 20 of this book.

perpetuity as a collective bulwark against future aggressors. (It may be noted that 'United Nations' had been the official name for the wartime alliance.) The UN therefore marked something of a return to the old Concert of Europe approach. The special status of the five major powers (the principal victors in the Second World War, of course) was formally reflected in their possession of permanent seats on the Security Council, together with the power of veto over its decisions.

The UN Charter went further than the League Covenant in restricting violence. It did this by prohibiting not only war as such, but also 'the use of force' in general–thereby encompassing measures short of war, such as armed reprisals. An express exception was made for self-defence. Regarding action against aggressors, the UN was both bolder and more timid than the League had been. It was bolder in that the Charter provided not only for economic sanctions but also for armed action against aggressors. The UN Charter was more timid than the League, however, in that sanctions (whether economic or military) were not mandatory and automatic, as in the League Covenant. The Security Council—dominated by the major powers–was to decide on an ad hoc basis when, or whether, to impose sanctions. The result was to make the UN a more overtly political body than the League had been.

Parallel to this security programme was another one for the promotion of global economic prosperity. The economic-integration effort of the nineteenth century, shattered by the Great War and by the Great Depression of the 1930s, was to be restructured and given institutional embodiments. The International Monetary Fund was founded to ensure currency stability, and the World Bank to protect and promote foreign investment and (in due course) economic development. Trade liberalization would be overseen by a body to be called the International Trade Organization (ITO).

In a host of other areas as well, the aftermath of World War II witnessed a huge increase in international cooperation. There scarcely seemed any walk of life that was not being energetically 'internationalized' after 1945—from monetary policy to civil aviation, from human rights to environmental protection, from atomic energy to economic development, from deep sea-bed mining to the exploration of outer space, from democracy and governance to transnational crime-fighting. The cumulative effect was to weld the States of the world in general—and international lawyers in particular—into a tighter global community than ever before. It is easy to understand that, amidst all this hub-bub of activity, a certain triumphalist spirit could pervade the ranks of international lawyers.

The euphoric atmosphere proved, alas, to be very short-lived. Scarcely had the UN begun to function than it became paralysed by Cold-War rivalry between the major power blocs—with the notable exception of the action in Korea in 1950–53 (only made possible by an ill-advised Soviet boycott of the Security Council at the relevant time). Nor did the new World Court find much effective use in its early decades. The ITO never came into being (because of a loss of interest by the USA). Plans for the establishment of a permanent international criminal court were also quietly dropped. Nor did the UN Charter's general ban against force have much apparent effect, beyond a cruelly ironic one: of propelling self-defence from a comparative legal backwater into the very forefront of international legal consciousness. Since self-defence was now the only clearly lawful category of unilateral use of force, the UN era became littered with self-defence claims of varying degrees of credibility, from the obvious to the risible. In particular, actions that previously would have been unashamedly presented as reprisals now tended to be deftly re-labelled as self-defence.[31]

---

[31] See Gray, Ch 21 of this book.

All was not gloom, though, by any stretch of the imagination. In non-political spheres, lawyers fared a great deal better, very much in the technocratic spirit of nineteenth-century positivism. The codification of international law, for example, made some major strides, in large part from the activity of a UN body of technical experts called the International Law Commission. The principal areas of law that received a high degree of codification included the law of the sea (with four related conventions on the subject in 1958, replaced in 1982 by a single, broader convention), diplomatic and consular relations (in the early 1960s), human rights (with two international covenants in 1966) and the law of treaties (in 1969).

At the same time, though, it was not so clear that the fundamentals of the subject had changed very much. The basic positivist outlook continued to have great staying power. Some of the most important political and intellectual upheavals of the twentieth century left strangely little mark on international law. Socialism, for example, far from being a major challenge to lawyers, was actually a conservative force. Socialist theorists tended to write more dogmatically in the positivist vein than their Western counterparts did, insisting with particular strength on the upholding of respect for State sovereignty (see Tunkin, 1974). Nor did the massive influx of developing States onto the world scene bring about any fundamental conceptual upheaval. For the most part, the developing countries readily accepted established ways, although they made some concrete contributions in specific areas. One was the establishment of self-determination as a fundamental, collective human right. Another was in the area of succession to treaties by newly independent States, with the States being given an option of choosing which colonial treaties to retain.

2. New challenges

Around the 1980s, a certain change of atmosphere in international law became evident, as something like the idealism of the early post-war years began, very cautiously, to return. There were a number of signs of this. One was a sharp upturn in the judicial business of the World Court. This included a number of cases of high political profile, from American policy in Central America to the Tehran hostages crisis to the Yugoslavian conflicts of the 1990s. In the 1990s, the ITO project was revived, this time with success, in the form of the creation of the World Trade Organization (WTO), which gave a significant impetus to what soon became widely, if controversially, known as 'globalization'.[32] Human rights began to assume a higher profile, as a result of several factors, such as the global campaign against South African apartheid and the huge increase in activity of non-governmental organizations.[33] The end of the Cold War led to tangible hopes that the original vision of the UN as an effective collective-security agency might, at last, be realized. The expulsion of Iraq from Kuwait in 1991 lent strong support to this hope. Perhaps most remarkable of all was the rebirth of plans for an international criminal court, after a half-century of dormancy. A statute for a permanent international criminal court was drafted in 1998, entering into force in 2002 (with the first conviction handed down in 2012).[34]

In this second round of optimism, there was less in the way of euphoria than there had been in the first one, and more of a feeling that international law might be entering an age of new—and dangerous—challenge. International lawyers were now promising, or threatening, to bring international norms to bear upon States in an increasingly intrusive manner. A striking demonstration of this occurred in 1994, when the UN Security Council authorized the use of force to overthrow an unconstitutional government in Haiti. In 1999, the

[32] See Loibl, Ch 24 of this book.   [33] See Rodley, Ch 27 of this book.
[34] See Cryer, Ch 26 of this book.

UN Security Council acquiesced in (although it did not actually authorize) a humanitarian intervention in Kosovo by a coalition of Western powers. It was far from clear how the world would respond to this new-found activism—in particular, whether the world would really be content to entrust its security, in perpetuity, to a Concert-of-Europe style directorate of major powers.

International legal claims were being asserted on a wide range of other fronts as well, and frequently in controversial ways and generally with results that were unwelcome to some. For example, lawyers who pressed for self-determination rights for various minority groups and indigenous peoples were accused of encouraging secession movements. Some human-rights lawyers were loudly demanding changes in the traditional practices of non-Western peoples. And newly found (or newly rejuvenated) concerns over democracy, governance, and corruption posed, potentially, a large threat to governments all over the world. Some environmental lawyers were insisting that, in the interest of protecting a fragile planet, countries should deliberately curb economic growth. (But which countries? And by how much?) Economic globalization also became intensely controversial, as the IMF's policy of 'surveillance' (a somewhat ominous term to some) became increasingly detailed and intrusive, and as 'structural adjustment' was seen to have potentially far-reaching consequences in volatile societies. Fears were also increasingly voiced that the globalization process was bringing an increase in economic inequality.

VII. CONCLUSION

How well these new challenges will be met remains to be seen. At the beginning of the twenty-first century, it is hard to see the UN 'failing' in the way that the League of Nations did and being completely wound up. No one foresees a reversion to the rudimentary ways of Herodotus's silent traders. But it is not impossible to foresee nationalist or populist backlashes within various countries against what is seen to be excessive international activism and against the élitist, technocratic culture of international law and organization. If there is one lesson that the history of international law teaches, it is that the world at large—the 'outside world' if you will—has done far more to mould international law than vice versa. But it is (or should be) sobering to think that the great forces of history—religious, economic, political, psychological, scientific—have never before been successfully 'managed' or tamed. And only a rash gambler would wager that success was now at hand. Perhaps the most interesting chapters of our history remain to be written.

REFERENCES

AGER, SL (1996), *Interstate Arbitrations in the Greek World, 337–90 B.C.* (Berkeley, Calif.: University of California Press).

ALLAIN, J (2011), 'Acculturation Through the Middle Ages: The Islamic Law of Nations and Its Place in the History of International Law,' in Orakhelashvili, A (ed) *Research Handbook on the Theory and History of International Law* (Cheltenham: Edward Elgar), pp 394–407.

ARISTOTLE (1941), 'Rhetoric', in McKeon, R (ed) *The Basic Works of Aristotle* ((New York: Random House), pp 1325–451.

BEDERMAN, DJ (2001), *International Law in Antiquity* (Cambridge: Cambridge University Press).

BHATIA, HS (ed) (1977), *International Law and Practice in Ancient India* (New Delhi: Deep and Deep).

BLUNTSCHLI, JC (1870), *Le droit international codifié* (Lardy, MC (trans)) (Paris: Guillaumin).

BONET, H (1949), *The Tree of Battles* (Coopland, GW (trans)) (Liverpool: Liverpool University Press).

BONFILS, H (1894), *Manuel de droit international public* (Paris: A Rousseau).

CALVO, C (1880-81), *Le droit international théorique et pratique précédé d'un exposé historique des progrès de la science du droit des gens*, 3rd edn, 4 vols (Paris: Pedone-Lauriel).

CICERO, MT (1998), *Republic* (Rudd, N (trans)) (Oxford: Oxford University Press).

COHN, G (1939), *Neo-neutrality* (Kellar, AS and Jensen, E (trans)) (New York: Columbia University Press).

CROOK, A (1975), *The Alabama Claims: American Politics and Anglo-American Relations, 1865–1872* (Ithaca, NY: Cornell University Press).

CRYER, R and BOISTER, N (2008), *The Tokyo International Military Tribunal* (Oxford: Oxford University Press).

De MARTENS, GF (1785), *Primae lineae iuris gentium Europaearum practici in usum auditorum adumbratae* (Göttingen: Johann Christian Dieterich).

De VATTEL, E (1916), *The Law of Nations* (Fenwick, CG (trans)) (Washington, DC: Carnegie Institution of Washington).

De VITORIA, F in Pagden, A and Lawrance, J (eds) (1991), *Political Writings* (Cambridge: Cambridge University Press).

DUPUIS, C (1909), *Le principe d'équilibre et le concert européen de la Paix de Westphalie à l'Acte d'Algésiras* (Paris: Perrin).

FALK, RA (1975), *A Study of Future Worlds* (New York: Free Press).

FRIEDMANN, W (1967), *Legal Theory*, 5th edn (London: Stevens and Sons).

FUNCK-BRENTANO, T and SOREL, A (1877) *Précis du droit des gens* (Paris: E. Plon).

GIERKE, O (1938), *Political Theories of the Middle Age* (Maitland, FW (trans)) (Cambridge: Cambridge University Press).

GROTIUS, H (1925), *The Law of War and Peace* (Kelsey, FW (trans)) (Oxford: Clarendon Press).

HAGGENMACHER, P (1983), *Grotius et la doctrine de la guerre juste* (Paris: Presses Universitaires de France).

HEFFTER, AW (1844), *Das Europäische Völkerrecht der Gegenwart, auf den bisherigen Grundlagen* (Berlin: EH Schroeder).

HERODOTUS (1954), *Histories* (De Sélincourt, A (trans)) (Harmondsworth: Penguin).

HINSLEY, FH (1986), *Sovereignty*, 2nd edn (Cambridge: Cambridge University Press).

HOBBES, T in Oakeshott, M (ed) (1957), *Leviathan; or The Matter, Forme and Power of a Commonwealth Ecclesiastical and Civil* (Oxford: Blackwell).

JESSUP, PC (1936), *Today and Tomorrow*, vol 4 of Jessup, PC and Deák, F (1935-37), *Neutrality: Its History, Economics and Law*, 4 vols (New York: Columbia University Press).

JOHN OF LEGNANO in Holland, TE (ed) (1917), *Tractatus de Bello, de Represaliis et de Duello* (Brierly, JL (trans)) (Oxford: Oxford University Press).

JOUANNET, E (1998), *Emer de Vattel et l'émergence doctrinale du droit international classique* (Paris: Pedone).

KEEN, M (1965), *The Laws of War in the Late Middle Ages* (London: Routledge and Kegan Paul).

KHADDURI, M (1955), *War and Peace in the Law of Islam* (Baltimore, Md: Johns Hopkins University Press).

KLEEN, R (1898-1900), *Lois et usages de la neutralité d'après le droit international conventionnel et coutûmier des États civilisés* 2 vols. (Paris: Marescq).

KNIGHT, WSM (1925), *Life and Works of Hugo Grotius* (London: Sweet & Maxwell).

KUNZ, J (1934), 'The "Vienna School" and International Law,' 11 *New York University Law Quarterly Review* 370-421.

LE FUR, L-E (1932), 'Le développement historique du droit international: De l'anarchie internationale à une communauté internationale organisée,' 41 *Recueil des Cours* (Academy of International Law) 501–602.

LORIMER, J (1883–4), *The Institutes of the Law of Nations: A Treatise of the Jural Relations of Separate Political Communities*, 2 vols (Edinburgh: W Blackwood).

LYONS, FSL (1963), *Internationalism in Europe, 1815-1914* (Leyden: A. W. Sythoff).

MANCINI, PS (1851), *Della Nazionalità come fondamento del diritto delle genti* (Turin: Eredi Botta).

MANUEL, FE (1956), *The New World of Henri St-Simon* (Notre Dame, Ind: University of Notre Dame Press).

NEFF, SC (1990), *Friends But No Allies: Economic Liberalism and the Law of Nations* (New York: Columbia University Press).

—— (2005), *War and the Law of Nations: A General History* (Cambridge: Cambridge University Press).

NIEMEYER, G (1940), *Law Without Force: The Function of Politics in International Law* (New Brunswick, NJ: Transaction Publications).

NIJMAN, JE (2004), *The Concept of International Legal Personality: An Inquiry into the History and Theory of International Law* (The Hague: TMC Asser Press).

OPPENHEIM, L (1908), 'The Science of International Law: Its Task and Method,' 2 *American Journal of International Law* 313–56.

PAGDEN, A (2001), *Peoples and Empires: Europeans and the Rest of the World, from Antiquity to the Present* (London: Phoenix Press).

PHILLIMORE, R (1854–61), *Commentaries upon International Law*, 4 vols (London: WG Benning).

PUFENDORF, S (1934), *On the Law of Nature and Nations* (Oldfather, CH and Oldfather, WA (trans)) (Oxford: Clarendon Press).

RUSSELL, FH (1975), *The Just War in the Middle Ages* (Cambridge: Cambridge University Press).

SCELLE, G (1932–34), *Précis de droit des gens*, 2 vols (Paris: Sirey).

SERENI, AP (1943), *The Italian Conception of International Law* (New York: Columbia University Press).

SIMPSON, G (2004), *Great Powers and Outlaw States: Unequal Sovereigns in the International Legal Order* (Cambridge: Cambridge University Press).

SUÁREZ, F (1944), 'A Treatise on Laws and God the Lawgiver', in *Selections from Three Works of Francisco Suárez*, (Williams, GL, Brown, A and Waldron, J (trans)) (Oxford: Clarendon Press), pp 19–660.

TAYLOR, T (1992), *The Anatomy of the Nuremberg Trials: A Personal Memoir* (Boston: Little, Brown).

TUCHMAN, B (1966), *The Proud Tower: A Portrait of the World Before the War* (Dobbs Ferry, NY: Ballantine).

TUCK, R (1999), *The Rights of War and Peace: Political Thought and the International Order from Grotius to Kant* (Oxford: Oxford University Press).

TUNKIN, GI (1974), *Theory of International Law* (Butler, WE (trans)) (Cambridge, Mass: Harvard University Press).

VERDROSS, A (1927), 'Le fondement du droit international', 16 *Recueil des Cours* (Academy of International Law) 247–323.

WATTERS, WE (1970), *An International Affair: Non-intervention in the Spanish Civil War* (New York: Simon and Schuster).

WHEATON, H (1866) in Dana, RH (ed) (1936), *Elements of International Law*, 8th edn (Oxford: Oxford University Press).

WOLFF, C (1737), *Cosmologia Generalis*, 2nd edn (Frankfurt: Officini Libraria Rengeriana).

—— (1934), *The Law of Nations Treated According to a Scientific Method* (Drake, JH (trans)) (Oxford: Clarendon Press).

FURTHER READING

BEDERMAN, DJ (2001), *International Law in Antiquity* (Cambridge: Cambridge University Press), very ably covers the ancient Near East, together with classical Greece and Rome.

DE VISSCHER, C (1968), *Theory and Reality in Public International Law*, 2nd edn (Princeton: Princeton University Press), has a section at the beginning, providing an excellent survey of the history of international law, focusing on doctrine and ideas.

EHRLICH, L (1962), 'The Development of International Law as a Science,' 105 *Recueil des Cours* (Academy of International Law) 173-265, provides a very good overview of the intellectual history of the field.

FASSBENDER, B and PETERS, A (eds) (2012), *Oxford Handbook of the History of International Law* (Oxford: Oxford University Press) is a massive collection of articles, more thematically than chronologically organized, largely on the post-medieval period.

GREWE, WG (2000), *The Epochs of International Law* (Byers, M (trans)) (Berlin: Walter de Gruyter), is a general historical survey of international law, focusing on State practice and having a generally political slant.

GUGGENHEIM, P (1958), 'Contributions à l'histoire des sources du droit des gens,' 94 *Recueil des Cours* (Academy of International Law) 1–84, is very enlightening on the key debates, and rival schools of thought, concerning the sources of international law through history.

HINSLEY, FH (1986), *Sovereignty*, 2nd edn (Cambridge: Cambridge University Press), is an excellent survey of the evolution of ideas and conceptions of sovereignty over the centuries. It is particularly strong on the medieval period.

JOHNSTON, DM (2008), *The Historical Foundations of World Order: The Tower and the Arena* (Leiden: Martinus Nijhoff), is a massive work that focuses chiefly on State practice.

JOUANNET, E (2012), *The Liberal-welfarist Law of Nations: A History of International Law* (Cambridge: Cambridge University Press) is an intellectual history, covering the period from the eighteenth century onwards.

KOSKENNIEMI, M (2001), *The Gentle Civilizer of Nations: The Rise and Fall of International Law 1870–1960* (Cambridge: Cambridge University Press) contains a vast wealth of information on continental European (particularly French and German) thought in the nineteenth and early twentieth centuries.

NUSSBAUM, A (1954), *A Concise History of the Law of Nations*, rev edn (New York: Macmillan) is a very broad-brush general historical survey of international law, concentrating largely on doctrine.

ORAKHELASHVILI, A (ed) (2011), *Research Handbook on the Theory and History of International Law* (Cheltenham: Edward Elgar), has more on theory than on history, but a broad survey of the subject, from the Middle Ages onward, is provided.

PAGDEN, A (2001), *Peoples and Empires: Europeans and the Rest of the World, from Antiquity to the Present* (London: Phoenix Press), is a sweeping survey of the historical (including the legal) evolution of imperialism, with careful attention to legal issues.

TUCK, R (1999), *The Rights of War and Peace: Political Thought and the International Order from Grotius to Kant* (Oxford: Oxford University Press), examines international law in the seventeenth and eighteenth centuries, concentrating on the doctrines of the major thinkers rather than on State practice.

The following works trace the history of certain topics:

ANAND, RP (1983), *Origin and Development of the Law of the Sea: History of International Law Revisited* (The Hague: Martinus Nijhoff).

DHOKALIA, RP (1970), *The Codification of Public International Law* (Manchester: Manchester University Press).

FREY, LS and FREY, ML (1999), *The History of Diplomatic Immunity* (Columbus, OH: Ohio University Press).

ISHAY, MR (2008), *The History of Human Rights: From Ancient Times to the Globalization Era* (Berkeley: University of California Press).

NEFF, SC (1990), *Friends But No Allies: Economic Liberalism and the Law of Nations* (New York: Columbia University Press).

—— (2000), *The Rights and Duties of Neutrals: A General History* (Manchester: Manchester University Press).

—— (2005), *War and the Law of Nations: A General History* (Cambridge: Cambridge University Press).

NIJMAN, JE (2004), *The Concept of International Legal Personality: An Inquiry into the History and Theory of International Law* (The Hague: TMC Asser Press).

RALSTON, JH (1929), *International Arbitration from Athens to Locarno* (London: Oxford University Press).

2

WHAT IS INTERNATIONAL LAW FOR?

Martti Koskenniemi

SUMMARY

The objectives of international law appear differently depending on one's standpoint. International law certainly seeks to realize the political values, interests, and preferences of various international actors. But it also appears as a standard of criticism and means of controlling those in powerful positions. Instrumentalism and formalism connote two opposite sensibilities of what it means to be an international lawyer, and two cultures of professional practice, the stereotypes of 'the advisor' to a powerful actor with many policy-alternatives and 'the judge' scrutinizing the legality of a particular international behaviour. Beyond pointing to the oscillation between instrumentalism and formalism as styles of legal thought and practice, however, the question 'what is international law for?' also invokes popular aspirations about peace, justice, and human rights, and thus acts as a platform for an international political community. Whatever its shortcomings, international law also exists as a promise of justice, and thus as encouragement for political transformation.

I. THE PARADOX OF OBJECTIVES

Attempting to answer the question in the title one first meets with a familiar paradox. On the one hand, it seems indisputable that international law 'has a general function to fulfil, namely to safeguard international peace, security and justice in relations between States' (Tomuschat, 1999, p 23). Or as Article 1 of the UN Charter puts it, the organization has the purpose to 'be a centre for harmonizing the actions of nations in the attainment of...common ends' such as international peace and security, friendly relations among nations, and international cooperation. Such objectives seem self-evident and have never been seriously challenged. On the other hand, it is hard to see how or why they could be challenged—or indeed why one should be enthusiastic about them—because they exist at such high level of abstraction as to fail to indicate concrete preferences for action. What do 'peace', 'security', or 'justice' really mean? As soon as such words are defined more closely, disagreement emerges. To say that international law aims at peace *between States* is perhaps already to have narrowed down its scope unacceptably. Surely it must also seek to advance 'human rights as well as the rule of law domestically inside States for the benefit of human beings...' (Tomuschat, 1999, p 23). But what if advancing human rights would call for the destruction of an unjust peace?

In the end, very little seems to depend on any general response to the question 'what is international law for?'. The real problem seems always to be less about whether international law should aim for 'peace', 'security', or 'human rights' than about how to resolve interpretative controversies over or conflicts between such notions that emerge when defending or attacking particular policies. There is no disagreement about the objective of peace in the Middle East between Israel and the Palestinian people. But if asked what 'peace' might mean for them, the protagonists would immediately give mutually exclusive answers. Nor is the 'Asian values' debate about being 'for' or 'against' human rights but about what such rights might be and how they should be translated into social practices in the relevant societies. Therefore, to inquire about the objectives of international law is to study the political preferences of international actors—what it is that *they* wish to attain by international law. And because those preferences differ, the answer to the question in the title can only either remain controversial or be formulated in such broad terms as to contain the controversy within itself—in which case it is hard to see how it could be used to resolve it.

It would thus be wrong to think of the paradox of objectives as a technical problem that could be disposed of by reflecting more closely on the meaning of words such as 'peace', 'security', or 'justice' or by carrying out more sophisticated social or economic analyses about the way the international world is or indeed by drafting definitions of such words in legal instruments. Such notions provide an acceptable response to the question 'what is international law for?' precisely because of their ability to gloss over existing disagreement about political choices and distributional priorities. If they did not work in this way, and instead permanently preferred some choices over other choices, they would no longer provide the neutral platform for peaceful political argument that we expect of them. In accordance with the founding myth of the system, the Peace of Westphalia in 1648 laid the basis for an agnostic, procedural international law whose merit consisted in its refraining from imposing any external normative ideal on the international society. The objectives of that society would now arise from itself and not from any religious, moral or political notions of the good given externally to it. If there is an 'international community', it is a practical association not designed to realize ultimate ends but to coordinate action to further the objectives of existing communities.[1] Sovereign equality builds on this: because there are no natural ends, every member of the international society is free to decide on its own ends, and to that extent, they are all equal. The law that governs them is not natural but artificial, created by the sovereigns through the processes that are acceptable because neutral (see eg Nardin, 1983). To say that international law is for 'peace', 'security', and 'justice' is to say that it is for peace, security, and justice *as agreed and understood between the members of the system.*[2]

What this means for international legal argument can be gleaned, for instance, from the opinion of the International Court of Justice in the *Reservations* case (1951). Here the Court was called upon to examine the admissibility of reservations to the 1948 Convention on the Prevention and Punishment of the Crime of Genocide. The Court first outlined what seemed a natural consequence of the principles of neutrality and sovereignty, namely

---

[1] This is why it is so easy to discuss it in terms of the ethics of Immanuel Kant, an ethics of universalizable principles of *right action* rather than as instrumental guidelines for attaining the Good. Cf, eg O'Neill, 2000.

[2] Henkin writes that instead of 'human values', the system is centred upon 'State values' (Henkin, 1989, p 109). This polemical contrast undermines the degree to which States—including principles of sovereignty and non-interference—find their moral justification in late-eighteenth century liberal individualism and the ideal of national self-rule: 'State values' persist because they channel 'human values' within a political community. See also Paulus, 2001, pp 69–97.

that no reservation should be effective against a State that has not agreed to it. To stay with this understanding, however, might have undermined the Convention by creating a system in which some reservations were in force in regard to some States (namely those accepting them) but not against others, while each non-accepting State would be free to regard the reservation-making State as not a party to the Convention at all. This would have gone against the universal nature of the Convention. Thus, the Court continued, a State having made a reservation that has been objected to by some of the parties, may still be held a party to the Convention if the reservation is compatible with the 'object and purpose' of the Convention. At this point, then, the Court moved to think of the law expressly in terms of its objectives. However, there were no objectives to the Convention that were independent from the objectives of the *parties* to the Convention. Thus, it was up to each party to make the determination 'individually and from its own standpoint'.[3]

Such an argument defines the objectives of international law in terms of the objectives of the (sovereign) members of the international society—in this case the society formed by the parties to the Genocide Convention—bringing to the fore two types of problems: what will happen in cases where States disagree about the objectives? And why would only State objectives count?

II. CONVERGING INTERESTS?

If no antecedent order establishes a firm priority between what States want, then any controversy about them either will have to remain open or we shall have to assume that the procedure in which the disagreement is revealed will somehow be able to dispose of it to the satisfaction of all. The latter suggestion embodies the idea of the 'harmony of interests', the presence of an underlying convergence between apparently conflicting State preferences. Under this view, any actual dispute would always be only superficial. At a deeper level, State interests would coalesce and the objective of international law would then be to lead from the former level to the latter.[4]

It is difficult to defend this view against realist criticisms. Why would harmony, instead of conflict, be the true nature of international politics? What evidence is there that, rightly understood, the interests of States are compatible? Might the harmony not rather seem a form of wishful thinking that prevents people from clearly seeing where their interests lie, and acting accordingly? Hans Morgenthau, one of the fathers of realist thought in international affairs, attacked the inter-war legalism precisely for having made this mistake. To believe in harmony under the League of Nations had left the world unprepared for Hitler's aggression in 1939 (Morgenthau, 1940, pp 261–84). EH Carr, another powerful realist thinker, described the harmony as an ideological smokescreen: 'Biologically and economically, the doctrine of the harmony of interests was tenable only if you left out of

---

[3] *Reservations to the Convention on the Prevention and Punishment of the Crime of Genocide*, Advisory *Opinion, ICJ Reports 1951*, p 15 at p 26.

[4] This argument, always implicit in moral objectivism and theories of natural law, was made in a dramatic way by Hersch Lauterpacht, speaking at Chatham House in 1941, as bombs were falling over Coventry and his family was being destroyed by the Nazis in Poland: 'The disunity of the modern world is a fact; but so, in a truer sense, is its unity. Th[e] essential and manifold solidarity, coupled with the necessity of securing the rule of law and the elimination of war, constitutes a harmony of interests which has a basis more real and tangible than the illusions of the sentimentalist or the hypocrisy of those satisfied with the existing *status quo*. The ultimate harmony of interests which within the State finds expression in the elimination of private violence is not a misleading invention of nineteenth century liberalism' (Lauterpacht, 1975, p 26).

account the interest of the weak who must be driven to the wall, or called in the next world to redress the balance of the present' (Carr, 1946, p 50).

International lawyers have responded to such criticisms in two ways. Some have accepted that only a marginal scope is left by power to law and defined any existing legal regimes as variables dependent on a central power (Schmitt, 1988; Grewe, 2001), or have developed purely instrumental accounts of the use of law in the defence of particular interests or preferences (McDougal, 1953, pp 137–259; Goldsmith and Posner, 2005). Others have sought to articulate the harmony under a more elaborate theory of interdependence or globalization: 'International trade and commerce, international finance, international communication—*all* are essential to the survival of States, and *all* require an international legal system to provide a stable framework within which they may function' (Watts, 2000, p 7). Institutional, procedural, and even linguistic theories have been used to argue that even the articulation of State interests is based on legal notions such as 'sovereignty', 'treaty', and 'binding force' that delimit and define what may count as State interests or even State identity in the first place.[5] In other words, many lawyers have in fact accepted the political realists' premise (that international law is completely determined by power) but seek to show either that power cannot have its way without international law or that it is in fact useful for everyone that some issues are left to be settled in a predetermined procedural framework.

A first thing to be said about this is that it does highlight that the opposition between 'realism' and 'idealism' is only of limited usefulness. The labels invoke contrasting political sensibilities and different jurisprudential techniques that often merge into each other. Even the hardest 'realism' reveals itself as a moral position (for example by highlighting the priority of the national interest) inasmuch as, 'philosophically speaking, realism is unthinkable without the background of a prior idealistic position deeply committed to the universalism of the Enlightenment and democratic political theory' (Guzzini, 1998, p 16). On the other hand, any serious idealism is able to point to aspects of international reality that support it, and needs such reference in order to seem professionally credible. Much of the realism-idealism controversy is in fact about what element of a many-faceted 'reality' should be chosen as the starting point of one's analysis. Progress in the discipline of international law has then occurred by a new generation of lawyers rejecting the previous one as either 'utopian' because excessively idealist or as 'apologist' because too impressed by sovereign power. These critiques are as available today as they were a century ago. Care must be taken not to associate any position or doctrine permanently with either: 'idealism' and 'realism' are best understood as forms of critique and channels for institutional reform in accordance with particular political sensibilities. They are crudely simplifying disciplinary labels, more useful for polemical than analytic purposes.

The second noteworthy aspect of this strategy is that in approving the realist premises it may in fact concede too much—namely that there are definable (political) interests or objectives that legal rules should only seek to realize. But this may often in fact not be the case (as will be discussed below). In such cases, there is no 'prior' realm of the political to which the law should always pay deference. In fact the determination of the political objective or interest is not independent from seeking to find the legally plausible way of dealing with a matter.[6]

---

[5] This is the 'constructivist' explanation of international law's impact on States, much used today in international relations studies. See, eg Finnemore, 1996. For a discussion, see Brunnee and Toope, 2000, pp 19–74; Kratochwil, 2000, pp 55–59.

[6] This is one of the central arguments in Koskenniemi, 2005.

Many lawyers—and increasingly often political theorists—have, however, made a more ambitious defence of international law. They have argued that, however neutral in regard to political principles, the structure of international law is not devoid of an autonomous normative direction. In their view, international law is accompanied by a cunning logic that slowly socializes initially egoistic States into the law's internationalist spirit.[7] It is possible (though not necessary) to picture this ethic as the 'inner morality of law' that accompanies any serious commitment to work in a legal system.[8] An alternative but parallel approach would be to characterize the system in terms of a 'culture of civility' shared by its administrators and excluding certain types of secrecy, dishonesty, fraud, or manipulation. Such an explanation resonates with international law's emergence in the late nineteenth century as an aspect of optimistic evolutionism among the liberal élites of Europe and North America. It is to assume that by entering into the processes it provides, States come to define not only their objectives but perhaps even their identity by principles offered by international law (Koskenniemi, 2001a).

III. THE SIGNIFICANCE OF STATEHOOD

But the Westphalian myth leaves also unexplained why only *State objectives* count. Ever since Immanuel Kant published his essay on the *Perpetual Peace* (1795), philosophers, political theorists, and lawyers have routinely challenged the State-centrism of the international system, arguing that whatever instrumental value States may have for the coordination of affairs of particular communities, the 'ultimate' members of those communities are individuals and that many other human groups apart from States ('peoples', 'nations', 'minorities', 'international organizations', 'corporations') also play important roles (Westlake, 1910, p 16). Globalization and the crisis of sovereignty have intensified the criticisms of international law as State law from sociological, functional, and ethical standpoints. These critiques have often sought to project a material value or an idea of social justice outside of statehood that they suggest should be enforced by international law (Koskenniemi, 1994, pp 22–9).

The universalizing vocabularies of human rights, liberalism, economic and ecological interdependence have no doubt complicated inter-sovereign law by the insertion of public law notions such as *jus cogens* and 'obligations owed to the international community as a whole' and by 'fragmenting' the international system into functional institutions (see Section VIII below). But no alternative to statehood has emerged. None of the normative directions—human rights, economic or environmental values, religious ideals—has been able to establish itself in a dominating position. On the contrary, what these values may mean and how conflicts between them should be resolved is decided largely through 'Westphalian' institutions. This is not to say that new institutions would not enjoy a degree of autonomy from their members. Human rights and many economic and environmental regimes provide examples of such. The EU has developed into an autonomous system that functions largely outside the frame of international law. How far these other regimes are

---

[7] A defence of the view that law socializes States not by constraint but by 'compliance strategies [that] seek to remove obstacles, clarify issues, and convince parties to change their behavior', as well as by 'various manifestations of disapproval: exposure, shaming, and diffuse impacts on the reputations and international relationships of a resisting party', is found in Chayes and Chayes, 1995, pp 109, 110. A more recent, proceduralist defence, insisting on the moral core of the international legal process is Habermas, 2004.

[8] The point about law necessarily containing certain 'aspirations of excellence' without which an order would not be recognized as 'law' in the first place, is made, of course, in Fuller, 1969, especially pp 41–94.

from that of the EU can, however, be gleaned from the characterization of the WTO system by the Appellate Body in the *Alcoholic Beverages* case (1996):

> The *WTO Agreement* is a treaty—the international equivalent of a contract. It is self-evident that in an exercise of their sovereignty, and in pursuit of their own respective national interests, the Members of the WTO have made a bargain. In exchange for the benefits they expect to derive as members of the WTO they have agreed to exercise their sovereignty according to commitments they have made in the *WTO Agreement*.[9]

This outlook was reaffirmed by the International Court of Justice in the *Nuclear Weapons Advisory Opinion* in 1996. In response to the question about the lawfulness of the threat or use of such weapons, the Court concluded that whatever the consequences, it could not exclude that such use would be lawful 'in an extreme circumstance of self-defence, when the very survival of a State would be at stake'.[10] 'Benefits' to the States and State survival remain the highest objectives of the system. Bodies such as the European Court of Human Rights or the UN Human Rights Committee recognize that the treaties they administer function in a State-centred world: the margin of appreciation and the wide scope of derogations allow for national security reasons if 'necessary in a democratic society' to operate with notions of 'security' and 'democracy' that are embedded in a world of States.[11]

The defence of international law's State-centredness is thoroughly practical. 'Stated quite simply', James Brierly once wrote, 'what [international law] tries to do is to define or delimit the respective spheres within which each of the... States into which the world is divided for political purposes is entitled to exercise its authority' (Brierly, 1944, p 3). Little of this justification has changed. A form and a process is needed that channels interpretative conflicts into peaceful avenues. This is not to say that non-State values such as 'human rights', 'efficient economies', 'clean environment', or 'democracy' would be unworthy objectives of political action. Disagreement about them provides the life and blood of international politics. The defenders of the State-system would only add that such values conflict and that 'States alone have provided the structures of authority needed to cope with the incessant claims of competing social groups and to provide public justice essential to social order and responsibility' (Schachter, 1997, p 22). States may be set aside, of course, by consent or revolution but there are dangers in such transformations, some of which are well known, and something about those dangers results from the single-mindedness of the teleologies pursued by the institutions seeking to replace statehood.

On the other hand, there is no doubt that international politics is far from the Westphalian ideal. The informal networks and epistemic communities that influence international developments beyond the rigid forms of sovereign equality are populated by experts from the developed West. It is hard to justify the attention given and the resources allocated to the 'fight against terrorism' in the aftermath of the attacks on New York and Washington in September 2001 in which nearly 3,000 people lost their lives, while simultaneously six million children under five years old die annually of malnutrition by causes

---

[9] *Japan—Taxes on Alcoholic Beverages*, Appellate Body Report (AB–1996–2) DSR 1996: I p 108 (4 October 1996).

[10] *Legality of the Threat or Use of Nuclear Weapons, Advisory Opinion, ICJ Reports 1996*, p 226, paras 96, 101(E).

[11] Or in other words, these mechanisms are only subsidiary: 'The [European Convention on Human Rights] leaves to each contracting State... the task of securing the rights and freedoms it enshrines', *Handyside v UK*, Judgment of 7 December 1976, Ser A, no 24, 1 *EHRR* 737, para 48. As Susan Marks points out, liberal reformers conceive of 'democratization' in terms of reform of *domestic* (and not international) institutions (Marks, 2000, pp 76–100).

that could be prevented by existing economic and technical resources.[12] What becomes a 'crisis' in the world and will involve the political energy and resources of the international system is determined in a thoroughly Western-dominated process (Charlesworth, 2002; Orford, 2003).

It is widely believed that the informal and fluid economic, technological, and cultural processes often termed 'governance' rather than 'government' strengthen the political position of the most powerful actors—transnational networks, large corporations, Western developed States—and marginalize public international law (eg Hurrell and Woods, 1999; Arnaud, 2003). Weak States despair over their inability to hold on to achieved positions and privileges by the antiquated rhetoric of sovereignty. But the latter's awkward defence of the conservative system of sovereign equality undermines the extent to which globalization may also open avenues for contestatory transgovernmental action within international civil society, or by what Hardt and Negri call the 'multitude' (Hardt and Negri, 1999, pp 393–413). There is room for conflict and consensus both *within* and *beyond* the Westphalian system and little political worth lies in deciding *a priori* in favour of either. Formal rules as well as anti-formal objectives and standards may each be used for progressive or conservative causes.[13] The choice of technique must reflect a historically informed assessment of the effect of particular institutional alternatives.

In the following sections I will try respond to the question 'what is international law for?' by describing its role in a world that is not one of pre-established harmony or struggle but of both cooperation *and* conflict simultaneously. I will argue that international law operates—and should operate—as an instrument for advancing particular claims and agendas *as well as* a relatively autonomous formal technique. This is not to claim political neutrality. Much instrumental thinking about international law today adopts the point of view of the decision-maker in a relatively prosperous State or transnational network, in possession of resources and policy-options and seeking guidance on how to fit their objectives within international legality—or to overrule legality with minimal cost. Clearly, international law exists 'for' such decision-makers. But it should not exist exclusively for them. My argument is that there is often a reason to adopt a 'formalist' view on international law that refuses to engage with the question of its objectives precisely in order to constrain those in powerful positions. The question 'what is international law for?' needs to be rescued from the context of legal routines and re-instated in the political arenas where it can be used to articulate claims by those who are sidelined from formal diplomacy and informal networks and feel that something about the routines of both is responsible for the deprivations they suffer. In other words, there is reason to defend a legal 'formalism' against a 'pragmatism' that views international law only in terms of the immediate objectives it serves. In order to do that, however, it is necessary first to outline the power of pragmatism.

IV. INTO PRAGMATISM?

The paradox of objectives shows that the formal law of Westphalia cannot be replaced by social objectives or ethical principles without invoking controversies that exist in regard to the latter. 'Whoever invokes humanity wants to cheat', Carl Schmitt once wrote (Schmitt,

---

[12] 'The State of Food Insecurity in the World 2002', http://www.fao.org/DOCREP/005/Y7352e/Y7352e00.HTM (last visited 24 October 2002).

[13] For the varying use of the rule/principle, opposition in self-determination arguments about change, participation, and community, see Knop, 2002, pp 29–49.

1996, p 54), citing the nineteenth-century French socialist Pierre Joseph Proudhon and making a useful point about the use of abstract humanitarianism to label one's political adversary as an enemy of humanity so as to justify extreme measures against him—a point that applied in today's context 'lacks neither lucidity nor relevance' (Kervégan, 1999, p 61). One need not think only of the extreme case of the 'war against terrorism' to canvass the slippery slope from anti-formal reasoning to human rights violation. Quite everyday legal argument assumes the analytical priority of the reasons for the law over the form of the law in a fashion that underwrites Stanley Fish's perceptive dictum: 'once you start down the anti-formalist road, there is no place to stop' (Fish, 1989, p 2).

For example, the right of self-defence under Article 51 of the Charter is formally conditioned by the presence of an 'armed attack'. But what about the case of a *threat* of attack by mass destruction weapons? Here we are tempted to look for guidance from the objective of Article 51. The rationale for allowing self-defence lies, presumably, in the objective of protecting the State. Surely we cannot expect a State to wait for an attack if this would bring about precisely the consequence—the destruction of the State—that the rule was intended to prevent. Because the rule itself is no more valuable than the reason for its existence, we erase the condition of prior armed attack and entitle the State to act in an anticipatory way.[14] Or the other way around: surely formal sovereignty should not be a bar for humanitarian intervention against a tyrannical regime; in oppressing its own population, the State undermines its sovereignty. We honour 'sovereignty' as an expression of a people's self-rule. If instead of self-rule there is oppression, then it would seem nonsensical to allow formal sovereignty to constitute a bar to intervention in support of the people.[15]

Such arguments are based on a thoroughly pragmatic-instrumentalist view of the law, a view that highlights that we do not honour the law because of the sacred aura of its text or its origin but because it enables us to reach valuable human purposes. We follow the emission reduction schedule of chlorofluorocarbons (CFCs) in Article 2 of the 1987 Montreal Protocol on the Protection of the Ozone Layer because we assume that it will reduce the depletion of the ozone layer and the incidence of skin cancer. We honour the domestic jurisdiction clause in Article 2(7) of the UN Charter because we assume it upholds the ability of self-determining communities to lead the kinds of life they choose. But what if it were shown that ozone depletion or skin cancer bears no relationship to the emissions of CFCs, or that domestic jurisdiction merely shields the arbitrary reign of tyrants? In such cases we would immediately look for an equitable exception or a counter-rule so as to avoid the—now unnecessary—costs that would be incurred by bowing to the empty form of the original rule. Article 10(1) of the European Convention on Human Rights provides for freedom of speech. If applying the right would enable the distribution of fascist propaganda, it is always possible to interfere and prohibit it by the counter-rule in Article 10(2) that enables the 'prevention of disorder or crime' and to ensure 'the protection of morals', with a margin of appreciation lying with State authorities. Enabling those authorities to protect 'national security' is indispensable if they are to secure the liberal rights-regime. Yet, because setting the 'balance' between security and rights lies with the authorities against whom the rights-regime was established, the door to abuse remains open (see Cameron, 2000, pp 62–8).

---

[14] This is the argument for the 'Bush doctrine' of pre-emptive self-defence, as made in the US security strategy, published on 20 September 2002. Cf the text in, eg *Financial Times*, 21 September 2002, p 4.

[15] This position is often combined with the argument for pro-democratic intervention. For useful analysis, see Chesterman, 2001, pp 88–111.

We often allow the reason for the rule to override the rule. We do this because we believe the rule itself has no intrinsic worth. If it fails to support the purpose for which it was enacted—or worse, prevents its attainment—why should it be honoured? In domestic society, abstract law-obedience can be defended in view of the routine nature of the cases that arise, and the dangers attached to entitling citizens to think for themselves. Such arguments are weak in the international realm where situations of law-application are few, and disadvantages of obedience often significant. Few States that were economically or politically dependent on Iraq fully implemented the sanctions set up in 1990. Though they were in formal breach of Articles 25 and 48 of the Charter, the UN preferred to look the other way. The EU is not going to give up the prohibition of importation of hormone-treated meat merely because a WTO dispute-settlement organ may have decided it should do so. The importance of the interest in living peacefully with a powerful neighbour and of deciding on national health standards vastly outweighs any consideration about the importance of abstract law-obedience (see Koskenniemi, 2001b).

And yet, there is a dark side to such pragmatic instrumentalism. A legal technique that reaches directly to law's purposes is either compelled to think that it can access the right purpose in some politics-independent fashion—in which case it would stand to defend its implicit moral naturalism—or it transforms itself to a licence for those powers in a position to realize their own purposes to do precisely that. In this way, pragmatism inculcates a heroic mindset: we *can* do it! It is the mindset of well-placed, powerful actors, confident in their possessing the 'right' purpose, the mindset that drove Stalin to collectivization, or Israel to destroy the Osiraq nuclear power plant in 1981. It is the mindset of the civilizing mission and of 'regime change' by force if necessary.

Instrumental action may or may not be acceptable in view of the circumstances and its advisability is typically the object of political controversy. But the instrumentalist mindset—the readiness to act as soon as that seems what one believes useful or good—creates a consistent bias in favour of dominant actors with many policy-alternatives from which to choose and sufficient resources to carry out their objectives.[16] To always look for reasons, instead of rules, liberates public authorities to follow their reasoning, and their purposes—hence their frequent aversion against rules in the first place: the International Criminal Court, disarmament or human rights treaties, environmental or law of the sea regimes, and so on (see Byers and Nolte, 2003).

The difficulty with the instrumentalist mindset is that there never are simple, well-identified objectives behind formal rules. Rules are legislative compromises, open-ended and bound in clusters expressing conflicting considerations. To refer to objectives is to tell the law-applier: 'please choose'. There is no doubt that Article 2(4) of the UN Charter aims towards 'peace'. Yet it is equally certain that most people disagree on what 'peace' might mean in a particular case. This is not only about semantic uncertainty. Even apparently unobjectionable objectives such as 'peace' contain a paradox. To be in favour of 'peace' cannot, for example, mean that nobody can ever take up arms. 'Perhaps the most serious problem with outlawing force is that sometimes it is both necessary and desirable' (Watts, 2000, p 10). The UN Charter expressly allows for the use of military force under the authority of the Security Council or in pursuance of the right of self-defence. The positive law of the Charter is both pacifist and militarist—and receives its acceptability by such schizophrenia. Without something like a right to use force in self-defence, aggression would always be rewarded. The European Convention on Human Rights seeks to protect individuals' rights to both freedom and security. But one person's freedom often conflicts

---

[16] For a description of instrumentalism as a culture, see Binder, 1988, pp 906–909.

with another's security. Whether or not authorities should be entitled to censor prisoners' letters or prohibit the publication of obscene materials, for instance, cannot be reached through instrumental reasoning that would be independent from a political choice (see Koskenniemi, 2000, pp 99–106). The will of the drafters *is* the language of the instrument. Beyond that, there is only speculation about what might be a good (acceptable, workable, realistic, or fair) way to apply it.

Practitioners usually understand international law as being more about routine application of standard solutions, ad hoc accommodation, and compromise than discourse about large objectives. Providing advice to a non-governmental organization or drafting judgments at the International Court of Justice are usually held to require pragmatic reconciliation of conflicting considerations, balancing between 'equitable principles', conflicting rights, or other prima facie relevant aspects of the case at hand. Settlement of the conflicts during the dissolution of the Former Yugoslavia in the early 1990s was understood to involve the balancing of conflicting considerations about stability of frontiers and expectations of just change, managing the *uti possidetis* principle together with minority rights for populations left on the wrong side of the boundary.[17] The balance struck between these considerations was in no way dictated by the law but reflected the negotiators' pragmatic assessment of what might work (Lâm, 2000, pp 141–51). At the European Court of Human Rights, individual freedoms are constantly weighted against the need for interference by public authorities. It is established case-law that 'an interference must achieve a "fair balance" between the demands of the general interests of the community and the requirements of the protection of the individual's fundamental rights'.[18] In a like manner, the law concerning the delimitation of frontier areas or the sharing of natural resources resolves itself into a more or less flexible cluster of considerations about distributive justice—sometimes described in an altogether open-ended fashion in terms of 'equitable principles' or 'equitable use'—in view of attaining a pragmatically acceptable end-result.[19] And hard cases within the laws of war invariably turn into a contextual assessment of what number of non-combatant casualties might still be within the limits of proportionality by reference to the military objective (military experts and humanitarian lawyers agreeing on the need to 'calculate' (see Kennedy, 2004)).

Few international lawyers think of their craft as the application of pre-existing formal rules or great objectives. What rules are applied, and how, which interpretative principles are used and whether to invoke the rule or the exception—including many other techniques—all point to pragmatic weighing of conflicting considerations in particular cases (Corten, 1997). What is sought is something practical, perhaps the 'fairness' of the outcome, as Thomas M Franck has suggested. Under this image, law is not about peace *or* justice, freedom *or* security, stability *or* change, but always about both one *and* the other simultaneously. 'The tension between stability and change, if not managed, can disorder the system. Fairness is the rubric under which the tension is discursively managed' (Franck, 1995, p 7). The lawyer's task is now seen in terms of contextual 'wisdom', or 'prudence', rather than the employment of formal techniques.[20] In a fluid, fragmented world,

---

[17] See Opinions 2 and 3 of the Arbitration Commission of the Peace Conference on the Former Yugoslavia (1992) 31 *ILM* 1497–1500.

[18] *Fredin* v *Sweden*, Judgment of 18 February 1991, Ser A, no 192, 13 *EHRR* 784, para 51; *Lopez Ostra* v *Spain*, Judgment of 9 December 1994, Ser A, no 303–C, 20 *EHRR* 277, para 51.

[19] See eg Separate Opinion of Judge Jiménez de Aréchaga, *Continental Shelf (Tunisia/Libyan Arab Jamahiriya), Judgment, ICJ Reports 1982*, p 18, pp 103–108 (paras 11–31) and, eg the International Convention on the Non-Navigational Uses of International Watercourses, A/RES/51/229 (8 July 1997). I have analysed this 'turn to equity' in, among other places, Koskenniemi, 1999b, pp 27–50.

[20] For a celebration of judicial creativity in this regard, see Lauterpacht, 1958.

everything hinges on the sensitivity of the practising lawyer to the pull of contextually relevant considerations.

V. A TRADITION OF ANTI-FORMALISM

The move to pragmatism emerges from a series of recurrent criticisms of international law's alleged 'formalism'. Pragmatism was supported in the last third of the nineteenth century by the use of a flexible notion of 'civilization' that enabled liberal lawyers to look beyond diplomatic protocol and an outdated natural law. The inter-war lawyers attacked the formalism of sovereignty they projected on pre-war doctrines and advocated (as conservatives) 'tradition' and (as progressives) 'interdependence' as bases for their prag- matic commitment. After the next war, reformist lawyers indicted what they described as the legalistic formalism of the League basing their 'realism' on Cold War themes, either expressly in favour of the West or in a more social-democratic way to support interna- tional institutions (see Kennedy, 2000, pp 380–87). Legal realism always had its Hawks and its Doves but for both, it seemed useful to criticize old law for its 'formalism' in order to support 'dynamic' political change.

Interdisciplinary studies in the 1990s highlighted the extent to which the formal validity of a standard was independent from its compliance pull (see, eg Shelton, 2000). As the law was seen instrumentally, its formality seemed to bear no particular merit: 'hard law' was just one choice among other possible regulative techniques, including soft standards or the absence of any standards at all in cases where the imposition of one's preference seemed within the limits of the possible and preferable given that it might 'minimise transaction and sovereignty costs'.[21] In such debates formal law has nobody speaking in its favour and is indicted as a utopianism supporting conservative causes. Anti-formalism is always a call for transformation: to overrule existing law either because it does not really exist at all, or if it does, because it should not. The debate on soft law and *jus cogens* in the 1980s and 1990s manifested both of these criticisms and Prosper Weil's famous analysis of the pathologi- cal problems (the 'dilution' and 'graduation' of normativity) introduced in international law by such notions were unpersuasive to anti-formalist critics who wanted to realize the good society *now* and had no doubt that they knew how to go about this (see Weil, 1983; Tasioulas, 1996). Avant-garde instrumentalism at the beginning of a new century reads like German public law conservatism a hundred years earlier: over every international rule hangs the sword of *clausula rebus sic stantibus* (see Kaufmann, 1911).

What makes the formalism/anti-formalism debate suspect is the extent to which *any- thing* may be and has been attacked as 'formalism' (see Kennedy, 2001). The following views, at least, have been so targeted:

(a) rationalistic natural-law theories;

(b) views emphasizing the importance of (formal) sovereignty;

---

[21] For a particularly straightforward instrumental approach, see Posner, 2003. An interdisciplinary research on the recent 'move to law' uses a method of assessing 'legalization' by reference to the standards' obligatory nature, precision, and the presence of a centralized authority. The project examines 'legalization' instrumentally, by concentrating on the conditions under which it constitutes a rational choice. See, eg, Abbott and Snidal, 2001, pp 37–72. Such instrumentalism is not neutral: to assess law from the perspective of rational choice is to occupy the perspective of a small number of actors that actually may choose their options by agendas they set. It celebrates the managerial culture of Western experts at work to advance Western interests.

(c)   views limiting international law's scope to treaties or other (formal) expressions of consent;

(d)   views highlighting the importance of international institutions;

(e)   views emphasizing 'rigour' in law-application;

(f)   views stressing the significance of formal dispute-settlement;

(g)   views insisting on a clear boundary between law and politics.

The list is by no means exhaustive. In fact, anything can be labelled 'formalism' because the term is purely relational. When a speaker advocates something (a norm, a practice) by its material fullness, the opposite view will inevitably appear to be holding fast to the dead weight of some 'form'. The almost uniformly pejorative use of the term 'formalism' in international law reflects the predominance of the instrumentalist mindset in diplomacy and international politics. The way the legal idiom constructs and upholds the structures of diplomacy and politics is left invisible.

The contrast between instrumentalism and formalism is quite fundamental when seeking to answer the question 'what is international law for?' From the instrumental perspective, international law exists to realize objectives of some dominant part of the community; from the formalist perspective, it provides a platform to evaluate behaviour, including the behaviour of those in dominant positions. The instrumental perspective highlights the role of law as social engineering; formalism views it as an interpretative scheme. The instrumental perspective is typically that of an active and powerful actor in possession of alternative choices; formalism is often the perspective of the weak actor relying on law for protection.

If instrumentalism today needs no particular defence, it may be useful to highlight the twin virtues of formalism. First, it is indispensable. Every standard is always substantive and formal at the same time. The very ideas of treaty and codification make sense only if one assumes that at some point there emerges an agreement, an understanding, a standard that is separate from its legislative background. When States enter an agreement, or when some behaviour is understood to turn from habit into custom, the assumption is that something that was loose and disputed crystallizes into something that is fixed and no longer negotiable. The point of law is to give rise to standards that are no longer merely 'proposed' or 'useful' or 'good', and which therefore can be deviated from if one happens to share a deviating notion of what in fact is useful or good. This is what it means to say that in addition to their acceptability and effectiveness, legal rules are should also possess 'validity'. To accept that positive law enjoys that property is not to say anything about how it is recognized in individual rules or standards, nor indeed of whether any actual standard so recognized would possess any particular meaning as against some other putative meaning. Validity indicates a formal property that leaves the norm so characterized a flat, substanceless surface—but a surface without which no 'law' could exist at all.

Secondly, the fact that the legal form is a 'flat substanceless surface' is not politically insignificant. It does something to those it accepts as legal subjects. In a world without or 'before' international law, the acting persons or entities exist as subjects of interests and preferences, both liberated and weighed down by their irreducible particularity. The logic of a social structure between them is a logic of instrumentalism, each subject a *homo economicus*, poised to perpetuate the realization of its idiosyncratic preference. Such actors are completely controlled by the environmental conditions that make interest-fulfilment possible. For them, the external world—including other actors—has no meaning beyond interest-fulfilment: on its own, it is chaotic, incomprehensible. Paradoxically, however, a single-minded instrumentalism is bound to be frustrated in the end: at the mercy of

a dangerous and incomprehensible world where every action creates unforeseen consequences, and always falls short of satisfying the ever intensifying interests (eg Foucault,
2005, pp 280–81). This is one of the tragedies of the continuing war in Afghanistan.

By contrast, as legal subjects, actors, as it were, give up their particularity in order to
participate in what is general. By recourse to the medium of law that claims 'validity', they
are lifted from the tyranny of subjective interests and preferences. The *homo juridicus* in a
way decentralizes its own perspective, opening itself to the world at large. In other words,
and as thinkers as diverse as Kant, Foucault, and Habermas have pointed out, the political significance of formal law—that is, of law irrespective of what interests or preferences
particular legislation might seek to advance—is that it expresses the universalist principle
of inclusion at the outset, making possible the regulative ideal of a pluralistic international
world. (See Kant, 1999, pp 24–5; Foucault, 2005, pp 280–81; Habermas, 2004. See also
Supiot, 2005.) '[O]nly a regime of non-instrumental rules, understood to be authoritative
independent of particular beliefs or purposes is compatible with the freedom of its subjects to be different' (Nardin, 1998, p 31). The form of law constructs political adversaries
as equals, entitled to express their subjectively felt injustices in terms of breaches of the
rules of the community to which they belong no less than their adversaries—thus affirming both that inclusion and the principle that the conditions applying to the treatment of
any one member of the community must apply to every other member as well. In the end,
competent lawyers may disagree about what this means in practice. But the legal idiom
itself reaffirms the political pluralism that underlies the Rule of Law, however inefficiently
it has been put into effect. In fact, the failures in the international legal system are always
recognized and constructive projects formulated by a prior (though often undisclosed)
acceptance of the idea of the rule of formal law. Without that idea, much of the criticisms
we all make of the international political world would no longer make sense.

Of course, formal law does not apply itself. Between that form and any decision to project on it meaning 'x' instead of 'y', is a professional technique that may be more or less successful in expressing these regulative ideals. In particular, there is a constant push and pull
in the professional world between a *culture of instrumentalism* and a *culture of formalism*.
It would be wrong to associate this dialectic with fixed positions representing particular
interests or preferences. Instrumental action by lawyers is a necessary part of the search
for good rules or institutions beyond the *status quo*. And any present rules are always also
mechanisms to support particular interests and privileges. 'Power' and 'law' are entangled
in such complex ways that it is often pointless to interpret particular events as manifesting
either one or the other: power works through 'formal rules'—just like instead of 'naked
power', we see everywhere power defined, delimited, and directed by rules.

But the two cultures do play distinct political roles in particular historical situations.
As the debates around the fluid dynamism of globalization have demonstrated, formal
standards and institutions are often called upon to provide protection for weak actors,
and to pose demands on powerful ones.[22] Irrespective of its philosophical justification,
there is no magic about formalism as a legal practice, however. It may also come to but-
tress privilege, apathy, or both. Hence it is important also to focus on instrumentalism
and formalism as 'cultures', sensibilities, traditions and frameworks, sets of rituals and
self-understandings among institutional actors. As pointed out earlier, the 'heroic' mindset of the *homo economicus* that sees law only as an instrument for *my objectives* often
leads to collateral damage, frustration and tragedy. Against it, I would invoke a practice
of formalism, with its associated tropes about valid law, rights, and constitutionalism, less

---

[22] Out of a burgeoning literature, see, eg, Tsagourias, 2000; Koskenniemi, 2009.

as definite institutional models than as regulative ideals for a profession without which no community could rule itself by standards it recognizes as its own (instead of those of some influential faction). The idea of a universal law needs servants that define themselves administrators (instead of inventors) of universal standards—the class of lawyers. The traditions and practices of this class are significant only to the extent they remain attached to the 'flat, substanceless surface' of the law.

VI. INSTRUMENTALISM, FORMALISM, AND THE PRODUCTION OF AN INTERNATIONAL POLITICAL COMMUNITY

Modern international law puts the international lawyer at the heart of the legal system. It is possible to represent that position schematically by reference to the two types of logic at play in the international rule of law. Here is the international relations theorist Hedley Bull:

> The special interests of the dominant elements in a society are reflected in the way in which the rules are defined. Thus the particular kinds of limitations that are imposed on resort to violence, the kinds of agreements whose binding character is upheld, or the kinds of right to property that are enforced, will have the stamp of those dominant elements. But that there should be limits of some kind to violence, and an expectation in general that agreements should be carried out, and rules or property of some kind, is not a special interest of some members of a society but a general interest of all of them. (Bull, 1977, p 55)

So described, law unites an *instrumentalist logic*, one that looks for the realization of objectives through law, with a *formalist logic*, one that establishes standards of behaviour. Now it is obvious that neither logic is fully constraining. The instrumental logic is indeterminate as the objectives always leave a number of possible choices: what does 'peace and security' mean and how should it be realized in the Middle East, for example? Nor is the formalist logic ever fully formal, but always in practice somehow partial and biased. However general the rules of law are, their equal application may appear unjust because the reality to which they are applied is profoundly unequal: should large and small States, democracies, and dictatorships really be treated alike? The form of law is realized in particular rules or decisions that are no longer formal but that always institute a bias in favour of some substantive preferences.

In the *Nuclear Weapons* case (1996), the ICJ was requested by the UN General Assembly to give an Advisory Opinion on the legal status of nuclear weapons. From the perspective of the instrumentalist logic, the relevant regulation (human rights law, environmental law, humanitarian law, and the law concerning the use of force) sought to accomplish several types of objectives: above all protection of human life and the environment, as well as the survival of States. These objectives proved indeterminate, however, and both opponents and supporters of nuclear weapons argued by reference to them: are people better protected with or without nuclear weapons? The instrumental logic did set some limits to what the Court could say, but it did not—indeed could not—fully constrain it. A decision by the Court was needed to bring the instrumental logic into a conclusion.

The formalist logic was equally under-determined. To decide that nuclear weapons were *illegal* would have created a consistent material bias in favour of States in possession of conventional weapons or in de facto possession of undisclosed nuclear weapons. To require the dismantling of disclosed nuclear arsenals would have revolutionized the existing military-political relationships in unforeseen ways. But to decide that nuclear weapons were *lawful* would have maintained the systemic bias in security policy in favour of the Great Powers and gone against the deep-rooted popular sense that the existence of such weapons constitutes a permanent hostage-taking by nuclear weapons States of most of the world's population. Neither illegality nor legality could remain fully within the formalist logic. Both broke through pure form and created one or another type of material preference. Indeed, it was impossible to decide either way without the decision seeming 'biased' from the opposed standpoints. And because the political choice in this case seemed too important for the Court to take, it chose the path of recognizing the insufficiency of both logics: 'the Court considers it does not have sufficient elements to enable it to decide with certainty that the use of nuclear weapons would be necessarily at variance with the principles and rules applicable in armed conflict in any circumstance'.[23]

I have defended elsewhere the Court's silence inasmuch as it protected the need for a sustained *political* condemnation of the killing of the innocent, lifting it from the banal instrumentalism and formalism of modern law (Koskenniemi, 1999a). Irrespective of that position, however, the case illustrates the indeterminacy of both of the two types of logic behind the Rule of Law, as outlined by Bull at the beginning of this section. Neither instrumental calculation nor a purely formal analysis could grasp the status of such weapons: a *decision* was needed that was irreducible to the two logics. Here the decision was silence. In other cases, the Court may have recourse to literalism, balancing, contextualization, and bilateralization, among a host of other techniques, to complete the instrumental and formal structures within which it works (Koskenniemi, 1989, pp 410–21). Each of such techniques is, again, indeterminate. None of them explain why *this* argument was held relevant, why *that* interpretation was chosen. The decision always comes about, as the political theorist Ernesto Laclau has put it, as a kind of 'regulated madness', never reducible to any structure outside it (Laclau, 1996, p 58).

A court's decision or a lawyer's opinion is always a genuinely political act, a choice between alternatives not fully dictated by external criteria. It is even a *hegemonic* act in the precise sense that though it is partial and subjective, it claims to be universal and objective (see further Koskenniemi, 2004a). But it is this very partiality and political nature of the decision that ensures that it is an aspect of, or even a creative moment of, a political community. Here finally is the significance of the under-determination of the two logics behind the Rule of Law. The society upheld by international law is not an effect of instrumental reason, nor even of (some conception) of formal reason *tout court*. It is an effect of decisions that invoke as their justification, and thus offer as valid points of criticism, an idea of (international) community beyond sectorial interests or preferences. An idea of solidarity informs that practice. Of course, such decisions are made under conditions of uncertainty and conflict. They are amenable for criticism from alternative standpoints: there is the solidarity of the lion and that of the antelope. But that this decision-making practice is not the passive reproduction of some globalizing (economic, environmental, humanitarian) structure, projects the international society as a *political community* that seeks to decide for itself what rules govern it. The practice of international law, as Bull suggested, seeks a union of 'dominant elements' with 'general interest'. As such, it remains a terrain in which the never-ending struggle between the two is being waged: hegemony, and critique of hegemony at the same time.

---

[23] *Legality of the Threat or Use of Nuclear Weapons, Advisory Opinion, ICJ Reports 1996*, p 226, para 95.

VII. BEYOND INSTRUMENTALISM
AND FORMALISM

In other words, although notions such as 'peace', 'justice', or 'human rights' do not fit well within the techniques of legal formalism, and are quite disappointing as behavioural directives, they give voice to individuals and groups struggling for spiritual or material well-being, fighting against oppression, and seeking to express their claims in the language of something greater than merely their personal interests. Law—including international law—has a 'utopian, aspirational face' (Cotterell, 1995, p 17) expressed in large notions such as 'peace', 'justice', or 'human rights' that in countless international law texts appeal to solidarity within community. They do this in three distinct, but related ways.

First, they redescribe individuals and groups as claimants of rights or beneficiaries of entitlements and in so doing provide them with an identity that they may assert against the homogenizing pull of society's dominant elements. As Karen Knop has pointed out, the treatment of claims of self-determination by marginalized groups such as indigenous peoples in legal institutions has sometimes enabled those groups to be represented by an identity 'that might resonate with those represented' and thus to 'equalize cultures in international law' (Knop, 2002, p 210). Secondly, legal principles give an international voice to communities by allowing them to read their particular grievances as claims of universal entitlement, at the same level as claims made by other members of the community. To be able to say that some act is an 'aggression' or that the deprivation of a benefit is a 'human rights violation' is to lift a private grievance to the level of a public law violation, of concern not only to the victim but to the community. Such notions—and the whole debate about the objectives of international law—act in the political realm to challenge what Norman Geras has termed the 'contract of mutual indifference'—the tendency to regard violations as a private matter between the victim and the perpetrator, and therefore not of concern to others (Geras, 1998). They challenge the way claims are blocked in the international realm as matters of 'security', 'economics', or, for example, 'private law', thus helping to contest dominant discourses and practices that seek to justify themselves by their apolitical self-evidence. And thirdly, to make those claims as *legal* claims (instead of moral aspirations or political programmes) is to imagine—and thus to create—the international world as a set of public institutions within which public authorities should use their power in roughly predictable ways and with public accountability to the community at large.

The fact that public law notions such as *jus cogens* or of obligations *erga omnes* tend to be formulated in such large terms as to restate the paradox of objectives has made them seem quite useless from an instrumental perspective. But, we may now assume, their role may be precisely to counteract the ideological effects of instrumentalism. Again, the *form* of those ideas—of an 'international legal community'—is important in allowing the articulation of the most varied types of claims as more than claims about personal preference, thus integrating the claimants as members of a pluralistic community. 'Self-determination', typically, may be constructed analytically to mean anything one wants it to mean, and many studies have invoked its extreme flexibility. Examined in the light of history, however, it has given form and strength to claims for national liberation and self-rule from the French Revolution to decolonization in 1960s, the fall of the Berlin Wall, and the political transitions that have passed from Latin America through Eastern Europe and South Africa. 'Peace', too may be an empty notion, perfectly capable of coexisting with economic deprivation and suppression of human rights. On the other hand, peace movements have been an invaluable aspect of political contestation inasmuch as they 'mobilise support and highlight the inconsistencies in international concepts of peace and security' (Charlesworth and Chinkin, 2000, p 272). Even if 'justice' does lie in the eye of the beholder, without a language of justice, the international struggles for resources, recognition, democracy, or, for instance, 'ending the culture of impunity', would have seemed like so many meaningless games played by diplomats.

In other words, though the question 'what is international law for?' is seldom useful as an aspect of the deliberations over particular problems among international lawyers, it is absolutely crucial as a focus for international law's emancipatory potential. This is why it was significant that the demonstrations against the war in Iraq in 2003 focused on the war's 'illegality'. In this way, the special scandal of Western military action could be articulated as not just the violation of the private interests of Iraqi citizens but as directed against the (legal) community, and thus everyone. The fabricated character of the justifications invoked for the war further highlighted the significance of the claim of the war's formal illegality: behind the contrast between a morality of 'freedom' and a morality of 'law', there was a deeper question about who should be entitled to rule us and what can we take on trust.

None of this deviates from the need to recognize that while the culture of formalism is a necessary though often misunderstood aspect of the legal craft, as a historical matter, it has often provided a recipe for indifference and needs to be accompanied by a live sense of its political justification. To lift the debate about objectives from diplomatic instruments or academic treatises to the level of political debates is a necessary counterweight to the bureaucratic spirit often associated with formalism. This will enable the reconstruction of international law as a political project. As modern international law arose in the last decades of the nineteenth century, it did so as a part of the élitist politics of European liberal internationalism that expected public opinion and democracy to pave the way for a rationally administered world (see Koskenniemi, 2001a; Pemberton, 2001). The last articulations of that spirit date from the first decade following the Second World War (see, eg, Lauterpacht, 1946). Since then, a gap has been created between the utopian and the pragmatic parts of international law, the former becoming a rather grandiose justification over the latter. But when formalism loses political direction, formalism itself is lost.[24] Hence the turn to pragmatism and instrumentalism surveyed earlier.

The question 'what is international law for?' needs to be resuscitated from the paralysis that it is infected with because of the indeterminacy of the responses given to it. But this necessitates a reformulation of the relationship of international law to politics, in either of its two guises, as principles and doctrines on the one hand, and as institutional practices on the other. Both political realism and institutional pragmatism arose as reactions to failed expectations about international law's autonomy: realists rejected legal institutions as a sham and told politicians to aim directly at their objectives. Institutionalists were wary of such objectives and instead relied on techniques of adjustment and compromise.

VIII. BETWEEN HEGEMONY AND FRAGMENTATION: A MINI-HISTORY

These reaction formations are intellectually disappointing and politically dubious. Neither provides space for anything but a most formal debate about 'what is international law for?' and no space at all for responding to that question by reference to popular aspirations

---

[24] For a useful reconstruction of Hans Kelsen's formalism in terms of the political project that inspired it, see von Bernstorff, 2001.

about peace, order, and justice. A first step in trying to account for such aspirations is to accept that these notions are subject to political controversy and that even as they are formulated in universal terms, they are constantly appropriated by particular agents and interests so as to support their agendas and causes. They are aspects of *hegemonic struggle*, that is to say, part of an argumentative practice in which particular subjects and values claim to represent that which is universal (see Mouffe and Laclau, 2001; Koskenniemi, 2004a). That the question 'what is international law for?' is a terrain of such controversy is a natural aspect of a pluralistic society and a precondition for conceiving its government in democratic terms.

The hegemonic nature of the debate about international law's objectives may be illustrated in terms of its history (see also Koskenniemi, 2004b; Supiot, 2005, pp 275–305). When Spain and Portugal at the end of the fifteenth century divided the non-European world between themselves by reference to a Papal directive, they claimed to be speaking as Christian powers on behalf of humankind as a whole. When the Spanish theologians, Vitoria or Las Casas later were claiming that God had given the Indians a soul just as He had given it to the Spanish, a particular form of Christian scholasticism—Dominican theology—came to speak in terms of universal principles, equally constraining on the Princes and the Indians. And when Hugo Grotius in 1608 challenged the Iberian claims, he was redefining the objectives of international law within a hegemonic struggle that opposed a Reformation-inspired commercial universalism against the *ancien régime* of (Catholic) Christianity. The narrative of international law from those days to the nineteenth century may be depicted as a succession of natural-law arguments that were united by their always emerging from some European intelligentsia that claimed it was speaking on behalf of the world as a whole. When de Emmerich Vattel in 1758 formulated his 'necessary law of nations' in terms of the commands of natural reason, and found that it consecrated a balance of power between European sovereigns, he already filled the category of the 'universal' with a profoundly particular understanding that was a part of the (European) Enlightenment.

Since the first appearance of the (modern) international law profession in Europe in the late nineteenth century, that profession imagined itself as, in the words of the Statute of the *Institut de droit international* (1873), the 'juridical conscience of the civilised world'.

This understanding, too, was born in a cultural environment that imagined its own experience—which it labelled 'civilization'—as universal and postulated it as the end-result of the development of societies everywhere. The civilizing mission enthusiastically propagated by late nineteenth-century international lawyers was a hegemonic technique, embedded in an understanding of the law as not simply a technical craft or a set of formal instruments and institutions. It was a spontaneous aspect of 'civilization' which had the natural tendency to become universal.

If the First World War destroyed whatever was left of the civilizing mission, it also gave rise to a series of efforts to articulate anew the universal basis of international law, sometimes in terms of a law-like movement of societies to ever more complex forms of division of labour and interdependence (eg, Huber, 1910), sometimes through a reinstatement of the hierarchical principles that were a natural part of legal systems (eg, Verdross, 1923). Most of the reconstructive scholarship of the inter-war period, however, simply generalized the legal experience of European societies into the international level, bringing into existence a universal international law through private law analogies, conceiving the Covenant of the League of Nations as a constitution of the world and by allocating to the juristic class the function of 'filling the gaps' in an otherwise primitive-looking legal system (see Lauterpacht, 1933; Koskenniemi, 1997). The particular European experience with the

Rule of Law became the placeholder for the aspirations of peace and justice that lawyers saw were demanded by populations struggling with industrialism and social conflict.

In the more recent post-war era, much of that kind of language—like the political liberalism with which it was associated—has lost credibility. When somebody today claims to be acting on behalf of the 'international community', we immediately recognize the hegemonic technique at work (see Klein, 2001; Feher, 2000; Koskenniemi, 2004a). As against the diplomatic antics of public international law, new specializations today often carry the ideals of universalism and progress. Recently, this has occasioned a lively debate about the 'fragmentation of international law'—the emergence and consolidation of special regimes and technical sub-disciplines: human rights law, environmental law, trade law, humanitarian law, and so on, each field projecting its preferences as universal ones. The result has been increasing normative and jurisdictional conflicts. In its *Tadić* judgment of 1999, the International Criminal Tribunal for the Former Yugoslavia (ICTY) expressly deviated from the practice of the International Court of Justice, as laid out in its *Nicaragua* case in 1986 concerning the attribution of conduct by military irregulars to a State. To move from a standard of 'effective control' to one of 'overall control' significantly enhanced the accountability of foreign States indirectly involved in internal conflicts, constituting a shift of normative preference with respect to one set of international problems.[25] The continuing debate about the relevance of environmental, human rights, or labour standards within the WTO system reflects a search for the relative priority of political objectives within WTO institutions as those priorities have not been set at the level of the relevant agreements themselves. The autonomy invoked by human rights regimes constitutes a subtle manoeuvre by human rights implementation organs to universalize their jurisdiction. 'Dynamic' arguments and the object and purpose test allow the creation of a systemic bias in favour of the protected individuals that could be difficult to justify under traditional law.

Such 'fragmentation' is not a technical problem resulting from lack of coordination. The normative preferences of environmental and trade bodies differ, as do preferences of human rights lawyers and international law 'generalists', and each organ is determined to follow its own preference and make it prevail over contrasting ones. The result is, sometimes, deviating interpretations of the general law, such preferences reflecting the priorities of the deciding organ, at other times the creation of firm exceptions in the law, applicable in a special field (Koskenniemi and Leino, 2002). Such fragmentation is also an aspect of hegemonic struggle where each institution, though partial, tries to occupy the space of the whole. Far from being a problem to resolve, the proliferation of autonomous or semi-autonomous normative regimes is an unavoidable reflection of a 'postmodern' social condition and a, perhaps at least to some extent, beneficial prologue to a pluralistic community in which the degrees of homogeneity and fragmentation reflect shifts of political preference (Stark, 2002).

IX. LEGAL FORMALISM AND INTERNATIONAL JUSTICE

Let me close by four responses to the question 'what is international law for?'. Two are rather straightforward. First, international law exists to advance the values, interests, and

---

[25] *Prosecutor* v *Dusko Tadić*, Judgment, Case No. IT-94-1-A, Appeals Chamber, 15 July 1999, 38 *ILM* 1518, para 137.

preferences that those in dominant positions seek to realize in the world. It is an instrument of power. Secondly, it also gives voice to those who have been excluded from powerful positions and are regularly treated as the objects of other peoples' policies; it provides a platform on which claims about violence, injustice, and social deprivation may be made even against the dominant elements. It is an instrument for the critique of power. To bring these two aspects of international law together means that there is no fixed set of objectives, purposes, or principles that would exist somewhere 'outside' or beyond international law itself, that they are always the objectives of particular actors involved in polemical confrontations. The law is instrumental, but what it is an instrument for cannot be fixed outside the political process of which it is an inextricable part.

This is why, thirdly, international law's objective is always also international law itself. For, as I have tried to argue in this chapter, it is international law's formalism that brings political antagonists together as they invoke contrasting understandings of its rules and institutions. In the absence of agreement over, or knowledge of, the 'true' objectives of political community—that is to say, in an agnostic world—the pure form of international law provides the shared surface—the *only* such surface—on which political adversaries recognize each other as such and pursue their adversity in terms of something shared, instead of seeking to attain full exclusion—'outlawry'—of the other. In this sense, international law's value and its misery lie in its being the fragile surface of political community among social agents—States, other communities, individuals—who disagree about their preferences but do this within a structure that invites them to argue in terms of an assumed universality.

But there is a fourth response as well: international law exists as a promise of justice. The agnosticism of political modernity has made the articulation of this teleological view extremely difficult. For the justice towards which international law points cannot be enumerated in substantive values, interests, or objectives. It has no predetermined institutional form. The lawyer's political advocacy and institutional reform-proposals express inadequate and reified images, (partial) points of view. Even when acceptable in their general formulation, as soon as they are translated into particular policies, and start to prefer some interests or values over others, they become vulnerable to the critique of 'false universalism'. For the *homo economicus*, none of this is too important. All that count are the external objectives projected upon the law. If law fails in realizing them, then it loses its authority. The image of law embodied in the metaphor of the *homo juridicus* is quite different. Now law itself—independently of the objectives projected upon it—has authority. This authority comes from the way it describes the international world as a (legal) community where questions of just distribution and entitlement are constantly on the agenda, where claims of legal subjects receive an equal hearing and where the acts of public officials are assessed by a language of community standards. For the instrumental view, the constraint received from law is justified only in view of the authority of the law's (external) objectives. In the formalist view, law is used to compel because the violations cannot coexist with the aspirations of universality embedded in the legal form. Such violations are singular until the law lifts them from the purely subjective into public illegality:

> Law is the name of the semblance of order—the assembling, the ordering, the establishing of commonality—that is made of our otherwise (subjective) differences when we take, or interpret them to be a world that can be judged, rather than mere subjective experiences. (Constable, 2000, p 95)

But the justice that animates political community is not one that may be fully attained. Not only is law never justice itself, the two cannot exist side by side. If there is justice, then no law is needed—and if there is law, then there is only a (more or less well-founded) *expectation* of justice. Here is the truth in instrumentalism about positive law being a pointer beyond itself. There is a Messianic structure to international law, the announcement of something that remains eternally postponed. It is this 'to-come' that enables the criticism of the law's own violence, its biases and exclusions. No doubt, law and justice are linked in the activity of lawyers, paradigmatically in the legal judgment. This is the wisdom grasped by legal pragmatism. But the judgment is always insufficiently grounded in law, just like positive law is always insufficiently expressive of justice. In the gap between positive law and justice lies the necessary (and impossible) realm of the politics of law. Without it, law becomes pure positivity, its violence a mere fact of power.

REFERENCES

ABBOTT, K and SNIDAL, D (2001), 'Hard and Soft Law in International Governance', in Goldstein, JL, Kahler, M, Keohane, RO, and Slaughter, A-M, *Legalization and World Politics* (Cambridge, Mass: MIT Press), pp 37–72.

ARNAUD, A-J (2003), *Critique de la raison juridique 2: Gouvernants sans frontiers. Entre mondialisation et post-mondialisation* (Paris: LGDJ).

BINDER, G (1988), 'Beyond Criticism', 55 *U Chi LR* 688–915.

BRIERLY, J (1944), *The Outlook for International Law* (Oxford: Oxford University Press).

BRUNNEE, J and Toope, SJ (2000), 'International Law and Constructivism: Elements of an Interactional Theory of International Law', 39 *Col J Transnat'l L* 19–74.

BULL, H (1977), *The Anarchic Society. A Study of Order in World Politics* (London: Macmillan).

BYERS, M and NOLTE, G (2003), *United States Hegemony and the Foundations of International Law* (Cambridge: Cambridge University Press).

CAMERON, I (2000), *National Security and the European Convention on Human Rights* (Stockholm: Iustus).

CARR, EH (1946), *The Twenty-years' Crisis 1919–1939* (London: Macmillan).

CHARLESWORTH, H (2002), 'International Law: A Discipline of Crisis', 65 *MLR* 377–92.

—— and CHINKIN, C (2000), *The Boundaries of International Law. A Feminist Analysis* (Manchester: Manchester University Press).

CHAYES, A and CHAYES, AH (1995), *The New Sovereignty. Compliance with International Regulatory Agreements* (Cambridge, Mass: Harvard University Press).

CHESTERMAN, S (2001), *Just War or Just Peace? Humanitarian Intervention and International Law* (Oxford: Oxford University Press).

CONSTABLE, M (2000), 'The Silence of the Law: Justice in Cover's "Field of Pain and Death"', in Sarat, A (ed), *Law, Violence and the Possibility of Justice* (Princetown, NJ: Princeton University Press).

CORTEN, O (1997), *L'utilisation du 'raisonnable' par le juge international. Discours juridique, raison et contradictions* (Brussels: Bruylant).

COTTERELL, R (1995), *Law's Community. Legal Theory in Sociological Perspective* (Oxford: Clarendon Press).

FEHER, M (2000), *Powerless by Design. The Age of the International Community* (Durham, NC: Duke University Press).

FINNEMORE, M (1996), *National Interests in International Society* (Ithaca, NY: Cornell University Press).

FISH, S (1989), *Doing What Comes Naturally. Change, Rhetoric, and the Practice of Theory in Literary and Legal Studies* (Oxford: Oxford University Press).

FOUCAULT, M (2005), *Naissance de la biopolitique. Cours au Collège de France 1978–79* (Paris: Gallimard/Seuil).

FRANCK, TM (1995), *Fairness in International Law and Institutions* (Oxford: Oxford University Press).

FULLER, LL (1969), *The Morality of Law*, 2nd rev edn (New Haven, Conn: Yale University Press).

GERAS, N (1998), *The Contract of Mutual Indifference. Political Philosophy after the Holocaust* (London: Verso).

GOLDSMITH, J and POSNER, E (2005), *The Limits of International Law* (Oxford: Oxford University Press).

GREWE, W (2001), *The Epochs of International Law* (Byers, M (trans)) (Berlin: De Gruyter).

GUZZINI, G (1998), *Realism in International Relations and International Political Economy* (London: Routledge).

HABERMAS, J (2004), *Der gespaltene Westen* (Frankfurt: Suhrkamp).

HARDT, M and NEGRI, A (1999), *Empire* (Cambridge, Mass: Harvard University Press).

HENKIN, L (1989), 'International Law: Politics, Values and Functions', 216 *Recueil des Cours* 9–416.

HUBER, M (1910/1928), *Die soziologischen Grundlagen des Völkerrechts* (Berlin: Rothschild).

HURRELL, A and WOODS, N (1999), *Inequality, Globalization and World Politics* (Oxford: Oxford University Press).

KANT, I (1999), *Critique of Practical Reason* (Gregor, M (ed), Introduction by Reath, A) (Cambridge: Cambridge University Press).

KAUFMANN, E (1911), *Das Wesen des Völkerrechts und die Clausula rebus sic stantibus* (Tübingen: Mohr).

KENNEDY, DAVID (2000), 'When Renewal Repeats: Thinking Against the Box', 32 *NYU JILP* 335–500.

—— (2004), *The Darker Side of Virtue. Reassessing International Humanitarianism* (Princeton, NJ: Princeton University Press).

KENNEDY, DUNCAN (2001), 'Formalism', in *The International Encyclopedia of Social & Behavioral Sciences* (The Hague: Kluwer).

KERVÉGAN, J-F (1999), 'Carl Schmitt and "World Unity"', in Mouffe, C (ed), *The Challenge of Carl Schmitt* (London: Verso), pp 54–74.

KLEIN, P (2001), 'Les problèmes soulevés par la référence à la communauté internationale comme facteur de legitimite', in Corten, O and Delcourt, B (eds), *Droit légitimation et politique exterieure: L'Europe et la guerre du Kosovo* (Brussels: Bruylant), pp 261–97.

KNOP, K (2002), *Diversity and Self-Determination in International Law* (Cambridge: Cambridge University Press).

KOSKENNIEMI, M (1989), *From Apology to Utopia. The Structure of International Legal Argument*, 2005 reissue with new Epilogue (Cambridge: Cambridge University Press).

—— (1994), 'The Wonderful Artificiality of States', 88 *ASIL Proc* 22–9.

—— (1997), 'Lauterpacht, The Victorian Tradition in International Law', 8 *EJIL* 215–63.

—— (1999a), 'The Silence of Law/The Voice of Justice', in Boisson de Chazournes, L and Sands, P (eds), *International Law, the International Court of Justice and Nuclear Weapons* (Cambridge: Cambridge University Press), pp 488–510.

—— (1999b) 'The Limits of International Law: Are There Such?', XXVIII *Thesaurus Acroasiarum: Might and Right in International Relations*, pp 27–50.

—— (2000), 'The Effect of Rights on Political Culture', in Alston, P (ed), *The EU and Human Rights* (Oxford: Oxford University Press), pp 99–116.

—— (2001a), *The Gentle Civilizer of Nations. The Rise and Fall of International Law 1870–1960* (Cambridge: Cambridge University Press).

—— (2001b), 'Solidarity Measures: State Responsibility as a New International Order?', 72 *BYIL* 339–56.

—— (2004a), 'International Law and Hegemony: A Reconfiguration', 17 *Cambridge Review of International Affairs*, 197–218.

—— (2004b), 'Legal Universalism: Between Morality and Power in a World of States', in Cheng, S (ed), *Law, Justice and Power: Between Reason and Will* (Stanford, NJ: Stanford University Press), 46–69.

—— (2005), 'International Law in Europe: Between Tradition and Renewal', 16 *EJIL* 113–24.

—— (2009), 'Miserable Comforters. International Relations as New Natural law', 15 *EJIR*, 395–422.

—— and LEINO, P (2002), 'The Fragmentation of International Law: Postmodern Anxieties', 16 *LJIL* 533– 579.

KRATOCHWIL, F (2000), 'How Do Norms Matter?', in Byer, M (ed), *The Role of Law in International Politics. Essays in International Relations and International Law* (Oxford: Oxford University Press), pp 35–68.

LACLAU, E (1996), 'Deconstruction, Pragmatism, Hegemony', in Mouffe, C (ed), *Deconstruction and Pragmatism* (London: Verso).

LÂM, MC (2000), *At the Edge of the State: Indigenous Peoples and Self-Determination* (Dobbs Ferry, NY: Transnational).

LAUTERPACHT, H (1933), *The Function of Law in the International Community* (Oxford: Oxford University Press).

—— (1946), 'The Grotian Tradition in International Law', 23 *BYIL* 1–53.

—— (1958), *The Development of International Law by the International Court* (London: Stevens).

—— (1975), 'The Reality of the Law of Nations', in *International Law, being the Collected Papers of Hersch Lauterpacht*, vol 2, pp 22–51.

McDOUGAL, MS (1953), 'International Law, Power and Policy. A Contemporary Conception', 82 *Recueil des Cours* 137–259.

MARKS, S (2000), *The Riddle of All Constitutions. International Law, Democracy and the Critique of Ideology* (Oxford: Oxford University Press).

MORGENTHAU, H (1940), 'Positivism, Functionalism, and International Law', 34 *AJIL* 261–84.

MOUFFE, C and LACLAU, E (2001), *Hegemony and Socialist Strategy*, 2nd edn (London: Verso).

NARDIN, T (1983), *Law, Morality and the Relations between States* (Princeton, NJ: Princeton University Press).

—— (1998), 'Legal Positivism as a Theory of International Society', in Mapel, DR and Nardin, T, *International Society. Diverse Ethical Perspectives* (Princeton, NJ: Princeton University Press), pp 17–35.

O'NEILL, O (2000), *Bounds of Justice* (Cambridge: Cambridge University Press).

ORFORD, A (2003), *Reading Humanitarian Intervention. Human Rights and the Use of Force in International Law* (Cambridge: Cambridge University Press).

PAULUS, A (2001), *Die internationale Gemeinschaft im Völkerrecht. Eine Untersuchung zur Entwicklung des Völkerrechts im Zeitalter der Globalisierung* (Munich: Beck).

PEMBERTON, J-A (2001), *Global Metaphors. Modernity and the Quest for One World* (London: Pluto Press).

POSNER, R (2003), 'Do States have a Moral Obligation to Obey International Law?', 55 *Stanford Law Journal* 1901–20.

SCHACHTER, O (1997), 'The Decline of the Nation-state and its Implications for International Law', *Col J of Transnat'l L* 7–23.

SCHMITT, C (1988), *Der Nomos der Erde im Völkerrecht des Jus Publicum Europaeum*, 3rd edn (Berlin: Duncker & Humblot).

—— (1996), *The Concept of the Political* (Schwab, G (trans and Introduction)) (Chicago: University of Chicago Press).

SHELTON, D (ed) (2000), *Commitment and Compliance. The Role of Non-Binding Norms in the International Legal System* (Oxford: Oxford University Press).

STARK, B (2002), 'After/Word(s): Violation of Human Dignity and Postmodernism in Law', 27 *Yale JIL* 336–47.

SUPIOT, A (2005), *Homo juridicus. Essai sur la fonction anthropologique de droit* (Paris: Seuil).

TASIOULAS, J (1996), 'In Defence of Relative Normativity: Communitarian Values and the Nicaragua Case', 16 *OJLS* 85–128.

TOMUSCHAT, C (1999), 'International Law: Ensuring the Survival of Mankind on the Eve of New Century', 23 *Recueil des Cours* 1–281.

TSAGOURIAS, N (2000), 'Globalization, Order and the Rule of Law', XI *FYBIL* 247–64.

VERDROSS, A (1923), *Die Einheit des rechtlichen Weltbildes* (Tübingen: Mohr).

VON BERNSTORFF, J (2001), *Der Glaube an das Universale Recht. Zur Völkerrechstheorie Hans Kelsens und seiner Schüler* (Baden-Baden: Nomos).

WATTS, SIR A (2000), 'The Importance of International Law', in Byers, M (ed), *The Role of Law in International Politics. Essays in International Relations and International Law* (Oxford: Oxford University Press), pp 5–16.

WEIL, P (1983), 'Towards Relative Normativity in International Law?', 77 *AJIL* 413–42.

WESTLAKE, J (1910), *International Law*, 2nd edn, vol 2 (Cambridge: Cambridge University Press).

3

A VIEW OF DELFT: SOME THOUGHTS ABOUT THINKING ABOUT INTERNATIONAL LAW

Iain Scobbie

Legal theory is always more or less closely connected with philosophical thinking, political conditions, and ideological currents. As these factors were vastly different in England, Germany and France during the nineteenth century, so legal theory took different directions in these three countries.

Karl Olivecrona, *Law as Fact*
(1971), p 27

[T]heories of law ... are one of the principal causes of low morale among students of international law.

Ian Brownlie, *International Law at the Fiftieth Anniversary of the United Nations* (1995), p 22

SUMMARY

International law does not exist in an intellectual vacuum. Our understanding of the nature of international law—of what it is and what it can and should do—is ultimately dependent on theoretical assumptions and presuppositions. These can be latent and unexamined, in which case they are likely to foster only an acritical complacency. As all law has a political dimension, because law attempts to provide authoritative models of how people should behave, it is not surprising that theoretical models of international law encode specific views of the world and of relations between States. These assumptions and presuppositions influence the analysis of substantive issues, thus active engagement with theory is a matter which should neither be ignored nor be simply left behind in the academy.

I THE PERILS OF PHILOSOPHY

Thinking can be dangerous, much more dangerous than the pseudo-danger envisaged in Professor Brownlie's fatuous assertion that 'there is no doubt room for a whole treatise on the harm caused to the business of legal investigation by theory' (Brownlie, 1983, p 627).[1] Examples of the dangers of thinking are not hard to find. For example, during the Cold War, there was a tendency for some Eastern European analytical legal theorists to focus on logic and formal modes of reasoning (see, eg Wróblewski, 1974). One supposes that at least partly the decision to do so was rooted in prudence because evaluative substantive or policy analysis could be personally, professionally, and politically dangerous.

Brownlie's assertion simply begs the question. How can one know what there is 'legal' to investigate unless one subscribes to some abstract conception of law? That is a matter for legal theory. It need not provide a watertight definition of what law is and what it is about, but it should at least give basic criteria which enable the identification of what counts as 'legal investigation' in the first place. Further, a disavowal of theory can also denote an unthinking and essentially conservative commitment to a hidden or latent theory that rests content with the status quo and seeks neither to question nor justify either the substance or practice of international law (Warbrick, 1991, pp 69–70).[2] This disinterest simply amounts to a complacent refusal to think about what one is doing, and constitutes an intellectual self-censorship which suppresses analysis and critical evaluation.

If being 'dangerous' takes things too far, thinking should at least be a 'challenge'. How do we know that our beliefs have value unless we examine them and, in particular, their underlying assumptions? These assumptions, these preconceptions, often colour our understanding of the content of international law. As Professor Koskenniemi has observed, a characteristic of contemporary international legal practice is specialization, where discrete sets of substantive issues are packaged into categories such as trade law or environmental law or human rights law and so on. These specializations 'cater for special audiences with special interests and special ethos'. Each contains structural biases in the form of dominant expectations about the values, actors and solutions appropriate to that specialization, which thus affect practical outcomes. The actors in these different fields conceptualize issues in ways which pull upon these preconceptions to reach solutions which are thought suitable for the specialization (Koskenniemi, 2009a and 2009b: see also Beckett, 2009, and Scobbie, 2009). For example, in discussing the relationship between the law of armed conflict and human rights, Professor Garraway underlines the importance of the analyst's own perspective and presuppositions:

> For human rights lawyers, human rights principles are those that provide the greatest protection to all by introducing a high threshold for any use of force and even if that threshold is crossed, a graduated use of force thereafter. On the other hand, international humanitarian lawyers see this as idealistic and impracticable. As they see it, it would become almost impossible to conduct hostilities legally to which many human rights lawyers would reply that that would be no bad thing! The difficulty is that such an attitude will not abolish armed conflict. (Garraway, 2010, p 509)

Similarly, Professor Kretzmer points out that the doctrine of proportionality employed by the law of armed conflict differs from that employed by human rights law. Proportionality

---

[1] For Brownlie's antipathy to theory, see further Brownlie, 1981, pp 5–8, and Brownlie, 1995, pp 22ff.

[2] See also Warbrick, 2000, p 621 passim, but especially at pp 633–6; and Lasswell and McDougal, 1943, p 207. This was their first co-authored work, and is reprinted as an appendix in Lasswell and McDougal, 1992, vol II at p 1265.

in the law of armed conflict concerns collateral damage, and thus permits civilian death and injury, an advance calculation which is an anathema to human rights law. He observes that Additional Protocol II, which regulates non-international armed conflict, makes no reference to proportionality, but that the International Committee of the Red Cross' customary international law study claims it is a principle which applies in this type of conflict (see Henckaerts and Doswald-Beck 2005, Vol I, pp 46–50). Kretzmer comments that this appears to assume that in an internal armed conflict proportionality protects potential victims, but its introduction could instead weaken the protection they might otherwise enjoy under a human rights regime because the armed conflict test of proportionality entrenches as a legitimate expectation that civilians may be killed and injured (see Kretzmer, 2009, pp 17–22).

These examples underline a point made, amongst others, by Professors Allott and Koskenniemi, that as lawyers we must conscious of what we are doing and why we are doing it and, above all, take responsibility for our arguments. We therefore owe it to ourselves to examine the assumptions and biases we bring with us to our work. As Gertrude Stein cautions, 'If you do write as you have heard it said then you have to change it' (Stein, 1936 (1998a), p 411). Don't worry about Gertrude: she will pop up again later. She often does.

II. THE PROLOGUE—THE VIEW FROM DELPHI

Probably the most widely-known fact about the ancient Greek philosopher Socrates, one of the founders of Western philosophy, is the manner of his death. He was condemned to commit suicide, by drinking hemlock, after being tried in Athens for impiety and corrupting youth. In the *Apology*, Plato's account of Socrates' own defence speech at his trial, Socrates recounts that one of his friends had once asked the oracle at Delphi if there was anyone wiser than Socrates, and the priestess replied that no-one was (see Plato, 1969, p 49). This was perhaps not the best way for the accused in a capital trial, essentially accused of thought crimes, to ingratiate himself with his jury. Nor, given the nature of the charges against him, was his assertion that he could not abandon philosophy as:

> to let no day pass without discussing goodness and all the other subjects about which you hear me talking and examining both myself and others is really the very best thing a man can do, and that life without this sort of examination is not worth living. (Plato, 1969, pp 71–2)

Socrates was as rashly audacious when, having been found guilty, the prosecutor proposed that he be sentenced to death. Socrates suggested an alternative 'penalty'. Because he had shunned material gain in order to devote himself to persuading Athenians to think of their moral well-being, he thought that Athens should not punish but rather reward him by paying for his upkeep (see Plato, 1969, pp 69–70). Perhaps, given the political context of his trial, he knew he was as good as dead (see, eg Hughes, 2010, pp 318–25; Waterfield, 2009, pp 173–90).

Pre-Socratic texts are few and fragmentary (see, eg Gagarin and Woodruff, 1995, and Waterfield, 2000) and no writings by Socrates survive, if indeed there ever were any in the first place. All we know or think we know about what Socrates thought and argued comes from secondary sources, from philosophers such as Plato and Xenophon, and from satirists like Aristophanes. As a result, some contemporary Socratic experts, such as Vlastos, argue that it is unclear what precise ideas should be ascribed to him (Vlastos, 1994).

In *Phaedrus*, Plato places in Socrates' mouth a discussion of the desirability of writing (see Plato, 2002, pp 68–70). He tells the fable of the Egyptian god Theuth who invented writing, and showed it to his fellow-god Thamous who asked him to explain what benefits it would bring. Theuth replied that it would increase the intelligence of Egyptians and improve their memories. Thamous dismissed this justification, arguing that Theuth was committed to writing because he had invented it, and that this commitment had blinded him to its true effect. It would shrivel people's memories. Their trust in the written word would make them remember things 'by relying on marks made by others' rather than on their own mental resources. Writing would simply be a mechanism for jogging the memory, and thus only furnish the appearance of, but not real, intelligence:

> Because your students will be widely read, though without any contact with a teacher, they will seem to be men of wide knowledge, when they will usually be ignorant. And this spurious appearance of intelligence will make them difficult company. (Plato, 2002, p 69)

Thus Socrates argued that anyone who thinks he can help a branch of knowledge to survive by reducing it to writing, or thinks 'that writing will give him something clear and reliable', is wrong:

> there's something odd about writing…which makes it exactly like painting. The offspring of painting stand there as if alive, but if you ask them a question they maintain an aloof silence. It's the same with written words: you might think they were speaking as if they had some intelligence, but if you want an explanation of any of the things they're saying and ask them about it, they just go on and on for ever giving the same single piece of information. (Plato, 2002, p 70)

There is an apparent paradox in criticizing the utility of written argument in the course of a written argument (see Waterfield's introduction to Plato, 2002, at pp xxxvii–xlii), but key to Socratic philosophical method is the technique known as *elenchus*, which is a search for truth using dialectic argument. Roughly this is a form of cross-examination where Socrates' interlocutor makes a claim which Socrates thinks is false and aims to disprove. To do so, Socrates secures agreement to an additional proposition or propositions which he then uses as the basis for further argument which aims at reaching a conclusion which his interlocutor will agree refutes or is incompatible with his initial claim. Accordingly, the optimum method of searching for the truth is by discussion in which claims and counter-claims may be tested and challenged. As Waterfield notes (Plato, 2002, p xxxix), Plato might have thought that the discursive nature of his dialogues should engage the reader in the conversation, which in any case was more concerned with provoking questions than providing answers.

The provocative nature of Socratic method is underlined in the *Apology*. Anytus, one of the prosecutors, had argued that Socrates must be condemned to death because, if not, Athenean youths 'would all immediately become utterly demoralised by putting the teaching of Socrates into practice' (Plato, 1969, p 61). The youths would be demoralized because the aim of Socrates' technique of *elenchus* was to leave his interlocutor in a state of *aporia*, an intellectual impasse which demonstrated to the interlocutor that he could not be sure that he really knew anything about the topic under discussion. To counter Anytus's censure, Socrates employed, again somewhat immodestly, what is sometimes known as the 'gadfly analogy':

> [If] you put me to death, you will harm yourselves more than me…If you put me to death, you will not easily find anyone to take my place…God has specially appointed me to this city, as though it were a large thoroughbred horse which because of its great size is inclined to be lazy and needs the stimulation of some stinging fly. It seems to me that God has attached me to this city to perform the office of such a fly; and all day long I never cease to settle here, there, and everywhere, rousing, persuading, reproving every one of you. You will not easily find another like me, gentlemen, and if you take my advice you will spare my life. (Plato, 1969, pp 62–3)

The gentlemen comprising the Athenian jury did not agree, and sentenced Socrates to death for impiety and corruption of youth.

This latter charge did not concern sexual impropriety. At that time, among some Athenians, sexual relations between adolescents and older men were socially acceptable. The idea was that the older man would act as a mentor to the younger, take him under his wing to show him how to be a proper Athenian citizen, and perhaps also take him to bed— although these relationships were not widespread but restricted essentially to the upper classes (see, eg Waterfield, 2009, pp 55–7). Some Victorian philosophers tried to cover this up. For example, in his introduction to *Phaedras*, which considers amongst other things the nature of love, Jowett counsels:

> In this, as in his other discussions about love, what Plato says of the loves of men must be transferred to the loves of women before we can attach any serious meaning to his words. Had he lived in our times he would have made the transposition himself. But seeing in his own age the impossibility of woman being the intellectual helpmate or friend of man ... seeing that, even as to personal beauty, her place was taken by young mankind instead of womankind, he tries to work out the problem of love without regard to the distinctions of nature (Plato, 1892, p 406).

The charge levied against Socrates that he had corrupted youth concerned, in particular, a young man named Alcibiades. In *Protagoras*, Plato has an unknown friend of Socrates exclaim:

> Hello, Socrates; what have you been doing? No need to ask; you've been chasing around after that handsome young fellow Alcibiades. Certainly when I saw him just recently he struck me as still a fine-looking man, but a man all the same, Socrates (just between ourselves), with his beard already coming. (Plato, 1996, p 3)

It was apparently an intimate relationship and, according to Plato's *Symposium*, they did sleep together. Alcibiades knew, or hoped he knew, what to expect, but these expectations were dashed. Plato has Alcibiades complain that when he and Socrates went to bed 'for all the naughtiness that we'd got up to, I might as well have been sleeping with my father or an elder brother' (Plato, 1994, p 66). Nothing physical took place. Alcibiades' hopes for sexual love were in vain.

This friendship was, nonetheless, one of the reasons why Socrates was sentenced to death as Alcibiades held less than democratic political ideas in the relentlessly democratic Athens of the fifth century BCE. Rather than be a true mentor and teach Alcibiades how to be a proper Athenian citizen, committed to its rather muscular and aggressive form of democracy, Socrates was thought to have corrupted him by encouraging him to challenge the established order and to favour oligarchy. This was the antithesis of Athenian democracy, and was associated with Athens' political rival, Sparta. Socrates, in one way or another, had corrupted young Athenian men because he encouraged them to question the ways and ideals of their fathers (see, eg Waterfield, 2009, especially Ch 11, and Hughes, 2010).

In this light, Professor Brownlie appears to be a modern Anytus who fears that law students and lawyers might be demoralized by being encouraged to think about the nature of law, and to think for themselves. Perhaps we should reformulate his criticism of legal theory to affirm that there is room for a whole treatise on the harm caused to the business of philosophical investigation by political repression. There are times when thinking, and encouraging thinking, can be dangerous, and which sometimes can be fatal. A more recent example than Socrates is that of Evgeny Pashukanis (1891–1937), the Soviet author of *The General Theory of Law and Marxism* (1924). He was denounced as an 'enemy of the people' and as a 'Trotskyist saboteur' in 1937 and executed without trial. Pashukanis' view that the State would gradually wither away under communism was incompatible with Stalin's claim that socialism had by then been achieved in the Soviet Union (see, eg Bowring, 2008, pp 146–58, and Head, 2004). Quite simply, the politic context may be toxic to a robust and independent evaluation of law's nature, proper aims, and substantive content.

III. LAW, POLITICS, AND INSTRUMENTALISM

It is beyond doubt that the content and conceptions of law, whether international or domestic, bear some relationship to the wider contemporary socio-political context. All law has a political dimension as it aims to provide authoritative models of how those subject to it should behave. Often an issue emerges that is perceived to require regulation, and the contours of its legal analysis are determined by recourse to broadly political values. An early example in international law is Francisco de Vitoria's (c. 1483–1546) *De Indis (On the American Indians)* (1537) which applied scholastic natural law reasoning to undermine the legitimacy of Spanish claims to sovereignty over its American possessions:

> Vitoria's writings on power and the rights of conquest effectively set the agenda for most subsequent discussions on those subjects in Catholic Europe until the late seventeenth century... [A]lthough it is clearly false to speak of Vitoria as the father of anything so generalized and modern as 'International Law', it is the case that his writings became an integral part of later attempts to introduce some regulative principle into international relations.(Vitoria, 1991, p xxviii: *De Indis* is at p 231: see also Brett, 2012, and Tuck, 1999, pp 72–5)

Law and legal theory do not exist in a value-free vacuum but are inevitably concerned with political concerns and conditions,[3] and law inevitably favours some values and interests while ignoring or prejudicing others. In the case of international law, the privileged entities are principally States. Since at least the time of the Peace of Westphalia,[4] global organization has been characterized by the primacy of States as the principal actors on its political stage, making international law in pursuit of their own interests and policies. As Professor Craven has noted:

> notions of State and sovereignty [are] the key architectural features of international relations, whose existence from the Peace of Westphalia onwards is taken to be both 'given' and historically 'constant'. (Craven, 2012, p 864)

Although, in recent years, international legal theory has started to examine the implications of globalization, global governance, and the constitutionalization of the international legal order (see, for instance, works as diverse as Allott, 2002, Berman, 2005, Dunhoff and Trachtman, 2009, Klabbers, Peters and Ulfstein, 2009, and Slaughter, 2004), the focus of

---

[3] For instance, for an overview of the political context of the development of jurisprudential ideas, see Olivecrona, 1971, Ch 1; and also Tuck, 1999.

[4] This was constituted by the Peace of Münster (Treaty of Peace between Spain and the Netherlands, signed 30 January 1648: (1648) 1 CTS 1), the Treaty of Münster (Treaty of Peace between the Holy Roman Empire and France, signed 24 October 1648: (1648) 1 CTS 271), and the Treaty of Onsnabrück (Treaty of Peace between the Holy Roman Empire and Sweden, signed 24 October 1648: (1648) 1 CTS 198). For an assessment of the influence of the Peace of Westphalia see, eg Gross, 1948, and Duchhardt, 2012, pp 629–34.

international law remains on the State. The substantive structure and content of international law is asymmetric: it privileges States' interests above all others, relegating those of non-State entities to, at best, a secondary consideration. This asymmetry of the international legal system is reflected in theoretical discussions of international law. While it should not be surprising that a great deal of international legal theory has been instrumental, aimed at elucidating and explaining the role and conduct of States in the international sphere, another tendency has been more idealistic and is critical of the international system we have.

On the one hand, international legal theory has frequently been employed to provide instrumental methodologies which aim at embedding States' political programmes into the substance of international law—'Legal doctrines dissolve far too easily into thin disguises for assertions of national interests' (Kennedy, 1985, p 371). Clear examples of an instrumental approach to international law are two schools of thought that are principally associated with the antagonistic world views of the USA and the Soviet Union as they each vied for supremacy and power during the Cold War—the New Haven School and Marxist-Leninist theory. Although Soviet theory changed radically after perestroika (see, eg McWhinney, 1990, and Vereshchetin and Mullerson, 1990, and Tunkin, 2003), instrumentalist approaches did not die with the Cold War, but remain alive and well in contemporary legal theory. Not only has there been a resurgence in interest in the New Haven School (see, eg Borgen, 2007, Dickinson, 2007, Hathaway, 2007, Koh, 2007, Levit, 2007, Osofsky, 2007, and Reisman, Wiessner and Willard 2007), but instrumentalism is also located in arguments that international law should, for instance, be liberal (see, eg Kennedy, 2003, and Slaughter, 1995; compare Alvarez, 2001), be hegemonic (eg Bolton, 2000, Goldsmith and Posner, 2005, and Rabkin, 2005; compare Carty, 2004, and Vagts, 2001), or be Marxist in one way or another (eg Chimni, 2004, Marks, 2008, and Miéville, 2004).

On the other hand, an instrumentalist concentration on the concerns of States has stimulated a counter-reaction which argues, in effect, that international law is something far too important to be left to States. Indeed for some theorists, particularly those associated with the New Stream or New Approaches to International Law group, this appears to amount to a manifesto: 'students of international law should reformulate their sense of cause and effect in international affairs: rejecting reliance upon visions both of State interests that we too often take to propel doctrine and of the law that we take to restrain statesmen' (Kennedy, 1985, p 381).[5]

Perhaps the most radical and extensive contemporary assault on the unchecked focus on the State in the formulation of international law and doctrine is Professor Allott's theory of Social Idealism.[6] For Allott, what matters is humanity rather than a collection of States, the pursuit of whose interests he thinks has all too often harmed people. The primacy of State concerns in the international arena has given rise to the perception that domestic and international affairs are 'intrinsically and radically separate' (Allott 2001, p 244, para 13.105(6)): morality is discontinuous between the domestic and international spheres. Citizens can only participate in international affairs through the mediation of

---

[5] See also Kennedy, 1999 and 2000. Good overviews of New Stream, or New Approaches to International Law, work are Cass, 1996, Paulus, 2001, Purvis, 1991, Rasulov, 2012, and Tushnet, 2005.

[6] For what might be his manifesto, see Allott, 1998, although the Preface to Allott, 2001 might provide an easier understanding of his enterprise; see also Scobbie, 2011, but compare Prager, 1998. The Eminent Scholars archive on the website of the Squire Law Library contains a video of Allott's 2013 lecture 'The True Nature of International Law', and also audio files and transcripts of conversations with him: the portal to this archive is at http://www.squire.law.cam.ac.uk/eminent_scholars/.

their governments. The State-centric nature of international unsociety (to use Allott's term) and its influence on the conduct of international relations greatly attenuates, if not eliminates, individual moral responsibility for the content and operation of international law. This allows State concerns to trump a demotic humanitarian impulse, as 'governments, and the human beings who compose them, are able to will and act internationally in ways that they would be morally restrained from willing and acting internally, murdering human beings by the million in wars, tolerating oppression and starvation and disease and poverty, human cruelty and suffering, human misery and human indignity' (p 248, para 13.105(16)). What we are left with is 'a world fit for governments' (p 249, para 13.109) in which 'international law is left speaking to governments the words that governments want to hear' (p 296, para 16.1).

Some contemporary theorists, however, deny the very existence of a discipline that we can identify as 'international law', as something distinct from other disciplines, particularly politics:

> Our inherited ideal of a World Order based on the Rule of Law thinly hides from sight the fact that social conflict must still be solved by political means and that even though there may exist a common legal rhetoric among international lawyers, that rhetoric must, for reasons internal to the ideal itself, rely on essentially contested—political—principles to justify outcomes to international disputes. (Koskenniemi, 1990, p 7)[7]

This effacement of international law as an entity distinct from politics is, of course, a critique of other theories which see international law as something separate, something distinctly 'legal': it has been challenged (see, eg Beckett, 2005 and, more generally, MacCormick, 1990). To understand the critique, we must first understand the orthodoxy which engendered it, as social institutions, such as law, often develop dialectically, where a new approach or doctrine emerges as reaction to, or against, the established order. For instance, in the nineteenth century, impressionism originated as a rejection of the historical tradition in French painting (see King, 2006). Théophile Gautier, a prominent and influential nineteenth century French art critic, was in despair, as he could not understand this new style—'One examines oneself with a sort of horror...to discover whether one has become obese or bald, incapable of understanding the audacities of youth' (King, 2006, p 231). This reaction mirrors that of the legal philosopher HLA Hart, who in a 1944 letter to Isaiah Berlin ruminated:

> I have pictures of myself as a stale mumbler of the inherited doctrine, not knowing the language used by my contemporaries (much younger) and unable to learn it...(quoted in Lacey, 2004, p 115)

Perhaps an appropriate place to start in considering orthodoxy in theories of international law is with Grotius, often celebrated as the father of international law, as his *De Iure Belli ac Pacis* (*On the Law of War and Peace*) (1625) 'played a decisive part in the emergence of international law as a separate legal discipline' (Haggenmacher, 2012, p 1098). It has been claimed that Grotius' ideas served as a theoretical blueprint for the Westphalian order of international organization, although he died a few years before its creation. Haggenmacher argues that this is only a 'piously nurtured foundational myth...[which] is not borne out by the text of Grotius' masterpiece' (ibid, p 1099). But if this is what he was not, what was he?

---

[7] See also, for instance, Kratochwil, 1989; and Koskenniemi, 1989: for a commentary on both, see Scobbie, 1990.

IV. THE VIEW FROM DELFT

Hugo Grotius was born on 15 April 1583 in Delft towards the start of the Eighty Years' War, the war of Dutch independence from Spain, which lasted from 1568–1648, and which was terminated by the Peace of Westphalia. Johannes Vermeer was born towards the end of the war, being baptized in Delft on 31 October 1632. We have no record of his birth date. These two top and tail the rest of this chapter, although our geography and time frame is cast wider than that of the Eighty Years' War.

Like Socrates, Grotius was a dangerous thinker, while Vermeer was socially marginalized as a convert to Catholicism in a predominantly Protestant community. As well as being a lawyer, Grotius was a theologian, and imprisoned for life in 1619 at least partly for his views on the proper relationship between the civil authorities and the church. He escaped from prison in 1621 hidden in a book chest. (Let's try doing that using a Kindle.) Grotius was also a poet, and perhaps one of his more singular poems was 'a *Proof of True Religion* (*Bewys van den Waren Godtsdienst*), designed particularly for the use of seafaring folk, to relieve the tedium of long voyages, and to furnish them with controversial armour to repel the assaults of heathens, Jews, and Mohammedans' (Lee, 1930, pp 35–6).

Hugo Grotius did not invent international law: as Professor Bederman has demonstrated, international law existed in antiquity (Bederman, 2001), but along with writers such as Vitoria and Alberico Gentili (1552–1608: see Scattola, 2012), Grotius is generally seen as one of its founding figures in the modern period. He was not insulated from the politics of his time and place, which were dominated by the protracted revolt of the Dutch United Provinces against their monarch (the king of Spain). A paramount Dutch concern in the early seventeenth century was trade with the East Indies. Grotius was commissioned to defend the military and commercial activity of the Dutch United East India Company in the Far East, including its resort to war as a non-State actor, which led him to write *De Iure Praedae* (*On the Law of Prize*), although this was first published in its entirety only in 1864. One chapter was published in 1609, entitled *Mare Liberum* (*The Free Sea*), at the request of the East Indies Company, in which some of Grotius' relations were directors, with the hope of influencing peace negotiations which were then underway. Subsequently, after his escape from prison, Grotius revised and expanded the theoretical part of *De Iure Praedae* which became *De Iure Belli ac Pacis*. Surviving working papers show that he wanted to contrast his ideas with those of Vitoria (see Haggenmacher, 1990, pp 142–5, and Tuck, 1999, pp 78–83).

Grotius' theory of law marked a break from the scholasticism of Francisco Suárez (1548–1617: see Brett, 2012) and Vitoria. Suarez had rejected the idea that there could be obligation without God, but scholastic natural law embodied an idea of God and the relationship between God and man which could only be considered 'natural' if it were persuasive outside Christian Europe, for instance in the new colonies in America (see Haakonssen, 1996, pp 21–4):

> One of the main points of modern scepticism was that this was not the case. Religious and moral notions were so relative to time and place that no theoretically coherent account could be given of them. Not least, such notions were relative to each person's interest or individual utility. (p 23)

This scepticism was noted by Grotius in the *Prolegomena* to *De Iure Belli Ac Pacis*. He attempted to formulate a theory of natural law which would be impervious to this scepticism, but in doing so he laid the foundations for a secular natural law, arguing that principles of natural law are binding 'though we should even grant, what without the greatest Wickedness cannot be granted, that there is no God, or that he takes no Care of Human Affairs' (*Prolegomena*, para XI, Grotius, 2005, p 38: see also Olivecrona, 1971, pp 13–14). He also rejected the notion that natural law could be identified with either the Old or New Testaments (*Prolegomena*, paras XLIX and LI, Grotius, 2005, pp 47–8). One of Grotius' central concerns was to prove that 'a legal, including an international, order was possible independently of religion' (Haakonssen, 1996, p 30).

Thus it may be argued that Grotius laid the foundations for the secularization of natural law (see Haakonssen, 1985, pp 247–53), although he was not himself irreligious or secular (see, eg Haggenmacher, 2012, p 1099). Further, he attempted to create an understanding of international law which was not dependent on the doctrine of a single Christian denomination for its validity:

> Grotius had to write outside a single denomination because he sought to fashion a law of nations that could appeal to and bind Catholics, various Protestants and even non-Christians alike. His theory of a law of nations based on the consent of sovereigns was meant to be more or less religiously neutral. (Janis, 1991, p 63, see pp 61–6 generally)

Grotius' conception of the law of nations contained two principal strands. It comprised the *ius gentium*, the law applied by many or all States concerning matters which had an international aspect, and which was rooted in nature and discovered by human reason or which had been disclosed by divine revelation, and the *ius inter gentes* which arose from States' express or tacit consent (see Bull, Kingsbury and Roberts, 1990, pp 28–32, and Olivecrona, 1971, pp 23–4). As Grotius stated:

> when many Men of different Times and Places unanimously affirm the same Thing for Truth, this ought to be ascribed to a general Cause; which...can be no other than either a just Inference drawn from the Principles of Nature, or an universal Consent. The former shews the Law of Nature, the other the Law of Nations...For that which cannot be deduced from certain Principles by just Consequences, and yet appears to be every where observed, must owe its rise to a free and arbitrary Will. (*Prolegomena*, para XLI, Grotius, 2005, p 45)

Accordingly, Grotius opened the avenue for consent-based accounts of law between nations which came to dominate subsequent accounts of the nature of international law as he argued:

> But as the Laws of each State respect the Benefit of that State; so amongst all or most States there might be, and in Fact there are, some Laws agreed on by common Consent, which respect the Advantage not of one Body in particular, but of all in general. And this is what is called the Law of Nations, when used in Distinction to the Law of Nature. (*Prolegomena*, para XVIII, Grotius, 2005, p 39)

Thus a consequence of Grotius' hypothetical rejection of the theological foundations of natural law was that the consent of States became accepted as the basis of the rules of international law. Grotius paved the way for a consensual and secular concept of international law. A theologically based explanation of international law, regardless of the dominant denomination or religion involved, would be radically different in form and content to the existing system. Could it, for example, contain room for human rights in matters such as gender equality, sexual orientation, and freedom of and from religion, and should we expect to find in it elaborate rules on when resort to war could be justified on religious grounds?

V. BUT WHAT IS A THEORY?

Kant provides a useful notion of a theory for our purposes. He defined a theory as:

> A collection of rules, even of practical rules, is termed a theory if the rules concerned are envisaged as principles of a fairly general nature, and if they are abstracted from numerous conditions which, nonetheless, necessarily influence their practical application. Conversely, not all activities are called practice, but only those realizations of a particular purpose which are considered to comply with certain generally conceived principles of procedure... [N]o-one can pretend to be practically versed in a branch of knowledge and yet treat theory with scorn, without exposing the fact that he is an ignoramus in his subject. He no doubt imagines that he can get further than he could through theory if he gropes around in experiments and experiences, without collecting certain principles (which in fact amount to what we term theory) and without relating his activities to an integral whole (which, if treated methodically, is what we call a system). (Kant, 1793 (1970), pp 61–2)

But what does this mean?

It means that the function of a theory is to formulate or guide practice; to provide a relatively abstract framework for the understanding and determination of action. A theory is necessary because it provides us with the intellectual blueprint which enables us to understand the world, or some specific aspect of human affairs. Kant's notion of a system, which comprises an integrated body of knowledge rather than simply a collection of essentially unrelated general rules, underlines the constitutive function of theory. Theory makes data comprehensible by providing a structure for the organization of a given discipline or body of knowledge.

Different types of legal theory have different aims and concerns. For example, analytical theory tends to deal with questions such as the structure of legal systems, its components (such as the nature of rights and duties), legal epistemology (what is legal knowledge?), and legal ontology (does, and how does, law exist?—see, for instance, Arend, 1999, Ch 1, especially at pp 28ff; and Franck, 1990, Ch 2). Traditionally the ontological argument has dogged international law because of the influence of Austinian imperative theory. Despite, in some quarters (eg Bolton, 2000, pp 2, 4–5, and 48), a lingering attachment to the classical Austinian positivist claim that, because there is no determinate sovereign superior to States capable of promulgating and enforcing its commands, international law is not law but merely amounts to positive morality (see Austin, 1832 (1995), Lecture V, pp 123–5), this view is no longer generally accepted. It seems somewhat bizarre to rely on a discredited nineteenth century legal philosophy which speaks of the 'sovereign' and is essentially pre-democratic (at least in terms of universal suffrage) as the foundation for a contemporary understanding of law, or for the expression of a hostility to—or even a fear of—the very notion of international law. With the posthumous publication of the works of Jeremy Bentham, it is clear that Austin owed much to Bentham's more sophisticated analysis of law. Further, '[a]lthough there is no question that Bentham had doubts about the law-like character of international law, he was by no means the skeptic that Austin was' (Janis, 2004, p 16, see pp 16-18 generally).

These doubts are now a thing of the past, although some vestiges of the ontological debate remain in theoretical investigations of the sources of international law—the identification of what counts, or should count, as international law, which is, for instance, exemplified in Professor d'Aspremont's examination of formalism and sources (d'Aspremont, 2011) and the debate about relative normativity (see, eg Beckett, 2001, Roberts, 2001, Tasioulas,

1996, and Weil, 1983). Nevertheless, as Professor Franck (1995, p 6) affirms: 'international law has entered its post–ontological era. Its lawyers need no longer defend the very existence of international law. Thus emancipated from the constraints of defensive ontology, international lawyers are now free to undertake a critical assessment of its content'.

The conceptual exegesis of distinct substantive themes or fields finds expression in works such as Franck's account of the emergence of individualism as a core concept in international law (Franck, 1999); in the numerous applications of New Haven analysis to such diverse topics as the law of the sea (McDougal and Burke, 1962), human rights (McDougal, Lasswell, and Chen, 1969 and 1980), and armed conflict (McDougal and Feliciano, 1994); and in Ragazzi's exegesis of obligations erga omnes as rooted ultimately in natural law (Ragazzi, 1997, pp 183–5). Another important strand of contemporary international legal theory is critical theory, that is the ideological critique of the structure and content of international law, often from a position of identity politics such as gender (eg Charlesworth and Chinkin, 2000), race, or Third World Approaches to International Law (eg Anghie, 2005). This can overlap with more normative theory which questions what is international law for and what it should do.

In this chapter, I do not propose to offer anything like a comprehensive account of the diverse theories of international law, or to offer some 'master' theory which trumps all others. We must bear in mind Koskenniemi's cautionary observation about personal predispositions and biases. This propounds that all theoretical positions are, to some degree, subjective. The aim here is much more modest: to offer an outline of some theoretical points and perspectives which should provide a basis for thinking about the nature and function(s) of international law. But we should be clear on one thing: because writers start from different, and often inarticulate, premises about the nature and function of international law, it is not surprising that adhesion to different theoretical presuppositions results in different conclusions about what counts as international law in the first place (Lauterpacht, 1933, p 57).

VI. PROVENANCE AND MEANING

Identifying authorial predispositions is crucial to evaluating the weight to be given to an argument. Indeed, identifying the very author of a text can be decisive in law, in a way alien to other disciplines. For instance, in literature, Foucault argues in favour of the death of the author—the idea that the identity and personality of the author of a work of fiction is irrelevant to the authority and interpretation of the text. He acknowledges:

> I seem to call for a form of culture in which fiction would not be limited by the figure of the author... All discourses, whatever their status, form, value, and whatever the treatment to which they will be subjected, would then develop in the anonymity of a murmur. We would no longer hear the questions that have been rehashed for so long: Who really spoke? Is it really he and not someone else? With what authenticity or originality? And what part of his deepest self did he express in his discourse... [W]e would hear hardly anything but the stirring of an indifference: What difference does it make who is speaking? (Foucault, 1998, p 222)

Foucault claims that the ascription of an author to a text entails that it 'is not ordinary everyday speech that merely comes and goes...On the contrary, it is a speech that must be received in a certain mode and that, in a given culture, must receive a certain status' (p 211). Yet the identity of the person or body promulgating some types of legal texts has precisely this function. The significance of the identity of the actor in law is akin to that of provenance in the art market. Provenance is the chain of proof that demonstrates that an artefact is not a forgery but may be safely attributed to a given artist. Provenance is crucial to valuation: a painting that cannot be shown to have been painted by, say, Manet, does not have the same value as a 'real' attested Manet. (Indeed, Gertrude Stein was displeased when, at the height of the cubist period, her friends Pablo Picasso and Georges Braque signed the other's name to their paintings, as she thought artists should bear responsibility for their own work—see Wagner-Martin, 1995, p 148.)

The value, or significance, of an ostensibly legal document or statement invariably depends on its author; because its author is a judge; because its author is a legislature; because its author is a foreign ministry; and so on. Legal documents and statements are not simply strings of words: rather, they are speech acts—words which are intended to have a practical impact. They are words which are meant to do things and not remain mere utterances. Like making a promise, they constitute an action (an illocutionary act) which does not describe but which is meant to change social reality (see Austin, 1996). When the Athenean jury sentenced Socrates to death, as it was legally empowered to do, its words were meant to have an effect in the real world, particularly for Socrates.

Legal texts, and their authors, only make sense within the context of the system that gives them authority and meaning. Literary, artistic, even philosophical texts, on the other hand, are a great deal more autonomous. At the extreme, as in the case of the fictitious Australian poet Ern Malley whose works were fabricated to satirize modernist poetry, but which now form part of the Australian literary canon, the 'author' need not even exist (see Heyward, 1993). Or reconsider Socrates: he left no writings, but would it matter if 'Socrates', like 'Ern Malley', never existed? Would it matter if he were only a literary device invented by Plato and Xenophon as a vehicle to present their thoughts?

In some circumstances, therefore, to gain a full understanding of a text, it must be located within a framework where it may be properly understood. Some, however, argue that all readings of a text are partial, and that a search for authorial intent, even in law, cannot generate a 'correct' interpretation (eg Balkin, 1986, p 772). There is a degree of truth in this, but it is equally true that legal texts, unlike literary texts, form part of an interlocking system of meaning and are not free radicals that bear the meaning anyone chooses to put upon them. There is a difference between a legal text such as Article 51 of the UN Charter, whose interpretation may be contested in regard to some matters, such as when it would allow a kinetic response (bullets, bombs, and things that go bang) as self-defence in response to a non-kinetic attack (cyber warfare) (see Tallinn Manual, 2013, Ch II, and Schmitt, 2012, pp 18–25), and a literary text which can bear any meaning one chooses, such as these lines from Gertrude Stein's poem 'Lifting belly':

> I say lifting belly and then I say lifting belly and Caesars. I say lifting belly gently and Caesars gently. I say lifting belly again and Caesars again. I say lifting belly and I say Caesars and I say lifting belly Caesars and cow come out. I say lifting belly and Caesars and cow come out. (Stein, 1998b, p 410 at 435)

While most literary critics interpret passages such as this as lesbian eroticism written by Stein for her lover Alice B. Toklas, with the 'cow' being an orgasm for Alice (but see Turner 1999, pp 24–31), reading early Stein, such as 'Lifting belly', generally involves a fruitless search for meaning, because it is an attempt to unlock the sense which she took pains consciously to erase (see Dydo, 2003):

> Stein's true radical legacy lay in her insistence on showing how words and their meanings could be undone; she took it as her right that she had the freedom to use words

exactly as she pleased, and in doing so she undermined the relation between words and the world...Janet Flanner remembered: 'A publisher once said to her, "We want the comprehensible thing, the thing the public can understand". She said to him: "My work would have been no use to anyone if the public had understood me early and first"'. (Daniel, 2009, p 190)

Indeed, one contemporary commentator thought that Stein had 'outdistanced any of the Symbolists in using words for pure purposes of suggestion—she has gone so far that she no longer even suggests' (Wilson, 1996, p 276, first published 1931). Does this matter? Stein's purpose in writing was to make manifest her 'genius': her work did, and does, not need to 'mean' anything. It exists in, and for, itself—as well as for the Greater Glory of Gertrude.

Legal texts, on the other hand, do need to have an identifiable meaning, or range of acceptable meanings, because the practice of law is an instrumental activity aimed at practical outcomes in the 'real' world. The Socratic (or at least Platonic) idea that the written word is like a painted image as it can only signify one thing entails that words are univocal, and bear one meaning and one meaning alone. This idea that written words 'just go on and on for ever giving the same single piece of information' is simply too reductive. Legal systems are expressed in natural language which cannot fulfil the requirement of univocity because natural language is inherently ambiguous (see, eg Perelman and Olbrechts-Tyteca, 1969, pp 13–14, para 1, pp 120ff, para 30, and pp 130ff, para 33, and Perelman 1976, pp 34–6, para 24 and pp 114–55, para 56bis). Perelman repeatedly illustrates the non-univocity of natural language using the apparent tautologies 'boys will be boys' or 'business is business'. To give these phrases meaning, different interpretations must be given to the repeated terms whereas in formal logical or mathematical systems such propositions would be meaningless because of the systemic requirement of the principle of identity, which necessitates that terms, or words, are univocal and unambiguous (see, eg Perelman and Olbrechts-Tyteca, 1969, pp 21ff, para 51, and pp 442–3, para 94, and Perelman, 1976, pp 115–16, para 56bis).

Perelman's theory of rhetoric aims at examining how arguments may persuade and thus assumes that legal arguments can communicate meaning. Drawing on the work of linguistic theorists such as Ferdinand de Saussure (1857–1913), particularly his *Course in General Linguistics* (*Cours de Linguistique Générale*, published posthumously in 1916), some legal theorists argue that all texts are inevitably and radically indeterminate and have no settled meaning (for an account and critique, see Solum, 1987). This has long been a tenet of US legal philosophy. One of the principal strands of American Legal Realism, rule scepticism, argued that this uncertainty lay in the very formulation of rules, and thus judicial decisions could not lay claim to being simply the inexorable application of the law to the issue in question (see Frank, 1949). This is reflected in McDougal and Lasswell's admonition that:

> From any relatively specific statements of social goal (necessarily described in a statement of low-level abstraction) can be elaborated an infinite series of normative propositions of ever increasing generality; conversely, normative statements of high-level abstraction can be manipulated to support any specific social goal. (Lasswell and McDougal, 1943, p 213)

It must be conceded that there cannot be hyper-reality in legal discourse because of the ambiguity of language, but that language must be able to communicate effectively. If law were radically indeterminate then no contract, statute, or treaty could have any determinable meaning, and every criminal conviction is unsafe because of the principle of legality—if all law is indeterminate, then how do we know if/when someone commits a criminal offence? How can there be an effective speech act, if the meaning of that speech cannot be discerned?

While extra-legal factors are undoubtedly taken into account in interpreting an ambiguous text, and in international law the influence of politics in this is well-nigh inescapable, to argue that this means that law inevitably collapses into politics might be to mistake the process for the outcome. Professor Raz draws a distinction between the deliberative and executive stages of legal reasoning. In the former, factors are evaluated to decide what the law should be, and then at the executive stage this solution is incorporated into the law (Raz, 1980, pp 213–14). The drafting of a treaty manifestly falls within the deliberative stage, as does a court's consideration of the proper interpretation of an instrument, but at the executive stage, once the treaty text is finalized, or once the judgment is issued, once the operative speech act takes place, then the political considerations in issue become subsumed within the law.

VII. LIBERAL DEMOCRACY V MARXISM-LENINISM—POLES APART?

It should be clear that the more overtly a writer uncovers his or her theoretical assumptions, the more honest is the writing, because his or her model of international law is exposed on the page for all to see.

To illustrate the formative power of theory, it is convenient to contrast two very different accounts of international law, namely the New Haven School which was elaborated principally by Myres McDougal and Harold Lasswell in Yale Law School, and the pre-perestroika Soviet theory of international law propounded by GI Tunkin. As products of the Cold War, these are primarily of historical interest, but they were distinctive theories of international law which clearly set out to bolster and justify the external projection of the political values of the USA and Soviet Union. Although they thus shared a similar purpose, they embodied profoundly different political aims and objectives: this is abundantly clear in their approach to sources and methodology.

It could be argued that the chasm between the two theories runs deeper, that there is an architectonic difference between the two, as the New Haven School sees law as facilitative whereas Soviet theory amounts to a constitutive theory. Posner explains the facilitative approach as claiming that law provides, 'a service to lay communities in the achievement of those communities' self-chosen ends rather than as a norm imposed on those communities in the service of a higher end' (Posner, 1990, p 94). The latter is, of course, the constitutive approach.

McDougal and Lasswell (1981, p 24) defined 'human dignity' as 'a social process in which values are widely and not narrowly shared, and in which private choice, rather than coercion, is emphasized as the predominant modality of power'. Accordingly, the New Haven goal of clarifying and implementing a world order of human dignity could be seen as falling squarely within Posner's notion of a facilitative theory. This is not the case. The raison d'être of the New Haven School was the pursuit of an imposed 'higher end', namely, the defence and maintenance of (American) liberal democracy as a bulwark against the spread of communism. This is manifestly a constitutive theory. It is ideological, the attempted globalization of the claim that the USA is morally exceptional and 'endowed by its creator with a special mission, a "manifest destiny", to "overspread" the North American continent and perhaps the world, so as to evangelize it with the twin gospels of American democracy and American capitalism' (Hodgson, 2005, p 20). As Falk observes, New Haven analysis is constructed around an:

> ideological bipolarity of a world order that pits totalitarian versus free societies as the essential struggle of our time, a view that anchors the McDougal and Lasswell jurisprudence in the history of the Cold War era. (Falk, 1995, p 2004)

For McDougal and Lasswell the choice was one between nuclear annihilation and the global promotion of US democratic values (Falk, 1995, p 2002; Duxbury, 1995, pp 195–8). They, in an act of 'ideological partisanship' (Falk, 1995, p 2003), chose the latter.

A. THE NEW HAVEN SCHOOL

The genesis of New Haven lay in the Second World War and the emergence of communism as an international political force. McDougal and Lasswell argued that, when US law schools reopened after the war, they should be 'a place where people who have risked their lives can wisely risk their minds' (Lasswell and McDougal, 1943, p 292). The aim of legal education was to provide systematic training for policy-makers attuned to 'the needs of a free and productive commonwealth':

> The proper function of our law schools is, in short, to contribute to the training of policy-makers for the ever more complete achievement of the democratic values that constitute the professed ends of American polity. (Lasswell and McDougal, 1943, p 206; see also Falk, 1995, p 1993)

These values should be reinforced so that the student applies them automatically to 'every conceivable practical and theoretical situation' (Lasswell and McDougal, 1943, p 244). As lawyers influence or create policy when indicating whether a proposed course of action is or is not lawful (p 209), the law school curriculum should aim towards the implementation of 'clearly defined democratic values in all the areas of social life where lawyers have or can assert responsibility' (p 207). Policy and value permeate law; there are no autonomous or neutral theories of law which can ignore the policy consequences of rules (McDougal and Reisman, 1983, p 122). Therefore:

> In a democratic society it should not, of course, be an aim of legal education to impose a single standard of morals upon every student. But a legitimate aim of education is to seek to promote the major values of a democratic society and to reduce the number of moral mavericks who do not share democratic preferences. The student may be allowed to reject the morals of democracy and embrace those of despotism; but his education should be such that, if he does so, he does it by deliberate choice, with awareness of the consequences for himself and others, and not by sluggish self-deception. (Lasswell and McDougal, 1943, p 212)

Although Lasswell and McDougal initially (1943, passim) envisioned the comprehensive application of their theory to reform the entire law school curriculum, it rapidly focused specifically on international law (Duxbury, 1995, p 191). The practical aim of the New Haven School is to advance 'a universal world order of human dignity' which secures the widespread enjoyment of values by individuals. A value is simply 'a preferred event' or, in other words, whatever an individual or decision-maker desires. A full enumeration of values is impossible—'if we were to begin to list all the specific items of food and drink, of dress, of housing, and of other enjoyments, we should quickly recognize the unwieldiness of the task'. McDougal and Lasswell claim that any given value will fall within one or more of the categories that they identify as enlightenment, respect, power, well-being, wealth, skill, affection, and rectitude (McDougal and Lasswell, 1981, p 20: see also Lasswell and McDougal, 1943, pp 217–32; McDougal and Reisman, 1983, p 118; Arend, 1999, p 72; and Duxbury, 1995, p 178). Human dignity, however, is not foundational, 'We postulate this goal, deliberately leaving everyone free to justify it in terms of his preferred theological or philosophical tradition' (McDougal and Lasswell, 1981, p 24: see also Lasswell and McDougal, 1943, p 213).

This goal reflects the New Haven School's basis in, and intended refinement of, the American Legal Realist school of jurisprudence and its intertwining of law and the social sciences, especially economics.[8] Realism rejected formalist accounts of law that claimed to be value-neutral and relied on the logical exegesis of legal principle to explain the operation of the courts and legal system.

Realism, contrary to formalism, laid stress on the social consequences of the law which should be taken into account in judicial decisions, and thus emphasized empiricism. This aimed at determining the real factors involved in judgments beyond the formal appeal to rules, and also at demonstrating the social impact that alternative judicial choices might have. Law was seen as a form of social engineering that could be used as a tool to attain desired societal goals. The New Haven School built on this tradition in American jurisprudence by rejecting the notion that law is merely a system of rules, by trying to achieve a more empirical account of the operation of law in society, and by postulating the instrumental aim of achieving human dignity (see Morison, 1982, pp 178–88).

The New Haven School displaces the conception of law as a system of rules in favour of one where law is a normative social system which revolves around trends of authoritative decisions taken by authorized decision-makers including, but not restricted to, judges. There is, after all, more to law than what happens in court rooms— 'If a legal system works well, then disputes are in large part *avoided* (Higgins, 1994, p 1, emphasis in original). International lawyers, giving legal advice that moulds policy and action, are more likely to be in foreign ministries than appearing before the International Court of Justice. Contemporary New Haven doctrine is more radical in its intentions. It claims that its methodology 'can be especially empowering for individuals not associated with the state, a class that classical international law all but disenfranchised'. Applying its techniques, either alone or as part of an interest group, individuals can be involved in influencing the decisions that affect their lives (see Reisman, Wiessner, and Willard, 2007, pp 576-578). Law is a continuing process of decisions involving choices aimed at realizing the common value of human dignity:

> the major systems of public order are in many fundamental respects rhetorically unified. All systems proclaim the dignity of the human individual and the ideal of a worldwide public order in which this ideal is authoritatively pursued and effectively approximated. (McDougal and Lasswell, 1981, p 19)

The New Haven process of decisions has been likened to Heraclitus' aphorism that one never steps into the same river twice, because the river moves on. For New Haven adherents, because the social context of decisions change, and because the trends and implications of past decisions can be unclear, the quest for human dignity necessitates the

---

[8] On American Legal Realism, see Duxbury, 1995, Chs 1 and 2; and Feldman, 2000, pp 105–15. More elementary accounts of this school may be found in standard textbooks on jurisprudence, such as Freeman, 2001, Ch 9.

rejection of a model of law that comprises simply the neutral or impartial application of rules. Rules are:

> inconsistent, ambiguous, and full of omissions. It was Mr. Justice Cardozo who aptly remarked that legal principles have, unfortunately, the habit of travelling in pairs of opposites. A judge who must choose between such principles can only offer as justification for his choice a proliferation of other such principles in infinite regress or else arbitrarily take a stand and state his preference; and what he prefers or what he regards as 'authoritative' is likely to be a product of his whole biography. (Lasswell and McDougal, 1943, p 236)

This, in itself, appears to be a New Haven refinement of the realist notion of the intuitive nature of judicial decision-making. Hutcheson had argued that, in hard cases, the judge does not decide by an abstract application of the relevant rules, but decides intuitively which way the decision should go before searching for a legal category into which the decision will fit—'No reasoning applied to practical matters is ever really effective unless motivated by some impulse' (Hutcheson, 1928–9, p 285). The New Haven School conceded that the application of its method could not overcome discretion or bias on the part of the decision-maker. As a bulwark against this, and thus the tendency to intuitive reductionism advanced by Hutcheson, it counselled that decision-makers should be as self-conscious as possible about their predispositions, and undertake a systematic and comprehensive assessment of policy choices relevant to their decisions as the state of available knowledge allowed (Falk, 1995, p 1999).

Rules are only 'shorthand expressions of community expectations' and thus, like any shorthand, are inadequate as a method of communication (Duxbury, 1995, p 194). Rules simply cannot be applied automatically to reach a decision because that decision involves a policy choice:

> Reference to 'the correct legal view' or 'rules' can never avoid the element of choice (though it can seek to disguise it), nor can it provide guidance to the preferable decision. In making this choice one must inevitably have consideration for the humanitarian, moral, and social purposes of the law. (Higgins, 1994, p 5)

Higgins continues that the New Haven School's articulation of relevant policy factors, and their systematic assessment in decision-making, precludes the decision-maker unconsciously giving preference to a desired policy objective under the guise of it being 'the correct legal rule'.

The realization of preferred values is not, however, the sole factor in decision-making: law does constrain. Recourse must be made to trends of past decisions; and how these relate to the goals the decision-maker wishes to achieve; and how these decisions may be deployed to realize these goals—'the task is to think creatively about how to alter, deter, or accelerate probable trends in order to shape the future closer to his desire' (Lasswell and McDougal, 1943, p 214). Further, these goals can only be achieved if the decision taken is both authoritative and controlling:

> Authority is the structure of expectation concerning who, with what qualifications and mode of selection, is competent to make which decisions by what criteria and what procedures. By control we refer to an effective voice in decision, whether authorized or not. The conjunction of common expectations concerning authority with a high degree of corroboration in actual operation is what we understand by law. (McDougal and Lasswell, 1981, p 22)

More succinctly, Higgins describes law as 'the interlocking of authority with power' (Higgins, 1994, p 5: see also Arend, 1999, pp 77–9).

Thus the New Haven School aims at providing a framework of values and matrix of effective and authoritative decision-making in pursuit of the democratic ideal it favours. In this matrix, the actual and desired distribution of values affects every authoritative decision. In turn, the future distribution of values which stems from these decisions aims to mould and secure community public order to maximize the realization of human dignity (McDougal and Reisman, 1983, p 118).

B. SOVIET THEORY

The other principal Cold War doctrine—the theory of international law sponsored by the Soviet Union, rooted in Marxism-Leninism, and reaching its apogee in the pre-perestroika works of Tunkin (but see Bowring, 2008 for a more nuanced account of Soviet legal theory)—was a diametrical opposite to the New Haven School, both in its professed structure and envisaged political outcome. This orthodoxy, enforced by the Soviet bloc, relied not on the values encompassed in human dignity to explain international law, but on the 'objective' rules of societal development and the historical inevitability of socialism:

> The foreign policy and diplomacy of socialist States is armed with the theory of Marxism-Leninism and a knowledge of the laws of societal development. Proceeding on the basis of a new and higher social system replacing capitalism, they adduce and defend progressive international legal principles which correspond to the laws of societal development and which are aimed at ensuring peace and friendly cooperation between states and the free development of peoples (Tunkin, 1974, p 277).[9]

Under Soviet theory, international law was 'under the decisive influence of the socialist States, the developing countries, and the other forces of peace and socialism', and was aimed at 'ensuring peace and peaceful co-existence, at the freedom and independence of peoples, against colonialism in all of its manifestations, and at the development of peaceful international cooperation in the interests of all peoples' (Tunkin, 1974, p 251). The role of international law was to promote human progress, which necessarily led to socialism. Indeed, Soviet writers argued that socialism was the inevitable outcome of social processes and, with its triumph, the State and law (including international law) would be eradicated as these are the products of class division, although there would still be rules of conduct (eg Tunkin, 1974, pp 42, 238: see pp 232ff generally). Until then, international law was 'immortalize[d] ... as an instrument of struggle between States belonging to opposed social systems' (Damrosch and Müllerson, 1995, p 4) in which the most that could be achieved was peaceful co-existence between capitalist and socialist States.

Soviet theory is squarely based in Marxist-Leninist theory to the extent that, at times, it seems simply to amount to taking the dogma for a walk. Perhaps paradoxically, Soviet theory is much more traditional, more conservative, than the New Haven School, placing its emphasis on rules and State consent to rules, rather than the New Haven realization of values by authorized decision-makers:

> both the Soviet government and Soviet doctrine consistently treated the existing corpus of international law as a system of sufficiently determinate principles and norms which all

[9] For an overview of Marxist theory of law, see Freeman, 2001, Ch 12: a clear, succinct, and critical introduction is Collins, 1984. For an account of the early formation of Soviet concepts of international law, see Macdonald, 1998.

States are obliged to observe in their mutual relations, in contrast to some Western scholars who find international law to be more or less adaptable and argue that law should fit
behaviour rather than the other way around. The Soviet preference for a relatively rigid
rule-bound approach was not merely an outgrowth of traditional jurisprudential conventions, but also served political and polemical functions. (Damrosch and Müllerson, 1995,
p 9, footnotes omitted)

Soviet theory was rooted in the class struggle, and the Marxist-Leninist tenet that the
mode of production within a society (the economic base) is the principal influence on the
will of the ruling class, and thus on the social institutions (the superstructure) of that society.
Only with the emergence of private property and social classes does the State emerge 'as
an organ of the economically dominant class', along with law which constitutes the will of
this ruling class in defence of its interests (Kartashkin, 1983, p 81).[10]

Capitalist and socialist States have different interests, and thus wills, given the difference
in their socio-economic organization—'the influence of the economic structure of society
and its societal laws affects the process of creating norms of international law through
the will of a state, since the content of this will basically is determined by the economic
conditions of the existence of the ruling class in a given state' (Tunkin, 1974, p 237). While
the dominant economic class determines the will of a capitalist State, in a socialist State,
this comprises 'the will of the entire Soviet people led by the working class' (p 249 and,
eg p 36). One clear consequence of this divergence in interest is Soviet theory's rejection of
'general principles of law recognized by civilised nations' (Article 38(1)(c) of the Statute of
the International Court of Justice) as an independent source of international law. Because
of the opposed nature of their socio-economic systems, Tunkin denied the possibility that
there could exist normative principles common to socialist and bourgeois legal systems.
Even if principles superficially appeared to be common to the two types of system, they
were 'fundamentally distinct by virtue of their class nature, role in society, and purposes'
(p 199).

A common ideology, however, is unnecessary for the development of international law,
but the existence of two opposed social systems places limits on the content of the norms
of international law. Because these must be agreed by States on the basis of equality—
'only those international legal norms which embrace the agreement of all states are norms
of contemporary general international law'—they can be neither socialist nor capitalist
(pp 250–51; see also 1974, Ch 2, passim, and Kartashkin, 1983, pp 96ff).

Consent between States, albeit reflecting the interests of their ruling classes, to specific rules is the keystone of Soviet theory which, furthermore, recognizes only treaties
and custom as sources of international law (Tunkin, 1974, pp 36, 291). There is no room
for some authoritative decision-maker to determine or influence the content of international law—for instance, 'The [International] Court does not create international law; it
applies it' (p 191). Norm creation necessarily requires State consent, whether express or
tacit (p 124 and Ch 4, passim):

the majority of states in international relations cannot create norms binding upon other
states and do not have the right to attempt to impose given norms on other states. This

---

[10] See also pp 79–83 generally; and Tunkin, 1974, pp 27, 36, 232ff. Kartashkin (1983, p 81) notes that
according to Marxist-Leninist theory, there are five socio-economic formations of society—primitive communal, slave, feudal, capitalist, and communist. Compare Smith's notion of the four stages of society found, for
instance, in Smith (1978, pp 14–16): 'in these several ages of society, the laws and regulations with regard to
property must be very different' (p 16).

proposition is especially important for contemporary international law, which regulates relations of states belonging to different and even opposed social systems. (p 128)

In its emphasis on consent which allows international law to bridge between different social systems, Soviet theory is redolent of Grotius' attempt to provide common rules for different 'denominations', although it is stripped of any thought of natural law. Tunkin argues that because natural law theorists of international law undermine its consensual basis, this creates a climate which increases the 'possibilities for an international legal justification of the imperialist policy of *diktat, coercion, and military adventurism*' (p 210).

Tunkin stresses that international law, as it exists between socialist and capitalist States, rests on consensual principles of peaceful co-existence which include the principles of the sovereign equality of States and non-interference in their domestic affairs (pp 29 and 251). The application and implications of these principles differ, however, in the international relations between States from opposed socio-economic systems and in the relations between socialist States *inter se*. Relations between socialist States are not predicated on the notion of peaceful co-existence but on the principle of socialist or proletarian internationalism (p 47: this doctrine is expounded at length at pp 427ff). Thus Kartashkin maintains that:

> principles of general international law, when applied in relations among socialist countries, expand their shape and acquire new socialist content. They go beyond general principles of international law. For example, the general principle of international law—the equality of states—acquires a new content when applied in relations among socialist states. Parallel to the respect for legal equality, its implementation presupposes the achievement of factual equality of all socialist states and the equalization of their economic level. The principles of socialist internationalism are used by socialist states to strengthen their relations, to protect them from anti-socialist forces, and to ensure the construction of socialism. Thus, in relations among socialist states two types of norms function—the socialist and general principles and the norms of international law. (Kartashkin, 1983, pp 82–3)

The principle of proletarian internationalism is that of 'fraternal friendship, close cooperation, and mutual assistance of the working class of various countries in the struggle for their liberation' (Tunkin, 1974, p 4: see also Butler, 1971, pp 796–7, but compare Hazard, 1971). This manifests itself in principles of socialist legality which, in the relations between socialist States, are *lex specialis* to the norms of general international law (Tunkin, 1974, pp 445–56: see also Osakwe, 1972, p 597). These principles are, 'first and foremost', those of 'fraternal friendship, close cooperation, and comradely mutual assistance' (Tunkin, 1974, pp 434–5: see also Butler, 1971, p 797, and Osakwe, 1972, p 598). Their implementation requires close cooperation between Socialist States in foreign and defence policy to secure 'the gains of socialism from possible feeble imperialist swoops' (Tunkin, 1974, p 430).

At its most stark, this aim was expressed in the Brezhnev doctrine, the claim that socialist States could, if necessary, use force to ensure that another socialist State did not divert from socialism and revert to capitalism. This doctrine asserted that a threat to socialism in one State was 'a threat to the security of the socialist community as a whole'[11] and thus a common problem. It therefore constituted 'the joint defense of the socialist system from

---

[11] Brezhnev doctrine as quoted in Schwebel, 1972, pp 816–17; see also Franck, 1970, pp 832–3. Franck argues that the USA foreshadowed the Brezhnev doctrine in its policy towards the Americas—see ibid, pp 833–5, and pp 822–35 generally.

any attempts of forces of the old world to destroy or subvert any socialist state of this system' (Tunkin, 1974, p 434). Although the Brezhnev doctrine was promulgated following the forcible suppression of moves towards democratization in Czechoslovakia in 1968 (see, eg Butler, 1971, p 797; Franck, 1970, p 833; and Schwebel, 1972, p 816), this principle of socialist internationalism was employed to justify the Soviet intervention in Hungary in 1956 (Tunkin, 1974, pp 435–6) and its 1980 invasion of Afghanistan (see Brezhnev, 1980, pp 6–9).

C. NEW HAVEN AND SOVIET APPROACHES COMPARED

Accordingly, just as New Haven has the teleological aim of achieving human dignity, and thus the external projection of democratic liberal values, so Soviet theory has the aim of realizing proletarian internationalism, and thus the global triumph of socialism. While New Haven rejects any foundational basis for human dignity, in that it is indifferent to the philosophical positions which individuals may use to justify human dignity, Soviet theory is foundational because it maintains that, by way of objective rules of societal development, the goal of proletarian internationalism is historically inevitable. In the meantime, according to Tunkin (1974, p 48) common ground must be sought in which competing social systems may peacefully co-exist. Despite opposed theories regarding the nature and function of international law, agreement on specific international legal norms was not impossible. For instance, the international regulation of human rights occurred despite the absence of a common ideology:

> Marxist-Leninist theory proceeds from the premise that human rights and freedoms are not inherent in the nature of man and do not constitute some sort of natural attributes. Rights and freedoms of individuals in any state are materially stipulated and depend on socio-economic, political and other conditions of the development of society, its achievements and progress. Their fundamental source is the material conditions of society's life. (Kartashkin, 1983, p 95)

McDougal and Lasswell would undoubtedly see this as an example where 'allegedly universal doctrines' such as sovereignty, domestic jurisdiction, and non-intervention are used 'to resist the institutional reconstructions which are indispensable to security'. In this case, the Soviet claim was that the content of internationally agreed human rights fell within the domestic jurisdiction of the implementing State (Tunkin, 1974, pp 82–3). McDougal and Lasswell (1981, p 18) resisted such 'false conceptions of the universality of international law', and argued that the discrediting of such false claims was necessary in order to clarify 'the common goals, interpretations, and procedures essential to achieving an effective international order'.

On the other hand, the policy science approach of New Haven was an anathema to Soviet thinking:

> Even though states may use international law as a support for foreign policy, this does not mean that international law is merged with policy. Mixing international law with policy inevitably leads to a denial of the normative character of international law, that is to say, to a denial of international law, which becomes buried in policy and vanishes as law.

> Professor McDougal's concept of the policy approach to international law is an example of this kind of mixing or blending of foreign policy and international law.

> …McDougal, while not denying the importance of international law in so many words and sometimes also stressing it, in fact drowns international law in policy. In consequence

thereof, international law in McDougal's concept is devoid of independent significance as a means of regulating international relations; it disappears into policy and, moreover, is transformed in to a means of justifying policies which violate international law. (Tunkin, 1974, p 297)

This criticism that New Haven analysis results in the eradication of international law is commonplace (see, eg Arend, 1996, p 290; Bull, 2002, pp 153–4; and Kratochwil, 1989, pp 193–200). Falk notes that, although not inevitable, the outcome of the application of New Haven analysis to a given issue 'had an uncomfortable tendency to coincide with the outlook of the US government and to seem more polemically driven than scientifically demonstrated' (Falk, 1995, p 2001, see also p 1997, and Koh 2007, p 563). It cannot be doubted that the same was true of Soviet international law, despite its reliance on 'norms'. As Damrosch and Müllerson (1995, pp 8–9) comment:

> The political climate of the Cold War undoubtedly contributed to the sense that the international legal order was far from approaching an optimal or perhaps even minimal level of determinacy. Especially in highly politicized areas such as the use of force or intervention, as well as in many aspects of human rights law, the content and clarity of principles and norms suffered from the fact that states proceeded from opposed interests; while they wanted to delineate parameters for the behaviour of the other side, they were wary of tying their own hands. The positions of the two sides were not only different but often irreconcilable; yet those positions were sometimes dictated more by ideological considerations than by real national interests.

The New Haven tendency to make law malleable in its pursuit of human dignity, McDougal and Lasswell's 'penchant for applying their theory in justification of US foreign policy' (Falk, 1995, p 1997), undoubtedly gives an impression of normative indeterminacy. Could it be argued, however, that this mistakes the anomaly for the paradigm? One of the criticisms of formalism made by realist scholars was that it focused on the judgments of appellate courts which concentrate on contestable points of law (Duxbury, 1995, pp 57, 135–7). Is this not also true of the common impression gained of the New Haven School (and equally of Soviet theory for that matter)? As Higgins (1994, pp 6–7) notes, New Haven does not require:

> one to find every means possible if the end is desirable. Trends of past decisions still have an important role to play in the choices to be made, notwithstanding the importance of both context and desired outcome. Where there is ambiguity or uncertainty, the policy-directed choice can properly be made.

Koskenniemi has observed that when he worked for the Finnish foreign ministry, politicians seeking international legal advice saw every situation as 'new, exceptional, [a] crisis'. The legal adviser's function was to link this back to precedents, to 'tell it as part of a history', and thus to present it as meshed in 'narratives in which it received a generalizable meaning' in order that the politician 'could see what to do with it' (Koskenniemi, 2005, p 120: compare Charlesworth, 2002b).

The application of most international law is not problematic: standardized rules are applied to standardized situations otherwise, as Franck (1990, p 20) points out, 'for example, no mail would go from one state to another, no currency or commercial transactions could take place... [V]iolence, fortunately, is a one-in-a-million deviance from the pacific norm'. Higgins' point appears to be that if ambiguity exists, then the decision-maker can make a choice which implements or is justified by existing legal material. Choice is inevitable in legal decision-making because rules are not fully determined. In these circumstances, Higgins (1994, p 5) thinks it:

> desirable that the policy factors are dealt with systematically and openly. Dealing with them systematically means that all factors are properly considered and weighed, instead of the decision-maker unconsciously narrowing or selecting what he will take into account in order to reach a decision that he has instinctively predetermined is desirable. Dealing with policy factors openly means that the decision-maker himself is subjected to the discipline of facing them squarely.

While one can disagree with the policy factors Higgins thinks relevant, at least this approach has the virtue of making these factors candid. Analysis and evaluation are easier because one knows the factors in play.

VIII. BEYOND THE STATE, ITS INTERESTS, AND INSTRUMENTALISM

Despite their differences, the New Haven and Soviet schools share a common approach: both are instrumental theories of law, aimed at guiding and informing practice while implementing a political programme. Not all legal philosophy has this focus, despite the fact that this might cause disappointment:

> Lawyers and law teachers...think (rightly) that legal practice is a practical business, and they expect the philosophy of law to be the backroom activity of telling front-line practitioners how to do it well, with their heads held high. When a philosopher of law asserts a proposition that neither endorses nor criticizes what they do, lawyers and law teachers are often frustrated...They cannot accept that legal philosophy is not wholly (or even mainly) the backroom activity of identifying what is good or bad about legal practice, and hence of laying on practical proposals for its improvement (or failing that, abandonment). (Gardner, 2001, p 204)

Much contemporary theory is non-instrumental, and thus detached from the practice of international law. This tendency towards detachment, a perceived disinclination to making clear commitments to anything but being 'critical', has caused adverse comment. For instance, Higgins (1994, p 9) argues that this approach 'leads to the pessimistic conclusion that what international law can do is to point out the problems but not assist in the achievement of goals'. This is precisely the criticism made of Kennedy by Charlesworth (Charlesworth, 2002a). Others have taken a more extreme view, denouncing critical scholars as engendering legal nihilism (eg Carrington, 1984).

Although these criticisms of the critics contain a degree of truth, they fail to give due weight to the idea that reason and knowledge are contextually embedded, that different discourses have different aims and functions. Consider Balkin's epistemologist who engages in a discussion with her colleagues in the philosophy department about the reliability of our knowledge of the passage of time. When, as a result of this discussion, she gets home later than she should and is upbraided by her husband because they are late for a dinner engagement, Balkin observes that it would be beside the point for her to respond using her philosophical arguments to question his knowledge of the passage of time—'in the context of dinner engagements, these speculations are irrelevant and philosophical scepticism is quite out of bounds' (Balkin, 1992, p 752).

Non-instrumental theories of international law are more akin to epistemological arguments regarding the passage of time than the more prosaic knowledge necessary to be prompt for dinner dates. Kennedy, for instance, is much more concerned with the critique of the practice and consequences of the practice of international law than in guiding that practice. As such, he could be seen as falling into an American intellectual tradition:

> Artists and writers began to conceive of themselves as refugees from the American mainstream, the specially endowed inhabitants of a transcendental region sealed off from the hurly-burly of the marketplace, the banality of popular opinion, and the grime of industrialized society. Alienation became the customary and most comfortable posture for American intellectuals; criticism rather than celebration of the dominant American institutions and attitudes became the accepted norm… [T]he voluntary withdrawal of American artists and intellectuals into a separate sphere was not peculiar; it was merely part of a major fragmentation that occurred as American society modernized. (Ellis, 1979, p 221)

Nevertheless, an important theme in Kennedy's work (eg 2004) is that individuals should shoulder responsibility for their actions in the international arena, eg in human rights activism. Unfortunately, he also seems to indicate that we can never know the full consequences of our action, which would suggest that we cannot even 'point out the problems'. This could lead to paralysis; a reluctance or refusal to act because we cannot assess the effects of any planned intervention (compare Finnis, 1980, pp 115–7). From Higgins' perspective as a New Haven lawyer, this is indeed a fatal flaw: decisions must be made on the basis of available knowledge with a view to action.

In contrast, Philip Allott, whose work is avowedly iconoclastic (for a range of views, see Allott et al, 2005, and Scobbie, 2011), is essentially a non-instrumentalist critical theorist who demands action. Unlike some tendencies within the New Stream, Allott is imbued with a regenerative idealism, and places his faith in the power of the human mind to reform the future by imagining what that future should be, and then use reason to implement this idea. Human consciousness thus provides the template for human action and human reality, 'We make the human world, including human institutions, through the power of the human mind. What we have made by thinking we can make new by new thinking' (Allott, 2001, p xxvii). Thus at the heart of Allott's project lies an elemental conviction in the power of ideas, of human consciousness, both to structure and to change— to restructure—the world. Allott seeks a 'revolution, not in the streets but in the mind' (p 257, para 14.9) in order to achieve 'a social international society [where] the ideal of all ideals is eunomia, the good order of a self-ordering society' (p 404, para 18.77).

Allott argues for the rejection of the State as the primary unit of authority, and thus for the reconstruction of world affairs. The emphasis in international relations on the centrality of the State is at least a mistake, if not a tragedy, because it encapsulates a fundamental misconception about what matters: it authorizes the pursuit of specifically State interests to the detriment of those of humanity. This structure of international relations, derived from Vattel:

> is not merely a tradition of international law. It implies a pure theory of the whole nature of international society and hence of the whole nature of the human social condition; and it generates practical theories which rule the lives of all societies, of the whole human race. It is nothing but mere words, mere ideas, mere theory, mere values—and yet war and peace, human happiness and human misery, human wealth and human want, human lives and human life have depended on them for two centuries and more. (p 243, para 13.105)

Just as the State is not co-extensive with society, international unsociety, where States dominate, is markedly less representative of humanity.

This was the inevitable outcome of the reception of Vattelian thought in international affairs, which played into the hands of ruling élites (pp 248–9, para 13.106). The conduct of international affairs through the conduit of the State made sovereignty, which projects 'an authority-based view of society', the structural premise of international affairs. This:

> tend[s] to make all society seem to be essentially a system of authority, and ... to make socie-ties incorporating systems of authority seem to be the most significant forms of society, at the expense of all other forms of society, including non-patriarchal families, at one extreme, and international society, at the other. (p 199, para 12.53)

Thus the notion of the State, organized as sovereign authority over specified territory, trumps membership of other possible societies which are not as exclusive, and whose con-sciousness and ideals may differ from those of the State (see also Franck, 1999). Moreover, the consciousness of the State is impoverished, concentrating on State rather than human interests. At least in some States, however, the notion of sovereignty has been surpassed by that of democracy which relocates power in society rather than in the simple fiat of authority. This introduces a profound shift in social consciousness as democracy 'seeks to make the individual society-member seek well-being in seeking the well-being of society. Democracy seeks to make society seek well-being in seeking the well-being of each indi-vidual society-member' (Allott, 2001, p 217, para 13.31).

International unsociety, on the other hand, has chosen 'to regard itself as the state exter-nalized, undemocratized, and unsocialized' (p 240, para 13.98). The purposes pursued in the world of States are those of States: 'purposes related to the survival and prospering of each of those state-societies rather than the survival and prospering of an international society of the whole human race' (p 247, para 13.105(13)). Morality thus becomes discon-tinuous between the domestic and international spheres (p 244, para 13.105(6)), and gov-ernments are able to act internationally free from the moral restraints that constrain them in domestic affairs, 'murdering human beings by the million in wars, tolerating oppression and starvation and disease and poverty, human cruelty and suffering, human misery and human indignity' (p 248, para 13.105(16)). 'This cannot be how the world was meant to be' (Allott, 2005). Allott's fundamental belief is that international society has the capacity to enable all societies to promote the ever-increasing well-being of themselves and their members:

> It is in international society that humanity's capacity to harm itself can achieve its most spectacular effects. And it is in international society that the ever-increasing well-being of the whole human race can, must, and will be promoted. (p 180, para 12.5)

The State system, and consequent discontinuity between international and domestic affairs, alienates people from international law which 'seems to be the business of a foreign realm, another world, in which they play no personal part' (pp 298–9, para 16.8). It is something, at best, imposed upon them and not something in which they participate, nor forge through the force of their consciousness. International law has not been integrated into the social process of humanity and is 'doomed to be what it has been—marginal, residual, and intermittent' (p 304, para 16.17). As things stand, international law can-not play its proper part in the realization of eunomia—'the good order of a self-ordering society'.

When Eunomia was first published, Allott's vision was criticized as utopian. It assumes that a fully socialized international society will be benevolent and eschew conflict, as conflict arises from the competing interests of States. Allott (p xxxii) denies that the criticism of utopianism has any force:

> In response to this criticism, it is surely only necessary to say that our experience of the revolutionary transformation of national societies has been that the past conditions the future but that it does not finally and inescapably determine it. We have shown that we can think ourselves out of the social jungle.

It is equally true that we can think ourselves into that jungle: the betrayal of the idealism of the 1917 Russian revolution by subsequent reigns of terror sometimes aimed, although often not, at the realization of socialism is only one case in point. Allott's presupposition that humanity would develop a more just, loving, and peaceful consciousness—and choose to implement this in its social reality were it allowed to do so—is difficult to accept without hesitation. His argument is predicated on the belief that bad or wicked choices have been made which have caused human misery. It might be that Allott does not believe in the possibility of 'pure' evil, of wicked acts done in and for themselves. For Allott, human evil might simply be a contingent possibility, the product of a perverted consciousness arising, for instance, from the asocial conduct of international affairs. Accordingly, for Allott, evil might not be a necessary part of the human condition and may be banished through the transformation of human consciousness in the strive for eunomia. This belief, nevertheless, appears to be more an act of faith than a demonstrable proposition (see Scobbie, 2011, pp 191–3).

On the other hand, one consequence of Allott's vision must surely be that of taking responsibility for international society and thus for international law. If Allott's inclusive international society were to be realized, international law would become a matter directly within individual consciousness. Accordingly, individuals (ultimately) rather than the State would determine and thus be responsible for the substantive content of international law. With that responsibility, Allott's hope is that morality would no longer be discontinuous between domestic and international society.

IX. A VIEW OF DELFT

The only landscape that we know Johannes Vermeer painted, *A View of Delft* (c 1660–61), lives in the Hague along with all those international courts and organizations. It hangs in the modest Dutch Classicist setting of the Mauritshuis, the Royal Cabinet of Paintings, and not, for instance, in the more exuberant neo-renaissance exterior, art nouveau interior, of the Peace Palace which houses the International Court of Justice, Permanent Court of Arbitration, and the Hague Academy of International Law. *A View of Delft* is perhaps not as well known as Vermeer's *Girl with a Pearl Earring* (c 1665), which is also in the Mauritshuis, but I think it is the better, and more interesting, painting. It is luminous, with the upper two-thirds of the canvas taken up with a darkening sky.

Art historians have pinpointed that Vermeer painted *A View of Delft* from the upper storey of a building on the Schieweg (Bailey, 2001, p 108). It is also thought that he probably made use of *camera obscura* as an aid in setting out the basic topography of the scene, but the final composition is not a 'photographic' representation of the view from the window on the Schieweg. He reorganized reality, changed perspective, and tonal contrast 'to reinforce the strong friezelike character of the city profile' (Wheelock and Broos, 1995, p 133, see also pp 120–24, Bailey, 2001, pp 109–11, and Westermann, 1996, pp 82–3). The conscious manipulation of elements of composition and perspective was not uncommon with Dutch artists in the eighteenth century (see, eg Westermann, 1996, pp 75–7). The aim was to highlight and emphasize some aspects at the expense of others in order to produce a more pleasing or dramatic image.

Legal theories are like this: their authors decide the aspects of law they want to discuss and in highlighting some, they downplay or ignore others. In rhetorical theory, this is known as 'presence':

> choice is…a dominant factor in scientific debates: choice of the facts deemed relevant, choice of hypotheses, choice of the theories that should be confronted with the facts, choice of the actual elements that constitute facts. The method of each science implies such a choice, which is relatively stable in the natural sciences, but is much more variable in the social sciences.
>
> By the very fact of selecting certain elements and presenting them to the audience, their importance and pertinency to the discussion are implied. Indeed, such a choice endows those elements with a presence, which is an essential factor in argumentation. (Perelman and Olbrechts-Tyteca, 1969, p 116; see pp 115–120.)

All theoretical discussions of international law are incomplete in one way or another because different theorists emphasize—give presence to—different aspects of the discipline. They have different concerns, different aims, and different presuppositions—in short, different perspectives—in their thinking about international law.

At the start of this chapter, I identified Socrates as 'one of the founders of Western philosophy', and this discussion has remained within that tradition. While Third World Approaches to International Law (TWAIL), to take one example, has been mentioned, it has not been discussed. That silence should be deafening. All theories distort reality through selection and simplification. Some contemporary—and not so contemporary—theorists argue that these differences are inevitable, because one's whole personality is inextricably involved in one's approach to and understanding of (international) law (see, eg Kennedy, 2004, and Koskenniemi, 1999; compare Frank, 1949, pp 146–56, and Lasswell and McDougal, 1943, p 236: see also Duxbury, 1995, pp 125–35). Accordingly, there can be no objectivity, no intellectual space beyond the individual analyst—'there is no there there' (Stein, 1938, p 251).

In one of his last books, published posthumously, Professor Judt adverted to the methodological solipsism of identity politics—'Why should everything be about "me"?'—and continued:

> If everything is 'political,' then nothing is. I am reminded of Gertrude Stein's Oxford lecture on contemporary literature. 'What about the woman question?' someone asked. Stein's reply should be emblazoned on every college notice board from Boston to Berkeley: 'Not everything can be about everything.' (Judt, 2010, pp 189–90)

REFERENCES

ALLOTT, PJ (1998), 'Out of the Looking Glass', 24 *Review of International Studies* 573.

—— (2001), *Eunomia: New Order For a New World* (Oxford: Oxford University Press) (first printed in 1990, reprinted 2001 with an extensive new preface).

—— (2002), *The Health of Nations: Society and Law Beyond the State* (Cambridge: Cambridge University Press).

ALLOTT, PJ et al (2005), 'Thinking Another World: "This Cannot Be How the World was Meant to Be"', 16 *EJIL* 255, including the following essays:

FRANCK, TM, 'The Fervent Imagination and the School of Hard Knocks', p 343;

HIGGINS, R, 'Final Remarks', p 347;

KNOP, K, 'Eunomia is a Woman: Philip Allott and Feminism', p 315;

KOSKENNIEMI, M, 'International Law as Therapy: Reading The Health of Nations', p 329; and

SCOBBIE, I, 'Slouching Towards the Holy City: Some Weeds for Philip Allott', p 299.

ALVAREZ, JE (2001), 'Do Liberal States Behave Better? A Critique of Slaughter's Liberal Theory', 12 *EJIL* 183.

ANGHIE, A (2005), *Imperialism, Sovereignty and the Making of International Law* (Cambridge: Cambridge University Press).

AREND, AC (1996), 'Toward an Understanding of International Legal Rules', in Beck, RJ, Arend, AC, and Lugt, RDV (eds), *International Rules: Approaches From International Law and International Relations* (New York: Oxford University Press), p 289.

—— (1999), *Legal Rules and International Society* (New York: Oxford University Press).

AUSTIN, J (1832) in Rumble, WE (ed) (1995), *The Province of Jurisprudence Determined* (Cambridge: Cambridge University Press).

AUSTIN, JL (1976), in Urmson JO, and Sbisà, M (eds), *How to do Things with Words: the William James Lectures Delivered in Harvard University in 1955* (Oxford: Oxford University Press).

BAILEY, A (2001), *Vermeer: a View of Delft* (New York: Henry Holt).

BALKIN, JM (1986), 'Deconstructive Practice and Legal Theory', 96 *Yale LJ* 743.

—— (1992), 'Just Rhetoric?', 55 *MLR* 746.

BECKETT, J (2001), 'Behind Relative Normativity: Rules and Process as Prerequisites of Law', 12 *EJIL* 627.

—— (2005), 'Countering Uncertainty and Ending Up/Down Arguments: Prolegomena to a Response to NAIL', 16 *EJIL* 213.

—— (2009), 'The Politics of International Law—Twenty Years Later: A Reply', http://www.ejiltalk.org/the-politics-of-international-law-twenty-years-later-a-reply/.

BEDERMAN, DJ (2001), *International Law in Antiquity* (Cambridge: Cambridge University Press) .

BERMAN, PS (2005), 'From International Law to Law and Globalization', 43 *Columbia Journal of Transnational Law* 485.

BOLTON, JR (2000), 'Is There Really "Law" in International Affairs?', 10 *Transnational Law and Contemporary Problems* 1.

BORGEN, CJ (2007), 'Whose Public, Whose Order? Imperium, Region, and Normative Friction', 32 *Yale Journal of International Law* 331.

BOWRING B, (2008), 'Positivism Versus Self-determination: the Contradictions of Soviet International Law', in Marks, S (ed), *International Law on the Left: Re-examining Marxist Legacies* (Cambridge: Cambridge University Press), p 133.

BRETT, A (2012), 'Francisco de Vitoria (1483–1546) and Francisco Suárez (1548–1617),' in Fassbender and Peters, *Handbook of History*, 1086.

BREZHNEV, L (1980), *On Events in Afghanistan: Leonid Brezhnev's Replies to a Pravda Correspondent* (Moscow: Novosti Press).

BROWNLIE, I (1981), 'The Reality and Efficacy of International Law', 52 *BYIL* 1.

—— (1983), 'Recognition in Theory and Practice', in Macdonald and Johnston, DM (eds), *The Structure and Process of International Law: Essays in Legal Philosophy Doctrine and Theory* (Dordrecht: Martinus Nijhoff), p 627.

—— (1995), 'International Law at the Fiftieth Anniversary of the United Nations: General Course on Public International Law', 255 *Recueil des Cours* 9.

BULL, H (2002), *The Anarchical Society: a Study of Order in World Politics*, 3rd edn (Basingstoke: Palgrave).

——, Kingsbury B, and Roberts, A (eds) (1990), *Hugo Grotius and International Relations* (Oxford: Clarendon Press).

Butler, WE (1971), ' "Socialist International Law" or "Socialist Principles of International Relations"?', 65 *AJIL* 796.

Carrington, PD (1984), 'Of Law and the River', 34 *J of Legal Education* 222.

Carty, A (2004), 'Marxism and International Law: Perspectives for the American (Twenty-First) Century', 17 *Leiden JIL* 247.

Cass, D (1996), 'Navigating the Newstream: Recent Critical Scholarship in International Law', 65 *Nordic JIL* 341.

Charlesworth, H (2002a), 'Author! Author!: A Response to David Kennedy', 15 *Harvard HRJ* 127.

—— (2002b), 'International Law: A Discipline of Crisis', 63 *MLR* 377.

—— and Chinkin, C (2000), *The Boundaries of International Law: A Feminist Analysis* (Manchester: Manchester University Press).

Chimni, BS (2004), 'An Outline of a Marxist Course on Public International Law', 17 *Leiden JIL* 1.

Collins, H (1984), *Marxism and Law* (Oxford: Oxford University Press).

Craven, M (2012), 'Colonialism and Domination' in Fassbender and Peters, *Handbook of History*, p 862.

Damrosch, LF and Müllerson, R (1995), 'The Role of International Law in the Contemporary World', in Damrosch, LF, Danilenko, GM, and Müllerson, R (eds), *Beyond Confrontation: International Law for the Post-Cold War Era* (Boulder, Colo.: Westview Press), p 1.

Daniel, L (2009), *Gertrude Stein* (London: Reaktion Books).

D'Aspremont, J (2011), *Formalism and the Sources of International Law: a Theory of the Ascertainment of Legal Rules* (Oxford: Oxford University Press).

Dickinson, LA (2007), 'Toward A "New" New Haven School of International Law', 32 *Yale Journal of International Law* 547.

Duchhardt, H (2012), 'From the Peace of Westphalia to the Congress of Vienna' in Fassbender and Peters, *Handbook of History*, 628.

Dufour, A, Haggenmacher, P, and Toman, J (eds) (1985), *Grotius et l'Ordre Juridique International: Travaux du Colloque Hugo Grotius, Genève, 10–11 Novembre 1983* (Lausanne: Payot).

Dunoff, JL, and Trachtman, JP (eds) (2009), *Ruling the World? Constitutionalism, International Law and Global Governance* (New York: Cambridge University Press).

Duxbury, N (1995), *Patterns of American Jurisprudence* (Oxford: Clarendon Press).

Dydo, UE (2003), *Gertrude Stein: The Language that Rises* (Evanston, Ill.: Northwestern University Press).

Ellis, JJ (1979), *After the Revolution: Profiles of Early American Culture* (New York: Norton).

Falk, RA (1995), 'Casting the Spell: The New Haven School of International Law', 104 *Yale LJ* 1991.

Fassbender, B and Peters, A (eds) (2012), *The Oxford Handbook of the History of International Law* (Oxford: Oxford University Press).

Feldman, SM (2000), *American Legal Thought from Premodernism to Postmodernism: An Intellectual Voyage* (New York: Oxford University Press).

Finnis, J (1980), *Natural Law and Natural Rights* (Oxford: Clarendon Press).

Foucault, M (1998), 'What is an Author?', in Faubian, JD (ed), *Essential Works 1954–84, vol 2, Aesthetics* (New York: New Press), p 203.

Franck, TM (1970), 'Who Killed Article 2(4)? or: Changing Norms Governing the Use of Force by States', 64 *AJIL* 809.

—— (1990), *The Power of Legitimacy Among Nations* (Oxford: Oxford University Press).

—— (1995), *Fairness in International Law and Institutions* (Oxford: Clarendon Press).

—— (1999), *The Empowered Self: Law and Society in the Age of Individualism* (Oxford: Clarendon Press).

FRANK, J (1949), *Courts on Trial: Myth and Reality in American Justice* (Princeton, NJ: Princeton University Press).

FREEMAN, MDA (2001), *Lloyd's Introduction to Jurisprudence* (London: Sweet & Maxwell).

GAGARIN, M and WOODRUFF, P (eds) (1995), *Early Greek Political Thought from Homer to the Sophists* (Cambridge: Cambridge University Press).

GARDNER, J (2001), 'Legal Positivism: 5½ Myths', 46 *American Journal of Jurisprudence* 199.

GARRAWAY, C (2010), ' "To Kill or not to Kill"—Dilemmas on the Use of Force', 14 *Journal of Conflict and Security Law* 499.

GOLDSMITH, JL, and POSNER, EA (2005), *The Limits of International Law* (New York: Oxford University Press).

GROSS, L (1948), 'The Peace of Westphalia, 1648–1948', 42 *AJIL* 20.

GROTIUS (2005) in Tuck, R (ed), *The Rights of War and Peace* (Indianapolis: Liberty Fund), available online at Liberty Fund, Online Library of Liberty, <http://oll.libertyfund.org/title/1425 >.

HAAKONSSEN, K (1985), 'Hugo Grotius and the History of Political Thought', 13 *Political Theory* 239.

——— (1996), *Natural Law and Moral Philosophy: from Grotius to the Scottish Enlightenment* (Cambridge: Cambridge University Press).

HAGGENMACHER, P (1983), 'Grotius et le Droit International–le Texte et la Légende', in Dufour *et al*, *Grotius*, 115.

—— (1990), 'Grotius and Gentili: a Reassessment of Thomas E. Holland's Inaugural Lecture', in Bull *et al*, *Hugo Grotius and International Relations*, 133.

——— (2012) 'Hugo Grotius (1583–1645)', in Fassbender and Peters, *Handbook of History*, 1098.

HATHAWAY, OA (2007), 'The Continuing Influence of the New Haven School', 32 *Yale Journal of International Law* 553.

HAZARD, J (1971), 'Renewed Emphasis Upon a Socialist International Law', 65 *AJIL* 142.

HEAD, M (2004), 'The Rise and Fall of a Soviet Jurist: Evgeny Pashukanis and Stalinism', 17 *Canadian Journal of Law and Jurisprudence* 269.

HENCKAERTS, J-M, and DOSWALD-BECK, L (2005), *Customary International Humanitarian Law* (Cambridge: Cambridge University Press).

HEYWARD, M (1993), *The Ern Malley Affair* (London: Faber and Faber).

HIGGINS, R (1994), *Problems and Process: International Law and How We Use It* (Oxford: Clarendon Press).

HODGSON, G (2005), 'The Other American Presidential Election: Choosing A President and Psychoanalyzing A Nation', (Oxford: Europaeum) available at http://www.europaeum.org/files/publications/pamphlets/GodfreyHodgson.pdf.

HUGHES, B (2010), *The Hemlock Cup: Socrates, Athens and the Search for the Good Life* (London: Jonathan Cape).

HUTCHESON, JC (1928–9), 'The Judgment Intuitive: The Function of the "Hunch" in Judicial Decision', 14 *Cornell LQ* 274.

JANIS, MW (2004), *The American Tradition of International Law: Great Expectations 1789-1914* (Oxford: Clarendon Press).

—— (1991), 'Religion and the Literature of International Law: Some Standard Texts', in Janis, MW (ed), *The Influence of Religion on the Development of International Law* (Dordrecht: Nijhoff), 61.

JUDT, T (2010), *The Memory Chalet* (London: Heinemann).

KANT, I (1793), 'On the Common Saying: "This May be True in Theory, But it Does Not Apply in Practice" ', in Reiss, H (ed) (1970), *Kant's Political Writings* (Cambridge: Cambridge University Press), p 61.

KARTASHKIN, V (1983), 'The Marxist-Leninist Approach: The Theory of Class Struggle and Contemporary

International Law', in Macdonald and Johnston, DM (eds), *The Structure and Process of International Law: Essays in Legal Philosophy Doctrine and Theory* (Dordrecht: Martinus Nijhoff), p 79.

KENNEDY, D (1985), 'International Legal Education', 26 *Harvard ILJ* 361.

—— (1999), 'The Disciplines of International Law and Policy', 12 *Leiden JIL* 9.

—— (2000), 'When Renewal Repeats: Thinking Against the Box', 32 *NYU JILP* 335.

—— (2002), 'The International Human Rights Movement: Part of the Problem?', 15 *Harvard HRJ* 101.

—— (2003), 'Tom Franck and the Manhattan School', 35 *NYU JILP* 397.

—— (2004), *The Dark Side of Virtue: Reassessing International Humanitarianism* (Princeton, NJ: Princeton University Press).

KING, R (2006), *The Judgment of Paris: the Revolutionary Decade that Gave the World Impressionism* (New York: Walker and Company).

KINGSBURY B and ROBERTS, A (1990), 'Introduction: Grotian Thought in International Relations', in Bull *et al*, *Hugo Grotius and International Relations* (Oxford: Clarendon Press), 1.

KLABBERS, J, PETERS, A, and ULFSTEIN, G (eds) (2009), *The Constitutionalization of International Law* (Oxford: Oxford University Press).

KRETZMER, D (2009), 'Rethinking Application of IHL in Non-International Armed Conflict', 42 *Israel Law Review* 1.

KOH, HH (2007), 'Is There a "New" New Haven School of International Law', 32 *Yale Journal of International Law* 559.

KOSKENNIEMI, M (1989), *From Apology to Utopia: The Structure of International Legal Argument* (Helsinki: Finnish Lawyers' Publishing Co).

—— (1990), 'The Politics of International Law', 1 *EJIL* 4.

—— (1999), 'Letter to the Editors of the Symposium', 93 *AJIL* 351.

—— (2005), 'International Law in Europe: Between Tradition and Renewal', 16 *EJIL* 113.

—— (2009a) 'The Politics of International Law—Twenty Years Later', 20 *EJIL* 7,

—— (2009b), 'The Politics of International Law—Twenty Years Later', <http://www.ejiltalk.org/the-politics-of-international-law-twenty-years-later>.

KRATOCHWIL, FV (1989), *Rules, Norms and Decisions: On the Conditions of Practical and Legal Reasoning in International Relations and Domestic Affairs* (Cambridge: Cambridge University Press).

LACEY, N (2004), *A Life of HLA Hart: the Nightmare and the Noble Dream* (Oxford: Oxford University Press).

LASSWELL, HD and McDOUGAL, MS (1943), 'Legal Education and Public Policy: Professional Training in the Public Interest', 52 *Yale LJ* 203.

—— and —— (1992), *Jurisprudence For a Free Society: Studies in Law, Science and Policy* (Dordrecht: Martinus Nijhoff).

LAUTERPACHT, H (1933), *The Function of Law in the International Community* (Oxford: Clarendon Press).

LEE, RW (1930), *Hugo Grotius* (Oxford: Oxford University Press).

LEVIT, JK (2007), 'Bottom-Up Lawmaking: Reflections on the New Haven School of International Law', 32 *Yale Journal of International Law* 393.

MACCORMICK, N (1990), 'Reconstruction after Deconstruction: A Response to CLS', 10 *Oxford JLS* 539.

MACDONALD, RSTJ (1998), 'Rummaging in the Ruins. Soviet International Law and Policy in the Early Years: Is Anything Left?', in Wellens, K (ed) *International Law: Theory and Practice. Essays in Honour of Eric Suy* (The Hague: Martinus Nijhoff), p 61.

—— and JOHNSTON, DM (eds) (1983), *The Structure and Process of International Law: Essays in Legal Philosophy Doctrine and Theory* (Dordrecht: Martinus Nijhoff).

McDougal, MS, and Burke, WT (1962), *The Public Order of the Oceans: A Contemporary International Law of the Sea* (New Haven, Conn.: Yale University Press).

—— and Feliciano, FP (1994), *The International Law of War: Transnational Coercion and World Public Order* (Dordrecht: Martinus Nijhoff).

—— and Lasswell, HD (1981), 'The Identification and Appraisal of Diverse Systems of Public Order', in McDougal, MS and Reisman, WM (eds), *International Law Essays* (Mineola, NY: Foundation Press), p 15; first published (1959) 53 *AJIL* 1.

——, ——, and Chen, LC (1969), 'Human Rights and World Public Order: A Framework for Policy-oriented Inquiry', 63 *AJIL* 237.

——, ——, and —— (1980), *Human Rights and World Public Order: The Basic Policies of an International Law of Human Dignity* (New Haven, Conn.: Yale University Press).

—— and Reisman, WM (1983), 'International Law in Policy-oriented Perspective', in Macdonald, RStJ and Johnston, DM (eds), *The Structure and Process of International Law: Essays in Legal Philosophy Doctrine and Theory* (Dordrecht: Martinus Nijhoff), p 103.

McWhinney, E (1990), 'The "New Thinking" in Soviet International Law: Soviet Doctrine and Practice in the Post-Tunkin Era', 28 *Canadian YIL* 309.

Marks, S (ed) (2008), *International Law on the Left: Re-examining Marxist Legacies* (Cambridge: Cambridge University Press).

Miéville, C (2004), 'The Commodity-Form Theory of International Law: An Introduction', 17 *Leiden JIL* 271.

Morison, WL (1982), *John Austin* (London: Edward Arnold).

Olivecrona, K (1971), *Law as Fact*, 2nd edn (London: Stevens).

Osakwe, C (1972), 'Socialist International Law Revisited', 66 *AJIL* 596.

Osofsky, HM (2007), 'A Law and Geography Perspective on the New Haven School', 32 *Yale Journal of International Law* 421.

Paulus, AL (2001), 'International Law After Postmodernism: Towards Renewal or Decline of International Law?', 14 *Leiden JIL* 727.

Perelman, C (1976), *Logique Juridique: Nouvelle Rhétorique* (Paris: Dalloz).

—— and Olbrechts-Tyteca, L (1969), *The New Rhetoric: a Treatise on Argumentation* (Notre Dame, Indiana: University of Notre Dame Press: translation of *La Nouvelle Rhétorique: Traité de l'Argumentation*, 1958).

Plato (1892), in Jowett, B (ed), *The Dialogues of Plato, Volume 1*, 3rd edn (Oxford: Oxford University Press), available at Liberty Fund, *Online Library of Liberty*, <http://oll.libertyfund.org/title/111>.

—— (1969), in Tredennick, H (ed), *The Last Days of Socrates* (Harmondsworth: Penguin, rev. edn).

—— (1994), in Waterfield, R (ed), *Symposium* (Oxford: Oxford University Press).

—— (1996), in Taylor, CCW (ed), *Protagoras* (Oxford: Oxford University Press).

—— (2002), in Waterfield, R (ed), *Phaedrus* (Oxford: Oxford University Press).

Prager, CAL (1998), 'Allott in Wonderland', 24 *Review of International Studies* 563.

Posner, RA (1990), *Cardozo: A Study in Reputation* (Chicago: University of Chicago Press).

Purvis, N (1991), 'Critical Legal Studies in Public International Law', 32 *Harvard JIL* 81.

Rabkin, JA (2005), *Law Without Nations? Why Constitutional Government Requires Sovereign States* (Princeton, NJ: Princeton University Press).

Ragazzi, M (1997), *The Concept of International Obligations Erga Omnes* (Oxford: Clarendon Press).

RASULOV, A (2012), 'New Approaches to International Law: Images of a Genealogy', in Beneyto JM and Kennedy D (eds), *New Approaches to International Law* (The Hague: TMC Asser Press), 151.

RAZ, J (1980), *The Concept of a Legal System: An Introduction to the Theory of Legal System*, 2nd edn (Oxford: Clarendon Press).

REISMAN, WM, WIESSNER, S, and WILLARD, AR (2007), 'The New Haven School: a Brief Introduction', 32 *Yale Journal of International Law* 575.

ROBERTS, AE (2001), 'Traditional and Modern Approaches to Customary International Law: A Reconciliation', 95 *AJIL* 757.

SCATTOLA, M (2012), 'Alberico Gentili (1552–1608)', in Fassbender and Peters, *Handbook of History*, 1092.

SCHMITT, M (2012), 'International Law in Cyber Space: the Koh Speech and the Tallinn Manual Juxtaposed', 54 *Harvard International Law Journal Online* 13 (2012), available at <http://www.harvardilj.org/2012/12/online-articles-online_54_schmitt/>.

SCHWEBEL, SM (1972), 'The Brezhnev Doctrine Repealed and Peaceful Co-existence Enacted', 66 *AJIL* 816.

SCOBBIE, I (1990), 'Towards the Elimination of International Law: Some Radical Scepticism about Sceptical Radicalism', 61 *BYIL* 339.

—— (2009) 'On the Road to Avila?: a Response to Koskenniemi', available at <http://www/ejiltalk.org/on-the-road-to-avila-a-response-to-koskenniemi.

—— (2011) ' "The Holiness of the Heart's Affection": Philip Allott's Theory of Social Idealism', in Orakhelashvili, A (ed), *Research Handbook on the Theory and History of International Law* (Cheltenham: Edward Elgar), 168.

SLAUGHTER, AM (1995), 'International Law in a World of Liberal States', 6 *EJIL* 1.

—— (2004), *A New World Order* (Princeton: Princeton University Press).

SMITH, A (1978), in Meek, RL, Raphael, DD, and Stein, P (eds) *Lectures on Jurisprudence*, (Oxford: Clarendon Press).

SOLUM, LB (1987), 'On the Indeterminacy Crisis: Critiquing Critical Dogma', 54 *University of Chicago Law Review* 462.

STEIN, G (1936) (1998a), 'The Geographical History of America or The Relation of Human Nature to the Human Mind', in Stimpson, CR and Chessman, H (eds), *Gertrude Stein: Writings 1932–1946* (New York: Library of America), p 365.

—— (1938), *Everybody's Autobiography* (London: Heinemann).

—— (1998b), in Stimpson, CR and Chessman, H (eds) *Gertrude Stein: Writings 1903–1932* (New York: Library of America).

TALLINN MANUAL (2013), Schmitt, M (general ed), *Tallinn Manual on the International Law Applicable to Cyber Warfare* (Cambridge: Cambridge University Press) available at <http://www.ccdcoe.org/249.html>.

TASIOULAS, J (1996), 'In Defence of Relative Normativity: Communitarian Values and the Nicaragua Case', 16 *Oxford JLS* 84.

TUCK, R (1999), *The Rights of War and Peace: Political Thought and the International Order from Grotius to Kant* (Oxford: Oxford University Press).

TUNKIN, GI (1974), *Theory of International Law* (Butler, WE (trans)) (London: Allen & Unwin).

—— (2003), *Theory of International Law* (Butler, WE (trans)), 2nd edn (London: Wildy, Simmonds and Hill).

TURNER, K (ed) (1999), *Baby Precious Always Shines: Selected Love Notes Between Gertrude Stein and Alice B. Toklas* (New York: St Martin's Press).

TUSHNET, M (2005), 'Survey Article: Critical Legal Theory (Without Modifiers) in the United States', 13 *Journal of Political Philosophy* 99.

VAGTS, D (2001), 'Hegemonic International Law', 95 *AJIL* 843.

VERESHCHETIN, VS and MÜLLERSON, R (1990), 'The Primacy of International Law in World Politics', in Carty, A and Danilenko, G (eds), *Perestroika and International Law: Current Anglo-Soviet Approaches to International Law* (Edinburgh: Edinburgh University Press), p 6.

VITORIA, F (1991) in Pagden, AR, Lawrance, J, and Lawrance, J (eds), *Vitoria: Political Texts* (Cambridge: Cambridge University Press).

VLASTOS, G (1994), 'The Historical Socrates and Athenian Democracy', in Vlastos (Burnyeat, M (ed)), *Socratic Studies* (Cambridge: Cambridge University Press), p 87.

WAGNER-MARTIN, L (1995), *'Favored Strangers': Gertrude Stein and her Family* (New Brunswick: Rutgers University Press).

WARBRICK, C (1991), 'The Theory of International Law: Is there an English Contribution?', in Allott, P *et al*, *Theory and International Law: an Introduction* (London: BIICL), p 49.

——— (2000), 'Brownlie's Principles of Public International Law: An Assessment', 11 *EJIL* 621.

WATERFIELD, R (ed) (2000), *The First Philosophers: the Presocratics and Sophists* (Oxford: Oxford University Press).

——— (2009), *Why Socrates Died: Dispelling the Myths* (New York: Norton).

WEIL, P (1983), 'Towards Relative Normativity?', 77 *AJIL* 413.

WESTERMANN, M (1996), *A Worldly Art: the Dutch Republic 1585–1718* (New Haven: Yale University Press).

WHEELOCK, AK, and BROOS, B (1995), 'The Catalogue', in Wheelock AK (ed), *Johannes Vermeer* (The Hague: Royal Cabinet of Paintings Mauritshuis), 85.

WILSON, E (1996), *Axel's Castle: A Study of the Imaginative Literature of 1870–1930* (New York: Modern Library, first published 1931).

WRÓBLEWSKI, J (1974), 'Legal Syllogism and Rationality of Judicial Decision', 5 *Rechtstheorie* 33.

FURTHER READING

In addition to the works cited in the bibliography, the following are useful in providing a variety of theoretical perspectives on international law, although this is an enormous and expanding field.

BECK, RJ, AREND, AC, and LUGT, RD (eds) (1996), *International Rules: Approaches From International Law and International Relations* (New York: Oxford University Press) is an excellent introductory collection of readings and commentary which covers the principal contemporary schools of international legal thought.

BESSON S, and TASIOULAS, J (eds) (2010), *The Philosophy of International Law* (Oxford: Oxford University Press) contains an excellent set of essays which are firmly rooted in philosophical concerns.

BYERS, M (ed) (2000), *The Role of International Law in International Politics: Essays in International Relations and International Law* (Oxford: Oxford University Press) is a collection of essays by distinguished authors which examines the interface between international law and politics. This is for a more advanced audience than Beck although it remains fairly accessible.

KOSKENNIEMI, M (2001), *The Gentle Civilizer of Nations: the Rise and Fall of International Law 1870–1960* (Cambridge: Cambridge University Press) is an extensive scholarly analysis of the intellectual history of modern international law.

ORAKHELASHVILI, A (ed) (2011), *Research Handbook on the Theory and History of International Law* (Cheltenham: Edward Elgar) is a useful collection of essays.

RUBIN, AP (1997), *Ethics and Authority in International Law* (Cambridge: Cambridge University Press) is a readable and slightly idiosyncratic account of the influence of the naturalist and positivist schools of legal theory on our understanding of international law.

PART II

THE STRUCTURE OF INTERNATIONAL LEGAL OBLIGATION

4

THE SOURCES OF INTERNATIONAL LAW

Hugh Thirlway

SUMMARY

A rule of international law must derive from one of the recognized sources, namely: (1) treaties and conventions; (2) international custom; (3) general principles of law; and (4) the 'subsidiary sources' of judicial decisions and legal teachings. Treaties are binding only on the parties to them; custom (which pre-supposes an established practice and a psychological element known as the *opinio juris*) is in principle binding on all States, unless it is a 'special' or 'local' custom, and save for the exceptional case of the 'persistent objector'. The general principles of law (principally as evidenced by national legal systems) may be appealed to if a point is not settled either by treaty or custom. Other sources, or alternative conceptions of how law comes into being, have from time to time been suggested, but the traditional analysis continues to be used in practice, in particular by the International Court.

I. INTRODUCTION: WHAT ARE SOURCES OF LAW?

The essence of every legal system is a body of principles and rules that lay down the rights and obligations of the subjects of that system.[1] These may for convenience be called the 'primary rules' of the system. However, each system also contains rules which can be applied to determine what are the primary rules, how they come into existence and how they can be changed; these we may term 'secondary rules'.[2] In municipal legal systems, ie the legal systems applicable within individual States, the presence of these secondary rules is easy to overlook in the actual practice of the law. The landowner suing his neighbour for trespass, or the prosecution in a criminal case, normally do not need to stop and ask

---

[1] The question whether international law is *solely* a set of principles and rules is controversial, but no-one denies that such principles and rules are comprised in it, and for present purposes it will be sufficient to limit our attention to those principles and rules. Cf the discussion of 'formalism' and 'anti-formalism' in Koskenniemi, Ch 2, Section V. The concept of 'sources' is in itself essentially formalist.

[2] The terminology is that employed by Hart, 1994 in the context of municipal systems; it is less commonly used in this context in international law, but makes for clarity. The distinction primary/secondary was also used by the International Law Commission in its study of State responsibility: the primary roles are those imposing specific obligations on States; the secondary rules determine how those obligations are to be implemented, or what consequences flow from their breach.

themselves, 'Why does encroachment on someone else's land invite legal consequences?', or 'Why is it an offence to do what the defendant has done?'—the law so provides, and that is all. The primary legal rules being applied in these cases did not, however, spring up from nowhere: they exist because the legislature passed particular legislation, or because a long line of judicial decisions has established that the common law is to this or that effect. Thus there exist secondary rules, to the effect that a Parliament, or other legislative body, has the power to make law; and that the common law as expressed in judicial precedents, constitutes the law of the land—the body of primary rules.

In international law, there exist similar secondary rules, but they are less clearly defined, for a number of reasons. There is, for example, at the international level neither a universal legislative body corresponding to a national Parliament, nor a system of universal judicial jurisdiction which has built up a wide-ranging body of precedent. At the municipal level, legal disputes are usually over the precise application or interpretation of rules, the exist- ence of which is generally recognized: do the circumstances of the case fall within the rule enunciated by the judges in a particular line of cases, or within the purview of a particular statute, as correctly interpreted? At the international level, disputes may frequently turn on whether the legal rule relied on by one State exists at all as a legal rule,[3] since there are controversial aspects of the workings of the secondary rules. There may also be recogni- tion of a rule, but dispute whether it is a rule binding on one or the other party to the dispute (since, as we shall see, not all rules of international law are binding on all States).

These secondary rules are referred to in international law as the *sources* of international law. This terminology highlights the idea that a rule must come *from* somewhere, as well as the idea that there is a flow, a process, which may take time: a rule may exist conceptually, as a proposal or a draft, and later come to be accepted as binding. The problem may then be to determine at what moment the rule acquired the status of a rule of existing, binding, law. Prior to that moment, it forms part of what is called *lex ferenda* (law which ought to be made, ie developing or embryonic law); thereafter it is part of the *lex lata* (law which has been made, positive law).

It is traditional to distinguish between what are called the *material sources* of interna- tional law, and the *formal sources*. In relation to a particular rule which is alleged to be a rule of international law, the material source is simply the place—normally a document of some kind—in which the terms of the rule are set out. This may be a treaty, a resolution of the UN General Assembly, a proposal of the UN International Law Commission, a judicial decision, a 'restatement' by a learned body, or even a statement in a textbook. In identify- ing a material source, no account need be taken of the legal authority of the textual instru- ment: for example, a treaty which has never come into force at all, and is thus not binding on anyone as a treaty, may still be the material source for a rule which has acquired the force of binding law by another route.[4]

The question of the authority for the rule as a rule of law, binding on States, is deter- mined by the *formal* source of the rule. The generally recognized formal sources are

---

[3] For example, the dispute between Hungary and Slovakia whether there exists in customary law a rule of automatic succession to a treaty by a successor State in case of dissolution of a State party to the treaty: *Gabčíkovo-Nagymaros Project (Hungary/Slovakia), Judgment, ICJ Reports 1997*, p 7, paras 116–21; and in a more narrow context, the *Dispute regarding Navigational and Related Rights (Costa Rica v Nicaragua), Judgment, ICJ Reports 2009*, p 21, paras 34–6.

[4] In this sense, *Oppenheims' International Law* 1992, p 23. For example, the 1933 Montevideo Convention on the Rights and Duties of States is regularly referred to as containing a convenient legal definition of a 'State', and of the conditions which must be met for that status to be acquired, despite the fact that for want of ratifica- tions it never came into force as a treaty.

identified in Article 38 of the Statute of the International Court of Justice (ICJ), to be examined in more detail later, but the two most important sources in practice are treaties and international custom. If a rule is laid down in a treaty, then it is binding on the States parties to that treaty, and the treaty is at once the material source and the formal source of the rule. The rule may, however, be taken over and applied in the practice of other States, not parties to the treaty, in such a way, and to such an extent, that it takes on the character of a customary rule. For these States, the material source of the rule will still be the wording of the original treaty, but the formal source will be international custom.

If the secondary rule defining the recognized sources of international law operates to make it possible to determine what are the primary rules, governing the actual conduct of States, what rule—presumably a tertiary rule—determines the identification of the secondary rules? If the question is asked, 'Why should I comply with this primary rule?', the answer may be, 'Because it is a rule of treaty-law, laid down in a treaty to which you are a party'; but what then is the answer to the question, 'Why must I comply with treaty-law?' The classic answer is that there is a principle *pacta sunt servanda*, that what has been agreed to must be respected; this is an example of a secondary rule, one which defines treaties and agreements as formal sources of international law. Theoretically one may then ask, 'But why should I respect the principle *pacta sunt servanda*? Is there a higher principle still requiring me to respect it?' Article 38 of the ICJ Statute, already referred to, provides that the Court, in deciding disputes in accordance with international law, is to apply international treaties and conventions in force; but that is no more than a recognition of treaties as one of the formal sources of primary rules. The Statute is in fact a material source of the secondary rule that treaties make law, but not a formal source of that rule.

Much legal ingenuity has been deployed to tackle this problem, by establishing, for example, a 'fundamental norm' on which all international law is based. None of the theories advanced commands universal assent; but nor are any of them actually essential to international legal relations in practice. The issue is fortunately one of purely academic interest. The realistic answer to the conundrum can probably only be that this is the way international society operates, and has operated for centuries, and probably the only way in which anything that can claim to be a society or community could possibly operate. This is particularly evident in the case of the principle *pacta sunt servanda*: if an agreement does not have to be respected, is there any point in making it?[5]

The doctrine of sources has attracted an enormous amount of discussion and criticism among international lawyers, and various proposals have been made for re-thinking the subject, or for getting rid of the idea of 'sources' altogether.[6] While the traditional view presents some anomalies and difficulties, it has so far proved the most workable method of analysing the way in which rules and principles develop that States in practice accept as governing their actions. At the present time, it seems unlikely that any other system will be able to replace the traditional approach. It is striking that such a comparatively recent

[5] Another approach would be to see *pacta sunt servanda* as one of the 'general principles of law'; but if these are a source parallel to treaties and custom, this merely produces a circular argument. There does of course exist a class of agreements not intended to be strictly legally binding: the obligations so created are known as 'soft law'. (See Boyle, Ch 5 and Shelton, Ch 6 Section IV in this book).

[6] In particular, in view of the greatly increased complexity and institutionalization of international legal relations today, some scholars have suggested either abandoning the traditional list of sources, and substituting for example a 'process-based' approach, or the recognition, alongside the sources, of such concepts as 'standard instruments for the exercise of international public authority' (Goldmann, 2008). Understanding of the traditional system of sources, however, remains essential, and newer philosophies have yet to take root in State practice.

development as international environmental law rests on the application of the traditional sources.[7]

II. ARTICLE 38 OF THE STATUTE OF THE INTERNATIONAL COURT OF JUSTICE

When the Permanent Court of International Justice was to be established in 1922, a Commission of Jurists was appointed to draw up its Statute, the legal instrument to govern its workings. The Permanent Court was to be the first standing international tribunal to decide disputes between States; if States were to be willing to accept it, one of the matters that had to be defined in advance was the nature of the law that the Court would apply. There was at the time an established tradition of referring inter-State disputes to binding arbitration, on an ad hoc basis, or of submitting groups of related disputes to a temporary standing body, usually called a Claims Commission; but the terms of reference of arbitral bodies or claims commissions were almost always defined in the international agreement (known as the *compromis*) by which they were established.

The text which was adopted as Article 38 of the Permanent Court Statute was re-adopted after the Second World War, when the Permanent Court was wound up and replaced by the International Court of Justice, with one change in the wording. The present text is as follows:

(1) The Court, whose function is to decide in accordance with international law such dis-putes as are submitted to it, shall apply:

  (a) international conventions, whether general or particular, establishing rules expressly recognized by the contesting states;

  (b) international custom, as evidence of a general practice accepted as law;

  (c) the general principles of law recognized by civilized nations;

  (d) subject to the provisions of Article 59, judicial decisions and the teachings of the most highly qualified publicists of the various nations, as subsidiary means for the determination of rules of law.

(2) This provision shall not prejudice the power of the Court to decide a case *ex aequo et bono*, if the parties agree thereto.

The clause in the first paragraph 'whose function is to decide in accordance with interna-tional law such disputes as are submitted to it' was added in 1946; its effect is to emphasize that, by applying what is mentioned in sub-paragraphs (a) to (d), the Court will be apply-ing international law, ie that the sources mentioned in those sub-paragraphs constitute recognized sources of international law, and (presumably) the sole sources of that law. That this was already the intention of the text is clear from the records of its drafting; but it also follows from the inclusion of paragraph 2. To decide a case *ex aequo et bono* is by definition to decide otherwise than in accordance with the applicable law: to decide sim-ply what seems to the judge or arbitrator the fairest solution in the circumstances.[8] Since

---

[7] See Redgwell, Ch 23, Section V.

[8] The Court has never been asked by the parties to a dispute to decide it in this way; but it has been suggested (by Judge Oda) that maritime delimitation cases, in view of the difficulty of basing any specified delimitation line on a framework of logically compelling legal argument, have in fact been decided on an unavowed *ex aequo et bono* basis, with the tacit consent of the parties.

the Court only possesses the power to decide in this way when the parties agree to it, all other decisions must be in accordance with law—and law as derived from the sources mentioned in paragraph 1.

Article 38 has been much criticized as a definition of the sources of international law, and it has often been suggested that it is inadequate, out of date, or ill-adapted to the conditions of modern international intercourse. As already noted, there have been suggestions that the whole concept of 'sources' should be thrown overboard, to be replaced by, for example, the 'recognized manifestations of international law'; it has also been suggested that the existence of additional sources should be accepted. Some of these latter suggestions will be addressed in Section IV; but the fact is that no new approach has acquired any endorsement in the practice of States, or in the language of their claims against each other; and the International Court has in its decisions consistently analysed international law in the terms of Article 38, which is generally regarded as an enumeration of the sources of international law, though it does not use the term.[9]

A. TREATIES AND CONVENTIONS IN FORCE

The principle *pacta sunt servanda* has already been mentioned as the basis for the binding nature of treaties. The whole point of making a binding agreement is that each of the parties should be able to rely on performance of the treaty by the other party or parties, even when such performance may have become onerous or unwelcome to such other party or parties. Thus a treaty is one of the most evident ways in which rules binding on two or more States may come into existence, and thus an evident formal source of law. The 1969 Vienna Convention on the Law of Treaties,[10] which is to a very large extent the codification of pre-existing general law on the subject, states the principle in Article 26, under the heading '*Pacta sunt servanda*': 'Every treaty is binding upon the parties to it and must be performed by them in good faith'.

It may seem strange that 'law' should be created simply by agreement.[11] Certainly the content of, let us say, a bilateral customs treaty, setting rates of duties and tariffs on various goods, does not look much like 'law'. At the other extreme, there are more and more examples in modern law of so-called 'law-making' treaties: multilateral conventions that lay down for the parties to them a whole regime, as for example the Geneva Conventions in the field of humanitarian law, the Genocide Convention, or the Vienna Convention on the Law of Treaties itself. The principle in each case is, however, the same: that the States parties accept a commitment to certain behaviour that would not be legally required of them in the absence of the treaty. They may indeed by treaty vary or set aside the rules that general international law imposes on all States, though such variation or exclusion is only effective between the parties; and this power is subject to the limits imposed by

---

[9] It may of course be objected that this is not necessarily significant, because whether or not Article 38 is obsolete as a general statement, the Court remains bound by it; but if there had really been a substantive change in international legal thinking on the question of sources, the Court might have been expected at the least to have taken note of it, while drawing attention to its inability to go beyond the terms of its own Statute.

[10] A multilateral convention adopted in 1969, on the basis of a draft prepared by the UN International Law Commission, and accepted by a large number of States. It codifies practically the whole of the law of treaties (see further Fitzmaurice, Ch 7).

[11] It has been argued that a treaty is better understood as a source of *obligation*, rather than as a source of law, See Fitzmaurice, 1958, but see also Mendelson (1990).

jus cogens.[12] The traditional approach that treaties are sources of law is therefore recommended by logic and convenience.

If it is axiomatic that a party to a treaty is committed to what has been agreed in the treaty, it is equally axiomatic that a State which is not a party to a treaty is under no such obligation. The principle *res inter alios acta nec nocet nec prodest* (a transaction between others effects neither disadvantage nor benefit) is as valid as *pacta sunt servanda* and can in fact be regarded as a corollary of that principle. As the Vienna Convention on the Law of Treaties (Article 34) expresses the point: 'A treaty does not create either obligations or rights for a third State without its consent'. The Vienna Convention being itself a treaty, its codifying provisions are thus themselves only applicable *as treaty-law* to the States which have ratified it.

There are two apparent exceptions to this principle—but they are only apparent. First, the situation in which an obligation stated in a treaty is or becomes an obligation of general customary law (a process to be examined later), in which case the non-party State may be bound by the same substantive obligation, but as a matter of customary law, and not by the effect of the treaty. This is in fact the case of the Vienna Convention on the Law of Treaties itself; its provisions have frequently been applied by the International Court, on the basis that such provisions state rules which apply to all States as customary law, to a State not party to the Convention. Secondly, it is possible for a State not a party to a treaty to accept an obligation stated in the treaty, or to derive a benefit from the treaty, if all States concerned—the parties to the treaty and the outsider State—are so agreed. In effect a new treaty is concluded extending the scope of the original treaty to the third State.[13]

The normal way in which a State becomes bound by the obligations provided for in a treaty is by becoming a party to it, through the processes to be described in Chapter 7, Section III. Where the treaty is a multilateral convention of the 'law-making' type, it has been suggested that a State could, simply by conduct, indicate its acceptance of the regime of the convention as applicable to itself. In the *North Sea Continental Shelf* case, the International Court did not accept the argument of Denmark and the Netherlands that Germany, which had signed but not ratified the 1958 Geneva Convention on the Continental Shelf, had 'by conduct, by public statements and proclamations, and in other ways, ... unilaterally assumed the obligations of the Convention'.[14] The Court rejected this contention on the facts of the case, but did not, however, absolutely rule out any possibility of such a process occurring.[15]

---

[12] This concept is examined in Section IV B below, and will be dealt with more fully in Shelton, Ch 6.: briefly, international law is regarded as divided into *jus dispositivum*, the rules of law from which States may freely contract out, by treaty; and *jus cogens*, a category composed of a limited number of norms which, because of their importance in and to the international community, remain binding notwithstanding any agreement to the contrary (see Articles 53 and 64 of the Vienna Convention on the Law of Treaties). The concept is generally accepted, but there remains considerable controversy as to its application, as to how rules of *jus cogens* acquire that status, and which rules have in fact acquired it.

[13] See Articles 35 and 36 of the Vienna Convention on the Law of Treaties.

[14] *North Sea Continental Shelf, Judgment, ICJ Reports 1969*, p 3, para 27.

[15] The Court did, however, make it clear, first that 'only a very definite, very consistent course of conduct on the part of [the] State' could have the effect suggested, and secondly that there could be no question of a State being permitted to claim rights or benefits under a treaty 'on the basis of a declared willingness to be bound by it, or of conduct evincing acceptance of the conventional regime': ibid, para 28. Underlying the distinction is of course the question of the consent of the original parties: they may be presumed to have no objection to other States accepting the *obligations* of the Convention, but if other States are to enjoy *benefits* under it there must

Article 38 of the ICJ Statute refers to 'treaties and conventions in force', thus excluding treaties which have not, or not yet, come into force, or which have ceased to be binding on the parties.[16] The question whether a particular treaty is 'in force' between a particular pair of States is, however, not an absolute one, to be answered simply by checking that each of them has ratified it. A new State may be bound by certain treaties concluded by its predecessor, without a formal act of accession thereto. A further complication is due to the possibility of reservations made by parties when signing or ratifying the treaty: in the case of a complex multilateral treaty, there may in effect be a number of parallel regimes operating between different pairs of States, depending on the extent to which a State may have excluded certain provisions of the treaty by reservation, and the extent to which the reservation has been accepted (or more precisely, not objected to) by other States parties.[17]

B. CUSTOM

1. Introduction

It is probably a universal characteristic of human societies that many practices which have grown up to regulate day-to-day relationships imperceptibly acquire a status of inexorability: the way things have always been done becomes the way things *must* be done. In treating custom as a source of legal rules, international law does not deviate from the pattern discernible in municipal legal systems.[18] Historically, at the international level, once the authority of natural law, in the sense of what was given by God or imposed by the nature of an international society made up of independent princes, had weakened, it was natural to derive legal obligations from the legitimate expectations created in others by conduct. The precise nature and operation of the process have, however, always presented obscurities.

One approach is to regard all custom as a form of tacit agreement: States behave towards each other in given circumstances in certain ways, which are found acceptable, and thus tacitly assented to, first as a guide to future conduct and then, little by little, as legally determining future conduct. The difficulty of this analysis is that if agreement makes customary law, absence of agreement justifies exemption from customary law. On that basis, a given rule would only be binding on those States that had participated in its development, and so shown their assent to the rule. Yet it is generally recognized that, subject to two exceptions, to be indicated in Section II.B.3, a rule of general customary international law is binding on all States, whether or not they have participated in the practice from which it sprang. This also includes new States, which take general customary law as they find it: during the period of decolonization after the Second World War, some attempt was made by the newly independent States to argue that they began life with a clean slate, so far as rules of customary law were concerned. This view was not accepted by other States, and later quietly abandoned by its adherents. It was probably realized that it could have been a two-edged sword; that most rules of general custom are such that a State which rejects

---

be positive consent of the original parties, as indeed the Vienna Convention requires. This point was also made by the ICJ in that case.

[16] The question whether neglected treaties cease to be binding through 'desuetude' was raised, but not answered, before the ICJ in the *Nuclear Tests* and *Aegean Sea Continental Shelf* cases; it remains controversial.

[17] The operation of the rules as to reservations will be explained more fully in Fitzmaurice, Ch 7, Section VI.

[18] For a valuable comparative study see Bederman, 2010.

one of them today in one dispute, may find it needs to invoke the same rule in its favour tomorrow in a different dispute.[19]

2. The two-element theory

The traditional doctrine is that the mere fact of consistent international practice in a particular sense is not enough, in itself, to create a rule of law in the sense of the practice; an additional element is required. Classical international law sees customary rules as resulting from the combination of two elements: an established, widespread, and consistent practice on the part of States; and a psychological element known as the *opinio juris sive necessitatis* (opinion as to law or necessity), usually abbreviated to *opinio juris*. The classic judicial statement *loc* on the point is the ICJ judgment in the *North Sea Continental Shelf* case; the Court was discussing the process by which a treaty provision might generate a rule of customary law, but its analysis is applicable to custom-creation generally:

> Not only must the acts concerned amount to a settled practice, but they must also be such, or be carried out in such a way, as to be evidence of a belief that this practice is rendered obligatory by the existence of a rule of law requiring it. The need for such a belief, ie the existence of a subjective element, is implicit in the very notion of the *opinio juris sive necessitatis*.[20]

The idea that State practice, to be significant, must be accompanied by a conviction of adhering to an *existing* rule of law, is here merely re-stated; it had long been recognized in international law. It has, however, been frequently pointed out that it is paradoxical in its implications: for how can a practice ever develop into a customary rule if States have to believe the rule already exists before their acts of practice can be significant for the creation of the rule?[21] Or is it sufficient if initially States act in the *mistaken* belief that a rule already exists, a case of *communis error facit jus* (a shared mistake produces law)?

The problem has been argued over endlessly by legal writers,[22] some of whom have sought to escape the dilemma by denying the two-element theory itself. It is clear that the elements of practice and *opinio* are closely intertwined: the Court spoke of the practice as 'evidence' of the existence of the *opinio juris*, and for some authors only the psychological element is essential, the role of State practice being merely to prove the existence of that element. This makes it possible to see a rule of international customary law where there is insufficient practice, or none, but there is other evidence that States believe in the existence of a rule of law; this is particularly relied on by those who see General Assembly resolutions as law-creating. An alternative approach is to see custom as essentially practice,

---

[19] The question of the application to a new State of treaties concluded by its predecessor, where each treaty could be considered independently, continued to cause controversy.

[20] *North Sea Continental Shelf, Judgment, ICJ Reports 1969*, p 3, para 77. See also *Continental Shelf (Libyan Arab Jamahiriya/Malta), Judgment, ICJ Reports 1985*, p 13, para 27; *Military and Paramilitary Activities in and against Nicaragua (Nicaragua v United States of America), Merits, Judgment, ICJ Reports 1986*, p 14, paras 183 and 207.

[21] In the case concerning *Jurisdictional Immunities of the State*, Italy asserted the existence of an exception to the generally accepted customary rules concerning such immunities, but the only practice it could point to was that of its own domestic courts (and, briefly, those of Greece). The Court rejected the Italian contention, essentially on the basis of the contrary practice of other States, accompanied by *opinio juris*; the question whether Italy held an appropriate contrary *opinio juris* was not raised: see *Jurisdictional Immunities of the State (Germany v Italy: Greece Intervening), Judgment of 3 February 2012*, paras 76-8.

[22] For an idiosyncratic modern re-statement of the difficulties, see Kammerhofer, 2004; and for a very thorough and original approach, Lepard, 2011.

the only relevance of the beliefs or intention of the States involved in the practice being to exclude practices rendered legally binding by a treaty obligation, or regarded by all concerned as dictated merely by courtesy or comity, without any legal commitment to continued observance.

Since the *opinio juris* is a state of mind, there is an evident difficulty in attributing it to an entity like a State; and in any event it has to be deduced from the State's pronouncements and actions, particularly the actions alleged to constitute the 'practice' element of the custom. It should not be overlooked that State practice is two-sided; one State asserts a right, either explicitly or by acting in a way that impliedly constitutes such an assertion, and the State or States affected by the claim then react either by objecting or by refraining from objection. The practice on the two sides adds up to imply a potential rule, supporting the claim if no protest is made, or excluding the claim if there is a protest. The accumulation of instances of the one kind or the other constitutes the overall practice required for establishment of a customary rule.

It also follows from the psychological requirement of *opinio juris*, the consciousness of conforming to a rule, that if the acts of practice are to be attributed to a motive other than such consciousness, they cannot show *opinio juris*. This point also arose in the *North Sea Continental Shelf* case: the Court, when considering whether a rule of maritime delimitation laid down in the 1958 Geneva Convention on the Continental Shelf had become a customary rule, noted that a number of instances of delimitation complying with the rule were delimitations effected by States parties to the Convention. Those States 'were therefore presumably...acting...in the application of the Convention', and thus 'From their action no inference could legitimately be drawn as to the existence of a rule of customary law...'[23]

Similar reasoning may be applied to the situation of States which, for one reason or another, cannot participate in a practice giving rise to a customary rule: an obvious example is that of land-locked States in relation to a rule concerning the delimitation of maritime areas off the coasts of coastal States. Such States may have a view as to the existence of such a rule, but one which cannot be demonstrated by acts of practice, and thus not a true *opinio juris*. It was probably this consideration that led the International Court, in the *North Sea Continental Shelf* case, to refer to the importance, in assessing the law-creative effect of State practice, of the participation in it of 'States whose interests are specially affected'.[24] More controversial was the question that arose in the case concerning the *Legality of the Threat or Use of Nuclear Weapons*:[25] was the practice of the States that actually possessed such weapons more significant than that of the States which did not? The Court did not, in its Advisory Opinion, comment directly on the point.

A further problem of a similar nature is the determination of customary law in a field in which there is no practice at all, because the subject matter is new. This was the case in the early stages of space exploration. Did a satellite, in orbiting the earth, infringe the sovereignty of the States whose territory it overflew? Were celestial bodies open to appropriation and sovereignty in the same way as unoccupied territories on earth? The problems were solved by international treaty;[26] but it was in this context that the suggestion was made that there had come into existence a new form of customary law, usually known as 'instant custom'. According to this view, first advanced in 1965 (Cheng, 1965),

---

[23] *North Sea Continental Shelf, Judgment, ICJ Reports 1969*, p 3, para 76.
[24] Ibid, para 74.
[25] *Legality of the Threat or Use of Nuclear Weapons, Advisory Opinion, ICJ Reports 1996*, p 226.
[26] Treaty on Principles Governing the Activities of States in the Exploration and Use of Outer Space, including the Moon and Other Celestial Bodies (1967), 610 UNTS, p 205.

custom could be deduced from declarations in General Assembly resolutions, such resolutions constituting at once elements of State practice and evidence of the necessary
opinio juris.

This theory, though influential for a time, never gained full acceptance, and eventually it
was implicitly rejected by the International Court in the cases of *Military and Paramilitary
Activities in and against Nicaragua*[27] and *Legality of the Threat or Use of Nuclear Weapons*,[28]
in which General Assembly resolutions were treated as evidence of *opinio juris*, but not
as acts of State practice. However, the approach of the Court to what amounts to practice
(in particular) may be becoming broader. In a recent case concerning the prohibition of
torture, the Court treated indiscriminately as both practice and *opinio juris* (along with a
number of international conventions), the fact that the prohibition had 'been introduced
into the domestic law of almost all States', and that 'finally, acts of torture are regularly
denounced within national and international fora'.[29] Nevertheless, the position appears
to be that in a field of activity in which there has not yet been any opportunity for State
practice, there is no customary law in existence.

3. Practice

Since international law, including custom, regulates the relationships between States, the
practice that is relevant for establishing a rule of customary law is essentially the practice
(action or inaction) of States in relation to each other, or in relation to other recognized
international actors, such as international organizations. This follows from the nature
of the process whereby custom grows from action by one subject of law which is either
accepted, rejected, or tolerated by the other subjects of law. Consequently, the practice
of a State in relation to its own citizens, a matter of 'domestic jurisdiction' within the
meaning of Article 2(7) of the UN Charter, was originally without significance for the
establishment of a customary rule.[30] This may appear to be in contradiction with the
corpus of the modern law of human rights, which prescribes numerous limitations on
the freedom of States in this domain. Human rights law has, however, grown very largely
through the adoption of wide-ranging international conventions, precisely because of
the difficulty in establishing a practice-based customary law.[31] Since many of these conventions have been ratified by almost all States, and in the view of the moral authority of
the principles which they embody, it is widely argued that the conventional provisions,
or some of those principles, are binding also on non-parties, and one of the grounds for
this contention is that there is, despite the theoretical problem just noted, a customary
law of human rights. The question remains controversial, though there are signs that
many States recognize a compromise approach which is workable, even if it may be difficult
to define legally.[32]

---

[27] *Military and Paramilitary Activities in and against Nicaragua (Nicaragua v United States of America),
Merits, Judgment, ICJ Reports 1986*, p 14, paras 184 and 188.

[28] *Legality of the Threat or Use of Nuclear Weapons, Advisory Opinion, ICJ Reports 1996*, p 226, para 73.

[29] *Questions relating to the Obligation to Prosecute or Extradite (Belgium v Senegal), Judgment of 20 July 2012*,
para 99.

[30] The treatment of foreign nationals, in particular those resident or present in the State's territory, may give
rise to a claim of diplomatic protection by the national State, and is thus very relevant to the development of
customary law in this field.

[31] The problem is not merely whether other States *may* legally object to actions by a State regarded as contrary to human rights, but also whether they will have any interest in doing so, and thus in carrying out acts
creative of State practice; the situation is very different in the field of, for example, international trade.

[32] See Byers, 1999, pp 43–5.

The controversy over customary human rights law also involves the problem whether non-binding resolutions of international bodies, particularly the UN General Assembly, rank as State practice.[33]

The settled practice required to establish a rule of customary law does not need to be the practice of every single State of the world, as long as it is widespread and consistent. A special problem is that of the divergence between States' assertion of the existence of a particular rule of customary law, and their practice inconsistent with it. In the field of human rights law, for example, it is probably the case that the municipal law of practically every State of the world prohibits torture, and States are generally agreed, in theory, that there is a rule of international law forbidding it; yet there is no doubt that torture continues to be widely practised. Can a rule which flies in the face of consistent practice still be said to have existence as one of customary law? An observation of the Intenational Court in the case of *Military and Paramilitary Activities in and against Nicaragua*, in connection with the question of the existence of customary rules forbidding the use of force or intervention, is in point here:

> It is not to be expected that in the practice of States the application of the rules in question should have been perfect, in the sense that States should have refrained, with complete consistency, from the use of force or from intervention in each other's internal affairs. The Court does not consider that, for a rule to be established as customary, the corresponding practice must be in absolutely rigorous conformity with the rule. In order to deduce the existence of customary rules, the Court deems it sufficient that the conduct of States should, in general, be consistent with such rules, and that instances of State conduct inconsistent with a given rule should generally have been treated as breaches of that rule, not as indications of recognition of a new rule. If a State acts in a way prima facie inconsistent with a recognized rule, but defends its conduct by appealing to exceptions or justifications contained within the rule itself, then whether or not the State's conduct is in fact justifiable on that basis, the significance of that attitude is to confirm rather than to weaken the rule.[34]

The Court here indicates that conduct inconsistent with an existing rule is not necessarily an indication of the recognition, or even the emergence, of a new rule; but it does at the same time recognize that this is a way in which a new rule may be discerned. Later in the same decision, discussing the principle of non-intervention, it observed that 'Reliance by a State on a novel right or an unprecedented exception to the principle might, if shared in principle by other States, tend toward a modification of customary international law'.[35] The paradox of *opinio juris* is of course here emphasized: if a State decides to act in a way inconsistent with a recognized rule of custom, it will no doubt have good and sufficient reason for doing so, and perhaps even for thinking that its approach should be generalized—that the rule needs to be modified consistently with its action. It will, however, almost by definition, not be acting because it is convinced that there is already a new rule. The process by which customary rules change and develop thus presents theoretical difficulties; but it is a process which does occur. Customary law, in the traditional conception of it, is not a rigid and unchangeable system, though it is sometimes criticized as being such.

---

[33] See Section IV B 3.

[34] *Military and Paramilitary Activities in and against Nicaragua (Nicaragua v United States of America)*, Merits, Judgment, ICJ Reports 1986, p 14, para 186.

[35] Ibid, para 207. Compare the attempt of Italy to establish a modification of the customary rules on State immunity, in the case of *Jurisdictional Immunities of the State (Germany v Italy: Greece Intervening)*, Judgment of 3 February 2012.

An important difference between customary law and law derived from treaties is that, as already observed, in principle customary law is applicable to all States without exception, while treaty-law is applicable as such only to the parties to the particular treaty. A State which relies in a dispute on a rule of treaty-law has to establish that the other party to the dispute is bound by the treaty; whereas if a claim is based on general customary law, it is sufficient to establish that the rule exists in customary law, and there is no need to show that the other party has accepted it, or participated in the practice from which the rule derives.[36] There are two exceptions to this principle: alongside general customary law there exist rules of *special* or *local* customary law, which are applicable only within a defined group of States; and it is in principle possible for a State which does not accept a rule which is in the process of becoming standard international practice to make clear its opposition to it, in which case it will be exempted from the rule when it does become a rule of law, having the status of what is generally called a *persistent objector*.

As regards *local customary law*, perhaps the only clear and well-known example is that relating to the practice of diplomatic asylum in Latin America, whereby the States of the region recognize the right of the embassies of other States of the region to give asylum to political fugitives.[37] The rule is purely local in that it is not asserted in favour of, or against, States outside the region: for example, neither the British Embassy in a South American capital, nor the Embassy of a South American State in London, would be regarded as entitled to offer asylum.[38] The International Court had to consider the detailed application of the rule in the *Asylum* and *Haya de la Torre* cases, in which Colombia relied, against Peru, on 'an alleged regional or local custom peculiar to Latin-American States'. In the *Asylum* case the Court observed that:

> The Party which relies on a custom of this kind must prove that this custom is established in such a manner that it has become binding on the other Party. The Colombian Government must prove that the rule invoked by it is in accordance with a constant and uniform usage practised by the States in question, and that this usage is the expression of a right appertaining to the State granting asylum and a duty incumbent on the territorial State.[39]

Further on in its judgment, the Court held that 'even if such a custom existed between certain Latin-American States only, it could not be invoked against Peru which, far from having by its attitude adhered to it, has on the contrary repudiated it...'.[40] This has been held by some commentators to constitute a finding that Peru had the status of 'persistent objector', to be discussed in a moment; but it can also be understood as a finding that the regional custom, at least on the specific point in dispute, applied to a group of States which did not include Peru.

It has even been held that a special custom may exist between two States only: in the *Right of Passage over Indian Territory* case, Portugal relied on such a custom as regulating

---

[36] If the dispute is subjected to arbitration or judicial settlement, there is theoretically no need even to establish the existence of the rule; according to the principle *jura novit curia* (the court knows the law), no proof of general rules of law is required. However, in practice litigant States do endeavour to prove the existence of the rules of law on which they base their claims.

[37] Another alleged rule of regional customary law was pleaded in the *Dispute regarding Navigational and Related Rights (Costa Rica v Nicaragua), Judgment, ICJ Reports 2009*, p 213, paras 34–6.

[38] Cf the asylum afforded to Julian Assange by the Ecuadorean Embassy in London, which the UK government rejects as unlawful.

[39] *Asylum, Judgment, ICJ Reports 1950*, p 266 at p 276.   [40] Ibid, pp 277–8.

the relationship between itself and India concerning access to certain Portuguese enclaves in Indian territory. The Court held that:

It is difficult to see why the number of States between which a local custom may be established on the basis of long practice must necessarily be larger than two. The Court sees no reason why long continued practice between two States accepted by them as regulating their relations should not form the basis of mutual rights and obligations between the two States.[41]

It would seem evident that two must be the minimum number of States to be subject to a special custom: if a single State claimed (otherwise than as a 'persistent objector'—see next paragraph) to be entitled in certain respects to rely on rules different from those generally in force, such a claim could only be maintained as the result of a general acceptance making it a matter of general customary law. Thus the suggestion that has from time to time been made that the USA, by reason of its position as sole remaining superpower, and self-appointed global policeman,[42] is not necessarily bound by such rules as that of non-intervention, cannot rest on the assertion of a special custom.

The notion of the 'persistent objector' has been identified in the reasoning in the Asylum case; but the idea is usually traced back to the earlier Fisheries case between the UK and Norway, which concerned the legality of the baselines drawn by Norway around its coasts in order to calculate the breadth of its territorial sea. The UK argued that the Norwegian baselines were inconsistent with a rule of customary law referred to as the 'ten-mile rule', but the Court was not satisfied that any such general rule of customary law existed. However, it then added, 'In any event the ten-mile rule would appear to be inapplicable as against Norway inasmuch as she has always opposed any attempt to apply it to the Norwegian coast'.[43]

Although there has been no confirmatory jurisprudence, it is generally accepted that a State which objected consistently to the application of a rule of law while it was still in the process of becoming such a rule—in other words, while practice consistent with the possible rule was still accumulating, but before the rule could be regarded as established—could continue to 'opt out' of the application of the rule even after it had acquired the status of a rule of general customary law.

This is an attractive theory, since if there were no possibility of dissent from a nascent rule, customary law would be created by the majority of States and imposed willy-nilly on the minority; but such State practice as there is to support it consists merely of express or implied assertions of disagreement with a current development, with a view to subsequent claims to such status; the existence of the rule has been questioned by commentators (Charney, 1993). What is certain is that customary law is not made simply by majority: in the case of Legality of the Threat or Use of Nuclear Weapons, the Court accepted that the opposition of the handful of nuclear States to any customary rule prohibiting such weapons blocked the creation of such a rule, even though it was favoured by a substantial majority of the States of the world.[44]

---

[41] *Right of Passage over Indian Territory, Merits, Judgment, ICJ Reports 1960*, p 6 at p 39. Cases of this kind are likely to be rare, since it would normally be more appropriate to analyse such a situation as one of tacit agreement, ie, in effect governed by treaty-law. In the *Right of Passage* case this interpretation would have raised problems of succession, the arrangement dating back to the Mughal period, and left undisturbed by the successive British and independent Indian governments.

[42] Cf the views of McDougal on hydrogen bomb testing, and (more recently) Murswiek, 2002, pp 195ff, rejecting the US approach as contrary to the principle of the sovereign equality of States.

[43] *Fisheries, Judgment, ICJ Reports 1951*, p 116 at p 131.

[44] *Legality of the Threat or Use of Nuclear Weapons, ICJ Reports 1996*, p 226, para 73.

C. THE GENERAL PRINCIPLES OF LAW

When Article 38 of the Statute of the Permanent Court was being drafted, the Commission of Jurists was concerned that in some cases the future Court might find that the issues in dispute before it were not governed by any treaty, and that no established rule of customary law either could be found to determine them. It was thought undesirable, and possibly inappropriate in principle, that the Court should be obliged to declare what is known as a *non liquet*—a finding that a particular claim could neither be upheld nor rejected, for lack of any existing applicable rule of law. This is to be distinguished from a finding that a particular claim is not supported by a positive rule of law, which is tantamount to a finding that there exists a negative rule of law. For example, in the *Barcelona Traction, Light and Power Co* case,[45] Belgium claimed that it could demand reparation from Spain for the economic loss suffered by Belgian shareholders in a Canadian company as a result of the bankruptcy of the company in Spain—allegedly brought about by unlawful action attributable to Spain. The Belgian claim was dismissed, on the ground that in customary law, only the national State of the company (Canada) could seek reparation; this was not a *non liquet*, a finding that there was no law on the point, but a finding as to the content of customary law.

The extent to which international legal relations were governed in the 1920s, at the time of the Commission's work, by anything beyond treaties and custom, was obscure, but the Commission was able to agree that, failing one of those sources, the Court should apply 'the general principles of law recognized by civilized nations'. Up to the present, while there have been judicial mentions of certain principles,[46] it seems that neither the ICJ nor its predecessor has based a decision directly on such general principles. There are decisions by arbitral bodies (to whom, of course, Article 38 of the ICJ Statute has no direct application) which have relied on the concept. There is, however, no unanimity among scholars as to the nature of the principles which may be invoked under this head. There are broadly two possible interpretations.

According to one interpretation, the principles in question are those which can be derived from a comparison of the various systems of municipal law, and the extraction of such principles as appear to be shared by all, or a majority, of them.[47] This interpretation gives force to the reference to the principles being those 'recognized by civilized nations'; the term 'civilized' is now out of place, but at the time it was apparently included inasmuch as some legal systems were then regarded as insufficiently developed to serve as a standard of comparison.[48] In line with this interpretation, parties to cases before the ICJ have at times invoked comparative studies of municipal law.[49] An alternative interpretation is to

---

[45] *Barcelona Traction, Light and Power Company, Limited, Second Phase, Judgment, ICJ Reports 1970*, p 3.

[46] See, for example, *Corfu Channel, Merits, Judgment, ICJ Reports 1949*, p 4 at p 22; *Reservations to the Convention on the Prevention and Punishment of the Crime of Genocide, Advisory Opinion, ICJ Reports 1951*, p 15 at p 23; *Nuclear Tests (Australia v France), Judgment, ICJ Reports 1974*, p 253 at p 268 and *(New Zealand v France), Judgment, ICJ Reports 1974*, p 457 at p 473.

[47] A pioneering and influential work on this subject was Lauterpacht, 1927. A clearer statement of the derivation of general principles from national systems is to be found in the Rome Statute of the International Criminal Court: 'general principles of law derived by the Court from national laws of legal systems of the world' (Article 21(1)(c)). On the dangers of analogy from municipal systems, see Thirlway, 2002.

[48] In the *Abu Dhabi* arbitration in 1951, 18 *ILR* 144, the arbitrator found that the law of Abu Dhabi contained no legal principles that could be applied to modern commercial instruments, and could not therefore be applied to an oil concession.

[49] In the case of *Right of Passage over Indian Territory*, Portugal argued that general principles of law supported its right to passage from the coast to its enclaves of territory, and adduced a comparative study of the provisions in various legal systems for what may be called 'rights of way of necessity'. When for the first time an

the effect that, while the Commission of Jurists may have had primarily in view the legal principles shared by municipal legal orders, the principles to be applied by the Court also include general principles applicable directly to international legal relations, and general principles applicable to legal relations generally. Many of these find expression in customary law, and therefore exist as rules derived from that source; others are in effect assertions of secondary rules (of the kind defined in the Introduction to this chapter), eg the principle *pacta sunt servanda*. Some are applied unquestioningly as self-evident: for example the principles already mentioned for determining the relationship between successive treaties (and possibly successive legal rules generally)—the principles that the special prevails over the general, and that the later prevails over the earlier. For some scholars, the 'general principles of law' justify appeal to ethical concepts, as deriving from 'the universal juridical conscience...as the ultimate material "source" of all law';[50] but this remains a minority view, and difficult to square with the origins of the concept.

There is a striking lack of evidence in international practice and jurisprudence of claims to a specific right of a concrete nature being asserted or upheld on the basis simply of the general principles of law.[51] It may be that such a phenomenon is inconsistent with the nature of such principles; in any event, this particular source of law is of less practical importance in determining the rights and obligations of States in their regular relations.

D. SUBSIDIARY SOURCES: JUDICIAL DECISIONS AND TEACHINGS

Paragraph 1(d) of Article 38 makes a clear distinction between, on the one hand, the sources mentioned in the preceding paragraphs, and on the other, judicial decisions and teachings, inasmuch as it refers to the latter as being merely 'subsidiary means for the determination of rules of law'. The reason for this is evident: if a rule of international law is stated in a judicial decision, or in a textbook, it will be stated as a rule deriving either from treaty, custom, or the general principles of law. The judge, or the author of the textbook, will not assert that the rule stated is law *because* he has stated it; he will state it because he considers that it derives from one of the three principal sources indicated in paragraphs (a) to (c) of Article 38. The first three sources of Article 38 are formal sources; those of paragraph (d) are material rather than formal sources, but material sources having a special degree of authority.

application was made by a State (Malta) to intervene in a case between two other States (Tunisia and Libya) on the basis of having an interest which might be affected by the decision in the case (a possibility referred to in Article 62 of the Court's Statute), Malta similarly relied on a comparative law study showing the conditions and modalities of intervention in judicial proceedings in various national courts.

[50] Separate opinion of Judge Cançado Trindade, *Pulp Mills on the River Uruguay (Argentina v Uruguay), Judgment, ICJ Reports 2010*, p 14 at p 156, para 42.

[51] One field in which the existence of a general principle of law has been asserted is on the controversial question of the binding effect of provisional measures (see Thirlway, Ch 20, Section VI A). When the question was examined by the ICJ in the *LaGrand* case, the Court dealt with it purely as a question of interpretation of the Statute, without recourse to 'general principles', *LaGrand (Germany v United States of America), Merits, Judgment, ICJ Reports 2001*, p 466, para 99. Greece invoked the *exceptio adimpleti contractus* as a general principle in the case of *Application of the Interim Accord of 13 September 1995*; the Court found it unnecessary to decide the point, which was, however, examined at length in the separate opinion of Judge Simma. See *Application of the Interim Accord of 13 September 1995 (the former Yugoslav Republic of Macedonia v Greece), Judgment of 5 December 2011, ICJ Reports 2011*, p 644 at para 161 and Judge Simma, p 695.

This was so even in the early days of the development of international law, when the opinions of the few, but widely respected, legal writers carried much more weight than do the authors of even the most respected textbooks of today. Those eminent authors based their views much more on natural law than on State practice or judicial decisions.[52] Natural law, by definition, as it were, is only visible in the form stated by legal authors; and the greater the authority of the author, the more trust is to be placed in his definition of what natural law prescribes. Nevertheless, the authority of the law stated as natural law rested on what would now be called the general principles of law, and not on the say-so of the writer, whatever his eminence.

Now that there exists a much greater body of judicial and arbitral decisions enunciating rules of law, the emphasis in practice has shifted to the contribution made by such decisions, and away from the views of 'the most highly qualified publicists of the various nations'. Furthermore, the judges and arbitrators are more often than not themselves eminent scholars and practitioners, so that the distinction between judicial precedent and teachings is not a sharp one. It remains the case, however, that States involved in a dispute, or their counsel, will cite the leading textbooks and monographs in support of their claims, as will arbitrators and individual judges of the ICJ in separate or dissenting opinions. The ICJ very rarely quotes teachings; it refers more frequently than it once did to arbitral decisions, and habitually cites its own previous decisions when deciding a point of customary law, to such an extent that it has been accused of paying these more attention than the actual State practice creative of the rules it is called upon to state.

There is of course no doubt that the judicial decisions referred to in Article 38 include the decisions of the ICJ itself, as being of the highest authority. The Court has, however, made clear that, in accordance with Article 59 of its Statute, it does not regard these as binding precedents. In a recent case in which one of the points in issue was directly covered by an earlier decision, the Court said in relation to that decision: 'It is not a question of holding [the parties to the current case] to decisions reached by the Court in previous cases. The real question is whether, in this case, there is cause not to follow the reasoning and conclusions of earlier cases'.[53]

The scope of Article 38(1)(d) is, however, not limited to the decisions of international courts and tribunals; they include the decisions of municipal courts also. Such decisions may play a dual role: on the one hand they may contain a useful statement of international law on a particular point (thus constituting a material source); on the other, the courts of a State are organs of the State and their decisions may also rank as State practice on a question of customary law. In the ICJ case concerning the *Arrest Warrant*, the question was whether Heads of State and Foreign Ministers enjoy absolute immunity from prosecution for crimes allegedly committed during their period of office, and whether there is an exception to this rule in the case of war crimes or crimes against humanity. The parties (Belgium and the Democratic Republic of the Congo) both relied on decisions on the point by the UK House of Lords in the *Pinochet* case[54] and the French *Cour de cassation* in the *Qadaffi* case.[55] The statements of international law in those decisions could have been regarded as 'subsidiary means' for the determination of the customary law on the subject;

---

[52] See Neff, Ch 1, Section III.

[53] *Land and Maritime Boundary between Cameroon and Nigeria, Preliminary Objections, Judgment, ICJ Reports 1998*, p 275, para 28.

[54] *R v Bow Street Metropolitan Stipendiary, ex parte Pinochet Ugarte (Amnesty International Intervening), (No 3)* [1999] UKHL 17; [2000] AC 147; [1999] 2 All ER 97.

[55] *SOS Attentat and Castelnau d'Esnault v Qadaffi, Head of State of the State of Libya*, France, Court of Cassation, criminal chamber, 13 March 2000, No 1414.

they were, however, presented as evidence of State practice, and the Court dealt with them as such.[56] The Court referred to the 'few' decisions of national courts on the question; the paucity of practice was obviously relevant to the question whether a customary rule had become established (as explained in Section II B). But if the decisions had been classified as 'subsidiary means' under Article 38(1)(d), the only question would have been whether they correctly stated the law, not whether they represented a widespread practice of national judicial bodies.[57]

III. THE RELATIONSHIPS BETWEEN THE SOURCES OF INTERNATIONAL LAW

A. RELATIONSHIP BETWEEN TREATY AND CUSTOM

The State practice which is required for the establishment of a rule of customary law has to take the form of action by a State on the international level, that is to say, in relation to one or more other States. An act of a State that has no impact outside its territory, or (saving the case of human rights[58]) in relation to any but its own subjects, is irrelevant as State practice. One of the most normal and essential acts of a State in relation to another State or States is, however, the conclusion of a treaty or agreement; and consequently treaties may well serve as acts of practice significant for the development of custom. The treaty in itself creates certain rights and obligations which are not of a customary nature; but if a number of States make a habit of concluding treaties containing certain standard provisions, then this may, in suitable circumstances, be taken to show that they recognize the existence of a custom requiring them to do so. The difficulty is of course that it can also be argued that the very fact that States have recourse to treaties to establish certain rules shows that they consider that those rules would not be applicable if no treaty were concluded, ie that there is *no* customary rule of that nature. This is a difficulty that has caused controversy, for example, over the question whether there is a customary rule to the effect that a State is not bound to extradite persons accused of political offences. A provision to that effect is almost always included in extradition treaties; does that signify the existence of a custom, or of a need which has to be met on each and every occasion by a special clause?

As already observed, as a result of the parallel existence of treaties and custom as sources of international law, the same question may be governed simultaneously by a treaty, as regards the relationships between the parties to the treaty, and by customary rules, as regards the relationship between non-parties, or between a party to the treaty and a non-party. It has even been held, by the International Court in the case of *Military and Paramilitary Activities in and against Nicaragua*, that where a customary rule has been replaced by a multilateral treaty, the customary rule continues to exist, not only for non-parties to the treaty, but also for the parties to it, 'behind' the treaty, as it were. Such continued existence will normally be of purely theoretical importance, so long as the treaty continues to bind, but in the case referred to, the customary rule rather than the treaty rule

---

[56] *Arrest Warrant of 11 April 2000 (Democratic Republic of Congo v Belgium), Preliminary Objections and Merits, Judgment, ICJ Reports 2002*, p 3, paras 57, 58.

[57] However, since they would only be subsidiary means of proving the law, it would have been necessary to show that there was *other* State practice supporting a customary rule.

[58] See Rodley, Ch 26.

fell to be applied by the Court (for special reasons connected with the nature of the Court's jurisdiction in the case).

The relationship between treaty and customary rules is not necessarily static, however. In the *North Sea Continental Shelf* case, the International Court identified three situations in which the existence or creation of a customary rule might be related to treaty provisions. In the first place, as already observed, a treaty may embody already established rules of customary law, so that it is, to that extent, simply declaratory of existing rules.[59] There are probably very few multilateral treaties of which every provision does no more than state existing customary law (since such a treaty would have little raison d'être).[60] Most such treaties contain a mixture of re-statement and new conventional rules, the problem being to determine to which category a given clause belongs. This is certainly the case of, for example, the Vienna Convention on Diplomatic Relations, or the Vienna Convention on the Law of Treaties, and the 1982 Montego Bay Convention on the Law of the Sea.

Secondly, it is possible that a multilateral treaty states rules and principles which can be found reflected in the practice of States prior to the adoption of the treaty, so that they can be regarded as *lex ferenda* which is ripe for transition to *lex lata*;[61] in such case, the processes of negotiation and adoption of the treaty may be regarded as having what the Court referred to as a 'crystallizing' effect on the nascent customary rules. This is probably particularly likely if the treaty results from the labours of the International Law Commission, whose methods of work allow for considerable input from governments, which is taken into account in the drafting of texts presented for incorporation in a convention.

Finally, it may be that, after the convention has come into force, States other than the parties to it find it convenient to apply the convention rules in their mutual relations, and this may constitute State practice leading to the development of a customary rule. The contention that this had occurred in relation to Article 6 of the 1958 Continental Shelf Convention signified, in the view of the Court:

> treating that Article as a norm-creating provision which has constituted the foundation of, or has generated a rule which, while only conventional or contractual in its origin, has since passed into the general *corpus* of international law, and is now accepted as such by the *opinio juris*, so as to have become binding even for countries which have never, and do not, become parties to the Convention. There is no doubt that this process is a perfectly possible one and does from time to time occur; it constitutes indeed one of the recognized methods by which new rules of customary international law may be formed. At the same time this result is not lightly to be regarded as having been attained.[62]

The Court pointed out that the rule in question would have to be 'of a fundamentally norm-creating character such as could be regarded as forming the basis of a general rule

---

[59] If the treaty does not re-state the customary rule exactly, the question may arise whether the omitted element still exists as part of the customary rule. On the basis of the *Military and Paramilitary Activities* ruling, mentioned in the preceding paragraph, it would seem that it should: *contra*, Judge Simma in the case of the *Application of the Interim Accord of 13 September 1995 (the former Yugoslav Republic of Macedonia v Greece), Judgment of 5 December 2011, ICJ Reports 2011*, p 644, p 695 at para 29.

[60] In the *Asylum* case, it was argued that the 1933 Montevideo Convention 'has merely codified principles which were already recognised by Latin-American custom' but the Court rejected this view: *ICJ Reports 1950*, p 266 at p 277.

[61] For these concepts, see Section I (Introduction) of this chapter.

[62] *North Sea Continental Shelf, Judgment, ICJ Reports 1969*, p 41, para 71. It is of course only the practice of the States not party to the treaty that will 'count' and, as noted earlier, they may be few in number, and treated as *potential* parties: ibid, p 43, para 76.

of law';[63] not every rule which finds a place in a multilateral convention is appropriate for general adoption. For a suitable rule to pass into customary law, 'it might be that, even without the passage of any considerable period of time, a very widespread and representative participation in the convention might suffice of itself', and it was in this respect that the Court emphasized, as already mentioned, the role of 'States whose interests were specially affected'.[64] What the Court regarded as 'indispensable' was that:

> within the period in question, short though it might be, State practice, including that of States whose interests are specially affected, should have been extensive and virtually uniform in the sense of the provision invoked;—and should moreover have occurred in such a way as to show a general recognition that a rule of law or legal obligation is involved.[65]

B. THE HIERARCHY OF SOURCES

In general, when there exists more than one rule that is prima facie applicable to a given situation, the choice between them can be made by the application of one or other of two principles: *lex specialis derogat generali* and *lex posterior derogat priori*: that is to say, the special rule overrides the general rule and the later rule overrides the earlier rule. However, when these principles are applied to the acts of a legislator, they may be regarded as ways of interpreting legislative intention: normally a new law is intended to replace or modify an older law, and legislation providing for a special case or regime is intended to constitute an exception to any general regime. There is normally no difficulty in applying these principles to treaties, which represent the shared intentions of the parties,[66] but it is less clear that they can operate in relation to custom.

Since, as explained earlier, it was the intention of the draftsmen of the PCIJ Statute that the 'general principles of law' should provide a fall-back source of law in the event that no treaty and no customary rule could be found to apply to a given situation, it is clear that to this extent there exists a hierarchy of sources. If a treaty rule or a customary rule exists, then there is no possibility of appealing to the general principles of law to exclude or modify it. The text of Article 38 does not, however, indicate whether there was a hierarchy of application between custom and treaty; a proposed provision, indicating specifically that the Court should apply the sources named in the order in which they were mentioned in that Article, was rejected during the drafting.

It will normally be the case that a treaty is *lex specialis*, and as such prevails over any inconsistent rules of customary law, or at least such as existed at the time of the conclusion of the treaty. It is to be presumed that the parties to the treaty were aware of the existing customary rule, and decided to provide otherwise in their treaty precisely in order to exclude the customary rule.[67] More difficult is the question whether a custom which arises subsequently to the conclusion of a treaty, and which might be regarded as *lex specialis* in relation to the regime established by the treaty, has the effect of overriding the treaty, or such part of it as is inconsistent with the customary rule, as between the parties. If the new customary norm is one accepted as *jus cogens*, then according to the Vienna Convention on the Law of

---

[63] Ibid, para 72.   [64] Ibid, para 73.   [65] Ibid, para 74.

[66] Article 30 of the Vienna Convention on the Law of Treaties, dealing with 'Application of successive treaties relating to the same subject-matter', in effect applies first the criterion of the actual intention of the parties, and then a combination of the two principles here discussed.

[67] See *Dispute regarding Navigational and Related Rights (Costa Rica v Nicaragua), Judgment, ICJ Reports 2009*, p 213, para 36 where the Court found it unnecessary to examine rules of customary law in the presence of a treaty that 'completely define[d] the rules applicable' to the matter.

Treaties, not merely is any inconsistent provision in the treaty overridden, but 'any existing treaty which is in conflict with that norm becomes void and terminates' (Article 64).

Assuming, however, that the new norm is not of that nature, what is the position? If the parties to the treaty have themselves contributed to the development of the new customary rule by acting inconsistently with the treaty, or have adopted the customary practice in their relations after the rule has become established, then the situation may be analysed as in effect a modification (or even perhaps an interpretation) of the treaty. There is a well-settled practice of the Security Council, treating as valid a resolution adopted over the abstention of one of the permanent members, despite the requirement in Article 27(3) of the Charter for the 'concurring votes' of the permanent members. This practice was upheld by the ICJ in the *Namibia* case,[68] in terms which left it obscure whether this was an agreed 'interpretation' of the Article, or an agreed amendment; no reference was made to any subsequently developed rule of custom.

The real problem arises when none of the parties, or only some of them, have participated in the new customary rule. Article 41 of the Vienna Convention on the Law of Treaties lays down a defined procedure for amendment of a multilateral treaty between certain of the parties only, thereby excluding a tacit amendment of this kind; but it is not certain that customary law is so exigent. At all events, the real question is whether the new customary rule can be asserted against those of the parties to the treaty that have not participated in it, or assented to it. One view of the matter is that the very existence of the distinction between *jus cogens* and *jus dispositivum* implies that a newly developed customary rule which is not *jus cogens* does not affect the operation of a pre-existing treaty; but the point must probably be regarded as unsettled.

IV. IS THE ENUMERATION OF ARTICLE 38 EXHAUSTIVE? POSSIBLE NEW OR ADDITIONAL SOURCES

A. HOW CAN NEW SOURCES COME INTO EXISTENCE?

On the basis that the enumeration of sources of international law indicated in Article 38 of the PCIJ Statute was complete and exhaustive at the time of its drafting, there is a certain difficulty in postulating that a new source has come into existence subsequently. The enumeration of sources is, as we have seen, a secondary rule of law, one of those that lays down how the primary rules, those that directly govern conduct, may be created or modified. As was explained in the Introduction to this chapter, the quest for what might be called a 'tertiary' rule, one that lays down how the secondary rules might be created or modified, for a 'fundamental norm' underlying all international law has proved to be vain. We must, it seems, be content to say that international society has established certain secondary rules that correspond to the nature of that society and are universally accepted.

Does it then follow that if the nature of international society changes, there may be a modification of the secondary rules, that is to say of the list of recognized sources of law? It is certain that the nature of international society has changed radically since, for example, the date of the preparation of the PCIJ Statute, in particular in view of the

---

[68] *Legal Consequences for States of the Continued Presence of South Africa in Namibia (South West Africa) notwithstanding Security Council Resolution 276 (1970), Advisory Opinion, ICJ Reports 1971,* p 16, paras 21–2.

great increase in number of sovereign States, and in the complexity of their relations with each other. One cannot exclude *a priori* the possibility of a modification of the secondary rules.

But by what process is such modification to occur? It is difficult to imagine any process that does not in effect involve invoking a secondary rule to effect a modification of a secondary rule. For example, let us suppose that it is contended that the resolutions of the UN General Assembly have become a new independent source of international law. How would one set about proving that this was so? Presumably, by showing that in their relations with each other States asserted rules stated in such resolutions, and accepted such rules as binding when asserted against them. This would, however, amount to saying that an international custom had arisen whereby such resolutions created binding international law. It would follow, either that a new source (resolutions) had arisen through the operation of an existing source (custom); or, perhaps more accurately, that the scope of custom as a source had become widened to include resolutions. On the latter view, a resolution would be (as it is now) a material source of law, but the formal source would be custom.

B. SOME ADDITIONAL SOURCES OR QUASI-SOURCES THAT HAVE BEEN SUGGESTED

1. Unilateral acts

Unilateral acts relevant in international law may be of two kinds. There are acts, unilateral in the sense that the State performing such an act chooses of its own will to do so, but the consequences of which are governed by general international law. In this category fall, for example, the ratification of a treaty, or protest at the action of another State. The question here to be considered is whether there exists a category of unilateral acts not directed to a specified addressee, and the effects of which are defined, not by pre-existing legal rules, but by the simple intention of the State performing them.

The place of unilateral acts of States of this kind in the structure of international law had been regarded as doubtful or somewhat marginal until the decision of the International Court in 1974 in the *Nuclear Tests* cases. In those cases, the Court held that France had assumed legally binding obligations through unilateral declarations, made to the world at large, to the effect that it would not hold any further atmospheric nuclear tests in the Pacific. The Court laid down a general rule in the following terms:

> It is well recognized that declarations made by way of unilateral acts, concerning legal or factual situations, may have the effect of creating legal obligations... When it is the intention of the State making the declaration that it should become bound according to its terms, that intention confers on the declaration the character of a legal undertaking.[69]

The Court recognized that 'Of course, not all unilateral acts imply obligation...'[70] but found on the facts that France had intended to enter into a binding commitment. As a result, the Court was able to hold that the purpose of the proceedings brought by Australia and New Zealand against France, namely a cessation of the atmospheric tests in the Pacific, had been achieved, and the case had therefore become 'without object' or moot.

---

[69] *Nuclear Tests (Australia v France), Judgment, ICJ Reports 1974*, p 253, para 43.
[70] Ibid, para 44.

The application of the traditional doctrine of sources to this decision posed problems. What was the formal source of France's obligation? It was not a treaty; neither of the other two States had indicated any acceptance of France's olive branch, so as to give rise to a contractual or conventional obligation. The Court had also made it clear that it was not ruling on the vexed question whether France had any obligation under customary law to stop its tests; if France was bound to do so, it was only because it had declared that it would do so. Was a unilateral act then to be treated as a new source of law?

This conclusion has been drawn by some scholars; but it does not seem to be an ineluctable one. Notwithstanding the Court's sweeping general statement, quoted earlier, the normal consequence of a unilateral declaration is either that it is accepted by the State or States to which it is addressed, and it will then become in effect part of a treaty settlement; or it will be ignored and rejected, and the other State or States will not seek to enforce it, so that it will become a dead letter. Even without any explicit acceptance, the moment that one of the addressees of the unilateral declaration seeks to rely on the legal obligation indicated in it, this will itself constitute the acceptance needed to convert it into a bilateral, conventional, relationship. The *Nuclear Tests* cases were exceptional in that, for reasons not relevant to the present discussion, the Court was seeking to impose on Australia and New Zealand a settlement of their claims on terms which they had not themselves accepted. Whatever view one may take of the specific *Nuclear Tests* decisions, to base a theory of sources on a decision in a case the special facts of which are very unlikely to be repeated, does not appear a sound approach.

2. Equity

Invocations of equity have played an increasing part in international legal discourse of recent years, but the exact nature of the concept is elusive. It has been said that 'Whatever the legal reasoning of a court of justice, its decision must by definition be just, and therefore in that sense equitable',[71] which, however, does not carry matters much further. The idea of 'equitable principles' or an 'equitable result' plays an important part in the specialized field of maritime delimitation, both in judicial and arbitral decisions and in Articles 74 and 83 of the 1982 UN Convention on the Law of the Sea.[72] Equity in many legal systems may play a moderating role in the sense that when the rigorous application of accepted rules of law leads to a result which appears unjust, equity may step in to adjust the outcome. This is in fact the way in which the concept has developed historically, from Aristotle to the distinction between common law and equity which still survives in the English legal system. Whether this is its role in international law, and if so whether it is its only role, is a controversial issue.

We are here concerned only with the question whether something bearing the label 'equity' can be considered to be a formal source of law: that is to say, whether a legal right or obligation can be asserted, which does not derive from any treaty or any rule of customary law, simply on the basis of being 'equitable'. There is little support for such a view either in State practice or in judicial decisions. In the *Barcelona Traction, Light and Power Co* case, the Court, having dismissed the Belgian legal claim against Spain (for injury to Belgian shareholders in the Canadian company), considered the possibility that 'considerations of equity might call for the possibility of protection of the shareholders in question by their own national State'; it took the view, however, that that hypothesis did not correspond to the circumstances of the case.[73] This might be read as implying that in

---

[71] *North Sea Continental Shelf, Judgment, ICJ Reports 1969*, p 3, para 88.
[72] See Evans, Ch 22, Section VI A.
[73] *Barcelona Traction, Light and Power Company, Limited, Second Phase, Judgment, ICJ Reports 1970*, p 3, para 93.

different circumstances a claim based on equity alone might have succeeded; but in fact it seems that the real point was that customary law on the point is equitable in its effects, so that the point does not arise.

Equity is probably best regarded, in words applied by the International Court to the comparable principle of good faith, as one of the basic principles governing the creation and performance of legal obligations, but 'not in itself a source of obligation where none would otherwise exist'.[74]

3. Resolutions of the UN General Assembly

Certain decisions of the UN Security Council are binding upon the member States, but this does not mean that they constitute an independent source of law: under Article 25 of the Charter the members agree to accept and carry out such decisions, so that their legal force derives from the Charter as a treaty. Resolutions of the UN General Assembly are not attributed such force by the Charter. Many Assembly resolutions are, however, convenient material sources of law, inasmuch as they state, with apparent authority, propositions of general law, and are often assented to by a very large majority of the Members, and thus of the States of the world.[75] It is therefore tempting to confer on them also the authority of a formal source of law, to look no further than the resolution itself in order to assert the binding quality of the rules enunciated. This is particularly so when the resolution in question is of a declaratory or 'law-making' type, and when it is difficult to discern a consistent practice of States in application of those rules, adequate to permit the conclusion that a customary rule exists, one may seek to equate the votes in favour of the resolution with *opinio juris*. This is, however, a too simplistic approach.[76] States vote as they do in the General Assembly (in particular) for a variety of reasons, only some of which may be declared or otherwise visible to the observer. Custom is also traditionally regarded as composed of two elements, practice and *opinio juris*; even if the voting may exhibit *opinio juris*, can it simultaneously be treated as an act of practice?[77]

The theoretical difficulties involved in seeing resolutions as an independent source of law have already been adverted to. When rules declared in resolutions have been relied on in international litigation, the resolutions have been judicially assessed as no more than declaratory of customary law, or at most as evidence of the existence of the *opinio juris*. In the case of *Military and Paramilitary Activities in and against Nicaragua*, the International Court declared that:

> The mere fact that States declare their recognition of certain rules is not sufficient for the Court to consider these as part of customary international law, and as applicable as such to those States.[78]

---

[74] *Border and Transborder Armed Actions (Nicaragua v Honduras), Jurisdiction and Admissibility, Judgment,* ICJ Reports 1988, p 12, para 94.

[75] For example, the Declaration on Principles of International Law Concerning Friendly Relations and Cooperation among States in Accordance with the Charter of the United Nations, GA Res 2625 (XXV); Declaration of Principles Governing the Sea-Bed and the Ocean Floor, and the Subsoil Thereof, Beyond the Limits of National Jurisdiction, GA Res 2749 (XXV); Declaration on the Establishment of a new International Economic Order, GA Res 3202 (S–VI).

[76] As was pointed out by an informed observer many years ago: see Higgins, 1970.

[77] For an interesting analysis whereby the legal significance of States' attitudes to resolutions of international bodies may be assessed in terms of each State's ability to manifest its practical interest in the question, defined as the 'cost' of such manifestation, see Byers, 1999, 151–3, 156–67.

[78] *Military and Paramilitary Activities in and against Nicaragua (Nicaragua v United States of America), Merits, Judgment, ICJ Reports 1986,* p 14, para 184. Similarly in the case concerning *Legal Consequences of the*

Had it considered that, independently of customary law, declarations in General Assembly resolutions were creative of law as a formal source, it would surely have so found. In the case concerning *Legality of the Threat or Use of Nuclear Weapons*, the Court interpreted the numerous General Assembly resolutions on the question of nuclear weapons as doing no more than revealing 'the desire of a very large section of the international community' to take steps toward nuclear disarmament.[79]

4. The problem of 'superior norms'

In the classical theory of international law, any priority of conflicting rules or norms was resolved simply according to the de facto hierarchy of the sources from which they derived, coupled with the principles of the overriding effect of *lex posterior* and *lex specialis* (see Section III B). For this purpose, the content of the rules in issue was irrelevant, except insofar as it was taken into account to judge whether there was in fact a conflict at all (the scope of each rule), and whether one rule was *specialis* in relation to the other, and if so, which was which.

In more recent years, however, more and more attention has been paid to the concept of *jus cogens*—the category of 'peremptory' legal norms, norms from which no derogation by agreement is permitted.[80] Exactly which norms can be so designated in modern international law is still subject to some controversy[81] but it is accepted that the status of peremptory norm derives from the importance of the *content* of the norm to the international community: an example is the prohibition of genocide. A further development is the attempt to assimilate such norms to those creating 'obligations *erga omnes*'[82]—obligations which are regarded as being owed to the whole international community, with the practical consequence that the right to react to any violation of the norm is not confined to the State or States directly injured or affected by the violation, but appertains to every State.[83] Another linked concept was that of the 'international crime' introduced by the

Construction of a Wall in the Occupied Palestinian Territory, ICJ Reports 2004, p 136, para 87, the Court referred to the principle excluding the acquisition of territory by the use of force, laid down in the 'Friendly Relations Declaration' (GA Res 2625 (XXV)) as a reflection of customary law.

[79] *Legality of the Threat or Use of Nuclear Weapons, ICJ Reports 1996*, p 226, para 73. See also the dissenting opinion of Judge Schwebel, ibid, p 319: 'The General Assembly has no authority to enact international law'.

[80] For a light-hearted, but well-reasoned, debunking of the whole concept, see d'Amato, 1991.

[81] The ICJ has specifically identified as *jus cogens*: the 'norm prohibiting genocide'. See *Application of the Convention on the Prevention and Punishment of the Crime of Genocide, Preliminary Objections, ICJ Reports 1996*, p 595, para 31; *Armed Activities on the Territory of the Congo (New Application: 2002) (Democratic Republic of the Congo v Rwanda), Jurisdiction and Admissibility, Judgment, ICJ Reports 2006*, p 6, para 64 'the prohibition of torture' *Questions relating to the Obligation to Prosecute or Extradite (Belgium v Senegal), Judgment of 20 July 2012*, para 99); in its Advisory Opinion on *Legality of the Threat or Use of Nuclear Weapons, Advisory Opinion, ICJ Reports 1996*, p 226, para 83 it found it unnecessary to determine whether certain rules of humanitarian law were *jus cogens*.

[82] The Latin phrase '*erga omnes*' means 'towards all' or 'in relation to all'. Consequently, a right *erga omnes* is not necessarily the counterpart of an obligation *erga omnes*: the one is a right which has to be respected by all States; the other an obligation which can be enforced by every State, whether or not it has suffered from the breach of the obligation. A number of writers have made this confusion, which seems also to have touched the ICJ: see the advisory opinion on *Legal Consequences of the Construction of a Wall in the Occupied Palestine Territory, Advisory Opinion, ICJ Reports 2004*, p 136, paras 154–9, and the critical comments of Judges Higgins, ibid, pp 216–17, paras 37–9, and Kooijmans, ibid, pp 231–4, paras 40–50. The counterpart of an obligation *erga omnes* is a right *omnium* (of all), as is recognized (for example) by Villalpando, 2005, pp 265ff.

[83] See the judgment in the *Barcelona Traction, Light and Power Company, Limited, Second Phase, Judgment, ICJ Reports 1970*, p 3, paras 33–5 and para 91. This assimilation is by no means self-evident; the Commentary to the ICL Articles on State Responsibility suggests that there is at least 'a difference in emphasis' (Commentary to Article 40, Part I, para (7)).

International Law Commission into its draft Articles on State Responsibility, but deleted again at a later stage of the Commission's work.

All these concepts will be examined more fully by Shelton, in Ch 6 they are mentioned here simply to draw attention to the theoretical and practical difficulties of analysing their development in terms of the classical theory of sources. A rule of *jus cogens* is normally (perhaps necessarily) a rule of customary law,[84] as is implied by the reference in Article 63 of the Vienna Convention of the Law of Treaties to the development of a new rule of this type after the conclusion of a treaty. To be such a rule at all, it has to be based upon the consistent practice of States, backed by the *opinio juris*. One would therefore expect that, for a rule to be one of *jus cogens*, or to give rise to obligations *erga omnes*, there would have been practice of such a kind as to show a conviction that the developing rule was of that specific nature, ie a sort of superior *opinio juris*. If a State endeavoured to rely on a treaty as justifying conduct otherwise flagrantly in conflict with a rule of international law, and the universal reaction of States was to assert that that rule was such that no derogation by treaty was permitted, this could be read as practice showing an *opinio* that the rule was one of *jus cogens*. Similarly, if a State not directly affected by a breach of international law took countermeasures against the offending State, and that State conceded its right to do so, this would show an *opinio* that an obligation *erga omnes* was involved. In fact, however, that has not been at all the way in which norms of *jus cogens* and obligations *erga omnes* have come to be identified; and the first hypothesis, of assertion of a treaty as justifying conduct universally condemned, is *a priori* somewhat unlikely to be realized.

Mention should finally be made of Islamic law (the *Shari'ah*). In some fields, particularly of human rights, there is for Islamic States a possibility of conflict of obligations under generally recognized international law, and the body of traditional Islamic law known as the *Shari'ah*.[85] So far as international human rights conventions are concerned, the matter can be dealt with by accession with suitably drafted reservations; the position in customary law is less clear. There is no doubt that in the eyes of Islamic jurists, in any conflict general international law must yield to the *Shari'ah*—a sort of specialized or local *jus cogens*. To date, however, the question has not arisen as a practical issue.

V. CONCLUSION

Ubi societas, ibi jus: wherever there is a social structure, you will find law. This is ultimately the only explanation for the development of international law, for the respect generally shown for it by States as international actors, and for the general recognition of the 'secondary rules' whereby law acquires binding effect. Historically, the more the individual States found it necessary to relate to each other, the greater the need for generally respected rules and guidelines. Even the concept of 'natural law' related to what was fitting and necessary for the good ordering of society; and the positivist approach, which sees all law as established by the express or tacit agreement of those subject to it, is in effect a prolongation of the 'social contract'.

The establishment of the Permanent Court of International Justice brought to a focus the ideas as to the sources of law that had, over the years, made their appearance in State practice, arbitral decisions, and the views of scholars. The definition given in Article 38 of the Statute of the Court has proved to embody a workable structure of recognized law-making processes. Modern scholarly criticisms of that structure have focused principally on two issues: the

---

[84] For an alternative view, that *jus cogens* is a matter of consensus, see the combative article by Kolb, 1998.
[85] See Baderin, 2003.

apparent illogicality of the rules as to creation and development of customary law (and thus the difficulty of its application); and the multiplicity of legal or quasi-legal instruments governing State action (declarations, resolution, regulations, understandings, etc) which, even if ultimately treaty-based, are at so many removes from specific State agreement as to be difficult to fit in to the traditional system of sources. Nevertheless, despite the criticisms made of it, and the multiplicity of new approaches to international law,[86] the definition supplied by Article 38 seems likely to continue to guide the international community and the international judge.

REFERENCES

BADERIN, MA (2003), *International Human Rights and Islamic Law* (Oxford: Oxford University Press).

BEDERMAN, DJ (2010), *Custom as a Source of Law* (Cambridge: Cambridge University Press).

BYERS, M (1999), *Custom, Power and the Power of Rules* (Cambridge: Cambridge University Press).

CHARNEY, R (1993), 'Universal International Law', 87 *AJIL* 529.

CHENG, B (1965), 'United Nations Resolutions on Outer Space: "Instant" Customary Law?', *Ind JIL* 23.

D'AMATO, A (1991), 'It's a Bird, it's a Plane, it's *Jus Cogens*', 9 *Conn JIL* (1991), 1; reprinted in D'Amato, A (2004), *International Law Sources: Collected Papers*, vol III (The Hague: Nijhoff).

FITZMAURICE, G (1958), 'Some Problems regarding the Formal Sources of International Law', Symolae Verzjil (The Hague: Nijhoff).

GOLDMANN, M (2008), 'Inside Relative Normativity: From Sources to Standard Instruments for the Exercise of International Public Authority', 9 *German Law Journal*, (2008), 1866–1908.

HART, H (1994), *The Concept of Law*, revised edn (Oxford: Oxford University Press).

HIGGINS, R (1970), 'The UN and Law-Making: the Political Organs', *Proceedings, American Society of International Law*, Vol 64, p 37.

KAMMERHOFER, J (2004), 'Uncertainty in the Formal Sources of International Law: Customary International Law and Some of its Problems', 15 *EJIL* 523–53.

KOLB, R (1998), 'The Formal Source of *Ius Cogens* in Public International Law', 53 *Zeitschrift für öffentliches Recht*, p 69.

LAUTERPACHT, H (1927), *Private Law Sources and Analogies of International Law* (London: Longmans, Green & Co).

LEPARD, BD (2011), *Customary International Law: a New Theory with Practical Applications* (Cambridge: Cambridge University Press).

MENDELSON, M (1990), 'Are Treaties Merely a Source of Obligation?', in Butler, WE (ed), *Perestroika and International Law* (Leiden: Martinus Nijhoff), p 81.

MURSWIEK, D (2002), 'The American Strategy of Pre-emptive War and International Law', XIII *FYBIL* 195.

OPPENHEIM, L (1992), JENNINGS, Sir R and WATTS, Sir A (eds), *Oppenheim's International Law*, 9th edn (Harlow: Longmans).

THIRLWAY, HWA (2002), 'Concepts, Principles, Rules and Analogies: International and Municipal Legal Reasoning', 294 *Recueil des Cours* 268–405.

VILLALPANDO, S (2005), *L'émergence de la communauté internationale dans la responsibilité des États* (IUHEI, Geneva: Presses Universitaires de France).

---

[86] A useful panoramic view of a number of modern methodologies will be found in a Symposium published in (1999) 93 *AJIL* 293.

FURTHER READING

D'AMATO, A (2004), *International Law Sources, Collected Papers*, vol III (The Hague: Nijhoff): a collection of papers from various dates, written in a vigorous and accessible style.

BOYLE, A and CHINKIN, C (2007), *The Making of International Law* (Oxford: Oxford University Press): the authors' approach is to leave aside the question of sources, and to survey 'the processes, participants and instruments employed in the making of international law'; a valuable supplement to the study of sources.

D'ASPREMONT, J (2011), *Formalism and the Sources of International Law: A Theory of the Ascertainment of Legal Rules* (Oxford: Oxford University Press): an important study of the question, advocating identification of law by formal criteria rather than, for example, intention; stylistically complex, and not easy reading.

HIGGINS, R (1994), *Problems and Process: International Law and How We Use It* (Oxford: Clarendon Press) (particularly Chs 1 and 2): for a study from a more 'policy-oriented' perspective.

KOLB, R (2006), 'Principles as Sources of International Law (with Special Reference to Good Faith)', 53 *Netherlands International Law Review* 1.

KOSKENNIEMI, M (1989), *From Apology to Utopia: the Structure of International Legal Argument*, 2005 reissue (Cambridge: Cambridge University Press): a highly original approach to international law, not easy reading, but still relevant after 20 years.

MENDELSON, M (1995), 'The Subjective Element in Customary International Law', 66 *BYIL* 177: an eloquent plea for the abandonment of the concept of *opinio juris*.

PERREAU-SAUSSINE, A and MURPHY, JB (eds) (2007), *The Nature of Customary Law: Legal Historical and Philosophical Perspectives* (Cambridge: Cambridge University Press): a collection of essays by various hands, generally taking a non-traditional view of the subject.

SCHACHTER, O (1989), 'Entangled Treaty and Custom', in Dinstein, Y (ed), *International Law at a Time of Perplexity: Essays in Honour of Shabtai Rosenne* (The Hague: Nijhoff), p 717: on the inter-relationship of the two sources in modern law.

SHELTON, D (2006), 'Normative Hierarchy in International Law', 100 *AJIL* 291.

THIRLWAY, HWA (2013), *The Law and Procedure of the International Court of Justice: Fifty Years of Jurisprudence*, (Oxford: Oxford University Press) pp 139–250, 1175-213: a survey of problems that have arisen before the ICJ concerning the various sources of international law.

5

SOFT LAW IN INTERNATIONAL LAW-MAKING

Alan Boyle

SUMMARY

From a law-making perspective the term 'soft law' is simply a convenient description for a variety of non-legally binding instruments used in contemporary international relations by States and international organizations. Soft law in this sense can be contrasted with hard law, which is always binding. Non-binding soft law instruments are not law per se, but they may be evidence of existing law, or formative of the *opinio juris* or State practice that generates new customary law. They may additionally acquire binding legal character as elements of a treaty-based regulatory regime, or constitute a subsequent agreement between the parties regarding the interpretation of a treaty or the application of its provisions. Thus the effect of non-binding soft law instruments may not be fundamentally different from those multilateral treaties which serve much the same law-making purposes. Both treaties and soft law instruments can thus become vehicles for focusing consensus on rules and principles, and for mobilizing a consistent, general response on the part of States. Other non-binding soft-law instruments are significant mainly because they are the first step in a process eventually leading to conclusion of a multilateral treaty, or because they provide the detailed rules and technical standards required for the implementation of a treaty. An alternative view of soft law focuses on the contrast between 'rules', involving clear and reasonably specific commitments which are in this sense hard law, and 'norms' or 'principles', which, being more open-textured or general in their content and wording, can thus be seen as soft even when contained in a binding treaty. Nevertheless, this form of soft law is also not without legal significance. For all these reasons it is a fallacy to dismiss soft law, properly understood: it can and does contribute to the corpus of international law.

I. THE SIGNIFICANCE OF SOFT LAW

Soft law is often misunderstood, although evidence of its importance as an element in modern international law-making is abundant, most notably in the declarations or resolutions adopted by States in international conferences or in the UN or other international organizations. Certainly, the concept has had its critics. Prosper Weil famously argued in his classic article 'Towards Relative Normativity in International Law?' that there is only law and non-law.[1] For him, soft law is a non-sequitur. Jan Klabbers has also dismissed

---

[1] Weil, 1983, p 411.

the concept of soft law as redundant.[2] It is true that soft law may appear to some as another example of the preference for 'informal regimes' which Martii Koskenniemi identifies with a 'managerialist' approach to international affairs, resulting in a dilution of their legal force.[3] But as Koskenniemi rightly observes, 'To believe that a commitment to "law" would be an automatically progressive choice is no less crude a directive to policy than the belief that all needs to be streamlined for the attainment of imperial preference.'[4] However, it is not necessary to indulge in high theory in order to make sense of soft law. As Rosalyn Higgins has observed in the context of UN General Assembly resolutions, '... the passing of binding decisions is not the only way in which law development occurs. Legal consequences can also flow from acts which are not, in the formal sense, "binding". And, further, law is developed by a variety of non-legislative acts which do not seek to secure, in any direct sense, "compliance" from Assembly members ....'[5]

Perhaps the most important point to make at the outset therefore is simply that some of the forms of 'soft law' under consideration here are potentially law-making in much the same way that multilateral treaties are potentially law-making. The proposition is not that non-binding declarations or resolutions of the General Assembly or any other soft law instrument are law per se, but that in appropriate cases such instruments may be evidence of existing law, or formative of the *opinio juris* or State practice that generates new customary law.[6] Widespread acceptance of soft law instruments will tend to legitimize conduct, and make the legality of opposing positions harder to sustain. They may additionally acquire binding legal character as elements of a treaty-based regulatory regime,[7] or constitute a 'subsequent agreement between the parties regarding the interpretation of the treaty or the application of its provisions',[8] or influence the development and application of treaties or general international law.[9]

It is certainly a fallacy to dismiss these forms of soft law as not law and therefore of no importance: they can and do contribute to the corpus of international law, as the examples considered next will show. Nor is reliance on soft law to be confused with the application of *lex ferenda* or 'evolving law'.[10] If it is true that some soft law instruments are—like treaties—part of the process by which customary law evolves, then it is equally true that in the evolutionary stage they have not yet generated actual law, and we should not pretend otherwise. Identifying when law in the making has become law is of course precisely the point on which States and international lawyers will often disagree, but it is precisely at that point that 'soft law' is in reality no longer soft. Our focus in this chapter is on soft law as one element in the law-making process precisely because it leads to law, not to something less than law.

II. WHAT IS SOFT LAW?

'Soft law' has a range of possible meanings.[11] From a law-making perspective the term 'soft law' is simply a convenient description for a variety of non-legally binding instruments

---

[2] Klabbers, 1996, pp 167–82.   [3] Koskenniemi, 2009, p 15. See also Koskenniemi, 1992, p 123.
[4] Koskenniemi, 2009, p 17.   [5] Higgins, 1995, p 24.
[6] Brownlie, 1979, p 261 refers to the 'decisive catalytic effect' of certain UNGA resolutions.
[7] Eg under the 1982 UN Convention on the Law of the Sea, Articles 210–11, or the 1994 Nuclear Safety Convention, on which see Section IV.
[8] See 1969 Vienna Convention on the Law of Treaties, Article 31(3)(a).
[9] See *Gabčíkovo-Nagymaros Project (Hungary/Slovakia), Judgment, ICJ Reports 1997*, p 7, para 140.
[10] *OSPAR Arbitration* (2003) PCA, 42 ILM 330, paras101–4. On the applicability of evolving law see the very sensible comments by McDorman, 2004.
[11] See generally Baxter, 1980; Chinkin, 1989; Sztucki, 1990; Dupuy, 1991; Hillgenberg, 1999.

used in contemporary international relations by States and international organizations. It encompasses, inter alia, inter-State conference declarations such as the 1992 Rio Declaration on Environment and Development; UN General Assembly instruments such as the 1948 Universal Declaration of Human Rights, the 1970 Declaration on the Principles of Friendly Relations Among States, or the 2007 Declaration on the Rights of Indigenous Peoples, or other resolutions dealing with outer space, the deep seabed, decolonization, or natural resources; or codes of conduct, guidelines and recommendations of international organizations, such as UNEP's 1987 Guidelines on Environmental Impact Assessment, FAO's Code of Conduct on Responsible Fisheries or many others adopted by IMO, IAEA, FAO and so on.

Soft law in this sense can be contrasted with hard law, which is always binding. Seen from this angle, the legal form is decisive: treaties which have entered into force are by definition hard law, at least for the parties. So, in principle, are UN Security Council Resolutions adopted under Chapter VII of the UN Charter, because all UN member States have agreed to accept and carry out these decisions.[12] If the form is that of a non-binding agreement, such as the Helsinki Accords (Schachter, 1977), or a UN General Assembly resolution or declaration,[13] it will not be a treaty for precisely that reason and we will have what is in effect a 'soft' agreement. Of course, the question whether an agreement is a binding treaty is not necessarily easy to answer, as we can observe in the *Qatar-Bahrain Maritime Delimitation* case.[14] The test is one of substance and intent; the label attached to the instrument is not decisive. Moreover, an agreement involving a State and another entity may be binding, even if it is not a treaty,[15] so the distinction between hard and soft agreements is not simply synonymous with the distinction between treaties and other instruments. Furthermore, once soft law begins to interact with binding instruments its non-binding character may be lost or altered.

As we have seen, reliance on soft law as part of the law-making process takes a number of different forms. While the legal effect of declarations, resolutions, guidelines and other soft law instruments is not necessarily the same, it is characteristic of nearly all of them that they are carefully negotiated, and often carefully drafted statements, which are in some cases intended to have some normative significance despite their non-binding, non-treaty form. There is at least an element of good faith commitment,[16] evidencing in some cases a desire to influence State practice or expressing some measure of law-making intention and progressive development. In this sense non-binding soft law instruments are in some cases not fundamentally different from those multilateral treaties which serve much the same law-making purposes. They may also be both an alternative to and part of the process of multilateral treaty-making. In the following sections we will explore the uses of soft law and consider what legal effect it may have.

---

[12] UN Charter, Article 25.

[13] In UN practice a 'declaration' is used in preference to a 'resolution' when 'principles of great and lasting importance are being enunciated'. See UN Doc E/CN.4/L.610 (1962), cited in Cheng, 1965, at p 32.

[14] *Maritime Delimitation and Territorial Questions between Qatar and Bahrain, Jurisdiction and Admissibility, Judgment, ICJ Reports 1994*, p 112.

[15] See *Anglo-Iranian Oil Co, Preliminary Objections, Judgment, ICJ Reports 1952*, p 93.

[16] *Voting Procedure on Questions relating to Reports and Petitions concerning the Territory of South West Africa, Advisory Opinion, ICJ Reports 1955*, p 4, Separate Opinion of Judge Lauterpacht, p 118: 'The State in question, while not bound to accept the recommendation, is bound to give it due consideration in good faith'. See also Virally, 1956, pp 85–91. A soft law declaration may result in binding unilateral obligations: see *OSPAR Arbitration* (2003) PCA, 42 ILM 330, para 90.

III. TREATIES OR SOFT LAW?

There are several reasons why soft law instruments may represent an attractive alternative to law-making by treaty. First, it may be easier to reach agreement when the form is non-binding. Use of soft law instruments enables States to agree to more detailed and precise provisions because their legal commitment and the consequences of any non-compliance are more limited. Secondly, it may be easier for some States to agree to non-binding instruments because they can avoid the domestic treaty ratification process, and perhaps escape democratic accountability for the policy to which they have agreed. Of course this may also make it comparably harder to implement such policies if funding, legislation, or public support, are necessary. Thirdly, soft law instruments are flexible. They will normally be easier to supplement, amend or replace than treaties, particularly when all that is required is the adoption of a new resolution by an international institution. Two good examples are the nuclear safety standards adopted by the International Atomic Energy Agency,[17] which amplify and interpret the basic obligations contained in the Nuclear Safety Convention, and FAO's Code of Conduct on Responsible Fisheries, which has itself been further developed by non-binding 'Plans of Action' adopted by the FAO Conference.[18] Treaties take time to replace or amend, and the attempt to do so can result in an awkward and overlapping network of old and new obligations between different sets of parties. One of the better examples of the confused state of the law which sometimes results from repeated treaty revisions is the 1929 Warsaw Convention Relating to International Carriage by Air (Gardiner, 1998). Lastly, soft law instruments may provide more immediate evidence of international support and consensus than a treaty whose impact is heavily qualified by reservations and the need to wait for ratification and entry into force. All of these points are well illustrated by some of the examples discussed in later sections of this chapter.[19]

Given the relative advantages of soft law over treaties, it is perhaps surprising that the multilateral treaty has until now been the International Law Commission's preferred instrument for the codification of international law.[20] One important advantage of the treaty as an instrument of codification is that States have significant input into the negotiations and they have sometimes made substantial changes to ILC drafts.[21] This renegotiation does not necessarily happen when the UN General Assembly simply adopts or takes note of a declaration of principles drafted by the Commission. A treaty basis may also be required when creating new international organizations or institutions, or for dispute settlement provisions. Nevertheless, in some situations soft law instruments appear to be just as useful a means of codifying international law as treaties. The Commission's draft articles on the law of State responsibility could equally well be codified using either a General Assembly resolution or a treaty.[22] Indeed a GA resolution may in this case be more effective than a treaty, which, like the Vienna Convention on the Law of Treaties, runs the

---

[17] See next section.   [18] See next section.

[19] Other examples include the UN Declaration on the Rights of Indigenous Peoples, UNGA Res 61/295 (13 September 2007), on which see Barelli, 2009.

[20] Articles 17 and 23 of the Statute of the Commission do refer expressly to the conclusion of conventions, but other possibilities are left open.

[21] Eg the 1969 Vienna Convention on the Law of Treaties and the 1997 International Convention on the Non-navigational Uses of International Watercourses. On the comparative advantages of different forms see Crawford, 2002, pp 58–60.

[22] The ILC recommended that the UNGA simply 'take note' of the draft articles.

risk of securing only a relatively small number of parties and taking many years to enter into force. The Vienna Convention is among the ILC's most successful and authoritative codifications, but it is difficult to suggest that this owes much to its treaty status, or to the number of States parties.[23]

The argument for using a treaty rather than a soft law instrument is stronger in the case of new law-making or the revision of existing law, such as the renegotiation of the law of the sea or the elaboration of human rights law, although in many of these cases institutions with extensive powers were also established at the same time and a treaty was thus desirable in any event. But even for new law, non-binding instruments may still be useful if they can help generate widespread and consistent State practice and/or provide evidence of *opinio juris* in support of a customary rule. There are good examples of UN General Assembly resolutions and intergovernmental declarations having this effect in the *Nicaragua* case,[24] the Nuclear Weapons Advisory Opinion,[25] and the *Western Sahara Advisory Opinion*.[26]

What all of this suggests is that the non-binding form of an instrument is of relatively limited relevance in the context of customary international law-making. Treaties do not generate or codify customary law because of their binding form but because they either influence State practice and provide evidence of *opinio juris* for new or emerging rules, or because they are good evidence of what the existing law is. In many cases this is no different from the potential effect of non-binding soft law instruments. Both treaties and soft law instruments can be vehicles for focusing consensus on rules and principles, and for mobilizing a consistent, general response on the part of States. Depending upon what is involved, treaties may be more effective than soft law instruments for this purpose because they indicate a stronger commitment to the principles in question and to that extent they may carry greater weight than a soft law instrument, but the assumption that they are necessarily more authoritative is misplaced. To take only one example, the 1992 Rio Declaration on Environment and Development both codifies existing international law and seeks to develop new law.[27] It is not obvious that a treaty with the same provisions would carry greater weight or achieve its objectives any more successfully. On the contrary, it is quite possible that such a treaty would, several years later, still have far from universal participation, whereas the 1992 Declaration secured immediate consensus support, with such authority as that implies. At the same time, it seems clear that agreements such as those on climate change and biological diversity adopted in 1992 could only be in treaty form, because of the combination of their status as new law, their more detailed terms, and their institutional provisions. For rather different reasons the ILC articles on State immunity were adopted as a treaty in order to facilitate giving effect to the necessary changes in the national law of those States with a monist view of the relationship between treaties and national law.[28] In these cases, because of the content and objective of the agreement, incorporation in a treaty was the right option and does carry a greater sense of commitment than a soft law instrument.

---

[23] As late as 2004, 35 years after adoption of the VCLT, there were still only 81 parties, but by the fortieth anniversary in October 2009 this had grown to 110 and has since risen to 113.

[24] *Military and Paramilitary Activities in and against Nicaragua (Nicaragua v United States of America), Merits, Judgment, ICJ Reports 1986*, p 14.

[25] *Legality of the Threat or Use of Nuclear Weapons, Advisory Opinion, ICJ Reports 1996*, p 226.

[26] *Western Sahara, Advisory Opinion, ICJ Reports 1975*, p 12.

[27] See *Legality of the Threat or Use of Nuclear Weapons, Advisory Opinion, ICJ Reports 1996*, p 226, paras 29–30 and Boyle and Freestone, 1999, Ch 1; Sands, 1993 Chs 1 and 3.

[28] See 2004 UN Convention on Jurisdictional Immunities of States and their Property.

IV. SOFT LAW AS PART OF THE MULTILATERAL TREATY-MAKING PROCESS

Some non-binding soft-law instruments are significant because they are the first step in a process eventually leading to conclusion of a multilateral treaty. Thus the non-binding Universal Declaration of Human Rights was adopted long before agreement on the 1966 Covenants became possible, but it was always intended by the Human Rights Commission that further binding agreements would follow. Examples are numerous, but they include General Assembly resolutions on outer space, the deep seabed, and climate change;[29] the IAEA Guidelines[30] which formed the basis for the rapid adoption of the 1986 Convention on Early Notification of a Nuclear Accident following the Chernobyl accident; UNEP Guidelines on Environmental Impact Assessment[31] which were subsequently substantially incorporated in the 1991 ECE Convention on Environmental Impact Assessment in a Transboundary Context; and UNEP's Guidelines on Land-based Sources of Marine Pollution,[32] which provided a model for regional treaties.[33]

Other soft law instruments are used as mechanisms for authoritative interpretation or amplification of the terms of a treaty, and to that extent must be taken into account. The ILC commentary to what is now Article 31(3)(a) of the Vienna Convention on the Law of Treaties notes simply that '...an agreement as to the interpretation of a provision reached after the conclusion of the treaty represents an authentic interpretation by the parties which must be read into the treaty for purposes of its interpretation.'[34] The ICJ has acknowledged the relevance of these instruments for the interpretation of treaty provisions.[35] There are well-known instances of General Assembly resolutions interpreting and applying the UN Charter, including the Universal Declaration of Human Rights and others dealing with decolonization or the use of force.[36]

The same task of giving guidance on or amplifying the terms of a treaty is performed more frequently by resolutions, recommendations and decisions of other international organizations, and by the conferences of parties to treaties. Thus it was a resolution of the parties to the Montreal Protocol to the Ozone Convention which first set out the terms of the non-compliance procedure provided for in the protocol.[37] The procedure was subsequently

---

[29] See 1963 Declaration of Legal Principles Governing the Activities of States in the Exploration and Use of Outer Space, UNGA Res 1962 (XVIII) (13 December 1963); 1970 Declaration of Principles Governing the Sea Bed and Ocean Floor and Subsoil Thereof Beyond the Limits of National Jurisdiction, UNGA Res 2749 (XXV) (12 December 1970); 1988 Resolution on Protection of Global Climate for Present and Future Generations of Mankind, UNGA Res 43/53 (6 December 1988).

[30] IAEA/INFCIRC/321 (1985).   [31] UNEP/GC14/25 (1987).   [32] UNEP/WG.120/3 (1985).

[33] See eg 1990 Kuwait Protocol for the Protection of the Marine Environment Against Marine Pollution from Land-based Sources.

[34] ILC, 'The Law of Treaties,' commentary to Article 27, at para (14), in Watts, 2000, vol II, p 689.

[35] See *Kasikili/Sedudu Island (Botswana/Namibia), Judgment, ICJ Reports 1999,* p 1045 at pp 1075–76, paras 47–51 and the case-law cited at para 50. See also Preliminary conclusions by the Chairman of the Study Group on the subject of Treaties over Time, ILC, Report on the Work of its Sixty-third Session (2011), *General Assembly, Official Records, Sup No 10* (A/66/10), pp 281–4.

[36] 1960 Declaration on the Granting of Independence to Colonial Countries and Peoples, UNGA Res 1514 (XV) (14 December 1960); 1970 Declaration on Principles of International law Concerning Friendly Relations and Co-operation Among States in Accordance with the Charter of the United Nations, UNGA Res 2625 (XXV) (24 October 1970). See *Western Sahara, Advisory Opinion, ICJ Reports 1975,* p 12; *Military and Paramilitary Activities in and against Nicaragua (Nicaragua v United States of America), Merits, Judgment, ICJ Reports 1986,* p 14.

[37] Decision II/5, UNEP/OzL.Pro/WG.3/2/2, Annex III (1990).

revised and then incorporated by amendment as an annex in the protocol, showing again how non-binding soft law can be transformed into binding form. Similarly, UNEP's Cairo Guidelines on the Transport of Hazardous Wastes[38] can be regarded as an amplification of the obligation of 'environmentally sound management' provided for in Article 4 of the 1989 Basel Convention on the Control of Transboundary Movements of Hazardous Wastes. Guidance of this kind helps ensure a common understanding of what a treaty requires and may provide the detailed rules and technical standards required for implementation.[39]

Environmental soft law is quite often important for this reason, setting standards of best practice or due diligence to be achieved by the parties in implementing their obligations. WHO and FAO standards may thus become 'international standards, guidelines or recommendations' for the purpose of judging compliance with the WTO Sanitary and Phytosanitary Agreement.[40] In the *Pulp Mills* case, the ICJ had to interpret references to 'guidelines and recommendations of international technical bodies' in Article 41 of the 1975 Statute of the River Uruguay. The parties relied, inter alia, on WHO standards for air and water pollution. These are not binding on States, but as the ICJ indicated '[they] are, to the extent they are relevant, to be taken into account by the State so that the domestic rules and regulations and the measures it adopts are compatible with those guidelines and recommendations'.[41] These 'ecostandards' are essential in giving hard content to the overly-general and open-textured terms of framework environmental treaties (Contini and Sand, 1972). The advantages of regulating environmental risks in this way are that the detailed rules can easily be changed or strengthened as scientific understanding develops or as political priorities change. Such standards could of course be adopted in binding form, using easily amended annexes to provide flexibility, but this is not always what parties want.

The IAEA has made particular use of non-binding standards, through its codes of conduct, guidelines, or safety recommendations. These generally represent an authoritative technical and political consensus, approved by the Board of Governors or General Conference of the Agency. Despite their soft law status it is relatively easy to see them as minimum internationally endorsed standards of conduct, and to regard failure to comply as presumptively a failure to fulfil the customary obligation of due diligence in the regulation and control of nuclear activities.[42] Although non-binding, these are obviously directly relevant to interpreting the phrase 'appropriate steps' used throughout the 1994 Nuclear Safety Convention to express the general obligation of due diligence.[43] Comparable examples in the outer space context include the 2007 Space Debris Mitigation Guidelines,[44] and the 2009 Safety Framework for Nuclear Power Source Application in Outer Space.[45] There

---

[38]   UNEP/WG.122/3.

[39]   Rose, 2012, gives a good account of how soft law guidance has been used by the OECD to help governments and national courts implement the 1997 Bribery Convention.

[40]   1994 SPS Agreement, Article 3.

[41]   *Pulp Mills on the River Uruguay (Argentina v Uruguay), Judgment, ICJ Reports 2010*, p 14, para 62. See also para 197. Unusually for an international organization, WHO may adopt 'regulations' which will be binding on all member states except those who register an objection, but this power is rarely used, and in practice non-binding recommendations have become the main regulatory instrument. 1948 WHO Constitution, Articles 21–3. See Fidler, 1998, 1079; Burci and Vignes, 2004, 124–55.

[42]   The preamble to the Nuclear Safety Convention recognizes that internationally formulated safety guidelines 'can provide guidance on contemporary means of achieving a high level of safety'. IAEA guidelines would be the obvious starting point for determining what constituted the 'appropriate steps' with regard to safety controls required by Articles 10–19 of the Convention.

[43]   See Birnie, Boyle, and Redgwell, 2009, Ch 9.

[44]   Endorsed by UNCOPUOS, Fiftieth Session, UN Doc A/62/20, annex.

[45]   Endorsed by UNCOPUOS, Fifty-second Session, UN Doc A/AC.105/934.

is no reason why these instruments should not be relied upon to assist in interpreting Article 9 of the Outer Space Treaty. They exemplify once again how soft law and treaties can interact in a complex regulatory framework.

Nor is IAEA unique in this respect. FAO has made use of a mixture of hard and soft law instruments to promote implementation of the fisheries provisions of the 1982 UN Convention on the Law of the Sea (1982 UNCLOS). The 1993 Agreement to Promote Compliance with Conservation Measures on the High Seas is a binding treaty, but it forms an integral part of the non-binding 1995 Code of Conduct on Responsible Fishing, which is itself further implemented by other measures including the 2001 Plan of Action on Illegal, Unreported and Unregulated Fishing, also a soft-law instrument. Negotiated in the same manner as treaties, and adopted by consensus in FAO,[46] these non-binding 'voluntary instruments' are aimed at regional fisheries organizations and the fishing industry as well as States, but in part they also reiterate, interpret and amplify relevant provisions of the 1982 UNCLOS and the 1995 Fish Stocks Agreement. The scope of the Code is much broader than either of these treaties, however. It contains some elements which are unlikely to find their way into a binding agreement, and others which could not be agreed on as part of the UN Fish Stocks Agreement. The 1993 Agreement and the 1995 Code were negotiated in parallel with the Fish Stocks Agreement, and all three 'can be viewed as a package of measures that reinforce and complement each other' (Moore, 1999, pp 91–2). Reviewing the effect of all these inter-related measures, a former FAO Legal Adviser concludes that 'There can be little doubt that the sum total of the changes introduced has substantially strengthened the regime of the 1982 UN Convention, leaving aside the question whether there has been a de facto amendment of it in some respect'(Edeson,1999, p 165. See also Edeson 2003, p 165).

Sometimes binding force is conferred on soft-law instruments by incorporating them into the terms of a treaty by implied reference. The 1982 UNCLOS makes use of this technique, impliedly incorporating recommendations and resolutions of IMO, as well as regulatory annexes to treaties such as the 1973/78 MARPOL Convention, under provisions variously requiring or permitting States to apply 'generally accepted rules and standards established through the competent international organization or general diplomatic conference'.[47] Thus although IMO has no general power under its constitution to adopt binding resolutions, for parties to the 1982 UNCLOS compliance with these soft-law instruments is no longer optional but provides a standard for compliance with the treaty itself.

Lastly, soft law instruments may operate in conjunction with a treaty to provide evidence of *opinio juris* for the possible emergence of a rule of customary international law. ICJ case law, including the Nicaragua case,[48] shows how the interplay between the UN Charter and resolutions of the General Assembly can have this effect.

These examples all point to the conclusion that the non-binding force of soft law can be over-stated. In many of the examples just described States are not free to disregard applicable soft-law instruments: even when not incorporated directly into a treaty, they may represent an agreed understanding of its terms. Thus, although of themselves these instruments may not be legally binding, their interaction with related treaties may transform their legal status into something more.

---

[46] However, some states expressed significant reservations when adopting the Plan of Action: see FAO, *Rept of the Committee on Fisheries*, Twenty-fourth Session (2001).

[47] 1982 UNCLOS, Articles 207–12.

[48] *Military and Paramilitary Activities in and against Nicaragua (Nicaragua v United States of America)*, Merits, Judgment, ICJ Reports 1986, p 14; *Western Sahara*, Advisory Opinion, ICJ Reports 1975, p 12.

V. TREATIES AS SOFT LAW

An alternative view of soft law focuses on the contrast between 'rules', involving clear and reasonably specific commitments which are in this sense hard law (eg 'No State may validly purport to subject any part of the high seas to its sovereignty'), and 'norms' or 'principles', which, being more open-textured or general in their content and wording, can thus be seen as soft.

The point was made many years ago by the late Judge Baxter that some treaties are soft in the sense that they impose no real obligations on the parties (Baxter, 1980). Though formally binding, the vagueness, indeterminacy, or generality of their provisions may deprive them of the character of 'hard law' in any meaningful sense. The 1992 Framework Convention on Climate Change provides another example. Adopted by consensus at the Rio Conference, this treaty does impose some commitments on the parties, but its core articles, dealing with policies and measures to tackle greenhouse gas emissions, are so cautiously and obscurely worded and so weak that it is doubtful whether any real obligations are created.[49] Moreover, whatever commitments have been undertaken by developing States are also conditional on performance of commitments by developed State parties to provide funding and transfer of technology.[50]

Such treaty provisions are almost impossible to breach and in that limited sense Judge Baxter is justified in calling them soft law. More of a political bargain than a legal one, these are 'soft' undertakings of a very fragile kind. They are not normative and cannot be described as creating 'rules' in any meaningful sense. This is probably true of very many treaties, a point recognized by the International Court in the *North Sea Continental Shelf* case when it specified that one of the conditions to be met before a treaty could be regarded as law-making is that it should be so drafted as to be 'potentially normative' in character.[51]

There is, however, a second and more significant sense in which a treaty may be 'soft' in character because it articulates 'principles' rather than 'rules' or 'obligations' but is nevertheless potentially normative. Here it is the formulation of the provision which is decisive in determining whether it is hard or soft, not its form as a treaty or binding instrument. An example of a soft formulation, which nevertheless has binding form, is Article 87(2) of the 1982 UNCLOS, which provides that high seas freedoms 'shall be exercised by all States with due regard for the interests of other States in their exercise of the freedoms of the high seas...' What is meant by 'due regard' for the interests of other States will necessarily depend on the particular circumstances of each case and in that sense the provision is more of a 'principle' than a rule.[52] The rule of customary law providing for equitable delimitation of maritime boundaries is another example of a comparably 'soft' formulation.[53]

---

[49] Especially Articles 4(1) and (2). The USA's interpretation of these articles was that 'there is nothing in any of the language which constitutes a commitment to any specific level of emissions at any time...'. The parties determined at their first meeting in 1995 that the commitments were inadequate and they agreed to commence negotiation of the much more specific commitments now contained in the 1997 Kyoto Protocol.

[50] Article 4(7).   [51] *North Sea Continental Shelf, Judgment, ICJ Reports 1969*, p 3, para 72.

[52] See *Fisheries Jurisdiction (United Kingdom v Iceland), Merits, Judgment, ICJ Reports 1974*, p 3; *(Federal Republic of Germany v Iceland), Merits, Judgment, ICJ Reports 1974*, p 175; *Nuclear Tests (Australia v France), Judgment, ICJ Reports 1974*, p 253; *(New Zealand v France), Judgment, ICJ Reports 1974*, p 457.

[53] 1982 UNCLOS, Article 74 and 83; *North Sea Continental Shelf, Judgment, ICJ Reports 1969*, p 3; *Delimitation of the Maritime Boundary in the Gulf of Maine Area, Judgment, ICJ Reports 1984*, p. 246; *Maritime Delimitation in the Area between Greenland and Jan Mayen, Judgment, ICJ Reports 1993*, p 38.

The Convention on Climate Change once again provides other good examples of such principles explicitly included in a major treaty. Indeed, given how weak the rest of the treaty is, the principles found in Article 3 are arguably the most important 'law' in the whole agreement because they prescribe how the regime for regulating climate change is to be developed by the parties. It is worth quoting the main elements of this provision:

Article 3: Principles

In their actions to achieve the objective of the Convention and to implement its provisions, the parties shall be guided, *inter alia*, by the following:

1. The Parties should protect the climate system for the benefit of present and future generations of humankind, on the basis of equity an in accordance with their common but differentiated responsibilities ...

3. The Parties should take precautionary measures to anticipate, prevent, or minimise the causes of climate change and mitigate its adverse effects ...

4. The Parties have a right to, and should, promote sustainable development ...

These elements of Article 3 are all drawn directly from the non-binding Rio Declaration on Environment and Development; they reflect principles which are not simply part of the Climate Change Convention, but which have been more widely endorsed and applied by States. They are not expressed in obligatory terms: the use of 'should' qualifies their application, despite the obligatory wording of the chapeau sentence. All of these principles are open-textured in the sense that there is considerable uncertainty concerning their specific content and they leave much room for interpretation and elaboration. They are not at all like rules requiring States to conduct an environmental impact assessment, or to prevent harm to other States.

Given their explicit role as guidance and their softer formulation, the 'principles' in Article 3 are not necessarily binding rules which must be complied with or which entail responsibility for breach if not complied with; yet, despite all these limitations they are not legally insignificant.[54] At the very least Article 3 is relevant to interpretation and implementation of the Convention as well as creating expectations concerning matters which must be taken into account in good faith in the negotiation of further instruments.

Article 3 takes a novel approach to environmental protection, but in the context of a dynamic and evolutionary regulatory regime such as the Climate Change Convention it has the important merit of providing some predictability regarding the parameters within which the parties are required to work towards the objective of the Convention. In particular, they are not faced with a completely blank sheet of paper when entering subsequent protocol negotiations or when the Conference of the Parties takes decisions under the various articles empowering it to do so. Thus it is significant that the relevance of Article 3 was reiterated in the mandate for negotiation of the Kyoto Protocol[55] and is referred to in the preamble to the Protocol. It is a nice question whether the parties collectively are entitled to disregard the principles contained in Article 3, or what the legal effect of decisions which do so may be,[56] but however weak it may seem, parties whose interests are affected do have a right to insist on having the principles of Article 3

---

[54] See the debate between Sands and Mann in Lang, 1995, pp 53–74.

[55] The so-called 'Berlin mandate': Decision 1/CP1, in *Report of the Conference of the Parties on its First Session*, UN Doc FCCC/CP/1995/7/Add.1.

[56] Arguably the principle of common but differentiated responsibility has been departed from in decisions of the parties to the Climate Change Convention taken in 2009–11. See Rajamani, 2012.

taken into account. As we shall see in the following section, sustainable development, intergenerational equity, or the precautionary principle, are all more convincingly seen in this sense: not as binding obligations which must be complied with, but as principles, considerations or objectives to be taken account of - they may be soft, but they are still law.

VI. SOFT LAW GENERAL PRINCIPLES

The idea that general norms or principles can affect the way courts decide cases or the exercise of discretionary powers by an international organization is not confined to treaty regimes. Indeed in modern international relations such general norms or principles are probably more often found in the form of non-binding declarations or resolutions of international organizations than in the provisions of multilateral treaties. The Universal Declaration of Human Rights remains one of the most influential examples of soft law of this kind. International courts have of course always had the power under Article 38(1)(c) of the ICJ Statute to refer to general principles of law. In most cases this entails borrowing by analogy from common elements of national law, such as non-discrimination or the right to a fair hearing.[57] In essence, resort to general principles of this kind is judge-made law.

However, it is also possible for States to adopt general principles not derived from national law, with the intention that courts and States should apply them when relevant. Such general principles do not have to create rules of customary law to have legal effect. Rather, their importance derives principally from the influence they can exert on the interpretation, application, and development of other rules of law. Article 31(3) of the 1969 Vienna Convention on the Law of Treaties requires subsequent agreements, practices and rules of international law to be taken into account when interpreting a treaty (McLachlan, 2005; Boyle, 2005, pp 572–4). This provision appears to include reference to general principles as an aid to treaty interpretation.[58] If that is correct, soft law declarations such as the 1992 Rio Declaration on Environment and Development or the 1948 Universal Declaration of Human Rights will have to be taken into account insofar as they articulate general principles agreed by consensus. The point is not confined to treaty interpretation, however. A general principle of this kind may also influence the interpretation and application of customary law.

The precautionary approach (or principle), endorsed by consensus in Principle 15 of the 1992 Rio Declaration on Environment and Development, is a case in point. The precautionary approach is a common feature of almost all the Rio and post-Rio global environmental agreements. Principle 15 of the Rio Declaration provides as follows:

Principle 15: In order to protect the environment, the precautionary approach shall be widely applied by states according to their capabilities. Where there are threats of serious or

---

[57] *South West Africa, Second Phase, Judgment, ICJ Reports 1966*, p 6, Dissenting opinion of Judge Tanaka, pp 250, 294–301; *Golder v UK*, Judgment of 21 February 1975, ECtHR, Ser A No 18, paras 10–6, 1 EHRR 524, but cf the Dissenting opinion of Judge Fitzmaurice, paras 18–46 and 48 and see generally Cassese, 1986, pp 170–4; Cheng, 1953; Friedmann, 1963.

[58] Thus in *Golder* the ECHR referred to access to a court as a 'general principle of law' when interpreting Article 6 of the European Convention on Human Rights. Note, however, that general principles cannot override or amend the express terms of a treaty: see *Beef Hormone Case*, Appellate Body Report, WT/DS26/AB/R, WT/DS48/AB/R (16 January 1998), paras 124–5.

irreversible damage, lack of full scientific certainty shall not be used as a reason for postpon-
ing cost-effective measures to prevent environmental degradation.

Its purpose is thus to make greater allowance for uncertainty in the regulation of environmental risks and the sustainable use of natural resources.

Some writers and governments have argued that the precautionary principle or approach
is a rule of customary international law, but international courts and most governments
have been noticeably hesitant to accept this characterization.[59] If, alternatively, the precautionary principle is viewed as a general principle of law, on which decision-makers
and courts may rely when deciding cases and interpreting treaties, then its subsequent
use by national and international courts, and by international organizations, is easier to
explain. In the *Pulp Mills* case both parties relied on 'sustainable development' and the
'precautionary approach' primarily as general principles whose significance lay in their
impact on the interpretation and application of the 1975 Statute of the River Uruguay. The
Court merely noted that 'a precautionary approach may be relevant to the interpretation
and application of the provisions of the Statute'.[60] Moreover, the same point may also apply
to interpretation and application of customary international law. Thus in the law relating
to transboundary harm, as Brownlie observes, 'The point which stands out is that some
applications of the principle, which is based on the concept of foreseeable risk to other
States, are encompassed within existing concepts of State responsibility' (Brownlie, 2008,
p 278). The ILC special rappporteur on transboundary harm has taken the same view,
concluding that the precautionary principle is already a component of customary rules
on prevention of harm and environmental impact assessment, 'and could not be divorced
therefrom'.[61]

Much the same could be said of sustainable development. Lowe (1999, p 31) makes the
essential point with great clarity:

> Sustainable development can properly claim a normative status as an element of the process
> of judicial reasoning. It is a meta-principle, acting upon other rules and principles - a legal
> concept exercising a kind of interstitial normativity, pushing and pulling the boundaries of
> true primary norms when they threaten to overlap or conflict with each other.

Sustainable development thus becomes a mediating principle between the right to development and the duty to control sources of environmental harm. Modifying norms or
principles need not impose obligations or regulate conduct, they do not depend on State
practice and they do not need the same clarity or precision as rules.

What gives general principles of this kind their authority and legitimacy is simply
the endorsement of States—*opinio juris* in other words.[62] Such principles have legal significance in much the same way that Dworkin (1977) uses the idea of constitutional

---

[59] See eg *Beef Hormone Case*, Appellate Body Report, WT/DS26/AB/R, WT/DS48/AB/R (16 January 1998),
paras 120–25; *Southern Bluefin Tuna (New Zealand v Japan; Australia v Japan)*, Provisional Measures, Order of
27 April 1999, ITLOS Reports 1999, p 280, paras 77–9; *Pulp Mills on the River Uruguay (Argentina v Uruguay)*,
Judgment, ICJ Reports 2010, p 14, para 164. Cf *Responsibilities and Obligations of States Sponsoring Persons and
Entities with Respect to Activities in the Area*, Advisory Opinion, ITLOS Reports 2011, nyr, para 131.

[60] *Pulp Mills on the River Uruguay (Argentina v Uruguay)*, Judgment, ICJ Reports 2010, p 14, para 164. See also
Southern Bluefin Tuna (New Zealand v Japan; Australia v Japan), Provisional Measures, Order of 27 April 1999,
ITLOS Reports 1999, p 280, paras 77–9 and see also Judges Laing at paras 16–19, Treves at para 9, and Shearer.

[61] Report of the International Law Commission, Fifty-second Session, A/55/10, para 716.

[62] Lowe, 1999, p 33, dispenses even with *opinio juris*, but unless such norms emerge from thin air at the
whim of judges the endorsement of states must be a necessary element. All the norms Lowe relies on do in fact
have such endorsement.

principles.[63] They lay down parameters which affect the way courts decide cases or how an international institution exercises its discretionary powers. They can set limits, or provide guidance, or determine how conflicts between other rules or principles will be resolved. They may lack the supposedly harder edge of a 'rule' or 'obligation', but they should not be confused with 'non-binding' or emerging law. That is perhaps the most important lesson to be drawn from the ICJ's references to sustainable development in the *Gabčíkovo-Nagymaros* and *Pulp Mills* cases.[64] Even if sustainable development is not in the nature of a legal obligation, it does represent a policy goal or principle that can influence the outcome of litigation and the practice of States and international organizations, and it may lead to significant changes and developments in the existing law.[65]

These examples show that subtle changes in the existing law and in existing treaties may come about through reliance on such general principles. In any system of law the ability to make changes on a systemic basis is important. How else could this be done in international law? New rules of customary law are not necessarily appropriate to the elaboration of general principles and could not be created quickly enough; moreover, a treaty endorsing the precautionary principle or sustainable development would only bind the parties. A binding resolution of the UNSC may be a possible option, but only where questions of international peace and security are at stake. Thus, the consensus endorsement by States of a general principle enshrined in a soft law declaration is an entirely sensible solution to such law-making challenges.

VII. SOFT LAW AND CUSTOMARY LAW

Resolutions of international organizations and multilateral declarations by States may be soft in the sense that they are usually not legally binding on States, but as we saw earlier this does not mean that they have no legal effect on customary law. Whether they do provide evidence of existing law, or of the *opinio juris* necessary for new law, or of the practice of States, will depend on various factors which must be assessed in each case.

A potentially law-making resolution or declaration need not necessarily proclaim rights or principles as law, but as with treaties, the wording must be 'of a fundamentally norm-creating character such as could be regarded as forming the basis of a general rule of law'.[66] The context within which soft law instruments are negotiated and the accompanying statements of delegations will also be relevant if assessing the *opinio juris* of States. Lastly, the degree of support is significant. A resolution adopted by consensus or by unanimous vote will necessarily carry more weight than one supported only by a two-thirds majority of States. Resolutions opposed by even a small number of States may have no law-making effect if those States are the ones most immediately affected.[67] The attempt by the General

---

[63] This argument is developed by Sands 1995, Ch 5.

[64] *Gabčíkovo-Nagymaros Project (Hungary/Slovakia), Judgment, ICJ Reports 1997*, p 7, para 140; *Pulp Mills on the River Uruguay (Argentina v Uruguay), Provisional Measures, Order of 13 July 2006, ICJ Reports 2006*, p 113, para 80; *Pulp Mills on the River Uruguay (Argentina v Uruguay), Judgment, ICJ Reports 2010*, p 14, paras 177 and 184.

[65] See for example the inclusion of provisions on sustainable use or sustainable development in the 1994 WTO Agreement, the 1995 UN Fish Stocks Agreement and the 1997 UN Convention on International Watercourses.

[66] *North Sea Continental Shelf, Judgment, ICJ Reports 1969*, p 3, para 72 and see Lowe, 1999; Brownlie, 1979, pp 260–2.

[67] See on this point the cautionary dissent of Schwebel in the *Legality of the Threat or Use of Nuclear Weapons, ICJ Reports 1996*, p 226, noting that: 'If a resolution purports to be declaratory of international law, if

Assembly in the 1970s to change the law on expropriation of foreign investments is a well-known example of the inability of majorities of States to legislate for minorities in this fashion.[68] The General Assembly's ban on deep seabed mining outside the framework of UNCLOS is another. In this case, the minority of objecting States established their own parallel regime, until eventually a compromise agreement was reached.[69]

In an international system where the consent or acquiescence of States is still an essential precondition for the development of new law or changes to existing law, these examples show that opposing votes matter. Even if such resolutions do change the law for States which vote in favour, it is clear that they do not do so for the dissenting minority. Moreover, even consensus adoption will not be as significant as it may at first appear if accompanied by statements which seriously qualify what has been agreed, or if it simply papers over an agreement to disagree without pressing matters to a vote. For all these reasons, the adoption of resolutions by international organizations or of declarations by States should not be confused with law-making per se.

Professor Cheng has argued that, if appropriately worded, General Assembly resolutions can create 'instant' customary law (Cheng, 1965). In his view the clearly articulated expression of *opinio juris* through the medium of a non-binding resolution or declaration may be enough, without further State practice, to afford evidence of a new rule of customary or general international law. For anyone seeking to use the UN General Assembly as a law-making instrument this is an attractive but generally unsustainable argument. Cheng himself rightly cautions against the facile assumption that UNGA resolutions make law, and his view of instant law-making is limited to very specific circumstances. Firstly, it depends on a strong consensus in favour of such a resolution.[70] Secondly, it requires appropriate wording. In his view, the principal UNGA resolutions on outer space fail this test, because they merely articulate principles by which States 'should be guided',[71] rather than potentially normative rules. In this respect they compare unfavourably with, for example, the rights proclaimed in the Universal Declaration of Human Rights or the Declaration on the Granting of Independence to Colonial Territories and Peoples. However, neither of these resolutions was adopted by consensus and it is very doubtful that their impact has ever been instantaneous. Cheng was also writing before any of the leading modern ICJ cases on the creation of customary law were decided, and even his cautious formulation may now be too generous. The jurisprudence is not favourable, it must be said, to notions of instant law-making, but stresses instead the need for subsequent confirmatory practice, or at least the absence of contrary practice.[72]

---

it is adopted unanimously (or virtually so, qualitatively as well as quantitatively) or by consensus, and if it corresponds to State practice, it may be declaratory of international law'.

[68] See 1974 Charter of Economic Rights and Duties of States, UNGA Res 3281 (XXX) (12 December 1974) and *Texaco Overseas Petroleum Co* v *Libyan Arab Republic* (1977) 53 ILR 422 at paras 80–91. 120 States voted for the resolution, 6 voted against, 10 abstained.

[69] The 1970 Declaration of Principles Governing the Seabed and Ocean Floor etc, UNGA Res. 2749 (XXV) (12 December 1970), was adopted by 108 votes in favour with 14 abstentions. For an account of the subsequent disagreements over the legal status of the deep seabed and the Reciprocating States regime established by Western States see Churchill and Lowe, 1999, pp 224–35.

[70] Resolutions 1721 (XV1)(20 December 1961) and 1962 (XVIII)(13 December 1963) were agreed first by the USA and USSR (the only space states at that time), then adopted unanimously by the Outer Space Committee, the First Committee and the UNGA.

[71] UNGA Res 1962 (XVIII)(13 December 1963). The wording of Resolution 1721 (XV1) (20 December 1961) is even weaker: 'The General Assembly….commends to States for their guidance…the following principles'.

[72] See especially *North Sea Continental Shelf, Judgment, ICJ Reports 1969*, p 3 and *Military and Paramilitary Activities in and against Nicaragua (Nicaragua* v *United States of America), Merits, Judgment, ICJ Reports 1986*,

If the resolutions on outer space did not make instant law, and were designed to be replaced by treaties,[73] why adopt them at all? Apart from important practical considerations of simplicity and speed of adoption compared to treaties, the importance of resort to the UNGA lies in the collective affirmation which is thereby provided for general principles otherwise only impliedly asserted by the space States. The resolutions provided both a record of what all States believed the relevant rules should be, and evidence of *opinio juris* demonstrating the law-making significance of their earlier practice. As Brownlie (1991, p 204) observes, 'In the face of a relatively novel situation the General Assembly provides an efficient index to the quickly growing practice of States'. Elsewhere he refers to the 'decisive catalytic effect' which such resolutions may have on State practice (Brownlie, 1979, p 261).

In those circumstances it would be safe for space States to proceed on the assumption that there would be no opposition to activities conducted in conformity with the principles endorsed by the resolutions. That these principles were subsequently reaffirmed in treaty form shows both the value of soft law precedents as a prelude to later agreement on a more detailed international regime, and the preference for treaties as a means of stabilizing the law within an appropriate institutional framework once the views and practice of States are settled. This may suggest a perception that soft law is too fragile an instrument to sustain the long-term regulation of common areas such as space or the deep seabed,[74] but it is certainly an effective starting point when States need reassurance before commencing novel and previously unregulated activities.

The adoption of non-binding resolutions or declarations can also lead to changes in the existing law, in some cases quite quickly. The termination of driftnet fishing on the high seas is a good example of the successful use of UNGA resolutions in this way.[75] Although the resolutions themselves have no legal force, and do not make 'instant' law, the widespread opposition to such fishing has been effective in pressuring the small number of States involved to comply with the resolutions and phase out the use of driftnets. Such changes in the law can of course only come about as a result of changes in practice by those States most closely involved. Moreover, even States which initially voted against such resolutions may eventually conform to the general will. The initial opposition of colonial powers to UN resolutions on self-determination soon faded, and as the *Western Sahara* and *East Timor* cases show,[76] former colonial States have become the principal advocates of self-determination for their former colonies.

Why use non-binding resolutions for such purposes? Negotiating a global treaty on driftnets would have taken as long or longer; it would not have entered into force until there were enough ratifications, and if the relevant States failed to become parties they would not be bound anyway. In the latter case the law would not change unless these States changed their practice, which is no less true of the non-binding resolutions adopted by UNGA. In such cases, if the consensus for a change in practice is strong enough, a treaty is not necessary. If it is not strong enough a treaty will not necessarily strengthen it.

---

p 14. But the *Gabčíkovo-Nagymaros Project (Hungary/Slovakia), Judgment, ICJ Reports 1997*, p 7 may be more favourably inclined to instant law-making.

[73] See now the 1967 Outer Space Treaty and the 1979 Moon Treaty.

[74] The USSR had from the start argued in favour of a treaty; Cheng, 1965, at p 31 surmises that it agreed to the adoption of a resolution out of concern that any treaty might be vetoed by the US Senate.

[75] UNGA Res 44/225 (22 December 1989) and UNGA Res 46/215 (20 December 1991) on Large Scale Pelagic Driftnet Fishing, and other instruments collected in FAO, *Legislative Study 47: The Regulation of Driftnet Fishing on the High Seas* (Rome, 1991). See Kaye, 2000, pp 188–94.

[76] *Western Sahara, Advisory Opinion, ICJ Reports 1975*, p 12; *East Timor (Portugal v Australia) Judgment, ICJ Reports 1995*, p 90.

Banning a specific form of fishing is a relatively simple change in the law. Soft law instruments may not be as useful when more complex changes are needed. When it became apparent that the provisions of the 1982 UN Convention on the Law of the Sea relating to the high seas would not be sufficient to ensure sustainable fishing, an additional treaty was negotiated. The 1995 Agreement on Straddling and Highly Migratory Fish Stocks in effect elaborates and amends the 1982 UNCLOS. It is an important and far-reaching instrument which makes notable changes in the law of high seas fishing. Inter alia, freedom of fishing is confined to States which operate within the rules of regional fisheries organizations; fisheries law is given a newly environmental focus, emphasizing sustainability and conservation of biological diversity and ecosystems; the enforcement powers of other States are extended, and regional agreements are brought within the UNCLOS dispute settlement system (see Freestone and Makuch, 1996; Davies and Redgwell, 1996). However strong the consensus in favour of these changes, given their far-reaching nature and impact on other treaties, a treaty was clearly the only possible instrument in this situation. In reality, some of these measures have been controversial, and some fishing States remain non-parties to the 1995 Agreement, but resort to soft law would not have been any more effective in such circumstances. But if the weakness of soft law is that States are not obliged to comply, the same is no less true of an unratified or poorly ratified treaty. Whether the 1995 Agreement changes the law will still depend on how far it influences the practice of States, rather than on its binding force.

VIII. CONCLUSIONS

Soft law is manifestly a multi-faceted concept, whose relationship to treaties, custom and general principles of law is both subtle and diverse. It is further explored in the following chapter by Dinah Shelton. At its simplest, soft law facilitates progressive evolution of customary international law. It presents alternatives to law-making by treaty in certain circumstances, at other times it complements treaties, while also providing different ways of understanding the legal effect of different kinds of treaty. Those who maintain that soft law is simply not law have perhaps missed some of the points made here; moreover those who see a treaty as necessarily having greater legal effect than soft law have perhaps not looked hard enough at the 'infinite variety' of treaties, to quote Baxter once more. Soft law in its various forms can of course be abused, but so can most legal forms, and it has generally been more helpful to the process of international law-making than it has been objectionable. It is inconceivable that modern treaty regimes or international organizations could function successfully without resort to soft law. Nor is it likely that the ICJ will take a different view, given the way soft law is used by parties to international litigation to legitimize their legal arguments. In the *Pulp Mills* case, for example, Argentina and Uruguay relied, inter alia, on the 1992 Rio Declaration on Environment and Development, UNEP's 1987 Goals and Principles of Environmental Impact Assessment, and the ILC's 2002 Draft Articles on Prevention of Transboundary Harm.[77] In the absence of hard law, litigators will inevitably turn to whatever best supports their case, even if it is soft law.

---

[77] The Court noted that the UNEP Goals and Principles, UNGA Res 42/184 (11 December 1987), constitute guidance issued by an 'international technical body' and therefore have to be taken into account under Article 41 of the Statute of the River Uruguay. See *Pulp Mills on the River Uruguay (Argentina v Uruguay), Judgment, ICJ Reports 2010,* p 14, para 205. Except when noting the submissions of the parties, the Court made no specific reference to the ILC draft articles or to the Rio Declaration, but its judgment affirms the legal status of the relevant provisions of both texts.

REFERENCES

BARELLI, M (2009), 'The Role of Soft Law in the International Legal System', 58 *ICLQ* 957.

BAXTER, RR (1980), 'International Law in "Her Infinite Variety"', 29 *ICLQ* 549.

BIRNIE, P, BOYLE, AE, REDGWELL, C (2009), *International Law and the Environment*, 3rd edn (Oxford: Oxford University Press).

BOYLE, AE (2005), 'Further Development of the Law of the Sea Convention: Mechanisms for Change', 54 *ICLQ* 563.

—— and FREESTONE, D (eds) (1999), *International Law and Sustainable Development: Past Achievements and Future Prospects* (Oxford: Oxford University Press).

BROWNLIE, I (1979), 'The Legal Status of Natural Resources', 162 *Recueil des Cours* 245.

—— (1991), *Basic Documents on International Law*, 3rd edn (Oxford: Oxford University Press).

—— (2008), *Principles of Public International Law*, 7th edn (Oxford: Oxford University Press).

BURCI, GL and VIGNES, C-H (2004), *World Health Organization* (The Hague: Kluwer Law).

CASSESE, A (1986), *International Law in a Divided World*, (Oxford: Oxford University Press).

CHENG, B (1953) 1987 reprint), *General Principles of International Law as Applied by International Courts and Tribunals* (Cambridge: Grotius).

—— (1965), 'United Nations Resolutions on Outer Space: "Instant" Customary Law?', 5 *Indian J Int L* 23–48 (reprinted in Cheng, B (ed) (1982), *International Law Teaching and Practice* (London: Stephens and Sons), p 237.

CHINKIN, CM (1989), 'The Challenge of Soft Law: Development and Change in International Law', 38 *ICLQ* 850.

CHURCHILL, RR and LOWE, AV (1999), *The Law of the Sea*, 3rd edn (Manchester: Manchester University Press).

CONTINI, P and SAND, P (1972), 'Methods to Expedite Environment Protection: International Ecostandards', 66 *AJIL* 37.

CRAWFORD, J (2002), *The International Law Commission's Articles on State Responsibility* (Cambridge: Cambridge University Press).

DAVIES, P and REDGWELL, C (1996), 'International Legal Regulation of Straddling Fish Stocks', 67 *BYIL* 199.

DUPUY, P-M (1991), 'Soft Law and the International Law of the Environment', 12 *Michigan JIL* 420.

DWORKIN, R (1977), *Taking Rights Seriously* (London: Duckworth).

EDESON, W (1999), in Boyle AE and Freestone, D (eds), *International Law and Sustainable Development: Past Achievements and Future Prospects* (Oxford: Oxford University Press), p 165.

—— (2003), 'Soft and Hard Law Aspects of Fisheries Issues,' in Nordquist, M, Moore, G and Mahmoudi, S (eds), *The Stockholm Declaration and Law of the Marine Environment* (The Hague: Nijhoff), p 165.

FAO (1991), *The Regulation of Driftnet Fishing on the High Seas: Legal Issues* (Rome: FAO).

FIDLER, S (1998), 'The Future of the WHO: What role for International Law?', 32 *Vand JTL* 1079

FREESTONE, D and MAKUCH, Z (1996), 'The New International Environmental Law of Fisheries', 7 *YBIEL* 3.

FRIEDMANN, W (1963), 'The Uses of General Principles in the Development of International Law', 57 *AJIL* 279.

GARDINER, R (1998), 'Revising the Law of Carriage by Air: Mechanisms in Treaties and Contract', 47 *ICLQ* 278.

HIGGINS, R (1995), *Problems and Process: International Law and How We Use It* (Oxford: Oxford University Press).

HILLGENBERG, H (1999), 'A Fresh Look at Soft Law', 10 *EJIL* 499.

KAYE, S (2000), International Fisheries Management (The Hague: Kluwer Law International).

KLABBERS, J (1996), 'The Redundancy of Soft Law', 65 *Nordic JIL* 167.

KOSKENNIEMI, M (1992), 'Breach of Treaty or Non-Compliance? Reflections on the Enforcement of the Montreal Protocol', 3 *YBIEL* 123.

—— (2009), 'The Politics of International Law', 20 *EJIL* 7.

LANG, W (ed) (1995), *Sustainable Development and International Law* (The Hague: Kluwer Law International).

LOWE, AV (1999), 'Sustainable Development and Unsustainable Arguments' in Boyle AE and Freestone, D (eds) (1999), *International Law and Sustainable Development: Past Achievements and Future Prospects* (Oxford: Oxford University Press), p 24.

MANN, H (1995), 'Comment' in Lang, W (ed) (1995), *Sustainable Development and International Law* (The Hague: Kluwer Law International), p 67.

McDORMAN, T (2004), 'Access to Information under Article 9 of the OSPAR Convention', 98 *AJIL* 330.

McLACHLAN, C (2005), 'The Principle of Systemic Integration and Article 31(3)(c) of the Vienna Convention', 54 *ICLQ* 279.

MOORE, G (1999) 'The Code of Conduct for Responsible Fisheries', in Hey, E (ed), *Developments in International Fisheries Law* (The Hague: Nijhoff), p 85.

RAJAMANI, L (2012), 'The Durban Platform for Enhanced Action and the Future of the Climate Regime', 61 *ICLQ* 501.

ROSE, C (2012), 'The UK Bribery Act 2010 and Accompanying Guidance', 61 *ICLQ* 485.

SANDS, P (ed) (1993), *Greening International Law* (London: Earthscan).

—— (1995), 'International Law in the Field of Sustainable 'Development', in Lang, W (ed) (1995), *Sustainable Development and International Law* (The Hague: Kluwer Law International), p 53.

SCHACHTER, O (1977), 'The Twilight Existence of Non-Binding International Agreements', 71 *AJIL* 296.

SZTUCKI, J (1990), 'Reflections on International "Soft Law"', in Ramberg, J et al (eds), *Festskrift till Lars Hjerner: Studies in International Law* (Stockholm: Norstedts), p 549.

VIRALLY, M (1956), 'Valeur juridique des recommandations', *Annuaire Français de Droit International*, p 66.

WATTS, AD (ed) (2000), *The International Law Commission*, vol II (Oxford: Oxford University Press).

WEIL, P (1983), 'Towards Relative Normativity in International Law', 77 *AJIL* 411.

FURTHER READING

BAXTER, RR (1980), 'International Law in "Her Infinite Variety"', 29 *ICLQ* 549: A classic account of the diversity of treaties and their legal effect.

CHARNEY, J (1993), 'Universal International Law', 87 *AJIL* 529: One of the best analyses of the evolution of general international law through soft law, although it does not use the term.

CHENG, B (1983), 'Custom: The Future of General State Practice in a Divided World', in Macdonald, R St J and Johnston, DM (eds), *The Structure and Process of International Law*

(Dordrecht: Martinus Nijhoff), p 5.
A sceptical treatment of idea that General
Assembly resolutions can be instant
customary international law.

CHINKIN, CM (1989), 'The Challenge of
Soft Law: Development and Change in
International Law', 38 *ICLQ* 850: This
remains one of the best discussions of the
subject.

SLOAN, B (1987), 'General Assembly
Resolutions Revisited', 58 *BYBIL* 39: The
classic account of the legal effect of
UN General Assembly resolutions, but
now dated.

6

INTERNATIONAL LAW AND 'RELATIVE NORMATIVITY'

Dinah Shelton

SUMMARY

'Relative normativity' concerns the nature and structure of international law. It involves issues of hierarchy and implicates the rules of recognition by which law is distinguished from norms that are not legally binding. There is general agreement that the main sources of international law do not imply a hierarchical relationship inter se, and debates have centred instead on three other topics. The first among these topics involves questions about the existence, content, and impact of superior or peremptory norms that override other norms and bind all States. Secondly, the expansion or 'fragmentation' of international law into many new subject areas, with a corresponding proliferation of international treaties and institutions, can produce conflicts in substantive norms or procedures within a given subject area or across legal regimes, necessitating the development and application of interpretive rules to reconcile or prioritize the competing norms. Thirdly, States and international institutions frequently adopt texts that contain norms or statements of obligation, but which are not in a legally binding form, constituting political commitments that can lead to law (custom, treaty, or general principle) or interpret or fill gaps in the law.

I. INTRODUCTION: THE CONCEPT OF RELATIVE NORMATIVITY

'Relative normativity' is a question of hierarchy of norms and the definition of law. As such, it concerns the nature, structure, and content of the international legal system. In practice issues of relative normativity arise in determining whether a legal rule exists to govern a problem, and in deciding whether priority must be given to a specific rule among several that may be applicable to a legal matter or dispute.

Systems of law usually establish a hierarchy of norms based on the particular source from which the norms derive. In national legal systems, it is commonplace for the fundamental values of society to be given constitutional status and afforded precedence in the event of a conflict with norms enacted by legislation or adopted by administrative regulation; administrative rules themselves must conform to legislative mandates, while written law usually takes precedence over unwritten law and legal norms prevail over non-legal (political or moral) rules. The mode of legal reasoning applied in practice is thus naturally hierarchical, establishing relationships and order among normative statements and levels of authority (Koskenniemi, 1997).

Since a seminal article highly critical of the concept appeared in 1983, the question of hierarchy or relative normativity in international law has been widely discussed (Weil, 1983). In practice, conflicts among norms and their interpretation are probably inevitable in the present, largely decentralized international legal system where each State is entitled initially and equally to interpret for itself the scope of its obligations and how to implement such obligations. The interpretations may vary considerably, making all international law somewhat relative, in the absence of institutions competent to render authoritative interpretations binding on all States.

Conceptual problems abound in determining relative normativity, in part because almost every purported principle of precedence (eg *lex specialis derogate lex generalis*) has exceptions and no rule establishes when to apply the principle and when to apply the exception.[1] There appears to be supremacy of process over content, however, because the identification of legal norms and their relative normativity occurs only through consideration of the procedural norms that allow recognition of substantive rules. Some scholars argue from the International Court of Justice (ICJ) Statute and from the sovereign equality of States that no hierarchy exists and logically there can be none: international rules are equivalent, sources are equivalent, and procedures are equivalent (Dupuy, 1995, pp 14–16) all deriving from the will of States. Others point to the concept of the community of States as a whole, expressed in Article 53 of the Vienna Convention on the Law of Treaties (VCLT) as an emerging limit on unilateral relativism (Salcedo, 1997, p 588).

Even identifying law can be problematic in the decentralized system of States. It is not always clear where law ends and non-law begins, or, to use the common terminology, where 'soft' law should be placed. The consequences can be significant. The jurisdiction of the ICJ in the dispute between Quatar and Bahrain,[2] for example, turned on whether or not 'minutes' taken 25 December 1990 constituted a legally binding agreement or a simple record of negotiations. On the merits, effective application of the principle *pacta sunt servanda*—that legal agreements should be carried out in good faith—necessitated some basic consensus about existence of a '*pacta*' or legal agreement. Is it necessary for a norm to be contained in a legally binding instrument in order for it to be accepted as binding (*pacta*)? Traditional international law clearly distinguished between binding and non-binding instruments, and this distinction seems to remain, despite the growing body and variety of 'soft law' instruments and without prejudice to the possibility that the norms contained therein may emerge in customary international law.

States have agreed on the means (or 'sources') to identify binding international obligations for the purpose of resolving their disputes, but they have not determined a hierarchy of norms. As formulated initially in the Statute of the Permanent Court of International Justice (PCIJ) and iterated in the ICJ Statute, the Court should decide an international dispute primarily through application of international conventions, international custom, and general principles of law.[3] The Statute makes no reference to hierarchy, except by listing doctrine and judicial decisions as 'subsidiary' and evidentiary sources of law. Although the Statute is directed at the Court, it is the only general text in which States have acknowledged the authoritative procedures by which they agree to be legally bound

---

[1] Compare for example the different approaches of the ICJ in *Legal Consequences for States of the Continued Presence of South Africa in Namibia (South West Africa) notwithstanding Security Council Resolution 276 (1970), Advisory Opinion, ICJ Reports 1971*, p 16 and *South West Africa, Second Phase, Judgment, ICJ Reports 1966*, p 6.

[2] *Maritime Delimitation and Territorial Questions between Qatar and Bahrain, Jurisdiction and Admissibility, Judgment, ICJ Reports 1994*, p 112.

[3] See ICJ Statute, Article 38 and Thirlway, Ch 4 of this book.

to an international norm. No mention is made of *jus cogens* as a source of obligation nor do non-binding instruments figure in the Statute.

Much recent debate has centred on whether or not State behaviour in adopting and complying with non-binding instruments evidences acceptance of new modes of law-making not reflected in the Statute of the Court. Of course, efforts to resolve social problems are not invariably in the form of law in any community. Societies strive to maintain order, prevent and resolve conflicts, and assure justice in the distribution and use of resources not only through law, but through other means of action. Issues of justice may be addressed through market mechanisms and private charity, while conflict resolution can be promoted through education and information, as well as negotiations outside legal institutions. Maintenance of order and societal values can occur through moral sanctions, exclusions, and granting or withholding of benefits, as well as by use of legal penalties and incentives. In the international arena, just as at other levels of governance, law is one form of social control or normative claim, but basic requirements of behaviour also emerge from morality, courtesy, and social custom reflecting the values of society. They form part of the expectations of social discourse and compliance with such norms may be expected and violations sanctioned.

Legal regulation, however, has become perhaps the most prevalent response to social problems during the last century. Laws reflect the current needs and recognize the present values of society. Law is often deemed a necessary, if usually insufficient, basis for ordering behaviour. The language of law, especially written language, most precisely communicates expectations and produces reliance, despite inevitable ambiguities and gaps. It exercises a pull toward compliance by its very nature. Its enhanced value and the more serious consequences of non-conformity lead to the generally accepted notion that fundamental fairness requires some identification of what is meant by 'law', some degree of transparency and understanding of the authoritative means of creating binding norms and the relative importance among them. A law perceived as legitimate and fair is more likely to be observed. This alone makes the issue of relative normativity an important topic, but recent evolution in the international legal system has fostered a burgeoning interest in the issue. Three developments appear particularly important.

The first development centres on the role of consent in determining legal obligation. Classical writers[4] claimed the existence of necessary law natural to and binding all States, overriding contrary treaties and custom. A distinction thus was made between consent-based law and universal, overriding norms which could not be amended or altered by the will of States. The rise of positivism largely repudiated this theory; instead, defining international law as a system of equal and sovereign States whose actions are limited only by rules freely accepted as legally binding.[5] Even today, *jus cogens*, or peremptory norms are seen as defined and recognized in positive international law by the international community of States as a whole.[6]

A problem remains for many, however, in determining whether there are substantive limits on law-making or only procedural constraints. The emergence of global resource crises such as the widespread depletion of commercial fish stocks, destruction of the

---

[4] H Grotius, *De Jure Belli Ac Pacis Libri Tres* (1625), 1, Ch 1, X, 5; E de Vattel, *Le Droit des Gens ou Principes de la Loi Naturelle* (1758), para 9; C Wolff, *Jus Gentium* (1764), para 5.

[5] See '*Lotus*', *Judgment No 9, 1927, PCIJ, Ser A, No 10* at p 18.

[6] The voluntarist approach to *jus cogens* is reflected in the report of the International Law Commission to the Vienna Conference on the Law of Treaties. It noted that 'it would clearly be wrong to regard even rules of *jus cogens* as immutable and incapable of modification in the light of future developments', a notion inconsistent with the natural law approach of classic writers. See *YBILC* (1966) Vol II (part two), pp 247ff.

stratospheric ozone layer, and anthropogenic climate change, has produced growing concern about the 'free rider', the holdout State that benefits from legal regulation accepted by others while enhancing its own profits through continued utilization of the resource or by on-going production and sale of banned substances. The traditional consent-based international legal regime lacks a legislature to override the will of dissenting States,[7] but efforts to affect their behaviour are being made, first through the doctrine of peremptory norms applicable to all States, and, secondly, through expanding the concept of international law to include 'soft law'. The same approach may be taken towards States seeking to denounce or acting to violate multilateral agreements that reflect widely and deeply held values, such as human rights or humanitarian law.

To press free riders or dissenting States into behaviour conforming to the needs of international society, States inside and outside international organizations may find it particularly useful to adopt normative statements in the form of non-legally binding instruments such as declarations, resolutions, and programmes of action. International law permits States to use political pressure to induce others to change their practices. In contrast, States generally cannot demand that others conform to legal norms the latter have not accepted. Non-binding commitments may be entered into precisely to reflect the will of the international community to resolve a pressing global problem over the objections of the one or few States causing the problem, while avoiding the doctrinal barrier of their lack of consent to be bound by the norm.[8]

The second development that spurs consideration of relative normativity is the substantial expansion of international law. Until the twentieth century, treaties were nearly all bilateral and the subject matter of international legal regulation mostly concerned diplomatic relations, the seas and other international waterways, trade, and extradition. Today, the number of international instruments has grown substantially, multilateral regulatory treaties are common, the topics governed by international law have proliferated, and non-State actors are increasingly part of the system. This complexity demands consideration and development of means to reconcile conflicts of norms within a treaty or given subject area, as well as across competing regimes, such as free trade and environmental protection.

New topics of regulation also require innovative means of rule-making with respect to non-State actors. Apart from some international organizations, non-State actors generally are not parties to treaties or involved in the creation of customary international law. The emergence of codes of conduct and other 'soft law' reflects this development.

Third, the emergence of international criminal law has led to considering the nature of international crimes and the relationship of this body of law to doctrines of obligations *jus cogens*, discussed later, and obligations *erga omnes*. The ICJ was the first to identify the category of obligations *erga omnes* in *dicta* in the *Barcelona Traction* case.[9] Unlike obligations arising in respect to specific injured States (eg in the field of diplomatic protection), obligations *erga omnes* are owed to the international community as a whole. The broad nature of the obligation could be based upon the fact that such obligations generally aim at

---

[7] Thus Salcedo argues that 'In principle...most rules of international law are only authoritative for those subjects that have accepted them' (Salcedo, 1997, p 584).

[8] The UN General Assembly actions on driftnet fishing were directed at members and non-members of the UN whose fishing fleets decimated dwindling fish resources through use of the driftnet 'walls of death'. The international community made clear its resolve to outlaw driftnet fishing and enforce the ban, albeit it was not contained in a legally binding instrument.

[9] *Barcelona Traction, Light and Power Company, Limited, Second Phase, Judgment, ICJ Reports 1970*, p 3, para 33.

regulating the internal behaviour of a State, such as in the field of human rights, and thus no States are likely to be materially affected by a breach. The principle of effectiveness thus supports broad standing, because without it violations could not be challenged. However, the rationale stated by the ICJ for recognizing this category of obligations appears more substantive: that 'in view of the importance of the rights involved, all States can be held to have a legal interest in their protection'.[10] This statement suggests that obligations *erga omnes* have specific and broad procedural consequences *because of* the substantive importance of the norms they enunciate. In addition, the fact that all States can complain of a breach may make it more likely that a complaint will be made following commission of a wrongful act, suggesting a higher priority accorded to these norms even if they are not considered substantively superior. The ICJ's examples of such obligations included the outlawing of aggression and genocide and the protection from slavery and racial discrimination. Nonetheless, the ILC has concluded that obligations *erga omnes* do not implicate normative hierarchy; while all *jus cogens* obligations have an *erga omnes* character, the reverse is not necessarily true.[11]

Similar to obligations *erga omnes*, international crimes are so designated because the acts they sanction are deemed of such importance to the international community that individual criminal responsibility should result from their commission.[12] Unlike obligations *erga omnes*, international criminal norms can raise problems of relative normativity. First, the question has been posed as to whether there is a hierarchy among the crimes. Secondly, it has been clear since the Nuremburg Trials that conforming to or carrying out domestic law is no excuse for breach of international criminal law; it would seem plausible as well, if unlikely to arise in practice, that a defence would fail based on carrying out norms of international law, such as those contained in a bilateral treaty, if those norms contradict the requirements of criminal law.[13] In this respect, norms of criminal law could be given supremacy over other international law in practice.

Other aspects of the inter-relationship of these categories of norms and the sources that create them are also significant. First, neither the designation of international crimes or obligations *erga omnes* involves a purported new source of law: crimes are created and defined through the conclusion of treaties; obligations *erga omnes* through treaty and customary international law. Secondly, it appears logical that all international crimes are obligations *erga omnes* because the international community as a whole identifies and may prosecute and punish the commission of such crimes. The reverse is not the case, however. Not all obligations *erga omnes* have been designated as international crimes. Racial discrimination, for example, is cited as an obligation *erga omnes*, but is not included among international crimes except in its most extreme forms (genocide and apartheid). Among those acts designated as international crimes, there appears to be no hierarchy. The International Criminal Tribunal for the Former Yugoslavia (ICTY) has rejected the

---

[10] Idem. See also *East Timor (Portugal v Australia), Judgment, ICJ Reports 1995*, p 90, para 29; *Application of the Convention on the Prevention and Punishment of the Crime of Genocide, Preliminary Objections, Judgment, ICJ Reports 1996*, p 595, para 31.

[11] International Law Commission, Report of the Study Group on Fragmentation of International Law: Difficulties arising from the Diversification and Expansion of International Law, A/CN 4/l.676, 29 July 2005, paras 48, 50.

[12] The collective nature of the State as subject of international law makes imposition of State criminal responsibility problematic. Although the International Law Commission included a provision on State crimes in early versions of its Articles on State Responsibility, the provision was eventually excluded.

[13] The treaty itself might be considered void as a violation of peremptory norms if it required or authorized the commission of an international crime.

notion of hierarchy, declaring in the *Tadić* judgment that 'there is in law no distinction between the seriousness of a crime against humanity and that of a war crime'.[14]

II. PEREMPTORY NORMS

Jus cogens or peremptory norms[15] are defined as rules from which no derogation is permitted and which can be amended only by a new general norm of international law of the same value. The only references to peremptory norms in positive law are found in the Vienna conventions on the law of treaties. Article 53 of the 1969 Vienna Convention on the Law of Treaties (VCLT), concerning treaties between States, provides that a treaty will be void 'if, at the time of its conclusion, it conflicts with a peremptory norm of general international law'. Such a norm is defined by the VCLT as one 'accepted and recognized by the international community of states as a whole as a norm from which no derogation is permitted and which can be modified only by a subsequent norm having the same character'. Article 64 adds that the emergence of a new peremptory norm of general international law will render void any existing treaty in conflict with the norm. No clear agreement was reached during the VCLT negotiations, nor has one emerged since then about the content of *jus cogens*.

In national legal systems, it is a general principle of law that individual freedom of contract is limited by the general interest, generally expressed in public law and policy.[16] Agreements that have an illegal objective are void and those against public policy will not be enforced.[17] Private agreements, therefore, cannot derogate from public policy of the community. The international community remains divided over the extent to which the same rules apply to the international legal system.

A. THEORETICAL APPROACHES

A strictly voluntarist view of international law rejects the notion that a State may be bound to an international legal rule without its consent and thus does not recognize a collective interest that is capable of overriding the will of an individual member of the society. States are deemed to construct the corpus of international law either through agreements or through repeated practice out of a sense of legal obligation (see Henkin, 1989, p 45; Weil, 1983; Danilenko, 1991, p 42; Lukashuk, 1989). The PCIJ, in one of its first decisions, stated that '[t]he rules of law binding upon States... emanate from their own free will as expressed in conventions or by usages generally accepted as expressing principles of law'.[18] As recently as 1986, the ICJ reaffirmed this approach in respect to the acquisition of weaponry by States.[19]

---

[14] *Prosecutor* v *Dusko Tadić*, Case No IT–94–1–A, Judgment in Sentencing Appeals, Appeals Chamber (26 January 2000), para 69. For a criticism of this view and discussion of the conflicting practice of the ICTY, see Danner, 2000.

[15] The terms *jus cogens* and peremptory norms are used interchangeably. VCLT Article 53 is entitled 'treaties conflicting with a peremptory norm of general international law (*jus cogens*)'.

[16] In Roman law, the maxim '*ius publicum privatorum pactis mutari non potest*' (D 2.14.38) made absolute the non-derogation from norms which were defined as *ius publicum*.

[17] Article 6 of the Code Napoléon is illustrative: '*On ne peut déroger, par des conventions particulières, aux lois qui intéressent l'ordre public et les bonnes moeurs*'.

[18] 'Lotus', Judgment No 9, 1927, PCIJ, Ser A, No 10 at p 18.

[19] *Military and Paramilitary Activities in and against Nicaragua (Nicaragua v United States of America), Merits, Judgment, ICJ Reports 1986*, p 14, para 269.

Some legal theorists have long objected that the source of international obligation cannot lie in consent, but must be based on a prior, fundamental norm that imposes a duty to comply with obligations freely accepted (Kelsen, 1935). Without a normative source outside consent there is an unavoidable circularity of reasoning. A natural law origin of international obligation was dominant among scholars until the nineteenth century, when positivism and an emphasis on the sovereignty of States emerged in theory and practice.[20]

Others object that positivism fails to describe adequately the reality of the current international order. According to Tomuschat: '[t]he fact is that the cohesive legal bonds tying States to one another have considerably strengthened since the coming into force of the United Nations Charter;...a community model of international society would seem to come closer to reality than at any time before in history' (Tomuschat, 1993, pp 210–211). The community consists of States that live within a legal framework of a few basic rules that nonetheless allow them considerable freedom of action. Such a framework has become necessary in the light of global problems threatening human survival in an unprecedented fashion. Recalcitrant States not only profit by rejecting regulatory regimes adopted by the overwhelming majority of States, they threaten the effectiveness of such regimes and pose risks to all humanity.

B. TEXTUAL REFERENCES

The extent to which the system has moved and may still move toward the imposition of global public policy on non-consenting States remains highly debated, but the need for limits on State freedom of action seems to be increasingly recognized. International legal instruments and doctrine now often refer to the 'common interest of humanity'[21] or 'common concern of mankind' to identify fundamental issues that could form part of international public policy. References also are more frequent to 'the international community' as an entity or authority of collective action.[22] In addition, multilateral agreements increasingly contain provisions that affect non-party States, either providing incentives to adhere to the norms, or allowing parties to take coercive measures that in practice require conforming behaviour of States not adhering to the treaty. The UN Charter itself contains a list of fundamental principles and in Article 2(6) asserts that these may be imposed on non-parties if necessary to ensure international peace and security.

It should be noted that the problem of dissenting States is not as widespread as might be assumed. First, the obligations deemed basic to the international community—to refrain from the use of force against another State, to settle disputes peacefully, and to respect human rights, fundamental freedoms, and self-determination—are conventional obligations contained in the UN Charter, to which all member States have consented. All States have accepted the humanitarian conventions on the laws of war which express customary international law. The multilateral regimes for the oceans, outer space, and key components of the environment (climate change, protection of the ozone layer, and biological diversity) are also widely accepted. Thus in most cases the problem is one of ensuring

---

[20] See Neff, Ch 1 of this book.

[21] See 1982 UN Convention on the Law of the Sea (UNCLOS), Article 137(2); 1967 Treaty on Principles Governing the Activities of States in the Exploration and Use of Outer Space, Including the Moon and Other Celestial Bodies, pmbl, para 2.

[22] See, eg VCLT Article 53; UNCLOS Articles 136–7.

compliance by States with obligations they have freely accepted and not one of imposing obligations on dissenting States.

The notion of *jus cogens* or peremptory norms as a limitation on international freedom of contract arose in the UN International Law Commission (ILC) during its work on the law of treaties. An early ILC rapporteur on the subject proposed that the ILC draft convention on the law of treaties include a provision voiding treaties contrary to fundamental principles of international law.[23] This proposal clearly constituted a challenge to the consensual basis of international law, which viewed States as having the right *inter se* to opt out of any norm of general international law. It also represented 'progressive development' of international law and not a codification of existing State practice.[24]

In addition to potentially invalidating treaties, the proposal raised difficulties for some in respect to the determination of norms *jus cogens*. If such norms could be created by general treaties, a treaty norm could become binding on non-parties. Even without peremptory norms, this could happen, however, because the VCLT provides that States can become bound by treaty norms if those norms are already or subsequently become rules of customary international law. Some scholars have suggested that it is only through the evolution of a treaty norm to custom that it can eventually emerge as *jus cogens*; for others the 'international community of states as a whole' could designate such a norm directly by treaty.

The proposal to include peremptory norms in the VCLT was controversial from the start and divided the Vienna Conference on the Law of Treaties. Strong support came from the Soviet bloc and from newly independent States, who saw it as a means of escaping colonial-era agreements. Western countries were less positive and several expressed opposition to the notion of peremptory norms, voting against the provision and withholding ratification of the treaty because of persisting objections to the concept. To date, the VCLT has been accepted by 113 States.

The drafting of the second treaty on treaties, the 1986 Vienna Convention on the Law of Treaties between States and International Organizations, indicated continued controversy over the concept of norms *jus cogens*. The text proposed by the ILC included provisions on *jus cogens* modelled after the 1969 VCLT. The commentary called the prohibition of the illegal use of armed force embodied in the UN Charter 'the most reliable known example of a peremptory norm' and also claimed that the notion of peremptory norms, as embodied in VCLT Article 53, 'had been recognized in public international law before the Convention existed, but that instrument gave it both a precision and a substance which made the notion one of its essential provisions'.[25] The representative of France disagreed during the plenary drafting session, expressing his government's opposition to VCLT Article 53 'because it did not agree with the recognition that article gave to *jus cogens*' while another government called *jus cogens* 'still a highly controversial concept which raised the fundamental question of how to recognize the scope and content of a peremptory norm of general international law', noting that time had revealed 'a divergence of views since 1969 regarding the nature of norms of *jus cogens*, which it had not been possible to define'.[26]

---

[23] Sir Humphry Waldock proposed the concept and three categories of *jus cogens*: (1) illegal use of force; (2) international crimes; and (3) acts or omissions whose suppression is required by international law. The categories were dropped by the ILC, because each garnered opposition from at least two-thirds of the Commission. See Kearney and Dalton, 1970, p 535.

[24] Robledo, 1982, p 17 called it 'une innovation profonde et un grand pas franchi'.

[25] According to the Commentary, 'it is apparent from the draft articles that peremptory norms of international law apply to international organizations as well as to states, and this is not surprising' (A/Conf 129/16/Add 1 (vol II), pp 39, 44).

[26] UN Conference on the Law of Treaties between States and International Organizations or Between International Organizations, Vienna, 18 February–21 March 1986, A/Conf 129/16 (vol I), 17. See also the

The text of the Convention was adopted by 67 to one, with 23 States abstaining; it has yet to enter into force. Several States explained their abstention by referring to the Articles concerning *jus cogens*, including the dispute settlement provisions on the topic.[27]

C. INTERNATIONAL JURISPRUDENCE

In practice, the concept has been invoked largely outside its original context in the law of treaties. At the ICJ the term initially appeared in separate or dissenting opinions;[28] States still rarely raise the issue,[29] and until recently the Court seemed to take pains to avoid any pronouncement on it.[30] The 1986 *Nicaragua* decision, most often cited for the Court's approval of *jus cogens*, does not in fact adopt either the concept or the content of such norms.[31] In a subsequent advisory opinion on nuclear weapons, the ICJ utilized descriptive phrases that could be taken to refer to peremptory norms, although the language is unclear. The ICJ called some rules of international humanitarian law so fundamental to respect for the human person and 'elementary considerations of humanity' that 'they constitute intransgressible principles of international customary law'.[32] Whether 'intransgressible' means the rules are peremptory or only that they are general customary international law legally binding on States not party to the conventions that contain them is uncertain.

The Court again avoided adjudicating the existence or impact of *jus cogens* in the *Arrest Warrant* judgment of 14 February 2002. The Court failed to mention *jus cogens* in deciding that 'certain holders of high-ranking office' enjoy immunity from civil and criminal process and concluded that no customary international law restricts diplomatic immunity when accused are suspected of having committed war crimes or crimes against humanity.[33]

In 2006, in its *Congo v Rwanda*[34] judgment, the Court affirmed both the existence of peremptory norms in international law, and asserted that the prohibition of genocide is 'assuredly' such a norm. Nonetheless, the Court emphasized that the *jus cogens* status of the prohibition of genocide did not have an impact on its jurisdiction, which remains governed by consent. A dissenting opinion questioned whether the *jus cogens* prohibition of genocide meant that a reservation to the Court's jurisdiction might be incompatible with

concerns expressed by Germany, and similar objections raised to Article 64 which concerns the emergence of a new peremptory norm of general international law (p 18).

[27] Ibid, pp 186–94.

[28] See, eg *Right of Passage over Indian Territory, Merits, Judgment, ICJ Reports 1960*, p 6 at pp 135, 139–40 (Judge ad hoc Renandes dissenting); *South West Africa, Second Phase, Judgment, ICJ Reports 1966*, p 6 at p 298 (Judge Tanaka dissenting).

[29] *Gabčíkovo-Nagymaros Project (Hungary/Slovakia), Judgment, ICJ Reports 1997*, p 7, para 112, noting that neither side had argued that new peremptory norms of environmental law had emerged.

[30] See *North Sea Continental Shelf, Judgment, ICJ Reports 1969*, p 3, para 72, declining to enter into or pronounce upon any issue concerning *jus cogens*.

[31] *Military and Paramilitary Activities in and against Nicaragua (Nicaragua v United States of America), Merits, Judgment, ICJ Reports 1986*, p 14 at para 190, citing the ILC assertion that the norm against aggression is a peremptory norm as evidence that it is an obligation under customary international law.

[32] *Legality of the Threat or Use of Nuclear Weapons, Advisory Opinion, ICJ Reports 1996*, p 226, para 79.

[33] Only one of the ten opinions in the *Arrest Warrant* case mentions the concept of *jus cogens* norms despite its obvious relevance to the issues in the case. The dissenting opinion of Judge Al-Khasawneh refers to *jus cogens*, linking immunity and impunity. *Arrest Warrant of 11 April 2000 (Democratic Republic of Congo/Belgium), Preliminary Objections and Merits, Judgment, ICJ Reports 2002*, p 3, Dissenting Opinion of Judge Al-Khasawneh, para 7.

[34] *Armed Activities on the Territory of the Congo (New Application: 2002) (Democratic Republic of the Congo v Rwanda), Jurisdiction and Admissibility, Judgment, ICJ Reports 2006*, p 6, para 64.

the object and purpose of the Genocide Convention, but the 'novelty and far-reaching implications' of declaring that *jus cogens* trumps reservations restrained the other judges.

After its 2006 judgment, the Court was confronted directly with the question of whether or not peremptory norms override other norms of international law. In December 2008, the Federal Republic of Germany filed an application against Italy at the ICJ, asserting that the Italian courts' exercise of jurisdiction over Germany in relation to claims of World War II forced labour and other war crimes constituted a wrongful denial of sovereign immunity. The application cited the Italian 'doctrine of non-invocability of sovereign immunity in cases of grave violations of human rights and humanitarian law'.[35]

In its judgment of 3 February 2012, the Court and the parties agreed that immunity is governed by international law and is not a mere matter of comity.[36] Unusually the Court evaluated at some length the evidence of customary international law on the scope of sovereign immunity, concluding that it holds an 'important place in international law, deriving from the principle of sovereign equality of States'.[37] Italy argued, inter alia, that in this case Germany was not entitled to immunity because its acts in question involved 'the most serious violations of rules of international law of a peremptory character for which no alternative means of redress was available'.[38] The Court found three strands to this argument. First that the claims constituted serious violations of the principles of international law applicable to the conduct of armed conflict, amounting to war crimes and crimes against humanity. Second, that the rules of international law thus contravened were peremptory norms (*jus cogens*). Finally that in the absence of other forms of redress, the exercise of jurisdiction by the Italian courts was necessary as a matter of last resort.

The Court rejected all three elements of the argument, first finding that 'there is almost no State practice which might be considered to support the proposition that a State is deprived of its entitlement to immunity' in a case of this type.[39] In addition, after reviewing treaty provisions, national legislation and the judgments of national and international courts, the Court found:

> there is a substantial body of State practice from other countries which demonstrates that customary international law does not treat a State's entitlement to immunity as dependent upon the gravity of the act of which it is accused or the peremptory nature of the rule which it is alleged to have violated.[40]

Assuming without deciding that the alleged violations rose to the level of *jus cogens*, the Court held that there was no conflict between that determination and the rule demanding respect for sovereign immunity: 'the two sets of rules address different matters', one substantive, one procedural.[41] There could be no conflict between the two. Notably, in dicta that appeared unnecessary to the disposition of the case, the Court added that it could not find a *jus cogens* norm requiring full compensation be paid to each and every individual victim of an armed conflict.[42] In sum, even on the assumption that the proceedings in the Italian courts involved violations of *jus cogens* rules, the applicability of the customary law on State immunity was not affected.

Neither *jus cogens* nor peremptory norms have been mentioned in decisions of the UN Tribunal for the Law of the Sea, nor were they referred to by the Iran or Iraq Claims Tribunals. Human rights tribunals until recently also avoided pronouncing on *jus cogens*.

---

[35] *Jurisdictional Immunities of the State (Germany v Italy)*, Application of 22 December 2008, p 12.
[36] *Jurisdictional Immunities of the State (Germany v Italy: Greece Intervening)*, Judgment of 3 February 2012, para 53.
[37] Ibid, para 57.   [38] Ibid, para 61.   [39] Ibid, para 83.   [40] Ibid, para 84.
[41] Ibid, para 93.   [42] Ibid, paras 100–101.

A Grand Chamber of the European Court of Human Rights, in its first judgment mentioning *jus cogens*, decided by a 9:8 majority in 2002, called the prohibition of torture a peremptory norm, but denied that a violation of the norm could act to deprive a State of sovereign immunity.[43] The court found that it was 'unable to discern' any basis for overriding State immunity from civil suit even where acts of torture are alleged. More recently, the Court followed the ICJ in calling the prohibition of genocide a peremptory norm.[44]

The Inter-American Court of Human Rights referred to *jus cogens* with some frequency between its 2003 advisory opinion on the juridical condition and rights of undocumented migrants[45] and 2008, but has done so far less often recently. In the 2003 Advisory Opinion, Mexico's fourth question to the court asked: 'What is the nature today of the principle of non-discrimination and the right to equal and effective protection of the law in the hierarchy of norms established by general international law and, in this context, can they be considered to be the expression of norms *jus cogens*?' Mexico also asked the court to indicate the legal effect of a finding that these norms are *jus cogens*.

The court's opinion, which it expressly stated applies to all OAS member States whether or not they are party to the American Convention on Human Rights, appears to view natural law as a source of obligation. According to the court, 'All persons have attributes inherent to their human dignity that may not be harmed; these attributes make them possessors of fundamental rights that may not be disregarded and which are, consequently, superior to the power of the State, whatever its political structure.' The court nonetheless cited 19 treaties and 14 soft law instruments on the principle of non-discrimination, finding that taken together they evidence a universal obligation to respect and guarantee human rights without discrimination.[46] The court concluded that non-discrimination is *jus cogens*, being 'intrinsically related to the right to equal protection before the law, which, in turn, derives "directly from the oneness of the human family and is linked to the essential dignity of the individual."' The court added that the principle belongs to *jus cogens* because the whole legal structure of national and international public order rests on it and it is a fundamental principle that permeates all laws. The court's opinion considerably shifts law-making from States to international tribunals, as the latter assess the demands of human dignity and international public order.

The court subsequently affirmed *jus cogens* norms in contentious cases, broadening the list to include the prohibition of torture,[47] access to justice,[48] the prohibition of forced

---

[43] *Al-Adsani v UK*, [GC], no 35763/97, ECHR 2001-XI, 34 *EHRR* 11. See also *Fogarty v UK* [GC], no 37112/97, ECHR 2001-XI, 34 *EHRR* 12 and *McElhinney v Ireland and UK* [GC], no 31253/96, ECHR 2001-XI, 34 *EHRR* 13 decided the same day as *Al-Adsani*. For a critique of the case, see Clapham, 2007.

[44] *Jorgic v Germany*, no 74613/01, ECHR 2007-XI, para 68.

[45] *Juridical Condition and Rights of the Undocumented Migrants*, Advisory Opinion, OC-18/03 Ser A, No 18 (17 September 2003).

[46] In stating that *jus cogens* has been developed by international case law, the court wrongly cited the ICJ judgments in the *Application of the Convention on the Prevention and Punishment of the Crime of Genocide, Preliminary Objections (Bosnia-Herzegovina v Yugoslavia)*, ICJ Reports 1996, p 595 and the *Barcelona Traction, Light and Power Company, Limited, Second Phase, Judgment*, ICJ Reports 1970, p 3, neither of which discusses the subject.

[47] See the Inter-American Court of Human Rights cases *Bayarri v Argentina, Preliminary Objection, Merits, Reparations and Costs*, Judgment of 30 October 2008, Ser C, no 187, para 81; *Martiza Urrutia v Guatemala, Merits, Reparations and Costs*, Judgment of 27 November 2003, Ser C, no 103, para 92; *Tibi v Ecuador, Preliminary Objections, Merits, Reparations and Costs*, Judgment of 7 September 2004, Ser C, no 114, para 143; *Bueno-Alves v Argentina, Merits, Reparations and Costs*, Judgment of 11 May 2007, Ser C, no 164, para 76; *Case of the Rochela Massacre v Colombia, Merits, Reparations and Costs*, Judgment of 11 May 2007, Ser C, no 163, para 132; *Case of the Miguel Castro-Castro Prison v Peru, Merits, Reparations and Costs*, Judgment of 25 November 2006, Ser C, no 160, para 271.

[48] Inter-American Court of Human Rights, case of *La Cantuta v Peru, Merits, Reparations and Costs*, Judgment of 29 November 2006, Ser C, no 162, para 160 ('... Access to justice constitutes a peremptory norm of

disappearance, and the duty to prosecute violations of *jus cogens* norms.[49] In its own juris-prudence, the Inter-American Commission on Human Rights has declared the right to life to be a norm *jus cogens*:

> derived from a higher order of norms established in ancient times and which cannot be contravened by the laws of man or nations. The norms of *jus cogens* have been described by public law specialists as those which encompass public international order…accepted…as necessary to protect the public interest of the society of nations or to maintain levels of public morality recognized by them.[50]

The International Criminal Tribunal for the Former Yugoslavia (ICTY), was the first tribunal to discuss *jus cogens* and declare the prohibition of torture as one such norm:

> Because of the importance of the values it protects, [the prohibition against torture] has evolved into a peremptory norm or *jus cogens*, that is, a norm that enjoys a higher rank in the international hierarchy than treaty law and even 'ordinary' customary rules. The most conspicuous consequence of this higher rank is that the principle at issue cannot be derogated from by states through international treaties or local or special customs or even general customary rules not endowed with the same normative force…. Clearly, the *jus cogens* nature of the prohibition against torture articulates the notion that the prohibition has now become one of the most fundamental standards of the international community.[51]

The discussion had no bearing on the guilt or innocence of the person on trial, nor on the binding nature of the law violated. It was not asserted that any treaty or local custom was in conflict with the customary and treaty prohibition of torture. The reference served a rhetorical purpose only. Similarly, an International Labor Organization (ILO) report on a 1996 complaint against Myanmar for forced labour referred to *jus cogens* although the State had long been a party to ILO Convention (No 29) concerning Forced or Compulsory Labour.[52] The Report's statement that the practice of forced labour violates a *jus cogens* norm appears intended to invite the criminal prosecution of individuals using forced labour, labelling the systematic practice of forced labour a 'crime against humanity'.[53]

International Law and, as such, it gives rise to the States' *erga omnes* obligation to adopt all such measures as are necessary to prevent such violations from going unpunished, whether exercising their judicial power to apply their domestic law and International Law to judge and eventually punish those responsible for such events, or collaborating with other States aiming in that direction…').

[49] Ibid, para 157; also *Ríos et al v Venezuela, Preliminary Objections, Merits, Reparations, and Costs*, Judgment of 28 January 2009, Ser C, no 194; *Tiu-Tojín v Guatemala, Merits, Reparations and Costs*, Judgment of 26 November 2008, Ser C, no 190, para 91 ('…[W]e should reiterate to the State that the prohibition of the forced disappearance of persons and the related duty to investigate them and, if it were the case, punish those responsible has the nature of jus cogens. As such, the forced disappearance of persons cannot be considered a political crime or related to political crimes under any circumstance, to the effect of preventing the criminal persecution of this type of crimes or suppressing the effects of a conviction. Additionally, pursuant with the preamble of the Inter-American Convention on Forced Disappearance, the systematic practice of the forced disappearance of persons constitutes a crime against humanity and, as such, entails the consequences established in the applicable international law.') See also *Perozo et al v Venezuela, Preliminary Objections, Merits, Reparations, and Costs*, Judgment of 28 January 2009, Ser C, no 195, *La Cantuta v Peru, Merits, Reparations and Costs*, Judgment of 29 November 2006, Ser C, no 162, para 157.

[50] OAS, Inter-American Commission on Human Rights, 81st Session, Annual Report of the Inter-American Commission on Human Rights, *Victims of the Tugboat '13 de Marzo' v Cuba*, Rep No 47/96, OR OEA/Ser.L/V/II.95/Doc.7, rev (1997) at 146–7.

[51] *Prosecutor v Furundzija*, Judgment, Case No IT-95–17/1-T, Trial Chamber (10 December 1998), para 153.

[52] 28 June 1930, 39 UNTS 55.

[53] Report of the Commission of Inquiry on Forced Labour in Myanmar (Burma), ILO Official Bulletin, 1998, Special Supp, vol LXXXI, Ser B, para 538.

Expert bodies have been willing to develop illustrative lists of *jus cogens* norms. The ILC's Commentary on its Articles on State Responsibility claims that peremptory norms 'that are clearly accepted and recognized' include the prohibitions of aggression, genocide, slavery, racial discrimination, crimes against humanity and torture, and the right to self-determination.[54] The Human Rights Committee addressed *jus cogens* in its General Comment No 29 on States of Emergency, issued 31 August 2001. According to the Committee, the list of non-derogable rights in Article 4(2) of the Covenant on Civil and Political Rights is related to, but not identical with the content of peremptory human rights norms. The Committee emphatically insists that 'States parties may in no circumstances invoke article 4 of the Covenant as justification for acting in violation of humanitarian law or peremptory norms of international law, for instance by taking hostages, by imposing collective punishments, through arbitrary deprivations of liberty or by deviating from fundamental principles of fair trial, including the presumption of innocence' (General Comment No 29, para 11). While this may appear to be adding new conditions to Article 4, in fact paragraph 1 explicitly provides that any measures taken by States in derogation of Covenant rights must not be 'inconsistent with their other obligations under international law'. In terms of consequences of this extension, the Committee asserts that one test of the legitimacy of measures in derogation of Covenant rights can be found in the definition of certain violations as crimes against humanity.

D. NATIONAL JURISPRUDENCE

The concept of norms *jus cogens* has been asserted most strongly, though largely without success in domestic courts. In the USA, lawyers initially sought to avoid US constitutional doctrine that considers treaties and custom equivalent to other federal law, allowing the President and Congress to enact US law inconsistent with international law. Obligations *jus cogens* thus were asserted in an effort to enforce the 1986 ICJ judgment against the USA in the *Nicaragua* case.[55] Lawyers argued that the constitutional precedents do not apply to norms *jus cogens*, which have a higher status that bind even the President and Congress. The Court accepted *arguendo* the theory, but held that compliance with a decision of the ICJ is not a *jus cogens* requirement.

Other domestic court cases involving *jus cogens* fall into one of two categories. First are cases in which sovereign immunity has acted to shield defendants from civil lawsuits for damages. The issue has arisen most often in courts of the USA and the UK.[56] In both fora lawyers argued that the foreign sovereign immunity must be interpreted to include an implied exception to sovereign immunity for violations of *jus cogens* norms. The argument posits that State agreement to elevate a norm to *jus cogens* status inherently results in an implied waiver of sovereign immunity. Every court thus far has rejected the argument and upheld immunity, although some judicial panels have split on the issue.[57]

In the case of former Chilean leader, Augusto Pinochet Ugarte, the issue of *jus cogens* was pressed in response to his claim of immunity from criminal prosecution. Among the many opinions in the case, Lord Millett stated that '[i]nternational law cannot be supposed

---

[54] Commentary to Article 26, para 5, Report of the ILC, GAOR, Supp No 10 (A/56/10) p 208.

[55] *Committee of US Citizens Living in Nicaragua v Reagan*, 859 F.2d 929, 940 (DC Cir 1988).

[56] *Al-Adsani v Kuwait* was litigated in English courts before it was submitted to the European Court of Human Rights.

[57] See, eg *Siderman de Blake v Republic of Argentina*, 965 F.2d 699 (9th Cir 1992), cert denied, 113 S Ct 1812 (1993).

to have established a crime having the character of a *jus cogens* and at the same time to have provided an immunity which is co-extensive with the obligation it seeks to impose'.[58] The judgment ultimately did not rely on *jus cogens* to determine the issue, however, because the situation was controlled by the relevant treaty.

Four cases from different national courts demonstrate the confusion over *jus cogens* and its relationship to issues of immunity. In all of the cases the courts held that the underlying violations constituted breaches of norms *jus cogens*—two cases involved war crimes and two concerned torture—but the courts split evenly on whether a finding of *jus cogens* violations results in overriding traditional immunity. The respective highest national courts in one case from Greece and another from Italy held that German crimes committed during World War II were not protected by sovereign immunity,[59] these being the decisions which the ICJ subsequently found to have been made in violation of international law.[60] In contrast, the Court of Appeal in Ontario, Canada and the UK House of Lords, have both held that the *jus cogens* prohibition of torture does not override sovereign immunity.[61]

A second category of domestic law cases in which the nature of norms as *jus cogens* has been asserted are cases filed pursuant to the US Alien Tort Claim Act (ATCA).[62] Some of the plaintiffs assert violations of norms *jus cogens*, often wrongly claiming that the landmark decision *Filartiga* v *Peña-Irala* held torture to be a violation of international *jus cogens*. In fact, the federal appellate court in that case held that official torture constitutes a violation of the law of nations and never mentioned the doctrine of *jus cogens*.[63]

No ATCA case has yet turned on the character of the norm as *jus cogens* or 'ordinary' custom, though there may soon be another opportunity. In 2010, the Supreme Court held in *Samantar* v *Yousef*,[64] that the Foreign Sovereign Immunities Act (FSIA) did not apply to the immunities of foreign officials and so decisions about official immunity instead continue to be governed by federal common law. Following this judgment, the State Department determined that Samantar—who was the former prime minister of the unrecognized Barre regime in Somalia—did not enjoy immunity. The District Court agreed and the Court of Appeals affirmed. The Fourth Circuit held, first, that State Department determinations of conduct-based immunity for official acts are entitled only to substantial weight, not absolute deference; second, that foreign officials are not entitled to conduct-based immunity for violations of *jus cogens* norms. Samantar filed a petition for the Supreme Court to review the Fourth Circuit judgment, arguing that the

---

[58] *R v Bow Street Metropolitan Stipendiary Magistrate and others, ex parte Pinochet Ugarte* [1999] 2 All ER 97 (HL) at 179.

[59] See *Prefecture of Voiotia v Federal Republic of Germany*, Case No 11/2000 (Areios Pagos, Supreme Court of Greece, 4 May 2000) and *Ferrini v Federal Republic of Germany*, Italian Court of Cassation, Judgment No. 5044 of 11 March 2004, 128 ILR 659; (2005) 99 *AJIL* 242. See De Sena & De Vittor, 2005.

[60] In *Jurisdictional Immunities of the State (Germany v Italy: Greece Intervening)*, Judgment of 3 February 2012, discussed in Section II C.

[61] See *Bouzari v Iran*, Ontario Court of Appeal, OJ No 2800 (2004), 1991–1 Feuille fédérale, pp 440–42 and *Jones v Ministry of Interior for the Kingdom of Saudi Arabia and Ors* [2006] UKHL 26; [2007] 1 AC 270.

[62] 28 USC §1350 ('The [federal] district courts shall have original jurisdiction of any civil action by an alien for a tort only, committed in violation of the law of nations or a treaty of the United States'). Judiciary Act of 1789, ch 20, §9(b) (1789), codified at 28 USC §1350.

[63] *Filartiga v Peña-Irala*, 630 F.2d 876 (2nd Cir 1980). Neither of the two US Supreme Court decisions to consider issues arising under the ATCA, *Sosa v Alvarez-Machain*, 542 US 692 (2004), and *Koibel v Royal Dutch Petroleum Co*, 133 S Ct 1659 (2013) mention *jus cogens* at all.

[64] *Samantar v Yousef*, 130 S Ct 2278 (2010).

decision conflicts with the decisions of other Circuits,[65] which have refused to recognize a *jus cogens* exception to the immunity at issue, which is currently pending. The Fourth Circuit's decision in *Samantar* was the first Court of Appeals decision to indicate that *jus cogens* violations cannot constitute official acts for purposes of conduct-based immunity. It should be noted that in *Samantar*, the question is now not whether to recognize a *jus cogens* exception to an immunity that had already attached, but the antecedent question of whether a *jus cogens* violation, by rendering the act no longer 'official', precludes immunity from attaching in the first place.

The ILC Articles on State Responsibility and accompanying Commentary acknowledge that the issue of hierarchy of norms has been much debated, but find support for *jus cogens* in the notion of *erga omnes* obligations, the inclusion of the concept of peremptory norms in the Vienna Convention on the Law of Treaties, in international practice and in the jurisprudence of international and national courts and tribunals.[66] Article 41 sets forth the particular consequences said to result from the commission of a serious breach of a peremptory norm. To a large extent Article 41 seems to be based on UN practice, especially actions of the Security Council in response to breaches of the UN Charter in Southern Africa and by Iraq.[67] The text refers to positive and negative obligations of all States. In respect to the first, '[w]hat is called for in the face of serious breaches is a joint and coordinated effort by all states to counteract the effect of these breaches'.[68] The Commentary concedes that the proposal 'may reflect the progressive development of international law' as it aims to strengthen existing mechanisms of cooperation. The core requirement, to abstain from recognizing consequences of the illegal acts, finds support in State practice, with precedents including rejection of the unilateral declaration of independence by Rhodesia,[69] the annexation of Kuwait by Iraq,[70] and the South African presence in Namibia.[71] Article 41 extends the duty to combat and not condone, aid, or recognize certain illegal acts beyond those acts that breach the UN Charter.

The primary purpose of asserting that a norm is *jus cogens* seems to be to override the will of persistent objectors to a norm of customary international law.[72] If *jus cogens* is 'a norm from which no derogation is possible' and its creation by 'the international community as a whole' means anything less than unanimity, then the problem arises of imposing the norm on dissenting States. It is not clear that the international community as a whole is

---

[65] See *Belhas v Ya'alon*, 515 F.3d 1279 (DC Cir 2008), abrogated on other grounds by *Samantar v Yousuf*, 130 S Ct 2278 (2010); *Bouzari v Islamic Republic of Iran*, [2004] 71 OR3d 675, 695 (CA); *Matar v Dichter*, 500 F. Supp 2d 284 (SDNY 2004), 563 F.3d 9 (2d Cir 2009); *Ye v Zemin*, 383 F.3d 620 (7th Cir 2004).

[66] Article 40, Commentaries, para 2.

[67] Eg UN SC Res 662 (9 August 1990), saying that the annexation of Kuwait had 'no legal validity and is considered null and void' and calling on the international community not to recognize the annexation and to refrain from any action or dealing that might be interpreted as a recognition of it. See also *Legal Consequences for States of the Continued Presence of South Africa in Namibia (South West Africa) notwithstanding Security Council Resolution 276 (1970), Advisory Opinion, ICJ Reports 1971*, p 16, para 126, declaring the illegality of South Africa's presence in Namibia as having *erga omnes* effects.

[68] Article 41, Commentaries, para 3.

[69] UN SC Res 216 (12 November 1965).

[70] UN SC Res 662 (9 August 1990).

[71] *Legal Consequences for States of the Continued Presence of South Africa in Namibia (South West Africa) notwithstanding Security Council Resolution 276 (1970), Advisory Opinion, ICJ Reports 1971*, p 16, para 126.

[72] Theoretically, of course, the concept would be applicable if two or more States actually decided to enter into an agreement to commit genocide or territorial acquisition by aggression and one of them later changed its mind. According to the VCLT, only a party to an illegal agreement can invoke the illegality to escape its treaty obligations. The ILC Articles on State Responsibility go further and impose obligations on all States to repress breaches of *jus cogens* norms.

willing to accept the enforcement of widely accepted norms against dissenters. In reality, the problem is likely to arise only rarely because those norms most often identified as *jus cogens* are clearly accepted as customary international law and there are no persistent objectors. Even if States violate the norms in practice, no State claims the right to acquire territory by the illegal use of force, to commit genocide, or to torture.

The question of dissenters could arise in the future if the number of purported norms *jus cogens* expands in an effort to further the common interests of humanity. The literature is replete with claims that particular international norms form part of the *jus cogens*. Proponents have argued for inclusion of all human rights, all humanitarian norms (human rights and the laws of war), the duty not to cause transboundary environmental harm, the duty to assassinate dictators, the right to life of animals, self-determination, and territorial sovereignty (despite legions of treaties transferring territory from one State to another).

The concerns raised are serious ones, for the most part, and the rationale that emerges from the literature is one of necessity: the international community cannot afford a consensual regime to address many modern international problems. Thus, *jus cogens* is a necessary development in international law, required because the modern independence of States demands an international *ordre public* containing rules that require strict compliance. The ILC Commentary on the Articles on State responsibility favours this position, asserting that peremptory rules exist to 'prohibit what has come to be seen as intolerable because of the threat it presents to the survival of states and their peoples and the most basic human values'.[73] The urgent need to act that is suggested fundamentally challenges the consensual framework of the international system by seeking to impose on dissenting States obligations that the 'international community' deems fundamental. State practice has yet to catch up with this plea of necessity and it has been international and national courts which have pushed the concept forward.

III. HIERARCHY AMONG CONFLICTING NORMS AND PROCEDURES

The expansion of international law in the past half century has led to wide discussions of fragmentation as a problem or challenge to unity and coherence in the law. Certainly the 'transposition of functional differentiations of governance from the national to international plane' has resulted 'in the creation of more or less complete regulatory regimes which may at times compete with each other' (Simma, 2009). There are potentially numerous problems of hierarchy posed by the need to apply or balance different rights and obligations contained within a single treaty, reconcile norms and procedures in multiple treaties governing the same topic, or resolve conflicts across regimes. International texts sometimes include terms that imply a hierarchy, for example, distinguishing 'fundamental' from other rights or 'grave' from ordinary breaches of law. Treaties also may contain 'savings clauses' that give express preference to other agreements or rules of customary international law. General rules of interpretation help resolve some problems of conflict but difficult issues remain of determining international priorities among areas of regulation that have developed independently of each other.[74]

---

[73] Article 40, Commentaries, para 3.

[74] See *Continental Shelf (Tunisia/Libyan Arab Jamahiriya), Judgment, ICJ Reports 1982*, p 18, para 38; *Military and Paramilitary Activities in and against Nicaragua (Nicaragua v United States of America), Merits, Judgment, ICJ Reports 1986*, p 14, para 274.

The ILC decided in 2000 to include the topic of fragmentation in its long-term program of work.[75] The topic involved discussion of hierarchy of norms, including *jus cogens* and *erga omnes* obligations, as well as the conflict of law rules applicable when competing norms may govern the same issue, and the impact of Article 103 of the UN Charter. After an initial discussion, the 2002 ILC Report cautioned that there is neither a well-developed and authoritative hierarchy of values in international law nor an institutional system to resolve conflicts (para 506). The lack of international institutional hierarchy alluded to has resulted in one well-known conflict between the ICJ and the ICTY concerning the standards on State responsibility for the activities of an armed military or paramilitary group.[76]

A. HIERARCHY WITHIN A SINGLE TREATY

The question of hierarchy and the need to balance or resolve conflicts of norms within a single treaty has arisen in a variety of contexts, from arbitral awards such as the *Beagle Channel Arbitration*[77] to the application of human rights treaties, where the exercise of one right may be deemed to conflict with another. Human rights tribunals attempt to resolve such conflicts by developing rules of interpretation. The European Court of Human Rights starts from the premise that the Convention 'must be read as a whole, and interpreted in such a way as to promote internal consistency and harmony between its various provisions'.[78] The court also utilizes the doctrine of *lex specialis*. In considering the relationship between Article 13 on the right an effective remedy before a national court and Article 5(4) that specifies that anyone deprived of liberty shall 'be entitled to take proceedings by which the lawfulness of his detention shall be decided speedily by a court and his release ordered if the detention is not lawful', it held that the stricter requirements of Article 5 must be considered *lex specialis*.[79] It has similarly held with respect to the relationship between Article 13 and the fair trial requirements of Article 6.[80]

Human rights texts are sometimes seen as establishing a hierarchy of human rights norms through the use of non-derogation provisions, limitation clauses, and restrictions on reservations to core rights. In respect to derogations, the International Covenant on Civil and Political Rights (ICCPR), Article 4, the American Convention on Human Rights, Article 27, and the European Convention for the Protection of Human Rights and Fundamental Freedoms, Article 15, permit States parties to take measures suspending certain rights 'to the extent strictly required by the exigencies of the situation provided that such measures are not inconsistent with their other obligations under international law and do not involve discrimination solely on the ground of race, color, sex, language, religion or social origin' (ICCPR, Article 4(1)). The African Charter on Human and Peoples'

---

[75] See Report of the International Law Commission on its Fifty-second Session, GAOR Fifty-fifth Session, Supp No 10, UN Doc A/55/10 (2000), ch IX.a. 1, para 729.

[76] Compare the 'effective control' test of the ICJ in the *Case concerning Military and Paramilitary Activities in and against Nicaragua (Nicaragua v United States of America), Merits, Judgment, ICJ Reports 1986*, p 14 at paras 106–16 with the ICTY's 'overall control' test in *Prosecutor v Dusko Tadić, Judgment, Case No IT-94-1-A*, Appeals Chamber, 15 July 1999, 38 ILM 1518, paras 115–45.

[77] *Case concerning a dispute between Argentina and Chile concerning the Beagle Channel*, UNRIAA, vol XXI (1997).

[78] *Demir and Baykara v Turkey* [GC], no 34503/97, Judgment of 12 November 2008, para 66.

[79] *Brannigan and McBride v UK*, Judgment of 26 May 1993, ECHR Ser A, no 258-B, para 76; see also *Nikolova v Bulgaria* [GC], no 31195/96, ECHR 1999-II, para 69.

[80] *Yankov v Bulgaria*, no 39084/97, ECHR 2003-XII, para 150.

Rights contains no derogation provision and the African Commission has interpreted the omission to mean that the Charter as a whole remains in force even during periods of armed conflict, suggesting a superior status for the entire instrument.[81]

Non-derogable rights common to the three instruments that discuss the matter are the right to life, the right not to be subjected to torture or to cruel, inhuman or degrading treatment or punishment, the right to be free from slavery, the right to be free from *ex post facto* criminal laws, and the right to be free from discriminatory treatment in respect to derogations. These non-derogable rights could provide the starting point for a hierarchy of positive norms, particularly when added to the provisions of the slavery conventions, the Genocide Convention, and the Torture Conventions, none of which contain derogations provisions. International humanitarian instruments further reinforce this thesis. In addition to the protections applicable during international armed conflicts, Common Article 3 to the four 1949 Geneva Conventions demands that in case of armed conflict not of an international character, all non-combatants must be treated humanely and without discrimination by race, colour, religion, sex, birth, wealth, or any similar criteria. Specifically protected are life and freedom from torture, humiliating and degrading treatment, hostage-taking, and fundamental due process.

In respect to economic, social, and cultural rights, global and regional bodies have through General Comments and other normative statements cautiously implied a hierarchy of norms. The International Committee on Economic, Social and Cultural Rights, General Comment No 3 (1990), expresses the view 'that a minimum core obligation to ensure the satisfaction of, at the very least, minimum essential levels of each of the rights is incumbent upon every State party. Thus, for example, a State party in which any significant number of individuals is deprived of essential foodstuffs, of essential primary health care, of basic shelter and housing, or of the most basic forms of education is, prima facie, failing to discharge its obligations under the Covenant'. In a separate General Comment (No 12) on the right to adequate food, the Committee established a core minimum obligation to ensure freedom from hunger, as distinguished from the more general right to adequate food.[82]

The Inter-American Commission on Human Rights (IACHR) also has adopted a 'basic needs' approach to economic, social, and cultural rights. According to the Commission, the obligation of member States to observe and defend human rights, set forth in the American Declaration and the American Convention, obligates them, 'regardless of the level of economic development, to guarantee a minimum threshold of these rights'.[83] States are obligated to immediately ensure 'a minimum level of material well-being which is able to guarantee respect of their rights to personal security, dignity, equality of opportunity and freedom from discrimination'. Finally, the European Social Charter and the ILO Declaration of Fundamental Rights of Workers also indicate that certain core rights are deemed of particular significance in the economic and social field.

---

[81] See *Commission Nationale des Droits de l'homme et des Libertés* v *Chad*, Comm 74/92, Ninth Annual Activity Report of the African Commission on Human and Peoples' Rights 1995/96, AGH/207 (XXXII), Annex VIII no 3; Murray and Evans, 2001, p 449.

[82] The International Covenant on Economic, Social and Cultural Rights (ICESCR) itself makes this distinction, speaking in Article 11(1) of the right of everyone to adequate food and in Article 11(2) of the 'fundamental right of everyone to be free from hunger'.

[83] IACHR, The Realization of Economic, Social and Cultural Rights in the Region, Annual Report of the Inter-American Commission on Human Rights, 1993, OEA/SerL/VII.85, doc 9, rev 11 February 1994, pp 519–34.

In some instances, the reference to a single right in a general treaty or repeated references in several agreements may be deemed to imply a hierarchy. The UN Charter mentions a single human right, non-discrimination, as it adds the phrase 'without distinction on the basis of race, sex, language or religion' to every reference to human rights and fundamental freedoms in the body of the Charter. The 1993 Declaration adopted at the conclusion of the Vienna Conference on Human Rights called non-discrimination 'a fundamental rule of international human rights law'. A possible preferred status for non-discrimination is supported by the Convention on the Suppression and Punishment of the Crime of Apartheid, the only international instrument apart from the Convention on the Prevention and Punishment of the Crime of Genocide to designate the acts covered by the treaty as a 'crime under international law'.[84]

The identification of certain human rights violations as crimes may also imply a hierarchy supremacy. In addition to genocide and apartheid, global and regional treaties against torture call upon each State party to 'ensure that all acts of torture are offences under its criminal law'.[85] Similarly, the Geneva Conventions of 1949 and the Protocols of 1977 require States parties to suppress and punish 'grave breaches' of the Conventions. In both the UN and the Inter-American systems, forced disappearances can be added to this category.[86] The establishment of ad hoc international tribunals for the former Yugoslavia and for Rwanda, as well as the conclusion of the Rome Statute for a permanent International Criminal Court reinforce the understanding that the international community places the commission of certain acts in a higher category for which individual criminal responsibility will be imposed in addition to State responsibility.

To a large extent, these provisions of positive law reflect theoretical approaches that posit maximum claims for equality, personal security, and subsistence rights. While there is some variety from one region to another in the number of rights deemed non-derogable, a minimum core does exist and supports the idea of a hierarchy of rights contained in each legal instrument.

B. HIERARCHY AMONG TREATIES GOVERNING THE SAME TOPIC

The proliferation of international law includes multilateral global and regional treaties, bilateral treaties, general and regional custom. The co-existence of these various forms of law results in multiple agreements and sources of law governing the same topic. Conflicts among treaties governing the same topic increase as global framework instruments are supplemented by regional arrangements or competing regimes within the same region apply to the same subject matter.[87]

The proliferation of treaties governing the same subject matter can raise particular difficulties for dispute settlement mechanisms. When global treaties comprehensively regulate a topic, such as the law of the sea, they usually establish a long-term regime and sometimes

---

[84] Convention on the Prevention and Punishment of the Crime of Genocide (1948), Article 1; International Convention on the Suppression and Punishment of the Crime of Apartheid (1973), Article 1. Earlier, the 1968 Proclamation of Teheran, para 7, called the policy of apartheid a 'crime against humanity'.

[85] Convention against Torture and Other Cruel, Inhuman and Degrading Treatment or Punishment (1984), Article 4(1); Inter-American Convention to Prevent and Punish Torture, Article 6.

[86] UN Convention for the Protection of All Persons from Enforced Disappearances, Articles (2006), Article 3. Inter-American Convention on Forced Disappearance of Persons (1994), Article 3.

[87] In Europe, three regional institutions address issues of human rights, sometimes with different interpretations of the same rights. See Shelton, 2003.

provide compulsory dispute settlement mechanisms. The problem of escaping jurisdiction through recourse to another, regional, treaty can arise. Usually the treaties do not expressly resolve the matter. In the first Annex VII arbitration under the 1982 UN Law of the Sea Convention, the arbitral tribunal decided that it lacked jurisdiction to adjudicate the claims because of an intervening regional agreement concluded by the three parties to the arbitration.[88]

Interpretive rules are sometimes suggested to reconcile the conflicts that emerge (Akehurst, 1974–5). The VCLT provides that generally the treaty later in time should prevail when the two instruments concluded by the same parties relate to the 'same subject-matter', subject to the primacy of the UN Charter. Determining when two or more instruments relate to the same subject matter can be problematic. The European Court of Human Rights made clear in 2008 that it 'has never considered the provisions of the Convention as the sole framework of reference for the interpretation of the rights and freedoms enshrined therein'. Instead, citing VCLT Article 31(3)(c), the Court indicated that it 'must also take into account any relevant rules and principles of international law applicable in relations between the Contracting Parties'.[89] This means it will determine the precise obligations imposed on the parties in the light of relevant international treaties on the same subject, in order to avoid inconsistencies with other international instruments and to make the Convention effective. Relevant rules also include 'general principles of law' which can be found in texts of universal scope and case law of human rights bodies. 'Intrinsically non-binding instruments' and the common practices or standards adopted by 'the vast majority of states' also are useful in interpreting the Convention consistent with other norms. This accumulation and comparison of normative instruments, if done on a consistent basis by the European Court and similar human rights tribunals, can solidify jurisprudence around progressive development of the law.

C. HIERARCHY AMONG REGIMES

As a general rule, the VCLT promotes a certain coherence and unity of international law by providing that treaties should be interpreted in the light of 'relevant rules of international law applicable in the relations between the parties' (VCLT, Article 31(3)(c)). These rules can derive either from treaty or from custom. The European Court of Human Rights has referenced VCLT Article 31(3)(c) in considering how to reconcile other norms of international law with those of the European Convention on Human Rights. Other tribunals, including the World Trade Organization (WTO),[90] the ICJ,[91] and the North American Free Trade Agreement (NAFTA) Tribunal[92] have also applied the VCLT to read treaty provisions in the light of customary norms. UNCLOS Article 293(1) indeed requires that the LOS Tribunal 'shall apply this Convention and other rules of international law not

---

[88] See *Southern Bluefin Tuna Case (Australia and New Zealand v Japan), Jurisdiction and Admissibility, Arbitral Tribunal constituted under annex VII of the United Nations Convention on the Law of the Sea*, Award of 4 August 2000 which concerned the Convention for the Conservation of Southern Bluefin Tuna (1993). See Oxman, 2002.

[89] *Demir and Baykara* v *Turkey* [GC], no 34503/97, Judgment of 12 November 2008, para 67.

[90] WTO United States: Import Prohibition of Certain Shrimp and Shrimp Products—Report of the Appellate Body (12 October 1998) WT/DS58/AB/R, (1999) 38 ILM 118. See also Korea—Measures Affecting Government Procurement, 1 May 2000, WT/DS163/R, para 7.96: 'customary international law applies generally to the economic relations between the WTO Members. Such international law applies to the extent that the WTO treaty agreements do not "contract out" from it'.

[91] *Oil Platforms (Islamic Republic of Iran v USA), Judgment, ICJ Report 2003*, p 161.

[92] Eg *Award on the Merits*, 10 April 2001; *Award in Respect of Damages*, 31 May 2002, (2002) 41 ILM 1347.

incompatible with this Convention'. It would appear that although a written agreement expresses concretely the will of the parties, there is a presumption that the parties do not intend to derogate from general international law.

Despite the general conciliatory approach of the VCLT, some institutions or treaties assert a hierarchical supremacy of one area of regulation over another or one treaty over others. The primacy of the UN Charter is set forth in Article 103 which provides that 'in the event of a conflict between the obligations of the members of the UN under the present Charter and their obligations under any other international agreement, their obligations under the present Charter shall prevail'. This 'supremacy clause' has been taken to suggest that the aims and purposes of the UN—maintenance of peace and security and promotion and protection of human rights—constitute an international public order to which other treaty regimes and the international organizations giving effect to them must conform. In addition, the VCLT Article 30(1) reiterates the priority of obligations under the UN Charter.

At the same time, the actions of UN organs themselves have come under increasing scrutiny from the perspective of hierarchy of norms. Judge Lauterpacht, in his separate opinion in *Application of the Convention on the Prevention and Punishment of the Crime of Genocide*, was the first jurist to suggest that a Security Council resolution will be void if it conflicts with a *jus cogens* norm, 'as a matter of simple hierarchy of norms'.[93] The courts of the EU have taken up this issue and provoked considerable controversy in doing so. In the *Yusuf* and *Kadi* cases,[94] the Court of First Instance (CFI) decided on an action for annulment of EU legislative acts implementing some UN Security Council actions for the suppression of international terrorism. The CFI declined to review these acts on the basis of EU law because the EC, it found, is bound by the obligations of the UN Charter, Article 103, in the same way as EC member States and cannot review the lawfulness of the Security Council resolutions indirectly. However, the CFI held that it could review the resolutions for compatibility with *jus cogens* because Security Council resolutions themselves must respect the fundamental peremptory norms of *jus cogens*.

On appeal, the European Court of Justice took a different tack, declaring that the CFI had no competence to engage in a review of the kind it did, but had to decide cases before it on the basis of EU law.[95] It held that the Community judicial organs must ensure the full review of the lawfulness of all Community acts, including those giving effect to Security Council resolutions under Chapter VII.

At the national level a decision by the Swiss Federal Supreme Court held that member States could annul Security Council resolutions in conflict with *jus cogens* norms.[96] Notably, both the CFI and the Swiss court found no *jus cogens* violations.

---

[93] *Application of the Convention on the Prevention and Punishment of the Crime of Genocide, Provisional Measures, Order of 13 September 1993, ICJ Reports 1993*, p 325 at p 440.

[94] Case T-306/91, *Yusuf* v *Council* [2005] ECR II-3533; Case T-315/01, *Kadi* v *Council* [2005] ECR II-3649. The court found the contents of *jus cogens* to be the 'mandatory provisions concerning the universal protection of human rights...intransgressible principles of international customary law', ibid at para 231.

[95] *Kadi and Al Barakaat International Foundation* v *Council*, Joined Cases 402/05 and 415/05 [2008] ECR I-6351. See also the decisions of the European Court of Human Rights in *Behrami and Behrami* v *France and Saramati* v *France, Germany and Norway* (Dec) [GC], nos 71412/01 and 78166/01, 2 May 2007 and *Beric and Others* v *Bosnia and Herzegovina* (Dec), no 36357/04 and others, ECHR 2007-XII. In the former cases, the European Court of Human Rights declared itself incompetent to judge the existence of human rights violations in Kosovo allegedly committed by forces whose presence was authorized by the Security Council. The latter case involved actions of the High Representative, a post established by Security Council Res 1031 (15 December 1995).

[96] *Nada* v *SECO*, Bundesgericht, 14 November 2007, 133 Entscheidungen des Schweizerischen Bundesgerickts II 450 (Switz).

Perhaps the most oft-cited regime conflict is that between trade and the environment, especially between WTO rules on free trade and the trade-restricting measures mandated or permitted under multilateral environmental agreements (Pauwelyn, 2001). Trade restrictions are imposed by the Convention on International Trade in Endangered Species, the Montreal Protocol on Ozone-Depleting Substances, and the Biosafety Protocol to the Convention on Biological Diversity (Safrin, 2002). While no dispute settlement body of the WTO has addressed the issue, various panels have found unilateral trade measures taken for environmental purposes to be contrary to WTO obligations.[97] The World Summit on Sustainable Development, held in Johannesburg, South Africa in 2002, seemed to lean towards favouring the free-trade regime over environmental protection; it suggested that means to balance or reconcile conflicts between the two areas of international regulation should be decided within the WTO bodies rather than by the UN Environment Program or a general forum like the UN General Assembly.[98]

Treaties sometimes contain specific choice of law provisions preserving rights and obligations under other treaties or regimes. The NAFTA contains obligations generally similar and additional to those imposed by the World Trade Organization 'Uruguay Round'. NAFTA Article 103 reaffirms the parties' 'existing rights and obligations with respect to each other under the General Agreement on Tariffs and Trade [GATT] and other agreements to which such Parties are party', but the Article also states that the NAFTA prevails over those agreements in the event of an inconsistency. The 'Objectives' Chapter (Chapter 1) similarly provides that in the event of an inconsistency, certain listed international environmental agreements take precedence over the NAFTA (Article 104), but parties must choose the actions least inconsistent with NAFTA obligations. The NAFTA also includes a preference for NAFTA dispute resolution procedures when disputes concern measures adopted or maintained to protect human, animal, or plant life or health, or the environment, and raise factual issues concerning the environment, health, safety, or conservation (NAFTA, Article (4)).

Other regimes more aggressively assert their primacy. Some human rights bodies have asserted the priority of human rights guarantees over other international law. The UN Committee on Economic, Social and Cultural Rights in a 1998 statement on globalization and economic, social, and cultural rights,[99] declared that the realms of trade, finance, and investment are in no way exempt from human rights obligations. The Committee's concerns were raised a second time in a statement urging WTO members to adopt a human rights approach to trade matters, recognizing the fact that 'promotion and protection of human rights is the first responsibility of Governments'.[100]

The former Sub-Commission on Promotion and Protection of Human Rights similarly affirmed the 'centrality and primacy' of human rights obligations in all areas of governance and development, including international and regional trade, investment and financial policies, agreements, and practices.[101] The Commission on Human Rights has asserted

---

[97] See eg *EC Measures Concerning Meat and Meat Products (Hormones)*, Panel Report, WT/DS26/R/USA, WT/DS48/R/CAN (18 August 1997) and *Beef Hormone Case*, Appellate Body Report, WT/DS26/AB/R, WT/DS48/AB/R (16 January 1998); *United States—Import Prohibition of Certain Shrimp and Shrimp Products*, Appellate Body Report, WT/DS58/AB/R (12 October 1998); *United States—Standards for Reformulated and Conventional Gasoline*, Appellate Body Report, WT/DS2/AB/R (29 April 1996); *United States—Restriction on the Imports of Tuna*, GATT Panel Report, (1991) 30 ILM 1594.

[98] See World Summit on Sustainable Development, Plan of Implementation (2002) para 91.

[99] Statement on Globalization (May 1998) (1999) 6 *IHRR* 1176.

[100] Statement to the Third Ministerial Conference of the World Trade Organization (1999), UN Doc E/C.12/1999/9 of 26 November 1999, para 6.

[101] *Human rights as the primary objective of trade, investment and financial policy*, E/CN.4/Sub.2/RES/1998/12, 20 August 1998.

that 'the exercise of the basic rights of the people of debtor countries to food, housing, clothing, employment, education, health services and a healthy environment cannot be subordinated to the implementation of structural adjustment policies and economic reforms arising
from the debt'.[102] The UN Special Rapporteurs on Globalization and Its Impact on the Full
Enjoyment of Human Rights forthrightly assert that 'the primacy of human rights law over
all other regimes of international law is a basic and fundamental principle that should not be
departed from'.[103]

The assertion of the primacy of human rights law has only limited support in State
practice and jurisprudence. The Inter-American Court of Human Rights held in the case
of *Sawhoyamaxa* v *Paraguay* that compliance with a bilateral investment treaty between
Paraguay and Germany could not provide a defence to alleged violations of the human
rights of an indigenous community. According to the Court: 'the enforcement of bilateral
commercial treaties...should always be compatible with the American Convention, which
is a multilateral treaty on human rights that stands in a class of its own and that generates
rights for individual human beings and does not depend entirely on reciprocity among
States'.[104] If such asserted primacy is more widely accepted, it means that there is no *lex
specialis* for trade or other fields where States can claim to be free from human rights obligations. It could also profoundly impact the work of all international organizations, which
commonly claim to be governed only by their constituting legal instruments and the mandate therein conferred.

Other treaties contain specific provisions establishing priorities of application or hierarchies. For example, UNCLOS Article 311 establishes the agreement of the parties to
maintain the basic principle of the common heritage of mankind 'and that they shall not
be party to any agreement in derogation thereof'. Article 311(3) further holds that States
parties may not conclude agreements that would derogate from a provision if the agreement would impact the effective execution of the object and purpose of the Convention
or affect the application of its basic principles. The Convention on Biological Diversity,
Article 22, establishes its relationship with other international conventions in force, providing that rights and duties under them shall not be affected, 'except where the exercise of
those rights and obligations would cause a serious damage or threat to biological diversity'.
Specific reference is made to implementing the Convention consistent with rights and
obligations of States under the law of the sea.

IV. 'SOFT LAW'

The use of non-binding normative instruments in several fields of international law is
widespread (Shelton, 2000). There is no accepted definition of 'soft law' but it usually refers
to any international instrument other than a treaty containing principles, norms, standards, or other statements of expected behaviour. The term 'soft law' is also sometimes
employed to refer to the content of a binding instrument. Some recent multilateral treaties
contain weak commitments that may be considered 'soft law' if the term is applied to the

---

[102] Effects of structural adjustment policies and foreign debt on the full enjoyment of all human rights,
particularly economic, social and cultural rights, E/CN4/RES/2000/821, 27 April 2000.

[103] 'Globalization and its impact on the full enjoyment of human rights', preliminary report submitted by J
Oloka-Onyango and Deepika Udagama, E/CN4/Sub2/2000/13, 15 June 2000.

[104] Inter-American Court of Human Rights, *Sawhoyamaxa Indigenous Community* v *Paraguay, Merits,
Reparations and Costs*, Judgment of 29 March 2006, Ser C, no 146, para 140.

content of the obligation.[105] In fact, the term 'soft law' seems more appropriate for use when referring to the more hortatory or promotional language of certain treaty provisions than when applied to instruments concluded in non-binding form, because treaties are legally binding even if specific commitments are drafted in general or weak terms.

In many cases, hard law instruments can be distinguished from soft law by internal provisions and final clauses, although the characteristics of each are increasingly difficult to identify. Recently, supervisory organs have been created to oversee compliance with non-binding norms. The Commission on Sustainable Development, for example, supervises implementation of Agenda 21, the plan of action adopted in 1992 at the Rio Conference on Environment and Development. In other instances, States have been asked to submit reports on compliance with declarations and programmes of action, in a manner that mimics if it does not duplicate the mechanisms utilized in treaties.

Some scholars have distinguished hard law and soft law by stating that breach of law gives rise to legal consequences while breach of a political norm gives rise to political consequences. Such a distinction is not always easy to make. Testing normativity based on consequences can be confusing since breaches of law may give rise to consequences that may be politically motivated. A government that recalls its ambassador can either be expressing political disapproval of another State's policy on an issue, or sanctioning non-compliance with a legal norm. Terminating foreign assistance also may be characterized either way. Even binding UN Security Council resolutions based on a threat to the peace do not necessarily depend upon a violation of international law.

Assertions that States are bound by law require identifying the process by which legal rules and principles are authoritatively created. If States expect compliance and in fact comply with rules and principles contained in soft law instruments as well as they do with norms contained in treaties and custom, then perhaps the concept of international law, or the list of sources of international law, requires expansion. Alternatively, it may have to be conceded that legal obligation is not as significant a factor in State behaviour as some would think. A further possibility is that law remains important and States choose a soft law form for specific reasons related to the requirements of the problem being addressed and unrelated to the expectation of compliance.

In respect to 'relative normativity', scholars debate whether binding instruments and non-binding ones are strictly alternative or whether they are two ends on a continuum from legal obligation to complete freedom of action, making some such instruments more binding than others. If and how the term 'soft law' should be used depends in large part on whether one adopts the binary or continuum view of international law. To many, the line between law and not-law may appear blurred. Treaty mechanisms are including more 'soft' obligations, such as undertakings to endeavour to strive to cooperate. Non-binding instruments in turn are incorporating supervisory mechanisms traditionally found in hard law texts. Both types of instrument may have compliance procedures that range from soft to hard. Some case law refers to UN resolutions as having 'a certain legal value' but one that 'differs considerably' from one resolution to another.[106]

Non-binding norms have complex and potentially large impact on the development of international law. Customary law, for example, one of the two main sources of international

---

[105] Eg ICESCR (1966), Article 2(1): each State party 'undertakes to take steps, individually and through international assistance and co-operation, especially economic and technical, to the maximum of its available resources, with a view to achieving progressively the full realization of the rights recognized...by all appropriate means, including particularly the adoption of legislative measures'.

[106] *Texaco Overseas Petroleum Co v Libyan Arab Republic*, Arbitral Award (1977) 53 ILR 422; (1978) 17 ILM 28–9.

legal obligation, requires compliance (State practice) not only as a result of the obligation, but as a constitutive, essential part of the process by which the law is formed. In recent years, non-binding instruments sometimes have provided the necessary statement of legal obligation (*opinio juris*) to evidence the emergent custom and have assisted to establish the content of the norm. The process of drafting and voting for non-binding normative instruments also may be considered a form of State practice.

The reality seems to be a dynamic interplay between soft and hard obligations similar to that which exists between international and national law. In fact, it is rare to find soft law standing in isolation; instead, it is used most frequently either as a precursor to hard law or as a supplement to a hard law instrument. Soft law instruments often serve to allow treaty parties to authoritatively resolve ambiguities in a binding text or fill in gaps. This is part of an increasingly complex international system with variations in forms of instruments, means, and standards of measurement that interact intensely and frequently, with the common purpose of regulating behaviour within a rule of law framework. The development of complex regimes is particularly evident in international management of commons areas, such as the high seas and Antarctica, and in ongoing intergovernmental cooperative arrangements. For the latter, the memorandum of understanding has become a common form of undertaking, perhaps 'motivated by the need to circumvent the political constraints, economic costs, and legal rigidities that often are associated with formal and legally binding treaties' (Johnston, 1997, p xxiv).

From the perspective of State practice, it seems clear that resolutions, codes of conduct, conference declarations, and similar instruments are not law, soft or hard, albeit they may be related to or lead to law in one manner or another. States and other actors generally draft and agree to legally non-binding instruments advertently, knowingly. They make a conscious decision to have a text that is legally binding or not. In other words, for practitioners, governments, and intergovernmental organizations, there is not a continuum of instruments from soft to hard, but a binary system in which an instrument is entered into as law or as not-law. The not-law can be politically binding, morally binding, and expectations can be extremely strong of compliance with the norms contained in the instrument, but the difference between a legally binding instrument and one that is not appears well understood and acted upon by government negotiators. Although a vast amount of resolutions and other non-binding texts includes normative declarations, so-called soft law is not law or a formal source of norms. Such instruments may express trends or a stage in the formulation of treaty or custom, but law does not have a sliding scale of bindingness nor does desired law become law by stating its desirability, even repeatedly.

Despite their limited juridical effect, non-binding instruments have an essential and growing role in international relations and in the development of international law. Such instruments may (1) precede and help form international customary and treaty law; (2) fill in gaps in international legal instruments and further define existing custom; (3) form part of the subsequent State practice that can be utilized to interpret treaties; and (4) substitute for legal obligation when on-going relations make formal treaties too costly and time-consuming or otherwise unnecessary. In the first three categories, non-binding instruments are often linked in one way or another to binding ones. The last category is perhaps the most interesting, because the extent to which members of the international community are willing to accept informal commitments and non-binding expressions of expected behaviour in their relations with others may reflect a maturing of the legal system and international society.

The first category posits that non-binding norms precede binding ones. It is evident that compliance with non-binding norms can lead to the formation of customary international law. In recent years, non-binding instruments sometimes have provided the necessary statement of legal obligation (*opinio juris*) to precede or accompany State practice, assisting in establishing the content of the norm.[107]

The adoption of non-binding normative instruments also can and often does lead to similar or virtually identical norms being codified in subsequent binding agreements. Indeed, the process of negotiating and drafting non-binding instruments can greatly facilitate the achievement of the consensus necessary to produce a binding multilateral agreement. In the human rights field, nearly all recent multilateral conventions have been preceded by adoption of a non-binding declaration. In environmental law, this has been the case with the Rotterdam Convention on Prior Informed Consent (1998).

The second category considers that non-binding instruments act interstitially to complete or supplement binding agreements. Sometimes this is foreseen in the agreement itself, eg the Bonn Convention on Migratory Species of Wild Animals (1979), the Antarctic Treaty (1959) regime, and agreements of the International Atomic Energy Agency (IAEA) concerning non-proliferation of nuclear weapons.[108] In other instances, the non-binding accords may appear relatively independent and free-standing, but upon examination make reference to existing treaty obligations, as is the case for example, with the Helsinki Accords that led to the Organization for Security and Cooperation in Europe (still lacking a treaty basis) and the Zangger Committee for multilateral weapons control.

In the third category are those non-binding instruments that are adopted by States parties to 'authoritatively interpret' broad and undefined treaty obligations. The examples of the Inter-American and Universal Declarations of Human Rights, as they relate to the human rights provisions of the OAS and UN Charters, and the more recent ILO Declaration on Fundamental Principles and Rights at Work can be cited here. One could add the General Comments[109] of various human rights treaty bodies, albeit the interpretation is accomplished by an independent treaty body conferred that authority and not by the States parties directly. While they are not legally-binding, General Comments are 'today one of the potentially most significant and influential tools available to each of the six UN human rights treaty bodies in their endeavours to deepen the understanding and strengthen the influence of international human rights norms.'[110] Some States have criticized particular General Comments, but national courts have looked to them in some cases[111] to understand and apply vague and broadly-worded human rights norms. The World Bank Operational Standards also seem intended to give guidance to employees in furthering the mandate of the World Bank.

Non-binding instruments are used by courts as well. The International Court of Justice often refers to texts adopted by the International Law Commission, especially the Articles on State responsibility. The European Court of Human Rights cites to resolutions and declarations adopted by the Council of Europe and other international organizations. National courts invoke the Universal Declaration of Human Rights and the Stockholm Declaration on the Human Environment, among other normative non-binding texts.

---

[107] Eg the UN General Assembly ban on Driftnet Fishing in UNGA Res 46/215 (20 December 1991).

[108] IAEA, The Structure and Content of Agreements Between the Agency and States Required in Connection with the Treaty on the Non-Proliferation of Nuclear Weapons, IAEA Doc INFCIRC/153 (May 1971).

[109] A General Comment is 'a formal statement of [a Committee's] understanding on an issue which arises out of the provisions of a treaty whose implementation it supervises', an understanding 'to which it attaches major importance'. See Alston, 2001, p 764.

[110] Ibid, at p 773.

[111] Eg *Government of the Republic of South Africa et al* v *Grootboom*, Constitutional Court of South Africa Case 11/00 (4 October 2000).

Finally, there are some instances of free-standing normative instruments that are neither related to nor intended to develop into binding agreements. The proliferating Memoranda of Understanding generally can be included here, along with non-binding export control guidelines developed by international weapons suppliers and the guidelines concerning money laundering adopted by the Financial Action Task Force (FATF).

States and other actors adopt non-binding normative instruments for a variety of reasons. In some cases that is all they can do in the given setting. International organizations in which much of the modern standard-setting takes place generally do not have the power to adopt binding texts. In addition, non-State actors can sign on, participate, and be targets of regulation, which is much more difficult to do with treaties. Non-binding instruments are faster to adopt, easier to change, and more useful for technical matters that may need rapid or repeated revision. This is particularly important when the subject matter may not be ripe for treaty action because of scientific uncertainty or lack of political consensus. Finally, non-binding texts serve to avoid domestic political battles because they do not need ratification.

In some instances, compliance with non-binding norms and instruments is extremely good and probably would not have been better if the norms were contained in a binding text. In fact, in many cases the choice would not have been between a binding and a non-binding text, but between a non-binding text and no text at all. In instances where the choice is presented, there is some evidence that there may be less compliance with non-binding norms, but that the content of the instrument is likely to be more ambitious and far-reaching than would be the product of treaty negotiations, so the overall impact may still be more positive with a non-binding than a binding instrument.

The considerable recourse to and compliance with non-binding norms may represent a maturing of the international system. The on-going relationships among States and other actors, deepening and changing with globalization, create a climate that may diminish the felt need to include all expectations between States in formal legal instruments. Not all arrangements in business, neighbourhoods, or in families are formalized, but are often governed by informal social norms and voluntary, non-contractual arrangements. Non-binding norms or informal social norms can be effective and offer a flexible and efficient way to order responses to common problems. They are not law and they do not need to be in order to influence conduct in the desired manner.

V. CONCLUSION

The growing complexity of the international legal system is reflected in the increasing variety of forms of commitment adopted to regulate State and non-State behaviour in regard to an ever-growing number of transnational problems. The various international actors create and implement a range of international commitments, some of which are in legal form, others of which are contained in non-binding instruments. The lack of a binding form may reduce the options for enforcement in the short term (ie no litigation), but this does not deny that there can exist sincere and deeply held expectations of compliance with the norms contained in the non-binding form.

What has been striking in recent years has been the growing role of international courts and quasi-judicial tribunals in aggregating to themselves a strong role in normative development and the creation of hierarchy among norms. International tribunals have begun identifying norms *jus cogens*, usually without pointing to or supplying evidence on which they have based their conclusion that the norm in question has been accepted as peremptory by the international community of States as a whole. It thus appears to be a rather subjective determination. For the most part States have not objected, although extreme efforts on the part of some in the Bush administration to re-define narrowly what constitutes torture challenged the very prohibition of the practice, whether or not it is prohibited by *jus cogens*. The Inter-American Court has been the most forceful in pressing its competence to identify peremptory norms and to add other norms to the prohibitions of genocide and torture accepted by other courts. International tribunals have also been willing to assess the extent to which norms contained in non-binding instruments have a juridical status as custom or general principles of law. The latter function seems more in keeping with the traditional role of international courts. In contrast, declaring *jus cogens* by judicial fiat seems to draw the courts into legislating unnecessarily, but thus far no consequences have followed from any of the declarations that have been made.

REFERENCES

AKEHURST, M (1974–5), 'The Hierarchy of the Sources of International Law', 47 *BYIL* 273.

ALSTON, P (2001), 'The Historical Origins of the Concept of "General Comments" in Human Rights Law', in Boisson de Chazournes, L and Gowlland-Debbas, V (eds), *The International Legal System in Quest of Equity and Universality: Liber Amoricum Georges Abi-Saab* (Leiden: Brill Publishers), p 763.

CASSESE, A (2008), 'The Italian Court of Cassation Misapprehends the Notion of War Crimes', 6 *Journal of International Criminal Justice* 1077.

CLAPHAM, A (2007), 'The *Jus Cogens* Prohibition of Torture and the Importance Sovereign State Immunity', in Kohen, MG (ed), *Promoting Justice, Human Rights and Conflict Resolution through International Law, Liber Amicorum Lucius Caflisch* (The Hague: Martinus Nijhoff), p 151.

DANILENKO, G (1991), 'International *Jus cogens*: Issues of Law-Making', 2 *EJIL* 42.

DANNER, AM (2000), 'Constructing a Hierarchy of Crimes in International Criminal Law Sentencing', 87 *Va L Rev* 415.

DE SENA, P and DE VITTOR, F (2005), 'State Immunity and Human Rights: The Italian Supreme Court Decision on the Ferrini Case', 16 *EJIL* 89.

DUPUY, P-M (1995), *Droit international public*, 3rd edn (Paris: Dalloz).

HENKIN, L (1989-IV), 'International Law: Politics, Values and Functions', 216 *Recueil des Cours* 9.

JOHNSTON, DM (1997), *Consent and Commitment in the World Community* (Irvington-on-Hudson, NY: Transnational).

KEARNEY, RD and DALTON, RE (1970), 'The Treaty on Treaties', 64 *AJIL* 495.

KELSEN, H (1935), 'The Pure Theory of Law', 51 *LQR* 517.

KOSKENNIEMI, M (1997), 'Hierarchy in International Law: A Sketch', 8 *EJIL* 566.

LUKASHUK, II (1989), 'The Principle Pacta Sunt Servanda and the Nature of Obligation under International Law', 83 *AJIL* 513.

MURRAY, R and EVANS MD (2001), *Documents of the African Commission on Human and Peoples' Rights* (Oxford: Hart Publishing).

OXMAN, B (2002), 'Complementary Agreements and Compulsory Jurisdiction', 95 *AJIL* 277.

PAUWELYN, J (2001), 'The Role of Public International Law in the WTO: How Far Can We Go', 95 *AJIL* 535.

ROBLEDO, AG (1982–III), 'Le Ius Cogens International: Sa Genese, Sa Nature, Ses Fonctions', 172 *Recueil des Cours* 17.

SAFRIN, S (2002), 'Treaties in Collision? The Biosafety Protocol and the World Trade Organization Agreements', 96 *AJIL* 606.

SALCEDO, JAC (1997), 'Reflections on the Hierarchy of Norms in International Law', 8 *EJIL* 583.

SHELTON, D (2003), 'Boundaries of Human Rights Jurisdiction in Europe', 13 *Duke JI & CL* 95.

—— (ed) (2000), *Commitment and Compliance: The Role of Non-Binding Norms in the International Legal System* (Oxford: Oxford University Press).

SIMMA, B (2009), 'Universality of International Law from the Perspective of a Practitioner', 20 *EJIL* 265.

TOMUSCHAT, C (1993), 'Obligations Arising for States Without or Against Their Will', (1993–IV) 241 *Recueil des Cours* 191.

WEIL, P (1983), 'Towards Relative Normativity in International Law?', 77 *AJIL* 413.

FURTHER READING

The following works provide useful amplification of the topics surveyed in this chapter.

D'AMATO, A (1990), 'It's a Bird, It's a Plane, It's Jus Cogens', 9 *Conn JIL* 1.

DE HOOGH, A (1996), *Obligations Erga Omnes and International Crimes* (The Hague: Kluwer Law International).

DE WET, E and VIDMAR, J (eds) (2012), *Hierarchy in International Law: The Place of Human Rights* (New York: Oxford University Press).

HANNIKAINEN, L (1988), *Peremptory Norms (Jus cogens) in International Law* (Lakimiesliiton Kustannus: Finnish Lawyer's Publishing Co).

RAGAZZI, M (1997), *The Concept of International Obligations Erga Omnes* (Oxford: Clarendon Press).

SZTUCKI, J (1974), *Jus Cogens and the Vienna Convention on the Law of Treaties* (Vienna: Springer).

TOMUSCHAT, C and THOUVENIN, J (eds) (2006), *The Fundamental Rules of the International Legal Order: Jus Cogens and Obligations Erga Omnes* (The Hague: Martinus Nijhoff).

7

THE PRACTICAL WORKING
OF THE LAW OF TREATIES

Malgosia Fitzmaurice

SUMMARY

This chapter considers key structural questions and fundamental problems relating to the law of treaties. The structural matters considered include: the concept of a treaty; the anatomy of treaties (including the making of treaties; authority to conclude treaties; expression of consent to be bound; invalidity of treaties (non-absolute grounds for invalidity of treaties, absolute grounds for invalidity of treaties, amendment and modification); suspension and termination.

The key issues addressed include the scope of legal obligation (the principle *pacta sunt servanda*, treaties, and third States); interpretation and reservation to treaties (including interpretative declarations); and finally, problems concerning the grounds for termination (supervening impossibility and material breach). The chapter takes into consideration the theory and practice of the law of treaties, with broad analysis of the case law of various international courts and tribunals, with special emphasis on jurisprudence of the International Court of Justice.

I. INTRODUCTION

Treaties are one of the means through which States deal with each other and a precise method of regulating relations between States. Treaties almost exclusively regulate some areas of international law, such as environmental law, while they are of the utmost importance in others, such as international economic relations, and play a decisive role in the field of human rights. International trade and international investments as well as international communication are unimaginable without treaties. Thus knowledge of the law of treaties is essential to an understanding of how international relations and international law work. That law is codified in the 1969 Vienna Convention on the Law of Treaties (the VCLT), the provisions of which will be presented and analysed in this chapter.

II. BASIC CONCEPTS AND STRUCTURES

A. WHAT IS A TREATY?

VCLT Article 2(2) defines a treaty as '[a]n international agreement concluded between States in written form and governed by international law, whether embodied in a single instrument or in two or more related instruments and whatever its particular designation'.

The term 'treaty' is used generically (Aust, 2013, p 10) and a treaty may be described in a multitude of ways. The International Law Commission (ILC) said:

> In addition to a 'treaty', 'convention', and 'protocol', one not infrequently finds titles such as 'declaration', 'charter', 'covenant', 'pact', 'act', '*statute*', 'agreement', 'concordat', whilst names like 'declaration', 'agreement', and '*modus vivendi*' may well be found given both to formal and less formal types of agreements. As to the latter, their nomenclature is almost illimitable, even if some names such as 'agreement', 'exchange of notes', 'exchange of letters', 'memorandum of agreement', or 'agreed minute', may be more common than others… there is no exclusive or systematic use of nomenclature for particular types of transaction.[1]

The Vienna Convention does not require that a treaty be in any particular form or comprise any particular elements so if there is a dispute concerning the status of a document— eg a joint communiqué—as a treaty, an objective test is used to determine the question, taking into account its actual terms and the particular circumstances in which it was made. For example, minutes of a meeting can comprise a treaty. In the *Qatar* v *Bahrain* case the International Court of Justice (ICJ) said:

> The Court does not find it necessary to consider what might have been the intentions of the Foreign Minister of Bahrain or, for that matter those of the Foreign Minister of Qatar. The two ministers signed a text recording commitment accepted by their Governments, some of which were to be given an immediate application. Having signed such a text, the Foreign Minister of Bahrain, is not in the position subsequently to say that he intended to subscribe only to a 'statement recording political understanding', and not to an 'international agreement'.[2]

The difficulty (if not impossibility) of formulating a firm definition of a treaty and consequently the reliance on the frequently inconsistent pronouncements of international courts and tribunals contributes to uncertainty for States regarding international obligations. Such a situation is exemplified by the recent Judgment of the International Tribunal for the Law of the Sea (ITLOS) in the *Bangladesh/Myanmar* case[3] where the legal character of minutes was again at issue. In this case, the ITLOS, having examined the two sets of Agreed Minutes in question, proceeded in an entirely different manner from the ICJ and reached the opposite conclusion. There are fundamental differences in reasoning relating to essentially very similar sets of documents. The ICJ was firmly of the view that the Agreed Minutes in question created rights and obligations for States and thus constituted an international agreement. The ITLOS, on the other hand, having

---

[1] *YBILC* (1966), vol II (part two), p 188.

[2] *Maritime Delimitation and Territorial Questions between Qatar and Bahrain, Jurisdiction and Admissibility, Judgment, ICJ Reports 1994*, p 112, para 27. See also *Land and Maritime Boundary between Cameroon and Nigeria (Cameroon v Nigeria; Equatorial Guinea Intervening), Judgment, ICJ Reports 2002*, p 303 in which the Court analysed two documents: 1975 Maroua Declaration and the 1971 Youndé II Declaration. On the basis of the manner in which these Declarations were concluded (signed by the Heads Cameroon and Nigeria), the Court stated as follows: '[t]he Court considers that the Maroua Declaration constitutes an international agreement concluded between States in written form and tracing a boundary; it is thus governed by international law and constitutes a treaty in the sense of the Vienna Convention on the Law of Treaties… and which in any case reflects customary international law in this respect' (para 263).

[3] *Delimitation of the Maritime Boundary in the Bay of Bengal (Bangladesh/Myanmar), Judgments*, ITLOS Reports 2012, nyr.

analysed two sets of fairly detailed and precise Agreed Minutes (dating from 1974 and 2008) was of the view they were nothing more than a record of two meetings. Such disparities in decisions regarding very similar cases must cause uncertainty and tension in inter-State relations.

Another fundamental difference between the findings relates to the question of the intention of the Parties. In the *Qatar* v *Bahrain* case the ICJ was adamant that the intentions of States as to the nature of an instrument was of no interest to the Court, which based its decision entirely on the objective text of the document before it. The ITLOS, however, took a different stand on this matter. It said:

> From the beginning of the discussions Myanmar made it clear that it did not intend to enter into a separate agreement on the delimitation of territorial sea and that it wanted a comprehensive agreement covering the territorial sea, the exclusive economic zone and the continental shelf.[4]

The ITLOS also stressed that the fact that both Parties not having submitted the Agreed Minutes to their domestic constitutional procedures in regard to the conclusion of treaties was an indication that the Agreed Minutes were not to be considered as legally binding.[5] According to VCLT Article 46, however, a State may not invoke the fact that its consent to be bound by a treaty has been expressed in violation of a provision of its internal law regarding competence to conclude treaties as invalidating its consent unless that violation was manifest and concerned a rule of its internal law of fundamental importance. This was confirmed by the ICJ in the *Cameroon* v *Nigeria* case.[6] Again, there seems to be a difference of approach between the ICJ and ITLOS on this point.

Since a treaty is a method of creating binding legal obligations, there must also be an intention to create legal relations. The Rapporteur of the ILC stated that the element is implicitly present in the phrase 'governed by international law'.[7] There are some international acts that may assume the form of international agreements but which were never intended to create legal obligations, such as the 1975 Final Act of the Conference on Security and Cooperation in Europe.[8]

Such Acts are sometimes called 'soft law'[9] and their legal status is not clear. However, as they are not legally binding, they are not enforceable in the courts. They cannot be ignored, however, since soft law may 'harden' into a treaty[10] or become a norm of international customary law. Some authors see 'soft law' as a more flexible alternative to treaty-making (Boyle, 2000) though others consider the whole concept misconceived, both in that if it is not binding, it is not law, and that it creates an expectation of compliance while simultaneously undermining the authority of law (Weil, 1983).

---

[4] Ibid, para 92.   [5] Ibid, para 97.

[6] *Land and Maritime Boundary between Cameroon and Nigeria (Cameroon v Nigeria: Equatorial Guinea Intervening), Judgment, ICJ Reports 2002*, p 303, para 265.

[7] Fourth Report on the Law Treaties, *YBILC* (1965), vol II, p 12.

[8] The Act stated that it was not eligible for registration under UN Charter Article 102 and was generally understood not to have binding force. The failure to register a treaty under UN Charter Article 102 does not mean that the instrument in question is not a treaty, whilst the act of registration does not mean that it is. For example, the 1957 Declaration by Egypt concerning the nationalization of the Suez Canal was registered by the Egyptian Government but was not a treaty.

[9] Other examples include the 1972 Stockholm Declaration on Human Environment and the 1992 Rio Declaration on Environment and Development. On soft law generally, see Ch 5 of this book.

[10] Eg the 1988 Baltic Sea Ministerial Declaration and the 1992 Baltic Sea Declaration hardened into the 1992 Convention on the Protection of the Baltic Sea and the Baltic Sea Area ('The Helsinki Convention').

Finally, in the *Nuclear Test* cases,[11] the ICJ made it clear that unilateral statements of States can have binding effect if the intention that they be legally binding is clear; that there is clear evidence regarding the circumstances in which they are made; and that the question is approached with due caution. However, it has been argued that there is little evidence to support the Court's view and, in any case, there was insufficient evidence of intent on the facts of the case.

B. THE VIENNA CONVENTIONS

The 1969 Vienna Convention on the Law of Treaties was opened for signature on 23 April 1969 and entered into force on 27 January 1980. It was the product of the International Law Commission[12] and the UN Conference on the Law of Treaties that met at Vienna from 26 March to 24 May 1968, and from 9 April to 22 May 1969. The subsequent 1986 Vienna Convention between States and International Organizations or Between Organizations adapts these rules to its subject matter and although not in force is considered to be applicable as law. Finally, the 1978 Vienna Convention on Succession of States in Respect of Treaties is in force but not all of its rules are considered to represent customary international law. The present chapter is based mainly on the provisions of the 1969 Vienna Convention.

1. The scope of the Vienna Convention

The Vienna Convention regulates treaties concluded between States (Article 1) and in written form (Article 2(1)(a)). This does not mean that oral agreements have no effect under international law or that principles found in the VCLT do not apply to such agreements, merely that they are not governed by the VCLT itself. Questions of succession to treaties, State responsibility, and the effect of the outbreak of hostilities on treaties are also excluded from its scope (Article 73). Furthermore, the Convention is not retroactive and only applies to treaties concluded after its entry into force (Article 4). It acts as a residual rule, ie it is applicable unless a particular treaty provides otherwise; or unless the parties agree otherwise; or if a different intention is otherwise established. Although the VCLT does not apply to treaties between States and international organizations *per se*, those of its provisions that reflect rules of international customary law do apply to such treaties (Article 3(b)). Moreover, the provisions of the VCLT apply as between States parties to the VCLT as regards treaties to which other forms of subjects of international law (such as international organizations) are also parties (Article 3(c)).

2. The Vienna Convention and customary law

There are two problems concerning the relationship between the Vienna Convention and international customary law: (i) which provisions of the Vienna Convention codified customary law and which constituted progressive development; and (ii) how does customary law relating to treaties operate?

It is difficult, if not impossible, to answer the first of these questions. Certain provisions of the Convention that represented progressive development at the time of its signing—such as reservations and modification of treaties—were probably already within the body of international customary law by the time of its entry into force (Sinclair, 1984, pp 10–21).

---

[11] *Nuclear Tests (Australia v France), Judgment, ICJ Reports 1974*, p 253, paras 42–3. The need for intention was reiterated by the Court in *Frontier Dispute, Judgment, ICJ Reports 1986*, p 554, para 39.

[12] The Special Rapporteurs of the Commission were Professors Briely and Lauterpacht, Sir G Fitzmaurice and Sir H Waldock.

In the *Gabčíkovo-Nagymaros Project* case the ICJ identified the rules concerning termination and suspension of treaties as codificatory[13] and in the *Kasikili/Sedudu Island* case said that the rules of interpretation reflected customary international law.[14]

As to the second problem, Articles 3(b), 4, 38, and 43 combine to provide that when the provisions of the Convention are inapplicable the rules of international customary law (or in some instances general principles of law) with the same legal content may be applicable. The most significant is Article 4 concerning the non-retroactive effect of provisions of the VCLT that were not reflective of customary law.

III. THE ANATOMY OF A TREATY

A. THE MAKING OF TREATIES

Treaties are by far the most important tools of regulating international relations. They may be concluded between States, States and international organizations, and between international organizations. International organizations, in particular the UN, play a most important role in international law-making as initiators of treaties and as a source of expertise.

B. AUTHORITY TO CONCLUDE TREATIES

VCLT Articles 7 and 8 concern the making of treaties. A most important issue is that of full powers,[15] the holder of which is authorized to adopt and authenticate the text of a treaty and to express the consent of the State to be bound by a treaty, although there are a growing number of treaties, particularly bilateral treaties, which are concluded in a simplified form that does not require the production of full powers (for example exchange of notes). The general rule expressed in the VCLT (Article 7 paragraph 1(a) and (b)) is that a person is considered as representing a State for the purpose of expressing the consent of the State to be bound by it if he or she produces appropriate full powers or it appears from the practice of the States concerned or from other circumstances that their intention was to consider that person as representing the State for such purposes and to dispense with full powers. There is, however, a group of persons who by virtue of their functions and without having to produce full powers, are considered to have such authority, these being: Heads of State, Heads of Government, and Ministers for Foreign Affairs; heads of diplomatic missions, for the purpose of adoption of the text of a treaty between the accrediting State and the State to which they are accredited; representatives accredited by States to an international organization or one of its organs, for the purpose of adopting the text of a treaty in that conference, organization, or organ (Article 7(2)). The ICJ in the *Cameroon v Nigeria* case confirmed this rule.[16] In 2006 in the *Democratic Republic of Congo v Rwanda* the Court examined the powers of the 'Big Three' (the Head of State,

---

[13] *Gabčíkovo-Nagymaros Project (Hungary/Slovakia), Judgment, ICJ Reports 1997*, p 7, para 46.

[14] *Kasikili/Sedudu Island (Botswana/Namibia), Judgment, ICJ Reports 1999*, p 1045, para 18.

[15] Defined in Article 2(1)(c) as a 'Document emanating from the competent authority of a State designating a person or persons to represent a State for negotiating, adopting or authenticating the text of a treaty, for expressing consent of the State by a treaty, or for accomplishing any other acts with respect to a treaty'. See also *Case Concerning the Land and Maritime Boundary between Cameroon and Nigeria (Cameroon v Nigeria; Equatorial Guinea Intervening), Judgment, ICJ Reports 2002*, p 303.

[16] *Land and Maritime Boundary between Cameroon and Nigeria (Cameroon v Nigeria; Equatorial Guinea Intervening), Judgment, ICJ Reports 2002*, p 303, para 265.

Head of Government and Minister for Foreign Affairs) to bind the States and, after having again confirmed the 'well established rule', went on to say that: 'The Court notes, however, that with increasing frequency in modern international relations other persons representing a State in specific fields may be authorised by that State to bind it by their statements in respect to matters falling within their purview. This may be true, for example, of holders of technical ministerial portfolio exercising powers in their field of competence in the area of foreign relations, and even of certain officials.'[17]

These developments in international law were not reflected in the approach taken by the ITLOS in the *Bangladesh/Myanmar* case where it adhered to the traditional rule, saying that:

> ...the head of the Burmese delegation, Commodore Hlaing, a naval officer, could not be considered as representing Myanmar for the purpose of expressing consent to be bound by a treaty as he was not one of the holders of high-ranking office in the State referred to in article 7, paragraph 2, of the Vienna Convention. Furthermore, the circumstances described in article 7, paragraph 1, of the Vienna Convention do not apply in the present case since Commodore Hliang did not have full powers issued by the Government of Myanmar and there were no circumstances to suggest that it was the intention of Myanmar and Bangladesh to dispense of full powers.[18]

Full powers have to be distinguished from credentials, which are submitted to an international organization or a government hosting an international conference by a delegate attending to negotiate a multilateral treaty. Credentials only authorize the delegate to adopt the text of a treaty and to sign a Final Act. Signing the treaty itself requires full powers or specific instructions from government. Full powers and credentials may be combined in one document.

Where an unauthorized person purports to conclude a treaty Article 8 provides that the action is without legal effect, unless subsequently confirmed by the State. On the other hand, Article 47 provides that where an authorized representative of a State expresses consent to be bound although instructed by their State not to do so, this does not invalidate that consent, unless the limitation on their authority was notified to other negotiating States beforehand.

C. EXPRESSION OF CONSENT TO BE BOUND

The role of the expression of consent by States to be bound by a treaty is to constitute a mechanism by which the treaty becomes a juridical act. According to Article 11, 'The consent of a state to be bound by a treaty may be expressed by signature, exchange of instruments constituting a treaty, ratification, acceptance, approval or accession, or by any other means if so agreed'. Article 11 lists a number of particular means of expressing consent to be bound, while also allowing parties to adopt any other means on which they agree. The precise method is, therefore, for the parties to a treaty to decide amongst themselves.

The legal effect of signature of a treaty depends upon whether or not it is subject to ratification, acceptance, or approval. If it is, then signature constitutes an intermediate step, indicating that the delegates have agreed upon the text and are willing to accept it. Signature

---

[17] *Armed Activities on the Territory of the Congo (New Application: 2002) (Democratic Republic of Congo v Rwanda) Jurisdiction of the Court and Admissibility of the Application, ICJ Reports 2006*, p 6, para 47.

[18] *Delimitation of the Maritime Boundary in the Bay of Bengal (Bangladesh/Myanmar), Judgments*, ITLOS Reports 2012, nyr, para 83.

under these circumstances does not express the final consent to be bound and the signing of a treaty does not impose any obligation on a State to ratify it or even, in the absence of an express term to this effect, to submit it to the national legislator for consideration. However, the initial signature also constitutes a juridical act in the sense that by its signature each State accepts certain legal consequences, for example under VCLT Articles 18, 24(4), and 25. The intermediate stage between signature and ratification enables States to promulgate necessary legislation or obtain necessary parliamentary approval. Ratification conforms to the democratic principle that the government should consult public opinion either in parliament or elsewhere before finally approving a treaty (Shearer, 1994, p 414).

1. Signature

Signature only expresses consent to be bound when it constitutes the final stage of a treaty-making process. Article 12 lists a variety of possible means to express consent to be bound by signature, including signature *ad referendum*. This commonly indicates either that the signatory State is currently unable to accept the terms of the treaty, or that the plenipotentiary concerned had no definitive instructions in the matter. Signature *ad referendum* becomes a full signature if subsequently confirmed by the State concerned. Article 12 also provides that initialling a treaty constitutes signature when it is established that the negotiating State so agreed.

2. Ratification

Ratification is understood as a formal, solemn act on the part of a Head of State through which approval is given and a commitment to fulfil its obligations is undertaken, although the significance of the act at the international level has changed over time. As Judge Moore said in 1924, the older view that treaties might be regarded as binding before they had been ratified was now 'obsolete, and lingers only as an echo from the past'.[19]

VCLT Article 2(1)(b) provides that: '"ratification", "acceptance", "approval" and "accession" mean in each case the international act so named whereby a state establishes on the international plane its consent to be bound by a treaty'. Despite the use of the word 'means', this does not define ratification, but indicates its effect. Article 14 provides that consent to be bound is expressed by ratification if: (a) the treaty expressly so provides; (b) the negotiating States otherwise agree that ratification is necessary; (c) the treaty has been signed subject to ratification; or (d) an intention to sign subject to ratification appears from the full powers or was expressed during negotiations.

Ratification is unconditional and, unless the treaty in question provides otherwise, is not dependent on the receipt or deposit of instruments of ratification by other States. Some support for a relatively relaxed approach to the formalities of ratification can be gleaned from the attitude of the ICJ in the *Nicaragua* case where Nicaragua's failure to ratify the Statute of the former Permanent Court of International Justice and convert 'potential commitment to effective commitment' was seen as being rectified by its ratification of the ICJ Statute.[20]

3. Accession

This means of consent to be bound is regulated by VCLT Article 15 and refers to the means by which a State expresses its consent to become a party to a treaty that it was not in a

---

[19] *Mavrommatis Palestine Concessions, Judgment No 2, 1924, PCIJ, Ser A, No 2*, at p 57.
[20] *Military and Paramilitary Activities in and against Nicaragua (Nicaragua v United States of America), Jurisdiction and Admissibility, Judgment, ICJ Reports 1984*, p 392.

position to sign.[21] A State can only accede to a treaty if the treaty so provides or the parties agree. Treaties setting up regional regimes may often permit accession by invitation.[22] Can a State accede to a treaty that is not yet in force? The International Law Commission has pointed out that:

> An examination of the most recent treaty practice shows that in practically all modern treaties which contain accession clauses the right to accede is made independent of the entry into force of a treaty, either expressly, by allowing accession to take place before the date fixed for the entry into force of the treaty, or impliedly, by making the entry into force of the treaty conditional on the deposit, *inter alia*, of instruments of accession.[23]

4. Acceptance and approval

These are recognized and widely used methods of expressing consent to be bound and are regulated by VCLT Article 14(2). There are no great differences between signature subject to acceptance or approval and signature subject to ratification. The use of these methods of consent to be bound was intended to simplify procedures by, for example, avoiding constitutional conditions that might require obtaining parliamentary authority prior to ratification. The rules applicable to ratification apply to acceptance and approval (Aust, 2013, p 100) and, unless provided otherwise, acceptance and approval have the same legal effect as ratification. Expressing consent to be bound by acceptance or approval without prior signature is analogous to accession. In many of the more recent conventions concluded under the auspices of the UN, such as the 1997 UN Convention on the Law of the Non-Navigational Uses of International Watercourses,[24] all means of consent to be bound are listed as available options.

Developments in treaty-making between States have resulted in the evolution of certain techniques, the legal character of which is unclear, but which may involve consent to be bound by a treaty being given in a more informal fashion. One such technique is the method of a 'tacit approval' which is based on a principle that a State is bound by a decision of an organ of established by a multilateral treaty unless it 'opts out'. This practice is adopted by many international agreements and has been particularly developed in treaties concluded under the auspices of the International Maritime Organization, such as the procedure of amending the annexes in the Convention on the Prevention of Pollution from Ships (MARPOL 73/78). At times, the changes to the obligations of States parties brought about by means of such informal amendment procedures can be very considerable. Therefore, in some States such changes may be submitted to a national approval procedure, as if they were a formal amendment to the treaty concerned.

Another new development regarding consent to be bound is connected to the advent of Multilateral Environmental Agreements (MEAs), which frequently empower their organs, known as the Conference of the Parties (COPs) or Meeting of the Parties (MOPs) to adopt the decisions which further develop or specify the obligations of State Parties, which were not agreed upon by the Parties at the time of the conclusion of the MEAs. The powers of the COPs/MOPS to do this are based on so-called 'enabling clauses' in the MEAs, which provide that certain obligations will be specified by these organs in such a fashion. In some cases COPs/MOPs have adopted decisions (such as the establishment of rather complex compliance mechanisms) even without an enabling clause. Therefore decisions of

---

[21] Very rarely it can be the principal means of expressing consent to be bound, as in the often cited yet isolated example of the 1928 General Act for the Pacific Settlement of International Disputes.

[22] Eg 1992 Convention on the Protection of the Marine Environment of the Baltic Sea Area.

[23] *YBILC* (1966), vol II (part two), p 199.   [24] (1997) 36 ILM 700.

COPs/MOPs can, in practice, reformulate the obligations of States without them giving their formal consent to be bound.

D. INVALIDITY OF TREATIES

The grounds for invalidity of treaties within the VCLT can be divided into two groups: relative grounds in Articles 46–50 and absolute grounds in Articles 51–3.[25] The main difference between these grounds is that the relative grounds render a treaty voidable at the insistence of an affected State whereas the absolute grounds means that the treaty is rendered void *ab initio* and without legal effect. The Vienna Convention does not differentiate between bilateral and multilateral treaties. However, in the case of bilateral treaties the legal effect of establishing a relative ground of invalidity has the same legal effect as establishing absolute invalidity: the treaty falls (Sinclair, 1984). In the case of multilateral treaties, however, establishing an absolute ground means that the treaty has no legal force at all whereas establishing a relative ground—meaning that the consent of a particular State to a multilateral treaty is vitiated—does not affect the validity of the treaty as a whole as between the other remaining parties (Article 69(4)).

Article 46 concerns the failure to comply with internal law regarding competence to conclude a treaty, and provides that this may only be a ground for invalidating consent to be bound if that failure was 'manifest'. In the *Cameroon* v *Nigeria* case, Nigeria argued that '... it should have been "objectively evident" to Cameroon, within the meaning of Article 46, paragraph 2 of the VCLT that the Nigerian Head of State did not have unlimited powers'[26] but the Court, while accepting that '[t]he rules concerning the authority to sign treaties are constitutional rules of fundamental importance', took the view that '... a limitation of a Head of State's capacity in this respect is not manifest in the sense of Article 46, paragraph 2, unless at least properly publicized. This is particularly so because Heads of States belong to the group of persons who, in accordance with Article 7, paragraph 2, of the Convention... are considered as representing the State'.[27]

Article 47 is similar, concerning cases in which the representatives purporting to conclude a treaty were acting beyond the scope of their instructions.[28] Article 48 concerns error as a vitiating ground, and follows the approach of the ICJ in the *Temple* case. In that case, Thailand argued that the boundary line indicated on a map annexed to a treaty was in error since it did not follow the watershed line that was prescribed by the treaty text. The Court rejected this argument, saying:

> It is an established rule of law that the plea of error cannot be allowed as a vitiating consent if the party advancing it contributed by its conduct or error, or could have avoided it, or the circumstances were such as to put party on notice of a possible error. The Court considers that the character and qualifications of persons who saw Annex I map on the Siamese side would alone made it difficult for Thailand to plead error in law...[29]

---

[25] Sinclair divides cases of invalidity into three groups, concerning: the capacity of the parties (Articles 46–7); the validity of consent to be bound (Articles 48–50); and the lawfulness of the object of the treaty (Articles 51–3) (Sinclair, 1984, p 160).

[26] *Land and Maritime Boundary between Cameroon and Nigeria (Cameroon* v *Nigeria; Equatorial Guinea Intervening), Judgment, ICJ Reports 2002*, p 303, para 258.

[27] *Land and Maritime Boundary between Cameroon and Nigeria (Cameroon* v *Nigeria; Equatorial Guinea Intervening), Judgment, ICJ Reports 2002*, p 303, para 265.

[28] *YBILC* (1966), vol II (part two), p 243.

[29] *Temple of Preah Vihear, Merits, Judgment, ICJ Reports 1962*, p 6 at p 26.

Articles 49 and 50 concern fraud and corruption. There is a paucity of materials relating to these Articles, though as far as corruption is concerned, the ILC observed that only an act calculated to exercise a substantial influence on the disposition of a representative to conclude a treaty could be invoked as a reason to invalidate an expression of consent that had subsequently been given.[30]

Turning from the relative to the absolute grounds for invalidity, Article 51 deals with the coercion of a representative, Article 52 the coercion of a State, and Article 53 the conflict with norms of *jus cogens*. In all these cases a treaty is void *ab initio*, in the latter case by virtue of its conflicting with international public policy (the consequences of which are addressed in Article 71). Practice in relation to all these Articles is limited. The classic example relating to Article 51, the coercion of a representative, concerns the pressure exerted by Göring and Ribbentrop upon President Hacha of Czechoslovakia to sign a treaty with Germany establishing a German protectorate over Bohemia and Moravia in 1939. There is a clear link between Article 52—the coercion of a State—and the prohibition of the use of force under international law. Iceland advanced a claim of this nature in the 1973 *Fisheries Jurisdiction* case and the ICJ stated that:

> There can be little doubt, as implied in the Charter of the United Nations and recognised in Article 52 of the Vienna Convention on the Law of Treaties, that under contemporary international law an agreement concluded under the threat or use of force is void...[31]

E. AMENDMENT AND MODIFICATION

The growth in number of multilateral treaties resulted in the necessity of devising amendment procedures and, in order to make amendment procedures more flexible, modification procedures. These are addressed in VCLT Articles 39–41. The ILC explained that amendment is a formal matter introducing changes into the treaty text whereas modification is a less formal procedure which affects only certain parties to a treaty.[32] However, in practice it is often difficult to distinguish between these two procedures (Sinclair, 1984, p 107).

Amendments to treaties should be distinguished from the revision of a treaty. Revision is a more comprehensive process resulting in changes to a treaty. However, a diplomatic conference is often needed both to revise and to amend a treaty, as, for example, in the case of the 1992 Convention on the Protection of the Marine Environment of the Baltic Sea (the '1992 Helsinki Convention').[33] Amendments are subject to approval by the parties to the treaty. However, some treaties—such as the Helsinki Convention—contain technical annexes, which may, if the treaty so provides, be amended by a simplified system whereby an amendment to an annex is deemed to have been accepted at the end of a specified period unless in the meanwhile any State party has submitted a written objection to the depositary.

---

[30] *YBILC* (1966), vol II (part two), p 244.
[31] *Fisheries Jurisdiction (United Kingdom v Iceland), Jurisdiction of the Court, Judgment, ICJ Reports 1973*, p 3, para 24. However, on the facts of the case the Court concluded that 'The history of negotiations which led up to the 1961 Exchange of Notes reveals that these instruments were freely negotiated by the interested parties on the basis of the perfect equality and freedom of decision on both sides'.
[32] *YBILC* (1966), vol II (part two), p 232.
[33] 'A conference for the purpose of a general revision of or an amendment to this Convention may be convened with the consent of the Contracting Parties or the request of the Commission' (Article 30).

F. TERMINATION AND SUSPENSION OF THE OPERATION OF TREATIES

The general provisions on suspension and termination of treaties are set out in VCLT Articles 54–9. Termination of a treaty may result from the grounds of termination that are internal to the treaty as well as from grounds external to the treaty. The 'internal' grounds will be considered here. The 'external grounds', concerning breach of obligations, will be considered later. As regards the 'internal' grounds for termination or suspension, the general rule in Article 54 is that a treaty may be terminated or a party may withdraw from a treaty in accordance with the provisions of the treaty itself or at any time by consent of all parties following consultations. Article 57 provides that the operation of a treaty with regard to all parties or to a particular party may be suspended in accordance with the provisions of the treaty in question.

Some treaties provide that they will remain in force only for a specific period of time whereas others provide for termination by a resolution of the contracting parties. As to withdrawal from a treaty, some treaties provide for a period of notice while others do not. For example, the 1992 Helsinki Convention provides that at any time after the expiry of five years from the date of its entry into force any party may, by giving written notification to the depositary, withdraw from the Convention. Withdrawal takes effect on the thirtieth day of June of the year following the year in which the depositary was notified of the withdrawal.

VCLT Article 58 provides for suspension of the operation of a multilateral treaty by agreement between certain parties only. This Article must be read in conjunction with Article 41 which provides for the modification of treaty provisions between certain parties only. Article 59 covers the case of tacit termination of a treaty. There is a particular problem concerning the relationship between tacit termination in accordance with Article 59 and Article 30, which concerns the effect of successive treaties relating to the same subject matter and which relates to cases in which the parties clearly intended the earlier treaty to be abrogated or its operation wholly suspended by the conclusion of the subsequent treaty.

IV. THE SCOPE OF LEGAL OBLIGATIONS

A. THE PRINCIPLE *PACTA SUNT SERVANDA*

The principle *pacta sunt servanda* is enshrined in Article 26 of the VCLT which provides that '[e]very treaty in force is binding upon the parties to it and must be performed by them in good faith'. Good faith is itself a legal principle and forms an integral part of the *pacta sunt servanda* principle.[34]

The fundamental importance of *pacta sunt servanda* was confirmed by the ICJ in the 1997 *Gabčíkovo-Nagymaros* case, which, generally speaking, advocated its strict observance. The case concerned the implementation of a 1977 treaty providing for the construction of a hydro-electric scheme along stretches of the Danube in Hungary and Slovakia. Hungary argued that the conduct of both parties indicated that they had repudiated this bilateral treaty, which, therefore, had come to an end. The Court, however, took the view that the reciprocal wrongful conduct of both parties 'did not bring the Treaty to an end nor justify its termination'.[35] The effect of breaching treaty obligations will be considered later,

---

[34] *YBILC* (1966), vol II (part two), p 211.
[35] *Gabčíkovo-Nagymaros Project (Hungary/Slovakia), Judgment, ICJ Reports 1997*, p 7, para 114.

but at this point it should be noted that, despite both parties being in fundamental breach of important elements of their treaty obligations, the Court thought the 1977 Treaty 'cannot be treated as voided by unlawful conduct'.[36]

The Court made a direct reference to the principle *pacta sunt servanda*, saying that 'What is required in the present case by the rule *pacta sunt servanda*, as reflected in Article 26 of Vienna Convention of 1969 on the Law of Treaties, is that the parties find solution within the co-operative context of the Treaty'.[37] The Court observed that the two elements in Article 26—the binding force of treaties and the performance of them in good faith—were of equal importance and that good faith implied that, 'in this case, it is the purpose of the Treaty, and the intentions of the parties in concluding it, which should prevail over its literal application. The principle of good faith obliges parties to apply it in a reasonable way in such a manner that its purpose can be realised'.[38]

These are far-reaching statements and, while they may have been particularly suited to the issues in the *Gabčíkovo-Nagymaros* case itself, it is still impossible to determine the extent to which they bear upon the application of the principle *pacta sunt servanda* in the law of treaties in general.

B. TREATIES AND THIRD STATES

The issue of treaties and non-State parties—third States—are addressed in VCLT Articles 34–8. The fundamental rule concerning the relationship between treaties and third States is expressed by the maxim *pacta tertiis nec nocent nec prosunt*, enshrined in Article 34. The Convention then deals with an obligation (Article 35) and a right (Article 36—often referred to as stipulations *in favorem tertii*) arising from a treaty for a third State. As to the obligation, the requirements are so strict that, when fulfilled, they in fact amount to the existence of a collateral agreement between the parties to the treaty and the third State and it is this collateral agreement, rather than the original treaty, which is the legal basis for the third State's obligation.

There are procedural differences in the establishment of an obligation and of a right. The third State must accept an obligation in writing, whereas in a case of the right, the assent of the third State(s) is presumed, unless the treaty provides otherwise or there are indications to the contrary. Any obligation arising for a third State can be revoked or modified only with the consent of the parties to the treaty and of the third State, unless it is established that they agreed otherwise. Any right arising for a third State can be revoked or modified only by the parties if it is established that the right was intended to be revocable or subject to modification without the consent of the third State. Caution is usually recommended when considering whether a treaty has given rise to stipulations *in favorem tertii*. As the PCIJ said:

> It cannot be lightly presumed that stipulations favourable to a third State have been adopted with the object of creating an actual right in its favour. There is, however, nothing to prevent the will of sovereign States from having this object and this effect. The question of the existence of a right acquired under an instrument drawn between other States is therefore one to be decided in each particular case: it must be ascertained whether the States which have stipulated in favour of the third State meant to create for that State an actual right which the latter has accepted as such.[39]

---

[36] Ibid, para 133.   [37] Ibid, para 142.   [38] Idem.
[39] *Free Zones of Upper Savoy and the District of Gex, Judgment, 1932, PCIJ, Ser A/B, No 46*, p 96 at pp 147–8.

Nothing in the VCLT prevents a rule set out in a treaty from becoming binding upon third States as a customary rule of international law if recognized as such (Article 37). However, the VCLT does not deal specifically with the question of whether the objective regimes created by treaties are binding only on States parties to those instruments or whether they are valid as against the entire international community—are valid *erga omnes*. Examples of such treaties would include those providing for the neutrality or demilitarization of a certain territory or area, or establishing freedom of navigation in international waterways such as the Suez Canal, Kiel Canal, and the Turkish Straits.[40]

V. GENERAL PRINCIPLES OF INTERPRETATION

A. GENERAL ISSUES

'There is no part of the law of treaties which the text writer approaches with more trepidation than the question of interpretation' (McNair, 1961). The complex issue of treaty interpretation will be discussed in the light of the work of the ILC during its codification of the law of treaties, the principles of interpretation included in the Vienna Convention, and the jurisprudence of the international and national courts and tribunals, with special regard to the case law of the ICJ. The purpose of interpretation is to establish the meaning of the text that the parties intended it to have 'in relation to circumstances with reference to which the question of interpretation has arisen' (Oppenheim, 1992).

Basing himself on the jurisprudence of the World Court,[41] the ILC's Rapporteur, Fitzmaurice (Fitzmaurice, 1951) drew up the following comprehensive set of principles of interpretation:

Principle I: actuality of textuality—that treaties are to be interpreted as they stand, on the basis of their actual texts.

Principle II: the natural and ordinary meaning—that, subject to principle of contemporaneity (where applicable), particular words and phrases are to be given their normal, natural, and unstrained meaning in the context in which they occur. This principle can only be displaced by direct evidence that the terms used are to be understood in manner different to their natural and ordinary meaning, or if such an interpretation would lead to an unreasonable or absurd result.

Principle III: integration—that treaties are to be interpreted as a whole. This principle is of fundamental importance and means that individual parts, chapters, or sections of a treaty are not to be interpreted out of their overall context.

The remaining principles take effect subject to the three principles outlined in the preceding paragraphs. There are:

Principle IV: effectiveness (ut magis valeat quam pereat)—that treaties are to be interpreted with reference to their declared or apparent objects and purposes; and particular provisions are to be interpreted so as to give them the fullest effect consistent with the

---

[40] The ILC took the view that Article 36(1) provided sufficient basis for rights to be accorded to all States and Article 38 a sufficient basis for the establishment of treaty rights and obligations *erga omnes*. For criticism see Chinkin, 1993.

[41] *YBILC* (1966), vol II (part two), p 220.

normal sense of the words and with the text as a whole in such a way that a reason and meaning can be attributed to every part of the text.

Principle V: subsequent practice—that recourse may be had to subsequent practice of parties relating to the treaty.

Principle VI: contemporaneity—that the terms of a treaty must be interpreted in the light of linguistic usage current at the time when the treaty was concluded.

In general, there are three main schools of interpretation: the subjective (the 'intention' of parties) approach; the objective (the 'textual') approach, and the teleological (or 'object and purpose') approach. These schools of interpretation are not mutually exclusive (Sinclair, 1984) and the VCLT draws on all three. It is the reconciliation of the objective and the subjective approaches that is the most difficult, controversial and, some would say, impossible, task (Koskenniemi, 1989). For the ILC, the starting point was the text rather than the intention of the parties,[42] since it presumed that the text represented a real expression of what the parties did in fact intend. It also appears that the ICJ's preferred method of interpretation is reliance on the text of a treaty.

B. PRACTICE

VCLT Article 31(1) provides:

A treaty shall be interpreted in good faith in accordance with the ordinary meaning to be given to the terms of the treaty in their context and in the light of its object and purpose.

The ICJ has acknowledged this to constitute international customary law.[43] The underlying principle is that a treaty will be interpreted in good faith. The 'rule' (in the singular) of interpretation is a procedure consisting of three elements: the text, the context, and the object and purpose. The context of a treaty is set out in some detail in Article 31(2) and embraces any instrument of relevance to the conclusion of a treaty, as well as a treaty's preamble and annexes. There is no hierarchy between the various elements of Article 31; rather, they reflect a logical progression, 'nothing more' (Aust, 2013, p 208).

The Court has consistently adhered to the textual interpretation as being the most important. In the *Libya/Chad* case, the Court stated that:

Interpretation must be based above all upon the text of a treaty. As a supplementary measure recourse may be had to means of interpretation such as the preparatory work of the treaty.[44]

Article 31 reflects the principle that a treaty has to be interpreted in good faith that is the embodiment of the principle *pacta sunt servanda*. The determination of that ordinary meaning of term is undertaken in the context of a treaty and in the light of its object and purpose. A good example is the Advisory Opinion *On the Interpretation of the Convention of 1919 Concerning Employment of Women During the Night*. Article 3 of that Convention ('women without distinction of age shall not be employed during the night in any public

---

[42] Idem.

[43] *Territorial Dispute (Libyan Arab Jamahiririya/Chad), Judgment, ICJ Reports 1994*, p 6, para 41; *Oil Platforms (Islamic Republic of Iran v United States of America), Preliminary Objections, Judgment, ICJ Reports 1996*, p 803, para 23; *Kasikili/Sedudu Island (Botswana/Namibia), Judgment, ICJ Reports 1999*, p 1045, para 18 (for which see Fox, 2010).

[44] *Territorial Dispute*, idem. The use of supplementary material is considered later in this chapter.

or private industrial undertaking, or in any branch thereof, other than an undertaking in which members of the same family are employed') left unclear its application to certain categories of women other than manual workers. The Court said:

> The wording of Article 3, considered by itself, gives rise to no difficulty; it is general in its terms and free from ambiguity or obscurity. It prohibits the employment during the night in industrial establishments of women without distinction of age. Taken by itself, it necessarily applies to the categories of women contemplated by the question submitted to the Court. If, therefore, Article 3 … is to be interpreted in such a way as not to apply to women holding posts of supervision and management and not ordinarily engaged in manual work, it is necessary to find some valid ground for interpreting the provision otherwise than in accordance with the natural sense of words. The terms of Article 3 … are in no respect inconsistent either with the title, or with the Preamble, or with any other provision of the Convention. The title refers to 'employment of women during the night'. The Preamble speaks of 'women's employment during the night'. Article 1 gives a definition of 'an industrial undertaking'. Article 2 states what is meant by the term 'night'. These provisions, therefore, do not affect the scope of Article 3, which provides that 'women shall not be employed during the night either in any public or private industrial undertaking, or in any branch thereof.[45]

This might be compared with the views of the Judge Anzilloti who argued that 'If article 3, according to the natural meaning of its terms, were really perfectly clear, it would be hardly admissible to endeavour to find an interpretation other than that which flows from the natural meaning of its terms'.[46] He thought that only the intention of the parties should have been used to determine the correct interpretation.

Another problem concerns what is to count as subsequent practice for the purposes of interpretation, the use of which is sanctioned as forming a part of the context of the treaty by Article 31(3). In the *Kasikili/Sedudu Island* case the Court adhered to the ILC's view that the subsequent practice of parties to a treaty constitutes an element to be taken into account when determining its meaning,[47] but it took a narrow approach to what comprises subsequent practice and did not take account of unilateral acts of the previous authorities of Botswana on the grounds that these were for internal purposes only and unknown to the Namibian authorities. The Court also considered the relevance of an alleged 'subsequent agreement' between the previous authorities in Namibia and Botswana as only amounting to 'collaboration' over matters concerning the border and not having any effect on the interpretation of the treaty in question.[48] However, the Court was prepared to accord such material some role, noting them as facts which supported the interpretation of the 1890 Treaty in accordance with the ordinary meaning of its terms.[49] This is a usage not explicitly foreseen by the VCLT.

The issue of the importance of subsequent practice of States arose in connection with the interpretation of the term '*comercio*' (commerce) in the 2009 *Costa Rica* v *Nicaragua* case. The Court said:

> This does not, however, signify that, where a term's meaning is no longer the same as it was at the date of conclusion, no account should ever be taken of its meaning at the time when the treaty is to be interpreted for purposes of applying it.

---

[45] *Interpretation of the Convention of 1919 Concerning Employment of Women During the Night, Advisory Opinion, 1932, PCIJ, Ser A/B, No 50,* p 365 at p 373.

[46] Dissenting Opinion of Anzilloti, ibid, p 383.

[47] *Kasikili/Sedudu Island (Botswana/Namibia), Judgment, ICJ Reports 1999,* p 1075, para 49.

[48] See generally ibid, paras 52–79.   [49] Ibid, para 80.

On the one hand, the subsequent practice of the parties, within the meaning of Article 31(3)(b) of the Vienna Convention, can result in a departure from the original intent on the basis of a tacit agreement between the parties. On the other hand, there are situations in which the parties' intent upon conclusion of the treaty was, or may be presumed to have been, to give the terms used—or some of them—a meaning or content capable of evolving, not one fixed once and for all, so as to make allowance for, among other things, developments in international law. In such instances it is indeed in order to respect the parties' common intention at the time the treaty was concluded, not to depart from it, that account should be taken of the meaning acquired by the terms in question upon each occasion on which the treaty is to be applied.[50]

C. *TRAVAUX PRÉPARATOIRES*

VCLT Article 32 makes it clear that supplementary means of interpretation—including *travaux préparatoires*, preparatory work—may be used either to confirm the meaning of the treaty or as an aid to interpretation where, following the application of Article 31, the meaning is ambiguous or obscure or leads to a result which is manifestly absurd or unreasonable. Both the *Employment of Women During the Night* Advisory Opinion and the *Kasikili/Sedudu* case, considered in n 48 in this chapter, illustrate the use of supplementary means to confirm an interpretation arrived at on the basis of Article 31. It is the use of preparatory work as a supplementary means of interpretation that gives rise to most difficulties, as is illustrated by the jurisdictional phases of the *Qatar v Bahrain* case.

The problem in this case centred on whether Qatar and Bahrain had ever entered into an agreement that would permit one of them to bring their case before the ICJ without the express approval of the other. The ICJ first decided that the fragmentary nature of the preparatory work meant that it could only be used with caution but noted that:

> ... the initial ... draft expressly authorised a seisin by one or other of the parties and that that formulation was not accepted. But the text finally adopted did not provide that the seisin of the Court could only be brought about by the two parties acting in concert, whether jointly or separately. The Court is unable to see why abandonment of a form of words corresponding to the interpretation given by Qatar ... should imply that they must be interpreted in accordance with Bahrain's thesis. As a result, it does not consider the *travaux préparatoires*, in the form in which they have been submitted to it—ie limited to the various drafts ... — can provide it with conclusive supplementary elements for the interpretation of the text adopted; whatever may have been the motives of each of the parties, the Court can only confine itself to the actual terms of the Minutes as the expression of their common intention, and to the interpretation of them which it has already given.[51]

The Court concluded that a unilateral application was legitimate. Judge Schwebel criticized this, arguing that the Court's interpretation did not reflect the common intention of the parties. He argued that the Court's view that the preparatory work did not provide conclusive supplementary elements was unconvincing, observing that:

> since deletion of the specification, 'either of the two parties may submit the matter to the International Court of Justice' in favour of the adopted provision 'the two parties may

---

[50] *Dispute regarding Navigational and Related Rights between Costa Rica and Nicaragua*, Judgment of 13 July 2009, para 64.
[51] *Maritime Delimitation and Territorial Questions between Qatar and Bahrain, Jurisdiction and Admissibility, Judgment, ICJ Reports 1995*, p 6, para 41.

submit the matter...' surely manifested Bahrain's intention that 'either of the two parties' may *not* submit the matter, the Court's inability to see so plain a point suggests to me an unwillingness to do so.[52]

He considered that 'the requisite common, ascertainable intention of the parties to author-ize unilateral reference to the Court is absent. Its absence is—or should be have been—determinative' [53] and concluded that:

> What the text and context of the Doha Minutes leaves unclear is, however, crystal clear when those Minutes are analysed with the assistance of the *travaux préparatoires*... the preparatory work of itself is not ambiguous; on the contrary, a reasonable evaluation of it sustains only the position of Bahrain.[54]

D. THE OBJECT AND PURPOSE OF A TREATY

Article 31 of the Vienna Convention stipulates that a treaty should be interpreted 'in the light of its object and purpose' but this is a vague and ill-defined term, making it an unreliable tool for interpretation. Indeed, the ILC itself voiced certain doubts as to the usefulness of this criterion, particularly as regards reservations[55] (a topic considered later in Section VI). A further problem concerns the relationship between the 'object and purpose' of a treaty and the principle of effectiveness which is considered in the following section.

E. THE PRINCIPLE OF EFFECTIVENESS

The principle of effectiveness, enshrined in the maxim *magis valeat quam pereat*, was acknowledged by the ILC, which observed that '[w]hen a treaty is open to two interpre-tations one of which does and the other does not enable the treaty to have appropriate effects, good faith and the objects and purposes of the treaty demand that the former interpretation should be adopted'.[56]

Although the principle of effectiveness can operate as an element within the 'object and purposes' test, it is not limited to this role and, as Thirlway notes, the ICJ has used it to ascertain the intention underlying the treaty and as a starting point for a broader discus-sion. It also operates in the broader context of giving effect to the terms of a text.

The principle of effectiveness has two meanings. The first is that all provisions of the treaty or other instrument must be supposed to have been intended to have sig-nificance and to be necessary to express the intended meaning. Thus an interpretation that renders a text ineffective and meaningless is incorrect. The second operates as an aspect of the 'object and purposes' test, and it means that the instrument as a whole and each of its provisions must be taken to have been intended to achieve some end, and that an interpretation that would make the text ineffective to achieve that object is also incorrect. Thirlway observes that this latter approach is similar to the 'object and purpose' criterion, and 'has therefore, like this criterion, to be employed with discretion' (Thirlway, 1992).

---

[52] Ibid, Dissenting Opinion of Judge Schwebel, p 27 at p 36.   [53] Ibid, at p 37.

[54] Ibid, at pp 38–9. For similar analyses see the Dissenting Opinions of Judges Shahabuddeen, ibid, p 51 and Koroma, ibid, p 67.

[55] First Report on the Law of Treaties, *YBILC* (1962), vol II, pp 65–6.

[56] *YBILC* (1966), vol II (part two), p 219.

F. THE DYNAMIC (EVOLUTIVE) INTERPRETATION OF TREATIES AND THE EUROPEAN COURT OF HUMAN RIGHTS (ECtHR)

One of the most contentious, disputed and discussed issues in treaty interpretation is so-called the dynamic (evolutive) interpretation of treaties, which in particular has been developed in the jurisprudence of the European Court of Human Rights. The basis for such as an interpretative method is predicated upon the principle that the treaty is a living instrument. There are several cases (such as *Tyrer* (1975), *Golder* (1978) and *Marckx* (1979)) in which the Court decided to override the consent of the Parties in the name of 'the interests served by the protection of the human rights and fundamental freedoms guaranteed by the Convention', which 'extend beyond individual interests of the parties concerned'. This resulted in the establishment by the Parties to the Convention of the 'standards forming part of the public law of Europe'. First of all, the interpretative method of the ECtHR derives from the special legal nature of this Convention and the obligations, which doctrinal basis was enunciated in the 1965 *Austria v Italy* case. The Court also stressed the 'essentially objective character' of the 'obligations undertaken by the High Contracting Parties'. The 'objective legal order' 'benefits from the 'collective enforcement'. However, such an interpretative method was a subject of much criticism (eg by Sinclair and Fitzmaurice) as overriding intention and the consent to be bound of the Parties to the Convention and introducing the element of uncertainty for the Parties due to much more extensive interpretation of the provisions of the Convention. There are other international judicial bodies, which to a certain degree adopted such a method, such as, eg within the World Trade Organization (WTO).

G. PLURILINGUAL TREATIES

A further problem concerns the interpretation of treaties drawn up in more than one language. The ILC observed that:

> ...the majority of more formal treaties contain an express provision determining the status of the different language versions. If there is no such provision, it seems generally accepted that each of the versions in which the text of the treaty was 'drawn' up is to be considered authentic, and therefore authoritative for the purpose of interpretation. Few plurilingual treaties containing more than one or two articles are without some discrepancy between the texts...the plurality of texts may be a serious additional source of ambiguity or obscurity in the terms of the treaty. On the other hand, when meaning of terms is ambiguous or obscure in one language, but it is clear and convincing as to the intentions of the parties in another, the plurilingual character of the treaty facilitates interpretations of the text the meaning of which is doubtful.[57]

In the *Mavrommatis Palestine Concession* case, the ICJ had to interpret the phrases 'public control' and 'contrôle public' in the French and English authentic languages texts of the Palestine Mandate. The Court said:

> ...Where two versions possessing equal authority exist one of which appears to have a wider bearing than the other, it is bound to adopt the more limited interpretation which can be

---

[57] *YBILC* (1966), vol II (part two), pp 224–5.

made to harmonise with both versions and which, as far as it goes, is doubtless in accordance with the common intention of the parties.[58]

The matter is covered by VCLT Article 33, which reflects these general approaches to the problem.

In conclusion it may be said that there are numerous examples of the difficulties concerning the treaty interpretation. Such an example is the interpretation of Article 18 of the 1929 Geneva Convention on the Treatment of Prisoners of War, which provides that prisoners were to salute the officers of the captor country. In 1944, this clause was a subject of an interpretative dispute. In the period between 1939 and 1944, allied prisoners of war in Germany saluted their German captors in a classical manner, by touching their hands to the visors of their caps. Articles 18 of the Convention is silent as to whether the salute be returned, which is a universal military tradition: 'a salute unreturned is like the sound of one hand clapping' (Vagts, 1993, at p 490). After the failed attempt at Hitler's assassination (20 July 1944), regular German army troops were ordered to salute prisoners of war in a Nazi style, which resulted in the protest of the British. Eventually, due to the services of the International Committee of the Red Cross, the issue was resolved and prisoners permitted to use the salute prevalent in their own army.[59]

VI. RESERVATIONS TO TREATIES

A. THE *GENOCIDE CONVENTION* CASE

Reservations to multilateral treaties are one of the most problematic issues in the law of treaties. According to VCLT Article 2(d) 'Reservation means a unilateral statement, however phrased or named, made by a State, when signing, ratifying, accepting, approving or acceding to a treaty, where, it purports to exclude or to modify the legal effect of certain provisions of the treaty in their application to that State'.

In its role as a treaty depository, the League of Nations had only allowed reservations that were accepted by all contracting parties to a treaty, otherwise it treated both the reservations and the signatures or ratifications to which they were attached as null and void. The Pan-American Union adopted a different, more flexible approach, the gist of which was that a treaty was considered to be in force as between a reserving State and States that accepted the reservation but not in force as between a reserving State and States that did not accepted the reservation.

The modern approach is derived from the 1951 Advisory Opinion of the ICJ in the *Reservation to the Convention on Genocide* case, the principal features of which were that:

> A State which has made and maintained a reservation which has been objected to by one or more of the parties to the Convention but not by others, can be regarded as being

---

[58] *Mavrommatis Palestine Concessions, Judgment No 2, 1924, PCIJ, Ser A, No 2*, p 19.

[59] Example from Vagts (1993, at p 490) who comments, 'Thus we find interpretation of the Convention being presented and considered by persons far away from the original negotiating process. Most of them were not lawyers and they had no access to *travaux préparatoires* (which, as so often happens, would not have been helpful). There was no decision-maker to force a solution upon the parties. Yet it is apparent that the parties in dispute, although coming from different and at the time violently hostile states, did share assumptions about what a "salute" was, and when and how one should be rendered. Indeed, it seems likely the professional and traditional German officers had more in common on this point with their British counterparts than with their Nazi colleagues'.

a party to the Convention if the reservation is compatible with the object and purpose of the Convention; otherwise, that State cannot be regarded as being a party to the Convention.[60]

The Court added that:

If a party to the Convention objects to a reservation which it considers to be incompatible with the object and purpose of the Convention, it can in fact consider that the reserving State is not a party to the Convention...if on the other hand, a party accepts the reservation as being compatible with the object and purpose of the Convention, it can in fact consider that the reserving State is a party to the Convention.[61]

It has to be said that although the Court's approach was subsequently reflected in the VCLT, the Court had made it clear that it was expressing its views on the operation of reservations only in relation to the Genocide Convention, noting that:

In such a Convention the contracting States do not have any interests of their own; they merely have, one and all, a common interest, namely the accomplishment of those high purposes which are the *raison d'être* of the convention. Consequently in a convention of this type one cannot speak of individual advantages or disadvantages to States, or of the maintenance of a perfect contractual balance between rights and duties.[62]

And that:

The object and purpose of the Genocide Convention imply that it was the intention of the General Assembly and of States which adopted it that as many States as possible should participate. The complete exclusion from the Convention of one or more States would not only restrict the scope of its application, but would detract from the authority of the moral and humanitarian principles which are its basis.[63]

It was for these reasons that the Court departed from the more rigid system operated by the League of Nations, which some judges had considered to reflect international customary law.[64] However, it was the General Assembly itself which requested that the UN Secretary-General adopt this new approach when acting in his capacity as depositary of multilateral treaties.[65]

The question of a reservation to Article IX of the Genocide Convention was a subject matter of the *Democratic Republic of Congo v Rwanda* case. The Democratic Republic of Congo (DRC) argued that the reservation made by Rwanda to Article IX of the Genocide Convention (ie to the submission of disputes arising from the interpretation of this Convention to the ICJ), was against the spirit of Article 53 of the 1969 VCLT as it prevented 'the...Court from fulfilling its noble mission of safeguarding peremptory norms'.[66] The Court, however, decided that 'the prohibition of genocide, cannot of itself provide a basis for jurisdiction of the Court to entertain that dispute. Under the Court's

---

[60] *Reservations to the Convention on the Prevention and Punishment of the Crime of Genocide*, Advisory Opinion, ICJ Reports 1951, p 15 at p 29. See also *Armed Activities on the Territory of the Congo (New Application: 2002), (Democratic Republic of the Congo v Rwanda), Jurisdiction of the Court and Admissibility of the Application*; see also Joint Separate Opinion of Judges Higgins, Kooijmans, Elaraby, Owada, and Simma, ICJ Reports 2006.

[61] Idem.   [62] Ibid, p 23.   [63] Ibid, p 24.

[64] See Joint Dissenting Opinion of Judges Guerrero, Sir Arnold McNair, Read, and Hsu Mo, ibid, p 31.

[65] GA Res 598 (VI), 12 January 1952.

[66] *Armed Activities on the Territory of the Congo (New Application: 2002) (Democratic Republic of Congo v Rwanda) Jurisdiction of the Court and Admissibility of the Application*, ICJ Reports 2006, p 6, para 56.

Statute that jurisdiction is always based on the consent of the parties'.[67] This prompted a powerful Joint Separate Opinion by Judges Higgins, Koojimans, Elaraby, Owada, and Simma who, in light of recent developments in relations to reservation in general and to human rights treaties, were of the view that '[i]t is thus not self-evident that a reservation to Article IX could not be regarded as incompatible with the object and purpose of the Convention and we believe that this is a matter that the Court should revisit for further consideration'.[68]

B. THE REGIME OF THE 1969 VIENNA CONVENTION

The Court's approach is reflected in VCLT Article 19 and so attempts to strike a balance between ensuring the integrity of a treaty while encouraging universal participation. Article 20(4) tips the balance towards widening participation by providing that even if a State party objects to a reservation attached to the signature or ratification of another State, the treaty will nevertheless enter into force and the reservation be effective between them unless 'a contrary intention is definitely expressed by an objecting State'. Moreover, the idea that the approach in the *Genocide Convention* case should be limited to those treaties where there was no particular advantage or disadvantage for an individual State was abandoned and Article 20(5) provides that, a reservation is considered to have been accepted by a State if it has not objected to it within 12 months of being notified of it, unless the reservation concerns the constituent instrument of an international organization, or the treaty in question provides otherwise.

Again following the *Genocide Convention* case, VCLT Article 19(c) provides that a State may not submit a reservation, which is 'incompatible with the object and purpose of the treaty'. This criterion is vague and difficult to grasp. However, reservations of general character are considered to be incompatible with the 'object and purpose' of a treaty.[69] While reservations to treaty provisions which codify international customary law are possible,[70] there is no doubt that reservations to provisions reflecting norms of *jus cogens* are not.

How are those reservations, which are incompatible with the object and purpose of a treaty, distinguished from those which are not? There are two schools of thought: the permissibility school and the opposability school. The permissibility school is based on a two-stage assessment procedure: first, the reservation must be objectively assessed for compatibility with the object and purpose of the treaty. If it is not compatible, acceptance by other States cannot validate it.[71] If, however, the reservation is compatible with the object and purpose of the treaty, the parties may decide whether to accept or object to the reservation on whatever other grounds they wish, such as for political reasons. The opposability school bases the validity of the reservation entirely upon whether it has

---

[67] Ibid, para 64.

[68] Ibid, Joint Separate Opinion of Judges Higgins, Koojimans, Elaraby, Owada and Simma, para 29.

[69] See, before the European Court of Human Rights, *Belilos v Switzerland*, Judgment of 29 April 1988, Ser A, No 132, para 55.

[70] See, eg *North Sea Continental Shelf, Judgment, ICJ Reports 1969*, p 3, paras 29 and 72 which seem to accept the possibility. But cf UN HRC General Comment No 24(52) on issues relating to Reservations made upon ratification or accession to the Covenant or Optional Protocols thereto, or in relation to declarations under Article 41 of the Covenant, 11 November 1994 (for text see (1995) 15 *HRLJ* 262) which argues that reservations to provisions in human rights treaties which represent customary international law are not permissible. This is considered further later.

[71] UN Doc A/CN.4/470 (30 May 1995) (First Report on Reservations), p 49, para 102. See also *YBILC* (1995), vol II (part two), p 101.

been accepted by other parties and sees the compatibility test as merely a guiding principle for the parties to contemplate when considering whether to accept or object to the reservation.[72]

Some treaties attempt to deal with this question on a treaty-by-treaty basis. For example, the 1965 International Convention on Elimination of All Forms of Racial Discrimination, Article 20 uses a mathematical test, providing that a reservation is incompatible with the 'object and purpose' of the treaty if at least two-thirds of the contracting parties object to it.

The *Restrictions to the Death Penalty* Advisory Opinion concerned a reservation made by Guatemala to the prohibition of the infliction of capital punishment 'for political offenses or related common crimes' found in Article 4(4) of the 1969 American Convention on Human Rights, which is a non-derogable provision. Faced with the question whether a reservation was permissible in the light of the object and purpose of the Convention, the Inter-American Court of Human Rights said that:

> ... a reservation which was designed to enable a State to suspend any of the non-derogable fundamental rights must be deemed incompatible with the object and purpose of the Convention and, consequently, not permitted by it. The situation would be different if the reservation sought merely to restrict certain aspects of a non-derogable right without depriving the right as a whole of its basic purpose. Since the reservation ... does not appear to be of a type that is designed to deny the right to life as such, the Court concludes that to that extent it can be considered, in principle, as being not incompatible with the object and purpose of the Convention.[73]

One unresolved question concerns the legal effect of having attached an impermissible reservation to a signature or ratification. There are two possible solutions: the first is that unless it is withdrawn, a State making an impermissible reservation will not be considered a party to a treaty. The second is that the impermissible reservation may be severed and the State be bound by the treaty in its entirety. Although, as will be seen in Section VII later in this chapter, there is some practice supporting the severability approach in the human rights sphere, it is difficult to see how the reservation can legitimately be severed if the consent to be bound is made expressly subject to such a reservation, albeit an impermissible one.

C. GUIDE TO PRACTICE ON RESERVATIONS TO TREATIES

At its 3125th Meeting on 11 August 2011 the International Law Commission completed its work on reservation to treaties, which had commenced in 1993, and recommended to the General Assembly that it take note of its Guide to Practice on Reservations to Treaties.[74] The Guide deals with all aspects of reservations—including in Section 4.5 the consequences of invalid reservations—and, unlike the 1969 VCLT, it also considers the meaning and effect of interpretative declarations.

The purpose of the Guide to Practice is to provide assistance to practitioners of international law—decision-makers, diplomats, and lawyers (including those who plead cases before national courts and tribunals), who are faced with problems concerning

---

[72] Idem.

[73] *Restrictions to the Death Penalty*, Advisory Opinion, Inter-American Court of Human Rights, AO OC-3/83, 8 September 1983, para 61, (1984) 23 *ILM* 320 at p 341.

[74] Sixty-third session (26 April–3 June and 4 July–12 August 2011), Suppl 10. The ILC Special Rapportuer on the topic, Professor Pellet, produced 17 Reports on the subject. For a full overview see http://legal.un.org/ilc/summaries/1_8.htm.

the permissibility and effects of reservations to treaties and interpretative declarations, explaining the VCLT and supplementing it by addressing some *lacunae*. Some sections of the Guide reproduce VCLT while some are *de lege ferenda*; in some cases, guidelines are based on practices that have develop in the margins of the Vienna Conventions; other guidelines are simply recommendations and are meant only to encourage.[75]

The Guide to Practice is divided into five parts. Part 1 is devoted to the definition of reservations and interpretative declarations and to the distinction between these two types of unilateral statement (it also includes an overview of various unilateral statements, made in connection with a treaty, that are neither reservations nor interpretative declarations). Part 2 sets out the form and procedure to be used in formulating reservations and interpretative declarations and reactions thereto. Part 3 concerns the permissibility of reservations and interpretative declarations and reactions thereto and sets out the criteria for the assessment of permissibility. Part 4 sets out the legal effects produced by reservations and interpretative declarations, depending on whether they are valid (in which case a reservation is 'established' if it has been accepted) or not; this part also includes the effects of objections to and acceptances of reservations. Part 5 supplements the only provision of the 1978 Vienna Convention on Succession of States in respect of Treaties that deals with reservations, this being Article 20 which provide for the continuity of a reservation to a treaty in the case of succession by a newly independent State. The Guide also addresses situations in which States unite or separate as well as issues raised by objections to or acceptances of reservations and by interpretative declarations in relation to succession of States.[76]

D. THE PROBLEM OF RESERVATIONS TO HUMAN RIGHTS TREATIES

The system of reservations found in the Vienna Convention was supposed to be comprehensive but it became clear in the 1980s that the system was difficult to apply particularly as regards the compatibility of reservations to human rights treaties with their 'object and purpose' and in 1993 the topic of the Law and Practice Relating to Reservations to Treaties was added to the ILC's agenda (see Section VI C in this chapter). Human rights treaties are not contractual in nature and do not only create rights and obligations between States on the traditional basis of reciprocity but they also establish relationships between States and individuals. Several undecided issues had to be solved: were all reservations made by States permissible?[77] If not, who decides on their permissibility? What are the legal effects of accepting or rejecting a reservation or of having made an impermissible reservation? Broadly speaking there are two main approaches: one illustrated by the approach of the UN Human Rights Committee (the HRC) that stresses the inadequacies of the VCLT regime and the other that considers that regime absolutely satisfactory.

There are very few international bodies, other than the European Court of Human Rights and the Inter-American Court of Human Rights, that have an institutionalized procedure to decide upon the permissibility of reservations. In the *Belilos* case the European Court of

---

[75] See 'Symposium: the International Law Commission's Guide to Practice on Reservations to Treaties', (2013) 24 *EJIL* 1055–1152.

[76] The Guide to Practice has prompted many comments from States, with particular concerns being expressed regarding Guideline 2.3.1 and 2.3.2 on the acceptance of, and objection to 'late reservations' and to Section 4.5 on the 'Consequences of an Invalid Reservation'.

[77] For further discussion of this see Pellet and Muller, (2011).

Human Rights decided that a declaration made by Switzerland when ratifying the ECHR was in fact a reservation of a general character and therefore impermissible under the terms of ECHR Article 64. The Court severed the reservation and decided that Switzerland was bound by the Convention in its entirety.[78] Similarly, in the *Lozidou* case the European Court of Human Rights considered that Turkish reservations to the jurisdiction of the Commission and Court to consider applications relating to activities in Northern Cyprus were invalid and severable, meaning that such applications could be considered by the Strasbourg organs, notwithstanding the intention of Turkey to prevent this.[79]

The question of reservations to human rights treaties was considered by the UN HRC in a controversial General Comment No 24 (1994).[80] The HRC is the body established under the 1966 ICCPR and has the task of overseeing compliance by States parties with their obligations under the Covenant. In its General Comment, the Committee took the view that the Vienna Convention provisions, which give a role to State objections in relation to reservations, are inappropriate in the context of human rights treaties, which do not comprise a web of inter-State reciprocal exchanges of mutual obligations but are concerned with endowing individuals with rights. The HRC took the view that reservations offending peremptory norms would not be compatible with the object and purpose of the Covenant and raised the question of whether reservations to non-derogable provisions of the Covenant were compatible with its object and purpose. It expressed the view that reservations to the system of individual communications to the Committee established under the first Optional Protocol to the Covenant would not be compatible with its object and purpose. The HRC also took the view that it was the Committee itself, which should determine whether a specific reservation was compatible with the object and purpose of the Covenant.

The General Comment provoked strong reaction, including from the UK and USA who considered VCLT Article 19(c) both adequate and applicable to reservations to human rights treaties and considered it for States parties to determine whether a reservation is compatible with the object and purpose of that treaty rather than the Committee. Moreover, the USA stressed that reservations formed an integral part of the consent to be bound and are not severable. The Committee, however, affirmed its General Comment in the *Rawle Kennedy* case, though it was questioned by a number of members who in a dissenting opinion observed that:

> The normal assumption will be that the ratification or accession is not dependent on the acceptability of the reservation and the unacceptability of the reservation will not vitiate the reserving State's agreement to be party to the Covenant. However, this assumption cannot apply when it is abundantly clear that the reserving State's agreement to becoming party to the Covenant is *dependent* on the acceptability of the reservation. The same applies with reservations to the Optional Protocol.[81]

However, in his Second Report as ILC Special Rapporteur Pellet, argued that the system of the Vienna Convention is adequate to address reservations in human rights treaties[82] and has recently noted that the practice of human rights bodies is not uniform and, eg the Committees of the Conventions on Elimination of Discrimination against Women

---

[78] *Belilos* v *Switzerland*, Judgment of 29 April 1988, Ser A, No 132, paras 52–5, 60.

[79] *Lozidou* v *Turkey (Preliminary Objections)*, Judgment of 23 March 1995, Ser A, No 310, paras 15, 27, 89, 90, 95.

[80] See, n 37.

[81] *Rawle Kennedy* v *Trinidad and Tobago*, Comm. No 845/1999, Decision, 2 November 1999, UN Doc A/55/40, vol II, Annex XI, A, Individual Dissenting Opinion of Ando, Bhagwati, Klein, and Kretzmer, para 16.

[82] For a summary see *YBILC* (1997), vol II, pp 53–4, 57.

and International Convention on the Elimination of All Forms of Racial Discrimination, attempt to persuade States to withdraw offending reservations rather than to decide on impermissibility.[83] It is, then, clear that there is a significant on-going controversy surrounding this question.

This was confirmed by the 2007 meeting between the ILC and human rights bodies regarding reservations to human rights treaties.[84] During this meeting the representatives of several human rights bodies as well as the members of the Commission presented their views on this issue. During the discussion several issues were raised, the most important being the invalidity of reservation to treaties. Although the special character of human rights treaties was noted, a view was expressed that there were other areas such as environmental protection which also had special characteristics. However, a distinctive feature of human rights treaties was the presence of the human rights bodies. It was observed, nevertheless, that the law of treaties generally and the regime set up under Article 19 of the VCLT were applicable and adequate to deal with reservations to human rights treaties but should be applied in 'an appropriate and suitably adopted manner'. The heart of the discussion was the issue of the delicate balance between the integrity and universality of treaties in respect of reservations. All participants were in agreement as to the competence of the human rights bodies to assess the validity of reservations. The most important issue was so-called 'reservation dialogue' between the reserving State and the human rights body. Taking a 'dialogue approach' best reflected the underlying political situation concerning reservations while giving human rights bodies the opportunity to exercise pragmatism (which is a particular feature of their policy towards reservations) and discretion. However, the question of the severance of an offending reservation from the consent to be bound by a treaty, remained an unresolved problem in cases where it was impossible to ascertain the intention of the States parties in this respect. On one hand, some human rights bodies supported their right to severe reservations; on the other hand, some participants adhered to the view that the principle of sovereignty must prevail.

In his final Report, Pellet further analysed the so-called 'reservations dialogue'.[85] According to Pellet, the reservations regime of the VCLT is so flexible that its leaves room for the dialogue between the key players (the author of the reservation on one hand, and the other contracting States or international organizations and any monitoring bodies, on the other). However, the VCLT does not provide a legal framework for such a dialogue, in which the Human Rights Treaty bodies have a leading role by drawing the attention of States parties to those reservations which they find dubious or outdated in order to encourage the reserving State to modify or withdraw them.[86] However, as Pellet says, such a dialogue does not often result in a satisfactory solution. Therefore, in the Addendum to his final, Seventeenth Report Pellet suggested that, following the precedent set by the Council of Europe, an impartial body—a 'reservations and objections to reservations assistance mechanism'—should be established to assist in a case of a stalemate.[87] However, after considering the matter in some depth, the ILC did not pursue this. It did, however,

---

[83] Pellet, A, *Eighth Report on Reservations to Treaties*, ILC, Fifty-fifth Session (2003), A/CN.4/535, paras 17–27.

[84] See Annex to Pellet, A. *Fourteenth Report on Reservation to Treaties*, ILC, Sixty-first Session (2009), A/CN.4/614, pp 27–34.

[85] Pellet, A, *Seventeenth Report of Reservations to Treaties*, ILC Sixty-third Session (2011), A/CN.4/647.

[86] The 'reservation dialogue' is frequently conducted during review of the periodic reports submitted to the Treaty Bodies by the State Parties, at which both are present.

[87] Pellet, A, *Seventeenth Report of Reservations to Treaties*, ILC sixty-third session (2011), A/CN.4/647/ Add. 1, paras 85–101.

include an Annex to the Guide to Practice, entitled 'Conclusions on the Reservations Dialogue', which offers guidance on how such a 'dialogue' might be facilitated and which recommends that 'The General Assembly call upon States and international organizations, as well as monitoring bodies, to initiate and pursue such a reservations dialogue in a pragmatic and transparent manner'.

E. INTERPRETATIVE DECLARATIONS

Interpretative declarations are not addressed by the VCLT. They are, however, frequently appended to treaties by governments at the time of signature, ratification, or acceptance. They are explanatory in character, setting out how a State understands its treaty obligation when expressing its consent to be bound. However, such declarations must be subject to close scrutiny. If they change the scope of the obligation, they cease to be declarations and become reservations. The legal effect of interpretative declarations depends upon whether they aim to offer an interpretation of the treaty that may subsequently be proved incorrect (a 'mere interpretative declaration') or whether they offer an interpretation that is to be accepted by others (a 'qualified interpretative declaration').

In practice, distinguishing between reservations and forms of interpretative declarations can be a very daunting task and the ILC Guide to Practice on Reservation to Treaties does now seek to provide some helpful guidance. First, is defines an interpretive declaration as a 'unilateral statement, however phrased or named, made by a State or an international organization, whereby a State or that organisation purports to specify or clarify the meaning or scope of a treaty or of certain of its provisions'.[88] It then says that 'The character of a unilateral statement as a reservation or as an interpretative declaration is determined by the legal effect that its author purports to produce'[89] and, in determining this, '….the statement should be interpreted in good faith in accordance with the ordinary meaning to be given to its terms, with a view to identifying therefrom the intention of its author, in light of the treaty to which it refers'.[90] While 'The phrasing or name of a unilateral statement provides an indication of the purported legal effect',[91] what it is called by the declaring State would not seem to be definitive, even though it the intention of the declaring State that is to be determined. Despite this additional guidance, distinguishing between a reservation and an interpretive declaration remains a difficult task.

VII. PROBLEMS CONCERNING THE GROUNDS FOR TERMINATION

This section will consider some specific issues concerning the external grounds for terminating or suspending a treaty, these being material breach, supervening impossibility of performance, and fundamental change of circumstances.

A. MATERIAL BREACH

VCLT Article 60 regulates the consequences of a breach of a treaty obligation deriving from the law of treaties, rather than from the law of State responsibility (see Simma and Tams, 2012). The guiding principle is that of reciprocity. The ILC took a cautious approach

---

[88] Guideline 1.2.   [89] Guideline 1.3.   [90] Guideline 1.3.1.   [91] Guideline 1.3.2.

to material breach, considering that a breach of a treaty, however serious, did not *ipso facto* put an end to a treaty but that within certain limits and subject to certain safeguards the right of a party to invoke the breach of a treaty as a ground for terminating it or suspending its operation must be recognized and Article 60 takes the same approach.

Taking a strict approach to the effect of a material breach aims at striking a balance between the need to uphold the stability of treaties and the need to ensure reasonable protection for the innocent victim of a breach, though it may appear that the stability of treaties is the first priority. It is certainly true that the ICJ takes a restrictive approach to the application of Article 60. For example, in the *Gabčíkovo-Nagymaros* case it responded to Hungary's claim that Slovakia's actions in relation to other treaties had a bearing upon the assessment of Hungary's own actions by saying that 'It is only material breach of the treaty itself, by a State party to that treaty, which entitles the other party to rely on it as a ground for terminating the treaty'.[92] The Court explained that, while the violation of any other treaty or rules of general international law might justify an injured State taking other measures, such as countermeasures, it did not constitute a ground for termination of the treaty under the law of treaties.

This case is also illustrative of what comprises a material breach. Hungary relied on the construction of a bypass canal in pursuance of a plan known as 'Variant C' by Czechoslovakia, and which was unauthorized by the original 1977 Treaty between the parties, as the basis for invoking material breach of that treaty. Czechoslovakia claimed that its plans were justified as a legitimate response to prior breaches of the treaty by Hungary. The Court found that Czechoslovakia had indeed violated the 1977 Treaty when it diverted the waters of the Danube into the bypass canal in October 1992 but that the construction of the works prior to this had not been unlawful. Thus the notification by Hungary in May 1992 that it was terminating the 1977 Treaty for material breach was premature, as no breach had yet occurred. Moreover, the Court took the view that by attempting to terminate the 1977 Treaty by means of a declaration issued on 6 May 1992 with effect as of some 19 days later on 25 May 1992, Hungary had not acted in accordance with the principle of good faith and therefore had by its own conduct prejudiced its right to terminate the 1977 Treaty. The Court stated that:

> This would still have been the case even if Czechoslovakia, by the time of the purported termination, had violated a provision essential to the accomplishment of the object or purpose of the Treaty.[93]

In the later case concerning the *Application of the Interim Accord of 13 September 1995* Greece attempted to invoke the material breach of a treaty obligation (VCLT Article 60(3)(b)) and countermeasures as subsidiary defences in order to justify its disregard for its obligations under the Interim Accord not to oppose the former Yugoslav Republic of Macedonia's application of membership of an international organization, in this case, NATO. Greece argued that the applicant was in material breach since it had displayed a particular symbol in contravention of Article 7(2) of the Interim Accord, but this was rejected by the Court.[94]

---

[92] *Gabčíkovo-Nagymaros Project (Hungary/Slovakia), Judgment, ICJ Reports 1997*, p 7, para 106.

[93] Ibid, para 110.

[94] The Court concluded that 'the only breach which has been established is the display of a symbol in breach of Article 7, paragraph 2, of the Interim Accord, a situation which ended in 2004. The Court considers that this incident cannot be regarded as a material breach within the meaning of Article 60 of the 1969 Vienna Convention'. See *Application of the Interim Accord of 13 September 1995 (the former Yugoslav Republic of Macedonia v Greece), Judgment of 5 December 2011, ICJ Reports 2011*, p 644, para 163.

The relationship between the material breach of a treaty and the law of State responsibility, and particularly with countermeasures, is extremely problematic. Although not resolved by the ILC in its work on the law of treaties it appears that its intention was that the two regimes should co-exist and the ILC's Commentary to its Articles on State Responsibility reflect this, indicating that State responsibility does not deal with the 'consequences of breach for the continual or binding effect of the primary rule (eg the right of an injured State to terminate or suspend a treaty for material breach, as reflected in Article 60 of the Vienna Convention on the Law of Treaties)'. The Special Rapporteur, James Crawford, explained that:

> There is thus a clear distinction between action taken within the framework of the law of treaties (as codified in the Vienna Convention) and conduct raising questions of State responsibility (which are excluded from the Vienna Convention). The law of treaties is concerned essentially with the content of primary rules and with the validity of attempts to alter them; the law of State responsibility takes as given the existence of primary rules (whether based on a treaty or otherwise) and is concerned with the question whether the conduct inconsistent with those rules can be excused and, if not, what consequences of such conduct are. Thus it is coherent to apply the Vienna Convention rules as to the materiality of breach and the severability of provisions of a treaty in dealing with issues of suspension, and the rules proposed in the Draft articles as to proportionality etc, in dealing with countermeasures.[95]

This finds reflection in the approach taken by the ICJ in the *Interim Accord* case, where it considered whether the actions of Greece might be justifiable as both under the law of treaties and as a countermeasure under the rules of state responsibility.[96]

B. SUPERVENING IMPOSSIBILITY OF PERFORMANCE

This ground for termination is well established and uncontested. VCLT Article 61 limits this ground to the 'permanent disappearance or destruction of an object indispensable for the execution of a treaty' and it cannot be invoked by a party that was itself instrumental in causing these circumstances to come about by the breach of its treaty obligations. Once again, the ICJ has taken a strict approach. In the *Gabčíkovo-Nagymaros* case Hungary argued that the essential object of the 1977 Treaty was a joint economic investment, which was inconsistent with environmental considerations and had ceased to exist, rendering the 1977 Treaty impossible to perform. The Court observed that if the joint exploitation of the investment was no longer possible, this was because of Hungary's failure to perform most of the works for which it was responsible under the 1977 Treaty and, as indicated, impossibility of performance cannot be invoked by a party as a ground for terminating a treaty when it is the result of that party's own failure to perform its treaty obligations.

---

[95] Third Report on State Responsibility, A/CN.4507/Add 3.

[96] Having rejected the argument based on material breach under the VCLT, the Court then rejected the argument based on countermeasures, 'the Court is not persuaded that the Respondent's objection to the Applicant's admission was taken for the purpose of achieving the cessation of the Applicant's use of the symbol prohibited by Article 7, paragraph 2'. See *Application of the Interim Accord of 13 September 1995 (the former Yugoslav Republic of Macedonia v Greece), Judgment of 5 December 2011, ICJ Reports 2011*, p 644, para 164).

C. FUNDAMENTAL CHANGE OF CIRCUMSTANCES

Fundamental change of circumstances as a ground for the termination of a treaty is controversial. The principle of stability of contractual obligations and the conviction that 'it is a function of the law to enforce contracts or treaties even if they become burdensome for the party bound by them' militates against it (*Oppenheim's International Law*, 1992) but this needs to be balanced against the view that 'One could not insist upon petrifying a state of affairs which had become anachronistic because it is based on a treaty which either does not contain any specific clause as to its possible termination or which even proclaimed itself to be concluded for all times to come' (Nahlik, 1971). VCLT Article 62 takes a particularly cautious approach. It accepts that termination on these grounds is possible, but it is of limited scope. It may not be invoked in relation to a treaty, which establishes a boundary; and, as with Article 61, a State may not invoke Article 62 if the change was caused by a breach of its own international obligations, either under the treaty in question or any other international agreement.

The ICJ has taken a very cautious approach to this principle. In the *Fisheries Jurisdiction* case it said:

> International law admits that a fundamental change of circumstances which determined the parties to accept a treaty, if it has resulted in a radical transformation of the extent of obligation imposed by it, may, under certain conditions, afford the party affected a ground for invoking the termination or suspension of a treaty. This principle, and the conditions and exceptions to which it is subject, have been embodied in Article 62 of the Vienna Convention on the Law of Treaties, which may in many respects be considered as a codification of existing customary law on the subject of termination of a treaty relationship on account of changed circumstances.[97]

The *Gabčíkovo-Nagymaros* case again illustrates the Court's approach. Hungary identified several 'substantive elements' that had been present when the 1977 Treaty had been concluded but which it claimed had changed fundamentally when it issued its notice of termination in May 1992, these being: the whole notion of socialist economic integration which underpinned the 1977 Treaty; the replacement of a joint and unified operational system with separate unilateral schemes; the emergence of market economies in both States; the Czechoslovakian approach that had turned a framework treaty into an immutable norm; and, finally, the transformation of a treaty inconsistent with environmental protection into a prescription for environmental disaster.[98]

The Court concluded that while the political situation was relevant to the conclusion of the 1977 Treaty, its object and purpose—the joint investment programme for the production of energy, the control of floods, and the improvement of navigation on the River Danube—were not so closely linked to political conditions that the political changes in central Europe had radically altered the extent of obligations still to be performed.[99] The Court drew the same conclusion regarding the changes in economic systems concluding that even if by 1992 the projected profitability of the scheme had declined, it had not done so to an extent that would transform the nature of the parties' obligations. Likewise, developments in environmental knowledge and environmental law were not completely unforeseen. Having analysed the parties' arguments the Court concluded that 'the changed

---

[97] *Fisheries Jurisdiction (United Kingdom v Iceland), Jurisdiction of the Court, Judgment, ICJ Reports 1973*, p 3, para 36 (see Fitzmaurice, 2012).

[98] *Gabčíkovo-Nagymaros Project (Hungary/Slovakia), Judgment, ICJ Reports 1997*, p 7, para 95.

[99] Idem.

circumstances advanced by Hungary are, in the Court's view, not of such nature, either individually or collectively, that their effect would radically transform the extent of the obligation still to be performed in order to accomplish the Project'.[100] The Court therefore interpreted VCLT Article 62 strictly, believing that a 'fundamental change of circumstances must have been unforeseen; the existence of the circumstances at the time of the Treaty's conclusion must have constituted an essential basis of consent of the parties to be bound by the Treaty' and that 'the stability of treaty relations requires that the plea of fundamental change of circumstances be applied only in exceptional cases'.[101]

VIII. CONCLUSION

This chapter has presented the main issues of treaty law found in the 1969 Vienna Convention on the Law of Treaties. It has attempted to illustrate the application and interpretation of the Convention in practice through the case law, in particular that of the International Court of Justice. Although rightly considered as one of the greatest accomplishments of the ILC, the Vienna Convention does not cover all possible areas and issues, particularly the question of reservation to human rights treaties and the relationship between State responsibility and material breach. The law of treaties is a classical yet constantly developing branch of international law. Treaties are the main tool of relations between States and therefore it is only to be expected that the rules that govern their application are not static but constantly evolve and reflect the development of other branches of international law. Indeed, the law of treaties has become a particularly dynamic subject and the International Law Commission has currently two projects on the law of treaties on its agenda. These are: 'subsequent agreements and subsequent practice in relation to the interpretation of treaties';[102] and 'the provisional application of treaties'.[103] It is clear, then, that there are further important developments to come.

REFERENCES

Aust, A (2007), *Modern Treaty Law and Practice*, 2nd edn (Cambridge: Cambridge University Press).

Boyle, A (2000), 'Some Reflections on the Relationship of Treaties and Soft Law', in Gowlland-Debbas, V (ed), *Multilateral Treaty Making* (The Hague: Martinus Nijhoff), p 25.

Chinkin, C (1993), *Third Parties in International Law* (Oxford: Oxford University Press).

Fitzmaurice, Sir G (1951), 'Treaty Interpretation and Certain Other Treaty Points, 1947–1951', 22 *BYIL* 1.

Fitzmaurice, M (2012), 'Exceptional Circumstances and Treaty Commitments', in Hollis, DB (ed), *The Oxford Guide to Treaties* (Oxford: Oxford University Press), p 605.

Fox, H (2010), 'Article 31(3)(a) and (b) of the Vienna Convention and the *Kasikili/Sedudu Island Case*', in Fitzmaurice, M,

---

[100] Ibid, para 104.   [101] Ibid.

[102] The ILC decided to commence work on this topic in 2008, which until 2012 was known as 'treaties over time', with Mr Georg Nolte as Special Rapporteur.

[103] The ILC decided to commenced work on this topic in 2012, with Mr Juan Gomez-Robledo as Special Rapporteur.

Elias, O and Merkouris, P, *Treaty Interpretation and the Vienna Convention on the Law of Treaties 30 Years On* (Leiden/Boston: Martinus Nijhoff), p 59.

KOSKENNIEMI, M (1989), *From Apology to Utopia; The Structure of International Legal Argument*, 2005 reissue (Cambridge: Cambridge University Press).

MCNAIR, AD (1961), *The Law of Treaties*, 2nd edn (Oxford: Clarendon Press).

NAHLIK, SE (1971), 'The Grounds of Invalidity of and Termination of Treaties', 65 *AJIL* 747.

OPPENHEIM, L (1992), Jennings, Sir R and Watts, Sir A (eds), *Oppenheim's International Law*, 9th edn (Harlow: Longman).

PELLET, A and MULLER, D (2011), 'Reservations to Treaties: An Objection to a Reservation is Definitely not an Acceptance', in Cannizzaro, E (ed),

The Law of Treaties Beyond the Vienna Convention (Oxford: Oxford University Press), p 37.

SHEARER, IA (1994), *Starke's International Law*, 11th edn (London: Butterworths).

SIMMA, B and TAMS, C (2012), 'Reacting to Treaty Breaches', in Hollis, DB (ed), *The Oxford Guide to Treaties* (Oxford: Oxford University Press), p 576.

SINCLAIR, SIR I (1984), *The Vienna Convention on the Law of Treaties*, 2nd edn (Oxford: Oxford University Press).

THIRLWAY, H (1992), 'The Law and Procedure of the International Court of Justice, 1960–1989', Part Three, 63 *BYIL* 1.

VAGTS, D (1993), 'Treaty Interpretation and the New American Ways of Law Reading', 4 *EJIL* 472.

WEIL, P (1993), 'Towards Relative Normativity in International Law', 77 *AJIL* 413.

FURTHER READING

AUST, A (2013), *Modern Treaty Law and Practice*, 2nd edn (Cambridge: Cambridge University Press). This book is a comprehensive study of the modern law of treaties written from the point of view of an experienced practitioner.

CORTEN, O and KLEIN, P (eds) (2011), *The Vienna Convention on the Law of Treaties: A Commentary* (New York: Oxford University Press): A detailed commentary on the Vienna Convention.

CANNIZZARO, E (2011), *The Law of Treaties Beyond the Vienna Convention* (Oxford: Oxford University Press): a collection of essays on challenging aspects of the law of treaties.

DÖRR, O and SCHMALENBACH, K (2012), *Vienna Convention on the Law of Treaties: A Commentary* (Berlin: Springer): an in-depth commentary on the VCLT.

FITZMAURICE, M and ELIAS, O (2005), *Contemporary Issues in the Law of Treaties* (Utrecht: Eleven International Publishing). This is a collection of essays dealing with some pertinent and often unresolved issues of the law of treaties.

FITZMAURICE, M, ELIAS, O and MERKOURIS, P (eds) (2010), *Treaty Interpretation and the Vienna Convention on the Law of Treaties 30 Years On* (Leiden/Boston: Martinus Nijhoff Publishers): an in-depth study on approaches to interpretation in the VCLT and on subsequent developments.

GARDINER, R (2008), *Treaty Interpretation* (Oxford: The Oxford International Law Library). This book is an in-depth study of treaty interpretation, based on meticulous analysis of Article 31 of the 1969 Vienna Convention on the Law of Treaties, including the historical development of treaty interpretation; the work of the International Law Commission; relevant case law and the views of doctrine.

HOLLIS, DB (ed) (2012), *The Oxford Guide to Treaties* (Oxford: Oxford University Press): this provides a comprehensive guide to treaties, on the rules and practices surrounding the making, interpretation, and operation of these instruments.

KLABBERS, J (1996), *The Concept of Treaty in International Law* (The Hague: Kluwer Law International). This book is a highly original study of the law of treaties, often controversial but very thought provoking. It includes an overview of relevant jurisprudence of the International Court of Justice.

LESTSAS, G (2007), *A Theory Interpretation of the European Convention on Human Rights* (Oxford: Oxford University Press).

McNAIR, AD (1961), *The Law of Treaties*, 2nd edn (Oxford: Clarendon Press). The classical treatise on the law of treaties.

ORAKHELASHVILI, A and WILLIAMS, S (eds) (2010), *40 Years of the Vienna Convention on the Law of Treaties* (London: British Institute Of International And Comparative Law). An evaluation of the VCLT, containing detailed analysis of unresolved issues.

PELLET, A and MÜLLER, DS (eds) (2011), 'Reservations to Human Rights Treaties: Not Absolute Evil…', in Fastenrath *et al* (eds), *From Bilateralism to Community Interest: Essays in Honour of Bruno Simma* (Oxford: Oxford University Press), p 521.

REUTER, P (1995), *Introduction to the Law of Treaties* (Moco, J and Haggenmacher, P (trans.)) (London: Kegan Paul International). This book presents an in-depth study of the 1986 Convention on the Law of Treaties between States and International Organizations or Between International Organizations.

SINCLAIR, SIR I (1984), *The Vienna Convention on the Law of Treaties*, 2nd edn (Manchester: Manchester University Press). This is a classical book on the 1969 Vienna Convention on the Law of Treaties that also includes practice of States and the overview of the ILC's work on the codification of the Convention.

VILLIGER, M (1997), *Customary Law and Treaties, A Manual on the Theory and Practice of the Interrelation of Sources*, 2nd edn (Zurich: Schulthess Polygraphisher Verlag and The Hague: Kluwer Law International). This book is a systematic and erudite study on written and unwritten international law.

——— (2009), *Commentary on the Vienna Convention on the Law of Treaties* (Leiden/Boston: Marinus Nijhoff Publishers): an in-depth commentary.

ZIEMELE, I (ed) (2004), *Reservations to Human Rights Treaties and the Vienna Convention Regime, Conflict, Harmony or Reconciliation* (The Hague: Martinus Nijhoff). This book gives a comprehensive overview of the practice of human rights bodies in relation to reservations, as well a theoretical background.

PART III

THE SUBJECTS OF
THE INTERNATIONAL
LEGAL ORDER

8

STATEHOOD,
SELF-DETERMINATION,
AND RECOGNITION

Matthew Craven

SUMMARY

The proposition that international law is largely concerned with States—what they do and how they behave in relation to one another—has long been one of the most axiomatic features of international legal thought. Yet the actual place occupied by the State in such thought and practice has always been equally elusive. In one direction, the existence of a society of independent States appears to be a necessary presupposition for the discipline—something that has to precede the identification of those rules or principles that might be regarded as forming the substance of international law. In another direction, however, statehood is also something that appears to be produced through international law following from a need to determine which political communities can rightfully claim to enjoy the prerogatives of sovereignty. Whereas in the past, this relationship between law and sovereignty could be mediated through an imperial 'standard of civilization' that differentiated between 'new' and 'old' States, or European and non-European forms of sovereignty, by the middle of the twentieth century such forms of discrimination were no longer tenable. The contradictions implicit in the idea of statehood (that it be both antecedent and a product of international law) were then to come to the fore demarcating debates as to the implications of self-determination (whether determining or determined) and of recognition (whether declaratory or constitutive). Intertwined within in such debates are an array of political commitments—to democracy and self-government, human rights, and the combating of violence—all of which relate thoroughly ambiguously to the role assigned to States within international legal thought in the sense that they remain both the source of the problem and the mode of emancipation.

I. INTRODUCTION

It is a remarkable feature of our contemporary understanding of the world that if forced to describe it, we would normally do so in one of two ways. One would be in terms of its physical and biological geography (a description of continents, oceans, climate and plant or animal life-forms); the other in terms of its political geography, as being a world divided systematically and uniformly by reference to the territorial parameters of States (as one would find marked by colours within an Atlas). That the second form of representation appears significant is to mark the extraordinary power that that idea of the State has come to play in the formation of our social, political, economic and cultural world view. Not only is it now an apparently universal institution, but one whose permanence is inscribed in a variety of discourses including, amongst others, international law.

Of course, we know the world has not always existed in this form, and States (if we like to identify them simply with the existence of 'political communities') have changed much over the centuries (Tilly, 1992; Spruyt, 1994). At one time political authority around the globe could largely be described in terms of its relative intensity: with high levels of loyalty and allegiance to the 'sovereign' concentrating in 'centres of power' within denser urban sites, and which shaded off in the more remote frontier zones that characterized the outer edges of the realm. In its place has emerged a global order framed in terms of a European model of the nation State marked by the possession of determinate and increasingly non-porous boundaries, centralized bureaucratic structures and a singular uniform system of law (Weber, 1978; Giddens, 1985). The purchase of this institution upon the political imagination has been such as to ensure not only that the daily routine of 'politics' remains firmly embedded within its frame (institutionalized, for example, in parliamentary debates, elections and campaigns for office), but that even the movements of resistance adopt it as the mode of their emancipation. The secessionist movements active in places as diverse as Bougainville, Chechnya, Nagorno-Karabakh, Somaliland, or West Irian almost invariably seek, as their objective, the establishment of an independent State. In some ways, it is hard to think what the alternative might be (Scott, 2009).

As much as movements for independence seem, in some respects, to affirm the singularity of the State as the primary mode of political organization, they are also evidently threatening to it. Not only do they put in question the authority of the State against which they assert their independence, but also appear to pose a challenge to the broader international order within which each State, as one of a plurality of political communities, necessarily locates itself. Not all such movements turn out in the same way of course. In some, claims to independence are given the definitive seal of Statehood by membership in the UN (eg Eritrea 1993), in others effective self-government continues yet the claim to independent statehood goes decisively unrecognized (eg Somaliland 1996–). Some, furthermore, survive in an apparent twilight zone of partial recognition (eg Kosovo 2009–, Palestine 1988–). At such moments, international lawyers are often asked for advice: is it right or proper for other States to recognize such claims? What are the implications for doing so, or indeed for refusing such recognition? How far does institutional membership go to determine the outcome in such cases? What consideration should be given to the democratic credentials of the new State or the role played by human rights? International lawyers seem to have some kind of expertise here, and one that is sought not only by those concerned with the distributional consequences of any political change, but by the public at large.

The answers, for the most part, are often hesitant: 'it depends' is usually a stock phrase. It 'depends' because as much as a community might be able to ground its claims to independence in a sense of ethnic, cultural or historic sense of self-identity, or in terms of its abuse at the hands of an 'alien' authoritarian elite, there may still be broader matters of stability or security to be addressed. It depends because as much as one or two States may have seen fit to recognize the new entity, this is not usually sufficient to pronounce upon its independent existence (albeit the case that it is hard to say quite what is sufficient). It depends because while we used to be quite clear about the conditions under which new States might come into being, things appear always to be changing, and practice coalescing around some new potential rule or principle. It depends because rule and practice rarely neatly align and one needs to attend to both the law and politics of recognition, and not one in isolation of the other. These, and many other common concerns, are such as to make definitive pronouncement a seemingly precarious business. Yet the fact remains that the creation or disappearance of States is not something about which international lawyers are, or indeed can be, entirely neutral. There are always legal consequences attendant to forms of political change that involve the alteration of borders. More than this, however, international lawyers also have an important linguistic and conceptual toolbox (which includes notions of sovereignty, territory, recognition, jurisdiction, personality, and self-determination) that provides a language for both projecting and evaluating claims made in respect of those processes of political and social change.

In some respects, however, the place assumed by the 'State' in international law is almost too self-evident. If international law is defined, as it tends to be, as the law that applies as between sovereign States, then some engagement with States, what they are, how they come into being, and how they change has to be part of the disciplinary orientation. Yet, the central position assumed by States in legal doctrine is also problematic. In the introduction to his *Principles of International Law* of 1895 Lawrence suggested that '[t]he meagre proposition that the Subjects of International Law are Sovereign States is often put forward as if it contained all the information that need be given about the matter.' (Lawrence, 1895, p 55) Of course, it wasn't all the information needed in his view, and for him, one needed to differentiate between different kinds of States and different forms of sovereignty. But in a very different sense, he might also have been aware that the figure of the sovereign State occupied such a central position within the discipline of international law that its presence or absence was not something that could be adequately conceptualized internally within that same framework. Since in absence of sovereign States there was no possibility of international law, their existence or demise could only be presupposed, or appreciated at some distance from the everyday discourse of a relational conception of law. One needed, in other words, to either postulate the existence of an international society prior to the legal relations that are generated within it (in which case regulation only reflects back on the pre-existent 'fact' of a State's existence) or to adjust the legal setting so as to conceive of the place occupied by States as being part of a much broader and diverse cosmopolitan legal order that somehow attributes legal competences to designated actors (which would include States or governments but would not necessarily be confined to them). In the event, Lawrence wanted to have it both ways—States were, for him, both a presupposition in the sense that they existed as factual orders of power quite independently of their legal relations, and simultaneously competent to regulate by way of international law the emergence of new States and their entry into the international family of nations.

For all the difficulties that Lawrence and other international lawyers had in grasping or conceptualizing the place of the sovereign State within their discipline, they were in no doubt as to its importance or of the central role assumed by it in international relations. A hundred years later, however, talk of both the exclusivity of States as subjects of international law and of States as primary actors in international relations is largely regarded as an antiquated, if not wholly, misleading proposition. Within international law itself, the recognition given to the rights and responsibilities of international organizations, to the rights and duties of individuals and a variety of different groups or communities of one form or another (minorities, indigenous peoples, corporations), has made the language of exclusive 'subjects' or 'objects' of international law largely redundant. Non-State actors (whether NGOs or International Organizations) are playing an increasingly important role in treaty-making, and the figure of the 'international community' is repeatedly invoked (in the context, for example, of the elaboration of *erga omnes* obligations) as an entity having some, albeit still rather vague, legal status.[1] Increasingly frequently, furthermore, the notion of 'sovereignty' has become seen as either redundant or as a dangerous fiction, and 'Statism' a derogatory label attached to any approach to international law that is seen to prioritize what States do or say at the expense of individuals and communities over whom they hold authority (see Marks, 2006)

Several considerations have informed this change in disciplinary orientation—some of which may be attributed to the somewhat elusive phenomenon of 'globalization', some to the dynamics of the post-cold war world. In an article written sometime before the attack on the World Trade Centre (which, of course, spawned several new reflections upon the role of non-State actors of one kind or another), Oscar Schachter (1998) was to reflect upon the 'decline of the Nation state' which he observed as being evidenced in four related developments:

(1) The growth, and increased mobility, of capital and technology (enhanced by global communications networks), coupled with a decreasing capacity to regulate foreign direct investment or protect national producers through tariff or non-tariff barriers, has undermined the centrality of the State in the organization of the economy. The age of capital-exporting imperialism or defensive mercantilism is over, and 'the superiority of markets over state control is almost universally accepted' (Schachter, 1998, p 10).

(2) The phenomenal growth of organized non-governmental movements operating across national borders in fields such as human rights, the environment and disarmament (but also including scientific and technical bodies) have become a force for mobilization and political change 'in areas long seen as domestic' and have fostered 'new social identities that cross national lines' (Schachter, 1998, p 13).

The enhanced role of this nascent international 'civil society' had also been paralleled in the emergence of a new transnational 'uncivil society' of drug traffickers, arms traders, terrorists and money launderers whose power had vastly increased as a consequence of the emergence of new communication networks and the deregulation of financial markets. All of these activities have underscored 'the weakness of nation-states and of the international legal system' (Schachter, 1998, p 15).

(3) The (re)emergence of a range of sub-State 'identities' have increasingly challenged the central authority of the juridical State. On one side, the old anti-colonial policy of self-determination has led to the emergence of a much broader array of secessionist movements demanding forms of autonomy or self-government the claims of which are located in a sense of historical, cultural, linguistic, or religious difference (Schachter, 1998, p 16). On the other side, as Franck attested, globalization has led to the emergence of new modes of loyalty and community that are neither 'genetic nor territorial', but rather focus upon a range of increasingly transnational agendas such as human rights, the environment, or feminism (Franck, 1996). This 'modern type of cosmopolitanism', in Schachter's view, marked the 'decline in the authority of the State' (Schachter, 1998, p 18).

(4) Finally, and for Schachter the 'most dramatic' example of the decline in State authority, is to be identified with the emergence of a new phenomenon of 'failed States'

---

[1] See, eg ILC Articles on the Responsibility of States for Internationally Wrongful Acts (2001), Arts 33, 42, 48.

(examples of which he cites as being Liberia, Somalia, and Afghanistan) in which government and civil order have virtually disappeared, and in which the survival of the State depends upon concerted international action. Thus in Cambodia a costly and elaborate 'rescue effort' was put in place involving UN oversight of a process of internal reconstruction that included elections, the creation of a reconciliation process and the establishment of constitutional government. For a period of two years, although Cambodia formally remained a State for international purposes, its government 'did not have full freedom to direct the internal affairs of the country' (Schachter, 1998, p 18).

All of these, in Schachter's view, posed challenges to an global order of States regulated by rules of international law, but were not in themselves sufficient to warrant fundamentally changing either our ideas about international society or of the way in which international law itself was conceptualized. Despite the trends, he concludes that 'it is most unlikely that the state will disappear in the foreseeable future'. Not only has the State provided the structures of authority needed to cope with the 'incessant claims of competing societal groups', but it still promises dignity and protection for the individual with access to common institutions and the equal protection of the law (Schachter, 1998, p 22). For Schachter, then, the key question was not so much whether the State as such would survive, but whether international law could adjust to such phenomena and respond to the changing demands of the environment in which it operated.

Whether or not one accepts Schachter's diagnosis, or indeed his confidence for the future, there are two broad themes interwoven here that are widely shared. One is a sociological reflection on the changing character of international society and the declining power or authority of the nation State, to which may be attributed the elaboration of new schemes of legal responsibility and control for purposes of buttressing or replacing that exercised by States themselves.[2] On the other side is an ethical variant which regards the tradition of State 'sovereignty' to be an archaic impediment to the pursuit of humanitarian or other cosmopolitan agendas (human rights, environmental protection, etc) and which has recommended various interventionist policies of a unilateral or multilateral character.[3] In some ways, of course, these two forms of reflection work against each other: the first believing States to be increasingly marginalized by social forces that escape their regulative or coercive capabilities; the second believing that States retain an authority that needs to be dismantled before emancipatory agendas may be put in place. Where they meet, however, is in an alarming vision of global order in which the State as political agent instructed with the task of 'mediating' between the individual and the general interest (as Hegel would put it) has neither the ability nor competence to resist a global civil society that claims both power and justice on its own side.[4]

---

[2] See, eg proposals relating to the development of 'Global Administrative Law' (Kingsbury, Krisch, and Stewart, 2005), and other initiatives directed towards the development of the accountability of non-State actors more generally (Clapham, 2006).

[3] See, for example, Orford's genealogical account of the relationship between the Responsibility to Protect and the development of international executive authority (Orford, 2011).

[4] See Hardt and Negri, 2000, p 15: 'Empire is formed not on the basis of force itself but on the basis of the capacity to present force as being in the service of right and peace'.

II. HISTORY

At the beginning of the Fourth Edition of his influential *Treatise on International Law* prepared for publication in 1895 shortly before his death, Hall was to start (much as he had in his earlier editions) with a succinct definition:

> International law consists in certain rules of conduct which modern civilised states regard as being binding on them in their relations with one another with a force comparable in nature and degree to that binding the conscientious person to obey the laws of his country, and which they also regard as being enforceable by appropriate means in case of infringement. (Hall, 1895, p 1)

This statement was remarkable in several respects. To begin with, there is the question of tone: this is not the beginning of an enquiry, or a speculation that has to be situated in some historical context. There is no attempt to locate his subject in contemporary debate or practice. This is international law written as science, beginning (as indeed seemed necessary) with a definition. International law is not merely a language, or a way of describing certain activities or practices. It is already a thing with definite content - there to be described. The description itself, of course, is significant. The content of international law is to be found, as far as Hall is concerned, in rules of conduct which States regard as binding upon them. This demands no access to a world of natural law (whether religious or rational), or engagement with the complex of social and political relations that constitute the authority of each of the States involved. Still less is there any requirement to speak about that complex idea—sovereignty—which John Austin had placed at the heart of his description of law. International law was simply to be located in an empirical practice of consent and obligation. At the heart of it, of course, was the 'modern civilized State' whose actions were both the object and measure of this science. One needed a community of civilized States for there to be rules of conduct. One needed also for those States to have a will, or consciousness, as to the binding force of their commitments. One needed, furthermore, for those States to understand that they had committed themselves to a system of law warranting the enforcement 'by appropriate means'. The figure of the State thus stood at centre stage around which an elaborate architecture of legal rules was to be described and generated.

At the time at which Hall was writing, nearly all treatises on international law began in similar manner and would be followed by one or more chapters containing an extemporized discussion of the State as the primary subject of international law (See Westlake, 1904; Twiss, 1884; Lawrence, 1895; Wheaton, 1866; Phillimore, 1871). Typically this section or chapter would seek to define what was meant by a State for purposes of international law, determine who or what would count for such purposes, and address matters of classification (distinguishing perhaps between 'sovereign' or 'semi sovereign' States, and identifying vassals, protectorates, condominia, and unions as particular classes). Comment would routinely be passed on difficulties of nomenclature, debating whether everything called a State could be treated as a State and whether States differed from 'nations'. In the process there would usually also be some associated reflections upon the notion of 'sovereignty' and what that might mean in the context of international relations, and of the putative role that 'recognition' might play.

This format was not merely a haphazard aesthetic choice, but reflected in large measure a desire to lay down in ordered manner the principle axioms or presuppositions of the discipline that could thereafter be employed in a variety of different particular contexts. Once in other words, one had established who the subjects of law were, and the framework for determining the extent and scope of their rights and obligations (ie sources), one could go on to apply those principles to a range of more concrete matters such as the law of the sea, the protection of nationals abroad or belligerent relations. The fact that this discussion of States and their character was always the starting point— almost a professional *a priori* as Koskenniemi has put it—was significant in more ways than one. In one respect, it bespoke of a changing attitude towards the sources of international law reflecting the determination to identify international law so far as possible with the specific determinants of State practice and consent rather than with the inherited tradition of natural rights. In another respect however, it also spoke of the central position that had come to be assumed by 'the State' understood as an idea quite distinct from many of its earlier designations—whether that be the people, the nation, civil society, the sovereign, the monarch, or the multitude. While Hall, like many others, continued to use Bentham's terminology in describing his subject matter (international law), he no longer attributed any significance to the 'nation' as such.

As much as Hall and others were to mark themselves out from their intellectual predecessors, they nevertheless uniformly saw themselves as working in a well-established tradition. This was a tradition understood to have its roots in the Roman Law notion of the *ius gentium* as subsequently received and modified through the work of those such as Suarez, Ayala, Gentili, Grotius, Bynkershoek, Pufendorf, Wolff, and de Vattel. In many respects what seemed to tie these classic works together as a tradition was not simply their espousal of the existence of a law that transcended the sovereign, but that the adumbrated *ius gentium* (or, in some works, the *ius inter gentes*) necessarily presupposed the existence of a plurality of sovereign subjects (whatever the particular terminology) all of which had 'external' relations that would be regulated by its terms. A key moment in this story, thus, was the development of a secular international society within Europe the inauguration of which was marked by the Peace of Westphalia of 1648, in which that community finally emerged from the shadow of the Holy Roman Empire and the coercive authority of the Catholic Church (Hall, 1895, pp 55–60).

The emphasis given to the Peace of Westphalia was significant at a systemic level since it sufficed to think of international society as a society of independent sovereigns. But this of course said very little about the State itself as an idea, the meaning and significance of which certainly did not stay stable over the ensuing centuries. As Machiavelli's account in *The Prince* suggested, the archetypal sixteenth century sovereign existed 'in a relationship of singularity and externality, of transcendence, to his principality' (Foucault, 2007, p 91). Since the Prince could receive his principality by inheritance, acquisition, conveyance or conquest, there was nothing but a synthetic link between the two. The principality, including both its territory and population, stood in a quasi-feudal relation to the Prince's authority; it had no separate meaning or significance. International relations could thus be understood almost exclusively in terms of the rights, possessions, and entitlements of the sovereign.

By the time at which Grotius and Pufendorf were writing in the following century, however, two new traditions of thought had started to emerge. One of these, marked by an invocation of the idea of the social contract (partially present in the work of Grotius, but later given much more concrete form in the work of Hobbes and Locke), sought to forge a definitive link between the people (understood as a community of individuals or as a 'multitude'), and the sovereign (the individual or group of people who were endowed with the right to rule). From this point on, the identification of the sovereign on the one hand, and the location of sovereignty on the other, could plausibly be separated. The other tradition, which was associated with the emergence of mercantilist thought in the seventeenth century, began conceptualizing the territory and people in terms of a unit of economic activity (Foucault, 2007). Since sovereignty, as Locke in particular was to aver, was underpinned by the appropriation and use of land,[5] the idea developed that the exercise of sovereign rights ought to be oriented in that direction: the people should be governed (put to work) and not merely ruled. This involved not only bringing the population as a productive resource within the boundaries of governmental action (eg through the regulation of migration and vagrancy and the introduction of 'poor laws'), but also led to a concern for the maximization of the productive output of land (leading, within Europe, to the 'clearing' of traditional land-holdings, and outside it, to the creation of new settler colonies).

Central to the development of this new 'art of government' (*raison d'état* as it became known), was an idea of the 'State' bearing two characteristics. On one side the State was to be framed by the respective components of territory, population and government, but yet assume an identity that was simultaneously independent of those elements. Governments might come and go, for example, but the State, so long as it retained the core elements, would remain the same. On the other hand, the State was not to be defined merely in terms of a relationship between its component parts, but in the idea also that it had some immanent end—whether that be simply to maintain common peace and security, or further the cause of society.

Both of these strands of thought came neatly to be expressed in Pufendorf's definition of the State as a 'compound Moral person, whose will being united and tied together by those covenants which before passed amongst the multitude, is deemed the will of all, to the end that it may use and apply the strength and riches of private persons towards maintaining the common peace and security' (Pufendorf, 1698, Bk VII, c 2, s 13). A significant feature of Pufendorf's definition, here, anticipated itself in Hobbes' description of the Leviathan, was the personification of the State as a moral entity in its own right. To describe the State as a 'person', a moral or jural entity, had several obvious consequences. In the first instance, it was to encourage the ascription to it, of certain passions, interests, and motivations that went beyond the strictly instrumental task of preserving peace and good order, or defending the realm from external attack. The State, as Wolff would later argue, was also to seek its own 'self-perfection' through the maximization of its wealth and prestige—a task which necessitated the development of new systems of knowledge (statistics) and the bureaucratic organization of social and economic affairs to that end (police). In the second place, it also encouraged the development, in the hands of Vattel in particular, of what has become known as the 'domestic analogy' in which States were to be understood as being in a position analogous to individuals prior to the establishment of civil society, seeking security and community in their relations with others. For Vattel, therefore, States existed in a state of nature, enjoying the same rights 'as nature gives to men for the fulfilment of their duties' (Vattel, 1758, p 4) and such natural liberties as befitted their character. The law of nations provided the structure by which that freedom and equality was to be preserve and promoted within the frame of a wider international society.

In many respects it is difficult to underestimate the enduring significance of Vattel's appealingly simplistic account of the State in international relations. However far international thought may have moved away from the idea of States enjoying certain natural

---

[5] Locke, *Second Treatise of Government*, 1690, pp 18–30. See also Vattel, *The Law of Nations*, 1758, pp 37–8: 'The whole earth is designed to furnish sustenance for its inhabitants; but it cannot do this unless it be cultivated. Every Nation is therefore bound by the natural law to cultivate the land which has fallen to its share'.

prerogatives, or of sovereignty being sharply demarcated between internal and external domains, the idea that the world could be described in terms of States as a sociological category, possessing a distinct 'will', 'mentality', or 'motivation' that may encourage them to interact with one another in certain determinate ways is one that endures to this day—and this no more clearly demonstrated than in the 'rational choice' analytics that is deployed, in some quarters, to detail the process and efficacy of international law (eg Goldsmith and Posner, 2005).

Nevertheless, for those receiving this tradition in the nineteenth century there were always evident complexities that had to be negotiated. To begin with, it was not exactly easy to translate this monadic description of international society as a society of 'free and independent' nations into practice at the time. Writing in the middle of the century, for example, Phillimore was to identify eleven different categories of State, four of which were 'peculiar' cases (Poland, Belgium, Greece, and Egypt), the rest of which included, in addition to States under one sovereign, two categories of Unions, States that took the form of Free Towns or Republics, Tribute-paying States (Vassals) and two further categories of States under different forms of Protectorate. Further to this, there was the complex phenomenon of the German Confederation (a loose alliance of 70 independent 'States') to be explained (Phillimore, 1871, p 101). This was, on no account, a uniform scheme of political organization.

By the end of that century, the picture had become still more complex and primarily as a consequence of a reflection upon the extent to which international law could be applied with equal ease in relation to the non-European world (a concern which had been explicitly taken up by the newly-formed Institut de Droit International in 1879[6]). The problem was this: in their desire to avoid the abstract rationalism of natural law and locate international rights and obligations instead in the empiricism of practice and custom, international lawyers had come to speak about international law in specifically European terms. At a time at which the idea of the nation as a cultural and linguistic community was emerging in a specifically political form (demanding an alignment between nation and State), it seemed obvious that the international relations of such a community of nation-States would be imbued with, or built upon, the same consciousness of history and tradition. Custom seemed to imply some kind of social consensus, and consensus a commonality of understanding and outlook (what Westlake referred to as a 'juridical consciousness') that could only readily be supposed in relation to 'civilized' communities in Europe (or those communities of 'European origin' elsewhere). For some, in fact, international law was actually more properly described as the Public Law of Europe as the work of those such as Martens (1864) and Klüber (1851) attests.

Yet for all this, international lawyers were also aware of the long history of treaty-making with all manner of local sovereigns in Asia, Africa and elsewhere the form of which seemed to suppose that those relations were to be governed by the terms of international law (Alexandrowicz, 1967; Anghie, 2005). Indeed the fact that from the early 1880s onwards European exploration of the interior of Africa was to be marked, amongst other things, by the systematic and widespread conclusion of treaties with local kings and chiefs providing for 'Protection' or for the cession of sovereignty was only to make the issue more pressing. How might an exclusively European system of public law conceive of such arrangements? And what might this imply as regards the status of those communities?

---

[6] Twiss, 1879–80, p 301. See generally Koskenniemi, 2001, pp 98–178.

In one sense the answer was obvious. Although few international lawyers at the time were explicitly to introduce into their definitions of the State a requirement that they be 'civilized',[7] the existence of an implicit 'standard of civilization' ran throughout most their work in relation to recognition or territorial title, or when describing the character of international law (Gong, 1985; Anghie, 2005). Thus, while Hall spoke in quite abstract terms about the 'marks of an independent state' (being permanently established for a political end, possessing a defined territory and being independent of external control) he was still to make clear that international law consisted of those rules of conduct which 'modern civilized states' regarded as being binding upon them (Hall, 1895, p 1). One could not, in other words, assume that simply because there existed treaty relations with non-European States such as China or Japan that those latter States were to be regarded as having the same rights and privileges as other European States. As Lawrence was to note:

> there are many communities outside the sphere of International Law, though they are independent states. They neither grant to others, nor claim form themselves the strict observance of its rules. Justice and humanity should be scrupulously adhered to in all dealings with them, but they are not fit subjects for the application of legal technicalities. It would, for instance, be absurd to expect the king of Dahomey to establish a Prize Court, or to require the dwarfs of the central African forest to receive a permanent diplomatic mission (Lawrence, 1895, p 58).

By and large, thus, international lawyers began to differentiate in their accounts between those 'normal' relations that pertained between European States and those that characterized relations with other political communities on the outside. Beyond Europe, the treaties that put in place regimes of Protection or for consular jurisdiction and extraterritoriality, or those that purported to 'cede' territory, took the form of agreements between sovereign States, the substance of which, however, was to deny any such pretension.

Yet there was also a paradoxical difficulty here. Even if such non-European States did not possess a sovereignty equivalent to that of European States, it was not convenient to deny them status of any kind, as to do so would have put in question the validity of the agreements upon which European privileges seemed to depend (Koskenniemi, 2005, pp 136–43). Some position within the broader frame of international law had to be found for them. They had to be simultaneously included yet excluded from the realm of international law.[8] In the event, there were several different ways in which this matter was approached. Some differentiated between legal relations as might exist between European States and non-legal, moral or ethical, propositions that governed relations with the non-civilized world (Westlake, 1894, pp 137–40), some differentiated between States enjoying full membership and those enjoying merely partial membership in the family of nations (Wheaton, 1866; Oppenheim, 1905), some differentiated between the plenary and partial recognition (Lorimer, 1883, pp 101–23). One point was clear, however, namely that in order to be admitted into the European family of nations, those aspirant States had to demonstrate their 'civilized' credentials. To be 'civilized' furthermore, largely meant

---

[7] See eg Phillimore, 1871, p 94. Occasionally, the point was made more explicit. See Westlake, 1984, pp 102–3; Lawrence, 1895, p 58.

[8] Schmitt, 1974, p 233, examining Rivier's *Lehrbuch des Volkerrechts* (1889) notes that his overview of 'current sovereign states' included 25 States in Europe, 19 in the Americas, then 'States in Africa' including the Congo Free State, the Free State of Liberia, the Orange Free State, the Sultanate of Morocco and the Sultanate of Zanzibar. Schmitt notes that in respect of the latter category these were called States but the word sovereign was avoided and in the case of Morocco and Zanzibar, Rivier had noted that 'obviously' they did 'not belong to the community of international law'. Schmitt asks pithily: 'Why were they even included in the enumeration?'

the creation of institutions of government, law, and administration modelled upon those found in Western Europe (Westlake, pp 141–3; Mill, 1859, pp 161–3). This was a message fully understood in Japan whose rapid process of 'Westernization' in the latter half of the nineteenth century eventually allowed it to rid itself of the regimes of consular jurisdiction that had been put in place in order to insulate Western merchants and traders from the application of local law. Only once this 'badge of imperfect membership' had been removed could it be said to have become a full member of international society (Westlake, 1894, p 46).[9]

These ideas, it has to be said, by no means disappeared overnight. Indeed many of them were remodelled and given institutional form in the League of Nations. Article 38(1)(c) of the statute of the Permanent Court of International Justice still referred to 'the general principles of law recognized by civilised nations' (a phrase also found in the statute of the ICJ) and the theme was maintained in the institutions of the Mandate system designed to deal with the situation of the colonies and territories extracted from Germany and the Ottoman empire under the terms of the various Peace Treaties. Under Article 22 of the Covenant on the League, 'advanced nations' (*viz* Britain, France, Belgium, Australia, New Zealand, South Africa, and Japan) were entrusted with the task of exercising 'tutelage' on behalf of the League over those colonies and territories which were 'inhabited by peoples not yet able to stand by themselves under the strenuous conditions of the modern world'. The purpose of this 'sacred trust' was to advance the 'well-being and development of such peoples' the precise implications of which depended upon a classification set out within that same Article. Certain territories (designated as Class A Mandates) were regarded as having 'reached a stage of development where their existence as independent nations can be provisionally recognized' in which case the Mandatory power was to provide administrative advice and assistance 'until such time as they are able to stand alone'. This category included those territories in the Middle East separated from the Ottoman Empire (Iraq, Palestine and Transjordan, Syria, and Lebanon). Class B territories (those in Africa with the exception of South-West Africa) were to be subject to significantly more intensive degrees of administrative control without any explicit expectation of independence, and Class C territories (Pacific Islands and South-West Africa) were those declared to be 'best administered under the laws of the Mandatory as integral portions of its territory', subject to certain safeguards 'in the interests of the indigenous population'. (See Anghie, 2005, pp 115–95.)

While, as Schwarzenberger suggested, the Mandate system came very close to being a mechanism for the continuation of colonialism 'by other means' (Schwarzenberger 1950, p 134), the very decision to employ 'other means' was significant. To begin with, the institution of an international trusteeship seemed to make clear that Mandate powers were not acquiring such territories as 'colonies', and therefore could not be taken to enjoy the normal rights of sovereignty in relation to such territories. But if that was the case, it posed the obvious question as to where sovereignty lay (Wright, 1930). The territories themselves, could barely be described as sovereign in their own right, as otherwise the restrictions on their

---

[9] A contrast might be drawn here with the rather slower progress made in the case of China. The Nine Power Treaty of 1922 sought to guarantee the 'Open Door' policy in China (by which was meant 'equality of opportunity in China for the trade and industry of all nations') to be secured by barring any agreement that might secure special commercial privileges for any one State. A special Commission was set up to examine the question as to whether the continuation of extraterritorial privileges was justified. It reported back in 1926 concluding that although progress had been made, more was needed before such regimes could be suspended. See Summary and Recommendations of the Report of the Commission on Extraterritoriality in China, 1926, in (1927) 21 *AJIL*, Supplement 58.

independence would have been inexplicable. Some other status had to be devised for them, or at least some language that avoided the problematic implications of the notion of 'sovereignty'. This, of course, was not a problem solely related to the institution of the Mandate, but was equally relevant to the authority exercised by the League of Nations itself—how might its powers be described within an international order comprising of sovereign States?

Whether or not as a consequence of reflecting upon such problems, international lawyers began to regard the notion of sovereignty and its correlates (sovereign equality and domestic jurisdiction) not as something integral to their understanding of international law, but as an obstacle to be overcome. For many, a fixation with the idea of sovereignty as both indicative of the absence of any higher authority, and as the source of law (understood, perhaps, as the will or command of the sovereign) had not only left the discipline in a condition of internal contradiction,[10] but ill-equipped to deal with a world of new international institutions and novel forms of governance. Writing in 1928, for example, Brierly joined the emerging chorus, dismissing the idea of sovereignty as 'an idolon theatre' that bore little relation to the way in which States actually related to one another in practice. (Brierly, 1924, p 13) If 'sovereignty' was to be retained as an idea it had, at the very least, to be re-packaged or re-shaped in some significant way.

One can turn to Hall's Treatise of 1895 as an early illustration of this change. One of the most significant features of the Treatise is its almost total avoidance of the term 'sovereignty' except in relation to those matters which were presumptively 'internal' such as might engage the relationship between the State and its subjects. In place of the word 'sovereignty' when describing the existence or authority of the State, he used the term 'personality'. Legal personality, of course, was a term that had already acquired a prominence in municipal law with the development of the limited liability corporation, but was not a term that had been extensively employed (at that time) in the context of international law. Its significance, however, lay in the fact that the idea of 'personality' assumed the existence of a systemic order that attributed a range of competences to certain designated actors. Just as a corporation, if duly brought into being, would then have the legal capacity to sue and be sued, so also one might think that States could similarly be understood to have been 'accorded' a certain capacity in international law. Statehood, in that context, was no longer something intrinsic, carrying with it certain natural rights or prerogatives (and one may think here, for example, of the 'inherent' right to self-defence), but descriptive of an abstract capacity accorded to certain entities fulfilling the requisite criteria.[11] In contrast to the Vattelian idea of States enjoying a natural liberty in a state of nature, for Hall this liberty of action was one 'subject to law' (Hall, 1895 p 24).

This semantic turn was one that may be appreciated not merely in a shift in linguistic usage from sovereignty to personality (as by no means everyone took that step), but also in an active reconceptualization of the idea of sovereignty itself.[12] Thus, in the *Wimbledon*

---

[10] Kennedy, 1997, p 114 associates a scepticism of sovereignty with positivism: 'To fulfil their polemical mission, to render plausible a legal order among sovereigns, the philosophy which sets this question, which makes sovereigns absolute or requires a sovereign for legal order, must be tempered, if not rejected. As a result, to inherit positivism is also to inherit a tradition of response to the scepticism and deference to absolute state authority, which renders legal order among sovereigns *implausible* in the first place.'

[11] See O'Connell,1970, Vol I, p 80: 'It is clear that the word "person" is used to refer to one who is a legal actor, but that it is of no assistance in ascertaining who or what is competent to act. Only the rules of international law may do this, and they may select different entities and endow them with different legal functions, so it is a mistake to suppose that merely by describing an entity as a "person" one is formulating its capacities in law.'

[12] For a more recent account of the transformation of sovereignty into a new global form of Empire see Hardt and Negri, 2000.

case, when presented with the claim by Germany that the granting of an unfettered right of passage to vessels of all nationalities through the Kiel canal would 'imply the abandonment by Germany of a personal and imprescriptible right, which forms an essential part of her sovereignty' the Permanent Court of International Justice responded by stating that it:

> declines to see in the conclusion of any Treaty by which a State undertakes to perform or refrain from performing a particular act an abandonment of its sovereignty. No doubt any convention creating an obligation of this kind places a restriction on the exercise of sovereign rights of the State, in the sense that it requires them to be exercised in a certain way. But the right of entering into international engagements is an attribute of State sovereignty.[13]

Sovereignty, in other words, was not to be understood as an unfettered freedom from external constraint, but rather as a way of describing a capacity for binding others to, and being bound by, international law. It was no longer something that had any innate content (such as describing certain natural rights or prerogatives), nor something that could be raised as an objection to those obligations once entered into.[14] It was merely a way of describing those remaining powers and liberties afforded to the State under international law.

This new way of thinking was undoubtedly helpful in several respects. To begin with, it allowed a dissociation between the possession of 'sovereign rights' on the one hand and the actual order of power on the other: territories under belligerent occupation,[15] subject to a treaty of Protection or placed under the administration of a Mandatory power could be conceived as being subject to the governmental authority of another yet not part of its territorial sovereignty. Sovereignty in such cases survived in suspended form. It also disposed of the problem of sovereign equality and domestic jurisdiction: States could regard themselves as equal, so long as it was clear that 'equality' meant an equal capacity to enjoy rights and bear obligations. They also retained a right of domestic jurisdiction so far as this described a residual domain of freedom left untrammelled by the constraints of external obligation.[16] It was only a short move from here to the position adopted by Kelsen, amongst others, who came to the conclusion that States were nothing but legal orders, described fully and completely in terms of propositions of law.[17] It was also only a short step to admitting that States were not the only legal subjects contemplated under the terms of the international legal order—there was nothing to exclude the possibility of other agents, whether that be international organizations, individuals or other groups, from being described as having some measure of international personality even if not on a par with that enjoyed by States.

Yet for all the determination to formalize statehood and oppose an inherited tradition that associated sovereignty with the possession of certain determinate rights and

---

[13] S.S. 'Wimbledon', Judgments, 1923, PCI, Series A, No 1, at p 25.

[14] See also *Military and Paramilitary Activities in and against Nicaragua (Nicaragua v United States of America), Merits, Judgment, ICJ Reports 1986*, p 14, para 259: 'A State... is sovereign for purposes of accepting a limitation of its sovereignty'.

[15] See Hague Regulations (1907), Article 43.

[16] See, eg *Nationality Decrees Issued in Tunis and Morocco, Advisory Opinion, 1923, PCIJ, Series B, No 4*, p 24: 'The question whether a certain matter is or is not solely within the jurisdiction of a State is an essentially relative question; it depends upon the development of international relations'.

[17] Kelsen, 1941—2, pp 64–5: 'The State is not its individuals; it is the specific union of individuals, and this union is the function of the order which regulates their mutual behaviour... One of the distinctive results of the pure theory of law is its recognition that the coercive order which constitutes the political community we call a state, is a legal order. What is usually called the legal order of the state, or the legal order set up by the state, is the state itself.'

obligations, there was a strongly resistant current in the shape of the principle of national self-determination. National self-determination, in the form advanced by President Wilson in 1918 (see Section IV of this chapter) implied a substantive conception of the State rooted in ideas of community and cultural homogeneity, determined perhaps by religious or linguistic markers. The sovereignty that this idea demanded was not one that could be regulated from outside, but that inhered in a determinate people with values and interests that required protection and advancement. To the extent that the promotion of national self-determination seemed to go hand in hand with the simultaneous juridification of sovereignty meant that legal doctrine was systematically cut through by an opposition between two ideas of statehood (one formal, the other substantive) and two ideas of sovereignty (one innate, the other attributed or delegated) neither of which could attain ascendency (Koskenniemi, 1989, pp 59–60, 224–33). This opposition, indeed, was to continue to infect the discourse on statehood through the period of decolonization and on into the new millennium—its presence being felt in debates as to the relationship between self-determination and *uti possidetis* (whether 'people' determined the territory, or the territory the people) and in discussions over the implications of recognition (whether it was 'constitutive or 'declaratory').

III. DEFINING THE STATE

The shift in legal thought described earlier from the idea of States existing in a Vattelian state of nature between whom a thin architecture of legal relations came to be established, to one in which States were understood to exist as legal entities endowed with certain competences under international law, was one that could be described in terms of an increasing concern to identify those 'marks' or 'criteria' by which statehood could be measured. For Vattel, describing or defining the State was primarily a matter of trying to capture, in as neutral as possible terms, the plurality of different kinds of political communities existing in Europe in the middle of the eighteenth century, but for those doing the same 100 or 200 years later, the project of description had taken on a different character.

For a period of time, it wasn't entirely clear whether what was being described in the process was a sociological fact or a legal category (one could construe a definition that merely outlined the 'marks' of a State in either way), but the terms of description became more explicitly exclusionary in nature as time went by. Thus when Wheaton in 1866 endorsed Cicero's classic definition of the State as 'a body political, or society of men, united together for the purpose of promoting their mutual safety or advantage by their combined strength' he was constrained to point out, at the same time, its limitations. It did not include, as far as he was concerned, corporations created by the State itself, nor 'voluntary associations of robbers or pirates', nor 'unsettled horde[s] of wandering savages', nor indeed nations since the State 'may be composed of different races of men' (Wheaton, 1866, s 17). The definition of the State thus became a vehicle not merely for purposes of description (providing an analytical framework for understanding the character of international society for purposes of law) but also for purposes of distinguishing between those political communities that might properly be regarded as subjects of international law and those that would not. For some, this shift in orientation was decisive. As O'Connell was later to suggest (1970, p 81): 'the proposition "France is a State" is not a description or a definition but merely a conclusion to a train of legal reasoning'.

Yet there was clearly a difficulty associated with this move from fact to law (or, if you prefer, from description to prescription). How, and in what way, might one conceive of international law participating in the establishment of territorial political communities? The title of Crawford's influential book on the subject—*The Creation of States in International Law*—would appear to attribute to international law a decisive role. Yet, it might be responded, States are surely not 'created' by international law in the same sense that a cabinet maker might craft a piece of furniture; rather they typically emerge through sustained political action and agitation—frequently violent—in which political independence is wrested from forces sustaining the political *status quo*. Indeed, that international lawyers (Crawford amongst them) rely upon the notion of 'effectiveness' for purposes of determining the existence or otherwise of a State is to suggest that the role of law is almost entirely *ex post facto*. 'Sovereignty' as Wade was to claim seemed to be 'a political fact for which no purely legal authority can be constituted' (Wade, 1955, p 196). But Crawford was not naïve in this sense. What he was arguing against was an exclusively 'empirical' notion of statehood. A State is not, as he puts it, 'a fact in the sense that a chair is a fact' it is rather 'a legal status attaching to a certain state of affairs by virtue of certain rules or practices' (Crawford, 2006, p 5). A closer analogy therefore might be the idea of the status of 'criminality' being generated through the institutions and structures of the criminal law, or of 'insanity' through the discipline of psychiatry (Foucault, 2006). Just as 'a thief' is a designation appropriate only once it has been determined that the person concerned has unlawfully appropriated the property of another, so also to call something a 'State' is to draw attention to the legal framework within which the powers and competences of a State may properly be acquired (Kelsen, 1941–2).

While this usefully directs our attention both to the relational aspect of statehood and the idea that its meaning is constituted in a range of ideas about authority and responsibility, it still doesn't quite deal with the problem. Crawford's assumption that the legal order that accords 'statehood' to those entities that possess the requisite characteristics might be meaningful so far as one may conceive of States being constituted through essentially consensual processes. The emergence of new Republics out of the defunct Soviet Union in the early 1990s, for example, posed relatively few problems on this score for the simple reason that Russia had effectively renounced, in the Alma Ata Declaration and Minsk Accord,[18] any legal interest or claims to sovereignty over those regions (Mullerson, 1993). Here, one could conceive of the parent State either 'delegating' sovereign authority to the nascent regime (much in the same way as Czechoslovakia, Poland, or the Serb-Croat-Slovene State were 'created' at the Peace Conferences in the aftermath of the 1914–18 War), or perhaps as creating the necessary legal 'space' through its evacuation of its claim to sovereignty, in order for the new State to then assert its rights over the territory and population concerned.[19] By and large, in fact, this has been the predominant means by which new States have emerged since 1945 even if many have done so under the rubric of 'self-determination'.

---

[18] Agreement Establishing the Commonwealth of Independent States (Minsk Accord), 8 December 1991, 31 *ILM* (1992) 143; Alma Ata Declaration, 21 December 1991, ibid, p 148.

[19] One may note here, that the answer often depends upon the stance adopted in relation to the role of recognition. See, eg Hall, 1895, p 88: 'Of course recognition by a parent state, by implying an abandonment of all pretensions over the insurgent community, is more conclusive evidence of independence than recognition by a third power, and it removes all doubt from the minds of other governments as to the propriety of recognition by themselves; but it is not a gift of independence; it is only an acknowledgement that the claim made by the community to have definitively established its independence.'

Yet it is also evident that in many cases the issue is not one of the consensual devolution of sovereign authority (*viz* the *granting* of independence) but of the emergence of a new State out of a condition of dispute or conflict. Here the question remains as to how one might conceive of a moment in which sovereign authority is created out of the mere fact of the forcible or violent seizure of power? In a lecture entitled 'Force of Law: the Mystical Foundation of Authority' Jacques Derrida (1989–90, p 927) posed the following question:

> How are we to distinguish between the force of law of a legitimate power and the supposedly originary violence that must have established this authority and that could not itself have been authorized by any anterior legitimacy, so that, in this initial moment, it is neither legal nor illegal—or, others would quickly say, neither just nor unjust?

Taking as his starting point, Walter Benjamin's distinction between 'constituted' and 'constitutive' force (between force authorized by law and force that originally establishes legal authority) Derrida's essay was concerned with highlighting how these two ideas converged, and to point out the continued presence within all schemes of law and legal thought of an originary (extra-legal) violence that necessarily accompanied the establishment of that legal authority. Of course, even if the authority of an original constitution cannot be thought to depend upon the law which it brings into effect, this may not preclude the possibility that international law may provide the means for validating that authority 'from the outside' so to speak. But once again we are presented with two difficulties. The first is that in order to sustain the argument that other States may authorize or validate the existence of a new State, one would still have to move back to determine the basis upon which those authorities claimed that ability. How might existing States bring into existence another State with 'law creating capacity' without the latter being seen, in some respects, as a subordinate authority? Does this not invoke a certain imperial mindset?

The second difficulty is that, as mentioned earlier, in a world already fully demarcated in terms of sovereign jurisdiction (in which there is no effective space for the emergence of an entirely new State like that of Liberia in 1847 or the Congo Free State in 1885) the process of 'creation' can only be achieved by way of displacing in some manner the prior claims to sovereignty of an existing State. Unless existing claims to territorial sovereignty are lifted or suspended in some way (such as by consent), the emergence of a new State could not be achieved without some measure of illegality.

Whatever the problems associated with this move from description to prescription, it was always evident that if States were to be regarded as actors endowed with personality by a superordinating legal order, it was necessary to set out somewhere the terms under which this 'attribution' of authority might take place and the consequences of it. Strange as it may seem, although the UN and the League of Nations before it were committed to a process of the codification of international law, they managed to accomplish neither of these tasks. In 1949 the International Law Commission did produce a Draft Declaration on the Rights and Duties of States,[20] which went some way towards summarizing what the implications of Statehood might be, albeit the case that this draft was not adopted by the General Assembly. Alongside a list of ten duties the Draft Declaration included four rights: 'the right to independence and hence to exercise freely, without dictation by any other States, all its legal powers, including the choice of its own form of government' (Article 1), 'the right to exercise jurisdiction over its territory and over all persons and things therein, subject to the immunities recognized by international law' (Article 2), the

---

[20] GA Res 375(VI) (6 December 1949), Annex.

right to 'equality in law with every other State' (Article 5), and the 'right of individual and collective self-defence against armed attack' (Article 12). Each of these, with some qualification, seems to describe those powers possessed only by States to which may be added, perhaps, a plenary competence to perform legal acts such as conclude treaties, a right not to be subject to compulsory international process or dispute settlement without consent, and the benefit of a presumption that they enjoy an 'unlimited freedom' subject only to those constraints determined by law (the '*Lotus*' principle) (Crawford, 2006, pp 40–41). These, in some respects at least, might suggest why Statehood remains an attractive proposition.

While drafting the Declaration, the International Law Commission also briefly discussed the merits of seeking to define the State for purposes of international law. The general reaction, at that time, was that such a project was either unnecessary as being self-evident or too controversial (the concern being that it would only have salience as regards 'new' rather than 'old' States). In some respects at least, this caution was probably informed by the fact that the Pan American Union (the predecessor of the Organization of American States) had already drafted the Montevideo Convention on the Rights and Duties of States 1933, Article 1 of which set out a basic definition which, if not definitive, could be taken as the starting point for most discussions of territorial status. Article 1 provides as follows:

> The State as a person of international law should possess the following qualifications:
>
> (a) a permanent population;
>
> (b) a defined territory;
>
> (c) government; and
>
> (d) capacity to enter into relations with other states.

For all its significance Article 1 is still treated with a certain degree of circumspection. The 'capacity to enter into relations with other states' seems to be a conclusion rather a starting point, and there is no mention of other putatively relevant matters such as independence, legitimacy, democracy, or self-determination. Precisely what Article 1 'declares', furthermore, is a little unclear. As a legal prescription, the terms of the Montevideo Convention appear to be either too abstract or too strict. They are too abstract in the sense that to say that an entity claiming to be a State needs to be able to declare itself as having people, territory and a form of government is really to say very little, and certainly does nothing to guide responses to claims by aspirant States such as Chechnya, Kosovo, Northern Cyprus, Palestine, or Quebec. Certainly it may exclude Wheaton's private corporation or his nomadic society, but one may ask what else? And to what end?

What appears to be needed here is one of two things. One possibility is that it requires a quantitative measure of intensity: so instead of merely necessitating the existence of a people, a territory and something that describes itself as a government, it requires that these qualities are possessed in sufficient degree. It must be large enough and effective enough to warrant being regarded as both self-sufficient and, as the final qualification suggests, have the capacity to enter into relations with other States. Another possibility is that it requires some qualitative evaluation—so rather than merely expecting a claim to be made in respect of a people or a territory, it expects those claims to be justified in some way for example on the basis that they respond to a principle of self-determination or are capable of substantiation without impinging upon the rights and duties of other sovereign States.

But both of these measures—of intensity and justification—seem then to demand too much. The measure of intensity seems to require the articulation of a 'threshold' evaluation the establishment of which would be virtually impossible in the abstract—who could say in advance how much territory, or how many people, are required in order to create a State? Surely what would matter is whether it is capable of surviving as an independent State, and that, presumably, is something to be determined after the fact so to speak? The measure of justification has a similar problem; it seems to rely upon the prior establishment of internationally recognized regimes of entitlement and responsibility (recognized claims over territory or in relation to nationals) the validity of which would assume that the State as a legal subject is already in existence. In either case, the problem is how one moves from fact to law, or from cognition of the existence of something that calls itself a State to its legal recognition without, in a sense, assuming that the thing being offered the imprimatur of 'legality' is not somehow already legally existent.

A. POPULATION

As suggested earlier, one of the critical ideas accompanying the development of the idea of the State was that the people were not merely the accidental objects of a sovereign's authority, but that they also partook of that sovereignty and were the immediate object of an emergent art of government (for which Lincoln's phrase 'government by the people, for the people, and of the people' was an obvious cumulative expression). A population was not merely a means of demonstrating the wealth and power of the sovereign, or a means by which the State could ultimately secure itself in competition with others (through the drafting of troops and the cooption of labour for the production of wealth). It also provided the rationality for government itself: the purpose of government (and hence of the State) was, amongst other things, the promotion of the prosperity and happiness of the populace.

That the State was to have this immanent end was to encourage the idea that, to be politically and economically viable, it needed to be of sufficient size (Hobsbawm, pp 29–39). The smaller, more backward, nationalities as Mill was to aver, were much better off being absorbed into larger nations, rather than 'sulk on [their] own rocks...cut off from the general movement of the World' (Mill, 1861, pp 363–4). Unification thus became the dominant theme of nation-building in the nineteenth century and the claims of those such as the Fenians in Ireland or the Bretons in France routinely disparaged. This was an idea not entirely shaken off in the early part of the twentieth century as doubt continued to be expressed as to whether small States such as Luxembourg or Liechtenstein, for example, could properly be regarded as independent States. Liechtenstein, indeed, was denied membership of the League of Nations in 1920 the formal reason for which was its lack of independence from Austria (to whom it had 'delegated' certain customs and postal duties under Agreement). Underlying that, however, was an evident concern over its size and the political implications of allowing microstates the same voting rights as other States in the organs of the League (Duursma, 1996, pp 173–4). Later practice in the context of the UN, however, has suggested that such a consideration is no longer quite what it used to be. Alongside Liechtenstein as members of the UN (for which, as Article 4 of the UN Charter makes clear, being a State is a prerequisite) sit States such as Andorra, Monaco, Brunei, Kiribati, Nauru, Palau, Vanuatu, and the Marshall Islands all of which have populations of under one million. As most conclude, whatever the Montevideo Convention says, there seems to be no minimum threshold population necessary in order to obtain statehood.

If the criterion of population seems not to relate to the notion of a threshold, then perhaps it refers instead to the idea that there must exist a population enjoying exclusive relations of nationality with the nascent State. While it is certainly true that in the early years of the twentieth century nationality did enjoy this aura of exclusivity—and hence, in some respects, represented a way of demarcating the populations of different States—this was merely an expectation rather than an obligation. The competence to confer and with-hold nationality was still regarded as a matter falling within the domain of domestic juris-diction in the sense that international law neither required such conferral in any particular case nor prohibited its withdrawal.[21] The only context in which international law seemed to be relevant was where one State sought to rely upon the bond of nationality when bring-ing a claim against another State alleging harm to one of its nationals and in which the reality of that 'bond' was open to dispute.[22] Not only did the conferral of nationality thus seem to be a competence that ensued from having legal capacity as a State (a consequence, that is, not a precondition), but as the toleration of multiple nationality has increased (see Franck, 1999, pp 61–75) even the theoretical possibility of it being regarded as an effec-tive condition for statehood has similarly disappeared. In fact the almost total conceptual separation between statehood and the idea of a constitutive population was marked in the second Opinion of the Badinter Commission in 1992 in which the Commission suggested, in the context of the collapse of the Socialist Federal Republic of Yugoslavia, that one of the possible implications of the principle of self-determination was that the individuals concerned should have a right to choose their own nationality.[23] That this offered the pos-sibility that a majority of the population of a new State might 'opt' for the nationality of a neighbouring State was treated as largely irrelevant for purposes of determining whether the new State met the conditions necessary for its own legal existence. Rather than a con-dition of statehood, thus, the existence of a 'population' seems to be cast in metaphorical terms—they must be exist 'as if' in relationship to an order of government over territory, in which their presence as objects of coercion is necessary, but their identity as partici-pants in that political community remains indeterminate.

B. TERRITORY

Much of the previous discussion also applies in relation to the criterion of territory. Just as there appears to be no threshold requirement for purposes of population, so also it is hard to discern any specific condition concerning possession of sufficient portions of land. Monaco has a territory of less than 1.95 km2 and the Vatican City (a 'non-member State' at the UN) less than 0.5 km2. (Duursma, 1996, 117) At the same time, it is clear that the real issue in most cases is not the issue of size, nor indeed the mere factual possession or control over territory (as, of course, possession may always be 'adverse' as in cases of bel-ligerent occupation), but rather the ability to rightfully claim the territory as a domain of exclusive authority. If, as Arbitrator Huber put it in the *Island of Palmas* case, sovereignty signifies independence, and independence 'in regard to a portion of the globe... the right to exercise therein, to the exclusion of any other State, the function of a State',[24] then the existence or absence of competing claims to sovereignty would appear to be key.

There is, however, an obvious difficulty here. If what is required of new States is the pos-session of territory that is otherwise 'unclaimed' or 'undisputed' then, unless one were to

---

[21] *Nationality Decrees Issued in Tunis and Morocco, Advisory Opinion, 1923, PCIJ, Series B, No 4*, p 24.

[22] *Nottebohm, Second Phase, Judgment, ICJ Reports 1955*, p 4.

[23] See also ILC Draft Articles on Nationality of Natural Persons in Relation to the Succession of States (1999), Articles 1 and 11.

[24] *Island of Palmas Case* (1928) 2 *RIAA* 829.

be able to identify the territory in question as *terra nullius* (unoccupied territory),[25] or territory which has been explicitly or tacitly 'ceded' to it, then it is very difficult to see how any such nascent State could fulfil such a criterion. This indeed, seems to be the condition of most secessionist enterprises and the extent cause for most to go unfulfilled. Yet the position is not quite as clear as this might suggest. It has long been accepted that the absence of clearly delimited boundaries is not a prerequisite for statehood. Albania, for example, was admitted to the League of Nations in 1920 despite the fact that its frontiers had yet to be finally fixed, the subsequent delimitation of which came to be the subject of an Advisory Opinion of the PCIJ in the *Monastery of Saint Naoum* case of 1924.[26] Reflecting upon this practice, the International Court of Justice subsequently affirmed in the *North Sea Continental Shelf* cases that:

> The appurtenance of a given area, considered as an entity, in no way governs the precise delimitation of its boundaries, any more than uncertainty as to boundaries can affect territorial rights. There is for instance no rule that the land frontiers of a State must be fully delimited and defined, and often in various places and for long periods they are not...[27]

Of course, one can rationalize this practice to the extent that one treats the border and the territory of the State as two different things. Borders seem to be the consequence of the possession of territory—their delimitation proceeding on the basis that there are legitimate entitlements on either side. Territory, in the context of statehood, however, seems incapable of being framed purely in terms of ownership or possession for the simple reason that it concerns the prior question as to the very existence of the legal person rather than merely its spatial parameters.

This distinction between the territory of a State and its boundaries is an appealing one in the sense that it allows for the disposal of ongoing disputes over the location of borders (often by reference to the classical 'modes' by which territory might be acquired such as discovery, cession, annexation, occupation or prescription[28]) without, at the same time, continually calling into question the identity of the States whose borders are the subject of dispute. It would be almost absurd to argue, for example, that the alteration of the UK's jurisdiction that occurred as a consequence of its assertion of sovereignty over the Island of Rockall in 1972 (following an earlier claim to its 'possession' in 1955) was such as to affect its legal identity and therefore require it to apply afresh for membership in the UN. At the same time, it is clear that radical changes to borders can have precisely that function—as was demonstrated, in particular, in the case of Yugoslavia/Serbia (see Blum, 1992). Borders, after all, are not merely lines on the ground, or ways of delimiting spheres of public jurisdiction, but serve also to delimit the existence of a political order by means of its separation from others—the 'non-democratic condition of democracy' as Balibar puts it (Balibar, 2004). The supposition, thus, that the lack of delimited borders is of no consequence is hard to maintain. In case of the emergence of Israel in 1948, for example, it was not merely the case that some of its borders were in question, but the entirety of its territory which had been carved out of the defunct Mandate for Palestine. In that context no small significance can be attributed to the general atmosphere of uncertainty generated, amongst other things, by the Security Council's failure to endorse the General Assembly's plan for partition outlined in Resolution 181(II) of 1947 and the apparent termination of

[25] For a discussion of this notion in the context of Western Sahara, see *Western Sahara, Advisory Opinion, ICJ Reports 1975*, p 12, paras 79–81.

[26] *Monastery of Saint-Naoum, Advisory Opinion, 1924, PCIJ, Series B, No 9.*

[27] *North Sea Continental Shelf, Judgment, ICJ Reports 1969*, p 3, para 46.

[28] For a classical account of the modes of acquisition of territory see Jennings, 1963.

the Mandate occasioned by the withdrawal of the British administration. The lack of an effective interlocutor able to claim that recognition of the new State constituted a violation of its own territorial sovereignty (even though there were clearly arguments to be made on the part of the Palestinian population generally) was such as to allow a critical space for recognition of the State of Israel without the kinds of qualms associated with premature recognition that would naturally arise in other contexts. Once again, thus, the criterion of territory like that of population, appears to principally subsist at the level of metaphor and fantasy: the 'reality' to which it seeks to direct our attention being one whose (contradictory) conditions of possibility are found in the performance of a belief that it is already 'the case'.

C. INDEPENDENT GOVERNMENT

To a large extent, those addressing the criteria for statehood are unified on one matter above all else: that the criteria are ultimately directed towards the recognition of 'effective' governmental entities. Governmental effectiveness understood as its power to assert a monopoly over the exercise of legitimate physical violence within a territory (to paraphrase Weber, 1994, pp 310–11) is taken to be central.[29] In a sense, the Weberian definition is evidently tautological—to say whether an entity enjoys a monopoly over the exercise of legitimate violence assumes the prior establishment of a distinction between legitimate and illegitimate violence (between the violence of the police and that of the insurgent). But what is clearly meant is that the government concerned must demonstrate unrivalled possession and control of public power (whatever the specificities of that might be in any particular setting), and that once that unrivalled possession is established recognition of statehood may follow. This emphasis upon governmental effectiveness forms a key part of Crawford's thesis. Given that 'nationality is dependent upon statehood, not vice versa' and that territory is defined 'by reference to the extent of governmental power exercised', 'there is a good case' he suggests 'for regarding government as the most important single criterion of statehood, since all the others depend upon it' (Crawford, 2006, p 56).

Crawford's argument doesn't stop here though. His purpose is not simply to point out that, as the Commission of Jurists maintained in the *Aaland Islands* case, a new State only comes into existence once it is 'strong enough to assert [itself] throughout the territories of the State without the assistance of foreign troops.'[30] Rather, it is to suggest that this criterion of effectiveness operates as a legal principle the effect of which is conditioned by other relevant principles such as that of self-determination or the prohibition on the use of force. He is thus able to maintain that, in some contexts, relatively effective political entities such as the Turkish Republic of Northern Cyprus or Southern Rhodesia have not come to be recognized as independent States for the reason that to offer such recognition would have violated other relevant norms of international law having the status of *jus cogens*. In the same sense, but to different effect, he also maintains that the criterion of effectiveness is, in practice, of relatively less significance if the State in question is one that enjoys a right of self-determination.

Crawford cites, by way of illustration, the case of the Belgian Congo which was granted a hurried independence in 1960 as the Republic of the Congo in circumstances in which

---

[29] Lauterpacht, 1947, pp 340–41: 'The principal and probably the only essential condition of recognition of States and governments is effectiveness of power within the State and of actual independence of other States. Other conditions are irrelevant to the true purposes and nature of recognition.'

[30] LNOJ, Sp Supp 4 (1920) pp 8–9.

little preparation had been made for independence and in which public order broke down shortly after (with secessionist factions seeking their own independence in Katanga and elsewhere). Belgian troops were reintroduced into the territory under the guise of humanitarian intervention and the UN responded by establishing ONUC for purposes of restoring order whose mission continued until 1964. As Crawford puts it '[a]nything less like effective government it would be hard to imagine. Yet despite this there can be little doubt that in 1960 the Congo was a State in the full sense of the term' (Crawford, 2006, p 57). Its admission to the UN for membership had already been approved and UN action had been taken on the basis of preserving the 'sovereign rights of the Republic of the Congo'. Crawford suggests ultimately that there were three possible ways of interpreting this practice: (i) that the international recognition of the Congo was simply premature because it did not possess an effective government; (ii) that international recognition of the Congo had the effect of creating a State despite the fact that it was not properly qualified (ie, that recognition was thereby 'constitutive'); or (iii) that the requirement of 'government' was, in certain particular contexts, less stringent than might otherwise be thought.

Crawford's clear preference is for the third of these three options and he explains the position as follows:

> by withdrawing its own administration and conferring independence on local authorities, Belgium was precluded from denying the consequences of its own conduct. Thereafter there was no international person as against whom recognition of the Congo could be unlawful. It is to be presumed that a new State granted full and formal independence by a former sovereign has the international right to govern its territory.... On the other hand, in the secessionary situation the position is different. A seceding entity seeks statehood by way of an adverse claim, and in general statehood can only be obtained by effective and stable exercise of governmental powers. (Crawford, 2006, pp 57–8)

It is important to understand the role assigned to the idea of effectiveness here. To begin with, it is presented as a general principle of international law—it is not, in that sense, a 'law creating fact' (as might be expressed in the phrase *ex factis ius oritur*), but simply a circumstantial trigger that produces certain legal consequences. Effectiveness, furthermore, is not sufficient on its own: just as some effective entities have not been recognized as States (such as Taiwan whose recognition as an independent State has been almost permanently deferred as a consequence of the claims made by China over its territory), so also other less-than-effective entities have continued to be regarded as States despite that condition (and one may mention here both States under a condition of belligerent occupation such as the Baltic Republics between 1940 and 1990 and Kuwait in 1990–91, and States which, like Lebanon and Burma in the 1970s, have experienced extended periods of internal turmoil). Effectiveness, in other words, is supposed to operate as a principle, the parameters of which are legally determined and may, at that level, interact with other relevant principles such as those of self-determination or of the prohibition on the use of force.

Yet it is equally clear that the further one goes in seeking to juridify the condition of 'effective government', the more clearly one exposes the inevitable tension between a legal principle that seeks to allow the recognition of new aspirant entities once they have become legal 'facts' so to speak, and one that prohibits any such recognition as being a violation of the territorial sovereignty of the State from which that entity is to emerge. In the nineteenth century, the criterion of effectiveness was intimately linked with the idea of premature recognition. If a third State were to recognize an insurgent movement as an independent State before the moment at which they had fully established themselves, that recognition would constitute 'a wrong done to the parent state' and, indeed, 'an act of intervention' (Hall, 1895, p 89).[31] European powers were, thus, very cautious when addressing the recognition of the new States in South America, frequently modulating their response by reference to what seemed to be happening on the ground. Usually the insurgent communities were initially recognized *de facto*, *de iure* recognition coming once it was clear that Spain had given up the fight. The importance of effectiveness, in such a context, was found in the way in which it served to definitively mark the moment at which the rights of the parent State gave way in face of those of the secessionist movement, much in the same way as it served to mark the point at which territory was acquired by way of annexation or occupation. This also meant that effectiveness was something of a movable feast in the sense that it never really meant quite the same thing in every place.[32] What was required in order to establish territorial sovereignty depended upon the nature and strength of rival claims such that a relatively ineffective Congo Free State could garner recognition in 1885 simply because of the apparent absence of any other recognized sovereign whose rights would be impeded in the process, yet considerably more was required for the recognition of the new Republics in Latin America. For all the subtle modulations of this early practice, however, such arguments clearly became more problematic in the course of the twentieth century once it came to be accepted that the use of force was no longer a legitimate means of acquiring title to territory.[33]

If the general prohibition on the use of force implies the illegality of the annexation of territory, it is very hard to see how one might legitimate the establishment of a State on the territory of another by that means (*ex inuria ius non oritur*). The now classic case of Manchukuo—cited mainly as an exemplar of the doctrine of non-recognition—is perhaps an example. When Japan engineered the establishment of the State of Manchukuo in China in 1931, the Lytton Commission, which had been dispatched by the League of Nations on a fact-finding mission, concluded that the Japanese action was inconsistent with both the Covenant and the Kellogg-Briand Pact and that Manchukuo itself remained largely under Japanese control. Its report underpinned the subsequent articulation of the 'Stimson doctrine' the substance of which affirmed the refusal of the USA (and those States which followed it) to 'admit the legality of any situation *de facto*. . . which may impair. . . the sovereignty, the independence, or of the territorial and administrative integrity of the Republic of China' that had been brought about by means contrary to the Pact of Paris.[34] Several League of Nations resolutions were adopted on this basis calling for non-recognition and the 'State' was finally dismantled in 1945. More recently than this, the establishment of the Turkish Republic in Northern Cyprus following the Turkish intervention in 1974 was denied recognition, principally again on the basis that its creation was the product of an unlawful military intervention.[35] Similar arguments were also put forward by Bosnia in its memorial in the *Genocide Case* which maintained that the Republica Srpska was not a

---

[31] In practice, even the intermediary step of recognizing insurgents as belligerents, as Britain and France did in relation to the secessionist States in the American Civil War of 1861–5, was frequently treated as an unjustified intervention.

[32] *Island of Palmas Case* (1928) 2 *RIAA* 829 per Huber: 'Manifestations of territorial sovereignty assume. . . different forms according to conditions of time and place. Although continuous in principle, sovereignty cannot be exercised in fact at every moment on every point of a territory. The intermittence and discontinuity compatible with the maintenance of the right necessarily differ according as inhabited or uninhabited regions are involved, or regions enclosed within territories in which sovereignty is incontestably displayed or again regions accessible from, for instance, the high seas.'

[33] See Article 2(4) UN Charter; Declaration of Principles of International Law Concerning Friendly Relations and Co-operation among States in Accordance with the Charter of the UN, GA Res 2625(XXV) (24 October 1970), Principle 1. See generally Korman, 1996.

[34] 1 Hackworth 334   [35] See *Cyprus v Turkey* [GC], no 2571/94, ECHR 2001-IV, 120 ILR 10.

State in part at least because its creation was associated with a violation of the prohibition on the use of force on the part of Serbian forces.[36]

It is worth noting, in this context, that the prohibition on the use of force has also been an idea instrumental not merely in resisting the establishment of puppet regimes, but of preserving the formal 'continuity' of States during periods of occupation. The Baltic Republics (Estonia, Latvia, and Lithuania), for example, were occupied by the Soviet Union in 1940 and incorporated within the Union. A good many States refused to recognize the legality of the incorporation (Ziemele, 2005, pp 22–27) and when in 1990 the Supreme Councils of the three Baltic States resolved to 're-establish' their independence (which involved the re-invocation of laws pre-dating the occupation and the rejection of obligations assumed on their behalf by the Soviet Union) the EC adopted a Declaration welcoming 'the restoration of sovereignty and independence of the Baltic States which they had lost in 1940' and resolving to re-establish diplomatic relations with them.[37] The prohibition on the use of force, in other words, seems to work not only as a way of denying the recognition of what might otherwise be regarded as effective entities, but as a way of keeping alive (as a formal idea at least) States which have been the subject of occupation and annexation and which are, to all intents and purposes, therefore 'ineffective'. In some respects at least, this seems to be unavoidable: one may recall the first Gulf War of 1990 was authorized by the Security Council in Resolution 678 (29 November 1990) on the basis of seeking to protect and secure the territorial integrity and political independence of Kuwait the continued existence of which had to be presupposed for purposes of authorizing the action despite the fact that its government had been effectively displaced by that of Iraq.

If this analysis is accurate, however, it does pose the question as to whether the principle of governmental effectiveness has any real meaning other than as a form of historical retrospection. If it is an idea that is systematically displaced by rules relating to the use of force or otherwise modulated by the principle of self-determination, its significance as a way of marking out the moment at which a State may be said to have come into legal existence seems to have significantly diminished. On one side, one may note an increased willingness to recognize as States (for one reason or another) entities that are in some respects ineffective—one may recall in recent years for example, that both Bosnia-Herzegovina and Croatia were recognized by the EC as independent States in 1992 at a time at which the governments concerned had effective control over only a portion of the territory in question (Rich, 1993). On the other side, it is also hard to think of many examples of new States emerging and being recognized simply because they have managed to secure their independence as a matter of fact. There are clearly several that have not (Katanga, Abkhazia, and the Republika Srpska for example) and for those that seem to be likely cases, some other explanatory framework is usually deployed (such as consent, self-determination, or disintegration) as a means of displacing the claims of the territorial sovereign. The most problematic cases are those of Bangladesh and Eritrea, the recognition of which could not easily be framed in terms of the standard understanding self-determination. Yet even here, commentators have tended to seek some other interpretive framework for explaining such practice: relying, for example, on the idea that Eritrea had been unlawfully seized by Ethiopia, and that Bangladesh had been effectively governed as a non-self-governing territory by Pakistan (a case 'approximating' colonial rule).

This tendency towards the promotion of an exclusively 'juridical' idea of statehood in which questions of effectiveness are routinely subordinated by reference to other legal

---

[36] *Memorial of the Government of the Republic of Bosnia and Herzegovina*, 15th April 1994, p 264.
[37] 7/8 Bull EC (1991) 1423.

principles has been noted in the work of those such as Jackson and Kreijen. For Jackson (1990, pp 21–31), decolonization marked the moment at which the notion of sovereignty increasingly took on a negative cast (as implying merely freedom from external interference as opposed to a positive capacity to act), leading to the recognition of what he calls 'quasi-States': States which, because of their precipitous independence, were given the imprimatur of statehood before developing the necessary internal capacity for political self-government and economic independence. Rather than be developed prior to independence, such States (mainly those in Africa it seems) have had to develop themselves after it. A similar stance is adopted by Kreijen who speaks of this change in terms of the 'transformation of the notion of independence from an inherently material concept based on internal sovereignty to a mere formal legal condition primarily depending on external recognition' (Kreijen, 2002, p 92). For Kreijen, this 'juridification of statehood' was a situation that demanded ameliorative action such as through the recognition of a right to development or the reintroduction of the notion of trusteeship into international law.

Such reflections draw upon themes that are common to recent debates over 'failed' or 'fragile' States, the significance of which goes someway beyond the narrow confines of a discussion as to the conditions under which a new State should be recognized, but nevertheless have resonance for an understanding of what the implications of statehood might be. In an influential article, Helman and Ratner (1992) commented upon what they saw to be a new phenomenon in international relations: the emergence of 'failed' or 'failing States'. Failed States were States such as Somalia, Sudan, Liberia, and Cambodia in which civil conflict, government breakdown and economic privation imperilled their own citizens and threatened their neighbours 'through refugee flows, political instability, and random warfare'. The designation of such States as 'failed', of course, was not simply a neutral exercise in description or diagnosis, but formed a necessary prelude for the adumbration of a series of policy recommendations the central feature of which was the proposed introduction of a system of 'United Nations Conservatorship' along the lines subsequently established in East Timor, Bosnia-Herzegovina, and Kosovo for purposes of national, post-conflict, reconstruction. While for Helman and Ratner, the notion was one that recommended reconstructive activity, in other hands, State failure has formed the basis for advocacy of a 'preventive' system including the imposition of sanctions upon such States and their exclusion from membership in international organizations (Rothberg, 2002). In some even, the notion has been employed as the basis for a refusal to recognize or implement treaty obligations.[38] As Simpson points out, such ideas are redolent of those abounding at the end of the nineteenth century in which critical differentiations were made between different kinds of State (such as, between civilized and uncivilized States) for purposes of legitimating a range of different kinds of intervention (Simpson, 2004, pp 240–42). On such a view the re-emergence of this 'liberal anti-pluralist' theme within international legal doctrine (in which the principles of territorial sovereignty and sovereign equality are routinely downplayed or excised) recalls the intellectual structures of nineteenth century imperialism (Gordon, 1997). Yet it is also run through with many of the same kinds of contradictions. Just as nineteenth century international lawyers struggled with the problem of having to both recognize and deny the status of political communities in the extra-European world, so those invoking the notion of State failure seem to maintain the idea that these are indeed still States for purposes of attributing responsibility for their condition, but yet not

---

[38] See Yoo, Memorandum, 9 January 2002 explaining that the Geneva Conventions did not apply because Afghanistan was a failed State.

entitled to the normal prerogatives of sovereignty that the intervening States would expect for themselves. As Crawford succinctly concludes, '[t]o talk of States as "failed" sounds suspiciously like blaming the victims' (Crawford, 2006, p 722).

IV. SELF-DETERMINATION

As observed earlier, one of the key characteristics of the idea of the State as it was to emerge in social and political thought from the time of Grotius onwards was that it was never solely reducible to the authority of the ruler or government of the time. The idea of the State was always organized by reference also to a community, society, or nation in relation to which governmental authority would be exercised. It is no accident, thus, that international law acquired the designation attributed to it by Bentham—it was always seen as the law between nations or societies as much as that between sovereigns, and the term civitas or respublica more often than not merely denoted the internal relationship between one thing and the other. Nevertheless, there were two immanent traditions of thought which informed this relationship between nation and State as they were to develop—one being what might be termed a tradition of civic republicanism that conceived of sovereign authority as being a product of relations between individuals existing within the frame of a pre-conceived society (exemplified most clearly in the theory of the social contract), the other a 'communitarian' tradition that emphasized the corporate character of the society or nation the institutional expression of which would be the State (exemplified in Pufendorf's characterization of the State as a 'moral person'). In both cases, the 'nation' remained an important idea—on one side as the social frame within which the contract of sovereignty would be formed, on the other side as a natural community endowed with certain innate ends and prerogatives (and, indeed, perhaps an independent 'will')—but in either case, the nation was never entirely reducible to the State itself.

In the course of the nineteenth century these two themes came to be summarized in a single verbal expression—that of 'national self-determination'—but which nevertheless merely internalized the two traditions. One form of self-determination, associated with emergent 'nationalist' thought in Germany and Italy (sustained in the work of Herder, Fichte, and Mazzini amongst others), conceived of the idea that nation and State should be made congruent. It was the perfection of national society (understood variously as a society determined by reference to racial, ethnic, religious, linguistic, or historic homogeneity) that was to be sought in the promotion of its self-determination. Another form of self-determination, associated with the tradition of civic republicanism (with roots in the work of those such as Kant), conceived of the idea of self-determination in terms of representative self-governance: it being the promotion of individual liberty through the technique of self-rule that was to be sought. Here, as Mill was to suggest, the frame of the 'nation' remained important if only because social uniformity and national homogeneity were necessary productive conditions for self-governance.[39] These two concepts of self-determination presented very different challenges to the existing order of sovereign States—the first as an 'external' challenge to the spatial ordering of a dynastic European society and its failure to map itself congruously with the geography of 'nations' as they were to perceive themselves; the second presenting a challenge to the authority of governments to represent externally the will of a people to whom they were not internally

---

[39] Mill, 1890, ch XVI: 'it is in general a necessary condition of the institutions, that the boundaries of governments should coincide in the main with those of nationalities'.

responsible. These were not identical claims by any means: the latter appeared to confront the sovereign's authority with a criterion of legitimacy founded upon a rationalistic conception of representation, whereas the former appeared to challenge even representative authority with a claim to power based upon group identity (Berman, 1987–8, p 58). In either sense, however, national self-determination was clearly the language of change and reform (see Cobban, 1945).

It was in the reconstruction of Europe in the aftermath of the 1914–18 War, however, that the principle of national self-determination was to obtain its most concrete institutional expression. The agenda had been set by President Wilson in his speech to Congress in 1918 in which he famously set out the 'Fourteen Points' which he believed should inform the peace process. None of these points referred explicitly to the principle of national self-determination, but it was nevertheless made clear that boundaries in the new Europe should be configured so far as possible by reference to 'historically established' relations of nationality and allegiance. The Polish State was resurrected, Czechoslovakia and a Serb-Croat-Slovene State created out of the former Austro-Hungarian Empire and various other border adjustments made with provision for plebiscites in various locations. In many respects, however, it was an imperfect plan. On the one hand, it was always evident that the task of aligning political boundaries around the various 'nations' of Europe would be impossible, not simply because of the difficulties of determining which 'nation' deserved a State, but also because of their dispersed character. This recommended two expedients—one being the forcible transfer of certain populations (such as between Greece and Turkey[40]), the other being the institution of minority agreements within the Peace Treaties in order to protect those residual national communities cut adrift from the 'kin State' to which they were naturally thought to belong (Claude, 1955, pp 12–30). On the other hand, it was also evident that the Wilsonian project of self-determination was destined to be geographically limited—national self-determination was not something that was envisaged as being applicable in relation to the victorious powers themselves (eg for the Flemish, Irish, or Basques), nor was it regarded as applicable to territories outside Europe which, in the terms of the time, had yet to discover their national consciousness (Hobsbawm, 1992, pp 131–41).

If national self-determination was merely the implicit premise behind the reorganization of Europe after the First World War, it became a very much more explicit part of the settlement after the Second World War, but in some ways on quite different terms. The UN Charter identified respect for the principle of equal rights and self-determination of peoples as being one of the purposes of the Organization (Article 1), Chapter XI of which made clear that the primary concern of which was to foster self-government, development and the political, economic, social and educational advancement of those peoples which had 'not yet attained a full measure of self-government'. That this was to be interpreted as meaning 'decolonization' was later made clear by the General Assembly in a series of resolutions beginning with the Declaration on the Granting of Independence to Colonial Territories of 1960[41]. Over the course of the next 30 years most of those territories identified as 'non-self-governing' by the UN were to acquire their independence and become, as an important marker of their new status, members of the Organization.

While decolonization was obviously to transform the membership of the UN, and radically re-shape the character and nature of its activities, its implications as an instance of the application of the principle of self-determination were somewhat less clear. In one

[40] Convention Concerning the Exchange of Greek and Turkish Populations, Lausanne, 30 January 1923.
[41] GA Res 1514 (14 December 1960). See also GA Res 1541 (15 December 1960).

direction, of course, it posed the question whether self-determination was a principle applicable only the context of decolonization, or whether it might also legitimate secession in other cases. UN practice seemed limited in that sense (Bangladesh remaining a problematic exception), but limited in a way that seemed to speak of pragmatism rather than principle. If what was in contemplation was the 'self-determination of 'all peoples' as Article 1(1) of the two UN Covenants on Human Rights affirmed,[42] then on what grounds might one want to restrict it only to those overseas territories that formed part of the maritime Empires of European States? Was it only in that context that one could speak of peoples being non-self-governing or subject to oppression or alien rule? But of course the practice was not one of 'national' self-determination in the sense that President Wilson had understood it at all. It was self-determination for those 'selves' that had been specifically designated as being entitled to determine their own political future through the plebiscite and ballot box. It did not extend to those other, self-selecting communities, such as the Ibo in Biafra or the Katangese in the Congo who demanded independence on their own initiative and whose claims to independence largely fell on deaf ears.

It was soon to become apparent that the primary means for this process of designation, or prior determination, was worked out through the medium of colonial administration. In some instances, the external boundaries of the colony defined the presumptive unit of self-determination— as, for example, in the case of Ghana or the Belgian Congo. In other cases, it was determined by reference to the internal boundaries that demarcated the different administrative units of a single colonial power (such as the boundary between Uganda and Tanganyika). The principle, in this second case, came to be expressed in the phrase *uti possidetis*—which referred to a concept having its origins in the somewhat hazy practice of boundary delimitation in South America, but which subsequently came to be affirmed as 'a general principle...logically connected with the phenomenon of obtaining independence, wherever it occurs'[43] (see generally Shaw, 1996). Precisely what 'logic' strictly required obeisance to the inherited parameters of colonial administration was not clear, but there did at least seem to be a need to determine who the people were before they were asked to decide upon their political future.

All of this, however, seems to be a long way away from the radical notion of self-determination as an idea which, as Berman puts it, challenges legal thought 'by posing the problem of law's relationship to sources of normative authority lying beyond the normal rules of a functioning legal system' (Berman, 1988–9, p 56). The more the principle could be described in terms of a prosaic institutional practice, or as a pragmatic obeisance to the determined character of existing boundaries, the less dangerous (and indeed less emancipatory) it seemed. Yet, fundamentally, there was still an inevitable tension between, on the one hand, the lofty proclamation of self-determination with its open-ended demand for self-government, and the simultaneous commitment to the principle of territorial integrity (which was almost invariably mentioned in General Assembly resolutions in the same breath as that of self-determination). Of course, preserving intact all external and internal administrative boundaries nodded in the direction of this idea of territorial integrity, and certainly served to secure the political integrity of the newly emergent States once they had become established. It is no great surprise, in that sense, that the member States of the Organization of African Unity pledged in Resolution 16(1) of 1964 to respect colonial frontiers as they existed at the moment of independence (Shaw,

---

[42] International Covenant on Civil and Political Rights (1966) Article 1(1); International Covenant on Economic, Social and Cultural Rights (1966), Article 1(1).

[43] *Frontier Dispute, Judgment, ICJ Reports 1986*, p 554, para 20.

1996, pp 97–105). But at the same time, it still evaded the larger question as to how, and on what basis, the colonies may have enjoyed a right of self-determination, rather than the different peoples that comprised those colonies or, as Belgium cynically insisted, other non-self-governing communities elsewhere in the world. Part of the answer must be found in the gradual prioritization during this period of the idea of self-determination as a principle associated with the republican notion of self-governance rather than as a vehicle for aligning the boundaries of the polis with that of the nation. In one direction, for example, one may note that the principle of self-determination had, by this stage, lost its prefix; 'peoples' had replaced 'nations' as the relevant subjects of the right, and the identification of a community as ethnically or linguistically homogenous increasingly became a marker of its status as a minority rather than as a people entitled to political independence. In another direction, this new alignment was also evident in the increased emphasis placed upon the intrinsic relationship between 'internal' self-determination and the protection of individual and collective human rights (Cassese, 1995, pp 101–40; McCorquordale, 1994).

Nevertheless, this still only answers half of the question: it may explain, for example, why self-determination took the shape it did, and why it was a right denied to other 'minority' communities, but still doesn't answer how it was that decolonization could be squared with the principle of territorial integrity. For some colonial powers, after all, the colony was still largely regarded as part of the Metropolitan State (very much more so for Portugal and France than for Britain) the separation of which necessarily implied some diminution of the sovereign claims of the colonial powers. The right of self-determination, furthermore, seemed to speak of a process of determining future status, rather than a status in its own right. This, as Berman puts it, posed the question as to how international law was able to 'recognize a right accruing to an entity which, by its own admission, lacks international legal existence?' (Berman, 1988–9, p 52). The answer to both questions seemed to be that self-determination had a suspensive capacity the effect of which was to displace claims to sovereignty on the part of the parent State, and affirm, somewhat obscurely, the nascent claims to sovereignty on the part of the people whose future had yet to be determined. There was, in fact, a model for this idea already in place and which had already informed some of the practice of the ICJ in its deliberations on the question of sovereignty in case of Protectorates (such as Morocco)[44] and Mandate territories. In the latter context, as McNair put it, the question of sovereignty seemed to lie in 'abeyance'.[45] The rights of the colonial power were not those of a sovereign, but those enjoyed in virtue of agreement, to be exercised by way of sacred trust. Independence thus in no way implied a loss of sovereignty, or a violation of the principle of territorial integrity, rather the fruition of a status temporarily subordinated by the fact of colonial administration. In that respect, the most remarkable feature of process of decolonization was the generalized, and quasi-legislative, statement found in the General Assembly's Declaration on Friendly Relations[46] which declared that 'the territory of a colony or other non-self-governing territory has, under the Charter of the UN, a status separate and distinct from the territory of the State administering it'. In virtue of this, any apparent tension that existed between its espousal of the principle of self-determination and simultaneous re-affirmation of the principle of territorial integrity largely evaporated.

---

[44] *Rights of Nationals of the United States of America in Morocco, Judgment, ICJ Reports 1952*, p 176, at p 188 where, despite the French Protectorate, Morocco was declared to be 'a sovereign State'.

[45] *International Status of South West Africa, Advisory Opinion*, ICJ Reports, p 128, Separate Opinion of Judge McNair, p 146 at p 150.

[46] GA Res 2625 (XXV) (24 October 1970).

If the principle of self-determination seemed to imply a suspension of claims to sovereignty on the part of the Metropolitan State, it also seemed to imply the non-recognition of attempts to subvert that process. Thus, for example, when a minority white regime in what was then Southern Rhodesia declared its independence from Britain in 1965 its unilateral declaration of independence was immediately condemned by both the UN General Assembly[47] and the Security Council which called upon States not to recognize the 'illegal racist minority regime', and provided for a regime of sanctions to be imposed.[48] Similarly, but in a different context, when the South African government in pursuit of its policy of apartheid established the Bantusans of Transkei, Ciskei, Venda, and Bophuthatswana in the years 1976–81 under the pretext that this constituted an implementation of the principle of 'self-government', those claims were again rejected with the General Assembly and Security Council condemning their establishment and calling for non-recognition.[49] Only in cases in which the subversion of self-determination came at the hands of another 'newly independent State' (Goa, West Irian, East Timor, and Western Sahara) was the reaction somewhat more muted or equivocal, and one may sense that this was probably informed by the idea that the rubric of anti-colonialism had somewhat less purchase in such cases.

Yet, for all its continuing associations with the process of decolonization, the story of self-determination does not end there. After the fall of the Berlin Wall in 1989 and the collapse of Soviet rule, the principle of national self-determination was once again to acquire a prominence in international legal thought and practice. Of the new States that were to emerge in the following decades, most did so on a platform of national self-determination, most also held plebiscites or national polls by way of authorization, some also sought to make as a determinant of subsequent citizenship a facility with the national language (Cassese, 1995, pp 257–7). Not all such cases, however, posed problems as far as the question of statehood was concerned. In some cases the change could be conceived as little more than a change of government (Hungary, Romania, Ukraine, Poland, Belarus, and Bulgaria for example), in some as the emergence from a condition of unlawful annexation (the Baltic Republics), in some as a basis for consensual re-unification (Germany) or of separation (the Czech and Slovak Republics, Serbia and Montenegro). In the cases of the former USSR and Socialist Federal Republic of Yugoslavia, however, the problem as to the implications of the process of disintegration and the role to be played by the principle of self-determination was to come to the fore.

The case of the Soviet Union, the problem was effectively resolved at two meetings in Minsk and Alma Ata (see Section III of this chapter) which, while by no means wholly consistently, put in place the idea that the independence of the new Republics in Central Asia and elsewhere had come about through the consensual secession of the administrative units of the Union leaving Russia as the rump State. If the language of national self-determination was relevant, here, it was not such as to challenge or disrupt the principle of sovereignty or territorial integrity in any profound way. The case of Yugoslavia, by contrast, was far more difficult (see Radan, 2002). Prior to 1989, Yugoslavia had been a Federal State comprising of six Republics representing the major 'nationalities' and two autonomous enclaves (Kosovo and Vojdvodina) each of which had representation in the administration of the Federation. The death of President Tito in 1980 was followed by a power-struggle within the Federation culminating in declarations of independence being

---

[47] GA Res 2379 (XXIII), (28 October 1968).
[48] SC Res 232 (16 December 1966); SC Res 235 (29 May 1968).
[49] GA Res 31/6A (26 October 1976); SC Res 402 (22 December 1976).

announced on the part of Slovenia and Croatia in 1991 recalling, in their terms, the principle of national self-determination (which itself had some recognition in the Federal Constitution). These initiatives, however, were forcibly resisted and the subsequent outbreak of violence was then to engulf Bosnia-Herzegovina, the severity of which led ultimately to the dispatch of peacekeeping forces (UNPROFOR), the establishment of the International Criminal Tribunal for the Former Yugoslavia and the later submission of claims of genocide to the International Court of Justice.

One of the key questions here for other European States was whether or not to recognize the Statehood of the entities emerging from the conflict. Doing so had several important implications as regards the characterization of the ongoing conflict (as international rather than merely internal (see Gray, 1996) and as to the justification for the arms embargo. It also, and more significantly for present purposes, would seem to bring into play the possibility that there might exist a 'post-colonial' right of secessionary self-determination, the implications of which would extend far beyond the confines of the conflict itself. Sensing that there were a number of delicate issues involved, the States participating in the Conference on Yugoslavia in 1991 established what became known as the 'Badinter Commission' (so named, after its Chairman Robert Badinter, President of the French Constitutional Court) to provide advice on the legal issues arising (see Craven, 1995, Terrett, 2000). In the Autumn of 1991 the Badinter Commission issued two significant Opinions that set the stage for the subsequent recognition of Croatia, Slovenia, Bosnia-Herzegovina and, somewhat later, that of Macedonia. The key advice given by the Badinter Commission, having specifically been asked about the implications of the principle of self-determination, was to declare that the former SFRY was 'in the process of disintegration' on the basis that the Federal organs could no longer wield effective power (it being hinted that those Federal organs such as the Yugoslav National Army that continued to operate had been effectively co-opted by the Serbian government). The significance of this should not be lost. What the Commission signally refused to say was that the 'nationalities' within the Federation had a right of secessionary self-determination. They could plausibly have linked such a claim to the provisions of the Constitution that spoke of self-determination, to the emerging idea that self-determination is legitimate in cases of abusive or totalitarian exercises of power, or indeed, more simply to the proclamations of independence on the part of the various Republics. Doing the latter would obviously have been a little awkward given the claims to independence on the part of the Serbian community in Bosnia,[50] but its general reluctance here, no doubt, was informed by the sense that the recrudescent ethnic nationalism that underpinned the claims to independence were a throwback to a pre-modern primitivism the function of which had merely been to exacerbate the conflict in the first place. Caught thus in a position of neither wanting to ally itself with the Milosevic regime whose campaign of violence had been pursued under the banner of the preservation of the territorial integrity of Yugoslavia (in whose name the government of Serbia and Montenegro continued to act), nor wanting to provide continuing justification for inter-ethnic violence in the name of national self-determination, the Commission's determination that the Federation was in the process of dissolution was an extraordinarily dextrous act. Its effect was to provide a necessary analytical space for the recognition of the emergent Republics (whether or not on the basis of the principle of

---

[50] In Opinion No 2, the Commission addressed the claim to self-determination on the part of the Serbs in Bosnia and decided that, as a minority, they were not entitled to independence. It did suggest, however, that self-determination might be reinterpreted as implying a right of each individual to the nationality of their choice.

self-determination[51]) without running the risk of undermining respect for the principle of territorial integrity. Indeed, on the latter score, the Badinter Commission reaffirmed, in its second Opinion, the principle of *uti possidetis*, making clear in the process that the entities emerging from the former Yugoslavia were to be those that already had enjoyed administrative recognition within the Federation.

This solution was always to leave a certain ambiguity as to the status of Kosovo, which of course had a degree of administrative independence within the Federal structure albeit not as a constitutive nationality, and perhaps goes some way to explain the ease by which the UN administration over the territory was established (UNMIK). It also explains, in some degree the effective 'blind-eye' turned to the 2008 Kosovo Assembly's Declaration of Independence by the International Court of Justice.[52] In its Advisory Opinion on the legality of the declaration of 2010, the International Court came to the surprising conclusion that there was nothing in international law that prohibited the issuance of declarations of independence of this kind. It did so, however, by carefully avoiding the issues of real contention. For, of course, in saying that international law did not prohibit the issuance of declarations of independence did not answer the question whether it might rightfully be acted upon, nor indeed whether other States were therefore entitled to recognize it as an independent State. Still less did it address what many saw to be the real cause of the claim—namely the persecution of the Kosovo Albanians throughout the 1990s as had been highlighted by the ICTY in the *Multinovic* case.[53]

For all the limitations of the International Court's Advisory Opinion, it might nonetheless be seen to have fulfilled an essential function: that of keeping in play two apparently contradictory ideas namely that international law both sustains the possibility of an emancipatory national self-determination, but yet also serves to protect and secure a stable, ordered, society of States. If these objectives seem, at moments, to be in tension, it is a tension that also discloses the fundamental secret of their mutual co-dependence. Self-determination not being something that invariably rubs against the grain of statehood, nor that necessarily stands in competition with the principle of territorial integrity, but a notion that takes both those ideas as its objective; statehood, for its part, finding its justification in the principle of national self-determination, and requiring the occasional visible re-affirmation of its import. What one finds in practice, therefore, is self-determination as an idea flourishing most visibly in the interstices of the existing order, occupying those spaces which have been opened up for it through the prior displacement of arguments about territorial sovereignty—whether that be through the idea that colonial territories had a status distinct from that of the metropolitan States, that independence was 'granted' rather than acquired, or that conflict had led to the dissolution of States from which the Republics were to emerge.

V. DEMOCRACY AND HUMAN RIGHTS

For all the normalizing characteristics of much of this practice, there has remained a strand in international legal thought that has resisted the implication that self-determination is nothing other than a process of describing how new States emerge. If 'national'

---

[51] See on this Koskenniemi, 1994a.

[52] *Accordance with International Law of the Unilateral Declaration of Independence in Respect of Kosovo, Advisory Opinion, ICJ Reports 2010*, p 403.

[53] *Prosecutor v Milutinovic*, Judgment, Case No IT-05-87-T, Trial Chamber III (26 February 2009).

self-determination understood in its ethnic, cultural, religious or linguistic sense has been carefully avoided (or perhaps subsumed within the discourse of minority rights), self-determination in its civic republican sense has not. Indeed events in recent decades have, if nothing else, given considerable impetus to the idea that there exists an emerging right to democratic governance in international law (Franck, 1996; Fox and Roth, 2000) the source of which is often traced to the linkage between the principle of self-determination and the individual rights of political participation (Article 25 International Covenant on Civil and Political Rights) and evidenced in the emerging practice of multilateral election monitoring and other initiatives designed to promote democracy and human rights ('low intensity democracy' as Marks (2003) puts it). At first glance, of course, the idea of a right to democratic governance has little obvious resonance for questions of statehood. Since it is concerned primarily with the issue of governmental rather than State legitimacy it may thus be thought to have salience in relation to a range of discretionary relations (diplomatic, financial, and trade relations for example), but not so in relation to the qualities of statehood itself. Yet it is clear that those advocates of the 'emerging' right to democratic government do not see it as so confined.

There are two plausible ways in which a concern for democracy and human rights may impinge upon the question of statehood: one as an additional 'condition' that needs to be met before independence may be recognized (one of the earliest examples being Fawcett's interpretation of the Southern Rhodesian crisis in 1965 (Fawcett, 1965–6)); the other as a basis for the exercise of self-determination on the part of a community suffering oppression or systematically excluded from access to government (sometimes referred to as 'remedial secession'). In respect of the first issue, as Murphy points out, elements of recent State practice seem to point towards a development in that direction. Shortly after the beginning of the conflict in Yugoslavia in 1991 the EC member States convened at an extraordinary EPC ministerial meeting to adopt a common policy on the recognition of States emerging from the Soviet Union and Yugoslavia. In the guidelines they were to produce, they affirmed 'their readiness to recognise, subject to the normal standards of international practice and political realities in each case, those new states which...have constituted themselves on a democratic basis'.[54] Further to this, they set out several conditions including: (1) respect for the provisions of the UN Charter and the Helsinki Final Act 'especially with regard to the rule of law, democracy and human rights'; (2) to guarantee the rights of ethnic and national groups and minorities; (3) to respect the inviolability of existing borders; (4) to accept all relevant arms control commitments; and (5) to commit to settle all questions of State succession and regional disputes by agreement. While clearly evidence of a potential shift in practice, these guidelines were nevertheless very loosely applied in the subsequent process by which the EC member States came to recognize the new Yugoslav Republics. The recognition of Croatia proceeded in early 1992 despite the fact that the Badinter Commission had found that it had not fully complied with the relevant conditions, whereas the recognition of Macedonia was held up as a consequence of an ongoing dispute with Greece over its name.[55] The guidelines, it seems, were simply what they declared themselves to be: merely guidelines. Commentators were thus doubtful as to whether such criteria had yet been definitively established (Murphy, 2000, p 139) even if there was considerable enthusiasm for the idea that the new States acquiring

---

[54] Declaration on the 'Guidelines on the Recognition of New States in Eastern Europe and in the Soviet Union', (1992) 31 *ILM* 1486.

[55] See *Application of the Interim Accord of 13 September 1995 (the former Yugoslav Republic of Macedonia v Greece), Judgment of 5 December 2011, ICJ Reports 2011*, p 644.

their independence would remain bound by all pre-existent human rights treaty commitments that were formally applicable to that territory (Kamminga, 1996; Craven, 2007, pp
244–56).

To some extent, however, this idea has been given a further lease of life in the
form of the recent regimes for international territorial administration (East Timor,
Bosnia-Herzegovina, and Kosovo) put in place, amongst other things, for purposes of
securing the rule of law and the protection of human rights (Wilde, 2008). As some
have argued, such regimes have seemed to function as institutional precursors to independence in such a way as to be evidence of a new emerging doctrine of 'earned sovereignty'—'earned' in the sense that independence will often be phased, conditional
and perhaps constrained (Williams, Scharf, and Hooper, 2002–3). On the face of it,
such arguments seem to promote a radical revision of the standard approach to statehood—forefronting the requirement of compliance with human rights and democratic
conditions, and relativizing the notion of sovereignty. Yet, whatever the perceived merits of such an agenda, and however far this may be thought to open out a new realm
of policy alternatives, it is hard to shake off the sense that this is anything other than
a highly selective reinstitution, under UN auspices, of the old Mandate/Trusteeship
arrangement in which territories were 'prepared' for independence under the tutelage
of colonial masters.

Just as there is a certain hesitancy about the role that considerations of democracy
and human rights might play in the recognition of new States, so also there is equivocation over the extent to which those considerations might serve as a basis for legitimating
secession. In its Advisory Opinion concerning the secessionist claims of Quebec, the
Canadian Supreme Court summarized what it saw to be the contemporary position:

> the international law right to self-determination [gives rise to]…a right to external
> self-determination in situations of former colonies; where a people is oppressed, as for
> example under foreign military occupation; or where a definable group is denied mean-
> ingful access to government to pursue their political, economic, social and cultural devel-
> opment. In all three situations, the people in question are entitled to a right to external
> self-determination because they have been denied the ability to exert internally their right
> to self-determination.[56]

Since Quebec 'did not meet the threshold of a colonial people or an oppressed people'
and since the Quebecers had not been denied 'meaningful access to government' the
Court concluded that they did not enjoy the right to effect the secession of Quebec from
Canada unilaterally. Rather, they enjoyed a (Constitutional) right to negotiate the terms
of a separation.

The most interesting feature of this Opinion, however, was the attempt by the Court to
run a thread through the three instances of secessionary self-determination outlined in its
Opinion by linking each one to a violation of 'internal self-determination'. There are two
ideas in play here: one is a three-fold association being forged between the fact of alien
rule, the denial of human rights (oppression) and the lack of access to government, each
of which is taken as expressive of the same denial of self-determination. The other, associated, idea is one that effectively makes conditional any claim to sovereignty (or territorial
integrity) upon the preservation and promotion of individual and collective rights and the
maintenance of a system of government by consent. One might conclude from this that in

---

[56] *Reference Re Secession of Quebec*, Canadian Supreme Court (1988) 37 ILM 1340, para 138.

cases where a determinate people have been oppressed, abused, or routinely denied their rights (treated, in some respects, as a non-self-governing territory), a claim for secessionary self-determination might be sustained simply by reason of the fact that the parent State is no longer in the position of being able to justify its claim to sovereignty. This 'remedial' notion of self-determination, on some accounts at least, goes some way to explain practice in the case of Eritrea, Bangladesh, and perhaps Kosovo (Crawford, 2006, p 126).

In the case of Kosovo, it is evident that in some instances, recognition of its independence was explicitly linked to the violence and abuse directed against the Kosovo Albanian population prior to the establishment of UNMIK, and to the consequential impossibility of it being 'returned' to Serbia. Yet one may also note that many other of the recognizing States were deeply equivocal on this score, making great play of the *sui generis* character of the situation—particular prominence being given to the 'suspensory' character of SC Resolution 1244 (1999) which authorized the establishment of an international civil administration in the territory, and the 'special role' played by the UN Special Envoy within the political process that had culminated in the development of the Comprehensive Proposal for the Kosovo Status Settlement (the Ahtisaari Plan). The apparently exceptional character of the position of Kosovo had two obvious implications. The first was to make clear that, whatever the outcome, the case of Kosovo should not set any kind of precedent for other aspirant communities. Far from reinforcing, therefore, the idea of a right to remedial secession, it appears to do the opposite. The second implication was that the asserted non-exemplary character of the Kosovan situation was such as to allow recognition to proceed unimpeded. Its apparent 'uniqueness' made it perfectly feasible for recognizing States to take a completely independent view on the matter.

Needless to say, it is evident that the kind of reasoning that tends to underpin this idea of remedial secession is not confined to that particular discourse. Precisely the same structure of argument is to be found in the debates over humanitarian intervention (and, more recently, the Responsibility to Protect[57]). In the view of those such as Reisman, for example, the abusive, totalitarian government is one that should no longer be allowed to enjoy the privilege of sovereignty as a defence against external intervention. Sovereignty, for him, is a relic of an absolutist past that has been profoundly reconfigured by the emergent law of human rights. And recent State practice - such as that exemplified in the interventions in Haiti (1994), Panama (1989) and Sierra Leone (1997) - were evidence of a beneficial shift in thought and practice (Reisman, 1990). Others, following this theme, have been cautious of its unilateralist bent, recommending in contrast, collective intervention under auspices of the UN in such circumstances (Franck, 2000). Yet for all the well-intentioned bravura associated with such 'muscular humanitarianism' (Orford, 2003), it poses all too many questions regarding the opacity of the conditions warranting intervention, the selective character of practice that underpins it and, if nothing else, its evidently imperial (and gendered) overtones. One may recall, after all, that the nineteenth century 'Scramble for Africa' was justified, in part at least, upon the basis that it was necessary in order to combat the slave trade—a claim that was almost immediately shown to be the merest figment given the subsequent violence that accompanied colonial rule in the Congo Free State and South West Africa.

---

[57] See 2005 World Summit Outcome, GA doc A/60/L.1 (2005) paras 138–39. See also Zifcak, Ch 17 of this book.

VI. STATEHOOD AND RECOGNITION

As has been suggested earlier, a key feature of the development of international law at the end of the nineteenth century was a certain critical ambivalence as to the process by which new States might come to acquire rights and obligations under international law. The Vattelian image of States existing in a state of nature in their relations with one another, subject only to such obligations as might have been voluntary accepted (through treaty or adherence to custom) seemed to place States in some respect prior to law. This, of course, had some enduring resonance: international law itself did not create States by way of some legislative fiat, rather they emerged through the spontaneous and concerted action of a community or society organizing itself internally as a sovereign political community. International law merely had a role in acknowledging the reality of something which already been put in place. A State 'is a State', as Wheaton put it, simply 'because it exists' (Wheaton, 1866, p 28).

In so far as the society of States remained entirely stable this might have sufficed, yet by the beginning of the nineteenth century the emergence of new States in South America and the establishment of Belgium and Greece within Europe, brought to prominence the practice of recognition, which had previously been employed largely for purposes of identifying a condition of belligerency or insurgency. This immediately posed the question as to the relationship between that practice and the general status of the communities being thereby recognized. Even if the existence of States was merely a question of fact, their claims to sovereignty often had to be judged by reference to the competing claims of other States. In case of secession, for example, it was understood that to recognize a new State before the moment at which it had fully established its independence was not merely to offend the sensibilities of the State attempting to suppress the rebellion, but also constituted an act of unlawful intervention. This was to subtly change, even if not to radically transform, the initial hypothesis. One could still think of the existence of States primarily in terms of their internal effectiveness, but the function of recognition came to determine the question of participation or membership in the wider international community. Wheaton (1866, s 21, p 28) thus distinguished between internal and external sovereignty for such purposes:

> So long, indeed, as the new State confines its action to its own citizens, and to the limits of its own territory, it may well dispense with such recognition. But if it desires to enter into that great society of nations, all the members of which recognize rights to which they are mutually entitled, and duties which they may be called upon reciprocally to fulfil, such recognition becomes essentially necessary to the complete participation of the new State in all the advantages of this society.

What this immediately put on the table was a distinction between the existence of States on the one hand, and their participation in the international community on the other. Questions of status and relations thus seemed separable: diplomatic recognition being relevant to the latter not the former. Of course, this only really made sense in a context in which international law was understood as occupying a specific geographical space. The hypothesis that there might be States possessing 'internal sovereignty' yet not participating in the 'great society of nations' had its concrete expression in the postulated divide between the European and non-European worlds at the time. This was precisely the way in which one could rationalize, in some degree at least, knowledge of the existence of the Ottoman Empire, China, and Japan as independent political communities yet not assume they were, as a consequence, subjects of international law in the fullest sense.

Nevertheless, the division between internal and external sovereignty, or between the existence of States and their participation in the international community was cause for a certain amount of (constructive) ambivalence. To begin with, there were two possible constructions of the position. One was that the State existed for legal purposes from the moment of its existence *de facto*, and that recognition and 'participation' were merely complementary benefits (see, eg Heffter, 1857, p 43). Another was that its existence for purposes of international law was determined by the moment of participation since it was only through recognition that legal relations with other members of the international community would be definitively established.[58] In some respects it seemed to be necessary to maintain both of these positions. On the one hand, in order for the society of nations to have determinate content, there needed to be a proximate relation between the subjects of law and the boundaries of that society understood as a legal order. On the other hand, it seemed equally necessary to admit the legal existence of unrecognized States in order to give legal effect to treaty relations with non-European States and societies. Colonization of the non-European world thus depended upon a simultaneous process of exclusion and inclusion: the native sovereign being excluded from the European legal order in order to justify the claims of the latter to be a society of civilized sovereigns, yet simultaneously included within the legal order in order to rationalize the treaty relations upon which colonization depended. The maintenance of an ambivalent relationship between recognition and statehood was the means by which that could be achieved.

Although by the beginning of the twentieth century, the project of 'land appropriation' in Africa had largely run its course, international lawyers were no clearer as to the nature or character of the process of recognition. In a remarkably obtuse passage Hall (1895, p 87) summarizes the position as follows:

> Theoretically a politically organized community enters of right...into the family of states and must be treated in accordance with law, so soon as it is able to show that it possesses the marks of a state. The commencement of a state dates nevertheless from its recognition by other powers; that is to say from the time at which they accredit ministers to it, or conclude treaties with it, or in some other way enter into such relations with it as exist between states alone. For though no state has a right to withhold recognition when it has been earned, states must be allowed to judge for themselves whether a community claiming to be recognised does really possess all the necessary marks, and especially whether it is likely to live. Thus although the right to be treated as a state is independent of recognition, recognition is the necessary evidence that the right has been acquired.

While overtly assuming what was to become known as a 'declaratory' approach to recognition (the essence of which insists that a State exists as a subject of international law at the moment at which it 'possesses the marks of a state' as defined by international law), this is immediately qualified in two ways. First, since international law is fundamentally relational, the 'theoretical' existence of the State remains precisely that—theoretical—until placed in a social context, and recognition thus marks the commencement of the State for practical purposes. Secondly, the fulfilment of the criteria for Statehood (which, of course, included such notions as to whether the State was sufficiently civilized) was in no circumstances either self-evident or self-expressive

---

[58] Wheaton, 1866, s 21: 'until such recognition becomes universal on the part of the other States, the new State becomes entitled to the exercise of its external sovereignty as to those States only by whom that sovereignty has been recognized.'; Lorimer, 1883, p 106: 'Though recognition is often spoken of as admission into the family of nations, it leaves the State which has claimed and obtained it from one State only, in the same position in which it formerly stood to every other State'.

but something that had to be subject to the judgement and appreciation. In absence of any other determining mechanism, the judgement and appreciation had to be that of existing States. Hall veers, at this point, towards the idea that recognition is, in fact, 'constitutive' in the sense that the legal existence of a State is thus dependent upon its recognition by others. But appreciating perhaps that this would fatally cut the ground from underneath his first assertion, Hall finally tries to regain his initial standpoint by insisting that this recognition is ultimately merely 'evidential' and that the 'right to be treated as a state' is independent of, such recognition. In a single paragraph, Hall thus seems to occupy all conceivable positions: recognition is both declaratory and constitutive; States exist prior to recognition but commence on recognition; recognition is a duty but also a privilege.

Hall's equivocation here summarizes in short form much of the ensuing debate over the character of recognition in the following century. For the most part those adopting a constitutive approach to recognition point to the speciousness of Hall's theoretical position—however confidently a political community might believe itself to have fulfilled the criteria for statehood, it is only through acceptance of that fact by other States, that one can say with any assurance that it has. It is meaningless to assert that Abkhazia, North Ossetia, or Taiwan are States if no one is prepared to accept them as such. Those, by contrast, adopting a declaratory approach point to the political and discretionary character of recognition— to the fact that, as in the *Tinoco Arbitration*, a State like the UK may refuse to recognize another (government in that case) not because of any perceived defect in origin or competence, but simply because it does not wish to have diplomatic relations with it.[59] The determinants of Statehood must, therefore, be posited as anterior to the practice of recognition even if the latter may be thought to provide evidence for the former.

To a large extent the respective positions on the question of recognition turn, not so much on the question as to whether the existence of a State is a self-expressive fact, or upon the fulfilment or lack thereof of the requisite criteria, but upon the analytical relationship between the two elements of 'status' and 'relations'. In one (the declaratory approach) these are kept distinct: the question of status has to be determined prior to the creation of relations with others. Only those entities fulfilling the requisite criteria can be said to have the capacity to enter into legal relations with others as States. In the other, the two issues are merged such that the existence or otherwise of such relations becomes the mode by which status is determined. Only those entities having relations with other States can be assumed to have the legal capacity to do so. The difficulty with the declaratory position is that it seeks to maintain both the idea that the creation of States is rule-governed, and that the conferral or withholding of recognition is an essentially political and discretionary act. To postulate the existence of a rule, but then deny it any ground for being applied is to rely rather heavily upon the self-executory character of formal rule. The difficulty with the constitutive position, by contrast, is that it seeks to maintain that the conferral or withholding of recognition is a legal act (or at least one with legal effects) but that in the absence of either a 'duty to recognize' (as asserted by Lauterpacht, 1947) or of the existence of an agency competent to adjudicate (as asserted by Dugard, 1987), then allows the question of status to become entirely dependent upon the individual position of the recognizing States. The best one could say, in any particular context, was that a political community was 'more or less' a State.

---

[59] *Tinoco Arbitration (Costa Rica v Great Britain)* (1923) 1 *RIAA* 369; (1924) 18 *AJIL* 147, at p 154.

For the most part, although many profess to prefer the 'declaratory approach' (support for which is found, once again, in the Montevideo Convention),[60] doctrine on recognition remains fundamentally ambivalent on most of these key questions.[61] There are two particular difficulties. To begin with, it is clear that recognition of another State will have certain legal implications: it implies, at the very least, a commitment to respect the sovereignty and territorial integrity of the State it has recognized and will also have a range of domestic legal consequences as might concern the recognition of its law and legal transactions occurring within its jurisdiction. By the same token, it is almost universally held that recognition will not necessarily imply a willingness to enter into diplomatic relations with that other State nor indeed, a recognition of its government (prior to 2001, for example, only three States recognized the Taliban as the government of Afghanistan, yet there was no doubt that all recognized the State of Afghanistan). The difficulty, however, is that it is frequently impossible to entirely dissociate the fact of recognition from the idea of political approval. This was typically a problem of particular acuteness in the context of governmental recognition (relevant primarily in case of those governments establishing their authority by unconstitutional means) and led to the enunciation by the Mexican Secretary of Foreign Relations of what became known as the 'Estrada Doctrine' the effect of which was to recommend the recognition of all effective governments irrespective of the means by which they came to power (Jessup, 1931). That this never quite avoided the problem (given that there would still be questions of interpretation in cases in which there were two rival governments competing for power) recommended a general abandonment of the policy of formally recognizing any governments at all (a policy which the British government belatedly adopted in 1980).[62]

The difficulty of separating law from policy, however, was not confined to governmental recognition, but also influenced practice in relation to the recognition of States. While non-recognition, as already observed has been employed as a way of signalling the international community's condemnation of attempts to subvert processes of self-determination or to establish new States by recourse to force, the fact that it is also still seen to be an essentially 'discretionary act that other States may perform when they choose and in the manner of their own choosing',[63] is such as to make it a somewhat haphazard semiotic device. In an enlightening typology, Warbrick (1997, pp 10–11) explains that the mere statement 'We (State A) do not recognize entity X as a State' has at least five possible meanings:

(1)   We take no decision, one way or another, about recognizing X [in A's eyes, X may or may not be a State];

(2)   We have chosen not to recognize X (although we could do) for political reasons not related to X's status [by implication, A does consider X to be a State];

(3)   We do not recognize X because it would be unlawful/premature for us to do so [A does not regard X as legally a State];

---

[60]   Article 3: 'The political existence of the State is independent of recognition by the other States'; and Article 6: 'The recognition of a State merely signifies that the state which recognizes it accepts the personality of the other with all the rights and duties determined by international law'. See also, Badinter Commission, Opinions 8 and 10, 92 ILR 201, 206 (1992).
[61]   See Brownlie, 1982, p 197: 'in the case of "recognition", theory has not only failed to enhance the subject but has created a *tertium quid* which stands, like a bank of fog on a still day, between the observer and the contours of the ground which calls for investigation'.
[62]   For a critique of this position see Talmon, 1998, pp 3–14.
[63]   Badinter Commission, Opinion No. 10 of 1992, 92 ILR 206, p 208.

(4) We do not recognize X, although it might (appear to) be a State, because there are customary law obligations or specific treaty obligations which prohibit us from doing so;

(5) We do not recognize X, although it might (appear to) be a State, because there is a specific obligation imposed by the Security Council not to do so.

Much would seem to depend, thus, upon how the recognizing State would characterize or understand its own actions. Only by looking behind the refusal to recognize might one determine a difference in stance, for example, between the refusal to recognize the Turkish Republic of Northern Cyprus (informed, it seems, by a reflection upon the illegality of the Turkish intervention in Cyprus) and the similar refusal to recognize the former Yugoslav Republic of Macedonia in early 1992 (informed, it seems, by an unwillingness to prejudice diplomatic relations with Greece). In some cases, however, the position is simply opaque. It was never entirely clear, for example, as to whether those Arab States which refused to recognize the State of Israel before 1993, really believed that Israel did not exist as a State (and hence was not bound by the various treaty obligations to which it was a party), or merely desired to make clear that it should not exist even if it did so in fact. This poses a particular problem since, just as it seems necessary to read recognition policy symptomatically (as being fundamentally an expression of something else), so also the result of such an enquiry might actually make it more, rather than less, difficult to disentangle those considerations that bear upon the question of legal status and those that apparently do not.

This relates to a second difficulty with the practice of recognition namely that even in cases in which States have taken a firm position in seeking to avoid recognition of a State (and hence avoid any sense of condoning its existence) they are not infrequently unable or unwilling to live with the consequences. As pointed out, it seemed unlikely that the Arab States, in refusing to recognize Israel, also believed that Israel was not therefore bound by the Geneva Conventions of 1949 in relation to its occupation of the West Bank and Gaza, or that it was otherwise free to ignore general principles of international law governing the use of force. Once again, their position was one of simultaneous inclusion and exclusion. In a more explicit sense, however, domestic courts have also frequently sought to avoid the consequences of non-recognition policies, and have resorted to a variety of different expedients to allow judicial cognition of the laws of what are formally unrecognized States. In the *Carl Zeiss* case, for example, the House of Lords avoided the obvious consequences of the British government's refusal to recognize the German Democratic Republic by treating the legislative acts of the GDR as essentially those of the USSR.[64] Similarly, in *Hesperides Hotels*, Lord Denning adopted a policy, already well established in the USA, of allowing recognition of the laws of unrecognized States (in that case the Turkish Republic of Northern Cyprus) insofar as they related to 'the day to day affairs of the people, such as their marriages, their divorces, their leases, their occupations and so forth'.[65] In the UK, in fact, this latter policy has come to find formal expression in the Foreign Corporations Act of 1991 which states that foreign corporations having status under the laws of an unrecognized State may nevertheless be treated as a legal person if those laws are 'applied by a settled court system in that territory'. In each of these cases, an important consideration seems to have been a concern to insulate the 'innocent' population from the 'illegalities' associated with the claims to authority on the part of their governments; but they also

---

[64] *Carl-Zeiss-Stiftung* v *Rayner & Keeler Ltd (No 2)* [1967] 1 AC 853.
[65] *Hesperides Hotels Ltd* v *Aegean Turkish Holidays Ltd* [1978] QB 205 at p 218.

illustrate in some ways a continued prevarication between the need, on the one hand, to recognize 'effective' entities while, on the other, to ensure at least the semblance of some commitment to the legal values that a refusal to recognize might have embodied.

More often than not, this dual commitment to admitting the reality of a situation while not accepting its 'legality' is spoken of in terms of 'pragmatism'. A pragmatist, in this sense, seems to be one who is not willing to commit to legal principle to the point at which it is disadvantageous either to the recognizing State or, as suggested earlier, to the population concerned. It bespeaks of an opposition to either a rigid commitment to the formal rule, or of a refusal to recognize the need to accept, in an imperfect world, imperfect solutions. Yet what this characterization of the situation misses is that the counterpoint is not between 'law' and 'reality' (or indeed any other alternative to 'law') but a counterpoint between the ethical and the factual that has always existed within international law itself. Just as, in the past, the distinction between recognition *de iure* and recognition *de facto*, allowed States the opportunity to have dealings with insurgent governments without, at the same time, being seen to implicate themselves overtly in an act of intervention, so also the practice of recognizing the acts of certain governments while not recognizing their claims to Statehood itself is one that really just goes to the point that legal doctrine has consistently sought to embed both law and fact within itself (however contradictory that might seem).

If doctrine on statehood and recognition seems to admit the necessity of a constructive ambiguity, perhaps the most obviously anomalous (or is that representative?) case is that of Taiwan (Crawford, 2006, pp 198–221). Having formerly been recognized as the government of China until 1971, Taiwan then was removed from the UN and replaced by the government of the People's Republic of China. Since then, it has never entirely renounced its claim to be the government of China, nor unequivocally asserted its existence as an independent State. Taiwan nevertheless has many dealings with other States largely on the same basis as any other State (but without the same diplomatic privileges). Taiwanese government agencies are often regarded as having legal status in other countries and a capacity to sue and be sued. It is a party to a number of treaties and has membership in the WTO (as a 'Separate Customs Territory' under the name 'Chinese Taipei'). In the UK, Taiwanese corporations are allowed to do business under the terms of the 1991 Foreign Corporations Act 'as if' Taiwan was a recognized State, and in the US relations have largely been 'normalized' under the terms of the Taiwan Relations Act 1979 which seeks to implement the policy of maintaining 'unofficial relations'. As Crawford observes '[i]t is surprising it does not suffer from schizophrenia' (Crawford, 2006, p 220). The same might be said of international lawyers more generally.

VII. CONCLUSION

In an article written in the early 1990s, Martti Koskenniemi reflected upon the contemporary resonance of Engel's notion of the 'withering away' of the State. In Koskenniemi's view, there were two versions of this thesis in circulation. One was a 'sociological' version that, on observing the recent globalization of politics, argues that 'states are no longer able to handle problems such as massive poverty, pollution of the atmosphere, or even their own security' without entering into forms of cooperation that entail the 'gradual dissolution of sovereignty' (Koskenniemi, 1994b, p 22). The other was an 'ethical' version that regards statehood as a form of 'morally indefensible egotism' that either serves to create and perpetuate 'artificial distinctions among members of the human community' or to justify the use of State apparatus for oppression. Each of these critiques stresses the artificiality of the State as an idea or institution; each also sees its withering away as essentially beneficial.

The point of Koskenniemi's article was not so much to defend the State as an institution as against these two critiques, but rather to defend the idea of the State as a place (or a language) in which various conceptions of justice, right, or economic efficiency might be worked out on an ongoing basis. What informs his argument here is that both versions of the thesis tend to take as 'given' that which they are using as the point of critique:

> The problem with the critiques of the state is their inability to reach into what is authentic and agree on what it requires in terms of political action. In suggesting that we must realize something that is already there—and in consequently de-emphasizing the decision pro-cesses needed to get there—the critiques function as political ideologies, and their claim to spontaneity, following Adorno, is 'a jargon of authenticity' instead of an expression of some hidden truth. [footnotes omitted] (Koskenniemi, 1994b, p 22)

To posit, in other words, the withering away of the state on the basis that it is either a socio-logical necessity or ethically desirable omits to reflect upon the unstable, or at the very least contestable, character of either the sociology or ethics that underpin them. The 'fact' of globalization or the 'justice' of certain rights claims may, after all, look very different in different parts of the world.

The resonance of Koskenniemi's observations here, however, relate to more than merely a reflection upon the debates over globalization, human rights or the survival of the State as an institution, but more generally to the question surrounding the relation-ship between international law and the condition of statehood. The two key standpoints that Koskenniemi highlights—the ethical and the sociological—operate not merely as standpoints external to the State, but rather run through the discourses on sovereignty, self-determination, legitimacy, and recognition that constitute the very idea of the State in the first place. There is a constant equivocation, in all such discussions, as to whether the world is to be taken 'as it is' (in which we might be inclined to treat statehood as a question of fact, effectiveness as the primary condition, recognition as declaratory and sovereignty as innate), or as something which must be engineered to correspond to those values which we take to be universal and necessary (in which case, we might treat statehood as being a matter of law, self-determination or democratic legitimacy as primary conditions, rec-ognition as quasi-constitutive, and sovereignty as delegated or conditional). To note the equivocation, here, however, is to advert to the untenable character of either position. We can no more rely upon the assumption that States simply exist independently of the rela-tions they have with others (the supposed 'authenticity of the real') than we can upon the assumption that justice always lies in the hands of those who have the capacity to speak its name (the supposed 'authenticity of the ethical'). On the one hand the ethics in ques-tion will always be situational, a product of certain social conditions arising at a particular point in time; on the other hand, what we call social reality itself 'is in the last resort an ethical construction' dependent upon our willingness to act 'as if' the world were really like that (Zizek, 1989, p 36).

One of the themes developed in this chapter, however, has been to explain how many of these seemingly abstract theoretical arguments about recognition, statehood, or sover-eignty had a definitive context, namely that which arose as a consequence of the European engagement with the non-European world in the late nineteenth century. The difficulties associated with both seeking to delimit, in a descriptive sense, the geographical orien-tation of international law by reference to the pre-existence of European nation-States, but simultaneously employ a prescriptive notion of statehood as a way of supervising the 'entry' of new States into the family of nations, have largely conditioned many of the theoretical puzzles that subsequently emerged. Statehood is both presumed and regulated, recognition both constitutive and declaratory, sovereignty both a source of right and a product of prior-regulation. Running through those debates has always been a dynamic of inclusion and exclusion which, in the past, served as a way of negotiating the relationship with the non-European world, but in more recent times has come to mark the various projects and proposals associated with the identification of new categories: failed States, rogue States, illiberal or illegitimate States. In many cases such projects have been initiated on the premise that they are seeking to avoid or cast aside the authoritarian characteristics of what they take to be a nineteenth century 'positivist' international law, but have strangely re-appropriated precisely the same structures of thought and argument.

In all of this, however, what may be remarked upon is the relative strength within international legal thought of what might be called a civic republican tradition that, recalling Kant's project of perpetual peace, forges a rough alignment between the idea of the State as a civic enterprise the object of which is to guarantee individual human rights and freedoms, of sovereignty as a set of entitlements conditioned by the government's democratic credentials (or ability to fulfil its mandate), of international law as a cosmopolitan order that supervises and regulates the relationship between those largely arbitrary collections of individuals and agencies, and of international organizations as the nascent institutional expression of the values and interests of the international community writ large. In this account, the place of community, culture or tradition is assigned no direct role and may occupy merely the spaces left available to it within that framework—as that which marks participation within a minority or indigenous community, or as that which is engendered by the State through the institutional apparatus of government (nationalism as a political agenda). In the same sense, the State as an institution becomes ultimately vulnerable to an essentially instrumentalist critique: either it does its job and can be justified on that basis, or it doesn't and can't. But if this may seem to represent the key shift in international legal thought over the past century, it is one that is strangely quiet on the questions Koskenniemi poses for it: how does it claim authenticity for the values it proclaims, and what kind of political action does it entail?

REFERENCES

ALEXANDROWICZ, C (1967), *An Introduction to the History of the Law of Nations in the East Indies* (Oxford: Clarendon Press).

ANGHIE, A (2005), *Imperialism, Sovereignty and the Making of International Law* (Cambridge: Cambridge University Press).

BALIBAR, E (2004), *We the People of Europe: reflections on Transnational Citizenship* (Princetown, Princetown University Press).

BERMAN, N (1988–89), 'Sovereignty in Abeyance: Self-Determination and International Law', 7 *Wisc ILJ* 51.

BLUM, Y (1992), 'UN Membership of the "New" Yugoslavia: Continuity or Break?', 86 *AJIL* 830.

BRIERLY, J (1924), 'The Shortcomings of International Law', 5 *BYIL* 13.

BROWNLIE, I (1982), 'Recognition in Theory and Practice', 53 *BYIL* 197.

CASSESE, A (1995), *Self-Determination of Peoples: A Legal Reappraisal* (Cambridge: Cambridge University Press).

CLAPHAM, A (2006), *Human Rights Obligations of Non-State Actors* (Oxford: Oxford University Press).

CLAUDE, I (1955), *National Minorities; an International Problem* (Cambridge, Mass: Harvard University Press).

COBBAN, A (1945), *National Self-Determination* (Oxford: Oxford University Press).

CRAVEN, M (1995), 'The European Community Arbitration Commission on Yugoslavia', 67 *BYIL* 333.

—— (2007), *The Decolonization of International Law: State Succession and the Law of Treaties* (Oxford: Oxford University Press).

CRAWFORD, J (2006), *The Creation of States in International Law*, 2nd edn (Oxford: Oxford University Press).

DERRIDA, J (1989–90), 'Force of Law: The Mystical Foundations of Authority', 11 *Cardozo Law Review* 921.

DUGARD, J (1987), *Recognition and the United Nations* (Cambridge: Cambridge University Press).

DUURSMA, JC (1996), *Fragmentation and the International Relations of MicroStates* (Cambridge: Cambridge University Press).

FAWCETT, JES (1965–66), 'Security Council Resolutions on Rhodesia', 41 *BYIL* 103.

FOUCAULT, M (2006), in Davidson, A (ed), *Psychiatric Power: Lectures at the College De France, 1973–1974* London: Palgrave Macmillan).

—— (2007), in Senellart, M (ed) *Security, Territory, Population: Lectures at the College de France 1977–1978* (London: Palgrave Macmillan).

FOX, GH and ROTH, BR (eds) (2000) *Democratic Governance and International Law* (Cambridge: Cambridge University Press)

FRANCK, T (1996), 'Clan and Superclan: Loyalty, Identity and Community in Law and Practice', 90 *AJIL* 359.

—— (1999) *The Empowered Self: Law and Society in an Age of Individualism* (Oxford: Oxford University Press).

—— (2000), 'Legitimacy and the Democratic Entitlement', in Fox, GH and Roth, BR (eds), *Democratic Governance and International Law* (Cambridge: Cambridge University Press), p 25.

GIDDENS, A (1985), *The Nation-State and Violence* (Cambridge: Polity Press).

GONG, G (1985), *The Standard of 'Civilization' in International Society* (Oxford: Clarendon Press).

GORDON, R (1997), 'Saving Failed States: Sometimes a Neo-colonialist Notion', 12 *American ULILP* 904.

GRAY, C (1996), 'Bosnia and Herzegovina: Civil War or Inter-State Conflict?', 67 *BYIL* 155.

HALL, WE (1895), *A Treatise on International Law*, 4th edn (Oxford: Clarendon Press).

HARDT, M and NEGRI, A (2000), *Empire* (Cambridge, Mass.: Harvard University Press).

HEFFTER, A-G (1857), *Le droit international publique de l'Europe* (Paris: Cotillon).

HELMAN, G and RATNER, S (1992–93), 'Saving Failed States', 89 *Foreign Policy* 3.

HOBBES, T (1957, first published 1651), in Oakeshott, M (ed), *Leviathan; or The Matter, Forme and Power or a Commonwealth Ecclesiastical and* (Oxford: Blackwell).

HOBSBAWM, E (1992), *Nations and Nationalism since 1780*, 2nd edn (Cambridge: Cambridge University Press).

JACKSON, R (1990), *Quasi-States: Sovereignty, International Relations and the Third World* (Cambridge: Cambridge University Press).

JENNINGS, R (1963), *The Acquisition of Territory in International Law* (Manchester: Manchester University Press).

JESSUP, P (1931), 'The Estrada Doctrine', 25 *AJIL* 719.

KAMMINGA, M (1996), 'State Succession in Respect of Human Rights Treaties', 7 *EJIL* 469.

KELSEN, H (1941–42), 'The Pure Theory of Law and Analytical Jurisprudence', 55 *Harv LR* 44.

KENNEDY, D (1997), 'International Law and the Nineteenth Century: History of an Illusion', 17 *Quinnipiac Law Review* 99.

KINGSBURY, B, KRISCH, N and STEWART, R (2005), 'The Emergence of Global Administrative Law', 68 *Law and Contemporary Problems* 15.

KLÜBER, J (1851), *Europaishes Völkerrecht*, 2nd edn (Schotthausen: Hurter).

KORMAN, S (1996), *The Right of Conquest: The Acquisition of Territory by Force in International Law and Practice* (Oxford: Oxford University Press).

KOSKENNIEMI, M (1989), *From Apology to Utopia: The Structure of International Legal Argument*, 2005 reissue (Cambridge: Cambridge University Press).

—— (1994a), 'National Self-Determination Today: Problems of Legal Theory and Practice', 43 *ICLQ* 241.

—— (1994b), 'The *Wonderful Artificiality* of States', 88 *ASIL Proceedings* 22

—— (2001) *The Gentle Civiliser of Nations: The Rise and Fall of International Law 1870–1960* (Cambridge: Cambridge University Press).

KREIJEN, G (2002) 'The Transformation of Sovereignty and African Independence: No Shortcuts to Statehood', in Kreijen, G (ed), *State Sovereignty and International Governance* (Oxford: Oxford University Press), p 45.

LAWRENCE, TJ (1895), *The Principles of International Law* (Boston: D C Heath and Co).

LAUTERPACHT, H (1947), *Recognition in International Law* (Cambridge: Cambridge University Press).

LOCKE, J, (1980) *Second Treatise of Government* (first published 1690) (McPherson, CB (ed)) (Indianapolis: Hackett Publishing Co).

LORIMER, J (1883), *The Institutes of the Law of Nations* (Edinburgh: W Blackwood).

MCCORQUODALE, R (1994), 'Self-Determination: A Human Rights Approach', 43 *ICLQ* 857.

MARKS, S (2003), *The Riddle of All Constitutions: International Law, Democracy and the Critique of Ideology* (Oxford: Oxford University Press).

—— (2006), 'State-Centrism, International Law, and the Anxieties of Influence', 19 *Leiden JIL* 339.

MARTENS, G DE (1864), *Précis du droit des gens moderne de l'Europe*, 2nd edn (Paris: Guillaume).

MILL, JS (1890) *Considerations on Representative Government* (London: Holt & Co).

MULLERSON, R (1993), 'The Continuity and Succession of States by Reference to the Former USSR and Yugoslavia', 42 *ICLQ* 473.

MURPHY, S (2000), 'Democratic Legitimacy and the Recognition of States and Governments', in Fox, G and Roth, B (eds), *Democratic Governance and International Law* (Cambridge: Cambridge University Press, 2000), p 123.

O'CONNELL, D (1970), *International Law*, 2nd edn (London: Stevens).

OPPENHEIM, L (1905), *International Law: A Treatise* (London: Longmans).

ORFORD, A (2003), *Reading Humanitarian Intervention: Human Rights and the Use of Force in International Law* (Cambridge: Cambridge University Press).

—— (2011), *International Authority and the Responsibility to Protect* (Cambridge: Cambridge University Press).

PHILLIMORE, R (1871), *Commentaries on International Law* (London: Butterworths).

PUFENDORF, S *On the Law of Nature and Nations* (first published 1698), (Oldfather, CH and Oldfather, WA (trans)) (Oxford: Clarendon Press).

RADAN, P (2002), *The Breakup of Yugoslavia and International Law* (London: Routledge).

REISMAN, W (1990), 'Sovereignty and Human Rights in Contemporary International Law', 84 *AJIL* 866.

RICH, R (1993), 'Recognition of States: The Collapse of Yugoslavia and the Soviet Union', 4 *EJIL* 36.

ROTHBERG, R (2002), 'Failed States in a World of Terror', 81 *Foreign Affairs* 127.

SCHACHTER, O (1998), 'The Decline of the Nation-State and its Implications for International Law', 36 *Col JTL* 7.

SCHMITT, C (1974), *The Nomos of the Earth* (Ulmen, G (trans) (2003)) (New York: Telos).

SCHWARZENBERGER, G (1950), *A Manual of International Law*, 2nd edn (London: Stevens).

SCOTT, J (2009), *The Art of Not Being Goverened: An Anarchist History of Upland Southeast Asia* (New Haven: Yale University Press).

SHAW, M (1986), *Title to Territory in Africa: International Legal Issues* (Oxford: Oxford University Press).

—— (1996), 'The Heritage of States: The Principle of *Uti Possidetis Juris* Today', 67 *BYIL* 75.

SIMPSON, G (2004), *Great Powers and Outlaw States: Unequal Sovereigns in the International Legal Order* (Cambridge: Cambridge University Press).

SPRUYT, H (1994), *The Sovereign State and its Competitors* (Princetown: Princetown University Press).

TALMON, S (1998), *Recognition of Governments in International Law* (Oxford: Clarendon Press).

TERRETT, S (2000), *The Dissolution of Yugoslavia and the Badinter Arbitration Commission* (Aldershot: Ashgate).

TILLY, C (1992), *Coercion, Capital and European States: AD 990–1992* (Oxford: Blackwell).

TWISS, T (1879–1880), 'Rapport', 3–4 *Annuaire Institut de Droit International*.

—— (1884), *Law of Nations Considered as Independent Political Communities*

(Oxford: Clarendon Press).

WADE, H (1955), 'The Basis of Legal Sovereignty', [1955] *Cam LJ* 172.

WARBRICK, D (1997), 'Recognition of States: Recent European Practice', in Evans MD (ed) *Aspects of Statehood and Institutionalism in Contemporary Europe* (Aldershot: Dartmouth Publishers), p 9.

WEBER, M (1978), *Economy and Society* (Berkeley: University of California Press).

—— (1994), 'The Profession and Vocation of Politics', in Lassman, P and Speirs, R (eds), *Weber: Political Writings* (Cambridge: Cambridge University Press), p 309.

WESTLAKE, J (1894), *Chapters on the Principles of International Law* (Cambridge: Cambridge University Press).

—— (1904), *International Law* (Cambridge: Cambridge University Press).

WHEATON, H (1866), in Dana, RH (ed) (1936), *Elements of International Law*, 8th edn (Oxford: Clarendon Press).

WILDE, R (2008), *International Territorial Administration: How Trusteeship and the Civilising Mission Never Went Away* (Oxford: Oxford University Press).

WILLIAMS, P, SCHARF, M, and HOOPER, J (2002–03), 'Resolving Sovereignty-Based Conflicts: the Emerging Approach of Earned Sovereignty', 31 *Denv JILP* 349.

WRIGHT, Q (1930), *Mandates under the League of Nations* (Chicago: The University of Chicago Press).

VATTEL, E DE, (1916) *The Law of Nations or the Principles of Natural Law* (first published 1758) (Fenwick, G (trans.)), (Washington DC: Carnegie Institute).

ZIEMELE, I (2005), *State Continuity and Nationality: The Baltic States and Russia* (Leiden: Martinus Nijhoff).

ZIZEK, S (1989), *The Sublime Object of Ideology* (London, New York: Verso).

FURTHER READING

ANGHIE, A (2005), *Imperialism, Sovereignty and the Making of International Law* (Cambridge, Cambridge University Press). An important corrective for all accounts of international law that fail to engage with the non-European world.

BERMAN, N (1988–89), 'Sovereignty in Abeyance: Self-Determination and International Law', 7 *Wisc ILJ* 51. The foremost author on the subject of nationalism and international law—here turning to the subject of self-determination.

CRAWFORD, J (2006), *The Creation of States in International Law*, 2nd edn (Oxford: Clarendon Press). A monumental, encyclopaedic, work that remains the key reference point on the subject of statehood.

KOSKENNIEMI, M (2005), *From Apology to Utopia: The Structure of International Legal Argument*, 2nd edn (Cambridge: Cambridge University Press). A challenging, structuralist, critique that lays out the indeterminacy of legal argumentation on the question of sovereignty (especially ch 4).

LAUTERPACHT, H (1947), *Recognition in International Law* (Cambridge, Cambridge University Press). Dated, and inevitably stamped with his own idiosyncrasies, yet still the best account of the doctrinal debate over recognition.

SIMPSON, G (2004), *Great Powers and Outlaw States: Unequal Sovereigns in the International Legal Order* (Cambridge: Cambridge University Press). Traces the persistence of the idea of sovereign inequality and imperialism in international law.

WILDE, R (2008), *International Territorial Administration: How Trusteeship and the Civilising Mission Never Went Away* (Oxford: Oxford University Press). The most comprehensive and effective account of the historic and contemporary practice of international territorial administration.

9

INTERNATIONAL ORGANIZATIONS

Dapo Akande

SUMMARY

This chapter examines the legal framework governing international organizations. It begins with an examination of the history, role, and nature of international organizations. It is argued in the chapter that although the constituent instruments and practices of each organization differ, there are common legal principles which apply to international organizations. The chapter focuses on the identification and exploration of those common legal principles. There is an examination of the manner in which international organizations acquire legal personality in international and domestic law and the consequences of that legal personality. There is also discussion of the manner in which treaties establishing international organizations are interpreted and how this differs from ordinary treaty interpretation. The legal and decision-making competences of international organizations are considered as are the responsibility of international organizations and their privileges and immunities. Finally, the chapter examines the structure and powers of what is probably the leading international organization—the United Nations (UN).

I. INTRODUCTION

A distinctive feature of modern international affairs is the large number of international organizations through which States seek to achieve cooperation. This chapter looks at the place occupied by international organizations within the international legal system and sketches the legal framework governing their activities. It also describes the structure and activities of the leading global international organization—the United Nations (UN).

A. HISTORY AND ROLE OF INTERNATIONAL ORGANIZATIONS

International organizations were first created in the nineteenth century as a means of conducting international relations and fostering cooperation between States. They evolved from the ad hoc multilateral conferences convened by States to deal with particular situations—such as the Congress of Vienna (1815) which settled issues arising from the end of the Napoleonic wars—into institutions in which member States not only met regularly but which also possessed organs that functioned on a permanent basis. The early international organizations dealt with technical, non-political matters and included Commissions regulating European rivers such as the Rhine, the International Telegraphic Union (1865), and the Universal Postal Union (1874). The League of Nations, created in 1919 after the First World War, was the forerunner of the UN and was the first international organization established to deal with general political and other relations between States and which aspired to universal membership.

International organizations now play a significant role in international affairs generally and in the development of international law specifically. They exist in practically all fields of endeavour ranging from general political cooperation to protection of the environment, defence, provision of humanitarian and development assistance, promotion of trade, etc. It is a reflection of the significant role that international organizations play in international affairs and in the exercise of public power that attention is now being paid to the question of what the limits of their powers are and the principles relating to when and how these organizations may be held accountable or responsible for the exercise of such powers.[1]

Within their diverse fields of operation, international organizations perform a number of functions. These include:

— Providing a forum for identifying and deliberating upon matters of common interests.

— Providing a forum for developing rules on matters of common interest.

— Acting as vehicles for taking action on international or transnational problems.

— Providing mechanisms for promoting, monitoring, and supervising compliance by States and non-State actors with agreed rules and policies as well as for gathering information regarding the conditions in and practices of States and non-State actors.

— Providing a forum for the resolution of international disputes.

B. DEFINITION, DISTINCTIONS, AND DIFFERENCES

Given the variety of organizations that are international in character, it is difficult to lay down a satisfactory and all-encompassing definition which distinguishes those organizations considered as 'international organizations' under international law from other types of organizations (Klabbers, 2009, p 6). Article 2(a) of the International Law Commission's 2011 Articles on the Responsibility of International Organizations (ARIO) provides that:

'international organization' means an organization established by a treaty or other instrument governed by international law and possessing its own international legal personality. International organizations may include as members, in addition to States, other entities;[2]

This definition embodies the key criteria for identifying whether an entity is an international organization. First, such an entity must be composed predominantly of States and/or other international organizations, though the membership may extend to other entities as well. Secondly, the entity must be established under international law. Although international organizations are usually created by treaty, they can also be created by other means, such as the resolution of another international organization, the resolution of a conference of States or by joint unilateral acts of States. Examples of organizations created

---

[1] See generally, Reinisch, 2001; Blokker, 2011, ILA Committee Report, 2004; ILA Study Group Report (2012), and ILC Report, 2011, Ch V, 'Responsibility of International Organizations'.

[2] ILC Report, 2011, p 54.

other than by treaty include the Organization for Security and Cooperation in Europe (OSCE) and the Organization of the Petroleum Exporting Countries (OPEC). Thirdly, for an entity to be an international organization it must have a will that is distinct and separate from that of the members. This is usually manifested in practice in at least one of the organs of the organization being autonomous from the members or possessing the ability to operate on a majority basis. It is having a 'distinct will' that justifies the conferral of separate legal personality.

The criteria set out in the preceding paragraph distinguish intergovernmental organizations which are the subject of this chapter from other types of international associations such as international non-governmental organizations and international public corporations. The key factor distinguishing international or intergovernmental organizations, such as the UN or the World Trade Organization (WTO), from international non-governmental organizations, such as Amnesty International or Greenpeace, is that the former are composed predominantly of States (and other intergovernmental organizations) while the latter are composed of private entities though they operate in more than one country. International public corporations or joint inter-State enterprises are entities jointly created by a number of States for the performance of commercial functions. Examples include the European Company for the Financing of Railway Rolling Stock (EUROFIMA) or Air Afrique (an airline established by 11 West African States). While international organizations are entities created under international law and have international legal personality, joint inter-State enterprises are formally established under the corporate law of one of the member States, even though the enterprise may have its roots in a treaty.

Despite sharing a common definition, there are many differences between international organizations. The most obvious differences concern membership and functions. Membership may either be universal (open) or closed. Universal organizations are open to all States and examples include the UN and its specialized agencies (see Section VII A.2 of this chapter). Closed organizations limit membership to those States fulfilling certain specified criteria. Examples of closed organizations include those whose membership is based on geographic criteria (eg regional organizations such as the Organization of American States (OAS) and the African Union (AU)) or economic criteria (eg OPEC and the Organization for Economic Cooperation and Development (OECD)). Some international organizations, such as the UN, have general functions within broad areas whereas the functions of others are restricted to particular fields, such as telecommunications, labour, health or trade. Membership and function can be combined in various ways: some closed regional organizations exercise general functions (eg the OAS and the Council of Europe), while some universal organizations only have competence in limited field (eg the UN specialized agencies and the WTO).

In considering whether or not a body or institutional structure qualifies as an international organization, one must consider the substance of the structure established by States rather than whether it is formally designated as an international organization. The key is whether the criteria outlined are fulfilled rather than the designation of the organization. Therefore, the more informal institutional arrangements established by some multilateral environmental treaties[3] and which are comprised simply of: (i) a conference of the parties to the relevant treaty (COP) which meet regularly; (ii) one or more subsidiary bodies of the COP; and (iii) a secretariat which services the work of the COP and subsidiary bodies,

---

[3] Eg, the London Convention on the Prevention of Marine Pollution by Dumping of Wastes and other Matter (1972); the UN Framework Convention on Climate Change (1992), and the Kyoto Protocol (1997). See further, Churchill and Ulfstein, 2000, pp 623–5.

may qualify as international organizations when they have a will distinct from those of the members. In some cases, these 'institutions' have even entered into treaties with States or other international organizations (Churchill and Ulfstein, 2000; Sands, 2003, pp 108–9).

C. IS THERE A COMMON LAW OF INTERNATIONAL ORGANIZATIONS?

Given their great diversity, the existence of a common law applicable to international organizations has been questioned. On one view, since the law governing each organization derives from its own constituent instrument and practices (its 'constitution'), each will be governed by different legal principles which can only be applied by analogy to other organizations. It is true that these 'constitutions' regulate many matters, such as membership, competences and financing, in differing ways. However, it is equally true that customary international law and, to a much lesser degree, treaties have generated principles of general application to international organizations. These common principles concern matters such as the legal personality of international organizations, implied competences, interpretation of constituent instruments, employment relations, immunities and privileges and the liability and responsibility of the organization and its member States (see ILC Report, 2011, Ch 5). These common principles apply in the absence of any contrary principle provided for in the law of the particular organization, and as regards liability and responsibility may even apply despite contrary provisions in the internal law of the organization. It is also accepted that the solutions adopted by one organization to a problem have a relevance to the approach to be taken to an analogous problem in another. The following sections outline the most important elements of this common law applicable to international organizations.

II. LEGAL PERSONALITY

In considering the legal position of international organizations it is useful to start by considering whether such entities possess legal personality and, if so, what the consequences of that legal personality are. Since international organizations usually operate on both the international plane and in national territories, one must consider whether these organizations possess international legal personality and legal personality in domestic law. Section II A examines the meaning of international legal personality and the sources of that personality for international organizations especially in cases in which it is not expressly provided for in the constituent instrument of that organization. It also examines the consequences for international organizations of the possession of international legal personality. Section II B considers whether non-member States of an international organization are bound to recognize its legal personality. Section II C examines the obligation of member States to confer personality in domestic law and the various techniques used by States to confer such personality.

A. PERSONALITY IN INTERNATIONAL LAW

1. The meaning of international legal personality

To say that an entity has international legal personality is to say that the entity is a bearer of rights and duties derived from international law. Although it was often asserted in the nineteenth and early twentieth centuries that States were the only subjects of international law it was decisively established in the *Reparation for Injuries* Advisory Opinion that other entities, particularly international organizations, also possess international legal personality. The case arose out of the murder of a UN mediator in Jerusalem by a Jewish group. The UN General Assembly requested an opinion from the International Court of Justice on whether the UN had the capacity to bring an international claim (against Israel) for the purpose of obtaining reparation for injuries done to the organization and its agents. While Article 104 of the Charter imposes an obligation on UN member States to confer legal personality on the Organization within their *domestic* legal systems, there is nothing in the Charter which expressly grants *international* personality to the UN. Nevertheless, the Court found that the UN possesses international legal personality, arguing that this was necessary for the fulfilment of its functions. The Court also deduced legal personality from the powers and rights that had been given to the UN (the power of decision-making, domestic legal personality, immunities, and privileges and treaty-making powers) under the Charter. The Court noted that the Organization 'occupies a position in certain respects in detachment from its members' and that:

> ...the Organization was intended to exercise and enjoy, and is in fact exercising and enjoying, functions and rights which can only be explained on the basis of the possession of a large measure of international personality and the capacity to operate on the international plane.[4]

To say that international organizations possess international legal personality tells us that they are capable of possessing international rights, capacities or duties. However, apart from a few specific capacities indicated in Section II A3 of this book, possession of international legal personality does not define the particular capacities, rights or duties that any particular organization possesses nor does it indicate that they possess the same capacities, rights or duties (Gazzini, 2011, p 43).

2. The sources of international legal personality for international organizations

Although treaties establishing universal international organizations do not usually provide expressly that they possess international legal personality, there are treaties dealing with closed international organizations which do so.[5] Where there is no express treaty basis, international personality may be deduced by other means.

There are two basic schools of thought regarding the method by which the personality is to be established in the absence of an express treaty provision. The first school—the will theory—asserts that the personality of an international organization is derived from the will of the members to confer such personality. This conferral is done expressly in the constitutive instrument of the organization or may be deduced from the capacities, powers, rights and duties bestowed to the organization (Schermers and Blokker, 2011, para 1565; Reinisch, 2000, pp 54–9; Sands and Klein, 2009, para 15-006). According to this school of thought, an international organization will only have personality if its members intended it to have such personality or if it can be asserted that such personality is necessary for the fulfilment of the functions ascribed to it by its members. The second school—the objective approach—asserts that an international organization has

---

[4] *Reparation for Injuries Suffered in the Service of the United Nations, Advisory Opinion, ICJ Reports 1949*, p 174 at p 179.

[5] Examples include Treaty on European Union (as amended by Lisbon Treaty), Article 47; EC Treaty, Article 210; European Coal and Steel Community Treaty, Article 6; Agreement Establishing the African Development Bank, Article 50.

international legal personality as long as certain objective criteria set out by law are fulfilled (Seyersted, 1964; Rama Montaldo, 1970). Thus personality is not derived from the will of the members but from the presence of the criteria stated earlier in the definition of an international organization.[6]

There has been much debate regarding which of these two approaches was taken by the Court in the *Reparation for Injuries* Advisory Opinion. It that case, the Court made reference on more than occasion to the intention of the parties in ascribing legal personality to the UN. However, this does not necessarily mean that the Court adopted the will theory.

What the Court seemed to be saying was that the intention of the members to ascribe certain rights, functions and characteristics to the UN could only be given effect if the organization possessed its own legal personality. This is not inconsistent with saying that the members had ascribed characteristics to the organization which satisfied the criteria required for conferring international personality. While the key factor is the possession of those characteristics, they necessarily arise out of the will of the members. Thus, there is no radical difference between the two schools if one accepts that the characteristics which confer international legal personality on international organizations must necessarily be conferred on it by its members. Once those characteristics are conferred (by the will of the members through its constituent instrument or subsequent practice), the rules of international law confer international personality on the organization with all the consequences that this entails. Arguably, all that the Court did in the *Reparation for Injuries* Advisory Opinion was to search to see if the characteristics necessary for international personality (and which are predetermined by international law) had been conferred on the UN by its members.[7]

3. The consequences of the possession of international legal personality by international organizations

Possessing international legal personality means that an organization possesses rights and duties in international law but this does not usually tell us the particular rights and capacities possessed by a particular organization. However, there are certain consequences which flow from the possession of international legal personality by an international organization.

(1) Personality distinguishes the collective entity (the organization) from the members. In particular, legal personality separates out the rights and obligations of the organization from those of the members (Lauterpacht, 1976, p 407).

(2) Personality entitles the organization to bring a claim in international law for the purpose of maintaining its own rights.[8] Such claims by international organizations will be brought through the mechanisms which exist in international law for the settlement of international disputes and can only be made in an international tribunal if that the tribunal has jurisdiction to deal with the case.

---

[6] Amerasinghe, 2005, p 83 tries to merge both schools by arguing that the intention required is not subjective but objective and to be found in the circumstances surrounding the creation of the organization.

[7] See text at n 4. In the sentences following that quote the Court states that the UN 'could not carry out the intention of its founders if it were devoid of legal personality. It must be acknowledged that its Members, by entrusting certain functions to it, with attendant duties and responsibilities, have clothed it with the compliance required to enable those functions to be effectively discharged'.

[8] Schermers and Blokker, 2011, para 1856 argue that this capacity is an implied power but one possessed by all international organizations.

(3) Personality entails the consequence that an international organization is responsible for the non-fulfilment of its obligations (Article 3, ARIO 2011). Personality also gives rise to a presumption that members of the organization are not liable with respect to the obligations *of the organization*, although this presumption can be displaced (see Section V of this book).[9] Members remain liable for *their own obligations* and that responsibility may arise in the same set of circumstances where the organization is also responsible.

These first three consequences are inherent in the very notion of international legal personality and apply to any international legal person. However, there are other consequences of the personality of international organizations which do not apply to all international legal persons but result from the nature of personality possessed by international organizations.

(4) Customary international law confers, at least within the host State, certain privileges and immunities on international organizations that are necessary for the efficient and independent functioning of the organization (see further Section VI of this book). As Higgins (1994, p 91) puts it, 'members—and *a fortiori* the headquarters State—may not at one and the same time establish an organization and fail to provide it with those immunities that ensure its role as distinct from that of the host State.'

(5) International organizations possess a power to conclude agreements which are subject to the law of treaties.[10] Although the question whether a particular type of treaty is within the competence of any particular organization depends on its implied powers, every organization at least has the competence (where not expressly denied) to enter into certain types of treaties. These include host State agreements and treaties for the purpose of settling claims by and against the organization.[11]

B. OBJECTIVE LEGAL PERSONALITY AND RELATIONS WITH NON-MEMBER STATES

Given that international organizations are created by treaties—which do not bind non-parties without their consent[12]—it might be argued that the personality of an international organization is only binding on members.[13] This would mean that non-members would only be bound to accept that personality where they have 'recognized' the organization as a legal person. However, the better view is that the personality of international organizations is in fact objective, which means that it is opposable to non-members and that non-members are bound to accept that organization as a separate legal person.[14]

In the *Reparation for Injuries* Opinion, the Court had to consider whether the UN could bring a claim against a State (Israel) which was not a member of the Organization. It took the view that:

> ... fifty States, representing the vast majority of the members of the international community, had the power, in conformity with international law, to bring into being an entity

---

[9] See ILC Commentary Article 62 ARIO, ILC Report, 2011, 163 (paras 2–3).

[10] Vienna Convention on the Law of Treaties between States and International Organizations or between International Organizations (1986), preambular para 11.

[11] See *Reparation for Injuries Suffered in the Service of the United Nations, Advisory Opinion, ICJ Reports 1949*, p 174 at p 181.

[12] Vienna Convention on the Law of Treaties (1969), Article 34.

[13] See *Third Restatement*, 1987, para 223.   [14] See ILC Reports, 2011, p 76 (para 9).

possessing objective international personality and not merely personality recognised by them alone....[15]

Thus, international organizations with a membership consisting of the vast majority of the international community possess objective international personality. However, it is important to note that the Court did not say that *only* such organizations possess objective personality and there are good reasons of practice and principle for concluding that the personality possessed by any international organization is objective and opposable to non-members. In practice, 'no recent instances are known of a non-member State refusing to acknowledge the personality of an organization on the ground that it was not a member State and had not given the organization specific recognition' (Amerasinghe, 2005, p 87). Furthermore domestic courts of non-member States do acknowledge the international personality of international organizations.[16] As a matter of principle, the personality of international organizations derives from the effect that customary international law (which is binding on all States) ascribes to their characteristics. Thus, once international law ascribes personality to an organization, a subject of international law is created with its own rights and its own duties.

C. PERSONALITY IN DOMESTIC LAW

1. The obligation to confer domestic legal personality

Since international organizations also operate within the territory of States, they usually need to possess domestic legal personality, including the capacity to perform legal acts in domestic law. For example, international organizations will need to be able to enter into contracts, own property and institute legal proceedings. Many treaties establishing international organizations provide that they are to have the necessary legal capacities in domestic law, for example, UN Charter, Article 104. Even where there is no express treaty obligation, there may be an implied obligation for members to provide the organization with such domestic capacities as are necessary to allow it to function effectively (Reinisch, 2000, p 44).

2. The manner in which domestic legal personality is recognized

States confer domestic legal personality on international organizations in various ways. The technique used depends in part on the relationship between international law and the national law of the State concerned. The technique also varies between member States of an organization and non-members. In member States which adopt a more monist tradition of the relationship between international law and national law, the domestic personality is often taken to flow directly from the treaty provision requiring the conferment of such personality. This position has been taken in: (i) the USA and Belgium[17] with respect to the UN; (ii) the Netherlands with respect to the UN Relief and Rehabilitation Administration;[18] and (iii) Italy with respect to the North Atlantic Treaty Organization (NATO).[19]

---

[15] *Reparation for Injuries Suffered in the Service of the United Nations, Advisory Opinion, ICJ Reports 1949*, p 174 at p 185.

[16] Eg, *International Tin Council v Amalgamet* (1988), 80 ILR 31; 524 NYS 2d 971.

[17] *Manderlier v Organisation des Nations Unies & Etat Belge (Ministre des Affaires Etrangères)* (1972), 45 ILR 446; *UN v B* (1952), 19 ILR 490.

[18] *UNRRA v Daan* (1949), 16 ILR 337.   [19] *Branno v Ministry of War* (1955), 22 ILR 756.

In member States in which treaties do not form part of domestic law such treaty obligations will usually need to be transformed into national law by a national instrument. This is the technique adopted in common law countries like the UK where the International Organizations Act 1968 provides that the Executive may by Order in Council confer the legal capacities of a body corporate on any international organization of which the UK is a member.[20]

Thus in the UK, the House of Lords in *JH Rayner (Mincing Lane) Ltd* v *Department of Trade and Industry* stressed that the legal persona of the International Tin Council (ITC) in English law was created not by the constituent agreement of the organization but by the domestic legislation. According to Lord Oliver:

> Without the Order in Council the I.T.C. had no legal existence in the law of the United Kingdom.... What brought it into being in English law was the Order in Council and it is the Order in Council, a purely domestic measure, in which the constitution of the legal persona is to be found and in which there has to be sought the liability of the members which the appellants seek to establish, for that is the act of the ITC's creation in the United Kingdom.[21]

The consequence of this was that the liability of members for the organization's debts depended on domestic legislation rather than on the position in international law.

The legal personality of international organizations will also be recognized by the courts of non-member States. Under private international law domestic courts will recognize the legal status and capacities of an organization created by foreign law. Similarly, since an international organization has personality under the law of its creation—international law—that personality will be recognized by domestic courts.[22]

In the UK, it has been held that the legal personality of an international organization of which the UK is not a member will be recognized where the organization has been accorded legal personality under the law of the host State or of another member State[23] rather than by virtue of international law and the relevant constituent treaty. Taken to its logical conclusion, this approach would have the unfortunate consequence that the law governing the status and capacities of the organization would be the foreign domestic law. Happily, the High Court in *Westland Helicopters Ltd* v *Arab Organization for Industrialization*[24] held that while the personality of an international organization of which the UK was not a member would only be recognized in the UK if a foreign State had accorded that organization personality in its domestic law, the law governing the status and capacities of the organization is international law, including the relevant treaties.

III. INTERPRETATION OF CONSTITUENT INSTRUMENTS

Treaties which establish international organizations set out both the purposes, structure and competences of the organization as a whole and the particular functions and powers

---

[20] International Organizations Act 1968, s 2(a). Similar legislation exists in the USA, Australia, Canada, and New Zealand.

[21] [1989] 3 WLR 969, 1012c.

[22] See *International Tin Council v Amalgamet* (1988), 80 ILR 31; 524 NYS 2d 971; *Arab Organization for Industrialisation and others v Westland Helicopters Ltd and others* (1987), 80 ILR 622.

[23] *Arab Monetary Fund v Hashim* [1990] 1 All ER 685. A similar approach was taken in the US case *In Re Jawa Mahmoud Hashim* (1995), 107 ILR 405.

[24] *Westland Helicopters Ltd v Arab Organization for Industralization* [1995] 2 All ER 387; 108 ILR 564.

granted to its individual organs. These treaties, define the position of the organization towards its members as well as the relationship between the individual organs. Although they are not party to such treaties, international organizations are bound by their constituent instruments.[25] In many cases, these treaties also create rights and impose obligations between the members. Finally, they may to some degree define the relationship between the organization and third parties. Consequently, the manner in which they are interpreted is of considerable importance. The following subsections consider: (i) who is empowered to interpret constituent treaties of international organizations; and (ii) the relevant principles of treaty interpretation.

A. WHO IS EMPOWERED TO INTERPRET?

Since the organs of international organization will need to have some appreciation of the scope of their functions and powers in order to carry them out, these organs will necessarily and routinely have to interpret the treaty setting up the international organization. In the *Certain Expenses* Advisory Opinion, the ICJ accepted that 'each organ [of the UN] must, in the first place at least, determine its own jurisdiction.'[26] Interpretations by organs will take place either formally and explicitly (eg in a legal act of the organ)—particularly in cases where dispute arises as to the meaning of particular provisions—or impliedly as a result of the practice of the organ in question. Some constituent treaties provide for formal and definitive interpretations by a particular organ. This is particularly common with respect to international financial institutions where there is often an obligation to submit questions of interpretation to the Executive Board, Board of Directors, or the Board of Governors of the institution for decision.[27] In such circumstances, the interpretations given by these organs are binding, at least on the parties to the dispute, if not on all members and other organs. Where there is no formal power of interpretation given, and interpretation arises simply in the course of the work of the organization, such interpretations are not binding on member States. In the same way that organs will have to interpret constituent treaties in the course of their functions, members will similarly have to do so (Tzanakopoulos, 2011, Ch 5).

Judicial or arbitral tribunals may also have occasion to interpret constituent instruments. Such bodies may be created to deal with legal issues which arise within the system of the international organization in question. Examples include the Court of Justice of the European Union and the International Tribunal for the Law of the Sea. International organizations do not have standing to be parties in contentious cases before the ICJ although UN organs and UN specialized agencies may request Advisory Opinions from the ICJ on legal questions arising within the scope of their competence, including the interpretation of their constituent instruments.[28] In the case of specialized agencies, this competence to request Advisory Opinions will be contained in agreements concluded with the UN or in their constituent instruments.[29] The ICJ may also have to interpret the constituent instrument

---

[25] *Interpretation of the Agreement of 25 March 1951 between the WHO and Egypt, Advisory Opinion, ICJ Reports 1980*, p 73, para 37.

[26] *Certain Expenses of the United Nations, Advisory Opinion, ICJ Reports 1962*, p 151 at p 168.

[27] Eg, IMF Articles of Agreement, Article XXIX(a); IBRD Articles of Agreement, Article IX(a); Agreement Establishing the Asian Development Bank, Article 59.

[28] Although there are implications to the contrary in the *Legality of the Use by a State of Nuclear Weapons in Armed Conflict, Advisory Opinion, ICJ Reports 1996*, p 66, para 28, the better view is that an authorized UN specialized agency is always entitled to request an Advisory Opinion on the interpretation of its constituent instrument. See Akande, 1998, pp 452–7.

[29] Eg, WHO Constitution, Article 76; IMO Constitution, Article 66.

of international organizations in contentious cases between States, where such a case raises questions relating to the rights and obligations of States arising from such treaties.

The constituent treaties may also provide for disputes arising thereunder to be referred to international arbitration.[30] Alternatively, an arbitral tribunal established under a treaty or contract between an international organization and a third party may have to interpret the constitution of that organization.[31] As has already been seen, national courts may also have to construe the constituent instruments of international organizations.

B. WHAT ARE THE RELEVANT PRINCIPLES OF INTERPRETATION TO BE APPLIED?

Since the constituent instruments establishing international organizations are usually treaties, interpretation is governed by Articles 31 and 32 of the Vienna Convention on the Law of Treaties (see Fitzmaurice, Ch 7 of this book). Article 5 of that Convention expressly states that the Convention applies to such treaties and in the *Nuclear Weapons Advisory Opinion (Request by WHO)* the ICJ stated that:

> From a formal standpoint, the constituent instruments of international organizations are multilateral treaties, to which the well-established rules of treaty interpretation apply.[32]

However, the ICJ has noted that constituent instruments have 'certain special characteristics'[33] and that:

> ...the constituent instruments are also treaties of a particular character; their object is to create new subjects of law endowed with a certain autonomy, to which the parties entrust the task of realizing common goals. Such treaties can raise specific problems of interpretation, owing, *inter alia*, to their character which is conventional and at the same time institutional; the very nature of the organization created, the objectives which have been assigned to it by its founders, the imperatives associated with the effective performance of its functions, as well as its own practice, are all elements which may deserve special attention when the time comes to interpret these constituent treaties.[34]

To the extent that constituent instruments are in some senses 'constitutions', the general rules of treaty interpretation have to be applied differently when such treaties are under consideration (Lauterpacht, 1976, p 416; Amerasinghe, 2005, p 59). It is these differences that are focused on next.

1. The role of objects and purposes—the principle of effectiveness

Article 31 of the Vienna Convention provides that:

> A treaty shall be interpreted in good faith, in accordance with the ordinary meaning to be given to the terms of the treaty in their context and in the light of its object and purpose.

---

[30] Eg Universal Postal Unison Constitution, Article 39.

[31] See *Westland Helicopters v Arab Organization for Industrialization et al* (1989), 80 ILR 595.

[32] *Legality of the Use by a State of Nuclear Weapons in Armed Conflict (Request by WHO), Advisory Opinion,* ICJ Reports 1996, p 66, para 19.

[33] *Certain Expenses of the United Nations, Advisory Opinion, ICJ Reports 1962,* p 151 at p 157.

[34] *Legality of the Use by a State of Nuclear Weapons in Armed Conflict, Advisory Opinion, ICJ Reports 1996,* p 66, para 19.

The ICJ has stated that 'interpretation must be based above all upon the text of the treaty'[35] and generally speaking, the objects and purpose of a treaty are subsidiary to the text (Aust, 2013, p 209). However, when interpreting constituent instruments of international organizations special prominence is given to the objects and purposes of the instrument and of the organization. In the *Nuclear Weapons* Advisory Opinion the Court spoke of 'the very nature of the organization created, the objectives which have been assigned to it by its founders, the imperatives associated with the effective performance of its functions' as elements which may 'deserve special attention' in interpreting the constituent instruments of international organizations. Likewise in the *Reparation for Injuries* Advisory Opinion, the Court stated that 'the rights and duties of an entity such as the Organization must depend on its purposes and functions as specified or implied in its constituent documents or developed in practice.'[36] Frequently, the Court 'will seek to determine what are the purposes and objectives of the organization and will give to the words in question an interpretation which will be most conducive to the achievement of those ends' (Lauterpacht, 1976, p 420). This is known as the principle of effectiveness. The primary example of this principle is the doctrine of implied powers, by which an organization is deemed to have those powers that are necessary for achieving its purposes even in the absence of words in the text which indicate that the organization is to have such a power (Section IV A of this book).

2. The role of subsequent practice

The practice of the organization is often given a special role, and is used not only in cases where the text of the agreement is ambiguous but also in cases of silence and to graft new rules on to the constituent instrument. The justification for this is that such treaties must be regarded as living instruments and be interpreted in an evolutionary manner, permitting the organization to fulfil its purposes in changing circumstances (Kadelback, 2012, p 79). A well-known example of this is the *Namibia* Advisory Opinion,[37] where the Court, relying on the consistent practice of the Security Council and its members, held that abstentions by a permanent member of the Security Council was a 'concurring vote' within the meaning of Article 27(3) of the UN Charter and not a veto. Similarly, in the *Reparation for Injuries* Advisory Opinion the Court referred to the practice of the UN and the fact that it had entered into treaties as confirming the legal personality of the organization.[38]

Reference to the practice of the parties as a means of treaty interpretation is permitted by the Vienna Convention, Article 31(3)(b). However, the Court has also drawn on the practice of the organs of the organization. This is significant since some organs are not composed of all the organization's members and, even if they are, many operate on a majority basis. Thus such practice may not reflect the position of all parties to the treaty. Where some members object to the practice of an organ, allowing that practice to influence interpretation or development of new rules amounts to imposing new obligations on the minority without their consent. This is contrary to the general principle of international law that obligations can only arise from express or implied consent and some

[35] *Territorial Dispute (Libya/Chad), Judgment, ICJ Reports 1994*, p 21, para 41.
[36] *Reparation for Injuries Suffered in the Service of the United Nations, Advisory Opinion, ICJ Reports 1949*, p 174 at p 180.
[37] *Legal Consequences for States of the Continued Presence of South Africa in Namibia (South West Africa) notwithstanding Security Council Resolution 276 (1970), Advisory Opinion, ICJ Reports 1971*, p 16, paras 20–22.
[38] *Reparation for Injuries Suffered in the Service of the United Nations, Advisory Opinion, ICJ Reports 1949*, p 174 at p 179.

judges of the ICJ have counselled against this approach.[39] Some authors claim there is an independent rule permitting the use of the practice of organs which members of organizations must be deemed to have accepted (Lauterpacht, 1976, p 460; Kadelbach, 2012, p 86). However, subsequent practice of a majority within an organ must not be used as a means of constitutional amendment (Amerasinghe, 2005, p 54; Lauterpacht, 1976, p 465). It is noteworthy that in practically all cases where the ICJ has referred to subsequent practice of organs it has simply been used as a means of confirming an interpretation already arrived at using other methods of interpretation. Subsequent practice of organs should therefore be confined to cases where it establishes the agreement of the parties, confirms a result already reached or to cases where other methods of interpretation lead to an ambiguity or an unreasonable result.

IV. POWERS OF INTERNATIONAL ORGANIZATIONS

In addition to the powers expressly conferred on international organizations by their constituent treaties these organizations also possess powers which are implied. This section examines the basis for those implied powers. It then surveys the kinds of decision-making powers possessed by international organizations and finally examines the legal consequences when organizations act beyond their powers.

A. IMPLIED POWERS

In the *Reparation for Injuries* Advisory Opinion, the ICJ stated that:

> Under international law, an Organization must be deemed to have those powers which, though not expressly provided in the Charter, are conferred upon it by necessary implication as being essential to the performance of its duties.[40]

This doctrine of implied powers has been applied by the ICJ in a number of cases. In the *Reparation for Injuries* Advisory Opinion, the Court held that the UN was entitled to present an international claim on behalf of its agents even though such a power is not stated in the Charter. Likewise, in the *Certain Expenses* Advisory Opinion,[41] the Court held that the UN Security Council and General Assembly were competent to establish peacekeeping operations although that concept is not mentioned in the Charter.

Implied powers are not restricted to those powers necessary for carrying out of express powers or functions. On the contrary, ICJ jurisprudence shows that powers can be implied whenever they are 'essential' for the fulfilment of the organization's objects and purposes. Furthermore, 'essentiality' does not mean that the power to be implied must be 'indispensably required' (Lauterpacht, 1976, pp 430–32). The Court has been rather liberal in its approach and has been willing to imply a power where it would 'promote the efficiency of the Organization'.[42] The main limitation is that the power must be directed at achieving

---

[39] See the Separate Opinion of Judge Spender in *Certain Expenses of the United Nations, Advisory Opinion, ICJ Reports 1962*, p 151 at p 197.

[40] *Reparation for Injuries Suffered in the Service of the United Nations, Advisory Opinion, ICJ Reports 1949*, p 174 at p 182.

[41] *Certain Expenses of the United Nations, Advisory Opinion, ICJ Reports 1962*, p 151 at p 177.

[42] Akande, 1998, p 444.

the aims and purposes of the organization. As the ICJ stated in *Certain Expenses* Advisory Opinion:

> When the Organization takes action which warrants the assertion that it was appropriate for the fulfilment of one of the stated purposes of the United Nations, the presumption is that such action is not *ultra vires* the Organization.[43]

B. DECISION-MAKING POWERS

International organizations are often given the power to take decisions relating to their spheres of activity. Some decisions relate to the internal workings of the organization itself and are directed at the organs of the organization—for example, decisions approving the budget, staff regulations, rules of procedure, or decisions establishing subsidiary organs. Other decisions are taken in the course of carrying out the tasks entrusted to the organization and are directed at the members of the organization or, exceptionally, at third parties such as individuals and other non-State entities. Examples include decisions of the World Health Organization (WHO) setting standards with respect to pharmaceutical and other products; decisions of the UN Security Council imposing sanctions on a State; decisions of the ICAO Council relating to safety standards for international aviation.

In determining whether or not a particular decision of an international organization is legally binding on its addressee one must consider, first, whether that organ or organization is empowered by its constitution (expressly or impliedly) to take binding decisions and secondly, whether the language of the decision reveals an intention on the part of the organ to issue a binding decision.

Some constituent treaties expressly confer on organizations the power to issue decisions binding on their members. For example, Article 25 of the UN Charter obliges members to carry out decisions of the Security Council and under Article 22 of the WHO Constitution regulations adopted by the World Health Assembly are binding, unless a member opts out of the regulation *ab initio*.

Since international organizations do not generally have law-making powers, they are usually given power to take non-binding decisions which may take a number of forms. The most common is the power to make *recommendations* to members concerning matters within the scope of the organization (eg UN General Assembly under Articles 10–14 of the UN Charter). Other decisions may be *determinations* consisting of findings of facts or characterizations or formal *declarations* of principles which the organ considers applicable in a particular area. Since these decisions are not binding, they do not, of themselves, create obligations for member States.

However, the non-binding nature of decisions does not mean that a particular decision is devoid of legal effect for members. Some constituent instruments oblige members to consider recommendations in good faith. For example, the International Labour Organization (ILO) and UN Educational, Scientific and Cultural Organization (UNESCO) Constitutions (Articles 19(6) and Articles 4(4) and 8 respectively) require member States to submit recommendations to their competent national authorities for consideration and are to report back to the organization on action taken. Furthermore, a separate international treaty may contain an obligation to have regard to (and possibly to comply with) non-binding decisions of an international organization. For example, the WTO Agreement on Sanitary and Phytosanitary Measures (SPS), Article 3 encourages members

---

[43] *Certain Expenses of the United Nations, Advisory Opinion, ICJ Reports 1962*, p 151 at p 168.

to base their SPS measures on standards adopted by other international organizations. Although members are not required to confirm these standards, measures in conformity are presumed to comply with the relevant WTO provisions.[44] Likewise a number of provisions of the UN Convention on the Law of the Sea require States to comply with standards adopted by the 'competent international organization' (usually the IMO). Additionally, it is arguable that there is a presumption that members acting in accordance with a relevant decision of an international organization are acting lawfully at least as between the members of that organization.

Finally, non-binding decisions of international organizations may contain rules of law which are or become binding through other processes of international law. Resolutions of the UN General Assembly which are couched in declaratory terms are a good example.[45] Where such declarations elaborate on rules contained in the constituent treaty of the organization or other treaties adopted within the organization they may be regarded as authoritative interpretations of the treaty in question or, alternatively, as subsequent practice establishing the agreement of the parties to the treaty.[46] Furthermore, such resolutions may be declaratory of pre-existing rules of customary international law. Alternatively, such resolutions may play a role in the formation of *new* customary rules so that the rules contained therein may come to be regarded as binding. As the ICJ noted in the *Nuclear Weapons* Advisory Opinion:

> ...General Assembly resolutions, even if they are not binding, may sometimes have normative value. They can, in certain circumstances, provide evidence important for establishing the existence of a rule or the emergence of an *opinio juris*. To establish whether this is true of a given General Assembly resolution, it is necessary to look at its content and the conditions of its adoption; it is also necessary to see whether an *opinio juris* exists as to its normative character. Or a series of resolutions may show the gradual evolution of the *opinio juris* required for the establishment of a new rule.[47]

Thus while some international organizations have the competence to adopt decisions which are binding on member States and others, most do not possess this power. However, non-binding decisions of international organizations are not without legal effect and the rules contained in those decisions may be binding through a link with other treaties or under customary international law.

C. *ULTRA VIRES* DECISIONS OF INTERNATIONAL ORGANIZATIONS

What is the effect of a decision that is beyond the powers (*ultra vires*) of the organ or the organization? Are these decisions legally effective, despite their illegal foundation or are such decisions nullities and therefore of no effect at all (void *ab initio*)? A middle position might perhaps be taken whereby such decisions are voidable, meaning that they are effective until they are set aside by a competent body. Whatever view is taken, the question arises how it is to be determined whether a particular decision is *ultra vires* or not. Very

---

[44] *Beef Hormone Case*, Appellate Body Report, WT/DS26/AB/R, WT/DS48/AB/R (16 January 1998).
[45] Eg, Universal Declaration of Human Rights, GA Res 217A (1948); Declaration of Principles of International Law Concerning Friendly Relations Among States, GA Res 2625 (1970).
[46] Article 31(3)(c) Vienna Convention on the Law of Treaties.
[47] *Legality of the Use by a State of Nuclear Weapons in Armed Conflict, Advisory Opinion, ICJ Reports 1996*, p 66, para 70. See also *Military and Paramilitary Activities in and Against Nicaragua (Nicaragua v United States), Merits, Judgment, ICJ Reports 1986*, p 14 at pp 99ff.

few international organizations have, like the EU, a judicial system competent to compulsorily adjudicate on the legality of acts of the organs of the organization. There is, for example, no general procedure by which the ICJ can consider the legality of decisions of the UN or its specialized agencies. However, such questions may be raised in ICJ Advisory Opinions requested by the organ or organization or may arise incidentally in a contentious case between States (Akande, 1997).

Review by the ICJ of the legality of decisions by the UN occurred in the *Certain Expenses* Advisory Opinion,[48] where the General Assembly requested an opinion from the Court on whether expenditures related to UN peacekeeping missions were expenses of the UN within the meaning of Article 17 of the Charter. If they were, member States had an obligation to contribute to the costs of such missions. In considering that question, the Court felt it necessary to consider whether the peacekeeping operations in question had been lawfully established by the Security Council and the General Assembly.

In the *Namibia* Advisory Opinion,[49] the Court was asked to consider the legal consequences for States of the continued presence of South Africa in Namibia following the termination of South Africa's mandate for the territory by the General Assembly and the decision by the Security Council in Resolution 276 that States had an obligation to refrain from dealing with South Africa in regard to that territory. The Court stated that while there was no established procedure of judicial review within the UN system, the Court was competent and would review the legality of the relevant decisions of the General Assembly and the Security Council. In both cases just referred to the Court found the relevant decisions to be lawful.

In addition to 'incidental' judicial review by international tribunals of the legality of acts of international organizations, there is the possibility that national and regional courts may also be called upon to decide, indirectly, on the legality of acts of international organizations (see Reinisch, 2010). This may happen when challenges occur in domestic legal systems to national measures implementing the decision of an international organization. There have been several cases where national courts and regional courts like the European Court of Justice or the European Court of Human Rights have been asked to invalidate, or find unlawful, national measures implementing decisions of the UN Security Council to impose sanctions under its powers under Chapter VII of the UN Charter.[50] In some cases, the national measure is challenged based on a lack of compliance with domestic law. However, in other cases the challenge is based on the failure of the challenged measure (the sanctions) to comply with international law standards, particularly those established by international human rights law. In these cases, the decision of the court is, in strict terms, about the legality of the domestic implementing act. However, since those acts are based on, and even mirror, decisions of the UN Security Council, the decision, in reality, constitutes a review of the Security Council's decision. The most extreme example of a tribunal engaging in such review is the decision of the Grand Chamber of the European Court of Justice (ECJ) in *Kadi II* that the imposition of targeted sanctions against a person alleged to have links with Al Qaeda was inconsistent with his fundamental rights as there was insufficient evidence of his involvement with Al Qaeda.[51]

---

[48] *Certain Expenses of the United Nations, Advisory Opinion, ICJ Reports 1962*, p 151 at pp 156–68.

[49] *Legal Consequences for States of the Continued Presence of South Africa in Namibia (South West Africa) notwithstanding Security Council Resolution 276 (1970), Advisory Opinion, ICJ Reports 1971*, p 16, paras 45–53.

[50] See Tzanakopoulos, 2010.

[51] See *Commission, Council, United Kingdom v Yassin Abdullah Kadi (Kadi II)* Joined cases C-584/10P; C-593/10P; C-595/10P (July 2013) (European Court of Justice). See also *Nada v Switzerland*, no 10593/08, Judgment of 12 September 2012, ECHR 2012.

The European Court of Human Rights has stated that since the UN Charter includes the achievement of international cooperation in promoting and encouraging respect for human rights and fundamental freedoms among its purposes, the court will presume that the Security Council does not intend to violate fundamental principles of human rights when interpreting resolutions of the Council which impose obligations on UN member states.[52] However, in one recent case, the Court has declared the actions of a State, acting in compliance with a decision of the Council to impose sanctions on a terrorist suspect, to be contrary to the provisions of the European Convention of Human Rights.[53] Although not quite a review of the Council's decisions, the Court has shown a willingness to disregard and not apply those aspects of a Security Council decision that do not conform to fundamental rights.

The dearth of established procedures for reviewing the legality, under international law, of decisions of international organizations makes the view that illegal decisions are voidable (Osieke, 1983, p 255) and problematic. In effect, it would mean that illegal decisions stand unless, by accident, there is the possibility of review. This is clearly unsatisfactory and the better view is that *ultra vires* decisions—but not those merely suffering some minor procedural defect—are a nullity.[54] As Judge Morelli said in the *Certain Expenses* case:

> In the case of acts of international organizations... there is nothing comparable to the remedies existing in domestic law in connection with administrative acts. The consequence of this is that there is no possibility of applying the concept of voidability to the acts of the United Nations. If an act of an organ of the United Nations had to be considered as an invalid act, such invalidity could constitute only the *absolute nullity* of the act. In other words, there are only two alternatives for the acts of the Organization: either the act is fully valid, or it is an absolute nullity, because absolute nullity is the only form in which invalidity of an act of the Organization can occur.[55]

Thus, where a decision is illegal, a State is free to depart from it.[56] However, there is always the risk that the decision might later be found to be lawful and the non-compliant State in breach of its obligations.

It must be noted that given the limited opportunities for judicial review, the principle that *ultra vires* acts are void *ab initio* might undermine the certainty of decisions of international organizations and permit States to seek to evade their treaty obligations. However, this danger is reduced by the presumption, already referred to, that acts of international organizations directed at the fulfilment of the purposes of the organization are valid, meaning that the burden of proof is on the State arguing otherwise. Additionally, mere procedural defects do not render decisions invalid. The combination of these principles is sufficient to ensure stability.

In addition to the prospect that a decision of an international organization which was adopted beyond the powers of that organization might be void, the organization might be responsible under international law for a breach of its obligations where the illegal decision is in violation of an international obligation owed by the organization (Tzanakopoulos, 2011, Part I).

---

[52] *Al-Jedda* v *the United Kingdom* [GC], no 27021/08, ECHR 2011; 53 *EHRR*; *Nada* v *Switzerland*, no 10593/08, Judgment of 12 September 2012, ECHR 2012

[53] *Al-Dulimi* v *Switzerland* no 5809/08, Judgment of 26 November 2013.

[54] The constitution of the organization might provide that wrongful decisions become void only following the determination of a competent body. See Osieke, 1983, pp 244–5.

[55] *Certain Expenses of the United Nations Advisory Opinion, ICJ Reports 1962*, p 151 at p 222.

[56] See Separate Opinion of Judge Gros, *Interpretation of the Agreement of 25 March 1951 between the WHO and Egypt, Advisory Opinion, ICJ Reports 1980*, p 73 at p 104.

V. RESPONSIBILITY OF INTERNATIONAL ORGANIZATIONS

International organizations are subjects of international law and therefore have their own obligations under international law. What happens when an international organization breaches these obligations? As was pointed out earlier, one of the consequences of the separate legal personality possessed by international organizations is that these organizations are responsible under international law for breaches of their international obligations. However, questions relating to the responsibility of international organizations become particularly tricky in cases where the act said to be in breach of the international organization was performed by an organ of a State that is acting, in the general context where the violation occurred, at the behest of the organization or as part of an operation of that organization. Such questions may arise, for example, in cases where State armed forces act as part of a peacekeeping or peace-enforcement operation that is authorized by an international organization.

As a result of the separate legal personality of international organizations, there is a presumption that members of the organization are not liable with respect to the obligations of the organization, although this presumption can be displaced.[57] The principle that members of the organization are not liable for its obligations is illustrated by the *International Tin Council* (ITC) cases. These cases arose out the failure of the ITC—an international organization established to control the price of tin on the world markets—to meet its commercial obligations. The ITC operated a buffer stock of tin and bought tin when prices were low (thus creating a demand) and sold when prices were high. The organization was empowered to borrow money to finance these transactions. As a result of a persistent drop in the price of tin, the organization was no longer in a position to carry out trading and defaulted on a number of contracts with tin brokers and commercial bankers. These parties brought an action in England (and elsewhere) seeking, amongst other things, to hold the members of the ITC liable for its debts. These actions were dismissed at all levels of the English courts on the ground that the personality of the organization precluded holding the members liable. The House of Lords relied primarily on English domestic law[58] while the majority in the Court of Appeal reached the same conclusion on the basis of international law.[59]

In 2011, the ILC adopted a set of Articles on the Responsibility of International Organizations (ARIO)[60] mapping out the field. The ARIO is modelled after the ILC's Articles on State Responsibility (see Crawford and Olleson, Ch 15 of this book). In most areas, the ILC has taken the same approach that it took with regard to State responsibility, even using similar wording in many of the corresponding articles. Article 3 of the ILC's Articles states that 'Every internationally wrongful act of an international organization entails the international responsibility of the international organization.' As is the case with State responsibility, an international organization commits an internationally wrongfully act when (i) conduct is attributable to that organization under international law and

---

[57] See ILC Commentary to Article 62 ARIO, ILC Report, 2011, 163 (paras 2–3).
[58] *JH Rayner* v *Department of Trade and Industry* [1988] 3 All ER 257; [1989] 3 WLR 969 (HL).
[59] [1988] 3 All ER 257 (CA), particularly Ralph Gibson LJ at 353. Likewise in the *Arab Organization for Industrialisation and others* v *Westland Helicopters Ltd and others* 80 ILR 622 Court of Justice, Geneva (1987); Swiss Federal Supreme Court (1988), the Swiss courts held the member States of the organization were not bound by the obligations undertaken by the organization towards a private entity.
[60] ILC Reports, 2011, Chapter V.

(ii) that conduct constitutes a breach of an international obligation of that international organization (Article 4, ARIO). The ILC has adopted similar rules (when compared with State responsibility) with regard to attribution, breaches of international obligations, circumstances precluding wrongfulness, the content of international responsibility and the implementation of the international responsibility of international organization.

The work of the ILC on the ARIO was the subject of a number of criticisms.[61] It was argued that since the mandates and functions of international organizations are very different, it is unreasonable to apply a single set of rules to all of them. Secondly, it is argued that the ARIO rely too greatly on the law of State responsibility and do not recognize sufficiently the differences between a State and international organization. Thirdly, it has been noted that in many areas, there is very little practice with regard to the responsibility of international organizations and it is therefore not clear where rules contained in the ARIO are derived from apart from the analogy with State responsibility. Some of these criticisms go too far, and were responded to by the ILC in its commentary to the ARIO (ILC Report 2011, pp 69–71).[62] Although international organizations are very different, the same is true for States (and individuals as well as corporations). It is not at all clear why the differences between international organizations should mean that there are different rules of responsibility for that category. Any justifiable differences can be preserved by making room for *lex specialis* regimes in particular cases (see ARIO, Article 64). In addition, though the ARIO follows the scheme for State responsibility, there are notable differences between States and international organizations that have warranted a different approach in some parts of the regime of responsibility of international organizations or which have required special attention.

One area which has required special attention is the division of responsibility between international organizations and their member States. Often, international organizations act through their members and this raises the question whether the acts of the members (or the organs of the members) when acting within the context of the organization will create responsibility for the State or for the organization. The general rule with regard to attribution of acts to an international organization is that the conduct of organs or agents of the organization are to be regarded as that of the organization when the organ or agent acts in the performance of their functions (Article 6, ARIO). However, there are circumstances when States lend their organs to an international organization, with the result that those organs become organs of the international organization, but they also remain organs of the lending State because they still act, in part, on behalf of the State. The question that arises in such a case is whether the act of the organ is to be attributed to the international organization or to the lending State. This question is of importance in the context of peacekeeping because, although UN peacekeeping forces are subsidiary organs of the UN, the troops are contributed by States and these States retain jurisdiction and some degree of control over their troops. Article 7 of the ARIO provides that:

> The conduct of an organ of a State or an organ of or agent of an international organization that is placed at the disposal of another international organization shall be considered under international law an act of the latter organization if the organization exercises effective control over that conduct.

---

[61] See, eg Blokker, 2011; Boon, 2011. See also *Legal Responsibility of International Organizations in International Law*, Meeting Summary, Chatham House, 11 February 2011, available at http://www.chathamhouse.org/publications/papers/view/109605.

[62] See Wood, 2013.

Therefore, whether the UN is legally responsible for the acts of peacekeeping or peace-enforcement forces will depend on the effectiveness of factual control exercised by the UN over the troops in question and over the conduct. The key test is not whether the organization has ultimate authority or control over the forces, as was held by the ECtHR in *Behrami v France* and *Saramati v France, Germany and Norway*,[63] but rather whether the organization has actual operational control of the activity in question. Since UN peace-keepers often continue to act within their national chain of command as well, the troop contributing State will be responsible in cases where it is that State that has directed the activities of the forces in question. To assert otherwise, as the European Court of Human Rights did, is to suggest that States 'can retain actual control over their forces [assigned to UN action] and at the same time have absolutely no liability for anything that these forces do, since their actions are supposedly attributable solely to the UN' (Milanović and Papić, 2009). This is an untenable position. Happily, in the later *Al-Jedda* case, the ECtHR recognized that the test of attribution of set out by the ILC is effective control (though it did not actually overrule its earlier decision in *Behrami*).[64] Also, there is no reason to assume that there may not be dual or multiple attribution. Attribution of conduct to an international organization on the basis of effective control does not mean that the act of the organ is not also attributable to the State.[65]

Member States may not escape responsibility for breaches of their own (ie the members') obligations simply by causing the organization to perform an act, which if performed by the member State would be a breach of the member's obligation (Article 60, ARIO). Thus, the ECtHR has held that States parties to the ECHR cannot free themselves from obligations under that Convention by transferring functions to an international organization. In such cases, 'the State is considered to retain Convention liability in respect of treaty commitments subsequent to the entry into force of the Convention'.[66] This principle is important as it prevents States circumventing their international obligations through the creation of an international organization which is then conferred with competence to act in the area in question.

Where an international organization is responsible for an internationally wrongful act it has an obligation to make reparation for the injury caused by the wrong (Article 30, ARIO). However, the mechanisms by which such responsibility can be established and through which injured parties can obtain redress against international organizations remain undeveloped. As will be seen in the following section, such organizations are usually immune from the jurisdiction of domestic courts. Furthermore, international organizations cannot be parties to contentious cases before the International Court of Justice and there are few standing tribunals with competence to decide cases involving international organizations. Therefore the quest for enhancing the accountability of these organizations must not only involve an elucidation of the relevant principles of responsibility but also the development of mechanisms through which that responsibility can be determined.

---

[63] *Behrami v France* and *Saramati v France, Germany and Norway* (Dec) [GC], nos 71412/01 and 78166/01, 2 May 2007; 45 *EHRR* 85.

[64] *Al-Jedda* v *the United Kingdom* [GC], no 27021/08, ECHR 2011; 53 *EHRR* 23, para 84.

[65] Ibid, para 80; See Dannenbaum, 2010, asserting that effective control is held by entity/entities with power to prevent violations. See now also the decision of the Netherlands Supreme Court in *Netherlands v Nuhanović*, 6 September 2013.

[66] *Bosphorus Hava Yollari Turizm ve Ticaret Anonim Sirketi* v *Ireland* [GC], no 45036/98 ECHR, 2005-VI, pp 157–8.

VI. PRIVILEGES AND IMMUNITIES

International organizations require certain privileges and immunities for the effective performance of their tasks. These immunities are granted to preserve the independence of the organization from its member States and to secure the international character of the organization. They ensure that no member State is able to interfere unilaterally through its legislative, executive, or judicial branches with the workings of an international organization set up to act in the common interests of members. This section considers the sources and content of the privileges and immunities of international organizations.

A. SOURCES OF PRIVILEGES AND IMMUNITIES

The privileges and immunities of international organizations may be derived from a number of sources.

1. Treaties

There are three types of treaties which deal with the privileges and immunities of international organizations. First, the constituent instrument of the organization often includes provisions requiring member States to grant the organization immunities. Such provisions are usually very basic and, like Article 105 of the UN Charter, only contain a general statement that the organization, its officials and representatives of members are to enjoy such privileges and immunities as are necessary for the exercise of their functions.[67]

Second, there are general multilateral agreements dealing with the immunities of particular international organizations or groups of organizations. These types of agreements are regarded as a necessary supplement to the more basic provisions in the constituent instruments. The leading examples include the 1946 General Convention on the Privileges and Immunities of the UN and the 1947 Convention on the Privileges and Immunities of the Specialized Agencies.[68]

The third type of treaties are bilateral agreements between international organizations and individual States which set out specific privileges and immunities. They are most commonly concluded between the organization and a State in which the former (or an organ of the organization) is situated (eg headquarters agreements) or with States in which the organization is to perform a particular mission, such as a peacekeeping or fact-finding activity (eg Status of Forces Agreements). Such States need not be members of the organization.[69]

2. Customary international law

In the absence of a treaty obligation, customary international law requires States to grant privileges and immunities to international organizations.[70] This has been recognized both by the domestic courts of member States of an organization and those of non-member

---

[67] See also ILO Constitution, Article 40; WHO Constitution, Article 12; Council of Europe Statute, Article 4(a); OAS Charter, Articles 133 and 134. However, the constitutional texts of international financial institutions contain fairly elaborate provisions. See, eg IBRD Articles of Agreement, Article VII; IMF Articles of Agreement, Article IX; EBRD Constitution, Articles 46–55.

[68] Similar treaties exist within the OAS, Council of Europe, European Communities, League of Arab States, and the OECD.

[69] For a long time Switzerland was not a member of the UN but had an agreement with the UN regarding the UN's office in Geneva.

[70] See Reinisch, 2000, pp 145ff; Higgins, 1994, pp 90–94; *Third Restatement*, 1987, para 467(1); Amerasinghe, 2005, pp 344–8; Möldner, 1995, p 1328. But see Sands and Klein, 2009, para 15–039 who only accepts such a

States which have consented to the organization functioning in their territory.[71] The obligation is one of good faith and only requires the 'provision of what is necessary for an organization to perform its functions' (Higgins, 1994, p 91).

3. National law

Since privileges and immunities are to be enjoyed within the national legal order (see generally Reinisch, 2013, many States have enacted domestic legislation governing their being granted. The relevant legislation in the UK is the International Organizations Act 1968 which provides that the Executive may by subsidiary legislation (Order in Council) grant the stated privileges and immunities to international organizations of which the UK is a member.

B. SCOPE OF PRIVILEGES AND IMMUNITIES

The particular privileges and immunities which a State is to grant an international organization flow from the source of the obligation which will most commonly be a treaty. Despite the impressive number of treaties providing for the privileges and immunities, there are remarkable similarities in their contents. This has permitted rules of customary international law to develop. However, these similarities relate to general matters and details vary from treaty to treaty.

Who is entitled to the immunity? Most treaties accord privileges and immunities to three categories of person: first, to the organization itself; secondly, to officials of the organization (including experts on mission for the organization); thirdly, to representatives of member States (or exceptionally of other bodies) to the organization. This chapter considers only the privileges and immunities of the organization itself since the personal immunities of international officials and State representatives are considered by Wickremasinghe in Chapter 13 of this book. The five main privileges and immunities conferred on international organizations are considered in the following sections.

1. Immunity from jurisdiction

International organizations are usually granted absolute immunity from the judicial jurisdiction of States.[72] This immunity from jurisdiction prevents law suits against organizations before domestic courts unless they have waived their immunity by consenting to the proceedings. As has been the case with State immunity, there has been pressure to restrict the absolute nature of the immunity granted to international organizations. It has been argued that according such immunity may cause injustice where individuals have no

---

customary obligation in some cases. For an extensive study which argues that customary international law does not provide immunity to international organizations (but which also cites several cases to the contrary), see Wood, 2014.

[71] See *X et al v European School Munich II* (Bavarian Administrative Court, Germany, 1995), referred to by Reinisch, 2000, pp 150–51; *Iran-United States Claims Tribunal v AS*, 96 ILR 321, 329 (Netherlands Supreme Court, 1985); *ESOC Official Immunity Case* 73 ILR 683 (Federal Labour Court, FR Germany, 1973); *Branno v Ministry of War*, 22 ILR 756 (Court of Cassation, Italy, 1954); *International Institute of Agriculture v Profili*, 5 ILR 413 (Court of Appeal, Italy, 1930). Courts of States other than the host State are not obliged to grant immunities to international organizations in the absence of a treaty. See *Bank Bumiputra Malaysia BHD v International Tin Council*, 80 ILR 24 (High Court, Malaysia, 1987); *International Tin Council v Amalgamet*, 80 ILR 31 (New York Supreme Court, 1988); *ECOWAS v BCCI*, 113 ILR 473 (Court of Appeal of Paris, France, 1993). See also *Tissa Amaratunga v Northwest Atlantic Fisheries Organisation*, 30 September 2010, 2010 Can LII 346 (Nova Scotia Supreme Court, Canada).

[72] For example, Article II, Section 2 of the 1946 Convention on the Privileges and Immunities of the UN.

other means of obtaining redress or may even lead to a violation of the human rights of individuals.[73] For these reasons, a number of domestic courts have applied to international organizations the concept of restrictive immunity, granting them jurisdictional immunity only in relation to acts *jure imperii* (in the exercise of sovereign authority) rather than acts *jure gestionis* (done privately).[74] Alternatively, it has been argued that the grant of immunity should be conditional on the presence of alternative methods of resolving disputes involving international organizations (Gaillard and Pingel-Lenuzza, 2002). The invocation of this obligation is intended to pressure the organizations and its member States to ensure that the organization provides adequate dispute-settlement obligations. The first approach, which relies on an analogy with State immunity, is based on the misapprehension that since international organizations are composed of States they are to be placed in the same position as foreign States. This approach is incorrect for at least two reasons. First, it is contrary to the express provisions of the relevant treaties. Secondly, international organizations are not sovereign entities and do not exercise sovereign authority. Their immunity is not granted to protect sovereign or public acts but is functional and granted in respect of acts done in the exercise of their functions. Such functions and acts may well be commercial and so classified as private if carried out by a State. Thus immunity may arise for an international organization in cases where a foreign State will be denied immunity. For example, employment disputes fall within the immunity of an international organization even if the relations with the particular employee might be classified as *jure gestionis*. The second approach, which conditions immunity on the existence of alternative dispute resolution mechanisms, is not in accordance with the treaties providing immunity. Although such treaties may provide an obligation for the organization to make provision for alternative modes of dispute settlement (eg Article 29, UN Convention discussed later) that obligation is not expressed as limiting the immunity of the organization before domestic courts. The two obligations (that of the organization to find alternative methods of dispute settlement and that of the State to accord immunity) are independent of each other.[75] However, in some cases, the ECtHR has held that where member States create an international organization and accord such organization immunity from domestic legal process without creating alternative methods of dispute settlement, this may amount to a violation, on the part of the members, of their obligation to provide access to a court.[76] In a more recent case, the ECtHR has declared that measures taken by a High Contracting Party which reflect generally recognized rules of international law on the immunity of international organizations cannot, in principle, be regarded as imposing a disproportionate restriction on the right of access to a court, since some restrictions on access to the courts are inherent in the right.[77] It may be that since the facts of that case arose out of the exercise by the UN Security Council of its powers to maintain international peace and security, the Court took the view that this aim was a sufficient counterweight to the denial of access to the Court. Alternatively, it may be thought that in cases where it is sought to hold international organizations responsible, in a domestic court, for acts occurring

---

[73] See the arguments advanced by the applicants in *Waite and Kennedy* v *Germany* [GC], no 26083/94, ECHR 1999-I and in *Association of Citizens 'Mothers of Srebrenica'* v *Netherlands & United Nations*, Rechtbank 's-Graveenhage [the Hague, District Court], 10 July 2008, 295247/HA ZA 07-2973.

[74] See Reinisch, 2000, pp 185–205 who notes that this trend is most common in Italy.

[75] *Association of Citizens 'Mothers of Srebrenica'* v *Netherlands & United Nations*, Rechtbank 's-Graveenhage, July 10, 2008, 295247/HA ZA 07-2973, para 5.15.

[76] *Waite and Kennedy* v *Germany* [GC], no 26083/94, ECHR 1999-I.

[77] *Stichting Mothers of Srebrenica and Others* v *The Netherlands*, ECtHR, App no 65542/12 (June 2013)

outside the territory of that State, and those acts are covered by immunity, the domestic forum does not have jurisdiction such as to be able to provide access to court.

It should be noted that some international organizations are not granted absolute immunity by the relevant treaties. In particular, constituent instruments of a number of international financial institutions such as the World Bank (IBRD) do not extend immunity to certain kinds of actions. This is because these organizations operate in the commercial world where it is felt necessary to permit creditors to institute actions in some instances.

2. Immunity from execution

International organizations also enjoy immunity from measures of execution. This prevents the seizure or even the pre-judgment attachment of its property or other assets. It is important to note that a waiver of jurisdictional immunity does not include a waiver of the enforcement jurisdiction which must be given expressly and separately. In some cases, particularly as regards international financial institutions, the immunity from execution granted by the relevant treaty only applies before the delivery of final judgment.

3. Inviolability of premises, property, and archives

Practically all relevant treaties provide that the premises of an international organization are to be inviolable and that its property and assets are to be immune from search, requisition, confiscation or other forms of interference by State authorities.[78] Thus, national authorities may not enter such premises without the consent of the international organization, even when a crime has been committed on the premises or a criminal is sheltering there. The treaties also impose an obligation on the national authorities to exercise due diligence in protecting those premises from acts of third parties.

The archives (documents) of an international organization are usually inviolable wherever located.[79] This ensures the confidentiality of communications within and with the international organization, enabling it to function effectively and independently. Consequently, international organizations are not obliged to produce their official documents, or other documents held by them, in proceedings before national courts. In one of the Tin Council cases—*Shearson Lehman Bros v Maclaine Watson & Co*[80]—the House of Lords held that documents issued by an international organization but which had been communicated to third parties by officials of the organization did not benefit from these principles. This decision has been criticized because the documents were sent by the organization to the States in their capacity as members—not as third parties—and in relation to the work of the organization. (Higgins, 1994, pp 93–4). Plainly, the confidentiality of such documents requires protection as otherwise the inviolability of the archives would relate only to documents prepared by the organization's secretariat and kept within it. It would fail to cover all the documents needed by an organization for work, since international organizations are made up of various organs.

4. Currency and fiscal privileges

Since many international organizations exercise their functions in a number of countries they will need to transfer funds. Several treaties provide that such transactions are to be free from financial restrictions. For example, the UN Convention provides that the organizations (a) 'may hold funds, gold or currency of any kind and operate accounts in any

---

[78] UN Convention 1946, Article II, Section 3; Specialized Agencies Convention 1947, Article III, Section 5.
[79] UN Convention 1946, Article II, Section 4; Specialized Agencies Convention 1947, Article III, Section 6.
[80] *Shearson Lehman Bros v Maclaine Watson & Co*, 77 ILR 107 (1987).

currency' and (b) may freely transfer their 'funds, gold or currency from one country to another or within any country and to convert any currency held by them into any other currency'.[81] International organizations are usually exempt from direct taxation of their assets, income and property as well as from custom duties and other import and export restrictions in respect of articles for official use.[82] However, this does not extend to charges for public utility services or excise duties or sales taxes.

5. FREEDOM OF COMMUNICATION

It is commonly provided that official communications by international organizations shall be accorded treatment at least as favourable as that accorded to foreign govern-ments.[83] In addition it is sometimes provided that no censorship shall be applied to official communications of the organization and that the organization shall have the power to use codes as well as couriers and bags having the same status as diplomatic couriers and bags.[84]

International organizations should not use their privileges and immunities to circum-vent either the domestic laws of States or their responsibility towards third parties. In order to prevent immunity being used to avoid legal responsibility, Article 29 of the UN Convention provides that 'The United Nations shall make provisions for appropriate modes of settlement of (a) disputes arising out of contracts or other disputes of a private law character to which the United Nations is a party...'. In practice international organiza-tions will often include arbitration clauses in contracts that they enter into. Furthermore, most organizations have a system for the settlement of employment disputes which includes recourse to an international administrative tribunal.

Finally, it must be remembered that international organizations remain responsible in international law for breaches of their obligations even if they are immune from process before domestic courts. As the ICJ has stated 'the question of immunity from legal process is distinct from the issue of compensation for any damages incurred as a result of acts performed by the UN or by its agents acting in their official capacity.'[85]

VII. THE UN SYSTEM

The remainder of this chapter will look at the structure and powers of what is perhaps the leading family of international organizations—the UN system. The UN was established after the Second World War with very broad aims, including: (i) the maintenance of inter-national peace and security; (ii) the development of friendly relations among nations; (iii) international cooperation in solving international problems of an economic, social, cul-tural or humanitarian character; and (iv) the promotion of human rights (Article 1, UN Charter). The work of the UN and its specialized agencies touches on practically every area of human life and endeavour.

---

[81] UN Convention, Article II, Section 5; Specialized Agencies Convention, Article III, Section 7.
[82] UN Convention, Article II, Section 7; Specialized Agencies Convention, Article III, Section 9.
[83] UN Convention, Article III, Section 9; Specialized Agencies Convention, Article IV, Section 11; IBRD Articles of Agreement, Article VII(7).
[84] UN Convention, Article III, Sections 9 and 10; Specialized Agencies Convention, Article IV, Section 12.
[85] *Difference Relating to Immunity from Legal Process, Advisory Opinion, ICJ Reports 1999*, p 62, para 66.

A. THE STRUCTURE OF THE UN

Like all international organizations, the UN is composed of a number of organs. In addition, the UN system comprises a family of international organizations which share certain common institutions and practices.

1. The UN organs

Article 7 of the UN Charter identifies two types of organs within the UN: principal organs and subsidiary organs. Article 7(1) lists the six principal organs of the UN: (i) the General Assembly; (ii) the Security Council; (iii) the Economic and Social Council (ECOSOC); (iv) the Trusteeship Council; (v) the International Court of Justice; and (vi) the Secretariat. The structure and powers of each of these organs shall be discussed later. Article 7(2) provides that 'such subsidiary organs as may be found necessary may be established in accordance with the present Charter'. While the list of principal organs is exhaustive and no such organs may be established or wound up except by amendment of the Charter, subsidiary organs can always be created by the principal organs. Their lifespan is determined by the principal organ that has established them.

The powers, functions and composition of the principal organs are determined by the Charter, while those of subsidiary organs are determined by the principal organ that establishes them. Subsidiary organs established by the General Assembly include the Human Rights Council, the International Law Commission, the UN Environment Programme (UNEP), the Office of the UN High Commissioner for Refugees (UNHCR), UNICEF, and the UN Development Programme (UNDP). Subsidiary organs set up by the Security Council include peacekeeping missions, Sanctions Committees, the International Criminal Tribunals for the Former Yugoslavia and Rwanda, and the UN Compensation Commission (UNCC).

In most cases, a principal organ will confer some of its powers on a subsidiary organ that it creates. However, a principal organ may be entitled to confer on the subsidiary organ powers which it does not itself possess where the power to establish such a subsidiary organ is necessary for the performance of the functions of the principal organ (Sarooshi, 1996, pp 426–31). Thus, both the General Assembly and the Security Council have established subsidiary organs that have judicial powers even though they themselves do not have such powers. The legality of their doing so was confirmed by the ICJ in the *Administrative Tribunal* Advisory Opinion[86] and by the Appeals Chamber of the International Criminal Tribunal for the Former Yugoslavia.[87] Moreover, in the *Administrative Tribunal* case it was held that the General Assembly was bound to give effect to the awards of the Administrative Tribunal thus confirming that a principal organ can establish a subsidiary organ with powers to bind the principal organ.

2. The specialized agencies

The Charter also refers to another type of body known as specialized agencies. Unlike the subsidiary organs, these are international organizations in their own right. They are established by separate treaties and brought into relationship with the UN by agreement (Articles 57 and 63). They operate in particular technical fields and, like the UN, are open

---

[86] *Effects of Awards of Compensation made by the United Nations Administrative Tribunal*, Advisory Opinion, *ICJ Reports 1954*, p 47.

[87] *Prosecutor v Tadić*, Decision on the Defence Motion for Interlocutory Appeal on Jurisdiction (Interlocutory Appeal), Case No IT–94–1–AR72 (2 October 1995); 105 ILR 419 at pp 470–1.

organizations with worldwide membership and responsibilities. There are currently 17 specialized agencies.[88]

Although they are independent international organizations, the UN Charter provides that the UN may coordinate their activities (Articles 57–60), principally through ECOSOC. In practice, coordination and cooperation are achieved through the UN System Chief Executives Board for Coordination (CEB), composed of the executive heads of the organizations within the UN, and its High Level Committees. Development assistance is coordinated by UNDP.

In the *Nuclear Weapons Advisory Opinion (WHO Request)*,[89] the ICJ, relying on what it termed the 'logic of the overall system contemplated by the Charter', appeared to suggest that overlap within the UN system should be avoided. According to the Court, the Charter 'laid the basis of a "system" designed to organize international co-operation in a coherent fashion by bringing the UN, invested with powers of a general scope, into relationship with various autonomous and complementary organizations, invested with sectorial powers'. The Court stated that the WHO 'cannot encroach on the responsibilities of other parts of the UN system'. Thus, since questions of disarmaments and arms regulations are within the competence of the UN itself they were held to be outside the competence of the specialized agencies.

However, the constitutions of the specialized agencies and their practice show that legitimate overlap can and does exist in the work of the specialized agencies. For example, both the WHO and the ILO are competent to deal with health of workers. Likewise IMO, UNEP and the International Atomic Energy Agency cooperate regarding transportation of nuclear fuel by sea (Akande, 1998).

3. Treaty bodies

A variety of treaties concluded under the auspices of the UN establish bodies which maintain very close relations with the UN and are considered as UN bodies. Examples include the various committees set up by human rights treaties to monitor compliance with the obligations they contain, such as the Human Rights Committee and the Committee Against Torture. These bodies only act in relation to those States which are parties to these treaties. They meet in the UN, are serviced by the UN Secretariat and submit reports to the General Assembly.

B. PRINCIPAL ORGANS OF THE UN

1. The General Assembly

The General Assembly is the plenary organ of the UN and is the only principal organ composed of all member States (Article 9). It is a deliberative not a legislative body and unlike the Security Council meets annually in regular session the main part of which

---

[88] These are: (1) The International Labour Organization (ILO); (2) The Food and Agriculture Organization (FAO); (3) The UN Educational, Scientific and Cultural Organization (UNESCO); (4) The World Health Organization (WHO); (5) The International Bank for Reconstruction and Development (IBRD or World Bank)—within the World Bank group are three agencies which are also specialized agencies but are run together with World Bank; (6) The International Development Association (IDA); (7) The International Finance Corporation (IFC); (8) The Multilateral Investment Guarantee Agency (MIGA); (9) The International Monetary Fund (IMF)—the IMF is separate from the World Bank but closely related as another 'Bretton Woods' Institution; (10) The International Civil Aviation Organisation (ICAO); (11) The Universal Postal Union (UPU); (12) The International Telecommunications Union (ITU); (13) The World Meteorological Organization (WMO); (14) The International Maritime Organisation (IMO); (15) The World Intellectual Property Organisation (WIPO); (16) The International Fund for Agricultural Development (IFAD); (17) The UN Industrial Development Organization (UNIDO).

[89] *Legality of the Use of Nuclear Weapons in Armed Conflict, Advisory Opinion, ICJ.*

usually takes place between September and December (Article 20). It may also meet in special session outside its regular sessions. At its regular sessions, most agenda items are allocated to one of the six main committees (eg Disarmament and International Security; Economic and Social; Financial; and Legal), where substantive discussion and decision-taking occurs.

There are also two procedural and two standing committees. The procedural committees, which unlike the main committee are not composed of all UN members, are the General Committee (responsible for organizing the work of the session and for deciding on the agenda) and the Credentials Committee (which examines the credentials of representatives of member States). The standing committees—the Advisory Committee on Administrative and Budgetary Questions and the Committee on Contributions—assist the Fifth Committee with financial matters and are composed of experts rather than representatives of member States.

The Assembly has competence to discuss and make recommendations upon the very broad range of matters falling within the scope of Charter (Article 10). However, it can only make binding decisions on internal administrative matters. Articles 11–17 of the Charter specifically provide that General Assembly has competence with regard to peace and security, promoting human rights, and international cooperation in political, economic, social, cultural, educational, and health fields. However, the Assembly may not make recommendations concerning disputes or situations in respect of which the Security Council is exercising its functions unless requested to do so by the Council (Article 12) and, together with UN as a whole, it may not intervene 'in matters which are essentially within the domestic jurisdiction of any State' (Article 2(7)). Voting in the Assembly is on the basis of one member one vote. Decisions on important questions must be adopted by two thirds of members present and voting. There is a non-exhaustive list of such important questions. Other decisions are to be taken by simple majority (Article 18).

2. The Security Council

The Security Council is composed of 15 member States of the UN. There are five permanent members of the Council (China, France, Russia, the UK, and the USA) and ten which are elected by the Assembly for two-year terms (Article 23). Its competence is mainly (though not exclusively) limited to issues concerning the maintenance of international peace and security, for which it bears primary responsibility within the UN system (Article 24). Although each member has one vote, decisions on non-procedural matters must be adopted by the affirmative vote of nine members and include the concurring vote of the permanent members who therefore possess a veto with respect to substantive decisions. Abstentions, however, are not deemed to be vetoes.[90] The powers of the Security Council with regard to the maintenance of peace and security and in regard to dispute settlement are explored by Merrills and Gray in Chs 19 and 21 of this book. It suffices here to note that the Council has the power to adopt decisions which are binding on members of the UN (Article 25).

3. The ECOSOC

ECOSOC is the primary organ responsible for economic and social matters within the UN. It is composed of fifty-four members who serve for three years; each member has one vote. ECOSOC can make or initiate studies in the area of its competence and make recommendations to the General Assembly, the member States or the specialized agencies

---

[90] *Legal Consequences for States of the Continued Presence of South Africa in Namibia (South West Africa) notwithstanding Security Council Resolution 276 (1970), Advisory Opinion, ICJ Reports 1971*, p 16, paras 20–22.

on such matters (Article 62). ECOSOC has special responsibility for the promotion of human rights. It has been active in preparing treaties in the human rights areas (eg the International Covenant on Civil and Political Rights). It also has responsibilities regarding the specialized agencies, concerning their relations with the UN and the coordination of their activities.

ECOSOC has created a number of subsidiary organs: five regional commissions—for Africa, Asia Pacific, Europe, Latin America and the Caribbean, and Western Asia—and nine functional Commissions dealing with particular topics, including the Commission on Sustainable Development and the Commission on the Status of Women. ECOSOC also has a few standing committees (eg the Commission on Human Settlements and the Commission on Transnational Corporations) and a number of standing bodies of experts.

4. The International Court of Justice

This is the principal judicial organ of the UN and is considered by Thirlway, Ch 20 of this book.

5. The Secretariat

The secretariat consists of the staff of the UN and is headed by the Secretary General. It services the work of the UN organs, except the ICJ, and carries out other functions that they assign to it. In addition, the Secretary General may bring to the attention of the Security Council any matter which he considers may threaten international peace and security (Article 99). Members of the secretariat are to be independent of governments and may not seek or receive instructions from them (Article 100).

6. Trusteeship Council

The Trusteeship Council was set up to administer the trusteeship system established by Chapter XII of the Charter. This concerned the administration of territories that had been League of Nations mandates (ie territories taken from Germany and Turkey following the First World War) and territories 'detached from enemy States as a result of the Second World War' (Article 77) with the objective of promoting the advancement of the inhabitants and their progressive development towards self-government and independence. The work of the Council was suspended in 1994 when the last of the Trust territories, Palau, achieved independence.

VIII. CONCLUSION

Despite the diversity in the nature and tasks of international organizations, it has proved possible to identify some common legal principles which govern these organizations. However, it cannot be forgotten that the structure, functions and powers of each organization are primarily to be derived from the treaty setting up the organization and the practice which has built up regarding that organization.

That States have created new international organizations to deal with emerging problems in international affairs is principally the result of three factors. First, there is the realization that a number of problems faced by States and their populations can only be resolved or can best be resolved through international cooperation. Secondly, there is the realization that such cooperation often needs to be multilateral. Thirdly, it is clear that such cooperation needs to be permanent. The heightened awareness by States of these points and the increasing emergence of 'global problems', means that there is likely to be an increase not only in the number of international organizations but also in the powers and functions accorded to those organizations. However, together with this increasing delegation of public powers by States to international organizations it is likely that greater attention will be paid to developing means to hold these organizations accountable for the exercise of such powers.[91] This is a process that has already generated much interest and will involve careful analysis of the limits of the powers of international organizations.

REFERENCES

AKANDE, D (1997), 'The International Court of Justice and the Security Council: Is there Room for Judicial Control of Decisions of the Political Organs of the United Nations?', 46 *ICLQ* 309.

——— (1998), 'The Competence of International Organizations and the Advisory Jurisdiction of the International Court of Justice', 9 *EJIL* 437.

AMERASINGHE, CF (2005), *Principles of the Institutional Law of International Organizations*, 2nd edn (Cambridge: Cambridge University Press).

AUST, A (2013), *Modern Treaty Law and Practice*, 3rd edn (Cambridge: Cambridge University Press).

BLOKKER, N (2011), 'Preparing Articles on Responsibility of International Organizations: Does the International Law Commission Take International Organizations Seriously? A Mid-Term Review', in Klabbers, J and Wallendahl, A (eds), *Research Handbook on the Law of International Organizations* (Cheltenham: Edward Elgar).

BOON, KE (2011), 'New Directions in Responsibility: Assessing the International Law Commission's Draft Articles on the Responsibility of International Organizations', 37 *Yale JIL Online* 8.

CHURCHILL, RR and ULFSTEIN, G (2000), 'Autonomous Institutional Arrangements in Multilateral Environmental Agreements: A Little-Noticed Phenomenon in International Law', 94 *AJIL* 623.

DANNENBAUM, T (2010), 'Translating the Standard of Effective Control into a System of Effective Accountability: How Liability Should be Apportioned for Violation of Human Rights by Member State Troop Contingents Serving as United Nations Peacekeepers', 51 *Harvard JIL* 113.

GAILLARD, E and PINGEL-LENUZZA, I (2002), 'International Organizations and Immunity from Jurisdiction: To Restrict or to Bypass', 51 *ICLQ* 1.

GAZZINI, T (2011), 'Personality of International Organizations', in Klabbers, J and Wallendahl, A (eds), *Research Handbook on the Law of International Organizations*, (Cheltenham: Edward Elgar).

HIGGINS, R (1994), *Problems and Process: International Law and How We Use It* (Oxford: Oxford University Press).

ILA Committee Report (2004), Final Report of the International Law Association Committee on Accountability of International Organization, *Report of the 71st Conference of the ILA held at Berlin*, p 164 (Previous reports of the Committee also available via http://www.ila-hq.org/en/committees/index.cfm/cid/9).

ILA Study Group Report (2012), Report of the International Law Association Study Group on the Responsibility of International Organization, (Sofia Conference) (available via http://www.ila-hq.org/en/committees/study_groups.cfm/cid/1019).

[91] See generally, Reinisch, 2001; ILA Committee Reports, 1996–2000; and ILC Reports 2009.

ILC Report (2011), *Report of the International Law Commission on the Work of its 63rd Session* (UN Doc A/66/10).

KADELBACH, S (2012), 'The Interpretation of the Charter', in Simma, B (ed), *The Charter of the United Nations: A Commentary* (Oxford: Oxford University Press).

KLABBERS, J (2009), *An Introduction to International Institutional Law*, 2nd edn (Cambridge: Cambridge University Press).

LAUTERPACHT, H (1976), 'The Development of the Law of International Organizations by the Decisions of International Tribunals', 52 *Recueil des Cours* 377.

MILANOVIĆ, M and PAPIĆ, T (2009), 'As Bad As It Gets: The European Court Of Human Rights' *Behrami and Saramati* Decision and General International Law', 58 *ICLQ* 267.

MÖLDNER, M (2012), 'International Organizations or Institutions, Privileges and Immunities', in Wolfrum, R (ed), *Max Planck Encyclopedia of Public International Law* (Oxford: Oxford University Press).

OSIEKE, E (1983), 'The Legal Validity of Ultra Vires Decisions of International Organizations', 77 *AJIL* 239.

RAMA MONTALDO, M (1970), 'International Legal Personality and Implied Powers of International Organizations', 44 *BYIL* 111.

REINISCH, A (2000), *International Organizations in Domestic Courts* (Cambridge: Cambridge University Press).

——— (2001), 'Securing the Accountability of International Organizations', 7 *Global Governance* 131.

——— (ed) (2010), *Challenging Acts of International Organizations Before National Courts* (Oxford: Oxford University Press).

——— (ed) (2013), *The Privileges and Immunities of International Organizations in Domestic Courts* (Oxford: Oxford University Press).

SANDS, P (2003), *Principles of International Environmental Law*, 2nd edn (Cambridge, Cambridge University Press).

——— and KLEIN, P (eds) (2009), *Bowett's Law of International Institutions (2009)*, 6th edn (London: Sweet & Maxwell).

SAROOSHI, D (1996), 'The Legal Framework Governing United Nations Subsidiary Organs', 67 *BYIL* 413.

SCHERMERS, HG and BLOKKER, N (2011), *International Institutional Law*, 5th rev edn (The Hague: Martinus Nijhoff).

SEYERSTED, F (1964), 'International Personality of Intergovernmental Organizations: Do their Capacities Really Depend upon their Constitutions?', 4 *IJIL* 1.

Third Restatement (1987), *Third Restatement of the Law: The Law of Foreign Relations of the United States*, vol 1 (St Pauls, Minn.: American Law Institute Publishers).

TZANAKOPOULOS, A (2010), 'Domestic Court Reactions to UN Security Council Sanctions' in Reinisch, A (ed), *Challenging Acts of International Organizations Before National Courts* (Oxford: Oxford University Press), p 54.

——— (2011), *Disobeying the Security Council: Countermeasures Against Wrongful Sanctions* (Oxford: Oxford University Press).

Wood, M (2013), ' "Weighing" the Articles on Responsibility of International Organisations', in Ragazzi, M (ed), *The responsibility of International Organisations. Essays in Memory of Sir Ian Brownlie* (The Hague: Martinus Nijhoff).

——— (2014), 'Do International Organizations Enjoy Immunity under Customary International Law', 10 *International Organizations Law Review*.

FURTHER READING

ALVAREZ, JE (2005), *International Organizations as Law-makers* (Oxford: Oxford University Press): this considers the law-making and dispute-settlement functions of international organizations.

AMERASINGHE, CF (2005), *Principles of the Institutional Law of International Organizations*, 2nd edn (Cambridge: Cambridge University Press): provides an excellent overview of the law relating to international organizations.

BEKKER, PHF (1994), *The Legal Position of Intergovernmental Organizations: A Functional Necessity Analysis of Their Legal Status and Immunities* (Dordrecht: Martinus Nijhoff): a good introduction to the legal status, privileges, and immunities of international organizations.

KLABBERS, J and WALLENDAHL, A (eds), (2011) *Research Handbook on the Law of International Organizations* (Cheltenham: Edward Elgar): a detailed examination of various issues relating to the law of international organizations.

RAGAZZI, M (ed)(2013), *The Responsibility of International Organizations. Essays in Memory of Sir Ian Brownlie* (The Hague: Martinus Nijhoff).

REINISCH, A (2000), *International Organizations in Domestic Courts* (Cambridge: Cambridge University Press): an excellent consideration of the legal issues which arise when international organizations sue and are sued in domestic courts.

SANDS, P and KLEIN, P (eds) (2009), *Bowett's Law of International Institutions* (2009), 6th edn (London: Sweet & Maxwell): this provides an excellent overview of the structure of the leading international organizations as well as of the common legal issues relating to these organizations.

SCHACHTER, O and JOYNER, J (eds) (1995), *United Nations Legal Order*, 2 vols (Cambridge: Cambridge University Press): a detailed examination of the structure of the UN and its specialized agencies, considering the competence of these organizations in a variety of areas.

SCHERMERS, HG and BLOKKER, N (2011), *International Institutional Law*, 5th rev edn (The Hague: Martinus Nijhoff): a detailed examination of the law relating to international organizations.

SIMMA, B (ed) (2012), *The Charter of the United Nations: A Commentary*, 3rd edn (Oxford: Oxford University Press): an article by article analysis of the Charter of the UN.

SLOAN, B (1991), *United Nations General Assembly Resolutions in Our Changing World* (Ardsley, NY: Transnational Publishers): a very good consideration of the status of UN General Assembly resolutions.

WELLENS, K (2002), *Remedies Against International Organizations* (Cambridge: Cambridge University Press): an overview of the law relating to responsibility of international organizations.

WHITE, N (2005), *The Law of International Organizations*, 2nd edn (Manchester: Manchester University Press): this provides an excellent overview of the law relating to international organizations.

10

THE INDIVIDUAL AND THE INTERNATIONAL LEGAL SYSTEM

Robert McCorquodale

SUMMARY

This chapter explores the role of the individual in the international legal system today. It considers the extent to which the individual, including groups of individuals, is an independent participant in this system. This participation is explored by reference to the direct rights and responsibilities of individuals under the international legal system, their capacity to bring international claims and their ability to participate in the creation, development, and enforcement of international law. Particular examples from a wide range of areas of international law, including international human rights law, international criminal law, and international economic law, will be used to show the conceptual and practical participation of individuals in the international legal system. The conclusion reached is that individuals are participants in that system, and are not solely objects that are subject to States' consent, though their degree of participation varies depending on the changing nature of the international legal system.

I. INTRODUCTION

The issue of the role of the individual in international law has been a part of the debate over the nature of the international legal system for centuries. In 1532 Francisco de Vitoria considered that the indigenous peoples of South America had some claim to protection under international law (Anaya, 2004, Paust, 2011) and, in the twenty-first century, the entry into force of the International Criminal Court confirmed the customary international law position of the direct responsibility of individuals under international law for certain actions (see Cryer, Ch 25 of this book), and the actions of individuals was significant in leading to constitutional changes and international actions in north Africa.

However, for much of this time the dominant view has been that individuals had no effective independent role in the international legal system. Their role was wholly determined by States and was entirely subject to States' consent (Remec, 1960; Tornaritis, 1972). The development of international law, particularly of international human rights law, in the second half of the twentieth century has been the main reason why the issue of the role of individuals in the international legal system has again come to prominence.

A. THE INDIVIDUAL

'The individual' is defined and conceived in a number of different ways in the international legal system. It clearly includes each human being. When human beings (usually known in law as 'natural persons') have any involvement in the international legal system, it is often as part of a group of natural persons acting together. For example, groups of indigenous people and groups who have the right of self-determination are natural persons who act together in regard to some international legal issues. As such, they should be considered to be 'individuals' within the international legal system. Natural persons do form groups due to common interests, such as non-governmental organizations (eg Amnesty International, Oxfam), although these groups are legally separate entities from natural persons. Corporations are also separate entities that are formed to further the common interests of natural persons and all legal systems recognize the existence and activities of corporations and acknowledge them as non-natural legal persons (Dine, 2000; Muchlinski, 2007). Therefore, the notion of 'individuals' could include all these types of legal person, natural and non-natural.

This chapter takes the concept of 'the individual' within the international legal system to include all those natural and non-natural persons acting separately and as groups.[1] The justification for taking such a view is that the international legal system is primarily a State-based system. The roles of any natural and non-natural persons (what may be termed 'non-State actors') in this system is compared with that of the State. Consequently, excluded from this concept of 'the individual' are States and also those entities who have authority and power that is State-like, such as intergovernmental organizations (eg the UN), armed opposition groups who control territory (see an example in *Elmi* v *Australia*),[2] or sub-State units in a federal State. In order to clarify as comprehensively as possible the role of the individual in the international legal system, this chapter considers as wide and as diverse a range of 'individuals' acting within that system as possible.

B. INDIVIDUALS IN THE INTERNATIONAL LEGAL SYSTEM

The international legal system is traditionally constructed as a State-based system with State sovereignty being supreme. The dominant positivist theories of international law confirm that construction, as their view is that '[s]ince the Law of Nations is a law between States only and exclusively, States only and exclusively are subjects of the Law of Nations' (Oppenheim, 1905, p 341). A 'subject' of the international legal system has direct rights and responsibilities under that system, can bring international claims and, it is argued, is able to participate in the creation, development, and enforcement of international law. Historically, under this dominant view, any role of the individual in the international legal system is purely as an 'object' of that system and not as a 'subject'.[3] In their view, individuals are objects, either in the same sense as territory or rivers are objects of the system because there are (State created) legal rules about them, or in the sense that they are beneficiaries

---

[1] This definition is similar to that adopted under the European Convention on Human Rights, see Committee of Ministers, 2001.

[2] *Elmi* v *Australia*, UN Committee Against Torture, No 120/1998, 7 *IHRR* 603.

[3] It was argued by the Chinese delegate (Mr Hsu) to the UN General Assembly's Sixth Committee in October 1954 that 'An individual who had no State to protect him was entitled to a direct international remedy. Moreover, while international delinquents, such as pirates or offenders against the peace and security of mankind, had been accepted as subjects of international law, it would be strange if stateless persons in need of protection would be regarded as outside its scope' (my thanks to Professor Sir Eli Lauterpacht for this material).

under the system, so that treaties on, for example, diplomatic persons or commerce, indirectly benefit individuals.

This traditional approach is now largely discredited. The reality is that there are many actors in the international legal system in addition to States and these actors have some international legal personality. The International Court of Justice (ICJ) clarified the issues of international personality, and what is a 'subject' of the international legal system, in its *Reparations for Injuries* Opinion:

> The subjects of law in any legal system are not necessarily identical in their nature or in the extent of their rights, and their nature depends on the needs of the community. Throughout its history, the development of international law has been influenced by the requirements of international life, and the progressive increase in the collective activities of States has already given rise to instances of action upon the international plane by certain entities which are not States... In the opinion of the Court, the [United Nations] Organisation was intended to exercise and enjoy, and is in fact exercising and enjoying, functions and rights which can only be explained on the basis of the possession of a large measure of international personality and the capacity to operate upon an international plane... That is not the same thing as saying that it is a State, which it certainly is not, or that its legal personality and rights and duties are the same as those of a State... It does not even imply that all its rights and duties must be upon the international plane, any more than all the rights and duties of a State must be upon that plane. What it does mean is that it is a subject of international law and capable of possessing international rights and duties, and that it has capacity to maintain its rights by bringing international claims.[4]

This is an important statement of international legal principles. It directly links being a subject of international law with international legal personality. It clarifies that there can be subjects of the international legal system that are not States. These subjects do not all possess the same rights and duties, and not all of these rights and duties need to be on the international plane alone. It also explains how the international legal system has developed, and continues to develop, in ways that allow non-States to have international legal personality and so to act independently in the international legal system (Nijman, 2004). In this Opinion the ICJ applied these principles to the position of the UN itself to decide that it did have international legal personality. A later ICJ decision[5] has applied these principles to other international (intergovernmental) organizations.

The Opinion clearly sets out broad principles that could be applied to any non-State actor (and thus applies to the individuals considered in this chapter) on the international plane. It recognizes that, while the State is the primary subject of the international legal system, the subjects of that system can change and expand depending on the 'needs of the [international] community' and 'the requirements of international life'. It does not say whether these 'needs' and 'requirements' are solely determined by States (as the dominant theories of international law would suggest) or by other means. After all, the term 'the international community' in the Opinion is expressly not limited to an international community of States alone (in comparison to the Vienna Convention on the Law of Treaties, Article 53) and so should include States and non-States. It certainly indicates that there can be subjects of the international legal system that are not States.

---

[4] *Reparation for Injuries Suffered in the Service of the United Nations, Advisory Opinion, ICJ Reports 1949*, p 174 at pp 178–9.

[5] *Legality of the Use of Nuclear Weapons in Armed Conflict, Advisory Opinion, ICJ Reports 1996*, p 66.

Some writers have argued that, rather than the State being the primary 'subject' of the international legal system, the primary 'subject' is the individual (Scelle, 1932). They argue, for example, that individuals are the real actors beneath the State, as the State itself does not exist without individuals. A variation on this idea is that of Hersch Lauterpacht, one of the most influential British international lawyers of last century, who argued that individuals could become subjects of the international legal system. He considered that the claim of the State to unqualified exclusiveness in the field of international relations was not tenable, especially as:

> Fundamental human rights are rights superior to the law of the sovereign State ... [and must lead to the] consequent recognition of the individual human being as a subject of international law. (Lauterpacht, 1950, p 72)

A middle path has been suggested in which individuals are objects when acquiring international rights and subjects when exercising them (Parlett, 2011). Philip Allott adopts a broader view in which he sees international society as not being comprised of States but as arising from the 'self-creating' of all human beings (Allott, 1992). So these writers would argue that the nature of the international legal system and the 'needs' of the international community have meant that individuals are subjects—the primary or only subjects—of the international legal system.

Of course, individuals are necessary for an entity to be recognized as a State, in the sense that an entity must have 'a population' to be a State (see Craven, Ch 8 of this book). In any event, the State is a legal fiction and so it cannot act by itself. Instead individuals and groups act on behalf of the State and in the State's name.[6] Thus individuals are at the very core of the international legal system, no matter how that system is defined. Yet this does not necessarily make them 'subjects' or 'objects' of this system.

The 'subject' v 'object' dichotomy has been criticized by a number of writers, not least because it privileges certain voices and silences others (eg Koskenniemi, 1989; Charlesworth and Chinkin, 2000). Rosalyn Higgins offers an alternative approach, arguing that:

> the whole notion of 'subjects' and 'objects' has no credible reality, and, in my view, no functional purpose. We have erected an intellectual prison of our own choosing and then declared it to be an unalterable constraint. (Higgins, 1994, p 49; see also Higgins, 1979)

Rather she prefers the idea of the 'participant' in the international legal decision-making process. She explains this by use of an example:

> The topics of minimum standard of treatment of aliens, requirements as to the conduct of hostilities and human rights, are not simply exceptions conceded by historical chance within a system that operates as between States. Rather, they are simply part and parcel of the fabric of international law, representing the claims that are naturally made by individual participants in contradistinction to state-participants. (Higgins, 1994, p 50)

Under this view, there are many participants in the international legal system, in the sense that there are many different entities, from States and international organizations to transnational corporations and natural persons, who engage in international activity (or 'upon an international plane' to use the ICJ's words set out earlier in this section in the *Reparations for Injuries* Opinion). Participation may be extensive and over a wide range of international matters or it can be limited to a few issues. Participation will depend on

---

[6] Though the individual, in his/her private capacity, remains distinct from the actions he/she takes on behalf of the State (Geuss, 2007).

the particular area of the international legal system concerned and the activity and involvement of entities in that area, rather than on the determination by States (and only States) as to whether any non-States are 'subjects' for a specific purpose. As the international community changes and the 'needs' or areas governed by international law develop, then so will participation in the international legal system.

This argument for considering individuals as 'participants' in the international legal system, rather than as 'objects' or 'subjects', is a compelling and practical one. Indeed, the notion of participation as a valuable framework to explore involvement in the international legal system (and thus as a means to determine if individuals have a voice in the system) has been applied effectively by Karen Knop from a different conceptual standpoint to that of Higgins (Knop, 2002). At the same time, this framework is still consistent with the dominant State-based concept of the international legal system, as participation in the system could be viewed as largely dependent on State consent and falls within the broad legal principles expressed by the ICJ in its *Reparations for Injuries* Opinion. Therefore, participation as a framework for considering the role of individuals in the international legal system is flexible and open enough to deal with developments in that system over the centuries and is not constricted to a State-based concept of that system or to appearances before international bodies. Accordingly, if it can be shown that individuals are exercising and enjoying 'in fact' (to use the ICJ's words) certain rights, privileges, powers, or immunities in the international legal system then they can be presumed to be acting as international legal persons (Meron, 2006; Boyle and Chinkin, 2007).

Of course, these individuals do not all share the same aims or values across the international community. They can reflect the hierarchies and political agendas within States, and can be captive to States and to power. Yet the decision to participate on the international plane is made by the particular individual and is not dictated by States' views, though it may be prompted by State action (eg to seek investment in a national industry) or State inaction (eg to fill the need for a secretariat of a treaty body). The degree of participation by an individual will vary, often depending on its own resources, its functions and on the attitude of other participants, including States (Puvimanasinghe, 2007).

It is the extent of that participation in the international legal system by individuals, and the State's role in determining the degree of participation, that will be considered in this chapter. This will be examined by reference to the direct rights and responsibilities of individuals under the international legal system, their capacity to bring international claims and their ability to participate in the creation, development, and enforcement of international law as independent participants.

II. INTERNATIONAL RIGHTS AND RESPONSIBILITIES

A. INDIVIDUAL RIGHTS

The Permanent Court of International Justice (PCIJ) had to consider in *Jurisdiction of the Courts of Danzig* whether it was possible for individuals to have rights under international law. They held:

> [I]t cannot be disputed that the very object of an international agreement, according to the intention of the contracting parties, may be the adoption by the parties of some definite rules creating individual rights and obligations and enforceable by the national courts.[7]

---

[7] *Jurisdiction of the Courts of Danzig, Advisory Opinion, 1928, PCIJ, Ser B, No 15,* pp 17–18.

While this Opinion confirmed that individuals can have rights in the international legal system, these rights will not all be of the same nature. As Wesley Hohfeld (1913) demonstrated, a 'right' can mean a claim-right, a privilege, a power, or an immunity (or a number of these at once). In some instances, the right of the individual within the international legal system is of the nature of the ability to bring a claim (a claim-right) against the State (see further later in this chapter). However, many of the rights of individuals in the international legal system are more in the nature of an immunity from action against them, such as those that arise due to their status as prisoners of war (see later in this section), or a privilege, such as the liberty to travel on the high seas without interference (see Evans, Ch 22 of this book). In the same way, States have a variety of rights within the international legal system, not all of which enable claims to be brought. The rights of individuals and the rights of States in the international legal system are not identical but, while they may overlap or interact (such as under international humanitarian law in relation to use of force on a territory affecting combatants and non-combatants—see Turns, Ch 27 of this book), they are distinct rights.

The area where individual rights are most developed is in relation to human rights, which include both rights of individuals and of groups, and which are now a matter of international law. At one time governments dealt with those within their jurisdiction as they wished and resisted all criticisms of their actions by claiming that human rights were matters of 'domestic jurisdiction' (under Article 2(7) UN Charter) and the responsibility of each State alone. However, human rights are now an established part of the international legal system with an institutional structure, including supervisory mechanisms to check compliance with legal obligations, and with a defined content of human rights (see Rodley, Ch 26 of this book). Every State has ratified at least one treaty containing legal obligations to protect human rights and all States have acknowledged that 'the promotion and protection of all human rights is a legitimate concern of the international community'.[8]

This acknowledgement that human rights are a legitimate concern of the international community has a direct effect on State sovereignty, in that one aspect of each State's control and authority over its activities on its territory and within its jurisdiction is now subject to international legal review. This applies when a State has expressly agreed to this review by ratifying a treaty protecting human rights. It also applies when the protection of a human right has become a matter of customary international law or *jus cogens*, which can happen without a State having any express practice on the issue. Some human rights create legal obligations on States that the State cannot evade by contrary practice. For example, the ICJ took the view that South Africa was bound by international obligations in relation to racial discrimination despite its clear contrary practice[9] and also that all States must comply with the right of self-determination.[10]

Thus States have, by treaty and other practice, placed human rights for individuals (including groups of individuals) within the international legal system. There are problems with the way international human rights law has been created, such as the conception that rights are only held in relation to a centralized State (Otto, 1997) and the general exclusion of individuals from direct responsibility for human rights violations (see later).

---

[8] Vienna Declaration (1993) 32 ILM 1661, para 4.

[9] *Legal Consequences for States of the Continued Presence of South Africa in Namibia (South West Africa) notwithstanding Security Council Resolution 276 (1970)*, Advisory Opinion, ICJ Reports 1971, p 16, paras 21–2.

[10] *East Timor Case (Portugal v Australia)*, Judgment, ICJ Reports 1995, p 90, *Legal Consequences of the Construction of a Wall in the Occupied Palestine Territory*, Advisory Opinion, ICJ Reports 2004, p 136, paras 118 and 122.

Nevertheless, international human rights law is significant in terms of demonstrating that individuals have rights within the international legal system.

Individuals also have rights in the international legal system outside the specific context of international human rights law. For example, within international humanitarian law, individuals have certain rights depending on their status as, for example, prisoners of war or non-combatants (see Turns, Ch 27 of this book), though some of these rights and protections are pursued through international human rights law due to the developed procedures of the latter (Henckaerts, 2007). Many of these individual rights are now considered to be customary international law or even *jus cogens*. Yet the rights of individuals within the international legal system were all initially determined and placed within that system by States. States decided and agreed that these rights were rights within that system and not solely rights within a national legal system. Martti Koskenniemi concludes from this that the creation of these rights of individuals by States, particularly within international human rights law, affirms the position of States as the sole rights-holder in the international legal system:

> By establishing and consenting to human rights limitations on their own sovereignty, states actually define, delimit, and contain those rights, thereby domesticating their use and affirming the authority of the state as the source from which such rights spring. (Koskenniemi, 1991, p 406)

Despite this view, each State, as demonstrated earlier, no longer has complete control over the continuance, development, and interpretation of individuals' rights, and the rights of individuals are distinct from the rights of States. Thus a number of the rights of individuals in the international system are now, to some extent, separate from the specific control and direction of States, at least as they are protected by customary international law (or by *jus cogens*), and are independent rights within the international legal system. It can be concluded, therefore, that, although originally based on the agreement of States, individuals now have some distinct rights in the international legal system, ranging from a person's right to freedom from torture to the protection of a group of individuals under the right of self-determination.

B. INDIVIDUAL RESPONSIBILITY

Responsibility in the international legal system is generally considered to mean a legal obligation that, if breached, can give rise to international consequences (see Crawford and Olleson, Ch 15 of this book). Even though individuals have been a part of international activity for centuries, from trading to colonizing, generally the actions of individuals did not give rise to any international responsibility on them; it only arose when those actions were attributed to the State and then the State was internationally responsible.[11]

The development of individual responsibility for certain crimes under both international criminal law and international humanitarian law illustrate the lineage of individual responsibility in the international legal system, with both piracy and slavery also widely seen as offences against the whole international community, for which individuals were directly responsible (Ratner and Abrams, 2009). The justification for this was that 'the pirate and the slave trader... [are each] *hostis humani generis*, an enemy of all mankind'.[12]

---

[11] See *United States Diplomatic and Consular Staff in Tehran, Judgment, ICJ Reports 1980*, p 3.

[12] *Filartiga v Peña-Irala*, 630 F.2d 876 (US 2nd Cir 1980).

Individuals, even when acting as part of the organs of the State and under orders from the State, are independently responsible within the international legal system for certain actions. This was neatly summarized by the Nuremberg International Military Tribunal:

> Crimes against international law are committed by men, not by abstract entities [of States], and only by punishing individuals who commit such crimes can the provisions of international law be enforced.[13]

This individual responsibility, which is based on both customary international law and treaties, is now enforced (where there is jurisdiction) through international criminal courts and tribunals (see Cryer, Ch 25 of this book). Prior to this, the individual responsibility still existed, and was occasionally enforced in national courts,[14] even though no international judicial body enforced it. In the same way, State responsibility exists even where no other State takes action to enforce it (such as seen in the lack of any legal action after the Chernobyl nuclear power plant explosion). Thus, even though it was necessary for States to agree to the decisions or treaties that created these recent international criminal tribunals and courts, the individual responsibility under international law still existed independently of these agreements.[15] The responsibility arose through customary international law and no one State now has the ability to limit this responsibility, at least with regard to acts such as piracy and genocide. However, the victims of actions that are contrary to international criminal law are not yet able to bring actions directly against the perpetrator to the international criminal courts and tribunals (where there is jurisdiction), as they must rely on States or on independent prosecutors to do so. However, victims of violations of international criminal law could seek reparations in some courts and tribunals, such as under Article 75 of the Statute of the International Criminal Court (Schabas, 2011; Henckaerts, 2007).

There has also been a development in international law in relation to the responsibilities of corporations for breaches of international law. The adoption by the UN Human Rights Council of the Guiding Principles on Business and Human Rights (UN Guiding Principles, 2011) makes clear that corporations have responsibilities for the harm that they do and must mitigate adverse human rights impacts. However, this is conceived by the Guiding Principles as being a voluntary responsibility and not a legally enforceable one (unless States create national laws to enforce it). However, it is possible that the breadth of the concept of 'due diligence' used in the Guiding Principles, together with actions by States and claims being brought by victims in this area, will lead to increased remedies for individuals affected by a corporation's actions (Mares, 2012; Lindsay, 2013).

There are limits to the responsibility of individuals under international law. For example, international human rights law is still crafted in terms of the responsibilities of States and actions by individuals that affect other individuals (such as actions by corporations) are not dealt with by international human rights law unless they can be attributed to the State (Joseph, 2010).

---

[13] *Nuremberg Judgment*, (1948) 22 Trial of the Major War Criminals before the International Military Tribunal 466.

[14] Eg, *Attorney-General of the Government of Israel* v *Eichmann* (1961) 36 ILR 5.

[15] Article 58 of the International Law Commission's Articles on State Responsibility, 2001, provides that 'These Articles are without prejudce to any question of the individual responsibility under international law of any person acting on behalf of a State'. See Clapham, 2010.

Yet a possibility of extending the responsibility of individuals under international law is seen in Security Council Resolution 1373 (2001), passed after the international terrorist actions in the USA in September 2001, where the Security Council declared that:

[A]cts, methods, and practices of terrorism are contrary to the purposes and principles of the United Nations and that knowingly financing, planning and inciting terrorist acts are also contrary to the purposes and principles of the United Nations.

As this paragraph (also repeated in later Resolutions) does not refer to crimes against humanity or other acknowledged areas of individual responsibility under international law, it must be asserting that terrorist actions *per se* give rise to individual responsibility. There is no requirement in the Resolution to link those activities to a State for there to be international responsibility. While Security Council Resolutions are not automatically international law, they can indicate the direction that international law may be headed. It appears, therefore, that certain actions by individuals (being terrorist actions) could be in breach of international law and so give rise to international responsibility by those individuals.

The importance of establishing responsibility of individuals for international crimes is that it demonstrates that there are some actions by individuals that lead to direct international responsibility on an individual. The individual is responsible without any need to link the individual with the State. This draws a clear distinction between the individual and the State in terms of international responsibility.

III. INTERNATIONAL CLAIMS

A. BRINGING INTERNATIONAL CLAIMS

The conceptual understanding that individuals have rights and responsibilities in the international legal system does not automatically mean that they have the ability to bring international claims to assert their rights or are able to claim an immunity to prevent their responsibilities being enforced (Hohfeld, referred to in Section II A of this chapter). Thus the PCIJ declared that 'it is scarcely necessary to point out that the capacity to possess civil rights does not necessarily imply the capacity to exercise those rights oneself'.[16] Instead, the conclusion reached by most writers is that 'individuals are extremely handicapped in international law from the procedural point of view' (Higgins, 1994, p 51). Many of the international institutions that determine claims, such as the ICJ, are barred to individuals, even though a significant number of their cases arise from actions by, or against, individuals. This was seen most starkly in the *East Timor* case,[17] where the claims of the East Timorese themselves could not be brought to, or directly considered by, the ICJ.

Traditionally, the only means available for individuals to bring a claim within the international legal system has been when the individual is able to persuade a government to bring a claim on the individual's behalf. Even then, it is not the individual's international rights that are being asserted but the State's own rights, as the PCIJ noted:

[I]n taking up the case of one of its nationals, by resorting to diplomatic action or international judicial proceedings on his behalf, a State is in reality asserting its own right, the right to ensure in the person of its nationals respect for the rules of international law.[18]

---

[16] *Appeal from a Judgment of the Hungaro/Czechoslovak Mixed Arbitral Tribunal, Judgment, 1933, PCIJ, Ser A/B, No 61, p 208 at p 231.*

[17] *East Timor Case (Portugal v Australia), Judgment, ICJ Reports 1995, p 90.*

[18] *Panevezys-Saldutiskis Railway, Judgment, PCIJ, Ser A/B, No 76, p 4. Cf LaGrand (Germany v United States of America), Merits, Judgment, ICJ Reports 2001, p 466, para 42.*

The justification that a State has to assert this type of claim is through the linkage of nationality.[19] The international legal system has developed intricate rules regarding the nationality of people in terms of their relationship to States, as determined by the degree of connection individuals have to the territory of a State (see Staker, Ch 11 of this book). Even then, this nationality connection may be insufficient if there are other international rules that override it or if the State chooses not to take action. Indeed, the ICJ has stated that:

> [t]he State must be viewed as the sole judge to decide whether its protection will be granted, to what extent it is granted, and when it will cease [and...] [s]hould the natural or legal persons on whose behalf it is acting consider that their rights are not adequately protected, they have no remedy in international law.[20]

This position was been challenged in the UK in a case arising from the clearly internationally unlawful detention by the USA of prisoners in Guantánamo Bay from the time of the Afghanistan conflict in 2001. In *Abbasi v Secretary of State for Foreign and Commonwealth Affairs*[21] the applicant (a British national) sought judicial review of the adequacy of the diplomatic actions of the British government with the US government. The UK Court of Appeal found that there was a legitimate expectation (though a limited one) by nationals that their government would make representations to another government to assist them and the courts could thus consider the diplomatic activity of the UK government. In this instance, the Court found that the UK government's actions were sufficient, yet it also expressed its very deep concern about the violation of international law that was occurring in Guantánamo Bay.

This position, by which the individual could not assert claims directly to international bodies, began to change during the twentieth century. A series of international bodies were established in the early part of that century as a means to settle conflicts between States and included in their powers was the ability to consider claims by individuals. These bodies included the Central American Court of Justice, the Mixed Arbitral Tribunals in Europe, the minority protections offered by the League of Nations, and the dispute mechanisms of the International Labour Organization (Butler, 2007; Parlett, 2011). In the second half of that century, the vast growth of international human rights supervisory bodies and international commercial arbitral bodies has taken the issue of individuals bringing international claims to a higher level.[22] Indeed, the fact that a dispute over territory between a State and an armed non-State actor could be determined by an international arbitration, as happened between the government of Sudan and the Southern Sudan People's Liberation Movement at the Permanent Court of Arbitration in 2009, is an example of this significant development.

Rather than set out the detailed provisions of the large number of treaties or other documents that enable individuals to bring claims in an international context, the rest of this section will summarize the main aspects of the key areas of international law in which individuals can bring claims: international human rights law and international economic

---

[19] There are some instances where a State might be able to bring a claim on behalf of the international community (of States and non-States): see International Law Commission (2001), Article 48.

[20] *Barcelona Traction, Light and Power Company, Limited, Second Phase, Judgment, ICJ Reports 1970*, p 3, paras 78–9.

[21] *Abbassi v Secretary of State for Foreign and Commonwealth Affairs* [2002] EWCA Civ 1316, 19 September 2002; (2003) 42 ILM 358.

[22] See the International Law Commission Reports on Diplomatic Protection and its changes over time: UN Doc A/CN.4/484 (1998) and UN Doc A/CN.4/506 (2000).

law. However, it should be noted that individuals can also bring international claims in other areas, for example, employees of some international organizations may bring claims against that organization to an international body (Hunt, 2010).

B. INTERNATIONAL HUMAN RIGHTS LAW

Within international human rights law, a number of treaties permit individuals to bring claims against a State, alleging violations of their human rights, before both international and regional bodies. This is an extraordinary development in the international legal system away from a position in which a State's actions on its own territory were not subject to international review. Claims can be brought by individuals against the State of which they are a national and against a State in whose jurisdiction they happen to be, even if temporarily, irrespective of whether they are a national of that State.[23] In most instances, the individual is a direct party to the proceedings before the international body (with most proceedings being conducted by written submissions). Decisions can be made, or 'views' given, by international bodies in which States are found to be in violation of their human rights obligations and remedies are indicated. These remedies range from monetary compensation to ordering the State to conduct investigations into the violations (Shelton, 2005).

Despite all of this, the State is still an intermediary, or directly involved in, these international claims by individuals. Such claims cannot be brought unless the relevant State has ratified the relevant treaty (whether a human rights treaty or a treaty establishing an international organization, such as the UN Charter, which facilitates claims by individuals), or the State has accepted the relevant Article of the treaty that allows individuals to bring the claim. In addition, no international claim can be brought by an individual unless he or she has exhausted domestic remedies in the relevant State. The reason for the latter is to enable States to resolve the issues at national level first, with the international bodies only being involved after all proceedings or other action at the State level have been effectively exhausted. Thus, in principle, there is no independent ability for individuals to bring claims before international human rights bodies.

Nevertheless, there are some aspects to these individual claims that show, in practice, some independent ability for individuals to bring international claims in this area. First, under the European Convention on Human Rights (ECHR) and the American Convention on Human Rights (ACHR) individuals can appear and bring their claims direct to the relevant Court. In addition, ratification of the ECHR is effectively required before a State can be a member of the EU (Douglas-Scott, 2011). Thus, in practice, European States are no longer able to prevent individual claims under that regional human rights system, which means that there are now about 800 million individuals who have the right to bring international claims under that treaty. Further, even if a State is not party to a particular human rights treaty, some international bodies, such as the Inter-American Commission on Human Rights and the UN Human Rights Council, can still, on the basis of individuals' claims revealing a consistent pattern of gross and reliably attested violations of human rights, make public conclusions about that State's human rights record.

Second, the link between nationality and the ability to bring claims is no longer essential. The link is now jurisdiction. If a State has jurisdiction over an individual, which power can include where that individual is not a national of that State and even where that State's jurisdiction over the individual is unlawful,[24] then an individual can bring a claim against

---

[23] Eg, *Soering* v *United Kingdom*, Judgment of 7 July 1989, Ser A, no 161, 11 *EHRR* 439.

[24] *Loizidou* v *Turkey (Preliminary Objections)*, Judgment of 23 March 1995, Ser A, no 310, 20 *EHRR* 99.

that State if that State has ratified a relevant human rights treaty. The State of which that individual is a national does not have to be a party to the treaty and the individual could be a stateless person. This has meant that, in practice, States are now subject to a wider number of claims by individuals before international bodies. This represents 'a momentous advance in the world community' (Cassese, 1986, p 102).

Third, these treaties give individuals the procedural capacity to bring international claims. While this is a restricted capacity as it is dependent on State consent (as seen earlier), it does have significant practical effects. States rarely ignore the individual's claim to an international body. Rather they often respond to the claim at some length (though the practice is by no means universal) especially as, if they do not respond, the international body will still consider the matter, as there is some onus on the State to prove that there has been no violation.[25] When an international human rights body reaches a conclusion in relation to an individual's claim then States usually treat this conclusion as a serious matter that requires some response. If the conclusion is that there is no violation of a human right then the State will ensure that the media is aware of this. If the conclusion is that there has been a violation, then the State will respond in some way, from amending the relevant law or practice to making a derogation from the relevant provision (should this be possible) or offering a justification for their actions. Sometimes a State will even seek to denounce the treaty and criticize the international body: Peru, for example, withdrew its acceptance of the jurisdiction of the Inter-American Court of Human Rights before later re-accepting it after a change of national government. Very rarely will the State not respond at all. So these individual claims are treated seriously by States, in the same way as a claim brought against a State by another State before an international body is treated seriously.

Finally, the conclusions reached by international human rights bodies about individual claims can have practical effects on a State through the adoption of those conclusions by national courts and by other international bodies whose decisions are legally binding on a State. The latter is seen in the approach taken by the European Court of Justice (now the Court of Justice of the European Union), which decided that 'respect for fundamental [human] rights forms an integral part of the general principles of [European] Community law protected by the Court of Justice',[26] and has applied this principle to restrict decisions by the UN Security Council on terrorism matters that did not take account of human rights.[27] Thus the practical effects of individuals being able to bring claims before international human rights bodies are such as to place effective limits upon a State's ability to control or restrict those claims. The State's role as an intermediary, or barrier, between the individual and an international human rights body, while still crucial for an individual to be able to bring a claim is, in practice, permeable.

C. INTERNATIONAL ECONOMIC LAW

One of the areas of significant growth in the international legal system since the latter part of the twentieth century has been international economic law. Part of this growth has included the creation and development of mechanisms by which individuals, usually corporations, can bring claims against States. These mechanisms were initially ad hoc arbitration bodies and inter-State bodies to which individuals have access, for example, the Iran-US Claims Tribunal and the UN Compensation Commission. They now include

---

[25] *Bleier* v *Uruguay*, decision of 29 March 1982 1 *Selected Decisions of the Human Rights Committee* 109.

[26] *Internationale Handelsgesellschaft* v *Einfur und Voratsstelle Getreide*, Case 11/70 [1970] ECR 1125, para 4.

[27] *Kadi and Al Barakaat International Foundation* v *Council*, Joined Cases 402/05 and 415/05, [2008] ECR I-6351.

institutional bodies (both treaty-based and non-treaty-based) with established procedures, such as under the International Chamber of Commerce and the International Centre for the Settlement of Investment Disputes and through the model law of the UN Commission on International Trade Law (see Subedi, Ch 24 of this book).

Each of these mechanisms allows individuals to bring claims against a State to an international body, which makes a decision, usually legally binding and enforceable, in relation to the claim (Redfern, 2009). The ability of an individual to bring an international claim against a State was considered by Arbitrator Dupuy in *Texaco* v *Libya* to show the international legal personality of an individual:

> [S]tating that a contract between a State and a private person falls within the international legal order means that for the purposes of interpretation and performance of the contract, it should be recognized that a private contracting party has specific international capacities. But, unlike a State, the private person has only a limited capacity and his quality as a subject of international law does enable him only to invoke, in the field of international law, the rights which he derives from the contract.[28]

While Dupuy's reasoning is consistent with that of the ICJ in the *Reparations for Injuries* Opinion in relation to the ability of individuals to have international legal capacity for specific purposes and functions, it does not completely reflect the position today. Most of the disputes between individuals and States in this area are now resolved by a combination of public and private international law, with decisions of international bodies enforced through national law, often as a consequence of a treaty obligation (such as the New York Convention on the Recognition and Enforcement of Foreign Arbitral Awards 1958).

In international economic law, as with international human rights law, it is the State that enables the individual to bring a claim either by ratifying the relevant treaty and/or through a contract agreed specifically by the State with the individual. However, in this area of law the ability of the State to refuse to allow individuals to bring international claims is often quite limited. In many instances the State, particularly a developing State, has little ability to resist an individual's (usually a transnational corporation) request to be able to bring an international claim (or to ratify the relevant treaty to enable such a claim to be made). This is because the economic power of such individuals is far greater than that of many States (McCorquodale, 2002). In addition, many economically powerful States will place pressure on other States to allow (eg by ratifying the relevant treaty) individuals to bring these claims due to the influence of the individual in that economically powerful State.

Many of the claims brought by States to international economic legal bodies, such as under the dispute settlement procedures of the World Trade Organization (WTO), are initiated, sponsored, and prosecuted in effect by the individual corporations—and individuals with the relevant nationality—that are affected by the trade action that is the subject of the claim (Croley and Jackson, 1996; Charnovitz, 2001). Examples of the driving role of corporations in directing litigation under the WTO, include Kodak and Fuji representatives being on the US and Japanese delegations on a case affecting them, and the large banana corporations convincing the USA and the EU to litigate about the trade in bananas from the Caribbean, despite the very few bananas produced in the USA and the EU (Tietje and Nowrot, 2004; Brown and Hoekman, 2005). Indeed, the drafting of key international economic treaties is often done at either the instigation of, or with the direct involvement of, transnational corporations, as seen in the Agreement on Trade-Related Aspects

---

[28] *Texaco Overseas Petroleum Company* v *Libyan Arab Republic* (1977) 53 ILR 389.

of Intellectual Property Rights 1994. Further, the World Bank has created an Inspection Panel, which allows individuals who believe that they will be affected detrimentally by a project in a State that is to be funded by the World Bank to ask the Panel to investigate their claim (Alfredsson and Ring, 2001). The Bank can do this even if the State is opposed to such investigation. A similar system is operated by the Asian Development Bank and the Inter-American Development Bank. This pressure from individuals for more control over international activity in the economic area will increase with globalization.

The major economic region of Europe provides the opportunity for individuals to bring claims to an international body. In *Van Gend en Loos* the European Court of Justice held:

> The European Economic Community [now European Union] constitutes a new legal order of international law for the benefit of which the States have limited their sovereign rights, albeit within limited fields, and the subjects of which comprise not only Member States but also their nationals. Independently of the legislation of Member States, Community law therefore not only imposes obligations on individuals but is also intended to confer upon them rights which become part of their legal heritage. These rights arise not only where they are expressly granted by the Treaty, but also by reason of obligations which the Treaty imposes in a clearly defined way upon individuals as well as upon the Member States and institutions of the Community.[29]

This decision highlights the limitations on the ability of States to prevent claims by individuals under European law. Though there are some situations in which the individual can bring a claim directly to the Court, in fact the main avenue for individuals to bring claims under the EU treaties is in their national courts. There is also indirect access to the Court of Justice, as most cases are brought to the Court by national courts seeking an interpretation from the Court in relation to EU treaty issues arising in the individual claim before that national court (Treaty Establishing the European Union, Article 267). While States can withdraw from these European treaties, the practical consequences of withdrawal from these foundational elements of the EU are such that a State's ability to do this has effectively now disappeared.

The ability of individuals (mainly corporations) to bring international claims in international economic law is now considerable. The main participants in a number of areas of international economic law are primarily States and corporations, and they are often acting on equal terms. In negotiation of contracts where a transnational corporation is involved, an agreement on a dispute settlement mechanism is vital. Invariably this will be an international body to which the corporation can bring a claim and obtain an enforceable judgment. That judgment by an international body can be affected by the nature of the claim being brought by the individual and their rights (McLachlan, 2007). For most States that seek to encourage foreign investment, such an agreement allowing international dispute settlement is necessary and is not able to be rejected. Indeed, the State of nationality is not even asserting its own rights, as has been acknowledged by investment arbitration tribunals:

> [W]hen a State claimed for a wrong done to its national [in international law] it was in reality acting on behalf of that national, rather than asserting a right of its own. The pretence that it was asserting a claim of its own was necessary, because the State alone enjoyed access to international dispute settlement and claims machinery. However, there is no need to continue that fiction in a case in which the individual is vested with the right to bring claims of

---

[29] *Van Gend en Loos*, Case 26/69 [1969] ECR 419.

its own [as in international economic law]. In such a case there is no question of the investor claiming on behalf of the State. The State of nationality of the Claimant does not control the conduct of the case. No compensation which is recovered will be paid to the State. The individual may even advance a claim of which the State disapproves or base its case upon a proposition of law with which the State disagrees.... It can be seen that the international protection for investment is really giving substantive rights to individuals that cannot be overridden by States, and a claim might not even be able to be prevented by the home State of the individual corporation.[30]

What now occurs is that the individual decides to file a claim, argues directly with the State, keeps the proceeds of the claim, has direct access to an international tribunal (usually without having to exhaust domestic remedies), and is the real actor in the international legal system. Thus, to all intents and purposes, individuals now have an independent capacity to ensure that they can bring an international claim in some areas of international economic law, which is a dramatic development in the last few decades.

D. IMMUNITIES

It is generally considered that, under the international legal system, only States have immunities from claims. These immunities can arise through non-acceptance of an international or a national legal mechanism. In addition, diplomats, Heads of State, representatives of international organizations, and others may have personal immunities arising from their relationship with the State or State-based bodies, even when acting outside their official roles. Even former Heads of State and former Foreign Ministers can have some personal immunity (see Wickremasinghe, Ch 13 of this book). These latter types of immunity are personal to the individual concerned and cannot be easily revoked by the State (though they are revocable). So it is possible to see an increasing recognition of the development of an immunity for individuals separate to that of the immunity of States.

Overall, the development of international law, particularly in the areas of human rights and economic law, has provided individuals with the ability of make claims to international bodies and have some personal immunities. In principle this ability is determined by States and their agreement to certain treaties that provide for individuals to make claims. Yet in practice many States are becoming less able to restrict, or to prevent, individuals having the ability to make international claims. There are at least some aspects of the international legal system that allow individuals an effective independent capacity to bring an international claim.

IV. CREATION, DEVELOPMENT, AND ENFORCEMENT OF INTERNATIONAL LAW

One of the essential aspects of an international legal person is 'the capacity to participate in international law-making and to enforce rules of international law' (Orakhelashvili, 2001, p 256). From the classical definition of the sources of international law found in Article 38 of the Statute of the ICJ, where State practice and State treaty-making are pre-eminent, to the laws on territory and jurisdiction being about State boundaries, it is the State that

---

[30] *Corn Products International, Inc v United Mexican States*, ICSID Case No ARB (AF)/04/1, *Decision on Responsibility*, Award,15 January 2008, paras 173–4.

appears to decide exclusively on the creation, development, and enforcement of international law. Even the definition of which entity is a State is decided (through the process of recognition) by other States. It is necessary to see the extent to which individuals have been involved in the creation, development, and enforcement of international law.

A. RIGHT OF SELF-DETERMINATION

One area where the role of the individual can be seen as a challenge to the State-based system and where individuals have been involved in the creation, development, and enforcement of international law is with respect to the right of self-determination. Article 1 of both the International Covenant on Economic, Social and Cultural Rights and the International Covenant on Civil and Political Rights provides that 'all peoples have the right of self-determination. By virtue of that right they freely determine their political status and freely pursue their economic, social and cultural development'. This right is a collective right, that is, a right of a group of individuals as a group. Its importance in relation to this chapter is that it is a part of the international legal system where the priority is given to groups of individuals and not to States. While the definition of the right of self-determination, including its limitations, have been drafted by States and a number of decisions about its exercise, such as whether to recognize a self-determining entity as a State, are decided by States, much of its development has been by individuals acting as a group.

This can be shown in a number of ways: from its original focus in the early part of the twentieth century on minorities within and across States; its development beyond a legal justification for decolonization (which operated largely within a State-based structure) to its application outside the colonial context to independent States and internal self-determination; and its emphasis on the right of the people to decide their own destiny (McCorquodale, 1994). Some of these aspects were explained by Judge Nagendra Singh in the *Western Sahara* Opinion, when he said that:

> [T]he consultation of the people of a territory awaiting decolonization is an inescapable imperative... Thus even if integration of territory was demanded by an interested State, as in this case, it could not be had without ascertaining the freely expressed will of the people— the very *sine qua non* of all decolonization.[31]

Indeed, the British government, one of the largest colonizers, went further when it stated: '[A]s the [United Nations] Charter and the two International Covenants expressly declare, [it is] a right of peoples. Not States. Not countries. Not governments. Peoples.'[32] It can be seen that 'the peoples in whom [the] right is vested are not inherently or necessarily represented by States or by governments of States' (Crawford, 1988, p 166).

In fact, so successful have groups of individuals been in relation to the right of self-determination that new States have arisen despite the expressed wish of some very powerful States that this should not happen (eg in the early stages of the break-up of the former Yugoslavia) and States are now forced to accept that self-determination applies to groups within States.[33] Indeed, it could be considered that the right of self-determination has changed the international legal system significantly as even the elements taken into

---

[31]   *Western Sahara, Advisory Opinion, ICJ Reports 1975*, p 12 at p 81.
[32]   Statement by the UK representative to the UN Commission on Human Rights (Mr H Steel), 9 February 1988 (1988) 59 *BYIL* 441.
[33]   *Reference Re Secession of Quebec*, Canadian Supreme Court (1998) 37 ILM 1340.

consideration as to whether an entity is a State now include whether that entity complies with the right of self-determination. With all the restrictions that States can bring to the exercise of the right of self-determination, its development has been beyond the control of States and its enforcement has frequently been due to the persistence of individuals and not of States, which largely remain unwilling participants in this area. While there remain concerns about the abuse of the right and the unequal impact of the right, especially on women (Charlesworth and Chinkin, 2000), the participation of peoples in this area opens the possibility of a less State-based and territorial idea of the right of self-determination (Knop, 2002; Saul, 2011; Wilde, 2011). The power of the people is expressed by Judge Ammoun in the *Namibia* Opinion:

> Indeed one is bound to recognize that the right of peoples to self-determination, before being written into charters that were not granted but won in bitter struggle, had first been written painfully, with the blood of the peoples, in the finally awakened conscience of humanity.[34]

B. INDIGENOUS PEOPLES

Another area of international law where the 'conscience of humanity' has been awakened is in relation to indigenous peoples. Although their international legal status had been acknowledged in the sixteenth century and some national courts considered them as communities distinct from States, it was not until late in the twentieth century that substantial renewed consideration was given to their position in the international legal system (Anaya, 2004). Most significantly, the Sub-Commission of the then UN Human Rights Commission (now the Human Rights Council) established a Working Group in Indigenous Populations in 1982. This Working Group comprised many representatives of indigenous peoples, who could participate fully in the drafting of (what became) the UN Declaration on the Rights of Indigenous Peoples 2007. This Declaration was adopted, after many years of delay, by the UN General Assembly with only four votes against (Australia, Canada, New Zealand, and the USA—though the governments of each of those States have since changed their stance). Its importance also lies in the fact that the process of the creation and development of this Declaration was largely outside the sole control of States. It was drafted with a significant degree of participation by indigenous peoples, who were, in the drafting process, acting on almost equal terms to State representatives. This process was revolutionary in the UN system (Lâm, 2000; Xanthaki, 2009).

Process and procedure, as discussed in relation to human rights, are significant aspects of the international legal system in terms of clarification of the participants in that system. In addition, the Declaration (even when it was a draft) assisted national and international courts in upholding the rights and separate status of indigenous peoples.[35]

C. NON-GOVERNMENTAL ORGANIZATIONS

The participation of individuals, usually as groups or peoples, in the creation, development, and enforcement of international law in the areas of self-determination and

---

[34] *Legal Consequences for States of the Continued Presence of South Africa in Namibia (South West Africa) notwithstanding Security Council Resolution 276 (1970), Advisory Opinion, ICJ Reports 1971*, p 16 at p 74.

[35] See *Cal v Attorney-General* (Claim 121/ 2007), Supreme Court of Belize, 18 October 2007, and Inter-American Court of Human Rights, *Case of the Saramanka People v Suriname*, Preliminary Objections, Merits, Reparations and Costs, Judgment of 28 November 2007, Ser C no 173.

indigenous peoples has been fostered by the growing role of non-governmental organizations (NGOs). These organizations, which are part of international civil society, have had an increasingly crucial effect on the creation, development, and enforcement of many parts of the international legal system. Even in earlier centuries their role was relevant, as seen in the activities of the Anti-Slavery Society being crucial to the abolition of slavery and the role of women's groups (Bianchi, 1997). In more recent times NGOs have been important in the creation of international law, with, for example, NGOs assisting in the drafting of the Convention on the Rights of the Child, as acknowledged in the *travaux préparatoires* of that treaty, and the Convention on the Conservation of Migratory Species of Wild Animals 1979 (Bowman, 1999), organizing a systematic campaign towards the adoption of the Convention Against Torture and other related documents (Van Boven, 1990), the creation of the International Criminal Court (Pace and Thieroff, 1999), the banning of landmines (Anderson, 2000), and reforming the environmental impacts of the World Bank's lending policies (Rossi, 2010), as well as fostering proposals for the establishment of a UN High Commissioner for Human Rights (Clapham, 1994).

There are two areas of the international legal system where the law has developed primarily as a response to the activities of NGOs. These are international humanitarian law, where the role of the International Committee of the Red Cross (ICRC)—though a hybrid NGO— has been crucial, and issues relating to labour conditions, where trade unions and employer organizations have played a significant role. The ICRC has the express acknowledgement of its role in the Geneva Conventions 1949 and the 1977 Protocols. For example, States can entrust the fulfilment of their duties to the ICRC (common Article 10 (or 11) of the Conventions), they must cooperate with the ICRC during conflicts (Article 81 Geneva Prisoner of War Convention) and before any proposed amendment by a State to the Protocols can be acted upon, the ICRC must be consulted (Article 97 Protocol I and Article 24 Protocol II). Similarly, trade unions and employer organizations are institutionally part of the International Labour Organization, which has adopted many treaties and other international documents. Of similar power, but with a less institutional role, have been the activities of environmental NGOs, who are a vital element in the creation and sustenance of international environmental law (Cullen and Morrow, 2001) and the roles of health foundations in the expansion of public/ private partnerships in international health law (Burci, 2009).

The roles that NGOs play in relation to the development of international law are numerous. They include 'elaborating further interpretative rules in connection with already existing international instruments…[which have come to be] referred to as…authoritative sources' (Van Boven, 1990, p 357). They are involved in international decision-making, usually indirectly, by their participation in international fora, from the UN itself to its agencies and as a distinct part of international conferences. Indeed, NGOs can be 'sought-after participants in a political process…that allow NGOs to move from the corridors to the sessions' (Knop, 1993). Sometimes this participation can be important as a balance against States' views, as seen in the Bangkok NGO Declaration on Human Rights that appeared successfully to reduce the impact of the Asian States' Declaration in relation to cultural relativism (Steiner and Alston, 2000, p 549), and sometimes NGOs act in opposing ways due to their different objectives (eg during the Beijing Conference on Women—Otto, 1999). Sometimes NGOs are essential to the continuing operation of some international bodies, as the African Commission on Human Rights has acknowledged (Motala, 2002), due to their provision of information, people, and resources. In the area of international environmental law the role of NGOs has been particularly crucial, for example, in relation to the protection of birds:

> [T]he role of [NGOs] has proved to be of vital importance. Not only have they regularly pressed for the adoption of agreements…they have frequently shown a willingness to

undertake much of the preliminary drafting work necessary to make such projects a reality. Insofar as these agreements, once concluded, have required to be sustained by technical resources and expertise, NGOs have been prominent in the provision of such support... [In relation to one treaty,] one such [NGO] has also provided the administrative infrastructure for the establishment of a secretariat. (Bowman, 1999, p 298)

The terms of the treaties that are eventually ratified are often drafted and negotiated by NGOs. The participation of NGOs in the treaty process itself also ensures greater transparency and accountability of States for their negotiating positions. To look solely at the end process (ie the ratified treaty) without any examination of the process by which that law is made, ignores the discursive context, power structures and interests involved in international law-making. This powerful role has been recognized at times, with NGOs being parties, with States, to Memoranda of Understanding (which are international agreements, though are not treaties) concerning conservation measures about particular species, with responsibilities being placed on both States and NGOs under these Memoranda (Bowman, 1999). NGOs, as part of civil society, are acknowledged in the Guiding Principles on Business and Human Rights as having a role in applying those Principles (McCorquodale, 2013).

NGOs are also active participants in the enforcement of international law. In many instances they assist individuals to bring international claims, or bring claims themselves, and they provide information to international bodies that will often not be provided by States (Charnovitz, 2006). These roles of NGOs are accepted now in practice by States, by the rules of procedure of the international bodies, and are even specifically referred to in some treaties (eg Article 45 of the Convention on the Rights of the Child) and in monitoring compliance (eg Aarhus Convention on Access to Information, Public Participation in Decision-Making and Access to Justice in Environmental Matters 1998—Ryngaert and Noortmann, 2010). NGOs have regularly brought *amicus curiae* information to international bodies, whereby they have sought to assist the international bodies in making decisions in cases brought by others against a State, and acted to implement State's policies, such as with development and humanitarian aid (Rossi, 2010).

At the same time, NGOs and individuals have used national legal systems to enforce international legal obligations of States (Vazquez, 1992). In addition, NGOs operate as fact-finding bodies, lobbyists, and advocates in a way that generates publicity about violations of international law. These can be a most effective means of enforcing compliance with international law by States in an international legal system where other forms of enforcement are often lacking or rarely operate. NGOs can also have such a powerful effect on States that some States will act directly against them, even if this is in breach of international law. For example, the persistent activities of Greenpeace, an environmental NGO, against French nuclear testing in the South Pacific led to the French government ordering some of its agents to sink the Greenpeace ship 'Rainbow Warrior' in a New Zealand harbour. As a consequence of this breach of international law, France had to pay compensation to New Zealand for interference in its sovereignty (but not to Greenpeace) and sending its agents to a remote Pacific island.[36]

It is beyond doubt that NGOs have participated in the creation, development, and enforcement of international law. They have brought new ideas, sustained focus and pressure, and effective means of action in the international legal system (Rajagopal, 2003; Lindblom, 2005). They offer an alternative voice to States, though they share the problems of lack of legitimacy, few democratic processes, and the limited representativeness

---

[36] *Rainbow Warrior (France/New Zealand)* (1990) 20 *RIAA* 217; 82 ILR 499.

of many States (Cullen and Morrow, 2001). They provide a means to hold States and State-based organizations to account and they seek to increase the transparency of international decision-making (Charnovitz, 2006). The importance of their roles has been acknowledged in the European Convention on the Recognition of the Legal Personality of International NGOs 1991 and the UN Declaration on the Rights of Human Rights Defenders 1998. Much of NGOs' activity is only possible because States allow it to happen, such as participation in international fora, but not all of it is controlled by, or controllable by, States. As a consequence a 'peculiar process of interaction between traditional law mechanisms and transnational social processes with the mediation of non-State actors has become a novel method of law-making and law enforcement' (Bianchi, 1997, p 201). NGO participation may be a novel method of international law-making but it is now an accepted method.

As mentioned, NGO activity is part of the individual's role in civil society. Individuals can also act without the legal framework of an NGO. For example, the inspiration behind the creation of the ICRC came from one individual's activity in response to an armed conflict, and groups of individuals can prompt international action, such as the international condemnation of South Africa's apartheid system. In more recent years, the role of social media, especially in the formation of protests against the State, can have an effect on international legal responses, including humanitarian intervention, as occurred in north Africa in 2011 (Cottle, 2011 and see Zifcak, Ch 17 of this book).

D. JURISTS

The role of jurists, or individual writers on international law, has had a long-term effect on international law. Jurists have been given a special position in the creation, development, and enforcement of international law with Article 38(d) of the ICJ Statute authorizing the ICJ to apply 'the teachings of the most highly qualified publicists of the various nations as [a] subsidiary means for the determination of rules of [international] law'. Their influence can be specific, such as their influence on the inclusion of persecutions on the basis of gender being considered as crimes against humanity (Bianchi, 1997), the drafting of the Siracusa Principles on derogations and the Limburg Principles on economic, social, and cultural rights, and on decisions of international bodies. It can also be general, such as the role of individual jurists on the various Draft Articles of the International Law Commission. The roles of jurists as experts on international law, from membership of international bodies, such as the ICJ and international human rights bodies, to advising States and being members of expert panels in international organizations (from the World Health Organization to the Atomic Energy Agency), is also important.

From the earliest philosophers, the understanding of what is the nature of international law has been a crucial part of the development of rules and principles in the international legal system. Allott has shown how the ideas of Vattel 'determined the course of history' (Allott, 1989, p 14) as Vattel propounded a sovereignty theory of the State (in contrast to the more inclusive 'all humanity' idea that had been expounded earlier), which now forms the basis of much of the dominant view of international law.

Indeed, much of our understanding of what is the international legal system, and the role of individuals in it, is affected by the writings of jurists. For example, jurists who adopt a positivist approach to the international legal system, although generally considering that the individual has no independent role from that of the State, have been important in identifying rules of customary international law and persuading States that these rules legally bind them (Oppenheim, 1905). Yet it has been argued that the positivist concept of international law as a State-based process 'is incapable of serving as the normative framework for present or future political realities...new times call for a fresh conceptual and ethical language' (Tesón, 1992, pp 53–4). Some of the fresh conceptual and ethical language that has been suggested includes the application of feminist theory to the international legal system, which shows the limitations of the State as a framework for engagement in gender issues (Charlesworth, Chinkin, and Wright, 1991) and a recognition that relying on constant binary oppositions, such as State v non-State, cannot produce a coherent international legal system (Koskenniemi, 1989). Other jurists consider that 'the burgeoning canon of individual rights has begun to crack open the previously encrusted [positivist] Vatellian system' (Franck, 1999, p 281) and that 'we should adjust our intellectual framework to a multi-layered reality consisting of a variety of authoritative structures...[in which] what matters is not the formal status of a participant...but its actual or preferable exercise of functions' (Schreuer, 1993, p 453). Others reject the current conceptual parameters and argue for a new understanding of international society (Allott, 2001).

Each of these conceptual approaches seeks to explain the law-making processes of the international legal system and, in so doing, offers reflections on the role of the individual in that system. These approaches have occasionally been taken up by States and others in ways that have affected the development of international law (eg in ICJ decisions and UN resolutions). A specific example is found in the speech of the UN Secretary-General, Kofi Annan, on the award of the Nobel Peace Prize 2001 to him and to the UN:

> Over the past five years, I have often recalled that the United Nations' Charter begins with the words: 'We the peoples'. What is not always recognized is that 'We the peoples' are made up of individuals whose claims to the most fundamental rights have too often been sacrificed in the supposed interests of the State or the nation...In this new century, we must start from the understanding that peace belongs not only to States or peoples, but to each and every member of those communities. The sovereignty of States must no longer be used as a shield for gross violations of human rights. Peace must be made real and tangible in the daily existence of every individual in need. Peace must be sought, above all, because it is the condition for every member of the human family to live a life of dignity and security...Throughout my term as Secretary-General, I have sought to place human beings at the centre of everything we do—from conflict prevention to development to human rights. Securing real and lasting improvement in the lives of individual men and women is the measure of all we do at the United Nations. (Annan, 2001, pp 2–3)

Therefore, it can be seen that, in various ways, individuals have had, and continue to have, an important part in the creation, development, and enforcement of international law. This has been by groups of individuals, from peoples with the right of self-determination and indigenous peoples, to NGOs, as well as the influence of jurists. It can also be seen in the contribution of women and men throughout the centuries, who offer new ideas and practical applications in relation to international law.

V. CONCLUSIONS

The role of the individual in the international legal system remains a contentious one. The extent of this role can depend on how the nature of the system is conceptualized and applied, as well as an understanding of diverse areas of international law. In most cases the crucial issue is whether the individual has an independent role in the system or whether the individual's role is solely dependent on State consent.

In approaching these issues, a broad definition of the 'individual' has been adopted, with the understanding that 'participation' in the international legal system (as against the 'subject' v 'object' stricture) is the relevant context for considering the role of the individual. This has opened up more possibilities to discover the conceptual and practical role of the individual in the system. It has been shown that individuals do have considerable international rights and responsibilities in the system, a number of which are independent from a State's ability to control or determine them. The vast array of international claims available to individuals are largely still within the control of States in principle, but not in practice.

It is clear that the individual has been a crucial factor in the creation, development, and enforcement of international law. As the ICJ noted in its *Reparations for Injuries* Opinion (see Section I B of this chapter), the 'needs of the [international] community' and 'the requirements of international life' have ensured that the individual has a continuing role in the international legal system. In addition, individuals, by their actions, influence not only the concept and content of international law but also the way it is applied by States and the extent and manner by which a State consents to rules of international law (McCorquodale, 2004). Individuals can begin to contribute to the development of customary international law as their participation affects the practice of international law, including the possibility that an agreement between a State and an individual may be considered to be an international law agreement or a treaty. Indeed, 'the proposal that individuals ought to be included in the process of customary international law formation is both theoretically grounded and technically feasible' (Ochoa, 2007, p 169; Müller, 2008). Yet this conclusion is a challenge to much of the current dominant view as Judge Cançado Trindade, then President of the Inter-American Court of Human Rights, noted:

> The doctrinal trend which still insists in denying to individuals the condition of subjects of international law is…unsustainable [and] that conception appears contaminated by an ominous ideological dogmatism, which had as the main consequence to alienate the individual from the international legal order. It is surprising—if not astonishing—besides regrettable, to see that conception repeated mechanically and ad nauseam by a part of the doctrine, apparently trying to make believe that the intermediary of the State, between the individuals and the international legal order, would be something inevitable and permanent. Nothing could be more fallacious.[37]

Individuals may not yet be participating in the international legal system to the same extent as States or on an equal footing to them but the trend is clear: the role of the individual in this system is continuing to expand, often despite the wishes of States. Indeed, it might be argued that this participation of the individual in the international legal system, 'reflects a strength in the system's potential to respond flexibly to the needs of the international community' (Parlett, 2011, p 369). If, as Annan asserts, the ultimate foundation of the international legal system is 'We, the Peoples', then the role of each State is not to ensure and perpetuate its own power but to enable every individual to live a life of dignity and security and so to ensure human flourishing. The interests of individuals must count for more than the interests of States.

---

[37] *Juridical Status and Human Rights of the Child*, Advisory Opinion OC-17/02 Ser A, No 17 (28 August 2002), (2004) 11 IHRR 510, Concurring Opinion of Judge Cançado Trindade, at paras 26–7.

REFERENCES

ALFREDSSON, G and RING, R (2001), *The Inspection Panel of the World Bank* (The Hague: Martinius Nijhoff).

ALLOTT, P (1989), *International Law and International Revolution: Reconceiving the World* (Hull: Hull University Press).

——— (1992), 'Reconstituting Humanity— New International Law', 3 *EJIL* 219.

——— (2001), *Eunomia: New Order for a New World*, rev edn (Oxford: Oxford University Press).

ANAYA, J (2004), *Indigenous Peoples in International Law*, 2nd edn (Oxford: Oxford University Press).

ANDERSON, K (2000), 'The Ottawa Convention Banning Landmines, The Role of International Non-Governmental Organisations and the Idea of International Civil Society', 11 *EJIL* 91.

ANNAN, K (2001), 'We Can Love What We Are Without Hating What—and Who—We Are Not', Nobel Peace Prize Lecture, 10 December 2001, http://www.un.org/News/Press/docs/2001/sgsm8071.doc.htm.

BIANCHI, A (1997), 'Globalization of Human Rights: The Role of Non-State Actors', in Teubner, G (ed), *Global Law Without a State* (Aldershot: Dartmouth).

BOWMAN, M (1999), 'The Global Protection of Birds', 11 *Journal of International Environmental Law* 87.

BOYLE, A and CHINKIN, C (2007), *The Making of International Law* (Oxford: Oxford University Press).

BROWN, C and HOEKMAN, B (2005), 'WTO Dispute Settlement and the Missing Developing Country Case: Engaging the Private Sector', 8 *J Int'l Econ. L* 861.

BURCI, GL (2009), 'Public/Private Partnerships in the Public Health Sector', 6 *International Organization LR* 359.

BUTLER, I (2007), *Unravelling Sovereignty: Human Rights and the Structure of International Law* (Groningen: Intersentia).

CASSESE, A (1986), *International Law in a Divided World* (Oxford: Clarendon Press).

CHARLESWORTH, H and CHINKIN, C (2000), *The Boundaries of International Law: A Feminist Analysis* (Manchester: Manchester University Press).

———, ———, and WRIGHT, S (1991), 'Feminist Approaches to International Law', 85 *AJIL* 631.

CHARNOVITZ, S (2001), 'Economic and Social Actors in the World Trade Organization', 7 *ILSA J of International and Comparative Law* 259.

——— (2006), 'Non-Governmental Organizations and International Law', 100 *AJIL* 348.

CLAPHAM, A (1994), 'Creating the High Commissioner for Human Rights: The Outside Story', 5 *EJIL* 556.

——— (2010), 'The Role of the Individual in International Law', 21 *EJIL* 25.

COMMITTEE of MINISTERS (2001), Report of the Evaluation Group on the European Court of Human Rights, 22 *HRLJ* 308.

COTTLE, S (2011), 'Media and the Arab Uprisings of 2011', 12 *Journalism* 647.

CRAWFORD, J (ed) (1988), *The Rights of Peoples* (Oxford: Oxford University Press).

CROLEY, S and JACKSON, J (1996), 'WTO Dispute Procedures, Standard of Review and Deference to National Governments', 90 *AJIL* 193.

CULLEN, H and MORROW, K (2001), 'International Civil Society in International Law: The Growth of NGO Participation', 1 *Non-State Actors in International Law* 7.

DINE, J (2000), *The Governance of Corporate Groups* (Cambridge: Cambridge University Press).

DOUGLAS-SCOTT, S (2011), 'The European Union and Human Rights after the Treaty of Lisbon', 11 *Human Rights Law Review* 645.

FRANCK, T (1999), *The Empowered Self: Law and Society in the Age of Individualism* (Oxford: Oxford University Press).

GEUSS, R (2007), *History and Illusion in Politics* (Cambridge: Cambridge University Press).

HENCKAERTS, J-M (2007), 'Concurrent Application of International Human Rights Law and International Humanitarian Law', 1 *Human Rights and International Legal Discourse* 95.

HIGGINS, R (1979), 'Conceptual Thinking about the Individual in International Law', 11 *New York Law School Law Review* 11.

—— (1994), *Problems and Process: International Law and How We Use It* (Oxford: Oxford University Press).

HOHFELD, W (1913), 'Fundamental Legal Conceptions as Applied to Judicial Reasoning', 23 *Yale LJ* 16.

HUNT, S (2010), 'Human Rights Accountability of International Organisations vis-à-vis their Staff: The United Nations', in Wouters, J, Brems, E, Smis, S and Schmitt, P (eds), *Accountability for Human Rights Violations by International Organizations* (Anterp: Intersentia), p 545.

International Law Commission (2001), *Articles on Responsibility of States for Internationally Wrongful Acts*, 53rd Session, UN Doc A/CN.4/L.602/Rev.1, 26 July 2001, available at http://www.un.org/law/ilc.

JOSEPH, S (2010), 'Scope of Application', in Moeckli, D, Shah, S, Sivakumaran, S (eds) *International Human Rights Law* (Oxford: Oxford University Press), p 150.

KNOP, K (1993), 'Re-statements: Feminism and State Sovereignty in International Law', 3 *Transnational and Contemporary Legal Problems* 293.

—— (2002), *Diversity and Self-Determination in International Law* (Cambridge: Cambridge University Press).

KOSKENNIEMI, M (1989), *From Apology to Utopia: The Structure of International Legal Argument*, 2005 reissue (Cambridge: Cambridge University Press).

—— (1991), 'The Future of Statehood', 32 *Harvard ILJ* 397.

LÂM, MC (2000), *At the Edge of the State: Indigenous Peoples and Self-Determination* (Ardsley, NY: Transnational Publishers).

LAUTERPACHT, H (1950), *International Law and Human Rights* (London: Stevens).

LINDBLOM, A-K (2005), *Non-Governmental Organisations in International Law* (Cambridge: Cambridge University Press).

LINDSAY, R, McCORQUODALE, R, BLECHER, L, BONNITCHA, J, CROCKETT A, and SHEPPARD, A (2013), 'Human Rights Responsibilities in the Oil and Gas Sector: Applying the UN Guiding Principles', 6 *Journal of World Energy Law and Business* 1.

McCORQUODALE, R (1994), 'Self-Determination: A Human Rights Approach', 43 *ICLQ* 857.

—— (2002), 'Human Rights and Global Business', in Bottomley, S and Kinley, D (eds), *Commercial Law and Human Rights* (Aldershot: Ashgate).

—— (2004), 'An Inclusive International Legal System', 17 *Leiden JIL* 477.

—— (2013), 'Pluralism, Global Law and Human Rights: Strengthening Corporate Accountability for Human Rights Violations', 2 *Global Constitutionalism* 287.

McLACHLAN, C, SHORE, l, WEINIGER, M (2007), *International Investment Arbitration* (Oxford: Oxford University Press).

MARES, R (ed) (2012), *Siege or Cavalry Charge? The UN Mandate on Business and Human Rights* (The Hague: Martinus Nijhoff).

MERON, T (2006), *The Humanization of International Law* (Boston: Brill Academic).

MOTALA, A (2002), 'Non-Governmental Organisations in the African System', in Evans, M and Murray, R (eds), *The African Charter on Human and Peoples' Rights*,

1st edn (Cambridge: Cambridge University Press), p 246.

MUCHLINSKI, P (2007), *Multinational Enterprises and the Law*, 2nd edn (Oxford: Oxford University Press).

MÜLLER, T (2008), 'Customary Transnational Law: Attacking the Last Resort of State Sovereignty', 15 *Ind J of Global Legal Studies* 19.

NIJMAN, J (2004), *The Concept of International Legal Personality* (The Hague: TMC Asser Press).

OCHOA, C (2007), 'The Individual and Customary International Law Formation', 48 *Va J Int'l L* 119.

OPPENHEIM, L (1905), *International Law*, vol 1 (London: Longmans).

ORAKHELASHVILI, A (2001), 'The Position of the Individual in International Law', 31 *California Western ILJ* 241.

OTTO, D (1997), 'Rethinking Universals: Opening Transformative Possibilities in International Human Rights Law', 18 *Aust YBIL* 1.

——— (1999), 'A Post-Beijing Reflection on the Limitations and Potential of Human Rights Discourse for Women', in Askin, K and Koenig, D (eds), *Women and International Human Rights Law*, vol 1 (Ardsley, NY: Transnational Publishers).

PACE, W and THIEROFF, M (1999), 'Participation of Non-Governmental Organisations', in Lee, R (ed), *The International Criminal Court* (The Hague: Kluwer).

PARLETT, K (2011), *The Individual in the International Legal System* (Cambridge: Cambridge University Press).

PAUST, J (2011), 'Nonstate Actor Participation in International Law and the Pretence of Exclusion', 51 *Virginia JIL* 977.

PUVIMANASINGHE, S (2007), *Foreign Investment, Human Rights and the Environment* (Leiden: Brill Academic).

RAJAGOPAL, B (2003), *International Law from Below* (Cambridge: Cambridge University Press).

RATNER, S and ABRAMS, J (2009), *Accountability for Human Rights Attrocities in International Law*, 3rd edn (Oxford: Oxford University Press).

REDFERN, A, HUNTER, M, BLACKABY, N, and PARTASIDES, C (2009), *Law and Practice of International Commercial Arbitration*, 5th edn (Oxford: Oxford University Press).

REMEC, P (1960), *The Position of the Individual in International Law According to Grotius and Vattel* (The Hague: Martinus Nijhoff).

ROSSI, I (2010), *Legal Status of Non-Governmental Organizations in International Law* (Antwerp: Intersentia).

RYNGAERT, C and NOORTMANN, M (2010), 'New Actors in Global Governance and International Human Rights Law', 4 *Human Rights and International Legal Discourse* 5.

SAUL, B (2011), 'The Normative Status of Self-Determination in International Law: A Formula for Uncertainty in the Scope and Content of the Right?', 11 *Human Rights Law Review* 609.

SCELLE, G (1932), *Précis de droit des gens* (Paris: Recueil Sirey).

SCHABAS, W (2011), *Introduction to the International Criminal Court*, 4th edn (Cambridge: Cambridge University Press).

SCHREUER, C (1993), 'The Waning of the Sovereign State: Towards a New Paradigm for International Law', 4 *EJIL* 447.

SHELTON, D (2005), *Remedies in International Human Rights Law*, 2nd edn (Oxford: Oxford University Press).

STEINER, H and ALSTON, P (2000), *International Human Rights in Context*, 2nd edn (Oxford: Oxford University Press).

TESÓN, F (1992), 'The Kantian Theory of International Law', 92 *Col LR* 53.

TIETJE, C and NOWROT, K (2004), 'Forming the Centre of a Transnational Economic Legal Order? Thoughts on the Current and Future Position of Non-State Actors in WTO Law', 5 *European Business Organization LR* 321.

TORNARITIS, C (1972), *The Individual as a Subject of International Law* (Nicosia: Public Information Office).

United Nations (2011), Special Representative to the Secretary-General's Report to the United Nations Human Rights Council, *Guiding Principles on Business and Human Rights: Implementing the United Nations 'Protect, Respect and Remedy' Framework* (21 March 2011), A/HRC/17/L.17/Rev.1.

VAN BOVEN, T (1990), 'The Role of Non-Governmental Organizations in International Human Rights Standard-Setting: A Prerequisite for Democracy', 20 *California Western ILJ* 207.

VAZQUEZ, C (1992), 'Treaty-Based Rights and Remedies of Individuals', 92 *Col LR* 1082.

WILDE, R (2011), 'Self-Determination, Secession, and Dispute Settlement after the Kosovo Advisory Opinion', 24 *Leiden Journal of International Law* 149.

XANTHAKI, A (2009), 'Indigenous Rights in International Law over the Last 10 Years and Future Developments', 10 *Melbourne Journal of International Law* 27.

FURTHER READING

It is in the nature of the topic that the vast amount of relevant literature in this area is found in articles and book chapters many of which are referred to in the text and listed in the References section. The publications of particular note are:

ALSTON, P (2005), *Non-State Actors and Human Rights* (Oxford: Oxford University Press).

CANÇADO TRINDADE, A (2011), *The Access of Individuals to International Justice* (Oxford: Oxford University Press).

CLAPHAM, A (2006), *Human Rights Obligations of Non-State Actors* (Oxford: Oxford University Press).

DUPUY, P-M and VIERUCCI, L (2008), *NGOs in International Law* (Cheltenham, Edward Elgar).

McCORQUODALE, R (2011), *International Law Beyond the State* (London: CMP Publishing). NØRGAARD, C (1962), *The Position of the Individual in International Law* (Copenhagen: Munksgaard).

PARLETT, K (2011), *The Individual in the International Legal System* (Cambridge: Cambridge University Press).

PORTMANN, R (2010), *Legal Personality in International Law* (Cambridge: Cambridge University Press).

PART IV

THE SCOPE OF SOVEREIGNTY

11

JURISDICTION

Christopher Staker

SUMMARY[1]

Each State has the right to regulate its own public order, and to that end it is entitled to legislate for everyone within its territory. But States are also entitled to legislate for their nationals, and some actions extend over national boundaries; and there are accordingly situations in which two or more States may seek to apply their laws to the same conduct. This chapter is concerned with the principles of international law that regulate the right of States to apply their laws to conduct, and with the resolution of disputes arising from overlapping jurisdictional claims, and also with the problems of enforcing national laws.

I. INTRODUCTION

A. THE MEANING OF 'JURISDICTION'

'Jurisdiction' is the term that describes the limits of the legal competence of a State or other regulatory authority (such as the European Community) to make, apply, and enforce rules of conduct upon persons. It 'concerns essentially the extent of each state's right to regulate conduct or the consequences of events'.[2]

States regulate conduct in this sense in various ways, which may involve any of the branches of government. Thus, the Legislature may lay down rules by statute, or the Executive may do so by order. Laws on the provocation of religious hatred, and statutory instruments forbidding the export of certain goods to certain countries, are obvious examples. Some laws are less obviously prescriptive, but are nonetheless equally part of the structure of the social order: for example, laws regarding the qualifications for the acquisition of a State's nationality or determining the circumstances in which contractual obligations may be avoided, or describing the conditions upon which a person will be liable to pay taxes to the State. States also regulate conduct by means of the decisions of their courts, which may order litigating parties to do or abstain from doing certain things. So, too, may the State's administrative bodies, which may apply rules concerning, for example, the issuance of licences to export goods to certain countries. The police, and other law-enforcement agencies, are also involved, in the arrest and detention of persons,

---

[1] Professor Vaughan Lowe was the sole author of this chapter as it appeared in the first and second editions, and co-author of the third edition, of this book. The present chapter retains substantial amounts of the original text.

[2] *Oppenheim's International Law*, 1992, p 456.

and the seizure of goods. All of these activities are in principle regulated by the rules of international law concerning jurisdiction.

The term 'jurisdiction' is also commonly used in international law to describe the scope of the right of an international tribunal, such as the International Court of Justice or the International Criminal Court, to adjudicate upon cases and to make orders in respect of the parties to them. In abstract terms, the jurisdiction of States and the jurisdiction of tribunals are both instances of the concept of the scope of the powers of a legal institution; but it is traditional, and practically useful, to distinguish between them and to treat them separately. The jurisdiction of international tribunals is, accordingly, not treated in this chapter.

B. THE SIGNIFICANCE OF THE PRINCIPLES OF JURISDICTION

The legal rules and principles governing jurisdiction have a fundamental importance in international relations, because they are concerned with the allocation between States, and other entities such as the EU, of competence to regulate daily life—that is, the competence to secure the *differences* that make each State a distinct society. Inasmuch as they determine the reach of a State's laws, they may be said to determine what the boundaries of that State's particular public order are. For instance, the rejection by western States of the *fatwah* issued against Salman Rushdie was, in essence, a denial that the jurisdiction of the Iranian authorities extended so far as to regulate conduct in the UK.[3] There are many other examples of contested jurisdictional claims, perhaps less spectacular but affecting a much wider range of interests. For example, the USA has at various times enacted laws that purport to forbid foreign businesses, based outside the USA, to trade with certain States such as the former Soviet Union, Iran, and Cuba. Those laws have imposed significant economic costs and disadvantages on non-US companies; and they raise the question of the propriety—indeed, the legality—of one State purporting to forbid persons in another State to do things that are perfectly lawful in the State where those persons are located.

Similarly, as the principles governing jurisdiction define the limits of the State's coercive powers, they effect one of the most important delineations of the different societies into which the world is divided. It is these principles that dictate that the executive and judicial authorities of one State have no right to operate in the territory of another State without the latter's consent. It was thus necessary, for instance, for France and the UK to conclude an agreement allowing the customs and immigration officers of each to operate in the territory of the other in relation to the Channel Tunnel,[4] and for the Netherlands and the UK to conclude an agreement to permit the Scottish court to sit at Camp Zeist in the Netherlands to hear the cases against the Libyan nationals accused of blowing up a US aeroplane in the skies above Lockerbie in Scotland.[5]

In view of their significance, it is not surprising that the principles governing jurisdiction have attracted considerable attention from jurists over the years. In fact, however, international controversy over the limits of jurisdiction, which was intense in the four or five decades after 1945, seems to have abated somewhat during recent years.

---

[3] It appears that it was technically a religious authority, rather than what in western terms would be thought of as a typically 'governmental' authority, that issued the *fatwah*. This raises the interesting question of the limits of the notion of 'the State' for the purposes of State responsibility. On this question see Part V of this book and see *United States Diplomatic and Consular Staff in Tehran, Judgment, ICJ Reports 1980*, p 3.

[4] See the Sangatte Protocol, 25 November 1991, Cm 1802; 62 *BYIL* 623–5 (1991).

[5] See the Agreement concerning a Scottish Trial in the Netherlands, 18 September 1998, UKTS No 43 (1999); 117 ILR 664, 666, 673. See also Aust, 2000.

Before turning to the examination of those principles in more detail, it is necessary to say a word about the framework within which jurisdictional principles are analysed by international lawyers.

C. THE DOCTRINAL ANALYSIS OF JURISDICTION

Jurisdiction, as a topic of international law, has a less solid and universal basis than is often supposed. English-language monographs typically devote a chapter to the topic,[6] as they have done since the late nineteenth century:[7] continental monographs, on the other hand, have tended to adopt a rather different approach, regarding jurisdiction as an aspect of statehood or territory or the law of the sea or of some other aspect of international law. There is, on this continental approach, no comprehensive, consolidated statement of all of the principles of jurisdiction.[8] It is notable that there is, for example, no volume devoted to jurisdiction in Verzijl's great treatise, *International Law in Historical Perspective*. That pattern appears to be changing. In 1968 the Council of Europe produced a *Model Plan for the Classification of Documents concerning State Practice in the Field of Public International Law*,[9] which distributed the treatment of jurisdiction under a number of different headings, including 'Personal Jurisdiction', 'State Territory and Territorial Jurisdiction', and 'Seas, Waterways, Ships', in line with the continental approach. In 1997, that plan was revised,[10] and jurisdiction now has its own separate chapter in the Model Plan, divided up as follows:

Part Eight: Jurisdiction of the State

    I. *Bases of jurisdiction*
        A. Territorial principle
        B. Personal principle
        C. Protective principle
        D. Universality principle
        E. Other bases

    II. *Types of jurisdiction*
        A. Jurisdiction to prescribe
        B. Jurisdiction to adjudicate
        C. Jurisdiction to enforce

    III. *Extra-territorial exercise of jurisdiction*
        A. General
        B. Consular jurisdiction
        C. Jurisdiction over military personnel abroad
        D. Others (artificial islands, *terrae nullius*, etc)

    IV. *Limitations upon jurisdiction (servitudes, leases, etc)*

    V. *Concurrent jurisdiction*

---

[6] See, eg the texts by Oppenheim, 1992; Crawford, 2012; O'Connell, 1970.
[7] See, eg the texts by Twiss, 1884 and Hall, 1895.   [8] See, eg Verhoeven, 2000.
[9] Council of Europe Res (68) 17 (28 June 1968). This scheme is used to arrange the survey of United Kingdom Materials on International Law, in each year's *British Yearbook of International Law (BYIL)*.
[10] Council of Europe Res (97) 11 (12 June 1997).

While European doctrine thus seems to be moving towards the traditional 'English' approach, there are signs of a different development in the USA. The great *Digests* of US practice, edited by Marjorie Whiteman, Marian Nash and others, had until 1988 separate chapters on jurisdiction, in accordance with the traditional approach. The more recent volumes, published (after a gap in publication) from 2001 onwards, do not. These volumes distribute material on jurisdiction under headings such as 'taxation', and 'international criminal court'. The shift may appear insignificant; and it may prove to be so. It may, however, signal a change in attitude to the very nature of jurisdiction. Whereas in the past jurisdiction was seen, both in the 'English' and the continental views, as a matter of the reach of the authority of a State, this development in US doctrine appears to treat jurisdiction as an aspect of the substantive topic that is regulated. If this trend persists the principles of jurisdiction may fragment, so that States may assert a more extensive jurisdiction over, say, tax matters and 'terrorist' offences than they do over unlawful arms sales and other crimes. Should that happen, and should the assertions of jurisdiction be recognized in international law, the near-inevitable result is that jurisdictional claims will steadily expand, and that the States most interested in regulating particular areas of conduct will increasingly apply their laws to activities outside their own borders and within the borders of other States—much in the manner of the Rushdie *fatwah*. For purposes of this chapter, however, the approach of the Council of Europe scheme will be adopted.

1. Types of jurisdiction

The first section of the Council of Europe Model Plan, 'Bases of jurisdiction', is concerned with the ambit of a State's laws: that is, with its jurisdiction to prescribe rules, or its 'legislative' or 'prescriptive' jurisdiction, as it is sometimes called. The second section, 'Types of jurisdiction', somewhat illogically steps up to a higher level of abstraction and distinguishes between, on the one hand, the jurisdiction to prescribe rules and, on the other hand, the jurisdiction to enforce them, or 'enforcement jurisdiction' as it is commonly known. Thus, the UK may enact a law forbidding, say, murder and make that law applicable to all British citizens wherever in the world they might be. That would fall within the UK's prescriptive jurisdiction, in accordance with what is called the 'nationality' or 'personal' principle (Section I B in the Council of Europe scheme). But if a British citizen were to commit murder in, say, Argentina, the UK authorities would have no right to enter Argentina and arrest the murderer; and if they did so they would violate Argentinean sovereignty.[11] The UK's enforcement jurisdiction, like that of every other State, is in principle limited to its own territory. That is why States need to seek the extradition of persons accused of committing crimes within their jurisdiction, in circumstances where the accused is living in another State.

There is another 'Type of jurisdiction' identified in the Council of Europe scheme, and in similar frameworks adopted elsewhere:[12] that is the 'jurisdiction to adjudicate', or 'adjudicative jurisdiction' or 'curial jurisdiction'. This refers to the right of courts to receive, try, and determine cases referred to them. However, problems arising where the courts of more than one State are seized of the same subject-matter (for instance where two disputing parties each commence proceedings against the other in different States in respect of the same dispute) are usually considered within the realm of private international law.

---

[11] For an example of such a violation see *Attorney-General of the Government of Israel* v *Adolf Eichmann* (1961), 36 ILR 5.

[12] See, eg the American Law Institute's *Restatement of the Law: the Foreign Relations Law of the United States*, 3rd edn, 1987; Akehurst, 1972–3, pp 145–217.

Insofar as parties choose to submit to the jurisdiction of a national court, there can be no cause for complaint unless one or more of the parties is subject to an order made under the law of another State, obliging them not to submit to the foreign court. If such an antisuit order is made, there is a clash of prescriptive jurisdictions, as there is if two or more courts hear the same case and issue conflicting orders.[13] For purposes of public international law, all of this can largely be analysed in terms of prescriptive and enforcement jurisdiction. A separate category of 'jurisdiction to adjudicate' is therefore not considered in this chapter.

2. Other jurisdictional issues

The third category in the Council of Europe scheme, 'Extra-territorial exercise of jurisdiction', is concerned with the exceptional circumstances in which a State is entitled to exercise its enforcement jurisdiction (and with it, by necessary implication its legislative jurisdiction) in the territory of another State. A common example in NATO States is the network of arrangements under which troops of one NATO State are stationed in another, but subject to the control of their home State authorities, so that, for instance, US military police will have the right to arrest and imprison members of US forces on military bases in the UK.

The fourth and fifth of the Council of Europe 'Types' are of a rather different kind. The 'Limitations upon jurisdiction' instanced by servitudes and leases are limitations that arise when a particular piece of territory is 'leased' to another State (as part of Hong Kong was leased by China to the UK from 1898 to 1997, as the Panama Canal Zone was leased by Panama to the USA from 1903 to 1977, and as Guantánamo Bay has since 1903 been, and still is, leased by Cuba to the USA), and under the terms of the lease the territorial sovereign permits the lessee to exercise exclusive jurisdiction over the area. This is not so much a 'type' of jurisdiction as a particular consequence of the temporary transfer or alienation of rights of sovereignty over areas of State territory, and it will not be further discussed here.[14] The final category, 'Concurrent jurisdiction', concerns the issues that arise when two or more States are entitled to exercise legislative (or, rarely, enforcement) jurisdiction in relation to the same factual circumstances.

II. PRESCRIPTIVE JURISDICTION

To whom may a State extend its laws? Whom may the State order to do this, or not to do that? Or, to ask a question of a slightly different kind, who may be deemed by a State to be, say, a citizen, or 'married', or 'an infant'; or how far may a State rule that a particular ceremony counts as a valid wedding, or divorce; what, in other words, are the limits of the right of a State to impose legal characterizations upon persons or events? These are all questions about the reach, the ambit or scope, of a State's laws; that is, about the limits of its prescriptive or legislative jurisdiction.

Before turning to the principles that explain the bases upon which States are entitled to exercise prescriptive jurisdiction, it is necessary to refer to a tiresome and oddly persistent fallacy that arose from an early case in the Permanent Court of International Justice (PCIJ). The case concerned a collision on the high seas (ie that part of the sea that is

---

[13] See 'The Principles for Determining When the Use of the Doctrine of *forum non conveniens* and Anti-suit Injunctions is Appropriate', Institut de Droit International, *Annuaire*, vol 70–I (2002–2003), p 14.

[14] See further Craven, Ch 8 in this book.

beyond the territorial jurisdiction of every State), between the French steamer, the *Lotus*, and the Turkish steamer, the *Boz-Kourt*, which resulted in eight deaths. When the *Lotus* entered Constantinople, the Turkish authorities prosecuted M Demons, the officer of the watch on the *Lotus*. Proceedings were also instituted against the captain of the Turkish ship. France objected to the proceedings against M Demons on the ground that no State is entitled to extend its law to foreign ships on the high seas, and that Turkey, accordingly, was not entitled to prosecute M Demons. The PCIJ held that Turkey was entitled to prosecute. The passage in question is so often quoted, and so much misunderstood, that it is worthwhile reproducing it here. The Court said:[15]

> the first and foremost restriction imposed by international law upon a State is that—failing the existence of a permissive rule to the contrary—it may not exercise its power in any form in the territory of another State. In this sense jurisdiction is certainly territorial; it cannot be exercised by a State outside its territory except by virtue of a permissive rule derived from international custom or from a convention.

That proposition is not controversial. It asserts that a State's *enforcement* jurisdiction is in principle confined to the State's territory (a point considered further in this chapter in Section III). In the *Lotus* case, this was not an issue. Turkish authorities had not gone out on to the high seas to arrest M Demons: they had waited until the *Lotus* entered a Turkish port and so came within Turkish territory and thus within Turkish enforcement jurisdiction. The question was whether having arrested M Demons in Turkey he, as a French citizen, could then be prosecuted by the Turkish authorities for his acts outside Turkish territory, on the high seas. The Court continued, addressing itself to this question, as follows:[16]

> It does not, however, follow that international law prohibits a State from exercising jurisdiction in its own territory, in respect of any case which relates to acts which have taken place abroad, and in which it cannot rely on some permissive rule of international law. Such a view would only be tenable if international law contained a general prohibition to States to extend the application of their laws and the jurisdiction of their courts to persons, property and acts outside their territory, and if, as an exception to this general prohibition, it allowed States to do so in certain specific cases. But this is certainly not the case under international law as it stands at present. Far from laying down a general prohibition to the effect that States may not extend the application of their laws and the jurisdiction of their courts to persons, property and acts outside their territory, it leaves them in this respect a wide measure of discretion which is only limited in certain cases by prohibitive rules...

That passage has been read as indicating that a State may extend the reach of its prescriptive jurisdiction as it chooses, except in circumstances where it can be shown that some rule of international law specifically prohibits it from doing so. A moment's thought will indicate that it is extremely improbable that this is what the Court meant to say. Suppose, for example, that Zimbabwe were to enact a law that made it an offence for anyone, of whatever nationality and wherever in the world they might be, to make a complaint to a UN body alleging that any State had violated its international human rights obligations; and suppose that a British citizen, on holiday in Zimbabwe, was arrested and charged with breaking that law by writing to the UN Human Rights Committee from his home in

---

[15] 'Lotus', Judgment No 9, 1927, PCIJ, Ser A, No 10, pp 18–19.   [16] Ibid, p 19.

Birmingham with a complaint that, say, Iraq had violated its obligations.[17] Could it really be supposed that the onus would be upon the UK to prove that some prohibitive rule of international law forbade such exercises of legislative jurisdiction by Zimbabwe?

There are many reasons for thinking that international law does not impose the burden of proof upon those objecting to egregious assertions of jurisdiction over foreigners outside the territory of the legislating State. Two are of particular relevance here. First, in more than a century of objections to exercises of extraterritorial jurisdiction, from the *Cutting* case[18] onwards, there seems to be not a single instance of an objecting State either seeking to prove that there existed a prohibitive rule forbidding the contested exercise of extraterritorial jurisdiction, or indicating that it might consider itself to be under any legal obligation to do so. When States object to exercises of jurisdiction, they simply assert that the other State has 'no right' to exercise jurisdiction in the way that it claims. State practice is consistently based upon the premise that it is for the State asserting some novel extraterritorial jurisdiction to prove that it is entitled to do so. Secondly, the argument in favour of the alleged presumption of freedom is fallacious. In the *Lotus* case the Court argued that:

> International law governs relations between independent States. The rules of law binding upon States therefore emanate from their own free will as expressed in conventions or by usages generally accepted as expressing principles of law and established in order to regulate the relations between these co-existing independent communities or with a view to the achievement of common aims. Restrictions upon the independence of States cannot therefore be presumed.[19]

Even if the characterization of international law as fundamentally consensual is accepted, it does not follow that a sovereign State is free to do what it wishes. The sovereign equality of States is equally a fundamental principle of international law. Claims by one State to prescribe rules for persons in another State encroach upon the right of the State where those persons are based to exercise jurisdiction itself over those persons within its territory.

There are two States—two 'co-existing independent communities'—involved, and there plainly can be no presumption that the one asserting extraterritorial jurisdiction is entitled to prevail in the event of a conflict, and to impose its laws on persons within the territory of another State.

The best view is that it is necessary for there to be some clear connecting factor, of a kind whose use is approved by international law, between the legislating State and the conduct that it seeks to regulate. This notion of the need for a linking point, which has been adopted by some prominent jurists,[20] accords closely with the actual practice of States. If there exists such a linking point, one may presume that the State is entitled to legislate; if there does not, the State must show why it is entitled to legislate for anyone other than persons in its territory and for its nationals abroad (who are covered by the territorial and the national principles respectively).

There are two of these linking points, or 'Bases of Jurisdiction', or 'principles of jurisdiction' (the terms mean the same thing) that are firmly established in international law: territoriality, and nationality.

---

[17] An extreme example: Zimbabwe has not, as far as I know, enacted any such law. The USA, however, has enacted a law in somewhat similar terms: see below, n 43.

[18] *Foreign Relations of the United States*, 1887, p 751; idem, 1888, II, pp 1114, 1180.

[19] 'Lotus', *Judgment No 9, 1927, PCIJ, Ser A, No 10*, p 18.

[20] See the discussion in *Attorney-General of the Government of Israel* v *Adolf Eichmann* (1961), 36 ILR 5.

A. THE TERRITORIAL PRINCIPLE

The territorial principle is a corollary of the sovereignty of a State over its territory. That sovereignty entails the right of the State to prescribe the laws that set the boundaries of the public order of the State. It is taken for granted that foreign visitors to a State are bound by the State's criminal law in the same way as everyone else in the State. It may be less obvious, but it is no less true, that States may impose the entirety of their laws—economic, social, cultural, or whatever—upon everyone within their territories. In practice, States generally exercise this power with moderation. While the basic principle is that everyone within the territory is equally obliged to obey the law, those laws may be drafted so as to exempt people who are merely visiting the State from certain obligations, such as obligations to pay income tax or to perform compulsory military service (and equally, so as to exclude them from certain rights, such as the right to vote, or to social security payments). Exactly how and where these lines are drawn is a matter for each State to decide, subject to its treaty commitments and its duty to respect basic human rights.

The 'territory' of the State includes not only its land territory but also both its territorial sea, which extends up to 12 n. miles from its coast, and the airspace above its land and sea territory. States may thus legislate for ships off their coasts, and for aircraft in their skies. It was the latter right that entitled the UK to prosecute the Libyan nationals accused of blowing up a US aircraft in the skies above Lockerbie, Scotland, in 1988. Again, in practice States usually leave the prescription of rules applicable on board ships or aircraft to the State of registry of the craft,[21] asserting jurisdiction only in exceptional cases. The routine application of the customs and excise laws of the territorial State is a common exception to this pattern, which is one reason why duty-free sales cease shortly before the craft arrives at its destination. States enjoy 'plenary' jurisdiction over their territory. That is to say, subject to their duties under human rights laws and similar constraints, they may legislate as they please, on any matter whatsoever. At sea, States enjoy an additional but functionally limited jurisdiction.

Beyond the 12 n. mile territorial sea they may claim a 12 n. mile contiguous zone, in which they can exercise jurisdiction in relation to customs, fiscal, sanitary, and immigration matters, and also in order to safeguard submarine archaeological sites. Subject to certain limitations, they may also assert jurisdiction over the exploration for and exploitation of living and non-living resources (such as fish and oil) and energy, over the establishment of artificial islands and structures, and over pollution and scientific research, in an Exclusive Economic Zone (EEZ) that extends up to 200 n. miles from the coast. And they may assert full civil and criminal jurisdiction over installations, such as oil rigs, set up on their continental shelves or in their EEZs in order to exploit seabed resources. These zones that lie beyond the territorial sea are not part of the territory of the State; but the coastal State is permitted to exercise limited jurisdiction in them, in contrast to the position on the high seas (and in outer space) where, in principle, craft and those on board them are subject to the jurisdiction only of the State of registry (the 'flag' State).[22]

Most acts, most bank robberies, weddings, and daily struggles to earn a living, take place squarely within the territory of a single State. The territorial principle is entirely adequate to sustain jurisdiction over such acts. Indeed, in the domestic law of many States

---

[21] See, for example, the handling of the problem of drunks on aircraft: 74 *BYIL* 681 (2003).

[22] See the UN Convention on the Law of the Sea, 1982, Articles 2, 33, 56, 60, 92, 303. For the case of ships having no nationality, see for instance *United States* v *Bravo*, 480 F.3d 88 (2007). Developments have been anticipated in relation to jurisdiction over activities in outer space with the emergence of private travel in that realm. See Hobe, 2007; Blount, 2007.

there is a presumption that the State's laws, in particular its statutes, apply throughout the State's territory but not outside that territory, unless there is clear indication that the law is intended to apply outside the territory. Some acts, however, straddle more than one jurisdiction. The Lockerbie bomb is said to have been loaded aboard the aircraft in Malta, before it entered the UK; the September 11th attacks are said to have been planned and prepared by people in a number of different countries. Which State has jurisdiction? One solution would be to allow each State to exercise jurisdiction over the particular fragment of the greater scheme that was located within its territory: one State might prosecute the offence of loading a bomb on board an aircraft, another the offence of causing an explosion on board an aircraft, another, murder, and so on. Whatever theoretical tidiness might be preserved by such an approach, it has no practical merits to commend it. It is more efficient if the investigation and prosecution of an offence is concentrated largely in the hands of a single State. That is what States in fact do. Territorial jurisdiction has spawned two variants to cope with such situations. They are commonly known as subjective territorial jurisdiction and objective territorial jurisdiction.

1. Subjective territorial jurisdiction

'Subjective territorial jurisdiction' is the name given to the exercise of prescriptive jurisdiction by a State in circumstances where it applies its law to an incident which is initiated within its territory but completed outside its territory. The prosecution for murder of bombers by the State in which they put the bomb on board an aircraft, even though the bomb exploded in the airspace of another State, is an example.

2. Objective territorial jurisdiction

'Objective territorial jurisdiction' is the name given to the exercise of prescriptive jurisdiction by a State in circumstances where it applies its law to an incident that is completed within its territory, even though it was initiated outside its territory. The prosecution for murder of bombers by the State in whose airspace a bomb on board an aircraft exploded, even though the bomb had been loaded onto the aircraft in another State, is an example. The *Lotus* case is another example. Ships (and aircraft) are treated for jurisdictional purposes much as if they are pieces of floating territory of the State of registration, although they are, in law, quite clearly not parts of the State's territory. The act of the *Lotus* in colliding with the Turkish ship was, therefore, an act completed within Turkish territorial jurisdiction—literally, within the Turkish ship—and accordingly liable to be prosecuted by the Turkish authorities.

Both subjective and objective territorial jurisdiction are routinely asserted by States, in order to secure the application of their laws to all elements of offences that they wish to prosecute. In English law, examples include *DPP* v *Doot*,[23] *DPP* v *Stonehouse*,[24] and *Liangsiriprasert* v *Government of the United States of America*.[25]

3. The 'effects' doctrine

Exercises of subjective territorial jurisdiction have not proved problematic; but the same cannot be said for exercises of objective territorial jurisdiction. There is little difficulty with cases where distinct physical elements of the overall crime take place within the jurisdiction of different States. But some States, notably the USA, have sought to extend

---

[23] *DPP* v *Doot* [1973] AC 807; [1973] 1 All ER 940 (HL).
[24] *DPP* v *Stonehouse* [1978] AC 55; [1977] 2 All ER 909 (HL).
[25] *Liangsiriprasert* v *Government of the United States of America* [1991] 1 AC 225; [1990] 2 All ER 866 (PC).

the concept much further. The clearest example of this is the so-called 'effects' doctrine, developed first in the context of US antitrust law. In the *Alcoa* case, *US v Aluminium Co of America*,[26] the USA asserted jurisdiction over the conduct of a non-US company that was a member of a cartel whose activities were intended to affect imports to or exports from the USA, and actually did so. The significance of the decision was that it did not depend upon the commission of physical acts within US territory: the intentional production of economic 'effects' within the USA was sufficient.

This idea reached what is perhaps its fullest expression in the *Uranium Antitrust* litigation, which surfaced in the English courts in *Rio Tinto Zinc Corp v Westinghouse Electric Corp*.[27] There, uranium producers in a number of States, including the UK, formed, with the knowledge or encouragement of their national governments, a cartel, primarily in order to maintain the world market price of uranium. This was in response to a protectionist US law that had effectively shut them out of the US market, which amounted to more than two-thirds of the world market. Meanwhile, Westinghouse, a US company, had contracted to sell uranium to a public utility in the USA, at a price set some years earlier, but needed to buy the uranium on the world market. The cartel's success in maintaining the market price of uranium was such that Westinghouse could not afford to fulfil the contract. Westinghouse was sued for $2bn; and it in turn sued some members of the cartel for $6bn, under a provision of US antitrust law that allows those injured by cartels to recover treble damages. Here, US law was to be applied to non-US companies, in respect of their acts outside the USA, at a time when they were forbidden by US law to trade in the USA. The only jurisdictional link was the 'effect' of the cartel upon the USA: there was no intraterritorial conduct in the USA at all. It is the reliance upon economic repercussions within the territory, rather than upon some element of intraterritorial conduct, that distinguishes the 'effects' doctrine in its pure form from objective territorial jurisdiction, which does require some intraterritorial conduct. The assertion of extraterritorial jurisdiction by the USA in this case was met with strong protests from many other States.

It is sometimes said that other States also assert jurisdiction on the basis of the 'effects' doctrine. There is some truth in this. States such as France and Germany, and the EC in cases such as *Woodpulp*,[28] have adopted laws or decisions that appear to involve such an assertion; but on a closer inspection it is clear that such laws are usually applied only in circumstances where there is some element of intraterritorial conduct. In cases where environmental pollution in one State causes physical damage in the territory of another, the jurisdiction of the latter in respect of the matter may be analysed in terms of objective territorial jurisdiction, rather than the 'effects' doctrine.[29]

B. THE NATIONAL PRINCIPLE

States have an undisputed right to extend the application of their laws to their citizens (that is, those who have the nationality of the State), wherever they may be. This type of jurisdiction has a longer history than jurisdiction based upon the territorial principle. Rulers asserted jurisdiction over those who owed allegiance to them even before the rulers' control over their land territory was consolidated to the point where they could be said

---

[26] *United States v Aluminium Co of America*, 148 F.2d 416 (1945).

[27] *Rio Tinto Zinc Corp v Westinghouse Electric Corp* [1978] 1 All ER 434 (HL); and see Lowe, 1983.

[28] *Ahlström Osakeyhtiö v Commission*, Cases 89/85 [1988] ECR 5193. In relation to India, see Chaudhry and Mahajan, 2011; Jain, 2012.

[29] Cf Ellis, 2012.

to assert territorial jurisdiction. Nonetheless, the advent of the European territorial State as the paradigmatic unit of the international legal order has long since given territorial jurisdiction pre-eminence. Jurisdiction based on nationality is used relatively infrequently.

States are in principle left free to decide who are their nationals, and to lay down the conditions for the grant of nationality in their own laws. One common basis for this has been to accord nationality to anyone born in the territory; except, perhaps, in cases where the mother's presence is merely transient—for example, as a passenger on a ship or aircraft transiting the State's territory. This basis of nationality is sometimes known as the *jus soli*. Another common basis is to accord nationality to children one or both of whose parents are themselves nationals of the State. This is sometimes known as the *jus sanguinis*. The nationality law of a State may apply a combination of variations of both of these principles.[30] States also commonly provide for the conferral of nationality by naturalization, the process in which those who fill whatever residential and other requirements the State may lay down apply to become nationals of the State. States typically also provide for the circumstances in which nationality is lost. For instance, a State's nationality legislation may provide that a person will cease to be a national of that State if they apply for and are granted the nationality of another State, and may provide for the possibility of voluntary renunciation of nationality. It is not uncommon for people to have two nationalities, one derived from the nationality of their parents, the other from the place where they were born, or one nationality that they acquired at birth and another that they subsequently obtained by naturalization. Such people are known as 'dual nationals'. Some people may have three, or even more, nationalities.

The nationality of companies is also a matter for each State to determine under its own laws; but here the practice is more complex. As the International Court noted in the *Barcelona Traction* case,[31] there is a divergence in State practice. Broadly speaking, there is a tendency for common law States to accord nationality to companies on the basis of their incorporation in the territory of the State, regardless of where the actual business or management of the company is carried out. In contrast, at least some civil law States confer their nationality not on the basis of the place of incorporation but rather on the basis of the place where the company has the seat of its management. As companies may be formally incorporated in one State for tax reasons, but maintain their actual business or management elsewhere, this is a significant point. In contrast to individuals it seems that companies cannot change their nationality, for example by naturalization. They can only achieve a comparable result, by dissolving the company and transferring all of its assets and responsibilities to a new company in another State. This is, however, more a matter of corporate succession than of a change of nationality.

The freedom of States to fix the conditions for the grant of nationality extends also to ships and aircraft. The same is true of comparable structures, such as offshore oil rigs (which appear to be regarded as having the nationality of the State of registry while they are in transit, even though they fall under the jurisdiction of the coastal State while they are actually operating on the continental shelf). Typical conditions might include a requirement that the vessel operates from a home port in the State, or has a certain proportion of the owners, or perhaps of the crew, having the nationality of the State. In this respect, many States tend to be more restrictive in granting nationality to ships and aircraft than they are in granting nationality to companies.

---

[30] See, for instance, the British Nationality Act 1981, s 1 (acquisition by birth or adoption), s 2 (acquisition by descent).

[31] *Barcelona Traction, Light and Power Company, Limited, Second Phase, Judgment, ICJ Reports 1970*, p 3.

This freedom to determine nationality is not absolute. The existence of limitations upon the international effectiveness of grants of nationality was discussed by the International Court in the *Nottebohm* case,[32] which is sometimes supposed to be authority for the proposition that a genuine and close link between the individual and the national State is necessary if nationality is to be effective: ie if other States are to be obliged to accept it as an adequate basis for the State to treat the individual as its national. The Court did not say that. It did hold that nationality should, in principle, be the juridical expression of a close factual link between the individual and the national State. But the Court was not concerned with the effectiveness of nationality in general, but only with the much narrower issue of its effectiveness as the basis for diplomatic protection. The Court was not even concerned with the general question of the right of a national State to exercise diplomatic protection. The Court limited itself to the particular question whether a State with which a naturalized citizen has no real links can exercise diplomatic protection on behalf of the citizen against another State with which the citizen, while not a national of that State (Nottebohm was not a dual national), does have close and real links. The decision was, accordingly, of no relevance whatever to the question of the efficacy of nationality for jurisdictional purposes. Indeed, as Nottebohm had himself chosen to become a naturalized citizen of a State, Liechtenstein, with which he had no real links, it is difficult to see any ground on which Liechtenstein could be denied the right to impose its laws upon Nottebohm in accordance with the nationality principle.

One may also note that on the one occasion, post-*Nottebohm*, when the International Court was invited to rule that grants of nationality not underpinned by some close factual connection with the putative national State were ineffective, it did not do so, but instead reaffirmed that it is for each State to fix the conditions for the grant of its nationality.[33] There are, no doubt, limits to this freedom. The mass imposition of nationality upon unwilling people, or nationality obtained by fraud or corruption, or a nationality acquired for vessels in order to circumvent legal regulations based upon the nationality of ships, for example, might in certain circumstances be held not to be effective. For practical purposes, however, States remain free to decide who are their nationals. (It should also be noted that it is arguable that the exercise of legislative jurisdiction based upon nationality is not a matter for international law at all. The way that a State treats its nationals is—questions of human rights apart—in general not a matter for international law. If a State were to legislate for persons who were indisputably its nationals, who could complain?)

In practice, States now rarely exercise legislative jurisdiction specifically on the basis of nationality.[34] They tend to do so in order to prohibit serious offences which not only disturb the peace of the place where they are committed, but also signal a characteristic of the offender in which the national State has an interest. For example, a State would plainly have an interest in forbidding its nationals to engage in bribery of officials of other countries while abroad, or to commit sexual crimes abroad.[35] A State might also for instance decide to tax its citizens resident abroad on their income earned abroad.[36]

There is an increasing tendency for States to extend the extraterritorial application of their laws not only to nationals but to residents, in order to make the repression of serious crimes more effective. The UK's Crime (International Co-operation) Act 2003

---

[32] *Nottebohm, Second Phase, Judgment, ICJ Reports 1955*, p 4.

[33] See the *Constitution of the Maritime Safety Committee of the Inter-Governmental Maritime Consultative Organization, Advisory Opinion, ICJ Reports 1969*, p 150.

[34] But see, for instance, *United States v Clark*, 435 F.3d 1100 (2006). For an argument that nationality jurisdiction should be used more frequently see Arnell, 2001.

[35] See the examples in n 38 in this chapter.   [36] The USA adopts this approach.

introduced such provisions into ss 63B and 63C of the Terrorism Act 2000.[37] States may also apply their own laws (including human rights law) to extraterritorial acts of their own governmental authorities, or persons contracted by or under the authority of their own governmental authorities.[38]

C. THE PROTECTIVE PRINCIPLE

It has long been recognized that when essential interests of the State are at stake States need to, and will, act in order to preserve themselves. Accordingly, when vital issues are threatened, even if by non-nationals acting outside the territory of the State, the State's interests are engaged and it may exercise its legislative jurisdiction over them.[39] The counterfeiting of a State's currency is a typical example, as is an extraterritorial conspiracy to evade the State's immigration laws.

The category of vital interests is not closed. The USA has asserted jurisdiction over foreigners on the high seas on the basis of the protective principle, in cases such as *US v Gonzalez*,[40] and in statutes such as the 1986 Maritime Drug Law Enforcement Act (see Murphy, 2003).[41] It argues that the illegal trade in narcotics constitutes so severe a threat to US society that the protective principle allows this extension of its jurisdiction. Other States have acquiesced in this US move; but they have tended not to follow it but rather to extend their jurisdiction by means of treaty arrangements concerning the suppression of unlawful drug trafficking.

The rationale of the protective principle is clearly linked to the protection of vital State interests. Accordingly, while the category is not closed, the potential for its expansion is limited. Whereas States could, in principle, apply any law that they might choose to their nationals, by no means every law could be given extraterritorial scope under the protective principle. That is why offences against, for example, a State's competition laws are not prosecuted on the basis of this principle but are instead explained as applications of the territorial principle or the 'effects' doctrine. That said, the overblown rhetoric with which governments from time to time describe their attempts to combat various 'threats' to the State, or to civilized values or to the world order or whatever, must take their toll. The pressure to expand the use of this principle, and the danger of unshackling it from the protection of truly *vital* interests and of permitting its use for the convenient advancement of important interests, is clear.

[37] See for instance the UK's Bribery Act 2010, extending the criminal provisions of that Act to persons having a 'close connection' with the UK, defined as persons with different types of British nationality, British subjects, British protected persons, UK residents, bodies incorporated in the UK and Scottish partnerships. A similar example is the US Foreign Corrupt Practices Act §78dd-2, applying the Act extraterritorially to US 'domestic concerns', defined to include US citizens, residents and corporations. See also the UK Sexual Offences Act 2003, ss 9, 72, which have application in relation to UK residents as well as UK citizens. See also Ratner, 2003. Cf Arnell, 2001 at p 984. See also, for instance, *XYZ v The Commonwealth* [2006] HCA 25 (High Court of Australia).

[38] See for instance *Al-Skeini and Others v the United Kingdom* [GC], no 55721/07, ECHR 2011; (2011) 53 EHRR 18 ; *Al-Jedda v the United Kingdom* [GC], no. 27021/08, ECHR 2011; 53 *EHRR* 23; *Smith v Ministry* of Defence [2013] UKSC 41; [2013] 3 WLR 69; cf *R v Hape* 2007 SCC 26, [2008] 1 LRC 551, 143 ILR 140; *Munaf v Geren* 553 US (2008); *United States v Passaro*, 577 F.3d 207 (2009); *R (Smith) v Oxfordshire Assistant Deputy Coroner* [2010] UKSC 29, [2011] AC 1. See also Ryngaert, 2008.

[39] See for instance German Criminal Code, Section 5.   [40] *US v Gonzalez* 776 F.2d 931 (1985).

[41] See also for instance *US v Reumayr*, 530 F.Supp 2d 1210 (2008), at 1221–2 and the cases there cited; *US v Yousef*, 327 F.3d 56 (2003) at 110–11.

D. THE UNIVERSAL PRINCIPLE

Some crimes are regarded as so heinous that every State has a legitimate interest in their repression. That is the traditional explanation of universal jurisdiction.[42] But given that the first, and one of the most firmly established, of the instances of crimes covered by the universal principle is piracy, one may wonder if the traditional explanation is entirely satisfactory.

It is probably more accurate to say that there are two strands running together to make up the universal principle. One is the strand that is indeed made up of heinous crimes, such as genocide, crimes against humanity, and serious war crimes,[43] all of which are subject to universal jurisdiction.[44] The second is crimes that are serious, and which might otherwise go unpunished. Piracy—which means simply an unauthorized act of violence or depredation committed by a private vessel on the high seas against another vessel, for private ends—may involve relatively minor uses of force; and not every act of piracy can properly be described as heinous. Yet for centuries, piracy was covered by universal jurisdiction, but murder, armed robbery, rape, and arson on land, which could surely be equally heinous, were (and are) not. The justification for universal jurisdiction over pirates is not so much that piracy is inherently heinous, and on a par with genocide and war crimes, as the fact that because pirates operate on the high seas it is very easy for them to evade the jurisdiction of any State that might have jurisdiction over them on some other basis (for example, the flag State of their ship, or their national State), unless any State that happens to have them within its jurisdiction is entitled to try them.[45]

This point is not trivial. One might argue that the principle could be extended to justify assertions of jurisdiction over others who commit serious crimes in places beyond the territorial jurisdiction of the State. Crimes committed in Antarctica would be one example (which the USA has in fact addressed by making certain acts, such as murder, committed by or against US nationals in Antarctica, subject to US jurisdiction).

Universal jurisdiction has undergone something of a renaissance in recent years.[46] Belgium is one of a number of States that have enacted laws providing for universal jurisdiction over particularly serious offences such as war crimes (see Reydams, 2003a). In the *Arrest Warrant* case[47] the Democratic Republic of the Congo complained that Belgium had issued a warrant for the arrest of the DRC's acting Minister of Foreign Affairs, Mr Yerodia, charging him with provoking massacres of Tutsi civilians, contrary to the Belgian War Crimes Act. There were no links between Belgium and the alleged offence or offender. The case was decided on grounds of the Foreign Minister's immunity, but some of the Separate and Dissenting Opinions discuss the validity of Belgium's claim to universal jurisdiction.

---

[42] See, eg *US* v *Yunis*, 681 F.Supp 896 (1988); *Arrest Warrant of 11 April 2000 (Democratic Republic of the Congo* v *Belgium), ICJ Reports 2002*, p 3; (2002) 41 ILM 563.

[43] The catalogue of crimes subject to universal jurisdiction is not yet definitively enumerated: for the view that it does not include terrorism, see *US* v *Yousef*, 327 F.3d 56 (2003) at 108.

[44] The extent to which crimes are subject to universal civil jurisdiction, in addition to universal criminal jurisdiction, may be an emerging issue: see, for instance, Donovan and Roberts, 2006.

[45] See again the *Yunis* case, idem. See further Goodwin, 2006. For a recent practical example of jurisdictional issues relating to piracy, see for instance Treves, 2009. The same argument might apply to any ship on the high seas that is without any nationality: compare *United States* v *Bravo* 480 F.3d 88 (2007).

[46] See *The Princeton Principles on Universal Jurisdiction* (2001), and the *Cairo-Arusha Principles on Universal Jurisdiction in Respect of Gross Human Rights Offences* (2002). However, the resurgence has not been without criticism: see, for instance Jalloh, 2010.

[47] *Arrest Warrant of 11 April 2000 (Democratic Republic of the Congo* v *Belgium), ICJ Reports 2002*, p 3.

The Opinions differ, but are mostly supportive of Belgium's claim.[48] The overlap between crimes of universal jurisdiction and treaty-based extensions of jurisdiction is considered further in the next section.

E. TREATY-BASED EXTENSIONS OF JURISDICTION

If the territorial principle, in all its variants, is overwhelmingly the most important principle in the day-to-day application of a State's laws, much the most important basis for the assertion of extraterritorial jurisdiction is now the large, and constantly growing, network of treaties in which States cooperate to secure the effective and efficient subjection to the law of offences of common concern.

Most of these treaties follow the same broad pattern. A particular offence or range of offences is defined. For example, Article 1 of the 1971 Montreal Convention for the Suppression of Unlawful Acts against the Safety of Civil Aviation (which was at the centre of the *Lockerbie* case in the International Court of Justice),[49] states that a person commits an offence if he unlawfully and intentionally performs an act of violence against a person on board an aircraft in flight if that act is likely to endanger the safety of that aircraft, or if he commits certain other specified acts. The Convention then goes on to require all States parties to make such acts punishable by severe penalties and to assert their jurisdiction over such offences if they are committed in certain specific circumstances, including offences committed in the territory of the State or on board an aircraft registered in the State, and offences committed in cases where the aircraft lands in the State's territory with the alleged offender still on board. Most significant of all is the obligation to provide for jurisdiction over offences in every case where the alleged offender is *found* within the State's territory, regardless of the offender's nationality or of the place where the offence was committed. This is a crucial element in what is often known as the *aut dedere, aut judicare* provision, which stipulates that in every case where an alleged offender is found within the State's territory the State must either extradite him to face trial in another State that seeks him for the purposes of prosecution (and for this purpose, the Convention offences are deemed by the Convention to be included in the lists of extraditable crimes that appear in any extradition treaties that may be in force between the two States), or if it does not extradite him, it must submit the case to its competent authorities for the purpose of prosecution. In *Questions relating to the Obligation to Prosecute or Extradite*,[50] the International Court found that Senegal had breached such an obligation found in Article 7 of the 1984 Torture Convention.

Thus, the aim is to ensure that alleged offenders do not escape prosecution; and the Convention does this in part by creating what is in essence a form of universal jurisdiction as between the parties (O'Keefe, 2004). (It is, strictly speaking, only applicable between the parties. In theory, if an alleged offender was prosecuted for an offence outside the territory of, and not on an aircraft registered in, the prosecuting State, and the national State of the alleged offender was not a party to the Convention, it could object to the assertion of jurisdiction over its citizen. There do not appear to have been any such protests, however.)

---

[48] See also for instance *Jorgic v Germany*, no 74613/01, ECHR 2007-III; (2008) 47 *EHRR* 6 at para 25, 48–54, 67–9; *Ould Dah v France* (Dec), no.13113/03, ECHR 2009; (2013) 56 *EHRR* SE17.

[49] See *Questions of Interpretation and Application of the 1971 Montreal Convention arising from the Aerial Incident at Lockerbie, Provisional Measures, Orders of 14 April 1993, ICJ Reports 1992*, pp 3, 114; 94 ILR 478; *Preliminary Objections, Judgment, ICJ Reports 1998*, pp 9, 115; 117 ILR 1.

[50] *Questions relating to the Obligation to Prosecute or Extradite* (*Belgium v Senegal*), Judgment of 20 July 2012.

There are many conventions that follow a similar pattern, most of them designed to counter various forms of terrorist activity or internationally organized crime. Some, such as the 1979 International Convention Against the Taking of Hostages, have introduced a different, wider range of circumstances in which States parties must establish their jurisdiction over offences defined in the convention. The 1979 Hostages Convention stipulates that States parties must establish their jurisdiction over convention offences committed: in the State's territory, or on board a ship or aircraft registered in the State; or by any of its nationals (and, if the State considers it 'appropriate' also by any stateless persons who have their habitual residence in its territory); or 'in order to compel that State to do or abstain from doing any act'; or with respect to a hostage who is a national of that State, 'if that State considers it appropriate'. The last two circumstances are particularly interesting.

In the last circumstance, jurisdiction is based on the nationality of the victim, a ground often known as the 'passive personality' principle, which will be discussed later in this chapter. It would allow a State to prosecute someone who took one of that State's citizens hostage in a foreign State. The other extension of jurisdiction, to States which are the target of the hostage-taker's pressure, would allow, for example, Israel to prosecute someone who took a non-Israeli Jew hostage in order to bring pressure upon Israel—a scenario similar to the hijacking of the *Achille Lauro* in 1985,[51] in which a Jewish US citizen was killed as part of a campaign to pressurize Israel. Striking as such bases of jurisdiction might be, in the context of the treaty their effect is less dramatic. The general *aut dedere, aut judicare* principle requires the State to prosecute *every* alleged offender found within its territory, if it does not extradite him. The law of States parties must therefore provide for jurisdiction over offenders whether or not the offence was committed within the State's territory or ships or aircraft, or by or against a national of the State, or in order to compel the State to do something. The broad grounds of treaty jurisdiction are all in effect swallowed up within the quasi-universal jurisdiction that the *aut dedere, aut judicare* principle requires. What the treaty regime does add, however, is a clear entitlement of States whose links with the offence fall within one of the specified grounds to seek the extradition of the alleged offender.[52] The treaty provisions have the important practical effect of extending the range of States acknowledged as having a legitimate interest in the prosecution of the alleged offender.

These extensions of jurisdiction treaty grounds have induced some parallel developments in the unilateral practice of States. For example, after the 1985 *Achille Lauro* incident, the USA followed the broad approach of these international treaties by enacting the 1986 Omnibus Diplomatic Security and Anti-Terrorism Act, which asserted jurisdiction over physical attacks on US citizens outside the USA. (It is interesting to note that this development was recorded in the *Cumulative Digest of United State Practice in International Law 1981–88* under the heading 'Jurisdiction Based on Universal and Other State Interests'—an indication of an increasingly robust approach to extraterritorial jurisdiction over terrorists.)

There is a discussion as to the extent to which instances of the principle of *aut dedere, aut judicare* are not merely treaty-based extensions of jurisdiction, but a part of customary international law (so that the obligation will apply to all States, whether or not the State

---

[51] See (1985) 24 ILM 1509. See also Cassese, 1989.

[52] In the case of an *aut dedere, aut judicare* provision in a human rights treaty for alleged violations of which there is a right of individual complaint, a victim of an alleged human rights violation may also be able to complain that the State in which the alleged perpetrator is present has failed to extradite or prosecute: see for example *Guengueng et al v Senegal*, Committee Against Torture, Communication No 181/2001, decision of 19 May 2006, CAT/C/36/D/181/2001.

is a party to a treaty which may merely reflect what is in any event a rule of customary international law).[53] Even in cases where the principle of *aut dedere, aut judicare* may not apply, there is still the question as to the extent to which customary international law still permits States to exercise criminal jurisdiction over crimes committed outside its territory by persons who are not its nationals, in exercise of the principle of universal jurisdiction.

For instance, the Statute of the International Criminal Court (ICC) gives that international court jurisdiction over genocide, war crimes and crimes against humanity, as set out in that statute. Some of those crimes also fall within the scope of earlier international treaties (such as the Geneva Conventions and Torture Convention), such that these crimes are subject to the principle of *aut dedere, aut judicare* by virtue of those earlier treaties. However, although the ICC Statute embodies a principle of 'complementarity' (the effect of which is that the ICC will deal with crimes within its jurisdiction only where national authorities are unwilling or unable to do so), it does not itself contain an express principle of *aut dedere, aut judicare* nor does it expressly provide that States have universal jurisdiction over such crimes. Nevertheless, various States have adopted legislation implementing the ICC Statute domestically, giving their national authorities and national courts some type of universal jurisdiction over such crimes.[54] Some States may even permit universal jurisdiction to be exercised in respect of conduct committed outside its territory where the alleged offender who is not a national of that State is not even present in that State, so that an exercise of universal jurisdiction requires a request for that person's extradition.[55] Other States have adopted more restrictive solutions.[56]

Some States appear to consider that unfettered exercises of universal jurisdiction may lead to difficulties in practice. In 2003 the Belgian legislation was amended so that prosecutions of serious violations of international humanitarian law committed extraterritorially require a link connecting the violations with Belgium, as the State exercising jurisdiction.[57] In 2011, the UK legislated to require the consent of the Director of Public Prosecutions for private prosecutions to be brought in respect of specified international crimes.[58] A Spanish court has also suggested that universal jurisdiction should be exercised only where the territorial State and the ICC fail to act.[59]

---

[53] See International Law Commission, Fourth report on the obligation to extradite or prosecute, Zdzislaw Galicki, Special Rapporteur, 31 May 2011, A/CN.4/648.

[54] For instance, the relevant national legislation in Australia, Canada, Germany, Netherlands, and New Zealand.

[55] For instance, Spain sought the extradition from the UK of former Chilean President Pinochet in respect of charges of crimes committed primarily in Chile: see *R v Bow Street Metropolitan Stipendiary Magistrate, Ex Parte Pinochet Ugarte (No. 3)* [2000] 1 AC 147, discussing universal jurisdiction under the Torture Convention. In the *Arrest Warrant* case (n 43 in this chapter), Belgium had issued an international arrest warrant for the former Minister for Foreign Affairs of the Democratic Republic of the Congo.

[56] For instance, the UK International Criminal Court Act 2001, especially ss 51, 58, 68, extends jurisdiction to UK citizens and residents, persons subject to UK service jurisdiction, as well as 'a person who commits acts outside the United Kingdom at a time when he is not a United Kingdom national, a United Kingdom resident or a person subject to UK service jurisdiction and who subsequently becomes resident in the United Kingdom'.

[57] See Reydams, 2003b. See also *Jiménez Sánchez and ors v Gibson and ors*, Appeal Judgment, No 1240/2006; ILDC 993 (ES 2006) (Spain, Supreme Court, Criminal Chamber) (but compare the earlier decision of the Spanish Constitutional Tribunal in the *Guatemala Genocide* case (2006) 100 *AJIL* 207). Such a link might be the nationality or residence of the victim or the presence of the accused person in the territory of the State exercising jurisdiction.

[58] Police Reform and Social Responsibility Act 2011, s 153. Cf *Re Gorbachev*, City of Westminster Magistrates Court, (2011) 82 *BYIL* 570.

[59] *Peruvian Genocide Case*, Spain, Supreme Court, 20 May 2003, 141 ILR 720.

In addition to universal criminal jurisdiction, in the USA the Alien Tort Statute ('ATS' or Alien Tort Claims Act) permits civil claims by aliens for damages in tort for 'violation of the law of nations or a treaty of the United States'.[60] Over the last decades numerous civil claims have been brought under this legislation in US courts, against defendants who are not US citizens in respect of conduct committed outside the USA in alleged breach of international law, in particular international criminal law or human rights law. However, in *Kiobel v Royal Dutch Petroleum Co*, the US Supreme Court recently held that the presumption against extraterritoriality applies to claims under the Alien Tort Statute, and that it did not in that case permit relief for violations of the law of nations occurring outside the USA. The Supreme Court said in that case that 'there is no indication that the ATS was passed to make the USA a uniquely hospitable forum for the enforcement of international norms'.[61] While the Supreme Court has thereby significantly reduced the scope of the ATS, it is too early to know exactly to what extent. The court stated in its conclusion that 'even where the claims touch and concern the territory of the USA, they must do so with sufficient force to displace the presumption against extraterritorial application' and that for this purpose 'it would reach too far to say that mere corporate presence suffices'.[62] As Justice Alito said in a concurring opinion, 'This formulation obviously leaves much unanswered'. Whether the 'touch and concern' test will prove to be something similar to the 'effects' doctrine discussed earlier, or something much narrower, remains to be seen.

F. CONTROVERSIAL BASES OF PRESCRIPTIVE JURISDICTION

The bases of jurisdiction described in the preceding section are generally accepted in State practice. There are certain other bases that have been advanced by States from time to time, which have not found general acceptance. These are instances of States considering that the link between them and the conduct that they seek to regulate is sufficient to warrant the exercise of prescriptive jurisdiction. The objections of other States, however, operate to preclude the emergence of a 'general practice accepted as law' and the consequent establishment of the claimed basis of jurisdiction in customary international law.

1. Passive personality

One of the oldest controversial bases of prescriptive jurisdiction is the so-called 'passive personality' principle: that is, the principle that would allow the national State of the victim of an offence to assert prescriptive jurisdiction. That principle lay behind the controversy that arose in 1885 when Mr AK Cutting, a citizen of the USA, was imprisoned in Mexico and charged with having libelled a Mexican citizen in a paper published in the USA. In his annual address to Congress in 1886, President Grover Cleveland recalled that the incident 'disclosed a claim of jurisdiction by Mexico novel in our history, whereby any offense committed anywhere by a foreigner, penal in the place of its commission, and of which a Mexican is the object, may, if the offender be found in Mexico, be there tried and punished in conformity with Mexican laws'. He went on to say that '[t]he admission of such a pretension would be attended with serious results, invasive of the jurisdiction of this Government and highly dangerous to our citizens in foreign lands. Therefore I have denied it and protested against its attempted exercise as unwarranted by the principles of

---

[60] See for instance Henner, *Human Rights and the Alien Tort Statute* (2009).
[61] *Kiobel v Royal Dutch Petroleum Co*, 133 S Ct 1659 (2013), at p 12.   [62] Ibid, p 14.

law and international usages.' It is a perfect example of a protest against an excessive jurisdictional claim. It will be noted that the USA assumed that the burden lay upon Mexico to prove its entitlement to exercise jurisdiction in this way; no attempt was made by the USA to establish a 'prohibitive rule' of the kind that is sometimes said to be required by the *Lotus* case.

Claims to jurisdiction based upon the passive personality principle have continued to be made. For example, in 1975 the USA again had cause to protest against assertions of passive personality jurisdiction, on that occasion by Greece.[63] There is, however, a trend in favour of accepting it. As one of the Separate Opinions in the *Arrest Warrant* case noted, '[p]assive personality jurisdiction, for so long regarded as controversial...today meets with relatively little opposition, at least so far as a particular category of offences is concerned.'[64] The qualification is important. Passive personality jurisdiction is indeed widely tolerated when used to prosecute terrorists. Whether it would be as acceptable if used to prosecute, for example, adulterers and defamers is another matter.

2. National technology

One of the most imaginative, and least successful, attempts to extend the scope of legislative jurisdiction was made by the USA in the 1980s. In the course of its attempts to prohibit trade with the Soviet Union, following the imposition of martial law in Poland, the USA made it a criminal offence for anyone, regardless of their nationality or State of residence, to export to the Soviet Union goods that contained more than a certain proportion of components of US origin or which had been created using US technology. This was an attempt to assert jurisdiction on the basis of the 'nationality' of technology (a concept unknown in international law); and it was vigorously resisted by the European States whose nationals bore the brunt of the prohibition. The main European protest appears in the Comments of the European Community dated 12 August 1982.[65] Again, however, the refusal of other States to accept the right of the USA unilaterally to impose its law on anyone who handles US technology has not prevented the acceptance of that basis of jurisdiction on an agreed basis in international treaties. For example, States appear to have been willing to conclude agreements relating to transfers of nuclear materials, under which the consent of the supplying State is required in the event of subsequent transfers of the material.

3. Unprincipled assertions of jurisdiction

From time to time, States are tempted to assert an extended extraterritorial jurisdiction in a manner that appears to be almost totally unprincipled. One of the most startling examples is to be found in the US Military Order of 13 November 2001, concerning the detention at a US base, Guantánamo Bay in Cuba, of 'international terrorists' seized by the USA in Afghanistan. Section 7 of that Order stipulates, in relation to detained individuals, that:

the individual shall not be privileged to seek any remedy or maintain any proceeding, directly or indirectly, or to have any such remedy or proceeding sought on the individual's behalf, in (i) any court of the United States, or any State thereof, (ii) any court of any foreign nation, or (iii) any international tribunal.[66]

---

[63] See the *Digest of United States Practice in International Law 1975*, p 339.

[64] *Arrest Warrant of 11 April 2000 (Democratic Republic of the Congo v Belgium), ICJ Reports 2002*, p 3, Joint Separate Opinion of Judges Higgins, Kooijmans, and Buergenthal, at p 11; *Lozano v Italy*, Appeal Judgment, Case No 31171/2008; ILDC 1085 (IT 2008) 24 July 2008.

[65] (1982) 21 ILM 891.

[66] http://georgewbush-whitehouse.archives.gov/news/releases/2001/11/20011113-27.html.

It is not clear whether this curiously drafted Order was intended to prevent the making of applications to bodies such as the Inter-American Commission of Human Rights;[67] but insofar as it is intended to forbid non-US citizens to make such applications, it is difficult to see that even the protective principle could be stretched so far as to justify this provision, even if it were otherwise compatible with the USA's international obligations.

G. INADEQUACIES OF THE TRADITIONAL APPROACH

The traditional approach to the bases of jurisdiction is beset by considerable difficulty in practice. Two problems stand out. First, the problem of locating acts; and second, the problem of reconciling conflicts when two or more States have concurrent jurisdiction.

1. The difficulty of locating acts

The territorial principle, both in its plain form and its objective and subjective variants, presupposes that it is clear *where* an act is committed; but that is far from always the case. Take, for example, the case of the hijacking of an aircraft. If control over an aircraft registered in State A is seized while the aircraft is in the airspace of State B, is the hijack 'committed' (or, rather, *still being* committed) when the aircraft lands in State C? And, to take another example, suppose that individuals in States L and M conspire by fax, telephone, and e-mail to import narcotics into State K, but that only one of them ever sets foot in State K. Could each of States K, L, and M assert jurisdiction over the entire conspiracy and all of the participants?[68]

As a matter of domestic law (the law under which the accused will, of course, be tried), it is evident that much will depend upon the particular way in which the crime with which they are charged is defined. The English courts have distinguished between 'conduct' crimes and 'result' crimes, the former focusing upon what is actually done and the latter upon the consequences of what is done, in a manner that lends itself respectively to the application of the subjective and objective variants of territorial jurisdiction.[69]

While such approaches may be sufficient to enable national courts to overcome any difficulties that they may have in determining the reach of the laws that they have to apply, it does not answer the question whether the jurisdictional reach asserted in those laws is in conformity with international law. Indeed, the drafting of national laws may aggravate the problem. It is quite possible to redraft every offence so as to make it a crime to enter the State having done *x*, *y*, or *z* before entry. For example, the customs laws of some Commonwealth States made it an offence for ships to enter the territorial sea *having broken* a bulk cargo into smaller parcels on the high seas (such breaking being almost invariably the prelude to smuggling of goods ashore). Was that an extension of the State's jurisdiction onto the high seas? Or was it an assertion of jurisdiction over acts that took place within the State's territory? A slightly different issue was raised in the 1920s by the US Prohibition Law, which sought to forbid the importation of alcohol into the USA. That law was applicable to foreign cruise ships entering US ports from the high seas. Did that therefore mean that the US was forbidding those ships to carry alcohol on the high seas?

---

[67] To its credit the Inter-American Commission acted anyway: see (2002) 41 ILM 532. So did the US Supreme Court: see *Rasul* v *Bush*, 542 US 466 (2004).

[68] See further Blackmore, 2006.

[69] See *DPP* v *Doot* [1973] AC 807; [1973] 1 All ER 940 (HL); *DPP* v *Stonehouse* [1978] AC 55; [1977] 2 All ER 909 (HL); *Liangsiriprasert* v *Government of the United States of America* [1991] 1 AC 225; [1990] 2 All ER 866 (PC). See Hirst, 2003.

That was certainly the practical effect of the enforcement of the Prohibition Law; but was it the proper juridical characterization of that law?

There is no clear theoretical answer to this problem. As usual, however, there is much to be said for falling back on common sense. Where other States consider that the jurisdictional claim has gone too far—as they did in relation to the application of the Prohibition Law to foreign cruise ships,[70] but not in relation to the laws on the breaking of bulk cargo—they will protest. Those protests generally hold jurisdictional claims within reasonable bounds. If other States choose to acquiesce in the claim, it will become established in customary law.[71]

There was much speculation that the internet would lead to near-unimaginable difficulties concerning jurisdiction. In fact international law appears to have accommodated crimes in cyberspace with barely the flicker of a monitor: the regime under the 2001 Council of Europe Convention on Cybercrime[72] is based upon the traditional territorial and national principles of jurisdiction. However, issues remain, and are likely to increase as technology evolves.[73]

2. The difficulty of overlapping jurisdiction

All of the examples cited in the previous section in fact involve overlapping jurisdiction: that is, more than one State can make out a claim on the basis of established principles of international law to apply its laws to the conduct in question. That is why the cases are problematic: it is unlikely that a State will complain about the assertion of jurisdiction over an individual unless there is some other State that might more appropriately assert jurisdiction. In the 'Prohibition' cases, for example, the protesting European States thought it right that the flag State, and not the State of each port at which a cruise ship might call, should decide whether or not the ship could carry alcohol on board.[74]

Instances of 'overlapping', or 'concurrent', jurisdiction give rise to the question of priority. If the applicable laws diverge, which is to prevail? In some cases it may appear clear which law is to yield. There is a considerable body of practice supporting the view that a State may not require anyone outside its territory to do an act that would violate the criminal law of the place where the act would be done. Thus, courts in the USA allow what is sometimes known as the 'foreign sovereign compulsion' defence. For example, the court may excuse a failure to produce documents in pursuance of an order of the court, if the failure results from a prohibition on disclosure under the criminal law of the State where the documents are located.[75] (This defence is not available in circumstances where the duty of non-disclosure arises under the civil, rather than the criminal, law of the territorial State.)[76]

---

[70] The dispute was largely settled by an accommodation in the series of bilateral 'Liquor treaties' made with the USA.

[71] For an application of acquiescence as a basis for jurisdiction see *US v Suerte*, 291 F.3d 36 (2002), *Digest of United States Practice in International Law 2002*, p 133.

[72] ETS No 185; 41 ILM 282 (2002). See Article 22.1.d.

[73] See, for instance, Bigos, 2005; Schultz, 2008; Levin, Doran, and Maria, 2012; Narayanan, 2011–12 (who considers the possible solutions to State jurisdiction over cloud computing to include extraterritorial application of domestic regulations, international cooperation, harmonization, and a sort of 'law of the cyber sea'). See also the *Tallin Manual on the International Law Applicable to Cyber Warfare*, 2013, 15–26.

[74] Compare that situation with the case of *US v Neil*, 312 F.3d 419 (2002), *Digest of United States Practice in International Law 2002*, p 131.

[75] See, eg *Société Internationale v Rogers*, 357 US 197 (1958).

[76] See, eg *US v First National City Bank*, 396 F.2d 897 (1968).

Some States have sought to utilize the foreign sovereign compulsion defence by enacting laws that oblige persons in their territory to do or not to do certain things. For instance, the UK enacted the Protection of Trading Interests Act 1980 (a more powerful successor to the Shipping Contracts and Commercial Documents Act 1964), under which the Secretary of State may order any person in the UK not to comply with orders from a foreign court for the production of evidence or, indeed, with substantive orders made on the basis of extraterritorial jurisdiction by a foreign State. The powers under the Act were invoked in 1982 in order to forbid British businesses to comply with US orders not to supply goods to the Soviet Union for use in connection with the construction of the Siberian gas pipeline, during the so-called 'pipeline' dispute[77]—an unusual example of one NATO State making it a criminal offence to comply with the law of another NATO State in respect of dealings with the Soviet Union during the Cold War. Similar laws, often known as 'blocking' statutes, have been adopted by a number of other States including Australia, Belgium, Canada, Denmark, Finland, France, Germany, Italy, Japan, the Netherlands, New Zealand, Norway, the Philippines, South Africa, Switzerland, and—the most dramatic measure of all—the European Community.[78]

Blocking statutes are no solution to jurisdictional conflicts. Quite apart from the fact that they represent a degree of friction in the international system that inevitably impairs its efficiency, they do nothing to overcome the problem of what might be called 'prudential compliance'. Even though an extraterritorial measure may be patently unlawful as a matter of international law, and though it is possible that a person may at some point be ordered not to comply with it, the risk of the legislating State imposing sanctions for non-compliance is so great that anyone caught by the extraterritorial claim must, if they are prudent, organize their affairs so as to comply with the law. European businesses, for example, often organize transactions so as to comply with US law, even though the USA may have no legitimate claim to jurisdiction over them; and the converse is increasingly true of US companies in relation to EU law.

Jurisdictional disputes continue to arise, though their forms change. Thus, in 1996 the USA enacted laws providing for sanctions against Cuba (the Helms-Burton Act) and against Iran and Libya (the D'Amato Act). Those laws contained a range of extraterritorial measures, including the imposition of sanctions upon non-US businesses which purchased, in good faith and for full value, property in Cuba that had been confiscated in the 1960s from US owners who had not been compensated for the takings. These measures provoked a strong response from the European Community, resulting in an uneasy stand-off when the full implementation of the American laws was suspended.[79]

The States that claim extraterritorial jurisdiction are by no means always and wholly insensitive to the views of other States. US courts, in particular, have developed what they call the 'balancing of interests' approach to jurisdiction of conflicts. This approach has a number of variants, which may be seen in the leading cases such as *Timberlane*, *Mannington Mills*, and *Hartford Fire Insurance*.[80] Broadly speaking, under this approach the court considers the nature and extent of the USA's interest in having its law applied, and the interests of the other State in not having US law applied, and also factors such as the nationalities of the parties involved and the nature of their links with the USA. It then

[77] See the symposium in (1984) 27 *German Yearbook of International Law* 11–142. Cf Killman, 2004.

[78] See European Community Council Regulation (EC) 2271/96, published in (1996) OJ L309. For other measures, see Lowe, 1983.

[79] See Lowe, 1997.

[80] The cases are discussed in *Hartford Fire Insurance Co v California*, 509 US 764;113 S Ct 2891 (1993); and Lowenfeld, 1995.

decides whether, on balance, it is right to apply US law or to exercise judicial restraint. Not surprisingly, it is practically invariably decided to apply US law. Nonetheless, there is no doubt that judges in US courts are now more sensitive to the constraints of international law and the demands of international comity than they were in the 1960s and 70s.[81]

There are more satisfactory approaches to a solution to jurisdictional conflicts than unilateral restraint and blocking statutes. Sometimes States may be able to harmonize their policies[82] so that even though their jurisdictional claims may overlap, individuals affected by those laws are not subjected to conflicting demands. Sometimes, States may be able to establish consultation procedures in order to seek to eliminate on a case-by-case basis extraterritorial applications of laws which would cause difficulty for the State in whose territory the regulated conduct occurs. A good example of this is the antitrust cooperation procedure established by the European Community and the USA.[83] Such steps have, in recent years, done much to defuse disputes over jurisdiction, which are now somewhat less common and less acute than they were in the 1980s—though whether this trend is anything more than temporary remains to be seen. Ultimately, however, it must be recognized that jurisdictional conflicts are conflicts over the right to prescribe the rules that make up the public order of the State. Whatever solution is adopted, it must be a solution that ensures the right of every State, as an equal sovereign, to decide for itself upon the precise nature of that public order, to the extent that it can do so without invading and subverting the right of other States to do likewise.

III. THE FUNDAMENTAL PRINCIPLE GOVERNING ENFORCEMENT JURISDICTION

In contrast to the principles governing the exercise of prescriptive jurisdiction, the international law governing the exercise of enforcement jurisdiction is clear and simple. There is one basic principle: enforcement jurisdiction may not be exercised in the territory of any other State without the consent of that State. In other words, enforcement jurisdiction is in principle limited to the territory of the State concerned. (In fact, those two propositions are not precisely the same: there are areas outside the territory of a State that do not fall within the territory of another State—for example, the high seas, and the exclusive economic zones of other States.)

One particular application of this principle is that the courts of one State will generally not enforce the public laws of another. 'Public laws', in this context, means not only criminal laws but also laws relating to matters such as taxation, that are quintessentially manifestations of the State's sovereign power, rather than laws that lay down the ground rules for the creation of rights and duties between individuals, in the way that, say, contract, family, and land law do. The most difficult laws to classify on this basis are tort laws. These are in some respects private, but may also be viewed as laws by which the State prescribes rules of conduct for society, in the same way that it does in its criminal law, but leaving the enforcement of those rules up to private parties. This dual nature of tort law is most

---

[81] See the decision of the Supreme Court in *F Hoffman-La Roche Ltd* v *Empagran SA*, 542 US 155; 124 S Ct 2359 (2004).

[82] For instance, through international treaties, or measures adopted in the context of regional organizations such as the EU: see for instance, Mitsilegas, 2009.

[83] EC-US Agreement on the Application of Positive Comity Principles in the Enforcement of their Competition Laws, OJ L173 of 18 June 1998.

evident in US antitrust laws, where those injured by unlawful anticompetitive practices are enabled to recover treble damages, as an incentive to act as 'private attorneys general' in the enforcement of the laws. For that reason, English courts have refused to enforce US antitrust laws.[84]

It is unusual, but not unknown, for one State to give another permission to exercise enforcement jurisdiction in its territory. Perhaps the most significant agreements of this kind in recent years are the so-called 'ship rider' agreements made, for example, by the USA with a number of Caribbean States, under which US navy vessels may in certain circumstances enter the territorial seas of the other party in order to pursue and arrest vessels suspected of being engaged in the illicit traffic in narcotic drugs. Similar agreements have been prepared on a multilateral basis in order to facilitate international action against narcotics traffic and (in the 2005 amendments to the 1988 Convention for the Suppression of Unlawful Acts Against the Safety of Maritime Navigation) against terrorism.

Ordinarily, where an alleged offender who is sought for the purposes of prosecution is within the territory of another State, the State that seeks him must request the State where he is found to surrender him. Many States are, under their own domestic law, bound not to surrender individuals except in accordance with an extradition agreement that is in force with the requesting State. In addition, some States are bound under their own law not to surrender their nationals to foreign States under any circumstances. There is a rich body of international law and practice concerning the interpretation and application of extradition treaties, but shortage of space precludes its discussion here.

It is not unknown for States to attempt to obtain custody of alleged offenders without going through the formalities of extradition procedures—or, indeed, any other formalities. For example, individuals are sometimes simply transported over national borders into the hands of law-enforcement officers on the other side. This appears, for example, to have been the way in which many members of the European terrorist organizations such as the Red Brigades and the Baader-Meinhof Gang were moved around Europe in the 1970s. On occasion, States have gone further, and themselves seized wanted persons from the territory of another State.[85] Such actions patently violate the territorial sovereignty of the State from which the persons are seized. If that State should retrospectively 'consent' to the seizure, that may cure the illegality; alternatively, the State may declare that it does not intend to pursue the question of the violation, and will regard the matter as closed. This seems to have happened, for instance, in relation to the seizure, apparently by agents of the government of Israel, of Adolf Eichmann from Argentina. Initially unaware of Eichmann's abduction, the government of Argentina subsequently agreed to abandon its claim for reparation for the violation of its territorial sovereignty.

What is the position if a State seizes an accused person, in violation of territorial sovereignty of another State, and then puts that person on trial in its own courts? As a matter of international law, one might say that the subsequent trial compounds the violation of the other State's territorial sovereignty; and even if that State acquiesces, as Argentina did in the trial of Eichmann, there is at least the possibility that the national State of the abducted individual might complain that its rights, too, have been violated. As far as the individual is concerned, the position is less clear. In some States the illegality of the abduction may, as a matter of the domestic law of the State, preclude the trial of the individual. In most States, however, it is likely that the illegality of the abduction will be regarded as a matter

---

[84] See the submissions of the Attorney-General in *Rio Tinto Zinc* v *Westinghouse Corp* [1978] AC 547 (HL). Cf *Lewis* v *Eliades* [2003] EWCA Civ 1758.

[85] Or tried to ship them abroad in wooden crates: see the two episodes noted in Harris, 2004, at p 369.

to be handled by the Executive, if and when the State from which the defendant is taken complains, but not a matter that the trial court needs to take into account. So, for example, in the USA the most egregious violation of international law appears to be insufficient to constitute a bar to the trial of the abducted defendant: even the sand-bagging of suspects and the smuggling of their comatose bodies back to the USA was held to be no obstacle to their trial before a US court, on the curious ground that the individuals did not enjoy the protection of US Constitutional safeguards while they were outside US territory.[86] The English courts adopt a somewhat different approach. Having long taken the view that it was no concern of the court how the defendant happened to have arrived before it, in more recent years the courts have moved towards the view that the forcible abduction of defendants in violation of agreed procedures may be so serious as to amount to an abuse of process, in which case their trial should not proceed.[87] Such a finding will, however, be unusual, and be made only where the British police or prosecuting authorities have themselves acted illegally or colluded in unlawful procedures in order to secure the presence of the defendant in the UK, or have violated international law or the law of a foreign State or otherwise abused their powers.[88]

IV. CONCLUSION

This chapter has surveyed, albeit briefly, the principles of international law governing exercises of legislative and enforcement jurisdiction. These are truly principles, and not rules. The difficulties of applying the principles rigidly have been noted, and are implicit in the nature of jurisdiction. It is not possible to devise strict rules that would divide jurisdiction between sovereign States in any practical manner. The solution to jurisdictional problems has to be found by increasing the sensitivity of States to the constraints imposed by international law, and also to the fact that the interests of other States demand respect. It should be clear that if in any case the exercise by one State of its jurisdiction threatens to subvert the laws that another State has enacted to regulate life in its own territory, in the exercise of its sovereign right to choose how to organize life within its borders, the boundaries of lawful jurisdiction have been over-stepped. If States wish to do more than they are able to do within the limits of the jurisdiction allowed to them, they must first seek the agreement and cooperation of other States.

REFERENCES

AKEHURST, M (1972–3), 'Jurisdiction in International Law', 46 *BYIL* 145–217.

ARNELL, P (2001), 'The Case for Nationality-Based Jurisdiction', 50 *ICLQ* 955.

AUST, AI (2000), 'Lockerbie: The Other Case', 49 *ICLQ* 278.

BIGOS, O (2005), 'Jurisdiction over Cross-boundary Wrongs on the Internet', 54 *ICLQ* 585.

---

[86] See *US* v *Toscanino*, 500 F.2d 267 (1974); *US* v *Verdugo-Urquidez*, 494 US 259 (1990); *US* v *Alvarez-Machain*, 504 US 655, 112 S Ct 2188 (1992). Cf *Sosa* v *Alvarez-Machain*, 542 US 692 (2004).

[87] *Bennett* v *Horseferry Road Magistrates' Court* [1994] 1 AC 42; [1993] 3 All ER 138 (HL). And see the South African case of *State* v *Ebrahim* (1992), 31 ILM 888.

[88] *R* v *Staines Magistrates Court, ex parte Westfallen* [1998] 4 All ER 210.

BLACKMORE, JDA (2006), 'The Jurisdictional Problem of the Extraterritorial Conspiracy', 17 *Criminal Law Forum* 71.

BLOUNT, P *et al* (2007), 'Jurisdiction in Outer Space: Challenge of Private Individuals in Space', 33 *Journal of Space Law* 299.

CASSESE, A (1989), *Terrorism, Politics and The Law* (Cambridge: Polity Press).

CHAUDHRY, S and MAHAJAN, K (2011), 'The Case for an Effective Extraterritorial Competition Commission of India in Light of International Practices', 32 *European Competition Law Review* 314.

CRAWFORD, J (2012), *Brownlie's Principles of Public International Law*, 8th edn (Oxford: Oxford University Press).

DONOVAN, D and ROBERTS, A (2006), 'The Emerging Recognition of Universal Civil Jurisdiction', 100 *AJIL* 142.

ELLIS, J (2012), 'Extraterritorial Exercise of Jurisdiction for Environmental Protection: Addressing Fairness Concerns', 25 *Leiden Journal of International Law* 397.

GOODWIN, J (2006), 'Universal Jurisdiction and the Pirate: Time for an Old Couple to Part', 39 *Vand J Transnat'l L* 973.

HALL, W (1895), *A Treatise on International Law*, 5th edn (Oxford: Clarendon Press).

HARRIS, DJ (2004), *Cases and Materials on International Law*, 6th edn (London: Sweet & Maxwell).

HENNER, P (2009), *Human Rights and the Alien Tort Statue* (Chicago: American Bar Association).

HIRST, M (2003), *Jurisdiction and the Ambit of the Criminal Law* (Oxford: Oxford University Press).

HOBE, S *et al* (2007), 'Space Tourism Activities: Emerging Challenges to Air and Space Law', 33 *Journal of Space Law* 359.

JAIN, A (2012), 'Extraterritorial jurisdiction of Competition Commission of India', 19 *Journal of Financial Crime* 112.

JALLOH, C (2010), 'Universal Jurisdiction, Universal Prescription? A Preliminary Assessment of the African Union Perspective on Universal Jurisdiction', 21 *Criminal Law Forum* 1.

KILLMAN, E (2004), 'Enforcement of Judgments and Blocking Statues', 53 *ICLQ* 1025.

LEVIN, D, DORAN, S, and MARIA, LA (2012), 'Megaupload and Criminal Charges', 4 *Revista Española de Relaciones Internacionales* 23.

LOWE, V (1983), *Extraterritorial Jurisdiction* (Cambridge: Grotius).

—— (1997), 'US Extraterritorial Jurisdiction: the Helms-Burton and D'Amato Acts', 46 *ICLQ* 378–390.

LOWENFELD, A (1995), 'Conflict, Balancing of Interests, and the Exercise of Jurisdiction to Prescribe: Reflections on the *Insurance Antitrust Case*', 89 *AJIL* 42.

MITSILEGAS, V (2009), 'The Third Wave of Third Pillar Law. Which Direction for EU Criminal Justice?', 34 *European Law Review* 523.

MURPHY, S (2003), 'Extraterritorial Application of US Laws to Crimes on Foreign Vessels', 97 *AJIL* 183.

NARAYANAN, V (2011–12), 'Harnessing the Cloud: International Law Implications of Cloud Computing', 12 *Chi J Int'l L* 783.

O'CONNELL, DP (1970), *International Law*, 2nd edn (London: Stevens).

O'KEEFE, R (2004), 'Universal Jurisdiction: Clarifying the Basic Concept', 2 *Journal of International Criminal Justice* 735.

OPPENHEIM, L (1992), JENNINGS, Sir R and WATTS, SIR A (eds), *Oppenheim's International Law*, 9th edn (Harlow: Longman).

RATNER, S (2003), 'Belgium's War Crimes Statute. A Postmortem', 97 *AJIL* 888.

REYDAMS, L (2003a), *Universal Jurisdiction: International and Municipal Legal Perspectives* (Oxford: Oxford University Press).

—— (2003b), 'Belgium Reneges on Universality: The 5 August 2003 Act on Grave Breaches of International Humanitarian Law', 1 *Journal of International Criminal Justice* 679.

RYNGAERT, C (2008), 'Litigating Abuses Committed by Private Military Companies', 19 *EJIL* 1035.

SCHULTZ, T (2008) 'Carving up the Internet: Jurisdiction, Legal Orders, and the Private/public International Law Interface', 19 *EJIL* 799.

TREVES, T (2009), 'Piracy, Law of the Sea, and Use of Force: Developments off the Coast of Somalia', 20 *EJIL* 399.

TWISS, SIR T (1884), *On the Rights and Duties of Nations in Times of Peace* (Oxford: Clarendon Press).

VERHOEVEN, J (2000), *Droit International Public* (Brussels: Larcier).

FURTHER READING

Curiously, there is no satisfactory modern monograph on jurisdiction. There are, however, some good articles that discuss the basic principles of jurisdiction in international law in the light of the various disputes that have arisen over the years:

AKEHURST, M (1972–73), 'Jurisdiction in International Law', 46 *BYIL* 145.

BOWETT, DW (1982), 'Jurisdiction: Changing Patterns of Authority over Activities and Resources', 53 *BYIL* 1.

LOWE, V (1981), 'Blocking Extraterritorial Jurisdiction: the British Protection of Trading Interests Act, 1980', 75 *AJIL* 257.

—— (1985), 'The Problems of Extraterritorial Jurisdiction: Economic Sovereignty and the Search for a Solution', 34 *ICLQ* 724.

MANN, FA (1964–I), 'The Doctrine of Jurisdiction in International Law', 111 *Recueil des Cours* 1.

—— (1984–III), 'The Doctrine of International Jurisdiction Revisited after Twenty Years', 186 *Recueil des Cours* 9.

SCHLOSSER, P (2000), 'Jurisdiction and International Judicial and Administrative Co-operation', 284 *Recueil des Cours* 9.

12

INTERNATIONAL LAW AND RESTRAINTS ON THE EXERCISE OF JURISDICTION BY NATIONAL COURTS OF STATES

Hazel Fox

SUMMARY

The three restraints—State immunity, act of State, and non-justiciability—operate as avoidance techniques and are based on the independence and equality which States enjoy under international law, by which States prevent their national courts from deciding disputes which relate to the internal affairs of another State. This chapter examines all three doctrines, in particular the operation of the restrictive doctrine of State immunity and concludes with an appraisal of the judgment relating to State immunity given by the International Court of Justice in 2012, the *Jurisdictional Immunities of the State* case.

I. OVERVIEW

A. INTRODUCTION

State practice, as illustrated by the practice in the UK with regard to claims against the Crown until the Crown Proceedings Act 1947, separated the settlement of claims arising from the conduct of States from the determination by the national courts of disputes between private persons. To keep lines of communication open and to preserve friendly relations with other States, agents of the State, including Heads of State themselves, were accorded a privileged position when present within the territory of another State. One method of conferring such privileges was to grant them immunity from criminal or civil proceedings in national courts (see Wickremasinghe, Ch 13 of this book). Similarly activities of governments and their departments were accorded immunity by the courts of other States, even though the conduct complained of might be categorized as breach of contract, defamation or expropriation.

The operation of a plea of immunity is in some way similar to that granted by national law to the legislature and its members; though of course the reasons for the conferment of immunity on a State or its officials differ. While, in the case of the legislature, the justification derives from the constitution of the country, the balance of powers between legislature, courts and the executive and the requirement that no attempt by the executive to use the power of the courts should prevent the proper exercise of the legislative function[1] in the case of diplomatic and State immunity the underlying purpose is the maintenance of peaceful relations between States and the settlement of disputes by consent rather than the diktat of one State. Thus, international law recognizes the independence and equality of States and accordingly requires restraint from subjecting one State to adjudication of its disputes in the national courts of another State. (For jurisdiction and its exercise by the State see Staker, Ch 11 in this book.)

Similarly, by the plea of act of State national common law courts of other States respect the legislation and public acts of other States; and, when a question relating to an international boundary, or State succession or State responsibility arises, national courts treat such international transactions between States as non-justiciable by municipal law and by accepting a plea of non-justiciability, refer any dispute to settlement by international law.

With the State's increasing engagement in commercial activities, State practice came to recognize that the immunities afforded to the State and its agents by international law need not be extended to commercial transactions into which the State entered in a manner similar to a private person. Thus, if a State failed to pay for goods or service ordered, immunity increasingly was held to provide no bar, though to enable the State to operate unhindered, special treatment continued to be afforded to the head and members of its diplomatic mission and to certain contracts of employment which it might make.

In the last ten years, with the development of the international law of human rights and the recognition of international crimes it has increasingly been asked why international law should not also permit national courts to exercise jurisdiction in respect of a breach of 'established rules of international law of fundamental importance'. In plain terms, why should a claim that a State or its official had tortured an individual or in the course of armed conflict had caused loss of life or property be barred by a claim of immunity from adjudication in the national court of another State, if it could be shown that the alleged acts were in breach of international law?

This chapter will discuss some of the complex issues which are involved in answering that question. But it is useful to point out at once difficulties which may arise. First, can a national court be relied on to determine a breach of international law, when that court is established by one State without any participation or consent of the defendant State? Second, acts of torture tend to be committed by the police or armed forces of a State—agencies which are closely concerned with defence and internal security of the State. To allow the national court of another State to review judicially the propriety of the conduct of such agencies would constitute a major intrusion into the internal administration of another State with consequent loss of independence.

The International Court of Justice's 2012 judgment in the *Jurisdictional Immunities of the State* case has now taken into account these obstacles to unilateral adjudication of inter-state disputes, in so far as the determination by a national court of acts committed in the course of international armed conflict by a State, when it declared that 'customary international law continues to require that a State be accorded immunity in proceedings for torts allegedly

---

[1] Cf UK Government green paper 'Parliamentary Privilege' 26 April 2012, proposing that it was 'wrong in principle to deny the courts access to any relevant evidence when the alleged act is serious enough to have been recognised as a criminal offence' (para 95), except where the alleged criminal offence 'related closely to the principal reason for the protection of privilege, ie the protection of freedom of speech and debate in parliament' (para 98).

committed on the territory of another State by its armed forces and other organs of State in the course of conducting an armed conflict.[2]

Let us now examine more closely the techniques which international law has evolved to deal with these problems.

B. STATE IMMUNITY, ACT OF STATE, AND NON-JUSTICIABILITY AS AVOIDANCE TECHNIQUES

International law limits the independence of any one over-powerful State by making legal equality a consequence of statehood with an accompanying obligation on all States to respect each other's independence and equality. That respect is given expression in an obligation of non-intervention in the internal affairs of another State and a prohibition on the settlement of disputes without the consent of all the States to whom such disputes relate. The obligation of non-intervention is given effect by the recognition accorded by other States to the validity of the legislative, adjudicative, and administrative acts of a State within its permitted area of jurisdiction. The consent requirement in dispute settlement is given effect by a rule of exhaustion of local remedies which provides an opportunity for a State to settle the claim in its own manner or by the removal of the dispute to the international plane, for diplomatic settlement. To honour this obligation of non-intervention in international law one State (known as the forum State by reason of the fact that the court before whom the proceedings are instituted is located in its territory) employs various methods to prevent its courts from deciding disputes which relate to the internal affairs of another State.

Some methods or avoidance techniques exist by virtue of the constitutional or municipal law of a State so as to restrict a particular court's competence or direct the case to a more appropriate forum; thus certain matters, such as the recognition of the existence of another State or government may be reserved to the executive branch of government; or a court of competence in civil and commercial matters may have no power to hear a matter relating to public administration; or a common law court may refuse to hear a case, exercising a discretion on a plea of *forum non conveniens* to rule that another forum, having competent jurisdiction is the appropriate forum for the trial of the case more suitably for the interest of the parties and the ends of justice.[3]

But the three avoidance techniques discussed and compared in detail in this chapter are more directly related to a State's obligation to respect the independence and equality of other States by not requiring them to submit to adjudication in a national court or to settlement of their disputes without their consent. These three avoidance techniques are immunity, act of State, and non-justiciability.

Immunity by reason of the sovereign independent status of a State is only available where proceedings are brought against a foreign State and is a preliminary procedural plea taken at the commencement of the proceedings. It serves two purposes: first, it debars the court of the State where proceedings are brought (the forum court or national court) from exercising jurisdiction to inquire further into the claim; and second, it removes the claim to another process of settlement, most frequently to settlement through diplomatic

---

[2] *Jurisdictional Immunities of the State (Germany v Italy: Greece Intervening), Judgment of 3 February 2012, ICJ Reports 2012*, para 78. See para 57 for the Court's reference to the principle of territoriality and 'the jurisdiction of the State over events and persons within that territory' which flows from that principle.

[3] *Spiliada Maritime Corporation v Cansulex Ltd* [1987] AC 460; [1986] 3 All ER 843 (HL) at 854; and see Collins (*Dicey, Morris and Collins*) 2012, Ch 12 and Fawcett, Carruthers and North (*Cheshire, North and Fawcett*), 2008, Chs 13, 15, and 16.

channels, though proceedings in the foreign State's own court are also a possibility. Because it brings a halt to proceedings it is, from a potential defendant's position, the most effective plea.

The other two pleas may be raised in proceedings where private persons or a foreign State is a party. Act of State is a defence to the substantive law requiring the forum court to exercise restraint in the adjudication of disputes relating to legislative or other governmental acts which a foreign State has performed within its territorial limits. Non-justiciability bars a national court from adjudicating certain issues, particularly international relations between States, by reason of their lacking any judicial or manageable standards by which to determine them.

In studying the subject it is important to keep a proper historical perspective. All three doctrines are based on a concept of the State, its changing role and increasing subjection to the rule of law in both its internal and external dealings. The doctrine of immunity in particular, has moved from an absolute to an increasingly restrictive phase, that is from total immunity to the recognition of exceptions to immunity permitting the institution of certain proceedings in a national court against a foreign State. The dualist approach of common law which treated international and municipal law as two separate systems has been considerably modified by the reception of international standards into common law, without express legislative enactment.

II. STATE IMMUNITY

A. ORIGINS OF THE PLEA OF STATE IMMUNITY

Following the Treaty of Westphalia 1648 the modern State emerged with its centralization of legislative, judicial, and enforcement powers. The need for protection of representatives of foreign States led to the development of diplomatic immunity for the Ambassador and members of a foreign embassy. The visits of personal sovereigns required development of a principle of inviolability of their person and immediate possessions and entourage as well as immunity from suit in the local court. The visits of warships of friendly States to national ports required the recognition of the ships' immunity from local jurisdiction.

B. DEVELOPMENT OF THE COMMON LAW RELATING TO STATE IMMUNITY

Indeed, for the common law it was in the course of formulating an immunity from the jurisdiction of the national court for warships that the general principle of State immunity was first established in the leading case of *The Schooner Exchange* v *McFaddon*.[4] The US Supreme Court rejected a creditor's claim for attachment and ordered the release of a vessel which by reason of bad weather was present undergoing repairs in the port of Philadelphia, having been seized under a decree of the French Emperor Napoleon and converted into a public armed ship. The court thereby established the immunity in common law courts of a ship of war of a State from arrest and process in the courts of another State. Marshall CJ stated the immunity to be based upon the consent of the territorial State to waive its exclusive jurisdiction but did so by reference to an implicit obligation so to do in the law of nations. His subtle reconciliation of the territorial State's jurisdiction and the

---

[4] *The Schooner Exchange* v *McFaddon* (1812) Cranch 116 (US).

foreign State's independence has been the source of much subsequent comment and was expressed as follows:

> This perfect equality and absolute independence of sovereigns and this common interest impelling them to mutual intercourse and an interchange of good offices with each other, have given rise to a class of case in which every sovereign is understood to waive the exercise of a part of that complete exclusive territorial jurisdiction, which has been stated to be the attribute of every nation.[5]

The English Court of Appeal in *The Parlement Belge* applied the ruling in the *Schooner Exchange* more widely to cover all ships of a foreign State regardless of whether they were engaged in public service or trade,[6] and despite growing dissatisfaction, the absolute rule, declared in *The Parlement Belge*, treating all acts of a foreign State as immune, continued to be observed in English law and applied by English courts until the 1970s.[7]

By the 1970s developments elsewhere, however, encouraged a bolder approach. In 1977, the Privy Council in *The Philippine Admiral*[8] reinterpreted *The Parlement Belge*, declaring that it had not laid down the wide proposition that 'a sovereign can claim immunity for vessels owned by him even if they are admittedly being used wholly or substantially for trading purposes'. It accordingly rejected a plea of immunity in respect of *in rem* proceedings (that is proceedings for attachment and sale directed against the vessel itself) brought for goods supplied to a vessel operated as an ordinary trading ship in which the Philippine government retained an interest. The next year the Court of Appeal in *Trendtex* v *Central Bank of Nigeria*[9] refused to allow a plea of immunity as a bar to proceedings against the Central Bank of Nigeria for failure to honour a commercial letter of credit;[10] the court, unanimously, held that the bank by the terms of its establishment was an independent entity and not to be treated as part of the State of Nigeria; and, by a majority, that English law recognized no immunity in respect of proceedings brought for a commercial activity such as the issue of a letter of credit. In accepting a restrictive doctrine of immunity in the common law—a move which was confirmed by the House of Lords in *I Congreso del Partido*,[11] the English courts were much influenced by legal developments elsewhere and these developments finally led to the enactment in 1978 of the State Immunity Act (SIA) providing for a restrictive scheme of immunity.

---

[5] The release of the Argentinian warship, the *Fragata Libertad*, after its arrest to enforce an outstanding commercial judgment given by both the New York and Ghana courts indicates this continued enforceability of the international law obligation to respect the immunity of a foreign State's warship. See 'ARA Libertad' (*Argentina* v *Ghana*), *Provisional Measures, Order 15 December 2012, ITLOS Reports 2012*; 27 September 2013, Agreement between Argentina and Ghana settling the dispute.

[6] *The Parlement Belge* (1879–90) 5 Prob Div 197 (CA); a packet boat owned by the King of the Belgians involved in a collision in the port of Dover was held to enjoy State immunity although at the time it was carrying both royal mail and passengers and merchandise for hire.

[7] *The Cristina* [1938] AC 485 (HL) per Lord Atkin at 491. Attempts to confine immunity to the central government of the State, or to exclude departments or agencies which enjoyed separate legal personality (*Baccus SRL* v *Servicio Nacional del Trigo* [1957] 1 QB 438; 28 ILR 160 (CA)), or to treat consent of the State given in an agreement prior to the dispute as constituting waiver of immunity (*Kahan* v *Pakistan Federation* [1951] 2 KB 1003; 18 ILR 210 (CA)), were all unsuccessful in the English courts.

[8] *The Philippine Admiral* [1977] AC 373; [1976] 1 All ER 78; 64 ILR 90 (PC).

[9] *Trendtex Trading Corporation* v *Central Bank of Nigeria* [1977] 1 QB 529; [1977] 1 All ER 881; 64 ILR 111 (CA).

[10] A letter of credit is an undertaking given by a bank to pay a certain sum of money on receipt of documents of title and transport relating to a particular consignment of goods; it may be enforced against the bank independently of the solvency or any refusal to pay on the part of the consignor.

[11] *I Congreso del Partido* [1983] 1 AC 244; [1981] 2 All ER 1064 at 1074; 64 ILR 307 (HL).

C. DEVELOPMENT IN CIVIL COURTS AND THE USA

With increased participation of States in trading activities following the First World War there was much dissatisfaction with the denial of legal redress against States for their commercial activities. Certain civil countries, notably in Italy, Belgium, and the Egyptian mixed courts, led the way in adopting a restrictive doctrine construing international law as requiring immunity for proceedings relating to acts committed in exercise of sovereign authority (*acta jure imperii*) and not for trading activities or acts which a private person may perform (*acta jure gestionis*); in 1963, in a magisterial decision surveying State practice, bilateral and multilateral treaties, and legal writing, the German Federal Constitutional Court declared that international law permits a restrictive doctrine of State immunity and that the proper criterion for the distinction between sovereign and private acts is the nature of the act, not its purpose. It allowed proceedings by a builder to recover the cost of repair carried out to the Iranian Embassy, holding the repair contract to relate to a non-sovereign act of the foreign State and hence not to be immune.[12]

Further support for the restrictive doctrine was given in the adoption in 1926 of the Brussels Convention for the Unification of Certain Rules concerning the Immunities of Government Vessels and later its 1934 protocol, providing that State-owned or operated ships used exclusively for non-governmental commercial purposes should enjoy no immunity and be subject to the same substantive legal rights and obligations as ships owned or operated by private persons for the purposes of trade; and in 1972 by the signature of the European Convention on State Immunity (ECSI) which introduced a number of exceptions to immunity from adjudication which were broadly based on the commercial or private law distinction and modified the absolute rule against coercive measures by an optional scheme. In 1952 the State Department of the USA announced in the Tate letter that in future US policy would be to follow the restrictive theory of sovereign immunity and in 1976, in part responding to the need of commercial banks financing sovereign States' debt to have legal recourse, Congress enacted the Foreign Sovereign Immunities Act (FSIA), being the first legislation to introduce the restrictive doctrine into the common law.

D. PRESENT DAY SOURCES OF THE INTERNATIONAL LAW OF STATE IMMUNITY

From 1976 and the enactment of the US FSIA onwards, with the legislation on State immunity of a number of other common law countries[13] and with their and other common law jurisdictions[14] along with the civil law systems of France, Austria and Germany,

---

[12] *Empire of Iran Case*, 45 ILR 57 at 80 (German Federal Constitutional Court, 30 April 1963).

[13] Foreign Sovereign Immunities Act 1976 (USA) (cited as FSIA); State Immunity Act 1978 (UK) (cited as SIA); Foreign States Immunities Act 1985 (Australia); Canadian State Immunity Act 1982; Immunities and Privileges Act 1984 (Malaysia); The Pakistan State Immunity Ordinance 1981; Singapore State Immunity Act 1979; The South African Foreign States Immunities Act 1981; Malawi Immunities and Privileges Act 1984 (No 16 of 1984). Other small common law jurisdictions have enacted similar legislation, eg St Kitts 1979. See also Israel Foreign States Immunity Law 2008; Argentina Immunity of Foreign States from the Jurisdiction of Argentinian Courts 1995.

[14] Kenya, *Ministry of Defence of Government of UK v Ndegna*, Kenya Court of Appeal, 17 March 1983, 103 ILR 235; Ireland, *Government of Canada v Employment Appeals Tribunal and Burke* [1992] ILRM 325; 95 ILR 467, Irish Supreme Court; New Zealand, *Governor of Pitcairn v Sutton* [1995] INZLR 426; 104 ILR 508; *Fang and Others v Jiang and Others* [2007] NZAR 420 (HC); Zimbabwe, *Barker McCormac (Private) Ltd v Government of Kenya* [1986] CR Comm (Const) 21; 84 ILR 18; Nigeria, *Kramer v Government of Kingdom of Belgium; Embassy of Belgium* [1989] 1 CLRQ 126; 103 ILR 299.

a considerable body of State practice was accumulated in support of the application of a restrictive doctrine in national courts.[15] With the dissolution of the Soviet Union and introduction of western capitalism other European countries, as members of the Council of Europe, and certain other developing economies also looked favourably on the adoption of the restrictive doctrine of immunity.

Until 2004, however, no universal international convention on State immunity had been adopted. The 1926 Brussels Convention, referred to in Section II C, and ratified by 29 States, merely removed immunity in respect of State-owned or operated ships and their cargoes engaged in trade. Only eight States (Austria, Belgium, Cyprus, Germany, Luxembourg, Netherlands, Switzerland, and the UK) are parties to the 1972 European Convention. Nor until 2002 was there any direct ruling on State immunity at the international level.

As the ICJ itself later confirmed, the State practice as described was:

> of particular significance to be found in the judgments of national courts faced with the question whether a foreign State is immune, the legislation of those States which have enacted statutes dealing with immunity, the claims to immunity advanced by States before foreign courts and the statements made by States, first in the course of the extensive study of the subject by the International Law Commission and then in the context of the adoption of the UN Convention. *Opinio juris* in this context is reflected in particular in the assertion by States claiming immunity that international law accords them a right to such immunity from the jurisdiction of other States; in the acknowledgment, by States granting immunity, that international law imposes upon them an obligation to do so; and, conversely, in the assertion by States in other cases of a right to exercise jurisdiction over foreign States.[16]

With the advent of the twenty-first century, however, the position has significantly changed in two respects; first by the International Court of Justice delivering a number of important decisions on the customary international law relating to State immunity:[17] in the *Arrest Warrant of 11 April 2000* the International Court made a ruling as to the immunity from criminal jurisdiction of an incumbent Minister for Foreign Affairs;[18] in the *Obligation to Prosecute or Extradite* it examined the extent to which universal jurisdiction was exercisable against a former Head of State accused of the international crime of torture who had sought refuge in a third State, Senegal;[19] and in the *Jurisdictional Immunities* case it reviewed the law of State immunity in a claim brought by Germany against Italy (with Greece intervening) for the disregard of its immunity by Italian courts in proceedings relating to war damage caused by Nazi Germany during the Second World War.[20]

---

[15] See Hafner, Kohen, Breau, 2006 (hereafter referred to as Hafner). This is a collection of the practice of all the member States of the Council of Europe as regards national legislation and judicial decisions relating to State immunity conducted under the supervision of its Committee of Legal Advisers on public international law (CAHDI).

[16] *Jurisdictional Immunities of the State (Germany v Italy: Greece Intervening), Judgment of 3 February 2012, ICJ Reports 2012,* para 55.

[17] The ICJ case *Certain Criminal Proceedings in France (Republic of the Congo v France)* concerned the immunities of the President and the Minister of the Interior of the Republic of the Congo, but the case was withdrawn at the request of the Republic of the Congo in 2010. See *Certain Criminal Proceedings in France (Republic of the Congo v France), Order of 16 November 2010, ICJ Reports 2010,* p 635.

[18] *Arrest Warrant of 11 April 2000 (Democratic Republic of Congo v Belgium), Preliminary Objections and Merits, Judgment, ICJ Reports 2002,* p 3.

[19] *Questions relating to the Obligation to Prosecute or Extradite (Belgium v Senegal), Judgment of 20 July 2012.*

[20] *Jurisdictional Immunities of the State (Germany v Italy: Greece Intervening), Judgment of 3 February 2012.* A full account of this judgment will be found in Section VII.

As to the second development, on 16 December 2004 the UN General Assembly adopted by resolution the first international convention on State immunity, entitled the UN Convention on the Jurisdictional Immunities of States and their Property (UN Convention on State Immunity, or UNCSI) based, after some 20 years work, on the International Law Commission's (ILC) 'Draft Articles on Jurisdictional Immunities of States and their Property' and further lengthy debate and revision in the UNGA Sixth Committee and its working party. This Convention adopts the restrictive doctrine of State immunity with regard to civil and commercial proceedings in national courts.

The UNCSI is not yet in force as a matter of treaty law: 30 ratifications are required to bring it into force (Article 30). Currently, 28 States, including China, India, and the UK have signed the Convention and as at 1 January 2014, 14 States have deposited ratifications or acceded to it.[21] Sweden and Japan have enacted legislation giving effect to the provisions of the Convention in their national systems and the ICJ, the European Court of Human Rights (ECtHR) and the UK courts have cited UNCSI favourably in their decisions but at the present time less support has come from the USA, Russia and the People's Republic of China (PRC).

Although both Russia and the PRC signed the UNCSI in 2005 and 2006 respectively, their national courts have subsequently abandoned the restrictive rule. President Yeltsin, and on several occasions the Russian Constitutional Court and the Supreme Commercial Court, have declared that restrictive immunity constituted a customary norm of international law. However, the repeated refusal by Russia to carry out arbitration awards and to permit enforcement orders against its property have resulted in rulings in the Swedish and German courts and in the ECtHR that Russia is in breach of international law and its treaty obligations in this regard.[22] In 2013, the ECtHR declared Russia to be in breach of its obligations regarding the right of access to a court under Article 6(1) of the ECHR as a result of the refusal by Russian courts to examine the applicant's claim, having 'applied absolute State immunity from jurisdiction without any analysis of the underlying transaction, the North Korea/Russia Trade Treaty 1960 and the applicable principles of customary international law, which under Article 15 (4) of the Constitution form an integral part of the Russian legal system'.[23] The PRC in 2005 enacted a national law providing for judicial immunity from execution of central banks of foreign States similar to the restrictive rule provided in the UN Convention[24] and, as a member of the WTO and signatory of other international conventions, indicated a willingness to adopt a restrictive rule in its courts (Dahai Qi, 2008). However, when confronted by the possibility of the Hong Kong Special Administrative Region (HKSAR) continuing to apply the restrictive State immunity ordinance which had been enacted under UK rule, mainland China hardened its support for a continuance of the absolute rule of immunity. The Standing Committee of the National People's Congress confirmed the decision of the Hong Kong Court of Final Appeal, by majority of three to two, deciding that:

> The HKSAR cannot, as a matter of legal and constitutional principle, adhere to a doctrine of state immunity which differs from that adopted by the PRC. The doctrine of state immunity

---

[21] Austria, France, Iran, Italy, Japan, Kazakhstan, Lebanon, Norway, Portugal, Romania, Saudi Arabia, Spain, Sweden, Switzerland.

[22] *Sedelmayer* v *Russian Federation*, Supreme Ct Sweden, 1 July 2011 (see Wrang, 2012); *Sedelmayer* v *Russian Federation*, German Federal Supreme Court, Case noVII ZB 8/05 and 9/05, 4 October 2005.

[23] *Oleynikov* v *Russia*, no 36703/04, Judgment of 14 March 2013, para 70.

[24] Law of the People's Republic of China on Judicial Immunity from Measures of constraint for the property of foreign central banks, adopted on 25 October 2005. See *FG Hemisphere Assoc* v *Congo*, HK App. Ct. (10.02.2010), [2010] 2 HKLRD 66.

practised in the HKSAR, as in the rest of China, is accordingly a doctrine of absolute immunity.[25]

The UNCSI provides a comprehensive code for the immunity of a State and its property from the civil and administrative jurisdiction of the courts of another State based on the restrictive doctrine of immunity, which is further elaborated upon in the commentaries which accompanied the 1991 ILC draft Articles. (As the UNGA resolution adopting the Convention makes plain, there is a general understanding that the Convention does not cover criminal proceedings, a point considered further in the next section.) The restrictive rule of immunity and the exceptions, which the Convention sets out as regards both the adjudication and the enforcement of judgments in national courts against a foreign State, reflect a balance between the legitimate interests of States as to the exercise of governmental powers and of private parties as regards commercial undertakings; the Convention thus provides 'a solid foundation on which States can base their domestic law' either by direct incorporation or harmonization (Stewart, 2005, p 206).

However, as the UN Convention does not yet have the number of ratifications needed to bring it into force, a degree of uncertainty remains. In the light of this uncertainly, the approach followed in this chapter is to ascertain the current law relating to State immunity by examining the provisions of the Convention in the light of the extent to which they are supported by State practice, as evidenced in the decisions of the ICJ, the European Court of Human Rights, other inter-State tribunals and the legislation and case law of the principal municipal jurisdictions.

E. THE ELEMENTS CONSTITUTING THE PLEA OF STATE IMMUNITY

1. The plea as a bar to the judicial power of the forum State in respect of proceedings before a court

The plea concerns immunity from the judicial power of another State, primarily the civil jurisdiction of the courts, though as regards the enforcement of that power it may also involve the executive power and the administrative authorities of that other State; with the exercise of criminal jurisdiction—by the arrest of the defendant by the police, his detention in State operated prisons, prosecution by the forum State's prosecutor—all treated as matters more closely connected with the executive of the forum State. The plea does not relate to the legislative power of the State—the State's jurisdiction to prescribe—which goes more to the plea of non-justiciability, act of State, and substantive liability (see later). A State may claim and enjoy other privileges and immunities from the forum State such as immunity for its nationals from military conscription or the privilege of payment of no import duties or preferential rates on petroleum fuel or alcoholic drinks, but these are not the direct concern of the plea of State immunity before a court.

The main significance of a plea of State immunity relates to its effect upon the jurisdiction of a national court of a State other than that of the defendant State,[26] including any tribunal exercising judicial or quasi-judicial powers, whether in criminal, civil, family, or other matters, including administrative tribunals. The position regarding arbitration

---

[25] *Democratic Republic of Congo and others* v *FG Hemisphere Associates LLC*, Hong Kong Court of Final Appeal, 8 June 2011 [2011] (FACV 5-7/2010) HKCFA 42.

[26] The Home State, as in respect of Crown privileges before UK courts, may enjoy certain privileges before its own national courts.

tribunals is different since they derive their authority directly from the consent of the parties and without that consent the arbitration tribunal has no competence to determine the dispute. However, given that the tribunal does not itself have any means through which to give effect to its award, it falls to the State and its courts to enforce an arbitral award, and so the plea of State immunity may have a relevance even as regards arbitratal proceedings (see Section II E 2).

International tribunals

State immunity primarily constitutes a bar to proceedings brought in national courts. It is not generally a bar to proceedings before an international tribunal where States enjoy equal standing and which is not operated within one State's legal system. Where the authority of the international tribunal derives from a Resolution of the UN Security Council made under Chapter VII which imposes binding obligations on all States, State immunity is no bar to prosecution of a State official. Thus the serving heads Milosevic of the former Yugoslavia, and Jean Kambanda, the former Prime Minister of Rwanda, were prosecuted in the International Criminal Tribunals for the former Yugoslavia (ICTY) and the International Criminal Tribunal for Rwanda (ICTR) respectively for international crimes and the International Criminal Court acting under UN SC Resolution 1593 (2005) has indicted a serving Head of State. On somewhat similar grounds Charles Taylor, the serving Head of State of Liberia, was held to enjoy no immunity from the jurisdiction of the Sierra Leone Special Court in respect of criminal proceedings, because that court ruled that it was not a national court but an international tribunal established by agreement between the UN and Sierra Leone pursuant to Security Council Resolution 1315 (2000) holding that: 'the principle of State immunity derives from the equality of States and therefore has no relevance to international criminal tribunals which are not organs of a State but derive their mandate from the international community'.[27] This is reinforced by the decision of the Special Tribunal for Lebanon (STL) Appeals Chamber on 24 October 2012, when it upheld the previous decision of the STL Trial Chamber rejecting a challenge to the legality of the Tribunal, finding that the Tribunal had no power to review the actions of the Security Council in establishing the Tribunal.

It may be necessary, however, to make a distinction between the accused State official whose claim to immunity will have no force before an international tribunal and the position of the State to which such official belongs when questions of enforcement of the tribunal's orders are concerned. Such distinctions may be particularly relevant in respect of 'mixed' or 'hybrid' courts which have been set up, that is courts whose constitution and powers are in some respects of an international character and in others of the character of the national law of a particular State; these include the Extraordinary Chambers in the Courts of Cambodia, East Timor Special Panels for Serious Crimes, the Bosnian and Serbian War Crimes Chambers, and the Special Tribunal for Lebanon (STL) (see Cryer, Ch 25, Section IV D and Wickremasinghe, Ch 13, Section VIII C in this book). The STL is an excellent illustration of the mixed international and national character of its constitution: although set up by a Chapter VII Security Council resolution, the jurisdiction conferred on the tribunal is over 'the persons responsible for the attack of 14 February

---

[27] *Prosecutor v Charles Taylor*, Appeals Chamber, No SCSL–2003–01–I, Judgment of 31 May 2004; 128 ILR 239. Liberia initially challenged this decision, filing an application against Sierra Leone before the International Court of Justice asserting that the Special Court was not a UN organ, nor established as an international criminal court, and that the Special Court 'cannot impose legal obligations on States that are not parties to the Agreement between Sierra Leone and the United Nations'. However, in 2006 Liberia requested that he be tried by the Special Tribunal and on 30 May 2012 Taylor was convicted of war crimes and supporting the commission of atrocities committed by rebel foces in the civil war in Sierra Leone. Taylor has lodged an appeal against his 50-year imprisonment sentence.

2005 resulting in the death of former Lebanese Prime Minister Rafiq Hariri and in the death or injury of other persons' and 'the provisions of the Lebanese Criminal Code relating to the prosecution and punishment of acts of terrorism, crimes and offences against life and personal integrity…' are made applicable to the prosecution of such persons for the attack.[28] It would seem that immunity is no bar to the prosecution of a crime under Lebanese law of any individual present in Lebanon and charged before the STL but enforcement against a State other than Lebanon may require its consent or a Chapter VII SC resolution.

Whether or not one characterizes the situation as one of immunity or not, that the effective operation of international tribunals remains dependent on the cooperation of States, a fact clearly recognized in the principle of complementarity and the need for an express provision relating to diplomatic and State immunity in the Rome Statute which established the International Criminal Court (ICC).[29]

2. Waiver

Since the plea of immunity acts as a personal bar *ratione personae* it may be removed with the consent of the defendant State. Accordingly, if the beneficiary State waives the immunity, the national courts of the other State will have jurisdiction to proceed against it. Modern law has broadened the occasions on which consent may be given; but three conditions remain—(a) that consent to waive the immunity must be given by the State itself not by the agency or individual performing the sovereign act on the State's behalf; (b) its expression be unequivocal and certain; (c) that waiver of immunity from execution requires a separate waiver from immunity from adjudication. US law interprets these requirements to permit implied as well as express consent to waive both immunity from jurisdiction and from execution, but waiver of immunity from prejudgment attachment of a State's property must be by express consent.[30] English law is narrower; it has abandoned the strict requirement that submission be made in the face of the court (to the judge hearing the case), but still requires that consents to both jurisdiction and execution to be given separately and in writing.[31] Waiver of immunity is to be distinguished from submission to the jurisdiction of a particular national court; thus a general waiver of immunity is not of itself to be construed as amounting to a submission to the jurisdiction of the English courts as required by the State Immunity Act 1978 (SIA) s 2(1).[32]

Implied consent: The facts or circumstances surrounding a claim have been used to imply consent and hence waiver by a State of its immunity. Consent to local proceedings has been used to develop the restrictive doctrine—if the State consents to trade then it is implied and deemed to consent to adjudication of disputes with private parties relating to such trade by the courts and to the law of the place where that trade is conducted. Similarly, reliance has been placed on the consent of a State contained in an arbitration agreement to support the recognition of the award by the national courts of the State where the arbitration takes place or whose State's law is the applicable law to the dispute; 'Arbitration is a consensual procedure and the principle underlying s 9 is that, if a State has agreed to

---

[28] UN SC Res 1757 (30 May 2007) and Agreement for the Special Tribunal for Lebanon annexed thereto.

[29] This situation arose in the case of the arrest warrant issued for President Al-Bashir of Sudan, which was not a party to the Rome Statute. Criticisms of the ICC Pre-Trial Chamber's rulings on this matter have resulted in uncertainties regarding the execution of the arrest warrant. See Wickremasinge, Ch 13, Section VIII C of this book.

[30] See US FSIA ss 1605(a)(1), 1610(a)(1) and (d)(1).

[31] Consent that UK law shall apply is not to be regarded as submission to jurisdiction (SIA s 2(2)).

[32] *Svenska Petroleum Exploration AB* v *Government of the Republic of Lithuania & Anor* [2006] EWCA Civ 1529; [2007] 2 WLR 876, confirming [2005] EWHC 2437 (Comm); [2006] 1 All ER 731 (Gloster J).

submit to arbitration, it has rendered itself amenable to such process as may be necessary to render the arbitration effective'.[33] More controversial is whether consent to arbitration can be construed as consent to the enforcement of the award against the State's property either by the courts of the State where the arbitration is held or by courts elsewhere.[34] To avoid such fictional extensions of consent, SIA, s 9, along with other common law legislation, has enacted an express exception to immunity for proceedings which relate to an arbitration. Implied consent has also be relied upon to justify the removal of immunity for claims arising from the commission of war crimes and crimes against humanity, the argument being that if the State consents to acts which contravene international obligations voluntarily assumed by treaty then it must be deemed to consent to the removal of immunity for such crimes.[35] However, this line of argument has been rejected. US courts have held that the provision in the FSIA relating to implied waiver is subject to an intentionality requirement. 'Implied waiver depends upon the foreign government's having at some point indicated its amenability to suit'.[36]

3. A procedural plea to the jurisdiction of the court, not an exemption from liability

The plea is one of immunity from suit, not of exemption from law. The ICJ has said that

> [t]he rules of State immunity are procedural in character and are confined to determining whether or not the courts of one State may exercise jurisdiction in respect of another. . . . It regulates the exercise of jurisdiction in respect of particular conduct and is thus entirely distinct from the substantive law which determines whether that conduct is lawful or unlawful.[37]

State responsibility concerns the extent to which the acts of a person, legal or human, may be attributed to a State whereas State immunity acts as a bar to acts of one State being subject to the jurisdiction of another. The entitlement to immunity is, therefore, not lost by reason of the gravity of the injury, its criminal nature under international law or the lack of alternative means of securing redress.[38] The underlying liability or responsibility of the defendant State remains unaffected by the grant of immunity, even though this may result in no remedy being available and liability avoided. Where immunity is waived the case can, of course, be decided by the application of the law in the ordinary way.[39]

---

[33] *Svenska Petroleum Exploration AB v Lithuania and Another* [2006] EWCA Civ 1529; [2007] 2 WLR 876 per Moore-Bick LJ at 913.

[34] *Creighton v Qatar*, France Court of Cassation, ch civ.1, 6 July 2000 (see Pingel, 2000). In *Orascom Telecom Holding SAE v Republic of Chad & Ors* [2008] EWHC 1841 (Comm); 2 Lloyds Rep [2008] 397, para 49 Stanley Burnton J refused to construe a foreign State's submission to arbitration and the signing of terms of reference containing express reference to ICC Rules Article 28(6) to constitute waiver so as to expand the waiver of immunity beyond the commercial purposes exception in SIA s 13(4).

[35] *Siderman de Blake v Republic of Argentina*, 965 F.2d 688 (9th Cir 1992); 103 ILR 454; *Princz v Federal Republic of Germany*, 26 F.3d 1166 (DC Cir 1994); 103 ILR 594.

[36] *Princz v Federal Republic of Germany*, 26 F.3d 1166 (DC Cir 1994); 103 ILR 594 at 1174.

[37] *Jurisdictional Immunities of the State (Germany v Italy: Greece Intervening), Judgment of 3 February 2012,* paras 58, 93.

[38] Ibid, para 101.

[39] This is well illustrated by the analogous case of diplomatic immunity where in *Dickinson v Del Solar* [1930] KB 376, the court held the company who insured a driver involved in a motor accident liable under the policy to pay damages for injuries caused, notwithstanding that the driver, as secretary of the Peruvian legation, enjoyed diplomatic immunity.

4 The nature of the proceedings in the national court

The plea affords to a varying degree immunity to one State in respect of criminal and civil proceedings in the court of another State.

Immunity from civil proceedings

A general rule of immunity from civil jurisdiction subject to exceptions for acts of a private law or commercial nature—the restrictive doctrine—is applied in the 2004 UN Convention on State Immunity and by the USA, common law countries, and Western European States. A distinction is applied by the restrictive doctrine between acts undertaken by the foreign State in the exercise of its sovereign authority—*acta jure imperii*, such as acts of the armed forces, police, diplomatic and political agents and agencies of the foreign State which continue to attract immunity—and the acts which it undertakes which are of a commercial or private law nature—*acta jure gestionis*, such as the sale of goods, contracts of employment, loans and financial arrangements—which do not attract immunity. The exceptions to immunity based on the restrictive doctrine are considered further in Section II G ('Exceptions to adjudication jurisdiction'). For the current position as to immunity from civil proceedings for acts in contravention of international law, see Section VI.

Immunity from criminal proceedings:

The immunity of a foreign State in respect of criminal proceedings brought in another State remains generally absolute. As regards the criminal position of State officials, however, the position in international law is less certain. The growing consensus that perpetrators of international crimes should not go unpunished has led to the prosecution of high ranking State officials *not only* before international criminal tribunals *but also* before national courts,[40] encouraged by the decision of the House of Lords in 1999 in the *Pinochet No 3* decision,[41] in which it decided that a former Head of State present in England had no immunity from extradition proceedings *in respect of the alleged offences*—torture, a crime involving violation of a fundamental human right—even though the acts in question were committed while the former Head was still in office and were official acts undertaken for the purposes of the State. In 2002, however, the International Court of Justice reaffirmed that the *Arrest Warrant* case that a Minister for Foreign Affairs (and other high officials), whether in office or no longer serving, enjoys the complete immunity from criminal proceedings in a court of another State, save for 'acts committed in a private capacity'.[42]

A distinction is made in the plea of immunity between 'adjudication jurisdiction' and 'enforcement jurisdiction'. The application of coercive measures to a State and its property involves different and more directly intrusive mechanisms than the ruling of a municipal court as to liability. Adjudication jurisdiction relates to the court's inquiry into the claim and its adjudication by means of a judgment or declaration of the rights and obligations of the parties; it extends to interlocutory proceedings and appeal. Enforcement jurisdiction

---

[40] However, such prosecutions have been unsuccessful as regards serving senior State officials: *SOS Attentat and Castelnau d'Esnault v Qadaffi, Head of State of the State of Libya*, France, Court of Cassation, criminal chamber, 13 March 2000, No 141, 124 ILR 508; the court quashed a ruling of the Paris court of appeal that absolute criminal immunity of a serving Head of State was subject to an exception in respect of a terrorist offence of use of explosives causing the destruction of an aircraft in flight and loss of life to French nationals.

[41] *R v Bow Street Metropolitan Stipendiary, ex parte Pinochet Ugarte (Amnesty International Intervening) (No 3)* [1999] UKHL 17; [2000] 1 AC 147; 119 ILR 135. See Fox, 1999.

[42] *Arrest Warrant of 11 April 2000 (Democratic Republic of Congo v Belgium), Preliminary Objections and Merits, Judgment, ICJ Reports 2002*, p 3. See further Wickremansinge Ch 13, Sections V A and VIII B of this book.

relates to the making and execution of mandatory orders or injunctions against the State in respect of, for example, attachment of property, restitution, damages, penalties, production of documents or witnesses, and accounts.

The distinction between the two, however, may not always be easily made; winding up proceedings in respect of proved liabilities, the order of a court to recognize a judgment given by the court of another State resemble proceedings for an order for attachment or other measures of constraint against State property but the better view is that they constitute new proceedings relating to the adjudicative stage.

The ICJ's treatment of the Italian court's decisions enforcing the judgment of the Greek court in respect of the German property—the Villa Vigoni—located in Italy in the *Jurisdictional Immunities* case illustrates the difference. At the first stage, adjudication, the issue was 'whether the Italian judgments declaring enforceable in Italy the pecuniary awards pronounced in Greece, did themselves—independently of any subsequent measure of enforcement—constitute a violation of the Applicant's immunity from jurisdiction'. At the second, enforcement, stage the question was '. . .to determine whether a measure of constraint—such as the legal charge on Villa Vigoni—violated Germany's immunity from enforcement'.[43] While the ICJ noted there to be a link between the two stages, since the measure of constraint against Villa Vigoni could only have been imposed on the basis of the judgment of the Florence Court of Appeal granting an *exequatur* in respect of the judgment of the Greek court in Livadia, it declared that the two issues remained distinct since they were governed by different sets of rules (see also Section II H of this chapter).

F. DEFINITION OF THE FOREIGN STATE FOR THE PURPOSE OF STATE IMMUNITY

Application of a restrictive doctrine has brought about a change in focus from the person of the State to the acts performed by the State or its agents, from status to function; the question is less whether an entity established, managed, or funded by the State is immune *ratione personae* and more whether the act performed by whosoever is of governmental nature and hence immune *ratione materiae* (see also Wickremasinghe, Ch 13, Section VI of this book). Nonetheless the personal nature of State immunity remains important, both for the State itself as regards its own position as a defendant in proceedings before a national court and also because the relationship between an agency and the foreign State is important in determining the extent to which immunity and its particular procedural requirements, apply to State agencies.

1. The State

Special procedural requirements concerning notice of proceedings, judgments and delayed time limits apply to proceedings against a State, which also has the option of waiving its immunity and submitting to the jurisdiction of the forum State.[44]

---

[43] *Jurisdictional Immunities of the State (Germany v Italy: Greece Intervening), Judgment of 3 February 2012,* para 124.

[44] It is worth noting, however, that by submitting to the jurisdiction a State may be deprived of the defences of *force majeure* and frustration, which private parties may raise, since these defences relate to matters within the control of the State as a contracting party. See *C Czarnikow Ltd v Centrala Handlu Zagranicznego 'Rolimpex'* [1979] AC 351.

2. State agencies

For the State agency, entitlement to immunity may afford it the special protection enjoyed by the State itself, as regards both the substantive law and special procedural requirements. The US FSIA goes so far as to treat all instrumentalities and agencies as coming within the definition of a foreign State for the purposes of immunity though with reduced restrictions as to procedure and enforcement against property held by the agency. Other jurisdictions distinguish between the central organs or departments of government which come within the protection of State immunity and other State agencies; but it remains controversial whether the appropriate criterion for attribution of the agency's act to the State is by authorization or performance in exercise of sovereign authority or whether both cumulatively should be applied, as in the 2004 UN Convention, Article 2.1(b)(iii) of which defines 'State' as including 'agencies or instrumentalities of the State or other entities, to the extent that they are entitled to perform and are actually performing acts in the exercise of sovereign authority'.

The UK SIA s 14(1)(c) limits the conferment of immunity to 'separate entities...distinct from the executive organs of the State and capable of suing and being sued', where such a 'separate entity' acts in the exercise of sovereign authority and the circumstances are such that the foreign State itself would be immune (SIA s 14 (2)). This requires an English court to engage in an extensive review of the past and present operations of an entity to determine which factor—the extent of the foreign State's control or the functions of the entity in conformity with private law of the forum State—is to prevail.[45] This can result in courts producing conflicting decisions, influenced in part by the extraneous consideration such of questions of sham, of fraud or the possibility of 'lifting the corporate veil'. In an attempt to clarify the position the Privy Council in the recent case of *Gecamines* has identified a separate entity as 'enjoying a hybrid status' and declared that in determining its status there should be applied a 'strong presumption...that its separate status should be respected'.[46] This approach would seem to differ from the European Convention on State Immunity, Article 27 and the UN Convention, Article 2.1(b)(iii), both of which require the application cumulatively of both factors.

3. Representatives of the State

The UN Convention's inclusion within its definition of 'State' 'representatives of the State acting in that capacity', Article 2.1(b)(iv), is likely to cause confusion, given that Article 3 states that the convention is without prejudice to the privileges of diplomatic missions, consular missions, special missions and missions to international organizations and the privileges and immunities accorded under international law to Heads of State *ratione personae*. The object would seem to bring official acts performed by officials on behalf of the State within the scope of the UN Convention, and to grant immunity *ratione materiae* for such acts, but to exclude, as governed by other international conventions or international customary law, the immunity *ratione personae* enjoyed by high ranking officials of the State by virtue of their office.

---

[45] See, for example, *Trendtex Trading Corporation* v *Central Bank of Nigeria* [1977] 1 QB 529, where such an exercise was with regard to the separate status of the Central Bank of Nigeria. Note that the SIA S 14(4) now provides that the central bank of a State, irrespective of whether it is a department or a separate entity, is to be treated as if it were the State for the purposes of enforcement.

[46] *La Générale des Carrières et des Mines ("Gécamines")* v *F.G. Hemisphere Associates LLC* [2012] UKPC 27, para 29.

In English law, the Court of Appeal has held that the word 'government' in SIA, s 14(1) has to be construed as affording to individual employees or officers of a foreign State protection under the same cloak as protected the State itself. The protection afforded to States by SIA would be undermined if employees or officers of the State could be sued as individuals for matters of State conduct in respect of which the State they were serving had immunity.[47] Thus the exceptions which apply in SIA to the State are applicable to officers of the State. In US law the definition of a 'foreign state' includes 'an agency or instrumentality of a foreign state', which in turn 'means any entity—(1) which is a separate legal person, corporate or otherwise' (FSIA s 1605 (a)-(b)). Conflicting decisions in the federal circuit courts whether the definition included 'natural persons' were resolved in 2010 by the Supreme Court determining that, there being no 'evidence of the intent to include individual officials within the meaning of "agency or instrumentality"', the FSIA had not replaced the common law with respect to the immunity of individual officials, according to which the Department of State, on the request of the foreign State, determines whether the official was acting in an official capacity (and so entitled to immunity) or not when undertaking the act in question.[48] In effect, while the conduct of a foreign official might still be construed as an act of the State for which there is no immunity (as it has been lifted by the FSIA), the State officials themselves might enjoy a greater degree of immunity than that of the State itself, including immunity from criminal prosecution for international crimes.[49]

Further confusion may be caused by the failure of the UN Convention Article 3 or the accompanying Understandings to make any reference to the exclusion from its scope of acts performed by the armed forces of a State, something which is widely found in State practice, as was shown by the examination of national legislation and case law by the ICJ in the *Jurisdictional Immunities* case. However, on introducing the Convention for adoption by the UNGA 6th (Legal) Committee, the Chairman of the *ad hoc* committee, Professor Gerhard Hafner, stated his belief that a general understanding had always prevailed that military activities were not covered by the Convention and referred to the 1991 ILC Commentary on draft Article 12 (the exception relating to personal injuries and damage to property) stating it did not apply to situations of armed conflict.[50]

G. EXCEPTIONS TO ADJUDICATION JURISDICTION

1. The exceptions to immunity from civil jurisdiction of a foreign State

Today there is widespread acceptance that the immunity of the foreign State from adjudication jurisdiction may properly be restricted by exceptions, whereas immunity from enforcement jurisdiction remains largely absolute.

---

[47] Cf *Propend Finance Pty* v *Sing* (1997), 111 ILR 611, affirmed in *Jones* v *Ministry of Interior for the Kingdom of Saudi Arabia and Ors* [2006] UKHL 26; [2007] 1 AC 270, paras 30, 78.

[48] *Samantar* v *Yousuf*, 130 S. Ct. 2278 (2010) at 2287–9.

[49] On remand in the *Samantar* case, the Fourth Circuit Court of Appeals, controversially, held the defendant was not entitled to immunity in respect of participation in torture and extrajudicial killing by the governing military regime, holding foreign official immunity did not extend to violations of *jus cogens*, even if the acts were performed in the defendant's official capacity (*Yousuf* v *Samantar*, 699 F.3d 763 (4th Cir 2012)). In March 2013 the defendant petitioned the Supreme Court to consider whether a foreign official's common law immunity for acts performed on behalf of a foreign State is abrogated if those official acts violate norms of *jus cogens*. A decision is pending. See further Wickremasinghe, Ch 13, Section VI of this book,

[50] The ratifications of Norway and Sweden contain a similar declaration which excludes military activities both during an armed conflict and activities performed in the course of official duties.

Widely recognized exceptions include proceedings relating to contracts which a private party may enter or which are of a commercial nature, contracts of employment other than those with nationals of the sending State engaged in public service, immoveable property, personal injuries, or damage or loss to property of a tangible nature, and proceedings relating to the operation of seagoing ships and their cargo. The US Act stands alone in removing immunity for claims in respect of expropriation of property contrary to international law.

Commercial transactions

The main exception in the restrictive doctrine relates to commercial transactions between a private party and the foreign State. It has proved difficult to find a workable criterion, particularly for borderline cases, by which to distinguish a commercial transaction from one in exercise of sovereign authority. As explained in the *Empire of Iran* case, 'the generally recognized sphere of sovereign activity' which remains immune 'includes the activities of the authorities responsible for foreign and military affairs, legislation, the exercise of police power and the administration of justice'. While the significance of the distinction was recognized by the ICJ in the *Jurisdictional Immunities* case, and that 'States are generally entitled to immunity in respect of *acta jure imperii*',[51] it provided no criteria for distinguishing between them, other than that 'the acts in question fall to be assessed by reference to the law governing the exercise of sovereign power *(jus imperii)* or the law concerning non-sovereign activities of a State, especially private and commercial activities *(jus gestionis)*'.[52] However, examples of the retention of immunity for acts in the exercise of sovereign immunity can be found in the careful drafting of enacted exceptions to State immunity.[53]

The competence of civil courts as in France is restricted to civil and commercial matters, and does not extend to public and administrative matters; it is, therefore, not too difficult to apply the civil court's criterion of an act or transaction in which an individual may engage, as opposed to '*un acte de puissance publique ou un acte qui a été accompli dans l'intérêt d'un service public*' to proceedings brought against a foreign State. A reflection of this approach is to be found in Article 4 of ECSI which allows an exception for proceedings relating to an obligation of a State by virtue of a *contract*—a contract being a legal transaction in which a private person may engage. Applying the same approach to non-contractual claims of a private law character, immunity was refused by the Austrian Supreme Court when sought by the USA in respect of a claim for damages arising out of a road accident due to the negligence of an embassy driver when collecting the mail of the US air attaché.[54] The court distinguished a sovereign act from a private one, such as the operation of a motor car and the use of public roads, where the relationship between the parties was on the basis of equality with no question of supremacy, rather than subordination; in

---

[51] *Jurisdictional Immunities of the State (Germany v Italy: Greece Intervening)*, Judgment of 3 February 2012, para 61.

[52] Ibid, para 60. Cf the Court's ruling in respect of immunity from enforcement that the cultural Centre Villa Vigoni 'intended to promote cultural exchanges between Germany and Italy', was 'being used for governmental purposes that are entirely non-commercial and hence for purposes falling within Germany's sovereign functions' (ibid, para 119).

[53] Thus agreements to which States are the sole parties are excluded from the exception for commercial transactions (SIA s 3(2), UNCSI Article 10(2)(a); contracts of employment with diplomats and agents excluded from the employment exception SIA s. 16(1)(a), UNCSI, Article 11(2)(b); warships and naval auxiliaries excluded from the exception for State ships SIA s 10 and UNCSI Articlce16(2)).

[54] *Holubek v The Government of United States*, Austrian Supreme Court, 10 February 1961, 40 ILR 73.

applying the distinction the court looked to the nature of the act of driving as opposed to its purpose, being the collection of mail between government departments.

Common law courts are generally not of limited competence and consequently have no national practice as to what constitutes an act performable by a private person as opposed to a State. But mindful of the underlying rationale of the restrictive doctrine—that States which engage in trade should be amenable to jurisdiction—they have applied a test of commerciality in determining the non-immune nature of the proceedings. Questions concerning contracts made in the territory of the foreign State and governed by its administrative law are expressly excluded from the commercial transaction exception in the UK SIA s 3(2).

Section 1605(a)(2) of the US FSIA removes immunity where claims are based upon a commercial activity and s 1603(d) provides that, 'The commercial character of an activity shall be determined by reference to the nature of the course of conduct or particular transaction or act, rather than by any reference to its purpose'. Commerciality is not defined by the US Act and conflicting and inconsistent decisions have been given in proceedings relating to development of natural resources, foreign assistance programmes, and government exchange control. Thus US courts have held immune the cancellation of an agreement licensing the export of rhesus monkeys,[55] and mistreatment by police resulting from a whistle-blowing complaint made in the course of employment under contract in a hospital;[56] and held non-immune a technical assistance contract under which the contractor enjoyed diplomatic immunities and tax exemption,[57] a foreign government's undertaking to reimburse doctors and the organ bank for kidney transplants performed on its nationals in US hospitals,[58] and a restriction on the payment of government-issued bonds due to a shortage of foreign reserves;[59] and evaded determining the issue whether the leasing of prisoners of war as slave labour by the Nazi regime to German industrial concerns constituted a commercial activity.[60]

To avoid such difficulties, the European Convention, the UK Act, and similar legislation of other Commonwealth States, have adopted a listing method by which proceedings relating to specific categories of commercial transactions are listed as non-immune; thus s 3 of the UK SIA lists as non-immune commercial transactions 'sale of goods or supply of services', and 'loans or other transaction for the provision of finance, guarantee or indemnity of any such transaction or of other financial obligation' (s 3(3)(a) and (b)) (such transactions are not qualified by the condition 'otherwise than in the exercise of sovereign activities);[61] and both that Act and the 1972 European Convention also make non-immune proceedings relating to certain contracts of employment, to participation in companies or associations, and to claims relating to patents, trademarks, and other intellectual property rights (ECSI Articles 5, 6, and 8; SIA ss 4, 7, and 8). The listing approach is also adopted by the UN Convention which sets out exceptions for commercial transactions (Article 10), contracts of employment (Article 11), ownership and use of property (Article 13), intellectual and industrial property (Article 14), companies (Article 15), and ships (Article 16).

[55] *Mol Inc* v *Peoples Rep of Bangladesh*, 736 F.2d 1326 (9th Cir 1994) cert denied 105 S Ct 513.

[56] *Saudi Arabia* v *Nelson*, 123 L Ed 2d 47 (Sup Ct 1993); 100 ILR 544.

[57] *Practical Concepts* v *Republic of Bolivia*, 811 F.2d 1543 (DC Cir 1987); 92 ILR 420.

[58] *Rush-Presbyterian-St Luke's Medical Center* v *the Hellenic Republic*, 877 F.2d 574 (7th Cir 1989) cert denied 493 US 937; 101 ILR 509.

[59] *Republic of Argentina* v *Weltover*, 504 US 607(1992); 100 ILR 509.

[60] *Princz* v *Federal Republic of Germany*, 26 F.3d 1166; (DC Cir 1994); 33 ILM 1483.

[61] *Orascom Telecom Holding SAE* v *Republic of Chad & Ors* [2008] EWHC 1841 (Comm) 2 Lll Rep [2008] 397, citing Lord Diplock in *Alcom Ltd* v *Republic of Colombia* [1984] 1 AC 580 at 603.

Even with this method, provision has to be made for a residuary category which turns on the application of the public/private act distinction, and the cases of *I Congreso del Partido* (whether disposal of a cargo by a State agency contrary to terms of the contract of carriage on orders of the State for political reasons was immune)[62] and *Kuwait Airways Corp v Iraqi Airways Co* (whether seizure and transfer of Kuwaiti aircraft to Iraq after the invasion of Kuwait with a view to incorporation in the Iraqi civil airfleet was immune),[63] demonstrate the difficulty of distinguishing a commercial transaction from an act in exercise of sovereign authority. The accepted solution applied by English courts is to determine the nature and not the purpose of the activity. But when applied to determine the nature of the funds held in a bank account of a diplomatic embassy this test proved arbitrary; such funds could be treated as being used for the purchase of goods and services—clearly commercial acts—or more broadly for the discharge of diplomatic functions, which were clearly activities in exercise of sovereign authority.[64]

Faced with these difficulties, Lord Wilberforce reformulated the test as requiring a court to consider:

> . . . the whole context in which the claim against the State is made, with a view to deciding whether the relevant act(s) on which the claim is based should, in that context, be considered as fairly within an area of activity, trading or commercial or otherwise of a private law character, in which the State has chosen to engage or whether the relevant activity should be considered as having been done outside the area and within the sphere of governmental or sovereign activity.[65]

Therefore, when deciding cases both under the statute[66] and under the common law, a purposive construction of the public/private criterion is now applied which takes account of the whole context, including the place where the persons are alleged to have committed the acts and those who were designed to benefit from the conduct complained of. Thus, for example, and although by their nature the acts in question were ones which a private person might have committed, proceedings brought against visiting US forces were barred since on the facts of the cases those acts had been performed in the exercise of sovereign authority by reason of their having been undertaken by service personnel and in pursuance of the purpose of maintaining an efficient fighting force.[67]

The relevance of purpose as well as the nature of the transaction was much debated by the ILC and its final formulation of the UN Convention, Article 2(2) reads as follows:

> In determining whether a contract or transaction is a 'commercial transaction' under paragraph 1 (c), reference should be made to the nature of the contract or transaction, but its purpose should also be taken into account if the parties to the contract or transaction

---

[62] *I Congreso del Partido* [1983] 1 AC 244; [1981] 2 All ER 1064; 64 ILR 307 (HL).

[63] *Kuwait Airways Corp v Iraqi Airways Co* [1995] 3 All ER 694; 103 ILR 340 (HL).

[64] In *Alcom Ltd v Republic of Colombia* the Court of Appeal adopted the first view [1983] 3 WLR 906; [1984] 1 All ER 1 and the House of Lords the second [1984] AC 580; [1984] 2 WLR 750; [1984] 2 All ER 6 (HL). See also *NML Capital Ltd v The Republic of Argentina* [2011] UKSC 31, where the Supreme Court was split on whether the commericial nature of the underlying transation rendered enforcement proceedings in respect of a judgment given in New York 'commericial' or 'sovereign' in nature.

[65] *I Congreso del Partido* [1983]1 AC 244; [1981] 2 All ER 1064 at 1074; 64 ILR 307 (HL).

[66] *Propend Finance Pty Ltd v Sing*, 111 ILR 611, 2 May 1997 (CA).

[67] *Holland v Lampen-Wolfe* [2000] 1 WLR 1573; [2000] 3 All ER 833; 119 ILR 367 (HL) concerning a complaint of libel contained in a report of a supervising officer of a civilian lecturer engaged to give a course to visiting US forces; *Littrell v USA (No 2)* [1994] 4 All ER 203; [1995] 1 WLR 82; 100 ILR 438 (CA) concerning a claim of medical negligence against a service doctor treating an airman on a US base in the UK.

have so agreed, or, if in the practice of the State of the forum, that purpose is relevant to determining the non-commercial character of the contract or transaction.

The reference to purpose, designed to accommodate developing States' wish to retain immunity for contractual transactions vital to their economy or for disaster prevention or relief, has resulted in a complex piece of drafting strengthening the defendant's immunity by which the national court may be required to engage in a four-stage exercise in determining whether it has jurisdiction in a commercial transaction under Article 2(1)(c)(iii).[68] The Annex of Understandings contains nothing specific with regard to this Article and it would seem that the ambiguities present in the Article constitute an open invitation for reservation or interpretative declaration to any State proposing to give effect to the Convention in its law by ratification. However, it should not be forgotten that the Working Group of the ILC itself in 1999, after an exhaustive review of the whole subject, concluded that 'the distinction between the so-called nature and purpose tests might be less significant in practice than the long debate about it might imply'.[69]

Non-commercial tort acts

In addition to the various exceptions which remove immunity for specified commercial activities, the UN Convention and State practice in legislation and court decisions allow an exception for certain non-contractual delictual activities of a foreign State. Thus, Article 12 of the 2004 UN Convention contains an exception from immunity in civil proceedings which 'relates to pecuniary compensation for death or injury to the person, or damage to or loss of tangible property, caused by an act or omission which is alleged to be attributable to the State, if the act or omission occurred in whole or in part in the territory of that other State, and if the author of the act or omission was present in that territory at the time of the act or omission'. Three comments are relevant to understanding the scope of this exception for delictual or tortious conduct of a foreign State. First, its scope is narrow, being confined to physical infliction of damage to the person or property with its origin derived from insurable risks arising from physical injuries and damage resulting from traffic accidents; proceedings relating to false, defamatory, or negligent statements are not included and this exclusion ensures that much delictual conduct arising from complaints as to the information or publications of a foreign State remains immune. Secondly, the exception only relates to wrongful conduct of a foreign State committed in the territory of the forum State: the UK SIA s 5 merely refers to '(a) the death or personal injury; or (b) damage to or loss of tangible property, caused by act or omission in the United Kingdom'; the US FSIA s 1605(a) (5) is similar with the personal injury, death or damage to or loss of property occurring in the USA (but excludes any claim based on failure of any State official or employee to exercise or perform a discretionary function); the UN Convention Article 12, following the 1977 European Convention on State Immunity, Article 11, is even stricter, limiting proceedings to where the author is present in the forum State at the time when the facts occurred. This territorial requirement present in all conventional or legislative formulations of the exception prevents the exception's application to personal injuries inflicted abroad and restricts the exercise of extraterritorial jurisdiction over a

---

[68] These stages being to consider the nature of the transaction, first in the absence and second in the presence of evidence of the purpose of the transaction; third, to take account of such purpose where an agreement of the parties so as to take such purpose into account is proved; and fourth to have regard to purpose if it is relevant in the practice of the forum State, *not* of its law, in determining the non-commercial character of the transaction.

[69] See A/CN.4/L.576, para 60.

foreign State in respect of such claims. Thirdly, the exception in the UN Convention and common law legislation contains no requirement that the personal injury or damage to property be caused in the course of commercial activity; injury or damage resulting from an act in exercise of sovereign authority is recoverable, as for example proceedings for State-ordered assassination of a political opponent which has been held non-immune under a similar tort exception in the US FSIA. Indeed the ICJ was careful in its latest judgment not to 'resolve the question whether there is in customary international law a "tort exception" to State immunity applicable to *acta jure imperii* in general'.[70]

Not all jurisdictions accept such a wide removal of State immunity for non-contractual claims; in a case relating to immunity in respect of an assault by a soldier of the foreign State while within the territory of the forum State, the European Court of Human Rights after a survey of State practice, concluded that a 'trend in international and comparative law towards limiting State immunity in respect of personal injury caused by an act or omission within the forum State' refers primarily 'to "insurable" personal injury, that is incidents arising out of ordinary traffic accidents, rather than matters relating to the core area of State sovereignty such as the acts of a soldier on foreign territory which, of their very nature may involve sensitive issues affecting diplomatic relations between States and national security'.[71]

The Greek and Italian courts in the *Voiotia* and *Ferrini* cases respectively sought to apply this territorial exception to claims relating to war damage: in *Voiotia*,[72] decided in 2000, the Greek Supreme Court awarded some $30 million in damages to Greek nationals for personal injuries and loss of property suffered at Distomo by reason of acts of the German occupying forces in 1944 and in 2004, in *Ferrini*[73] the Italian Supreme Court awarded damages for forcible deportation and forced labour of an Italian national by German military authorities during the Second World War disregarding Germany's immunity and enforcing the German judgment against the Villa Lagoni, a German property located in Italy.[74]

Germany referred to the International Court of Justice its claim against Italy for breach of international law by violation of its immunity by *Ferrini* and similar decisions of the Italian courts. Basing its jurisdiction on the European Convention for the Peaceful Settlement of Disputes 1957, by which the two States had conferred jurisdiction on the Court in respect of disputes after 1961, and applying customary international law, the International Court upheld Germany's claim in its entirety. In respect of the claims

---

[70] *Jurisdictional Immunities of the State (Germany v Italy: Greece Intervening), Judgment of 3 February 2012*, para 65.

[71] *McElhinney v Ireland and the UK* [GC], no 31253/96, para 38, ECHR 2001-XI, 34 *EHRR* 13.

[72] *Prefecture of Voiotia v Federal Republic of Germany*, Case No 11/2000, Supreme Court, 4 May 2000, 123 ILR 513. Subsequently, somewhat undermining the authority of the earlier proceedings, a specially convened Greek Constitutional Court competent to decide issues of international law, in a judgment of 17 September 2002, ruled that international law continues to vest foreign States with immunity when sued for acts which take place in the territory of the forum and in which its armed forces were implicated, whether or not these acts violated *jus cogens*. See *Margellos v Federal Republic of Germany*, Case No 6/2002, Supreme Court, 17 September 2002, 129 ILR 526.

[73] *Ferrini v Federal Republic of Germany*, Italian Court of Cassation, Judgment No 5044 of 11 March 2004, 128 ILR 659.

[74] In Greece enforcement was refused by the Greek Minister of Justice and in Germany by the the German court, and on application for a violation of ECHR Article 6(1) the ECtHR held that Greece, in refusing to authorize enforcement, enjoyed a wide margin of appreciation, particularly in matters of foreign relations, and that Germany's responsibility was in no way engaged for lack of enforcement of the judgment. *Kalogeropoulou v Greece and Germany* (Dec), no 59021/00, ECHR 2002-X, 129 ILR 537: see also *Distomo Massacre Case*, Germany Federal Constitutional Court, 15 February 2006, 135 ILR 185.

relating to immunity from adjudication, it rejected the application of any territorial tort exception to State immunity as regards the deportation to Germany and enforced labour in German factories of Italian nationals entitled to prisoner of war status: 'State practice in the form of judicial decisions supports the proposition that State immunity for *acta jure imperii* continues to extend to civil proceedings for acts occasioning death, personal injury or damage to property committed by the armed forces and other organs of a State in the conduct of armed conflict, even if the relevant acts take place on the territory of the forum State'.[75]

The International Court's rulings as to the legality of the Italian courts' orders relating to the German Villa Lagoni usefully clarified the law both as regards the extent to which an exception to immunity from adjudication exists in respect of a foreign judgment made by a third State relating to immunity, and as regards enforcement, with regard to the criterion for the removal of immunity in respect of measures of constraint against foreign State property (see also Section II H of this chapter). As regards Germany's claim that its immunity was infringed by the Italian courts' grant of *exequatur* to enforce of the *Voiotia* judgment, the ICJ pointed out that it was not necessary to determine whether the *Greek* courts had violated German immunity in the *Voiotia* case. Rather, the correct question was whether the *Italian* courts had respected Germany's immunity from jurisdiction in allowing the application for *exequatur*. For the same reasons as it upheld German immunity in respect of the Italian claims relating to war damage, the ICJ concluded that the Italian courts would have been obliged to grant immunity to Germany if they had been seized of the merits of a case such as *Voiotia*. Therefore, they could not grant *exequatur* without violating Germany's jurisdictional immunity.

The wider significance of the *Jurisdictional Immunities* judgment and the acceptability of the force of the public/private criterion on which it rests as the sole determinant of relevance of a plea of State immunity is examined in the final section of this chapter.

2. Jurisdictional connection of non-immune proceedings with the forum State

The limitation of the personal injuries exception to acts committed in the forum territory highlights the general question whether the jurisdiction of national courts over foreign States is conditional on some close link with the territory of the forum State, and whether such a link is the same or stricter than that which principles of private international law provide for civil litigation between private parties. Both the European Convention on State Immunity and the US FSIA require as regards the removal of State immunity that there be a nexus or jurisdictional connection with the forum State in respect of each of the recognized exceptions to State immunity. That jurisdictional connection for some exceptions, as with employment contracts and personal injuries, is stricter than those recognized in private international law for private party litigation. The UK and other common law jurisdictions which follow the SIA have also accepted additional jurisdictional links for the employment, tort and other exceptions; only in respect of the commercial transaction exception, the arbitration and State ships exceptions is there an absence of a connection other than those required in ordinary litigation for the exercise of extraterritorial personal jurisdiction under Civil Procedure Rules, r 6.26 (formerly RSC Order 11, r 1) or like common law procedures. Recently the UK Supreme Court in *NML* v *Argentina* endorsed the omission in s 3(1)(a) of a jurisdictional link between the foreign State's commercial

---

[75] *Jurisdictional Immunities of the State (Germany v Italy: Greece Intervening), Judgment of 3 February 2012,* para 77.

transaction and the UK jurisdiction. In the leading judgment Lord Phillips said, and which point all their Lordships concurred:

> I can see no justification for giving section 3(1)(a) a narrow interpretation on the basis that it is desirable to restrict the circumstances in which it operates to those where the commercial transaction has a link with the United Kingdom. The restrictive doctrine of sovereign immunity does not restrict the exemption from immunity to commercial transactions that are in some way linked to the jurisdiction of the forum.[76]

The UN Convention adopts a neutral position, referring in Article 10(1) to the determination of jurisdiction over the commercial transaction exception to 'the applicable rules of private international law' of the forum State.[77]

For proceedings which are clearly identical to those brought in private litigation, there may be no need to require any special additional jurisdictional link where the defendant is a foreign State. But for proceedings which relate to conflicts of jurisdiction between States, as further discussed in Section VI, the plea of immunity at the present time serves to demarcate the limits of State jurisdiction exercisable over the public acts of another State. Until agreed rules for the allocation of jurisdiction replace the present exclusive jurisdiction of the State over acts in exercise of sovereignty performed within its own territory, the restriction of the exception to immunity for non-contractual delictual acts to the performance of those within the territory of the forum State and indeed the general bar of State immunity is likely to remain.

H. IMMUNITY FROM ENFORCEMENT

Unlike its immunity from adjudication which is subject to exceptions, a foreign State continues largely immune from forcible measures of execution against its person or property; as the ICJ has said, the rules of customary international law governing immunity from enforcement are distinct from and go further than those governing jurisdictional immunity, and must be separately applied.[78]

1. Immunity of the person of the State or representatives from coercive measures

Immunity from measures against the personal representative of the State remains absolute. As recently confirmed by the International Court of Justice in the *Arrest Warrant* case, no Head of State, head of government, or Minister for Foreign Affairs while in office may be arrested by order of the national court of another State or preliminary measures such as the issue or international circulation of an arrest warrant taken against such persons.[79] The personal immunity enjoyed by such persons while in office is an important element of the

---

[76] *NML Capital Ltd* v *The Republic of Argentina* [2011] UKSC 31, para 39.

[77] See also ILC Commentary to Article 10(1), para (3) and (4).

[78] *Jurisdictional Immunities of the State (Germany* v *Italy: Greece Intervening), Judgment of 3 February 2012,* para 113. Hence Professor Sucharitkul, the ILC's Special Rapporteur's has described immunity from execution as 'the last fortress...the last bastion of State immunity' (*YBILC* (1991), vol II (Part two), p 13, Commentary to ILC Draft Articles, Article 18, para 1).

[79] *Arrest Warrant of 11 April 2000 (Democratic Republic of Congo* v *Belgium), Preliminary Objections and Merits, Judgment, ICJ Reports 2002,* p 3, paras 62–71. In the case concerning *Certain Criminal Proceedings in France (Republic of Congo* v *France)* brought in 2003 the applicant State claimed that the initiation of a criminal investigation by the French court without service on the foreign State constituted a violation of a serving Head of State's immunity. This case was discontinued in 2010. See *Certain Criminal Proceedings in France (Republic of the Congo* v *France), Order of 16 November 2010, ICJ Reports 2010,* p 635.

State's own immunity enabling it to function effectively. In the *Djibouti v France* case the Court laid down a requirement that 'the State which seeks to claim immunity for one of its organs is expected to notify the authorities of the other State concerned, whether through diplomatic exchanges or before a French judicial organ', and explained that 'this would allow the court of the forum State to ensure that it does not fail to respect any entitlement to immunity and might thereby engage the responsibility of that State. Further the State notifying a foreign court that judicial process should not proceed, for reasons of immunity against its State organs, is assuming responsibility for any internationally wrongful act at issue committed by such organs'.[80] It would thereby effect a warning that any failure to respect immunity might engage the international responsibility of the forum State and further inform that State that the notifying State assumes its own responsibility for any internationally wrongful act committed by such organs.

No injunction or order for specific performance may be directed by a national court against a foreign State on pain of penalty if not obeyed. Thus the Netherlands Supreme Court has ruled that it has no jurisdiction to declare a foreign State bankrupt:

> Acceptance of this jurisdiction would imply that a trustee in bankruptcy with far-reaching powers could take over the administration and the winding up of the assets of a foreign power under the supervision of a Dutch public official. This would constitute an unacceptable infringement under international law of the sovereignty of the foreign State concerned.[81]

For this same reason the UK SIA s 13(1) prohibits the imposition of any penalty by way of committal or fine in respect of any failure or refusal by the State to disclose information or produce any document, and s 13(2) the giving of any relief against a State by way of injunction or order for specific performance or recovery of land or other property.

2. Immunity of State property from coercive measures

Some relaxation of immunity would seem appropriate where a judgment is rendered in respect of a non-immune commercial or private law transaction; one might expect that the restrictive doctrine would permit the local court to have jurisdiction to execute such a judgment against the property of the foreign State, by forcible means if necessary. The practice of the Swiss courts in fact endorses such an approach stressing 'the overall unity of substantive law', and that 'a judgment imports enforceability'. The Swiss Federal Tribunal has held that to refuse execution would mean that the judgment would lack its most essential attribute, namely that it will be executed even against the will of the party against which it is rendered.[82]

The practice of other States, however, remains more cautious and reflects underlying political realities that there is no international law of insolvency to resolve a State's general inability to meet its financial commitments. Rescheduling of State debt continues today as largely a political process.[83] Short of resort to war there is, therefore, little alternative

---

[80] *Certain Questions of Mutual Assistance in Criminal Matters (Djibouti v France)*, Judgment of 4 June 2008, para 196.

[81] *WL Oltmans v The Republic of Surinam*, Netherlands Supreme Court, 28 September 1990 (1992) 23 *NYIL* 442 at 447.

[82] *Kingdom of Greece v Julius Bar and Co*, Swiss Federal Tribunal, 6 June 1956, 23 ILR 195. See also *United Arab Republic v Mrs X*, Swiss Federal Tribunal, 10 February 1960, 65 ILR 384.

[83] Following the insolvency of the Republic of Argentine creditor, States showed little enthusiasm to adopt the proposals put forward by the International Monetary Fund for a sovereign debt restructuring mechanism (EDREM).

where property in the control of the debtor State is concerned but to reach a settlement of judgment debts with its cooperation and by diplomatic means.

In consequence, as declared in another decision of the German Federal Constitutional Court in *The Philippine Embasssy* case '...Whilst the general rules of international law imposed no outright prohibition on execution by the State of the forum against a foreign State....there is an established general custom among States backed by legal consensus, whereby the State of the forum is prohibited from levying execution, under judicial writs against a foreign State, on property of the foreign State which is situate or present in the State of the forum and is used for sovereign purposes except with the latter's consent'.[84] In accordance with this decision, State practice and the UN Convention on State Immunity now recognize an exception to the general rule of immunity from execution in respect of State property in use for commercial purposes. English law now permits the recognition and enforcement of a foreign judgment given against a State, (other than the UK or the State to which that court belongs) provided the foreign court would have had jurisdiction if it had applied the UK rules on sovereign immunity set out in SIA ss 2 to 11,[85] but execution without the consent of the State remains solely in respect of State property shown to be 'in use or intended for use for commercial purposes' (SIA s,13(4)). The UN Convention draws a distinction, also generally recognized, between measures of enforcement against the property of a State prior to adjudication from those taken post-judgment; while as regards both prior and post judgment the rule of immunity is absolute unless the State has consented, or allocated or earmarked the property for the satisfaction of the claim. An additional exception to immunity, somewhat narrower than SIA s. 13(4), is permitted in respect of post judgment measures for State property in use for commercial purposes, Article 19(c) (see Section II H 6 of this chapter).

In the *Jurisdictional Immunities* case the ICJ, when deciding whether Germany's immunity from enforcement had been infringed by the Italian court's imposition of a legal charge on the German Villa Lagoni, referred to Article 19 of the UN Convention and, without deciding whether it reflected current customary international law, noted that it provided for three exceptions to immunity—express consent, allocation by the State, and the use of State property 'for an activity not pursuing governmental non-commercial purposes'. Finding that Villa Vigoni was used for wholly cultural purposes, it concluded that it was used entirely for non-commercial governmental purposes and so was immune from measures of constraint.[86]

3. State property generally recognized as immune

Diplomatic and military property have generally been recognized in State practice as categories of State property used for sovereign purposes and consequently have enjoyed immunity from seizure, even in the event of a general waiver by the State of its immunity from enforcement, and the category of the property of central banks, though not as well established, had also been recognized as enjoying immunity in the US FSIA and UK SIA

---

[84] *The Philippine Embassy Bank Account* case, German Federal Constitutional Court, 13 December 1977, 46 *BverfGE*, 342; 65 ILR 146 at 184.

[85] Civil Jurisdiction and Judgments Act 1982 s 31, *NML Capital Ltd* v *The Republic of Argentina* [2009] 1 Lloyd's Rep 378, reversed [2010] EWCA Civ 41; appeal allowed [2011] UKSC 31. For registration of a judgment against the UK see SIA Part II ss 18–19; no procedure is available for registration of a judgment given by a court against a State to which that court belongs *AIC Ltd* v *Federal Government of Nigeria and Attorney-General of Federation of Nigeria* [2003] EWHC 1357 (QB); 129 ILR 871.

[86] *Jurisdictional Immunities of the State (Germany* v *Italy: Greece Intervening), Judgment of 3 February 2012*, paras 118–20.

and more recently by China. The UN Convention on State Immunity adds two relatively new categories, property forming part of the cultural heritage of a State or of its archives, and property forming part of an exhibition of objects of scientific, cultural, or historical interest (Articles 21(1)(d) and (e)).[87]

Property of the diplomatic mission

In *The Philippine Embassy* case (referred to in n 84 in this chapter) immunity was recognized when attachment was sought of the account of the Philippine diplomatic mission in Bonn to satisfy a judgment for unpaid rent of an office. The 1961 Vienna Convention on Diplomatic Relations, Article 22(3) explicitly provides:

> The premises of the mission, their furnishings and other property thereon and the means of transport of the mission shall be immune from search, requisition, attachment or execution.

Although the bank account of the mission is not expressly mentioned in the Vienna Convention, State practice, confirmed by Article 21(1)(a) of the 2004 UN Convention which expressly refers to 'any bank account', overwhelmingly recognizes that an account of a diplomatic mission held in a bank in the forum State enjoys immunity unless it can be affirmatively shown that the sums deposited have been specifically allocated to meet commercial commitments.

Military property

Ships of war were recognized to be immune from local jurisdiction from the eighteenth century or earlier, but the modern category of military property, as defined in the UN Convention on State Immunity as 'property of a military character or used or intended for use in the performance of military functions' (Article 21(1)(b)), is capable of a wider meaning.[88] The US Act adopts a similar definition of property used or intended to be used 'in connection with a military activity', which, the House Report explains, includes not only all types of armaments and their means of delivery but also basic commodities such as food, clothing and fuel to keep a fighting force operative.[89] The existence of such an immune category exposes sales of military equipment to a plea of immunity from jurisdiction. Such a possibility would seem to be avoided in English law and come within the SIA s 3 definition of a commercial transaction provided the sale is in ordinary private law form and not pursuant to an agreement between States.

Central bank property

As regards the property of a central bank, the practice under US and UK legislation and some other States, though some countries have no specific rules on the matter, supports immunity from execution of property of a central bank where that bank performs the functions of a central as opposed to commercial bank; China recently has adopted legislation conferring similar immunity from 'measures of constraint such as attachment and execution' on the property of foreign central banks unless there has been express waiver

---

[87] The immune categories may lose their immunity by express consent or specific allocation.

[88] The UNGA Ad Hoc Committee decided in view of the uncertainty of the law to exclude aircraft and space objects by stating in Article 3 that the 2004 UN Convention is without prejudice to the immunities enjoyed by a State under international law with respect to aircraft and space objects owned or operated by a State. This would seem to exclude this type of State property from the category of military property declared immune in Article 19(1)(c).

[89] FSIA s 1611(b)(2); Legislative History of the Foreign Sovereign Immunities Act 1976, House Report No 94–1487, 94th Cong, 2nd Sess 12 reproduced in (1976) 15 ILM 1398 at 30–31.

in writing or allocation of the property.[90] Article 19(1)(c) of the UN Convention on State Immunity is in line with this practice when it provides that property of the central bank or other monetary authority of the State shall be immune and not treated as property in use or intended commercial use unless the State has expressly consented in writing or specifically allocated or earmarked such property to satisfy the judgment. In a case relating to the of State property held by a private corporation in the name of the State's central bank the English court construed the term 'property of the State' in the SIA 'include all real and personal property and will embrace any right, interest, legal, equitable or contractual in assets that might be held by a State or any "emanation of the State" or central bank or other monetary authority that comes within sections 13 and 14 of the Act'.[91] Recently the placing of excess foreign exchange reserves in Sovereign Wealth Funds by certain States, often with a declared purpose of their 'use for future generations', has raised issues relevant to their enjoyment of immunity from execution, particularly where invested in equities, derivatives or short term commercial assets (Truman, 2007). Such Funds, whether held in the name of the State or its central Bank, currently enjoy, under US, UK, and Chinese legislation and the UN Convention, complete immunity from enforcement measures. Where, however, such a fund is deployed for the purpose of wealth enhancement by 'playing the markets', it would seem, at least as regards the fees of brokers, banks and other third parties which such transactions generate, that for the purposes of attachment these credits in the funds might be treated as for commercial purposes despite the overall long term intention of the fund to serve as a reserve for the State and its people.

Cultural heritage of the State

The two new categories in the UN Convention—relating to protection of property 'forming part of the cultural heritage of a State or part of its archive and not intended for sale', and to property 'forming part of an exhibition of objects of scientific, cultural, or historical interest and not placed or intended to be placed on sale'—would seem designed to deter pillage and illegal export of a country's scientific, cultural or historical treasures. As to the first category, the subject is complicated by applicable laws of ownership, State regulation of privately owned national treasures, and claims of individuals to property expropriated in time of armed conflict.[92] Where the presence of cultural objects is restricted to their temporary public exhibition State practice seems more favourable to conferment of immunity; in 2004 the Swiss Ministry of External Affairs declared that cultural property of a State on exhibition was immune and overruled a court order on the application of a creditor of Russia, the Swiss trading company NOGA for the seizure of paintings from the Moscow's Pushkin Museum on exhibition in Switzerland and ordered their return to Russia.[93] The US Immunity Seizure Act of 1966 and the UK Tribunals and Courts Act 2007 Part 6 confer protection from seizure or attachment on objects in possession of a foreign State sent for exhibition subject to prior notification of their intended exhibition,

---

[90] Law of the People's Republic of China on Judicial Immunity from Measures of Constraint for the property of foreign central banks adopted on 25 October 2005.

[91] *AIG Capital Partners Inc & Anor* v *Kazakhstan (National Bank of Kazakhstan intervening)* [2005] EWHC 2239 (Comm); [2006] 1ALL ER (Comm) 1; [2006] 1 WLR 1420; 129 ILR 589.

[92] The ruling by the US Supreme Court in *Republic of Austria* v *Altmann* (2004) 541 US 677 that there was no limitation on the retroactive operation of the FSIA, renders applicable the restrictive doctrine including the expropriation exception to State immunity in s 1605(a)(3) to such claims for war damage. In that case Austria sought to rely on the rule of absolute immunity in force prior to 1952 as a bar to a claim by the owner of several Klimt paintings confiscated by the Nazis and exhibited by the Austrian national gallery.

[93] RSDIE 14 (2004) 674.

though the UK Act does not bar museums in the UK or lenders being subject to proceedings, other than specific restitution, in respect of exhibited works of art.

Apart from these accepted categories of immune property State practice in determining when a foreign State's property is in commercial use and subject to execution remains diverse. Whereas it is relatively easy to determine that a seagoing vessel equipped with guns and manned by personnel of a State's navy is not to be treated as property in commercial use, it is much more difficult to ascertain the character of funds held in the name of a State. Three particular problems arise—what evidence is available to establish intended commercial use of State property? How are mixed funds held both for commercial and sovereign purposes to be treated? And is the property to be attached to have a connection with the subject matter of the claim which it is sought to satisfy?

4. Proof of use for sovereign purposes

In answer to the first question, the evidence and burden of proof, in the *Philippine Embassy* case the German court considered that it would constitute interference contrary to international law in matters within the exclusive competence of the sending State for any inquiry, beyond obtaining the Ambassador's certificate, to be instituted as to the intended use of funds held in a mission's bank account. A similar position prevails in English law. By s 13(4) of the UK SIA, property in use or intended use for commercial purposes is made subject to attachment; s 17 defines 'commercial purposes' to mean 'purposes of such transactions or activities as are mentioned in section 3(3)', that is, use in relation to a sale of goods or supply of services, a transaction for provision of finance or a commercial, industrial, professional, or industrial activity. In a case seeking attachment of a diplomatic mission's account for unpaid surveillance equipment, the English Court of Appeal construed the statutory words 'intended use for commercial purposes' as covering commercial transactions entered into by the Ambassador; but the House of Lords declared the current account of a foreign diplomatic mission was held for the sovereign purpose of meeting the expenses of the mission and was not susceptible of anticipatory dissection into the various uses, commercial as well as sovereign, to which monies drawn on it might be used in the future. Only specific earmarking of a fund for present or future commercial use, the House of Lords held, would meet the exception to immunity from execution provided in the SIA for commercial property in use or intended use for commercial purposes (SIA s 13(4)).[94] A modification of this strict requirement was permitted in *Orascom*; a London bank account (not of the diplomatic mission) into which the oil revenues of a foreign State were paid for the purpose of discharging a commercial debt owed to World Bank with the surplus, if any, to be held for general use including sovereign purposes, was treated as an account for commercial purposes and non-immune.[95]

5. Mixed bank accounts

This English decision also provides the answer to the second question relating to mixed accounts: funds held for both sovereign and commercial purposes in a mission's bank account remain immune unless a specific account is opened or specific allocation made for a commercial purpose. This ruling has had its critics. Although arguments that UN Security Council Resolutions freezing Iraq's assets overrode Iraq's control of its assets and that amounts in an account held in the name of the Iraq diplomatic mission exceeded the

[94] *Alcom v Republic of Colombia* [1984] AC 580; [1984] 2 WLR 750; [1984] 2 All ER 6 (HL).

[95] *Orascom Telecom Holding SAE v Republic of Chad & Ors* [2008] EWHC 1841 (Comm); 2 Lll Rep [2008] 397. To the same effect, *EM Ltd v Republic of Argentina* 473 F 3d 463 (2d Cir 2007).

reasonable amount required to meet the mission's expenses were entertained at first by Belgian and French courts, on appeal they were rejected and the presumption that assets of a diplomatic mission were in use or intended use for sovereign purposes was applied and hence immunity from execution granted.[96] A US District Court allowed attachment of a mixed diplomatic bank account; exemption of mixed accounts would in the court's view create a loophole, for any property could be made immune by using it, at one time or other, for some minor public purpose.[97] A later court, however, refused attachment of a mixed bank account holding that such attachment would be contrary to the USA's obligation under Article 25 of the Vienna Convention on Diplomatic Relations to afford full facilities to the diplomatic mission of a sending State; and the US President, even in the face of federal legislation removing immunity from execution of property where judgment was obtained against commercial property of a foreign State designated as a State sponsor of terrorism, has by exercise of his waiver, preserved the immunity of mixed accounts of diplomatic missions in the USA.[98]

6. The requirement of a connection between the State property to be attached and the subject matter of the proceedings

On the third issue, there is a division in State practice. In addition to being located within the USA and used for commercial activity, the US FSIA requires that the State property 'is or was used for the commercial activity upon which the claim was based' (s 1610(a)(2)). This restriction, which is not one the UK SIA requires, serves two purposes; it ensures that execution of State property only takes place in respect of commercial activity which pursuant to an earlier section in the FSIA is within an exception to immunity and for which consequently the US courts have jurisdiction. Secondly it limits the property to satisfy the judgment to resources of the State already committed to the non-immune transaction. This requirement of a connection between the property and the claim restricts considerably the scope of the execution permitted against the property of a foreign State. It is to be noted that the US FSIA only imposes the connection condition when execution is sought against a State, but not as against a State agency or instrumentality. In this event all property used for commercial activity is permitted.[99] Where, however, the acts are of a tortious nature as in the exception for personal injuries, there is unlikely to be any prior commitment of resources of the State to those acts, with the consequence that, as the Second Circuit Appeals Court held, the connection requirement in the FSIA 'create[s] a right without a remedy'.[100]

In respect of State property but not the property of a State agency, French law imposes a similar requirement of a connection between the property to be attached and the subject matter of the claim, but enlarges it to include prejudgment by 'saisie conservatoire'.[101] As confirmed in Sonatrach 'the assets of a foreign State are in principle not liable (subject to) seizure, subject to exceptions in particular where they have been allocated for

---

[96] *Leica AG* v *Central Bank of Iraq*, 15 February 2000, Brussels Ct of Appeal, J des trib (2001) 6; *Iraq* v *Vinci Constructions*, 4 October 2002, Brussels Ct of Appeal, J des trib (2003) 318; 127 ILR 101; *Dumez* v *Iraq*, French Ct of Cassation, 15 July 1999; 27 ILR 144.

[97] *Birch Shipping Corp* v *Embassy of United Republic of Tanzania*, 507 F.Supp 311 (DDC 1990); 63 ILR 524.

[98] *Flatow* v *Republic of Iran*, 74 F.2d Supp 18 (DDC 19 December 1999). See Murphy, 2002, pp 70–77 and Murphy, *Hemisphere Assoc* v *Congo*, Vol II 2005, pp 66–81.

[99] US FSIA s 1610(b)(2).

[100] *Letelier* v *Republic of Chile*, 748 F.2d 790 (2nd Cir 1984) at 798; 63 ILR 378.

[101] *Islamic Republic of Iran* v *Eurodif*, Court of Appeal, Paris, 21 April 1982, 65 ILR 93, Court of Cassation, 14 March 1984, JDI 1984 598; 77 ILR 513.

an economic or commercial activity under private law which is at the origin of the title of the attaching debtor'.[102] The provisions in the UN Convention dealing with this issue was much debated and Article 19(c) makes post-judgment measures against the property of the State subject to three requirements: the property is to be (i) in use or intended use by the State for other than governmental non-commercial purposes; (ii) the property is to be in the territory of the forum State; and (iii) the property to have a connection with the entity against which the proceeding was directed. This article is accompanied by three annexed Understandings, defining 'entity' as one enjoying independent legal personality, 'property' as 'broader than ownership or possession' and in order to prevent evasion of the State of its liability to meet its judgments, reserves the position under national laws as to 'piercing the veil'. The sum total of these provisions would seem to broaden the scope of State property over which measures of constraint are allowed beyond the narrow confines found in the US FSIA of State property which is the subject matter of the proceedings.

III. THE OTHER TWO AVOIDANCE TECHNIQUES

A. ACT OF STATE

In accordance with the principles of private international law the applicable law will generally be the law of the State in whose territory the act takes place and the defence of act of State broadly provides an application of those principles to legislative or governmental acts affecting title to private property, moveable or immoveable, located within the territory of another State.

The principle enunciated in *Underhill v Hernandez*[103] that the courts of one State will not sit in judgment on the acts of the government of another done within its territory provides a further ground for imposing restraint on the English court. Thus in the leading case of *Luthor v Sagor* the English court upheld the validity of an expropriatory decree relating to timber situated in Russia of the newly established Soviet government. The governmental nature of the act performed by a foreign sovereign State was clearly a factor deterring the court from inquiry into the validity of the expropriation, with Scrutton LJ considering it would be 'a serious breach of international comity' to postulate that its legislation is 'contrary to essential principles of justice and morality'.[104] Later cases held the rule of recognition of foreign decrees applied to aliens as well as to nationals of the foreign State.[105] The act of State defence is subject to exceptions, which are comprehensively covered by the general statement that the English court will not enforce a foreign government act if it is contrary to public policy. It is established that public policy prevents the court from enforcing the penal or fiscal laws of another country[106] or discriminatory legislation directed against particular individuals or a particular class of individuals. In *Oppenheimer v Cattermole*[107] a Nazi decree of 1941 which deprived all Jews outside Germany of their German nationality, was declared *obiter dicta* to be contrary to public policy as legislation in contravention of fundamental human rights. At this point questions of non-justiciability

---

[102] *Société Sonatrach v Migeon*, France, Court of Cassation, 1 October 1985 rev crit 1986, 526, (1987) 26 ILM 998; 77 ILR 525.

[103] *Underhill v Hernandez* 168 US 250 (1897).

[104] *Luther v Sagor* [1921] 3 KB 532 (CA).

[105] *In re the Claim of Helbert Wagg & Co Ltd* [1956] 1 Ch 323; [1956] 1 All ER 129.

[106] *Government of India, Ministry of Defence (Revenue) Division v Taylor* [1955] 1 All ER 292.

[107] *Oppenheimer v Cattermole* [1976] AC 249; [1975] 1 All ER 538.

impinge; whether an exception to the act of State rule is permitted depends not merely on the issue being contrary to public policy but also a justiciable issue. More recently, in *Kuwait Airways Corp* v *Iraqi Airways Co (No 2)*, to be discussed later, the House of Lords have confirmed that the exception to the act of State rule as contravening public policy is not confined to a foreign State's acts in contravention of fundamental human rights but also extends to and even overrides legislation of a foreign State contrary to fundamental and well-established principles of international law.

The judgment breaks new ground, being 'the first decision to hold that acts of a foreign State within its territory may be refused recognition because they are contrary to international law'.[108] The consequences of that refusal of recognition go beyond a mere declaration of invalidity; the Lords refused to recognize the law which private international law rules identified as the proper law to determine both the tortious nature of the act and the ownership of the aircraft, being the law where the act was committed and the *lex situs*, the law where the title was transferred.

The judgment in *Kuwait Airways*, in its application to expropriation in time of armed conflict, raises difficult issues of applicable law relating to property. While there were strong grounds of public policy to give effect to the international condemnation of Iraq's action in looting the aircraft, the application of public international law, unlike private international law rules, provides little guidance as to the detailed consequences in municipal law on acts held contrary to international law. It may be that the proper law of the whole transaction, once the Iraqi legislation was struck down, was the law of Kuwait. But the Lords' decision made no reference to the law of Kuwait. The English court, which itself had no substantive connection with the claim—the original taking was from Kuwait, the alleged conversion in Iraq—it would seem, by reference to English law, construed the conduct of IAC (Iraqi Airways Corporation) as tortious and a deprivation of property although Iraqi law held it to be lawful and IAC to be the owner.

B. NON-JUSTICIABILITY

Non-justiciability remains today a doctrine of uncertain scope. It may be raised as a plea in proceedings whether or not a foreign State is itself made a party to them, and may be dealt with as a preliminary issue, but being highly fact specific it may not be possible to decide such issues until after disclosure or even until trial. In origin it operated in a manner similar to a plea of immunity barring further inquiry into matters falling within another State's jurisdiction or for international settlement. In the *Buttes Gas* case Lord Wilberforce sought to formulate non-justiciability into a distinct doctrine. The *Buttes Gas* case concerned a defamation action between companies in which, if it were to proceed, in the House of Lords' view, the English court would have to make a determination on a disputed maritime boundary between foreign States, involving a series of inter-State transactions from 1969 to 1973, of States' motives and the lawfulness of actions taken by Sharjah, and possibly Iran and the UK. The House of Lords held, there were 'no judicial or manageable standards by which to judge these issues, or to adopt another phrase, the court would be in judicial no man's land; the court would be asked to review transactions in which four foreign States were involved, which they had brought to a precarious settlement, after diplomacy, and the use of force'. Lord Wilberforce, who gave the single judgment of the House, after a review of particular rules, and reference to proceedings in

---

[108] *Op cit* per Lord Steyn at para 114.

US federal courts on the same international incident, declared there to be a general principle, 'not one of discretion but inherent in the very nature of process' that 'There exists in English law a more general principle that the courts will not adjudicate on the transactions of foreign sovereign States'.[109]

Lord Wilberforce's ruling that courts must declare certain matters non-justiciable continues to apply to matters of international relations which depend on diplomacy, countermeasures, sanctions and the use of force for their resolution. However, in situations where State practice has been reduced to a generally accepted and certain rule, even though it be a rule of international rather than municipal law, English courts may find sufficient judicial and manageable standards to determine the issues. In the words of Lord Nicholls in *Kuwait Airways No 2*, the principle of non-justiciability does not 'mean that the judiciary must shut their eyes to a breach of an established principle of international law committed by one State against another when the breach is plain and indeed acknowledged'. And as Lord Hope in the same case said, 'restraint is what is needed, not abstention'.[110]

In *Kuwait Airways No 2* the applicant, Kuwait Airways, claimed damages against the IAC for conversion of ten Kuwati aircraft which, following the Iraqi invasion of Kuwait in 1993, had been seized subsequently incorporated into the IAC's commercial fleet. While accepting that the situation fell within the scope of the act of State doctrine, given that the validity of Iraqi legislation within the territory of Iraq was at issue the Lords took the view that public policy required an exception to be made because Resolution 369, along with Iraq's seizure of the planes, constituted 'a gross violation of established rules of international law of fundamental importance'. On the facts there was universal consensus as to its illegality and clear evidence that recognition of its validity would be contrary to the UK's international obligations. Accordingly, the House of Lords determined that IAC's acts incorporating the aircraft into its civil airline fleet constituted conversion of assets belonging to KAC.[111] In doing so the House of Lords narrowed the scope of the plea of both the act of State doctrine and of non-justiciability.

Recently, however, there have been now two further developments which may narrow the distinction between issues subject to international law and those subject to municipal law: the first is where 'a foothold in domestic law' is established so as to permit an English court to make a ruling on international law; and the second is where State immunity barring the exercise of jurisdiction of a national court conflicts with the procedural right of access to court which is now enacted in international and regional human rights conventions to which the UK is a party. Where the facts support one or other of these two developments—that is, where there exists 'a foothold in domestic law', or where the denial of jurisdiction amounts to a disproportionate disregard of right of access to court of the private claimant, there will be no dismissal of a claim on the basis of either act of State or non-justiciability.

---

[109] *Buttes Gas and Oil Co v Hammer* [1982] AC 888 at 931–2, 938; 64 ILR 331; [1981] 3 All ER 616 at 628. Cf *Petrotimor Companhia de Petroleos SARL v Commonwealth of Australia* [2003] 126 FCR 354 where the Australian High Court held non-justiciable a challenge by an oil company relying on a concession granted by Portugal to the validity of the Seas and Submerged Lands Act 1973 which, in disregard of those concessionary rights, purported to vest Australia's sovereign rights at international law in the continental shelf in the Commonwealth of Australia.

[110] *Kuwait Airways Corp v Iraqi Airways Co* [2002] UKHL 19, 16 May 2002, paras 26 and 141.

[111] *Kuwait Airways Corp v Iraqi Airways Co* [2002] UKHL 19, 16 May 2002.

The first development is illustrated by a number of cases. The first is *Abbasi*, which concerned a request relating to a British national captured in Afghanistan and detained by the USA as an illegal combatant at Guantánamo Bay in Cuba without charge or legal representation. In that case, while the Court of Appeal was prepared to find, on the facts of the case, that there was a legitimate expectation that the government would provide diplomatic protection and that this could give rise to a justiciable issue, it also concluded that the government enjoyed a wide discretion as to the decision whether and in what manner to grant such protection and that the Court could not order the Secretary of State to make any particular representations since 'this would have an impact on the conduct of foreign policy'.[112] Where, however, the determination of rights, interests or duties under domestic law requires the court to consider issues of international law non-justiciability may provide no bar to the court's exercise of jurisdiction, as in the case of the *AY Bank* where the issue was the correct valuation according to principles of English banking law of a debt in an English bank, the sharing of which between the successors to Yugoslavia had been determined by an international treaty.[113]

A further example of such a possible 'foothold in domestic law' is where the facts support an application for the issue of the writ of *habeas corpus*.[114] Thus in *Rahmatullah*, where the detention of the claimant was believed to be within the control of the UK authorities because of a MOU between the USA and the UK relating to his custody at Bagram Airbase in Afghanistan, it was considered appropriate to issue the writ, with the result that the executive was required to request his return from US custody, which they duly did.[115]

The second area of development relating to situations in which a claim may not be dismissed on the basis of either act of State or non-justiciability concerns the procedural right of access to justice granted by Article 14 of the 1966 International Convention on Civil and Political Rights 1966[116] and by Article 6 of the 1950 European Convention on Human Rights.[117] State immunity has been challenged on the grounds that it infringes the right of access to a court in a number of different situations, including alleged torture committed abroad in a prison of the foreign State in *Al-Adsani* v *UK*; assault by a soldier

---

[112]　*R (Abbassi)* v *Secretary of State for Foreign and Commonwealth Affairs* [2002] EWCA Civ 1598; [2003] UKHRR 76 and see para 107 (ii).

[113]　*AY Bank Ltd (in liquidation)* v *Bosnia and Herzegovina & Ors* [2006] EWHC 830; [2006] 2 All ER Comm 463. See also *Occidental Exploration & Production Company* v *Republic of Ecuador* [2005] EWCA Civ 1116; [2006] QB 432; [2006] 2 WLR 70, para 37, where, with regard to the interpretation of an arbitral award which, in turn, turned on the interpretation of a treaty between the USA and Ecuador, Mance LJ said 'The case is not concerned with an attempt to invoke at a national legal level a Treaty which operates only at the international level. It concerns a Treaty intended by its signatories to give rise to rights in favour of private investors capable of enforcement, to an extent specified by the Treaty wording, in consensual arbitration against one or other of its signatory States'.

[114]　The writ of *habeas corpus* may be issued at the suit or on behalf of any prisoner unlawfully detained so as to bring him (now more often just the facts of the case) before the High Court, and his release ordered; 'the object of the writ is not to punish previous illegality, but to release from present illegal detention' (*per* Scrutton LJ in *Ex p. O'Brien* [1923] 2 KB 361, 391).

[115]　*Secretary of State for Foreign and Commonwealth Affairs* v *Rahmatullah* UKSC 48; [2012] 3 WLR 1087. Prior to the Supreme Court hearing the the case on appeal, the USA replied to the UK's letter, refusing to relinquish control of the detainee to the UK. In the light of this, the majority concluded that, although the Court of Appeal had been correct to issue the writ, the UK had done all it could to comply with the writ and it was now evident that the UK did not have the degree of control upon which its issuance had been premised.

[116]　This provides that, in the determination of a criminal charge, there is a right to 'a fair and public hearing by a competent, independent and impartial tribunal established by law'.

[117]　This provides that 'in the determination of his civil rights and obligations and of any criminal charge against him' confers on everyone a right to 'a fair and public hearing within a reasonable time by an independent and impartial tribunal'.

of the foreign State while within the territory of the forum State in *McElhinney* v *Ireland*; and discrimination on the basis of sex in connection with an appointment to a post in a foreign embassy in *Fogarty* v *UK*. In all three cases it was contended that the national courts had wrongly applied immunity to bar access to a national court and its exercise of jurisdiction. Relying on Article 6(1) of the European Convention of Human Rights, the Court in all three cases confirmed its previous ruling that 'a State could not, without restraint or control by the convention enforcement bodies, remove from the jurisdiction of the courts a whole range of civil claims or confer immunities from civil liability on large groups or categories of persons'. But it distinguished State immunity from immunities imposed by a single municipal law: in *Al-Adsani* v *UK* it held that State immunity was a part of the body of relevant rules of international law which the Convention as a human rights treaty must take into account; the Convention 'cannot be interpreted in a vacuum' and must 'so far as possible be construed in harmony with other rules of international law of which it forms part including those relating to the grant of State immunity'. The Court declared:

> Sovereign immunity is a concept of international law, developed out of the principle *par in parem non habet imperium*, by virtue of which one State shall not be subject to the jurisdiction of another State. The court considers that the grant of immunity to a State in civil proceedings pursues the legitimate aim of complying with international law to promote comity and good relations between States through the respect of another State's sovereignty.[118]

However, while holding that State immunity could not be struck down as contrary to the right of access to a court, the European Court held it to be always necessary to ensure that the barring of a civil right was not disproportionate to the legitimate aim which State immunity pursues. The Court held that none of the individual claims came within recognized exceptions to State immunity and that the plea on the facts in each case was legitimate and proportionate: the exception for proceedings for personal injuries was generally intended to cover 'insurable' business acts of a State such as traffic accidents occurring within the forum State's territory, and not to torture in a foreign prison; in regard to *McElhinney*, an act of a visiting member of the armed forces of another country was clearly an act *jure imperii*; and in regard to *Fogarty* a claim for discrimination in recruitment of staff to an embassy, as opposed to a claim for compensation for wrongful dismissal, equally fell within a State's exercise of sovereignty.

Account must now be taken of a thorough and authoritative analysis by the unanimous Court of Appeal in 2013 in *Yukos Capital*. Rix LJ has now stated that Lord Wilberforce's principle of non-justiciability has to subsume the act of State doctrine as the 'paradigm principle' preventing adjudication on the validity, legality, lawfulness, acceptability, or motives of State actors. However, the Court in formulating the revised plea of act of State/non-justiciability has declared it subject to five qualifications. The Court concludes that the act of State doctrine does not prevent adjudication of 'the judicial acts of a foreign State', which 'are judged by judicial standards, including international standards regarding jurisdiction...'.[119]

---

[118] *Al-Adsani* v *UK* [GC] no 35763/97, ECHR 2001-XI, 34 *EHRR* 11, paras 54–5. The other two decisions are *Fogarty* v *UK* [GC], no 37112/97, ECHR 2001-XI, 34 *EHRR* 12 and *McElhinney* v *Ireland and the UK* [GC], no 31253/96, ECHR 2001-XI, 34 *EHRR* 13.

[119] *Yukos Capital* v *OJSC Rosneft Oil* [2013] 3 WLR 1329 at [40]–[104].

IV. COMPARISON AND EVALUATION OF
THE THREE AVOIDANCE TECHNIQUES

From the account given it will be clear that the pleas are related one to the other. Respect for the independence and equality of a foreign State when it is a party to proceedings is achieved by a plea of State immunity which brings the case to a halt. Where the proceeding is between private parties such an immediate halt will only take place if by reason of the non-justiciability of the issues to be determined the court decides that it had no competence to decide them. In cases where the proceedings between private parties progresses to examination of the substantive law, the court may also conclude that it has no judicial or manageable standards by which to decide the issues and declare them non-justiciable; alternatively it may accept a plea of act of State and decide that the recognition of the validity of a foreign State's governmental act deprives the claim of any basis for its assertion. Thus by accepting a plea of act of State the English court goes some way to endorsing the validity of the act of the foreign State whereas in immunity the court remains neutral, merely deciding that it is not the appropriate forum.

As regards fundamental human rights violations, the choice of an applicable municipal law may be less acute in that for States which have ratified them international human conventions provide a set of rules for the consequences of such violations and, in some instances, international or regional tribunal to which complaints may be referred. But in direct proceedings against a foreign State problems still remain as to the jurisdiction of, and cause of action exercisable by, a national court in respect of such violations committed within the territory of another State, as illustrated by the case of *Jones v Minister of Interior for the Kingdom of Saudi Arabia* considered further in Section VI of this chapter.

V. THE ARGUMENTS FOR AND AGAINST
THE USE OF AVOIDANCE TECHNIQUES

Three main grounds are given for the grant of immunity to foreign States: first, that the national court has no power of enforcement of its judgments against a foreign State; secondly, that the independence and equality of States prevents the exercise of jurisdiction by the courts of one State over the person, acts, and property of another State; and thirdly, that foreign States ought properly to enjoy a like immunity to that accorded by national courts to their own forum State. Additional grounds are found in the territoriality of the jurisdiction of the courts of the receiving State and on reciprocity and international comity.

As shown, the first ground is in part contradicted by modern State practice whereby the forum State authorities execute validly obtained judgments against State property in commercial use and is supported by a general view that States should honour their commercial undertakings. While the third ground provides support for a general application of the rule of law, to impose on another State without its consent the constitutional restraints of municipal law which the forum State accepts, smacks of a new sort of paternal imperialism.

This leaves as the main justification of State immunity and the consequent bar of measures of constraint against such a State and its property, the second ground, the independence and equality of States with the consequent bar of forcible measures of constraint against the State and its property. These attributes of the State were a foundation of the Westphalian system of international law which was built on the recognition and equal status of countries with defined territorial boundaries exercising State power. While the competing interests of States, who differ sharply as to their internal policies, religion or culture, may be met by the use of the avoidance techniques which we have been discussing, such techniques arguably take little account of the interests of the individual or the larger concerns of the international community as a whole. International immunities of States and the pleas of State immunity and non-justiciability based on them have consequently come under attack both as contrary to the administration of justice of national courts and as conferring impunity from violations of international law.

VI. CHALLENGES TO IMMUNITY AND JUDICIAL RESTRAINT

A number of challenges to the pleas of non-justiciability and State immunity have been made on the ground that such pleas have the effect of conferring impunity for violations of international human rights law. As far as the plea of non-justiciability is concerned, it we have shown that English courts have responded to these pressures by providing some form of remedy where, on the facts, 'a foothold in domestic law' can be discerned. As regards the bar of State immunity, challenges have been made in a number of ways. One way has been in terms of *jus cogens*, claiming that a fundamental human right as a peremptory norm of general international law which by reason of its superior status overrides the bar of immunity so as to permit the adjudication of its violation by national courts. Another way has been to assert that universal jurisdiction requires the forum State courts to exercise jurisdiction, while a third has been to rely on the right of access to court pursuant to ECHR Article 6(1), which has already been considered. (See further Wickremasinghe, Ch 13, Section VIII of this book for the conflicting priorities regarding immunity and impunity and their resolution by criminalization of the gravest excesses before international tribunals and also before national courts as regards State officials claiming immunities *ratione materiae*.)

As far as the challenge based on *jus cogens* is concerned, it is claimed that because of their superior status, such norms not only to override conflicting treaty obligations but also to trump the bar of State immunity, meaning that their violation can be adjudicated upon by national courts. The extent of such primacy or overriding effect remains uncertain. In *Jones* v *Ministry of Interior for the Kingdom of Saudi Arabia* the court refused to set aside a plea of State immunity in a relation to a claim brought by British nationals for alleged acts of torture committed in a Saudi prison on the orders of the Minister of Saudi Arabia.[120] This illustrates the continued nature of the conflict between the immunity of the foreign defendant State and pressure to provide national remedies for breaches of international human rights obligations. Nevertheless, Lord Hoffman explained how, in the view of the Supreme Court, no conflict arose: 'To produce a conflict with state immunity, it is therefore necessary to show that the prohibition on torture has generated an ancillary procedural rule which, by way of exception to State immunity entitles or perhaps requires states to assume civil jurisdiction over other states in cases in which torture is alleged. Such a rule may be desirable... [b]ut contrary to the assertion of the minority in Al-Adsani, it is not entailed by the prohibition of torture.'[121] As Lord Bingham in the same

---

[120] *Jones v Ministry of Interior for the Kingdom of Saudi Arabia and Ors* [2006] UKHL 26; [2007] 1 AC 270. This is currently pending before the European Court of Human Rights. See *Jones v the UK*, no 34356/06 (application lodged 26 July 2006).

[121] Ibid, para 45.

case succinctly stated: 'The International Court of Justice has made plain that breach of a *jus cogens* norm of international law does not suffice to confer jurisdiction (*Democratic Republic of the Congo* v *Rwanda*, ICJ, 3 February 2006, para 64)'.[122]

Universal jurisdiction has also been proposed as another way to circumvent State immunity in domestic proceedings. A number of multilateral conventions impose an obligation requiring State parties to exercise universal jurisdiction in respect of specific offences defined in the Convention and provide an obligation *aut dedere, aut judicare* where an alleged offender is within the territory of a State party; that is, that the case is either submitted to the prosecuting authorities or the suspect is extradited to face prosecution elsewhere.[123] It has also been claimed that the State has an obligation under customary international law to prosecute on the basis of universal jurisdiction a person present in its territory who has been granted asylum and who has been accused of committing grave international crimes, and that other States would be in breach of their obligations under international law if they attempted to prevent this.[124] This, it is said, 'trumps' the right of other States to assert immunity in respect of such acts and has the practical effect of entitling, in some cases, the exercise of universal jurisdiction in respect of an individual accused of the *jus cogens* violation. However, in the *Obligation to Extradite or Prosecute* case, the International Court of Justice, and individual judges in their separate opinions, failed to give support to there being a customary law obligation to prosecute crimes under international law committed by foreign nationals abroad.[125]

Over the last 20 years all three forms of challenge to State immunity has received considerable encouragement by the exercise of extraterritorial civil jurisdiction by US courts handing down judgments based on the 1787 Alien Claims Tort Act and the Anti-terrorism and Effective Death Penalty Act (AEDPA) 1996, which gives a civil remedy against State officials in respect of crimes under the law of nations and by the grant of a similar extraterritorial jurisdiction for such crimes against the foreign State itself by amending the FSIA to provide an express exception to immunity in the case of States designated as 'state sponsors or terrorism'.[126] Lately, however, the US Supreme Court has been reining in these expansionary tendencies, confining the reach of the 1787 ATCA to 'rights already

---

[122] Ibid, para 24. Had the alleged acts of torture taken placed within the UK, rather than in a Saudi prison, the territorial tort exception in SIA s 5, which is also found in Article 12 of the UN Convention, might have been applicable. Expanding the tort exception to include international crimes causing death or injuries to the person attracted considerable support at the 2009 Naples Session of the Institut de droit international, but was not, however, included in the final Resolution adopted. See Institut De Droit, Naples, 2009 Resolution on International Crimes and Immunities from Jurisdiction of States and their Agents (Rapporteur Lady Fox), ADI vol 73 and see Salmon, 2009.

[123] There may be a question concerning which countries may request extradition. See, for example, the US reservation to the UN Convention against Torture which only requires extradition to the State in which the alleged offence occurred, or of which the alleged offender is a national.

[124] The basis for this being Article 41 of the ILC's Articles on the Responsibility of States for Internationally Wrongful Acts, which requires States to 'co-operate to bring to an end through lawful means' serious breaches arising under a peremptory norm. Cf *Jurisdictional Immunities of the State* (*Germany* v *Italy: Greece Intervening*), *Judgment of 3 February 2012*, Dissenting Opinion of Judge Gaja, para 10.

[125] *Questions relating to the Obligation to Prosecute or Extradite* (*Belgium* v *Senegal*), *Judgment of 20 July 2012*, para 54.

[126] The State Department has designated Cuba, Iran, Iraq, Libya, North Korea, Syria, and Sudan as terrorist States and also the Federal Republic of Yugoslavia under President Milosevic's regime. After the invasion of Iraq the designation of Iraq as a State sponsor of terrorism was lifted and all previously blocked Iraqi assets were vested 'in the Department of the Treasury' to be used 'to assist the Iraqi people and to assist in the reconstruction of the Treasury'. Emergency Supplemental Appropriations Act, 16 April 2003 and the Presidential determination of 7 May 2003; Murphy, p 970.

recognized by international law'[127] and, most recently and most remarkably, by deciding that the ACTA does not have extraterritorial effect and so only provides a cause of action in respect of acts committed within the jurisdiction of the USA.[128]

VII. THE EXCLUSIONARY PROCEDURAL NATURE OF THE PLEA OF STATE IMMUNITY

These challenges to State immunity on the basis of *jus cogens*, universal jurisdiction and a right of access to court in civil proceedings have further been slowed by the 2012 decision of the International Court of Justice. In the *Jurisdictional Immunities* case the International Court upheld Germany's claim that its State immunity had been breached by the Italian courts' adjudication of claims relating to war damage caused by German armed forces in 1943–5, and also enforcing judgments of Italian and Greek courts in respect of German government property in Italy.

This recent judgment is of great value and requires close study. As has already been seen earlier in this chapter, it contains valuable rulings on numerous aspects of customary international law concerning State immunity: for example, in respect of immunity from adjudication, that the territorial tort exception to State immunity has no application to acts 'committed by the armed forces and other organs of the State in the conduct of armed conflict', even if the relevant acts take place on the territory of the forum State; and, in respect of immunity from enforcement, rulings as to the recognition and enforcement by the forum State of foreign judgments given against a foreign State in the national courts of a third States and the immunity from measures of constraint of the German Villa Lagioni as a cultural property.

In excluding the territorial tort exception the Court was careful to confine its ruling to State immunity. It stressed that:

> In reaching that conclusion, the Court must emphasize that it is addressing only the immunity of the State itself from the jurisdiction of the courts of other States; the question of whether, and if so to what extent, immunity might apply in criminal proceedings against an official of the State is not in issue in the present case.[129]

The extent to which the judgment impacts on State officials and their immunity in criminal and civil courts proceedings in national courts will be considered by Wickremasinghe (see Ch 13 of this book) but it should not be overlooked that an official's immunity is derived from the immunity of the State and it is the State alone which can confer or remove the immunity of its officials.

The 2012 judgment also sets out a general ruling of the nature of State immunity which has wider implications. In response to Germany's application, Italy responded by supporting her position with three strands of argument: first, that there is no immunity in international law when a State has committed serious violations of international humanitarian law amounting to war crimes and crimes against humanity; second, that there is

---

[127] *Sosa v Alvarez Machain* 542 US 692 (2004).

[128] *Kiobel v Royal Dutch Petroleum Co*, 133 S Ct 1659 (2013), in the context of an attempt to extend extraterritorial jurisdiction under the ATCA to companies who in their overseas operations were 'aiders and abetters' of human rights violations by foreign States.

[129] *Jurisdictional Immunities of the State (Germany v Italy: Greece Intervening), Judgment of 3 February 2012*, para 91.

no State immunity for violations of norms of *jus cogens* character; third, that the denial of immunity is justified because all other attempts to obtain reparations for the victims had failed.[130] The ICJ in deciding against Italy's claim dismissed all three arguments and also rejected Italy's contention that the combined effect of the three lines justified an exception to State immunity. In doing so the ICJ based its reasoning on the straightforward exclusionary proposition that the plea of immunity was a procedural plea independent of the issues raised in the Italian claim relating to State responsibility and their determination. The Court stated:

> The rules of State immunity are procedural in character and are confined to determining whether or not the courts of one State may exercise jurisdiction in respect of another State. They do not bear upon the question whether or not the conduct in respect of which the proceedings are brought was lawful or unlawful.[131]

Earlier, the Court had noted:

> ...that Italy, in response to a question posed by a member of the Court, recognized that those acts had to be characterized as *acta jure imperii*, notwithstanding that they were unlawful. The Court considers that the terms '*jure imperii*' and '*jure gestionis*' do not imply that the acts in question are lawful but refer rather to whether the acts in question fall to be assessed by reference to the law governing the exercise of sovereign power (*jus imperii*) or the law concerning non-sovereign activities of a State, especially private and commercial activities (*jus gestionis*). To the extent that this distinction is significant for determining whether or not a State is entitled to immunity from the jurisdiction of another State's courts in respect of a particular act, it has to be applied before that jurisdiction can be exercised.[132]

This exclusionary force attributed to the immunity plea as a procedural plea invites close scrutiny. Similar distinctions between procedure and substance have been made in private international law in determining whether the issue is one of remedy or consequential damage, in application of ECHR Article 6(1) which permits no challenge of substantive rules in a State party's domestic law, and in the ILC Draft Article of State Responsibility between primary rules relating to different obligations and universal secondary rules relating to breach of such obligations, have been applied by national courts, international tribunals and jurists. But over time they have been found to produce inconsistent results at variance with the intended purposes for which they were adopted (Fox and Webb, 2013, Ch 2).

The ICJ did not define the distinction into public *acts jure imperii* and private acts *jure gestionis* and the meaning of 'commercial or private law acts' remains open to interpretation. It is progressively being expanded in some areas. For example, in the application of the exception for employment contracts the notion that 'public service' has been abandoned as a sufficient description to identify a whole sector of employment in the public sector as acts in exercise of sovereign authority; in consequence routine provisions relating to terms of employment and pensions which are found in commercial employment when applied to terms in the public service are now treated as within the exception to immunity for employment contracts. Similarly, where human rights violations can be characterized as occurring in a commercial or employment context, as intimidation sexual harassment, or as causing personal injuries (mental as well as physical) as a result of an act committed on

---

[130] Italy also had an arguments based on the territorial tort exception to immunity.

[131] *Jurisdictional Immunities of the State (Germany v Italy: Greece Intervening), Judgment of 3 February 2012*, para 93.

[132] Ibid, para 60.

the State's behalf within the forum territory there may also be potential to bring the resulting complaints within the commercial or tort exceptions and to set aside State immunity.

In addition, although the ECtHR's requirements of legitimate aim and proportionality was cited in paragraph 96 in support of the ICJ's judgment, when applied to the bar of immunity it may yet be shown to be subject to application by way of review of the limits of State immunity. It may be, as referred to in dicta by the French Court of Cassation in *Reunion Aerienne* v *Libya*, that the 'legitimate aim and proportionality test' could provide a route for breaking down the procedural/substantive distinction.[133] Thus the ECtHR has ruled that where a question arises as to the hierarchy between the obligations arising under the Human Rights Convention on the one hand and under the UN Charter on the other, 'for a measure to be regarded as proportionate and as necessary in a democratic society, the possibility of recourse to an alternative measure that would cause less damage to the fundamental right at issue while fulfilling the same aim must be ruled out'.[134] An Egyptian national barred for some six years from transiting Swiss territory by Switzerland's compliance with UN Security Council Resolutions listing him as a person associated with Al-Qaeda, applied this maxim to support a claim for breach of his right to private and family life pursuant to ECHR Article 8 by reason that the implementation of this listing imposed disproportionate restrictions for six years on his freedom of movement. The ECtHR found that the Swiss compliance with the UNSC resolutions did not strike a fair balance between the applicant's right to the protection of his private and family life, on the one hand, and the legitimate aims of the prevention of crime and the protection of Switzerland's national security and public safety on the other.[135]

This decision has relevance to the application of State immunity as a bar to human rights complaints. Just as the ECtHR ruled that reliance on the overriding effect of a Security Council Chapter VII resolution did not exempt Switzerland from seeking alternative ways of compliance to accommodate the applicant's claim, so a State's reliance on a plea of State immunity does not exempt it from seeking alternative ways of disposal of a violation of fundamental human rights compatible with respect for the legitimate aim and proportionality of its immunity plea.

In sum, it is suggested that the procedure/substance distinction as applied to the plea of State immunity (Nollkaemper, 2012) may prove less impenetrable than the ICJ *Jurisdictional Immunities* judgment suggests. It is well to bear in mind that the court itself was careful to restrict the scope of its judgment to 'the time being'. The ICJ's use of the procedural exclusionary nature of a plea of State immunity as a resort to internal rules of the structure of making a claim may come to be regarded as a 'distinction of expedience rather than principle' (Sloane, 2012, pp 491–2), as a clarification of the correct way to process a

---

[133] *Reunion Aerienne* v *Libya*, Court of Cassation, No. 09-14743, 9 March 2011, *Bull. civ.*, March 2011, No. 49, p 49 where insurers challenged the bar of immunity in order to seek recovery of losses incurred in consequence of the Libyan terrorist bombing of a French registered aircraft. See also *Jurisdictional Immunities of the State (Germany* v *Italy: Greece Intervening)*, *Judgment of 3 February 2012*, Dissenting Opinion of Judge Gaja.

[134] *Nada* v *Switzerland*, no 10593/08, Judgment of 12 September 2012, para 183 referring to *Ahmed and others* v *HM Treasury*.

[135] The Court found that Switzerland 'could not validly confine itself to relying on the binding nature of Security Council resolutions, but should have persuaded the Court that it had taken—or at least had attempted to take—all possible measures to adapt the sanctions regime to the applicant's individual situation' (ibid, para 126) and that this finding 'dispensed the Court from determining the question of the hierarchy between the obligations of the States arties to the Convention under that instrument, on the one hand, and those arising from the UN Charter, on the other. In the Court's view, the important point is that the respondent Government have failed to show that they attempted, as far as possible, to harmonize the obligations that they regarded as divergent' (ibid, para127).

foreign State's claim in order to exclude the disposal of awkward issues of substantive law. As Nollkaemper (2012) writes, it gives rise to questions as to 'the normative choices that courts inevitably have to make and reflects on the question of whether, and to what extent, the shaping of these connections is properly part of the international judicial function, taking into account problems of legitimacy that may arise when judge-made procedures undo State-made substantive law'.[136]

VIII. CONCLUSION

At the present day the three avoidance techniques, immunity, act of State, and non-justiciability, by application of the restrictive doctrine of State immunity as now set out in the UN Convention, are subject to close scrutiny. The pendulum continues to swing between preserving the independence of foreign States and their freedom from judicial review by the Court of other States on the one hand, and claims to provide remedies and reparation for violations of international law on the other. As a result, the recognition of 'a foothold in private law' as a means of modifying the plea of non-justiciability alternates with the ICJ's reminder that State immunity is a procedural exclusionary bar to the exercise of domestic jurisdiction.

Much is written about the replacement of the club of sovereign States by an international community representing the interests of all, particularly individuals, yet States remain the main source of authority and implementation of the law in international relations. In consequence their qualities of independence and equality encapsulate three principles which are given effect in the plea of immunity: the principle of domestic jurisdiction by which the organization and legal relations of the State are exclusively or primarily matters for that State to determine; the principle that certain disputes involving States are to be settled on the international plane, not subjecting the State to the compulsory jurisdiction of a municipal court of another State; and the rule of exhaustion of the local remedies which provides an opportunity for the foreign State to settle the dispute in accordance with its own laws. Reduced to its simplest, the justification for use of avoidance techniques, particularly of the plea of immunity, is to allocate in the most appropriate manner suitable to all interests and the ends of justice jurisdiction between the forum and the foreign States.

REFERENCES

COLLINS, L (Gen ed) (2012), *Dicey, Morris and Collins on Conflicts of Laws*, 15th edn (London: Thomson Sweet & Maxwell).

DAHAI, QI (2008), 'State Immunity, China and its Shifting Position', 7 *Chinese J Int Law* 307.

FAWCETT, J, CARRUTHERS, J and NORTH, P (2008), in *Cheshire, North and Fawcett: Private International Law*, 14th edn (Oxford: Oxford University Press).

Fox, H (1999), 'The *Pinochet Case No 3*', 48 *ICLQ* 687.

—— and WEBB P (2013), *The Law of State Immunity*, 3rd edn (Oxford: Oxford University Press).

HAFNER, G, KOHEN, M, and BREAU, S (eds) (2006), *State Practice regarding State Immunities: La pratique des Etats concernant les immunités des Etats in English and French* (Strasbourg: Council of Europe).

---

[136] See also Keitner, 2013.

HIGGINS, R (1982), 'Certain Unresolved Aspects of the Law of State Immunity', 29 *Netherlands ILR* 265.

INSTITUT DE DROIT, NAPLES (2009), *Resolution on International Crimes and Immunities from Jurisdiction of States and their Agents* (Rapporteur Lady Fox), ADI vol 73.

KEITNER C (2013), 'Germany v Italy and the Limits of Horizontal Enforcement: Some Reflections from a United States Perspective', 11 *Journal of International Criminal Justice* 167.

McGREGOR, L (2013), 'State Immunity and Human Rights Is There a Future after Germany v. Italy?', 11 *Journal of International Criminal Justice* 25.

MURPHY, SD (2002), *United States Practice in International Law, Vol I 1999–2001* (Cambridge: Cambridge University Press).

—— (2003) 'Terrorist-State Litigation in 2000-3', 97 *AJIL* 966.

—— (2005), *United States Practice in International Law, Vol II, 2002-2004* (Cambridge: Cambridge University Press).

NOLKAEMPER, A (2012), 'International Adjudication of Global Goods: The Intersection of Substance and Procedure', 23 *EJIL* 770.

PINGEL, N (2000), '*Creighton v Qatar*', *JDI* 1054.

SALMON, J (2009) 'La Résolution de Naples de L'Institut de droit international sur les immunités de juridiction de l'Etat et de ses agents en cas de crimes internationaux (10 Septembre 2009)', *Belg Rev DI* 316.

SLOANE, RD (2012), 'On the Use and Abuse of Necessity in the law of State Responsibility', 106 *AJIL* 446.

STEWART, DP (2005), 'The UN Convention on Jurisdictional Immunities of States and their Property', 99 *AJIL* 194.

TRUMAN, EM (2007), 'Sovereign Wealth Funds: the Need for Greater Transparency and Accountability', *Peterson Institute Policy Brief* BP 07-6.

WARBRICK, C (2004), 'Immunity and International Crimes in English Law', 53 *ICLQ* 769.

WRANGE, P (2012), '*Sedelmayer v Russian Federation*', 106 *AJIL* 347.

FURTHER READING

ALEBEEK, R VAN (2008), *The Immunities of States and Their Officials in International Criminal Law and International Human Rights Law* (Oxford: Oxford University Press).

AKANDE, D and SHAH, S (2010), 'Immunities of State Officials, International Crimes, and Foreign Domestic Courts', 21 *EJIL* 815.

BRADLEY, CA (2013), 'Supreme Court Holds That Alien Tort Statute Does Not Apply to Conduct in Foreign Countries', *American Society of International Law, Insights*, Vol 17 (12).

BROWNLIE, I (2008), *Principles of Public International Law*, 7th edn (Oxford: Oxford University Press): setting out his proposed alternative solution to the application of the *jure imperii/ jure gestionis* dichotomy with two sets of countervailing criteria which were to be balanced in determining the nature of the act of the foreign State.

BYHOVSKAYA, E (2008), *State Immunity in Russian Perspective 2008* (London: Wildy, Simmonds and Hill).

CASSESE, A (2002), 'When may Senior State Officials be Tried for International Crimes? Some Comments on the *Congo v Belgium* Case', 13 *EJIL* 853.

——, GAETA, P et al (2008), *Cassese's International Criminal Law*, 3rd edn (Oxford: Oxford University Press).

CATALDI, G (2013), 'The Implementation of the ICJ's Decision in the *Jurisdictional Immunities* Case in the Italian Domestic Order: What Balance Should Be Made between Fundamental Human Rights and International Obligations', *European Society of Int Law Reflections* Vol 2, Issue 2.

CRAWFORD, J, (ed), *Brownlie's Principles of Public International Law*, 8th edn (Oxford: Oxford University Press). See in particular Chs 21 on Jurisdictional Competence and 22 on Privileges and Immunities of States.

CRYER, B, FRIMAN, H, ROBINSON, D and WILMSHURST, E (2010), *An Introduction to International Criminal Law and Procedure*, 2nd edn (Cambridge: Cambridge University Press), Ch 21 Immunities.

DAMROSCH, L, HENKIN, L, MURPHY, S, and SMIT, H (2009), *International Law Cases And Materials*, 5th edn (West Academic Publishers).

DICKINSON, A, LINDSAY, R, and LOONAM, JP (2004), *State Immunity: Selected Materials and Commentary* (Oxford: Oxford University Press). A useful collection of the texts of the 1926 Brussels Convention, 1972 European Convention on State Immunity and the 2004 UN Convention on Jurisdictional Immunities of States and their Jurisdiction, and of US, UK and other national legislation on State immunity with commentaries.

FOX, H and WEBB, P (2013), *The Law of State Immunity*, 3rd edn (Oxford: Oxford University Press). A survey of the entire field of law covered by State immunity including an analysis of the 1991 Draft Articles on Jurisdictional Immunities of States and their Property as proposed by the International Law Commission and debated in the UN Sixth Committee and its working parties.

GALLAGHER, K (2010), 'Civil Litigation and Transnational Business: an Alien Tort Statute Primer', 8 *Journal of International Criminal Justice* 745.

GATTINI, A (2008), 'The International Customary Law Nature of Immunity from Measures of Constraint for State Cultural Property on Loan', in Buffard, I, Crawford, J, Pellet, A, and Wittich, S (eds) (2011), *International Law between Universalism and Fragmentation: Festschrift in honour of Gerhard Hafner* (The Hague: Martinus Nijhoff), p 421.

LAUTERPACHT, H (1951), 'The Problem of Jurisdictional Immunities of Foreign States', 28 *BYIL* 220: the seminal article which greatly influenced US and UK lawyers in the adoption of a restrictive doctrine of State immunity.

McGOLDRICK, D (2010), 'The Boundaries of Justiciability', 59 *ICLQ* 981.

MEYER-FABRE (2000), 'Enforcement of Arbitral Awards against Sovereign States: a New Milestone..', *Mealey's International Arbitration Report*, Vol 15(9).

MIZUSHIMA T (2010), 'The Enactment of Japan's State Immunity Act in 2009', 53 *Jap YBIL*.

NESI, G (2013), 'The Quest for a Full Execution of the ICJ Judgment between Germany and Italy' 11 *Journal of International Criminal Justice* 185.

NOBUMORI, T (2010), 'Recent Sovereign Immunity Legislation in Japan from the Perspective of Central Banks', 53 *Jap YBIL* 275.

O'KEEFE, R (2008), 'The Doctrine of Incorporation Revisited', 78 *BYIL* 2-85.

—— and TAMS, C J (eds) (2013), *The UN Convention on Jurisdictional Immunities of States and Their Property: A Commentary* (Oxford: Oxford University Press). A thorough analysis of the meaning and force of this UN Convention article by article.

PROVOST, R (2012), 'Canada's Alien Tort Statute', *EJIL Talk*, 29 March 2012.

REINISCH, A (2006), 'Recent Practice of European Courts with Regard to State Immunity from Enforcement Measures', 17 *EJIL* 4.

WAIBEL, M (2011), *Sovereign Defaults before International Courts and Tribunals* (Cambridge: Cambridge University Press).

WOLFRUM, R (Gen ed) (2011), *Encyclopaedia of Public International Law*, edn, 'Acts of State Doctrine'. This short piece provides a convenient summary and comparison of the scope of US and English approaches to acts of State.

13

IMMUNITIES ENJOYED BY OFFICIALS OF STATES AND INTERNATIONAL ORGANIZATIONS

Chanaka Wickremasinghe

SUMMARY[1]

This chapter seeks to explain the immunities enjoyed by various categories of officials of States and international organizations involved in the conduct of international relations. It sets out the broad rationale underlying these immunities as being to facilitate the processes of communication between States on which international relations and cooperation rely. The law relating to the various categories of officials is then considered in turn, noting in particular the extent of the immunities from jurisdiction which they enjoy.

Finally the question of the inter-relation of the law on immunities (which developed largely as a 'self-contained regime') with recent developments in the field of international criminal law is considered. The discussion focuses on the challenges to immunities which are presented by measures to end the impunity of those who commit the most serious international crimes, such as through the development of extraterritorial jurisdiction and the establishment of international criminal courts and tribunals. A range of judicial decisions, such as the House of Lords decision in the *Pinochet No 3* case, the judgments of the International Court of Justice in the *Arrest Warrant*, and *Jurisdictonal Immunities of the State* cases, and the decisions of the International Criminal Court relating to the arrest warrant in the *Al Bashir* and *Qadhafi* cases are reviewed in order to consider how international law has sought to reconcile these apparently conflicting priorities.

I. INTRODUCTION

The primary focus of this chapter is on the immunities which officials of States and international organizations enjoy from the jurisdiction of other States, which are broadly

[1] The views expressed here are purely personal. I am grateful to Sir Michael Wood, Sir Daniel Bethlehem, Chris Whomersley, Diana Brooks, Doug Wilson, and Malcolm Evans for helpful suggestions and improvements to earlier drafts.

contained within the framework of diplomatic law.[2] For these purposes diplomatic law means the law by which international relations are conducted, and the processes of communication at the public international level are facilitated. Such communication can occur by a variety of means and in a number of settings. It includes both eye-catching, single events such as State visits and summits between Heads of States, as well as the more everyday work of foreign ministries, diplomatic missions, consular posts, and international organizations (James, 1991). The setting for such international communication ranges from simple ad hoc bilateral meetings of State officials, to the permanent institutionalized cooperation in large international organizations such as the UN and its specialized agencies.

Diplomatic law has ancient roots, and today comprises a large and, in many respects, highly developed body of law, derived from a variety of sources. For present purposes these include the 1961 Vienna Convention on Diplomatic Relations (VCDR), the 1963 Vienna Convention on Consular Relations (VCCR), and the 1969 Convention on Special Missions. Additionally, in relation to international organizations there is a large number of treaties which deal with both the privileges and immunities of representatives of States to international organizations and the privileges and immunities of officials and experts of those organizations. The best known examples of these treaties are the 1946 Convention on the Privileges and Immunities of the UN, and the 1947 Convention on the Privileges and Immunities of the Specialized Agencies. A further important component of diplomatic law is the Convention on the Prevention and Punishment of Crimes against Internationally Protected Persons, including Diplomatic Agents 1973.[3]

However, diplomatic law is not fully codified, and certain categories of those engaged in the conduct of international relations therefore enjoy immunity only by virtue of customary international law. For example, as we shall see, the law governing the privileges and immunities of foreign Heads of State and other senior government officials remains largely uncodified at the international level. In addition to this body of treaties and custom which set out the primary rules of diplomatic law, it is also important to review the extensive body of judicial decisions of both international and national courts and tribunals in which those rules have been interpreted and applied.

In earlier eras, when the range of diplomatic communication was less developed, its governing law was less sophisticated and the rationales on which that law rested were broad approximations. In the modern era, however, the legal fiction of extraterritoriality of foreign missions has now been discredited (Crawford, 2012, pp 397). The 'representative theory' (ie the identification of representatives of a sending State with the State itself) has been subjected to more rigorous rationalization, but continues to contribute to the rationale of jurisdictional immunities.[4] However, it is now the 'functional necessity' theory which provides the most convincing explanation of much of the modern law of

---

[2] Whilst the primary focus will be on diplomatic law, its interaction with other more recent developments in international law, including in human rights law and international criminal law will be considered in a number of the subsequent sections of this chapter.

[3] For text see (1974) 13 *ILM* 41. This Convention comprises an important aspect of the duty of protection States owe to officials of States and international organizations engaged on international business, providing for broad extraterritorial jurisdiction in respect of crimes relating to attacks on these persons. For a commentary on its drafting and negotiation see Wood, 1974.

[4] The representative theory suggests that diplomats, as representatives of the sending State should enjoy the same immunities as the State does itself. The preamble of the VCDR states that: '...the purpose of such privileges and immunities is not to benefit individuals but to ensure the efficient performance of the functions of diplomatic missions as representing States...'. In any event it might also be noted that the immunities of States themselves are now more limited and are increasingly based on function rather than simply on status.

diplomacy.[5] This recognizes that international cooperation between States, from which political, economic, social, and cultural benefits flow, is entirely dependent on effective processes of communication. It is therefore essential that international law should protect and facilitate those processes, and it is to that end that modern diplomatic law seeks to ensure an appropriate balance between the interests of the sending and receiving States. Professor Denza (2008, p 2) observes:

> Diplomatic law in a sense constitutes the procedural framework for the construction of international law and international relations. It guarantees the efficacy and security of the machinery through which States conduct diplomacy, and without this machinery States cannot construct law whether by custom or by agreement on matters of substance.

The primary aspect of diplomatic law on which this chapter will concentrate is the grant of immunity from local jurisdiction. In this respect it is important to note that international law recognizes two basic types of immunity from jurisdiction in relation to officials of States and international organizations.

The first is immunity *ratione personae*, ie immunity enjoyed by certain categories of State officials by virtue of their office. The functions of certain key offices of State are so important to the maintenance of international relations that they require immunity for their protection and facilitation.[6] These immunities cover both the official and the private acts of such office-holders, since interference with the performance of the official functions of such a person can result from the subjection of either type of act to the jurisdiction of the receiving State (eg if a diplomat is arrested it will interfere with his ability to perform his official functions whatever the reason for his arrest). These categories of official enjoy complete personal inviolability (including freedom from arrest and/or detention) and absolute immunity from criminal jurisdiction. Immunity from civil jurisdiction may also be recognized (though given the less coercive nature of civil jurisdiction, this immunity may be limited in respect of certain purely private actions of members of certain categories of official).[7] However, because immunities *ratione personae* attach only to enable the proper functioning of particular offices of State, rather than to benefit the office-holder individually, they lapse when the office-holder leaves office.

The second type of immunity is immunity *ratione materiae*—these immunities attach to the official acts of State officials. They are derivative from the principle of State immunity, which precludes the courts of one State adjudicating upon the acts of another State without its consent. Such immunities are, therefore, determined by reference to the nature of the acts in question rather than by reference to the particular office of the official who performed them. As such they cover a narrower range of acts than immunities *ratione personae*, but cover a wider range of actors—indeed they potentially apply to the official acts of all State officials. Furthermore because they relate to the nature of the act in question, the immunity for such official acts subsists even after the individual who performed has ceased to have any official functions. Thus a former State official can benefit from such immunity in respect of his official acts performed while in office, even after he has left office.

[5] See introductory comments to Section II, of the ILC Commentary on its final draft Articles, 1958 *YBILC* vol II, pp 94–5; see also comments of Sir Gerald Fitzmaurice, *YBILC* (1957), vol I (part two), at para 10.

[6] See, eg the preamble to the VCDR and the judgment of the ICJ in *Arrest Warrant of 11 April 2000 (Democratic Republic of Congo v Belgium), Preliminary Objections and Merits, Judgment, ICJ Reports 2002*, p 3.

[7] Denza, 2008, pp 280–83 notes how, historically, the immunities of diplomats from civil jurisdiction were less readily accepted than immunities from criminal jurisdiction.

It is important to note that both of these types of immunity operate simply as procedural bars to jurisdiction, and can be waived by appropriate authorities of the sending State, thus enabling the courts of a foreign State to assert jurisdiction.

The related, but conceptually distinct, doctrines of non-justiciability and/or act of State are not dealt with here. Non-justiciability is sometimes confusingly described as 'subject-matter immunity', but is in fact distinct from procedural immunity, since it essentially asserts that the subject matter of the claim is in fact governed by international law (or, in some cases, foreign public law) and therefore falls outside the competence of national courts of other States to determine.[8] A plea of non-justiciability requires the court to give closer examination to the basis of the proceedings than when it deals with a procedural immunity. However, further confusion may arise from the fact that these various forms of objection to jurisdiction are not mutually exclusive, but can in fact exist simultaneously (see Barker, 1998). Cases where different grounds for objection to jurisdiction coexist will usually be dismissed on the basis of a procedural immunity, since that question must be decided at the outset of proceedings, and will often be the simplest means of bringing the proceedings to an end.[9]

Despite the considerable constraint which procedural immunities (and other privileges of foreign diplomatic missions) place on the territorial jurisdiction of a receiving State, States generally observe them scrupulously. Perhaps more surprisingly, despite certain notorious cases of their abuse, there is no substantial body of opinion which advocates their abolition or restriction. For example, in response to the *St James's Square Incident* of 1984 (in which a police officer was killed by a shot fired from within the Libyan People's Bureau in London, while she was patrolling a political demonstration outside the Bureau), both the Foreign Affairs Committee of the UK Parliament and the UK government considered whether amendment of the VCDR should be sought, but rejected this on the grounds that it was neither practicable nor desirable.[10]

The generally high level of compliance with diplomatic law is usually ascribed to the reciprocal nature of diplomatic exchange (see, eg Higgins, 1985). Since each State is both a sending State and a receiving State, each State has an interest in maintaining the proper equilibrium between the rights of sending and receiving States. This explains the restraint shown both by receiving States in respecting the privileges and immunities of foreign missions, and by members of diplomatic missions in their conduct while abroad.

It should be noted that diplomatic law has grown up largely as a 'self-contained regime', setting out the rights and obligations of receiving States and sending States, and with its own remedies available in cases of abuse. This has been observed by the ICJ[11] and is also reflected in the ILC Articles on State Responsibility, Article 50 of which provides that

---

[8] See *Buttes Gas and Oil Co v Hammer* [1982] AC 888 (HL). For the limits of this doctrine see the case of *Kuwait Airways Corp v Iraqi Airways Co (No 2)* [2002] UKHL 19, 16 May 2002. For the application of the doctrine of non-justiciability alongside questions of the immunity of a former State official see the dissenting speech of Lord Lloyd in the *Pinochet (No 1)* case [1998] 3 WLR 1456 at pp 194–6 and discussed by Denza, 1999, pp 956–8.

[9] Procedurally non-justiciability/act of State is considered more as a substantive defence rather than simply a procedural bar to the jurisdiction of the court, and may therefore be considered at a later stage of proceedings—eg the judgment of Lord Goff in *Kuwait Airways Corp v Iraqi Airways Co (No 1)* [1995] 1 WLR 1147 (HL). For the obligation of a court to consider the plea of immunity *in limine litis* see *Difference Relating to Immunity from Legal Process of a Special Rapporteur of the Commission on Human Rights, Advisory Opinion, ICJ Reports 1999*, p 62.

[10] See *Abuse of Diplomatic Privileges and Immunities*, FAC First Report 1984–5 (HC 127), at paras 53–7, and the Government's Reply (Misc No 5 (1985), Cmnd 9497), at paras 9–11.

[11] See *United States Diplomatic and Consular Staff in Tehran, Judgment, ICJ Reports 1980*, p 3, at paras 86–7.

States are not permitted to infringe the inviolability of diplomatic and consular agents, premises, archives, and documents when taking countermeasures (Crawford, 2002, pp 50 and 288–93). However, as will be seen in Section VII of this chapter, the interaction of diplomatic law with recent developments in other areas of international law, and particularly in international criminal law, has raised difficult problems which have yet to be fully answered.

II. DIPLOMATIC RELATIONS

The primary, though not exclusive, means of communication between governments is through the establishment of diplomatic relations, usually involving the exchange of permanent diplomatic missions. A diplomatic mission is of course in a position of considerable vulnerability, being located in territory over which another State exercises jurisdiction, and thus having limited means available to it for ensuring its own security. From the earliest times, therefore, international society has recognized the need to protect diplomatic agents so as to enable diplomatic exchange (Young, 1964; Barker, 1996, pp 32–55). The rules of international law which govern the establishment and maintenance of such diplomatic relations are now codified in the 1961 Vienna Convention on Diplomatic Relations (VCDR). With over 180 parties, the VCDR is amongst the most widely ratified of all international conventions, and it is probable that even those of its aspects which were originally progressive development of the law now reflect customary international law.[12] The VCDR has thus been extraordinarily successful in its aim to create a comprehensive legal framework for the conduct of diplomatic relations.[13]

A. THE SCHEME OF THE VIENNA CONVENTION ON DIPLOMATIC RELATIONS

The VCDR seeks to establish a proper balance of the rights of sending and receiving States. The founding principle set out in Article 2 is that diplomatic relations take place by mutual consent. Article 3 then sets out the primary functions of a diplomatic mission:

(a) to represent the sending State;

(b) to protect the interests of the sending State and its nationals;

(c) to negotiate with the government of the receiving State;

(d) to ascertain and report to the government of the sending State the conditions and developments within the receiving State;

(e) to promote friendly relations between the sending State and the receiving State, and to develop their relations in economic, cultural, and scientific fields.

---

[12] Ibid, paras 45 and 62. For a summary of the main issues on which the VCDR represented progressive development of the law at the time of its negotiation, see Denza, 2008, pp 3–6.

[13] Denza, 2008, pp 2–3 suggests three reasons to explain the success of the VCDR. First, that the law in this area is both long-established and has been relatively stable for a considerable time. Secondly, the important role played by reciprocity in the maintenance of the rules. Thirdly, the careful attention paid in the drafting processes of the ILC and in the Vienna Conference itself to producing a text which could command the general approval of States.

The next part of the Convention (Articles 4–19) deals with various procedural questions in relation to the establishment of diplomatic relations, and in particular the appointment and accreditation of diplomatic agents. The consent of the receiving State is required in the form of a prior *agrément* for the appointment of the head of mission. Denza (2008) observes:

> The justification for the requirement lies in the particular sensitivity of the appointment of a head of mission and the need, if a head of mission is effectively to conduct diplomacy between two States, for him to be personally acceptable to both of them.

In relation to other diplomatic agents (except defence attachés) the sending State does not have to obtain the prior consent of the receiving State (Article 7). Nevertheless the sending State must provide to the receiving State notification (and, as far as possible, prior notification) of the arrival and final departure (or termination of the functions) of all members of missions (Article 10).[14] Furthermore the receiving State is, at any time (including before their arrival in the receiving State), entitled to inform the sending State that the head of the mission or any other member of a mission is *persona non grata*, or unacceptable, without giving reasons for doing so (Article 9).[15] In such cases the sending State must recall the person or terminate his functions. If the sending State fails to respond the receiving State may, after a 'reasonable period', treat the person as no longer enjoying diplomatic privileges and immunities.

Articles 20–28 concern the privileges and facilities which the sending State must grant to the mission itself. Thus under Article 22 the premises of the mission are inviolable, and agents of the receiving State are not entitled to enter them without the consent of the head of the mission. During the drafting work of the ILC and also during the negotiation of the VCDR, it was considered whether there should be any exceptions to this rule in times of extreme emergency. However, such proposals were overwhelmingly rejected on the grounds that the power of appreciation as to whether one of the exceptions was applicable to a given situation would belong to the receiving State, and that this might lead to abuse. In 1984 during the *St James's Square Incident* the UK government scrupulously respected the inviolability of the Libyan Mission throughout, notwithstanding the outrage that had been perpetrated from there, and the premises were not entered until after the severance of diplomatic relations and the vacation of the premises.[16]

---

[14] It now appears that the UK courts will not consider that notification is a prerequisite to the entitlement of diplomatic status, *R v Home Secretary, ex parte Bagga* (1990) 88 ILR 404: but see also the earlier cases of *R v Governor of Pentonville Prison, ex parte Teja* (1971) 52 ILR 368, *R v Lambeth Justices, ex parte Yusufu* (1985) 88 ILR 323, and *R v Governor of Pentonville Prison, ex parte Osman (No 2)* (1988) 88 ILR 378—in relation to the latter see also the certificate of the Foreign and Commonwealth Office in (1988) 59 *BYIL* 479.

[15] In its Reply to the Foreign Affairs Committee (n 10 of this chapter at paras 689–90) the Government set out its policy in respect of the kinds of behaviour which would lead to a declaration of *persona non grata*, which included matters such as espionage and incitement to violence, as well as other criminal offences. In addition a serious view would be taken of reliance on diplomatic immunity to evade civil liabilities. Finally the Government also stated a new policy in relation to parking offences, under which persistent failure to pay parking fines would lead to a review of a person's acceptability as a member of a mission. Denza, 2008, p 86 notes how the numbers of parking tickets cancelled on grounds of diplomatic immunity fell from over 100,000 in 1984, to just over 2,300 in 1993.

[16] During the inquiry into the incident by the Foreign Affairs Committee two possible grounds of entry into the mission were examined. First, whether there had been a material breach of treaty by Libya entitling the UK to repudiate it and enter the premises. This was rejected on the basis that the VCDR is a self-contained regime, with its own remedies in case of breach. The second question was whether the UK would have had a right to enter the premises under the doctrine of self-defence. The Legal Adviser to the Foreign and Commonwealth Office told the Committee that self-defence would in principle be available in respect of both action directed against

Furthermore under Article 22(2) the receiving State is under a special duty to take all appropriate steps to protect the premises of the mission against all intrusion, and to prevent disturbances to the peace of the mission or impairment of its dignity. Thus in the *Tehran Hostages* case, although those who attacked the US Embassy and Consulates were not acting on behalf of Iran in the initial phase, Iran was nonetheless responsible for having failed to take appropriate steps to protect the premises and their occupants.[17]

In relation to the duty to prevent any disturbance of the peace of the mission or impairment of its dignity in normal times, the question of whether to allow peaceful political demonstrations outside diplomatic missions may require the receiving State to strike a balance between rights of political expression and the maintenance of its obligations towards the sending State.[18]

Similarly under Article 24 the archives of the mission are inviolable.[19] In addition, Article 27 provides for the free communication of the mission, including the inviolability of official correspondence, free use of diplomatic bags for diplomatic documents and articles for official use, and the protection from interference of diplomatic couriers.

Articles 29–39 deal with the immunities enjoyed by members of the mission. As well as jurisdictional immunities (considered later in this chapter), these include other matters such as the inviolability of the private residence of a diplomatic agent, exemption from taxes and customs duties, and exemption from national service requirements in the receiving State. Thus members of diplomatic missions enjoy wide protections from interference by the receiving State, which must be given effect in national law, this being done in the UK by the Diplomatic Privileges Act 1964. However, it is important to emphasize that the rights and privileges are not granted for the personal benefit of the individuals concerned, but to ensure the efficient performance of the functions of the diplomatic mission.

By way of *quid pro quo* for the enjoyment of privileges and immunities, members of diplomatic missions owe certain duties towards the receiving State. These are:

(a)   the duty to respect the laws and regulations of the receiving State (Article 41(1));

(b)   the duty not to interfere in the internal affairs of the receiving State (Article 41(1));

---

the State and action directed against its nationals. However, he believed the circumstances of this case did not justify forcible entry on the grounds of self-defence, as the criteria specified in the *Caroline* case were not met. The Committee accepted the latter conclusion but made no comment on the general point as to the applicability of self-defence as a ground for entering diplomatic premises (n 9 of this chapter, at paras 94–5). Mann (1990, pp 333–7) argued that the inviolability of premises is conditioned by the lawfulness of their use, and so the Government had the right, and the duty, to enter the premises, to search for and remove any weapons held there.

[17]   *United States Diplomatic and Consular Staff in Tehran, Judgment, ICJ Reports 1980*, p 3, paras 62–8. During the second period when the Court found that through its support of the hostage-takers, Iran was directly responsible for their actions, it violated, *inter alia*, paras (1) and (3) of Article 22 VCDR (ibid, para 77).

[18]   In its Reply to the Foreign Affairs Committee, (n 10 of this chapter, para 39(e)) the government explained that in most cases this was left to the police who tended to manage such situations by, for example, keeping demonstrators on the opposite side of the road to the mission premises.

[19]   A violation of Article 24 was found in *United States Diplomatic and Consular Staff in Tehran, Judgment, ICJ Reports 1980*, p 3. For the question of whether inviolability extends to documents which have been removed from the mission and are subsequently used in legal proceedings see *Shearson Lehman Brothers Inc v Maclaine Watson and Co, International Tin Council Intervening* [1988] 1 WLR 16 and Mann, 1990, pp 328–9. See also the pre-VCDR Canadian case of *Rose v The King* (1947) 3 DLR 710 in which documentary evidence of espionage against accused persons in criminal proceedings was held to be admissible notwithstanding that it had been stolen from the Russian Embassy and inviolability had not been waived. In the case of *Fayed v Al-Tajir* (CA [1987] 3 WLR 102) an internal memorandum of an Embassy in London was found to be protected by absolute privilege as a diplomatic document, leading to a dismissal of a libel action based on the contents of the document. In the recent case of *R (Bancoult) v Secretary of State for Foreign and Commonwealth Affairs (No 3)* [2013] EWHC 1502 (Admin), the Administrative Court ruled that a reporting cable from the US Embassy in

(c) all official business of the communication by the mission with the receiving State should be through the Ministry of Foreign Affairs of the receiving State, or with such other ministries as may be agreed (Article 41(2));

(d) the premises of the mission must be not be used in any manner incompatible with the functions of the mission (Article 41(3));

(e) a diplomatic agent must not practice for personal profit any professional or commercial activity in the receiving State (Article 42).

Finally in Articles 43–6 the Convention deals with arrangements on the termination of diplomatic functions and on severance of diplomatic relations.

B. JURISDICTIONAL IMMUNITIES

The VCDR recognizes various categories of staff members of diplomatic missions, each enjoying immunity from jurisdiction to a different extent:

(a) diplomatic agents (ie the head of the mission and other members of the diplomatic staff) and their families (provided that they are not nationals of the receiving State (Article 37(1)) enjoy immunities *ratione personae*, ie by virtue of their office. Thus they are granted personal inviolability, including freedom from arrest and detention (Article 29),[20] and absolute immunity from criminal jurisdiction (Article 31). A diplomatic agent is also immune from civil and administrative jurisdiction,[21] except in three types of case:

   (i) a real action relating to immovable property situated in the territory of the receiving State, unless he holds it on behalf of the sending State for the purposes of the mission;[22]

   (ii) an action relating to succession in which the diplomatic agent is involved as executor, administrator, heir, or legatee as a private person and not on behalf of the sending State;

   (iii) an action relating to any professional or commercial activity exercised by the diplomatic agent in the receiving State outside his official functions.

(b) Administrative and technical staff and their families, who are not nationals or permanent residents of the receiving State, enjoy similar personal inviolability and immunity from criminal jurisdiction to diplomatic agents. However, their

---

London back to the State Department, which had been leaked through the 'wikileaks' website (ie without the consent of the USA), was not admissible by virtue of the inviolability that attached to the cable under Articles 24 and 27(2) of the VCDR (see paras 37–51). This decision was under appeal at the time of writing.

[20] A further aspect of inviolability is the duty to protect diplomatic agents, on which see also the Convention on the Prevention and Punishment of Crimes against Internationally Protected Persons—see n 3 of this chapter. For clear breaches of both limbs of Article 29 see *United States Diplomatic and Consular Staff in Tehran, Judgment, ICJ Reports 1980*, p 3, paras 62–3 and 77. Self-defence or an overriding duty to protect human life appears to provide a limited exception. See ibid, para 86 and Denza, 2008, pp 265–9.

[21] This includes civil proceedings concerning private matters. See, eg the Australian case of *De Andrade v De Andrade* (1984) 118 ILR 299, in which the immunity of a diplomat was upheld in relation to divorce and custody proceedings.

[22] See Denza, 2008, at pp 289–99. On the difficult issue of whether the private residence of a diplomat is included within the exception, see *Intpro Properties v Sauvel* [1983] 2 WLR 908. The private residence of a diplomat is, however, inviolable by virtue of Article 30.

immunity from civil jurisdiction does not extend to acts performed outside the course of their duties (Article 37(2)).

(c) Service staff who are not nationals or permanent residents of the receiving State enjoy immunity *ratione materiae*, in respect of acts performed in the course of their duties (Article 37(3)).

(d) Diplomatic agents representing the sending State but who are in fact nationals or permanent residents of the receiving State, also enjoy immunity *ratione materiae* in respect of official acts performed in the exercise of their functions (Article 38(1)).

(e) All members of diplomatic missions who enjoy immunities while in office enjoy a subsisting immunity *ratione materiae* with respect to acts performed in the exercise of their functions as members of the mission even after they have left office (Article 39(2)).[23]

It might be noted that generally immunities under the VCDR operate only in respect of the jurisdiction of the receiving State. However, the provisions of Article 40 can be distinguished in that third States must accord diplomatic agents (and their family members) inviolability and such immunities as may be required to ensure their transit or return while en route to and from post.[24]

C. REMEDIES IN CASES OF ABUSE

While the immunities set out in the previous section impose a considerable derogation from the jurisdiction of receiving States, the VCDR seeks to redress the balance, at least partially, by providing for certain remedies in cases of abuse. Jurisdictional immunities operate purely at the procedural level, by barring the adjudicative powers of the local courts in respect of the holder, but they do not in themselves amount to substantive exemptions from the law itself. Indeed as we have seen members of diplomatic missions are under a duty to respect the law of the receiving State. Therefore where such immunity is waived, the local courts may enjoy jurisdiction within the usual bounds set by international law. Article 32 of the VCDR deals with the question of waiver setting out: (a) that waiver is a prerogative of the sending State (not the diplomatic agent in question) (Article 32(1)); (b) that waiver must always be express (Article 33(2)); and (c) that waiver from jurisdiction in respect of civil or administrative proceedings does not, in itself, imply waiver from execution of the judgment (Article 33(4)).[25]

However, waivers remain in the discretion of the sending State,[26] and in the event that it refuses, the receiving State must rely on the broader remedy of withdrawing its consent, either in respect of a particular member of the mission by declaring him or her *persona non grata* or, in a particularly egregious case, by breaking off diplomatic relations.

---

[23] See the German Constitutional Court case of the *Former Syrian Ambassador to the GDR* (1997) 115 ILR 596, see also the *Pinochet* case discussed later in this chapter. For further explanation see Dinstein, 1966.

[24] See the Netherlands case, *Public Prosecutor* v *JBC* (1984) 94 ILR 339. In a recent UK case, a diplomat accredited to the Ethiopian Embassy in Washington was prosecuted and convicted of the importation of drugs whilst on a holiday in Europe. The judge of the Crown Court rejected the defendant's plea of immunity as she was not travelling through London to resume her diplomatic functions in Washington (*R* v *Wondemagegne* 12 July 2012—ruling on file with the author).

[25] By way of an exception to Article 32(1) and (2), Article 32(3) provides that a waiver will be implied in respect of counterclaims which are directly related to the principal claim in proceedings commenced by the holder of the immunity.

[26] For examples of practice see also Denza, 2008, p 345–7.

III. CONSULAR RELATIONS

The role of consuls is to represent the sending State, and to promote and/or protect its interests in the receiving State, but with the emphasis of that role on technical and administrative matters rather than political matters (in which diplomatic staff specialize). Consuls often deal with private interests, such as assistance to nationals of the sending State in the receiving State and the promotion of trade, rather than the public interests of the sending State. Nevertheless, generalizations about consular relations must be treated cautiously since the range of consular functions, as set out in VCCR, Article 5, is very broad. It can include:

(a) protecting in the receiving State the interests of the sending State and its nationals;[27]

(b) assisting nationals of the sending State in need of help in the receiving State;

(c) obtaining appropriate legal assistance for nationals of the sending State before tribunals and other authorities of the receiving State;

(d) assistance to vessels and aircraft of the sending State and their crews, as well as exercising rights of supervision and inspection thereof;

(e) promoting trade between the two States;

(f) issuing passports and/or visas and other notarial functions;

(g) promoting cultural exchange.

Though international law on consular relations has ancient roots, the modern law first developed in a vast web of bilateral consular treaties in the nineteenth and twentieth centuries. Yet so varied were these treaty provisions, that it was believed that (unlike the law of diplomatic relations prior to 1961) customary international law played only a very limited role in the establishment and maintenance of consular relations. However, following work by the ILC in the late 1950s and early 1960s, the 1963 Vienna Convention on Consular Relations (VCCR) sought to consolidate and codify a basic body of rules. While the VCCR does establish a widely accepted benchmark for consular relations[28] it expressly states that it shall not affect existing agreements between States, or prevent States from varying its provisions in their future agreements (Article 73).[29]

The scheme of the VCCR is not unlike the VCDR, dealing with: the establishment and conduct of consular relations (Articles 2–24); the end of consular functions (Articles 25–7); facilities, privileges, and immunities relating to a consular post (Articles 28–39); facilities, privileges, and immunities relating to consular officers and other members of a consular post (Articles 40–57); the regime relating to honorary consuls (Articles 58–68); and general provisions (Articles 69–73).

---

[27] On the VCCR system of consular protection of nationals of the sending State, see *LaGrand (Germany v USA), Merits, Judgment, ICJ Reports 2001*, p 466 at para 74. In the context of UK public law see also *R (Abbasi) v Secretary of State for Foreign and Commonwealth Affairs* ([2002] EWCA Civ 1598).

[28] For example in *United States Diplomatic and Consular Staff in Tehran, Judgment, ICJ Reports 1980*, p 3, para 62 the ICJ found the protection of consular staff and property under the VCCR also reflected rules of customary international law.

[29] Similarly under the UK implementing legislation, the Consular Relations Act 1968, the relevant provisions of the VCCR are implemented by and scheduled to the Act, but by virtue of s 3 any international agreement of the UK, under which consular privileges and immunities differ from the VCCR standard, may be given effect by Order in Council.

The differences in the functions of consuls, as compared to diplomats, explain the differences in the extent of immunities from jurisdiction that are generally granted to consuls.[30] Consular officers enjoy a more limited personal inviolability—they may not be arrested or detained pending trial, except in the case of a grave crime[31] and pursuant to a decision by the competent judicial authority (Article 41). In relation to immunity from jurisdiction, consular officers enjoy only immunity *ratione materiae*, ie in respect of acts performed in the exercise of their consular functions (Article 43).[32]

IV. SPECIAL MISSIONS

In addition to the communication between governments that is enabled through the establishment of permanent diplomatic missions, an important means of carrying out particular items of inter-governmental business is through the use of special missions (sometimes called ad hoc diplomacy). The advantages of conducting international relations in this way are various. One is that it is a way of enabling direct contact between senior office-holders or those with particular specialisms or expertise in the respective countries (eg the UK currently has a number of roving special representatives including one for climate change whose interlocutors in other States will include individuals beyond the classical diplomatic channel between an Embassy and the Ministry of Foreign Affairs of the receiving State). Another aspect for some countries may be that ad hoc diplomacy may contribute to saving some of the costs of maintaining an extensive network of large diplomatic missions overseas. Special missions offer an important degree of flexibility to States in maintaining their international relations. In practice therefore special missions may vary considerably in appearance—ranging from missions involving the Head of State in person on matters of great political moment, to missions consisting of relatively junior officials concerned with a purely technical matter between the sending and receiving State.

While the use of ad hoc diplomacy of this sort in fact pre-dates the establishment of the present system of permanent diplomatic missions, the legal status of such missions has begun to attract greater attention in recent years. There is a growing body of State practice including national legislation, decisions from national courts and governmental statements (Wood, 2012).

The ILC considered the topic of special missions following its work on diplomatic and consular relations, resulting in the 1969 UN Convention on Special Missions. The Convention seeks to set out in some detail norms for the conduct of *ad hoc* diplomacy, including the privileges and immunities which attach to special missions. The Convention does not have wide participation[33] and there is some dispute as to whether all of its provisions reflect customary international law. While the basic principles are not in doubt, Sir

---

[30] Though in its practice with certain States, the UK has been willing to agree that the diplomatic standard of privileges and immunities should be extended to consular officers—see, eg Consular Relations (Privileges and Immunities) (People's Republic of Bulgaria) Order 1970 (SI 1970/1923); Consular Relations (Privileges and Immunities) (People's Republic of China) Order 1984 (SI 1984/1978); Consular Relations (Privileges and Immunities) (Polish People's Republic) Order 1978 (SI 1978/1028); and Consular Relations (Privileges and Immunities) (USSR) Order 1970 (SI 1970/1938). For comparable US practice see Lee and Quigley, 2008, pp 463–9

[31] The term 'grave crime' is not defined under the VCCR. However, the UK Consular Relations Act 1968 defines it as any crime punishable by up to a term of five years' imprisonment (s 1(2)).

[32] Determining what constitutes an 'official act' for these purposes can raise difficult questions of characterization. See Lee and Quigley, 2008, pp 440–61.

[33] There are currently 38 parties. The UK signed the Convention on 17 December 1970, but has not ratified it.

Arthur Watts has suggested that the main reason for the limited success of the Convention appears to be its inflexibility, in that it seeks to apply a single standard of treatment to all kinds of missions (see Watts, 1999, pp 344–5). There may also have been some concerns arising from the definition of special missions, as well as some practical difficulties arising from the temporary nature of such missions.

The Convention broadly follows the familiar scheme of the VCDR and VCCR. It sets out firmly the principle of mutual consent as underlying ad hoc diplomacy (Articles 2 and 3), and then deals with procedural questions for the sending and conduct of special missions (Articles 2–19). It sets out the facilities, privileges, and immunities of missions (Articles 22–8) and of their members and other staff (Articles 29–48).

Substantive aspects of the Convention also resemble the VCDR; hence for the purposes of jurisdictional immunities the staff are divided into broadly similar categories enjoying immunities to a similar extent.[34] Members of special missions are under an obligation to respect local law (Article 47). Also in cases of abuse the remedies of the receiving States are similar to those under the VCDR, including seeking waiver (Article 41), declaration of *persona non grata* (Article 12), or bringing the mission to an end (Article 20(1)(e)). Finally it might be noted that the Convention provides that such additional privileges and immunities as may be required under international law apply to the Head of the sending State, the Head of its Government, its Minister for Foreign Affairs, or other persons of high rank when on a special mission (Article 21).[35]

The fact that relatively few States are parties to the Special Missions Convention means that a good part of the caselaw and other State practice pertains to the customary international law of special missions. Crawford sums up the position as follows:

> The Convention has influenced the customary rules concerning persons on official visits (special missions) which have developed largely through domestic caselaw. The Convention confers a higher scale of privileges and immunities upon a narrower range of missions than extant customary law, which focuses on the immunities necessary for the proper conduct of the mission, principally inviolability and immunity from criminal jurisdiction. (Crawford, 2012, p 414)[36]

Thus the members of a special mission will enjoy personal inviolability and unqualified immunity *ratione personae* from criminal jurisdiction, as well as such immunity from civil and administrative jurisdiction as is necessary for them to carry out the functions of their mission. Such immunity should in principle last only for so long as is functionally necessary for the achievement of the special mission, but not longer. In addition immunity *ratione materiae* will attach to the official acts of the members of the special mission

---

[34] Under Articles 29 and 31 'representatives of the sending State in the special mission and members of its diplomatic staff' enjoy personal inviolability and jurisdictional immunities equivalent to those of diplomatic agents under the VCDR (save that in respect of immunity from civil jurisdiction a further exception is made in relation to road traffic accidents outside the official functions of the person concerned). Family members, administrative and technical staff, service staff, and members of the mission who are nationals of the receiving State, all enjoy equivalent immunities to those under the VCDR (see Articles 39, 36, 37, and 40 respectively). Temporally immunities are limited to the duration of the mission, save that immunity *ratione materiae* in relation to official acts continues to subsist even after the mission has come to an end (Article 44(2)).

[35] However, it is not clear what additional privileges and immunities this might entail. See *Satow's Diplomatic Practice* (2009, p 190).

[36] See also Wood 2012 for a survey of State practice from Austria, Belgium, Finland, France, Germany, the Netherlands, the UK, and the USA, leading to the conclusion that '[t]here now appears to be a "settled answer" to the question of the customary law on the immunities of special missions'.

performed during the mission, which will in principle subsist even after the special mission has been completed.

It may be of interest to dwell for a moment on some recent UK practice in relation of special missions. In the UK there have been a number of recent cases in which a court of first instance has had to consider whether a foreign visitor enjoys immunity under customary international law as being on a special mission. Among these, one concerned a visiting Minister of Commerce and International Trade who was a member of a visiting delegation on a State Visit led by the Head of State, and another concerned a visiting Defence Minister attending high-level meetings with members of the UK government.[37] However, the issue of special mission immunity was given its most thorough examination to date by the High Court (on appeal from the Magistrate's Court) in the case of *Khurts Bat v Investigating Judge of the Federal Court of Germany*.[38] In that case a Mongolian official visiting the UK in the hope of arranging official meetings once there, but without having obtained UK consent to his presence in the UK for those purposes, claimed that he was immune from extradition proceedings in the UK on the basis that he was on a special mission. The High Court accepted that special mission immunity was governed by customary international law, which for these purposes was part of the common law. The Court started from the definition of a special mission in Article 1 of the 1969 Convention:

> A 'special mission' is a temporary mission, representing the State, which is sent by one State to another State *with the consent of the latter* for the purposes of dealing with it on specific questions or performing in relation to it a specific task (emphasis of the Court).[39]

The Court found that it was vital that the consent of the receiving State must be previously obtained, and must be consent to a special mission as such. As neither of these conditions was satisfied in the instant case, the Court rejected the claim for special mission immunity. In doing so the Court held that the question of consent by the UK (ie as the receiving State) was—like the question of whether or not the UK had agreed to the accreditation of a member of a permanent diplomatic mission—a matter that was exclusively for decision by the government and not the courts. It was therefore a question on which the government could provide conclusive evidence to the Court by means of a certificate.

The issue of special mission immunity arose again, though in a different context, some months later in a during a visit to London of the then Israeli Leader of the Opposition, Tzipi Livni, on an invitation for official talks from the British Foreign Secretary, William Hague. A would-be private prosecutor sought the consent of the Director of Public Prosecutions (DPP) to the issue of an arrest warrant in respect of Ms Livni in relation to allegations of war crimes committed during the time that she was Foreign Minister of Israel. Following

---

[37]   See judgment of the Bow Street Magistrates' Court in the case of *Bo Xilai* (2005) 128 ILR 713 (8 November 2005), and that of the Westminster Magistrates' Court in *Re: Ehud Barak*, 29 September 2009, (not yet reported). See also the unreported cases in the City of Westminster Magistrates' Court of *Court of Appeal of Paris v Durbar* (16 February 2008) and *Re Mikhael Gorbachev* (2011) 82 *BYIL* 570 (30 March 2011). Other references to special missions in the English courts have been in *obiter dicta*, where the case has been decided on other grounds; see, eg *Fenton Textiles Association v Krassin et al* (1921) 6 BILC 247; *R v Governor of Pentonville Prison, ex parte Teja* [1971] 2 QB 274; and *R v Governor of Pentonville Prison, ex parte Osman (No 2)* (1988) 88 ILR 378. See also the contrasting *dicta* of Lord Millett and Lord Phillips in *R v Bow Street Metropolitan Stipendiary, ex parte Pinochet Ugarte (Amnesty International Intervening) (No 3)* (hereafter *Pinochet No 3*) [1999] 2 WLR 827 at 905E and 918E respectively.

[38]   *Khurts Bat v Investigating Judge of the Federal Court of Germany* [2011] EWHC 2029 (Admin). For comment see Sanger, 2013.

[39]   Ibid, para 29.

the issue of certificate by the Foreign and Commonwealth Office (FCO) confirming that it had consented to her visit as a special mission, the DPP declined to consent to the issue of the warrant, issuing a statement explaining that the FCO certificate was conclusive evidence that Ms Livni was on a special mission.[40]

The UK government has recently sought to set out a clearer process for decision-making on the question of special missions, initially on a pilot basis. Prior to the *Khurts Bat* decision the question of special mission status had often been left to be implied from the circumstances of each case, leading to the potential for some uncertainty, of which, indeed, that case might itself be said to be an illustration. In a Written Ministerial Statement to Parliament,[41] the Foreign Secretary therefore set out the government's view of what a special mission was but, referencing the *Khurts Bat* case, also noted that not all official visitors would necessarily be entitled to special mission status. The intention was to establish a new procedure so that the question of the government's consent to a visit as a special mission could be expressly addressed before its arrival in the UK. To that end foreign diplomatic missions in London were invited to submit details of forthcoming official visits from their respective sending States, where those States required clarity on whether the UK would consent to the visit as a special mission. This administrative procedure has already been used in a number of cases, but it is perhaps too soon to assess how effective it has been in providing greater clarity and certainty in this area.[42]

V. HOLDERS OF HIGH-RANKING OFFICES, SUCH AS HEADS OF STATE, HEADS OF GOVERNMENT, AND MINISTERS FOR FOREIGN AFFAIRS

A. HEADS OF STATE

In previous eras when most States were governed by personal sovereigns such as monarchs or emperors, there was a close identity in international law between such persons and their States. However, modern international law tends to consider the rights and competences of Heads of State as attaching to them in their capacity as the highest representatives of their States, rather than inherently in their own right (Watts, 1994, pp 35–7). That said, international law recognizes that the Head of State may exercise a number of important powers in international relations *ex officio*, including the sending and receiving of diplomats and consuls, and the conclusion of treaties.[43]

The immunity of Heads of State from the jurisdiction of foreign States remains largely uncodified at the international level, but it has undergone some important changes in modern times. During earlier times when international law closely identified a Head

---

[40] See CPS statement of 6 October 2011 at http://blog.cps.gov.uk/2011/10/cps-statement-in-relation-to-ms-tzipi-livinis-visit-to-the-uk.html.

[41] Hansard HC Deb, 4 March 2013, Col 55–6WS.

[42] Hansard HC Deb, 12 July 2013, Col 427–30W. Coincidentally, in a recent development in the Netherlands, the Dutch Government wrote to the Dutch Parliament setting out its view of its obligations under customary international law to grant immunity to members of foreign official missions (see letter of 26 April 2012 from the Minister of Foreign Affairs and the State Secretary for Security and Justice to the Senate and House of Representatives on the immunity of members of foreign official missions).

[43] See, eg 1969 VCLT, Article 7 and *Land and Maritime Boundary between Cameroon and Nigeria (Cameroon v Nigeria: Equatorial Guinea Intervening)*, ICJ Reports 2002, paras 263–8.

of State with his or her State, the absolute doctrine of 'sovereign immunity' prevailed. However, more recently, as the restrictive doctrine of immunity in relation to States has developed, more distinct rules in relation to Heads of State have also developed (Watts, 1994, pp 52–66).[44]

The International Court of Justice has recently reaffirmed aspects of the law as regards personal inviolability and immunity from criminal jurisdiction, in the following terms:

> ...A Head of State enjoys in particular 'full immunity from criminal jurisdiction and inviolability' which protects him or her 'against any act of authority of another State which would hinder him or her in the performance of his or her duties'. Thus the determining factor in assessing whether or not there has been an attack on the immunity of the Head of State lies in the subjection of the latter to a constraining act of authority...The Court recalls that the rule of customary international law reflected in Article 29 of the Vienna Convention on Diplomatic Relations, while addressed to diplomatic agents, is necessarily applicable to Heads of State. This provision reads as follows:

> > "[t]he person of a diplomatic agent shall be inviolable. He shall not be liable to any form of arrest or detention. The receiving State shall treat him with due respect and shall take all appropriate steps to prevent any attack on his person, freedom or dignity."

> This provision translates into positive obligations for the receiving State as regards the actions of its own authorities, and into obligations of prevention as regards possible acts by individuals. In particular, it imposes on receiving States the obligation to protect the honour and dignity of Heads of State, in connection with their inviolability.[45]

Further evidence of the relevant principles of customary international law can also be found in the practice of national courts, as well as in relevant national legislative provisions.[46]

In the UK, s 20 of the State Immunity Act 1978 essentially equates the position of a foreign Head of State with the head of a diplomatic mission. Thus a foreign Head of State

---

[44] For a US perspective on this development see *Tachiona and others* v *Mugabe and others* 169 F.Supp 2d 259 (2001) (although the Court of Appeals (2nd Circuit) did not follow the same line of reasoning in its decision of 6 October 2004, 386F.3d 205). See also *Wei Ye* v *Jiang Zemin* 383F.3d 620. More recently, following the decision of the Supreme Court in *Samantar* v *Yousuf*, 130 S Ct 2278 (2010) that the immunity of individuals is not governed by the Foreign Sovereign Immunities Act, this issue will now usually focus on any 'suggestion of immunity' filed by the State Department—see for example *Habyarimana* v *Kagame*, Court of Appeals 696 F.3d 1029 (10th Circuit, 2012) and *Manoharan* v *Rajapaksa*, Court of Appeals (DC Circuit), 29 March 2013.

[45] *Case concerning Certain Questions of Mutual Assistance in Criminal Matters (Djibouti* v *France)* Judgment of 4 June 2008, at paras 170 and 174. On the facts of the case the Court found that an invitation to a Head of State to testify in the course of criminal proceedings (without any suspicion attaching to him) did not violate his inviolability. However, the Court also found that had the French authorities passed confidential information regarding the witness summons to the Press, in the context of an official visit by the Djiboutian Head of State, this could constitute a failure in its obligation to protect his honour and dignity. On the other hand see *Aziz* v *Aziz and others* [2007] EWCA Civ 712 in which the English Court of Appeal rejected an application by a Head of State for parts of a judgment to which he was not a party to be kept secret, in order to avoid the revelation of personal information about him. In similar vein see *Harb* v *King Fahd* [2005] EWCA Civ 632, discussed in n 48 in this chapter.

[46] In this respect, it is interesting to note the recent proposal of Equatorial Guinea to France to refer to the International Court of Justice the question of whether actions of the French authorities in relation to the assets of President Obiang in part of an anti-corruption investigation.

The recent complaints of President Morales of Bolivia about the refusal of some European States to allow the overflight of his personal flight on its way from Moscow, were based on his legal status as a serving Head of State.

(whether on an official or a private visit) will enjoy complete personal inviolability and absolute immunity from criminal jurisdiction *ratione personae*.[47] Immunity from civil jurisdiction is more complex in that it involves determining whether the act in question was performed by the Head of State in his or her official capacity as an organ of the State, or whether it was performed in his or her personal capacity. In relation to the acts of a Head of State performed in his public capacity, the provisions in Part I of the Act (relating to the immunity of State itself, and considered in the previous chapter) will be applicable. For all other acts Heads of State will enjoy immunity from civil jurisdiction subject to the three exceptions noted in respect of Article 31(1) VCDR.[48] Finally it should be noted that the immunities of a Head of State can be waived, either by the Head of State himself or herself, or by his or her State.

On the other hand when a Head of State leaves office, the House of Lords has found that he or she will enjoy immunities on the same basis as a former diplomat, and in particular subsisting immunity *ratione materiae* for his or her official acts (as per Article 39(2) VCDR). The extent of this immunity was of course the subject of detailed scrutiny in the *Pinochet* case (examined later in this chapter).

B. HEADS OF GOVERNMENT AND MINISTERS FOR FOREIGN AFFAIRS

Heads of Government and Ministers for Foreign Affairs enjoy immunity from jurisdiction *ratione personae* under international law to the same extent as Heads of State, since they perform comparable functions in representing their States in international relations.[49] The position in relation to the personal inviolability and immunity from criminal jurisdiction of serving Foreign Ministers was clarified by the International Court of Justice in the *Arrest Warrant* case.[50]

---

[47] See, eg judgment of the Bow Street Magistrates' Court in *Mugabe* of 14 January 2004 (2004) 53 *ICLQ* 770.

[48] See, eg Laddie J in *BCCI v Price Waterhouse* [1997] 4 All ER 108, in which certain acts of Sheikh Zayed of Abu Dhabi were immune from suit under s 20 as he was Head of State of the UAE, notwithstanding that the acts in question were not performed in that capacity. This was so even though Shiekh Zayed was simultaneously head of one of the constituent units of the UAE, and his acts may have been performed in a public capacity in that respect. In the case of *Harb v HM King Fahd bin Abdul Aziz*, [2005] EWCA Civ 632 the President of the Family Division of the High Court upheld a Head of State's assertion of immunity in relation to proceedings for ancillary relief in matrimonial proceedings. The applicant appealed, but King Fahd died before the Court of Appeal could hear the appeal, thus bringing the proceedings to an end (see [2005] EWCA Civ 1324). However, the Court of Appeal had already by that stage ruled that the duty of the forum State to protect a Head of State from 'any attack on his person, freedom or dignity' (Article 29 VCDR) did not entail that the proceedings in which King Fahd was asserting immunity must be held in private.

Another aspect of the assimilation of a Head of State with the position of a head of a diplomatic mission, namely the extension of immunities to members of the family was considered in the case of *Apex Global Management Ltd v Fi Call Ltd and others* [2013] EWHC 587(Ch)). A half-brother of the current King of Saudi Arabia (and son of the former King) and his son both claimed immunity in civil proceedings on the basis they were 'members of the family forming part of the household' of the King, as per s 20(1)(b) of the State Immunity Act. The Court found that they could not be considered as 'forming part of the household' of the King for these purposes.

[49] In principle their official acts, like those of other State officials, will also be protected by immunity *ratione materiae* which subsists even after they have left office: see Sections VI and VIII B of this chapter.

[50] *Arrest Warrant of 11 April 2000 (Democratic Republic of Congo v Belgium), Preliminary Objections and Merits, Judgment, ICJ Reports* 2002, p 3. For comments see Cassese, 2002; Wirth, 2002; Spinedi, 2002; Sir Robert Jennings, 2002; Stern, 2002; Schreuer and Wittich, 2002; McLachlan, 2002.

The case concerned the issue by a Belgian magistrate of an international warrant for the arrest of the incumbent Congolese Foreign Minister[51] for his alleged involvement in grave breaches of the Geneva Conventions and the Additional Protocols thereto, and crimes against humanity. The relevant Belgian statute provided for universal jurisdiction in the Belgian courts over these crimes (ie wherever and by whomsoever they were committed) and provided that 'the immunity attaching to the official capacity of a person shall not prevent the application of the present law'.[52]

The ICJ upheld Congo's complaint that the issue of the arrest warrant was a violation of the immunity from criminal jurisdiction and the personal inviolability which an incumbent Foreign Minister enjoys under international law. The Court based this conclusion chiefly on the functions exercised by a Foreign Minister in international relations. The Court noted that he or she is in charge of his or her government's diplomatic activities, and represents it in international negotiations and meetings, as well as his powers under international law to act on behalf of and to bind the State in for example treaty relations, simply by virtue of his or her office. Such functions required that a Foreign Minister should be able to travel internationally freely and to be able to be in constant communication with his or her government and its diplomatic missions around the world. Such considerations led the Court to consider that Foreign Ministers enjoyed complete personal inviolability and absolute immunity from criminal jurisdiction *ratione personae*, throughout the duration of their office. In that respect it was irrelevant whether the acts in question were private or official, or that they were performed prior or subsequently to the Foreign Minister in question assuming office, or whether the Foreign Minister was in the forum State on a private or an official visit.

Three further points should be noted about the extent of the immunity from jurisdiction of an incumbent Foreign Minister under the judgment.[53] First, it might be noted that Foreign Ministers may rely upon their immunities in any State, whereas for example diplomatic immunity is largely limited to immunity from the courts of the receiving State. Secondly, attention might be drawn to the fact that the Court found specifically that there was no exception to the immunity of a serving Foreign Minister from the criminal jurisdiction of national courts in respect of war crimes or crimes against humanity. Thirdly, the immunity of a Foreign Minister can be waived by his own State.

Though the Court's findings are strictly speaking confined to the immunities enjoyed by Foreign Ministers, it seems clear that similar immunities apply, perhaps *a fortiori*, to Heads of Government.[54] How far such immunities can also be extended to other Ministers or officials may depend on analogous reasoning, based on the involvement of such persons in international relations.[55] Thus, for example in the UK, decisions at first

---

[51] In fact whilst he was the incumbent Foreign Minister at the material time, ie at the point the arrest warrant was issued, he subsequently left that office to become the Minister of Education and by the time of the judgment he held no ministerial portfolio at all.

[52] *Act concerning the Punishment of Grave Breaches of International Humanitarian Law* of 10 February 1999 (1999) 38 ILM 921. The Act has since been substantially amended and this provision removing immunity has been repealed.

[53] The Court's comments, strictly speaking obiter dictum, on the extent of the subsisting immunity *ratione materiae* of a Foreign Minister after he has left office are considered in Section VIII of this chapter.

[54] See, eg the US case of *Saltany v Reagan and others* (1988) 80 ILR 19, affirmed (1989) 87 ILR 680. For a contrasting view on immunity scope of immunity *ratione materiae* see Douglas, 2012.

[55] In this respect the Second Report of Special Rapporteur Escobar Hernandez on the 'Immunity of State Officials from Foreign Criminal Jurisdiction' 4 April 2013 (A/CN.4/661) has proposed limiting immunity *ratione personae* in this respect to the so-called 'Troika' ie the Head of State, Head of Government and Minister of Foreign Affairs, leaving other high-ranking official visitors to be protected only by special mission immunity which would not extend therefore to visits in a private capacity (see paras 59–68). This position has been endorsed by the ILC: see ILC Report 2013, Ch V.

instance have recognized that such immunities extend to a visiting Defence Minister,[56] and to a visiting Minister of Commerce (whose portfolio included responsibility for international trade).[57] On the other hand in the *Khurts Bat* case the administrative head of the National Security Office of Mongolia was found to be outside the 'narrow circle' of those entitled to immunity *ratione personae*, as his position was simply not sufficiently senior in the structure of the Mongolian State. Nevertheless it is not yet clear where the lines should properly be drawn, and the task is not made easier by the different ways in which different governments organize themselves internally. In any event other ministers or senior officials will enjoy immunities when on official visits as members of special missions.

VI. THE IMMUNITIES OF OTHER STATE OFFICIALS

The immunities discussed in Sections II–V of this chapter appear to be the principal regimes of immunities which international law requires should be granted *ratione personae* in respect of particular categories of State official.[58] However, under the doctrine of State immunity, all State officials (and former State officials[59]) enjoy immunity *ratione materiae* for their official acts. The rationale for this is that a State as an entity can only act through the agency of individuals working on its behalf. The official acts of those individuals can engage the international responsibility of the State, and they can only be challenged in a way that is consistent with international law. In broad terms a national court of one State is therefore precluded from adjudicating upon the official acts of State officials of another State.

It is convenient to examine this proposition first in relation to civil jurisdiction and then criminal jurisdiction. It seems clear that the immunity of State officials in respect of their official acts from the civil jurisdiction of the courts of other States should be upheld, where the effect of proceedings would be to undermine or render nugatory the immunity of the employer State.[60] In other words it prevents an applicant from seeking to circumvent the impediment of State immunity by adopting the tactic of suing the individual carrying out the business of State. This is reflected in the 2004 UN Convention on the Jurisdictional Immunities of States and Their Property.[61]

In the UK this proposition finds support in both the common law[62] and in some recent cases under the State Immunity Act 1978. Thus in *Propend Finance v Sing* the

---

[56] See judgment of the Bow Street Magistrates' Court in the case of *Mofaz*, 12 February 2004 (2004) 53 *ICLQ* 771–3. See also *Re: Ehud Barak*, 29 September 2009, (not yet reported).

[57] See judgment of the Bow Street Magistrates' Court in the case of *Bo Xilai* (2005) 128 ILR 713 (8 November 2005).

[58] Additional categories would be State officials who staff permanent representations to international organizations. Their status, privileges, and immunities will depend on the particular arrangements made under relevant treaties on privileges and immunities as well as the Headquarters Agreement of the organization in question, see for example El-Erian and Scobbie, 1998, pp 857–67.

[59] See for example Article 39(2) VCDR in relation to former members of diplomatic missions, and the treatment of the immunities of former Heads of State in *Pinochet No 3* [1999] 2 WLR 827, discussed in Section VIII B of this chapter.

[60] See Lord Browne-Wilkinson in *Pinochet No 3* [1999] 2 WLR 827 at 847F.

[61] Thus in defining the 'State' (the beneficiary of immunity under the convention) it includes in Article 1(b)(iv) 'representatives of the State acting in that capacity'.

[62] See, eg *Twycross v Dreyfus* (1877) 5 Ch D 605; *Rahimtoola v Nizam of Hyderabad* [1958] AC 379; also *Zoernsch v Waldock* [1964] 2 QB 352. See Whomersley, 1992.

Commissioner of the Australian Federal Police (AFP) was permitted to claim State immunity, in connection with contempt proceedings for an alleged breach of an undertaking committed by an AFP officer accredited as a diplomatic agent to the Australian High Commission in London. The Court of Appeal held:

> The protection afforded by the Act of 1978 [ie the State Immunity Act 1978] to States would be undermined if employees, officers or (as one authority puts it) 'functionaries' could be sued as individuals for matters of State conduct in respect of which the State they were serving had immunity. Section 14(1) must be read as affording individual employees or officers of a foreign State protection under the same cloak as protects the State itself.[63]

The House of Lords approved this formulation of the principle in the case of *Jones v Ministry of the Interior of the Kingdom of Saudi Arabia*, in the context of civil proceedings relating to allegations of torture against Saudi Arabia and certain of its officials.[64] Lord Bingham drew the following conclusions as relevant: (1) that the individual defendants were at the material times acting or purporting to act as servants or agents of the State; (2) that their acts were accordingly attributable to the State; (3) that no distinction could be made between the claim against the State and the claim against the individual defendants; and (4) none of the claims fell within any exception to immunity under the State Immunity Act 1978.[65] The Court went on to find that the *jus cogens* nature of the prohibition of torture did not of itself operate to enable a third State to assert civil jurisdiction in the face of State immunity, and that there was currently no generally accepted exception to State immunity from civil jurisdiction in relation to breaches of international law.

In contrast to the interpretation by the UK courts of the State Immunity Act in this respect, the US Supreme Court has recently reversed the practice of a number of lower courts[66] and found that the immunity *ratione materiae* enjoyed by individuals (whether current or former officials) is not governed by the US Foreign Sovereign Immunities Act (1976).[67] Instead the immunity of individuals in US law remains regulated by the common law, and in this respect it is open to the US government to make a 'suggestion of immunity' which the courts will invariably follow.[68] The *Samantar* case concerned a former Prime

---

[63] *Propend Finance v Sing* 111 ILR 611 at 669. For criticism see Barker, 1998. But see also the US cases of *Chuidian v Philippine National Bank* (1990) 92 ILR 480 and *Herbage v Meese* (1990) 98 ILR 101. Also the Canadian cases of *Jaffe v Miller* (1993) 95 ILR 446 and *Walker v Baird* (1994) 16 OR (3d) 504. Other cases from the UK include *Re P (No 2)* (1998) 114 ILR 485, and under the common law of State immunity *Holland v Lampen-Wolfe* [2000] 1 WLR 1548.

[64] *Jones v Ministry of Interior for the Kingdom Saudi Arabia and Ors* [2006] UKHL 26; [2007] 1 AC 270. The plaintiff has a complaint against the UK pending in the European Court of Human Rights that in upholding the claims to immunity the House of Lords' decision contravened his right of access to a court under Article 6 of the European Convention on Human Rights.

[65] Ibid at para 13.

[66] See for example the case of *Belhas v Ya'alon*, US Court of Appeals (DC Circuit), 515 F.3d 1279, 15 February 2008, which had found that a former senior member of the Israeli Defence Force enjoyed immunity under the FSIA in respect of civil proceedings arising from alleged war crimes.

[67] See the case of *Samantar v Yousuf*, 130 S Ct 2278 (2010).

[68] For some other recent examples of suggestions of immunity in this respect see the Suggestion of Immunity filed on 7 September 2012 in the case *Jane Doe v Ernesto Zedillo Ponce de Leon* in US District Court of Connecticut, providing that the former Mexican President Zedillo enjoyed continuing immunity for his official acts whilst he was in office. The District Court upheld his immunity in line with the Suggestion in a judgment of 18 July 2013. See also the Suggestion of Immunity of 17 December 2012 filed in the case of *Rosenberg et al v Lashkar e Taiba*, in which the immunity of two former Directors of Pakistan's Inter-Service Intelligence Directorate in a suit concerning the terrorist attacks in Mumbai in 2008 was at issue. See also Koh, 2011; Bellinger, 2011.

Minister of Somalia accused of serious human rights abuses during his period in office. After the Supreme Court's judgment, the case was remitted for further determination, and the State Department issued a Suggestion of Immunity finding that Samantar did not enjoy immunity because there was currently no government of Somalia recognized by the USA able to assert the immunity on his behalf. The State Department also offered the view that, given Samantar's adoption of US residence, it was incumbent on him to accept the values of American society. Interestingly the Court of Appeals of the Fourth Circuit subsequently held that it was not bound by the terms in the Suggestion of Immunity, but rather found that Samantar did not enjoy immunity because the allegations against him were of breaches of norms of *ius cogens*, and that there was an exception to immunity in this respect. Samantar has subsequently sought certiorari in the Supreme Court, and at the time of writing it remains to be seen whether the Supreme Court will take a further appeal in this matter. One interesting factor if they do so will be that the USA now recognizes the government of Somalia, and that government has asserted immunity on Samantar's behalf.

Turning to the application of immunity *ratione materiae* in relation to criminal jurisdiction, a useful starting point is the ongoing work of the International Law Commission. The first Special Rapporteur on the topic (Ambassador Kolodkin) addressed the law and practice on immunity *ratione materiae* in some detail. In his Second Report the Special Rapporteur set out the traditional rationale for immunity *ratione materiae*, but then considered whether as a matter of customary international law there were any exceptions to this form of immunity for example in relation to international crimes or human rights abuses.[69] He noted that there were various attempts at justifying such an exception: (i) that such objectionable acts could not be considered to be 'official acts' for the purposes of immunity; (ii) that official act immunity is incompatible with individual criminal responsibility in international criminal law; (iii) that the *ius cogens* nature of these prohibitions in question prevailed over immunity; (iv) that there is a customary international law exception to immunity in relation to international crimes; (v) that the availability of universal jurisdiction for the gravest crimes was incompatible with immunity. However, he found none of these propositions persuasive. The only case in which he found there was an absence of immunity was 'where criminal jurisdiction is exercised by a State in whose territory an alleged crime has taken place, and this State has not given its consent to the performance in its territory of the activity which led to the crime and to the presence in its territory of the foreign official who committed the alleged crime'.[70]

In his Third Report the Special Rapporteur considered some of the modalities of immunity. Of particular interest is his finding that the because immunity *ratione materiae* is an immunity of the State and not of the individual, the State which the official serves must assert immunity *ratione materiae* in any case before it can be given effect. An assertion by an individual official alone is not sufficient. Nor is there any obligation on the court to raise immunity *ratione materiae* proactively or *proprio motu* in relation to criminal proceedings. Interestingly he suggests that a waiver of immunity *ratione materiae* could be implied as well as express, and, despite subjecting the proposition to some scrutiny, he appears to accept a waiver by consenting to be bound by a relevant international agreement is possible.

It is pertinent to note that in broad terms the applicability of immunity *ratione materiae* in criminal proceedings appears to be accepted by the UK courts. To the extent that the immunities *ratione materiae* of a former Head of State are a manifestation of this more

---

[69] Respectively UN Doc A/CN.4/631 and A/CN.4/646.

[70] Second Report of Special Rapporteur Kolodkin (UN Doc A/CN.4/646) at para 94. For a review of relevant practice see Franey, 2011, pp 157–285.

general immunity, it might be noted that in *Pinochet No 3* it was suggested that such immunity could be asserted successfully to bar proceedings in respect of most crimes (with the important exception of torture contrary to the UN Convention against Torture) where these are committed in the performance of the functions of government.[71]

The point was given further consideration by the High Court in the case of *Khurts Bat*. The case arose in relation to extradition proceedings commenced by Germany in respect of an alleged abduction and serious bodily injury, which in large part took place on German soil. Mongolia intervened (a) indicating that it had accepted responsibility for Khurts' actions on the plane of international law (an official apology had been submitted to Germany), and (b) asserting immunity *ratione materiae* on his behalf. The Court accepted the broad principle of immunity *ratione materiae*, but noted the finding of Special Rapporteur Kolodkin that an exception to immunity from criminal jurisdiction existed, where the acts in question took place on the territory of the forum State, in circumstances where the forum State had neither given its consent to the presence of the official on its territory nor to the activities under investigation. Finding that the authorities were broadly, but not unanimously, supportive of that proposition, the Court found that Khurts did not benefit from immunity *ratione materiae* in the instant case.

VII. OFFICIALS OF INTERNATIONAL ORGANIZATIONS

While the immunities of international organizations have been inspired by the immunities granted to States and their officials, they differ in some respects, reflecting the important differences between international organizations and States.[72] In the normal course of events an international organization will not have its own territory, but rather be based on territory over which a State exercises jurisdiction (special cases of international administration as, for example, the UN administration of Kosovo or in East Timor are not considered here). An international organization will not have its own population, from which its officials are chosen, but instead will employ persons who hold the nationality (with its attendant rights and obligations) of a State. Finally an international organization will not generally perform all the functions of government, with a full legal system of its own. Rather it will have its own institutional law, but will have to rely upon the local law in respect of other matters such as, for example, the maintenance of public order through the exercise of criminal jurisdiction.

Both diplomatic immunities and the immunities of international organizations arise from considerations of functional necessity, and as we shall see the former have inspired the latter in some respects. However, it does not follow that they should be identical in extent. Jenks suggests that there are three major differences between diplomatic immunities and those of international officials (Jenks, 1961, p xxxvii). First, it is unusual for a diplomatic agent to have the nationality of the receiving State and in such situations as we have seen the scope of the immunities he enjoys can be restricted by the receiving

---

[71] Thus Lord Hope found that immunity *ratione materiae* of a former Head of State could be relied upon in relation to charges of conspiracy to murder—see [1999] 2 WLR 827 at 881 and 887. See also the speeches of Lords Browne-Wilkinson and Hutton, ibid, at 848 and 888 respectively. On the other hand Lord Millett expressly found that immunity *ratione materiae* is not available in respect of an offence committed in the forum State (ibid, at 913). See also *Wei Ye v Jiang Zemin* 383F.3d 620.

[72] See para 7 of the General Commentary on the ILC *Draft Article on the Responsibility of International Organisations with commentaries* (2011) http://legal.un.org/ilc/texts/instruments/english/commentaries/9_11_2011.pdf.

State to his or her official activities only. On the other hand for officials of international organizations[73] it may be especially important that they enjoy immunities against their own States of nationality.[74] Secondly, whereas a diplomatic agent may be immune from legal process in the receiving State, he or she will remain subject to legal process in the sending State. In relation to officials of international organizations there is no sending State as such, and thus appropriate procedures may have to be adopted, either through some international disciplinary procedure established by the organization, or through waiver of immunity. Thirdly, the principle of reciprocity, which plays such an important role in the maintenance of diplomatic law between States, cannot operate in the same way in respect of international organizations. Thus Jenks rejects a simple assimilation of the immunities of international organizations with diplomatic immunities, in favour of looking at the former on their own merits as based upon their particular functional needs.

It is of course impossible to survey the range of international organizations, and the immunities of each will be governed by their own treaty provisions.[75] Only the immunities of personnel of the UN are considered here, as illustrative rather than generally applicable (see further, Michaels, 1971). In broad terms the Convention on the Privileges and Immunities of the UN 1946 divides staff members of the UN into three categories:

(a) the Secretary-General and the Assistant Secretaries-General shall be accorded ambassadorial status, and enjoy equivalent immunities *ratione personae* (Article V, s 19);

(b) all other officials of the Organization enjoy immunity from legal process in respect of their official acts, ie immunity *ratione materiae* (Article V, s 18(a)); and

(c) experts on mission (ie, persons who undertake temporary missions for the UN) who enjoy immunity from suit for their official acts (*ratione materiae*), as well as— in view of their need to travel freely in performance of their mission—a specific grant of personal inviolability (Article VI, s 22).[76]

The Convention makes clear that the immunities of officials and experts are granted not for their personal benefit, but for the benefit of the Organization. The Secretary-General thus has the right *and the duty* to waive immunity of any official where the immunity would in his or her opinion impede the course of justice and can be waived without prejudice to the interests of the Organization (Article V, s 20).

---

[73] Under relevant instruments additional categories of persons may benefit from similar immunities (though not identical in every respect) see for example the position of 'experts on mission' under the 1946 Convention on the Privileges and Immunities of the UN.

[74] Not all States accept that their own nationals when employed by international organizations enjoy the full range of immunities enjoyed by the officials who hold other nationalities. However, such limitations often concern fiscal immunities or exemptions from national service rather than immunity from legal process. For examples of the general rule see the ICJ Advisory Opinions in the *Applicability of Article VI, Section 22 of the Convention on the Privileges and Immunities of the United Nations, Advisory Opinion, ICJ Reports 1989*, p 177 ('*Mazilu*') and *Difference Relating to Immunity from Legal Process of a Special Rapporteur of the Commission on Human Rights, Advisory Opinion, ICJ Reports 1999*, p 62 ('*Cumaraswamy*').

[75] Though in relation to most officials of international organizations there is considerable uniformity in the relevant treaty provisions, that they enjoy immunity from jurisdiction *ratione materiae*, ie in relation to their official acts, whilst provision is often made for certain high officials to be granted a wider immunity *ratione personae* whilst in office. In relation to international organizations of which the UK is a member their immunities may be given effect in the UK by Order in Council made under the International Organizations Act 1968.

[76] At the time of writing a ruling is awaited form the Central Criminal Court (Old Bailey) in London, in the case of *R v Lama* in which the defendant, a Nepalese army office and member of a UN Observer Mission in South Sudan, claims that his arrest in the UK was a violation of his immunity from arrest as an expert on mission.

Given that most officials and experts of the UN only enjoy immunity *ratione materiae* in respect of their official acts, an important question is who should determine whether any particular act is an 'official act'. In many of the cases which might concern the exercise of ordinary criminal jurisdiction it will be possible to say that the offence is not an official act, and so the question of immunity does not arise. Thus for example when during the Cold War there were a number of cases in which international officials were accused of espionage in the USA, they were unable to claim immunity as the activities in question were not official activities.[77] However, in other cases, where there may be some dispute as to the nature of an act, it is necessary to ask whether that issue should be determined by the Secretary-General on behalf of the Organization, or the relevant national court as part of its task in applying the immunity. In the *Cumaraswamy* case, the ICJ gave a rather nuanced answer to the question, stating that:

> When national courts are seised of a case in which the immunity of a UN agent is in issue, they should immediately be notified of any finding by the Secretary-General concerning that immunity. That finding and its documentary expression creates a presumption which can only be set aside for the most compelling reasons and is thus to be given the greatest weight by the national courts.[78]

The Court thus sought to balance interests of the organization and the local jurisdiction, though, in the final analysis, it is the local court which must decide whether there are compelling reasons to rebut the presumption established by the Secretary-General's finding.

VIII. THE SCOPE OF IMMUNITIES FOR SERIOUS CRIMES UNDER INTERNATIONAL LAW—IMMUNITY AND IMPUNITY DISTINGUISHED

None of the immunities which have been considered are for the benefit of any particular individual or group of individuals, but rather are for the benefit of the State/international organization which they represent. Thus the sending State/employer international organization can waive any of these immunities, thereby consenting to the jurisdiction of the courts of another State over the official in question. This applies whether the immunity in question arises *ratione personae* or *ratione materiae*.

However, in a parallel development, the scope of international law has now broadened from an almost exclusive concern with the rights and duties of States, so that it now also imposes a considerable body of obligations in respect of individuals. Of particular interest for present purposes is the evolution of individual criminal responsibility under international law for a number of serious international crimes which offend international public order. As Sir Arthur Watts (1994, p 82) points out:

> For international conduct which is so serious as to be tainted with criminality to be regarded as attributable only to the impersonal State and not to the individuals who order or perpetrated it is both unrealistic and offensive to common notions of justice.

---

[77] See, eg *US v Coplon* 84 F.Supp 472 (1949); *US v Melekh* 190 F.Supp 67 (1960); and *US v Egorov* 222 F.Supp 106 (1963). In another context see also the case of *Westchester County v Ranollo* (1946) 13 ILR 168.

[78] *Difference Relating to Immunity from Legal Process of a Special Rapporteur of the Commission on Human Rights, Advisory Opinion, ICJ Reports 1999, p 62, para 61.* For comment see Wickremasinghe, 2000.

Furthermore, recent years have seen a determination within international society to put an end to the impunity of the perpetrators of such crimes, through the development of extraterritorial jurisdiction and the establishment of international criminal tribunals. In a further development, and in line with the general trend to seek to rationalize all regimes of privilege or immunity (which is observable in other areas of international and national law), the immunities of State officials in respect of international crimes have been subject to particularly keen scrutiny in recent years.[79]

Exactly how these apparently conflicting priorities in the law should be integrated is still being worked out. Simple attempts at seeking to choose between them on the basis of hierarchy by means of the *jus cogens* or *erga omnes* nature of the primary prohibitions of the criminalized conduct appear not to provide answers, particularly in respect of procedural obligations of States—a point that has recently been underlined by the decision of the International Court of Justice in the *Jurisdictional Immunities* case.[80] Nevertheless in recent years the law has undergone, and may still be undergoing, considerable re-examination and some significant revisions. What follows therefore does not attempt to prescribe what the law ought to be, but simply seeks to describe the law as it is in its current stage of development.

A. IMMUNITIES *RATIONE PERSONAE*

In the *Arrest Warrant* case the ICJ was concerned with the immunity *ratione personae* of a serving Foreign Minister, and concluded that under customary international law no exception to that immunity exists in respect of war crimes or crimes against humanity. The Court based this upon its review of national legislation[81] and those few decisions of higher courts in national legal systems on the point.[82] One of these was the decision of the French *Cour de Cassation* in the *Qadaffi* case (Zeppala, 2001), in which the immunity of a serving Head of State was found to operate in respect of allegations of his involvement in international terrorism.[83] The other major case referred to is the decision of the House of Lords in the *Pinochet* case, in which in a number of dicta their Lordships suggested that the immunity *ratione personae* of serving Heads of States and serving Ambassadors (unless waived) could be relied upon in proceedings for international crimes.[84]

---

[79] In this respect it is to be welcomed that the International Law Commission have adopted the topic of 'Immunity of State officials from foreign criminal jurisdiction'. The Preliminary report of the Special Rapporteur Amb. Kolodkin (UN Doc A/CN.4/601), and the Memorandum of the Secretariat (UN Doc A/CN.4/596) contain a wealth of information and insight.

[80] See, eg the ECtHR case of *Al-Adsani v UK* [GC], no 35763/97, ECHR 2001-XI, 34 *EHRR* 11, which dealt with the question of the immunity of the State itself from civil jurisdiction. See also Article 98(1) of the Statute of the International Criminal Court at n 98 of this chapter.

[81] In this respect the former Belgian Act of 10 February 1999 under which immunities were not admissible in respect of war crimes, crimes against humanity, and genocide, appeared exceptional and so could not be relied upon as sufficient evidence in itself of an emerging rule of general international law. A point underlined by the fact that this provision was repealed and the Act as whole was substantially amended following the Court's judgment and diplomatic pressure from other States.

[82] Subsequent cases which also support the findings of the ICJ are *Tachiona and others v Mugabe and others* 169 F.Supp 2d 259 (2001) and *Wei Ye v Jiang Zemin* 383F.3d 620; similarly the trio of cases from the Bow Street Magistrates' Court, *Mugabe* of 14 January 2004 (2004) 53 *ICLQ* 770, *Mofaz*, 12 February 2004 (2004) 53 *ICLQ* 771–3 and *Bo Xilai*, 8 November 2005 (128 ILR 713) as well as the case of *Re Ehud Barak* from the Westminster Magistrates' Court (*Re Ehud Barak*, 29 September 2009 (not yet reported)).

[83] *Qadaffi* case, (2001) 125 ILR 490.

[84] See the speeches of Lord Browne-Wilkinson at 844E–G; Lord Hope at 886G–H; Lord Saville at 903F–G; Lord Millett 913 E–G; and Lord Phillips at 924C–D.

Thus it seems that based on general principle the immunity *ratione personae* of certain incumbent high State officials, including Heads of State, Heads of Government, Foreign Ministers, as well as diplomatic agents and members of special missions, are, in the absence of waiver by the sending State, an absolute bar to the criminal jurisdiction of the national courts for the duration of their office/mission,[85] even in relation to these serious international crimes. The reason for this is that the functions which these officials serve in maintaining international relations are such that they should not be endangered by the subjection of such officials (while they are in office) to the criminal jurisdiction of another State.

However, in the *Arrest Warrant* case the ICJ also stressed that immunity was not the same as impunity. In this respect it noted four circumstances in which the availability of immunity *ratione personae* of incumbent office-holders would not prevent their prosecution:

(i)   where the office-holder in question is prosecuted by the courts of his or her own State;

(ii) where immunity is waived by the office-holder's State;

(iii) when the office-holder leaves office, he or she may be prosecuted by the court of another State (provided that in other respects it has jurisdiction in accordance with international law) in respect of his or her acts prior to or subsequent to his or her period of office, or for his or her private acts during his period of office; and

(iv) by certain international criminal courts, provided that they have jurisdiction.

The first two of these circumstances are relatively uncontroversial and are well-established in international law, and need little further comment here.[86] However, the latter two circumstances form the basis of the consideration of the following subsections.

B. IMMUNITIES *RATIONE MATERIAE*

The prelude to the re-examination of immunities *ratione materiae* in relation to serious crimes under international law was the arrest of the former President of Chile, General Pinochet, in 1998. As is well-known Pinochet was arrested while temporarily in London for medical treatment, following a request by Spain for his extradition in connection with charges of *inter alia* the widespread use of torture during his period of office as Head of State of Chile. Eventually the House of Lords had to consider whether Pinochet could resist extradition by relying on his subsisting immunity *ratione materiae*, ie in respect of official acts he performed while he was Head of State, notwithstanding that he was no longer in office.

Trying to distil the *ratio decidendi* of the judgment of the House of Lords is complicated not only by the nature of the case, but also by the fact the reasoning in each of the speeches of the six judges in the majority differs. A full treatment is therefore beyond the scope of this chapter.[87] The court was faced on the one hand with allegations of the crime of torture

---

[85] Heads of State, Heads of Government, and Foreign Ministers appear to enjoy immunities in respect of all foreign States (ie *erga omnes*), whereas the immunities under the VCDR and the Special Missions Convention are primarily enjoyed only in the receiving State (though they also provide for privileges and immunities whilst in transit).

[86] It might be noted in respect of (i) that the immunities *ratione personae* of certain high officials of international organizations can be opposed to the jurisdiction of the courts of their own State of nationality.

[87] The case is the subject of a considerable literature, including: Warbrick, Salgado, and Goodwin, 1999; Fox, 1999; Barker, 1999; Denza, 1999; Dupuy, 1999; Dominicé, 1999; Cosnard, 1999; Chinkin, 1999; Van Alebeek, 2000.

under the Torture Convention, which is defined so as to require official involvement,[88] and on the other with Pinochet's claim to immunity *ratione materiae*. By a majority of six to one the House rejected the plea of immunity in respect of the torture allegations.

Put briefly, three of their Lordships relied upon an implied waiver of the immunity *ratione materiae*, which it found States parties to the Torture Convention must have intended.[89] If this were otherwise the international criminalization of torture under the Convention would have been rendered largely ineffective, as anybody charged with torture would (in the absence of waiver) be able to rely on official act immunity.

However, the speeches of the other three of their Lordships in the majority appear to have been more broadly based. They suggest that individual responsibility for serious crimes in international law cannot be opposed by reliance upon the immunity *ratione materiae* of former Heads of State. That form of immunity only covers official acts in order to ensure that the immunities of the State itself are not undermined by proceedings against its former Head. The purpose of the immunity is therefore to ensure that the national courts of one State do not adjudicate on the responsibility of another State without the consent of the latter. However, these judges found that as such immunity is concerned with the responsibility of the State, it cannot be invoked in respect of an individual's own criminal responsibility in international law.[90]

For now what can be said with certainty is that the *Pinochet* case is authority in English law for the proposition that there is an exception to immunity from criminal jurisdiction *ratione materiae* enjoyed by former Heads of State in respect of acts of official torture. It might also be noted that their Lordships found that since the development of individual criminal responsibility in respect of torture represents a distinct basis of responsibility to which official act immunity does not extend, Pinochet's immunity *ratione materiae* from civil process was unaffected. Beyond this it is difficult to draw further conclusions. Whether the exception to immunity found in this case can be extended in respect of other international crimes and/or in respect of other immunities *ratione materiae* enjoyed by officials or former officials has been much debated, but firm conclusions cannot be drawn.

It should also be recalled that the International Court of Justice in its judgment in the *Arrest Warrant* case also commented on this issue, though these comments are strictly speaking *obiter* since this case was concerned with the immunities *ratione personae* of a serving Foreign Minister. The majority of the Court found that a former Foreign Minister would be liable to prosecution in the courts of another State for the acts he performed during his period of office in his private capacity.[91] If this is taken as a broad statement of the

---

[88] See Article 1(1) of the UN Convention Against Torture and other Cruel, Inhuman or Degrading Treatment of Punishment 1984, which defines torture as the intentional infliction of pain or suffering for various purposes, 'when such pain or suffering is inflicted by or at the instigation of or with the consent or acquiescence of a public official or other person acting in an official capacity'.

[89] See the speeches of Lord Browne-Wilkinson at 847; Lord Hope (who found the exception to immunity *ratione materiae* applied only in respect of a systematic or widespread torture) at 882–7; and Lord Saville at 904.

[90] Lord Hutton accepted the fact that the allegations of torture concerned acts in the performance of public functions, but found that 'certain crimes are so grave and so inhuman that they constitute crimes against international law and that the international community is under a duty to bring to justice a person who commits such crimes'. He then held that individual criminal liability in respect of such crimes was quite distinct from the question of State responsibility which underlay immunities *ratione materiae* (at 887–902). Lord Millett found the existence of immunity *ratione materiae* simply inconsistent with the development of serious crimes of *jus cogens* nature for which extraterritorial jurisdiction was available (at 909–14). Lord Phillips similarly found that the development of international crimes and extraterritorial jurisdiction could not co-exist with immunity *ratione materiae* (at 924).

[91] *Arrest Warrant of 11 April 2000 (Democratic Republic of Congo v Belgium), Preliminary Objections and Merits, Judgment, ICJ Reports 2002*, p 3, para 61.

principle that a former Foreign Minister enjoys a subsisting immunity *ratione materiae* for his official acts, it may be unsurprising. However, this passage of the judgment has been the subject of criticism for the narrowness of its formulation (McLachlan, 2002) and some have even drawn from it the implication that the subsisting immunity of a former Foreign Minister would be applicable in respect of serious international crimes such as war crimes and crimes against humanity (Wirth, 2002; Spinedi, 2002). If this latter point is what the Court intended then it might suggest that a narrow reading should be given to the decision of the House of Lords in the *Pinochet* case.[92] On the other hand, it should be noted that in their Joint Separate Opinion Judges Higgins, Kooijmans, and Buergenthal suggest that the current trend of State practice is that serious international crimes are not covered by the immunities *ratione materiae* of former State officials.[93]

More recently the Swiss case of *Nezzar*[94] concerned an Algerian accused of atrocities amounting to crimes against humanity and war crimes during his service as an Army General, the Defence Minister and part of the collective Presidency of Algeria in the early 1990s. A criminal complaint was brought in Switzerland during the temporary presence of the accused there. When the Swiss Ministry of Foreign Affairs were asked for their view on immunity they provided an answer in line with the *Arrest Warrant* judgment to the effect that as a former State official he enjoyed an ongoing immunity for his official acts. The Swiss Federal Criminal Court, however, rejected the claim to immunity *ratione materiae* on the basis that it would be inconsistent with the international criminalization of crimes as serious as those charged in the instant case.

Despite the apparent breadth of the ruling in this case, Professor Wuerth points out that it may be distinguishable in that Algeria did not assert immunity on behalf of Nezzar, and as we have seen there is some authority for saying that in the case of immunity *ratione materiae* the State must assert that immunity. Thus she concludes that *Pinochet* remains the only case where immunity has been denied in criminal proceedings in the face of an assertion of immunity by the State in whose service the defendant official or former official was acting at the time of the allegations (Wuerth, 2012 and 2013).

C. IMMUNITIES BEFORE INTERNATIONAL CRIMINAL COURTS

The development of international criminal courts has clearly been a major step in combating impunity for serious international crimes. While a detailed discussion of the question of immunities before such courts is beyond the scope of this chapter, the broad principles will be outlined. As we have noted the ICJ suggested that immunities would not in principle be available before international courts providing that they have jurisdiction. An apparently similar finding was made by the Appeals Chamber of the Special Court of Sierra Leone.[95] Indeed the Statutes of the Nuremberg and Tokyo Tribunals, the International Criminal Tribunal for the Former Yugoslavia (ICTY), the International Criminal Tribunal

---

[92] In *Jurisdictional Immunities of the State (Germany v Italy: Greece Intervening), Judgment of 3 February 2012, para 87*, the ICJ certainly seem to have given the *Pinochet* judgment a narrow reading based on the particular language of the Torture Convention.

[93] *Arrest Warrant of 11 April 2000 (Democratic Republic of Congo v Belgium), Preliminary Objections and Merits, Judgment, ICJ Reports 2002*, p 3, Joint Separate Opinion, para 85. See also Akande (2004, p 415) who concludes that 'immunity *ratione materiae* does not exist with respect to domestic criminal proceedings for any of the international crimes set out in the Statute of the ICC'.

[94] *A v Ministère public de la Confédération, Swiss Federal Criminal Court*, 25 July 2012.

[95] See *The Prosecutor v Charles Taylor*, Case No SCSL-2003-01-I (31 May 2004).

for Rwanda (ICTR), the Rome Statute of the International Criminal Court (ICC), and the Statute of the Special Court for Sierra Leone (SCSL) all contain express provisions to the effect that the official capacity of an individual shall in no case exempt him from criminal responsibility.[96] Such provisions would appear to suggest that neither immunity *ratione personae* nor immunity *ratione materiae* would in principle be a bar to the jurisdiction of these international criminal courts.

Nevertheless as Akande has persuasively argued this picture requires some further elaboration in view of the range of different international criminal tribunals which currently exist (Akande, 2004). In particular the question of whether an individual can rely on immunities in international law before an international court will, as a first step, require a consideration of the basis on which the court was established as well as the provisions of its constitutive statute. Moreover, since these international courts will require the assistance of national authorities and national courts in matters such as arresting and transferring suspects, providing evidence and other forms of cooperation, there are also questions as to the availability of immunities before relevant national authorities in these situations.

In this respect the ICTY and ICTR, which were established by the Security Council pursuant to its mandatory powers under Chapter VII of the UN Charter, may be distinguished from tribunals established by treaty. The removal of the immunity of defendants in the Statutes of these two Tribunals not only entitles the Tribunals themselves to adjudicate over such individuals, but it also provides a legal basis for all member States of the UN not to afford immunity to such persons when arresting or transferring them pursuant to Orders of the Tribunals. At the same time however, it should also be noted that the Appeals Chamber of the ICTY has for example recognized the immunities of State officials *ratione materiae*, exempting them from a requirement to produce documents in evidence which they held by virtue of their official position.[97]

As a body established by treaty, the ICC is in a different position, since States must consent to be bound by the Rome Statute before they are bound by it. While the Rome Statute appears to limit the immunities available to defendants in proceedings before the ICC itself (Article 27), it is not clear that this provision can restrict the immunities of officials of States that are not parties to the Rome Statute, unless, of course, there is a waiver by the relevant State, or a binding resolution of the Security Council to this effect. In relation to the availability of immunities to proceedings before national authorities and national courts, relating to requests by the ICC for surrender and assistance, it should be noted that Article 98(1) of the Rome Statute also preserves the State and diplomatic immunities of officials and property of third States.[98] In other words, officials of a State which is not a party to the Rome Statute may be able to claim immunity in respect of their arrest and transfer to the Court, whereas a State party to

---

[96] See Article 7 of the Charter of the International Criminal Tribunal of Nuremberg and Article 6 of the Charter of the Tokyo Tribunal. See Article 7(2) of the Statute of the ICTY; Article 6(2) of the Statute of the ICTR; Article 27 of the Statute of the ICC; and Article 6(2) of the Statute of the Special Court for Sierra Leone.

[97] See *Prosecutor v Blaskić*, Judgment, Case No IT-95-14-T, Trial Chamber (3 March 2000); 110 ILR 609. However, see also the case of *Prosecutor v Krstić*, Judgment, Case No IT-98-33-A, Appeals Chamber (19 April 2004). For comment see Akande, 2004, p 418.

[98] Thus Article 98(1) states: 'The Court may not proceed with a request for surrender or assistance which would require the requested State to act inconsistently with its obligations under international law with respect to the State or diplomatic immunity of a person or property of a third State, unless the Court can first obtain the cooperation of that third State for the waiver of the immunity.'

the Rome Statute has in effect waived such immunities in respect of its own officials both before the ICC itself and in the courts of other States parties in respect of their cooperation with the ICC. However, there may be a further layer of complexity in cases which are referred to the Court by the Security Council, depending on the terms of such referral.

The first decision of the ICC to deal with these issues, was the decision of the Pre-Trial Chamber on the arrest warrant sought by the Prosecutor in the case of *The Prosecutor* v *Omar Hassan Ahmad Al Bashir*.[99] As is well-known the Prosecutor sought the arrest of President Al Bashir, the serving Head of State of Sudan, for war crimes, crimes against humanity, and genocide. In the event the Court issued two warrants in respect of 5 counts of crimes against humanity, 2 counts of war crimes and 3 counts of genocide.[100] It dealt with the immunity issue in a short passage that found that the position of Al Bashir, as Head of a State which was not a party to the Rome Statute, had no effect on the jurisdiction of the Court over the case. In support of this finding it considered: (i) that putting an end to impunity was a core goal of the Rome Statute; (ii) Article 27 of the Rome Statute sought to give effect to this goal with specific language limiting exemptions and immunities attaching to persons by reason of their office; (iii) on the basis of the clear language of Article 27, there was no need to examine other sources of law; and (iv) in referring the situation in Darfur to the ICC, the Security Council accepted that the investigation and any resulting prosecutions would accord with the provisions of the Rome Statute as a whole. Thus it was clear that Al Bashir's position as Head of State was not a bar to the jurisdiction of the Court.

The more complex issue seems to be what steps States may or must take in execution of the warrants.[101] Although the Court did not expressly address the application of Article 98(1), it did consider that Sudan was obliged 'to cooperate fully with and provide any necessary assistance to the Court' by virtue of Security Council Resolution 1593 (2005), a binding resolution under Chapter VII of the UN Charter and given primacy over other obligations by virtue of Article 103 of the Charter.[102] The Court ordered that the arrest warrant be served on all States parties to the Rome Statute, and all members of the Security Council that are not States parties to the Rome Statute, with a request for the arrest and surrender of Al Bashir. While the reasoning of the Court is concise, it might suggest that the effect of Resolution 1593 (2005) is to assimilate the position of Sudan with that of a State party, which by virtue of Article 27 cannot assert immunity to oppose arrest proceedings at the national level. If that is the case, then clearly States parties are under an obligation to comply with request for arrest and surrender under Article 89 of the Rome Statute.[103]

    [99] *The Prosecutor* v *Omar Hassan Ahmad Al Bashir*, 4 March 2009, Case No ICC-02/05-01/09.

    [100] See decisions of Pre-Trial Chamber I of 4 March 2009 (ref. ICC 02/05 – 01/09 - 3) and 12 July 2010 (ref. ICC 02/05 - 01/09 – 94) respectively.

    [101] Gaeta, 2009 and Akande, 2009.

    [102] Paragraph 2 of UNSCR 1593 provides: '*Decides* that the Government of Sudan and all other parties to the conflict in Darfur, shall cooperate fully with and provide any necessary assistance to the Court and the Prosecutor pursuant to this resolution and, while recognizing that States not party to the Rome Statute have no obligation under the Statute, *urges* all States and concerned regional and other international organizations to cooperate fully'.

    [103] In this respect see the Judgments of the Pre-Trial Chamber in relation to Malawi (13 December 2011) and Chad (13 December 2011), finding that these States had failed in the obligation of cooperation in failing to arrest Bashir when he visited them.

    It might be noted that following the Court's decision in 2009, the UK made an Order in Council based on the enabling powers in both s 23(5) of the International Criminal Court Act 2001 and s 1 of the United

The effect on non-States parties other than Sudan would depend upon the interpretation of relevant Security Council resolutions.[104]

IX. CONCLUSION

Thus we have seen that in modern diplomatic law there has been considerable movement towards the rationalization of immunities, so that it is now clear that they are not granted for the personal benefit of their holders. Instead they are granted on a functional basis, to facilitate the processes of communication and cooperation in international relations. Carefully considered legal regimes have been created in which the interests of sending and receiving States have been balanced. There is a general acceptance that without these immunities their holders could be impeded from effective performance of these important functions, the purpose of which serves the international public interest. Following its codification in the 1960s diplomatic law has, for the most part, constituted a well-observed and stable body of rules.

At the same time greater consensus has developed and continues to develop on the standards of governance of those exercising public power, and in particular recently on the criminalization of the gravest excesses in this respect. The wholesale exemption of those who commit such crimes in connection with public purposes would clearly be contradictory. The establishment of the International Criminal Court, in relation to which immunities are not available (except as provided for in Article 98 of the Rome Statute), is clearly a hugely significant step for international law.

However, the resolution of these conflicting priorities at the national level is still being worked out, and an authoritative statement of the law is not possible at this point. Nevertheless if the perspectives expressed here are accepted, international law currently appears to be moving towards compromise. The immunities *ratione personae* attaching to certain offices will render their holders immune from national proceedings, but not necessarily from international proceedings. On the other hand once they have left office, such persons will enjoy a general immunity in respect of their official acts *ratione materiae*, but exceptionally it appears that in respect of certain international crimes, notably torture, they might not be so immune.

Nations Act 1946, providing that State or diplomatic immunities will not prevent proceedings in the UK for the arrest and delivery of persons alleged to have committed an ICC Crime as a result of the referral of the situation in Darfur under UNSCR 1593 (see the International Criminal Court (Darfur) Order 2009, SI 699/2009).

[104] A full treatment of all the issues raised (both legal and diplomatic) is beyond the scope of this chapter. It should be noted that the case has resulted in considerable diplomatic activity. President Bashir's ability to travel internationally has been severely curtailed. On the other hand, there is an ongoing process of discussion in the African Union which touches on many of the issues raised here (see most recently 'Recommendations of the Ministerial Meeting on the Rome Statute of the International Criminal Court', 6 November 2009). There have also been calls from some quarters for the Security Council to invoke its powers under Article 16 of the Rome Statute to defer the proceedings, but to date no State has made a formal proposal to the Council in this respect.

REFERENCES

AKANDE, D (2004), 'International Law Immunities and the International Criminal Court', 98 *AJIL* 407.

—— (2009), 'The Legal Nature of Security Council Referrals to the ICC and its Impact on Al Bashir's Immunity', 7 *J Int'l Crim Just* 333.

BARKER, JC (1996), *The Abuse of Diplomatic Privileges and Immunities: A Necessary Evil?* (Aldershot: Dartmouth).

—— (1998), 'State Immunity, Diplomatic Immunity and Act of State: A Triple Protection Against Legal Action', 47 *ICLQ* 950.

—— (1999), 'The Future of Former Head of State Immunity after *ex parte Pinochet*', 48 *ICLQ* 937.

BELLINGER, J (2011), 'The Dog that Caught the Car: Observations on the Past, Present and Future Approaches of the Office of the Legal Adviser to Official Acts Immunities', 44 *Vanderbilt Journal of Transnational Law* 819

—— (2008), 'The Italian Court of Cassattion Misapprehends the Notion of War Crimes: the *Lozano* case', 6 *J Int'l Crim Just* 1077.

CHINKIN, C (1999), 'Ex Parte Pinochet Ugarte (No 3), Casenote', 93 *AJIL* 703.

COSNARD, M (1999), 'Quelques Observations sur les Décisions de la Chambre des Lords dans l'Affaire *Pinochet*', 103 *RGDIP* 309.

CRAWFORD, J (2002), *The International Law Commission's Articles on State Responsibility* (Cambridge: Cambridge University Press).

CRAWFORD, J (2012), *Brownlie's Principles of Public International Law*, 8th edn (Oxford: Clarendon Press).

DENZA, E (1999), '*Ex Parte Pinochet*: Lacuna or Leap?', 48 *ICLQ* 949.

—— (2008), *Diplomatic Law*, 3rd edn (Oxford: Clarendon Press).

DINSTEIN, Y (1966), 'Diplomatic Immunity from Jurisdiction *Ratione Materiae*', 15 *ICLQ* 76.

DOMINICÉ, C (1999), 'Quelques Observations sur l'immunité de Jurisdiction Pénale de l'ancien Chef d'État', 103 *RGDIP* 297.

DOUGLAS, Z (2012), 'State Immunity for the Acts of State Officials', 82 *BYIL* 281.

DUPUY, P-M (1999), 'Crimes et immunités', 103 *RGDIP* 289.

EL-ERIAN, A and SCOBBIE, I (1998), 'International Organisations and International Relations', in Dupuy, R-J (ed), *A Handbook on International Organisations*, 2nd edn (Dordrecht: Martinus Nijhoff).

FOX, H (1999), 'The *Pinochet No 3* Case', 48 *ICLQ* 687.

FRANEY, E (2011), *Immunity, Individuals and International Law* (Saarbrücken: Lambert Academic Publishing).

GAETA, P (2009), 'Does President Al Bashir Enjoy Immunity from Arrest?', 7 *J Int'l Crim Just* 315.

HIGGINS, R (1985), 'The Abuse of Diplomatic Privileges and Immunities: Recent United Kingdom Experience', 79 *AJIL* 641.

JAMES, A (1991), 'Diplomatic Relations and Contacts', 62 *BYIL* 347.

JENKS, CW (1961), *International Immunities* (London: Stevens).

JENNINGS, SIR ROBERT (2002), 'Jurisdiction and Immunity in the ICJ Decision in the *Yerodia* case', 4 *International Law Forum* 99.

KOH, HH (2011), 'Foreign Official Immunity after *Samantar*: A United States Government Perspective', 44 *Vanderbilt Journal of Transnational Law* 1141.

LEE, LT and QUIGLEY, J (2008), *Consular Law and Practice*, 3rd edn (Oxford: Clarendon Press).

McLACHLAN, C (2002), '*Pinochet* Revisited', 51 *ICLQ* 959.

MANN, FA (1990), ' "Inviolability" and other problems of the Vienna Convention on Diplomatic Relations', in Mann, FA, *Further Studies in International Law* (Oxford: Clarendon Press).

MICHAELS, DB (1971), *International Privileges and Immunities: a Case for a Universal Statute* (The Hague: Martinus Nijhoff).

ROBERTS, I (ed) (2009), *Satow's Diplomatic Practice*, 6th edn (Oxford: Oxford University Press).

SANGER, A (2013), 'Immunity of State Officials from the Criminal Jurisdiction of a Foreign State', 62 *ICLQ* 193.

SCHREUER, C and WITTICH, S (2002), 'Immunity v Accountability: the ICJ's Judgment in the *Yerodia* case', 4 *International Law Forum* 117.

SPINEDI, M (2002), 'State Responsibility v Individual Responsibility for International Crimes: *Tertium Non Datur*', 13 *EJIL* 895.

STERN, B (2002), 'Les Dits et non Dits de la Cour Internationale de Justice dans l'affaire RDC contre Belgique', 4 *International Law Forum* 104.

VAN ALEBEEK, R (2000), 'The *Pinochet* case: International Human Rights Law on Trial', 71 *BYIL* 29.

WARBRICK, CJ, SALGADO, EM, and GOODWIN, N (1999), 'The *Pinochet* Cases in the United Kingdom', 2 *YIHL* 1.

WATTS, SIR ARTHUR (1994), 'The Legal Position in International Law of Heads of States, Heads of Governments and Foreign Ministers', 247 *Recueil des Cours* 9.

―――― (1999), *The International Law Commission 1949–1998 Vol I* (Oxford: Oxford University Press).

WHOMERSLEY, C (1992), 'Some Reflections on the Immunity of Individuals for Official Acts', 41 *ICLQ* 848.

WICKREMASINGHE, C (2000), 'The Advisory Opinion on the Difference Relating to Immunity from Legal Process of Special Rapporteur of the Commission on Human Rights', 49 *ICLQ* 724.

WIRTH, S (2002), 'Immunity for Core Crimes? The ICJ's Judgment in the *Congo* v *Belgium* case', 13 *EJIL* 877.

WOOD, M (1974), 'The Convention on the Prevention and Punishment of Crimes against Internationally Protected Persons, including Diplomatic Agents', 23 *ICLQ* 791.

―――― (2012), 'The Immunity of Official Visitors' 16 *Max Planck Yearbook of UN Law* 35.

WUERTH, I (2012), '*Pinochet*'s Legacy Reassessed', 106 *AJIL* 731.

―――― (2013), 'Foreign Official Immunity: Invocation, Purpose and Exceptions', 23 *Swiss Review of International and European Law* 207.

YOUNG, E (1964), 'The Development of the Law of Diplomatic Relations', 40 *BYIL* 141.

ZEPPALA, S (2001), 'Do Heads of State Enjoy Immunity from Jurisdiction for International Crimes? The *Ghaddafi* case before the French *Cour de Cassation*', 12 *EJIL* 595.

FURTHER READING

CONSULS

LEE, LT and QUIGLEY, J (2008), *Consular Law and Practice*, 3rd edn (Oxford: Clarendon Press): the standard guide to consular law.

DIPLOMATS

DENZA, E (2008), *Diplomatic Law*, 3rd edn (Oxford: Clarendon Press): the definitive guide to the Vienna Convention on Diplomatic Relations.

ROBERTS, I (ed) (2009), *Satow's Diplomatic Practice*, 6th edn (Oxford: Oxford University Press): an up-to-date and very readable edition of a classic work, containing a wealth of information and practice.

SPECIAL MISSIONS

WOOD, M (2012), 'The Immunity of Official Visitors', 16 *Max Planck Yearbook of UN Law* 35: A thorough and thoughtful survey of customary international law and recent State practice on this under-explored subject—an important addition to the literature.

HEADS OF STATE, HEADS OF GOVERNMENT, AND FOREIGN MINISTERS

WATTS, SIR ARTHUR (1994), 'The Legal Position in International Law of Heads of State, Heads of Governments and Foreign Ministers', 247 *Recueil des Cours* 9: a very readable survey of the law and its underpinning at that date.

OFFICIALS OF INTERNATIONAL ORGANIZATIONS

ZACKLIN, R (1998), 'Diplomatic Relations: Status Privileges and Immunities' and SCOBBIE, I (revising El-Erian, A), 'International Organisations and International Relations', both in Dupuy, R-J (ed), *A Handbook on International Organisations*, 2nd edn (Dordrecht: Martinus Nijhoff), at pp 293–313 and 831–67, respectively.

THE INTERPLAY OF INTERNATIONAL CRIMINAL LAW AND THE LAW OF IMMUNITIES

VAN ALEBEEK, R (2008) *The Immunity of States and their Officials in International Criminal Law and International Human Rights Law* (Oxford: Clarendon Press): an interesting attempt to bring coherence to the various legal strands of the issues.

WORK OF THE INTERNATIONAL LAW COMMISSION ON 'IMMUNITY OF STATE OFFICIALS FROM FOREIGN CRIMINAL JURISDICTION'

Preliminary Report of the Special Rapporteur, Amb. Kolodkin (UN Doc A/CN.4/601); Second Report (UN Doc A/CN.4/631); and Third Report (UN Doc A/CN.4/646).

Preliminary Report of Special Rapporteur Madam Escobar Hernandez A/CN 4/654; and Second Report A/CN 4/661.

Memorandum of the Secretariat (UN Doc A/CN.4/596).

PINOCHET

There is an abundance of literature on this case, a starting point might be:

WARBRICK, CJ, SALGADO, EM, and GOODWIN, N (1999), 'The *Pinochet* cases in the United Kingdom', 2 *YIHL* 1.

For some of the legal policy issues at stake see:

BIANCHI, A (1999), 'Immunity versus Human Rights: the *Pinochet* Case', 10 *EJIL* 237.

DENZA, E (1999), '*Ex parte Pinochet*: Lacuna or Leap', 48 *ICLQ* 949.

IMMUNITIES BEFORE THE ICC

AKANDE, D (2004), 'International Law Immunities and the International Criminal Court', 98 *AJIL* 407.

14

THE RELATIONSHIP BETWEEN INTERNATIONAL AND NATIONAL LAW

Eileen Denza

SUMMARY

Enormous growth in the substance of international law implies that it is now mostly applied and enforced by national authorities and courts. International tribunals are clear that in case of conflict the international rule prevails, but they will not invalidate national law and have traditionally regarded as a domestic matter how the correct international result is achieved. For national legislatures and courts by contrast, their mandate derives from their national constitution. Constitutional provisions are complex and infinitely varied and do not give clear answers to many problems which arise in national courts. There is no prospect of a harmonized approach to the relationship between international and national law, but it is possible to identify factors conducive to the avoidance of conflict. These include close involvement of international lawyers in the treaty-making and ratification process, attention at the time of ratification to implementation questions, teaching of international law as part of professional training of judges, and expert assistance to national courts when international law questions arise.

I. INTRODUCTION

The law of nations was until the twentieth century concerned mainly—though never exclusively—with the conduct of sovereign States and the relations between those States. Now, however, it permeates and radically conditions national legal orders, its rules are applied and enforced by national authorities, and national courts are asked to resolve its most fundamental uncertainties. Yet international law does not itself prescribe how it should be applied or enforced at the national level. It asserts its own primacy over national laws, but without invalidating those laws or intruding into national legal systems, requiring a result rather than a method of implementation. National constitutions are therefore free to choose how they give effect to treaties and to customary international law. Their choice of methods is extremely varied. Can it be shown that certain constitutional approaches are based on greater deference to international law or help to reduce conflict between legal orders? If not, are there other general factors conducive to greater mutual understanding and to resolving the practical problems of co-existence?

II. THE APPROACH OF INTERNATIONAL COURTS AND TRIBUNALS

The jurisdiction given to international courts and tribunals is normally limited to the determination of questions of international law. In theory, there is nothing to prevent two States from referring to international arbitration or adjudication an issue of national law. Given the nature of international relations, however, questions of national law usually arise before international tribunals only if relevant to the construction of an international agreement or to the establishment of breach of an international obligation.

The Permanent Court of International Justice in the cases of *The Serbian Loans*[1] and *The Brazilian Loans*[2] explored the nature of its competence, under a Special Agreement between France and the Kingdom of the Serbs, Croats and Slovenes, to construe the terms of a loan contract between the Kingdom and French bondholders. The Court observed that while its main function was to decide disputes between States on the basis of international law, it also had jurisdiction to determine 'the existence of any fact which, if established, would constitute a breach of an international obligation'. This jurisdiction included questions of municipal law.

The Court made clear, however, that it was not entitled to undertake its own construction of national laws, with the danger of contradicting rulings of national tribunals. It said that:

> It would be a most delicate matter to do so, especially in cases concerning public policy and in cases where no relevant provisions directly relate to the questions at issue. It is French legislation, as applied in France, which really constitutes French law...

In the *Nottebohm* case[3] the International Court of Justice had to determine whether Liechtenstein was entitled to exercise a right of diplomatic protection of Nottebohm—a German national by birth who had become a naturalized citizen of Liechtenstein but without having any real connections with that State. As a general rule, States are entitled to exercise diplomatic protection of their nationals, and international law does not impose limitations on the right of a sovereign State to determine who are its nationals. The Court emphasized, however, that the issue in the case was not the domestic law validity of Nottebohm's naturalization, but whether the grant of nationality by Liechtenstein produced international legal effects which must be recognized by Guatemala.

A. WHERE NATIONAL LAW CAUSES BREACH OF INTERNATIONAL LAW

International tribunals have consistently held that in the event of conflict between international obligations and national law, the international rule prevails. The position was set out in the draft Declaration on Rights and Duties of States prepared by the International

---

[1] *Serbian Loans, Judgment No 14, 1929, PCIJ, Ser A, No 20.*
[2] *Brazilian Loans, Judgment No 15, 1929, PCIJ, Ser A, No 21.*
[3] *Nottebohm, Second Phase, Judgment, ICJ Reports 1955, p 4.*

Law Commission and endorsed in 1949 by the UN General Assembly. Article 13 provided that:

> Every state has the duty to carry out in good faith its obligations arising from treaties and other sources of international law, and it may not invoke provisions in its constitution or its laws as an excuse for failure to perform this duty.[4]

The rule was restated in Article 27 of the Vienna Convention on the Law of Treaties[5] as follows:

Internal law and observance of treaties

> A party may not invoke the provisions of its internal law as justification for its failure to perform a treaty. This rule is without prejudice to Article 46.

Article 46 permits a State to argue that its consent to a treaty was invalidated by violation of its internal law only where 'that violation was manifest and concerned a rule of its internal law of fundamental importance'.

The Permanent Court of International Justice, in the *Exchange of Greek and Turkish Populations* case,[6] stated that it was self-evident that a State which had assumed valid international obligations was bound to make such modifications in its legislation as were necessary to ensure their fulfilment. The need for effective implementation of international human rights obligations in national law so that they can be relied on by individuals is particularly obvious, and the primacy of international obligations over conflicting national law has often been reaffirmed by human rights tribunals. The Inter-American Court of Human Rights, for example, in an Advisory Opinion on *International Responsibility for the Promulgation and Enforcement of Laws in Violation of the Convention* said:

> Pursuant to international law, all obligations imposed by it must be fulfilled in good faith; domestic law may not be invoked to justify non-fulfilment. These rules may be deemed to be general principles of law and have been applied by the Permanent Court of International Justice and the International Court of Justice even in cases involving constitutional provisions...[7]

International tribunals will not, however, declare national laws invalid—merely that these laws or the way in which they have been applied are inconsistent with international law. Thus the Inter-American Court of Human Rights, in the Advisory Opinion just cited made clear that its Opinion related:

> ...only to the legal effects of the law under international law. It is not appropriate for the Court to rule on its domestic legal effect within the State concerned. That determination is within the exclusive jurisdiction of the national courts and should be decided in accordance with their laws.[8]

The International Court of Justice in the *LaGrand* case[9] was required to consider the consequences of the admitted failure by the USA to give timely notification to two German nationals of their right to consular protection under Article 36 of the Vienna Convention on Consular Relations. Notwithstanding a provisional order from the ICJ asking the USA

---

[4] GA Res 375 (IV).   [5] UKTS No 58 (1980), Cmnd 7964.

[6] *Exchange of Greek and Turkish Populations, Advisory Opinion, 1925, PCIJ, Ser B, No 10.*

[7] *Advisory Opinion, OC-14/94, Ser A, No 14 (9 December 1994), para 35, 116 ILR 320.*

[8] Para 34.

[9] *LaGrand (Germany v United States of America), Merits, Judgment, ICJ Reports 2001*, p 466. See Mennecke and Tams, 2002.

to 'take all measures at its disposal' to stay execution of Walter LaGrand until the case brought by Germany had been decided,[10] he was executed as scheduled. On the merits Germany later argued, *inter alia*, that the US constitutional rule of 'procedural default' (under which a procedural failing which had not been raised at State level could not be argued at federal level) violated Article 36 of the Vienna Convention, which required the USA to give full effect to the purposes for which the rights to notification and consular access are intended. The ICJ rejected the suggestion by the USA that in pronouncing on the application of Article 36 it was acting as 'a court of appeal of national criminal proceedings'. It further emphasized that:

> In itself, the rule does not violate Article 36 of the Vienna Convention. The problem arises when the procedural default rule does not allow the detained individual to challenge a conviction and sentence by claiming, in reliance on Article 36, paragraph 1 of the Convention, that the competent national authorities failed to comply with their obligation to provide the requisite consular information 'without delay', thus preventing the person from seeking and obtaining consular assistance from the sending State.[11]

The Court held that an apology for any future violations of Article 36 would be inadequate reparation, and that the USA must allow review and reconsideration of a conviction and sentence in the light of the violation of the rights in the Convention. They stressed, however, that this obligation could be carried out in various ways, and that 'The choice of means must be left to the United States'.[12]

In the case of *Avena* in 2004 the Court noted that the procedural default rule had not been revised, and it refined its views on adequate reparation, saying:

> It follows that the remedy to make good these violations should consist in an obligation on the United States to permit review and reconsideration of these nationals' cases by the United States courts...with a view to ascertaining whether in each case the violation of Article 36 committed by the competent authorities caused actual prejudice to the defendant in the process of administration of criminal justice.[13]

Responding to the Court's judgment, President Bush ordered courts in the USA to review the cases of 49 Mexicans under sentence of death. But on a further application by one of those covered by the *Avena* decision and again in the face of an order from the International Court calling for a stay of execution, the US Supreme Court in the case of *Medellin v Texas*[14] by majority ruled that the ICJ ruling did not constitute enforceable US federal law and that the President had no constitutional authority to alter this position so as to overrule the procedural default rule. Texas executed Medellin in full knowledge that this represented a violation of the international obligations of the USA.[15]

---

[10] *LaGrand (Germany v United States of America), Provisional Measures, Order of 3 March 1999, ICJ Reports 1999*, p 9.

[11] *LaGrand (Germany v United States of America), Merits, Judgment, ICJ Reports 2001*, p 466, paras 79–91.

[12] Ibid, para 125.

[13] *Avena and Other Mexican Nationals (Mexico v United States of America), Judgment, ICJ Reports 2004*, p 12, para 121. See Shelton, 2004.

[14] *Medellin v Texas* (2008) 552 US 491, noted in (2008) 102 AJIL 859.

[15] For the restrained reaction of the ICJ, see judgment in *Request for Interpretation of the Judgment of 31 March 2004 in the Case concerning Avena and Other Mexican Nationals (Mexico v United States of America)*, Judgment of 19 January 2009 paras 47–59. It follows that in the US legislation would be required to ensure compliance with the obligations of consular notification and access, and neither Congress nor the executive has so far seriously pursued this course.

B. INTERNATIONAL LAW LOOKS MAINLY TO THE RESULT

Traditionally, international tribunals and supervisory bodies have concerned themselves only with the result in the specific case where there has been a complaint of breach. The method of national implementation of international obligations has been regarded as an internal affair. There are, however, signs of a more intrusive approach.

In the European Community law context, the European Court of Justice from the outset, went beyond asserting the primacy of a European Community treaty or secondary obligation. In the case of *Costa* v *ENEL*,[16] the ECJ did not limit itself to saying that Italy was in breach of its Community law obligations because its courts upheld a later national measure which was inconsistent with these obligations. It held that:

> By contrast with ordinary international treaties, the EEC Treaty has created its own legal system which, on the entry into force of the Treaty, became an integral part of the legal systems of the Member States...

and that:

> ...the law stemming from the Treaty, an independent source of law, could not, because of its special and original nature, be overridden by domestic legal provision, however framed, without being deprived of its character as Community law and without the legal basis of the Community itself being called into question.

This formulation of the supremacy of Community law—not self-evident on the face of the European Community Treaties—is among the features distinguishing European Community law from international law (Craig and de Búrca, 2007, Ch 8; Slaughter and Burke-White, 2007). In consequence of the more intrusive nature of the Community legal order member States may be accountable for the methods by which they implement regulations and directives. The European Commission is charged with ensuring that the provisions of the Treaty are applied, and has vigorously monitored methods of national implementation of Community legal obligations.

In the field of international criminal law, it is now common for treaties not merely to permit but to require the assumption of criminal jurisdiction at national level, and to set out a uniform definition of certain criminal offences in such a way that detailed changes in national law are required. Under the 1984 UN Convention Against Torture and Other Cruel, Inhuman or Degrading Treatment or Punishment,[17] for example, there is first a uniform definition of torture for the purposes of the convention. Secondly, there is a requirement for each party to take effective legislative, administrative, judicial, or other measures to prohibit torture within its own jurisdiction and to ensure that all acts of torture are offences under its criminal law. Thirdly, a party must establish a wider extraterritorial jurisdiction on grounds such as the nationality of the alleged offender and where it does not extradite an alleged offender taken into custody in its territory. The requirements imposed on national laws by successive treaties in the field of international criminal law have become increasingly detailed. Even the 1948 Convention on the Prevention and Punishment of the Crime of Genocide[18] however—the precursor of these treaties—provided in Article V that:

> The Contracting Parties undertake to enact, in accordance with their respective Constitutions, the necessary legislation to give effect to the provisions of the present

---

[16] *Costa* v *ENEL* Case 6/64 [1964] ECR 585.   [17] UKTS No 107 (1991), Cm 1775.
[18] UKTS No 58 (1970), Cmnd 4421; 78 UNTS 277.

Convention and, in particular, to provide effective penalties for persons guilty of genocide or any of the other acts enumerated in Article III.

The Statute of the International Criminal Court does not impose express requirements on Parties to incorporate international criminal offences in domestic law, but the principle of complementarity (whereby the ICC assumes jurisdiction only where Parties fail in their primary responsibility to prosecute) ensures that Parties give close attention to national implementation of substantive rules of criminal law.[19]

The Convention against Torture, like earlier human rights conventions, establishes a Committee whose functions include monitoring national implementation. Parties must report to the Committee against Torture, within one year of becoming bound by the convention and subsequently at four-yearly intervals, on the measures taken to give effect to their undertakings. The Committee comment on the effectiveness of national implementing measures, and may make any criticisms public (along with observations by the State concerned) in its own annual report. Governments should therefore give careful thought to implementation before ratification rather than simply leave to their courts the task of giving effect to the convention within the context of national criminal law and procedure. Other modern conventions—on for example non-proliferation of biological or chemical weapons or protection of the environment—may also require for proper implementation administrative supervision or inspection mechanisms at national level for which no international model law can be prescribed.[20]

The need for precise national implementation in criminal matters has been highlighted by the difficulty in controlling piracy off the coast of Somalia. Customary international law permits national arrest and punishment of any pirates apprehended on the high seas—but in addition to problems in the arrest of pirates sheltering in a State lacking effective participation in the international legal system, it has been found that other States willing to try and to punish pirates lack the necessary national criminal jurisdiction. The international maritime community regard it as urgent that international conventions which plug this gap are widely ratified and effectively enforced at national level.[21]

III. THE APPROACH OF NATIONAL PARLIAMENTS AND NATIONAL COURTS

While the principles applied by international tribunals to the relationship between international and national law are uniform and reasonably straightforward, this is not the case with the approaches taken by national parliaments or by national courts. For each national legislature and court, the starting point for any examination of the relationship is its own constitution. National bodies do not dispute what is said by international tribunals as to the position in international law, or dispute the existence or binding character of international law, but they perceive the way in which international law is integrated into and applied within their own legal order as being their own constitutional affair. Other States do not question this autonomy, and even international tribunals—as was illustrated in Section II of this chapter—regard national laws and constitutional methods as outside their competence.

---

[19] See Third Report of ICC Committee of the International Law Association, Rio de Janeiro (2008).
[20] See generally Ulfstein, 2007.
[21] UN SC Res 1846 (2 December 2008) has addressed these problems.

Scholars have put forward various theories to explain the relationship between international and national law. Most persistent have been the theories of monism and of dualism. In the view of the monists, there is a single legal system with international law at its apex and all national constitutional and other legal norms below it in the hierarchy. There is no need for international obligations to be 'transformed' into rules of national law, and in case of any apparent conflict, the international rule prevails. The fact that national organs do not behave according to such rules indicates the weakness of international law, but does not invalidate the theory, since the State will incur international responsibility where it permits violations of international legal rules to occur. According to Kelsen, the leading exponent of the monist theory, it could not be based on scientific observation, but was dependent on ethical considerations (Kelsen, 1920).

Under the dualist theory, international law and national law operate on different levels. International law is a horizontal legal order based on and regulating mainly the relations and obligations between independent and theoretically equal sovereign States. To the extent that to be effective it requires to be applied at national level, it is for each State to determine how this is done. If the international rule confers rights or obligations on individuals or entities created under national law, the national legislature may 'transform' it into a rule of national law, and the national judge will then apply it as a rule of national, or domestic law.

Neither theory has had a significant input into the development or revision of national constitutions, into national debates about ratification of international agreements, or into decisions of national courts on questions of international law. Except as shorthand indications of the general approach within a particular State to implementation or application of international rules, the theories are not useful in clarifying the relationship between international law and national laws. They suggest—at least to law students—that there are only two methods of approach and that one or other theory must be 'correct' or at least preferable. Neither of these impressions is helpful. There are almost as many ways of giving effect to international law as there are national legal systems. To classify a State as 'monist' or 'dualist' does not greatly assist in describing its constitutional approach to international obligations, in determining how its government and parliament will proceed in order to adopt or implement a new treaty, or in predicting how its courts will approach the complex questions which arise in litigation involving international law.

IV. THE SPECTRUM OF CONSTITUTIONAL RULES

Six States have been chosen as examples spanning the spectrum from monism to dualism and as reflecting constitutions emerging, or undergoing revision, at different historical periods. They are the Netherlands, Germany, France, Russia, the USA, and the UK. In each of these, the approach to international law reflects the historical background to the adoption, or revision of the constitution.[22]

These necessarily brief accounts of constitutional frameworks can give only a partial account of rules which have been extensively interpreted and supplemented by the practice of national legislative, executive, and judicial organs. Only in the light of that practice and jurisprudence can one assess how practical problems are dealt with in each national context.

---

[22] For a wider cross-section of approaches see Nijman and Nollkaemper (eds), 2007 (in particular Peters, 2007, pp 254–70; Sloss, 2009 and Shelton, 2011).

A. THE NETHERLANDS

The provisions in the Netherlands Constitution, as revised in 1953 and most recently in 2002 are based on two elements—a very strong degree of parliamentary control of the approval of all treaties before the Netherlands becomes bound, and a clear hierarchical superiority of treaties thus ratified over both prior and subsequent laws and statutory regulations. Article 94 of the Constitution provides for the supremacy of treaties binding on all persons in the Netherlands over prior and subsequent national law, but Article 91 makes this supremacy conditional on the treaty having been approved by the States-General. Such approval may be express or tacit. Some categories of treaties are exempted by statute from the requirement of parliamentary approval. Where any provision in a treaty conflicts or may conflict with the Constitution, a two-thirds majority in the States-General is required for approval. Under Article 120, Netherlands courts may not review the compatibility of a treaty with the Constitution, though in other respects they interpret and apply the treaty as national law. Article 93 further provides that treaties and resolutions of international organizations become binding after they are published. These provisions do not apply to customary international law which is not given the same precedence over national law.

Article 90 of the Constitution requires the government to promote the development of the international legal order. This, however, gives the government no mandate to override careful scrutiny by the States-General, and before approval of treaties, lawyers and other negotiators are cross-examined in Parliamentary Committees over the detail of their texts to an extent unparalleled elsewhere in Europe. Van Dijk and Tahzib comment on this system of scrutiny:

> Thus a fair balance is achieved between the primary duty of the Government to promote the international legal order and Parliament's control over the way this duty is exercised.[23]

B. GERMANY

The 1949 German Basic Law (Grundgesetz), reflecting the German experience of National Socialism and the Second World War, provides in Article 25 that:

> The general rules of public international law shall be an integral part of federal law. They shall take precedence over the laws and shall directly create rights and duties for the inhabitants of the federal territory.

Articles 23 and 24 of the Basic Law permit the Federation by legislation to transfer sovereign powers to intergovernmental institutions, in particular to the EU established by the Treaty on European Union signed at Maastricht in 1992, and to a system of mutual collective security in order to 'bring about and secure a peaceful and lasting order in Europe and among the nations of the world'. Article 26 makes it unconstitutional to carry out acts with the intention of disturbing peaceful relations between nations, especially preparation of an aggressive war.

Article 59, however, provides that:

> (2) Treaties which regulate the political relations of the Federation or relate to matters of federal legislation shall require the consent or participation, in the form of a federal law, of the bodies competent in any specific case for such federal legislation . . .

---

[23] Van Dijk and Tahzib, 1994, p 125. See also van Panhuys, 1953; Schermers, 1987; Leigh, Blakeslee, and Ederington (eds), 1999; Peters, 2007, pp 304–5; Shelton, 2011, p. 407.

Under German constitutional practice, Parliament may be involved in treaty negotiations, and policy issues may be discussed in the Foreign Affairs Committee of the Bundestag or in that of the Bundesrat. The treaties regarded as regulating the political relations of the Federation are those which might affect the existence, independence, status, or role of the German State. Ultimate control of new treaties lies with the Federal Constitutional Court (Bundesverfassungsgericht) and its decision in the matter binds all State organs. The Court has stated that a fundamental objective of the Grundgesetz is to enable fulfillment of Germany's obligations under international law.

The role of the Federal Constitutional Court was of central importance to Germany's position as the last member State to ratify the Maastricht Treaty in 1993. Even following adoption of the new Article 23 of its Basic Law as the basis for participation in the new EU, Germany was unable to ratify until the Constitutional Court had ruled in the case of *Brunner v European Union Treaty*. Brunner argued that the integration to be effected by the Treaty would lead to 'development towards the covert and irrevocable institution of a European federal state'. On this, the court said:[24]

> Germany is one of the 'Masters of the Treaties' which have established their adherence to the Union Treaty concluded 'for an unlimited period'... with the intention of long-term membership, but could also ultimately revoke that adherence by a contrary act. The validity and application of European law in Germany depend on the application-of-law instruction of the Accession Law. Germany thus preserves the quality of a sovereign State in its own right and the status of sovereign equality with other States...

A similar review of the implications of the 2007 Treaty of Lisbon was carried out by the Constitutional Court, and the Court insisted on further national legislation to elaborate parliamentary rights of control before German ratification.[25]

In the *Görgülü* Case, the Federal Constitutional Court clarified that international agreements—and in particular the European Convention on Human Rights (ECHR)—have the status of a federal statute but do not prevail in case of conflict with the Basic Law. The Basic Law must, however, be construed in accordance with the ECHR as interpreted by the European Court of Human Rights.[26]

C. FRANCE

The 1958 Constitution of the Fifth Republic also requires careful control of the ratification of treaties. Article 53 provides that:

> Peace treaties, commercial treaties, treaties or agreements concerning international organizations, those which impose a financial burden on the State, those which modify legislative provisions, those concerning personal status, those which effect cession, exchange or addition of territory, may not be ratified or approved except by virtue of a law.

Under Article 54, if the Constitutional Council (*Conseil Constitutionnel*) declares that an international commitment contains provision adverse to the Constitution, authorization to ratify may be given only after amendment of the Constitution. Amendment under the

---

[24] *Brunner v European Union Treaty*, [1994] 1 CMLR 57, at para 55. See also Schwarze, 1994, 1995, 2001; Treviranus and Beemelmans, 1995.

[25] *BVerfG*, 2 BvR 2/08, 30.6.2009 and Press Release no 72/2009. On the 'cooperative relationship' between German and international courts, particularly on human rights, see Paulus, 2007.

[26] *Görgülü* case, BVerfGE 111, 307, 2 BvR 148/04 (Order of 14 October 2004); 1BvR 1664/04 (Order of 5 April 2005); 1BvR 2790/04 (Order of 10 June 2005); Shelton, 2011, p 240.

terms of this provision has been made for the ratification of the Treaties of Maastricht and Amsterdam, and more recently for the ratification of the Statute of the International Criminal Court.[27] In 1985 the Constitutional Council concluded that Protocol No 6 to the European Convention on Human Rights and Fundamental Freedoms on the Abolition of the Death Penalty was not in conflict with the Constitution and, in particular, that it was not inconsistent with the essential conditions for national sovereignty (Favoreu, 1985). Article 55 provides that treaties duly ratified have, after publication, an authority superior to legislation. Only in 1989, however, did the Conseil d'Etat accept that this superiority applied not only to earlier but also to later national legislation (Eisemann and Kessedijan, 1995). In this context a specific treaty provision must be shown to have direct effect before it may be invoked by a party to litigation in French courts (Errera, 2008).

Under French practice, the Minister for Foreign Affairs may issue an interpretation of a treaty provision to a court, and this interpretation can be relied on in later cases involving the same provision if it is of general application and binding on the court.[28] In the case of *Kandyrine de Brito Paiva*,[29] the Conseil d'Etat invited submission of an *amicus curiae* brief from Gilbert Guillaume[30] to assist in resolution of a conflict between ECHR—which prohibits discrimination on the basis of nationality in regard to the right to property—and the Agreement of 1997 between France and Russia which settled pre-1917 claims but limited distribution of assets to French nationals. The claimant had inherited a claim in respect of a loan from his French great-uncle but was himself Portuguese. The Court held that there was no conflict between the two treaties since the ECHR had to be interpreted in the light of the bilateral treaty whose purpose was to resolve a long-standing dispute. But it also held that if there were conflict between treaties, this should be resolved in the light of national constitutional rules and principles.

D. RUSSIA

In 1993, after a prolonged internal battle between the Constitutional Commission and President Yeltsin, the Russian Federation adopted a new constitution to reflect the newly democratic character of Russia and a new acceptance of the international legal order. Article 86 of the Constitution gives the President of Russia the power to negotiate and conclude treaties. Article 106 provides for both Chambers of Parliament (the Duma and the Federal Council) to give consent to treaties by federal law. Some uncertainties as to the meaning of these provisions were later resolved by the 1995 Federal Law on International Treaties which reflected accession by Russia to the Vienna Convention on the Law of Treaties. As with most national constitutions, publication is essential for a treaty to carry binding force in Russian law, and the treaty must be binding under international law.[31]

Under Article 15.4 of the 1993 Constitution:

The generally recognized principles and norms of international law and the international treaties of the Russian Federation shall constitute part of the legal system. If an international

---

[27] Constitutional Law of 8 July 1999, No 99–568. See Errera in House of Lords EU Committee, 6th Report 2003–04, HL Paper 47 *The Future Role of the European Court of Justice*, QQ 161–8 and Supplementary Notes, 2008; Bell, 2005.

[28] *Affaire Barbie*, 100 ILR 330.

[29] Conseil d'Etat No. 3036/78, 28 Revue française de droit administrative 17 (2012); (2012) 106 *AJIL* 353.

[30] Former Legal Adviser to the Ministry of Foreign Affairs, Judge of the ICJ and member of the Conseil d'Etat.

[31] Decree No 10 of the Plenum of the Supreme Court of the Russian Federation, 5 October 2003.

treaty of the Russian Federation establishes other rules than those stipulated by the law, the rules of the international treaty shall apply.

This provision gives clear priority to both customary international law and treaties in force for Russia over both earlier and later national laws. It marked a radical change from the position under the 1977 Constitution of the Soviet Union which did not permit treaties to be invoked before domestic courts. The numerous treaties on human rights which the Soviet Union had so freely ratified without reservation suddenly became enforceable in Russian courts. Russian courts are increasingly applying principles of international law directly—particularly the ECHR and its case law—though they have been hampered by the limited experience of judicial independence, the lack of professional training in international law, and the shortage of relevant materials in Russian translation.

Article 15.4 does not, however, give international law priority over the Russian Constitution. The Constitutional Court may review the compatibility with the Constitution of treaties not yet in force for Russia, and probably also of treaties already in force (Danilenko, 1994; Butler, 1997; Danilenko, 1999; Zimnenko, 2007; Petrov and Kalinchenko, 2011). This was emphasized by the Chairman of the Russian Constitutional Court in response to the judgment of the Grand Chamber of the European Court of Human Rights in the case of *Markin* v *Russia*[32] finding that Russia was in breach of Article 14 of the ECHR in refusing equal treatment regarding parental leave to a military serviceman. The President recommended that Russia should follow the approach taken by the German Constitutional Court in the *Görgülü* case.[33]

Russian courts interpret treaties in accordance with the Vienna Convention on the Law of Treaties, but may apply for assistance from the Ministry of Foreign Affairs or the Ministry of Justice.[34]

E. THE USA

Under Article II s 2 of the Constitution of the USA, adopted in 1787 when the original confederal system was replaced by a fully federal system, the President:

> ...shall have Power, by and with the Advice and Consent of the Senate, to make Treaties, provided two thirds of the Senators present concur...

It is clear that the 'advice and consent' was intended to require consultation of the Senate during negotiations, but following one unhappy experience, the first President, George Washington, limited consultation to the approval of treaties before their ratification. The independent power of the Senate to reject or delay approval of treaties submitted by the executive is substantial.

Article VI s 2 further provides that:

> This Constitution, and the Laws of the United States which shall be made in Pursuance thereof; and all Treaties made, or which shall be made, under the authority of the United States, shall be the Supreme Law of the Land, and the Judges in every State shall be bound thereby, any Thing in the Constitution or Laws of any State to the Contrary notwithstanding.

International law was accepted as part of the law of the individual States, and following the formation of the USA it was also accepted as part of federal law without the need for

---

[32] Application No 30078/06. See analysis and comment at (2013) 106 *AJIL* 836.
[33] See n 26 in this chapter.   [34] Shelton, 2011, p 523.

incorporation by Congress or by the President. International law is, however, regarded as subject to the Constitution and thus, at national level, to 'repeal' by later law of the USA. Wherever possible a US statute will be construed in such a way as not to conflict with international law or US treaty obligations.[35] Where no such reconciliation is possible, it is accepted that the change in domestic law does not relieve the USA of its international obligation or the consequences of violation of that obligation.

International law and international agreements binding on the USA may be interpreted and enforced by US courts. According to the Third Restatement of the Foreign Relations Law of the United States:

(2) Cases arising under international law or international agreements of the United States are within the Judicial Power of the United States and, subject to Constitutional and statutory limitations and requirements of justiciability, are within the jurisdiction of the federal courts.

(3) Courts in the United States are bound to give effect to international law and to international agreements of the United States, except that a 'non-self-executing' agreement will not be given effect as law in the absence of necessary implementation.[36]

Determinations of international law by the Supreme Court, including review of State laws on grounds of inconsistency with international law, are binding on the States and on State courts. There are complex rules of constitutional law and practice determining whether an agreement is 'self-executing' in the USA, and these have little regard to international rules of treaty interpretation. They were applied by the Supreme Court in the case of *Medellin* v *Texas*, described in Section II A (n 14) of this chapter, where the majority held that a judgment of the International Court of Justice did not constitute a self-executing obligation in the USA.[37] In response, a Joint Task Force of the American Bar Association and the American Society of International law on Implementing Treaties under US Law studied *Medellin* and in its Report recommended expedited legislation where there was imminent risk of treaty-breach by the USA and, for future treaties, better identification by the executive and the Senate of self-executing provisions and delay in bringing a treaty into force until other provisions were implemented by legislation.[38]

On ratifying the International Covenant on Civil and Political Rights in 1992, the US government attached a declaration stating that Articles 1 through 27 of the Covenant were not self-executing, and there has been no implementing legislation. The US Senate, in giving 'advice and consent' to a treaty, now states which of its provisions are self-executing. Where an agreement is given effect in US law, it is the implementing legislation, not the agreement, which is regarded as US law.[39]

Under US judicial practice, great weight is given to views on questions of international law expressed by the US government, whether by way of *amicus curiae* briefs, interventions as a party or 'executive suggestions'. This is done on the grounds that it is desirable that the USA should speak with one voice on such questions and that the executive branch will have to answer for any alleged breach of international law by the USA.

---

[35] In *Al Bihani* v *Obama*, US Court of Appeals No 09-5051, (2010), however, the Court found that Congress did not intend the international laws of war to constrain the President's war powers as defined under statute.

[36] Chapter 2 Status of International Law and Agreements in United States Law, s 111.

[37] See nn 15 and 16 of this chapter.

[38] Report at http://www.americanbar.org/content/dam/aba/migrated/leadership/2010/midyear/daily_journal/108C.authcheckdam.pdf.

[39] Third Restatement of the Foreign Relations Law of the US. See also Jackson, 1987; Riesenfeld and Abbott, 1994; Aust, 2013, pp 174–6.

The receptiveness of the USA to international law has, however, been challenged both at federal and at State level by a series of bills which would prohibit use of international and foreign law. A typical example was the Oklahoma 'Save our State' resolution which would have prohibited the State courts from considering international law. Most of these bills have been or are likely to be struck down as unconstitutional, but they betray ignorance of their practical implications and send a damaging message abroad.[40]

F. THE UK

Under the unwritten constitution of the UK, Parliament has the supreme power to establish and to change the law of the UK. The conduct of foreign affairs, including the conclusion and termination of treaties, remains under the royal prerogative—which means that it is carried out by the government of the day. The government are broadly accountable to Parliament for their conduct of foreign affairs.

Customary international law has long been regarded as part of the law of England and of Scotland without any need for specific incorporation, and this rule has also applied in Commonwealth States as part of the common law.[41] Treaties, however, are not regarded as a source of rights or obligations in domestic law. The reason is that otherwise it would be open to the monarch and now to the executive to alter national law by a treaty instead of through the enactment of legislation and thus to bypass the supremacy of Parliament. It is in theory open to the executive to assume international legal commitments, but these will not be given effect within the national legal system if they require changes in the law or the jurisdiction of the UK or the payment of money (which must be voted by Parliament). The executive may conclude treaties which do not involve changes in domestic law—for example Treaties of Friendship or Investment Promotion and Protection Agreements.

The position was expressed succinctly by Lord Templeman thus in one of the cases which followed the collapse in 1985 of the International Tin Council and the attempts of its creditors through UK courts to recover their losses from its member States:

> A treaty is a contract between the governments of two or more sovereign States. International law regulates the relations between sovereign States and determines the validity, the interpretation and the enforcement of treaties. A treaty to which Her Majesty's Government is a party does not alter the laws of the United Kingdom. A treaty may be incorporated into or alter the laws of the United Kingdom by means of legislation. Except to the extent that a treaty becomes incorporated into the laws of the United Kingdom by statute, the courts of the United Kingdom have no power to enforce treaty rights and obligations at the behest of a sovereign government or at the behest of a private individual.[42]

Under Part 2 of the Constitutional Reform and Governance Act 2010,[43] which replaced the constitutional convention, formerly known as the Ponsonby rule, all treaties subject to ratification are laid before Parliament for 21 days on which it is sitting. It has, however, almost never happened that for a treaty—even an important one—not requiring any change in UK law, Parliament has pressed for a debate. The

---

[40] See Fellmeth, 2012; Shelton, 2011, esp. pp 655–9.
[41] For the position in Canada, for example, see *R v Hape* [2008] 1 LRC 551 at paras [34]–[46].
[42] *JH Rayner* v *Department of Trade and Industry* [1988] 3 All ER 257; 81 ILR 670.
[43] C 25.

2010 Act prohibits the government from ratifying if the House of Commons vote against it, and imposes conditions if the House of Lords vote against.[44] The Foreign and Commonwealth Office since 1996 accompany the treaty text with an Explanatory Memorandum which enables issues of significance to be identified.[45] Where the treaty will require changes in UK law or payment of money, the government also secure passage of the necessary changes—whether by Act of Parliament or by secondary legislation—before the treaty is brought into force for the UK. The government never deliberately assumes international commitments without being able to give internal effect to them. These constitutional constraints make the UK a demanding partner in international negotiations, but rigorous scrutiny of national implementation before ratification has meant that it has rarely been found in breach of its commitments.[46] There have been violations of the ECHR found against the UK—but they are a very small proportion of the individual complaints brought, and the Human Rights Act 1998[47] was deliberately designed to reduce their number by providing a more effective system of domestic application.

Parliament may, however, decide as sovereign to violate treaty commitments. This was made clear by the Lord Chancellor in the context of the question of the response by the UK to a judgment of the European Court of Human Rights declaring unlawful the total ban on allowing prisoners to vote. The government did not dispute its international legal duty to implement this decision, but draft legislation presented to Parliament permitted it the choice of non-compliance.[48]

The UK government does not direct the courts on questions of international law. On request from the court or from a party to litigation, however, the Foreign and Commonwealth Office issues certificates on points of fact peculiarly within the knowledge of the government. These relate, for example, to whether an entity is recognized as a State or government and to whether an individual has been notified and received as a diplomat. Where a point of international law of interest to the government is in issue in litigation, the Attorney-General may nominate counsel to assist the court as *amicus curiae*. But although counsel so nominated may be assisted by government legal advisers, he or she is not directly instructed and remains an independent 'friend of the court'.

These brief and superficial surveys illustrate that at the stage of national acceptance as well as of national judicial application of international law obligations, the methods employed do not turn on any universally applicable theory of the relationship. They turn rather on the relationship between the executive, legislative, and judicial organs of each State, on how a potential new international obligation is to be democratically scrutinized, on how its subsequent application can be effectively guaranteed, and on whether the national courts are judicially independent of the executive in determining issues of international law.

---

[44] For detail, see Barrett, 2011. House of Commons Note SN/1A/5855, Parliament's new statutory role in ratifying treaties

[45] For the new arrangements, see *Hansard*, HC, vol 576 (16 December 1996) WA 1101, 1996 *BYIL* 746 and 753.

[46] For UK practice see Aust, 2013, pp 168–71.   [47] C 42, especially s 3.

[48] Evidence to HL Select Committee on the Constitution 21 November 2012, QQ 2–7. The Lord Chancellor cited Lord Hoffmann's judgment in *R v Secretary of State for the Home Department ex parte Simms* [2000] 2 AC 115.

V. SOME PROBLEMS WHICH ARISE IN
NATIONAL COURTS

Examination of a few of the cases in national courts where the question of the relationship between international and national law has been raised shows the extreme
diversity of the issues which present themselves. In many cases these issues are not
capable of easy resolution in terms of national constitutions, far less in terms of general
theories.

A. DOES A RULE OF CUSTOMARY INTERNATIONAL LAW
PREVAIL OVER CONFLICTING NATIONAL LAW?

It seems that all national legal systems—even those of the UK and of the Commonwealth
States whose constitutions have followed the same approach as regards treaties—accept
customary international law as an integral part of national law. Incorporation is specifically provided for in some constitutions, but in others which make no express provision
the result is the same. The nature of customary international law as part of Scots law was
examined for the first time in 1999 by the Appeal Court of the High Court of Justiciary in
two criminal cases where the defendants, charged with sabotage against Britain's nuclear
weapons, argued as 'reasonable excuse' for their conduct the international illegality of the
holding of these weapons. The court held, without citing Scottish authority since there was
none, that a 'rule of customary international law is a rule of Scots law'. It was not a fact to
be established (like foreign law) by expert evidence, but was to be argued by submission
and decided by the judge.[49]

English courts, however, found themselves for many years precluded from applying
modern customary international law rules on restricted State immunity because the old
rule of absolute State immunity had become embedded, or 'transformed' into English
common law by a series of judicial decisions. Under the English rules on precedent, the
judges maintained that the old rule could be reversed only by the House of Lords as the
supreme appellate body. Eventually Lord Denning, presiding over the Court of Appeal in
the case of *Trendtex Trading Corporation Ltd* v *Central Bank of Nigeria* persuaded one of
his two judicial colleagues that this attitude was wrong. Customary international law was
incorporated into English law so that when its rules changed, English law also changed.
Lord Denning said:

> International law does change, and the courts have applied the changes without the aid of
> any Act of Parliament. Thus, when the rules of international law were changed (by the force
> of public opinion) so as to condemn slavery, the English courts were justified in applying the
> modern rules of international law...[50]

There are few examples of national courts setting aside national law because of its conflict with customary international law, but the Court of Justice of the EU—functioning at
a level intermediate between the international legal order and national legal orders—set
out criteria under which it might review Union law as regards its consistency with rules of

---

[49] Cases of *John* v *Donnelly* and *Lord Advocate's Reference No 1, 2000,* 2001 SLT 507 (*Greenock anti-nuclear
activists*), described in Neff, 2002.
[50] *Trendtex Trading Corporation Ltd* v *Central Bank of Nigeria* [1977] 1 QB 529; [1977] 1 All ER 881. For
critical comment, see Collier, 1989.

customary international law. In the *Air Transport Association of America* Case,[51] the Court held that customary rules could be relied on by an individual as against an EU act insofar as, first, the rules were capable of calling into question the competence of the Union to adopt the act challenged and, secondly, the act was liable to affect rights or to create EU obligations. It held, however, that application of the EU's carbon-trading scheme to international flights by non-EU airlines landing or taking off from territory of the member States was not inconsistent with customary international law principles regarding sovereignty or jurisdiction.

B. WHAT IS THE MEANING OF AN INTERNATIONAL LAW RULE IN THE CONTEXT OF DOMESTIC LAW?

In most cases, the national court does not merely have to decide whether to apply a rule of international law on its own, but on the meaning and effect of the international rule in the domestic law context where it arises. Thus, in the Scottish nuclear weapons protesters cases described in Section V A (n 50) of this chapter, holding that international law was part of Scots law was not the end of the matter. The court had then to consider whether the holding of nuclear missiles was lawful under international law—a question which had been carefully avoided by the International Court of Justice[52]—and further whether international law gave individuals a right of forcible intervention to stop international crimes such as would amount to a defence of 'necessity' under Scottish criminal law. The Appeal Court held that the conduct of the UK government was not illegal and that international law conferred no right of forcible intervention on individuals. The UK House of Lords, dismissing claims by protesters against the impending conflict in Iraq that they were 'preventing crime', held in the case of *R* v *Jones*,[53] that although a crime of aggression existed in international law, it did not follow automatically that 'aggression' was an offence in domestic law. Aggression was a crime committed by a State, not precisely defined under international law, and it would be contrary to modern constitutional practice for English courts to treat it as a crime in English law without specific statutory authority. As to the argument that the crime under international law had been tacitly assimilated into domestic law, Lord Bingham maintained that it was 'very relevant not only that Parliament has so far refrained from taking this step but also that it would draw the courts into an area which, in the past, they have entered, if at all, with reluctance and the utmost circumspection'.

In 2004 the US Supreme Court in *Rasul* v *Bush*,[54] in order to determine whether they had jurisdiction to review the legality of the detention of prisoners in the Guantánamo Bay Naval Base in Cuba, applied the terms of the Lease Agreement of 1903 under which Cuba conferred on the USA 'complete jurisdiction and control' over the Base while retaining ultimate sovereignty. The majority inferred from the Agreement that the relevant statute should be construed to give US federal courts jurisdiction.

In 2010 The US Supreme Court in the case of *Abbott* v *Abbott* had to construe the term 'rights of custody' in the Hague Convention on the Civil Aspects of Child Abduction to determine whether a father with a *ne exeat* right under Chilean law restricting removal

---

[51] *Air Transport Association of America, American Airlines Inc, Continental Airlines Inc, United Airlines Inc* v *Secretary of State for Energy and Climate Change*, Case C-366/10, [2012] 2 CMLR 4; Denza, 2012.

[52] *Legality of the Threat or Use of Nuclear Weapons, Advisory Opinion, ICJ Reports 1996*, p 226.

[53] *R* v *Jones* [2006] UKHL 16. See also remarks of US Court of Appeals in *Hamdan* v *US*, Judgment of 16 October 2012, No 11-1257.

[54] *Rasul* v *Bush* (2004) 542 US 466.

of his son from Chile without his consent was entitled to demand his return under the Convention. The Supreme Court had regard to the object and purpose of the Convention, the negotiating history, the views of the State Department and decisions of courts in other Contracting States in deciding that a *ne exeat* right amounted to a right of custody.[55]

US courts were authorized directly to determine questions of international law by the Alien Tort Statute 1789,[56] which confers original jurisdiction on federal district courts to determine 'any civil action by an alien for a tort only, committed in violation of the law of nations or a treaty of the United States'. After the rediscovery of this statute in the celebrated case of *Filartiga* v *Peña-Irala*,[57] where the plaintiff claimed damages for the torture of his son in Paraguay, the courts were invited in many cases to decide whether conduct which had taken place abroad violated modern rules of international law. The Supreme Court, however, in 2004, in the case of *Sosa* v *Alvarez-Machain*,[58] placed a narrow construction on the statute. They held that it was intended to be a jurisdictional statute covering causes of action where in 1789 the common law imposed personal liability—offences against ambassadors, violation of safe-conducts and piracy. New violations of international law were not entirely excluded, but the courts should be cautious in finding new private rights on the basis of the law of nations. In the case of *Kiobel* v *Royal Dutch Petroleum*[59] the Supreme Court held further that the statute was not intended to have extraterritorial application and could not be invoked by Nigerian nationals in regard to conduct abroad by the Nigerian subsidiary of a Dutch/British oil company. The majority said that the Alien Tort Statute was intended to avoid friction for the US in foreign relations and was not meant to make the USA a forum for litigating violations of international law in the territory of foreign sovereigns.

C. IS THE INTERNATIONAL RULE DIRECTLY APPLICABLE AND DIRECTLY EFFECTIVE?

International courts often have to determine whether an international rule—usually a treaty provision—is directly applicable, so that no further implementing action is required for it to be legally binding at national level. This question is often cast in terms of whether the treaty is 'self-executing'—an expression which may under national law depend solely on construction of the treaty or may also (particularly in the USA) turn on internal constitutional practice. A different question is whether the rule is directly effective—so that an individual may rely on it as a source of rights at national level. The distinction between direct applicability and direct effect has been clarified by the jurisprudence of the European Court of Justice. Contrary to what is sometimes suggested, the ECJ did not invent the doctrine of direct effect, which can be traced back to rulings of the Permanent Court of International Justice and to cases in European jurisdictions, but it did lay down criteria to be uniformly applied throughout the European Community. It is this uniformity which is one of the most striking features distinguishing European Community from public international law.

The cases of *Breard* v *Pruett, Breard* v *Greene* were almost identical to the *LaGrand* case described in Section II A of this chapter.[60] Breard was a national of Paraguay convicted of

---

[55] 130 S Ct 1983. See (2010) 59 ICLQ 1158; (2011) 105 *AJIL* 108.   [56] 28 USC §1350.

[57] *Filartiga* v *Peña-Irala*, 630 F.2d 876 (1980); 577 F.Supp 860.

[58] *Sosa* v *Alvarez-Machain* 124 S Ct 2739, 29 June 2004. For a full account and comment see Roth, 2004.

[59] US S Ct, 17 April 2013. See earlier discussion in (2012) 106 *AJIL* 509–71 and 862–5. For comprehensive analysis of the case and its implications see Wuerth, 2013b.

[60] See text at n 10 of this chapter.

murder by a Virginia court in the USA. A few days before he was to be executed, Paraguay brought proceedings before the International Court of Justice, on the ground that the authorities had failed to inform him of his rights to consular protection under Article 36 of the Vienna Convention on Consular Relations. The ICJ issued an interim order requesting that the USA should take all measures to suspend the execution pending its final decision.[61] On the day of the execution, the Supreme Court considered petitions seeking a stay. Among the issues was whether Article 36 of the Vienna Convention requiring notification to a person arrested of his rights to consular access and protection, was directly effective in a national court. On this, the Supreme Court held that:

> ...neither the text nor the history of the Vienna Convention clearly provides a foreign nation a private right of action in United States courts to set aside a criminal conviction and sentence for violation of consular notification provisions.[62]

The Supreme Court denied the petitions by a majority of six to three and Breard was executed in the face of the ICJ's order. The Supreme Court followed the *Breard* ruling in the case of *Sanchez-Llamas* v *Oregon*[63] notwithstanding the intervening decisions of the International Court of Justice casting doubt on the application of domestic procedural rules where Article 36 had been violated. Chief Justice Roberts denied that the interpretation of the International Court was binding on US courts, saying:

> If treaties are to be given effect as federal law under our legal system, determining their meaning as a matter of federal law 'is emphatically the province and duty of the judicial department' headed by the 'one supreme Court' established by the Constitution.

In *Medellin* v *Texas*, described in Section II A (n 14) of this chapter,[64] the Supreme Court held further that a judgment by the International Court of Justice in the *Avena* case[65] did not create directly enforceable domestic law. The conflict between entitlement under international law and US State law has continued and been confirmed by the case of *Leal Garcia* v *Texas*.[66]

A similar issue was raised in the case of *US* v *Alvarez-Machain* in 1992. Alvarez-Machain, a national of Mexico, was abducted in an operation for which the US Drug Enforcement Administration (DEA) was responsible. Charged with kidnap and murder of a DEA agent he argued that his forcible abduction constituted outrageous conduct in violation of customary international law and that US courts therefore lacked jurisdiction to try him. The Supreme Court, reversing by majority the decision of the Court of Appeals, accepted that the abduction, against which Mexico had protested, violated general international law principles. This violation did not, however, give the defendant a free-standing right to contest jurisdiction. Nor could the US–Mexico Extradition Treaty be read as including an implied term prohibiting abduction or prosecution when the defendant's presence was obtained by means outside the Treaty.[67]

In the following year a similar situation arose in the English case of *Bennett* v *Horseferry Road Magistrates' Court*. There the presence of the accused resulted from abduction by South African police in collusion with English police. The House of Lords by majority held

---

[61]   *Vienna Convention on Consular Relations (Paraguay v United States of America), Provisional Measures, Order of 9 April 1998, ICJ Reports 1998*, p 248.

[62]   134 F.3d 615 (1998); 118 ILR 23.   [63]   *Sanchez-Llamas* v *Oregon* (2006) 548 US 331.

[64]   *Medellin* v *Texas* (2008) 552 US 491.   [65]   See n 14 of this section.

[66]   131 S Ct 2966 (2011); Charnovitz, 2012.

[67]   *US* v *Alvarez-Machain* (1992) 504 US 655. For the sequel, see *Sosa* v *Alvarez-Machain*, in the previous section.

that the courts should decline as a matter of discretion to exercise criminal jurisdiction. Lord Bridge said:

> Where it is shown that the law enforcement agency responsible for bringing a prosecution has only been enabled to do so by participating in violations of international law and of the laws of another state in order to secure the presence of the accused within the territorial jurisdiction of the court, I think that respect for the rule of law demands that the court take cognisance of that circumstance.[68]

D. DOES A TREATY PREVAIL OVER INCONSISTENT NATIONAL LAW?

On the whole, national constitutions give clear directions to their courts on questions of priority, though they differ. For the UK and for its former dependencies which continued to follow its constitutional approach on becoming independent States within the Commonwealth, an unincorporated treaty cannot prevail over a conflicting statute, whether the statute is earlier or later in time. Under Article 55 of the French Constitution, by contrast, duly ratified and published treaties take precedence over national laws, whether earlier or later. The Constitutional Council in 1988 examined a complaint by candidates in elections to the National Assembly requesting annulment of elections in a particular constituency on the ground that the French Law of 11 July 1986 prescribing the procedure for elections violated Article 3 of the First Additional Protocol to the European Convention on Human Rights and Fundamental Freedoms, signed in 1950. This requires that elections should take place 'under conditions which will ensure the free expression of the opinion of the people in the choice of the legislature'. The Constitutional Council held, however, that taken as a whole, the 1986 Law was not inconsistent with Protocol No 1.

The Russian Constitution of 1993, as explained earlier, gives priority to customary international law and treaties over inconsistent Russian national laws. Article 17 of the Constitution further guarantees human rights in conformity with generally recognized principles of international law. In the *Case Concerning Certain Normative Acts of the City of Moscow and Some Other Regions*,[69] the Constitutional Court reviewed the legality of local acts reintroducing a residence permit requirement in the light of Article 17. The court held that they were inconsistent with the right to freedom of movement and choice of place of residence guaranteed under Article 12 of the International Covenant on Civil and Political Rights, by Protocol No 4 to the ECHR and by general principles of international law.

Under the US Constitution an act of Congress supersedes an earlier rule of international law if it is clear that this was the intention of the domestic law and the two cannot fairly be reconciled. Thus in the *Breard* case, described in Section V C of this chapter, the Supreme Court found that to the extent that Breard had a right to consular assistance on the basis of Article 36 of the Vienna Convention on Consular Relations, it had been superseded in 1996 by the express terms of the Antiterrorism and Effective Death Penalty Act, providing that a petitioner in federal courts alleging that he was held in violation of treaties of the USA would not, as a general rule, be afforded an evidentiary hearing on his claim if he had failed to develop the factual basis of his claim in State courts.[70]

---

[68] *Bennett v Horseferry Road Magistrates' Court* [1993] 3 All ER 138 at 155.

[69] VKS 1996 No 2, described in Danilenko, 1999, pp 57, 64.

[70] 118 ILR 23, at 33–4.

The courts of the US, like those of other States, will usually go to considerable effort to avoid conflict between national rules and international obligations. The approach of English courts was set out by Lord Denning in *Saloman* v *Commissioners of Customs and Excise*, where he said of a treaty which could not directly be relied on but which formed part of the background to the statutory provision in issue:

> I think we are entitled to look at it because it is an instrument which is binding in international law and we ought always to interpret our statutes so as to be in conformity with international law.[71]

The case of *Alcom* v *Republic of Colombia and others*[72] in 1984 raised the question whether execution of a judgment could take place against the ordinary bank account of a diplomatic mission. The question had not been expressly regulated by the UK State Immunity Act 1978. The House of Lords accepted, largely on the basis of a 1977 judgment of the German Constitutional Court in proceedings against the Philippine Republic that international law required such immunity from enforcement. Lord Diplock observed that the position in international law at the date of the State Immunity Act did not conclude the question of construction, and said:

> It makes it highly unlikely that parliament intended to require United Kingdom courts to act contrary to international law unless the clear language of the statute compels such a conclusion; but it does not do more than that.

A similar approach was taken in 1988 by the Southern District Court of New York in *US* v *The Palestine Liberation Organization and others*, which held that the US Anti-Terrorism Act 1988 did not supersede the 1946 Headquarters Agreement between the UN and the USA. The District Court emphasized that precedence of a later statute over a treaty occurred only where the two were irreconcilable and Congress had clearly shown an intent to override the treaty in domestic law, stating that:

> ...unless this power is clearly and unequivocally exercised, this court is under a duty to interpret statutes in a manner consonant with existing treaty obligations. This is a rule of statutory construction sustained by an unbroken line of authority for over a century and a half.[73]

E. CAN A TREATY PREVAIL OVER A NATIONAL CONSTITUTIONAL NORM?

There are many instances where a national constitutional court has reviewed the compatibility with the national constitution of a treaty before its ratification. The French and German Constitutions were each amended to ensure the compatibility of the Treaty on European Union signed at Maastricht with the national constitutional order. It may be argued that by the European Communities Act 1972 the UK also amended its constitution in order to accept features of the Community legal order—in particular direct applicability and direct effect—which were inconsistent with its own general approach to the implementation of international obligations.

---

[71] *Saloman* v *Commissioners of Customs and Excise* [1967] 2 QB 116. See also Lord Denning in *Corocraft Ltd and another* v *Pan American Airways Inc* [1969] 1 QB 616.
[72] *Alcom* v *Republic of Colombia and others* [1984] 2 All ER 6.
[73] *US* v *The Palestine Liberation Organization and others*, 695 F.Supp 1456 (1988); 82 ILR 282.

With the possible exception of the Netherlands Constitution, there appears on the other hand to be no example of a national legal order requiring the supremacy of international legal obligations over the national constitution. The transparent procedures used before the acceptance of ground-breaking treaties by most States have ensured that direct conflicts between national constitutions and treaties in force have been rare. In 1974, however, the German Federal Constitutional Court in the *Internationale Handelsgesellschaft* case[74] considered the possibility that European Community law might infringe the constitutional rights guaranteed under the German Constitution. The court said that so long as [solange] the Community did not have its own catalogue of fundamental rights, the German courts must reserve the right to examine the compatibility of Community law with the fundamental rights in the German Constitution. The judgment (known colloquially as the *Solange* judgment) appeared to challenge the doctrine of the supremacy of European Community law, and it gave rise to successive and prolonged attempts by the Commission of the European Communities, by Germany and some other member States to secure accession by the Community to the European Convention on Human Rights. It shows clearly that for German courts, their own constitution, as amended to provide for acceptance of specific treaties, is their supreme law. This approach has been confirmed by the *Görgülü* case described in Section IV B of this chapter.[75]

While European law may be compared with international law so far as national legal systems are concerned, in its implementation of its international obligations it is to be compared with national legal systems. The European Court of Justice in its judgment in the *Kadi* case,[76] considering the relationship between the international legal order and the Community legal order, in order to decide whether it could review the legality of Community measures implementing a Security Council resolution on sanctions, also began with its own basic constitutional charter, the European Community Treaty and fundamental rights as general principles of law guaranteed by the Court. They stressed that:

> ...the obligations imposed by an international agreement cannot have the effect of prejudicing the constitutional principles of the EC Treaty, which include the principle that all Community acts must respect fundamental rights, that respect constituting a condition of their lawfulness...

Review of a Community implementing instrument would, however, not entail any challenge to the primacy of the Security Council resolution in international law.

F. SHOULD THE EXECUTIVE DIRECT OR GUIDE THE NATIONAL COURT?

In most States this question is not dealt with in constitutional provisions, but is clear from practice. It cannot be expected that national judges will have up-to-date knowledge of international law, even where it forms part of their legal education. Except where there are practising lawyers with this expertise, or the possibility of international law teachers appearing as advocates, the main source of expert advice will be the lawyers working continuously for the government on international law questions. As explained earlier, national

---

[74] *Internationale Handelsgesellschaft* v *Einfur und Voratsstelle Getreide*, Case 11/70 [1970] ECR Reports 1125; [1974] 2 CMLR 540.

[75] N 26.

[76] *Kadi and Al Barakaat International Foundation* v *Council*, Joined Cases 402/05 and 415/05, Judgment of 3 September 2008, nyr, at paras 280–330. See comment on *Kadi* in Denza, 2013, pp 185–7.

courts generally seek to avoid conflicts with international obligations which would embarrass their governments. They accept that it is highly desirable that on questions of recognition, jurisdiction, and immunity the State should speak with one voice.

In a surprisingly large number of States—notwithstanding any principle of separation of powers—the executive will direct a national court on questions of international law—particularly on diplomatic and State immunity. In France, for example, the Conseil d'Etat would until recently normally seek guidance from the Ministry of Foreign Affairs on the construction of an international agreement, particularly if it saw a danger of embarrassment to the government. French courts may, however, decide that a reference is unnecessary because the treaty is clear (*acte clair*) and may dissent from the advice given (de la Rochère, 1987).[77] In the USA, although the courts have general powers to determine questions of international law, it is usual for the executive to give assistance in sensitive cases, either through *amicus curiae* briefs, interventions or 'executive suggestions'. In the legal battles over Concorde's access to Washington and New York, culminating in the case of *Air France and British Airways* v *Port Authority of New York and New Jersey* in the US District Court of New York and the US Court of Appeals, *amicus curiae* briefs from the USA government to the courts on its international obligations under the bilateral air services agreements with the UK and with France were crucial to the airlines' success and so to Concorde's entry into commercial service (Owen, 1997, Ch 10). In passing the Foreign Sovereign Immunities Act,[78] the US government sought to delegate to its courts determination of questions of State immunity which had often proved politically sensitive or embarrassing. But the State Department has made clear that residual common law State immunity remains in some areas and that in these areas it may still file *amicus curiae* briefs and will expect US courts to defer to its views.[79] In *Habyarimana* v *Kagame*[80] the US Court of Appeals, citing justifications in earlier cases, accepted as conclusive the determination of the executive that the Head of State of Rwanda was immune from suit even for acts committed prior to assuming office.

In the UK, the executive are constrained by the independence of the courts from offering direction on questions of law. On questions of fact peculiarly within the knowledge of the government it has, however, long been practice to provide certificates on request, and statutes such as the Diplomatic Privileges Act 1964[81] and the State Immunity Act 1978,[82] expressly provide for such certificates to be given 'by or under the authority of the Secretary of State' and for their conclusive effect. In cases of importance for the government, the Attorney-General may nominate counsel to act as *amicus curiae*, although the *amicus* will act in a more independent role than under US procedure. Nominations were made in the case of *Alcom* v *Colombia* described in Section V D of this chapter and in the *Pinochet* case.[83]

Although international law does not generally prescribe what guidance the executive should give a domestic court, some assistance may be derived from the Advisory Opinion of the International Court of Justice in the *Cumaraswamy* case.[84]

---

[77] See *Gisti* case, Conseil d'Etat, 29 June 1990, 111 ILR 499; *Agyepong* case, Conseil d'Etat, 2 December 1994, 111 ILR 531. In the case of *Beaumartin* v *France*, Judgment of 24 November 1994, Ser A, no 296-B; 19 *EHRR* 485 the European Court of Human Rights held that the practice was incompatible with the right, under Article 6 of the ECHR, of access to 'an independent and impartial tribunal established by law'.

[78] 28 USC § 1603.   [79] See US *amicus* brief in *Matar* v *Dichter*, No. 07–2579-cv, 19 December 2007.

[80] 821 F. Supp 2d 1244.   [81] C 81, s 4. For examples, and for US practice see Denza, 2008, pp 308–11.

[82] Section 21.

[83] *R* v *Bow Street Metropolitan Stipendiary, ex parte Pinochet Ugarte (No 1)* [1999] UKHL 52; [1998] 3 WLR 1456. On the contrasting approaches of US and UK courts, see Collins, 2002.

[84] *Difference Relating to Immunity from Legal Process of a Special Rapporteur of the Commission on Human Rights, Advisory Opinion, ICJ Reports 1999*, p 62, paras 60–2 and in Separate Opinion of Judge Oda.

G. SHOULD A NATIONAL COURT APPLY A FOREIGN LAW WHICH CONFLICTS WITH INTERNATIONAL LAW?

The six questions described in preceding Sections A-F raise questions about the application of international law within each national legal order and, generally speaking, answers are provided for national courts by national constitutional law and practice. Two other questions often arise for which no direct answers are given in national constitutions. The first concerns the effect of a foreign law or executive action which is alleged to contravene international law. To answer this question the national court is required not merely to ascertain the content of international law but to decide whether it has been violated by the act of another State and, if so, what will be the effect of that illegal act within its own legal order.

The doctrine of judicial restraint in scrutiny of the acts of another sovereign has been most extensively developed by the courts of the USA. The classic statement of the rule, in 1897, was in *Underhill* v *Hernandez*, where the Supreme Court said:

> every sovereign state is bound to respect the independence of every other sovereign state, and the courts of one country will not sit in judgment on the acts of the government of another, done within its own territory.[85]

The rule has often been applied in the context of acts of expropriation alleged to violate international law, and US courts have adopted a flexible approach designed not to hinder the executive and legislative branches in their conduct of foreign policy. The 'act of State' doctrine was re-examined by the Federal Court of Appeals in 1983 in the context of claims of corruption and anti-competitive practices in the context of an award of a concession to exploit offshore oil. In the case of *Clayco Petroleum Corporation* v *Occidental Petroleum Corporation and others* the court confirmed the applicability of the doctrine. The grant of a concession to exploit natural resources was inherently a sovereign act which no private person could perform, and 'the purpose of the doctrine is to prevent the judiciary from interfering with the political branch's conduct of foreign policy'.[86] By contrast, the US Court of Appeals refused to apply the doctrine in the case of *Republic of the Philippines* v *Marcos and others*, where the successor government of the Philippines sought to prevent further misappropriation of real properties in New York illegally acquired by Marcos when he was President. The court emphasized that any misappropriation had been a purely private act, that Marcos was no longer President of the Philippines, and that the present government of the Philippines actively sought the assistance of the US courts. This action by the new government was not expropriation:

> The complaint seeks recovery of property illegally taken by a former head of state, not confiscation of property legally owned by him.[87]

The House of Lords re-examined the scope of the rule in the case of *Kuwait Airways Corporation* v *Iraqi Airways*.[88] The case resulted from the taking by Iraqi forces during their invasion of ten commercial aircraft belonging to Kuwait Airways Corporation (KAC) and their transfer, by decree of the Revolutionary Command Council, to the State-owned

---

[85] *Underhill* v *Hernandez* 168 US 250, 18 S Ct 83n (1897).

[86] *Clayco Petroleum Corporation* v *Occidental Petroleum Corporation and others* 712 F.2d 404 (1983); 81 ILR 522.

[87] *Republic of the Philippines* v *Marcos and others* 806 F.2d 344 (1986); 81 ILR 581.

[88] *Kuwait Airways Corporation* v *Iraqi Airways Co (No 2)* [2002] UKHL 19; [2002] 3 All ER 209. See Note in (2002) 73 *BYIL* 400. The reasoning was criticized by Carruthers and Crawford, 2003.

Iraqi Airways Company. Some of the aircraft were later destroyed by coalition bombing during the conflict to liberate Kuwait and others were flown to and sheltered by Iran. KAC claimed the return of the aircraft or payment of their value, and damages. To determine liability under English law for the events of 1990 and 1991 it was necessary to apply the law of Iraq and thus to determine the validity of the decree of the Revolutionary Command Council. It was clear that the invasion of Kuwait and the seizure of its assets violated fundamental rules of international law including binding Security Council Resolutions. Lord Nicholls went on to say, at paragraph 29:

> Such a fundamental breach of international law can properly cause the courts of this country to say that, like the confiscatory decree of the Nazi government of Germany in 1941, a law depriving those whose property has been plundered of the ownership of their property in favour of the aggressor's own citizens will not be enforced or recognized in proceedings in this country. Enforcement or recognition of this law would be manifestly contrary to the public policy of English law. For good measure, enforcement or recognition would also be contrary to this country's obligations under the UN Charter. Further, it would sit uneasily with the almost universal condemnation of Iraq's behaviour and with the military action, in which this country participated, taken against Iraq to compel its withdrawal from Kuwait. International law, for its part, recognizes that a national court may properly decline to give effect to legislative and other acts of foreign states which are in violation of international law...

Although the US and English cases on this form of 'act of State' have developed on parallel tracks, a comparison shows that the US cases are based more closely on deference to the views of the executive, so that the State may speak with a single voice, while the English courts are seeking rather to apply international law themselves.

H. ARE THERE QUESTIONS OF INTERNATIONAL LAW WHICH NATIONAL COURTS SHOULD DECLINE TO ANSWER?

Generally speaking, where questions of international law arise before national courts, they are either (as with immunity) an essential preliminary to assumption of jurisdiction over the claim or criminal charge, or they are incidental to the construction of a national statute or a claim brought under national law. The court, with whatever assistance it can secure from counsel or from its ministry of foreign affairs, must do the best it can. Sometimes, however, where a question of international law is central to the claim, English and US courts have held that they are in effect not competent to answer it. The classic statement of this principle of 'judicial restraint' was the judgment of Lord Wilberforce in the House of Lords in the case of *Buttes Gas and Oil Co* v *Hammer*.[89] On its face the claim was one of defamation and the defence was justification. But the underlying dispute was over the extent of the territorial waters of Sharjah in the Persian Gulf and the right to exploit natural resources below these waters, and could not be decided without investigation of the conduct of Umm al Qaiwain, Iran, and the UK as well as Sharjah. Lord Wilberforce, with the support of his judicial colleagues, found that for an English court there were no judicial standards to judge the issues of international law and that:

> ...the court would be in a judicial no-man's land; the court would be asked to review transactions in which four sovereign states were involved, which they had brought to a precarious

---

[89] *Buttes Gas and Oil Co* v *Hammer* [1982] AC 888; 64 ILR 273 and 331.

settlement, after diplomacy and the use of force, and to say that at least part of these were 'unlawful' under international law.

The principle of judicial restraint was considered in the successive *Pinochet* cases before the House of Lords. In the first case Lord Slynn and Lord Lloyd—both of whom held that General Pinochet was immune as a former Head of State—also maintained that the rule was applicable. Lord Lloyd said assumption of jurisdiction would imperil relations between governments and that:

> ...we would be entering a field in which we are simply not competent to adjudicate. We apply customary international law as part of the common law, and we give effect to our international obligations so far as they are incorporated in our statute law; but we are not an international court.[90]

Lord Nicholls and Lord Steyn held, however, that the doctrine did not apply. Lord Steyn maintained that the charges against General Pinochet were already in 1973 condemned as high crimes by customary international law and that it would be wrong for English courts to extend the doctrine of judicial restraint in a way which ran counter to customary international law at the relevant time. In the third *Pinochet* case before the House of Lords[91] judicial restraint was given short shrift.

The English High Court also gave a narrow interpretation to non-justiciability in 2005 in *The Republic of Ecuador* v *Occidental Exploration and Production Company*.[92] Aikens J described the doctrine as establishing 'a general principle that the municipal courts of England and Wales do not have the competence to adjudicate upon rights arising out of transactions entered into independent sovereign States between themselves on the plane of international law.' He held that it did not apply to prevent the court from determining a challenge by Ecuador under the UK Arbitration Act 1996 to an Award made pursuant to a Bilateral Investment Treaty between the USA and Ecuador. The Court of Appeal agreed with his analysis.

In *Mbasogo (President of the State of Equatorial Guinea)* v *Logo*,[93] the English Court of Appeal dismissed a claim for damages arising from an attempted private coup, holding that it was non-justiciable since it involved the exercise or assertion of a sovereign right. English courts had no jurisdiction to enforce the public law of a foreign State. The English Administrative Court also declined to review the UK government's decision to ratify the Treaty of Lisbon without a referendum in the case of *R (Wheeler)* v *Office of the Prime Minister*, denying the existence of an implied promise giving rise to a legitimate expectation. The Court held that 'The subject-matter, nature and context of a promise of this kind took place in the realm of politics, not of the courts, and the question whether the government should be held to such a promise is a political rather than a legal matter.'[94]

The *Buttes* case was highly unusual and the doctrine of judicial restraint has been strongly criticized by Rosalyn Higgins (Higgins, 1991, pp 273–4). But the approach is parallel to the

---

[90] *R* v *Bow Street Metropolitan Stipendiary, ex parte Pinochet Ugarte (No 1)* [1998] UKHL 41; [2000] AC 61; [1998] 4 All ER 897; [1998] 3 WLR 1456 at 1495.

[91] *R* v *Bow Street Metropolitan Stipendiary, ex parte Pinochet Ugarte (Amnesty International Intervening) (No 3)* [1999] UKHL 17; [2000] 1 AC 147; [1991] 2 All ER 97; [1999] 2 WLR 827; 119 ILR 135. See, on the question of act of State, Denza, 1999. See also *Campaign for Nuclear Disarmament* v *The Prime Minister* [2002] EWHC 2759 (QB) and Note in (2002) 73 *BYIL* 444.

[92] *The Republic of Ecuador* v *Occidental Exploration and Production Company* [2005] EWHC 774 (Comm). See also the judgment of the Court of Appeal at [2007] EWCA Civ 456.

[93] *Mbasogo (President of the State of Equatorial Guinea)* v *Logo* [2006] EWCA Civ 1370, [2007] QB 846.

[94] [2008] UKHL 20. See also McGoldrick, 2010.

restraint shown by the Permanent Court of International Justice in the extract from *The Serbian Loans* and *Brazilian Loans* cases cited at the outset of this chapter. It may also be seen as similar to the rule of *forum non conveniens* in private international law whereby courts defer to domestic courts of another State. A solution for some cases would be for the International Court of Justice to be given an advisory jurisdiction to determine questions of international law referred to it by national courts and thus to ensure the uniform development and application of the law.

VI. CONCLUSION: ELEMENTS OF A HAPPY RELATIONSHIP

Several of the constitutional provisions described in this chapter have been revised in recent years in order more effectively to integrate international law into the national legal order. There is continuous cross-fertilization in attempts to remedy perceived weaknesses. The extent to which this now happens in the superior courts in the UK has been vividly described by Lord Bingham, who summed up as follows:

> If we believe, as we probably do, that peace and good order in the world depend to a large extent on the observance of legal rules, on the international as on the national place, the contribution made by national courts, not least our own, is one of which we.....may be proud.[95]

But on the other hand there have been signs in a few States—Germany, Russia, the USA, and the UK are mentioned in this chapter—of renewed emphasis on the supremacy of national constitutions and of popular suspicion of adverse judgments from international courts.

It is unrealistic to suggest that any fundamental harmonization of national constitutional provisions is practicable. So long as national constitutions reflect the history and identity of independent States, and so long as international law itself remains in general non-intrusive as to how it is applied and enforced at national level, there will be infinite variety in national systems.

It is difficult even to suggest criteria on which a 'scoreboard' of impressive and failing performers could be drawn up. If, for example, the criterion is the production of judgments on general questions of international law which carry weight in other jurisdictions, one would rate Germany at the highest level. The laconic judgments of French courts, however correct, lack wider appeal because there is little evidence of the legal reasoning behind them. Judgments of the UK House of Lords and the US Supreme Court probably carry less weight abroad because the courts have so often been openly divided on fundamental questions—*Breard, Alvarez-Machain, Pinochet*, to name only three discussed in this chapter.[96] Receptiveness to decisions in other States could be a criterion—in most jurisdictions there is increasing readiness to take into account cases from other jurisdictions, even though primary reliance on national precedents has led to some divergence of international law into separate streams.[97] Adverse judgments from international tribunals might be another criterion—and for the UK this was undoubtedly a factor in changing its system of enforcing the European Convention on Human Rights in its domestic legal order. But an objective assessment on this basis would need to take in readiness to

---

[95] Bingham, 2010, p 54.   [96] On *Pinochet's* influence, see Wuerth, 2013a.
[97] See Roberts, 2011.

accept exposure to international assessment. The UK accepted the right of individual petition under the Convention at an early stage and is now the only Permanent Member of
the Security Council to accept the compulsory jurisdiction of the International Court of
Justice.

In the absence of any identification of the ideal relationship between international law
and national law, or the best of the alternatives, five factors will be proposed as generally
conducive to the avoidance of conflict. They are:

(1) close involvement in the treaty-making process of lawyers with knowledge both of
     their own legal systems and of international law—in particular the fundamental
     norms of each;

(2) close attention to questions of national implementation during the treaty-making
     process and before ratification;

(3) detailed parliamentary scrutiny of important treaties before national ratification;

(4) teaching of international law as a compulsory element of a law degree and of pro-
     fessional training; and

(5) involvement of specialist international lawyers as counsel and as *amici curiae*
     whenever difficult questions of international law arise in national courts.

Some of these suggestions go to 'the reality of legal culture' (Higgins, 1991, pp 266–8). All
of them call for openness to international law, including its imperfections, its uncertainties and its rapid shifts. The motto for national law-makers and judges might well be 'only
connect'.

REFERENCES

Aust, A (2013), *Modern Treaty Law and Practice*, 3rd edn (Cambridge: Cambridge University Press).

Barrett, J (2011), 'The United Kingdom and Parliamentary Scrutiny of Treaties: Recent Reforms', 60 *ICLQ* 225.

Bell, J (2005), 'French Constitutional Council and European Law', 54 *ICLQ* 735.

Bingham, T (2010), *Widening Horizons: The Influence of Comparative Law and International Law on Domestic Law* (Hamlyn Lectures, Cambridge: Cambridge University Press).

Butler, W (1997), *The Russian Law of Treaties* (London: Simmonds and Hill).

Carruthers, JM and Crawford, EB (2003), 'Kuwait Airways Corporation *v* Iraqi Airways Company', 52 *ICLQ* 761.

Charnowitz, S (2012), 'Correcting America's Continuing Failure to Comply with the Avena Judgment', 106 *AJIL* 572.

Collier, J (1989), 'Is International Law Really Part of the Law of England?', 38 *ICLQ* 924.

Collins, L (2002), 'Foreign Relations and the Judiciary', 51 *ICLQ* 485.

Craig, P and De Búrca, G (2007), *EU Law: Text, Cases and Materials*, 3rd edn (Oxford: Oxford University Press).

Danilenko, G (1994), 'The New Russian Constitution and International Law', 88 *AJIL* 451.

—— (1999), 'Implementation of International Law in CIS States: Theory and Practice', 10 *EJIL* 51.

De La Rochere, D (1987), in Jacobs and Roberts (eds), p 39.

Denza, E (2008), *Diplomatic Law*, 3rd edn (Oxford: Oxford University Press).

—— (1999), 'Ex parte Pinochet: Lacuna or Leap?', 48 *ICLQ* 687.

—— (2012), 'International Aviation and the EU Carbon Trading Scheme: Comment on the *Air Transport Association of America Case*', 37 *European Law Review* 314.

—— (2013), 'Placing the European Union in International Perspective', in Adams, Meeusen, Straetmans and de Waele (eds), *Judging Europe's Judges: The Legitimacy of the Case Law of the European Court of Justice Examined* (Oxford, Hart).

EISEMANN, P-M and KESSEDIJAN, C (1995), in Leigh and Blakeslee (eds), p 1.

ERRERA, R (2008), 'Domestic Courts and International Law, the Law and Practice in France', paper given to Colloquium on International Law in Domestic Courts, organized by Amsterdam Center for International Law.

FAVOREU, L (1985), XXXI *Annuaire Français de Droit International* 868.

FELLMETH, A (2012), 'U.S. State Legislation to Limit Use of International and Foreign Law', 106 *AJIL* 107.

HIGGINS, R (1991–V), 'International Law and the Avoidance, Containment and Resolution of Disputes', *Recueil des Cours* 273–4.

JACKSON, J (1987), in Jacobs and Roberts (eds), p 141.

JACOBS, F and ROBERTS, S (eds) (1987), *The Effect of Treaties in Domestic Law* (London: Sweet & Maxwell).

KELSEN, H (1920), *Das Problem der Souveränitat und die Theorie des Völkerrechts-Beitrag zu einer reinen Rechtslehre* (Tübingen: JC Mohr).

LEIGH, M and BLAKESLEE, MR (eds) (1995), *National Treaty Law and Practice*, vol 1, (Washington, DC: ASIL).

——, ——, and EDERINGTON, LB (eds) (1999), *National Treaty Law and Practice*, vol 2 (Washington, DC: ASIL).

McGoldrick, D (2010), 'The Boundaries of Justiciability', 59 *ICLQ* 981.

MENNECKE, M and TAMS, C (2002), 'The LaGrand Case', 51 *ICLQ* 449.

NEFF, S (2002), 'International Law and Nuclear Weapons in Scottish Courts', 51 *ICLQ* 171.

NIJMAN, J and NOLLKAEMPER, A (eds) (2007), *New Perspectives on the Divide Between National and International Law* (Oxford: Oxford University Press).

OWEN, K (1997), *Concorde and the Americans* (Shrewsbury: Airlife Publishing).

PAULUS, A (2007), 'The Emergence of the International Community and the Divide Between International and Domestic Law', in Nijman and Nollkaemper (eds), p 216.

PETERS, A (2007), 'The Globalization of State Constitutions', in Nijman and Nollkaemper (eds), p 251.

PETROV, R. and KALINCHENKO, P. (2011), 'The Europeanization of Third Country Judiciaries through the Application of the EU Acquis: the Cases of Russia and Ukraine', 60 *ICLQ* 325.

RIESENFELD, S and ABBOTT, F (eds) (1994), *Parliamentary Participation in the Making and Operation of Treaties* (The Hague: Nijhoff/Kluwer).

ROBERTS, A (2011), 'Comparative International Law? The Role of National Courts in International Law', 60 *ICLQ* 57.

ROTH, B (2004), 'Note on *Sosa* v *Alvarez-Machain*', 98 *AJIL* 798.

SCHERMERS, H (1987), in Jacobs and Roberts (eds), p 109.

SCHWARZE, J (1994), 'La ratification du traité de Maastricht en Allemagne, l'arrêt de la Cour constitutionnelle de Karlsruhe', 1994 *Revue du Marché Commun* 293.

—— (1995), 'Towards a Common European Public Law', 1995 *European Public Law* 227.

—— (ed) (2001), *The Birth of a European Constitutional Order* (Baden-Baden: Nomos).

SHELTON, D (2004), 'Note on *Avena and Other Mexican Nationals*', 98 *AJIL* 559.

—— (2011) *International Law and Domestic Legal Systems*, Oxford, New York, Oxford University Press.

SLAUGHTER, A-M and BURKE-WHITE, W, (2007), 'The Future of International Law is Domestic (or, The European Way of Law)' in Nijman and Nollkaemper (eds), p 110.

SLOSS, D (ed.) (2009), *The Role of Domestic Courts in Treaty Enforcement: A Comparative Study* (Cambridge, New York, Cambridge University Press).

TREVIRANUS, H and BEEMELMANS, H (1995), in Leigh and Blakeslee (eds), p 5.

ULFSTEIN, G (ed, in collaboration with Marauhn, T and Zimmermann, A) (2007), *Making Treaties Work* (Cambridge: Cambridge University Press)

VAN DIJK, P and TAHZIB, BG (1974), in Riesenfeld and Abbott (eds), p 109.

VAN PANHUYS, JHF (1953), 'The Netherlands Constitution and International Law', 47 *AJIL* 537.

WUERTH, I (2013a), '*Pinochet*'s Legacy Reassessed', 106 *AJIL* 731.

—— (2013b), *Kiobel* v. *Royal Dutch Petroleum Co*: The Supreme Court and the Alien Tort Statute', 107 *AJIL* 601.

ZIMNENKO, BL (2007), *International Law and the Russian Legal System*, Butler, WE (ed and trans) (Utrecht, Eleven International Publishing).

FURTHER READING

AUST, A (2007), *Modern Treaty Law and Practice*, 2nd edn (Cambridge, Cambridge University Press), Ch 10, 'Treaties and Domestic Law'. A clear introduction.

CASSESE, A (2005), *International Law*, 2nd edn (Oxford: Oxford University Press), Ch 12, 'The Implementation of International Rules within National Systems'. An up-to-date, thorough account of theory and practice in a large number of States.

GARDINER, RK (2003), *International Law* (Harlow: Longman), Ch 4, 'International Law and National Laws'. This focuses particularly on approaches to treaty interpretation.

LEIGH, M, BLAKESLEE, MP, and EDERINGTON, LB (eds) (1999), *National Treaty Law and Practice* (Washington, DC: ASIL). The most extensive comparative survey.

NIJMAN, J and NOLLKAEMPER, A (eds) (2007), *New Perspectives on the Divide Between National and International Law* (Oxford: Oxford University Press). A wide variety of critical analyses of theories.

RIESENFELD, S and ABBOTT, F (eds) (1994), *Parliamentary Participation in the Making and Operation of Treaties* (The Hague: Nijhoff/Kluwer).

SHELTON, D (ed) (2011), *International Law and Domestic Legal Systems* (Oxford, New York: Oxford University Press). A wide-ranging survey of constitutional provisions and practice.

PART V

RESPONSIBILITY

15

THE CHARACTER AND FORMS OF INTERNATIONAL RESPONSIBILITY

James Crawford and Simon Olleson

SUMMARY

On the international plane, responsibility is the necessary corollary of obligation: every breach by a subject of international law of its international obligations entails its international responsibility. This chapter starts by giving an overview of different forms of responsibility/liability in international law before examining the general character of State responsibility. Due to the historical primacy of States in the international legal system, the law of State responsibility is the most fully-developed branch of responsibility and is the principal focus of the chapter. In contrast, although the International Law Commission, broadly following the scheme of the 2001 Articles on State Responsibility, adopted Articles on Responsibility of International Organizations in 2011, the responsibility of international organizations remains an under-developed area; it is considered only briefly, as is the potential responsibility under international law of other international actors.

The law of State responsibility deals with three general questions: (1) has there been a breach by a State of an international obligation; (2) what are the consequences of the breach in terms of cessation and reparation; (3) who may seek reparation or otherwise respond to the breach as such, and in what ways? As to the first question, this chapter discusses the constituent elements of attribution and breach, as well as the possible justifications or excuses which may preclude responsibility. The second question concerns the various secondary obligations which arise upon the commission of an internationally wrongful act by a State, and in particular the forms of reparation. The third question concerns issues of invocation of responsibility, including the taking of countermeasures.

I. THE SCOPE OF INTERNATIONAL RESPONSIBILITY: INTRODUCTION AND OVERVIEW

Article 1 of the Articles on Responsibility of States for Internationally Wrongful Acts ('ARSIWA' or 'the Articles on State Responsibility'), adopted by the International Law

Commission in 2001,[1] provides: 'Every internationally wrongful act of a State entails the international responsibility of that State'.[2] Due to the historical development of international law, its primary subjects are States. It is on States that most obligations rest and on whom the burden of compliance principally falls. For example, human rights conventions, though they confer rights upon individuals, impose obligations upon States. If other legal persons have obligations in the field of human rights, it is only by derivation or analogy from the human rights obligations accepted by States (see Alston, 2005; Clapham, 2006; McCorquodale, Ch 10 in this book). State responsibility is the paradigm form of responsibility on the international plane.

But there can be international legal persons other than States, as the International Court of Justice (ICJ) held in *Reparation for Injuries*.[3] Being a subject of any legal system involves having responsibilities as well as rights. Thus it would seem unproblematic to substitute the words 'international organization' or 'international legal person' for 'State' in Article 1 of the Articles on State Responsibility; that basic statement of principle would seem equally applicable by definition to all international legal persons.

In relation to international organizations, at least, a corollary of their undoubted capacity to enter into treaties with States or with other international organizations is that they are responsible for breaches of the obligations undertaken; this follows from the principle *pacta sunt servanda*.[4] The same is true for breaches of applicable general international law.

The potential responsibility of international organizations under general international law was affirmed by the International Court in the *Cumaraswamy* Advisory Opinion.[5] But there are serious difficulties of implementation, since the jurisdiction of international courts and tribunals has been developed largely by reference to States and not international organizations.[6]

Between 2002 and 2011, the ILC attempted to pull together the relatively sparse international practice in relation to the responsibility of international organizations. In doing so, it to a large extent based itself upon the model of the Articles on State Responsibility; the Articles on Responsibility of International Organizations ('ARIO'), adopted by the ILC

---

[1] Articles on the Responsibility of States for Internationally Wrongful Acts, adopted by the ILC on 10 August 2001: Report of the International Law Commission, Fifty-third Session, A/56/10, Chapter IV. The General Assembly took note of the Articles, recommended them to the attention of governments, and annexed them to GA Res 56/83 (10 December 2001). For subsequent consideration, see Crawford, 2013, pp 42–4 and GA Res 68/104 (16 December 2013). The Articles and the Commentaries are reproduced in Crawford, 2002 (the Articles at pp 61–73) and the Articles alone in Evans, 2013, pp 524–31.

[2] See the often quoted dictum of the Permanent Court of International Justice in *Factory at Chorzów, Jurisdiction, Judgment No 8, 1927, PCIJ, Ser A, No 9* at p 21: 'It is a principle of international law that the breach of an engagement involves an obligation to make reparation'.

[3] *Reparation for Injuries Suffered in the Service of the United Nations, Advisory Opinion, ICJ Reports 1949,* p 174 at p 179.

[4] See Vienna Convention on the Law of Treaties between States and International Organizations or Between International Organizations (1986), Article 26; cf Morgenstern, 1986, pp 13–16, 32–6, 115.

[5] *Difference Relating to Immunity from Legal Process of a Special Rapporteur of the Commission on Human Rights, Advisory Opinion, ICJ Reports 1999*, p 62, para 66.

[6] Thus special provision has had to be made for the EU, which is not a State, so that it could be a party to contentious proceedings under the 1982 UN Convention on the Law of the Sea (see Article 305 and Annex IX) and under the WTO dispute settlement mechanism. See generally Wellens, 2002; Klabbers, 2009. Similarly, Article 17 of Protocol 14 to the European Convention of Human Rights (2004) provided for the amendment of Article 59 of the Convention so as to permit the EU to become a party by accession. A draft accession agreement was finalized on 5 April 2013; prior to signature, the draft text is to be submitted to the Court of Justice of the European Union for its opinion.

in 2011,[7] adopt and adapt many of the formulations of the Articles on State Responsibility. But there are also some major differences, reflecting the differences in structure and function as between States and international organizations.[8]

The position so far as the international responsibility of individuals, corporations, non-governmental organizations, and other groups are concerned is far less clear. Despite the fact that international law may confer rights directly upon individuals, even outside the field of international human rights law,[9] it is doubtful whether they are in any meaningful sense 'subjects' of international law and so far no general regime of responsibility has developed to cover them.

The international responsibility of individuals has only developed in the criminal field, and then only in comparatively recent times. True, piracy has been recognized as a 'crime against the law of nations' for centuries. But it is better to see this as a jurisdictional rule allowing States to exercise criminal jurisdiction for pirate attacks on ships at sea rather than a rule conferring 'legal personality' on pirates.[10] One does not acquire international legal personality by being hanged at the yardarm.

Since the Second World War, by contrast, real forms of individual criminal responsibility under international law have developed. First steps were taken with the establishment of the Nuremberg and Tokyo war crimes tribunals and the conclusion of the Genocide Convention in the immediate post-war period; after the end of the Cold War there followed, in rapid succession, the creation by Security Council resolution of the International Criminal Tribunal for Yugoslavia (ICTY) (1992) and the International Criminal Tribunal for Rwanda (ICTR) (1994), and the adoption of the Rome Statute of the International Criminal Court (ICC) (1998), which entered into force on 1 July 2002. Further, various 'mixed' or 'hybrid' international criminal tribunals have been set up for, *inter alia*, Bosnia-Herzegovina (2004–), East Timor (2000–2006), Sierra Leone (2002–2013), Cambodia (2003–), and Lebanon (2007–).

By contrast, so far there has been no development of corporate criminal responsibility in international law. Under the two ad hoc Statutes and the Rome Statute only individual persons may be accused. The Security Council often addresses recommendations or demands to opposition, insurgent, or rebel groups—but without implying that these have separate personality in international law. Any international responsibility of members of

---

[7] Articles on Responsibility of International Organizations ('ARIO'), Report of the International Law Commission, Sixty-third Session, A/66/10 (2011), Chapter V. The ARIO are reproduced in Evans, 2013, pp 558–569.

[8] In addition, Part Five ARIO (Articles 58–63) deals with the question of State responsibility in connection with the act of an international organization. It attempts to frame rules dealing with questions, paralleling those in Part One, Chapter IV of the Articles on State Responsibility, as regards aid or assistance, direction and control, and coercion by a State in relation to the internationally wrongful act of an international organization (Articles 58–60). In addition, it contains rules applicable to the situation in which a member State seeks to avoid compliance with its own international obligations by procuring an act of the international organization to do what it itself is unable to do (Article 61), and a provision in relation to the acceptance of responsibility by a State for the internationally wrongful act of an international organization (Article 62). Article 63 is a saving clause, which makes clear that the preceding provisions of Part Five are 'without prejudice to the international responsibility of the international organization which commits the act in question, or of any State or other international organization'. These provisions undoubtedly constitute progressive development, rather than codification.

[9] *Jurisdiction of the Courts of Danzig, Advisory Opinion, 1928, PCIJ, Ser B, No 15* at pp 17–21; *LaGrand (Germany v United States of America), Merits, Judgment, ICJ Reports 2001*, p 466, para 77; *Avena and Other Mexican Nationals (Mexico v United States of America), Judgment, ICJ Reports 2004*, p 12, para 40.

[10] See the Separate Opinion of Judge Moore in *The 'Lotus', Judgment No 9, 1927, PCIJ, Ser A, No 10* at p 70; United Nations Convention on the Law of the Sea 1982, Arts 101–107; Rubin, 1998; *Oppenheim's International Law*, 1992, vol 1, pp 746–55.

such groups is probably limited to breaches of applicable international humanitarian law or even of national law, rather than general international law. If rebel groups succeed in becoming the government of the State (whether of the State against which they are fighting, or of a new State which they succeed in creating), that State may be responsible for their acts (ARSIWA, Article 10; Commentary, Crawford, 2002, pp 116–20). But if they fail, the State against which they rebelled is in principle not responsible, and any possibility of collective responsibility for their acts fails with them.

It is also very doubtful whether 'multinational corporations' are subjects of international law for the purposes of responsibility, although steps are being taken to develop voluntary adherence to human rights and other norms by corporations.[11] From a legal point of view, so-called multinational corporations are better regarded as groups of corporations, each created under and amenable to the national law of their place of incorporation as well as to any other national legal system within which they operate.

Thus although Article 58 of the ILC's Articles on State Responsibility reserves in general terms the possibility of 'individual responsibility under international law of any person acting on behalf of a State',[12] a reservation which is not limited to criminal responsibility, so far there has been virtually no development in practice of civil responsibility of individuals or corporations for breaches of international law. Only the USA has legislation dealing (in a very uneven way) with this issue; in recent years the scope of application of that legislation has been severely curtailed.[13] As the dissenting judges in the *Arrest Warrant*

---

[11] See, eg the *ILO Tripartite Declaration of Principles Concerning Multinational Enterprises and Social Policy 1977* (adopted by the Governing Body at its 204th Session), 17 ILM 416; the OECD's '*Guidelines for Multinational Enterprises*' (2000), 40 ILM 237; the 'Nine Principles' of the UN Global Compact Initiative (2000) (relating to human rights, labour standards, and the environment), and see most recently, the work of John Ruggie (the Special Representative of the Secretary General on Business and Human Rights), including in particular the *Guiding Principles on Business and Human Rights: Implementing the United Nations "Protect, Respect and Remedy" Framework* (2011) A/HRC/17/31, Annex, endorsed by the Human Rights Council by HRC Res 17/4 (16 June 2011). Generally, see De Schutter, 2006. On the problems of establishing international responsibility of corporations, see Ratner, 2001.

[12] See likewise ARIO, Art 66.

[13] Private parties (US or foreign) can in principle be sued for torts occasioned 'in violation of the law of nations' committed against aliens, under the unusual jurisdiction created by the Alien Tort Claims Act (28 USC §1350). The US cases have distinguished between corporate complicity with governmental violations of human rights, and those violations (eg genocide, slavery) which do not require any governmental involvement or State action. See, eg *Kadić* v *Karadžić* 70 F.3d 232 (1995) (2nd Cir 1995); 104 ILR 135. The existence of jurisdiction under ATCA to hear claims of breach of fundamental human rights norms survived scrutiny by the Supreme Court in *Sosa* v *Alvarez-Machain* 124 S Ct 2739; 542 US 692 (2004), although its scope was somewhat reduced. Its scope of application was severely limited in *Kiobel* v *Royal Dutch Petroleum Company* 133 S Ct 1659; 569 US (2013), which held that, in light of the presumption against extraterritorial application of statutes, ATCA does not provide a cause of action in relation to conduct in breach of international law occurring outside the USA, at least where both parties are not US nationals. The Supreme Court did not in the end decide in *Kiobel* the question (for which certiorari was originally granted) whether, in any event, corporations can be liable under ATCA, and there remains a split in the decisions on that issue in the lower courts.

The Torture Victims Protection Act 1991 (PL 102–256, 106 *Stat* 73) creates a cause of action against individuals in relation to torture or extrajudicial killing 'under actual or apparent authority, or color of law, of any foreign nation'; after a divergence of views among the Courts of Appeals, the question whether the TVPA can be applied to corporations has been finally resolved in the negative by the decision of the Supreme Court in *Mohamad* v *Palestinian Authority*, 132 S Ct 1702; 566 US (2012). The Supreme Court held that, in light of its use of the word 'individual', the scope of the TVPA is restricted to natural persons, and claims thereunder cannot be brought against organizations or corporations.

Finally, §1605A of the Foreign Sovereign Immunities Act confers jurisdiction, removes sovereign immunity and creates a cause of action against 'rogue' States which have been designated as State sponsors of terrorism, as well as against individual agents and officials, in respect of claims by US nationals, members of the armed forces or employees of the USA in respect of personal injury or death caused by an act of torture, extrajudicial killing, aircraft sabotage, or hostage taking by an official, employee, or agent of the foreign state acting in the course of their duties.

case pointed out in 2002, at a time when the interpretation of the jurisdiction under the Alien Tort Claims Act (ATCA) was perhaps at its highest point, that legislation could be seen as 'the beginnings of a very broad form of extraterritorial jurisdiction'[14] in civil matters; however, they added that although 'this unilateral exercise of the function of guardian of international values has been much commented on, it has not attracted the approbation of States generally'.[15]

The development of international criminal law is considered by Cryer in Ch 25. In this chapter we examine the foundational rules of State responsibility—in particular the bases for and consequences of the responsibility of a State for internationally wrongful acts. Questions of the implementation of such responsibility by an injured State or by other interested parties, as well as possible responses (retorsion, countermeasures, sanctions) are dealt with only briefly; they are discussed in greater detail in other chapters (see Okowa, Ch 16 and White and Abass, Ch 18). To a large extent, similar principles apply to the responsibility of international organizations, with appropriate adjustments to take account of their particular nature; to the extent that the applicable rules differ significantly, they are likewise noted below.

II. STATE RESPONSIBILITY: ISSUES OF CLASSIFICATION AND CHARACTERIZATION

The category 'State responsibility' covers the field of the responsibility of States for internationally wrongful conduct. It amounts, in other words, to a general law of wrongs. But what is a breach of international law by a State depends on what its international obligations are, and especially as far as treaties are concerned, these vary from one State to the next. There are a few treaties (the United Nations Charter, the 1949 Geneva Conventions and some international human rights treaties) to which virtually every State is a party; otherwise each State has its own range of bilateral and multilateral treaty obligations. Even under general international law, which might be expected to be virtually uniform for every State, different States may be differently situated and thus *de facto* may have different responsibilities—for example, upstream States rather than downstream States on an international river, capital importing and capital exporting States in respect of the treatment of foreign investment, or States on whose territory a civil war is raging as compared with third parties to the conflict. There is no such thing as a uniform code of international law, reflecting the obligations of all States.

On the other hand, the underlying concepts of State responsibility—attribution, breach, excuses, consequences—seem to be general in character. Particular treaties or rules may vary these underlying concepts in particular respects, otherwise they are assumed and they apply unless excluded.[16] These background or standard assumptions of responsibility

---

[14] *Arrest Warrant of 11 April 2000 (Democratic Republic of Congo v Belgium), Preliminary Objections and Merits, Judgment, ICJ Reports 2002*, p 3, Separate Opinion of Judges Higgins, Kooijmans, and Buergenthal, para 48.

[15] Ibid.

[16] ARSIWA, Article 55 (*lex specialis*). For examples of a *lex specialis* see, eg the provisions of the WTO Agreements excluding compensation for breach and focusing on cessation, and (perhaps) Article 41 of the European Convention on Human Rights which appears, at least in some circumstances, to give States an option to pay compensation rather than providing restitution in kind; nevertheless they remain bound by Article 46 of the European Convention to abide by the judgments of the European Court, and in that regard, to take, under the supervision of the Committee of Ministers, 'the general and/or, if appropriate, individual measures to be adopted in their domestic legal order to put an end to the violation found by the Court and to redress so far as possible the effects' (*Scozzari and Giunta v Italy* [GC], nos 39221/98 and 41963/98, para

on the basis of which specific obligations of States exist and are applied are set out in the ILC's Articles on State Responsibility. The Articles are the product of more than 40 years' work by the ILC on the topic, and in common with other ILC texts they involve both codi-fication and progressive development (Crawford, 2013, pp 35-42; and *Symposium*, 2002, 96 *AJIL* pp 773–890). They are the focus of what follows.

A. RESPONSIBILITY UNDER INTERNATIONAL OR NATIONAL LAW?

Evidently State responsibility can only be engaged for breaches of international law, that is, for conduct which is internationally wrongful because it involves some violation of an international obligation applicable to and binding on the State. A dispute between two States concerning the breach of an international obligation, whether customary or treaty-based, concerns international responsibility, and this will be true whether the remedy sought is a declaration that conduct is wrongful, cessation of the conduct, or com-pensation for damage suffered. On the other hand, not all claims brought against a State involve international responsibility, even if international law may be relevant in some way. For example, if a State is sued on a commercial transaction in a national court, interna-tional law helps to determine the extent of the defendant State's immunity from jurisdic-tion and from measures of enforcement, but the underlying claim will derive from the applicable law of the contract. There is thus a distinction between State responsibility for breaches of international law, and State liability for breaches of national law. One does not entail the other.[17]

Even at the international level, not all claims brought by one State against another necessarily involve State responsibility; in addition to claims alleging breach of an obliga-tion or as to the reparation required for a breach, the category of international claims also covers, *inter alia*, disputes relating solely to the proper interpretation of a treaty, and dis-putes as to sovereignty over territory or maritime delimitation.[18] Claims of responsibility

---

249, ECHR 2000-VIII). After initial hesitations (see eg, *Ireland* v *UK*, Judgment of 18 January 1978, para 187, Ser A no 25), the recent practice of the European Court of Human Rights appears to be evolving, at least in relation to certain types of breach, towards a requirement of real restitution by way of just satisfaction, rather than merely the payment of compensation: see eg *Assanidze* v *Georgia* [GC], no 71503/01, paras 202–3 ECHR 2004-II; *Ilaşcu and Others* v *Moldova and Russia* [GC], no 48787/99, para 490, ECHR 2004-VII; *Sejdovic* v *Italy* [GC], no 56581/00, paras 125–6, ECHR 2006-II; *Verein gegen Tierfabriken Schweiz (VgT)* v *Switzerland (No 2)* [GC], no 32772/02, paras 85–90, ECHR 2009; *Al-Saadoon and Mufdhi* v *United Kingdom*, no 61498/08, paras 170–1, ECHR-2010; *Laska and Lika* v *Albania*, nos 12315/04 and 17605/04, 20 April 2010, paras 73–7; *Hirsi Jamaa* v *Italy* [GC], no 27765/09, paras 209–11, ECHR 2012; and *Savriddin Dzhurayev* v *Russia*, no 71386/10, paras 247–9 and 252–5, ECHR 2013.

[17] ARSIWA, Articles 1, 3, 27; *Elettronica Sicula SpA (ELSI), Judgment, ICJ Reports 1989*, p 15, paras 73 and 124. See also *Compañía de Aguas del Aconquija and Vivendi Universal* v *Argentine Republic* (ICSID Case No ARB/97/3), Decision on Annulment, 3 July 2002, 41 ILM 1135; *ICSID Reports*, vol 6, p 340, paras 93–103; *SGS Société Générale de Surveillance SA* v *Islamic Republic of Pakistan* (ICSID Case No ARB/01/13), Decision on Objections to Jurisdiction, 29 January 2004, *ICSID Reports*, vol 8, p 483, paras 146–8.

[18] In setting out (apparently exhaustively) the categories of disputes as to which a State may choose to accept the jurisdiction of the Court, Article 36(2) of the Statute of the International Court of Justice (the Optional Clause), mentions, in addition to disputes involving questions of responsibility (ie 'the existence of any fact which, if established, would constitute a breach of an international obligation'; and 'the nature or extent of the reparation to be made for the breach of an international obligation' (paragraphs (c) and (d)), disputes as to 'any question of international law' and disputes relating to 'the interpretation of a treaty' (paragraphs (a) and (b)), Neither of the latter types of dispute necessarily involve questions of responsibility (although claims of respon-sibility may form part of the wider dispute in a particular case).

were traditionally brought directly between States at the international level, or (much less often) before an international court or tribunal. Both these avenues remain but there is now a further range of possibilities. For example in some cases individuals or corporations are given access to international tribunals and can bring claims of State responsibility in their own right, eg for breach of the European Convention on Human Rights before the European Court of Human Rights, or for breach of a bilateral investment treaty (or multilateral investment protection treaty) before an arbitral tribunal established under the relevant treaty. Whether such international claims could also be enforced in national courts depends on the approach of the national legal system to international law in general (see Denza, Ch 14) as well as on the rules of State immunity (see Fox, Ch 12). In certain circumstances it is possible for responsibility claims to be 'domesticated', and the principles of subsidiarity and complementarity indicate an increasing role for national courts in the implementation and enforcement of international standards.[19] But the interaction between rules of jurisdiction and immunity and the relation between national and international law make this a complex area. For the sake of simplicity, this chapter will be confined to claims of State responsibility brought at the international level.

B. TYPOLOGY OF STATE RESPONSIBILITY

National legal systems often distinguish types or degrees of liability according to the source of the obligation breached—for example, crime, contract, tort, or delict.[20] In international law it appears that there is no general distinction of this kind. As the arbitral tribunal said in the *Rainbow Warrior* case:

> the general principles of International Law concerning State responsibility are equally applicable in the case of breach of treaty obligation, since in the international law field there is no distinction between contractual and tortious responsibility, so that any violation of a State of any obligation, of whatever origin gives rise to State responsibility.[21]

To this extent the rules of State responsibility form the basis for a single system, having no precise equivalent in national legal systems. The reason is that international law has to address a very wide range of needs on the basis of rather few basic tools and techniques. For example, treaties perform a wide range of functions in the international system—from establishing institutions in the public interest and rules of an essentially legislative character to making specific contractual arrangements between two States. Unlike national law, there is no categorical distinction between the legislative and the contractual. The characterization of a particular treaty (or particular obligations contained in a treaty) as 'legislative' or

---

[19] For consideration of the extent to which domestic courts may contribute to the development of the law of international responsibility, including consideration of application of the Articles by domestic courts, see Olleson, 2013 and Wittich, 2013.

[20] Cf the division of sources of obligation in Roman law into contract, delict, and quasi-contract/unjust enrichment: D.1.1.10.1 (Ulpian): 'Iuris praecepta sunt haec: honeste vivere, alterum non laedere, suum cuique tribuere' ('the principles of law are these: to live honourably, not to harm any other person, and to render to each his own').

[21] *Rainbow Warrior (France/New Zealand)*, (1990) 20 *RIAA* 217, para 75; for the arguments of the parties, see ibid, paras 72–4. See also the ICJ in *Gabčíkovo-Nagymaros Project (Hungary/Slovakia), Judgment, ICJ Reports 1997*, p 7, paras 46–8, especially para 47: 'when a State has committed an internationally wrongful act, its international responsibility is likely to be involved whatever the nature of the obligation it has failed to respect', citing what is now ARSIWA, Article 12: 'There is a breach of an international obligation by a State when an act of that State is not in conformity with what is required of it by that obligation, *regardless of its origin or character*' (emphasis added).

'contractual' is to a large extent a question of degree and analysis, and *per se* has no consequences in the international legal sphere; what is crucial is the structure of the specific obligations imposed (that is, whether, on analysis they are owed bilaterally between pairs of States or multilaterally to all States parties), and whether they can be characterized as having been established for the protection of some collective interest (whether of the group of States parties to the treaty, or the international community as a whole).

The Tribunal in the *Rainbow Warrior*[22] arbitration and the International Court in the *Gabčíkovo-Nagymaros Project*[23] case both held that in a case involving the breach of a treaty obligation, the general defences available under the law of State responsibility coexist with the rules of treaty law, laid down in the 1969 Vienna Convention on the Law of Treaties.[24] But the two sets of rules perform different functions. The rules of the law of treaties determine when a treaty obligation is in force for a State and what it means, that is, how it is to be interpreted. The rules of State responsibility determine when a breach of such an obligation has occurred and what the legal consequences of that breach are in terms of such matters as reparation. There is some overlap between the two but they are legally and logically distinct. A State faced with a material breach of a treaty obligation can choose to suspend or terminate the treaty in accordance with the applicable rules of treaty law, thus releasing itself from its obligation to perform its obligations under the treaty in the future (VCLT, Article 60). But doing so does not prevent it also from claiming reparation for the breach.[25]

In addition, national legal systems also characteristically distinguish 'civil' from 'criminal' responsibility, with the latter characteristically involving repression and punishment. By contrast there is little or no State practice allowing for 'punitive' or 'penal' consequences of breaches of international law. For instance, in 1976, Chilean agents killed a former Chilean minister, Orlando Letelier, and one of his companions by a car bomb in Washington, DC. The US courts subsequently awarded both compensatory and punitive damages for the deaths, acting under the local torts exception of the Foreign State Immunity Act.[26] But the local judgment was practically unenforceable.[27] Subsequently, as part of the restoration of relations between the USA and Chile following the latter's return to democracy, it was agreed that a bilateral commission would determine the amount of compensation payable as an *ex gratia* settlement without admission of liability. Under the terms of reference of the Commission, the damages were to be assessed 'in accordance with applicable principles of international law, as though liability were established'.[28] The Commission awarded sums

---

[22] *Rainbow Warrior (France/New Zealand)*, (1990) 20 *RIAA* 217, para 75.

[23] *Gabčíkovo-Nagymaros Project (Hungary/Slovakia), Judgment, ICJ Reports 1997*, p 7, paras 46–8.

[24] See also *Application of the Interim Accord of 13 September 1995 (the former Yugoslav Republic of Macedonia v Greece), Judgment of 5 December 2011, ICJ Reports 2011*, p.644, in which the Court (at paras 144–65) rejected various arguments put forward by the respondent State based on alleged breaches by the applicant state of its international obligations under both the law of treaties (the so-called *exceptio inadimpleti contractus* and material breach of treaty under Article 60 VCLT) and the law of State responsibility (countermeasures) by which the respondent state had attempted to justify its own failure to comply with its international obligations.

[25] In other words a State can terminate a treaty for breach while claiming damages for breaches that have already occurred: see VCLT, Articles 70(1)(b), 72(1)(b), 73.

[26] See *Letelier et al v The Republic of Chile et al:* see 488 F.Supp 665 (1980); 19 ILM 409; 63 ILR 378 (District Court, DC) for the decision on State immunity, and see 502 F.Supp 259 (1980); 19 ILM 1418; 88 ILR 747 (District Court, DC) for the decision as to quantum; the Court awarded the plaintiffs approximately $5 million, of which $2 million were punitive damages.

[27] The Court of Appeals for the 2nd Circuit, reversing the District Court, refused to allow enforcement against the Chilean national airline: 748 F.2d 790 (1984); the Supreme Court denied certiorari: 471 US 1125 (1985).

[28] *Re Letelier and Moffitt* (1992), 88 ILR 727 at 731.

only on a compensatory basis for loss of income and moral damage; the separate opinion of the Chilean member of the Commission made clear that punitive damages were not accepted in international law.[29]

The draft of the ILC's Articles on State Responsibility adopted on first reading in 1996 sought to introduce the notion of 'international crimes' of States.[30] It was not envisaged that States could be fined or otherwise punished—no State has ever been accused of a criminal offence before an international court, even where the conduct involved aggression or genocide. In 1998, the concept of 'international crimes of States' was set aside, contributing to the unopposed adoption of the Articles on State Responsibility by the ILC in 2001. The episode suggests that State responsibility is an undifferentiated regime, which does not embody such domestic classifications as 'civil' and 'criminal'; the International Court endorsed this approach in the *Bosnian Genocide* case.[31]

But this does not prevent international law responding in different ways to different kinds of breaches and to their different impacts on other States, on individuals and on international order. First, individual State officials have no impunity if they commit crimes under international law, even if they may not have been acting for their own individual ends.[32] Secondly, the Articles on State Responsibility make special provision for the consequences of certain serious breaches of peremptory norms of general international law (*jus cogens*). A breach is serious if it involves a 'gross or systematic failure by the responsible State to fulfil' such an obligation (Article 40(2)). The major consequence of such a breach is not any form of penal consequence for the responsible State, but rather the obligation on all other States to refrain from recognizing as lawful the situation thereby created or from rendering aid or assistance in maintaining it (Article 41(2)). In addition, States must cooperate to bring the serious breach to an end 'through any lawful means' (Article 41(1)); the principal avenues for such cooperation are through the various international organizations, in particular the Security Council, whose powers to take measures to restore international peace and security substantially overlap with these provisions (Koskenniemi, 2001).

In the Advisory Opinion on *Legal Consequences of the Construction of a Wall in the Occupied Palestine Territory*, the ICJ discussed the existence of such consequences for third States as a result of the breaches by Israel the right of self-determination and certain obligations of international humanitarian law. The Court made no express reference to

[29] Ibid, p 741. The resulting award was paid to the victims' heirs on condition that they waived their rights under the domestic judgment.

[30] For the text of former Article 19 see Crawford, 2002, pp 352–3.

[31] *Application of the Convention on the Prevention and Punishment of the Crime of Genocide (Bosnia and Herzegovina v Serbia and Montenegro), Merits, Judgment, ICJ Reports 2007*, p.43, paras 65 and 66.

[32] At the international level see the Statute of the ICTY, Articles 7(2), 7(4); the Statute of the ICTR, Articles 6(2), 6(4); Rome Statute of the ICC, Articles 27, 33. At the national level see *R v Bow Street Metropolitan Stipendiary, ex parte Pinochet Ugarte (Amnesty International Intervening) (No 3)* [1997] UKHL 17; [2000] 1 AC 147. However, the ICJ has held that serving foreign ministers (and by implication, serving Heads of State and other senior ministers) while in office are inviolable and have absolute jurisdictional immunity from prosecution in the national courts of other States: *Arrest Warrant of 11 April 2000 (Democratic Republic of Congo v Belgium), Preliminary Objections and Merits, Judgment, ICJ Reports 2002*, p 3, paras 51–61. The Court protested that this immunity did not involve impunity, *inter alia*, because of the possibility of prosecution at the international level, or prosecution by the national State. The jurisdictional immunity apparently lasts only so long as the individual holds office: cf, however, ibid, paras 60–61, and compare with the Separate Opinion of Judges Higgins, Kooijmans, and Buergenthal, ibid, para 89. As a matter of English law, officials of a foreign State who, in the performance of their functions, commit crimes abroad contrary to international law enjoy immunity before the English courts when faced with *civil* claims in relation to those acts, even if the acts of which they are accused constitute a breach of a peremptory norm of international law (*jus cogens*): *Jones v Ministry of Interior for the of Kingdom of Saudi Arabia and Ors* [2006] UKHL 26; [2007] 1 AC 270.

Articles 40 and 41 of the Articles; rather it reasoned first that the norms in question constituted rights and obligations *erga omnes* (ie owed to the international community as a whole) and then held that '[g]iven the character and the importance of the rights and obligations involved', other States were under obligations not to recognize the illegal situation resulting from the construction of the Wall, and not to render aid and assistance in maintaining the situation thereby created, as well as an obligation 'while respecting the United Nations Charter and international law to see to it that any impediment, resulting from the construction of the wall, to the exercise by the Palestinian people of its right to self-determination is brought to an end'.[33] In addition, the Court was of the view that the 'United Nations, and especially the General Assembly and the Security Council, should consider what further action is required to bring to an end the illegal situation resulting from the construction of the wall...'[34]

By contrast, in *Jurisdictional Immunities of the State*, the Court openly referred to Article 41 of the Articles and appeared to endorse the norms it contains imposing obligations on third States as reflecting customary international law, observing that

> recognizing the immunity of a foreign State in accordance with customary international law does not amount to recognizing as lawful a situation created by the breach of a jus cogens rule, or rendering aid and assistance in maintaining that situation, and so cannot contravene the principle in Article 41 of the [Articles].[35]

Quite apart from collective enforcement and the obligations which may arise for third states, the possibility remains of unilateral action by individual States against States responsible for such serious breaches as genocide, war crimes, or denial of fundamental human rights.[36] Further, as discussed further below, at least as regards certain categories of obligations which protect fundamental 'community' interests, it is possible that States to which the obligation is owed may invoke the responsibility of the wrongdoing State even if they have themselves suffered no injury save the legal injury resulting from the violation of the norm in question.

III. THE ELEMENTS OF STATE RESPONSIBILITY

As already noted, the international responsibility of a State arises from the commission of an internationally wrongful act. An internationally wrongful act presupposes that there is conduct, consisting of an action or omission, that: (a) is attributable to a State under international law; and (b) constitutes a breach of the international obligations of the State (ARSIWA, Article 2). In principle, the fulfilment of these conditions is a sufficient basis for international responsibility, as has been consistently affirmed by international courts and tribunals.[37] In some cases, however, the respondent State may claim that it is justified

---

[33] *Legal Consequences of the Construction of a Wall in the Occupied Palestine Territory, Advisory Opinion, ICJ Reports 2004*, p 136, para 159.

[34] Ibid, para 160.

[35] *Jurisdictional Immunities of the State (Germany v Italy; Greece Intervening)*, Judgment of 3 February 2012, nyr, para 93.

[36] For instance States may adopt measures which are not inconsistent with their international obligations (retorsion). Further, in the case of breach of certain types of obligation, a right *may* exist allowing States which themselves are not injured to take countermeasures; see, for instance, the catalogue of State practice discussed in the Commentary to ARSIWA, Article 54, which may be evidence of such a customary international rule. The ILC left the question open in Article 54 for future development,

[37] See the Permanent Court of International Justice in *Phosphates in Morocco, Preliminary Objections, Judgment, PCIJ, Ser A/B, No 74*, p 10, and the International Court of Justice in *United States Diplomatic and*

in its non-performance, for example, because it was acting in self-defence or was subject to a situation of *force majeure*. In international law such defences or excuses are termed 'circumstances precluding wrongfulness'. They will be a matter for the respondent State to assert and prove, not for the claimant State to negative.

The three elements—attribution, breach, and the absence of any valid justification for non-performance—will be discussed in turn before we consider the consequences of State responsibility, in particular for the injured State or States.

A. ATTRIBUTION OF CONDUCT

Although they seem real enough to their citizens (and, normally, to others), States are juridical abstractions. Like corporations in national law, they necessarily act through organs or agents.[38] The rules of attribution specify the actors whose conduct may engage the responsibility of the State, either generally or in specific circumstances. It should be stressed that the issue here is one of responsibility for breaches of international obligations of the State. It does not concern the question which officials can enter into those obligations in the first place. Only senior officials of the State (the head of State or government, the minister of foreign affairs, and diplomats in certain circumstances: see VCLT, Article 7) have inherent authority to bind the State; other officials act upon the basis of express or ostensible authority (VCLT, Article 46).[39] By contrast, any State official, even at a local or municipal level, may commit an internationally wrongful act attributable to the State—the

Consular Staff in Tehran, Judgment, ICJ Reports 1980, p 3, para 56; *Military and Paramilitary Activities in and against Nicaragua (Nicaragua v United States of America), Merits, Judgment, ICJ Reports 1986*, p 14, para 226; *Gabčíkovo-Nagymaros Project (Hungary/Slovakia), Judgment, ICJ Reports 1997*, p 7, para 78; and *Application of the Convention on the Prevention and Punishment of the Crime of Genocide (Bosnia and Herzegovina v Serbia and Montenegro), Merits, Judgment, ICJ Reports 2007*, p 43, para 385, where the Court referred to 'the well-established rule, one of the cornerstones of the law of State responsibility, that the conduct of any State organ is to be considered an act of the State under international law, and therefore gives rise to the responsibility of the State if it constitutes a breach of an international obligation of the State'; see also ibid, para 149. See also the decision of the Mexico-United States General Claims Commission in *Dickson Car Wheel Company* (1931) 4 *RIAA* 669, 678.

[38] *German Settlers in Poland, Advisory Opinion, 1923, PCIJ, Series B, No 6*, at p 22.

[39] See also *Maritime Delimitation and Territorial Questions between Qatar and Bahrain, Jurisdiction and Admissibility, ICJ Reports 1994*, p 112, paras 26–7; *Land and Maritime Boundary between Cameroon and Nigeria (Cameroon v Nigeria: Equatorial Guinea Intervening), Merits, Judgment, ICJ Reports 2002*, p 303, paras 264–8. For an analogous question as to whether the position taken by organs of the constituent entities of a federal State is capable of giving rise to a 'dispute as to the meaning or scope' of a prior judgment sufficient to form the basis for a request for interpretation under Article 60 of the Statute of the ICJ, see *Request for Interpretation of the Judgment of 31 March 2004 in the Case concerning Avena and Other Mexican Nationals (Mexico v United States of America), Provisional Measures, Order of 16 July 2008, ICJ Reports 2008*, p 311. The Court held that the refusal of the courts of certain constituent states of the USA to give effect to the Court's prior judgment in *Avena*, as well as the decision of the Supreme Court that the judgment was not directly enforceable as a matter of domestic constitutional law, were sufficient to give rise to the appearance of the existence of a 'dispute' within the meaning of Article 60 as to the meaning of the Court's judgment; this was held to be the case despite the statement of the federal executive authorities that they did not dispute the meaning and effects of the ICJ's judgment in *Avena* to the effect that the USA was under an obligation to allow reconsideration and review of the convictions (ibid, paras 55–6). Subsequently, the Court refused the request for interpretation on other grounds: see *Request for Interpretation of the Judgment of 31 March 2004 in the Case concerning Avena and Other Mexican Nationals (Mexico v United States of America), Judgment, ICJ Reports 2009*, p 3, paras 43–6; although in doing so it did not expressly depart from its finding made at the provisional measures stage as to the existence of a dispute, its discussion of the issue casts some doubt on whether the position taken by the courts of the USA were in fact sufficient in that regard given the position taken by the federal executive: paras 11–42 (in particular paras 31–42).

local constabulary torturing a prisoner or causing an enforced disappearance,[40] for example, or the local mayor requisitioning a factory.[41]

A clear example of attribution of conduct performed by State agents vis-à-vis another State was the sinking on 10 July 1985 of the Greenpeace ship *Rainbow Warrior* in Auckland harbour. The French Government subsequently admitted that the explosives had been planted on the ship by agents of the Directorate General of External Security, acting on orders received. New Zealand sought and received an apology and compensation for the violation of its sovereignty.[42] This was quite separate from the damage done to Greenpeace, a non-governmental organization, and to the Dutch national who was killed by the explosion; separate arrangements were made to provide compensation for these interests.

A State does not normally guarantee the safety of foreign nationals on its territory, the security of their property or the success of their investments. In terms of any injury suffered, there has to be some involvement by the State itself—in effect, by the government of the State, in the conduct which is complained of. A State will generally only be liable for the conduct of its organs or officials, acting as such (ARSIWA, Article 4; Commentary, Crawford, 2002, pp 94–9). Purely private acts will not engage the State's responsibility, although the State may in certain circumstances be liable for its failure to prevent those acts, or to take action to punish the individuals responsible.[43] On the other hand, the scope of State responsibility for official acts is broad, and the definition of 'organ' for this purpose comprehensive; it includes 'all the individual or collective entities which make up the organization of the State and act on its behalf'.[44] There is no distinction based on the level of seniority of the relevant officials in the State hierarchy; as long as they are acting in their official capacity, responsibility is engaged. In addition, there is no limitation to the central executive; as noted earlier, responsibility may be engaged for acts of federal, provincial or even local government officials. The classification of powers is also irrelevant: in principle, the concept of 'organ' covers legislatures, executive officials and courts at all levels.[45]

Under Article 4, the primary consideration for characterization of a person or entity as an organ is their formal status under the State's domestic law (so-called '*de jure* organs'). In addition, the International Court of Justice has made clear that the conduct of what it referred to as '*de facto*' organs[46] may, exceptionally, be attributable to the State in the same manner:

> [...] persons, groups of persons or entities may, for purposes of international responsibility, be equated with State organs even if that status does not follow from internal law, provided that in fact the persons, groups or entities act in 'complete dependence' on the State, of

---

[40] See, eg *Velásquez-Rodríguez* v *Honduras, Merits, Judgment of 29 July 1988, Ser C no 4*, 95 ILR 259, para 183 ('not all levels of the Government of Honduras were necessarily aware of those acts, nor is there any evidence that such acts were the result of official orders. Nevertheless, those circumstances are irrelevant for the purposes of establishing whether Honduras is responsible under international law'). See also ibid, 296, para 170.

[41] *Elettronica Sicula SpA (ELSI), Judgment, ICJ Reports 1989*, p 15.

[42] *Rainbow Warrior (No 1)* (1986), 74 ILR 256.

[43] *Janes* (US v *Mexico*) (1926) 4 RIAA 82; cf *Noyes* (US v *Panama*) (1933) 6 RIAA 308.

[44] Commentary to Article 4, paragraph (1). ARSIWA, Article 4 itself and this passage from the Commentary were cited with approval by the ICJ in *Application of the Convention on the Prevention and Punishment of the Crime of Genocide (Bosnia and Herzegovina* v *Serbia and Montenegro), Merits, Judgment, ICJ Reports 2007*, p 43, para 388.

[45] ARSIWA, Article 4. See also *LaGrand (Germany* v *United States of America), Provisional Measures, Order of 3 March 1999, ICJ Reports 1999*, p 9, para 28: 'Whereas the international responsibility of a State is engaged by the action of the competent organs and authorities acting in that State, whatever they may be'.

[46] *Application of the Convention on the Prevention and Punishment of the Crime of Genocide (Bosnia and Herzegovina* v *Serbia and Montenegro), Merits, Judgment, ICJ Reports 2007*, p 43, para 390.

which they are ultimately merely the instrument. In such a case, it is appropriate to look beyond legal status alone, in order to grasp the reality of the relationship between the person taking action, and the State to which he is so closely attached as to appear to be nothing more than its agent: any other solution would allow States to escape their international responsibility by choosing to act through persons or entities whose supposed independence would be purely fictitious.[47]

In addition to the acts or omissions of organs (whether *de jure* or *de facto*), the conduct of persons or entities exercising elements of governmental authority is attributable to the State, provided that they were acting in exercise of the governmental authority conferred on them (ARSIWA, Article 5); a State cannot avoid responsibility for particular conduct by privatizing or delegating what are properly governmental functions to persons or individuals which do not formally constitute its organs. The touchstone for attribution in this context is that the person or entity was in fact exercising governmental authority in carrying out the conduct in question.

Acts or omissions of any State organ (*de jure* or *de facto*) or of persons or entities exercising elements of governmental authority, are attributable to the State provided they were acting in that capacity at the time; that is the case even if they may have been acting *ultra vires* or in contravention of instructions.[48] Indeed, the State may be responsible for conduct which is clearly in excess of authority, if the official has made use of an official position. For example, in the *Caire* case, a French national in Mexico was shot and killed by members of the Mexican army after he had refused their demands for money. The tribunal held that, for the *ultra vires* acts of officials to be attributable to the State, 'they must have acted at least to all appearances as competent officials or organs, or they must have used powers or methods appropriate to their official capacity.'[49] In the circumstances the responsibility of the State was engaged 'in view of the fact that they acted in their capacity of officers and used the means placed at their disposition by virtue of that capacity'.[50] Similarly, in *Youmans*, US citizens cornered in a house by a mob were killed after soldiers sent to disperse the crowd, contrary to orders, opened fire on the house, forcing the inhabitants out into the open. The Tribunal held that there was State responsibility given that 'at the time of the commission of these acts the men were on duty under the immediate supervision and in the presence of a commanding officer'. The Tribunal went on to comment that:

> Soldiers inflicting personal injuries or committing wanton destruction or looting always act in disobedience of some rules laid down by superior authority. There could be no liability whatever for such misdeeds if the view were taken that any acts committed by soldier in contravention of instructions must always be considered as personal acts.[51]

By contrast, a State is not responsible for the acts of mobs or of private individuals as such. Their conduct will only be attributable to the State if they were in fact acting on the instructions, or under the direction or control of the State in carrying out the particular conduct (ARSIWA, Article 8),[52] or if the State acknowledges adopts (or in common law terminology 'ratifies') their acts as its own (ARSIWA, Article 11). In the *Tehran Hostages*

---

[47] Ibid, para 392.
[48] Article 7 ARSIWA; see also the final words of Article 5 ARSIWA. For an illustration, see *Union Bridge Company (USA v Great Britain)* (1924) 6 *RIAA* 138.
[49] *Caire (France v Mexico)* (1929) 5 *RIAA* 516 at p 530.   [50] Ibid, at p 531.
[51] *Youmans (USA v Mexico)* (1926) 4 *RIAA* 110; (1927) 21 *AJIL* 571, para 14.
[52] Cf *Application of the Convention on the Prevention and Punishment of the Crime of Genocide (Bosnia and Herzegovina v Serbia and Montenegro)*, Merits, Judgment, *ICJ Reports 2007*, p 43, para 400.

case, the International Court held that although initially the students who took control of the US Embassy in Tehran were not acting as agents of Iran, a subsequent decree of Ayatollah Khomeini endorsing the occupation of the embassy:

> translated continuing occupation of the Embassy and detention of the hostages into acts of [Iran]. The militants, authors of the invasion and jailers of the hostages, had now become agents of the Iranian State for whose acts the State itself was internationally responsible.[53]

Similarly, the State will be responsible if the authorities act in collusion with the mob, or participate in the mob violence. However, international tribunals generally require strong evidence of such collusion.[54]

In addition, conduct which is not attributable to a State because it was carried out by persons acting in a purely private capacity may nonetheless result in the State's international responsibility because the State failed in some obligation to prevent the conduct in question. However, in such a case, responsibility arises as a result of the State's own failings, rather than directly as a result of the conduct of the private individuals. For instance, in the *Tehran Hostages* case, Iran was held to have breached its special obligation of protection of the embassy and consular premises and personnel, even prior to its adoption of the acts of the occupying students.[55] The duty to control a mob is particularly important when the mob is in some way under the control of the authorities.[56]

Like other systems of law, international law does not limit attribution to the conduct of the regular officials or organs of the State; it also extends to conduct carried out by others who are authorized to act by the State or at least who act under its actual direction or control. In the *Nicaragua* case, the International Court stated that:

> For this conduct [of the *contra* rebels] to give rise to legal responsibility of the USA, it would in principle have to be proved that that State had *effective control* of the military or paramilitary operations in the course of which the alleged violations were committed.[57]

The Articles on State Responsibility follow this approach: under Article 8, conduct of a person or group of persons is attributable to the State 'if the person or group of persons is in fact acting on the instructions of, or under the direction or control of, that State in carrying out the conduct' (ARSIWA, Article 8; Commentary, Crawford, 2002, pp 110–13); and it was reaffirmed by the International Court in *Bosnian Genocide*, as concerns the attribution to the FRY of the conduct of the Bosnian Serb forces and paramilitary groups.[58] There the Court disapproved the test of 'overall control' proposed by the Appeals Chamber of the ICTY in *Tadić*,[59] observing that:

> the 'overall control' test has the major drawback of broadening the scope of State responsibility well beyond the fundamental principle governing the law of international responsibility: a State is responsible only for its own conduct, that is to say the conduct of persons acting, on whatever basis, on its behalf... [T]he 'overall control' test is unsuitable, for it

---

[53] *United States Diplomatic and Consular Staff in Tehran, Judgment, ICJ Reports 1980*, p 3, paras 73–4.

[54] *Janes (USA v Mexico)* (1926) 4 *RIAA* 82.

[55] *United States Diplomatic and Consular Staff in Tehran, Judgment, ICJ Reports 1980*, p 3, para 63.

[56] See, eg *The Zafiro (Great Britain v USA)* (1925) 6 *RIAA* 160.

[57] *Military and Paramilitary Activities in and against Nicaragua, Merits, Judgment (Nicaragua v United States of America), ICJ Reports 1986*, p 14, para 115 (emphasis added).

[58] *Application of the Convention on the Prevention and Punishment of the Crime of Genocide (Bosnia and Herzegovina v Serbia and Montenegro), Merits, Judgment, ICJ Reports 2007*, p 43, paras 402–7.

[59] *Prosecutor v Tadić, Judgment*, Case No IT-94-1-A, Appeals Chamber, 15 July 1999, 38 ILM 1518, para 145.

stretches too far, almost to breaking point, the connection which must exist between the conduct of a State's organs and its international responsibility.[60]

As this passage illustrates, the governing principle is that of independent responsibility: the State is responsible for its own acts, ie for the acts of its organs and agents, and not for the acts of private parties, unless there are special circumstances warranting attribution to it of such conduct.

The same applies where one State is somehow implicated in the conduct of a third State, whether by aiding or assisting the other State in breaching an obligation owed by both of them, or by coercing or exercising direction and control over the other State to that end—indeed it applies a *fortiori*, since the third State will ordinarily be responsible for its own acts in breach of its own international obligations (ARSIWA, Articles 16–19). But there is another facet to the principle of independent responsibility: a State cannot hide behind the involvement of other States. It is responsible if and to the extent that it contributed to that wrongful conduct by its own acts. Thus in *Nicaragua*, the acts of the *contras* were not as such attributable to the USA, but the USA was responsible for its own conduct (in itself internationally wrongful) in training and financing the *contras* and in carrying out some specific operations, including the mining of a Nicaraguan harbour.[61] Likewise if a number of States act together in administering a territory, each will be responsible for its own conduct as part of the common enterprise.[62]

In another and rather special form of parallelism, the State will be responsible for the conduct of an insurrectional movement which subsequently becomes the government of that State (or, if they are a secessionary movement, of the new State they are struggling to create). The rule is to some extent anomalous, since it determines the attribution of conduct not by events at the time of that conduct but by reference to later contingencies—the success or failure of the revolt or secession. But the principle is established, and is reflected in Article 10 of the ILC Articles. Further, in *Yeager*,[63] immediately after the revolution in Iran in 1979 the claimant had been detained for several days by 'revolutionary guards' and had then been evacuated from the country. The US–Iran Claims Tribunal held that, although the guards were not recognized under internal law as part of the State apparatus, they were in fact exercising public functions in the absence of the previous State apparatus: Iran was thus held responsible for their acts.[64]

The question of attribution of conduct in the field of responsibility of international organizations has somewhat different contours. As just discussed, in the law of State responsibility, there are a number of ways in which the conduct of organs, instrumentalities and even, in some circumstances, private parties may be attributed to the State. By

---

[60] *Application of the Convention on the Prevention and Punishment of the Crime of Genocide (Bosnia and Herzegovina v Serbia and Montenegro), Merits, Judgment, ICJ Reports 2007*, p 43, para 406.

[61] *Military and Paramilitary Activities in and against Nicaragua (Nicaragua v United States of America), Merits, Judgment, ICJ Reports 1986*, p 14, in particular paras 75–80, 238, 242, 252, 292(3)–(6).

[62] Cf *Certain Phosphate Lands in Nauru (Nauru v Australia), Preliminary Objections, ICJ Reports 1992*, p 240 where the International Court left the question of possible apportionment of any compensation found to be due between the other implicated States to the merits stage. See also the *Legality of the Use of Force* cases between Yugoslavia and the NATO States (eg, *Legality of the Use of Force (Yugoslavia v Belgium), Provisional Measures, Order of 2 June 1999, ICJ Reports 1999*, p 124); the Court eventually held that it did not have jurisdiction over the claims (eg, *Legality of the Use of Force (Yugoslavia v Belgium), Preliminary Objections, Judgment, ICJ Reports 2004*, p 279).

[63] *Yeager v The Islamic Republic of Iran* (1987), 82 ILR 178.

[64] Cf, however, *Short v The Islamic Republic of Iran* (1987) 82 ILR 148 and *Rankin v The Islamic Republic of Iran* (1987) 82 ILR 204 (decided on the basis that the claimants had failed to prove that their departure was caused by actions attributable to Iran, rather than the general turmoil accompanying the revolution).

contrast, given the different structure of international organizations—which are functional entities, not territorial communities—the 'general rule' is that conduct must be that of an organ or agent of the international organization, acting in the performance of its functions (ARIO, Article 6). This 'functional' criterion underlying attribution of conduct to an international organization has parallels in other areas of the law, in particular as concerns the immunity from jurisdiction of the officials or agents of international organizations.[65]

The addition of the notion of agents to that of organs substantially widens the basis of attribution as compared to the corresponding rules under the law of State responsibility. As a result it substantially subsumes the other bases of attribution. For instance, an individual who does not have any official status within an international organization but carries out conduct upon its instructions or under its direction and control will be regarded as its agent and the conduct will be attributable to the organization on that basis.

As a result of the dominant role played by the rule permitting attribution of the conduct of organs and agents of international organizations, the Articles on Responsibility of International Organization contain only two alternative bases for the attribution of conduct to an international organization: first, in a similar fashion to the position under the law of State responsibility, conduct will be attributable if it has been acknowledged and adopted by the international organization as its own (ARIO, Article 9); second, conduct may be attributed to an international organization on the basis that the conduct is that of the organ of a State or the organ or agent of another international organization, which has been placed at the disposal of the international organization and over which the international organization exercises 'effective control' (ARIO, Article 7). However, in contrast to the other provisions dealing with attribution, the purpose of this rule is not to determine *whether* particular conduct is attributable as such, but rather it addresses the question of to which of two entities (the 'borrowing' international organization or the 'lending' State (or international organization)), the conduct is to be attributed.

That provision is of particular relevance in the context of the attribution of the conduct in breach of applicable international obligations of national contingents assigned to United Nations peacekeeping missions. Whether or not the conduct in question is to be attributed to the United Nations or to the contributing State turns on the relative degree of 'effective control' in fact exercised by those entities over the conduct in question. That in turn depends upon a number of factors, including the character of, and basis for, the

---

[65] See eg Article 105, UN Charter; Convention on the Privileges and Immunities of the United Nations, 13 February 1946, (the General Convention), Article V, Section 18 (as regards UN officials) and Article VI (as regards experts on mission), and Convention on the Privileges and Immunities of the Specialized Agencies, 21 November 1947, Article VI, Section 19. See also *Applicability of Article VI, Section 22, of the Convention on the Privileges and Immunities of the United Nations*, Advisory Opinion, ICJ Reports 1989, p 177, in which the ICJ, in concluding that Special Rapporteurs of the (now-defunct) Sub-Commission on the Prevention on Discrimination and the Prevention of Minorities of the Human Rights Commission enjoyed the privileges and immunities accorded to an expert on mission under the General Convention (para 55), observed that '[t]he essence of the matter lies not in their administrative position, but in the nature of their mission' (para 47). Similarly, in the *Cumaraswamy* advisory opinion, the Court held that Special Rapporteurs of the Human Rights Commission are entitled to the privileges and immunities accorded to experts on mission under the General Convention, observing that: 'what is decisive is that they have been entrusted with a mission by the United Nations and are therefore entitled to the privileges and immunities provided for in Article VI, Section 22, that safeguard the independent exercise of their functions': *Difference Relating to Immunity from Legal Process of a Special Rapporteur of the Commission on Human Rights*, Advisory Opinion, ICJ Reports 1999, p 62, para 43. Whether the agent was carrying out functions on behalf of an organization is also the criterion on the basis of which the question of whether an international organization may bring a claim by way of 'functional protection' in relation to injuries caused to the agent is to be determined: see *Reparation for Injuries Suffered in the Service of the United Nations*, Advisory Opinion, ICJ Reports 1949, p 174 at pp 177, 180, 181–4. See further ARSIWA, Article 9.

mandate under which the peacekeeping mission has been set up, any agreements between the United Nations and the contributing State as to the terms on which troops were to be placed at the disposal of the United Nations, the extent to which the troops remain subject to the command and jurisdiction of the contributing State, and whether (operational) United Nations command and control was in fact effective.

The appropriate test to be applied in these circumstances has given rise to controversy. In 2007, the Grand Chamber of the European Court of Human Rights, in its joined decision in *Behrami and Behrami v France* and *Saramati v France, Germany and Norway*, determined that the United Nations exercised a sufficient degree of control over troops forming part of KFOR in Kosovo that their actions were to be attributed to the United Nations, such that the Court had no jurisdiction *ratione personae* over the applicant's claims; in doing so, it, applied a test of whether the United Nations Security Council 'retained ultimate authority and control so that operational command only was delegated'.[66]

Subsequently, a similar question, whether the actions of UK troops forming part of the multinational force in Iraq authorized by SC Res 1546 (8 June 2004) were to be attributed to the United Nations, rather than the UK, came before the House of Lords in *R (Al-Jedda) v Secretary of State for Defence*.[67] While apparently accepting the correctness of the 'ultimate authority and control' approach enunciated by the Grand Chamber in *Behrami*, the House distinguished the case before it on the facts, and held, on the basis of the wording of the relevant Security Council resolutions, that UK troops in Iraq could not realistically be said to be subject to UN authority and control.

In its Commentary on the Articles on Responsibility of International Organizations, adopted in 2011, the ILC noted that the UN Secretary-General had distanced himself from the approach taken in *Behrami*, and gently criticized the approach of the European Court on the basis that 'when applying the criterion of effective control, "operational" control would seem more significant than "ultimate" control, since the latter hardly implies a role in the act in question'.[68]

Subsequently, when *Al-Jedda* in due course came before the European Court, the Grand Chamber appears to have retreated somewhat from its previous position in *Behrami*, albeit without explicitly acknowledging that it was doing so. In rejecting the argument of the UK Government that the actions of UK troops should be regarded as attributable to the United Nations, the Grand Chamber followed the approach of the House of Lords in distinguishing the decision in *Behrami* on the facts, although it appeared to continue to endorse the actual result in *Behrami*.[69] At the same time it avoided taking a firm position on whether the applicable test was that of ultimate authority and control (as suggested in *Behrami*), or effective operational control over the relevant conduct of troops (as suggested by the ILC), merely finding that, in the circumstances, neither test was fulfilled.[70]

---

[66] *Behrami and Behrami v France* and *Saramati v France, Germany and Norway* (Dec) [GC], nos 71412/01 and 78166/01, 2 May 2007, para 133. See also subsequently *Kasumaj v Greece* (Dec), no 6974/05, 5 July 2007; *Gajić v Germany* (Dec), no 31446/02, 28 August 2007; and *Beric and Others v Bosnia and Herzegovina* (Dec), no 36357/04 and others, ECHR 2007-XII.

In *Behrami*, the Court did not go on to address the extent to which the conduct in question might be attributable to both the UN and the contributing States.

[67] *R (Al-Jedda) v Secretary of State for Defence* [2007] UKHL 58; [2008] 1 AC 332.

[68] ARIO, Commentary to Article 7, para (10); Report of the International Law Commission, Sixty-third Session, A/66/10, 90-91.

[69] *Al-Jedda v the United Kingdom* [GC], no. 27021/08, ECHR 2011, para 83.

[70] Ibid, para 84. Notably, the decision of the Grand Chamber continued to refer only to the ILC's 2004 draft commentary (ibid, para 56), and made no reference to the ILC's criticism of the decision in *Behrami*, which had already appeared in the Commentary to draft Article 6 (as it then was) adopted on first reading in 2009: see

The matter was taken further by the decision of the Dutch Supreme Court of 6 September 2013 in the so-called *Dutchbat* case.[71] A Dutch battalion serving as part of UNPROFOR in Bosnia was involved in a decision to expel three Bosnian men from a compound they controlled at Srebrenica. Despite attempts to negotiate safe passage with the commander of the Bosnian Serb militia (Mladić) the three men were shortly afterwards murdered by the militia. The Dutch Government relied on *Behrami* and argued that responsibility lay with the United Nations exclusively. Affirming on cassation the decision of the Hague Court of Appeal, the Supreme Court held that the Dutch Government was civilly responsible for their deaths. It said:

> ...international law, in particular article 8 [ARIO] in conjunction with article 48(1) [ARIO], does not exclude the possibility of dual attribution of given conduct. For the purpose of deciding whether the State had effective control it is not necessary for the State to have countermanded the command structure of the United Nations by giving instructions to Dutchbat or to have exercised operational command independently. It is apparent from the Commentary on article 7 [ARIO] that the attribution of conduct to the seconding State or the international organization is based on the factual control over the specific conduct, in which all factual circumstances and the special context of the case must be taken into account.[72]

In the circumstances it was unnecessary to determine whether the United Nations was also responsible. The Court robustly rejected the argument that its decision would deter governments from engaging in peacekeeping operations and that a policy of restraint should be followed. On that basis, the Court said:

> [t]here would be virtually no scope for the courts to assess the consequences of the conduct of a troop contingent in the context of a peace mission, in this case the conduct of which Dutchbat and hence the State are accused. Such far-reaching restraint is unacceptable. Nor is this altered by the fact that the State expects this to have an adverse effect on the implementation of peace operations by the United Nations, in particular on the willingness of member States to provide troops for such operations. This should not, after all prevent the possibility of judicial assessment in retrospect of the conduct of the relevant troop contingent.[73]

B. BREACH OF AN INTERNATIONAL OBLIGATION

The second element of responsibility is breach of an international obligation of the State. Here an initial distinction is drawn between State responsibility arising in the context of direct State-to-State wrongdoing and State responsibility arising in the context of diplomatic protection (injury to aliens or their property). This is so even though the relevant obligations may be contained in a treaty, the breach of which in principle engages direct State-to-State responsibility. The International Court was careful to preserve the distinction in the *ELSI* case, where the USA sought to base its action on breach of a bilateral treaty: nonetheless, the Chamber said, its claim was in the nature of diplomatic protection

---

Commentary to draft Article 6, paras (9)-(11), Report of the International Law Commission, Sixty-first Session, A/64/10, 67-69.

[71] *State of the Netherlands* v *Nuhanović*, First Chamber, Supreme Court of the Netherlands, 6 September 2013.
[72] Ibid, paras 3.11.2–3.   [73] Ibid, para 3.18.3.

and was thus subject to the normal requirements applicable to such a claim, including the exhaustion of local remedies.[74]

Many of the problems which arise in the context of diplomatic protection (nationality of claims, exhaustion of local remedies) do not arise in the context of direct State-to-State disputes. The only issue in these direct State-to-State cases is whether conduct attributable to State B causes legal harm to State A in violation of international law. If so, responsibility is *prima facie* engaged.

On its face, the requirement that there should be a breach of an international obligation of the State seems obvious enough. However, a number of questions arise: for example, causation, the notion of injury, the time factor (rules concerning non-retrospectivity of international law and acts continuing in time), and so on.

An important preliminary point should be made: international law is a distinct system, separate from national legal systems. In its own terms it prevails over national law in the event of conflict, and this is so irrespective of the approach taken by the national legal system. Several consequences follow. First, a State cannot invoke its own municipal law as a justification for refusal or failure to comply with its international obligations, whether under a treaty or otherwise.[75] The fact that an act or omission is lawful (or unlawful) under national law does not prejudge the question of its lawfulness or otherwise under international law.[76] Second, the content of municipal law is considered a matter of fact for international law;[77] in theory, the two live in distinct spheres, communicating via the rules of evidence. Third, a State cannot seek to invalidate the entry into force of international obligations by reference to municipal law constraints which it failed to observe.[78]

Of course, conduct attributable to a State may consist of both actions and omissions; breach of international obligations by omission (or by a combination of acts and omissions) is relatively common.[79] For instance in the *Tehran Hostages* case, the International Court

---

[74] *Elettronica Sicula SpA (ELSI), Judgment, ICJ Reports 1989*, p 15, para 52. Compare *Arrest Warrant of 11 April 2000 (Democratic Republic of Congo v Belgium), Preliminary Objections and Merits, Judgment, ICJ Reports 2002*, p 3, para 40. In *Armed Activities on the Territory of the Congo (Democratic Republic of the Congo v Uganda), ICJ Reports 2005*, p 168 it was held, in relation to counterclaims of mistreatment of persons within the grounds of the embassy of the respondent State, that to the extent that the claims were based on alleged breaches of the Vienna Convention on Diplomatic Relations due to mistreatment of diplomats of the respondent State and violations of the inviolability of its embassy, they were not claims having the character of diplomatic protection as they sought reparation for direct injury to the respondent State itself (paras 330–1). By contrast, insofar as the counterclaims were brought in respect of individuals not having diplomatic status, they fell under the rubric of diplomatic protection.

[75] *Greco-Bulgarian 'Communities', Advisory Opinion, 1930, PCIJ, Ser B, No 17* at p 32; ARSIWA, Articles 3, 32. For a slightly different manifestation of the same principle in relation to the obligation to comply with a judgment of the ICJ, see also *Request for Interpretation of the Judgment of 31 March 2004 in the Case concerning Avena and Other Mexican Nationals (Mexico v United States of America), Judgment, ICJ Reports 2009*, p 3, para 47: 'considerations of domestic law which have so far hindered the implementation of the obligation incumbent upon the United States, cannot relieve it of its obligation'.

[76] *Elettronica Sicula SpA (ELSI), Judgment, ICJ Reports 1989*, p 15, at para 73. *Compañía de Aguas del Aconquija and Vivendi Universal v Argentine Republic (ICSID Case No ARB/97/3), Decision on Annulment, 3 July 2002*, 41 ILM 1135.

[77] *Certain German Interests in Polish Upper Silesia, Merits, Judgment No 7, 1926, PCIJ, Ser A, No 7* at p 19.

[78] *Free Zones of Upper Savoy and the District of Gex, Judgment, 1932, PCIJ, Ser A/B, No 46*, p 96 at p 167 and see ibid, at p 170; *Legal Status of Eastern Greenland, Judgment, 1933, PCIJ, Ser A/B, No 53*, p 22 at p 71, and the Dissenting Opinion of Judge Anzilotti, ibid, pp 91–2. In relation to the law of treaties, see Vienna Convention on the Law of Treaties, Articles 27, 46; and see *Land and Maritime Boundary between Cameroon and Nigeria (Cameroon v Nigeria: Equatorial Guinea Intervening), Judgment, ICJ Reports 2002*, p 303, paras 264–8.

[79] Cf ARSIWA, Article 2, and Commentary to Article 1, paras 1 and 8; Commentary to Article 2, para 4.

held that the responsibility of Iran was due to the 'inaction' of its authorities which 'failed to take appropriate steps' in circumstances where such steps were evidently called for.[80]

1. Fault, harm, and damage

There has been a major debate about whether international law has a general requirement of fault. The debate is between those who maintain that international law requires some fault on the part of the State if it is to incur responsibility and supporters of so-called 'objective responsibility'. The case law tends to support the objective school. Thus in *Caire*, the arbitral tribunal affirmed 'the doctrine of the "objective responsibility" of the State, that is, the responsibility for the acts of its officials or organs, which may devolve upon it despite the absence of any *'faute'* on its part'.[81] However, there are statements which may be seen as going the other way. In the *Corfu Channel* case, the International Court held that:

> It is clear that knowledge of the minelaying cannot be imputed to the Albanian Government by reason merely of the fact that a minefield discovered in Albanian territorial waters caused the explosion of which the British warships were victims... [I]t cannot be concluded from the mere fact of the control exercised by a State over its territory and waters that that State necessarily knew, or ought to have known, of any unlawful act perpetrated therein, nor yet that it necessarily knew, or should have known, the authors. This fact, by itself and apart from other circumstances, neither involves *prima facie* responsibility nor shifts the burden of proof.[82]

In that case Albania's responsibility was upheld on the basis that (according to the evidence gathered, including by an expert commission) Albania must have known that the mines had been recently laid and nonetheless, in breach of its international obligations, failed to warn ships passing through the strait of their presence.

When scholarly debate bogs down around some dichotomy such as 'responsibility for fault'/'objective responsibility', something has almost always gone wrong. Here the problem is one of level of analysis: there is neither a rule that responsibility is always based on fault, nor one that it is always independent of it—indeed, there appears to be no presumption either way. This is hardly surprising in a legal system which has to deal with a wide range of problems and disposes of a limited armoury of techniques. But in any event circumstances alter cases, and it is illusory to seek for a single dominant rule. Where responsibility is essentially based on acts of omission (as in *Corfu Channel*), considerations of fault loom large. But if a State deliberately carries out some specific act, there is less room for it to argue that the harmful consequences were unintended and should be disregarded. Everything depends on the specific context and on the content and interpretation of the obligation said to have been breached.

Thus the ILC Articles on State Responsibility endorse a more nuanced view. Under Articles 2 and 12, the international law of State responsibility does not require fault before an act or omission may be characterized as internationally wrongful. However, the interpretation of the relevant primary obligation in a given case may well lead to the conclusion

---

[80] *United States Diplomatic and Consular Staff in Tehran, Judgment, ICJ Reports 1980*, p 3, paras 63, 67. See also *Velásquez-Rodríguez v Honduras, Merits, Judgment of 29 July 1988, Ser C no 4*, 95 ILR 259, para 170: 'under international law a State is responsible for the acts of its agents undertaken in their official capacity and for their omissions...'; *Affaire relative à l'acquisition de la nationalité polonaise (Germany v Poland)* (1924) 1 RIAA 425.

[81] *Caire (France v Mexico)* (1929) 5 RIAA 516 at p 529.

[82] *Corfu Channel, Merits, Judgment, ICJ Reports 1949*, p 4 at p 18. See also the decision in *Home Missionary Society (USA v Great Britain)* (1920) 6 RIAA 42.

that fault is a necessary condition for responsibility in relation to that obligation, having regard to the conduct alleged.[83]

Similarly, there has been an intense debate concerning the role of harm or damage in the law of State responsibility. Some authors (and some governments) have claimed that the State must have suffered some form of actual harm or damage before responsibility can be engaged (Bollecker-Stern, 1973). Once more, the ILC Articles leave the question to be determined by the relevant primary obligation: there is no *general* requirement of harm or damage before the consequences of responsibility come into being. In some circumstances, the mere breach of an obligation (which may be seen as involving 'legal' injury) will be sufficient to give rise to responsibility; this is the case, for instance, of even a minor infringement of the inviolability of an embassy or consular mission. On the other hand, in the context for example of pollution of rivers, it is necessary to show some substantial impact on the environment or on other uses of the watercourse before responsibility will arise.[84]

A corollary of this position is that there may have been a breach of international law but no material harm may have been suffered by another State or person in whose interest the obligation was created. In such cases international courts frequently award merely declaratory relief on the ground that nothing more is required.[85] However, in such circumstances, the main point of asserting responsibility may be for the future, to avoid repetition of the problem, rather than to obtain compensation for the past.

2. Continuing wrongful acts and the time factor

The basic principle is that a State can only be internationally responsible for breach of a treaty obligation if the obligation is in force for that State at the time of the alleged breach. It is therefore necessary to examine closely at what point an obligation entered into force, or at what point the obligation was terminated or ceased to bind the State.

For example in the *Mondev* case,[86] a claim was brought by a Canadian company alleging breach of the NAFTA Chapter 11 investment protection provisions by the USA. The claimant alleged that by various actions of the Boston city authorities the value of the applicant's interests in building and development projects had effectively been expropriated. But all of these actions took place before NAFTA's entry into force on 1 January 1994: the only later events were decisions of US courts denying Mondev's claims under US law. The tribunal held that NAFTA could not be applied retrospectively to actions prior to its entry into force. This left open the possibility of a claim of denial of justice in respect of the court decisions after NAFTA came into force, but the tribunal concluded that the courts had not in any way acted improperly, and thus that there had been no denial of justice.

The relevant principle is stated in Article 13 of the ILC Articles: 'An act of a State does not constitute a breach of an international obligation unless the State is bound by the

---

[83] ARSIWA, Articles 2 and 12; Commentary, Crawford, 2002, pp 83–5, 125–30. See further, Crawford, 2013, pp. 93, 113–14, 217–20.

[84] Thus the mere risk of future harm was held not to constitute a sufficient basis for responsibility in the *Lac Lanoux Arbitration* (1957), 24 ILR 101. In *Gabčíkovo-Nagymaros Project (Hungary/Slovakia), Judgment, ICJ Reports 1997*, p 7, the ICJ held that preparations for the diversion of the Danube on the territory of one State did not involve a breach of treaty until the diversion went ahead (and caused damage to the other State). See further, Crawford, 2013, pp. 233–35.

[85] *The 'I'm Alone'* (1935) 3 *RIAA* 1609 at p 1618; see also *Corfu Channel, Merits, Judgment, ICJ Reports 1949*, p 4 at pp 35–6, in which the ICJ made such a declaration in relation to Albania's claim of violation of its sovereignty as the result of the mine-sweeping operations carried out within its territorial waters by British warships.

[86] *Mondev International Ltd v United States of America* (Case No ARB(AF)/99/2), award of 11 October 2002, *ICSID Reports*, vol 6, 192.

obligation in question at the time the act occurs'. The principle is clear enough, but its application may cause problems, in particular regarding changes in customary international law obligations, when it will not be clear precisely when an old customary rule was replaced by a new one.[87] For example, slavery was not always unlawful under international law, yet claims are sometimes made for reparation for persons or groups whose lives are said to have been affected by slavery and the slave trade.[88]

Another problem in applying Article 13 involves determining exactly when, or during what period, a wrongful act occurs. Wrongful acts can continue over a period of time—for instance the continued detention of diplomatic and consular personnel in the *Tehran Hostages* case, or the forced or involuntary disappearance of a person contrary to human rights norms.[89] Other wrongs may be instantaneous, even though their effects may continue after the point of breach. For example, an unlawful killing or a law expropriating property have effect at a specific moment; the breach occurs at the moment the victim is killed or the property passes, and this even though the effects of these breaches are enduring. In general such continuing consequences concern the scope of reparation, not whether there has been a breach in the first place.[90]

These distinctions may also be significant when it comes to issues of the jurisdiction of courts in cases concerning responsibility. For example under the European Convention on Human Rights (ECHR), claims can only be brought against a State party concerning breaches occurring after the Convention entered into force for that State. But it may be—depending on how one characterizes the conduct—that a breach which was initially committed by a State before it became a party continues thereafter and to that extent falls within the jurisdiction *ratione temporis* of the tribunal in question. For example, the circumstances of the *Loizidou* case before the European Court of Human Rights went back to the Turkish intervention in Cyprus in 1974, after Turkey became a party to the European Convention but long before it accepted the right of individual petition. But the continuing exclusion of Mrs Loizidou from access to her property in the Turkish-controlled north continued after that date and could be dealt with by the Court.[91]

C. CIRCUMSTANCES PRECLUDING WRONGFULNESS: DEFENCES OR EXCUSES FOR BREACHES OF INTERNATIONAL LAW

Although conduct may be clearly attributable to a State, and be clearly inconsistent with its international obligations, it is possible that responsibility will not follow. The State may be able to rely on some defence or excuse: in the Articles on State Responsibility these are collected under the heading of 'Circumstances precluding wrongfulness' in Chapter V

---

[87] See, eg *Fisheries Jurisdiction (United Kingdom v Iceland), Merits, Judgment, ICJ Reports 1974*, p 3.

[88] *Le Louis* (1817) 2 Dodson 210.

[89] See, eg the judgment of the Inter-American Court of Human Rights in *Blake v Guatemala, Merits, Judgment of 24 January 1998, Ser C, no 36* (1998).

[90] ARSIWA, Article 14; Commentary, Crawford, 2002, pp 135–40. See further, Crawford, 2013, pp 253–65.

[91] See *Loizidou v Turkey (Preliminary Objections)*, Judgment of 23 March 1995, Ser A, no 310, 20 *EHRR* 99 and *Merits, RJD 1996–VI*, 23 *EHRR* 513: see also *Papamichalopoulos and others v Greece*, Judgment of 24 June 1993, Ser A, no 260–B (European Court of Human Rights). For cases dealing with similar issues before other human rights bodies, see, eg the decision of the Human Rights Committee in *Lovelace v Canada*, decision of 30 July 1981, UN Doc A/36/40, p 166 under the individual petition provisions of the Optional Protocol to the ICCPR; and the judgments of the Inter-American Court of Human Rights in *Blake v Guatemala, Preliminary Objections, Judgment of 2 July 1996, Ser C, no 27* (1996) and *Blake v Guatemala, Merits, Judgment of 24 January 1998, Ser C, no 36* (1998), affirming the continuing character of forced disappearances.

of Part One. Chapter V is essentially a catalogue or compilation of rules that have been rec-ognized as justifying or excusing non-compliance by a State with its international obliga-tions, and it is not exclusive.[92] It should be noted that none of the circumstances precluding wrongfulness can operate to excuse conduct which violates a peremptory norm (ARSIWA, Article 26): one cannot plead necessity to justify invading Belgium, for example.[93]

1. Consent

Valid consent by a State to action by another State which would otherwise be inconsist-ent with its international obligations precludes the wrongfulness of that action as against the consenting State (ARSIWA, Article 26). This is consistent with the role of consent in international relations generally: thus a State may consent to military action on its ter-ritory which (absent its consent) would be unlawful under the United Nations Charter. More mundanely, a State may consent to foreign judicial inquiries or arrest of suspects on its territory.[94] However, the scope of any consent in fact given by a State needs to be carefully examined and normally will be strictly construed.[95] Further, consent only goes so far: a State cannot waive the application of what in national law would be called manda-tory rules and in international law are called peremptory norms. Thus a State cannot (by treaty or otherwise) consent to or legitimize genocide, a situation expressly provided for in the ILC's formulation of the defence of consent; consent must be 'valid' (ARSIWA Article 20; cf Article 26). Further, consent will only preclude the wrongfulness of conduct with regard to the consenting State; if the obligation breached is owed in parallel to more than one State, the wrongfulness of the act will not be precluded with regard to those States that have not consented.[96]

2. Self-defence

In certain circumstances, a State may permissibly disregard other international obliga-tions while acting in self-defence in accordance with the Charter of the United Nations (ARSIWA, Article 21). The point was implicitly recognized by the International Court in the *Nuclear Weapons* Advisory Opinion, when it distinguished between *per se* restric-tions on the use of force, whatever the circumstances—in another formulation, 'obliga-tions of total restraint'—and considerations which, even if mandatory in time of peace, might be overridden for a State facing an imminent threat and required to act against it in self-defence.[97]

3. *Force majeure*

In common with most legal systems, international law does not impose responsibility where the non-performance of an obligation is due to circumstances entirely outside the

---

[92] Specific defences or excuses may be recognized for particular obligations: eg, Article 17 of the 1982 Convention on the Law of the Sea. Cf ARSIWA, Article 55.

[93] As Chancellor von Bethmann-Hollweg did before the Reichstag in 1914: see Crawford, 2002, p 178. See further, Crawford, 2013, Ch 9.

[94] See, eg *Savarkar (Great Britain v France)* (1911) 11 *RIAA* 243.

[95] See, eg the careful consideration given by the ICJ to the scope and extent of the DRC's consent to the pres-ence of Ugandan troops on its territory in *Armed Activities on the Territory of the Congo (Democratic Republic of the Congo v Uganda)*, Judgment, ICJ Reports 2005, p 168.

[96] See, eg *Customs Régime between Germany and Austria, 1931, Advisory Opinion*, PCIJ, Ser A/B, No 41, p 37.

[97] On *per se* restrictions see *Legality of the Threat or Use of Nuclear Weapons, Advisory Opinion*, ICJ Reports 1996, p 226, paras 39, 52; on 'obligations of total restraint', see ibid, para 30.

control of the State. This defence obviously needs to be tightly circumscribed, and the language of Article 23(1) of the ILC Articles provides that *force majeure* is a defence only where 'the occurrence of an irresistible force or of an unforeseen event, beyond the control of the State, [makes] it materially impossible in the circumstances to perform the obligation'. The defence of *force majeure* is further circumscribed by the limitations in Article 23(2), which provide that *force majeure* will not apply if either the situation 'is due, either alone or in combination with other factors, to the conduct of the State invoking it', or if, as a result of assessment of the situation and the obligation in question, the State seeking to invoke *force majeure* is to be regarded as having assumed the risk of the situation occurring.

4. Distress and necessity

The two circumstances of distress and necessity have much in common in that they both excuse conduct which would otherwise be wrongful because of extreme circumstances. According to Article 24, distress operates to excuse conduct where the author of the act 'had no other reasonable way...of saving the author's life or the lives of other persons entrusted to the author's care'. By contrast, necessity operates to excuse conduct taken which 'is the only means for the State to safeguard an essential interest against a grave and imminent peril'. Distress and necessity are to be distinguished from *force majeure* in that violation of the obligation in question is theoretically avoidable, although absolute compliance of the State with its international obligations is not required; a State is not normally required to sacrifice human life or to suffer inordinate damage to its vital interests in order to fulfil its international obligations.

The possibilities of abuse are obvious, in particular for invocation of necessity, and in the ILC Articles both circumstances are narrowly confined. Thus reliance on them is precluded if the State has in some way contributed to the situation which it is seeking to invoke to excuse its conduct. Further, the invoking State can only excuse conduct which is not unduly onerous for other States. Reliance on distress is precluded if the act in question 'is likely to create a comparable or greater peril' (ARSIWA, Article 24(2)(b)). Likewise, the invocation of a state of necessity is precluded if the action would 'seriously impair an essential interest of the State or States towards which the obligation exists, or of the international community as a whole' (ARSIWA, Article 25(1)(b)).

In recent years, Argentina has sought to rely on a state of necessity as justifying the measures it adopted to deal with the Argentine financial crisis between 1999 and 2002; those measures have given rise to a large number of claims by foreign investors under bilateral investment treaties. In the majority of cases, the plea of necessity has been rejected on the grounds that the financial crisis and its potential consequences were not sufficiently serious to be regarded as imperilling an 'essential interest' and the situation did not involve a 'grave and imminent peril'; in any case, the measures adopted were not the 'only way' for Argentina to deal with the crisis, there were other lawful means at its disposal in that regard, and Argentina had contributed to the situation.[98]

---

[98] See eg *CMS Gas Transmission Company* v *Argentine Republic (ICSID Case No ARB/01/8)*, Award of 12 May 2005; *Enron Corporation and Ponderosa Assets LP* v *Argentine Republic (ICSID Case No ARB/01/3)*, Award of 22 May 2007; *Sempra Energy International* v *Argentine Republic (ICSID Case No ARB/02/16)*, Award of 28 September 2007; *BG Group plc* v *Republic of Argentina*, Final Award of 24 December 2007. Cf *LG&E Energy Corp, LG&E Capital Corp, LG&E International Inc* v *Argentine Republic (ICSID Case No ARB/02/1)*, Decision on Liability of 3 October 2006, in which the Tribunal concluded that a state of necessity had existed for at least part of the period in question. The Award in *CMS* was the subject of an application for annulment; the ad hoc Committee, although finding various defects in the reasoning of the Tribunal, declined to annul the Award: *CMS Gas Transmission Company* v *Argentine Republic (ICSID Case No ARB/01/8)*, Decision on Annulment of 25 September 2007.

Although where either distress or a state of necessity is found to have been established the wrongfulness of the act is precluded, other States are not necessarily expected to bear the consequences of another State's misfortune; the invoking State may have to pay compensation for any material loss caused to the State or States to which the obligation breached was owed (Article 27(b)).[99]

5. Countermeasures

As the International Court affirmed in the *Gabčíkovo-Nagymaros Project* case, counter-measures taken by a State in response to an internationally wrongful act of another State are not wrongful acts, but are recognized as a valid means of self-help as long as certain rather stringent conditions are respected.[100] Countermeasures as described in the ILC Articles only cover the suspension of performance by a State of one or more of its obligations; they are to be distinguished from acts of retorsion which, since they are by definition not a breach of the obligations of the State, cannot give rise to State responsibility and therefore require no justification. Certain obligations, such as that to refrain from the use of force, those protecting fundamental human rights and of a humanitarian character prohibiting the taking of reprisals, and those under other peremptory norms may not be suspended by way of countermeasure.

6. Consequences of invoking a circumstance precluding wrongfulness

Although the wrongfulness of an act may be precluded by international law, that is not the end of the question. First, the wrongfulness of the act will only be precluded so long as the circumstance precluding wrongfulness continues to exist. For instance, if State A takes countermeasures in response to a breach by State B of obligations owed to State A, if State B recommences performance of its obligations State A must terminate its countermeasures; if it does not, it will incur responsibility for the period from which the countermeasure was no longer justified (ARSIWA, Article 27(a); and see Articles 52(3)(a) and 53). Secondly, the preclusive effect may be relative rather than general: again, this is obviously true of coun-termeasures, where conduct which is justified *vis-à-vis* a wrongdoing State will not or may not be justified *erga omnes*.

IV. THE CONTENT OF INTERNATIONAL
RESPONSIBILITY

Upon the commission of an internationally wrongful act, certain secondary obligations arise by operation of law. These are codified in Part Two, Chapter I of the ILC Articles, which identifies two main categories, the obligations of cessation and reparation. The

---

[99] Cf *LG&E Energy Corp, LG&E Capital Corp, LG&E International Inc* v *Argentine Republic (ICSID Case No ARB/02/1)*, Decision on Liability of 3 October 2006, in which the Tribunal held that no compensation was payable to the investor in relation to the period during which it held that a state of necessity had existed.

[100] The conditions required by the ARSIWA, in order for countermeasures to be lawful are: they must be taken to induce compliance with the obligations contained in Part Two of the Articles (reparation, cessation...) (Article 49(1)); they must be as far as possible reversible (Article 49(3)); they must be proportionate (Article 51); and there must have been a request to the State to fulfil its obligations, and notification of the decision to take countermeasures accompanied by an offer to negotiate (Article 52(1)). For the recognition of these conditions as customary see *Gabčíkovo-Nagymaros Project (Hungary/Slovakia), Judgment, ICJ Reports 1997*, p 7. Generally see Crawford, 2013.

equal emphasis on these involves an important insight. Issues of State responsibility are not only backward-looking, concerned at obtaining compensation for things past. They are at least as much concerned with the restoration of the legal relationship which has been threatened or impaired by the breach—ie with the assurance of continuing performance for the future. This is particularly clear where the individual breach may not have in itself caused any great amount of harm but where the threat of repetition is a source of legal insecurity. It can be seen in matters as diverse as the protection of embassies or of the environment. In these and other contexts, the relevant rules exist to protect ongoing relationships or situations of continuing value. The analogy of the bilateral contract, relatively readily terminated and replaceable by a contract with someone else, is not a useful one even in the context of strictly bilateral inter-State relations, and *a fortiori* where the legal obligation exists for the protection of a wider range of (non-synallagmatic) interests.

Thus the fact that the responsible State is required to make reparation for a breach does not mean that it can disregard its obligation for the future, effectively buying its way out of compliance; when an obligation is breached, it does not disappear of its own accord. The obligation continues to bind the responsible State, and the State therefore remains obliged to perform it (ARSIWA, Article 29). As a corollary, in the case of a continuing wrongful act, the responsible State is under an obligation to bring that act to an end (Article 30(a)). Indeed in certain circumstances it will be appropriate for—and may be incumbent upon— the responsible State to offer appropriate assurances and guarantees of non-repetition of the act in question to the State to which the obligation is owed (Article 30(b)).

The point was made by the International Court in the *LaGrand* case, which concerned the USA's non-observance of obligations of consular notification under Article 36 of the Vienna Convention on Consular Relations. The particular occasion of Germany's complaint was the failure of notification concerning two death row inmates who (notwithstanding their German nationality) had hardly any connection with Germany; but there was a wider concern as to USA's compliance with its continuing obligations of performance under the Consular Relations Convention. Indeed the USA accepted this, and spelled out in detail the measures it had taken to ensure compliance for the future. In consequence the Court held:

> that the commitment expressed by the United States to ensure implementation of the specific measures adopted in performance of its obligations under Article 36, paragraph 1(b), must be regarded as meeting Germany's request for a general assurance of non-repetition.[101]

But of course questions of reparation also arise, especially where actual harm or damage has occurred, and under international law the responsible State is obliged to make full reparation for the consequences of its breach, provided that these are not too remote or indirect. The linkage between breach and reparation is made clear, for example, in Article 36(2) of the Statute of the International Court of Justice, which specifies among the legal disputes as to which a State may accept the Court's jurisdiction:

(c) the existence of any fact which, if established, would constitute a breach of an international obligation;

(d) the nature or extent of the reparation to be made for the breach of an international obligation.

---

[101] *LaGrand (Germany v United States of America), Merits, Judgment, ICJ Reports 2001*, p 466, para 124; see also the dispositif, para 128(6).

This link was spelled out in a classic passage by the Permanent Court in the *Factory at Chorzów* case, in the context of a jurisdictional provision conferring jurisdiction on the Court over 'differences of opinion arising from the interpretation and the application' of particular treaty provisions:

> It is a principle of international law that the breach of an engagement involves an obligation to make reparation in an adequate form. Reparation therefore is the indispensable complement of a failure to apply a convention and there is no necessity for this to be stated in the convention itself. Differences relating to reparations, which may be due by reason of failure to apply a convention, are consequently differences relating to its application.[102]

Thus there is no need for a specific mandate to an international court or tribunal to award reparation, if it has jurisdiction as between the parties in the matter: a dispute as to the interpretation or application of a treaty covers a dispute as to the consequences of its breach and thus the form and extent of reparation.

The underlying principle is that reparation must wipe out the consequences of the breach, putting the parties as far as possible in the same position as they would have been if the breach had not occurred. In order to achieve that, reparation may take several forms, including but not limited to monetary compensation. Again, both points were made by the Permanent Court in a later stage of the *Chorzów* case:

> The essential principle contained in the actual notion of an illegal act—a principle which seems to be established by international practice and in particular by the decisions of arbitral tribunals—is that reparation must, so far as possible, wipe out all the consequences of the illegal act and reestablish the situation which would, in all probability, have existed if that act had not been committed. Restitution in kind, or, if this is not possible, payment of a sum corresponding to the value which a restitution in kind would bear; the award, if need be, of damages for loss sustained which would not be covered by restitution in kind or payment in place of it—such are the principles which should serve to determine the amount of compensation due for an act contrary to international law.[103]

As this passage suggests, in theory at least, international law has always placed restitution as the first of the forms of reparation; it is only where restitution is not possible that other forms are substituted. This contrasts with the common law approach, under which money was taken to be the measure of all things and specific performance or restitution in kind were historically somewhat exceptional. In practice the two approaches are tending to converge—on the one hand, it is not infrequently found that specific restitution is not possible or can only be made in an approximate form in international law, while courts in the common law tradition have been expanding the scope of non-pecuniary remedies.

The basic requirement of compensation is that it should cover any 'financially assessable damage' flowing from the breach (ARSIWA, Article 36). In many cases (especially those involving loss of life, loss of opportunity, or psychiatric harm), the process of quantification is approximate and may even appear arbitrary; however, as in domestic legal systems, the difficulty in quantifying intangible loss has never had as a consequence that no compensation is payable.[104] By contrast in cases involving loss of property (including expropriation) a

---

[102] *Factory at Chorzów, Jurisdiction, Judgment No 8, 1927, PCIJ, Ser A, No 9* at p 21.

[103] *Factory at Chorzów, Merits, Judgment No 13, 1928, PCIJ, Ser A, No 17* at p 47.

[104] See eg the classic statement by Umpire Parker in relation to non-material damage in *The S.S. 'Lusitania' (USA v Germany)*, (1923) 7 *RIAA* 32 at p 40: 'That one injured is, under the rules of international law, entitled to be compensated for an injury inflicted resulting in mental suffering, injury to his feelings, humiliation, shame, degradation, loss of social position or injury to his credit or to his reputation, there can be no doubt, and such

market for the property may exist which will give greater guidance. In addition, issues such as loss of profits may arise and, provided they are clearly established, may be compensable. Compensation may be supplemented by the award of interest (including, if this is justified, compound interest); after some prevarication, the ILC decided to treat the issue of interest in a separate article (ARSIWA, Article 38; Commentary, Crawford, 2002, pp 235–9).

Although international tribunals have gradually been moving towards a more realistic appreciation of issues of compensation (Gray, 1987, pp 77–95; Crawford, 2002, pp 218–30; Crawford, 2013, Ch 17)—and of remedies more generally—it remains the case that many international disputes have a distinctly symbolic element. The claimant (whether a State or some other entity) may seek vindication more than compensation, and this is recognized in the international law of reparation by way of the protean remedy of 'satisfaction'. According to Article 37(2) of the ILC Articles, satisfaction 'may consist in an acknowledgement of the breach, an expression of regret, an apology or another appropriate modality'. In many cases before international courts and tribunals, an authoritative finding of the breach will be held to be sufficient satisfaction: this was the case in terms of Albania's claim that the UK had violated its sovereignty by conducting certain mine-sweeping operations in its territorial waters in the *Corfu Channel* case,[105] and it has been held to be the situation in innumerable human rights cases, including some where more substantial remedies might have seemed justified (Shelton, 2005, pp 255–68). Similarly, in the *Bosnian Genocide* case, the ICJ held that the FRY had breached its obligation to prevent genocide in relation to the massacre at Srebrenica. Having recognized that restitution was not possible and that compensation was not appropriate given the lack of the necessary 'sufficiently direct and causal nexus' between the breach by the FRY of the obligation and the massacre,[106] it held that a declaration constituted 'in itself appropriate just satisfaction'.[107]

On the other hand, in a situation in which the breach is a continuing one, a declaration of breach and that the responsible State is under a duty to put an end to it may take on some of the characteristics of an injunction, albeit that there are few mechanisms to ensure enforcement or compliance. Thus in *Avena*, the ICJ held that the USA had breached its obligations under the Vienna Convention on Consular Relations in relation to a number of Mexican nationals who had been convicted and sentenced to death by failing to inform them of their right to have the consular authorities notified. The Court made declarations as to the specific violations of the Vienna Convention,[108] and further held that appropriate reparation consisted in a declaration that the USA was 'to provide, by means of its own choosing, review and reconsideration of the: convictions and sentences of the Mexican nationals'.[109] Similarly, in *Bosnian Genocide*, the Court concluded that there had been a failure to comply with the obligation to punish genocide. The Court in that regard made a declaration not only of the fact of the breach, but also ordered that Serbia 'should immediately take effective steps to ensure full compliance' with its obligation to punish, and 'to transfer individuals accused of genocide [...] for trial by the International Criminal Tribunal for the former Yugoslavia, and to co-operate fully with that Tribunal'.

---

compensation should be commensurate to the injury. Such damages are very real, and the mere fact that they are difficult to measure or estimate by money standards makes them none the less real and affords no reason why the injured person should not be compensated therefore as compensatory damages.'

[105] *Corfu Channel, Merits, Judgment, ICJ Reports 1949*, p 4 at p 25 and pp 35–6.

[106] *Application of the Convention on the Prevention and Punishment of the Crime of Genocide (Bosnia and Herzegovina v Serbia and Montenegro), Merits, Judgment, ICJ Reports 2007*, p 43, paras 460–62.

[107] Ibid, paras 463 and 471(5) and (9).

[108] *Avena and Other Mexican Nationals (Mexico v United States of America), ICJ Reports 2004*, p 12, paras 153(4)–(8).

[109] Ibid, para 153(9).

As was noted above in Section II B, if the conduct in question constitutes a serious breach of an obligation arising under a peremptory norm of general international law certain additional consequences arise for all other States under Article 41—in particular, the obligation not to recognize as lawful the situation created and not to render aid or assistance in its maintenance.

V. INVOCATION OF RESPONSIBILITY: RESPONSES BY THE INJURED STATE AND OTHER STATES

Although international responsibility is deemed to arise directly by operation of law on the occurrence of a breach, for practical purposes that responsibility has to be invoked by someone. It may be invoked by the injured State or other party, or possibly by some third State concerned with the 'public order' consequences of the breach. Part Three of the ILC Articles deals with this important issue but in a non-exclusive way. In particular, while it acknowledges that the responsibility of a State may be invoked by an injured party other than a State (eg by an individual applicant to the European Court of Human Rights), Article 33(2) leaves issues of the rights of persons or entities other than States (including the right of invocation) for treatment elsewhere. The scope of Part Three is thus narrower than that of Parts One and Two of the Articles: these deal with the conditions for and consequences of *all* breaches of international law by a State in the field of responsibility, whereas Part Three only deals with the invocation of the responsibility of a State by another State or States.

Even so, the subject of Part Three is a large and controversial one. To what extent is a State to be considered as injured by a breach of international law on the part of another State? And if not individually injured, to what extent might it demand remedies for the breach—with the inferential consequence of countermeasures if such remedies are not forthcoming? Given that international law includes not only bilateral obligations analogous in national systems to contract and tort (or delict), but also obligations intended to protect vital human interests of a generic kind (peace and security, the environment, sustainable development), the questions dealt with in Part Three could scarcely be more important.

They are primarily addressed through two articles. One (Article 42) defines in relatively narrow and precise terms the concept of the 'injured State', drawing in particular on the analogy of Article 60(2) of the Vienna Convention on the Law of Treaties.[110] The second (Article 48) deals with the invocation of responsibility in the collective interest, in particular with respect to obligations owed to the international community as a whole, giving effect to the

---

[110] Article 60(2) provides as follows:
  2. A material breach of a multilateral treaty by one of the parties entitles:
    (a) the other parties by unanimous agreement to suspend the operation of the treaty in whole or in part or to terminate it either:
      (i) in the relations between themselves and the defaulting State; or
      (ii) as between all the parties;
    (b) a party specially affected by the breach to invoke it as a ground for suspending the operation of the treaty in whole or in part in the relations between itself and the defaulting State;
    (c) any party other than the defaulting State to invoke the breach as a ground for suspending the operation of the treaty in whole or in part with respect to itself if the treaty is of such a character that a material breach of its provisions by one party radically changes the position of every party with respect to the further performance of its obligations under the treaty.

Court's dictum in the *Barcelona Traction* case, set out below. The former category covers the breach of an obligation owed to a State individually. Also treated as 'injured States' are those which are particularly affected by the breach of a multilateral obligation, either because they are 'specially affected' or because the obligation is integral in character, so that a breach affects the enjoyment of the rights or the performance of the obligations of all the States concerned.

The contrast is with the 'other States' entitled to invoke responsibility, which are specified in Article 48(1):

Any State other than an injured State is entitled to invoke the responsibility of another State... if:

(a) the obligation breached is owed to a group of States including that State, and is established for the protection of a collective interest of the group; or

(b) the obligation breached is owed to the international community as a whole.

Article 48(1)(b) reflects the distinction drawn by the International Court in *Barcelona Traction* between 'bilaterizable' obligations and obligations owed to the international community as a whole (sometimes called obligations '*erga omnes*'), a category that encompasses most, if not all, peremptory norms of international law,. In the case of the latter type of obligations:

By their very nature [they] are the concern of all States. In view of the importance of the rights involved, all States can be held to have a legal interest in their protection...[111]

The Court in 1970 gave a number of examples of such obligations, including the prohibition of acts of aggression and genocide and 'the principles and rules concerning the basic rights of the human person, including protection from slavery and discrimination.'[112] Since then, the Court has also recognized the right of self-determination,[113] those obligations of international humanitarian law which it had previously described as 'intransgressible principles of international customary international law,'[114] as well as the prohibition of torture[115] as falling within the category.

Article 48(1)(a) covers obligations owed to a group of States and 'established for the protection of a collective interest of the group'; the prime examples are obligations under multilateral treaties protecting 'community' interests, for instance obligations under human rights treaties, and certain treaty obligations in the field of environmental law. The primary

---

[111] *Barcelona Traction, Light and Power Company, Limited, Second Phase, Judgment, ICJ Reports 1970*, p 3, para 33.

[112] Ibid, para 34. For reaffirmation of the *erga omnes* nature of the prohibition of genocide, see *Application of the Convention on the Prevention and Punishment of the Crime of Genocide, Preliminary Objections, ICJ Reports 1996*, p 595, para 31; *Armed Activities on the Territory of the Congo (New Application: 2002) (Democratic Republic of the Congo v Rwanda), Provisional Measures, Order of 10 July 2002, ICJ Reports 2002*, p 219, para 71.

[113] See *East Timor (Portugal v Australia), Judgment, ICJ Reports 1995*, p 90, para 29. See also *Legal Consequences of the Construction of a Wall in the Occupied Palestine Territory, Advisory Opinion, ICJ Reports 2004*, p 136, para 155.

[114] Ibid, para 157; the quoted passage is from the *Legality of the Threat or Use of Nuclear Weapons, Advisory Opinion, ICJ Reports 1996*, p 266, para 79. In *Jurisdictional Immunities of the State (Germany v Italy; Greece Intervening)*, Judgment of 3 February 2012, nyr, paras 93–7, the Court deliberately abstained from taking a position as to whether the 'rules of the law of armed conflict which prohibit the murder of civilians in occupied territory, the deportation of civilian inhabitants to slave labour and the deportation of prisoners of war to slave labour' constitute rules of *jus cogens*, reasoning that, even assuming that were so, in any case there was no conflict between the *jus cogens* character of the relevant norms and the rules on State immunity.

[115] *Questions Relating to the Obligation to Prosecute or Extradite (Belgium v Senegal)*, Judgment, of 20 July 2012, nyr, para 99.

beneficiaries of such obligations are either individuals in the case of the former, or the group of States as a whole in the case of the latter.[116] Obligations of this type are sometimes referred to as obligations *erga omnes partes*.

By definition the States falling within the situations covered by Article 48(1), will not normally have suffered any injury, save the purely 'legal' injury resulting from the very violation of the norm in question. As a consequence, the ILC proposed that in invoking the responsibility of the wrongdoing State on this basis, they should be limited to claiming cessation of continuing wrongful acts and assurances and guarantees of non-repetition, as well as performance of the obligation of reparation 'in the interest of the injured State or the beneficiaries of the obligation breached' (Article 48(2)(a) and (b)).

As yet, the ILC's proposal as to obligations *erga omnes*, although founded on the dictum of the Court in *Barcelona Traction*, has found no concrete support in State practice.[117] However, as concerns obligations *erga omnes partes*, in *Questions Relating to the Obligation to Prosecute or Extradite*, a dispute arising under the Convention Against Torture (one of the paradigm examples of a multilateral treaty establishing obligations in the collective interest), the International Court substantially endorsed the approach proposed by the ILC in Article 48(1)(b) although it did so without expressly referring to the Articles.

In rejecting the objection to the admissibility of Belgium's claim invoking the responsibility of Senegal for failure to comply with its obligations under the Convention in respect of Hissene Habré, who was accused of various acts of torture, the Court observed:

> The States parties to the Convention have a common interest to ensure, in view of their shared values, that acts of torture are prevented and that, if they occur, their authors do not enjoy impunity. The obligations of a State party to conduct a preliminary inquiry into the facts and to submit the case to its competent authorities for prosecution are triggered by the presence of the alleged offender in its territory, regardless of the nationality of the offender or the victims, or of the place where the alleged offences occurred. All the other States parties have a common interest in compliance with these obligations by the State in whose territory the alleged offender is present. That common interest implies that the obligations in question are owed by any State party to all the other States parties to the Convention. All the States parties 'have a legal interest' in the protection of the rights involved [...]. These obligations may be defined as 'obligations erga omnes partes' in the sense that each State party has an interest in compliance with them in any given case.
>
> The common interest in compliance with the relevant obligations under the Convention against Torture implies the entitlement of each State party to the Convention to make a claim concerning the cessation of an alleged breach by another State party. If a special interest were required for that purpose, in many cases no State would be in the position to make such a claim. It follows that any State party to the Convention may invoke the responsibility of another State party with a view to ascertaining the alleged failure to comply with its obligations *erga omnes partes* [...], and to bring that failure to an end.[118]

---

[116] This does not exclude the possibility that one or more States may be injured in the sense of ARSIWA, Article 42 by a breach of an environmental protection norm. Rather, as demonstrated by the fact that cessation is sought in the interests of the beneficiaries of the obligation, Article 48 seeks, without prejudice to that possibility, to articulate the possible interest of other States in compliance with the obligation in question.

[117] Although cf the comments of Judge Simma in *Armed Activities on the Territory of the Congo (Democratic Republic of the Congo v Uganda)*, Judgment, ICJ Reports 2005, p 168, Separate Opinion of Judge Simma, paras 32–41.

[118] *Questions Relating to the Obligation to Prosecute or Extradite (Belgium v Senegal)*, Judgment of 20 July 2012, nyr, paras 68–9.

The Court's reference to the 'legal interest' in protection of the rights involved, in support of which the Court provided a reference to its *dictum* in the *Barcelona Traction* case, implies an acceptance of the same approach in respect of obligations *erga omnes*.

Part Three of the ILC Articles goes on to consider a number of related questions, for example, the consequences of invocation of responsibility by or against several States, circumstances such as waiver or delay where a State may be considered to have lost the right to invoke responsibility, as well as that ultimate form of invocation, the taking of countermeasures in response to an international wrongful act which remains unredressed and unremedied. Some of these issues are dealt with elsewhere in this book.

VI. FURTHER DEVELOPMENT OF THE LAW OF INTERNATIONAL RESPONSIBILITY

As we have seen, there has traditionally been a tendency to view international responsibility as, in the first place, essentially a bilateral matter, without wider consequences for others or for the international system as a whole, and, in the second place, as quintessentially an inter-State issue, separated from questions of the relations between States and individuals or corporations, or from the rather unaccountable world of international organizations. This approach works well enough for bilateral treaties between States or for breaches of general international law rules which have an essentially bilateral operation in the field of intergovernmental relations. But international law now contains a range of rules which cannot be broken down into bundles of bilateral relations between States but cover a much broader range. How can these be accommodated within the traditional structure of State responsibility? The attempt to develop the law beyond traditional paradigms was the greatest challenge facing the ILC, and constitutes one of the more fascinating fields of a rapidly developing—and yet precarious—international order. In the decade or so since the adoption of the Articles, at least some of the progressive steps proposed by the ILC are now becoming accepted.

REFERENCES

ALSTON, P (2005), *Non-State Actors and Human Rights* (Oxford: Oxford University Press).

BOLLECKER-STERN, B (1973), *Le prejudice dans la théorie de la responsabilité internationale* (Paris: Pedone).

CLAPHAM, A (2006), *Human Rights Obligations of Non-State Actors* (Oxford: Oxford University Press).

CRAWFORD, J (2002), *The International Law Commission's Articles on State Responsibility; Introduction, Text and Commentaries* (Cambridge: Cambridge University Press).

—— (2013), *State Responsibility. The General Part* (Cambridge: Cambridge University Press).

DE SCHUTTER, O (2006), *Transnational Corporations and Human Rights* (Oxford: Hart Publishing).

EVANS, MD (2013), *Blackstone's International Law Documents*, 11th edn (Oxford: Oxford University Press).

GRAY, C (1987), *Judicial Remedies in International Law* (Oxford: Clarendon Press).

JENNINGS, RY and WATTS, A (1992), *Oppenheim's International Law*, 9th edn (London: Longman).

KLABBERS, J (2009), *An Introduction to International Institutional Law*, 2nd edn (Cambridge: Cambridge University Press).

KOSKENNIEMI, M (2001), 'Solidarity Measures: State Responsibility as a New International Order?', 72 *BYIL* 337.

MORGENSTERN, F (1986), *Legal Problems of International Organizations* (Cambridge: Grotius).

OLLESON, S (2013), 'Internationally Wrongful Acts in the Domestic Courts: The Contribution of Domestic Courts to the Development of Customary International Law Relating to the Engagement of International Responsibility', 26 *LJIL* 615.

RATNER, SR (2001), 'Corporations and Human Rights: A Theory of Legal Responsibility', 111 *Yale LJ* 443.

RUBIN, AP (1998), *The Law of Piracy*, 2nd edn (Irvington-on-Hudson, NY: Transnational Publishers).

SHELTON, D (2005), *Remedies in International Human Rights Law*, 2nd edn (Oxford: Oxford University Press).

WELLENS, K (2002), *Remedies against International Organizations* (Cambridge: Cambridge University Press).

WITTICH, S (2013), 'Domestic Courts and the Content and Implementation of State Responsibility', 26 *LJIL* 643.

FURTHER READING

BODANSKY, D, CROOK, J, ROSENSTOCK, R, BROWN WEISS, E, BEDERMAN, DJ, SHELTON, D, CARON, DD, and CRAWFORD, J (2002), 'Symposium: The ILC's State Responsibility Articles', 96 *AJIL* 773–890: a collection of responses to the adoption of the ILC's Articles on State Responsibility.

CRAWFORD, J (2002), *The International Law Commission's Articles on State Responsibility; Introduction, Text and Commentaries* (Cambridge: Cambridge University Press): the ILC's Articles on State Responsibility and authoritative commentaries adopted in 2001, together with an introduction and analytical tools, including an index and table of cases.

—— (2013), *State Responsibility: The General Part* (Cambridge: Cambridge University Press): comprehensive account of the law and practice; appends the main texts.

—— and OLLESON, S (2005), 'The Continuing Debate on a UN Convention on State Responsibility', 54 *ICLQ* 959: an account of the debate in the Sixth Committee of the General Assembly in late 2004 as to whether the ILC's Articles on State Responsibility should be transformed into a multilateral convention.

——, PELLET, A and OLLESON, S (eds) (2010), *The Law of International Responsibility* (Oxford: Oxford University Press): a collection of essays by expert academics and practitioners, covering an overview of the entirety of the field of international responsibility.

DUPUY, P-M, NOLTE, G, SPINEDI, M, SICILIANOS, L-A, WYLER, E, TAMS, CJ, GATTINI, A, SCOBBIE, I, ALLAND, D, and KLEIN, P (2002), 'Symposium: Assessing the Work of the International Law Commission on State Responsibility', 13 *EJIL* 1037–1256: a stimulating collection of essays on the ILC's Articles on State Responsibility, with particular emphasis on the 'serious breaches' provisions and the multilateral aspects of invocation.

OLLESON, S (2013), 'Internationally Wrongful Acts in the Domestic Courts: The Contribution of Domestic Courts to the Development of Customary International Law Relating to the Engagement of International Responsibility', 26 *LJIL* 615.

RAGAZZI, M (2005), *International Responsibility Today. Essays in Memory of Oscar*

Schachter (Leiden: Nijhoff): a useful collection of 36 essays by specialists covering general and special issues in the field of responsibility.

WITTICH, S (2013), 'Domestic Courts and the Content and Implementation of State Responsibility', 26 *LJIL* 643.

WEBSITES

http://www.lcil.cam.ac.uk/projects/state-responsibility-project
Collection of materials on State responsibility, including the reports of the last Special Rapporteur, and various articles.

http://www.un.org/law/ilc
Official website of the International Law Commission, maintained by the United Nations Secretariat. Collection of materials on the codification of State responsibility by the Commission.

16

ISSUES OF ADMISSIBILITY AND THE LAW ON INTERNATIONAL RESPONSIBILITY

Phoebe Okowa

SUMMARY

This chapter examines the legal regime governing the admissibility of claims in international adjudication. A central element in the admissibility of claims is the requirement that a litigant should be able to establish a legal interest in respect of the claim brought before an international tribunal. Specific attention is therefore paid to the modalities of establishing a legal interest in respect of claims brought by States in their own right and on behalf of their nationals. The role of nationality is examined and the problems posed by competing claims in relation to multiple nationalities are explored. The unique nature of the problems raised in extending diplomatic protection to corporations and shareholding interests is considered in light of the jurisprudence of international tribunals. The emergence of a large category of obligations designed to protect community values and which do not fit within a private rights model pose particular problems for an international adjudication framework, which is largely bilateral in character. Special consideration is therefore given to the perennial difficulties involved in establishing legal interest in the case of obligations *erga omnes*, or those designed to protect collective interests and therefore owed to a multiplicity of States. These difficulties, it is suggested are compounded by the fact that the development of obligations *erga omnes* have not been accompanied by any discernible refinement of the mechanisms for their enforcement. The final section considers the extent to which the operation of the rule on exhaustion of local remedies may operate to affect the admissibility of a claim. The parameters of the rule are explored and circumstances when, as a matter of policy, it ought to be regarded as inapplicable are discussed.

I. INTRODUCTION

The legal premises for the imposition of responsibility as well as the excuses that may exonerate a State from responsibility have already been discussed in the previous chapter. The concern in this chapter is essentially twofold. First, to identify the State or States that could be described as having *locus standi* in relation to a given wrong. Second, to consider the application of other rules of international law that may operate to preclude the admissibility of a claim before an international tribunal even if a cause of action and legal interest are clearly established. Although the basis of responsibility and issues of admissibility generally tend to be treated as discrete topics in much of the literature, there is nevertheless a close relationship between them. The admissibility of a claim is inexorably linked with substantive grounds for the imposition of responsibility. For who has standing to sue in respect of a wrong is to a large extent determined by the nature and content of the obligation, manner of breach, and the range of interests the obligation is designed to protect. As a preliminary matter, a litigant State must be able to establish that an obligation owed to it has been breached. In theory, where the obligation breached is designed to protect community values, it is much easier for a claimant State to establish legal interest by demonstrating that it is within the zone of protection afforded by that obligation (Thirlway, 1995, pp 49–58; Crawford, Pellet and Olleson, 2010, p 1024).[1] But as will be immediately apparent from the following discussion, the legal regime for protecting community obligations lacks intellectual coherence and the modalities for their implementation are fraught with practical difficulties.

II. LEGAL INTEREST AS A PRE-REQUISITE TO ADMISSIBILITY OF CLAIMS

In general, international law like most other legal systems insists that only those claimants who have a demonstrable interest may bring an action in respect of a wrong. A good illustration is in the *South West Africa* cases. The International Court of Justice (ICJ) rejected the applicants' claim principally on the basis that they had no legal right or interest in respect of the subject matter of the dispute brought by them.[2] Ethiopia and Liberia had argued that South Africa's policy of racial discrimination in South West Africa was an express violation of its obligations as trustee under the League mandate. The Court took the view that the obligations in respect of which Ethiopia and Liberia were bringing claims were owed to the League of Nations and not to its individual members, and as such the applicant States had no *locus standi* in respect of the matter. Although the correctness of the interpretation of the mandate by the Court has been doubted (Dugard, 2004, para 38), there is nevertheless a consensus that apart from obligations *erga omnes*, only those who are designated as beneficiaries of international obligations have a right to enforce them.[3] In the *Nicaragua* case, the International Court denied that the USA could rely on alleged breaches of obligations which Nicaragua owed to the Organization of American States (OAS) rather than to the USA itself as a justification for imposing countermeasures on Nicaragua. In the event, the obligations in question were found to

---

[1] The practice of the ICJ unfortunately paints a different picture. In its jurisprudence, the Court has maintained a distinction between the existence of legal interest and the ability to invoke the jurisdictional provisions of the Court. The existence of a legal interest does not necessarily mean that a State will be entitled to bring a claim and other jurisdictional factors may operate to exclude the claim. See *East Timor* case (*Portugal* v *Australia*), *Judgment, ICJ Reports 1995*, p 90 at para 29.

[2] *South West Africa, Second Phase, Judgment, ICJ Reports 1966*, p 6, para 99; see ILC Commentary to Draft Article 48 (para 7), Official Records of the General Assembly, Fifty-sixth Session, Supplement No 10 (A/56/10) Chapter V.

[3] *Barcelona Traction, Light and Power Company, Limited, Second Phase, Judgment, ICJ Reports 1970*, p 3, para 35. See also Crawford, 2013, p 542.

be in the nature of a political pledge rather than a legal commitment. The Court nevertheless pointed out that:

> even supposing that such a political pledge had the force of a legal commitment it could not have justified the United States insisting on the fulfilment of a commitment made not directly towards the United States but towards the organisation, the latter alone being empowered to monitor the implementation.[4]

A. RATIONALE OF INTERNATIONAL LAW RULES ON *LOCUS STANDI*

Several reasons may be detected in the various rules underpinning *locus standi* in international law. The first and most obvious can in part be explained by the nature of international law as a law primarily between States, and as a consequence only States in general have procedural capacity to bring an action before an international tribunal. Thus in the absence of special treaty arrangements granting individuals, corporations, or other legal entities access to international tribunals, their claims must be channelled through the State of their nationality.[5] In this respect, there is something artificial about international law rules on *locus standi*, for even when it is the individual who has been injured, the traditional view proceeds on the premise that it is the State of which that individual is a national that is wronged and who can therefore bring an action in respect of the wrong (Leigh, 1971, p 453; Crawford, *Brownlie's Principles*, 2012, p 702).

Second, general international law rules on standing are premised on a particular view of the role of international tribunals, this being that their function is primarily that of settling disputes between States on a private rights model. They are in large measure concerned with discretely bilateral disputes. Although there has been a consistent jurisprudence recognizing that a large number of obligations do not fit into the private rights model, in particular those designed to protect community values, international law has tended to exclude standing where an applicant State's interest is a general vindication of community values or upholding the principles of legality.[6] A related rationale of the rules on *locus standi*, it could be argued, is to provide an orderly framework for the resolution of disputes and to avoid wherever possible overlapping claims or those that are entirely unmeritorious. Nationality in this context provides a convenient basis for channelling claims.

Thirdly, the rules on admissibility attempt to strike a balance between the need for international supervision of obligations and respect for the sovereign power of States to adjudicate on matters within their jurisdiction. Jurisdiction in respect of matters occurring on their territory is an attribute of sovereignty, and in general national courts have a right of first recourse, with international tribunals possessing something akin to a default power, exercisable in large measure where domestic tribunals have failed to grant a remedy. Thus rules on exhaustion of local remedies can in part be explained by reference to

---

[4] *Military and Paramilitary Activities in and against Nicaragua (Nicaragua v United States of America), Merits, Judgment, ICJ Reports 1986*, p 14, para 262.

[5] The many jurisdictional issues that arise in this context are strictly speaking beyond the scope of the present inquiry and have been extensively dealt with in the literature on jurisdiction of international tribunals. See Fitzmaurice, 1986, pp 427–575; Rosenne, 1997.

[6] See *Barcelona Traction, Light and Power Company, Limited, Second Phase, Judgment, ICJ Reports 1970*, p 3 and *East Timor (Portugal v Australia), Judgment, ICJ Reports 1995*, p 90.

the territorial character of jurisdiction. The decisions in the *Nottebohm*[7] and *Barcelona Traction* cases[8] also manifest a particular sensitivity to the right of the territorial State to deal with matters occurring on its territory.

The emergence of a large category of obligations designed to protect community values and interests, which do not fit within a bilateral or private rights framework, pose a particular challenge for the traditional rules on admissibility of claims. These obligations transcend individual State interests, and the need to protect them through international claims has long been recognized as necessary to protect the underlying community interests.[9] The obligations, principally in the field of human rights, protection of the environment and the preservation of peace and security, may affect the interests of the international community at large without affecting the interests of any one particular State.[10] Extended notions of *locus standi* have been proposed *de lege ferenda* in order to make the protection of these values a reality. Thus, there is increasingly a presumption that all States have a general interest in the legality of actions that affect community values, even if the precise implications are yet to be worked out.[11]

B. MODALITIES OF ESTABLISHING LEGAL INTEREST

Given international law's conception of standing as a vindication of primarily private rights, it comes as no surprise that for a claim to be admissible, the applicant State must demonstrate that it has a legal interest in the matter. At a general level, legal interest is defined by reference to the obligation breached; not quite a distinct issue but part of the definition of the cause of action—the party to whom the obligation is owed is the party entitled to claim. However, two broad propositions provide the basic framework for determining legal interest in international litigation. First, in determining the *locus standi* of a State, a distinction is usually maintained between injury to direct interests and those that affect indirect interests (principally injury to nationals whether natural, corporate, or other legal entity recognized by municipal law). There is a presumption that State protection of its sovereign rights is inherent and a State must be taken to have a legal interest in respect of those wrongs that affect its direct interests. Although the distinction between direct and indirect interests is well established in the literature, and in the jurisprudence of international tribunals, the dividing line between them is not always easy to determine, especially with regard to mixed claims where there are elements of direct injury to a State's own interests as well as injury to its nationals (Meron, 1959, pp 87–8; Wittich, 2001, pp 121–87). In practice, it is accepted that damage to a State's warships, diplomatic missions, members of its armed forces, the executive (including the Head of State) and damage to State property are examples of injuries which qualify as direct interests.

---

[7] *Nottebohm, Second Phase, Judgment, ICJ Reports 1955*, p 4.

[8] *Barcelona Traction, Light and Power Company, Limited, Second Phase, Judgment, ICJ Reports 1970*, p 3.

[9] See, for example, SS '*Wimbledon*', *Judgments, 1923, PCIJ, Series A, No 1* in which the UK, France, Italy, and Japan were able to bring a claim against Germany for denying access to the Kiel Canal. Of the applicant States, Italy and Japan were not directly injured themselves but they were allowed to bring the claim because of the collective interests that all maritime States had in the Kiel canal.

[10] Although there has been a general recognition of obligations *erga omnes*, there is not a single case in which an applicant State has successfully brought a claim designed to enforce community values.

[11] See ILC Articles on the Responsibility of States for Internationally Wrongful Acts (ARSIWA), Article 48; Crawford, 2013, p 370; Simma, 1994, p 217.

III. THE BASES OF DIPLOMATIC PROTECTION

A. NATIONALITY AS THE BASIS OF LEGAL INTEREST IN INDIRECT CLAIMS

Where injury is suffered by a natural person or other legal entity recognized by municipal law, the general view is that the right to bring a claim in respect of the wrong lies with the State of the victim's nationality. It is the bond of nationality that creates the necessary link between a State and the injury in respect of which a claim is brought.

In the *Mavrommatis* case, the Permanent Court observed that:

> It is an elementary principle of international law that a State is entitled to protect its subjects, when injured by acts contrary to international law committed by another State, from which they have been unable to obtain satisfaction through ordinary channels. By taking up the case of one of its subjects and by resorting to diplomatic protection or international judicial proceedings on his behalf, a State is in reality asserting its own rights—rights to ensure, in the person of its subjects, respect for the rules of international law.[12]

Since the exercise of diplomatic protection is generally viewed as the right of the State, the argument has consistently been made that reliance on the right is within the absolute discretion of States (Borchard, 1915, p 29; Oppenheim, 1992, p 934; Malanczuk, 1997, p 257; Dugard, 2000, p 213; ILA, Report of the 96th Conference, 2000; Crawford, 2013, p 571). It is further accepted that the decision whether to exercise the discretion or not is invariably influenced by political considerations rather than the legal merits of the particular claim. The International Court in the *Barcelona Traction* case succinctly made the point when it noted that:

> ...within the limits prescribed by international law, a State may exercise diplomatic protection by whatever means and to whatever extent it thinks fit, for it is its own right that the State is asserting. Should the natural or legal person on whose behalf it is acting consider that their rights are not adequately protected, they have no remedy in international law. All they can do is resort to municipal law, if means are available, with a view to furthering their cause or obtaining redress. The municipal legislator may lay upon the State an obligation to protect its citizens abroad, and may also confer upon the national a right to demand the performance of that obligation, and clothe the right with corresponding sanctions. However, all these questions remain within the province of municipal law and do not affect the position internationally.
>
> The State must be viewed as the sole judge to decide whether its protection will be granted, to what extent it is granted, and when it will cease. It retains in this respect a discretionary power the exercise of which may be determined by considerations of a political or other nature, unrelated to the particular case. Since the claim of the State is not identical with that of the individual or corporate person whose cause is espoused, the State enjoys complete freedom of action.[13]

---

[12] *Mavrommatis Palestine Concessions, Judgment No 2, 1924, PCIJ, Ser A, No 2* at p 12.

[13] *Barcelona Traction, Light and Power Company, Limited, Second Phase, Judgment, ICJ Reports 1970*, p 3, paras 78–9.

In *Abbasi* v *Secretary of State for Foreign and Commonwealth Affairs*,[14] the applicant, who was detained by the US authorities at Guantánamo Bay, sought judicial review to compel the UK foreign office to take up his case and make appropriate representations on his behalf to the US government. In the alternative, he asked that the UK government be compelled to give an explanation as to why representations on his behalf had not been undertaken. The English Court of Appeal, after an extended review of authorities confirmed the orthodox position that diplomatic protection was a right of States and that it did not as such give rise to an enforceable duty under English law. However, it noted that this discretion was subject to judicial oversight, especially if it could be shown that the decision was irrational or contrary to the rules of natural justice.

Moreover, it follows from the discretionary nature of diplomatic protection that there is in principle no obligation on the part of the State to transmit the damages obtained to any of the individuals concerned. Furthermore, in so far as the right of protection is characterized as that of the State, the State espousing a claim may choose to do so even in the face of opposition from the injured individual. It is principally for this reason that those tribunals and jurists who have considered the issue have rejected the so-called *Calvo clause*, the terms of which allowed certain natural and corporate persons to waive the right of diplomatic protection (Shea, 1955).

The discretionary character of diplomatic protection has in recent years been subjected to trenchant criticism, as incompatible with an international system committed to human rights. It has therefore been proposed that the right of diplomatic protection should be seen as a legal duty exercisable by the State on behalf of the injured individual.[15] This position finds some support in national constitutions which provide for a right of protection which is enforceable even against the State of which the person is a national.[16] In practice though, constitutional entrenchment does not radically improve the position of aggrieved individuals. The right as interpreted in domestic cases still grants the executive a wide discretion and in many cases the individual is entitled to no more than an expectation that his request for diplomatic represen- tation will be treated fairly by the executive. For instance, in *Kaunda and others* v *President of the Republic of South Africa and others*[17] the South African Constitutional Court recognized that the right to request diplomatic protection was a constitutional entitlement under the South Africa constitution but it went on to hold that its actual exercise was a matter of foreign policy and therefore within the discretion of the executive branch. The decision in *Kaunda* has been confirmed in two subsequent decisions of the Supreme Court of South Africa. In *Rootman* v *President of the Republic of South Africa*,[18] the Supreme Court refused a request

[14] *Abbasi* v *Sec of Foreign and Commonwealth Affairs and Sec of Home Office* [2002] EWCA Civ 1598, 6 November 2002.

[15] Bennouna, *Preliminary Report on Diplomatic Protection*, 1998, paras 34–7, 65–6; Dugard, 2000, paras 17 and 61–74.

[16] Examples include the constitutions of Albania, Belarus, Bosnia and Herzegovina, Bulgaria, Cambodia, China, Croatia, Estonia, Georgia, Guyana, Hungary, Italy, Kazakhstan, Lao People's Democratic Republic, Latvia, Lithuania, Poland, Portugal, Republic of Korea, Romania, Russian Federation, Spain, the Former Yugoslav Republic of Macedonia, Turkey, Ukraine, Vietnam, and Yugoslavia. See Dugard, 2000, para 80.

[17] *Kaunda and others* v *President of the Republic of South Africa and others*, Case CCT 23/04, 2005 (4) SA 235 (CC).

[18] *Rootman* v *President of the Republic of South Africa*, Case 016/06, [2006] SCA 80 (RSA). See also *Van Zyl* v *Government of the Republic of South Africa*, Case 170/06, [2007] SCA 109 (RSA), rejecting the applicant's argument that they had a constitutional right to diplomatic protection and the government a corresponding obligation to provide such protection, including the submission of claims to international arbitration or adjudi- cation before the international court. The court, although conceding that the exercise of diplomatic protection remained the prerogative of state, was prepared to accept that this may in fact entail a duty to exercise such

by the applicant that the South African Government be compelled to take steps to assist him in securing the execution of a money judgment in his favour, granted by the Pretoria High Court, against the government of the Democratic Republic of Congo (DRC). The applicant had argued that the rule of law created an expectation that the State would assist a citizen enforce his or her rights. The Court, however, noted that although the State may engage in diplomatic negotiations with a foreign State to secure the rights of its citizens, it could not be compelled to do so.

In *Omar Khadr v The Prime Minister of Canada*, the applicant argued that the failure of the Canadian Government to make representations to the US government that he be released from Guantánamo Bay was a violation of his rights under the Canadian Charter of Rights and Freedoms. This was contested by the Canadian government, which argued that it had an 'unfettered discretion to decide whether to request the return of a Canadian citizen detained in a foreign country, this being a matter within its exclusive authority to conduct foreign affairs'. The Court was therefore called upon to examine whether Canada had a legal duty to protect Mr Khadr and what the ambit of that duty might be. The Canadian Supreme Court concluded that, in general, the right of protection was not enforceable as it fell within the executive's conduct of foreign policy. However, the Court would intervene if the government's position was irrational or contrary to a legitimate expectation. The Court concluded that in the specific circumstances of the case, the failure to exercise diplomatic protection was a violation of the applicant's rights to life, liberty, and security of the person.[19] The Supreme Court explained that, in Canada, the rule of law entailed an expectation that all government action was potentially subject to the Charter and the individual rights which it guaranteed. The crown prerogative in the conduct of foreign affairs was also subject to the Charter.[20]

The decisions of national courts on these constitutional provisions support the thesis that general international law as it stands does not contain an enforceable legal duty of diplomatic protection.[21] Human rights obligations and treaties protecting the economic interests of individuals have nevertheless substantially eroded the centrality of diplomatic protection as a mechanism for the protection of aggrieved individuals by creating directly enforceable rights even as against the State of which the individual is a national (ILA Reports, 2000, p 634). When contrasted with its traditional role, it is probably accurate to say that diplomatic protection is today more of a default mechanism for the enforcement

protection where the fundamental rights of the citizen was involved. In deciding whether or not to take up the case of one of its nationals, the government was expected to act rationally. The Court also noted that as the right of diplomatic protection was derived from the constitution as an aspect of citizenship, the South African government could not be expected to intervene where the wrong had been done not to South African citizens but to a foreign company in respect of which they had an interest.

[19] *Omar Khadr v The Prime Minister of Canada* 2009 FCA 246.

[20] However, in *Ilaşcu and Others v Moldova and Russia* [GC], no 48787/99, ECHR *2004-VII* the European Court of Human Rights took the view that duty to make representations including judicial claims may be legally mandatory as a consequence of a State's obligations in Article 1 of the ECHR to 'secure to everyone within its jurisdiction' the rights guaranteed by the convention. In relation to the detention of the applicants in the Transdniestrian Republic controlled by the separatists, the Court took the view that Moldova was under an obligation to make representations to Russia and the separatists to try and secure their release. Failure to do so was a violation of the obligations in Article 1 of the ECHR.

[21] *Kaunda and others v President of the Republic of South Africa and others*, Case CCT 23/04, 2005 (4) SA 235 (CC). In the *Hess Decision*, BverfGE, 55, 349, 90 ILR 386, the German Federal Constitutional Court upheld the existence of a federal constitutional right to diplomatic protection but denied that it was required by customary international law. See also *Abbasi v Sec of Foreign and Commonwealth Affairs and Sec of Home Office* [2002] EWCA Civ 1598, 6 November 2002. Federal Court of Australia in *Hicks v Ruddock* [2007] FCA 299, para 93, did not rule out the possibility that a right of diplomatic protection may in fact be enforceable.

of claims where there are no direct avenues provided for by international law. A better view, it is suggested, is to see diplomatic protection and enforcement mechanisms in human rights instruments as operating in parallel, serving related—but at times discrete—objectives. For example, vindication of the rule of law may require that an action be brought on the international plane by a State even in the face of opposition by the wronged individual (Brierly, 1928, p 48; Dugard, 2000, para 73; Crawford, 2013, pp 584–7). It must also be accepted that States may have wider concerns going beyond the immediate interests of the wronged individual; these interests will at times be better served by exercising the discretion not to bring an action on the international plane. Where the exercise of its discretion results in the denial of a fundamental right, it is suggested that the right of the State should be subordinated to the rights of the aggrieved individual. The existence of a human rights obligation, it is suggested, creates a strong expectation that the State will exercise its discretion in support of the aggrieved individual.

B. ESTABLISHING NATIONALITY FOR PURPOSES OF DIPLOMATIC PROTECTION

1. Natural persons

It is generally accepted that the conferment of nationality is *prima facie* a matter which falls within the jurisdiction of States as an attribute of its sovereignty, and in general there is a presumption that nationality granted by a State in accordance with its domestic law is valid for all purposes, including entitlement to bring a claim on the international plane. There is nevertheless considerable, if not universal, support for the view that the validity of any nationality so conferred on the international plane is a question of international law, and will only be opposable to other States if it has been granted in a manner that conforms to international law criteria.[22] In particular, for nationality to provide a valid basis for the exercise of diplomatic protection, it must have been granted in a manner consistent with principles of international law. For this reason, a grant of nationality may be disregarded on the international plane or treated as a nullity, if it has been made in excess of jurisdictional limits placed by international law, such as the extension of nationality laws to foreigners who owe no allegiance to the State granting nationality. Dugard has also suggested that international law retains a reserve power to disregard nationality laws that are discriminatory in character, or inconsistent with fundamental principles of human rights.[23] Most authorities also agree that nationality will be invalid if it has been acquired *mala fides*, or on the basis of a tenuous connection, such as extending nationality laws to aliens in transit.[24]

The precise role of international law in determining nationality for purposes of diplomatic protection is, however, not free from controversy (Crawford, 2013, pp 574–80). In general, two diametrically opposed positions seem to have emerged in the literature. The first proceeds on the premise that questions of nationality must be settled by way of *renvoi* to municipal law, and in principle the validity of nationality conferred by a State in accordance with the requirements of its internal law must be treated as conclusive since

---

[22] See *Nottebohm, Second Phase, Judgment, ICJ Reports 1955*, p 4.
[23] According to Dugard, nationality laws should be disregarded if they discriminate on the basis of race, gender, or religious affiliation. Dugard, 2000, para 104. See also Oppenheim, 1992, pp 856 and 874; Brownlie, 2008, pp 386 and 388.
[24] Dugard, 2000, para 104.

international law does not as such have a law on nationality.[25] The second position denies conclusiveness to municipal law criteria, and takes as its starting point the view that the validity of nationality on the international plane is a question of international law. In particular, for nationality to be valid on the international plane it must be firmly grounded on the existence of a genuine link between the claimant State and the individual on whose behalf he claims (Brownlie, 2008, p 398; Fitzmaurice, 1957, pp 196–201).

Proponents of the second position argue that although the grant of nationality is a prerogative of States and therefore a question of domestic law, like most unilateral acts performed on the municipal plane, questions of ultimate validity on the international plane must be determined by reference to international standards if the rule of law is to be maintained.[26] This position received explicit support in Article 1 of the 1930 Hague Convention on certain Questions Relating to the Conflict of Nationality Laws, which provided that 'It is for each State to determine under its own law who are its nationals'—but with the proviso that:

> This law shall be recognized by other States in so far as it is consistent with international conventions, international custom, and the principles of law generally recognized with regard to nationality.[27]

Although most writers agree that international law must retain some quality control in matters of nationality, the precise nature of this oversight is the subject matter of disagreement. There is consensus that international law must retain a reserve power to disregard nationality claims that are fraudulent in origin, discriminatory, or in clear violation of generally accepted jurisdictional principles. Beyond that, it is controversial whether—at least in the context of diplomatic protection—international law requires that there should be a genuine or effective link between the State and the national on whose behalf it is claiming (Crawford, *Brownlie's Principles*, 2012, p 706).

2. The requirement of the genuine link

In the *Nottebohm* case the International Court was of the view that for nationality to be a valid basis of diplomatic protection on the international plane, it must be based on a genuine link between the wronged individual and the State on whose behalf it was claiming. It said that:

> A State cannot claim that the rules [pertaining to the acquisition of nationality] which it has thus laid down are entitled to recognition by another State unless it has acted in conformity with this general aim of making the legal bond of nationality accord with the individual's genuine connection with the State which assumes the defence of its citizens by means of protection as against other States.

The Court listed the following as indispensable elements of valid nationality for purposes of diplomatic protection:

> A legal bond having as its basis a social fact of attachment, a genuine connection of existence and sentiments, together with the existence of reciprocal rights and duties. It may be said to constitute a juridical expression of the fact that the individual upon whom it is conferred, either directly by the law or as a result of an act of the authorities, is in fact more

---

[25] *Nottebohm* case, *Second Phase, Judgment, ICJ Reports 1955*, p 4, Dissenting Opinions of Judges Klaestad (p 30), Reid (p 42), and Guggenheim (p 54).
[26] *Flegenheimer Claim* (1958) 25 ILR 91 at pp 96–112; Oppenheim, 1992, p 855.
[27] 179 LNTS 89.

closely connected with the population of the State conferring nationality than with that of any other State.[28]

In State and arbitral practice, the requirement of a genuine link was not without precedent, and had been applied to cases of diplomatic protection involving dual or multiple nationality as a mechanism for prioritizing the claim of the State with the most effective connection. (Brownlie, 2008, p 407). In the *Nottebohm* case, the Court refused to confine its application to those situations. The majority were of the view that a genuine link was a general requirement, a necessary condition for all claims grounded on nationality.[29]

This decision has been controversial and in the literature and subsequent judicial decisions attempts have been made either to distinguish it, or to limit its application to the facts of the case. In the *Flegenheimer* case, the Italian–USA Commission confined the application of the genuine link requirement to cases involving dual nationals.[30] In the *Barcelona Traction* case, the International Court refused to extend the genuine link requirement to corporations, and further, refrained from expressing an opinion on the correctness of the genuine link requirement as a matter of general international law.[31] A number of reasons have been advanced in support of the view that the *Nottebohm* case was not laying down general rules of international law applicable to all cases of nationality. First, there was considerable evidence before the Court that the processes of naturalization by which Nottebohm had acquired his citizenship were probably in bad faith. Dugard has therefore suggested that finding the links between Nottebohm and Liechtenstein to be tenuous provided the Court with a convenient excuse to avoid acknowledging a nationality claim that was tainted by bad faith without having to pass judgment on a government's competence to confer nationality under its own domestic law (Dugard, 2000, para 108).

Secondly, there is no doubt that the Court was influenced by the unique factual context of the dispute. Nottebohm's links with Guatemala were close and long-standing, spanning over a period of some 34 years. On the other hand his connections with Liechtenstein were weak and transitory and, given the circumstances, the Court thought it inequitable to allow Liechtenstein to exercise diplomatic protection as against Guatemala.[32] It is for this reason that in much of the subsequent literature the argument has been made that the Court was not dealing with the question of the validity of Nottebohm's application as against the whole world but more specifically against Guatemala. Indeed many authorities have doubted whether the Court would have reached the same conclusion if the case had been brought by Liechtenstein against some third State with whom Nottebohm had no connection (Crawford, 2013, p 574; Harris, 1998, p 594).

It is also possible to argue that although in formal terms the Court was faced with a claim of a person possessing only one nationality, it approached the case as if Nottebohm was a national of both States but with his real and effective nationality being that of Guatemala. If this were so, the *Nottebohm* decision is in keeping with the long-held view that where a person possesses two nationalities, it is the effective nationality that is determinant[33] and the State of second nationality cannot bring a claim against the State of effective first nationality where a genuine link exists.

---

[28] *Nottebohm, Second Phase, Judgment, ICJ Reports 1955*, p 4 at p 23.   [29] Ibid.

[30] *Flegenheimer Claim* (1958), 25 ILR at 148–50.

[31] *Barcelona Traction, Light and Power Company, Limited, Second Phase, Judgment, ICJ Reports 1970*, p 3, para 70.

[32] *Nottebohm, Second Phase, Judgment, ICJ Reports 1955*, p 4 at p 26.

[33] *Canevaro* case (Permanent Court of Arbitration) (1912) 11 *RIAA* 397; *Merge* claim (1955) 22 ILR 443; *Esphanian* v *Bank Tejarat* (1983) 2 Iran-USCTR 157.

The Court's formal conclusion that nationality must be supported by a 'genuine link' in order to be opposable in the field of diplomatic protection has also been criticized for two reasons. First, it has been argued that as a matter of policy, it is desirable that the test for nationality be capable of objective determination. The requirement of a genuine link introduces into this area of law a vague and uncertain test and is therefore open to abuse.[34] Second, that by denying the validity of certain forms of nationality, it has the practical effect of severely restricting the scope of diplomatic protection. It has been argued that it is undesirable as a matter of policy that a wrong should go without redress simply because the links between the State and the national on whose behalf he is claiming are weak.[35] In its decision in the *Ahmadou Sadio Diallo* case,[36] the International Court was not particularly troubled by the genuine link requirement when treating as admissible Guinea's claims against the Democratic Republic of Congo (DRC). Guinea had instituted proceedings by way of diplomatic protection on behalf of Ahmadou Sadio Diallo, a businessman of Guinean nationality who had been resident in the DRC for 32 years. His connections with Guinea were at best tenuous, yet the court's approach to the nationality question was in marked contrast to that taken in the *Nottebohm* case.[37] That Guinea was able to bring this action without any challenge by the respondent State or adverse comment by the Court is a further indication of the prevailing uncertainty as to the exact reach of the 'genuine link' requirement. Until his expulsion from the DRC, it appears that all of Mr Diallo's links for a period of 32 years were with that State—a period not dissimilar to the 34-year link between Nottebohm and Guatemala in the *Nottebohm* case. The *Diallo* decision lends some support to the view that the *Nottebohm* decision should be confined to its own facts and not treated as laying down rules of general application (Douglas, 2009, p 313; Okowa, 2008).

3. Some conclusions

Notwithstanding the authoritative decision of the majority judgment in the *Nottebohm* case, there is no general support for the genuine link requirement in State practice. This is not to say that there is no role for international law in matters of nationality. A limited reserve power to exclude certain nationality claims is generally argued for in cases of manifest fraud, instances where nationality has been extended in bad faith or where the grant of nationality is incompatible with fundamental principles, such as those prohibiting racial discrimination (Crawford, *Brownlie's Principles*, 2012, p. 706).

C. THE NATIONALITY OF CORPORATIONS

As in the case of individuals, international law proceeds on the premise that it is the State of which it is a national which may exercise diplomatic protection on behalf of a company. The general difficulty in this area is in deciding what criteria may be employed to determine the nationality of corporations. The difficulty is not helped by the existence of largely contradictory and incompatible principles in both the literature and in the jurisprudence of international tribunals.

---

[34] Dissenting Opinion of Judge Reid, *Nottebohm, Second Phase, Judgment, ICJ Reports 1955*, p 4 at p 46.

[35] See Dissenting Opinion of Judge ad hoc Guggenheim, ibid, at pp 63–4 and see Brownlie, 2008, pp 417–18.

[36] *Ahmadou Sadio Diallo (Republic of Guinea v Democratic Republic of Congo), Preliminary Objections,* Judgment of 24 May 2007.

[37] Ibid, para 41. Although it is perhaps significant that Mr Diallo, unlike Nottebohm, was born in Guinea of Guinean parents and lived there for his first 17 years. See application instituting proceedings, p 31.

In the *Barcelona Traction* case, the International Court concluded that the nationality of a company had to be determined by reference to the laws of the State in which it was incorporated or had its registered office. The majority were of the view that the simple fact of incorporation under the law of a State was conclusive. Moreover, the majority thought that it was not necessary to lift the corporate veil in order to determine the economic reality of a company, even if this indicated that it had links with a State other than that of incorporation. The Court thus denied Belgium the right to bring an action in respect of wrongs done to a Canadian company, in circumstances where the majority of the share-holders were Belgian. In rejecting Belgium's claim, the Court noted that a company, as an institution of municipal law, was an entity distinct from its shareholders. As such, where a wrong was done to the company, while the interests of the shareholders might be affected it was the company alone that had the right to maintain an action in international law. It noted that:

> whenever shareholder's interests are harmed by an act done to the company, it is to the lat-ter that he must look to institute appropriate action; for although two separate entities may have suffered from the same wrong, it is only one entity whose rights have been infringed.[38]

However, the majority of the Court thought there were a number of instances in which the State of which the shareholders were nationals might be entitled to bring a claim on the international plane. This included those situations where the direct rights of shareholders were affected. Examples given by the Court included: (a) their rights to dividends; (b) the right to attend and vote at general meetings; and (c) the right to share in the assets of the company after liquidation.[39]

Some judges thought that shareholders may be entitled to diplomatic protection in cases where the company had the nationality of the respondent State. The Court refrained from expressing an opinion on the correctness of this proposition, noting that the issue did not arise on the facts of the case since it was Canada, not Spain, which was the coun-try of nationality of the company.[40] However, the correctness of the proposition is in any event open to challenge. First, it ignores the traditional rule that a State is not guilty of violating international law when it harms one of its own nationals.[41] Secondly, it is difficult to reconcile it with the argument advanced by the majority that, when a wrong is done to a company, the interests of the shareholders may be affected but only the company has rights which are capable of legal protection. If shareholders are entitled to protection in the situation where the wrong is done to the company by the state of incor-poration and therefore to its own national, what is the precise legal basis of the protec-tion? Is there a process here by which mere interests are transformed into rights capable of legal protection?

The Court also thought that shareholders may be entitled to protection where the com-pany had ceased to exist.[42] On the facts, the Court took the view that although the Barcelona Traction Company was in receivership, it was formally still in existence, and for this rea-son Belgium could not exercise protection on behalf of the shareholders. Other judges

---

[38] *Barcelona Traction, Light and Power Company, Limited, Second Phase, Judgment, ICJ Reports 1970*, p 3, para 44.

[39] Ibid, para 47. See also Lowe, 2002, p 275; Watts, 1996, p 435.

[40] Ibid, para 92. There is, however, support for this view in the jurisprudence of the Iran-USA Claims tribunal, eg *Starrett Housing Corporation, et al v Government of the Islamic Republic of Iran, et al* (1983) 4 Iran-USCTR 122.

[41] See ibid, Separate Opinion of Judge Jessup, p 162 at p 192 (para 52).   [42] Ibid, paras 64–8.

were prepared to extend diplomatic protection in those instances where, although a company was still formally in existence, it had become practically paralysed.[43]

The Court advanced some policy-based justifications to support its conclusions.[44] In rejecting the claims of Belgium, the Court denied that shareholders were vested with any general right of protection. It noted that extension of protection to shareholders, by exposing the allegedly wrong-doing State to a wide range of claimants, could introduce an element of uncertainty and insecurity in international economic relations. The Court was also concerned with the practical difficulty of ascertaining shareholding interests since such shares frequently change hands, and in many instances it could be difficult to determine which State was entitled to exercise protection, especially where the nominee and beneficiaries were from different States.[45] Moreover, given the fluid character of the shares, ascertaining the legal interest may be particularly difficult, since for a right of protection to exist nationality must be continuous (a point examined subsequently). In the *Barcelona Traction* case itself, there was some doubt whether the Belgian interest in the shares had been continuous and in particular whether Belgium could have satisfied the test at the time of the injury. The decision is therefore an unequivocal authority in support of the view that, when a company is injured, it is the national State of the company alone that may bring an action and shareholders as a category are not entitled to diplomatic protection. However, it is clear that some judges were prepared to extend protection to shareholders. Moreover, a number of them favoured a different test for corporations and would have applied the genuine link test as formulated in the *Nottebohm* case, with the result that the State of incorporation would not have an automatic right of protection in the absence of some tangible connection. Such a genuine link could be demonstrated by proving that the majority of shareholders were from the State asserting the right of diplomatic protection. Furthermore, there is evidence that in practice, States have been prepared to extend diplomatic protection to shareholding interests in foreign corporations, and such a right has been unequivocally advocated by the ILA in its 2000 report on the law of diplomatic protection (Douglas, 2009, p 397). There is also evidence that States have been reluctant to extend protection to companies incorporated in their territory in the absence of substantial link with the national economy. However, the law in this area cannot be stated with certainty. In the *Oil Platforms Case*, Iran denied that the USA had the right as a matter of international law to extend diplomatic protection to US flagged but foreign owned merchant ships, on the basis that there was an absence of a genuine link between the ships and the US government as required by international law.[46] The Court's judgment, however, does not suggest that it was particularly troubled by the absence of a genuine link with the USA.[47]

The protection of corporations and shareholding interests received extended consideration by the ICJ in the *Case Concerning Ahmadou Diallo*, its first significant decision on this point since the *Barcelona Traction* case.[48] Mr Diallo, it will be recalled, had been settled in Zaire for 32 years. During this time, he had established two companies which

---

[43] See, eg ibid, Separate Opinion of Judge Fitzmaurice, p 65 at pp 72–5 (paras 14–20).

[44] Ibid, paras 94, 96.

[45] There was some evidence before the Court that the ultimate beneficiaries of the shareholding interest in the *Barcelona Traction* case were themselves non-Belgian.

[46] See *ICJ Pleadings, Oil Platforms (Islamic Republic of Iran v United States of America)*, Reply and Defence to Counter Claim submitted by the Islamic Republic of Iran, vol I, pp 202–14 (10 March 1999).

[47] *Oil Platforms (Islamic Republic of Iran v United States of America), Judgment, ICJ Reports 2003*, p 161, passim.

[48] *Ahmadou Sadio Diallo (Republic of Guinea v Democratic Republic of Congo), Preliminary Objections*, Judgment of 24 May 2007.

were at the centre of the dispute: Africom-Zaire and Africontainers-Zaire. In the course of their business dealings, the DRC, as well as several mining and oil companies operating in the DRC, became indebted to Mr. Diallo's companies. The attempts by Mr Diallo and his companies to sue and recover the monies owed received unfavourable treatment from the Congolese authorities and his attempts at litigation in the Congolese courts were largely fruitless. Guinea argued that the decision of the Congolese authorities to expel Mr Diallo in November 1995 was taken in order to irrevocably frustrate his efforts to enforce a judgment obtained by him against Zaire Shell for the sum of 60 billion dollars. The DRC raised a number of preliminary objections. It argued that Guinea lacked standing to bring the application, in so far as it related to wrongs allegedly done to Africom-Zaire and Africontainers-Zaire, these being Congolese companies. The DRC relied directly on the *Barcelona Traction* case in support of its arguments that the two companies were corporations under Zairean law, with rights distinct and separate from those of Mr. Diallo, a shareholder. DRC argued that positive international law did not entitle a State to bring an action in respect of a wrong done to a shareholder in a company registered in another State. It further denied that international law recognized a process of 'substitution' whereby the rights of a company could be assigned to a shareholder for purposes of litigation, when the State whose responsibility is at issue is also the national State of the company.

The Court accepted that that Mr Diallo's direct rights as a shareholder in the two companies were affected and as a result Guinea had *locus standi* to bring the claims. It drew a distinction between Mr Diallo's rights and those of the company, and concluded that Guinea as the national State was entitled to exercise diplomatic protection in relation to his shareholding interests. The right to protect shareholders' direct interests was explicitly recognized by the majority in the *Barcelona Traction* case.

As noted already, the judgment of the ICJ in the *Barcelona Traction* case left unresolved the question whether shareholders were entitled to diplomatic protection if the company had the nationality of the wrong-doing State. In the *Diallo* case, Guinea's third claim rested squarely on the alleged existence of this exception, claiming a right of diplomatic protection by way of substitution on the ground that the wrong-doing State was the State of nationality of Africom-Zaire and Africontainers-Zaire, the companies concerned.

The Court categorically denied the existence of this exception as a matter of customary international law.[49] In support of its claim for a right of diplomatic protection by way of substitution, Guinea had relied on arbitral awards, decisions of the European Commission on Human Rights, ICSID jurisprudence, and bilateral treaties for the promotion and protection of investment disputes, which had recognized protection of shareholding interests, where the respondent State was also the national State of the company (Douglas, 2009, p 397). The court regarded these arbitral awards and treaty provisions as *lex specialis* and that they did not support a broad right of diplomatic protection by way of substitution.[50] It distinguished its earlier decision in the *Electtronica Sicula* case, where a chamber of the Court had allowed the USA to bring a claim in respect of a wrong done to an Italian company, the shares of which were held by two American corporations,[51] on the grounds that it was not based general international law but on treaty provisions which allowed protection of shareholding interests in the circumstances that had arisen.

In its draft articles on diplomatic protection, the ILC had considered a more limited exception, allowing protection of shareholding interests only where a company's

---

[49] Ibid, para 89. This aspect of the judgment was followed by the South African Supreme Court in *Van Zyl* v *Government of the Republic of South Africa*, Case 170/06, [2007] SCA 109 (RSA).
[50] Ibid, para 90.   [51] *Elettronica Sicula SpA (ELSI), Judgment, ICJ Reports 1989*, p 15.

incorporation in a respondent State was a mandatory condition of doing business in that country. The Court noted that, on the facts before it, there was no evidence that Africom-Zaire and Africontainers-Zaire had been incorporated in Zaire (DRC) as a condition of doing business there. It therefore expressed no opinion on the validity of the ILC's proposed exception as a matter of customary law.

Thus more than 40 years after its landmark decision in the *Barcelona Traction* case, the court has reaffirmed that judgment in almost all respects. The significance of the Court's judgment should not, however, be exaggerated. The Court itself noted that the role of diplomatic protection has largely fallen into disuse since most issues relating to diplomatic protection of corporations and shareholding interests are now dealt with comprehensively in international treaties.[52] The significant delays that accompany claims arising by way of diplomatic protection also account for the lack of interest in this process. The litigation in the *Barcelona Traction* case lasted almost two decades, while in the *Diallo* case, it took more than ten years to reach the final judgment.

D. APPLYING THE NATIONALITY RULE

1. Nationality must be continuous

To the extent that the State exercising the right of diplomatic protection is acting on its own behalf and not as agent of the injured national, it is generally said to be a requirement that the nationality must be continuous. This is logical, since it is the bond of nationality which establishes the State's interest in the claim. Thus the claim must belong to a person or group of persons, having the nationality of the claimant State from the time of the injury until the making of the award. Therefore, in cases of subrogation and assignment, it is arguable that the nominee or assignee should have the same nationality as the original holder of the title. Many authorities nevertheless state that the rule should have no application where there has been a forced or involuntary change of nationality, for instance through a process of State succession or changes in a State's frontiers (Crawford, *Brownlie's Principles*, 2012, p 703; Crawford, 2013, p 577). The argument has also been made that the rule should be applied flexibly where the protection of financial interests is at issue as these frequently change hands and the ties of nationality are unlikely to be of much significance. It is also suggested that the rule should have no application in proceedings which have as their object the protection of fundamental human rights.

2. Diplomatic protection and the problem of multiple nationality

Cases of multiple nationalities present particular problems, for they involve decisions concerning which of the potentially competing claimants should be entitled to exercise diplomatic protection. They also raise the problem of whether one State of nationality can maintain a claim against a second State of nationality. A number of rules have emerged in State practice to deal specifically with such problems.

Two broad principles are widely accepted as regulating diplomatic protection in this area. First, diplomatic protection of dual or multiple nationals is governed by the principle of real or dominant nationality, and where there is a conflict, the nationality based on an effective link is to be treated as decisive.[53] This principle has been explicitly endorsed in the jurisprudence of international tribunals, including the Iran–USA Claims Tribunal.[54] It has also been

---

[52] Ibid, para 88.   [53] Eg *Canevaro* case (1912) 11 *RIAA* 397.
[54] *Esphanian* v *Bank Tejarat* (1983) 2 Iran-USCTR 157 at p 166. The decision in the *Salem* case (1932) 2 *RIAA* 1161 provides an isolated example rejecting the dominant/effective nationality test.

adopted without qualification in claims brought before the UN Compensation Commission, which considered claims against Iraq arising out of its invasion of Kuwait in 1991:[55] applying the effective nationality test, the Commission was prepared to admit claims by Iraqi nationals who also possessed valid and therefore the effective nationality of another State.

Secondly, where the application of the test indicates that the national has equally strong ties with two or more States, neither should be permitted to exercise diplomatic protection on his behalf against the other State of which he is a national, the rule of international law being that one does not have a remedy on the international plane against one's own State.[56] Moreover, to allow protection in circumstances where the national has strong ties with both States would undermine the sovereign equality of States. In deciding which of the nationalities is to be treated as dominant or effective, tribunals have paid regard to factors such as whether the nationality was acquired at birth, the residence or domicile of the national, date of naturalization, language, employment and financial interests, whether the nationality was acquired *bona fides*, and whether the national was precluded from denying a nationality that he had in everyday dealings held out as his own.[57]

3. Claims against third States

There is authority for the view that the principle of dominant or effective nationality has no application where any of the national States of a dual national wish to protect that national against a third State (Crawford, *Brownlie's Principles*, 2012, p 710). In the *Salem* case, the tribunal held that:

> the rule of international law [is] that in the case of dual nationality a third power is not entitled to contest the claim of one of the two powers whose national is interested in the case by referring to the nationality of the other power.[58]

It is difficult to mount a principled defence for the exclusion of the effective nationality rule in these circumstances, unless one believes the rule is no more than a vehicle for resolving competing claims in cases involving dual nationals and there is no justification for its application outside those contexts. However, it may be taken as another indication that international *lex lata* is not too wedded to the requirement of a genuine link.

4. Some issues concerning protection of shareholding interests

In the *Barcelona Traction* case, several judges thought shareholders had an independent right of protection under international law but there were fundamental differences concerning the precise nature of that right. Some thought that shareholders should be regarded as having a secondary right of protection which could be activated if the national State of the company had failed to act on its behalf.[59] The majority, however, rejected this, arguing that a secondary right could only come into existence once the primary right had been extinguished, and the failure of a State to exercise a primary right did not necessarily extinguish it.[60] Furthermore, the Court noted that the national State of the company is

---

[55] UN Doc S/AC.26/1991/7 Rev1, para 11.

[56] See *Merge* claim (1955) 22 ILR 443 and see Dugard, 2000, p 53; Brownlie, 2008, p 400–2.

[57] See the *Hein* case, *Annual Digest and Reports of Public International Law Cases 1919–22*, Case No 148, p 216; *Canevaro* case (1912) 11 *RIAA* 397.

[58] *Salem* case (1932) 2 *RIAA* 1161 at p 1188.

[59] *Barcelona Traction, Light and Power Company, Limited, Second Phase, Judgment, ICJ Reports 1970*, p 3, Separate Opinion of Judge Fitzmaurice, p 65 at p 96 (para 53).

[60] *Barcelona Traction, Light and Power Company, Limited, Second Phase, Judgment, ICJ Reports 1970*, p 3, para 96.

perfectly free to decide on the method and extent of protection it should grant to a company having its nationality. It may for instance decide to settle the claim, and to re-open these settlements by granting shareholders either a parallel or subsidiary right would substantially undermine the security of international economic transactions.[61]

Another argument in support of extending protection to shareholders is that the genuine link requirement formulated in the *Nottebohm* case also applies to the protection of companies, so that only in cases where there is such a link, can the State of incorporation bring a claim. The existence of a shareholding interest, it is then argued, provides the best evidence of the genuine link requirement, especially in those instances where the shareholders are from the State claiming a right of protection or where the board of directors has ties of nationality with the claimant State. In the *Barcelona Traction* case, for instance, Judge Jessup denied that Canada had a right to exercise diplomatic protection by virtue of the company's incorporation in that State, in the absence of some demonstrable link. He noted that:

> If a State extends its diplomatic protection to a corporation to which it has granted a charter of convenience while at the same time similar diplomatic assistance is being extended by another State whose nationals hold 100% of the shares, the situation might be considered analogous to cases of dual nationality of natural persons—*Nottebohm* principle applies equally here.[62]

In State practice and the jurisprudence of international tribunals there are numerous instances where States have been prepared to intervene and exercise diplomatic protection in respect of shareholding interests in foreign corporations (Douglas 2009, p 397; Oppenheim, 1992, p 322). In the *Barcelona Traction* case the ICJ treated these instances as *lex specialis*, based as it were on the terms of the instruments establishing them. However, in a curious judgment in the 1989 *ELSI* case, and without any reference to the *Barcelona Traction* case, the USA was permitted to exercise diplomatic protection in respect of injury to an Italian company, which was wholly owned by two US subsidiaries. Although Italy raised objections, the Court was untroubled by them, and preferred to dispose of the claim on the basis that there had been no violation of the treaty obligations relied on by the USA.[63]

It would therefore seem that notwithstanding the opinion of the majority in the *Barcelona Traction* case, there is a substantial body of international practice and jurisprudence in support of the protection of shareholding interests. However, a number of problems remain, in particular, with regard to the precise circumstances when shareholders may be entitled to protection, the range of interests capable of protection and the modalities of reconciling competing claims (Lowe, 2002).

5. Exclusion of the nationality rule

The nexus of nationality is not required in all instances and its application may be waived by treaty or other *ad hoc* arrangements, such as delegation of the right of protection to another sovereign. Treaties may also extend a general right of protection to non-nationals. The most significant development in this respect relates to Article 8C of the Treaty of the EU which creates a treaty-based right of diplomatic protection for all EU nationals within the jurisdiction of a member State irrespective of nationality (Dugard, 2004, para 8). Other subjects of international law, such as international organizations, may be entitled

---

[61] Ibid, para 97.   [62] Ibid, Separate Opinion of Judge Jessup, p 162 at p 170 (para 19).
[63] *Elettronica Sicula SpA (ELSI), Judgment, ICJ Reports 1989*, p 15, para 101. But cf the Dissenting Opinion of Judge Oda, ibid, p 83 who questioned the right of the USA to exercise diplomatic protection on behalf of shareholders in an Italian company when that company had not ceased to exist.

to exercise such functional protection for those in their service unencumbered by considerations of nationality (Crawford, 2013, p 593). In the *Reparations* case, the ICJ thought
nationality irrelevant in cases where the UN brings a claim in respect of injuries to agents
of the organization incurred in the course of their duties. The Court justified the right of
protection in the following terms:

> In order that the agent may perform his duties satisfactorily, he must feel that this protec-
> tion is assured to him by the Organization, and that he may count on it. To ensure the
> independence of the agent, and, consequently, the independent action of the organiza-
> tion itself, it is essential that in performing his duties he need not have to rely on any
> protection than that of the organization...In particular, he should not have to rely on the
> protection of his own State. If he had to rely on that State, his independence might well
> be compromised.[64]

The claim in these instances could even be addressed to the State of the victim's nationality.
Examples of other instances where the nationality of claims rule has been regarded as generally inapplicable include situations where claims have been brought on behalf of aliens in
the service of the claiming State;[65] Stateless persons; non-nationals forming a minority in
a group of national claimants; refugees and non-nationals with long-term residence in the
State espousing diplomatic protection (Oppenheim, 1992, p 515). In *Al-Rawi and Others* v
The Secretary of State for Foreign and Commonwealth Affairs[66] the English Court of Appeal
denied that a sovereign State possessed standing to exercise diplomatic protection on
behalf of resident aliens or refugees. It concluded that Article 8 of the ILC draft articles
on diplomatic protection,[67] which envisaged protection for stateless persons and refugees
habitually resident in a claimant State, was, strictly speaking, *lex ferenda* and an exercise
in the progressive development of the law and not its restatement. *Al-Rawi* is, however, a
decision of a domestic court and, to the extent that it is at odds with the weight of authority
in public international law, cannot be regarded as decisive on this point. Article 48 (2)b of
the ILC Articles on State Responsibility entitle States to bring claims and seek reparation
including on behalf of non-nationals in respect of *erga omnes* obligations unencumbered
by the requirements of nationality.

IV. ADMISSIBILITY IN CASES CONCERNING OBLIGATIONS OWED TO A PLURALITY OF STATES

A. INTRODUCTION

The obligations forming the basis of claims considered in the previous sections have
been in the nature of distinct bilateral duties; they are either owed directly to the State or

---

[64] *Reparation for Injuries* case (*Advisory Opinion*), *ICJ Reports 1949*, p 174 at pp 179, 181–4.

[65] See for example *The M/V Saiga No 2 (Saint Vincent and the Grenadines v Guinea)*, ITLOS Case No 2,
Judgment of 1 July 1999, in which the International Tribunal for the Law of the Sea accepted that the flag State
had the right to protect non-national crew members.

[66] *Al-Rawi and Others v The Secretary of State for Foreign and Commonwealth Affairs* [2006] EWCA Civ
1279, paras, 63, 64, 89, and 115 ff.

[67] See Seventh Report of the ILC Rapporteur on Diplomatic Protection, 7 March 2006, Fifty-eighth Session,
A/CN.4/567.

indirectly through persons having its nationality. In both instances, the legal interest takes the form of a private law claim; the wronged State must demonstrate either a direct injury to its interests or those of its nationals. Much of the traditional law on State responsibility has been concerned precisely with the enforcement of these bilateral rights and duties. The category of obligations considered in this section takes two forms. The first are obligations *erga omnes partes* owed to a State under a treaty instrument, and which have the objective of protecting the collective interests of all the parties. As long as the injury or violation is within the scope of the protected interests, any of the States parties to the treaty instruments has a prima facie right to make representations or bring a claim. For instance, States parties to regional human rights treaties invariably have a right to make representations even if the affected individuals are not their nationals. Other treaties creating zones of collective interests include regional nuclear-free zone treaties, regional environmental treaties, and regional instruments for economic integration.[68]

The second variation concerns the so-called *erga omnes* obligations *stricto sensu* which are owed to the international community as a whole. There has long been a consensus, at least since the Second World War, that international law may have an interest in creating obligations for the benefit of individuals and other non-State entities, such as units of self-determination, international organizations, etc. Other obligations in this category rest on the premise that certain values are fundamental, and are therefore owed to the international community as a whole. The protection of these values may coincide with individual State interests, as in the case of aggression, but in most cases they usually transcend such interests. As a result, the international system may recognize a role for third States in their enforcement even if they are not directly injured. An implicit feature of this category of obligations is that the specific requirements of legal interest based either on direct injury or ties of nationality are dispensed with.

In an often cited passage, the International Court of Justice in the *Barcelona Traction* case accepted that there were gradations of obligations in the international system, and that implicitly these qualitative differences may call for or justify different responses by members of the international community. It observed that:

> An essential distinction should be drawn between obligations of a State towards the international community as a whole and those arising vis-à-vis another State in the field of diplomatic protection. By their very nature the former are the concern of all States in view of the importance of the rights involved, all States can be held to have a legal interest in their protection, they are obligations *erga omnes*. Such obligations derive for example in contemporary international law, from the outlawing of aggression, and of genocide, as also from the principles and rules concerning the basic rights of the human person, including protection from slavery and racial discrimination. Some of the corresponding rights of protection have entered into the body of general international law[69] while others are conferred by international instruments of a universal or quasi-universal character.[70]

The Court's pronouncements on the *erga omnes* character of obligations was, strictly speaking, *obiter* since no such rights were involved on the facts, but the literature accepted

---

[68] For relevant treaties see for instance South Pacific Nuclear Treaty (Raratonga, 1985) (1985) 24 ILM 1442; Treaty of Tlatelolco on the Prohibition of Nuclear Weapons in Latin America (1967) 634 UNTS at 281; Africa Nuclear Free Zone Treaty (1996) 35 ILM 698; ASEAN Nuclear Free Zone Treaty 1996, 35 ILM 635.

[69] See *Reservations to the Convention on the Prevention and Punishment of the Crime of Genocide, Advisory Opinion, ICJ Reports 1951*, p 23.

[70] *Barcelona Traction, Light and Power Company, Limited, Second Phase, Judgment, ICJ Reports 1970*, p 3, paras 33–4.

that, at least at the level of primary rules, international obligations fell into two distinct categories; those in the nature of a civil law right and which were owed to individual States, and those which created a regulatory framework for dealing with public order concerns and were therefore owed to the international community as a whole (Tams, 2005; Ragazzi, 1997).

The court's declaration has unfortunately not been matched with practical mechanisms for the enforcement of these collective duties. In particular, there is no consensus on whether a distinct category of secondary rules has also come into operation which deals with the enforcement and legal consequences of *erga omnes* obligations as opposed to those relating to ordinary breaches. It remains a moot point whether international law recognizes litigation in the public interest, and in particular whether States have a legal interest to enforce community values through the processes of adjudication.

B. TREATY INSTRUMENTS PROTECTING COLLECTIVE INTERESTS

It has long been recognized that States may have an interest in the observance of treaty instruments to which they are a party even without being directly affected. For example, Article 60 of the Vienna Convention on the Law of Treaties entitles States parties to terminate a treaty on account of material breach. Similarly, Article 42 of the ILC's Articles on State Responsibility explicitly recognizes the interests of States in ensuring compliance with treaty instruments to which they are a party. The obligations are described as interdependent with the result that non-compliance by any one party automatically affects the interests of all other parties to the treaty instrument. The Commission's approach is to create different degrees of 'affectedness', and the forms of responses that States may be entitled to adopt are determined by the degree to which they are affected by the breach.[71]

Arguably, there is no reason in principle why a State should not bring an action for the sole purpose of enforcing the rule of law on the basis of a treaty instrument or customary law. It should in principle have the right to do so even if it has suffered no material injury itself, or in the person of its national. Thus, leaving aside the problematic question whether international law recognizes an *actio popularis*, it could be said that at least in respect of those obligations contained in multilateral treaties, to which a large number of States are parties, the public interests concerns are readily met by the recognition that all parties to such instruments may bring an action for their enforcement. The International Court has explicitly endorsed *locus standi* in the case of *erga omnes partes* (as opposed to *erga omnes, stricto sensu*) in *Questions relating to the Obligation to Prosecute or Extradite (Belgium v Senegal)* under the UN Convention against Torture. Referring to obligations under the Torture Convention the Court noted that:

> The common interest in compliance with the relevant obligations under the Convention against Torture implies entitlement of each State Party to the Convention to make a claim concerning the cessation of an alleged breach by another State Party. If a special interest were required for that purpose, in many cases no State would be in a position to make such a claim. It follows that any State Party to the Convention may invoke the responsibility of another State Party with a view to ascertaining the alleged failure to comply with its

---

[71] ILC ARSIWA Articles 42 and 48 envisage a distinct role for States in enforcing obligations *erga omnes* including a right to bring an action and obtain compensation on behalf of an injured State.

obligations *erga omnes partes*, such as under Article 6, paragraph 2, and Article 7, para 1, of the Convention, and to bring that failure to an end.[72]

C. LITIGATION IN THE PUBLIC INTEREST AND THE ENFORCEMENT OF *ERGA OMNES* OBLIGATIONS *STRICTO SENSU*

In Roman law it was always accepted that a plaintiff could bring an action before the court if it was in the public interest, and there was no requirement that the plaintiff should demonstrate a specific injury to its own interests. Most systems of law have adopted in some form mechanisms for protecting community values. In the *South West Africa* cases, the International Court indirectly considered the question whether general international law recognized the right of States to bring an action in vindication of the public interest. The applicant States, Liberia and Ethiopia had argued that in order to be effective, the mandate for South West Africa should be interpreted in a way that would recognize their own right to bring an action, even though the obligations in question was not owed to them as individuals members of the League but rather to the League itself. The Court rejected this argument and observed that:

> Looked at in another way moreover, the argument amounts to a plea that the Court should allow the equivalent of an *actio popularis*, or right resident in any member of a community to take legal action in vindication of public interest. But although a right of this kind may be known to certain municipal systems of law, it is not known to international law as it stands at present: nor is the Court able to regard it as imported by the general principles of law referred to in Article 38, paragraph 1 (c) of its Statute.[73]

Moreover, there are further indications in the *Barcelona Traction* case itself that the Court did not regard the existence of *erga omnes* obligations as necessarily importing recognition of an *actio popularis*. The right of enforcement in the Court's view only existed in those instances where the obligation was strictly speaking binding *erga omnes partes*. It observed that:

> With regard more particularly to human rights, to which reference has already been made in paragraph 34 of this judgment, it should be noted that these include protection against denial of justice. However, on the universal level, the instruments which embody human rights do not confer on States the capacity to protect the victims of infringements of such rights irrespective of their nationality. It is therefore still on the regional level that a solution to this problem has had to be sought; thus within the Council of Europe, of which Spain is not a member, the problem of admissibility encountered by the claim in the present case has been resolved by the European Convention on Human Rights, which entitles each State which is a party to the Convention to lodge a complaint against any other contracting State for the violation of the Convention, irrespective of the nationality of the victim.[74]

---

[72] *Questions relating to the Obligation to Prosecute or Extradite* (*Belgium v Senegal*), *Judgment of 20 July 2012*, nyr, paras 69–70.

[73] *South West Africa, Second Phase, Judgment, ICJ Reports 1966*, p 6, para 88. Judge Jessup who delivered a strong dissent was nevertheless disinclined to accept a general right of *actio popularis*.

[74] *Barcelona Traction, Light and Power Company, Limited, Second Phase, Judgment, ICJ Reports 1970*, p 3, para 91.

The conclusion is problematic because it has the effect of depriving the *erga omnes* regime of much practical value. There are few instruments of general application which provide for the enforcement of *erga omnes* obligations. This lack of realistic mechanisms for enforcement has the unfortunate effect of rendering these obligations largely theoretical.

Even assuming that the case for *actio popularis* as a general rule of international law is defensible in principle, it will still be subject to the jurisdictional rules that regulate access to international tribunals. Thus, in absence of a jurisdictional nexus with the Court on the part of the claimant and respondent State, the Court will invariably be unable to entertain the claim notwithstanding its *erga omnes* character (Schachter, 1991, p 210; Crawford, *Brownlie's Principles*, 2012, pp 596–7). This much is clear from the ICJ decision in the *East Timor* case.

In this case Portugal brought an action against Australia arguing that by entering into a treaty with Indonesia regarding the delimitation of the East Timorese continental shelf, Australia had interfered with the right of East Timorese people to self-determination, a right whose *erga omnes* character was impeccable. Yet a substantive judgment on the matter required the Court to rule on the legality of Indonesia's invasion of East Timor and the subsequent jurisdictional authority enjoyed by Indonesia over the East Timorese. Indonesia was not a party to the dispute, nor had it accepted the Court's jurisdiction. It was therefore immediately apparent that the Court was being asked to rule on the rights and obligations of a third party to the dispute contrary to its previous jurisprudence as laid down in the *Monetary Gold* case. Portugal argued that limitations on the Court's jurisdiction under the *Monetary Gold* principle had no application in view of the *erga omnes* character of the obligations involved. The Court rejected the claim and observed that:

> ...Portugal's assertion that the right of people's to self-determination as it evolved from the Charter and from the UN practice has an *erga omnes* character is irreproachable. The principle of self-determination of peoples has been recognised in the United Nations Charter and in the jurisprudence of the Court. It is one of the essential principles of contemporary international law. However, the Court considers that the *erga omnes* character of a norm and the rule of consent are two different things. Whatever the nature of the obligations invoked, the Court could not rule on the lawfulness of the conduct of a State when its judgment would imply an evaluation of the lawfulness of the conduct of another State which is not a party to the case. Where this is so, the court cannot act even if the right in question is a right *erga omnes*.[75]

In the *Armed Activities in the Territory of the Congo (DRC v Rwanda)*, the Court confirmed its previous jurisprudence. It noted that the *erga omnes* character of the obligations under the Genocide Convention did not give the Court jurisdiction to entertain a dispute in the absence of the parties' consent.[76]

Nevertheless, in its Advisory Opinion on the *Legal Consequences of the Construction of a Wall in the Occupied Palestinian Territory* the Court came quite close to recognizing the existence of an *actio popularis*. Referring to Israeli violations of the rights of the Palestinian people to self-determination, it observed that:[77]

> Given the character and importance of the rights and obligations involved, the Court is of the view that all States are under an obligation not to recognize the illegal situation resulting

---

[75] *East Timor (Portugal v Australia), Judgment, ICJ Reports 1995*, p 90, para 29.

[76] *Armed Activities on the Territory of the Congo (New Application: 2002) (Democratic Republic of the Congo v Rwanda), Jurisdiction and Admissibility, Judgment, ICJ Reports 2006*, p 6, paras 28–70.

[77] *Legal Consequences of the Construction of a Wall in the Occupied Palestine Territory, Advisory Opinion, ICJ Reports 2004*, p 136, para 159.

from the construction of the wall...They are also under an obligation not to render aid or assistance in maintaining the situation created by such construction. It is also for all States, while respecting the United Nations Charter and international law, to see to it that any impediment, resulting from the construction of the wall, to the exercise by the Palestinian people of its right of self-determination is brought to an end.

The right of all States to enforce community norms was eloquently advanced by Judge Simma two years later in *Armed Activities in the Territory of the Congo (DRC v Uganda)*. The Court had refused to entertain Uganda's counterclaim concerning the alleged mistreatment by Congolese soldiers of persons whose nationality had not been established. Judge Simma argued that the Court should have entertained the claim since the obligations in question were binding *erga omnes*. He said that:[78]

...the question of standing of a claimant state for violations of human rights committed against persons which might or might not possess the nationality of that state, the jurisdiction of the Court not being at issue, the contemporary law of state responsibility provides a positive answer as well...The obligations deriving from the human rights cited above and breached by the DRC are instances *par excellence* of obligations that are owed to a group of States including Uganda, and are established for the protection of a collective interest of the States parties to the Covenant.

Further obstacles in the path of litigation *actio popularis* have been noted. Schachter, for instance, has suggested that States are reluctant to set precedents which could be used in future litigation against them and so they are unlikely to lodge claims even in respect of *erga omnes* obligations unless their direct interests were involved. Moreover, he warns that there is a real risk that an expansive concept of *actio popularis* is likely to deter even further State acceptance of the International Court's compulsory jurisdiction; and those States who accept compulsory jurisdiction will invariably protect themselves from its consequences by making reservations against *actio popularis* suits (Schachter, 1991, p 212). In any case, it is abundantly clear from the few occasions that the International Court has considered the matter that it has been particularly reticent to acknowledge public interest litigation as a means of enforcing *erga omnes* obligations (Tam, 2005).

The Articles finally adopted by the ILC in 2001 explicitly recognize the right of States other than those directly injured to bring an action in the public interest.[79] The Special Rapporteur in the commentary to Article 48 acknowledged that the Article involved elements of progressive development of the law insofar as it entitled States to bring claims

---

[78] *Armed Activities on the Territory of the Congo (Democratic Republic of the Congo v Uganda), Judgment, ICJ Reports 2005*, p 168, Separate Opinion of Judge Simma, pp 347–8.

[79] Article 48 provides:
  1. Any State other than an injured State is entitled to invoke the responsibility of another in accordance with Para 2 if:
      (a) the obligation breached is owed to a group of States including that State, and is established for the protection of a collective interest of the group; or
      (b) the obligation breached is owed to the international community as a whole.

  2. Any State entitled to invoke responsibility under paragraph 1 may claim from the responsible State:
      (a) cessation of the internationally wrongful act, and assurances and guarantees of non-repetition in accordance with Article 30; and
      (b) performance of the obligation of reparation in accordance with the preceding articles, in the interest of the injured State or of the beneficiaries of the obligation breached.

  3. ...

for restitution and reparation on behalf of the beneficiaries of the obligation even when they were not directly affected. The Articles were commended to States by the UN General Assembly in GA Resolution 56/83 (12 December 2001), but it remains an open question whether this positive endorsement will be reflected in actual State behaviour (Crawford and Olleson, 2005).

V. ADMISSIBILITY OF CLAIMS AND THE RULE ON EXHAUSTION OF LOCAL REMEDIES

A. INTRODUCTION

There is almost universal consensus that in the absence of an agreement to the contrary, a claim is inadmissible on the international plane unless the alien or legal person on whose behalf a claim has been brought has exhausted local remedies in the putative respondent State. The rule has been endorsed in the literature as a rule of customary law and its normative quality has been accepted by international tribunals.[80]

A number of reasons have been put forward in support of the rule. The first is a logical consequence of the sovereignty of States in respect of matters occurring on their territory.

It is therefore generally accepted that out of respect for sovereignty, a State must be given the first opportunity to exercise jurisdiction in respect of matters occurring in its territory. There is here also a presumption that the wronged national by voluntarily bringing himself within the jurisdiction of the respondent State, must be taken to have assumed the risk, of having local law applied to him.

The second reason rests on considerations of practical convenience. It would be both expensive and futile to bring small claims before an international forum when there is a possibility of expeditious redress before local tribunals. It has also been suggested that in these instances the local courts are better placed to evaluate the facts and the evidence, as well as deciding on the appropriate methods of compensation (Crawford, *Brownlie's Principles*, 2012, pp 710–11). They are therefore clearly more appropriate fora for the settlement of these disputes than the international arena.

Thirdly, in a number of instances, it is the failure to provide local redress for breach of an international obligation that engages the responsibility of the State. There can be no claim on the basis of denial of justice until local remedies have been exhausted. In this instance failure to exhaust local remedies is not so much a bar to the admissibility of the claim; rather it operates to determine the existence of responsibility, since until such remedies have been exhausted and found to be wanting no case for violation of international law can be made.

B. THE CONTENT OF THE RULE

What are the parameters of the rule requiring exhaustion of local remedies and when and in what circumstances is it discharged? The first general observation is that the rule only applies in those instances where the State brings a claim on behalf of a national. As a matter of principle, a State bringing a claim to protect its direct interests is not obliged to

---

[80] See for instance *Ahmadou Sadio Diallo (Republic of Guinea v Democratic Republic of Congo), Preliminary Objections*, Judgment of 24 May 2007, paras 42–4.

exhaust such remedies. Although there is nothing to preclude it from doing so, and in particular circumstances it may in fact be convenient to explore the availability of remedies in the local courts.

Second, there is considerable support for the view that the obligation to exhaust local remedies relates only to legal remedies, and would exclude remedies that are discretionary or that are available as a matter of grace (Brownlie, 2008, p 495; Brierly, 1963, p 281). It also seems to be a general requirement that the national in question must exhaust the remedies available to their fullest extent. In particular, they must raise before local courts all the arguments that they may wish to bring before international tribunals,[81] as well as appeal procedures provided for under local law.[82]

It seems perfectly logical that as a corollary there is no obligation to exhaust local remedies where these are unavailable in practice or are unlikely to yield any concrete results. Nevertheless the decision whether legal remedies are unavailable in a particular legal system is a contentious one, and it remains unclear how far the foreign national is expected to test the options under national law before reaching the conclusion that they are bound to be futile. In the *Interhandel* case, brought by Switzerland before the International Court, the Court concluded that as Interhandel's suit was still pending before US courts, local remedies had not been exhausted.[83] The conclusion on the face of it appeared harsh, since the corporation had been involved in litigation in US courts for a period of almost ten years before proceedings were commenced by Switzerland before the International Court.

The jurisprudence of international tribunals indicate that local remedies will generally be regarded as unavailable if the applicant, although granted a right of appeal on a point of law, chooses not to exercise it, because the precise point raised has previously been decided by a higher court to the detriment of a litigant. Similarly, local remedies are treated as unavailable if an appeal would lie on a point of fact, but appellate courts lack the power to review points of fact.[84] In other words, the remedy available must present a reasonable possibility of redressing the personal claim of the litigant (Crawford, 2013, p 581; Dugard, 2002, para 45).

C. THE APPLICATION OF THE RULE IN THE CONTEXT OF MIXED CLAIMS

The rule requiring the exhaustion of local remedies only applies in those instances where the State brings forward a claim on behalf of a national, and not when it claims on its own behalf. The rule therefore rests on the assumption that it will always be easy to distinguish between these two situations. While it is usually possible to maintain the distinction, there are many cases where the dividing line is not so clear, especially when the wrong simultaneously injures both the national and the State's own direct interests. In these instances, it becomes difficult to decide whether the rule requiring the exhaustion of local remedies applies. Moreover, it is not uncommon for applicant States to seek a declaration or an interpretation of a treaty and damages in respect of an injury to their nationals in the same proceedings. Dugard, in his second report on diplomatic protection, has suggested

---

[81] *Finnish Ships Arbitration*, 1934, 3 *RIAA* 1479; *Elettronica Sicula SpA (ELSI), Judgment, ICJ Reports 1989*, p 15.

[82] *Ambatielos Claim*, 1956, 12 *RIAA* 83.

[83] *Interhandel, Preliminary Objections, Judgment, ICJ Reports 1959*, p 6.

[84] *Finnish Ships Arbitration*, 1934, 3 *RIAA* 1479; *Panevezys-Saldutiskis Railway, Judgment, 1939, PCIJ, Ser A/B, No 76*, p 4 at p 18.

that in respect of such mixed claims, the exhaustion of local remedies rule should only apply if the claim is overwhelmingly concerned with injury to the national (Dugard, 2001, paras 19–24).

There is some support in the jurisprudence of international tribunals for the *preponderance* of interests test in the case of mixed claims. In the *Interhandel* case, Switzerland had insisted on the non-applicability of the local remedies rule, arguing that its claim concerned the failure of the US authorities to apply the terms of an applicable treaty, that had caused it direct harm. In rejecting the claim, the Court noted that the dispute was essentially one in which:

> the Swiss Government appears as having adopted the cause of its national Interhandel, for the purpose of securing restitution to that company of assets vested by the government of the USA.

It further observed that:

> ...one interest, and one alone of Interhandel has induced the Swiss Government to institute proceedings, and that this interest is the basis for the present claim and should determine the scope of the action brought before the Court by the Swiss Government in its alternative as well as principal form.[85]

In the *ELSI* case, the Chamber of the International Court of Justice rejected the argument of the USA that, insofar as the claim was founded on breach of a treaty obligation, it should be treated as an instance of direct injury to State interests rather than a claim made on behalf of a national for purposes of the local remedies rule. In rejecting the argument, the Chamber observed that:

> ...the matter which colours and pervades the United States Claim as a whole is the alleged damage to Raytheon and Machlett [United States Corporations].[86]

This surely is correct because even claims brought exclusively on behalf of nationals usually originate in some kind of non-compliance with a treaty obligation owed to the applicant State. The fact that a breach of a treaty is at issue cannot therefore be regarded as a reliable test (if at all) for distinguishing between direct injury to a State's interests and those cases where it claims on behalf of a national.

Theodore Meron suggested that in deciding on the nature of the claim, it is necessary to have regard to the real interests and goals of the litigant State. Is the State primarily pursuing its own interests or is the action really a claim brought on behalf of a national? If the claim is primarily concerned with injury to a national, then the rule will operate to exclude the admissibility of the claim including any secondary elements, which strictly speaking are in the nature of inter-State claims (Crawford, 2013, p 584; Meron, 1959, p 87). There is also general recognition that claims, which are primarily about treaty interpretation and application, are direct State claims even if they arise in circumstances also affecting the rights of a private person[87] (Oppenheim, 1992, p 523). The subject matter of the dispute may also provide a useful guide to the true character of the claim. Thus injuries to diplomatic or consular staff,[88] or State property[89], will generally be regarded as direct

---

[85] *Interhandel, Preliminary Objections, Judgment, ICJ Reports 1959*, p 6 at p 29.

[86] *Elettronica Sicula SpA (ELSI), Judgment, ICJ Reports 1989*, p 15, para 91.

[87] See *Avena and other Mexican Nationals (Mexico v United States of America), Judgment, ICJ Reports 2004*, p 12, paras 35–6.

[88] *United States Diplomatic and Consular Staff in Tehran, Judgment, ICJ Reports 1980*, p 3.

[89] *Corfu Channel, Merits, Judgment, ICJ Reports 1949*, p 4.

claims and therefore not subject to the local remedies rule. Although not conclusive, the nature of the remedy sought may also be a useful indicator in claims presenting mixed elements (Adler, 1990, p 652; Dugard, 2001, paras 29–30). There is considerable justification in looking at the essence of the claim and characterizing it by paying regard to its principal objectives. However, a rigid application of the predominance test may preclude valid claims by governments, especially when in the circumstances they are unlikely to obtain any local remedies for breach of their treaty rights (Fitzmaurice, 1961, p 37; Thirlway, 1995, pp 85–90). Moreover the *dominance test* ignores the fact that a State may have a legal interest of its own to protect, such as vindicating the values underpinning the treaty regime, and which are unlikely to be satisfied by any material compensation or restitution of property in national courts.

D. A RULE OF SUBSTANCE OR PROCEDURE?

Is the rule requiring exhaustion of local remedies a rule of procedure or substance? There has been considerable discussion in the literature as to the precise character of the rule requiring exhaustion of local remedies, and in particular whether it is a rule of substance or procedure. This seemingly sterile debate on a closer analysis has important normative consequences, and therefore merits close attention.

A number of different positions have been adopted. The first characterizes the rule as one of substance and proceeds from the premise that the exhaustion of local remedies is not so much a condition of admissibility of claims; rather, it determines the very existence of responsibility. On this view until local remedies have been exhausted and found wanting, there can be no international 'delict' to engage the responsibility of the State.[90]

The second position treats the rule as a procedural pre-requisite to the admissibility of a claim. On this view the responsibility of a State is engaged and complete from the time of the wrongful act, but redress on the international plane cannot be effected until local remedies have been exhausted.

The third position distinguishes between different kinds of wrongs that may cause injury to a national on whose behalf a claim is subsequently brought. On this view, where the national is injured by a violation of a rule of domestic law, no question of international responsibility arises, until local remedies have been exhausted. Only then can a claim be brought on the international plane for denial of justice. Here exhaustion of local remedies is substantive, for until such remedies have failed there can be no question of responsibility on the international plane. Proponents of this third position distinguish the situation where the national is injured by what is clearly a rule of international law. Here, the responsibility of the respondent State is activated from the time of the injury. In this instance, the requirement that local remedies have to be exhausted must be seen as no more than a procedural pre-requisite to the admissibility of a claim on the international plane, and does not as such affect the origin of responsibility.

This debate as to the nature of the local remedies rule may have implications for other related rules of admissibility, such as the requirement that the applicant State must demonstrate the continuous nationality of the claim. It has been noted that for a claim to be admissible on the international plane it must be national in origin. In other words, from the time of the injury until the making of the award, the claim must belong to persons having the nationality of the claimant State. The exact time when a wrong ripens for purposes of

---

[90] Ago, R, 'Sixth Report on State Responsibility', *YBILC* (1977), vol II (part one), pp 22–3.

responsibility also depends on whether one adopts the procedural or substantive position and therefore has implications for rule on continuous nationality of claims.

Second, if the rule determines the origin of responsibility, it operates as a bar to States wishing to seek declaratory judgments or interpretation of treaties in circumstances where injured nationals have not exhausted local remedies since, until such remedies have been exhausted, there can be no question of responsibility.

Finally, Dugard has suggested that the rule may also affect the *temporis* jurisdiction of international tribunals in those instances where States have stated that their acceptances of the Court's jurisdiction will only be effective after a specified date. (Dugard, 2001, para 33). On the procedural view, the effective time for jurisdictional purposes is the occurrence of the injury. On the substantive view, the effective time will be after the exhaustion of local remedies. Thus a claim may be admissible or inadmissible depending on which view of the rule one adopts.

E. WHICH VIEW REPRESENTS THE LAW?

The answer to this question must surely be speculative, and has to be approached as a matter of principle rather than on the basis of State and arbitral practice since no international decision has explicitly addressed the issue and the positions adopted by governments have been largely partisan and influenced by the exigencies of litigation. However, the decisions in the *German Interests in Polish Upper Silesia*,[91] *Chorzow Factory*,[92] and *Phosphates in Morocco*[93] cases provide strong evidence in support of the procedural position. In both cases the Court reached the conclusion that responsibility was incurred immediately following on the wrongful act, rather than after the exhaustion of local remedies.

As a matter of principle, it is difficult to mount a spirited defence of the substantive position. It proceeds on the premise that the determination of whether a breach of international law takes place depends not on the international norm but on the procedures of local tribunals. This potentially undermines the values that inform the applicable legal regime. (Dugard, 2001, paras 56 and 63; Amerasinghe, 1990, p 328). Non-compliance with an obligation threatens the integrity of the applicable norm irrespective of whether local remedies have been exhausted or not. As Judge Lauterpacht noted in the *Norwegian Loans* case:

> …the exhaustion of local remedies cannot itself bring within the province of international law a dispute which is otherwise outside its sphere. The failure to exhaust local remedies may constitute a bar to the jurisdiction of the court; it does not affect the intrinsically international character of a dispute.[94]

Secondly, it is generally accepted that States may agree by treaty to exclude the operation of a rule. The validity of such agreements was accepted without qualification in the *ELSI* case. Dugard has suggested that the validity of such waiver is difficult to defend, if one adopts the substantive view, since it is tantamount to saying that States can agree to make something delictual when ordinarily it would not be a breach unless and until it has given rise to subsequent denial of justice (Dugard, 2001, para 33). For this reason most authorities consider the exhaustion of local remedies to be a rule of procedure. The State incurs

---

[91] *Certain German Interests in Polish Upper Silesia, Merits, Judgment No 7, 1926, PCIJ, Ser A, No 7.*
[92] *Factory at Chorzow, Merits, Judgment No 13, 1928, PCIJ, Ser A, No 17.*
[93] *Phosphates in Morocco, Judgment, 1937, PCIJ, Ser A/B, No 74,* p 10.
[94] *Certain Norwegian Loans, Judgment, ICJ Reports 1957,* p 9, Separate Opinion of Judge Lauterpacht, p 34 at p 38.

international responsibility from the moment of the wrongful act but the right to bring an international claim is suspended until the State has had the opportunity to remedy the situation.

F. THE EXCLUSION OF THE LOCAL REMEDIES RULE

There can be no obligation to exhaust local remedies if there are no local remedies to exhaust (Fitzmaurice, 1961, p 59). In order to be considered effective, the local remedy must have the capacity to remedy the complaint. Clearly, when the conduct giving rise to the injury does not violate local law, there will be no local remedies and the matter can immediately be taken up on the international plane. The argument has also been made that there is no obligation to exhaust local remedies in cases where public international law does not permit the respondent State to exercise jurisdiction in the first place (Brownlie, 2008, p 495; O'Connell, 1970, p 951). Thus an attempt to exercise jurisdiction over an alien in circumstances where international law does not grant jurisdiction would clearly be a nullity, and there is considerable merit in the argument that no obligation to exhaust local remedies arises.[95]

Many authorities argue that there is no obligation to exhaust local remedies where there is no voluntary link between the injured individual and the respondent State (Dugard, 2002, para 83). Thus the argument has been made that in principle there should be some degree of connection between the injured individual and the respondent State and that the obligation is therefore dispensed with, where the links are transitory or clearly involuntary. Examples would include air crash victims involuntarily or fortuitously injured by events in the respondent State. On the other hand, it can be argued that it is precisely such cases that local courts are particularly suitable for, given the multiple character of the claims and the clear local interest in the dispute.

Finally, the requirement to exhaust local remedies may be formally dispensed with by a treaty. Many international treaties provide that in the event of a dispute between the State and foreign legal person, the dispute is to be referred to arbitration. Tribunals considering the issue have reached the conclusion that where provision is expressly made for arbitration, then there will clearly be no obligation to exhaust local remedies (Crawford, *Brownlie's Principles*, 2012, p 715).

VI. CONCLUSION

The preceding discussion has attempted to isolate the main legal grounds governing the admissibility of claims. These conditions operate across the board irrespective of the particular circumstances of the case. The requirement of exhaustion of local remedies will invariably govern the admissibility of most claims unless on the facts, a specific waiver is in operation. Unfortunately the development of *erga omnes* obligations has not been accompanied by any discernible refinement of the mechanisms for their enforcement. The work of the International Law Commission, completed in 2001, represents the most significant advance yet, insofar as it provides for a coherent regime for the enforcement of these obligations. Yet even the Commission's proposals especially in Article 48 are clearly stated in

---

[95] See *Barcelona Traction, Light and Power Company, Limited, Second Phase, Judgment, ICJ Reports 1970*, p 3, Separate Opinion of Judge Fitzmaurice, p 65 at pp 103–10 (paras 66–83).

de lege ferenda terms and their effectiveness will ultimately depend on their reception in State practice.

It is to be regretted though that despite a fairly extensive jurisprudence, the rules governing the nationality of claims, in particular the criteria for nationality, in the context of diplomatic protection cannot be stated with certainty. The work then of the International Commission on the law governing diplomatic protection has consolidated and clarified the law on many important issues and is to be welcomed.

This brief survey does not purport to be a complete account of the infinite variety of circumstances that may legally operate to preclude the admissibility of a claim. Some of these, such as inadmissibility on account of 'waiver' have received attention in the literature, including in the work of the International Law Commission (Crawford, 2002, pp 266–9). Other grounds of preclusion—such as a finding that the dispute is without object;[96] that the applicant State has itself indulged in the same wrongful act in respect of which it now complains (the 'clean hands' doctrine);[97] that the applicant has acquiesced in wrongful conduct forming the subject matter of the dispute;[98] or that the chosen forum is inappropriate (especially where the applicant State has instituted proceedings in a forum other than that nominated by the treaty)—are closely intertwined with the merits, and may therefore be treated either as issues of admissibility or as substantive grounds for defeating the claim at the merits stage. Moreover, in certain cases, the operation of estoppel may preclude the examination of a particular issue even in circumstances when the claim itself has been found to be admissible.[99] The survey is also undertaken without prejudice to the *lex specialis* regimes governing the protection of corporations or their shareholders under international economic treaties and protection mechanisms in human rights instruments.[100]

REFERENCES

ADLER, M (1990), 'The Exhaustion of the Local Remedies Rule after the International Court of Justice's Decision in ELSI', 39 *ICLQ* 641.

AMERASINGHE, CF (1990), *Local Remedies in International Law* (Cambridge: Grotius).

BORCHARD, EM (1915), *The Diplomatic Protection of Citizens Abroad* (New York: Banks Law Publishing Co).

BRIERLY, JL (1928), 'The Theory of State Complicity in International Claims', 9 *BYIL* 48.

[96] *Northern Cameroons, Preliminary Objections, Judgment, ICJ Reports 1963*, p 15.

[97] See *ICJ Pleadings, Oil Platforms (Islamic Republic of Iran v United States of America)*, Counter Memorial and Counter Claim Submitted by the United States of America, Part VI, pp 161–79 (23 June 1997) and Reply and Defence to Counter Claim submitted by the Islamic Republic of Iran, vol I, pp 187–98 (10 March 1999); *Gabčíkovo-Nagymaros Project (Hungary/Slovakia), Judgment, ICJ Reports 1997*, p 7, para 133; Dugard, 2005, passim.

[98] *ICJ Pleadings, Passage through the Great Belt (Finland v Denmark)*, Counter-memorial of the Government of the Kingdom of Denmark, Vol I, p 248 (May 1992).

[99] Eg *Temple of Preah Vihear, Merits, Judgment, ICJ Reports 1962*, p 6 at pp 22–3.

[100] In many cases these contain express provisions where parties agree to waive their right to diplomatic protection. Article 27 of the 1965 Convention on the Settlement of Investment Disputes, 575 UNTS 159, is particularly apt. It reads that: 'No Contracting State shall give diplomatic protection, or bring an international claim, in respect of a dispute which one of its nationals and another Contracting State shall have consented to submit or shall have submitted to arbitration under this Convention, unless such other Contracting State shall have failed to abide by and comply with the award rendered in such dispute'.

—— (1963), *The Law of Nations*, 6th edn (Oxford: Clarendon Press).

BROWNLIE, I (2008), *Principles of Public International Law*, 7th edn (Oxford: Clarendon Press).

CRAWFORD, J (2002), *The International Law Commission's Articles on State Responsibility* (Cambridge: Cambridge University Press).

—— (2012), *Brownlie's Principles of Public International Law*, 8th edn (Oxford: Clarendon Press).

—— (2013), *State Responsibility: The General Part* (Cambridge: Cambridge University Press).

——, PELLET, A, and OLLESON S (2010), *The Law of International Responsibility* (Oxford: Oxford University Press).

—— and OLLESON, S (2005), 'The Continuing Debate on a UN Convention on State Responsibility', 54 *ICLQ* 959.

DOUGLAS, Z (2009), *The International Law of Investment Claims* (Cambridge: Cambridge University Press).

DUGARD, J (2000), *First Report on Diplomatic Protection*, UN Doc A/CN.4/506.

—— (2001), *Second Report on Diplomatic Protection*, UN Doc A/CN.4/514.

—— (2002), *Third Report on Diplomatic Protection*, UN Doc A/CN.4/523.

—— (2004), *Fifth Report on Diplomatic Protection*, UN Doc A/CN.4/538.

—— (2005), *Sixth Report on Diplomatic Protection*, UN Doc A/CN.4/546.

FITZMAURICE, G (1957), 'The General Principles of International Law, Considered from the Standpoint of the Rule of Law', 92 *Recueil des Cours* 1.

—— (1961), 'Hersch Lauterpacht—The Scholar as Judge', 38 *BYIL* 37.

—— (1986), *The Law and Procedure of the International Court of Justice*, vol II (Cambridge: Grotius).

HARRIS, DJ (1998), *Cases and Materials on International Law*, 5th edn (London: Sweet & Maxwell).

LEIGH, GIF (1971), 'Nationality and Diplomatic Protection', 20 *ICLQ* 453.

LOWE, AV (2002), 'Shareholders Rights from Barcelona to ELSI', in Ando, N, McWhinney, E, and Wolfrum, R (eds), *Essays in Honor of Judge Oda* (The Hague: Kluwer), p 65.

—— and FITZMAURICE, M (1996), *Fifty Years of the International Court of Justice* (Cambridge: Cambridge University Press).

MALANCZUK, P (1997), *A Modern Introduction to International Law* (London: Routledge).

MERON, Y (1959), 'The Incidence of the Rule of Exhaustion of Local Remedies', 35 *BYIL* 83.

O'CONNELL, DP (1970), *International Law*, 2nd edn (London: Stevens).

OKOWA, P (2008), 'Case Concerning Ahmadou Sadio Diallo (Republic of Guinea v DRC), Preliminary Objections', 57 *ICLQ* 219.

OPPENHEIM, L (1992), *Oppenheim's International Law*, 9th edn (London: Longman).

RAGAZZI, M (1997), *The Concept of International Obligations Erga Omnes* (Oxford: Oxford University Press).

ROSENNE, S (1997), *The Law and Practice of the International Court, 1920–1996*, 3rd edn (The Hague: Nijhoff).

SCHACTER, O (1991), *International Law in Theory and in Practice* (Dordrecht: Martinus Nijhoff).

SHEA, D (1955), *The Calvo Clause* (Minneapolis, Minn.: University of Minnesota Press).

SIMMA, B (1994), 'From Bilateralism to Community Interest in International Law', 250 *Recueil des Cours* 217.

TAMS, C (2005), *Enforcing Obligations Erga Omnes in International Law* (Cambridge, Cambridge University Press).

THIRLWAY, H (1995), 'Law and Procedure of the International Court of Justice', 66 *BYIL* 4.

WATTS, A (1996), 'Nationality of Claims: Some Relevant Concepts', in

Lowe, AV and Fitzmaurice, M (eds), *Fifty Years of the International Court of Justice* (Cambridge: Cambridge University Press), p 424.

WITTICH, S (2001), 'Direct Injury and the Incidence of the Local Remedies Rule', 5 *Austrian Rev of Int'l and European L* 121.

FURTHER READING

AMERASINGHE, CF (1990), *Local Remedies in International Law* (Cambridge: Grotius). A comprehensive survey of the law including an in-depth study of the main doctrinal controversies.

CANCADO TRINDADE, AA (1983), *The Application of the Rule of Exhaustion of Local Remedies in International Law* (Cambridge: Cambridge University Press). A useful account of the rule with detailed illustrations from the jurisprudence of human rights tribunals, but rather dated.

DE HOOGH, AJJ (1996), *Obligations Erga Omnes and International Crimes: A Theoretical Inquiry into the Implementation and Enforcement of the International Responsibility of States* (The Hague: Kluwer). A detailed inquiry into the perennial difficulties surrounding the enforcement of *erga omnes* obligations.

INTERNATIONAL LAW ASSOCIATION (2000), *Committee on Diplomatic Protection of Persons and Property, Report of the Sixty-Ninth Conference* (London). A comprehensive and interesting examination of a wide range of issues relating to diplomatic protection.

PARRY, C (1956), 'Some Considerations Upon the Protection of Individuals in International Law', 90 *Recueil des Cours* 657. A good analysis of the law on diplomatic protection and includes some consideration of claims brought by international organizations.

TAMS, C (2005), *Enforcing Obligations Erga Omnes in International Law* (Cambridge, Cambridge University Press).

WARBRICK, C (1988), 'Protection of Nationals Abroad: Current Legal Problems', 37 *ICLQ* 1002. A useful analysis of some of the problematic aspects of diplomatic protection.

17

THE RESPONSIBILITY TO PROTECT

Spencer Zifcak

SUMMARY

The responsibility to protect has succeeded humanitarian intervention as the primary conceptual framework within which to consider international intervention to prevent the commission of mass atrocity crimes. First conceived in 2001, the doctrine has obtained international recognition in a remarkably short time. Its acceptance by the UN World Summit of political leaders in 2005, and later by the UN Security Council, provided the foundation for its further elaboration in international relations theory and political practice. This chapter provides the background to the new doctrine's appearance with a survey of the existing law and practice with respect to humanitarian intervention. It traces the responsibility to protect's subsequent intellectual and political development both before and after the adoption of the World Summit resolutions that embodied it. This analysis discloses that debate about the doctrine has been characterized by significant differences of opinion and interpretation between nations of the North and the South. In that context, the chapter concludes with a detailed consideration of the contemporary standing of the doctrine in international law.

I. INTRODUCTION

The genocide in Rwanda and ethnic cleansing in the Balkans left the international community's political leadership with a formidable dilemma. Plainly, the international community could no longer stand by while mass atrocities were committed. The cost in human rights and human life was simply too great. At the same time, however, the UN Charter's core commitment to national sovereignty seemed an insuperable obstacle to international intervention in conflicts that took place entirely within the boundaries of a State. Non-interference in a nation's domestic affairs remained the cardinal rule underpinning the global legal order. If, therefore, the call 'never again' were to be made meaningful, new thinking and greater resolve were needed to chart the perilous waters between these apparently irreconcilable legal principles and political commitments.

The dilemma itself was not new. Debates about humanitarian intervention had taken place over centuries (Chesterman, 2001). Nevertheless, the impetus had seemed greater, and the scale of recent atrocities not least in Kigali and Srebrenica, had shocked the world's conscience. The widespread and rapid acceptance of the understanding that individuals, just as much as States, should be regarded as the subjects of international law and, therefore, that they were deserving of its protection, had elevated human rights concerns to the top table of international political, legal and academic deliberation (Alston and MacDonald, 2008; Fabri, 2008; Peters, 2009; Teitel 2011).

It was largely by way of cracking that seemingly intractable problem that the idea that nations individually have a responsibility to protect their own citizens and that collectively they may take action to protect those in peril elsewhere has recently been developed and elaborated.[1] As I will argue, the 'responsibility to protect' (R2P) has not yet crystallized into a norm of international law. Yet its advance as a widely considered and broadly accepted political doctrine has been remarkably rapid. In the remainder of this chapter, I trace this advance and assess the doctrine's contemporary legal and political standing. To do that effectively, it may help to contextualize the issue by examining briefly the legal position with respect to its predecessor conception—humanitarian intervention (Evans, 2006).

II. HUMANITARIAN INTERVENTION IN INTERNATIONAL LAW

The *prima facie* position with respect to military interventions undertaken for humanitarian purposes appears to be as follows.[2] Pursuant to Article 2(4) of the UN Charter:

> All states shall refrain in their international relations from the threat or use of force against the territorial integrity and political independence of any state, or in any other manner inconsistent with the purpose of the United Nations.

This injunction against the use of force is reinforced by the terms of Article 2(7) which declares: 'Nothing in the present Charter shall authorize the UN to intervene in matters which are essentially within the domestic jurisdiction of any state'. The principle of non-intervention, together with that of the sovereign equality of States, is designed to ensure that each State respects the prerogatives and entitlements of every other State.

There are only two exceptions in the Charter to the Article 2(4) prohibition. First, Chapter VII of the Charter empowers the Security Council to authorize the use of force in response to threats and breaches of international peace and security. Pursuant to Article 39, therefore, the Security Council may make recommendations as to what measures, including the use of armed force, should be taken to address an identified threat to international peace and security or to any act of aggression. Secondly, in accordance with Article 51, member States of the UN may take measures, whether individually or collectively, in pursuit of their inherent right to self-defence should they be subject to armed attack. Such action in self-defence may continue until the Security Council itself has instituted whatever further measures are necessary to maintain international peace and security.

When laid down plainly in this way, it is apparent that the express terms of the Charter do not readily embrace either humanitarian intervention or a responsibility to protect.

---

[1] See the International Commission on Intervention and State Sovereignty (2001), *The Responsibility to Protect: Report of the International Commission on Intervention and State Sovereignty*, Ottawa: International Development Research Centre.

[2] See generally, Chesterman, 2001, Ch 2; Wheeler, 2004; Welsh, 2004.

The principle of non-intervention stands steadfastly in their path. The UN Declaration on Friendly Relations of 1970 states the duty in similar and compelling fashion:[3]

> No State or group of states has the right to intervene directly, or indirectly, for any reason whatsoever in the international external affairs of any other State. Consequently, armed intervention and all other forms of interference or attempted threats against the personality of the state or against its political, economic and cultural elements are in violation of international law.

Of course, the Charter's provisions are capable of competing interpretations. These can occupy the full spectrum from the literal to the liberal. International lawyers, for example, have argued that, despite what appear to be the plain words of the Charter text, a doctrine of humanitarian intervention may be insinuated into its interstices (Chesterman, 2001, p 47; Holzgrefe, 2003, p 53). One argument made is that Article 2(4) prohibits the use of force only against 'the territorial integrity or political independence of a state'. If, therefore, force is used in the pursuit of some other objective, particularly one that is consistent with the objects of the Charter, it may be permissible. A humanitarian intervention, properly conducted, may pose no long-term threat either to the territorial integrity or political autonomy of a State. Its sole purpose may be said to be to prevent the further commission of atrocities pending the restoration of stability.

Such an interpretation faces great difficulty, however, because it creates the prospect of a damaging ambiguity in the Charter's interpretation. Even a brief look at the *travaux préparatoires*, as a means of resolving such an ambiguity, demonstrates clearly that such an adventurous interpretation of the qualification has little if any plausible foundation. Instead, the original aim of the non-intervention principle appears to have been to protect smaller States and the words 'territorial integrity and political independence' were added as supplements to, not as detractions from, the general prohibition on the use of force.

Next, it may be suggested that the use of force is permitted so long as it is not, in the terms of Article 2(4), 'in any other manner inconsistent with the purposes of the United Nations'. Clearly, if the objective of the intervention is to prevent gross violations of human rights, it could not be said to be anything other than consistent with the Charter's fundamental purposes. The argument runs into immediate problems, however, not the least of which is that even if the disputed intervention is aimed at protecting and preserving the human rights of the afflicted people of a nation, the Charter's express prohibition of infringements upon the territorial integrity and political independence of a sovereign State still stands. It is unlikely that a vague reference to humanitarian purpose is sufficient to displace it.

Alternatively, a right or obligation of humanitarian intervention may arise in consequence of its progressive acceptance as part of customary international law (Cassese, 1999; Chesterman, 2001, Ch 2; Corten, 2008). There are significant methodological and practical problems, however, that stand in the path of humanitarian intervention's recognition as a customary rule. The International Court of Justice, for example, has had only limited opportunity to develop the rules governing the use of force.[4] In so far as the Court has considered the matter, it has come down steadfastly against any broadly applicable doctrine of permissible intervention. Nations themselves are not often clear or straightforward about

---

[3] Declaration on Principles of International Law Concerning Friendly Relations and Co-operation among States in accordance with the Charter of the UN (GA Res 2625(XXV), 24 October 1970), Article 1.

[4] See in particular *Military and Paramilitary Activities in and against Nicaragua (Nicaragua v United States of America), Merits, Judgment, ICJ Reports 1986*, p 14; *Legality of Use of Force (Yugoslavia v Belgium), Provisional Measures, Order of 2 June 1999, ICJ Reports 1999*, p 124.

their motivations for acting, and mix legal justifications with political and security concerns in a way that makes the interpretation of State action an uncertain exercise. The UN's norm-creating bodies, in particular the Security Council and General Assembly, may not always be at one in their judgment of events, raising complex questions about the weight to be given to the opinions of each and the relative merits of both.

Such methodological difficulties have plainly been present in the most recent examples of international military interventions claimed to have had a humanitarian foundation. These are worth examining more closely. Two classes of case may be identified: those where the UN Security Council has sanctioned purported humanitarian interventions and those where it has not.

A. INTERVENTION WITH SECURITY COUNCIL AUTHORIZATION

In the first category are the cases of international intervention in Somalia, Rwanda, and Bosnia (see Weiss, 2007; Evans, 2008). The Somali operation was justified principally on the basis that the obstacles being placed in the way of urgently required humanitarian assistance to the country's distressed population were, in the opinion of the Security Council, such as to constitute a threat to international peace and security. The Council, therefore, authorized the international community pursuant to Chapter VII to use all necessary means to establish a secure environment for international relief operations.[5] The UN Secretary-General later expressed his opinion that the Somali operation constituted a new precedent for the Council. It had, for the first time, authorized a military intervention for purely humanitarian purposes.[6]

All too late, the Security Council authorized French military intervention to prevent further mass atrocities in Rwanda. It had previously determined that the Rwandan genocide had constituted a threat to international peace and security and therefore that safe-havens were therefore required for those fleeing the genocide. In its primary resolution the Council also referred specifically to the wider disruption to cross-border security that had been created by the mass internal displacement of Rwandan citizens. Again, the Council authorized all necessary means to achieve the primary humanitarian objective. To that end, it instructed the French interveners to create a safe haven in which those fleeing the wider conflict could find security.[7] The French were also clear that any intervention on their part had to be founded upon the Security Council's mandate, even if delay were the result.[8]

The Security Council's many resolutions in relation to Bosnia-Herzegovina were directed principally at ending civil conflict consequent upon the dissolution of the former Yugoslavia rather than having a primarily humanitarian objective, although the latter remained significant. Resolution 770 (1992), for example, called upon States to take the measures necessary to facilitate the delivery of humanitarian aid and assistance to Sarajevo and other parts of the country as needed. It went further to authorize the UN intervention force to act in self-defence where necessary in order to reply to bombardments of established safe-havens or to armed incursion into them and to take all necessary measures, including the use of air power in and around the internationally protected safe areas, to support its protective objective.[9] Again these resolutions proceeded from the Council's

---

[5] SC Res 794 (3 December 1992).   [6] [1993] *UNYB* 51.   [7] SC Res 929 (22 June 1994).
[8] 40 *Annuaire Français de Droit International Public* (1998) 429–30.
[9] SC Res 770 (13 August 1992) and see further SC Res 814 (26 March 1993); SC Res 816 (31 March 1993); SC Res 844 (19 June 1993); and SC Res 871 (2 October 1993).

earlier determination that the conflict in Bosnia-Herzegovina constituted a threat to international peace and security.

These three cases suggest that since 1990, a highly circumscribed recognition of a right of humanitarian intervention may have been developing gradually within customary international law. The legal preconditions for such a nascent right were first that an existing or potential humanitarian catastrophe must be identified. Secondly, the catastrophe and its wider effects must be such as to constitute, in the opinion of the Security Council, a threat to international peace and security. Thirdly, the Security Council must explicitly authorize any subsequent military intervention. Fourthly, and implicitly, the authorization and conduct of the intervention must be an act of last resort (see Gazzini, 2005, p 174; Corten, 2008, p 106).

B. INTERVENTION WITHOUT SECURITY COUNCIL AUTHORIZATION

Following the defeat of the Iraqi army in Kuwait and its subsequent withdrawal from that country, in 1991 the Kurdish peoples in the north of the country sought to assert their right to political independence. This uprising was met with brute military force by troops loyal to the Hussein regime and, after it was put down, the government embarked upon further, genocidal, repression of the Kurdish population. In response, the Security Council adopted Resolution 688. The resolution condemned the repression of the Iraqi civilian population, demanded that Iraq end this oppression and insisted that Iraq allow international humanitarian organizations immediate access to all those in need of assistance. The Council also appealed to all member States and humanitarian organizations to continue their humanitarian relief efforts. Despite its strong language, however, the resolution did not contain any express authorization for military action pursuant to Chapter VII.[10]

Nevertheless, on the same day, the US administration announced that it would commence dropping food and other forms of material aid over Northern Iraq in partnership with France and the UK. Then, 11 days later when it appeared as if the aid effort was being substantially compromised by mountainous and inhospitable terrain into which the aid was being delivered, President Bush announced unilaterally that US troops would enter Northern Iraq in order to establish safe-havens for the beleaguered Kurdish population.

When these interventions were challenged by Iraq in the Security Council, the coalition partners contended that their actions were justified on purely humanitarian grounds. They also sought to establish legal legitimacy for their interventions by arguing that Resolution 688 had provided implicit legal authorization for them. The argument that humanitarian intervention might legally be supported by such implicit authorization was difficult to justify. This was because the express terms of the relevant resolution did not appear to allow for such an expansive interpretation. The resolution itself was the first of 14 that had not been adopted under Chapter VII. And in the Council debates that led to its adoption, the prospect of military intervention had never explicitly been contemplated. However strongly based on humanitarian concern, then, the arguments put in favour of the right of a State or States to engage unilaterally in humanitarian intervention without express Security Council authorization seemed, at least at that stage, to have only the most tenuous foundation.

The question as to the legality of unilateral humanitarian intervention emerged for consideration again in 1999 in relation to the controversial intervention by NATO in defence

---

[10] SC Res 688 (5 April 1991).

of the ethnic Albanian people of Kosovo.[11] So as to protect the Kosovar Albanians from violence and ethnic cleansing at the hands of Serbian forces, NATO conducted some thousands of bombing raids on Kosovo and surrounding areas over several months. Prior to this, the Security Council had adopted three resolutions concerning the deteriorating military and humanitarian situation.

Resolution 1160 condemned the use of excessive force by Serbian police, imposed an arms embargo and expressed support for a political solution based on the territorial integrity of the Former Republic of Yugoslavia (FRY) with greater autonomy for the Kosovar Albanians.[12] Resolution 1199 recognized the deteriorating humanitarian situation, one that had already resulted in numerous civilian casualties and the displacement of 230,000 people from their homes. It declared the situation as one constituting a threat to international peace and security and, acting under Chapter VII, demanded a ceasefire and action to improve the humanitarian position.[13] In Resolution 1203, finally, the Council decided that should the concrete measures it had demanded not be taken, and should Serbia not comply with the terms of the agreement reached with NATO and the Organization for Security and Co-operation in Europe (OSCE) to end the hostilities, it would *consider* further action and additional measures to maintain or restore peace and stability in the region.[14] These resolutions fell far short of authorizing any international military intervention to achieve that aim.

Certainly, the Council had determined that the deterioration of the situation in Kosovo threatened regional peace and security. And, in Resolution 1199, the Council had demanded an immediate end to hostilities and the maintenance of a ceasefire. It had also demanded immediate measures to avert an imminent catastrophe. Not once, however, had the Council authorized the use of force by the international community in order to advance these objectives. Instead, in Kosovo, NATO took upon itself the task of pursuing and achieving them without further reference to the Council.

The bones of NATO's legal argument were straightforward. The Security Council had adopted resolutions under Chapter VII that demanded that the Yugoslavian authorities halt their brutal repression of ethnic Albanians. The authorities had refused to comply with these resolutions and the prior, brokered agreements to which they referred. Consequently, NATO member States presumed unilaterally to act in support of those resolutions by intervening to prevent further violations.

However forcefully legal arguments in favour of the NATO action were put, formidable obstacles remained in the path of their acceptance. The argument that NATO's intervention was implicitly justified as a means of enforcing prior Security Council resolutions again was weak. This was because the wording of the resolutions did not at all appear to authorize any subsequent unilateral military action and it left for the Council's further consideration any decision as what additional measures might be necessary to pursue and enforce its demands (Corten, 2008). Quite apart from this, the idea that a State or group of States could or should act unilaterally to enforce Council resolutions without any subsequent Council involvement or authorization could open the door to opportunistic interventions of any and every kind.[15] Finally, even if it had been accepted prior to Kosovo that the protection of non-derogable human rights had achieved the status of *jus cogens* and therefore obliged the UN to protect them, it by no means followed that the unilateral

---

[11] See Simma, 1999; Chinkin, 2000; Thakur, 2011a.   [12] SC Res 1160 (31 March 1998).
[13] SC Res 1199 (23 September 1998).   [14] SC Res 1203 (24 October 1998).
[15] See to similar effect the statement by the Permanent Representative of India during Security Council debate, SC/1035 (24 March 1999).

employment of military force, outside the UN, to secure them, had also become part of customary international law (Alston and MacDonald, 2008).

Considering this, the conclusion of the Independent Commission Report on Kosovo (2000) is apt:

> Far from opening up a new era of humanitarian intervention the Kosovo experience seems, to this Commission at least, to teach a valuable lesson of skepticism and caution. Sometimes, and Kosovo is such an instance, the use of military force may become necessary to defend human rights. But the grounds for its use in international law urgently need clarification and the tactics and rules of engagement for its use need to be improved. Finally, the legitimacy of such use of force will always be controversial, and will remain so, as long as we intervene to protect some people's lives but not others.

III. THE BIRTH OF THE 'RESPONSIBILITY TO PROTECT'

In the decade following Kosovo, there had been no significant instances of humanitarian military interventions in which the international community engaged. State practice, therefore, provided no further guidance as to the doctrine's development in international law. At the same time, however, conceptual and political developments have been quick. These political developments have focused not upon humanitarian intervention per se, but rather on a bold endeavour, by those concerned to prevent mass atrocity crimes, to craft a new, more thoughtful and more measured doctrine to build upon and at the same time differentiate it from its humanitarian predecessor. In just a few years the idea of humanitarian intervention has been displaced by what has come to be known as the 'responsibility to protect' (R2P).

Speaking in an address to the UN General Assembly in 1999, then UN Secretary-General Kofi Annan challenged member States to resolve what he saw as the conflict between the principle of non-interference with State sovereignty, embodied in Article 2(4) of the Charter, and the responsibility of the international community to respond to massive human rights violations and ethnic cleansing. He posed what he described as a tragic dilemma:

> To those for whom the greatest threat to the future of the international order is the use of force in the absence of a Security Council mandate, one might ask...in the context of Rwanda: if in those dark days and hours leading up to the genocide a coalition of states had been prepared to act in defence of the Tutsi population, but did not receive prompt Security Council authorization, should such a coalition have stood aside and allowed the horror to unfold?

To those for whom the Kosovo action heralded a new era when States and groups of States can take military action outside the established mechanisms for enforcing international law, one might ask: is there not a danger of such interventions undermining the imperfect, yet resilient, security system created after the Second World War, and of setting dangerous precedents for future interventions without a clear criterion to decide who might invoke these precedents, and in what circumstances?[16]

---

[16] Address by Kofi Annan to the Fifty-fourth Session of the UN General Assembly, 20 September 1999.

To steer between the Scylla and Charybdis of the problem, Annan argued that the Security Council must be able to agree on effective action to defend fundamental human rights. He proposed that the core challenge to the Council in the twenty-first century was: 'To forge unity behind the principle that massive and systematic violations of human rights—wherever they may take place—should not be allowed to stand.'[17]

The Secretary-General's call to action met with a mixed, and in some quarters hostile, response in the General Assembly. Nevertheless, it prompted the Canadian Government, in a singular initiative, to form an international panel of experts, the International Commission on Intervention and State Sovereignty (ICISS), to address the problem. The Commission consulted widely with governments, non-governmental organizations, inter-governmental organizations, universities and think-tanks. On the basis of these extensive consultations, it produced its final report, *The Responsibility to Protect*.[18] The report radically altered the terms of the ensuing political debate in three inter-related ways.

First, it re-conceptualized forcible international action in defence of peoples at risk of mass atrocity. The international community would no longer engage in 'humanitarian intervention' but would instead exercise a broader 'responsibility to protect' nations at risk of failure and descent into violence. Secondly, the new approach attributed primary responsibility for taking action to prevent humanitarian disaster upon the sovereign government of the nation in which might occur. Only if and when that responsibility had not been exercised would the larger global community's parallel responsibility to intervene in the national and international interest be engaged. Thirdly, new rules of engagement should be developed to ensure that any such intervention would have the maximum possible opportunity for success.

The Commission asserted, more in hope than expectation given its novelty, that the 'responsibility to protect' reflected an emerging norm of international law and behaviour:

> Based on our reading of state practice, Security Council precedent, established norms, guiding principles, and evolving customary international law, the Commission believes that the Charter's strong bias against military intervention is not to be regarded as absolute when decisive action is required on human protection grounds.[19]

As to the vexed question of military intervention, ICISS recommended that it should take place pursuant to authorization by the Security Council and only then after the careful consideration of five criteria of legitimacy. These were that:

- The threatened harm must be serious, ie it must involve genocide, war crimes, crimes against humanity, or ethnic cleansing.
- The primary purpose of the intervention must be to halt the threatened humanitarian catastrophe.
- Military intervention must be adopted only as a measure of last resort.
- The proposed military action must be proportionate to the threat.
- The adverse consequences flowing from the military intervention should clearly be less than the consequences of inaction (see Evans, 2008, p 139).

---

[17] Ibid.

[18] International Commission on Intervention and State Sovereignty (2001), *The Responsibility to Protect: Report of the International Commission on Intervention and State Sovereignty*, Ottawa, International Development Research Centre.

[19] Ibid, p 16.

Finally, ICISS developed its conceptual framework by proposing that three different forms of responsibility were engaged. R2P should best be exercised initially through prevention. This *responsibility to prevent* spoke to the need to take every reasonable step to ensure that predicted humanitarian catastrophes would not occur. Preventive strategies such as good governance and human rights, together with international aid and development assistance should be the first to be deployed. Next, *the responsibility to react* emphasized that in the exercise of its preventive role, the international community should always prefer non-forcible measures, such as diplomatic negotiations and economic sanctions, to instigating armed intervention. Once a crisis had been averted, whether militarily or otherwise, a *responsibility to rebuild* would be assumed. In this, the international community would involve itself in peacekeeping, economic and social reconstruction and other similar developmental initiatives.

The central thrust of the report, then, was upon the prevention of conflict through a range of non-military measures that would likely entail significant transfers of wealth, expertise and opportunity from developed to developing countries. It would involve taking Third World development seriously. Only once such measures had failed to avert an anticipated humanitarian crisis would more coercive means be considered.

IV. THE 2005 WORLD SUMMIT

A. TOWARDS THE 2005 WORLD SUMMIT

Three years after ICISS had reported, its recommendations received powerful endorsement from the Secretary-General's High-Level Panel on Threats, Challenges and Change (HLP). The Panel adopted the conceptual framework embodied in the idea of the 'responsibility to protect'. It favoured the ICISS's conclusion that any such responsibility should be exercised only with the endorsement of the Security Council. And it incorporated, with some minor alterations, the legitimacy criteria that had been set down in the original report.[20]

Addressing the relevant legal issues, the Panel observed that the Charter reaffirmed a fundamental faith in human rights but did not do much to protect them. Article 2(7) prohibits intervention in matters which are essentially within the jurisdiction of any State. Nevertheless, the Panel asserted that the principle of non-intervention embodied in that Article could not be used to shield nations from the consequences of state-sponsored genocidal acts or other atrocities. These should properly be considered as threats to international peace and security under Article 24 and, as such, might with legal justification provoke a response from the Security Council.

> We endorse the emerging norm that there is a collective international responsibility to protect, exercisable by the Security Council, authorizing military intervention as a last resort, in the event of genocide and other large-scale killing, ethnic cleansing or serious violations of international humanitarian law which sovereign governments have proved powerless or unwilling to prevent.[21]

---

[20] *A More Secure World: Our Shared Responsibility*, the Report of the High-Level Panel on Threats, Challenges and Change, UN Doc A/59/565, 2004.

[21] Ibid; and for an analysis of the assertion see Corten, 2008, p 127.

Taking his lead from the Panel, the Secretary-General recommended that the World Leaders' Summit in 2005 adopt the responsibility to protect.[22] Even so, it was unclear whether his recommendation would survive the exhaustive and exhausting negotiations that would occur in six months preceding the Summit. The principal line of objection was clear. Some States would argue strongly in favour of the international community's entitlement to intervene in the face of genocide, crimes against humanity and other mass atrocities committed by a State. Others, however, would maintain that the Security Council was prohibited legally from authorizing coercive action against sovereign nations in relation to any matter that occurred within their borders. As the Permanent Representative of Algeria stated in an early discussion on the Secretary-General's report:

> ...interference can occur with the consent of the State concerned...we do not deny that the United Nations has the right and duty to help suffering humanity. But we remain extremely sensitive to any undermining of our sovereignty, not only because sovereignty is our last defence against the rules of an unequal world, but because we are not taking part in the decision making process of the Security Council...[23]

Generally speaking, the Western Europe and Others Group (WEOG) nations supported the inclusion of a resolution in favour of the responsibility to protect in the World Summit outcome document. The USA, however, had significant reservations. A powerful bloc in the Non-Aligned Movement (NAM) either opposed its inclusion or sought significant amendments to the basic principles that had been set down. Several Latin American nations also expressed their disquiet. The most interesting and crucial aspect of these pre-Summit discussions was the strong support for the doctrine provided by the nations of Africa. In a sense, this was not surprising. It has been in Africa—perhaps more than in any other region of the world—that mass violations of human rights of the kind sought to be prevented here, have occurred. African nations had first-hand, or near-hand, experience of the atrocities and consequent human suffering with which the doctrine was concerned, and an intimate and devastating knowledge of the consequences of both State and international failure.[24] In this context, the Tanzanian President had made the case plainly:

> We must now stop misusing the principles of sovereignty and non-interference in the internal affairs of states to mark incidences of poor governance and unacceptable human rights abuses...In the aftermath of the genocide in Rwanda, and in light of the massive influx of refugees in the Great Lakes Region, it is inevitable to conclude that the principle of non-intervention in the internal affairs of a state can no longer find unqualified, absolute legitimacy...Governments must first be held responsible for the life and welfare of their people. But, there must also be common agreed rules and benchmarks that would trigger collective action through our regional organizations and the United Nations against governments that commit unacceptable human rights abuses.[25]

---

[22] *In Larger Freedom: Towards Development, Security and Human Rights for All*, Report of the Secretary-General, UN Doc A/59/2005, 2005, p 35.

[23] Abdallah Baali, Permanent Representative of Algeria, Statement to the Informal Thematic Consultations of the General Assembly to Discuss the Four Clusters Contained in the Secretary-General's Report 'In Larger Freedom', Cluster III: Freedom to Live in Dignity, 19 April 2005.

[24] For that reason the African Union had previously inserted a provision embodying a doctrine resembling the responsibility to protect into its Constitutive Act. See Article 4(h).

[25] President of Tanzania, Benjamin Mkapa, Address to the First Summit of the International Conference of the Great Lakes, Dar-es-Salaam, November 2004.

B. THE WORLD SUMMIT RESOLUTION

Under heavy pressure to adopt some form of the 'responsibility to protect' formula, diplomatic representatives in New York haggled into the last week before the Summit to try to find the words that might permit a compromise text to go to the world's leaders for endorsement.[26] After frenzied last minute negotiations, the final text was concluded. It was hedged with qualifications and therefore weaker than that which had been proposed in the ICISS and HLP reports. Nevertheless, the very fact that the concept and principle had been agreed to at the World Summit represented a substantial success. The concluded wording was as follows:

> 138. Each individual State has the responsibility to protect its populations from genocide, war crimes, ethnic cleansing and crimes against humanity. This responsibility entails the prevention of such crimes, including their incitement, through appropriate and necessary means. We accept that responsibility and will act in accordance with it...
>
> 139. The international community, through the United Nations, also has the responsibility to use appropriate diplomatic, humanitarian and other peaceful means, in accordance with Chapters VI and VII of the Charter, to help protect populations from genocide, war crimes, ethnic cleansing and crimes against humanity. In this context, we are prepared to take collective action, in a timely and decisive manner, through the Security Council, in accordance with the Charter, including Chapter VII, on a case-by-case basis and in cooperation with relevant regional organizations as appropriate, should peaceful means be ineffective... We stress the need for the General Assembly to continue considerations of the responsibility to protect populations from genocide, war crimes, ethnic cleansing and crimes against humanity and its implications, bearing in mind the principles of the Charter and international law. We also intend to commit ourselves, as necessary and appropriate, to helping states build capacity to protect their populations from genocide, war crimes, ethnic cleansing and crimes against humanity and to assisting those which are under stress before crises and conflicts break out.[27]

Despite this success, a close look at the Summit resolution makes it plain that several of the doctrine's underlying principles are likely to be qualified heavily in practice. In the process of negotiating the final text, victory went to those favouring the acceptance of the new doctrine. However, those opposing it, whether absolutely or conditionally, managed to extract substantial concessions. A close reading of the text reveals the following qualifications:

- The crimes in relation to which a responsibility to protect may arise are limited to genocide, war crimes, ethnic cleansing and crimes against humanity.
- The international community is enjoined in the first instance to exercise its responsibility by using all appropriate diplomatic, humanitarian and other peaceful means in accordance with the Charter. Collective action will be triggered only when such peaceful means are considered to have been inadequate.
- The international community, in its Summit embodiment, has indicated that it is 'prepared to take collective action'. Following from an American recommendation, the words 'we recognize our shared responsibility to take collective action' were removed.

---

[26] As to the General Assembly Debate prior to the World Summit see Bellamy, 2008a; Zifcak, 2009, Ch 6.
[27] 2005 World Summit Outcome, UN Doc A/60/L.1.

- Collective action by the international community must be authorized by the Security Council in accordance with the terms of Chapter VII of the Charter. The idea, referred to briefly by the High-Level Panel, that there may be certain circumstances in which intervention may be countenanced without such authorization did not make its way into the text.

- No criteria of legitimacy are set down. Instead, the international community, through the UN, will determine on a 'case-by-case' basis whether collective action to defend populations from criminal activities is required. This was a late insertion, at the behest of the USA and China.

- Collective action under Chapter VII will be considered only where national authorities 'manifestly fail to protect their populations' from the relevant crimes. This is a standard considerably higher than that initially suggested.

A recommended constraint—that the permanent members of the Security Council should refrain from exercising the veto in cases of genocide, war crimes, ethnic cleansing, and crimes against humanity—was rejected.

There is no doubt that the formal recognition of the new doctrine of the responsibility to protect by the world's political leadership stood as one of the principal achievements of the World Summit. And for such a doctrine to achieve consensus agreement within five years of its first formulation is almost unprecedented. However, as is plain from this analysis of the resolution's text, there remains ample room for argument as to its meaning, standing, and exercise (Focarelli, 2008).

V. POST WORLD SUMMIT RECOGNITION OF THE DOCTRINE

Since the World Summit, the most significant development with respect to the responsibility to protect has been its recognition by the Security Council. In the context of a debate upon the protection of civilians in armed conflict, the Security Council approved Resolution 1674 dealing with all aspects of that question, including the promotion of economic growth, poverty eradication, national reconciliation, good governance, democracy, the rule of law and the protection of fundamental human rights.[28] This resolution reaffirmed 'the provisions of paragraphs 138 and 139 of the 2005 World Summit Outcome Document regarding the responsibility to protect populations from genocide, war crimes, ethnic cleansing and crimes against humanity'. Apart from the normative importance of this reaffirmation, the adoption of the resolution marked the first occasion upon which the Security Council acknowledged expressly that its role may extend not just to the prevention of threats to international peace and security but also to the cessation of mass atrocities taking place within State borders.

Soon after, without any further elaboration of the doctrine, the Security Council invoked the new norm for the first time—in relation to the situation in Darfur. In Resolution 1706, the Council resolved, among other things, to deploy a UN peacekeeping force in Darfur and sought the consent of the Sudanese Government to do so.[29] In its preliminaries, the resolution recalled Resolution 1674 and its endorsement of the terms of the World Summit Outcome in this respect. It reaffirmed the Council's strong commitment to the

---

[28] SC Res 1674 (28 April 2006).   [29] SC Res 1704 (25 August 2006).

sovereignty, unity, independence and territorial integrity of Sudan but made clear its view that the nation's sovereignty would not be adversely affected by the transition to a UN force devoted to the cause of peace.

Even more recently, in the preamble of Resolution 1973 with respect to the Libyan intervention, the Council reiterated the responsibility of the Libyan authorities to protect the population and reaffirmed that the parties to the conflict bore the primary responsibility for ensuring the protection of civilians.[30] A similar reaffirmation followed in the Council resolution on Côte D'Ivoire.[31]

VI. THE SECRETARY-GENERAL'S ELABORATION OF THE RESPONSIBILITY TO PROTECT

The resolutions with respect to R2P, although adopted by consensus, were highly general in nature and much work remained to be done to put flesh on their bones. To assist with this task Ban Ki-Moon appointed Professor Edward Luck to be his special adviser on the subject, and Luck went to work to make the doctrine comprehensible and concrete. The product was the Secretary-General's report to the General Assembly on the implementation of the responsibility to protect,which was tabled in January 2009.[32]

The report was a detailed encapsulation and explication of the new doctrine's principal parameters. It drew heavily on the work of ICISS and the HLP but its cast was much more pragmatic. The report made clear that Kofi Annan's successor was also committed to the doctrine. In elaborating upon it, a three-pillar approach to its implementation was proposed.

In the first, the nation in which a humanitarian catastrophe is in prospect must assume responsibility for taking timely and appropriate preventative measures. These may include intensive diplomatic steps to mediate impending conflict, the adoption of anti-corruption strategies, the early prosecution of those engaging in violent activity, the promotion of human rights and efforts to establish more effective governance. The second pillar involves a calibrated reaction by the international community. Here, concerted and directed assistance in the form of development aid, foreign investment, technical assistance, economic incentives, rapid police responsiveness, and more general capacity building will be crucial. Under the third pillar, these measures may be supplemented initially by 'soft' coercion which may include international fact finding, the deployment of peacekeepers, the imposition of arms embargoes, the application of diplomatic and economic sanctions and the creation of safe-havens and no-fly zones. Then, when all else has failed, the Security Council may authorize military intervention as the measure of last resort.

The Secretary-General sought to clarify certain issues about which there had been considerable confusion or dissension since the World Summit. He made clear that the R2P applies only in relation to cases of genocide, war crimes, crimes against humanity and ethnic cleansing. It does not detract from existing international commitments under international humanitarian law, human rights law or refugee law. Collective action in the use of force must be undertaken with the authority of the Security Council and in accordance with Chapter VII of the Charter. The responsibility to protect provides no support, therefore, for unilateral military interventions. The doctrine is to be distinguished from

---

[30] SC Res 1973 (17 March 2011).   [31] SC Res 1975 (30 March 2011).
[32] Report of the Secretary-General, *Implementing the Responsibility to Protect*, UN Doc A/63/677; Luck, 2009.

'humanitarian intervention'. Humanitarian intervention, the report said, posed a false choice between either standing by in the face of catastrophe or deploying coercive military force to protect populations that were threatened. The responsibility to protect seeks to overcome this binary divide by recasting sovereignty as responsibility and then defining in some detail what the respective duties and obligations of nations and the international community to prevent humanitarian disaster should be.

The UN Secretary-General presented three further reports on R2P from 2010–12. The first of these focused on early warnings of possible genocide, crimes against humanity, war crimes and ethnic cleansing.[33] It outlined a series of institutional innovations that would assist in the primary tasks of detection and prevention. Within the UN the key innovation was the establishment of a joint office for special advisers on genocide and the responsibility to protect. The report recommended that regional organizations and civil society should create similar advisory offices directed towards the monitoring and evaluation of potential conflict situations.

The second report focused more specifically on the role of regional inter-governmental organizations in implementing the responsibility to protect.[34] The Secretary-General proposed a global-regional partnership in the implementation of all three pillars of R2P. He committed the UN to collaboration with all major regional organizations, including the African Union, the Economic Community of West African States (ECOWAS), the Organization of American States (OAS), the Association of Southeast Asian Nations (ASEAN) and the Arab League in the development of the doctrine's conceptual framework and in its practical implementation.

The most important of these reports was the third on 'timely and decisive response'.[35] This report was significant because it was the first in the UN system to be directed at illuminating the parameters and practice of coercive intervention. It was also the first in which the Secretary-General could address disagreements that had emerged in the course of the UN sanctioned NATO intervention in Libya.

The report set down five key lessons that had been learnt from the experience of the doctrine's implementation to date.

- While each instance of its application had been distinct, the doctrine's principles could and should be applied uniformly. Its mechanisms and methods, however, had necessarily to be shaped by circumstances on the ground.

- The Security Council had become more engaged than previously when responding to gross human rights violations.

- A more integrated and nuanced understanding of how the three pillars related to one another was required. None of the pillars was likely to stand on its own. The purpose of pillar 3 intervention, for example, was directed primarily to enabling national authorities to resume their responsibility to protect their own peoples in conformity with the legal obligations inherent in pillar 1.

- Any effective and integrated strategy is likely to involve elements of response and prevention. Capacity building, through the establishment of independent commissions of inquiry, for example, embraces elements of both.

---

[33] Report of the Secretary-General, *Early Warning, Assessment and the Responsibility to Protect*, UN Doc A/64/864.

[34] Report of the Secretary-General, *The Role of Regional and Sub-Regional Arrangements in Implementing the Responsibility to Protect*, UN Doc A/65/877–S/2011/393.

[35] Report of the Secretary-General, *Responsibility to Protect: Timely and Decisive Response*, UN Doc A66/874/ - S/2012/578.

- Finally, the value of partners, in particular regional inter-governmental organizations, had been invaluable. Every effort should be made to strengthen the ties between the two in the joint battle to prevent mass atrocities.

Treading onto the more uncertain territory of coercive intervention, the Secretary-General's report was at pains to point out that pillar 3 interventions did not necessitate the application of military force. A comprehensive range of less intensive measures was available including sanctions, the restriction of scientific and technical cooperation, the constraint or severance of diplomatic ties, and the control of the availability of high value commodities or weapons. Even under Article 42 of the UN Charter, military intervention could be left as a last resort in favour of the establishment of security and no-fly zones.

As for the NATO intervention in Libya, the Secretary-General explained diplomatically that:

> ...the Security Council decided to authorize the use of force after most of its members had come to the conclusion that a series of peaceful measures had proven inadequate. Some member states, however, have contended that non-coercive measures were not given sufficient time to demonstrate results...Others have expressed the view that those charged with implementing Council Resolution 1973 exceeded the mandate they were given by the Council. Whatever the specific merits of the arguments, it is important that the international community learn from these experiences and that concerns expressed by member states are taken into account in the future.[36]

This third report, like that in 2009, was valuable for its illumination of key theoretical and practical issues that had emerged since the responsibility to protect's introduction. At the same time, the report implicitly acknowledged that the Libyan intervention had acted to disrupt the doctrine's steady and incremental evolution and acceptance. Soon after, disruption turned to convulsion as the catastrophe in Syria unfolded. To understand the present content and standing of the responsibility to protect, therefore, a brief assessment of the nature and effects of these two conflicts is required (Zifcak, 2012).

VII. R2P IN LIBYA AND SYRIA

A. LIBYA

The fact of military victory on the ground was sufficient to justify the initial conclusion that the Libyan R2P operation had succeeded (Evans, 2011, 2012; Thakur, 2011b). This is despite strong protests as to its methods, lodged not without reason, by those members of the Security Council who abstained from the vote on Resolution 1973.[37]

It was not just the military win that seemed to secure R2P as an international political doctrine of considerable importance. The Libyan success had a number of novel aspects, each of which seemed to consolidate the doctrine's gains (Bellamy, 2011; Adams, 2012). Unlike preceding humanitarian interventions, the Libyan one was founded upon a resolution of the UN Security Council with explicit preambular reference to its conformity with R2P. This was not a unilateral intervention by Western forces such as that which had created such enormous legal controversy in Kosovo. The role of regional organizations was

---

[36] UN Doc A/66/874 (25 July 2012), para 54.   [37] UN Doc S/PV.6498 (17 March 2011).

even more important.[38] The Arab League in particular, took firm action against Libya, condemning the government's attitudes and actions and expelling the country from its membership. Importantly, success in Libya also came without the imposition of 'boots on the ground'.

At the same time, the intervention revealed deficits in the manner of its implementation. The most severe criticism of the Libyan case related to 'mission creep'. Those members of the Security Council who abstained from the vote on Resolution 1973 attacked forcefully what they saw as the abuse of the Council's mandate. In their view there was no way in which the relevant resolution could have permitted the transformation of the mission from the protection of civilians to the objective of regime change.

Consequently, reservations were expressed as to the legality of the transformation. Here, the argument was that Resolution 1973 could not be stretched to cover actions such as intervention in a civil war, the assassination of a government's leadership and the overthrow of the regime.[39] Security Council endorsement was critical to underpin the legality of the intervention but the actions of the coalition forces were said by the BRICS countries, Russia and China, to take the intervention beyond the resolution's terms and, therefore, possibly beyond what the UN Charter could be interpreted to allow. Further, Russia, China, India, and Brazil all objected strongly to the alteration of NATO's military stance from the relative neutrality of civilian protection to evident partiality in taking the rebel side.[40]

B. SYRIA

It was partly owing to such reservations that three draft resolutions recommending various degrees of condemnation and action in response to the Syrian crisis were vetoed by Russia and China.[41] The reality, however, was that for political and strategic reasons it would in any case have been unlikely that the Council would have endorsed a coercive military action at any time during the first two years of the conflict. The balance of consequences always told against such a course.

The fundamental question that Security Council members had to address when considering their response to the Syrian disaster was whether or not a direct military intervention of the kind undertaken in Libya and contemplated in Syria was likely to achieve its protective objective—without causing more harm to the civilian population than might otherwise have occurred. The likely answer to that question would have been 'yes' in the Libyan case but 'no' in the Syrian.

Militarily, the Libyan regime was in a considerably weaker position than its Syrian counterpart. Its army was divided, thus opening up the prospect of large-scale defections, Gaddafi himself was haemorrhaging political support, and opposition forces had already made significant gains particularly in the East. Because the regime was effectively isolated, there was no likelihood that neighbouring States would enter the fray to defend an erratic and discredited dictatorship.

None of these favourable conditions existed in Syria. It had substantial military resources; its military command and security intelligence services were, with the exception of some

---

[38] SC Res 1973 (17 March 2011).

[39] UN Doc S/PV.6566 (27 June 2011), Mr Mashabane (South Africa).

[40] See, eg UN Doc S/PV.6528 (4 May 2011), Mr Churkin (Russian Federation) & Mr Baodong (China).

[41] UN Doc S/2011/612 (4 October 2011); UN Doc S/2012/77 (4 February 2012); UN Doc S/2012/538 (19 July 2012); and see Gifkins, 2012.

notable defections, cohesive and loyal to the government; and the President still retained the confidence of a substantial proportion of the population, particularly in Damascus and Aleppo. Recruits and advisers from Palestine, Lebanon, Iran, and Iraq bolstered government forces. A steady flow of weapons continued to arrive from Russia and Iran.

At the same time, the Syrian rebellion also strengthened. The opposition counted many thousands of fighters amongst its number. Swathes of the north and central regions became no-go areas for regime combatants. The major cities of Homs and Hama were hostile to President Al-Assad. The rebels launched wave after wave of attacks upon suburban areas of Damascus and Aleppo. Government troops and *shabbiha* militia respond in kind with aerial bombing, shelling and indiscriminate killing. Atrocities were committed on all sides.[42] The Syrian conflict had become a war of attrition.

In this connection, a significant barrier to an R2P intervention was the critically divided nature of the Syrian rebel movement. Any possibility of a Western or Arab incursion in favour of the rebels was set back by profound concern as to the composition and agenda of the many different military and militia factions of which the opposition was comprised. At the heart of that concern was the fundamentalist character of Syrian and foreign rebel groups alike. Principal amongst the latter were Jabhat al-Nusra, a jihadist element closely connected to Al-Qaeda; Kata'ib Ahrar Al-Sham, whose principal aim was the establishment of an Islamic state and Liwa al-Islam, a radical jihadist group committed to the introduction of a Salafi version of Sharia law.[43] The problem for those advocating intervention, therefore, was that the armed opposition lacked cohesion and that none of the countries who might participate, whether Western or Arabic, wished the outcome of a rebel victory to be hard-line Islamist rule.

At the political level, the civilian Syrian National Coalition, formed in November 2012 as a notionally representative grouping of Syrian opposition actors, was moderate and received substantial political support from Western nations and the Arab League alike.[44] It made initial attempts to engage the Syrian government, minus President Al-Assad, in peace negotiations. However, it had next to no control of the military and militant groups doing the fighting on the ground. And its members too were often at odds. This was unhelpful to potential interveners and, in the end, it was likely to be people with the guns, rather than the more distantly involved and largely symbolic political leadership, that would determine the final shape of the Syrian State when the fighting finally ended.[45]

Syria, unlike Libya, was intensely enmeshed in its region. Until, and for a long time after, the protests began, the Al-Assad government was perceived by its neighbours as a strong and stable country in the midst of a volatile region. Not all of its policies may have been endorsed but Middle Eastern governments regarded Syria as an important trading partner, an influential political force, and in many cases, an essential strategic ally. Syria's web of alliances in the Arab world served as a strong disincentive to Security Council condemnation and action.

Further, military intervention, even if directed only at the protection of civilians, was likely to have severe, adverse effects on the stability of the entire Middle East. That consequence arose principally from Syria's geographical position, bordering five other nations almost all of which were volatile.

---

[42] Charles Glass, 'Aleppo betrayed by attacks that are foreign to its nature', *The National*, 13 February 2012.

[43] 'An Interview with Jabat-Al-Nusra', *The Economist*, Pomegranate Blog, May 23 2013.

[44] Patrick Seale, 'Syria's New Opposition Coalition Still has its Old Problems', *The Guardian*, 14 November 2012.

[45] Ramzy Mardini, 'After Assad. Chaos?', *The Guardian*, 3 February 2013.

Western intervention would certainly incite Syria's ally Hezbollah in Lebanon thousands of whose members had already crossed the border to fight. It would fan the flames of sectarianism in Lebanon thereby risking the downfall of the fragile Lebanese government, and possibly prompting civil war there.[46] Syria's relations with Turkey had worsened as a result of huge cross-border refugee flows from Syria's North. Early in 2013, approximately 170,000 Syrians had fled to camps in Turkey. The Turkish Prime Minister, Mr Erdogan, made it clear that Turkey would not make the smallest concession in its oppositional stance on Syria. In Iraq, rebel victory could embolden the country's Sunni minority and exacerbate tensions with its Shia majority. There was not yet a civil war in Iraq but the signs of enduring sectarian conflict were increasing and persistent. Jordan was already home to nearly three million Palestinian and Iraqi refugees and was stretched to the limit by the arrival of a further 300,000 Syrians. This had the potential to create significant political instability in Jordan, whose ruling royal family had become increasingly unpopular.[47]

If there were a Western-led military intervention, the probability that Iran may engage, whether indirectly through its Lebanese and Palestinian allies, or directly would be high. Iran had much at stake in Syria. Should the Assad regime fall, its likely replacement by a Sunni-led government would mean that Syria could move closer to Tehran's adversaries in the Gulf. The Syrian conflict had metamorphosed into a highly dangerous proxy war between Iran and its principal regional antagonists, Saudi Arabia, Qatar, and Turkey. Israel, meanwhile, had become extremely concerned about Syria's arsenal of chemical weapons, particularly since Al-Qaeda and other extremist militants had joined the war against President Al-Assad. Both Israel and the USA drew a red line under the use and distribution of chemical weapons, threatening military intervention should such weapons be deployed.

At the time of writing, a Western-led military intervention, even under the R2P banner, could have extensive, adverse effects upon many countries and governments in the Middle East in a way that was not, and was never likely to be replicated in the Libyan situation. Intervention there had been an altogether less perilous enterprise.

The self-interest of major global powers also played its part in discouraging Security Council endorsed intervention in Syria. No member of the Council on either side of the debate neglected its strategic interests entirely in order to assume a purely humanitarian stance. To state the obvious, the closer a Security Council member's ties with the Al-Assad regime had been, the less likely it was that that the State would favour an external intervention into the country's domestic affairs.[48]

The clearest example in this instance was Russia. Russia was the principal opponent of any direct international action against Syria.[49] Most often, its arguments against an R2P intervention were delivered at the level of principle. It was not difficult, however, to discern the country's significant political, economic and strategic investment in Syria. Syria remained a major purchaser of exports of Russian arms and defence equipment. It hosted a strategically positioned Russian naval base at Tartus on the west coast, its only one outside the former Soviet Union. Russia's largest intelligence gathering organization situated on foreign soil was located in Latakia also on Syria's west coast. The Russian government continued to send weapons to Syria throughout the period of the crisis. It was unsurprising

---

[46] Roula Khalaf, 'Lebanon's Complex Part in Syrian Conflict', *Financial Times*, 29 October 2011.

[47] Nicholas Pelham, 'Jordan Starts to Shake', *The New York Review of Books*, 8 December 2011.

[48] See Charles Glass, 'Syria's many new friends are a self-interested bunch', *The National*, 11 July 2012.

[49] David Herszenhorn and Nick Cumming-Bruce, 'Putin Defends Stand on Syria and Chastises U.S. on Libya Outcome', *Financial Times*, 20 December 2012.

given these important connections that the Russians did not wish to see them disturbed by the replacement of the Al-Assad regime. Its veto at the Security Council, exercised on three separate occasions, provided it with political power it needed to forestall any such possibility.

Russia was not the only global power involved. The USA's substantial economic, political and strategic interests in Israel provided the most obvious counter-instance. It was clearly in the USA's interests to ensure the stability and viability of the Israeli State and take such actions as may be opportune to alter the political configuration of the region so as best to ensure that objective was achieved. The removal of the Al-Assad regime would play into that agenda. The fall of Al-Assad would also constitute a huge setback for Iranian influence and would also remove a significant barrier to more concerted attempts by Israel and the USA to deprive Iran of nuclear capability.

In summary, in the Middle East, Syria was of enormous strategic significance. Libya was not. The Syrian regime's military capacities and alliances were strong. The Libyans' were much weaker. Libya possessed a fairly cohesive political and military opposition. No such cohesion existed in Syria. The Libyan conflict was relatively self-contained. The Syrian civil war threatened the stability of the Middle East. In Libya, the principal regional organization, Arab League, intervened early on the side of intervention. In Syria, the League dragged its feet. The major global powers had a great deal invested politically, economically, and militarily in the outcome of the Syrian conflict. There was not so much at stake in the Libyan uprising.

The way was clearer and surer, then, for steps to be taken by the West to displace Gaddafi in a manner that would be far more fraught and dangerous in the case of Al-Assad. Syria is a complex, diverse and regionally significant nation in which a Western or Arab military intervention, even for the protection of civilians, might risk destroying all that the potential intervenors claimed to support.

VIII. PILLAR 3 INTERVENTION:
KEY PRINCIPLES

The Security Council's paralysis with respect to Syria clouded R2P's future considerably. Nevertheless, several propositions encapsulating the current state of play regarding the character and content of pillar 3 intervention may be derived from the lessons of the Libyan and Syrian experience. These are as follows:[50]

- Prior to approving a coercive pillar 3 intervention, in the interests of underpinning national sovereignty and independence, the Security Council will need to be satisfied that every feasible diplomatic solution to a crisis has been exhausted.

- Prior to approving a coercive intervention, the Security Council is likely in future to insist that its objectives be made clear and that its mandate be spelt out with precision.

- It is highly unlikely that the Security Council will approve a pillar 3 intervention if its explicit or implicit objective is regime change.

---

[50] By way of comparison see a comparable list of propositions (the Responsibility While Protecting) set forth by the Permanent Mission of Brazil to the UN at: *Letter dated 9 November 2011 from the Permanent Representative of Brazil to the United Nations addressed to the Secretary-General*, UN Doc A/66/551-S/2011/701 (11 November 2011), Annex 1 [10]; Kenkel, 2012.

- A Security Council resolution mandating a coercive intervention is likely, in future, to require continuous monitoring of the intervention's implementation on the ground. If the mandate is no longer regarded as sufficient or if the Council determines that it has been exceeded, the conduct of the intervention would return to the Security Council for further discussion and review.

- Given that a Security Council mandate for a pillar 3 intervention is likely to have as its principal objective the protection of civilians, it is probable that the Security Council will in future require that the position of an intervening force be one of strict neutrality as between the contending parties.

- A pillar 3 intervention should, in all aspects, conform to the dictates of international law, and in particular, international humanitarian law.

- Before approving a pillar 3 intervention, the Security Council will clearly need to be satisfied:

  — first, that the intervention is likely to achieve its protective objective within the country concerned;

  — secondly, that an intervention is likely to result in the maintenance or creation of a stable and legitimate government; and

  — thirdly, that intervention is highly unlikely to result in wider regional destabilization.

- Where a contemplated coercive intervention runs contrary to the core political or strategic interests of a member of the P-5, it is highly unlikely to proceed.

- However inadequate, engagement in pillar 3 intervention which includes action under Article 41 but excludes it under Article 42 may still be preferable to provoking Security Council gridlock. This is because, as in Syria, the outcome of gridlock may be seen by antagonists in a conflict as an international licence for the commission of further crimes against humanity.

- Finally and alternatively, in response to mass atrocities coalitions of the willing could decide to take action outside the legal framework of the UN Charter. Should this become common, however, R2P may wither to the great detriment of the international rule of law.

IX. THE RESPONSIBILITY TO PROTECT AS INTERNATIONAL LAW

Politically speaking, it is fair to say that until the point at which NATO forces intervened in the Libyan conflict there had been a progressive convergence of opinion amongst member States of the UN that they bear a responsibility individually and collectively to protect their peoples from the commission of mass atrocity crimes. That broad consensus, at least in relation to pillar 3 intervention, was partially fractured by events in Libya and Syria. Despite this, whether R2P in whole or in part may be regarded as having attained the status of a norm of international law remains a matter of interest and contention in diplomatic and academic circles (Stahn, 2007). For the following reasons, the preferable conclusion is that it has not (see Thakur, 2011c; Burke-White, 2012).

The responsibility to protect is not embodied in any treaty.[51] Consequently, the most likely way that it could be considered as a norm of international law would be by way of its acceptance as part of customary international law. A doctrine or principle will form part of customary law if two broad conditions are met. First, it must be a matter of State practice and that practice must be recurrent and widely observed. Secondly, there must be a conviction among nations that the practice is sufficiently consistent and of sufficiently general application as to be regarded as a compulsory rule.[52] In other words, it should come to be understood that the practice is dictated by international law (*opinio juris*).

A. STATE PRACTICE

Applying these conditions to the responsibility to protect it is evident immediately, first, that State practice in conformity with the doctrine is nascent and that, secondly, following the Security Council disagreements concerning the Libyan and Syrian cases such State practice as there is, is neither recurrent nor widely observed.

It could perhaps be argued that State practice in relation to prior humanitarian interventions should also be taken into account thereby providing a stronger foundation for a claim for R2P's normative standing. Given, however, that the new doctrine's sponsors have been at great pains to distinguish it from humanitarian intervention, and that many in the General Assembly have repudiated the latter, the argument cannot be accorded much weight.[53]

Still, there is one current of thought that suggests that the existence of well-settled State practice may not be absolutely critical in the formation of customary rules. So for example, within the framework of international humanitarian law, an imperative of moral behaviour and the dangers attendant upon its abuse may be such as to make the observance of a particular rule of war absolutely necessary even prior to recurrent State practice having been established. In this case, 'the laws of humanity' and the 'dictates of public conscience' are put on the same footing as State practice in the formation of international law (see Cassese, 2005, pp 160-61).

In that context it might reasonably be accepted that the principle that States have an individual and collective responsibility to protect their peoples from genocide, war crimes, crimes against humanity and ethnic cleansing is a 'law of humanity' of a similar kind and standing (see Teitel, 2011). But that is still far from affirming that in its practical operation R2P will be accorded similar force and legal effect.

B. *OPINIO JURIS*

The second condition to be met is that there should be a mutual conviction among nations that the doctrine or principle in question should have the character of a binding rule of law. In the present case, the existence of this '*opinio juris*' is difficult to discern or to justify. Certainly, the responsibility to protect has been the subject of consideration, elaboration,

---

[51] The doctrine, however, is closely related to the objectives and provisions of existing international treaties including for example, the International Convention on the Prevention and Punishment of the Crime of Genocide (1948), the Geneva Conventions (1949), and the Rome Statute of the International Criminal Court (2002).

[52] *North Sea Continental Shelf, Judgment, ICJ Reports, 1969, p 3*, para 77.

[53] See Ban Ki-Moon, 'Responsible Sovereignty: International Co-operation for a Changed World', Speech delivered in Berlin, 15 July 2008; Sahnoun, M, 'Africa: Uphold Continent's Contribution to Human Rights', *AllAfrica.com*. 21 July 2009; Evans, G, Statement delivered to the UN General Assembly Interactive Thematic Dialogue on the Responsibility to Protect, 23 July 2009.

and recommendation by international commissions of stature. It has been embodied, though not without considerable prior political division, in the resolutions of the most important summit of world leaders held in the past decade. It has been referred to and endorsed in general terms in subsequent Security Council resolutions. And at least in relation to its core components, it has generated a surprising measure of acceptance at all four General Assembly dialogues on R2P.

Yet the idea that it might constitute a legal rule that binds nations to it by common consent is not a position that has yet been reached. This has been demonstrated clearly by the reservations expressed within the Security Council in the aftermath of the Libyan intervention and the Council's paralysis in relation to the adoption of any resolution at all with respect to Syria.

It is clear, further, that although the three-pillar model for R2P's operation is now widely accepted, there remain significant areas of uncertainty as to its scope, meaning and effect. Many conceptual as well as operational questions remain to be addressed and resolved in the light of practical experience. It is difficult to contend in such circumstances that some new, generally accepted legal norm governing the conduct of nations has come to fruition.

On this basis the best that can be said, in my view, is that R2P is a political doctrine that at most constitutes but a fledgling rule of international customary law. It has quite some considerable way to go before it can be regarded as having been adopted in practice and obtained the requisite international acceptance to be considered as fully formed.

C. SECURITY COUNCIL PRACTICE

One final legal matter should be considered. As explained at the commencement of this chapter, the UN Charter's provisions, and in particular the terms of Articles 2(4) and 2(7), have proven exceptionally difficult to reconcile with any doctrine of external intervention in a nation's domestic affairs. Article 2(7) relevantly provides, however, that this principle of non-interference is not to prejudice the application of enforcement measures under Chapter VII. Chapter VII enforcement measures may be pursued where the Security Council has determined the existence of any threat to the peace, breach of the peace or act of aggression. It has generally been assumed that any such threat must be to international peace and security as Chapter VII measures are authorized in accordance with Articles 41 and 42 only to restore international peace and security.

However, the sole arbiter of whether there exists a threat to international peace and security remains the Security Council itself. And in recent years it has become apparent that the Council is now more willing than it has been previously to determine the existence of such a threat even where conflict or strife is taking place entirely within the boundaries of one State.

Generally speaking the Council has made such a determination only where, for example, the 'international dimension' is constituted by some cross-boundary ramification of the primary conflict such as massive consequential refugee flows. In the past two decades or so, however, it has seemed prepared to go one step further where a humanitarian disaster is in prospect and declare a threat even where cross-boundary consequences have not plainly been in evidence. The Council's resolutions in relation to Somalia, Rwanda, Bosnia-Herzegovina and, more recently, Libya and Côte D'Ivoire provide relevant examples.[54]

---

[54] See SC Res 794 (3 December1992) (Somalia); SC Res 770 (13 August 1992) (Bosnia-Herzegovina); SC Res 929 (22 June 1994) (Rwanda); SC Res 1973 (17 March 2011) (Libya); SC Res 1975 (30 March 2011) (Côte D'Ivoire); and see Chesterman, 2001, pp 140-51.

In the absence of a power of judicial review of Security Council decision-making, the Council will continue to have very considerable flexibility when determining whether threats to international peace and security are present. And, further, it does not need to give reasons for its decisions.

This broad exercise of Security Council discretion in humanitarian cases suggests, consequently, that there may be one further, legally recognized way in which the competing demands of sovereignty and the prevention of atrocity may eventually be capable of reconciliation within the framework of the UN Charter. On the basis of the emerging trend, it could over time become standard Security Council practice to interpret the threshold requirement of a threat to peace and security as existent in situations of humanitarian crisis, even where the crisis is contained entirely within a State. Were this practice to become recurrent and internationally recognized as necessary and appropriate, a new customary rule, as embodied in Council practice, may eventually crystallize as part of international law.[55] This rule would allow for an exception to Article 2(4) by sanctioning intervention by the international community to prevent a humanitarian catastrophe occurring entirely within the boundaries of one State pursuant, first, to a preliminary determination by the Security Council under Article 39 of a threat to international peace and security followed, secondly, by authorized international intervention in accordance with Articles 41 and 42.

This is not to suggest that international law has arrived at such a normative recognition yet. Security Council practice in the relevant respect has neither solidified nor attained the requisite measure of consistency and international acceptance. And to achieve recognition as institutional custom, a large stretch in the interpretation of the language of the Charter would still be required. Nevertheless, it is not unreasonable to observe that in an increasingly interconnected and interdependent world, few conflicts or catastrophes remain entirely local in their ramifications.

The promise of eventual legal recognition remains but, for the moment, that hope rests on fragile and uncertain foundations.

REFERENCES

ADAMS, S (2012), *Libya and the Responsibility to Protect* (New York: Global Centre for the Responsibility to Protect).

ALSTON, P and MACDONALD, E (2008), 'Sovereignty, Human Rights, Security: Armed Intervention and the Foundational Problems of International Law', in Alston, P and MacDonald, E (eds), *Human Rights, Intervention, and the Use of Force* (Oxford: Oxford University Press), p 1.

BELLAMY, A (2008a), *The Responsibility to Protect* (Cambridge: Polity Press).

—— (2011) 'Libya and the Responsibility to Protect: The Exception and the Norm', 23 *Ethics and International Affairs* 263.

BURKE-WHITE, W (2012), 'Adoption of the Responsibility to Protect' in Genser, J and Kotler, I (eds), *The Responsibility to Protect: The Promise of Stopping Mass Atrocities in Our Time* (Oxford: Oxford University Press).

CASSESE, A (1999), 'Follow Up: Forcible Humanitarian Countermeasures and *opinio necessitas*', 10 *EJIL* 791.

—— (2005), *International Law* (Oxford, Oxford University Press).

---

[55] In an analogous case, the International Court of Justice determined in an Advisory Opinion that the UN had international legal personality partly based on the practice of the UN in concluding international conventions: *Reparation for Injuries Suffered in the Service of the United Nations, Advisory Opinion, ICJ Reports 1949*, p 174.

CHESTERMAN, S (2001), *Just War or Just Peace: Humanitarian Intervention and International Law* (Oxford: Oxford University Press).

CHINKIN, C (2000), 'The Legality of NATO Action in the Former Republic of Yugoslavia (FRY) under International Law', 49 *ICLQ* 910.

CORTEN, O (2008), 'Human Rights and Collective Security: Is there an Emerging Right to Humanitarian Intervention?', in Alston, P and MacDonald, E (eds), *Human Rights, Intervention, and the Use of Force* (Oxford: Oxford University Press), p 87.

EVANS, G (2006), 'From Humanitarian Intervention to the Responsibility to Protect', 24 *Wisconsin International Law Journal* 703.

—— (2008), *The Responsibility to Protect: Ending Mass Atrocity Crimes Once and for All* (Washington: The Brookings Institution Press), Ch 1.

—— (2011), 'End of the Argument', (December 2011) *Foreign Policy*.

—— (2012) 'R2P and RWP after Libya and Syria', Keynote Address to Global Centre for the Responsibility to Protect and the Stanley Foundation, *The Responsibility While Protecting: What Next?*, Rio De Janeiro, 23 August 2012.

FABRI, H (2008), 'Human Rights and State Sovereignty: Have the Boundaries been Significantly Redrawn?', in Alston, P and MacDonald, E (eds) (2008), *Human Rights, Intervention, and the Use of Force* (Oxford: Oxford University Press), p 33.

FOCARELLI, C (2008), 'The Responsibility to Protect and Humanitarian Intervention: Too many Ambiguities for a Working Doctrine', 13 *Journal of Conflict and Security Law* 191.

GAZZINI, T (2005), *The Changing Rules on the Use of Force in International Law* (Manchester: Manchester University Press).

GIFKINS, J (2012), 'Briefing—The UN Security Council Divided: Syria in Crisis', 4 *Global Responsibility to Protect* 377.

HOLZGREFE, J (2003), 'The Humanitarian Intervention Debate', in Holzgrefe, J and Keohane, R (eds), *Humanitarian Intervention* (Cambridge: Cambridge University Press), p 53.

INDEPENDENT INTERNATIONAL COMMISSION ON KOSOVO (2000), *Kosovo Report, Conflict, International Response, Lessons Learned* (Oxford: Oxford University Press).

KENKEL, K (2012), 'Brazil and R2P: Does Taking Responsibility Mean Using Force?', 4 *Global Responsibility to Protect* 5.

LUCK, E (2009), 'Sovereignty, Choice and the Responsibility to Protect', 1 *Global Responsibility to Protect* 1.

PETERS, A (2009), 'Humanity as the Alpha and Omega of Sovereignty', 20 *EJIL* 513.

SIMMA, B (1999), 'NATO, the UN and the Use of Force: Legal Aspects', 10 *EJIL* 1.

STAHN, C (2007), 'Responsibility to Protect: Political Rhetoric or Emerging Legal Norm?', 101 *AJIL* 99.

TEITEL, R (2011), *Humanity's Law* (Oxford: Oxford University Press).

THAKUR, R (2011a), 'Kosovo, Humanitarian Intervention and the Challenge of World Order', in Thakur, R, *The Responsibility to Protect: Norms Laws and the Use of Force in International Politics* (Abingdon: Routledge).

—— (2011b), 'R2P, Libya and International Politics as the Struggle for Competing Normative Architectures', in Stark, A (ed), *The Responsibility to Protect: Challenges and Opportunities Following the Libyan Intervention*, e-International Relations, 13 (December 2011) *Foreign Policy*.

—— (2011c), 'Normative Contestation, Incoherence and Inconsistency', in Thakur, R (ed), *The Responsibility to Protect: Norms Laws and the Use of Force in International Politics* (Abingdon: Routledge).

WEISS, T (2007), *Humanitarian Intervention* (Cambridge: Polity Press).

WELSH, J (2004), 'Conclusion: The Evolution of Humanitarian Intervention in International Society', in Welsh, J (ed), *Humanitarian Intervention and*

International Relations (Oxford: Oxford University Press), Ch10.

WHEELER, N (2004), 'The Humanitarian Responsibilities of Sovereignty: Explaining the Development of a New Norm of Military Intervention for Humanitarian Purposes in International Society', in Welsh, J (ed), *Humanitarian*

Intervention and International Relations (Oxford: Oxford University Press), Ch 3.

ZIFCAK, S (2009), *United Nations Reform: Heading North or South?* (London: Routledge).

—— (2012), 'The Responsibility to Protect after Libya and Syria', 13 *Melbourne Journal of International Law* 59.

FURTHER READING

INTERNATIONAL COMMISSION ON INTERVENTION AND STATE SOVEREIGNTY (2001), *The Responsibility to Protect: Report of the International Commission on Intervention and State Sovereignty*, Ottawa, International Development Research Centre. The Canadian Commission Report in which the Responsibility to Protect doctrine was first formulated.

REPORT OF THE SECRETARY-GENERAL, *Implementing the Responsibility to Protect*, UN Doc A/63/677 (2009). The UN Secretary-General's most comprehensive elaboration of the core elements of the Responsibility to Protect.

ALSTON, P and MACDONALD, E (2008), (eds), *Human Rights, Intervention, and the Use of Force* (Oxford: Oxford University Press). A fine contemporary overview of the inter-relationship between sovereignty, armed intervention and human rights under international law.

CHESTERMAN, S (2001), *Just War or Just Peace: Humanitarian Intervention and International Law* (Oxford: Oxford University Press). The most extensive overview of the law with respect to humanitarian intervention.

EVANS, G (2008), *The Responsibility to Protect: Ending Mass Atrocity Crimes Once and for All* (Washington: The Brookings Institution Press). The key text in the field written by one of the co-authors of the ICISS report in which the Responsibility to Protect was first formulated.

THAKUR, R (2011), *The Responsibility to Protect: Norms, Laws and the Use of Force in International Politics* (Abingdon: Routledge). A collected series of articles from the last decade by the second co-author of the ICISS report conceptualizing and contextualizing the Responsibility to Protect.

PART VI

RESPONDING TO BREACHES OF INTERNATIONAL OBLIGATIONS

18

COUNTERMEASURES AND SANCTIONS

Nigel D White and Ademola Abass

SUMMARY

The issue of enforcement by means of non-forcible measures is one of the least developed areas of international law. Two legal regimes are relatively clear—non-forcible countermeasures taken by States (countermeasures) and non-forcible measures taken by international organizations (sanctions). The development of a restricted doctrine of countermeasures as the modern accepted form of self-help is considered, along with the partial centralization of coercion in international organizations. The problems within each of these regimes are examined, along with the limitations that have been placed upon their application. The co-existence of countermeasures based on a traditional view of international relations, alongside the post-1945 development of centralized institutional responses, is explored. Moreover, the range of State and institutional practice that seems to lie somewhere between the basic right of a State to take countermeasures to remedy an internationally wrongful act, and the power of international organizations to impose sanctions in certain circumstances, is considered. The legality of the continued use by States of non-forcible reprisals, retorsion, and wider forms of economic coercion is explored, as is the issue of collective countermeasures imposed either multilaterally or institutionally.

I. INTRODUCTION: SELF-HELP IN INTERNATIONAL LAW

Traditionally, States co-exist in a legal system that is essentially consensual. States, no matter their disparities in size or strength, are sovereign and equal. Obligations are accepted by States either in treaty or custom by consent, they are not imposed by any higher authority. In its purest form such a legal condition existed in the eighteenth and nineteenth centuries. This period was one of self-help, in that if a State breached one of its obligations, the victim State(s) of such a breach could take both non-forcible and forcible measures to remedy or to punish that breach. Forcible measures could range from measures short of war, such as armed reprisals,[1] or could take the form of war. War itself could be a relatively minor exchange of fire, even mere confrontation without hostilities, or it could be a full-scale bloody conflict the causes of which could be relatively minor.

---

[1] *Naulilaa* case (1928) 2 *RIAA* 1052.

Before this period of absolute sovereignty and its accompanying self-help regime of enforcement, theories of natural law argued for a hierarchy of norms within the concept of an international society (Bull, 1992, pp 71–2). Moving forward to the advent of the League of Nations in 1919, created in the aftermath of the failure of the system of self-help, there emerged structures as well as norms that were again suggestive of a more hierarchical approach. The Covenant of the League of Nations purported to regulate, if not prohibit, war, and the organization it established potentially had weak authority over States. Brierly argued that the League was based on the principles of consensuality and voluntarism (Brierly, 1946, p 92), a view that would suggest that the organization did not upset the pre-existing order. McNair on the other hand thought that the League marked a move away from a system of purely private law between consenting States towards a system of public law (McNair, 1930, p 112) indicating a more vertical system of regulation.

The idea of an international organization, with some measure of authority over States, took an even firmer grip on the imagination of States during the Second World War. The UN was created in 1945, its Charter containing in Article 2(4) a basic rule prohibiting the threat or use of force in international relations, and creating machinery to promote and restore international peace and security. The prohibition of force, which itself formed a core norm in an emerging corpus of peremptory norms of international law (*jus cogens*) from which States could not derogate, immediately cut back on the type of measures a State could take in response to a breach of international law. Self-help was reduced to half its former size by the UN Charter. Although States were still permitted to take forcible action in self-defence in response to an armed attack against them, forcible measures beyond that were prohibited by the new legal regime initiated by the Charter. Although some States and writers have repeatedly tried to resurrect the concept of armed reprisals (Bowett, 1972a) there does not appear to be any general acceptance of an erosion of the statement of law made by member States of the UN in 1970—'States have a duty to refrain from acts of reprisal involving the use of armed force'.[2]

The prohibition in 1945 of forcible measures of self-help left the position of non-forcible measures untouched but at the same time unclear. Clarity was lacking because the doctrines that had emerged over the centuries were inevitably subject to many interpretations. In addition, the UN itself was given significant power to impose on member States obligations to impose non-forcible measures against miscreant member States by virtue of Article 41 of the Charter. The developing Inter-American system of collective security also provided for the application of such measures,[3] a trend that was to be followed by some other regional organizations. A self-help system of non-forcible measures deriving from an earlier period of international relations, had to co-exist with a system of centralized 'sanctions' based on notions of hierarchy and governance. In addition to the uncertainty that existed between the institutional level and the customary level, there was also a lack of clarity in the relationship between the universal organization (the UN) and other organizations. Article 53(1) of the UN Charter seems to provide that any non-forcible measures taken by regional organizations that amounts to 'enforcement action' requires the authorization of the Security Council.

The concept of lawful non-forcible measures survived the new world order of the post-1945 period. Article 2(4) of the Charter prohibited the 'threat or use of force', and this was clearly construed as military force (but see Paust and Blaustein, 1974, p 417). State

---

[2] *Declaration on Principles of International Law concerning Friendly Relations and Co-operation among States in Accordance with the Charter of the United Nations*, UN Res 2625 (XXV) (24 October 1970).

[3] Articles 8, 17, 20 Rio Treaty, 1947, 21 UNTS 77.

practice in the immediate post-1945 period provided evidence of the continuation of the concept of non-forcible measures. As Elagab states '[r]egardless of whether the conditions of legality had been complied with in each case, the crucial feature was the very fact of such claims being staked at all. This provides a presumption of continuity of counter-measures as a viable mode of redress' (Elagab, 1988, p 38). In the first decade after the UN Charter the USA adopted, *inter alia*, measures freezing the assets of China, Bulgaria, Romania, and Hungary. The coinage of the term 'countermeasures' in the *Air Services Agreement* case of 1978[4] and the codification of countermeasures by the International Law Commission (ILC), culminating in Chapter III of the Articles on State Responsibility of 2001,[5] represent its consolidation in the structures of international law.

Despite the proliferation of international institutions since 1945, the ILC was confident in asserting in 2001 that countermeasures are inherent in a decentralized system where 'injured States may seek to vindicate their rights and to restore the legal relationship with the injured State which has been ruptured by' an unlawful act.[6] As noted by Alland—'countermeasures are a mechanism of private justice', the result of which are 'contradictions inherent in a self-assessed (ie auto-interpreted or auto-appreciated) decentralized policing of an international *ordre public*' (Alland, 2002, pp 1223, 1235). Provost is even more explicit in depicting the weaknesses of such a system when he writes that 'the right of states unilaterally to assess a breach by another state and to validate what would otherwise be an illegal act has the potential of significantly destabilizing international relations' (Provost, 2002, p xv).

Nevertheless, as has been stated earlier, a totally decentralized system no longer exists (but see Zoller, 1984, p xiii). While injured States are entitled to take certain non-forcible actions within a bilateral context against States responsible for a breach of international law, sanctions imposed by the UN and other international organizations create a vertical relationship between the organization and the implementing States (Gowlland-Debbas, 2001, p 2). Essentially the horizontal system of self-help has been supplemented by the creation of organization(s) with the competence to create vertical relationships. After 1945, and arguably in a weaker sense, after 1919 (but see Brierly, 1932, p 68), there no longer exists a pure system of self-help, and this has affected practice as shall be seen. States wanting to take measures against a responsible State may go to international bodies for authority/legitimacy, indeed it could be argued that they ought to do this when they are not the direct victims of the unlawful act.

II. COUNTERMEASURES

A. DEFINITION OF COUNTERMEASURES

Since the first use of the term in 1978 by the arbitral tribunal in the *Air Services Agreement* case, the term countermeasures has been used to indicate non-forcible measures. However, the following discussion will illustrate that this has not necessarily clarified the matter, for the related doctrines of retorsion, reprisals (in a non-forcible sense), economic coercion,

---

[4] *Air Services Agreement* case (1978), 54 ILR 303.
[5] See Report of the International Law Commission on the work of its Fifty-third Session, UN Doc A/56/10, adopted 9 August 2001. The Articles and the Commentary are found in Crawford, 2002. The Articles will be referred to as ARSIWA (Articles on Responsibility of States for Internationally Wrongful Acts). The references to the Commentary are to Crawford's text.
[6] Crawford, 2002, p 281.

and economic sanctions remain. In effect, after the ILC Articles of 2001 the concept of countermeasures is a fairly narrow one at one end of a spectrum of non-forcible measures that may
be taken in international relations. At the other end of the spectrum are sanctions undertaken
by international organizations. In between there is something of a grey area where regulation is rudimentary, indeed, arguably, non-existent. In this section, the focus is on countermeasures on the grounds that they have become perhaps the most clearly defined type of
non-forcible measures, having been the subject of many years of study by the ILC. The ILC's
concept of countermeasures is the one portrayed here, though it must be noted that it may
well constitute an example of the ILC progressively developing international law. It should
be noted that the ILC's Special Rapporteur on the matter, James Crawford, commented only
a few years before the adoption of the Articles that 'at present there are few established legal
constraints on non-forcible counter-measures' (Crawford, 1994, p 65). As Bederman suggests
'the central conceptual mission' of the ILC's articles on countermeasures, is 'the search for a
polite international society' (Bederman, 2002, p 819). Further he contends that the countermeasures articles represent a 'profound impulse toward social engineering for international
relations...imagining a time in international life when unilateral and horizontal means of
enforcement through robust self-help will be a thing of the past' (Bederman, 2002, p 831).
Nevertheless, while the ILC does purport to define and constrain countermeasures, in so
doing it leaves question marks hanging over the legality of a large segment of State practice on
wider non-forcible measures.

Countermeasures 'are intrinsically unlawful, but are justified by the alleged failing to which
they were a response' (Alland, 2002, p 1221). In its final Articles on State Responsibility of
2001, the ILC defined countermeasures as non-forcible measures taken by an injured State in
response to a breach of international law in order to secure the end of the breach and, if necessary, reparation.[7] Non-forcible countermeasures may only be taken in response to an internationally wrongful act, and only against the State responsible for that act.[8] If such measures
are taken without fulfilling these conditions, they themselves will constitute an internationally
wrongful act, giving rise to State responsibility and possible countermeasures. According to
the ILC, countermeasures are limited to the temporary non-performance of one or some
of the international obligations of the injured State owed to the responsible State.[9] Cassese's
summation is perhaps stronger than that of the ILC, but useful nonetheless. He states that 'in
the event of a breach of international law, the injured State is legally entitled to disregard an
international obligation owed to the delinquent State' (Cassese, 2005, p 302). In ILC terms,
countermeasures are not intended to be punishment for illegal acts but as 'an instrument
for achieving compliance with the obligations of the responsible State'. Countermeasures are
taken 'as a form of inducement, not punishment'. The ILC's definition does not restrict States
taking countermeasures to suspension of performance of the same or very similar obligation.
Countermeasures though are more likely to accord with the conditions of proportionality and
necessity if they are so taken. Such measures which correspond to the obligation breached by
the responsible State are sometimes called 'reciprocal countermeasures'.[10]

The suspension or temporary non-performance of a treaty obligation, quite often the
suspension of a trade agreement, and the freezing of the assets of a State under international
obligations, are primary examples of countermeasures.[11] In ILC terms the paradigmatic
case is the *US-French Air Services Arbitration* of 1978. This case concerned the application

---

[7] Ibid, p 281.

[8] Article 49(1) ARSIWA. See also *Gabčíkovo-Nagymaros Project (Hungary/Slovakia), Judgment, ICJ Reports 1997*, p 7, paras 83–5.

[9] Article 49(2)(3) ARSIWA.   [10] Crawford, 2002, pp 282–6.   [11] Ibid, p 286.

of the bilateral air services agreement that existed between the two countries. France had objected, as being incompatible with the treaty, to the so-called 'change of gauge' or change of type of aircraft by PanAm on its flight from the USA to Paris via London. The French authorities prevented PanAm passengers from disembarking in Paris. By the time of arbitration, the USA had initiated (but had not implemented), measures which would have prohibited certain French flights to the USA. The arbitral tribunal found that the change of gauge by PanAm was permitted under the treaty and that the US retaliatory measures were permissible countermeasures, which were not disproportionate to the violative actions taken by France. The arbitral tribunal stated '[i]f a situation arises, which in one State's view, results in the violation of an international obligation by another State, the first State is entitled, within the limits set by general rules of international law, pertaining to the use of armed force, to affirm its rights through "countermeasures".'[12] Of course, the case reveals the inherent problem with countermeasures, indeed with measures of self-help more generally, in that the crucial element, the determination of the initial wrongful act, is a subjective one. As Alland makes clear it is this 'self-assessed' aspect of countermeasures, which 'manifests the danger they represent in the international legal order: they open the possibility to all States to take prejudicial measures contrary to the obligations incumbent on them on the basis of subjective unilateral claims' (Alland, 2010, p 1129).

Countermeasures are distinct from suspension or termination of treaty obligations due to material breach within the meaning of Article 60 of the 1969 Vienna Convention on the Law of Treaties (VCLT). Measures taken under Article 60 affect the substantive legal obligations of the State parties while countermeasures are concerned with the responsibility that has arisen as a result of the breach. The aim of countermeasures is to rectify the legal relationship and their application should always be temporary.[13] Article 60 of the VCLT deals with 'material breach' of the treaty, countermeasures may be taken in response to any breach, as long as they are proportionate. Article 60 specifies a procedure for suspension or termination of treaty obligations for material breach, which differs from the procedures required to take countermeasures. Action under Article 60 of the VCLT must be confined to the treaty being breached, while countermeasures are not so confined (Elagab, 1988, p 164). Article 60 of the VCLT provides for the possibility of termination of the treaty, or obligation, while, in principle, countermeasures are only temporary.

It is possible that a non-forcible measure taken by a State can be classified as both a response to a material breach and a countermeasure if it meets the different set of requirements for each. The International Court of Justice considered arguments concerning countermeasures and material breach in 2011 in a case involving a dispute between the Former Yugoslav Republic of Macedonia (FYR Macedonia) and Greece over violations of an Interim Accord agreed in 1995 by the two States in the context of the dissolution of Yugoslavia. The Court found that Greece had violated the Accord by objecting to FYR Macedonia's admission to NATO in 2008. Greece attempted to justify this action as a response to a material breach of the Interim Accord by FYR Macedonia and as a countermeasure to the same breach. The Court did find that FYR Macedonia had breached the Accord by the use of a symbol (the 'Sun of Vergina'). The Court dismissed the argument that Greece's actions could be justified as a response to a material breach under Article 60 of the Vienna Convention on the basis that it was not a serious enough breach, and also because the violation by FYR Macedonia had ceased in 2004 so that Greece's action in 2008 could not be seen as a response to that breach. Neither could Greece's actions be

---

[12] *Air Services Agreement* case (1978) 54 ILR 303 at p 337.   [13] Crawford, 2002, p 282.

justified as a countermeasure because such measures are taken for the purposes of achieving a cessation of a wrongful act, and Macedonia had ceased its wrongful act in 2004.[14]

Given the growth of international organizations possessing international legal personality, with rights and duties under international law, there appears no reason why countermeasures cannot be taken by States or other organizations against international organizations that have committed internationally wrongful acts, or by organizations that are the victims of internationally wrongful acts. In principle countermeasures should be available to any entity possessing international legal personality, though in the current state of international legal development such actors are generally confined to States and a significant number of inter-governmental organizations. The ILC's work on the responsibility of international organizations, started in 2002, made good progress until it came to the issue of countermeasures in its 2008 report.[15] Although certain draft articles on countermeasures were posited in the report,[16] there was clearly some disagreement among the members of the ILC as to the value of including articles on countermeasures by and against international organizations.[17]

Nonetheless, the final Articles, adopted in 2011 and taken note of by the General Assembly, contain articles on countermeasures against and by international organizations,[18] most of which are similar in content to those governing State responsibility. The final articles try to balance the logic of countermeasures being available to counter unlawful acts committed by international organizations (as international legal persons) and the desire to prevent member States precipitously taking unilateral countermeasures against the organization for perceived internationally wrongful or *ultra vires* acts. Given the problems the UN has been faced with in the past, with France and the Soviet Union withholding their peacekeeping contributions on the basis of the alleged *ultra vires* actions of the General Assembly in mandating peacekeeping forces in the Middle East and the Congo in the late 1950s and early 1960s, and the US practice of withholding financial contributions in the 1980s and 1990s, there is clearly a potential problem in recognizing that member States can take countermeasures against organizations in response to perceived unlawful acts.

Arguably, however, States that believe they are victims of unlawful actions by an organization (for example being subjected to economic sanctions) have very limited options to challenge the legality of such measures (with no access to the International Court of Justice for instance). Without giving member States means of holding organizations to account, arguably they should have the right to take countermeasures against the organization (O'Connell, 2008, pp 267, 271). Organizations, on the other hand, normally possess a number of means of controlling their members—expulsion, suspension, other non-forcible measures such as sanctions and, as international legal persons, countermeasures (Dopagne, 2011, pp 178–91).

Ultimately, the 2011 Articles on the Responsibility of International Organizations came down on the side of the organization by providing a number of restrictions on when countermeasures can be taken against it. The Articles permit an injured State or organization to take countermeasures against an international organization for an internationally wrongful act, but contain a number of limitations in addition to the normal conditions attaching

---

[14] *Application of the Interim Accords of 13 September 1995 (the Former Yugoslav Republic of Macedonia v Greece), ICJ Reports 2011*, p 644, paras 162–4.

[15] ILC Report of Sixtieth Session (2008), A/63/10.   [16] Ibid, paras 141–4.

[17] Ibid, paras 148, 163.

[18] Articles on the Responsibility of International Organizations, Articles 51–7, UN Doc A/66/10 (2011); taken note of in GA Res 66/100 (2011).

to countermeasures. A number of those additional limitations are aimed at reducing the over-use of countermeasures by disgruntled member States of the UN and other organizations. These limitations are a general one that provides that 'countermeasures shall, as far as possible, be taken in such a way as to limit their effects on the exercise by the responsible international organization of its functions'. For member States of a responsible organization countermeasures: shall not be inconsistent with the rules of the organization; shall not be used where appropriate means are available for inducing compliance; and, most significantly, shall not be taken by an injured State which is a 'member of a responsible international organization against that organization in response to a breach of an international obligation under the rules of the organization unless such countermeasures are provided for by those rules'.[19] The 'rules of the organization' are defined as 'the constituent instruments, decisions, resolutions and other acts of the international organization adopted in accordance with those instruments, and established practice of the Organization'.[20] This would clearly include the obligation to pay expenses under Article 17(2) of the Charter and equivalent provisions in the constituent treaties of the UN's specialized agencies. Certainly, the views of UNESCO on these restriction suggest that UN organizations are not too concerned that the Articles will open them up to a rash of countermeasures by disgruntled member States: 'for international organizations of quasi-universal membership such as those of the United Nations system, the possibility for their respective Member States to take countermeasures against them would either be severely limited by the operation of the rules of those organizations, rendering it largely virtual, or would be subject to a *lex specialis*—thus outside the scope of the draft articles—to the extent that the rules of the organization concerned do not prevent the adoption of countermeasures by its Member States'.[21]

B. REPRISALS AND RETORSION

The ILC's definition of countermeasures has internal coherency. But its failure to address the related concepts of non-forcible reprisals and retorsion leaves the impression that other types of non-forcible action taken by States (as opposed to institutions) remain unregulated and, on one view of international law, therefore permitted.[22] This means that in reality while States can engage in countermeasures that are quite specific, they may also be able to engage in wider non-forcible measures. The aim of these measures may be to punish the responsible State (reprisals) as opposed to inducing it into compliance (countermeasures); or which are not limited to the suspension of international obligations owed to the responsible State (retorsion). On the other hand, it could be argued that this approach, essentially permitting other non-forcible measures to be taken by States makes something of a nonsense of the painstaking process of defining countermeasures. Why spend so many years defining lawful countermeasures, unless it is based on a presumption that wider action by States is unlawful? There was certainly a move by the ILC away from conflating countermeasures and reprisals, and countermeasures and sanctions.[23] The separation of these concepts though is not, by itself, concrete evidence that unilateral non-forcible measures, not coming within the ILC's doctrine of countermeasures, are

---

[19] Articles 51(1) 51(4), 52(1), 52(2), Articles on the Responsibility of International Organizations, 2011.
[20] Ibid, Article 2(b).   [21] ILC Report of the Sixty-third Session, UN Doc 66/10 (2011), pp 151–2.
[22] See 'Lotus', Judgment No 9, 1927, PCIJ, Ser A, No 10 at p 18.
[23] See the writings of earlier ILC Rapporteurs where these terms were used without real distinction; Arangio-Ruiz, 1994, p 21; Ago, 1979, p 47.

unlawful. This issue will be returned to in particular when looking at the wider concept of economic coercion.

Retorsion is conduct that does not involve the suspension of international obligations owed by the injured State to the responsible State, even though usually taken in response to unlawful acts on the part of the responsible State. 'Acts of retorsion may include the prohibition of or limitations upon normal diplomatic relations or other contacts, embargoes of various kinds or withdrawal of voluntary aid programs'.[24] Countermeasures could take the form of a suspension of a trade agreement; whereas acts of economic retorsion are based on a State's freedom to trade or not to trade (or deal more generally) with other States. 'An act of retorsion is an unfriendly but nevertheless lawful act by the aggrieved party against the wrongdoer. As such retorsion is not circumscribed by the international legal order' (Zoller, 1984, p 5). Some writers, however, see countermeasures as encompassing both non-forcible reprisals and retorsion (Abi-Saab, 2001, p 38, citing Schachter, Virally, and Leban in support). In general Abi-Saab sees them as 'reactions permitted in international law to illegality' (Abi-Saab, 2001, p 37). However, that view was not adopted by the ILC, which, at least in its final Articles, keeps the concepts distinct and only concerns itself with delimiting countermeasures, keeping them apart from retorsion. Furthermore, the ILC, together with the International Court of Justice, distinguish countermeasures from reprisals by saying that countermeasures are instrumental while reprisals are punitive.[25]

Thus, non-forcible measures taken by a State may constitute countermeasures if they arise as a result of the suspension of international obligations owed to the responsible State. If they are not the result of the non-fulfilment of an international obligation owed to the responsible State then they may be acts of retorsion. Whether this means that victim States have freedom to impose sanctions against States that have violated international law will be considered later. At first sight it seems odd that acts of retorsion which could be more damaging than countermeasures may be acceptable but this seems to reflect the under-developed state of international law in this area. It is the case that acts of retorsion, while not governed by a specific bilateral legal relationship between the responsible State and the injured State, are still governed by the limitations of necessity and proportionality, and by general principles of international law, such as those prohibiting intervention or violation of basic human rights norms. Furthermore, if the ILC's doctrine of countermeasures is to make complete sense, retorsion arguably should be viewed as a residual remedy in the case of a State injured by a breach of international law where the injured State does not have any existing specific obligations to the responsible State that it is able to suspend. It may, in these circumstances, take limited proportionate non-forcible measures of retorsion that are an attempt to remedy that breach.

Cassese defines retorsion as 'any retaliatory act by which a State responds, by an unfriendly act not amounting to a violation of international law, to either (a) a breach of international law or (b) an unfriendly act, by another State'. He gives examples of the breaking off of diplomatic relations, discontinuance or reduction of trade/investment, withholding economic assistance, expulsion of nationals, heavy fiscal duties on goods from the offending State, or strict passport regulations. As can be seen these measures may be much more damaging than the fairly restrictive doctrine of countermeasures (Cassese, 2005, p 310).

---

[24] Crawford, 2002, p 281.
[25] *Gabčíkovo-Nagymaros Project (Hungary/Slovakia), Judgment, ICJ Reports 1997*, p 7, paras 83–5.

C. LIMITATIONS UPON COUNTERMEASURES AND OTHER NON-FORCIBLE MEASURES TAKEN BY STATES

The doctrine of countermeasures as defined by the ILC is specific. First of all the response to an unlawful act can only be the suspension of an international obligation owed to the responsible State. This distinguishes countermeasures from reprisals and retorsion. Further, there are numerous other limitations governing the form and extent of that suspension. Whether some or all of these limitations are also applicable to acts of retorsion and reprisal is unclear though it may be suggested that a number are. These will be mentioned later. Of course this assumes that such judgments taken by themselves are lawful, an issue that will be returned to.

Countermeasures must not be forcible. This clearly applies to other types of non-forcible measures.[26] Furthermore, 'anticipatory non-forcible counter-measures are unlawful; since by definition they precede actual occurrence of breach' (Elagab, 1988, p 63). The same principle must be applicable to all non-forcible measures taken by States, since they are based on the occurrence of unlawful or unfriendly acts. Countermeasures should be directed against the responsible State and not third party States.[27] This too seems applicable to other non-forcible measures.

Countermeasures are temporary and should, whenever possible, be reversible so the future legal relations between victim State and responsible State can be restored.[28] If the measures taken punish the responsible State by inflicting irreparable damage on it, then they are not countermeasures.[29] Such punitive measures would appear to be non-forcible reprisals, the legality of which is not discussed by the ILC, but that body's movement away from the notion of punishment as the rationale for countermeasures, indicates uncertainty about the legality of reprisals. This is supported by the International Court's statement in the *Gabčíkovo* case that the purpose of countermeasures is to 'induce the wrong-doing State to comply with its obligations under international law, and that the measures must therefore be reversible'.[30] It is noticeable that James Crawford, then Rapporteur, stated that the 'international community has moved away from the classical terminology of reprisals and towards the notion of countermeasures as temporary, reversible steps' (Crawford, 2001, p 66). As with many changes in international law it is not possible to draw a clear line between the demise of one concept or principle and the emergence of another; the transition is gradual.

Countermeasures must be proportionate. According to the ILC, they 'must be commensurate with the injury suffered, taking account of the gravity of the internationally wrongful act and the rights in question'.[31] Disproportionate countermeasures give rise to the responsibility of the State taking them.[32] Taking a different approach Franck asserts that the response must be proportionate to the initial unlawful act, equivalent to the biblical eye for an eye, tooth for a tooth approach (Franck, 2008, pp 715, 763). However, there appears to be difficulties in both the approaches of the ILC and Franck. The issue ought not to be one of proportionality to the unlawful act or the injury it causes, because this would

---

[26] Article 50(1)(a), ARSIWA; Article 2(4) UN Charter; *Declaration on Principles of International Law Concerning Friendly Relations and Co-operation among States in Accordance with the Charter of the United Nations*, UN Res 2625 (XXV) (24 October 1970).

[27] Article 49(1)(2), ARSIWA.   [28] Articles 49(2)(3), 53, ARSIWA.   [29] Crawford, 2002, p 287.

[30] *Gabčíkovo-Nagymaros Project (Hungary/Slovakia), Judgment, ICJ Reports 1997*, p 7, paras 56–7.

[31] Article 51, ARSIWA.

[32] Crawford, 2002, p 294. See *Naulilaa* case (1928) 2 *RIAA* 1052 (disproportionate); *Gabčíkovo-Nagymaros Project (Hungary/Slovakia), Judgment, ICJ Reports 1997*, p 7, para 87 (disproportionate); *Air Services Agreement* case (1978) 54 ILR 303 (proportionate).

suggest that countermeasures are taken to punish the responsible State, thus confusing countermeasures with reprisals. As Cassese states 'in current international law the purpose of countermeasures must be seen...in impelling the offender to discontinue its wrongful conduct or to make reparation for it. If this is so, the proportionality must be appraised by establishing whether the countermeasure is such as to obtain this purpose'. This should mean that in certain cases a weak State may be subject to countermeasures that are quantitatively less than the injury suffered by a powerful State, if the measures are sufficient to bring an end to the illegal act (Cassese, 2005, p 306). The International Court has found that non-forcible countermeasures were disproportionate in the *Gabčíkovo-Nagymaros* case, though it provided little by way of explanation of why Czechoslovakia's assumption of control of part of the Danube in response to Hungary's violation of a treaty obliging it to undertake construction to aid shipping, energy development and flood control on the section of the Danube shared by both countries, was disproportionate.[33] This adds to the impression of indeterminacy in the principle of proportionality despite its elevation to a general principle of international law (Franck, 2008, p 716).

According to the ILC, countermeasures must not violate basic obligations under international law (namely those prohibiting the threat or use of force, protecting fundamental human rights,[34] concerning obligations of a humanitarian character), and those arising under *jus cogens*. Countermeasures should not affect dispute-resolution procedures that are applicable. Countermeasures cannot be taken to impair consular or diplomatic inviolability.[35] Diplomatic law provides its own legal regime for dealing with illicit activities by members of diplomatic or consular missions.[36] 'If diplomatic or consular personnel could be targeted by way of countermeasures, they would in effect constitute resident hostages against perceived wrongs of the sending State, undermining the institution of diplomatic and consular relations'.[37] Countermeasures must follow an unsatisfied demand by the injured State that the responsible State comply with its international obligation(s). The injured State must also notify the responsible State that it intends to take countermeasures and offer to negotiate, except in the case of urgent countermeasures necessary to preserve the injured State's rights (eg temporary staying orders or the temporary freezing of assets).[38] Further they must be suspended if the wrongful act has ceased and the dispute has been submitted to a tribunal with binding authority.[39]

The limitations discussed in this section are arguably applicable to other more controversial claims to non-forcible measures, with the exception of the suspension of diplomatic relations that seems to be an accepted act of retorsion in international relations. This seems to contradict the 'resident hostages' argument mentioned earlier. This is illustrative of the problem in defining countermeasures without addressing the issue of retorsion. In general Elagab states that in the case of a 'self-contained regime' where such a regime 'possesses its own mechanism for redressing the wrongful conduct, countermeasures should not be

---

[33] *Gabčíkovo-Nagymaros Project (Hungary/Slovakia), Judgment, ICJ Reports 1997*, p 7, para 87. See also Scobbie, 2004, p 1129 for discussion as to whether Israel's construction of a security wall is better analysed as a purported non-forcible countermeasure rather than the purported exercise of the right of self-defence, dismissed by the International Court in *Legal Consequences of the Construction of a Wall in the Occupied Palestinian Territory, ICJ Reports 2004*, p 136 at paras 139–40.

[34] Especially the non-derogable rights contained in the International Covenants—Crawford, 2002, p 289. See also CESCR General Comment No 8 (1997), UN Doc E/C.12/1997/8, 5 December 1997, paras 1 and 5.

[35] Article 50(1)(2) ARSIWA.

[36] *United States Diplomatic and Consular Staff in Tehran, Judgment, ICJ Reports 1980*, p 3, paras 84–6.

[37] Crawford, 2002, pp 292–3.   [38] Ibid, p 299.

[39] ARSIWA, Article 52. See also *Application of the Interim Accord of 13 September 1995 (the Former Yugoslavia Republic of Macedonia v Greece), ICJ Reports 2011*, p 644, para 164.

imposed' (Elagab, 1988, p 218). He refers to diplomatic law, but the same can be said of the WTO's procedures for dispute settlement, followed, if necessary by a form of institutionalized countermeasures. Although they look like countermeasures, they are not measures imposed by dint of custom but by reason of the GATT treaty regime. They are thus similar in appearance to countermeasures but the source of the rights and duties is the special treaty regime, and the limitations may be different (but see Gazzini, 2006, pp 737–41).

Thus, countermeasures may be excluded by special rules (eg a treaty which states that its provisions cannot be suspended)[40] or a regime which dictates the way in which measures are taken by victim States (the primary example is the WTO).[41] Countermeasures are thus said to be 'residual' remedies,[42] reflecting the fact States may choose to move away from a decentralized system of self-help by developing treaty regimes with their own processes of enforcement.

D. COUNTERMEASURES AND THIRD STATES

We turn now to the question of whether countermeasures as defined by the ILC can be taken by States other than the State directly injured. According to the ILC, countermeasures are normally taken by a State injured by an internationally wrongful act of another State. However, responsibility may be invoked by States other than the injured State acting in the collective interest.[43] Responsibility is not invoked by these third States as a result of injury to themselves but as a result of breach of an obligation to a group of States of which it is a member—obligations *erga omnes partes* (eg regional environmental or human rights regimes), or to the international community as a whole—obligations *erga omnes* (eg laws prohibiting genocide, aggression, slavery, racial discrimination, self-determination).[44]

However, the ILC is careful to distinguish third States invoking responsibility from them taking countermeasures. The latter issue is left much more open. Such third States can demand cessation and performance in the interests of the injured States or the beneficiaries of the obligation breached.[45] 'The question is to what extent these States may legitimately assert a right to react against unremedied breaches',[46] *viz* by taking countermeasures against the responsible State. One problem in taking collective countermeasures is that of proportionality, though it is difficult to prove a violation of this principle if the aim is to stop a breach of an obligation owed *erga omnes*. In the absence of institutional sanctions imposed for example by the UN Security Council under Chapter VII of the Charter,[47] the legality of such measures is in doubt, though there seems to be some State and institutional practice to support the proposition that such measures are allowed. However, practice is inconsistent, making the drawing of any conclusions as to *opinio juris* extremely difficult if not impossible.

Further, it is inaccurate to portray such 'collective' countermeasures as a replacement for centralized collective action through an international organization. The term 'collective countermeasures' gives the 'illusion of concerted action when in reality such

---

[40] EU treaties provide for their own system of enforcement—Crawford, 2002, p 291.

[41] The WTO system requires authorization from the Dispute Settlement Body before a member can take measures against another—Crawford, 2002, p 291.

[42] Crawford, 2002, p 283.   [43] Ibid, p 276.

[44] Article 48(1) ARSIWA. See *Barcelona Traction, Light and Power Company, Limited, Second Phase, Judgment, ICJ Reports 1970*, p 3, paras 33–4; *East Timor (Portugal v Australia), Judgment, ICJ Reports 1995*, p 90, para 29.

[45] Article 48(2) ARSIWA.   [46] Crawford, 2002, p 302.   [47] Ibid.

collective countermeasures are individual initiatives—even though there is more than one such initiative at the same time' (Alland, 2002, p 1222). In addition, the subjective assessments of States as to whether to impose such countermeasures undermines the enforcement of these crucial norms (Alland, 2002, p 1237). However, it is true to say that to expect international institutions such as the UN Security Council to replace this subjective assessment with something more objective when considering whether to impose non-forcible measures under Chapter VII of the UN Charter would, in reality, 'be replacing one subjectivity (of states) by another (of the Security Council)' (Klein, 2002, p 1249). It is thus premature to argue that the UN Security Council's sanctioning machinery has, or indeed should, replace a system of collective countermeasures even though that system is very weak. In reality there currently exist two weak systems of non-forcible sanctions, one decentralized and one (partly) centralized, for the enforcement of community norms.

Indeed, the practice coming from the decentralized system mentioned in its commentary by the ILC leads it to conclude that 'the current state of international law on countermeasures taken in the general or collective interest is uncertain. State practice is sparse and involves a limited number of States. At present there appears to be no clearly recognized entitlement of [third] States…to take countermeasures in the collective interest'[48] (but see Sicilianos, 2010, p 1148). Hence Article 54 of the ILC Articles states that a third State's right to take 'lawful' measures is not prejudiced by any of its other provision on countermeasures. What are lawful measures in this context is an issue that is, in effect, left open (Klein, 2002, pp 1253–5; but see Alland, 2002, p 1233). Bederman's summary of the ILC's position on collective countermeasures characterizes it as the 'only possible political solution' was 'to defer debate to another day and to allow customary international lawmaking processes to elaborate any conditions on the use of collective countermeasures' (Bederman, 2002, p 828).

The ILC[49] mentions the US prohibition in 1978 of export of goods and technology to Uganda and all imports from Uganda in response to alleged genocide by the government of Uganda. This certainly appears to be a response to a breach of an obligation owed *erga omnes*, but it did not only concern the suspension of US treaty obligations, and therefore goes beyond countermeasures as defined by the ILC. The US response appears to be unilateral non-forcible measures, in effect sanctions, imposed to enforce community norms. The ILC also refers to measures taken by Western States against Poland and the Soviet Union in 1981 in response to internal repression by the Polish government. Measures included suspension of treaty landing rights for scheduled civilian aircraft. These actions seemed to take the form of countermeasures but were they a response to a breach of an obligation owed *erga omnes*? It is still difficult, though not impossible, to argue for a right to democracy in the twenty-first century, but in 1981 such an argument was mainly a political, not legal, one. The US countermeasures in the form of the suspension of treaty landing rights against South African airlines in 1986 seem to be a clearer example given the odium attached to the system of apartheid, and its categorization as a crime against humanity.

The examples cited by the ILC of non-forcible measures imposed by regional organizations, mainly the EC, illustrates the even greater legal confusion when the analysis of such measures is elevated from the purely bilateral. In 1982 the EC, along with Australia, Canada, and New Zealand adopted trade sanctions against Argentina in response to its invasion of the Falklands. Before the GATT, the EC justified these as measures taken by

---

[48] Ibid, p 305.   [49] Ibid, pp 302–4.

the 'Community and its Member States' on the basis of their 'inherent rights', meaning the right of self-defence (Zoller, 1984, p 105). In 1990 (before the UN Security Council imposed sanctions) the EC and USA imposed trade sanctions and froze Iraqi assets in response to Iraq's invasion of Kuwait. In both of these episodes the non-forcible measures were in response to a breach of an obligation owed *erga omnes* (not to commit aggression) but they seemed to extend beyond mere countermeasures to take the form of multilateral economic sanctions. In 1998, in response to the crimes against humanity being committed in Kosovo, the EC imposed a flight ban and froze Yugoslav assets in response to the humanitarian crisis in Kosovo. In some countries the flight ban was a product of the suspension of treaty rights. The suspension of treaty rights and the freezing of assets seem to be clear examples of countermeasures undertaken in response to a breach of a fundamental norm. Nevertheless, the EC does not limit itself to clear countermeasures in other instances. In response to violence and human rights violations that marred the run-up to the Presidential elections in Zimbabwe in March 2002, the EU imposed a travel ban, a freeze on financial assets, and an arms embargo. The Commonwealth, on the other hand, simply suspended Zimbabwe from membership, a power that is purely institutional. Both institutional responses do show, however, that there is practice that suggests that denial of democracy/democratic rights could now be seen as a breach of an obligation owed *erga omnes*. It is too early to state that this has crystallized into a rule of customary law given the uncertainty about the legal status of third party countermeasures.

What the examples we have described illustrate is that State and institutional practice is confused in a number of ways. First the wrongful acts involved are not always clearly breaches of obligations owed *erga omnes*. Secondly, non-forcible measures, especially trade sanctions are not always a product of non-performance of existing obligations. Thirdly, some of the practice is institutional rather than by individual States, though the line between them is not clear. Zoller expresses doubts about the imposition of sanctions by regional organizations, in the sense of whether they are actually deploying sanctions as international legal persons, or whether, in reality 'the organization acts less as an organization than as a collectivity of the member States as a whole. When countermeasures are undertaken under these circumstances, it is legally hazardous to consider that they can genuinely be attributed to the organization as such' (Zoller, 1984, p 104). Zoller views the EC measures taken against Argentina in 1982 following its invasion of the Falklands, and against the Soviet Union in 1981 following the imposition of martial law in Poland, as a product of political cooperation by States, despite the fact that the measures against Argentina were imposed by a regulation adopted under Article 113 of the EEC Treaty (Zoller, 1984, pp 104–5). The line between countermeasures and sanctions can be unclear though the justification for the latter 'does not derive from general international law' (as with countermeasures) 'but from the constituent instrument of the organization' (Alland, 2010, p 1135).

Crawford casts further doubts on the role in international law of obligations *erga omnes*. The ICJ inspired the concept in the *Barcelona Traction* case but in a dictum wholly inapplicable to the case. When the Court was faced in the *Second South West Africa*[50] and the *East Timor* cases with concrete arguments based on *erga omnes*, it shied away from the application of the concept (Crawford, 2001, p 64). This may indicate doubts about whether collective measures taken outside the UN, by other organizations or third States, can constitute lawful countermeasures. In reality they are a modern form of non-forcible measure or sanction that are outside the narrowly defined countermeasures regime. They are in

---

[50] *South West Africa, Second Phase, Judgment, ICJ Reports 1966*, p 6.

essence, in the grey area between the doctrine of countermeasures as defined by the ILC, and the imposition of centralized sanctions.

Cassese suggests that in the case of countermeasures taken by third States in response to 'aggravated responsibility' (ie breach of fundamental rules), a precondition is that they have sought to bring the matter before an international organization. This can be the UN or a regional organization, with a view to settlement or the adoption of sanctions. This precondition is 'dictated by the inherent nature of this class of responsibility. This responsibility arises out of a gross attack on community or "public" values. The response to the wrongdoing must therefore be as much as possible public and collective'. However, 'if those bodies take no action, or their action has not brought about cessation of the wrong or adequate reparation…all States are empowered to take peaceful countermeasures on an individual basis' (Cassese, 2005, p 274). Although this seems to be a useful suggestion, it is more by way of *de lege ferenda*, given that States do not always report to IGOs first. It also shows that Cassese certainly does not think that regional or indeed individual countermeasures are subject to any need for prior UN *authorization*.

It certainly seems to be the case that regional organizations have in their practice taken non-forcible measures against member and non-member States without seeking authority from the Security Council. Practice by the OAS against Cuba and Venezuela in the early 1960s and against Haiti in the early 1990s, as well as the measures taken by the EC against Yugoslavia in the 1990s, all without UN authority or preceding UN measures, suggest that the requirement in Article 53 of the UN Charter that 'enforcement action' needs the authorization of the Security Council does not cover non-military, as opposed to military, coercive measures. Of course, if the Security Council goes on to take non-forcible measures under Article 41 of the UN Charter after determining that the situation is a threat to the peace, the Security Council 'takes over', and individual States may only take action to the extent allowed by the UN Charter (individual or collective self-defence), or recommended, authorized, or decided upon' by the Security Council (Cassese, 2005, p 275). This is achieved by dint of Article 25 of the Charter, which makes Security Council decisions binding on members of the UN. Article 103 gives obligations arising out of the UN Charter pre-eminence over obligations arising under any other international treaty, though it is not clear that this affects member States' customary duties.

III. ECONOMIC COERCION

While the ILC has defined lawful countermeasures with a high degree of abstraction and in quite a narrow way thereby implicitly excluding reprisals, the reality of international relations seems to be very different. Powerful States do not always appear to be constrained by the niceties of the requirements of countermeasures, they do not simply suspend obligations, they do not simply seek to remedy the illegality, what they seek is coercion and punishment by the application of sanctions often of an economic nature. While preferring a collective umbrella for these actions if possible, the USA, for example, is prepared to go it alone if necessary. Its sanctions regimes against Iran first imposed in 1979 and those against the Soviet Union in 1980 are cases in point. Neither could be authorized by the Security Council, and so the USA imposed them unilaterally. This has led one leading US commentator to state that 'the suggestion that economic sanctions are unlawful unless approved by the Security Council (or by a regional organization such as the OAS) is obsolete'. Furthermore, he states that 'sanctions have become sufficiently common—and often better than the alternatives—to have become tolerated (not to say accepted) as a tool of foreign relations' (Lowenfeld, 2001, p 96). Furthermore US practice includes the imposition of extraterritorial sanctions.[51] Even when the Security Council does agree on sanctions, for instance against North Korea for WMD proliferation,[52] the USA's own non-forcible measures, though largely similar, make no reference to them.[53]

This reflects a view of international law that existed before 1945. Writing in 1933 Lauterpacht stated that 'in the absence of explicit conventional obligations, particularly those laid down in commercial treaties, a state is entitled to prevent altogether goods from a foreign state from coming into its territory'. The prevention of trade going the other way from the victim State to the responsible State seemed equally permissible in the pre-Charter period. Further, this is justified on the basis that 'in a community from which war in its technical sense has been eliminated and which has not reached the stage of moral perfection, pacific means of pressure are unavoidable. To prohibit them would mean to court the more radical remedy of war' (Lauterpacht, 1933, pp 130, 140). In a modern sense this still appears to be the case, subject to the requirements of the multilateral regime of the WTO. Non-forcible measures, ranging from countermeasures in the ILC sense to punitive economic sanctions, can be justified under the view that 'restrictions upon the independence of States, cannot be presumed',[54] in other words on the basis of a State's freedom to trade. However, this basic tenet of sovereignty has to be balanced against another tenet—that of non-intervention. The sovereign freedom of a State must always be balanced against the infringement of the sovereignty of other States.

To take two obvious instances—the Arab oil embargo of 1973–4, and the US embargo against Cuba in place since 1960. These were much more coercive, hurtful, and intrusive than the regime of countermeasures suggested by the ILC. Their motivations were political—to support the Palestinians and to undermine a communist regime respectively—they were not simply about the suspension of obligations in response to an illegal act in order to try and remedy that act.

Such embargoes appear to breach the law as stated in several General Assembly resolutions that prohibit coercive economic intervention that is intended to undermine the territorial integrity or political independence (and arguably other sovereign rights) of the target States.[55] It is interesting to note too that the General Assembly has regularly called for the ending of the US economic, commercial, and financial embargo against Cuba and in so doing, it recalls the principle of non-intervention.[56] The problem is that State practice does not appear in conformity with this law (Bowett, 1972b, p 4). Lillich outlines a 'general principle that serious and sustained economic coercion should be accepted as a form of permissible self-help only when it is also compatible with the overall interests of the world community, as manifested in the principles of the UN Charter or in decisions taken or documents promulgated thereunder' (Lillich, 1975, p 366). However, this is suggested by way of *de lege ferenda*. Furthermore, the approach advocated by Lillich and Bowett is that non-forcible, principally economic activity and measures must be presumed to be lawful unless there is evidence of intent by the sanctioning State—'measures not illegal *per se* may become illegal only upon proof of an improper motive or purpose' (Bowett, 1972b, pp 3–7).

---

[51] See US Helms-Burton Act 1996 and the D'Amato-Kennedy Act 1996 discussed in Cassese, 2005, p 305.
[52] See, for example, SC Res 1874 (12 June 2009).
[53] Executive Order 13466, promulgated by President Bush on 26 June 2008, renewed by President Obama on 24 June 2009.
[54] 'Lotus', Judgment No 9, 1927, PCIJ, Ser A, No 10 at p 18.
[55] GA Res 2131 (21 December 1965: Non-intervention); GA Res 2625 (24 October 1970: Friendly Relations); GA Res 3171 (17 December 1973: Permanent Sovereignty over Natural Resources); GA Res 3281 (12 December 1974: Charter of Economic Rights and Duties of States).
[56] Starting with GA Res 47/19 (24 November 1992).

Given the unclear state of international law, that presumption could equally be replaced by the opposite proposition that such measures that interfere with the sovereign rights of another State are unlawful—that is certainly the General Assembly's view.[57]

Elagab considers State practice and Assembly resolutions and concludes rather ambivalently (but perhaps accurately) that 'there are no rules of international law which categorically pronounce either on the prima-facie legality or prima-facie illegality of economic coercion'. However, he is of the opinion that this does not leave economic coercion unregulated by international law, rather that 'individual rules of international law may be applied to determine the legality of economic conduct on a given occasion'. He seems to suggest that while non-forcible measures may involve some element of coercion, their regulation is subject to a separate legal regime (Elagab, 1988, pp 212–13), though this regime is subject to limitations including principles of international law. Thus the sanctions against Cuba by the USA go far beyond countermeasures (and, indeed, reprisals and retorsion); they amount to coercion. This is then subject to applicable rules of international law, such as *jus cogens* and fundamental human rights standards, and, it is argued here, by the principle of non-intervention, which (despite significant erosion over the years) has a core element, prohibiting coercion of political independence (Boisson de Chazournes, 2010, pp 1209–11).

If a State wishes to overcome the principle of non-intervention and subject another State to sanctions then it has to seek authority from an international organization, even in the case of breaches of obligations owed *erga omnes*, unless the State confines itself to countermeasures. The UN Security Council clearly has the competence to override the domestic jurisdiction limitation in Article 2(7) when acting under Chapter VII of the UN Charter. The issue of whether other international organizations have this competence will be turned to.

IV. SANCTIONS

A. DEFINITION OF SANCTIONS

Non-forcible countermeasures, reprisals, and acts of retorsion clearly continue to exist in international relations. Analysis so far has raised a presumption against the legality of non-forcible measures wider than countermeasures as defined by the *Air Services* case, unless they are imposed for breaches of community norms (*erga omnes*), normally through institutional mechanisms. Reprisals are therefore illegal if they are imposed with the purpose of punishment or coercion of the sovereign will of the target State, and by means that are designed to achieve these ends. Punitive measures and deeper coercion than necessary to force the responsible State to stop its illegal act are best seen as sanctions. Of course, in a general sense all measures designed to enforce the law can be seen as sanctions.

There does exist sanction behind the law. Kelsen sees law as essentially a coercive order, an organization of force, a system or norms providing for sanctions (Kelsen, 1945). Brown-John argues that 'in a juristic sense a sanction is a hyphen between prescribed law and law enforcement, although certainly sanctions tend to be more closely related to enforcement than a prescribed law' (Brown-John, 1975, p 2). But despite the fact that sanctions exist under international law, their nature is less precise compared to sanctions

---

[57] For US justifications for the Cuban embargo see Krinsky and Golove, 1993, pp 37, 135, 233.

under the domestic system, a disparity that has led to controversy about whether sanction exists at all in international law.

Brierly notes the 'real difference...between municipal and international law is not that one is sanctioned and the other is not, but that in the one the sanctions are organized in a systematic procedure and that in the other they are left indeterminate. The true problem for consideration is therefore not whether we should try to create sanctions for international law, but whether we should try to organize them in a system' (Brierly, 1932, p 68). Similarly Kunz observes that 'the alleged absence of sanctions has been and is today the principal argument of those who deny that the rules of international law have the character of legal rules. But general international law *has* sanctions...This is not a unique feature of international law, but it is common to all primitive, highly decentralized legal orders, whether municipal or international. Such legal orders have no central organs either for the making or application of legal rule or for the determination of the delict or the execution of sanctions. All these functions must be left to the members of the legal community; in international law, to the sovereign states. There are no collective but only individual sanctions, carried out by way of self-help; there is no monopoly of force at the disposal of a central law-enforcing organ; there is no distinction between criminal and civil sanctions; the sanctions are based on collective, not individual responsibility' (Kunz, 1960, p 324). While Kunz was writing at the height of the Cold War, with no real practice by the UN on sanctions, in the post-Cold War period it might be argued that there now exists a central sanctioning organ—the Security Council.

Schachter attributed the decentralized nature of sanctions under international law to an indifferent attitude in the international legal community to enforcement in general rather than to a formal system of structuring between law and politics. Accordingly, 'for a long time compliance and enforcement were on the margins of UN concern. Like somewhat backward members of a family, their place was vaguely recognized, but not much was expected from them. The busy world of UN law-making and law applying carried on pretty much without serious consideration of means of ensuring compliance. Some prominent international lawyers dismissively referred to enforcement as a political matter outside the law. Within UN bodies comfort was taken in the pious hope that governments which acknowledged their legal obligations would carry them out, at least most of the time. It was far from evident that they generally did so in some areas, but measures such as compulsory jurisdiction, mandatory fact finding and coercive sanctions were not considered acceptable or feasible' (Schachter, 1994, pp 9–10). Schachter, though, also points to the progress made on enforcement and compliance in the post-Cold War period.

Sanctions are different from countermeasures. Zoller is clear on this when she states that '[a]s opposed to countermeasures, sanctions are very specific measures. A countermeasure is a measure which has temporary effects and a coercive character, while a sanction has final effects and a punitive character. Moreover, sanctions have an exemplary character directed at other countries which countermeasures do not have' (Zoller, 1984, p 106). For instance, the Security Council through Resolution 1343, imposed sanctions on Liberia in 2001 following its determination that its government was supporting the Revolutionary United Front (RUF), in Sierra Leone, in violation of SC Resolution 1132 which had imposed sanctions against the rebel group. This was the first time the Security Council had imposed sanctions against a country because of its refusal to comply with sanctions against another country (Cortright and Lopez, 2002, p 82). Zoller further argues that '...countermeasures should always be temporary measures, they draw a line between the consequences of unlawful conduct in international law; they underline the difference between them and those measures which impose a final harm on the defaulting party and which could properly be designated by the term "sanctions". For this reason, '[c]ountermeasures…have to be placed within reparation and outside punishment' (Zoller, 1984, p 75).

The adoption of unilateral sanctions in the sense used by Zoller is unlawful. To be lawful, sanctions have to be pursued by international organizations, representing the 'centralized mechanisms' hinted at by Brierly (Gowlland-Debbas, 2001, p 6). The issue is not simply how many States were involved in the decision to impose sanctions but rather whether the decision was taken by those States acting under the auspices of an organization competent to do so. The British Royal Institute of International Affairs recognized the element of collectivity when in 1938 it defined sanctions as 'action taken by members of the international community against an infringement, actual or threatened, of the law' (Brown-John, 1975, p 5), though it is uncertain whether 'international community', as used in this context, equates to international organizations for the purpose of establishing the legality of sanctions. Abi-Saab defines sanctions as 'coercive measures taken in execution of a decision of a competent social organ, ie an organ legally empowered to act in the name of the society or community that is governed by the legal system'. He distinguishes them sharply from 'coercive measures taken individually by States or group of States outside a determination and a decision by a legally competent social organ', including countermeasures. These 'are manifestations of "self-help" or "private justice", and their legality is confined to the very narrow limits within which "remnants" of "self-help" are still admitted in contemporary international law' (Abi-Saab, 2001, p 32).

Cassese notes the trend in the 'international community is for international bodies, and principally international organizations, to react to gross breaches of international law' by means of sanctions (Cassese, 2005, pp 310–11). This practice became more evident after the end of the Cold War. One common trait of this practice is the utilization of sanctions by international organizations to counter unconstitutional removals of governments among their membership. Witness the use of sanctions by the OAS against the military junta in Haiti in 1992 and similar scenarios with regard to ECOWAS in Liberia (1989–97) and Sierra Leone (1997–2001). This practice has been further entrenched by the use of sanctions by ECOWAS to reverse an unconstitutional governmental take-over in Togo in February 2005.

While countermeasures are taken by individual States, sanctions are imposed within a collective context, normally an international organization. This development corresponds to the growth in recognition of community interests, representing the 'creation of international institutional responses to violations of such core norms' (Gowlland-Debbas, 2001, p 7). However, the distinction between countermeasures and sanctions should not be read as suggesting that countermeasures can only be taken on an individual basis. Certainly, countermeasures, like sanctions, can also be taken collectively. Elagab recognizes this possibility with regard to countermeasures taken by international institutions although he doubted that there is a 'generalized theory of countermeasures taken by international institutions' (Elagab, 1988, p 1).

Sanctions imposed by the Security Council under Article 41 of the Charter can include full or partial trade, financial, commercial, and arms embargoes, and are therefore, generally, of an economic nature. Schachter states that 'sanctions under Article 41 have come to be seen as quintessential type of international enforcement. The language of Article 41 is broad enough to cover any type of punitive action not involving use of armed force' (Schachter, 1994, p 12). Gowlland-Debbas argues that although Chapter VII measures imposed by the Security Council were not intended to be restricted to cases of non-compliance with international law, the practice of the Council has moved considerably towards dealing with responsibility of States for breaches of international law

(Gowlland-Debbas, 2001, p 9; cf Zoller, 1984, pp 106–7). The determination of Iraq's guilt for its invasion of Kuwait, and the requirement for it to pay compensation is a case in point.[58] Before taking action under Chapter VII, the Council is required by Article 39 of the UN Charter to determine the existence of a 'threat to the peace', 'breach of the peace', or 'act of aggression'. The Council can thus deal with threats to or breaches of the peace that do not constitute internationally wrongful conduct. Aggression would appear to be more a determination of breach of international law, although the history of the definition of aggression shows that there is a reluctance to delimit the Security Council's competence in purely legal terms. Thus it is true to say that sanctions imposed by the UN serve much wider purposes than the concept of unilateral, or even collective, countermeasures as defined by the ILC.

It is relevant to ask whether economic measures taken by regional organizations are subject to the legal regime governing sanctions (as with the UN) or the legal regime governing countermeasures. Economic sanctions based on Chapter VII are to be distinguished from economic countermeasures in that, unlike sanctions, the latter are bilateral, imposed in peacetime, and generally considered to be lawful unless prohibited by national law (Kondoch, 2001, p 269). Countermeasures are not punitive, they are taken to ensure that the responsible State ceases its violation, and, if applicable, provides reparation. They are instrumental—their aim is to achieve a restitution of a legal relationship (Crawford, 2001, p 61). Thus there is clear autonomy for regional organizations to authorize the imposition of countermeasures against a State for breach of either regional or international community norms. Action taken by the regional organization outside its membership must be justified as countermeasures for breach of an international community rule, not merely a regional one.

Given the requirements of Article 53 of the UN Charter, question marks may be raised against action beyond countermeasures, for example measures taken by regional organizations that are designed to be punitive or aimed at achieving a change in regime. Such actions beyond countermeasures are a slippery slope that threatens to blur the distinction between sanctions and countermeasures. The imposition of measures designed to achieve a regime change in another country is an action beyond the doctrine of countermeasures since the original action by the target State may not necessarily constitute a breach of an obligation owed to any of the imposing States. In March 2005, ECOWAS imposed sanctions against Togo in order to reverse the unconstitutional take-over of government in that country. Clearly these were coercive measures designed to achieve regime change, albeit, in response to an earlier unconstitutional regime change in that country. It could be argued, however, that the sanctions imposed by ECOWAS on Togo were not illegal under Article 53 of the Charter since Togo, as an ECOWAS member State, had agreed to an ECOWAS treaty that entitles ECOWAS to take such measures against any member State under specific circumstances (see Abass, 2004, p 163). This is different to a situation where a regional organization imposes sanctions on a non-member State. The imposition of sanctions by the EU on Zimbabwe in 2002 seems to depart from Article 53 given that Zimbabwe is not an EU member State, although there may be arguments of violations of obligations owed *erga omnes*. However, there is institutional practice by the EC and OAS, reviewed earlier in this section, on which it may be argued that Article 53 does not pose an absolute prohibition on unauthorized regional action of a non-forcible kind, subject to the caveat that the Security Council still has the power to condemn autonomous regional activity as a breach of the Charter.

---

[58] SC Res 687 (3 April 1991).

B. LIMITATIONS UPON SANCTIONS

One effect of Article 103 of the UN Charter seems to be that mandatory sanctions resolutions adopted by the Security Council under Article 41 of the UN Charter result in obligations for member States that prevail over obligations arising under other international treaties. The Security Council has adopted Article 41 sanctions in a number of instances (eg Southern Rhodesia, South Africa, Iraq, the Federal Republic of Yugoslavia, Libya, Somalia, Haiti, Sudan, UNITA areas of Angola, Liberia, Sierra Leone, Rwanda, Afghanistan, and more lately North Korea and Syria) (Conforti, 2000, pp 185–94). Sanctions regimes have proliferated since the end of the Cold War, with the comprehensive regime against Rhodesia (1966–79) and the arms embargo against South Africa (1977–94) being the only instances of *mandatory* sanctions imposed by the Security Council during the Cold War. It has also adopted measures directed at stopping assistance to terrorists in the wake of the attacks against the USA on 11 September 2001,[59] and has followed this up with general measures aimed at preventing the spread of weapons of mass destruction, especially to non-State actors.[60] These measures are binding on all States and are directed at *activities* (for example financing terrorists) rather than the past sanctions regimes that were binding on all States but were targeted at *certain States*, including those allegedly supporting terrorism (Libya, Sudan, and Afghanistan). This apparent expansion in the legislative powers of the Security Council has caused considerable discussion (Happold, 2003; Talmon, 2005).

As a consequence of UN sanctions regimes, member States may be required to suspend some of their treaty relations with the target State—eg trade treaties or civil aviation treaties. Article 103 of the Charter provides a dispensation for implementing States from the performance of these treaty obligations (Gowlland-Debbas, 2001, p 18). The justification for this must be that the UN was established, or has become recognized, as having the competence to uphold and protect community norms, and can therefore direct a collection of States to take measures which would otherwise be unlawful. This partial constitutionalization would also suggest that non-members should also comply with UN directives, certainly to the extent that the Council requires them to take action to combat breaches of fundamental rules. Requiring non-member States to take action beyond that is problematic, although Article 2(6) of the Charter suggests that non-member States should comply if this is deemed necessary to maintain international peace and security. It is questionable whether other organizations have this competence in theory, though they may take collective countermeasures within their region on the basis of regional laws (*erga omnes partes*). In practice, regional organizations have taken wider non-forcible measures or sanctions to enforce obligations owed *erga omnes* as well as *erga omnes partes*, though this practice can be said to have only taken hold because the UN has ultimately not condemned it either specifically or in a general sense.

If the Security Council or the General Assembly only recommend sanctions, it is questionable whether this entitles States (if they choose) to suspend treaty obligations. Since there are no legal obligations created by a recommendatory resolution (except perhaps a duty to consider), Articles 25 and 103 do not come into play, although some commentators argue that the authority of the UN is sufficient to entitle member States to breach trade agreements (Lowenfield, 2001, p 97). Even mandatory sanctions imposed by the Security Council do not *ensure* that all members comply. The sanctions committees established by

---

[59] SC Res 1373 (28 September 2001).   [60] SC Res 1540 (28 April 2004).

the Council to oversee implementation try to ensure this but there has been little attempt to force non-complying States into action.

There is generally no real investigation into the effective execution of sanctions by those States purportedly complying with Council decisions though there are indications that more supervision is occurring. In 2001, Charles Taylor's government in Liberia reported that it was no longer supporting the RUF following SC Resolution 1343 (see Section IV A). Liberia's claim was independently confirmed by an ECOWAS delegation which reported that Liberia 'seemed serious in meeting the demands of the Security Council' (Cortright and Lopez, 2002, p 84). Furthermore, with respect to the effect of the sanctions imposed by SC Resolutions 1127 and 1178 on Angola/UNITA, both the mission headed by the Canadian Representative to the UN, Robert Fowler, and the panel of experts, reported the effectiveness of the sanctions against UNITA (Cortright and Lopez, 2002, p 63). Additionally, in relation to the non-forcible measures directed against terrorism after 11 September 2001, the Counter Terrorism Committee established by the Security Council is actively supervising their implementation (Ward, 2003).

It is only with the adoption of comprehensive regimes, especially that imposed against Iraq in the period 1990–2003, that the focus has turned to the limitations upon sanctions in terms of their effects. The Committee on Economic, Social and Cultural Rights produced an opinion in 1997 that stated that sanctions regimes should not violate basic economic, social, and cultural rights, on the basis that unlawfulness of one kind should not be met with unlawfulness of another.[61] In 2000, the Bossuyt Report, which emerged at the behest of Sub Commission on the Promotion and Protection of Human Rights, proposed six tests for evaluating the effectiveness of sanctions.[62] Like a study commissioned by the UN Department of Humanitarian Affairs in 1998,[63] the Bossuyt Report recommended that sanctions be based on a valid reason, specifically target the parties responsible for the threat or breach of peace, exclude the targeting of humanitarian goods, and be imposed for a limited time.

The UN may impose sanctions not on the basis of a breach of international law but with the aim of restoring peace and security. It must be the case that in these situations, *a fortiori*, it must protect the human rights of the target State's population.[64]

If the International Court actively reviews a sanctions regime in the future—a possibility raised by the *Lockerbie* cases, 'considerations of proportionality might be examined by the Court'. 'If a particular form of sanctions results in injury to innocent civilians or causes serious harm to the environment and has no discernible impact on the targeted delinquent regime, would it be improper for the Court to say that the measures taken are disproportionate to the goals to be achieved?' (Dugard, 2001, pp 88–9). In reality there are two limitations here, namely those of human rights norms as well as the general principle of proportionality, although the two are closely related. Sanctions regimes must not cause serious human rights violations, though causation is notoriously difficult to

[61] General Comment No 8, UN Doc E/C.12/1997/8, (1998) 5 *IHRR* 302.

[62] The Adverse Consequences of Economic Sanctions on the Enjoyment of Human Rights (The Bossuyt Report), E/CN4/Sub.2/2000/33, 21 June 2000.

[63] Bruberlin, 1998; cited by Kondoch, 2001 at p 273.

[64] So, for example, SC Res 1267 (15 October 1999) and 1989 (17 June 2011) established what is now the UN Security Council Al Qaeda Sanctions Committee to oversee an 'Al Qaeda sanctions list', comprised of individuals and entities which it considers pose threats to international peace and security due to their links with Al Qaeda. The most recent revision, on 31 May 2013, resulted in the Syrian rebel group, Al-Nusra Front, being added to the sanctions list. See http://www.un.org/sc/committees/1267/aq_sanctions_list.shtml.

prove in these situations, especially when sanctions regimes always contain an exception for humanitarian supplies. In addition, they must be proportionate to the end being aimed at, either the restoration of peace and security by the withdrawal of an aggressor State,[65] or some specific acts that would lead to the termination of a threat to the peace. For example in the case of Libya, this amounted to the handing over of the two suspects and the renunciation of terrorism by Libya.[66] In the case of Rhodesia, the first attempt by the UN at a comprehensive sanctions regime,[67] the aim was to end white-minority rule in that country.

However, to adapt Zoller's words, it is true to say that '[i]n the field of countermeasures and law enforcement, the international legal order has not yet reached a very advanced stage. Most of the time, as the rain in the New Testament, [sanctions] draw no distinction between the just and the unjust; they affect both the state and its citizens, or more precisely the state through its citizens. This situation is a direct result of the primitive doctrine of collective responsibility' (Zoller, 1984, p 101). The Iraqi citizens suffered from the effects of sanctions in the period 1990–2003 because of the guilt of their government. The response has been to modify and target sanctions more accurately on those who are really responsible—the leaders of the regimes, or non-State actors responsible, for example, for acts of terrorism or for supporting terrorism. The irony is that while the Security Council has tempered its general sanctions regimes out of concern for the human rights of the general population, preferring instead targeted or smart sanctions against individuals, those more directed measures can also be seen as falling foul of human rights protections of the targeted individuals. Since 1999, starting with Resolution 1267, the Security Council has in place a scheme of targeted measures, under Chapter VII of the Charter, [68] whereby an individual whose name is placed on the Security Council's list of individual members, or supporters, of the Taliban or Al-Qaeda has his assets and funds frozen by relevant member States, as well as being subject to a travel embargo. Though there is some debate as to whether these sanctions are 'administrative' rather than 'criminal', 'preventive' rather than 'punitive' (Bianchi, 2006, pp 905–7); thereby causing uncertainty as to the human rights of the individuals listed, there seems to be increasing judicial recognition that such measures, without any safeguards, violate the human rights of the individuals concerned (Keller and Fischer, 2009, p 257). In the *Kadi* judgment of 2008 the European Court of Justice found that the EU's incorporation of obligations under SC Resolution 1267 violated European fundamental rights of Mr Kadi who had been listed by the Council's 1267 Committee and therefore had his assets frozen without recourse to a remedy, but the Court gave the European bodies the chance to redraft the regulations in a way that was human-rights compliant.[69] The argument that Article 103 of the Charter means that the obligations created by Resolution 1267 prevailed over human rights treaty obligations did not prevail, at least in that case (Cardwell, French, and White, 2009, p 237).

---

[65] SC Res 661 (6 August 1990) (Iraq).   [66] SC Res 748 (31 March 1992).

[67] SC Res 253 (29 May 1968).

[68] SC Res 1267 (15 October 1999, against the Taliban) and SC Res 1333 (19 December 2000, against Al-Qaeda).

[69] See decision of the European Court of Justice in *Kadi and Al Barakaat International Foundation* v *Council*, Joined Cases 402/05 and 415/05, [2008] ECR I-6351. See also the decision of the Human Rights Committee in *Sayadi and Vinck* v *Belgium* (2009) 16 IHRR 16; and the decision of the European Court of Human Rights in *Nada* v *Switzerland*, no 10593/08, Judgment of 12 September 2012, ECtHR.

The development of 'smart sanctions' (Cortright and Lopez, 2000, pp 4–5) is a recent one, and the question of whether they will be effective in achieving their aims by targeting the regimes and leaders of States as well as individuals such as terrorist suspects while alleviating the suffering of the civilian population remains to be seen. Indeed, in terms of success, sanctions in their raw form rarely achieve their primary purposes. Sometimes it is the combination of economic and military measures that produces the required change in the targeted State; for example Rhodesia in 1979 (guerrilla campaign); Haiti in 1994 (threat of force by the USA); Serbia in 1995 (use of force by NATO and Muslim/Croat army); and Iraq in 1991 (Coalition action). On other occasions it is the combination of sanctions plus diplomacy, as in the majority of other cases of sanctions mentioned in this section. Thus it appears that economic sanctions are not by themselves an alternative to military coercion (or indeed diplomacy), but must be used in combination with other foreign policy tools. Normally, they must be used in combination with diplomacy, only exceptionally should they be used in combination with military action when States are acting under the right of self-defence or under the authority of the UN. The UN Secretary-General recognized this when he observed that 'sanctions, as preventive or punitive measures, have the potential to encourage political dialogue, while the application of rigorous economic and political sanctions can diminish the capacity of the protagonists to sustain a prolonged fight' (Cortright and Lopez, 2000, p 2).

V. CONCLUSION

This chapter has demonstrated that there are only two areas of legal clarity here. These are that countermeasures taken under the doctrine enunciated by the ILC and the *Air Services* case are lawful (subject to limitations concerning, *inter alia*, human rights and proportionality). Non-military sanctions imposed by the UN Security Council under Chapter VII are lawful (subject to the limitations of human rights and proportionality). This would suggest that the topic dealt with under the title of this chapter 'Countermeasures and Sanctions' is straightforward—unfortunately it is not. The clashes between the continuance (at least in the non-forcible realm) of self-help with greater centralization in the post-Charter era, combined with the perennial clash between States' freedom of action and the principle of non-intervention, means that much of the area in the middle between countermeasures and UN sanctions is unclear. However, this chapter's analysis shows that measures in that space are, on balance, illegal, with the probable exceptions of countermeasures imposed by third States for breaches of obligations owed *erga omnes* or *erga omnes partes*, and retorsion in a residual sense. Such measures can be taken through organizations other than the UN as can more punitive or coercive economic sanctions, subject to censure by the Security Council, or arguably, the General Assembly. In convincing the world of the legality and therefore the legitimacy of non-forcible measures, States are best advised to stick to the doctrine of countermeasures. If they want to take deeper, more punitive or coercive measures, they should seek authority of a regional organization, and preferably, though not necessarily, the UN. The requirement of convincing an organization helps to ensure that such measures are taken for the purpose of protecting a community norm, and are not taken out of pure self-interest. Thus, although there may be remaining doubts about some of the legal conclusions drawn here, there is no doubt that the legitimacy of non-forcible measures in international relations is vastly increased if they are channelled through a competent international organization.

REFERENCES

ABASS, A (2004), *Regional Organisations and the Development of Collective Security. Beyond Chapter VIII of the UN Charter* (Oxford: Hart Publishing).

ABI-SAAB, G (2001), 'The Concept of Sanction in International Law', in Gowlland-Debbas, V (ed), *United Nations Sanctions and International Law* (The Hague: Kluwer), p 38.

AGO, R (1979), 'Eighth Report', *YBILC*, vol II, part one, 47.

ALLAND, D (2002), 'Countermeasures of General Interest', 13 *EJIL* 1221.

ALLAND, D (2010), 'The Definition of Countermeasures', in Crawford, J, Pellet, A, and Olleson, S (eds), *The Law of International Responsibility* (Oxford: Oxford University Press), p 1127.

ARANGIO-RUIZ, G (1994), 'Countermeasures and Dispute Settlement: The Current Debate within the ILC', 5 *EJIL* 20.

BEDERMAN, DJ (2002), 'Counterintuiting Countermeasures', 96 *AJIL* 817.

BIANCHI, A (2006), 'Assessing the Effectiveness of the UN Security Council's Anti-terrorism Measures: The Quest for Legitimacy and Cohesion', 17 *EJIL* 881.

BOISSON DE CHAZOURNES, L (2010), 'Other non-derogable rights', in Crawford, J, Pellet, A, and Olleson, S (eds), *The Law of International Responsibility* (Oxford: Oxford University Press), p 1205.

BOWETT, DW (1972a), 'Reprisals Involving Recourse to Armed Force', 66 *AJIL* 1.

—— (1972b), 'Economic Coercion and Reprisals by States', 13 *Virginia JIL* 1.

BRIERLY, JL (1932), 'Sanctions', 17 *Transactions of the Grotius Society* 68.

—— (1946), 'The Covenant and the Charter', 23 *BYIL* 83.

BROWN-JOHN, LC (1975), *Multilateral Sanctions in International Law: A Comparative Analysis* (New York: Praeger).

BRUBERLIN, C (1998), 'Coping with the Humanitarian Impact of Sanctions', http://www.reliefweb.int/ocha_ol/pub/sanctions.html.

BULL, H (1992), 'The Importance of Grotius in the Study of International Relations', in Bull H *et al* (eds), *Hugo Grotius and International Relations* (Oxford: Oxford University Press), p 65.

CARDWELL, PJ, FRENCH, D, and WHITE, ND (2009), 'Yassin Abdullah Kadi', 58 *ICLQ* 229.

CASSESE, A (2005), *International Law*, 2nd edn (Oxford: Oxford University Press).

COLLINS, R and WHITE, ND (eds), *International Organizations and the Idea of Autonomy: Institutional Independence in the International Legal Order* (Abingdon: Routledge, 2011).

CONFORTI, B (2000), *The Law and Practice of the United Nations*, 2nd edn (The Hague: Kluwer).

CORTRIGHT, D and LOPEZ, GA (2000), *The Sanctions Decade: Assessing UN Strategies in the 1990s* (Boulder, Colo.: Lynne Rienner).

—— (2002), *Sanctions and the Search for Security: Challenges to UN Action* (Boulder, Colo.: Lynne Rienner).

CRAWFORD, J (1994), 'Counter-Measures as Interim Measures', 5 *EJIL* 65.

—— (2001), 'The Relationship between Sanctions and Countermeasures', in Gowlland-Debbas, V (ed), *United Nations Sanctions and International Law* (The Hague: Kluwer), p 57.

—— (2002), *The International Law Commission's Articles on State Responsibility* (Cambridge: Cambridge University Press).

——, PELLET, A, and OLLESON, S (eds) (2010), *The Law of International Responsibility* (Oxford: Oxford University Press, 2010).

DOPAGNE, F (2011), 'Sanctions and countermeasures by international organizations', in Collins and White (eds), *International Organizations and the Idea of Autonomy: Institutional Independence in the International Legal Order* (Abingdon: Routledge), p 178.

DUGARD, J (2001), 'Judicial Review of Sanctions', in Gowlland-Debbas, V (ed), *United Nations Sanctions and International Law* (The Hague: Kluwer), p 8.

ELAGAB, OY (1988), *The Legality of Non-Forcible Counter-Measures in International Law* (Oxford: Clarendon Press).

FRANCK, TM (2008), 'On Proportionality of Countermeasures in International Law', 102 *AJIL* 715.

GAZZINI, T (2006), 'The Legal Nature of WTO Obligations and the Consequences of their Violation', 17 *EJIL* 723.

GOWLLAND-DEBBAS, V (ed) (2001), *United Nations Sanctions and International Law* (The Hague: Kluwer).

HAPPOLD, M (2003), 'Security Council Resolution 1373 and the Constitution of the United Nations', 16 *Leiden JIL* 593.

KELLER, H and FISCHER, A (2009), 'The UN Anti-terror Sanctions Regime under Pressure', 9 *Human Rights Law Review* 257.

KELSEN, H (1945), *General Theory of Law and State* (Cambridge, Mass.: Harvard University Press).

KLEIN, P (2002), 'Responsibility for Serious Breaches of Obligations Deriving From Peremptory Norms of International Law and United Nations Law', 13 *EJIL* 1241.

KONDOCH, B (2001), 'The Limits of Economic Sanctions under International Law: The Case of Iraq', 7 *International Peacekeeping* 267–94, also available at http://www.casi.org.uk\info\kondoch01.pdf.

KRINSKY, M and GOLOVE, CD (eds) (1993), *United States Economic Measures against Cuba* (Northampton, Mass.: Aletheia Press).

KUNZ, LK, (1960) 'Sanctions in International Law', 54(2) *AJIL* 324.

LAUTERPACHT, H (1933), 'Boycott in International Relations', 14 *BYIL* 125.

LILLICH, RB (1975), 'Economic Coercion and the International Legal Order', 51 *International Affairs* 358.

LOWENFELD, AF (2001), 'Unilateral versus Collective Sanctions: An American Perception', in Gowlland-Debbas, V (ed), *United Nations Sanctions and International Law* (The Hague: Kluwer), p 95.

McNAIR, AD (1930), 'The Functions and Different Legal Character of Treaties', 11 *BYIL* 100.

O'CONNELL, ME (2008), *The Power and Purpose of International Law* (Oxford: Oxford University Press).

PAUST, J and BLAUSTEIN, AP (1974), 'The Arab Oil Weapon—A Threat to International Peace', 68 *AJIL* 410.

PROVOST, R (2002), *State Responsibility in International Law* (Aldershot: Ashgate).

SCOBBIE, I (2004), 'Smoke, Mirrors and Killer Whales: the International Court's Opinion on the Israeli Barrier Wall', 5 *German Law Journal* 1107.

SCHACHTER, O (1994), 'United Nations Law' 88 *AJIL* 1.

SICILIANOS, L-A (2010), 'Countermeasures in Response to Grave Violations of Obligations Owed to the International Community', in Crawford, J, Pellet, A, and Olleson, S (eds), *The Law of International Responsibility* (Oxford: Oxford University Press), p 1137.

TALMON, S (2005), 'The Security Council as World Legislature', 99 *AJIL* 175.

WARD, CA (2003), 'Building Capacity to Combat International Terrorism: The Role of the United Nations Security Council', 8 *Journal of Conflict and Security Law* 289.

ZOLLER, E (1984), *Peacetime Unilateral Remedies: An Analysis of Countermeasures* (Dobbs Ferry, NY: Transnational).

FURTHER READING

CORTRIGHT, D and LOPEZ, GA (2000), *The Sanctions Decade: Assessing UN Strategies in the 1990s* (Boulder, Colo.: Lynne Rienner). A very good examination of the issues and problems of recent and current UN sanctions regimes.

CRAWFORD, J (2002), *The International Law Commission's Articles on State Responsibility: Introduction, Text and Commentaries* (Cambridge: Cambridge University Press). An essential collection of International Law Commission materials necessary for an understanding of the nature, role, and function of countermeasures.

ELAGAB, OY (1988), *The Legality of Non Forcible Counter-Measures in International Law* (Oxford: Clarendon Press). A very thorough exposition of the history and development of countermeasures.

FARRALL, JM (2007), *United Nations Sanctions and the Rule of Law* (Cambridge: Cambridge University Press). A thorough review of sanctions practice by the Security Council and an evaluation of its legal shortcomings.

GOWLLAND-DEBBAS, V (ed) (2001), *United Nations Sanctions and International Law* (The Hague: Kluwer). An excellent collection of essays, exploring, *inter alia*, the boundaries between countermeasures and sanctions.

O'CONNELL, ME (2008), *The Power and Purpose of International Law* (Oxford: Oxford University Press). A clear reconsideration of the theory and practice of the enforcement of norms of international law, by both forcible and non-forcible means.

SICILIANOS, L-A (1990), *Les Réactions Décentralisées Á L'Illicite: Des Contre-Mesures Á La Légitime Défense* (Paris: Librarie Générale de Droit et de Jurisprudence). Leading non-English text on the subject matter of countermeasures.

ZOLLER, E (1984), *Peacetime Unilateral Remedies: An Analysis of Countermeasures* (Dobbs Ferry, NY: Transnational). A useful conceptual analysis of countermeasures.

19

THE MEANS OF DISPUTE SETTLEMENT

John Merrills

SUMMARY

The peaceful settlement of disputes occupies a central place in international law and international relations. A range of methods of handling international disputes has been developed and this chapter explains what the relevant techniques and institutions are, how they work, and when they are used. Because important distinctions are to be found between the various diplomatic means of settlement (negotiation, mediation, inquiry, and conciliation) and the legal means of arbitration and judicial settlement, the two categories are examined separately. Also considered is the role of the UN and regional organizations.

In the light of current international practice two main conclusions emerge: first that enormous progress has been made in refining and developing the means available for dealing with disputes; and secondly that while the various methods have distinctive features which determine how and when they are likely to be used, the key to resolving disputes often lies in their use in combination and interaction.

I. INTRODUCTION

The idea that international disputes should be settled by peaceful means rather than by the use of force has a long history. The attempt to construct institutions and develop techniques with this objective is a more recent phenomenon, however, much of what exists today having been created in the twentieth century and a significant proportion since 1945. This chapter is concerned with the result of that effort in the form of the means currently available for resolving international disputes peacefully. Initially, though, and to put the present arrangements in context, two questions need to be considered: what we mean by an 'international dispute', and what the law has to say about States' obligations.

A 'dispute' is a disagreement about something and an 'international dispute' is a disagreement, typically but not exclusively between States, with consequences on the international plane. However, a dispute is not just any disagreement, but a disagreement about something fairly specific. So the Arab-Israeli problem, for example, is not really a dispute, but because it is so complex is better described as a 'situation'. Of course, 'situations' generally contain specific disputes within them and the international community has to be concerned with both.[1] Nevertheless this chapter is mainly concerned with

---

[1] On the significance of 'situations' with particular reference to the role of the UN, see Koufa, 1988.

methods for dealing with disputes, rather than situations, so the distinction is worth bearing in mind.

What sort of specific disagreements qualify as disputes? Or to put the question another way, what is the subject matter of disputes? This is easily answered. International disputes can be about almost anything. A dispute within the EU, for instance, about the need for closer political integration, would be a dispute about policy. In contrast, most disputes about boundaries or territorial issues involve a disagreement about legal rights. Disputes can also sometimes be about issues of fact. Where was State A's ship when it was intercepted by State B? What was it doing there? Did it have permission? And so on. Clearly these various sources of disagreement (fact, law, and policy) are not mutually exclusive and in many disputes are mixed up together. Separating the different elements, as we shall see, may be a key move in dealing with such disputes effectively.

What, then, are States' legal obligations in this field? A comprehensive statement can be found in an important resolution of the UN General Assembly, the 1982 Manila Declaration on the Peaceful Settlement of International Disputes,[2] which confirms and elaborates the relevant provisions of the UN Charter and the General Assembly's earlier Declaration on Principles of International Law concerning Friendly Relations and Co-operation among States of 1970.[3] Thus paragraph 2 of Section I of the Manila Declaration, like Article 2(3) of the Charter, requires every State to 'settle its international disputes exclusively by peaceful means in such a manner that international peace and security and justice, are not endangered'. And paragraph 5, echoing Article 33, lists the means available, calling for States to 'seek in good faith and in a spirit of co-operation an early and equitable settlement of their international disputes by any of the following means: negotiation, inquiry, mediation, conciliation, arbitration, judicial settlement, resort to regional agencies or arrangements or other peaceful means of their own choice including good offices'. Acknowledging the range of contingencies, the paragraph then concludes, 'In seeking such a settlement the parties shall agree on such peaceful means as may be appropriate to the circumstances and the nature of their dispute'.

It should also be noted that the Declaration says that in the event of the failure of the parties to reach an early solution 'they shall continue to seek a peaceful solution' and 'consult forthwith on mutually agreed means' (paragraph 7), adding in the next paragraph that the parties to a dispute and other States 'shall refrain from any action whatsoever which may aggravate the situation so as to endanger the maintenance of international peace and security and make more difficult or impede the peaceful settlement of the dispute The obligation, then, is not just to give peaceful methods a try, but to persevere for as long as necessary, while at the same time avoiding action which could make things worse. In other words, if a dispute cannot be settled, States must at least manage it and keep things under control. What the various methods are and how they are used will therefore now be considered.

II. DIPLOMATIC METHODS

A. NEGOTIATION

The methods of peaceful settlement listed in the Manila Declaration are not set out in order of priority, but the first mentioned, negotiation, is the most widely used way of dealing

---

[2] GA Res 37/10 (15 November 1982) 21 ILM 449.
[3] GA Res 2625 (XXV) (24 October 1970) 9 ILM 1292. See further Merrills, 1994.

with international disputes.[4] In fact, negotiation is used more often in practice than all the other methods put together. Often, indeed, negotiation is the only means employed, not just because it is normally the first to be tried and is often successful, but also because its advantages may appear so great as to rule out other methods, even where the chances of a negotiated settlement are slight. When other methods are chosen, negotiation is not supplanted but used to resolve instrumental issues, the terms of reference for an inquiry commission, for instance, or the arrangements for implementing an arbitral award.

Since negotiation allows the parties to retain control of a dispute without involving third parties, it is not surprising that governments find it so attractive. However, the decision to negotiate can itself be controversial, acknowledging as it does both the other party's standing and the legitimacy of its interests. Consequently, on sensitive subjects such as sovereignty, if it is possible to negotiate at all, it may be necessary to restrict discussions to relatively uncontentious issues at least to start with, leaving the bigger problems until later. In 1973, for example, the UK succeeded in negotiating an Interim Agreement during its fishing dispute with Iceland[5] and following the Falklands War of 1982 was likewise able through diplomatic contact to establish a *modus vivendi* with Argentina (Evans, 1991; Churchill, 1997). It would therefore be a mistake to see negotiation as concerned only with settling international disputes. Its function in 'managing' disputes, ie containing them in order to preserve other aspects of the parties' relationship, may be equally significant.

Because negotiation is fundamental it should be thought of not so much as a first stage in the conduct of virtually all disputes, but rather as an option available to the parties at any time, for use either alongside, or as part of, other processes. Thus, as the International Court indicated in the *Aegean Sea Continental Shelf* case, the fact that negotiations are being pursued during litigation is no bar to the exercise of the Court's powers and *vice versa*.[6] As a result, it is not at all uncommon for cases to be resolved by negotiation in the course of litigation, as happened in 1996 in the Iran-USA *Aerial Incident* case.[7] Similarly, a State may decide to take a dispute to a political body like the Security Council or General Assembly but at the same time continue bilateral discussions. Such twin-track approaches, employing both public and private diplomacy, are perfectly permissible and show the adaptability of negotiation.

Important though negotiation is, it cannot guarantee that a dispute will be settled, or even managed, because it is limited in various ways. It may be impossible if the parties refuse to speak to each other and it will be ineffective if their positions are too far apart, although in both situations, as we shall see, mediation or good offices can help. If a procedure for dealing with the dispute, such as arbitration, has already been agreed, one party may see no point in further negotiation, especially if it is confident of its legal position. More generally, the objective of resolving disputes 'equitably' and in accordance with justice, which are what the Manila Declaration prescribes, sits uneasily with the prospect of having to negotiate in a situation of grossly unequal political power. Accordingly, though negotiation is often called for by the strong, the weak may be justified in declining the invitation.

Negotiation, however, is not always a matter of free choice. Quite apart from the force of circumstances which may mean that refusing to negotiate is not an available option, a State may bind itself to negotiate in a treaty, or find that an obligation to negotiate

---

[4] For more detailed discussion of negotiation see Merrills, 2011, Ch 1.

[5] See *Fisheries Jurisdiction (United Kingdom v Iceland), Merits, Judgment, ICJ Reports 1974*, p 3, paras 37–9.

[6] See *Aegean Sea Continental Shelf, Judgment, ICJ Reports 1978*, p 3, para 29.

[7] See *Aerial Incident of 3 July 1988, Order of 22 February 1996, ICJ Reports 1996*, p 9. See also (1996) 90 *AJIL* 278.

arises under the general law. In the *North Sea Continental Shelf* cases, for instance, the International Court decided that according to customary international law the delimitation of continental shelf boundaries between neighbouring States 'must be effected by agreement in accordance with equitable principles'.[8] Of course, an obligation to negotiate on this or any other subject is not the same as an obligation to agree, nor does it exclude recourse to other procedures. What the Court wished to emphasize here was simply that as each party had rights in the disputed area, the boundaries in question were not subject to unilateral determination, and unless resolved by another procedure, had to be settled by negotiation.

The duty to negotiate sometimes laid down in treaties may be compared with related, but lesser, obligations which are an alternative. The 1994 World Trade Organization (WTO) Agreement requires its parties to 'enter into consultations' over trade issues when requested by another party,[9] which is an obligation to negotiate, whereas the 1982 Law of the Sea Convention calls only for the parties to a dispute to 'proceed expeditiously to an exchange of views' as to the means of settlement to be used.[10] It is, however, worth stressing that just as there is no general duty to consult before taking action which may affect others, so there is no general duty to seek negotiated settlements. The various methods of settlement available in international law are listed as alternatives. Negotiation is simply one possibility and in the absence of a specific duty to negotiate, such as in the WTO Agreement, States can use it or not as they see fit.

Despite this essential qualification, negotiation is an extremely important means of dealing with disputes and international relations would be unimaginably different without it. In almost all cases diplomatic exchanges will have to take place before a disagreement becomes specific enough to be described as a dispute—that is in order for the parties to establish what, if anything, they disagree about. And once it is clear a dispute exists, negotiation will often provide the best prospect of a solution, whether permanent or provisional, and for cases involving major differences as well as routine friction. It is evident, however, that although negotiation must be regarded as basic, it may not be sufficient, without more, either to resolve a dispute, or even supply a *modus vivendi*. The other methods mentioned in the Declaration must therefore now be considered.

B. MEDIATION

Mediation is essentially an adjunct of negotiation and involves a third party. If the latter does no more than encourage the protagonists to resume negotiations, or simply acts as a channel of communication, the role is described as one of 'good offices'. A mediator, on the other hand, is an active participant, authorized, and indeed expected, to advance fresh ideas and to interpret, as well as to transmit, each party's proposals to the other.[11] Mediation therefore has much in common with conciliation, although a mediator usually makes proposals informally and on the basis of information supplied by the parties, rather than through independent investigations which are a feature of conciliation. In practice,

---

   [8] *North Sea Continental Shelf, Judgment, ICJ Reports 1969*, p 3, para 85.
   [9] WTO Understanding on Rules and Procedures Governing the Settlement of Disputes (1994), Article 4(3). Text in (1994) 33 ILM 1226.
   [10] United Nations Convention on the Law of the Sea (1982), Article 283(1). Text in (1982) 21 ILM 1245.
   [11] For more detailed discussion of mediation see Bercovitch and Rubin, 1992; Greenberg, Barton, and McGuiness, 2000; Merrills, 2011, Ch 2.

however, these distinctions tend to be blurred. In a given case it may therefore be difficult to draw the line between mediation and conciliation, or to say exactly when good offices ended and mediation began.

Mediation can only take place if the parties to a dispute consent and a mediator willing to act in that capacity is available. The UN and several regional organizations are charged with the resolution of disputes as an institutional objective and as a result the Secretary-General and his regional counterparts often find themselves providing good offices and mediation. Non-governmental organizations too, such as the International Committee of the Red Cross, can act as mediators. Since it offers an opportunity to become involved in a dispute and to influence its outcome, the role of mediator also has attractions for States, or individuals, with the necessary qualifications. Accordingly, it is not unusual for the course of significant international disputes to be punctuated by offers of mediation from one or more outside sources.

Since mediation cannot be forced on the protagonists, unless they take the initiative and invite outside involvement, an unwillingness even to consider this form of assistance may frustrate the efforts of would-be mediators. If a party is unwilling to negotiate, or to contemplate any modification of its position, its acceptance of mediation (which would imply the opposite) is clearly very unlikely. On the other hand, States normally have an interest in resolving their disputes and while the terms of any settlement are plainly important, intransigence may be too expensive politically for a blank refusal of mediation to be feasible. In 1982, for example, Argentina and the UK were willing to accept good offices from the UN Secretary-General, and then mediation from the USA, because neither government could afford to alienate potential supporters.[12] It was clear at the time that something of a miracle would be needed to avoid further conflict, but for the sake of appearances, if for no other reason, they had to show willing.

Once mediation has been accepted, the task of the mediator is to devise or promote a solution which both sides can accept. Here much can be achieved by simply providing good offices and facilitating communication, especially if the parties are unable to deal with each other directly. This was the situation in both the Falklands crisis and the Diplomatic Hostages dispute of 1980, where Algeria acted as intermediary between Iran and the USA (Sick, 1985). As well as acting as a channel for information, a mediator can remind the parties of their real objectives, or encourage rethinking, and devise suitable compromises, as the Papal mediator in the Beagle Channel dispute eventually succeeded in doing (Laudy, 2000). A powerful mediator may also be able to influence the parties by exploiting the role, offering inducements to agree in the form of rewards, or indicating that a failure to do so will be costly.

Normally, a mediator's main concern is only to find terms the parties can accept; in some types of mediation, however, any settlement must also meet certain external criteria. Thus according to Article 38 of the European Convention on Human Rights, one of the functions of the European Court of Human Rights is to 'place itself at the disposal of the parties concerned with a view to securing a friendly settlement of the matter *on the basis of respect for human rights*' as defined in the Convention and its Protocols. In this provision, which has its counterpart in other human rights treaties, the Court is, in effect, required to act as mediator, while at the same time respecting the Convention's basic values. A significant number of individual claims have been resolved using the friendly settlement

---

[12] For an account of these initiatives and the subsequent efforts of the President of Peru, see Freedman and Gamba-Stonehouse, 1990, pp 150–323.

procedure,[13] demonstrating that mediation with a substantive dimension is both workable and appropriate in the human rights field.

As a means of dispute settlement mediation is clearly subject to important limitations. A mediator must be available and the parties must be willing to accept mediation. When mediation has begun the prospects of success rest largely on the parties' readiness to compromise which means that timing is often crucial. In both the Diplomatic Hostages crisis and the Beagle Channel dispute mediation occurred at an opportune moment and a peaceful resolution of the situation was achieved. In the Falklands crisis, on the other hand, the aims of Britain and Argentina were diametrically opposed and as neither was willing to yield on the crucial issue of sovereignty, the matter was eventually resolved by armed conflict.

Mediation, then, is as effective as the disputants allow it to be and their attitudes are likely to be governed by their immediate situation. This restricts the possibilities of mediation, but does not destroy its value. A mediator does more than perfect an inchoate settlement. By facilitating the parties' dialogue, providing them with information and suggestions, identifying and exploring their aims, and canvassing possible solutions, intercession may be vital in moving them towards agreement. Success will often be incomplete and failure sometimes unavoidable. The mediator, however, must spare no effort and trust that the parties reciprocate.

C. INQUIRY

Inquiry in the context of dispute settlement is a term used in two distinct, but related senses. In the broader sense it refers to the process performed whenever a court or other body attempts to resolve a disputed issue of fact. Since most international disputes raise such issues, even if questions of law or policy are also present, it is clear that inquiry in this operational sense must play a large part in arbitration, conciliation, the work of international organizations, and other methods of peaceful settlement. Inquiry can, however, also be used in a narrower sense, not as a process of general relevance and application, but as a specific institutional arrangement which may be selected instead of arbitration or other techniques to establish the facts. In its institutional sense, then, inquiry refers to a particular type of international tribunal, known as the commission of inquiry and introduced by the 1899 Hague Convention.[14]

The delegates to the first Hague Peace Conference were prompted to address the issue of fact-finding by an incident the year before in which the unexplained destruction of the US battleship *Maine* had precipitated a Spanish-American war. In an effort to minimize such problems in the future the Conference suggested the appointment of international commissions of inquiry for impartial fact-finding and arrangements to this effect were incorporated in the 1899 Hague Convention. Soon afterwards in 1904 they were used for the first time in a curious episode known as the Dogger Bank incident when the Russian fleet, wrongly believing it was under attack, fired on and damaged a number of British trawlers. A commission of inquiry appointed by the two governments established that a mistake had been made and on payment of suitable compensation the incident was declared closed (Bar-Yaacov, 1974, pp 72–81).

The Dogger Bank episode was a striking example of the value of fact-finding in the settlement of international disputes. However, it also revealed certain weaknesses in the provisions of the Hague Convention which were conspicuously lacking in detail.

---

[13] For an account of practice under Article 38 (ex 28) of the European Convention, see Merrills and Robertson, 2001, pp 279–82, 318–19. See also Koopmans, 2008, pp 184–99.

[14] For more detailed discussion of inquiry see Bar-Yaacov, 1974; Merrills, 2011, Ch 3.

Accordingly, the Hague Convention of 1907 expanded the earlier scheme with a series of Articles devoted to organization and procedure. These arrangements were then used in a group of cases over the next two decades involving incidents at sea, where once again establishing the facts enabled the disputes to be disposed of.[15] This was also the outcome in the *Red Crusader* case[16] in 1962 in which the UK and Denmark set up an inquiry commission to deal with a dispute arising out of an attempt to arrest a British trawler.

Following the 1907 Hague Convention the USA concluded treaties with France and Great Britain, known as the Taft treaties, providing for commissions of inquiry with expanded powers and a further series, known as the Bryan treaties, featuring further variations. A number of other States concluded agreements along similar lines. All this treaty practice failed to produce a sequence of inquiries like those generated by the Hague Conventions, although in 1992 one of the Bryan treaties was used in the *Letelier and Moffitt* case[17] to resolve a dispute over compensation between the USA and Chile. But if in terms of case law the significance of these bilateral treaties was negligible, they were important more generally because the idea of combining inquiry with the power to make recommendations produced the institutional arrangement known as conciliation described further in the next section.

Inquiry is clearly a very flexible method having been used both for 'pure' fact-finding, as in some of the early cases, and for situations where legal questions were prominent, as in *Letelier and Moffitt*. Why, then, is it so rarely used? One explanation is that today when an inquiry is needed it can sometimes be carried out through an international organization without using the Hague Conventions. The Security Council, for example, sets up fact-finding commissions from time to time, as do the Specialized Agencies and in 1993 the World Bank introduced a unique Inspection Panel procedure[18] to investigate development projects. These institutional developments account, at least in part, for the relatively small number of cases using the Hague procedure. There is, however, a more fundamental explanation.

All forms of third party settlement have proved less popular than was once anticipated. The root of the problem is that States are often less interested in settling a dispute than in having their own views prevail. It is therefore only when certain special conditions are satisfied that there is usually scope for setting up an inquiry commission. These are that the disputed issue is largely one of fact, that no other procedure is being employed and, most important of all, that the parties are willing to accept that their version of events may be shown to be wrong. Such a combination evidently does not occur very often. When it does, the highly satisfactory outcome of the *Red Crusader* episode shows that the international commission of inquiry can still produce useful results.

D. CONCILIATION

Conciliation has been defined as:

> A method for the settlement of international disputes of any nature according to which a Commission set up by the Parties, either on a permanent or an ad hoc basis to deal with

[15] For a summary of these cases see Bar-Yaacov, 1974, pp 141–79.

[16] The text of the Commission's Report can be found in 35 ILR 485. For discussion of the case see Bar-Yaacov, 1974, pp 179–96.

[17] *Letelier and Moffitt* case (Chile-USA), 88 ILR 727 and (1992) 31 ILM 1. For comment see Merrills, 2011, Ch 3.

[18] See Gowlland Gualtieri, 2001; Koopmans, 2008, pp 212–17; and French and Kirkham, 2010, pp 68–72. The Inter-American Bank and the Asian Development Bank have established similar panels.

a dispute proceeds to the impartial examination of the dispute and attempts to define the terms of a settlement susceptible of being accepted by them, or of affording the Parties with a view to its settlement, such aid as they may have requested.[19]

If mediation is essentially an extension of negotiation, conciliation puts third party intervention on a formal footing and institutionalizes it in a way comparable, but not identical, to inquiry or arbitration. For the fact-finding exercise that is the essence of inquiry may or may not be present in conciliation, while the search for terms 'susceptible of being accepted by the parties' but not binding on them, contrasts sharply with arbitration and forms a link between conciliation and mediation.

Like other institutional methods, conciliation is normally entrusted to commissions containing several members. However, it is also possible to refer a dispute to a single conciliator and this procedure was adopted in 1977 when Kenya, Uganda, and Tanzania asked the experienced Swiss diplomat, Dr Victor Umbricht, to make proposals for distributing the assets of the former East African Community (EAC). As the extent of the assets was unknown, the conciliator had to begin by conducting a wide-ranging inquiry, first to identify and then to value the assets, after which he could consider their distribution. Although in the final negotiated settlement the division of assets differed slightly from that proposed by Dr Umbricht, it is clear that his activities, which included mediation as well as conciliation and inquiry, and extended over seven years, made a vital contribution to the eventual settlement (Umbricht, 1984).

A more straightforward dispute which was resolved at about the same time involved a commission of the type familiar from previous conciliations. In 1980 Iceland and Norway set up a commission to make recommendations with regard to the dividing line for the area of continental shelf between Iceland and Jan Mayen Island. The Commission was instructed to take into account Iceland's 'strong economic interests' in the sea areas in question, along with various other factors. Following a detailed investigation of geological and other evidence, the Commission proposed both a boundary line and a joint development agreement for the area where oil deposits might exist (Richardson, 1988). This recommendation, typical of the kind of constructive compromise which conciliation can generate, was accepted by the parties and in 1981 was incorporated in a treaty which ended the dispute.

Bilateral agreements providing for the reference of future disputes to conciliation were quite common in the League of Nations era after the First World War, but are now quite rare. When States use conciliation in a bilateral treaty today it is therefore usually in order to deal with a specific dispute, as in the two cases just mentioned. Multilateral treaties, however, show a quite different pattern and in recent practice agreements providing for conciliation, often in conjunction with other procedures, have been concluded on a variety of topics. Among treaties demonstrating the relevance of conciliation to dispute settlement in different fields are the 1969 Vienna Convention on the Law of Treaties, the 1981 Treaty establishing the Organization of Eastern Caribbean States, the 1982 Convention on the Law of the Sea, and the 1992 Convention on Biological Diversity.[20]

The 1987 Montreal Protocol on Substances that Deplete the Ozone Layer is also worth mentioning here as it establishes a novel 'non-compliance procedure', constituting a special kind of conciliation. Under the procedure an Implementation Committee consisting

---

[19] The quotation is from Article 1 of the Regulations on the Procedure of International Conciliation, adopted by the Institute of International Law in 1961. For more detailed discussion of conciliation see Cot, 1972; Bar-Yaacov, 1974, pp 198–248; Merrills, 2011, Ch 4; and Koopmans, 2008.

[20] See also the 1997 UN Convention on the Law of the Non-Navigational Uses of International Watercourses, Article 33 of which provides for Commissions charged with inquiry and conciliation.

of ten parties to the Protocol hears submissions relating to a party's non-compliance which may be put forward by the Secretariat or any other party. The Committee may then make recommendations 'with a view to securing an amicable solution of the matter on the basis of respect for the provisions of the Protocol'. Chinkin (1998, p 129) points out that a process such as this, dealing as it does with disputes both 'in-house' and informally, is particularly suitable for an evolving regulatory regime, as it can reflect the expectations and understandings of the parties, but at the same time avoid crystallizing the law in a fast changing area. Following the example of the Montreal Protocol, non-compliance procedures have been included in a number of other environmental treaties, including the 1997 Kyoto Protocol, the 1998 Aarhus Convention and the 2000 Cartagena Protocol on Biosafety (Scott, 2010).

The Law of the Sea Convention, which includes conciliation as part of elaborate arrangements for the settlement of disputes, lays down the procedure to be followed in setting up commissions, together with details of their organization and jurisdiction.[21] Other multilateral treaties contain similar provisions, though with various differences of detail. For States wishing to establish an ad hoc commission the UN General Assembly has produced a set of model rules covering all aspects of conciliation which were approved in 1995. In the following year the Permanent Court of Arbitration produced its own optional rules for States wishing to use the Court and the UN Commission on International Trade Law (UNCITRAL) adopted rules in 1980 for conciliation in international commercial disputes.[22]

Although conciliation is now regularly included in provisions on dispute settlement, the number of cases in which it has actually been used remains very small. Moreover, since a commission's proposals are not binding, even when conciliation is attempted, there can be no guarantee it will be successful. Conciliation, nevertheless, has a value. Compulsory procedures of any kind, by their very existence, tend to discourage unreasonable claims, while conciliation in practice has proved particularly useful for disputes like the *Jan Mayen* case where the main issues are legal, but the parties are seeking an equitable compromise. Like inquiry, the process from which it developed, conciliation offers a procedure adaptable to a variety of needs and shows the advantage to be gained from a structured involvement of outsiders in the settlement of international disputes.

III. LEGAL METHODS

A. ARBITRATION

The oldest of the legal methods of dispute settlement is arbitration, the origins of which in current international practice can be traced back to the 1794 Jay Treaty between Great Britain and the USA. A distinctive feature of arbitration is that the parties themselves set up a tribunal to decide a dispute, or a series of disputes, usually on the basis of international law, and agree to treat its decisions as binding. Since form is subordinate to function in international relations, variations on the basic pattern are possible, but the standard form of arbitration is now well-established and regularly used for many kinds of international disputes.[23]

---

[21] For analysis of these arrangements and their relation to the Convention's other provisions see Merrills, 2011, Ch 8.

[22] See the Annex to GA Res 35/52 (4 December 1980) and Collier and Lowe, 1999, p 31.

[23] For useful surveys of the development and current role of arbitration see: Simpson and Fox, 1959; Gray and Kingsbury, 1992; Collier and Lowe, 1999, pp 189–279; Merrills, 2011, Ch 5.

   Traditionally, arbitration has been used for disputes in which the issues are legal and
the need to remove an obstacle to good relations makes the idea of a binding settlement
attractive. Territorial and boundary disputes, for example, often fall into this category.
Because the parties define the question to be answered and can specify the basis of the
decision, they exercise a degree of control over the process which is a further advantage.
Moreover, the parties are entitled to choose the arbitrators. Although this, like other elements of an arbitration, requires agreement and so may cause delay, it means that the
dispute will eventually be decided by a tribunal which the parties believe they can trust, a
factor of fundamental importance in international litigation. Over the years the reference
of disputes to arbitration has generated a significant and influential case law, prominent
awards including those in the *Tinoco* case (1923),[24] the *Island of Palmas* case (1928),[25]
and the *Trail Smelter* case (1938–41).[26] More recently, the value of arbitration has been
further demonstrated in the *Abyei* case (2009),[27] where a land boundary was in issue, the
Guyana/Suriname case (2007)[28] involving a maritime boundary, and the two-stage *Red
Sea Islands* case (1998–9)[29] between Eritrea and Yemen, where territorial sovereignty and
maritime delimitation were both in issue. Among notable arbitrations where boundary
issues were not involved are the two arbitrations in the *Rainbow Warrior* case (1986 and
1990)[30] between France and New Zealand, the *OSPAR (Article 9)* case (2003)[31] between
Ireland and the UK and the *Iron Rhine Railway* case (2005) between Belgium and the
Netherlands.[32]
   Arbitration, like conciliation, is a method which can be employed ad hoc when a dispute
arises, or provided for in advance by appropriate arrangements in a treaty. It is therefore
to be found in the dispute settlement provisions of multilateral and bilateral conventions
on a wide variety of subjects, as either an optional or a compulsory procedure, and often
in combination with other methods. The 1982 Law of the Sea Convention, for example,
gives a very prominent role to arbitration, as do the 1992 Stockholm Convention on
Conciliation and Arbitration within the CSCE and a number of recent conventions concerned with the environment.[33] In the WTO's dispute settlement system, similarly, though
the general emphasis is on panel proceedings (described in Section C Other Courts and
Tribunals), arbitration is also an option and for certain disputes is even mandatory.
   The use of arbitration to decide inter-State disputes must be distinguished from its
use in a related context, to deal with disputes between a State on one side and an individual or corporation on the other. In cases of this type, known as mixed arbitrations,[34]
the tribunal's jurisdiction may derive from a contract rather than a treaty, but in either
event has international implications that are likely to be significant. The Iran-USA Claims
Tribunal,[35] for example, was set up in 1981 to handle a large number of disputes arising
from the Islamic revolution in Iran and has jurisdiction over both inter-State and private
claims. Its decisions, which now run to more than 30 volumes, not only show the value
of arbitration as a procedure for resolving serious and complex disputes of a commercial
character, but because the Tribunal has had to address issues such as expropriation and
State responsibility, have also made a significant contribution to international law.

---

[24] 1 *RIAA* 369.   [25] 2 *RIAA* 829.   [26] 3 *RIAA* 1905.   [27] (2009) 48 ILM 1254.
[28] (2008) 47 ILM 164.   [29] (2001) 40 ILM 900 and 983.   [30] 74 ILR 241 and 82 ILR 499.
[31] (2003) 42 ILM 330.   [32] 140 ILR 130.   [33] See Merrills, 2011, Chs 5 and 8.
   [34] For a good account of mixed arbitration, including the work of the International Centre for the Settlement
of Investment Disputes (ICSID), and the related topic of international commercial arbitration, see Collier and
Lowe, 1999, pp 45–84.
   [35] For a more detailed account of the Tribunal and its work see Brower, 1998.

Arbitration, then, is an important means of handling international disputes. It does, however, have significant limitations. As we shall see in the next section, States are reluctant to make general commitments to judicial settlement and for much the same reasons often resist the idea of arbitration. When a specific dispute arises, however, negotiation or another diplomatic method may be preferred on the ground that it keeps the solution firmly in the hands of the parties. Another limitation concerns enforcement. Although arbitration produces a binding decision, it can be difficult to ensure that the losing party carries out the award. This does not mean that arbitral decisions are widely disregarded, but nonetheless is a real weakness. Ways of encouraging compliance are available and can be useful, but the answer really lies with the protagonists. Arbitration, like other means of settling disputes in a world of sovereign States, relies for its effectiveness on responsible behaviour from the parties.

B. THE INTERNATIONAL COURT OF JUSTICE

Judicial settlement involves the reference of disputes to permanent tribunals for a legally binding decision. It is listed in the Manila Declaration after arbitration, from which it developed historically, and is currently available through a number of courts with general or specialized jurisdiction. The only court of general jurisdiction is the International Court of Justice (ICJ) at The Hague (for a detailed consideration see Thirlway, Ch 20 of this book). Courts with specialized jurisdiction include human rights courts and various tribunals considered in the next section and the European Court of Justice (ECJ), a regional organ with extensive powers over the member States of the European Community, Community organs, and natural or legal persons. It is interesting to note that the ECJ and the other specialized courts have all been created since 1945 and reflect the increasing complexity of international relations. Our review must begin, however, with the ICJ.[36]

The Court's authority to decide cases is conferred by its Statute and is based on the principle of consent. It is therefore open to States to agree to take future disputes, or any particular dispute, to the Court by concluding a treaty in appropriate terms, or to make a unilateral acceptance of jurisdiction in the form of a declaration under Article 36(2) of the Statute, known as the Optional Clause.[37] In the event of a disagreement as to whether jurisdiction has been accepted the matter is decided by the Court, whose decision, according to Article 36(6), is final. Only States may be parties in cases before the Court, although under Article 65 it may also give advisory opinions on legal questions for the benefit of international organizations.

The Court is composed of 15 judges who are elected for nine-year terms by the Security Council and General Assembly of the UN. The Statute requires the judges to be broadly representative of 'the main forms of civilization and of the principal legal systems of the world', but they sit as independent judges, not as representatives of their national States. However, if a party to a dispute does not currently have a judge of its nationality on the Bench, it is entitled to appoint an ad hoc judge who becomes a member of the Court for that case only. Cases are normally heard by the full Court, but if the parties wish, they can instead refer it to a smaller chamber (normally five judges). The composition

---

[36] For more detailed treatment of the International Court and its work see Merrills, 2011, Chs 6 and 7; Collier and Lowe, 1999, pp 124–89 and the essays in Muller, Raic, and Thuranszky, 1997.

[37] For discussion of the Optional Clause, with particular reference to recent State practice, see Merrills, 2009 and for an earlier survey, Merrills, 2002.

of a chamber is in practice determined by the parties, making the process similar in this respect to arbitration.[38]

The Court's function is described in Article 38(1) of the Statute as 'to decide in accordance with international law such disputes as are submitted to it and the list of materials which follows, beginning with 'international conventions' and ending with 'judicial decisions' and 'the teachings of publicists', has come to be seen as the core of modern international law. As well as interpreting and applying the law, the Court must, of course, also resolve any issues of fact that may be necessary and for this purpose receives and assesses documentary or other evidence brought forward by the parties, the quantity of which may sometimes be extremely large. This may include the evidence of witnesses or experts and the Court itself may decide to visit the scene, as happened in 1997 in the *Gabčíkovo-Nagymaros Project* case.[39]

Under Article 38(2) of the Statute the Court may at the request of the parties give a decision *ex aequo et bono* instead of on the basis of law. However, this provision, which blurs the distinction between adjudication and conciliation, has never been used. A less drastic alternative is to refer a case to the Court for a decision on an agreed basis. Like the chambers procedure, this again brings adjudication close to arbitration, although the Court's powers must always be exercised within the Statute. A further possibility is for the Court to extend its function on its own initiative by utilizing equitable considerations of various kinds. While this is not a licence for freewheeling judicial legislation, it introduces an element of flexibility into the Court's decisions which can sometimes be useful.

When the Court decides a case, its judgment is binding on the parties and is final and without appeal. Whether it actually resolves the dispute, however, depends partly on whether the parties accept it, that is are prepared to treat it as binding, and partly on the precise question referred. States may, for example, decide to use the Court only to obtain a ruling on applicable rules and principles,[40] or to determine whether a dispute is subject to compulsory arbitration[41] and in cases such as these further steps may be needed to achieve a final settlement. As regards the acceptance of decisions, difficulties can sometimes arise, especially where the unsuccessful party has sought to challenge the Court's jurisdiction. On the other hand, disputes are often taken to the Court and resolved there without acrimony because the States concerned want a settlement. In such cases repudiation of the decision would merely return the dispute to the political arena and therefore be self-defeating.

C. OTHER COURTS AND TRIBUNALS

Among the various courts with specialized jurisdiction the most spectacular developments have unquestionably been those associated with human rights tribunals, notably the European Court of Human Rights at Strasbourg and the Inter-American Court in San José. Before 1970 the former was rarely employed and the American Court was not inaugurated until 1979. Today, however, the European Court, which was reconstructed in 1998, has a flourishing jurisprudence[42] and although the American Court is not as busy,

---

[38] For discussion of this and other aspects of the chambers procedure see Ostrihansky, 1988.

[39] *Gabčíkovo-Nagymaros Project (Hungary/Slovakia), Order of 5 February 1997, Judgment, ICJ Reports 1997*, p 7.

[40] As in the *North Sea Continental Shelf, Judgment, ICJ Reports 1969*, p 3.

[41] As in *Ambatielos, Merits, Judgment, ICJ Reports 1953*, p 10.

[42] For an account of the Court and its work, including the changes made in 1998, see Merrills and Robertson, 2001.

it has made its mark with both contentious cases and advisory opinions (Pasqualucci, 2003). The work of these courts stems mainly from cases brought by individuals, but both courts have jurisdiction over inter-State disputes and deal with such cases from time to time. More importantly, as human rights are now an international issue, procedures for adjudicating claims help to promote friendly relations whether or not they are brought by States. The activities of human rights courts thus certainly fall within the Manila Declaration.

Courts with specialized jurisdiction of a quite different type are to be found in the 1982 Law of the Sea Convention. For among several new institutions created by the Convention is a new court, the International Tribunal for the Law of the Sea (ITLOS), and a separate subsidiary organ, the Sea-Bed Disputes Chamber (SBDC).[43] ITLOS reflects the preference which many States had for a special tribunal to handle disputes arising out of the new law contained in the 1982 Convention, and the Court has begun to develop its own distinctive jurisprudence. In the same way the SBDC was set up because the complex arrangements in the Convention for exploiting the deep sea-bed were thought unsuitable for adjudication in the main Tribunal. In 2011 the SBDC decided its first case when it gave an advisory opinion at the request of the International Seabed Authority.[44]

The arrangements pertaining to the organization and jurisdiction of ITLOS and the SBDC and the choice of law to be applied are set out in great detail in the 1982 Convention and show the thinking behind their creation. Among points particularly worth noting are that the jurisdiction of ITLOS is based on the principle of free choice of means, since it depends upon States making a declaration nominating the Tribunal as their preferred option. The SBDC, on the other hand, has a jurisdiction which is automatically accepted by all the parties to the Convention. Both tribunals, unlike the International Court, are open not just to States, but also to other entities, including organizations, and each is permitted to split into smaller chambers, in order to provide the parties, if they wish, with some of the advantages of arbitration.

Functioning in a quite different sphere of operation is the dispute settlement system of the WTO, set up when the Organization was created in 1994. This complex system exists to deal with disputes concerned with trade agreements and utilizes consultations between the parties, mediation, conciliation, and arbitration in elaborate provisions details of which must be sought elsewhere.[45] At the centre of the system is an arrangement for referring disputes to panels made up of independent experts whose role resembles that of arbitrators. Panel reports are then liable to review by the members of an organ called the Appellate Body, which further emphasizes the juridical nature of the process.

A feature of the WTO system is that the principle of free choice of means, normally so important in dispute settlement, is largely absent. While States are encouraged to settle disputes by agreement, if they fail to do so, the complaining party is entitled to request a panel. When the panel has reported, recourse to the Appellate Body is again a matter of right, and when the litigation stage is complete, a political organ, called the Dispute Settlement Body, takes over to ensure implementation. Notice also that by subscribing to the WTO Agreement States not only forgo the remedy of self-help, but also undertake

---

[43] On the arrangements relating to ITLOS and its place in the dispute settlement arrangements of the Convention, see Klein, 2005; and Merrills, 2011, Ch 8.

[44] *Responsibilities and Obligations of States Sponsoring Persons and Entities with Respect to Activities in the Area, Advisory Opinion, ITLOS Reports 2011*, nyr, (2011) 50 ILM 458.

[45] There is already a large literature on the WTO system, including Palmeter and Mavroidis, 2004 and a detailed treatment by Petersmann, 1997. For a more concise treatment see Merrills, 2011, Ch 9.

to use its procedures exclusively. So, for example, if a dispute could be dealt with either through the WTO, or through a regional system, the former should be given priority.

Although the WTO system is relatively new, it is in constant use and regularly proves its worth. Trade disputes are complex, often involve shifts in economic and political forces and are capable of arousing strong passions. If this makes peaceful methods for resolving such disputes essential, it also means that methods which encourage accommodation are no less important than those that seek to enforce rules. That is why the WTO system features diplomatic as well as legal processes. Moreover, in international trade law, as elsewhere, adjudication works best when rules are not just applied impartially, but also command general acceptance. As the fairness of trade rules depends on the policies of the major players in the WTO, their responsibility as legislators underpins its system for dealing with disputes.

D. THE PLACE OF LEGAL METHODS

To understand the significance of arbitration or other legal methods and how they are used in practice it is important to appreciate at the outset that courts and tribunals do not operate in isolation, but regularly interact with political institutions and processes. So, for example, the reference of a dispute to the ICJ may be prompted by the efforts of a regional organization, negotiations may be necessary to establish the question asked, and may well continue on substantive matters once litigation is in progress. At the post-adjudication stage, likewise, technical assistance from the UN, or further negotiations, perhaps assisted by a mediator, may be needed to deal with boundary demarcation, or similar issues concerning implementation.[46]

When considering the role of adjudication it is also as well to recognize that courts and tribunals have no all-embracing ability to solve international problems, but occupy a specialized place among the instruments of dispute settlement. Not only are they limited to deciding disputes and so lack competence to deal with broader 'situations', but as their normal function is to decide cases by applying law, many problems are unsuited to adjudication because they do not raise legal issues. Thus the International Court has indicated that as a general rule it cannot deal with issues requiring, say, a political or economic assessment, rather than a legal decision, and by the same token it will decline to answer questions which are moot or only of historical interest.[47]

What, then, is the value of legal methods? Because the decisions of courts and tribunals are binding, litigation is a good way of disposing of troublesome issues the resolution of which is considered to be more important than the actual result. Conversely, when the result is all-important adjudication is likely to be unattractive because it is simply too risky, a point which is reinforced by the fact that adjudication is not merely dispositive, but tends to produce a winner-takes-all type of solution. This explains why States are notoriously reluctant to make a general commitment to take their disputes to the International Court, but may be willing to do so in individual cases. It also explains the popularity of ITLOS and the WTO panels system, which are designed for a specific purpose, where the parties' commitments are defined and the judges have special expertise. It is worth bearing

---

[46] For discussion of the issue of compliance and implementation generally see Paulson, 2004 and Schulte, 2004. For a wider perspective Shany, 2012.

[47] See *Haya de Torre, Judgment, ICJ Reports 1951*, p 71; *Northern Cameroons, Preliminary Objections, Judgment, ICJ Reports 1963*, p 15; *Nuclear Tests (Australia v France), Judgment, ICJ Reports 1974*, p 253, and *Nuclear Tests (New Zealand v France), Judgment, ICJ Reports 1974*, p 457. See also Lowe, 2012.

in mind, however, that when arrangements of this kind are set up they are not mutually exclusive. Consequently, an unavoidable effect is to create situations of overlapping competence, where several courts or tribunals may have jurisdiction over the same dispute, or different aspects of it. If, as may happen in such circumstances, the parties elect to refer a dispute to different legal bodies, difficult questions can arise as to which, if either, should have priority (Shany, 2003; Merrills, 2007; Crawford and Nevill, 2012).

Are international courts capable of deciding disputes with a strong political element? The answer is to be found in a firmly established principle which is really quite basic to international adjudication. It is that courts and tribunals are set up to resolve legal issues and so, provided a case presents a legal issue, they are not prevented from deciding it merely because it also has political elements.[48] It is easy to see that such an attitude is essential if adjudication is to function. All disputes between States have political elements because States are political bodies. Therefore to concede that a case could not be decided if it had political elements would be to enable any case to be blocked. Quite rightly, this absurd conclusion has been rejected.

Since international disputes often have both a legal and a political dimension, it is no surprise to find that on occasion disputes are referred to legal and political institutions simultaneously. The Tehran hostages dispute, for example, between the USA and Iran was considered by both the ICJ and the UN Security Council in 1980 and there have also been cases involving regional organizations. Such cases clearly raise the question of the relation between the legal and the political process, on which the Court's view, as might be expected, is that each has its own sphere and neither is entitled to priority as a matter of principle.[49] This is useful as far as it goes, but leaves open questions such as how far the legality of the Security Council's actions may be challenged before the Court, a problem to which as yet there is no clear answer.[50]

When the parties to a dispute decide to employ adjudication by, for example, concluding an arbitration agreement, or jointly referring a case to the International Court they are, in effect, agreeing that the legal and political aspects of the dispute should be separated. When, on the other hand, a case is referred unilaterally, it may be because the parties view the dispute differently, the applicant seeing the legal aspect as paramount, but the respondent emphasizing its political aspects and so regarding it as unsuitable for adjudication. As already noted, a court can decide such a case, notwithstanding the conflict of characterization, but does so by isolating the legal element, thereby effecting a 'depoliticization' which the parties were unable to achieve consensually.

The point just made is critical because it means that although courts and tribunals are competent to deal with disputes which present legal issues, however complex their political background, the party whose concerns are with the non-legal elements of the dispute may be unwilling to accept the decision. This clearly limits the contribution which adjudication can make to the resolution of international disputes in practice. It is also why appreciating the interaction of legal and political processes is so vital and why, when describing the WTO system, we noticed the role of consultation and the need for trade rules which all States can regard as legitimate. It is not enough to have courts and tribunals capable of

---

[48] For discussion of the cases in which this point has been made, including the *Diplomatic Staff in Tehran* case and the *Nicaragua* case, see Merrills, 2011, Ch 7.

[49] For discussion of the 1993 *Genocide* case and earlier cases in which this point has been made see Merrills, 2011, Ch 10.

[50] For discussion of the *Lockerbie* cases which raised this point see Akande, 1997; White, 2002, pp 119–30; Merrills, 2011, Ch 10.

handing down legal decisions. Persuading States to use them, and making their decisions effective, are problems grounded in the political context.

IV. INTERNATIONAL ORGANIZATIONS AND DISPUTE SETTLEMENT

A. REGIONAL ORGANIZATIONS

The reference in the Manila Declaration to 'resort to regional agencies or arrangements' relates to bodies such as the Organization of American States (OAS), the African Union (AU), formerly the Organization of African Unity (OAU), NATO, and the EEC, which are recognized in Article 52(2) of the UN Charter as relevant to the settlement of local disputes.[51] There is no reference in the Declaration's list to the UN's own procedures, although these are covered in some detail in later provisions which, as well as mentioning the ICJ, deal also with the Security Council and the General Assembly. Thus the Declaration acknowledges the role of international political organizations in dispute settlement at both the regional and universal levels.

One of the main functions of regional organizations is to provide governments with opportunities for diplomatic contact in a structured setting. Although such contact serves many purposes, it is something which may be particularly useful when there are disputes between member States because it can provide them with an opportunity to discuss their differences when tension may have disrupted normal communication. Such contact, moreover, is by no means restricted to the speech-making and formal proceedings of the organization, but also includes behind the scenes activity where the real work is often done. Indeed, informal contact of this kind may well be more valuable for parties with a dispute since it enables other States to use their influence without having to take a public position.

Negotiations, whether formal or informal, are the basic method of dealing with disputes, but, as noted earlier, may benefit from the presence of an outsider to encourage the dialogue and keep it going, or to make an independent contribution. Regional organizations provide opportunities for both good offices and mediation, as may be seen, for example, in the OAU which frequently provided these services in disputes between African States (Maluwa, 1989) and the EU which attempted mediation during the break-up of Yugoslavia. Some of these efforts, including the last, were unsuccessful, but then mediation, it will be recalled, is about facilitating negotiations, not imposing solutions.

More formal than mediation are the other diplomatic methods—inquiry and conciliation—and these too can be used by regional organizations. Inquiry, as we have seen, is essentially a fact-finding exercise, whereas conciliation involves presenting the parties with specific recommendations. Both processes need an individual or a commission to do the necessary fact-finding or conciliation and the two can sometimes be combined. In 1929, for example, the Conference of American States established a body called the Chaco Commission to investigate a dispute between Bolivia and Paraguay and to make proposals for a settlement. This involved both inquiry and conciliation and the Commission produced recommendations which the parties accepted, so demonstrating the value of this type of initiative (Bar-Yaacov, 1974, pp 199–211). So far we have really been considering

---

[51] On the role of regional organizations in general see Fawcett and Hurrell, 1995 and in relation to disputes specifically Merrills, 2011, Ch 11.

ways in which disputes can be handled *through* regional organizations, rather than ways in which they can be handled *by* them. Negotiation and the other diplomatic methods are all processes which States can, and often do, employ on their own initiative without involving a regional organization at all. This does not make such organizations irrelevant because they may provide the spur to make things happen. It does, however, prompt the question whether there is action in relation to disputes which only organizations can take. Is there, in other words, a contribution from regional organizations that is uniquely their own?

The answer is yes, as may be seen from the following examples. First, a collective declaration of policy, such as the OAU's 1964 Declaration on respecting African boundaries,[52] can both reduce the likelihood of disputes and provide a basis for dealing with them when they arise. Secondly, though the powers of regional organizations are subject to international law and not unlimited, in some circumstances they are entitled to impose sanctions on a recalcitrant member.[53] And thirdly, regional organizations can play a role in international peacekeeping,[54] or in support of action by the Security Council under Chapter VII of the Charter. Such measures show how collective action may be used to pursue goals not open to States acting separately and the variety of ways in which regional organizations may be involved in international dispute settlement.

B. THE UNITED NATIONS

Article 1 of the UN Charter sets out the purposes of the UN which are: to maintain international peace and security; to develop friendly relations among nations; to achieve international cooperation in solving problems of an economic, social, cultural, or humanitarian character and in promoting human rights; and to be a centre for harmonizing the actions of States in attaining these ends. These are inter-related purposes, but the maintenance of international peace and security occupies a primary place, the UN having a responsibility to bring about cessation of conflict whenever it occurs and to assist the parties to international disputes to settle their disputes by peaceful means. Clearly, then, dealing with disputes is a central function of the Organization according to the Charter.[55]

How is this to be done? The Charter assigns a key role to the Security Council and gives it the relevant powers in Chapter VI, which is wholly concerned with the peaceful settlement of disputes. Although the Council may make recommendations with a view to the settlement of any dispute, if all the parties so request, and under Article 34 can investigate any dispute or threatening 'situation', its general competence is limited to disputes 'the continuation of which is likely to endanger the maintenance of international peace and security'. It is therefore clear that although Article 2(3) imposes a quite general obligation on member States to settle disputes by peaceful means, only the more serious disputes, or those which may become serious, are regarded as the Council's concern.

The particular role of the Security Council is further emphasized in Article 33(1) which provides that the parties to a dispute within its remit should 'first of all' seek a solution by negotiation or another peaceful means of their own choice, and Article 52(2),

---

[52] See on the declaration Zartman, 1991. Another example is the adoption in 1991 of a common policy on recognition towards the States of Eastern Europe by the members of the EU on which see Warbrick, 1992.

[53] For an example see Macdonald, 1963–4, pp 367–72.

[54] For a general survey see McCoubrey and Morris, 2000. An interesting illustration of such activity is provided by the operations carried out by the Commonwealth of Independent States (CIS) in several parts of the former Soviet Union, which are described by Webber, 1996.

[55] From the vast literature on the UN the following relate specifically to the issues discussed in the text: Peck, 1996; White, 1997; Merrills, 2011, Ch 10.

which provides that members of regional arrangements or agencies 'shall make every effort to achieve peaceful settlement of local disputes' through such arrangements or agencies before referring them to the Security Council. However, despite these priorities, the Council has the right under Article 36(1) to recommend appropriate procedures at any time. Moreover, its authority to consider these issues comes from the relevant provisions of the Charter. Thus, unlike a court of arbitration or conciliation commission, the Security Council does not require the consent of the States concerned in order to become involved.

A final point to make about Chapter VI is that the provisions in this part of the Charter, which are all concerned with encouraging States to use peaceful methods of settlement, need to be read alongside those of Chapter VII, which give the Security Council power to impose sanctions. The structure of the Charter can therefore be seen as designed first and foremost to help States with their problems, but in the last resort to back this up with coercive measures in disputes or situations which lead to a 'threat to the peace, breach of the peace or act of aggression'. How well this has worked in practice is another matter, but in theory at least the Charter equips the Security Council with enforcement powers to use when they are needed.

Because the Charter envisages the Security Council playing the main role in UN dispute management, there is nothing as elaborate as Chapter VI or Chapter VII conferring powers on the General Assembly or Secretary-General. However, these organs too are given a role. Thus the General Assembly has broad powers of discussion and recommendation under Articles 10 to 14. These are wide enough to cover, for example, the recommendation of 'measures for the peaceful adjustment of any situation, regardless of origin, which it deems likely to impair the general welfare or friendly relations among nations' (Article 14), although this provision, like others relating to the General Assembly, is subject to Article 12, which preserves the primacy of the Security Council.

The role of the Secretariat is set out in Articles 98 and 99 of the Charter which, though brief, are very important. Article 98 speaks of the Secretary-General performing secretarial (ie administrative) functions for the General Assembly, the Security Council, and the other principal organs and performing 'such other functions as are entrusted to him by these organs'. Under this provision, then, tasks relating to disputes and other matters may be delegated to the Secretariat. Article 99, on the other hand, refers to the Secretary-General bringing 'to the attention of the Security Council any matter which in his opinion may threaten the maintenance of international peace and security'. Here therefore the Secretary-General is given a power of initiative which, as will be seen, has proved highly significant.

C. THE CHARTER SYSTEM IN PRACTICE

The UN is often criticized for failing to solve the world's problems and the validity of this criticism, at least in relation to disputes, is something we must consider. Before doing so, however, something should be said about what the UN has been able to achieve, beginning with the work of the political organs. As noted earlier, both the General Assembly and the Security Council are entitled to make recommendations and both organs have used this power extensively, to try to calm disputes, to urge the use of particular methods, or in some cases to recommend specific terms for a settlement. As these are merely recommendations, they can be, and often are, ignored. On the other hand, such UN involvement has the effect of bringing diplomatic pressure to bear and is sometimes helpful in providing States which may be locked on a collision course with a way out of their difficulty.

It was pointed out earlier that the existence of regional organizations stimulates negotiation by bringing States together in a setting where diplomatic contact is easy and can be encouraged by others. The UN functions in a similar way with the advantage that at the UN diplomacy is possible not just among States which are neighbours, but on a worldwide scale. Providing a setting for diplomatic contacts is useful in itself, but it is often possible to go further and use the Organization's own machinery to facilitate negotiations. One rather formal method is to appoint a committee of selected member States to assist negotiations, as was done for discussions on Indonesia's independence in 1947. Another is to use individuals as mediators or conciliators, which has been one of the Secretariat's most significant activities.

The contribution which fact-finding can make to the resolution of certain types of disputes has also already been mentioned. This too is a matter on which the UN may be able to help and there are many examples of the Security Council or the General Assembly creating subsidiary organs for this purpose.[56] As we have seen, this is something which the States concerned could do for themselves utilizing the inquiry procedure of the Hague Conventions, but this requires the parties to agree and by the time a dispute reaches the UN it is usually plain they are not going to do so. The Organization's contribution is therefore to fill this gap by promoting the necessary investigation, in an attempt to bring the parties closer together.

If the political organs cannot help directly, or do not wish to do so, they can refer a dispute to another body, a regional organization, for example, or another UN organ. So long as it is not merely a way of evading responsibility (as it can sometimes be), passing a dispute on in this way may be a desirable step. A case in point is legal disputes, which Article 36(3) says should 'as a general rule' be referred to the International Court. The General Assembly and the Security Council may also ask the Court for advisory opinions and this power is potentially very important in disputes like that in the *Western Sahara* case[57] which involve decolonization or other UN policies. Accordingly, the Court responded positively to the requests from the General Assembly for advisory opinions on the effects of Kosovo's declaration of independence and on the legal consequences of Israel's construction of a security barrier in the occupied Palestinian territory.[58] It cannot be said, however, that the political organs use the Court as often as they might with the result that opportunities to engage it in their work have been somewhat neglected.

The political organs, and the Security Council in particular, though active in the ways described, have frequently been slow to act; however, the same cannot be said for the Secretary-General, whose work under Articles 98 and 99 has often formed the main, or even the only element in a UN response (Chesterman, 2007). As regards Article 98, one of the most important contributions has been to provide good offices and mediation when the authorizing organ perceives a need to help the parties with negotiations (Franck and Nolte, 1993; Skjelsbaek and Fermann, 1996). In such cases introduction of the Secretary-General as a neutral third party, supported by the Security Council or the General Assembly can be a constructive move. Among the many examples of such involvement are the Secretary-General Waldheim's creation of a fact-finding and conciliation

---

[56] For a review of early UN practice, see Plunkett, 1968–9. For recent practice see White and Saul, 2010.

[57] *Western Sahara, Advisory Opinion, ICJ Reports 1975,* p 12. See also the *Namibia* case, *Legal Consequences for States of the Continued Presence of South Africa in Namibia (South West Africa) notwithstanding Security Council Resolution 276 (270), Advisory Opinion, ICJ Reports 1971,* p 16.

[58] *Accordance with International Law of the Unilateral Declaration of Independence in Respect of Kosovo, Advisory Opinion, ICJ Reports 2010,* and *Legal Consequences of the Construction of a Wall in the Occupied Palestinian Territory, Advisory Opinion, ICJ Reports 2004,* p 136.

commission, together with the provision of good offices, in the Diplomatic Hostages crisis of 1979, and the good offices of Secretary-General Boutros-Ghali, following the invasion of Kuwait in 1990.

The powers of initiative possessed by the Secretary-General under Article 99 have been interpreted broadly which has made this provision just as important in practice as Article 98. Consequently, a similar range of activities has been undertaken. It is important to appreciate, however, that even when exercising initiative under Article 99, the Secretary-General has always been careful to coordinate his work with that of the political organs, especially the Security Council (Perez de Cuellar, 1993). This underlines the point that the primary responsibility for making the UN system work lies with the member States. If they fail to play their part it is pointless expecting the Secretary-General to fill the gap and blaming him when things go wrong. The Secretary-General has a key role, but cannot carry the whole burden of dispute management for the UN.

D. THE VALUE AND LIMITATIONS OF ORGANIZATIONS

Enough has been said to indicate that political organizations can make a useful contribution to the management and resolution of international disputes. However, various factors which can limit their activity must now be noted. To take regional organizations first, one very obvious limitation is that they are unlikely to be very effective in disputes which cross regional boundaries, ie in disputes between States from different regions. Another, no less significant, limitation is that regional organizations are often reluctant to become involved in disputes within States, for example, civil wars and other internal conflicts. A further limitation is that most regional organizations lack resources and so may simply be unable to undertake the more expensive kinds of institutional activities such as peacekeeping.

Turning to the UN, its involvement in disputes has tended to reflect the extent to which the major States have seen UN action as something which is in their interests. This means that in many disputes there has been little UN involvement, or its contribution has been only marginal. Where the UN has been involved, the record underlines the point made at the beginning about the need to manage international disputes when they cannot be settled. Not many disputes have been settled through the UN, compared with the large number which have been managed, in the sense of being dealt with in some way, through the Organization's processes. This is particularly clear in the case of peacekeeping operations, for example, which have almost always been concerned with stabilizing situations, so as to create conditions in which other processes can be used.

To see why all this is so is to begin to understand the nature and limitations of the UN system. The Organization is a reflection of the social and political relations of States. Although constructive steps have sometimes been taken, effective action is usually possible only insofar as States are prepared to relinquish claims to exclusive control and seek assistance. When things become sufficiently serious, a UN presence or other initiative may be acceptable, but unless what is wanted is simply a face-saving arrangement, settling the basic problem is likely to be much more difficult. As a consequence, in very many cases prophylactic measures may be all that is politically possible, yet the fact that a festering dispute remains unresolved will be accounted another failure of the Organization.

In *An Agenda for Peace*,[59] his 1992 report to the Security Council, Secretary-General Boutros-Ghali examined the potential of the UN in the fields of preventive diplomacy,

---

[59] SC Doc S/24111, 17 June 1992. Text in (1992) 31 ILM 953.

peacekeeping, peacemaking, and post-conflict peacebuilding. The report described what the Secretary-General saw as the contribution which regional organizations could make to resolving disputes, emphasizing, as might be expected, that they must act in a manner consistent with the Charter and that the Security Council has primary responsibility for maintaining international peace and security. However, provided these constitutional limitations are respected, regional action could lighten the Security Council's burden and 'contribute to a deeper sense of participation, consensus and democratization in international affairs'.[60]

As the Secretary-General indicated, cooperation between regional organizations and the UN is particularly useful in situations which call for peacekeeping forces or related action and recent events have demonstrated how institutions can perform complementary functions when the political atmosphere is favourable. In the complex situation in Central America in the 1980s, for example, the main diplomatic work was carried out through the regional Contadora process, but when security arrangements were needed, a UN force (ONUCA) was established by the Security Council (White, 1993, pp 226–7). Similarly, in the Liberian crisis of 1990 peacekeeping forces were supplied by the local sub-regional organization (ECOWAS) and subsequently supported both politically and on the ground by the UN (White, 1996, pp 217–19). It is scarcely necessary to add that cooperation between organizations presents many difficulties and is not a panacea. But if there is still far to go before we can speak of a global-regional peacemaking system, what *An Agenda for Peace* calls 'this new era of opportunity',[61] makes it worth working for.

The Charter, as already noted, puts the Security Council at the centre of the collective security system. It was therefore fitting that following the controversial invasion of Iraq in 2003, which lacked explicit authorization from the Council, Secretary-General Kofi Annan established a High Level Panel to bring forward new ideas on collective security, including a re-evaluation of the role of the principal organs of the UN (Slaughter, 2005). The Panel's report,[62] which appeared in 2004, adopted a radical approach, proposing, among other steps, that the Security Council should employ five criteria to guide its decisions on the use of force. In response, the Secretary-General produced his own report, *In Larger Freedom: Towards Development, Security and Human Rights for All*,[63] in which he largely endorsed the Panel's conclusions. However, the UN World Summit in September 2005 did not support the five criteria, although another of the Panel's proposals, the concept of a 'responsibility to protect' was accepted (Gray, 2007). Collective security is, of course, only one aspect of dispute settlement. Likewise, the prominence of the Security Council in this field should not prevent the potential of other organs from being recognized. The report of the High Level Panel and the response of the Secretary-General are nonetheless important for both their content and as a reminder of how hard it can be to secure political support for institutional changes.

One final point. Institutions exist to help with disputes which States are incapable of dealing with themselves. It follows that these will tend to be the more difficult cases and it should be no surprise if even moderate success is often elusive. However, whether a dispute is referred to an organization or not, the primary responsibility remains with the governments concerned. Organizations are valuable and worth improving, but institution building is no more a substitute for responsible behaviour internationally, than it is in domestic affairs.

---

[60] Ibid, para 64.   [61] Ibid, para 63.
[62] *A More Secure World: Our Shared Responsibility*, UN Doc A/59/565.   [63] UN Doc A/59/2005.

V. CONCLUSION

International law requires States to resolve their disputes peacefully and the primary means available for them to do so remains negotiation, sometimes assisted by good offices and mediation from third parties, and including today new forms of diplomacy associated with the ever-expanding role of international organizations. With the introduction of inquiry and conciliation we find third party assistance formalized in processes which provide the benefit of independent findings or recommendations, but with no prior commitment to accept the result. The non-binding character of these methods means they should be thought of more as ways of moving a dispute forward than of settling it, but their value and flexibility may be seen in international practice.

States which are prepared to relinquish control over their disputes can reap the additional advantages of judicial settlement or arbitration. Legal means, including the dispute settlement system of the WTO, and an increasing number of specialized courts, provide a way of obtaining binding decisions for individual cases, or whole classes of disputes. Moreover, access to such procedures need not, as hitherto, be confined to States, but is now sometimes available to international organizations, companies, or individuals. Important as they are, however, courts and tribunals are not suitable for all disputes and even when available, may not always be utilized, or be effective. Thus legal methods must be seen in their political context.

Organizations are also important. However, the UN is not a world government, but essentially a body through which pressure and influence can be exerted on States when their disputes come before the Organization. Of course, many disputes never reach the UN, while many of those that do remain unsettled. Regional organizations can sometimes help by providing a diplomatic forum, or involving regional neighbours in the capacity of mediators or conciliators. There is also now the possibility of combining regional action with action by the UN. In both fora though, institutional action will often be less important in practice than the parties' own initiatives. Organizations, then, bring new possibilities, but for much of the time are no more than a further arena in which the sovereign State can exercise its traditional power to settle, or not to settle, its international disputes.

No student of current affairs needs to be told that dispute settlement is a subject on which the gulf between rhetoric and reality is conspicuously wide. All too often governments express support for general propositions like those to be found in the UN Charter, the Declaration on Friendly Relations, and the Manila Declaration, only to follow quite different precepts in their international behaviour. But realism is not cynicism and any dispassionate observer must recognize that since the landmark 1899 Hague Convention enormous progress has been made in refining the methods available for resolving international disputes and in developing States' obligations. The challenge for the twenty-first century is to see that current arrangements, which unquestionably provide the means for dealing with disputes, continue to be used in international practice.

REFERENCES

AKANDE, D (1997), 'The International Court of Justice and the Security Council: Is there Room for Judicial Control of Decisions of the United Nations?', 46 *ICLQ* 309.

ANDO, N, McWHINNEY, E, and WOLFRUM, R (eds) (2002), *Liber Amicorum Judge Shigeru Oda* (The Hague: Kluwer).

BAR-YAACOV, N (1974), *The Handling of International Disputes by Means of Inquiry* (Oxford: Oxford University Press).

BERCOVITCH, DJ and RUBIN, JZ (eds) (1992), *Mediation in International Relations* (London: St Martin's Press).

BERCOVITCH, J (ed) (1996), *Resolving International Conflicts: The Theory and Practice of Mediation* (London: Lynne Rienner).

BROWER, CN (1998), *The Iran-United States Claims Tribunal* (The Hague: Kluwer).

CHESTERMAN, S (ed) (2007), *Secretary or General? The UN Secretary-General in World Politics* (Cambridge: Cambridge University Press).

CHINKIN, C (1998), 'Alternative Dispute Resolution under International Law', in Evans, MD (ed), *Remedies in International Law: The Institutional Dilemma* (Oxford: Hart Publishing), p 123.

CHURCHILL, RR (1997), 'Falkland Islands: Maritime Jurisdiction and Co-operative Arrangements with Argentina', 46 *ICLQ* 463.

COLLIER, J and LOWE, AV (1999), *The Settlement of Disputes in International Law* (Oxford: Oxford University Press).

COT, J-P (1972), *International Conciliation* (London: Europa).

CRAWFORD, J and NEVILL, P (2012), 'Relations between International Courts and Tribunals The "Regime Problem"', in Young, MA (ed), *Regime Interaction in International Law* (Cambridge: Cambridge University Press), p 260.

DENG, FM and ZARTMAN, IW (eds) (1991), *Conflict Resolution in Africa* (Washington, DC: The Brookings Institute).

EVANS, MD (1991), 'The Restoration of Diplomatic Relations between Argentina and the United Kingdom', 40 *ICLQ* 473.

—— (ed) (1998), *Remedies in International Law: The Institutional Dilemma* (Oxford: Hart Publishing).

FAWCETT, L and HURRELL, A (eds) (1995), *Regionalism in World Politics* (Oxford: Oxford University Press).

FRANCK, TM and NOLTE, G (1993), 'The Good Offices Function of the Secretary-General', in Roberts, A and Kingsbury, B (eds) (1993), *United Nations, Divided World. The UN's Roles in International Relations*, 2nd edn (Oxford: Clarendon Press), p 143.

FREEDMAN, L and GAMBA-STONEHOUSE, V (1990), *Signals of War: The Falklands Conflict of 1982* (London: Faber & Faber).

FRENCH, D and KIRKHAM, R (2010), 'Complaint and Grievance Mechanisms in International Dispute Settlement', in French, D, Saul, M, and White, ND (eds) (2010), *International Law and Dispute Settlement* (Oxford: Hart Publishing), p 57.

FRENCH, D, SAUL, M, and WHITE, ND (eds) (2010), *International Law and Dispute Settlement* (Oxford: Hart Publishing).

GOWLLAND GUALTIERI, AN (2001), 'The Environmental Accountability of the World Bank to Non-State Actors: Insights from the Inspection Panel', 72 *BYIL*, 213.

GRAY, C (2007), 'A Crisis of Legitimacy for the UN Collective Security System?', 56 *ICLQ* 157.

—— and KINGSBURY, B (1992), 'Developments in Dispute Settlement: Inter-State Arbitration since 1945', 63 *BYIL* 97.

GREENBERG, MC, BARTON, JH, and McGUINESS, ME (eds) (2000), *Words over War. Mediation and Arbitration to Prevent Deadly Conflict* (Lanham, Md.: Rowman and Littlefield).

KLEIN, N (2005), *Dispute Settlement in the UN Convention on the Law of the Sea* (Cambridge: Cambridge University Press).

KOOPMANS, SMG (2008), *Diplomatic Dispute Settlement* (The Hague: TMC Asser Press).

KOUFA, KK (1988), 'International Conflictual Situations and their Peaceful Adjustment', 18 *Thesaurus Acroasium* 7.

LAUDY, M (2000), 'The Vatican Mediation of the Beagle Channel Dispute', in Greenberg, MC, Barton, JH, and McGuiness, ME (eds) (2000), *Words over War. Mediation and Arbitration to Prevent Deadly Conflict* (Lanham, Md.: Rowman and Littlefield), p 293.

LOWE, V (2012), 'The Function of Litigation in International Society', 61 *ICLQ* 209.

—— and WARBRICK, C (eds) (1994), *The United Nations and the Principles of International Law* (London: Routledge).

MCCOUBREY, H and MORRIS, J (2000), *Regional Peace-keeping in the Post Cold War Era* (The Hague: Kluwer).

MACDONALD, RStJ (1963–4), 'The Organisation of American States in Action', 15 *University of Toronto LJ* 359.

MALUWA, T (1989), 'The Peaceful Settlement of Disputes among African States, 1963–1983: Some Conceptual Issues and Practical Trends', 38 *ICLQ* 299.

MERRILLS, JG (1994), 'The Principle of Peaceful Settlement of Disputes', in Lowe, AV and Warbrick, C (eds), *The United Nations and the Principles of International Law* (London: Routledge), p 49.

—— (2002), 'The Optional Clause at Eighty', in Ando, N, McWhinney, E, and Wolfrum, R (eds), *Liber Amicorum Judge Shigeru Oda* (The Hague: Kluwer), p 435.

—— (2007), 'The Mosaic of International Dispute Settlement Procedures: Complementary or Contradictory?', 54 *Netherlands ILR* 361.

—— (2009), 'Does the Optional Clause Still Matter?', in Kaikobad, KH and Bohlander, M (eds) (2009), *International Law and Power. Perspectives on Legal Order and Justice* (Leiden: Martinus Nijhoff).

—— (2011), *International Dispute Settlement*, 5th edn (Cambridge: Cambridge University Press).

—— and ROBERTSON, AH (2001), *Human Rights in Europe*, 4th edn (Manchester: Manchester University Press).

MULLER, AS, RAIC, D, and THURANSZKY, JM (eds) (1997), *The International Court of Justice* (The Hague: Kluwer).

OSTRIHANSKY, R (1988), 'Chambers of the International Court of Justice', 37 *ICLQ* 30.

PALMETER, D and MAVROIDIS, PC (2004), *Dispute Settlement in the World Trade Organization. Practice and Procedure* 2nd edn (Cambridge: Cambridge University Press).

PASQUALUCCI, JM (2003), *The Practice and Procedure of the Inter-American Court of Human Rights*, (Cambridge: Cambridge University Press).

PAULSON, C (2004), 'Compliance with Final Judgments of the International Court of Justice since 1987', 98 *AJIL* 434.

PECK, C (1996), *The United Nations as a Dispute Settlement System* (The Hague: Kluwer).

PEREZ DE CUELLAR, J (1993), 'The Role of the UN Secretary-General', in Roberts, A and Kingsbury, B (eds) (1993), *United Nations, Divided World. The UN's Roles in International Relations*, 2nd edn (Oxford: Clarendon Press), p 125.

PETERSMANN, E-U (1997), *The GATT/WTO Dispute Settlement System* (Dordrecht: Kluwer).

PLUNKETT, EA (1968–9), 'UN Fact-Finding as a Means of Settling International Disputes', 9 *Virginia JIL* 154.

RICHARDSON, EL (1988), 'Jan Mayen in Perspective', 82 *AJIL* 443.

ROBERTS, A and KINGSBURY, B (eds) (1993), *United Nations, Divided World. The UN's Roles in International Relations*, 2nd edn (Oxford: Clarendon Press).

SCHULTE, C (2004), *Compliance with Decisions of the International Court of Justice* (Oxford: Oxford University Press).

SCOTT, KN (2010) 'Non-Compliance Procedures and Dispute Resolution Mechanisms under International Environmental Agreements' in French, D, Saul, M, and White, ND (eds) (2010), *International Law and Dispute Settlement* (Oxford: Hart Publishing), p 225.

SHANY, Y (2003), *The Competing Jurisdictions of International Courts and Tribunals* (Oxford: Oxford University Press).

—— (2012), 'Assessing the Effectiveness of International Courts: A Goal-Based Approach', 106 *AJIL* 225.

SICK, G (1985), 'The Partial Negotiator: Algeria and the US Hostages in Iran', in Touval, S and Zartman, IW (eds), *International Mediation in Theory and in Practice* (Boulder, Colo.: Westview Press), p 21.

SIMPSON, JL and Fox, H (1959), *International Arbitration: Law and Practice* (London: Stevens).

SKJELSBAEK, K and FERMANN, G (1996), 'The UN Secretary-General and the Mediation of International Disputes', in Bercovitch, J (ed), *Resolving International Conflicts: The Theory and Practice of Mediation* (London: Lynne Rienner), p 75.

SLAUGHTER, AM (2005), 'Security, Solidarity and Sovereignty: The Grand Themes of UN Reform', 99 *AJIL* 619.

TOUVAL, S and ZARTMAN, IW (eds) (1985), *International Mediation in Theory and in Practice* (Boulder, Colo.: Westview Press).

UMBRICHT, V (1984), 'Principles of International Mediation. The Case of the East African Community', 187 *Hague Recueil des Cours* 307.

WARBRICK, C (1992), 'Recognition of States', 41 *ICLQ* 473.

WEBBER, M (1996), 'Coping with Anarchy: Ethnic Conflict and International Organisations in the Former Soviet Union', 13(1) *International Organisation* 1.

WHITE, ND (1993), *Keeping the Peace* (Manchester: Manchester University Press).

—— (1996), *The Law of International Organisations* (Manchester: Manchester University Press).

—— (1997), *Keeping the Peace*, 2nd edn (Manchester: Manchester University Press).

—— (2002), *The United Nations System* (London: Lynne Rienner).

—— and SAUL, M (2010), 'Legal Means of Dispute Settlement in the Field of Collective Security. The Quasi-Judicial Powers of the Security Council', in French, D, Saul, M, and White, ND (eds) (2010), *International Law and Dispute Settlement* (Oxford: Hart Publishing), p 191.

YOUNG, MA (ed) (2012), *Regime Interaction in International Law* (Cambridge: Cambridge University Press).

ZARTMAN, IW (1991), 'Conflict Reduction: Prevention, Management and Resolution', in Deng, FM and Zartman, IW (eds) (1991), *Conflict Resolution in Africa* (Washington, DC: The Brookings Institute), p 320.

FURTHER READING

COLLIER, J and LOWE, AV (1999), *The Settlement of Disputes in International Law* (Oxford: Oxford University Press). A wide-ranging survey with the focus on institutions and procedures for dealing with disputes involving individuals, corporations, and other non-State actors, as well as States.

FRENCH, D, SAUL, M, and WHITE, ND (eds) (2010), *International Law and Dispute Settlement* (Oxford: Hart Publishing). A collection of essays which focuses

upon the growth of the various legal methods for handling international disputes. Ranging from key conceptual issues such as proliferation and the associated risks of fragmentation through to innovations in dispute settlement mechanisms in many topical areas of international law, including international trade law, environmental law and collective security law.

MERRILLS, JG (2011), *International Dispute Settlement*, 5th edn

(Cambridge: Cambridge University Press).
A review of dispute settlement in its legal
and political context, explaining what techniques and institutions exist for dealing
with disputes involving States, how they
work and when they are used, and
containing many practical examples.

PECK, C (1996), *The United Nations
as a Dispute Settlement System* (The
Hague: Kluwer). A comprehensive study of
the characteristics of the UN system from
a dispute settlement perspective with some
perceptive observations about its potential
for further development.

20

THE INTERNATIONAL COURT OF JUSTICE

Hugh Thirlway

SUMMARY

The International Court of Justice, the principal judicial organ of the UN, is a standing tribunal to which States may bring their disputes, and which is empowered to give advisory opinions to UN organs and specialized agencies. Its jurisdiction derives from the consent of the States parties to the case, which may be given either directly in respect of a specific dispute, or in advance in respect of a defined class or category of disputes; the Statute of the Court also provides for acceptance of a general 'compulsory' jurisdiction by simple declaration, which may, however, be subject to reservations. Decisions of the Court, given after an extensive written and oral procedure, are binding on the parties in respect of the case, but not otherwise.

I. INTRODUCTION

The International Court of Justice (ICJ) is often referred to in non-technical contexts as the 'World Court', but this is perhaps misleading. Such an appellation may suggest the international equivalent of a national supreme court, a body of worldwide jurisdiction, empowered to pass judgment on the legal rights and duties of all States from a position of superiority and supervision. No such tribunal, however, exists. The International Court can better be seen as a standing mechanism available for the peaceful settlement of disputes between States, to the extent that they wish to make use of it. No dispute can be the subject of a decision of the Court unless the States parties to it have consented to the Court's jurisdiction over that specific dispute, or over a class of disputes of which that dispute is one. Access to the Court is enjoyed by all members of the UN, but its 'compulsory jurisdiction' (also a somewhat misleading term) is accepted by only a fairly small number of States, and for the most part with reservations that limit effective jurisdiction to certain classes of dispute.

The Court is defined in the UN Charter (Article 92) as the 'principal judicial organ' of the Organization, but here also the term 'judicial' simply serves to distinguish the role of the Court from that of the political organs, the General Assembly and Security Council. It does not signify that the Court enjoys, within the Organization, any position resembling that of the supreme court or constitutional court of a State. It has, for example, no overriding power to interpret the Charter, and the question whether it is entitled to examine the legality of a decision adopted by one of the other principal organs is controversial.[1]

Despite these limitations, the Court has an important role to play in the maintenance of international peace through the settlement of disputes, and in the development of international law. Its function is defined by its Statute (Article 38) as being 'to decide, in accordance with international law, such disputes as are submitted to it'. It is further empowered to give advisory opinions on legal questions at the request of the Security Council or the General Assembly; subject to certain limitations (to be examined later in this chapter), such opinions may also be requested by other organs and agencies authorized by the General Assembly.

II. HISTORY

The present Court was established by the UN Charter, and came into existence with the election of the first members in February 1946. It was, however, created as the successor to the Permanent Court of International Justice (PCIJ), established pursuant to Article 14 of the Covenant of the League of Nations in 1921, and was modelled closely on that body.

The move towards the creation of a standing international judicial body came as the culmination of the trend, throughout the nineteenth and early twentieth centuries, to make increasing use of arbitration as a means of settling international disputes. (The development of arbitration, its operation, and its advantages and disadvantages, are dealt with in Merrills, Ch 19 of this book.) Two practical problems, however, stood in the way of implementing proposals for the establishment of such a permanent body. When an existing dispute was taken to arbitration, the arbitrators were appointed by the States parties to the dispute (or by a third party nominated by them), and the expenses of the arbitration were borne by the parties. If a standing tribunal were set up to try *future* disputes, how were its judges to be appointed, and how should it be financed? The Permanent Court of Arbitration, created in 1899, had gone some way to meet the difficulty, by establishing a large panel of potential arbitrators from among whom States could make a choice for a particular dispute, and by establishing a small standing secretariat, but this did not amount to a true court. With the creation of the League of Nations, it became possible to set up a system of election of members of the new Court by the League Council and Assembly, and for the expenses of the Court to be met out of the budget of the League.

It was originally hoped that the new Court would have a status approximating to that of a 'World Court' as described in the preceding paragraphs, and in particular that it would have universal compulsory jurisdiction, at least over members of the League. This proved over-optimistic; the new Court's jurisdiction had to be the subject of general acceptance, and it was too much to expect States to give a new and untried body such a wide mandate. Jurisdiction could be conferred ad hoc by agreement, or accepted by treaty in advance for defined categories of disputes; and the 'optional clause' of Article 36(2) of the PCIJ Statute, whose operation will be explained later, went as far as was possible for the time in the direction of compulsory jurisdiction.

The history of the Permanent Court during the inter-war period was generally a satisfactory one; it gave a number of judgments and advisory opinions, some on matters of

---

[1] The question has been debated before the Court in the cases of the *Aerial Incident at Lockerbie* (*Libya* v *United Kingdom, Libya* v *United States*), but the cases were discontinued by agreement before the Court had ruled on the point.

acute political or legal delicacy, and its operation inspired increasing confidence. The fact of its existence was also a force for peaceful settlement, since the possibility that a dispute might be brought before it, with the attendant publicity, was an inducement to reach a negotiated settlement. However, although it was not formally an organ of the League, its fortunes were bound up with those of the League; and the paralysis of the League caused by the outbreak of the Second World War had already impeded the Court's work even before the German invasion of the Netherlands, where the Court had its seat, brought it completely to a halt.

The Allies' plans for a new post-war international organization included provision for a judicial body; the possibility of keeping the Permanent Court in being was considered, but it was thought better to let it disappear with the League of Nations, and set up a new Court to continue its work. However, the new International Court of Justice was not only to take over the premises and archives of the pre-war Court, but also, so far as possible, to inherit its jurisdiction. Numerous treaties had been concluded providing for settlement of disputes by the Permanent Court; the Statute of the new Court provided that, as between parties to that Statute, such treaties should be read as referring to the new Court.[2]

III. STRUCTURE AND COMPOSITION

The Court consists of 15 judges, elected by the Security Council and the General Assembly (voting separately) for terms of nine years; the elections are staggered so that five judges complete their terms of office every three years. A judge may be re-elected (and this has frequently occurred), but the system thus ensures that a regular renewal of the Bench is possible, while at the same time preserving continuity. Judges are elected as individuals, not as representatives of their countries, and are required to make a solemn declaration in open court of impartiality in the exercise of their functions. Article 16 of the Statute requires that they do not engage in any other occupation 'of a professional nature' during their period of office.[3]

No two members of the Court may be of the same nationality.[4] The Statute (Article 9) directs that the election be such as to ensure the representation of 'the main forms of civilization and of the principal legal systems of the world'. There is no official allocation of seats on this (or any other) basis, but it is a long-standing convention that the candidate of each of the permanent members of the Security Council will always be elected, and the other seats are unofficially distributed between various regions of the world.

The salaries of the judges, and the other expenses of the Court, are borne by the UN, as part of the regular budget. The seat of the Court is at The Hague, in the Peace Palace, where the Court occupies premises under an agreement between the UN and the Carnegie

---

[2] Similarly, pre-war 'optional clause' jurisdiction was preserved, so far as possible: see n 22 in this chapter. These provisions of the Statute did not specifically regulate the position of States parties to the Statute of the Permanent Court who did not become members of the UN, and thus parties to the Statute of the new Court, until many years after the Permanent Court had ceased to exist. For the handling of lacunas of this kind, see *Temple of Preah Vihear, Preliminary Objections, ICJ Reports 1961*, p 17; *Barcelona Traction, Light and Power Company, Preliminary Objections, ICJ Reports 1964*, p 6.

[3] During a period when the Court had few cases before it, it became accepted that a Member of the Court could properly sit as an arbitrator, or member of an arbitral tribunal. Some concern may be felt that this practice has continued, notwithstanding the fact that the number and size of the cases being handled by the Court would suggest that the full participation of every Member is now continuously required.

[4] But a judge ad hoc (see later) may have the same nationality as an elected member of the Court.

Foundation, the owner of the building. The President of the Court (elected triennially by his or her colleagues) is to 'direct the work and supervise the administration of the Court' (Rules, Article 12). The day-to-day administration of the Court is the responsibility of the Registry, headed by a Registrar, elected by the Court for a seven-year term.

Cases are heard by the full Court unless the parties to a case agree that it shall be heard by a chamber of the Court (see later). A judge is not required to withdraw if a case is brought by the State of which he is a national; on the contrary, he is bound to sit in all cases before the full Court, unless there are special reasons, other than the mere fact of nationality, why it would be inappropriate for him to sit. (If, however, the President of the Court is a national of one of the parties to a case, he does not preside in the case, but hands over the presidency to the Vice-President or senior judge.) The disqualification or withdrawal of a judge from a case is dealt with by Articles 17 and 24 of the Statute: the commonest reason for exclusion is that the judge has, prior to his election, already been involved in the case, for example, as having advised one of the parties.

The possible presence on the Bench of a judge of the nationality of one of the parties was seen, when the Statute was drafted, as suggestive of inequality, despite the fact that members of the Court are required to act impartially. This view is defended on the ground that the presence of a 'national judge', even one bound to decide impartially, is still valuable for ensuring justice for the State of which he is a national, since he can ensure that the case presented by his country is fully understood. Rather than requiring withdrawal of the judge in such circumstances, the Statute ensures equality by enabling the other party to a case of this kind to nominate a person to sit as judge solely for that case, with the title of judge ad hoc.[5] The Statute also provides, consistently with the idea of the benefit of a 'national judge', that in a case where neither party has a judge of its nationality on the Bench, and thus there is no inequality between the parties, each party still has the right to choose a judge ad hoc. In such cases, the parties, however, quite often agree that neither of them will exercise this right.

Elected members of the Court not infrequently vote against the State of their nationality, but to date judges ad hoc have nearly always voted in favour of the State that appointed them; and it is often too much to expect that they should do otherwise.

In addition to certain standing chambers (in practice virtually never used),[6] a chamber may be formed by the Court to deal with a specific case, if the parties so request. The number of judges to constitute such a chamber is determined by the parties, but the individual judges to be members of it are elected by the Court, and the composition of the chamber is thus, theoretically, outside the control of the parties. In practice, however, it has become accepted that if the parties indicate that certain names would be acceptable, the Court is virtually certain to elect them, if only because the creation of a chamber composed otherwise than as desired by the parties would be likely to result in the case being withdrawn and referred to some other method of settlement.[7]

---

[5] There is, however, no requirement that the judge ad hoc be of the nationality of the party appointing him, and this is frequently not the case. For an analysis of the function of a judge ad hoc, see the dissenting opinion of Judge ad hoc Franck in the case of *Sovereignty over Pulau Ligitan and Pulau Sipadan*, *ICJ Reports 2002*, p 625, paras 9–12, quoting the Separate Opinion of Judge ad hoc Elihu Lauterpacht in the *Application of the Convention on the Prevention and Punishment of the Crime of Genocide, Provisional Measures, Order of 13 September, ICJ Reports 1993*, p 325, at pp 408–9, paras 4–6.

[6] The experience with special chambers suggests that the reason for the neglect of the standing chambers is probably that their composition is determined in advance by the Court, and the parties have no say in it.

[7] The first request for a special chamber, by the USA and Canada in the *Gulf of Maine* case, was made pursuant to a treaty which provided explicitly that the case would be transferred to arbitration if the Chamber was not formed as the parties wished. Subsequent approaches to the Court have been more tactful.

Reference of a case to a special chamber of the Court, a procedure long neglected, became more popular between 1984 and 2002, but may now be in decline.[8] To some extent the use of chambers makes for greater flexibility and thus tends toward speedier settlement of cases; but simultaneous operation of two chambers is only practicable for this purpose if no member of one chamber is also a member of the other. In tribunals where the chambers are established by the tribunal itself, as sub-units (eg the International Criminal Tribunal for the Former Yugoslavia and the International Criminal Court), this can be arranged; but where the membership of chambers is in effect left to the parties to determine, experience shows that overlapping membership is often inevitable. The use of chambers has thus not appreciably accelerated the procedure of the International Court.

IV. PROCEDURE

The procedure before the Court is regulated primarily by its Statute. Under Article 30 of the Statute the Court has power to make rules 'for carrying out its functions', including rules of procedure. The Rules of Court adopted in 1946 were modelled closely on those drawn up by the Permanent Court; they were revised in part in 1972, and more radically in 1978. Further revisions of detail have been effected in more recent years. The Court has recently found it useful to regulate detailed matters of procedure in a more informal way, by issuing 'Practice Directions' interpreting and implementing the Statute and Rules. The hierarchy of norms is of course that Practice Directions cannot be inconsistent with the Rules or the Statute, and the Rules cannot depart from the Statute.[9] Generally, the extent to which the broad lines of the procedure laid down in the Statute of the Permanent Court, and in the Rules adopted by that body, have been found satisfactory and thus maintained, is a tribute to the work of the jurists of the inter-war period. The official languages of the Court are French and English.

The proceedings in contentious cases are set in motion in one of two ways. If the parties have concluded an agreement (*compromis* or special agreement) to bring the dispute before the Court, the case begins with the notification of this to the Court. If not, one State may file an application instituting proceedings against another State, and the Registrar communicates this to that State. In either event, all other States entitled to appear before the Court are notified of the institution of proceedings. The procedure thereafter represents something of a blend of the continental system of extensive written pleadings, and the Anglo-American common law system in which the hearing, the 'day in court', is the essential element. In a first stage, the parties exchange written pleadings (Memorial by the applicant, Counter-Memorial by the respondent; in some cases followed by a Reply (applicant) and a Rejoinder (respondent), but these additional pleadings are now exceptional). There then follows a series of hearings, which in the past might take up several weeks, but are usually limited to a few days, at which the parties address their arguments to the Court in the same order: a presentation by the applicant, followed by a presentation by the respondent, and a much briefer 'second round' devoted to refutation of the opponent's

---

[8] The following cases have been decided by chambers: *Gulf of Maine* (1984); *Frontier Dispute (Burkina Faso/Mali)* (1986); *Elettronica Sicula* (1989); *Land, Island and Maritime Frontier Dispute* (1992); *Application for Revision of the Judgment of 11 September 1992 in the Land, Island and Maritime Frontier Dispute* (2003); *Frontier Dispute (Benin/Niger)* (2005).

[9] For an example of a challenge to a provision in the Rules on the ground that it was inconsistent with the Statute, see the dissenting opinion of Judge Shahabuddeen in the *Land, Island and Maritime Frontier Dispute, (El Salvador/Honduras), Application to Intervene, Order of 28 February 1990, ICJ Reports 1990*, p 3 at pp 18ff.

contentions. When the case is brought by special agreement, rather than by a unilateral application filed by one State against another, neither party is, strictly speaking, in the position of applicant or respondent; the order of speaking is determined by the Court, taking into account the views of the parties.[10] The hearing is open to the public, and is usually broadcast on the Court's website and the UN television channel; the Court has power to hold a closed hearing (Statute, Article 46), but has done so only on two occasions.[11] The written pleadings are normally made available to the public (in particular, on the Court's website) at the time of the opening of the oral proceedings (Rules, Article 53(2)), and transcripts (and a videocast) of the hearings are also available.

Evidence is normally submitted in the form of documents, though it may of course take other forms (eg photographs, physical objects); witnesses may give written evidence, or appear at the hearing to give their evidence orally, in which case they may be cross-examined by the other party. The procedure in this respect is modelled broadly on Anglo-American practice. Hearsay evidence does not carry weight;[12] and in the case of *Military and Paramilitary Activities in and against Nicaragua* the Court expressed some reservations as to the value of evidence of government ministers and other representatives of a State, who could be taken to have some personal interest in the success of their government's case.[13]

The burden of proof of fact, in accordance with general procedural principles, rests upon the party alleging the fact. In accordance with the principle *iura novit curia* (the law is known to the Court), the parties are not required to prove the existence of the rules of international law that they invoke; the Court is deemed to know such rules. An exception to this is where a party relies on a customary rule which is not one of general law (local or special custom): in this case, the party must 'prove that this custom is established in such a manner that it has been binding on the other Party'.[14] In practice, particularly where the existence of a particular rule of general law is controversial, States will devote much argument to demonstrating that it does, or does not, exist, citing the facts of State practice in support.

The sources of international law to be applied by the Court, enumerated in Article 38 of the Statute, have been discussed in Chapter 4 of this book: international treaties and conventions; international custom; general principles of law; and the subsidiary sources, ie decisions of tribunals[15] and opinions of jurists.

The decision of the Court is adopted by majority vote; a judge is not permitted to abstain. The President of the Court has a casting vote in the event of a tie. Every judge has the right to append to the decision an individual statement of his views, normally entitled 'separate opinion' if he agrees in the main with the decision, or 'dissenting opinion' if he does not (the term 'declaration' is also used). Until 1978, the way in which a judge had voted would not become public unless he chose to attach such an opinion; but the revised Rules of Court adopted in that year provided that in future the decision would indicate

---

[10] The order of speaking is different in proceedings on preliminary objections or requests for the indication of provisional measures; these proceedings are explained later.

[11] *South West Africa, Pleadings, Oral Arguments, Documents*, Vol VIII, p 4; *Legal Consequences for States of the Continued Presence of South Africa in Namibia (South West Africa) Notwithstanding Security Council Resolution 276 (1970) Pleadings, Oral Arguments, Documents*, Vol II, p 3. In the latter case, the verbatim record of the closed sitting was later made public (ibid).

[12] Cf *Corfu Channel, Merits, Judgment, ICJ Reports 1949*, p 4 at pp 16–17; *Military and Paramilitary Activities in and against Nicaragua (Nicaragua v USA), Merits, Judgment, ICJ Reports 1986*, p 42, para 68.

[13] Ibid, para 70.

[14] *Asylum, Judgment, ICJ Reports 1950*, p 266 at p 276. For the distinction between general and special custom, see Thirlway, Ch 4 of this book, Section II B.

[15] For the treatment by the Court of its own decisions, see Section VII of this chapter.

not only the numbers of the votes on each side, but also the names of the judges voting for and against.

V. THE COURT'S JURISDICTION

Emphasis has already been laid on the fact that the jurisdiction of the Court, like that of any international judicial or arbitral body, is based upon the consent of States. The application of this principle is, however, complicated as a result of the fact that the Court is a permanent institution.

In the first place, the Court is a treaty-based institution, created and regulated by the UN Charter and the Statute of the Court (which is in fact an 'integral part' of the Charter: see Article 92); this means that the general scope of its jurisdiction, and the conditions of its exercise, are defined *ne varietur* by those instruments. Jurisdiction in this sense, relating to access to the Court, and to the general nature of the powers it possesses, is thus a function of the will of the body of States parties to the Charter and Statute, not of the will of the specific parties to a given dispute. The consent of the parties to the dispute cannot therefore abrogate or modify statutory provisions of this kind;[16] it is in fact those provisions that determine how, for example, the necessary consent may be given for the creation of jurisdiction in specific cases.

Secondly, the jurisdiction of the Court may be, and frequently is, asserted on the basis of treaty instruments of a general nature conferring future jurisdiction over a range or category of disputes. When the instrument was concluded, no such disputes may yet have been in existence, but the possibility that such might arise will have been foreseen, and consent given in advance to the binding determination of them by the Court. When a dispute is subsequently brought before the Court on the basis of a clause of this kind, that advance consent creative of jurisdiction is still operative (assuming that the treaty has not been denounced), but it may well not be accompanied, at the time that the matter is brought to the Court, by actual contemporary consent or willingness to have that particular dispute settled by decision of the Court. The respondent State may therefore seek to deny that the general consent given in the past applies to the specific dispute, because, for example, it does not really fall within the category of disputes contemplated, or because any conditions attached to it have not been met in the specific case. The Court, in order to be satisfied that consent to its dealing with the dispute has actually been given, will have to analyse, in sometimes painstaking detail, the provisions of the relevant instruments in order to trace a link between the consent given, often in wide general terms, by the respondent and the facts of the particular case. The principle remains simple: has the respondent State given consent to jurisdiction? Its application may, however, involve much subtle and complex argument.

A. JURISDICTION: STRUCTURAL LIMITATIONS

The most basic limitation on the Court's jurisdiction is that provided in Article 38 of the Statute: 'Only States may be parties to cases before the Court'. The reference is of course to

---

[16] Discussing Article 35, para 2, of the Statute, the Court has observed that 'it would have been inconsistent with the main thrust of the text to make it possible in the future for States to obtain access to the Court simply by the conclusion between themselves of a special treaty…': *Legality of the Use of Force (Serbia and Montenegro v Belgium), Judgment, ICJ Reports 2004*, p 319, para 102.

sovereign States in the sense of the principal category of subjects of international law, and excludes the component States of federations, for example. A case could not be brought by or against a non-State entity, such as an individual, a non-governmental organization, or a multinational, even if the other party were a State and consented to the case being brought.[17] Nor can an intergovernmental international organization (not even the UN itself) be a party, though the major ones are empowered to ask the Court for advisory opinions.

To be a party to a case, a State must also be one of those to which the Court is 'open', or having 'access' to the Court, under Article 35 of the Statute. The principal category of States with such access is that of parties to the Statute of the Court (Article 35(1)); this category automatically includes the members of the UN.[18] There is also provision, in Article 93(2) of the UN Charter, for a State to become a party to the Statute without joining the UN, but the quasi-universal membership of the UN has made this practically obsolete.[19] The application of these requirements is normally simple, inasmuch as it is generally evident at the outset of a case whether the parties are States, and States having access to the Court;[20] and if one of them is not, then the case cannot proceed, even with the consent of the other party. If for example an individual attempts to bring a case before the Court (as frequently

---

[17] The position is apparently different in advisory proceedings, in which there are strictly speaking no 'parties': cf the participation by Palestine in the case concerning *Legal Consequences of the Construction of a Wall in the Occupied Palestinian Territory*, ICJ Reports 2004, p 136, para 4; Order of 17 October 2008 in the case of *Accordance with International Law of the Unilateral Declaration of Independence by the Provisional Institutions of Self-Government of Kosovo*. The Court has also indicated in Practice Direction XII that where an international non-governmental organization submits a statement in advisory proceedings, while 'it is not to be considered part of the case-file', the Court may refer to it as 'a publication readily available', and it may thus be referred to by, and before, the Court.

[18] UN Charter, Article 93, para 1. Paragraph 2 of Article 35 of the Statute contains an obscure reference to 'the special provisions contained in treaties in force'. At the provisional measures stage of the *Bosnia v Yugoslavia* case, the Court took the view that this might authorize proceedings against a State which was not a party to the Statute and had not complied with the conditions laid down by the Security Council: *Application of the Convention on the Prevention and Punishment of the Crime of Genocide, Provisional Measures, Order of 8 April 1993*, ICJ Reports 1993, p 3, paras 18–19. The Court, however, took the opposite view in the NATO cases: see for example *Legality of the Use of Force (Serbia and Montenegro v Belgium), Judgment*, ICJ Reports 2004, p 279, paras 113–14.

[19] Article 93(2) of the Charter provides that the conditions for this are to be laid down by the General Assembly, on the recommendation of the Security Council. Furthermore, under Article 35(2) of the Statute, the Security Council is empowered to lay down the conditions on which other States not parties to the Statute may have access to the Court. Security Council Resolution 9 (1946) implements this provision, and provides for the deposit with the Secretary-General of a declaration accepting the jurisdiction of the Court and undertaking to comply with its decisions.

[20] An exception is the case of the *Application of the Convention on the Prevention and Punishment of the Crime of Genocide*. Following the break-up of the former Socialist Federal Republic of Yugoslavia, for a time the new Republic of Yugoslavia (Serbia and Montenegro) was treated by the UN as the successor of the old Yugoslavia, and on that basis it was made respondent to the proceedings before the Court. On 1 November 2002, however, after the Court had indicated certain provisional measures in the case, and had given judgment dismissing certain preliminary objections, the new Yugoslavia was admitted to the UN as a new member. Yugoslavia filed an Application for Revision of the Court's judgment on the preliminary objections on the basis that this admission showed that it had not previously been a party to the Statute. The Court, however, dismissed the Application on the ground that this event was not a 'new fact' within the meaning of Article 61 of the Statute (see Section VI C of this chapter). The question then arose again in the cases brought by Yugoslavia against 10 member States of NATO: at a late stage in the proceedings, Yugoslavia withdrew its claim to have been a party to the Statute (and to the Genocide Convention) and invited the Court 'to decide on its jurisdiction'. The Court ruled that Yugoslavia had not been a member of the UN when its Application was filed, and consequently declined jurisdiction: *Legality of the Use of Force*, eight judgments dated 15 December 2004.

happens), the Registrar draws his attention to the provisions of Article 38, and no further action is necessary.

A similar limitation is imposed by the provisions of the Statute concerning the nature of the Court's judgment, which is 'final and without appeal'. The Court cannot, even at the request of the parties, give a provisional or conditional judgment (though it can give a declaratory judgment, confined, for example, to certain aspects of a dispute). For example, parties to a case before the Permanent Court of International Justice requested the Court to give an informal and non-binding indication of how it was minded to decide, so that they could negotiate a settlement on that basis; but the Court declined, on the basis that it had no power to give a ruling of this kind, which would be dependent for its implementation on the wishes of the parties.[21]

B. JURISDICTION IN PARTICULAR CASES

1. Special agreements and compromissory clauses

The simplest means of putting into effect the principle that jurisdiction is conferred on the Court by the consent of the parties is for two States that wish a dispute to be settled by the Court to enter into an agreement to that effect. This is the classic *compromis* or special agreement, used for many years prior to the establishment of the Court for the submission of a dispute to arbitration. Such an agreement will define the dispute and record the agreement of the parties to accept the Court's decision on it as binding—this last being theoretically unnecessary in view of the provisions of the Charter and Statute. It may also contain provisions as to the procedure to be followed (number and order of written pleadings, possibly waiver of the right to appoint judges ad hoc, etc). Normally no jurisdictional problems arise in a case brought before the Court by special agreement, since the consent of the parties is real and contemporaneous, rather than given in advance and in general terms.[22] When a special agreement has been concluded, the procedural step by which a case is brought before the Court—in technical language the 'seising' of the Court—is the notification of the agreement to the Court. Whether this is done by one party or by both parties jointly, the essence of a case of this kind is that it is a joint approach to the Court, not an action commenced by one party against the other.

Where jurisdiction is asserted on the basis of some instrument other than a special agreement, the Court is seised unilaterally, by an application, indicating the subject of the dispute and the parties. The applicant State claims that the other party to the dispute has in the past consented to settlement of disputes of a particular category being referred unilaterally to the Court for settlement, and that the current dispute falls into that category. In a case of this kind, the consent creative of jurisdiction will, according to the applicant, have been given in advance. It may take the form of a compromissory clause, that is to say a clause in a treaty providing that all disputes relating to the application or interpretation of the treaty may be brought by one or the other party before the Court by unilateral

---

[21] *Free Zones of Upper Savoy and the District of Gex, Order of 6 December 1930, PCIJ, Ser A, No 24*, at p 14. In a more modern case, however, concerning a treaty contemplating a complex project, which had not been completed, each party asserting breach of the treaty by the other, the Court decided (*inter alia*) that the parties 'must negotiate in good faith in the light of the prevailing situation, and must take all necessary measures to ensure achievement of the objectives' of the treaty: *Gabčíkovo-Nagymaros Project, (Hungary/Slovakia), Judgment, ICJ Reports 1997*, p 7, para 155(2)(c).

[22] There may, however, be limitations on the exercise of jurisdiction: see the *Monetary Gold Removed from Rome in 1943, Judgment, ICJ Reports 1954*, p 19; Section VII of this chapter.

application. Alternatively, the treaty itself may have been concluded for the purpose of making advance provision for the settlement by the Court of all disputes (or certain categories of disputes) that may subsequently arise between the parties: a treaty of judicial settlement (often combined with a treaty of friendship or commercial relations).

If a case is brought before the Court by unilateral application, there is thus normally a pre-existing title of jurisdiction in the form of a treaty between the parties of this kind, or in the form of acceptances of jurisdiction under the 'optional clause', to be discussed later. This does not mean, however, that an application that fails to specify such a pre-existing title is invalid; the Statute of the Court (Article 40) only requires an application to specify 'the subject of the dispute and the parties', and the Rules of Court (Article 38(2)) only require that it indicate 'as far as possible' the basis of jurisdiction relied on. Consequently, an application may be made which in effect invites the State named as respondent to consent to jurisdiction simply for the purposes of that particular case, a process known as *forum prorogatum*. At one time this possibility was being abused for political ends, applications being made simply for publicity purposes against States whose known attitude to judicial settlement made it certain that no such consent would be forthcoming. As a result, a special provision (Article 38(5)) was included in the Rules of Court in 1978 whereby an application of this kind is treated for procedural purposes as ineffective until the consent of the named respondent is forthcoming—usually it is not, but in two recent cases, both brought against France, following applications on this basis, France later gave its consent to ad hoc jurisdiction.[23] *Forum prorogatum* can in theory also result from the simple participation in the proceedings of a respondent State which has not previously accepted jurisdiction, but only if such participation amounts to 'an unequivocal indication' of acceptance of jurisdiction in a 'voluntary and indisputable' manner.[24]

2. The 'optional clause' system

At the time of the drafting of the Statute of the Permanent Court in 1920, it was first envisaged that the new Court would have universal compulsory jurisdiction, in the sense that any State party to the Statute could bring before the Court, by unilateral application, any dispute whatever with another State party to the Statute. The necessary consent conferring jurisdiction would thus be given simply by accession to the Statute. However, as noted earlier, it was soon realized that the majority of States were not ready for so radical an innovation, and the optional clause system was devised as being the furthest that it was then possible to go in the direction of compulsory jurisdiction. This system was carried over, without change of substance, into the Statute of the post-war Court, and it is in that context that it will be examined here.[25]

Under Article 36(2) of the Statute, a State may deposit with the UN Secretary-General a declaration that it accepts the jurisdiction of the Court for disputes in respect of all or

---

[23] See *Certain Criminal Proceedings in France (Republic of the Congo v France)*, (2003), which was later withdrawn (see *Certain Criminal Proceedings in France (Republic of the Congo v France), Order of 16 November 2010, ICJ Reports 2010*, p 635) and *Certain Questions of Mutual Assistance in Criminal Matters (Djibouti v France), Judgment, ICJ Reports 2008*, p 177; see paras 39–43 and 63–95 for the complications involved in ascertaining the precise extent of such jurisdiction.

[24] *Armed Activities on the Territory of the Congo (New Application: 2002) (Democratic Republic of the Congo v Rwanda), Jurisdiction and Admissibility, Judgment, ICJ Reports 2006*, p 6, paras 19–22.

[25] Article 36(5) of the Statute of the post-war Court preserves, as between parties to that Statute, any declarations of acceptance of jurisdiction made under the PCIJ Statute: cf *Military and Paramilitary Activities in and against Nicaragua (Nicaragua v USA), Jurisdiction and Admissibility, Judgment, ICJ Reports 1984*, p 392, para 14. (See also n 2 in this chapter.)

some of a number of matters enumerated in Article 36 (in effect, all international legal disputes), 'in relation to any other State accepting the same obligation'. The intended effect of this was that those States that were ready to accept compulsory jurisdiction could do so among themselves, while other States would have to rely on obtaining the consent ad hoc of any State with which they might have a dispute, if that dispute were to be brought before the Court. There would be two classes of 'clients' of the Court, those within the 'optional clause' system and those outside it. This simple vision became complicated, however, as a result of the recognition by Article 36 of the possibility of making reservations to an optional clause declaration. Specifically, the reservations foreseen were 'a condition of reciprocity on the part of several or certain States' and acceptance 'for a certain time'. The simplicity of the system was already compromised by this facility; but the question soon arose whether any *other* reservations were effective (eg the exclusion of disputes of a specified type, or of disputes arising before or after a specified date). No reservation was challenged before the Permanent Court as being unauthorized by the Statute, and the inclusion of reservations became standard State practice. The prevailing view became that, since a State was free to decide to accept or not to accept the optional clause jurisdiction in its entirety, it was also free to accept it subject to whatever reservations it saw fit to make.[26]

Furthermore, Article 36(2) of the Statute employed the term 'reciprocity', and provided for acceptances of jurisdiction 'in relation to any other State accepting *the same obligation*'. If a State which had made a reservation to its acceptance brought proceedings against a State which had made none, was the jurisdiction of the Court affected by the reservation? The Permanent Court held that it was; that the respondent State could invoke the applicant State's reservation, or to put it another way, that the Court's jurisdiction was defined by the narrower of the two acceptances.[27] Some of the cases concern reservations that must necessarily operate bilaterally, for example the reservation limiting jurisdiction to disputes arising after a certain date: if a dispute arises after such date for one party to it, then it must equally do so for the other.[28] A more striking example of the application of this principle is afforded by the *Certain Norwegian Loans* case, in which the reservation made by France, the applicant, excluding disputes within the domestic jurisdiction of France could be turned against it by Norway, the respondent, so as to exclude a dispute on the ground that it was within the domestic jurisdiction of Norway.[29]

The consequence was that, instead of the simple system of universal compulsory jurisdiction within a limited group of States, foreseen by the draftsmen of the Statute, the

---

[26] See the statement in the report of Subcommittee IV/1/D of the San Francisco Conference that drafted the Statute of the post-war Court: UNCIO, vol 13, pp 391, 559. The League Assembly had taken the view as early as 1928 that reservations were not limited to those specifically contemplated in the Statute: see the resolution of the Assembly quoted in *Aerial Incident of 10 August 1999 (Pakistan v India), Jurisdiction, ICJ Reports 2000*, p 12, para 37.

[27] *Electricity Company of Sofia and Bulgaria, Judgment, 1939, PCIJ, Ser A/B, No 77*, p 64 at p 81; see also *Certain Norwegian Loans, Judgment, ICJ Reports 1957*, p 9 at p 24. For a fuller examination of the problem, see Thirlway, 1984.

[28] See, eg the Orders on provisional measures in the cases concerning the *Legality of Use of Force*, brought by Yugoslavia against the member States of NATO: eg *Yugoslavia v Belgium, Provisional Measures, Order of 2 June 1999, ICJ Reports 1999*, p 124, paras 22ff.

[29] *Certain Norwegian Loans, Judgment, ICJ Reports 1957*, p 9: the reservation was in fact of the 'Connally' type (see later). Cf also the *Aegean Sea Continental Shelf, Judgment, ICJ Reports 1978*, p 3, where a reservation made by Greece (applicant) excluding matters of the 'territorial integrity' of Greece applied to exclude a matter concerning the territorial integrity of Turkey (respondent), though this case related, not to Article 36(2) of the Statute, but to the 1928 General Act for the Pacific Settlement of International Disputes.

jurisdiction of the Court under Article 36(2) became a complex network of bilateral relationships. The fact that two States have each made a declaration of acceptance no longer signifies that any dispute between them can be brought by either of them unilaterally before the Court, unless both acceptances are entirely without reservations. If that is not so, it is necessary to find the lowest common denominator of the jurisdiction *not* excluded by reservations on each side, and consider whether the particular dispute falls within it.

Another disruptive development, though one that has now more or less passed out of use, was the invention of the 'self-judging' reservation, designed to retain control of the extent of the jurisdictional obligation in the hands of the State making the declaration. In the form pioneered by the USA, and known as the 'Connally reservation', this was a reservation excluding matters within the domestic jurisdiction of the reserving State *as determined by the reserving State.* This reservation apparently enabled the reserving State to declare, even after the Court had been seised of a dispute on the basis of the optional clause declaration, that the dispute was a matter of domestic jurisdiction, and that the Court had therefore no jurisdiction. It was generally felt that a reservation of this kind was objectionable as being incompatible with the system of Article 36, and in particular with the principle of the *compétence de la compétence* stated in Article 36(6) (see later), but the Court nevertheless gave effect to the reservation. It has been convincingly argued that to rule that the reservation was invalid would lead to the consequence that the whole declaration of acceptance was invalid, so that the reserving State would still be able to escape the jurisdiction of the Court.[30]

There is, however, nothing illicit about attaching even extensive reservations to an acceptance of jurisdiction. The Court has had occasion to emphasize the 'fundamental distinction between the acceptance by a State of the Court's jurisdiction and the compatibility of particular acts with international law'.[31] The fact that a reservation to an optional clause declaration excludes jurisdiction over acts of which the legality may be doubtful does not render the reservation invalid; the reservation may have been made specifically because there is doubt about the matter, and this does not mean that the reserving State is claiming a licence to commit wrongful acts with impunity. This is another application of the principle that, since a State is free not to accept the jurisdiction of the Court at all, it must also be free to decide for itself what limitations it will impose on such acceptance as it does consent to make.

C. JURISDICTION AND ITS EXERCISE

In principle, if the Court finds that it has jurisdiction to entertain a particular case, it is under a duty to exercise that jurisdiction, to the extent that it has been conferred and to the extent of the claims of the parties before it (the rule *ne ultra petita*). In a few cases, the Court has, however, found that, even before inquiring into the existence of jurisdiction, it sees reasons for not exercising it. One example of a category of cases of this kind is

[30] See *Certain Norwegian Loans, Judgment, ICJ Reports 1957*, p 9, Separate Opinion of Judge Lauterpacht, p 34 at pp 56ff. This was on the basis that it would not be proper to 'sever' the reservation from the acceptance, since to do so would be to impose on the State concerned an obligation that it had clearly not consented to accept. The European Court of Human Rights, on the basis of a virtually identical provision in its constituent instrument, has, however, taken a different view on this point: see *Belilos v Switzerland*, Judgment of 29 April 1988, Ser A, no 132; 10 *EHRR* 418, and *Loizidou v Turkey (Preliminary Objections)*, Judgment of 23 March 1995, Ser A, no 310, 20 *EHRR* 99.

[31] *Fisheries Jurisdiction (Spain v Canada), Jurisdiction of the Court, Judgment, ICJ Reports 1998*, p 432, para 55.

where to decide the case would involve deciding the legal situation of a State not a party to the case (the *Monetary Gold* principle, examined further in Section VII of this chapter). Another is where any judgment given would be ineffective, because the legal situation is such that the decision would have no 'forward reach',[32] or because the claims of the applicant have in effect been satisfied, so that the case has become 'without object' or 'moot'.[33] Since a refusal to exercise jurisdiction would normally be a renunciation of the very function of the Court, these cases are, however, highly exceptional.[34]

D. VERIFICATION OF JURISDICTION AND ADMISSIBILITY: PRELIMINARY OBJECTIONS

A well-established principle of the law relating to international arbitral and judicial proceedings is that a tribunal (arbitral or judicial) has power to decide, with binding effect for the parties, any question as to the existence or scope of its jurisdiction.[35] This principle is known as that of the *compétence de la compétence*, the jurisdiction to decide jurisdiction. It is in fact inherent in the concept of consensual jurisdiction: if a party, having consented to dispute-settlement by a third party, were then to claim the right to determine for itself the extent of the third party's jurisdiction, it would be in effect withdrawing the consent given.

The principle is stated as applicable to the Court by Article 36(6) of the Statute: 'In the event of a dispute as to whether the Court has jurisdiction, the matter shall be settled by the decision of the Court'. The text makes it clear that if the two parties agree on the extent of jurisdiction, the Court can and must accept that agreement (provided the question is one of consensual jurisdiction—see earlier); and that the decision of the Court on a jurisdictional question is binding on the parties.[36] The matter is, however, not merely one of application of the Statute: the principle of the *compétence de la compétence* is a general one, which would operate even if Article 36(6) were not included in the Statute.[37]

The Court must exercise this power in any case in which the existence of its jurisdiction is disputed. It is not merely debarred from *deciding* a case in which the parties have not conferred jurisdiction upon it by consent: it may not even entertain it, that is to say begin to receive written or oral argument upon it. The existence of a special agreement will of course guarantee jurisdiction; in the case of an application, the ground of jurisdiction relied on will normally be indicated (and if it is conceded that there is no pre-existing jurisdiction, the case will not proceed, as explained earlier). Sometimes the attitude of the respondent State in disputing jurisdiction is fully justified: the applicant State may be trying to extend a limited acceptance of jurisdiction by its opponent to cover a dispute of a kind that was never contemplated in the instrument relied on. Sometimes,

[32] *Northern Cameroons, Judgment, ICJ Reports 1963*, p 15 at p 37.

[33] *Nuclear Tests (Australia v France), Judgment, ICJ Reports 1974*, p 253, paras 55ff.

[34] When a point of this kind was raised in the cases concerning the *Aerial Incident at Lockerbie*, the Court declined to deal with it as a preliminary issue (and the cases were subsequently discontinued). See *Questions of Interpretation and Application of the 1971 Montreal Convention arising from the Aerial Incident at Lockerbie (Libyan Arab Jamahiriya v United Kingdom), Preliminary Objections, Judgment, ICJ Reports 1998*, p 9, paras 46–50.

[35] It even extends to ruling on a claim that the tribunal itself has no legal existence: see the decision of the Appeals Chamber of the ICTY in *Prosecutor v Dusko Tadić, Decision on the Defence Motion for Interlocutory Appeal on Jurisdiction (Interlocutory Appeal)*, Case No IT-94-1-AR72 (2 October 1995).

[36] Note that the matter is 'settled' by a 'decision', and under Article 59 of the Statute the decision has 'binding force' for the parties in respect of that particular case.

[37] Consequently it is equally applicable in advisory proceedings: cf the PCIJ advisory opinion on *Interpretation of the Greco-Turkish Agreement of December 1 1926, PCIJ Ser B, No 16*, p 20.

on the other hand, the respondent is trying to evade its obligation to accept settlement of the dispute by the Court because the ruling, or even any discussion of the matter before the Court, is likely to cause political embarrassment. The Court has also indicated that if the jurisdictional issue is one that cannot be waived by agreement of the parties (tacit or otherwise), then it is 'one which the Court is bound to raise and examine, if necessary, *ex officio*'.[38]

A State named as respondent that considers that the case has been brought without a jurisdictional title will normally raise this at an early stage, and the usual procedure is to file a 'preliminary objection', defined by the Rules of Court as 'Any objection by the respondent to the jurisdiction of the Court or to the admissibility of the application, or other objection the decision upon which is requested before any further proceedings on the merits..' (Article 79(1)).[39] Such an objection is usually presented in response to the Memorial filed by the applicant (though it may be filed earlier). Objections to jurisdiction are of course denials that the respondent State ever gave its consent to the particular dispute being brought before the Court, or denials that the particular dispute falls within a category of disputes for which it did accept jurisdiction. Objections to admissibility are less easy to define, except negatively, as contentions that are neither matters of jurisdiction, nor questions of the merits. Examples are the contention that the applicant lacks *locus standi* (ie has no legally protected interest), that remedies available within the respondent State (local remedies) have not been exhausted; that the case is, or has become, 'without object' or moot; that the presence as a party of a third State is essential to the proceedings (see Section VII of this chapter), etc.

In accordance with the principle mentioned in this section, the effect of a preliminary objection is that the proceedings on the merits of the case (the actual dispute brought before the Court) are suspended (Rules, Article 79(3)), and will never be resumed if an objection to jurisdiction is upheld (some objections to admissibility may be 'curable' and make the continuation of the proceedings possible after certain steps have been taken). A separate phase of the proceedings is opened to deal with the objection: the applicant has the opportunity of responding in writing to the objection, in a pleading entitled 'Observations', and in the subsequent oral proceedings the respondent speaks first to present its objection, and the applicant replies. This is the application of a principle of procedural law, *in excipiendo reus fit actor* (by submitting an objection the defendant becomes the plaintiff). The Court may uphold an objection or reject it; but it may also 'declare that the objection does not possess, in the circumstances of the case, an exclusively preliminary character' (Article 79(7)). This possibility, introduced in the revision of the Rules of 1978, was at first somewhat obscure, but it is now clear that its effect is that the objection is not determined at the preliminary stage, but may be re-presented and re-argued along with the merits.[40]

---

[38] *Application of the Convention on the Prevention and Punishment of the Crime of Genocide (Bosnia and Herzegovina v Serbia and Montenegro), Judgment, ICJ Reports 2007*, p 43, para 122. The Court had, however, in that case not in fact done so, or at least not explicitly. Cf Article 79, para 8, of the Rules of Court.

[39] It was at one time unclear whether a State that failed to present a timely preliminary objection was to be taken to have renounced the objection; but in the *Avena* case the Court made it clear that 'a party failing to avail itself of the [preliminary objection] procedure may forfeit the right to bring about a suspension of the proceedings on the merits, but can still argue the objection along with the merits' (*Avena and other Mexican Nationals (Mexico v United States of America), ICJ Reports 2004*, p 12, para 24).

[40] See the Judgments on preliminary objections in the cases concerning *Questions of Interpretation and Application of the 1971 Montreal Convention arising from the Aerial Incident at Lockerbie (Libyan Arab Jamahiriya v United Kingdom) (Libyan Arab Jamahiriya v United States of America), ICJ Reports 1998*, pp 9, 115.

VI. OTHER INCIDENTAL PROCEEDINGS

A. REQUESTS FOR THE INDICATION OF PROVISIONAL MEASURES

The power of a tribunal to determine its own jurisdiction is one that belongs to all national judicial bodies, and its attribution to international judicial and arbitral organs is not in doubt. More controversial is the question whether the power, also enjoyed by most, if not all, municipal courts, to issue binding interim injunctions, that is to say directives requiring or prohibiting certain action pending settlement of the case before the court, is also a necessary and essential part of the armoury of international courts and of the International Court of Justice in particular. The Statute (Article 41) does in fact include a power of the Court to 'indicate, if it considers that circumstances so require, any provisional measures which ought to be taken to preserve the respective rights of either party'; the debate is therefore in this instance not about the existence of *some* power of this kind, but whether the measures so indicated create an obligation to respect them, binding on the States addressed. The wording of the Statute is, to say the least, ambiguous, inasmuch as it uses such mild terms as 'indicate' and 'measures which ought to be taken' (rather than 'direct' or 'order', and 'measures which shall be taken'); and the trend of the *travaux préparatoires* of the drafting of the PCIJ Statute is rather such as to suggest that, like universal compulsory jurisdiction, a power of the new Court to indicate binding measures at a preliminary stage may have been regarded as more than States were ready to accept. Some scholars have been ready to appeal to the idea that a power to indicate binding measures is bound up with the power to settle disputes by binding final decisions, and thus belongs in principle to all international judicial bodies; from this they conclude that the power conferred by Article 41 must be interpreted in this sense.

The question long remained unsettled; but in the *LaGrand* case, the Court decided that provisional measures addressed to the USA, which had not been complied with, had created a legal obligation, the breach of which gave rise to a duty of reparation, independently of the rights and duties of the parties in respect of the original dispute.[41] It did not, however, base this conclusion on any general principle, analogous to that of the *compétence de la compétence*, but on an interpretation of Article 41 as having been intended to achieve that result.[42] The finding that an Order indicating measures is binding has been welcomed in many quarters. However, it should not be overlooked that the fact that an Order (or, indeed, a Judgment) is binding on the parties does not ensure that it will in fact be complied with; and as explained later in this chapter (Section VII) there is no procedure for enforcement of decisions of the Court.

There is no doubt that the Court has incidental jurisdiction under Article 41 to indicate measures; but a question that has given rise to some difficulty is the relationship between this incidental jurisdiction and the jurisdiction of the Court to hear and determine the merits of the case in which measures are requested. The problem only arises at the international level, because of the principle that international jurisdiction rests on consent, and consent has therefore to be proved in each case. If an indication of measures is requested in a case in which the respondent State has already made it clear that it denies the existence of jurisdiction over the merits, what is the relevance of this circumstance to the exercise

---

[41] *LaGrand (Germany v United States of America), Merits, Judgment, ICJ Reports 2001*, p 466, paras 98ff.

[42] In the light of the *travaux préparatoires* and of the general trend of interpretation of the text in practice, this view of Article 41 may be regarded as somewhat revolutionary: see Thirlway, 2001, at pp 114ff.

of the power to indicate measures? At one extreme, it might be argued that if the Court has no jurisdiction to hear the case at all, then it has no power to indicate measures; at the other extreme, it might be said that, since Article 41 confers an independent power (and contains no reference to the question of merits jurisdiction), the Court could indicate measures, if it saw fit, in a case where it was very doubtful whether it had any jurisdiction over the merits, or even where it was almost certain that it had none.

The first view has the obvious defect that it tends to rob the provisional measures procedure of all meaning: if no measures can be indicated until the disputed question of merits jurisdiction has been thrashed out, then the measures cannot serve to meet the urgent needs that they were designed for.[43] The second view may, however, be seen as a threat to the principle of consensual jurisdiction, or even to the sovereign independence of States, if a State can be subjected to an order indicating measures that it is bound to comply with, in a case in which it asserts (justifiably, as it later turns out) that it has never consented to the Court having any jurisdiction at all.[44]

A middle solution has therefore become established in the jurisdiction of the Court: the possibility or probability of establishing jurisdiction over the merits is one of the factors to be weighed by the Court when considering whether to indicate measures. A number of different formulae has been employed to express this relationship. It is, however, clear that, on the one hand, the Court is not debarred from indicating measures by the existence of an objection to jurisdiction, even one which seems *prima facie* likely to be upheld; and on the other, that it is open to the Court to decline to indicate measures because there is a 'manifest lack of jurisdiction', or even a serious doubt as to the existence of merits jurisdiction. In some of the cases brought by Yugoslavia against members of NATO, the Court found, when examining the request for provisional measures, that it 'manifestly lack[ed] jurisdiction' to entertain the application instituting proceedings; it not only rejected the request for measures, but decided to remove the case from the list at that stage.[45] If the Court's eventual finding on jurisdiction contradicts the expectations on which its decision on provisional measures was founded, this will not retrospectively invalidate that decision: thus if it considers it justified to indicate measures on the basis of a likelihood of jurisdiction over the merits, a subsequent finding against jurisdiction will simply cause the measures to lapse, but they will have been valid until then.[46] If the Court refuses measures because of doubts as to jurisdiction, a subsequent finding upholding jurisdiction might justify a renewed request for measures, but the original refusal would not be undermined.

The purpose of the indication of provisional measures is, as stated in Article 41, 'to preserve the respective rights of either party'; and this has been understood to mean the

---

[43] This view was nevertheless put forward by dissenting judges in the *Nuclear Tests* case in 1974, but has not been heard of since.

[44] The difficulty is exacerbated by the ruling in *LaGrand* that the measures indicated constitute an independent legal obligation, one which exists even in face of a later finding of lack of jurisdiction, at least up to the moment that that finding is made. Provisional measures lapse when judgment on the merits is given, the obligations of the judgment being substituted for those under the measures. In the *Avena (Interpretation)* case, provisional measures were indicated forbidding the execution of five named individuals, and in its judgment refusing the Request the Court unanimously found that the execution of one of them had been a breach of the obligations of the USA under the provisional measures Order (see Judgment of 19 January 2009, para 61(2)).

[45] See, eg *Legality of Use of Force (Yugoslavia v United States of America), Provisional Measures, Order of 2 June 1999, ICJ Reports 1999*, p 916, para 29. Removal of a case from the list, without any decision even on jurisdiction, is an exceptional step, only taken in particular circumstances: see, eg *Legality of the Use of Force (Serbia and Montenegro v Belgium), ICJ Reports 2004*, p 279, para 33.

[46] See the 2009 decision on the Request for Interpretation in the *Avena* case.

rights that are in issue in the proceedings, and no others. Thus in a case concerning the formal validity of an arbitral award defining a maritime boundary, the Court declined to indicate measures directed to the conduct of the parties in the maritime areas concerned, since the only question before the Court was the validity or otherwise of the award, not the legal correctness of the boundary indicated.[47] However, in cases where measures were requested in the context of a request for interpretation of an earlier decision (where it might be thought that the only relevant rights were limited to obtaining an interpretation) the Court has shown itself ready to adopt a wider interpretation of its powers, especially where hostilities or other threat to human life was concerned.[48]

The indication of measures is an interlocutory measure justified by urgency: there must be a threat to the rights of a party that is immediate in the sense that the final decision in the case may come too late to preserve those rights. If therefore it is to be expected that the case will have been decided before irreparable injury is caused, no measures will be indicated.[49] The workload of the Court is currently such that this is a much less likely situation than in the past; and pending a decision the respondent may not better its legal position by making modifications to the status quo, of which the Court might thus, if it upheld the applicant's claim, order the reversal.

B. PARTIES: JOINDER OF CASES; INTERVENTION BY THIRD STATES

Contentious proceedings before the Court are normally brought either by two States jointly (by special agreement), or by one State against another (by application); in either case there are only two parties to the proceedings. It is, however, possible for two or more States to bring proceedings as joint applicants against another State. In practice, it has been more frequent for two States to bring independent proceedings against the same respondent; and the Court then has power, if it sees fit, to 'direct that the proceedings...be joined' (Rules, Article 47). The cases are then heard and determined together, by a single judgment; and the Court may 'direct that the written or oral proceedings...be in common'. A joinder of this kind was ordered in the two *South West Africa* cases (*Liberia v South Africa*; *Ethiopia v South Africa*), and in the two *North Sea Continental Shelf* cases (brought by two special agreements: *Denmark/Federal Republic of Germany*; *Netherlands/Federal Republic of Germany*). Joinder has, however, become less common: it was not ordered in the two *Fisheries Jurisdiction* cases (*UK v Iceland*; *FRG v Iceland*), the two *Nuclear Tests* cases (*Australia v France*; *New Zealand v France*), or in subsequent 'pairs' of cases.

Similarly, it is possible for a State to bring proceedings against two or more States as joint respondents, though this has never yet occurred. The legal claim of Nauru against Australia in the case of *Certain Phosphate Lands in Nauru* was in fact asserted also against New Zealand and the UK, who had constituted, jointly with Australia, the administering authority under a UN Trustee Agreement for Nauru; but Nauru did not choose to bring proceedings against all three States, probably because it was uncertain of being able to

---

[47] *Arbitral Award of 31 July 1989, Provisional Measures, Order of 2 March 1990, ICJ Reports 1990*, p 64.

[48] See the orders made in the *Avena (Interpretation)* and *Temple of Preah Vihear (Interpretation)* cases cited in n 59 in this chapter.

[49] When Finland complained that the construction by Denmark of a bridge over a particular seaway would block the passage of ships and thus prevent Finland from exercising its rights to pass through the seaway, the Court declined to indicate measures because the timetable for the bridge-works was such that there would be no interference with passage within the time likely to be required for the Court to decide the case: *Passage through the Great Belt, Provisional Measures, Order of 29 July 1991, ICJ Reports 1991*, p 12.

establish jurisdiction against the other two. The absence of the other two States was in fact raised by Australia as an objection to the admissibility of the claim, but the Court ruled it admissible.[50] In the two cases concerning the *Lockerbie* incident,[51] and the ten cases brought by Yugoslavia against the NATO States,[52] the contentions against each respondent in each set of cases were virtually identical, but the applicants nevertheless chose to bring parallel cases, and the Court did not see fit to join them.[53]

Where cases are brought in parallel in this way, but no formal joinder is effected, the Court does, for example, hold hearings in quick succession, deliberate on both cases, and issue several judgments on the same day; and the judgments are often identical in much of their reasoning and construction.

The choice of States to be parties is normally therefore in the hands of the State or States commencing proceedings; but it may happen that another State wishes to become involved in the case. The Statute provides two possibilities in this respect. Under Article 63, 'Whenever the construction [ie interpretation] of a convention to which States other than those concerned in the case are parties is in question' in a case, the other parties to the convention have to be notified, and may choose to intervene in the proceedings: however, it is provided that if they do so, the interpretation of the convention given by the Court will be binding upon them. Possibly as a result of this provision, the faculty of intervention under Article 63 has been very little used. In any event, the interpretation by the Court of a multilateral convention will enjoy authority beyond the parties to the case in which it is given.

Under Article 62, a State may request the Court to permit it to intervene in a pending case if it 'consider[s] that it has an interest of a legal nature which may be affected by the decision in the case'. One specific type of dispute has made intervention under this Article particularly attractive to third States. In a number of cases the Court was asked to rule on the delimitation of seabed areas in a dispute between two States, but in a geographical situation in which the possible rights or interests of other States might be infringed in some way—even if in strict law the decision of the Court would be *res inter alios acta* for those States. These cases showed that application of Article 62, which had long remained virtually unused, gives rise to a number of problems. First of all, what sort of interest is contemplated, and how may it be 'affected' by the decision, given that the judgment is only binding on the parties? Secondly, must the original parties agree to the intervention, and if not, does an objection on their part affect the matter? Thirdly, does the State permitted to intervene become a 'party' to the case, and as such bound by the judgment; or if it is not a party, may it still be bound by the decision? The most controversial question has, however, been that of the 'jurisdictional link'.

The problem was illustrated by the attempted intervention of Fiji in the *Nuclear Tests* cases. Australia and New Zealand had brought proceedings against France asserting the illegality of atmospheric nuclear tests in the Pacific, and had been able to cite as bases

---

[50] *Certain Phosphate Lands in Nauru (Nauru v Australia), Preliminary Objections, Judgment, ICJ Reports 1992*, p 240, para 457.

[51] *Questions of Interpretation and Application of the 1971 Montreal Convention arising from the Aerial Incident at Lockerbie (Libya v UK, Libya v USA)*.

[52] *Legality of Use of Force (Yugoslavia v Belgium, Yugoslavia v Canada, Yugoslavia v France, Yugoslavia v Germany, Yugoslavia v Italy, Yugoslavia v Netherlands, Yugoslavia v Portugal, Yugoslavia v Spain, Yugoslavia v UK, Yugoslavia v USA)*.

[53] A controversial question is whether the existence of parallel cases which have not been joined affects the right to appoint a judge ad hoc: see the Joint Declaration of Judges Bedjaoui, Guillaume, and Ranjeva in the *Lockerbie* cases, ibid, *ICJ Reports 1998*, pp 32ff.

of jurisdiction the French acceptance under the 'optional clause', and a 1928 Treaty. Fiji sought to join in the proceedings, in effect as co-plaintiff, but could not point to any jurisdictional title available to it: it was not a party to the 1928 Treaty, and it could not rely on the optional clause declaration because it had not deposited one of its own. Accordingly, Fiji could not validly have brought a separate case against France; could it therefore be allowed to jump on the bandwagon, as it were, to reach the same result by taking advantage of the fact that Australia and New Zealand had brought proceedings? The cases came to a premature end before the Court was called upon to decide the point, but some of the judges felt strongly enough to indicate their views upon it in separate or dissenting opinions.[54]

After some judicial hesitation, a chamber of the Court ruled, in the case of the *Land, Island and Maritime Boundary Dispute* between El Salvador and Honduras, that no jurisdictional link was required for an intervention which did not confer the status of party; and that the objection of the original parties was to be taken into account, but was not decisive.[55] These findings were approved by the full Court in the subsequent cases of *Land and Maritime Boundary between Cameroon and Nigeria*[56] and *Sovereignty over Pulau Ligitan and Pulau Sipadan*.[57] It appears that intervention as a party is also possible, either with the consent of the original parties,[58] or if there exists a jurisdictional title such that the intending intervener could have brought independent proceedings against each of them.[59] If, however, the intervener is not a party, the chamber in the *El Salvador/Honduras* case held that it is not bound by the judgment, but similarly cannot invoke it against the original parties.[60] These decisions have also clarified the significance of the 'legal interest' and how it was to be 'affected'.

C. INTERPRETATION AND REVISION OF JUDGMENTS

Article 60 of the Court's Statute provides that 'The judgment is final and without appeal'. The text, however, continues: 'In the event of dispute as to the meaning or scope of the judgment, the Court shall construe it upon the request of any party'.[61]

---

[54] A further complication was introduced by the introduction into the new Rules of Court, adopted in 1978, of a text which was (apparently deliberately) ambiguous on the issue (Article 81(2)(c)).

[55] *Land, Island and Maritime Frontier Dispute (El Salvador/Honduras), Application to Intervene, Judgment,* ICJ Reports 1990, p 92.

[56] *Land and Maritime Boundary between Cameroon and Nigeria, Application to Intervene, Order of 21 October 1999,* ICJ Reports 1999, p 1029.

[57] *Sovereignty over Palau Ligitan and Pulau Sipidan (Indonesia/Malaysia), Application to Intervene, Judgment of 23 October 2001,* ICJ Reports 2001, p 575, paras 35–6.

[58] In the *Land and Maritime Boundary between Cameroon and Nigeria (Cameroon v Nigeria: Equatorial Guinea Intervening), Judgment,* ICJ Reports 2002, p 303, para 12, the Court took note of the fact that the parties had no objection to the intervention of Equatorial Guinea, but that State was not seeking to intervene as a party.

[59] The only case to date in which intervention as a party has been specifically requested was the intervention applied for by Honduras in the *Territorial and Maritime Dispute (Nicaragua v Colombia), Application of Honduras to Intervene, Judgment of 4 May 2011,* ICJ Reports 2011.

[60] The intending intervener (Nicaragua) had in fact announced in advance that it would accept the judgment as binding, but the chamber did not find this acceptance legally effective.

[61] *Request for Interpretation of the Judgment of 20 November 1950 in the Asylum case, Judgment,* ICJ Reports 1950, p 395; *Application for Revision and Interpretation of the Judgment of 24 February 1982 in the Case concerning the Continental Shelf (Tunisia/Libyan Arab Jamahiriya) (Tunisia v Libyan Arab Jamahiriya), Judgment,* ICJ Reports 1985, p 192; *Request for Interpretation of the Judgment of 11 June 1998 in the Case concerning the Land and Maritime Boundary between Cameroon and Nigeria (Cameroon v Nigeria), Preliminary Objections (Nigeria v Cameroon), Judgment,* ICJ Reports 1999, p 31; *Request for Interpretation of the Judgment of 31 March 2004 in the*

Article 61 further qualifies the finality of a judgment, by providing that:

An application for revision of a judgment may be made only when it is based upon the discovery of some fact of such a nature as to be a decisive factor, which fact was, when the judgment was given, unknown to the Court and to the party claiming revision, always provided that such ignorance was not due to negligence.

The fact is then referred to in paragraph 2 as 'the new fact'; this expression has been a source of confusion, as the fact must be an old fact newly discovered. In the case between Bosnia and Yugoslavia, the Court distinguished between a fact of this kind and 'the legal consequences' as to a pre-existing state of affairs drawn from 'facts subsequent to the Judgment';[62] but the distinction is not entirely convincing.

Requests for interpretation or for revision were formerly comparatively rare, but recent years have seen an increase in their frequency.[63] In particular, requests for interpretation have been employed to bring an issue before the Court which would not be covered by any existing title of jurisdiction, as no independent title is required for such a request, which is treated as ancillary to the original proceedings leading to the judgment to be interpreted. A remarkable example is the request made for interpretation of the Judgment in the case of the *Temple of Preah Vihear*, made nearly 50 years after the Judgment was given![64]

VII. EFFECT OF THE DECISIONS OF THE COURT

A judgment of the Court is binding upon the parties to the case in which it is given. As noted earlier, under Article 60 of the Statute, the judgment is 'final and without appeal', and Article 59 provides that 'The decision of the Court has no binding force except between the parties and in respect of that particular case', implying *a contrario* that, between the parties and in respect of the particular case, it is binding. Furthermore, under Article 94(1), of the Charter, 'Each Member of the United Nations undertakes to comply with the decision of the International Court of Justice in any case to which it is a party'.[65]

Case concerning Avena and Other Mexican Nationals (Mexico v United States of America), Judgment, ICJ Reports 2009, p 3;. Request for Interpretation of the Judgment of 15 June 1962 in the case concerning the Temple of Preah Vihear (Cambodia v Thailand), Order of 18 July 2011.

[62] *Application for Revision of the Judgment of 11 July 1996 in the Case concerning Application of the Genocide Convention (Bosnia and Herzegovina v Yugoslavia), Preliminary Objections (Yugoslavia v Bosnia and Herzegovina), ICJ Reports 2003, p 7, para 69.*

[63] *Application for Revision and Interpretation of the Judgment of 24 February 1982 in the Case concerning the Continental Shelf (Tunisia/Libyan Arab Jamahiriya) (Tunisia v Libyan Arab Jamahiriya), Judgment, ICJ Reports 1985, p 192; Application for Revision of the Judgment of 11 July 1996 in the Case concerning Application of the Genocide Convention (Bosnia and Herzegovina v Yugoslavia) (Yugoslavia v Bosnia and Herzegovina), Judgment, ICJ Reports 2003, p 7; Application for Revision of the Judgment of 11 September 1992 in the Case concerning the Land, Island and Maritime Frontier Dispute (El Salvador v Honduras: Nicaragua Intervening) (Honduras/El Salvador), Judgment, ICJ Reports 2003, p 392.*

[64] The unsuccessful party in the original proceedings, Thailand, had never accepted the Court's decision to allocate the Temple to Cambodia; and the situation had become acute as a result, ironically enough, of the proposal to adopt the Temple as a World Heritage Site! See the Court's Order of 18 July 2011 on the request of Cambodia for the indication of provisional measures.

[65] This commitment does not, as such, apply to parties to the Statute that are not UN members, or to States admitted to appear without being parties to the Statute. However, when the General Assembly admits a State, under Article 93 of the Charter, to become a party to the Statute, it always attaches as a condition 'Acceptance of all the obligations of a Member of the United Nations under Article 94 of the Charter' (see GA Res 91 (I)), 11 December 1946 (Switzerland); 3 GA Res 63 (IV), 1 December 1949 (Liechtenstein); GA Res 806.

If, however, a judgment is not complied with, there is no possibility for the winning party to come back to the Court to compel the other party to comply. The only provision for what might be termed enforcement is Article 94(2) of the Charter:

> If any party to a case fails to perform the obligations on it under a judgment rendered by the Court, the other party may have recourse to the Security Council, which may, if it deems necessary, make recommendations or decide upon measures to be taken to give effect to the judgment.

Very little use has been made of this faculty, which does not confer any additional powers on the Security Council; the political implications of any attempt to enforce a judgment by this means need not be gone into here.

There is a clear obligation of treaty law to treat a judgment of the Court as binding and to comply with it. In legal theory, however, the judgments of the Court are in principle declaratory of the rights and obligations of the parties, not creative of new rights and obligations.[66] If therefore the Court decides, for example, that under a provision in a treaty, the correct interpretation of which is disputed, one of the parties is under a particular obligation, that obligation results from the treaty (as authoritatively interpreted), but is backed by the obligation to comply with the judgment. The only special status that the existence of the judgment confers on the original obligation is confirmation that it exists, in the sense that no alternative interpretation of the treaty provision is legally possible. The fact that the judgment is binding on the parties does not mean that they may not, by agreement between themselves, depart from it—unless of course the obligation found by the Court to exist is one of *jus cogens*.[67] All it means is that neither party may unilaterally act as though the legal situation were other than as declared by the Court.

Some of the relevant texts refer to the 'judgment' of the Court (Statute, Article 60; Charter, Article 94(2)) and others to the 'decision' of the Court (Statute, Article 59; Charter, Article 94(1)). The question has therefore sometimes been raised whether an Order of the Court is binding on the parties. Most orders are procedural, and any sanction for compliance is also procedural: if a party fails to file a pleading within the time-limit fixed by an Order, it may lose the right to file that pleading. A special case is, however, that of provisional measures, which are invariably indicated in the form of an Order. Now that the Court has decided (see Section VI A of this chapter) that the measures themselves constitute a legal obligation, the formal question of the effect of the order as a 'decision' has perhaps lost much of its pertinence.

Article 59 thus excludes any formal impact of the judgment on third parties; and on this basis the Court has, for example, been willing to draw a boundary line between two States in an area where a third State might have valid claims, reasoning that the decision of the Court, like a delimitation agreement between the two States before the Court, would be *res inter alios acta* for the third State, and could not therefore prejudice its position.[68] Other cases, however, have given rise to a distinction: if the Court finds that the rights and obligations of a third State would not merely be affected by the decision, but would form the very subject matter of the decision, the Court takes the view that it should decline to exercise its jurisdiction. The classic case on the point was that of the *Monetary Gold*

---

[66] With the possible exception of Orders indicating provisional measures: see Section VI A of this chapter.

[67] On the concept of *jus cogens*, see Thirlway, Ch 4 of this book, Section III B, and Shelton, Ch 6 passim.

[68] *Frontier Dispute, ICJ Reports 1986*, p 554, paras 46ff. The position is apparently different in the case of maritime delimitations: see, eg *Land and Maritime Boundary between Cameroon and Nigeria (Cameroon v Nigeria: Equatorial Guinea Intervening) ICJ Reports 2002*, p 424, para 245.

Removed from Rome in 1943.[69] The parties to the case were Italy as applicant, and the UK, France, and the USA as respondents. The disputed gold had been removed from Rome by the Germans during the Second World War, but was subsequently found by an arbitrator to have belonged to Albania. Italy and the UK, however, each claimed that gold, on the basis of legal claims by those two States against Albania. The Court found that in order to determine the validity of Italy's claim, it would have to 'determine whether Albania has committed any international wrong against Italy', and thus to 'decide a dispute between Italy and Albania'. However, Albania was not before the Court as a party to the proceedings, and had not consented to the dispute being settled by the Court:

> To adjudicate upon the international responsibility of Albania without her consent would run counter to a well-established principle of international law embodied in the Court's Statute, namely that the Court can only exercise jurisdiction over a State with its consent.[70]

It was urged that, under Article 59 of the Statute, the decision would not be binding on Albania; but the Court held that where 'the vital issue to be settled concerns the international responsibility of a third State, the Court cannot, without the consent of that third State, give a decision on that issue binding upon any State, either the third State, or any of the parties before it'.[71]

The possibility of intervention (see Section VI B of this chapter) has been raised in connection with the principle laid down in the *Monetary Gold* line of cases. If a State, not a party to a case, did not wish its rights and duties to be discussed before the Court in its absence, it was open to such a State, it was said, to intervene. The Court, however, drew a distinction: if the interests of the absent State would merely *be affected* by the decision, then if that State chose not to exercise its right to request intervention, the proceedings could continue to judgment; but if the legal interests of the absent State 'would form the very subject matter of the decision', then the Court could not exercise its jurisdiction in the absence of that State.[72]

VIII. ADVISORY PROCEEDINGS

In addition to its function of settling international disputes in accordance with international law, the Court is empowered by its Statute to give advisory opinions. The provision to that effect included in the Statute of the Permanent Court was something of an innovation: some, but by no means all, national supreme courts possessed a power of this kind; and on the international level, arbitration proceedings, from which the concept of an international tribunal sprang, were essentially means of reaching a binding settlement of a dispute. It was the organs of the League of Nations that were expected to feel a need for such an opinion, and from the beginning it was only such international organs, and not States, that were to be entitled to ask for advice in this form.

The essence of an advisory opinion is that it is advisory, not determinative: it expresses the view of the Court as to the relevant international legal principles and rules, but does not oblige, any State, nor even the body that asked for the opinion, to take or refrain from any action. The distinction, clear in theory, is less so in practice: if the Court advises, for example, that a certain obligation exists, the State upon which it is said to rest has not

---

[69] *Monetary Gold Removed from Rome in 1943, Judgment, ICJ Reports 1954*, p 19.
[70] Ibid, p 32.   [71] Ibid, p 33.   [72] Ibid, p 32.

bound itself to accept the Court's finding, but it will be in a weak position if it seeks to argue that the considered opinion of the Court does not represent a correct view of the law.

The essentially non-binding character of an advisory opinion has in the past given rise to some doubts as to the legal effect of a treaty commitment whereby an opinion of the Court is to be accepted, by the parties to the treaty, as binding. One field in which treaty provisions of this kind have proved useful is the relations between international organizations, particularly the UN itself, and States. Since an international organization cannot be a party to proceedings before the Court, a dispute between an organization and a State cannot be settled by contentious proceedings. A device that has been used to meet the difficulty is to provide in a convention (for example the 1946 Convention on the Privileges and Immunities of the UN) that, in the event of a dispute of this kind, the General Assembly (or other organ concerned) will ask the Court for an advisory opinion on the point at issue, and that it is agreed in advance that the Court's opinion will be accepted as 'decisive' by the State and the organization. It is established that since the essentially non-binding character of the opinion itself is not affected, there is no legal obstacle to the conclusion of an agreement of this kind.

Under the Charter, Article 96(1), the General Assembly and the Security Council are entitled to request the Court 'to give an advisory opinion on any legal question'. This is purely a faculty: nowhere in the Charter is there any obligation to seek the advice of the Court, and the Court has no power to offer it unasked. A proposal during the drafting of the Charter to give the Court responsibility for authoritative interpretations of the Charter was not adopted.

Article 96(2) provides that 'Other organs of the United Nations and specialized agencies, which may at any time be so authorized by the General Assembly, may also request advisory opinions of the Court on legal questions arising within the scope of their activities'.[73] Such authorizations have in fact been given to the Economic and Social Council and to practically all the specialized agencies. The restriction as to the type of questions to be put was, however, held to debar the World Health Organization, which had received a general authorization from the General Assembly to request opinions, from asking for an opinion on the question whether the use of nuclear weapons by a State would be a breach of its obligations under international law 'including the WHO Constitution'. The Court held that under the 'principle of speciality' the WHO could not deal with matters beyond what was authorized by its Constitution; that the question of the legality of nuclear weapons was outside that Constitution; and accordingly the question was not one 'arising within the scope' of the activities of the Organization.[74] In another case, the question was raised whether a subsidiary organ of the General Assembly, whose sole function was in fact to ask for advisory opinions (on the validity of judgments of the UN Administrative Tribunal), had any 'activities' of its own for the purposes of this text; the Court ruled in the affirmative.[75]

The provision in the Statute that corresponds to this Charter text is Article 65, which provides that 'The Court may give an advisory opinion on any legal question' at the request

---

[73] The wording of paras 1 and 2 of Article 96 suggests that a request from the Security Council or General Assembly can relate to a question not 'within the scope of their activities', but there are dicta of the Court suggesting that this approach may be too wide: see *Legal Consequences of the Construction of a Wall in the Occupied Palestinian Territory, Advisory Opinion, ICJ Reports 2004*, p 136, para 16, and references there cited.

[74] *Legality of the Use by a State of Nuclear Weapons in Armed Conflict, Advisory Opinion, ICJ Reports 1996*, p 66.

[75] *Application for Review of Judgment No 158 of the United Nations Administrative Tribunal, Advisory Opinion, ICJ Reports 1973*, p 166.

of any authorized body. The use of the word 'may' signifies, as the Court has repeatedly emphasized, that the Court is not bound to give an opinion, but may decline to do so if it considers that course appropriate. It has never in fact done so,[76] but has on a number of occasions considered the possibility of refusal. From the resulting jurisprudence it is clear that the reply of the Court, itself an organ of the UN, 'represents its participation in the activities of the Organization and, in principle, should not be refused'; and that only compelling reasons would justify a refusal.[77]

A special problem, however, arises if the question put to the Court is related to an inter-State dispute, and one of the States concerned in that dispute objects to the Court giving the opinion. The consent of the States parties to a dispute is the basis of the Court's jurisdiction in contentious cases; but since the Court's reply to a request for an advisory opinion has no binding force, 'it follows that no State...can prevent the giving of an Advisory Opinion which the United Nations considers to be desirable in order to obtain enlightenment as to the course of action it should undertake'.[78] The consent of any State party to a dispute underlying a request for advisory opinion is thus not necessary for the opinion to be given; but, as the Court declared in a later case, that concerning *Western Sahara*, 'lack of consent might constitute a ground for declining to give the opinion requested', in the exercise of the Court's discretion, 'if, in the circumstances of a given case, considerations of judicial propriety should oblige the Court to refuse an opinion'.[79] The Court offered as an instance of this (and probably the most compelling instance), 'when the circumstances disclose that to give a reply would have the effect of circumventing the principle that a State is not obliged to allow its disputes to be submitted to judicial settlement without its consent'.[80] This might be so if the object of the requesting organ (*in casu* the General Assembly) were 'to bring before the Court, by way of a request for advisory opinion, a dispute or legal controversy, in order that it may later, on the basis of the Court's opinion, exercise its power and functions for the peaceful settlement of that dispute or controversy'.[81] This criterion appears, however, to have been tacitly abandoned in the *Wall* case.[82] In no case up to the present has the Court declined to give an opinion on this ground, or any other discretionary ground. It did not even refuse in the case of a dispute between the General Assembly and a State, in which the Assembly, unable to obtain a binding advisory opinion under the provisions of the Convention on the Privileges and Immunities of the UN, because of a reservation to that Convention made by the State concerned, sought and obtained a non-binding opinion of the Court on the point in dispute.[83]

---

[76] The refusal, referred to in the preceding paragraph, of the opinion requested by WHO was not a matter of discretion but a matter of lack of jurisdiction following the lack of competence of WHO to ask for an opinion on the subject.

[77] See, eg *Western Sahara, Advisory Opinion, ICJ Reports 1975*, p 12, para 23.

[78] *Interpretation of Peace Treaties with Bulgaria, Hungary and Romania, First Phase, Advisory Opinion, ICJ Reports 1950*, p 65 at p 71.

[79] *Western Sahara, ICJ Reports 1975*, p 12, para 32.

[80] Ibid, para 33. This passage was later criticized, by Judge Kooijmans in the *Wall* case, as containing 'purely circular reasoning': *Legal Consequences of the Construction of a Wall in the Occupied Palestinian Territory, ICJ Reports 2004*, p 227, para 27.

[81] *Western Sahara, Advisory Opinion, ICJ Reports 1975*, p 12, para 29.

[82] See the Separate Opinion of Judge Higgins, *Legal Consequences of the Construction of a Wall in the Occupied Palestinian Territory, Advisory Opinion, ICJ Reports 2004*, p 136 at p 210, paras 12–13.

[83] *Applicability of Article VI, Section 22, of the Convention on the Privileges and Immunities of the United Nations, Advisory Opinion, ICJ Reports 1989*, p 177, para 38.

A further difficulty that has arisen in connection with requests for advisory opinions in cases involving, or related to, existing international disputes is the extent to which a party, or the parties, to such a dispute should be treated as though they were parties to a contentious case, and in particular should be able to appoint a judge ad hoc. Article 68 of the Statute provides that:

> In the exercise of its advisory functions the Court shall further be guided by the provisions of the present Statute which apply in contentious cases to the extent to which it recognizes them to be applicable.

The Permanent Court had recognized that in some cases States should be treated as 'parties' to the extent of appointing judges ad hoc. The Rules of Court make no direct provision for this, but Article 102(2) repeats the text of Article 68, and adds: 'For this purpose, it shall above all consider whether the request for the advisory opinion relates to a legal question actually pending between two or more States'.

Practice has shown that the implementation of these texts in specific cases in relation to the appointment of judges ad hoc is not always straightforward. In the *Namibia* case, South Africa, which had a very special interest in the proceedings, and could claim that there was a 'legal question actually pending' between itself and nearly every other State, was not permitted to appoint a judge ad hoc.[84] In the *Western Sahara* case, Morocco and Mauritania each claimed the existence of special legal ties with the territory, and contested the arguments of Spain, the former colonial power: Morocco was permitted to appoint a judge ad hoc, but Mauritania was not.[85] In the *Wall* case one of the parties to the dispute (Palestine) was not a State for the purposes of the Statute.[86]

IX. THE COURT PAST AND PRESENT: AN ASSESSMENT

For the first 20 years of its existence, the International Court of Justice seemed destined to play a part on the international scene similar to that played by its predecessor, the Permanent Court of International Justice. Cases were submitted to it in a small but regular flow, and a series of requests were made by the General Assembly for advisory opinions; the decisions and advisory opinions given were on the whole well received, and the Court's contribution to the development of law, though necessarily marginal, was significant. While the creators of the Permanent Court, and their successors at the San Francisco Conference in 1946, might have hoped for a more spectacular contribution to international dispute-settlement, the experiment begun in 1920 could be regarded as successful.

In the 1960s and 1970s, a marked change was observed. For reasons which need not be gone into here, but which must include the Court's 1966 decision in the *South West Africa* case (which had a devastating effect on the Court's reputation with the developing

---

[84] *Legal Consequences for States of the Continued Presence of South Africa in Namibia (South West Africa) notwithstanding Security Council Resolution 276 (1970), Order of 29 January 1971, ICJ Reports 1971*, p 12, and *Advisory Opinion*, ibid, p 16, paras 35ff.

[85] *Western Sahara, Order of 22 May 1975, ICJ Reports 1975*, p 6.

[86] See the Separate Opinion of Judge Owada, *Legal Consequences of the Construction of a Wall in the Occupied Palestinian Territory, Advisory Opinion, ICJ Reports 2004*, p 136 at p 267, para 19. The problem remained hypothetical, as Israel did not claim the right to appoint a judge ad hoc.

countries), doubts began to be expressed about the future of the Court, as fewer and fewer States seemed inclined to bring their disputes before it. For a brief period, the Court had no cases whatever on its list. Little by little, however, the situation improved, particularly as a result of the increasing need for impartial settlement of seabed delimitation disputes, where the Court had shown the way in the *North Sea Continental Shelf* case (1969). The formation of a special chamber according to the wishes of the parties in the *Gulf of Maine* case (1984) offered an attractive alternative to submission to the full Court, and it was striking that the next request for such a chamber came from two developing countries in sub-Saharan Africa (Burkina Faso and Mali in the *Frontier Dispute*, 1986).

Today, the Court is busier than it has ever been before. Disputes have been submitted to it not only by its more established 'clients', but by States of: Latin America;[87] Eastern Europe;[88] Asia;[89] and Africa.[90] On the other hand, China has so far remained aloof, and the USA now shows distinct coolness toward the Court, marked by the withdrawal of various long-established bases of jurisdiction, avowedly in response to what it regards as unjustifiedly extensive interpretation by the Court of its jurisdiction over the USA.[91] There has, however, been increasing use of the possibility of requesting an advisory opinion, including the request by both WHO and the General Assembly for an opinion on the legality of nuclear weapons,[92] and by the General Assembly on an aspect of the Israel/Palestine problem.[93]

On the practical level, there are signs that the Court is becoming a victim of its own success. The principle that all cases are heard by the full Court unless the parties agree to a chamber means that there is a limit to the number of cases that can be heard and determined each year; and although the Registry has been enlarged and some of the Court's working methods improved, there are signs of an overload. Judicial settlement has never been a speedy means of resolving disputes, but it is to be feared that States considering bringing a case to the Court may be put off by the likely delay before a decision is given, due to the presence of so many other cases in the queue.

---

[87] *Military and Paramilitary Activities in and against Nicaragua (Nicaragua v USA), Border and Transborder Armed Actions (Nicaragua v Honduras, Nicaragua v Costa Rica), Land, Island and Maritime Frontier Dispute (Honduras/El Salvador, Nicaragua intervening), Territorial and Maritime Dispute (Nicaragua v Colombia); Maritime Delimitation between Nicaragua and Honduras in the Caribbean Sea; Avena and other Mexican Nationals (Mexico v USA); Territorial and Maritime Dispute (Nicaragua v Colombia).*

[88] *Gabčíkovo-Nagymaros Project (Hungary/Slovakia), Application of the Convention on the Prevention and Punishment of the Crime of Genocide (Bosnia and Herzegovina v Serbia and Montenegro), Legality of Use of Force (Yugoslavia against 10 NATO countries); Application of the Convention on the Prevention and Punishment of the Crime of Genocide (Croatia v Serbia); Maritime Delimitation in the Black Sea (Romania v Ukraine).*

[89] *Aerial Incident of 10 August 1999 (Pakistan v India); Sovereignty over Pulau Ligitan and Pulau Sipadan (Indonesia/Malaysia); Sovereignty over Pedra Blanca/Pulau Batu Pateh, Middle Rocks and South Ledge (Malaysia/Singapore).*

[90] *Frontier Dispute (Benin/Niger); Ahmadou Sadio Diallo (Republic of Guinea v Democratic Republic of the Congo); Armed Activities on the territory of the Congo (Democratic Republic of the Congo v Rwanda); Arrest Warrant of 11 April 2000 (Democratic Republic of the Congo v Belgium); Armed Activities on the Territory of the Congo (Democratic Republic of the Congo v Burundi; v Rwanda; v Uganda); Certain Criminal Proceedings in France (Republic of the Congo v France).*

[91] The cases of *Armed Activities in and against Nicaragua, Oil Platforms*, and *Avena and other Mexican Nationals* may be mentioned.

[92] Opinions differ, however, as to the wisdom of using the advisory opinion procedure in an area of this kind (see, eg *Legality of the Threat or Use of Nuclear Weapons, Advisory Opinion, ICJ Reports 1996*, p 226, Dissenting Opinion of Judge Oda, p 330).

[93] *Legal Consequences of the Construction of a Wall in the Occupied Palestinian Territories, Advisory Opinion, ICJ Reports 2004*, p 136.

A consistently high standard has, however, been maintained in the quality of the Court's decisions, even though they have, as always, been exposed to healthy criticism. The bringing of more cases has meant more opportunities for contribution to the development of the law; on a number of occasions, for example, the Court has been able to supplement the work of the International Law Commission by settling authoritatively the customary-law status of a rule embodied in a treaty or other text emanating from the ILC.

Considerable use has been made of the possibility of requesting the indication of provisional measures, *inter alia* in situations of armed hostilities. It remains to be seen, however, whether the ruling in the *LaGrand* case, that provisional measures give rise to a binding obligation of compliance, may conceivably have a negative influence on advance acceptance of jurisdiction. The provisional measures procedure has always offered a temptation to States to commence proceedings on a shaky jurisdictional foundation in the hope of getting at least the short-term benefit of an order for provisional measures, and this is all the more attractive when the order is recognized to be immediately binding, even if unenforceable. The only defence against such tactics is to limit generalized acceptances of jurisdiction that may be misused; but there is no sign at present of any generalized flight from potential jurisdiction, in terms of withdrawal of acceptances or denunciation of settlement treaties.

Nevertheless, the prospects as regards acceptance of jurisdiction must otherwise be regarded as mixed: existing treaties for dispute-settlement, compromissory clauses, and optional dispute-settlement protocols continue to provide a background of potential jurisdiction, but there seem to be few fresh treaties of this kind concluded, and such clauses seem to appear less frequently in new multilateral treaties.[94] Nor does the optional clause system seem to be thriving. The number of States having filed declarations of acceptance (currently 67 out of 193 UN members) is not increasing, and the declarations that have been filed are much qualified by reservations. Some disquiet has also been caused by what is perceived as a trend whereby the Court, in order to comment on legal questions of substantial current importance, has been over-generous in its interpretation of texts conferring jurisdiction. The decision in the *Oil Platforms* case[95] in particular has been criticized on this ground.[96] The development of a coherent system of intervention has been valuable, since many modern international disputes are plurilateral rather than bilateral. The Court is clearly alive to the need to review its own procedures, as is shown by the recent revision of Articles 79 and 80 of the Rules, and the use of Practice Directions.

All in all, the prospects for the future role of the Court in the settlement of international disputes are encouraging. While it may not be such a World Court as idealists might like to envisage, in its present structure and operation it remains a real force for peaceful settlement of disputes, and the furthest extension of judicial power to the affairs of States that is likely to be acceptable to the members of the present-day international community.

---

[94] According to the information on the Court's website, derived from registrations of treaties with the UN Secretariat, only three new bilateral treaties providing for ICJ jurisdiction have been concluded since 1991; and no multilateral treaties with such provisions have been registered since 2003.

[95] *Oil Platforms (Islamic Republic of Iran v United States of America), Judgment, ICJ Reports, 2003*, p 161.

[96] Cf the opinion of Judge Kooijmans in that case, ibid, p 257, para 35, and Small, 2004.

CITATION OF ICJ CASES

Although cases brought before the Court are numbered consecutively on the Court's General List (Rules, Article 26(1)(b)), these numbers are not used for purposes of citation. The official title of each case is determined by the Court at the outset of the proceedings, on the basis of the document instituting proceedings; considerations of avoiding any appearance of pre-judgment lead to such titles often being somewhat unwieldy. The names of the parties are sometimes included in the official title, particularly when the same title is used for more than one case. Abbreviated titles are therefore often used by scholars in books and articles; unfortunately, there is no generally recognized system for these.

REFERENCES

THIRLWAY, H (1984), 'Reciprocity in the Jurisdiction of the International Court', 15 *NYBIL* 97.

—— (2001), 'The Law and Procedure of the International Court of Justice 1960–1989, Part Twelve', 72 *BYIL* 37.

SMALL, D (2004), 'The Oil Platforms case; Jurisdiction through the Closed Eye of the Needle', 3 *Law and Practice of International Courts and Tribunals* 113.

FURTHER READING

AMR, MSM (2003), *The Role of the International Court of Justice as the Principal Judicial Organ of the United Nations* (The Hague: Kluwer Law International).

BOWETT, D *et al* (1997), *The International Court of Justice: Process, Practice and Procedure* (London: BIICL (British Institute of International and Comparative Law)). Based on the work of a Study Group set up by the British Institute of International and Comparative Law, this study focuses on the practical aspects of the Court's work and procedures.

KOLB, R (2013), *The International Court of Justice* (Oxford: Hart Publishing). An up-to-date and encyclopedic survey of the Court and its work. Although probably too detailed for student use, it is valuable for the clarity with which it is written.

ROSENNE, S (1997), *The Law and Practice of the International Court, 1920–1996* (The Hague:

Martinus Nijhoff). This is the most complete and authoritative survey of the Court.

THIRLWAY, H (2013), *The Law and Procedure of the International Court: Fifty Years of Jurisprudence* (Oxford: Oxford University Press). An assemblage of the articles contributed by this author to the British Year Book of International Law, 1989–2012.

A Commentary on the Statute of the International Court of Justice (April 2006), a joint publication of the Max-Planck-Institut, Heidelberg, the Institut für Völker- und Europarecht, Humboldt University, Berlin, and the Walter-Schücking-Institut, University of Kiel.

International Court of Justice: Yearbook. This annual publication contains a wealth of information on current cases and on points of practice and procedure.

The International Court of Justice (1996), 4th edn. This useful handbook is published by the Court and distributed jointly by the Court and the UN Department of Public Information.

The International Court of Justice: Questions and Answers about the principal judicial organ of the United Nations (2000), UN Sales No E.99.I.25. This sets out basic facts concerning the Court.

WEBSITES

http://www.icj-cij.org

The Court's website contains the text in the two official languages (English and French) of the Statute, Rules of Court and Practice Directions, the other texts governing jurisdiction, and full texts of all recent decisions, press releases, and other materials. Once the Court has decided that the pleadings in a case are to be made public, these and the oral arguments will also be on the website, but only in the language in which they were presented. The translations of judges' separate and dissenting opinions may also not be available until some time after the decision itself is given.

21

THE USE OF FORCE AND THE INTERNATIONAL LEGAL ORDER

Christine Gray

SUMMARY

This is one of the most controversial areas of international law. States are divided as to the interpretation of the fundamental rules on the use of force in the UN Charter. The prohibition of the use of force in Article 2(4) is directed at inter-State conflicts; there is disagreement as to whether this allows the use of force for humanitarian intervention or 'responsibility to protect'. The application of Article 2(4) to civil wars is also problematic. The main exception to the prohibition on the use of force is the right to self-defence under Article 51. It is controversial whether this is a narrow right, available only in response to an armed attack, or whether it allows force in protection of nationals abroad or in response to terrorist attacks. The UN Charter also establishes a collective security system whereby the Security Council may respond to threats to the peace, breaches of the peace and acts of aggression. This chapter examines the use of enforcement action and the institution of UN peacekeeping as well as the power of regional organizations to assist in peacekeeping and enforcement action.

I. INTRODUCTION

The law on the use of force is one of the most controversial areas of international law and one where the law may seem ineffective. The UN Charter prohibits the use of force by States in Article 2(4), but this has not prevented the occurrence of over 100 major conflicts since 1945 and the deaths of over twenty million people. Difficult questions arise as to how far international law in fact influences State behaviour. In practice States are clearly anxious to avoid condemnation for their use of force and they generally use the language of international law to explain and justify their behaviour—not as the sole justification but as one of a variety of arguments. Thus NATO based its use of force in 'humanitarian intervention' over Kosovo on a mixture of political, moral, and legal arguments. It is tempting to dismiss legal arguments in justification of the use of force by States, especially powerful States, as merely self-interested manipulation of the rules, but in the absence of clear empirical evidence about the nature of decision-making within States this remains an assumption. It may underestimate the genuine differences of viewpoint between opposing States and the commitment of the vast majority of States, especially small, weak States, to the prohibition on the use of force.

A. THE UN CHARTER SCHEME

The UN Charter is the starting point for any discussion of international law on the use of force (Simma, 2012). It was concluded after, and in response to, the experiences of the Second World War, in the same way as the League of Nations Covenant was a response to the First World War. There is disagreement as to whether the prohibition of the use of force in the UN Charter was a revolutionary new provision or whether customary law had already developed along the lines of Article 2(4) by the time of the creation of the UN (Brownlie, 1963, p 66). The Charter aims not only to prohibit the unilateral use of force by States by Article 2(4), but also to centralize control over the use of force in the Security Council, acting under Chapter VII.

The Preamble of the Charter begins 'We the peoples of the United Nations determined to save succeeding generations from the scourge of war', and the first purpose of the UN set out in Article 1 is 'To maintain international peace and security, and to that end: to take effective collective measures for the prevention and removal of threats to the peace and for the suppression of acts of aggression or other breaches of the peace'. The original scheme was that the Security Council should respond to threats to the peace, breach of the peace, and acts of aggression, if necessary through its own standing UN army. However, this plan foundered during the Cold War because the veto possessed by the five permanent members of the Security Council—the USA, the USSR (now succeeded by Russia), China, France, and the UK—obstructed effective decision-making by the Security Council (Patil, 1992).

The original Charter scheme has not been implemented; the action taken by the Security Council under Chapter VII has been different from that originally planned. 'Coalitions of the willing' have replaced the plan for a standing UN army: member States have been authorized to use force in major enforcement operations which are perceived to be beyond the resources of the UN. Also the institution of peacekeeping which grew up as a partial substitute for Security Council enforcement action during the Cold War did so without express provision in the Charter.

There is broad agreement between States on the core of the law on the use of force, as set out in the UN Charter and also in regional and collective self-defence treaties. However, early divisions between developed and developing States emerged on the interpretation of the brief provisions of the Charter. The UN General Assembly adopted resolutions on the use of force to elaborate on the Charter, and where these were adopted by consensus they are generally regarded as statements of customary international law or as authoritative interpretations of the UN Charter. But often these resolutions were deliberately ambiguous. The consensus in favour of the *Definition of Aggression*,[1] the *Declaration on Friendly Relations*,[2] and the *Declaration on the Non-Use of Force*[3] masked the divisions between States on questions such as the scope of the right of self-defence. These divisions were apparent in the debates leading up to the resolutions. The central concerns of developing States have been with disarmament, nuclear weapons, and economic coercion; in general they have favoured a stricter interpretation of the prohibition of the use of force than developed States.

---

[1] *Definition of Aggression*, GA Res 3314 (XXIX) (14 December 1974).

[2] *Declaration on Principles of International Law concerning Friendly Relations and Co-operation among States in Accordance with the Charter of the United Nations*, GA Res 2625 (XXV) (24 October 1970).

[3] *Declaration on the Enhancement of the Effectiveness of the Principle of Refraining from the Threat or Use of Force in International Relations*, GA Res 44/22 (18 November 1987).

Also important in the interpretation and application of the UN Charter rules on the use of force are the resolutions of the General Assembly and of the Security Council passed in reaction to specific instances of the use of force by States. Of course these are political bodies, but it is generally accepted that a condemnation of a use of force is strong evidence of its illegality. In contrast, a failure to condemn may not be conclusive evidence that the action in question was lawful, given the variety of motives influencing States. The International Court of Justice (ICJ) has also played a significant part in the identification and development of the rules on the use of force in the *Nicaragua* case,[4] the *Legality of the Threat or Use of Nuclear Weapons* Advisory Opinion,[5] the *Oil Platforms* case,[6] and the *Case Concerning Armed Activities on the Territory of the Congo (DRC v Uganda)*.[7]

II. THE PROHIBITION OF THE USE OF FORCE IN ARTICLE 2(4) UN CHARTER

Article 2(4) is the basic prohibition on the use of force by States. It provides that 'All Members shall refrain in their international relations from the threat or use of force against the territorial integrity or political independence of any State, or in any other manner inconsistent with the Purposes of the United Nations'. Clearly this is directed at the inter-State use of force, although as it has turned out civil conflicts have been more common than traditional inter-State conflicts since the Second World War. Under Article 2(6) there is a duty on the UN to ensure that even States which are not UN members act in accordance with these principles so far as may be necessary for the maintenance of international peace and security. This brief prohibition of the use of force in Article 2(4) is accepted as representing customary international law, as was acknowledged by the ICJ in the *Nicaragua* case.[8] But its interpretation has given rise to much debate. General Assembly resolutions give some limited guidance, but gloss over the more fundamental disagreements.

A. THE USE OF FORCE IN 'INTERNATIONAL RELATIONS'

Article 2(4) prohibits the use of force in 'international relations'; certain States have therefore tried to argue that they were justified in the use of force to recover what they claimed to be their own territory. Thus, Argentina invaded the Falkland Islands in 1982 in order to seize them back from the UK whose title to the territory it rejected.[9] Iraq invaded Kuwait in 1990 on the basis that it had pre-colonial title and therefore was not violating Article 2(4) because the territory belonged to it.[10] These invasions were strongly condemned by the international community; the actions of Argentina and Iraq were inconsistent with the duty under Article 2(3) of the UN Charter to settle disputes,

---

[4] *Military and Paramilitary Activities in and against Nicaragua (Nicaragua v United States of America), Merits, Judgment, ICJ Reports 1986*, p 14.

[5] *Legality of the Threat or Use of Nuclear Weapons, Advisory Opinion, ICJ Reports 1996*, p 226.

[6] *Oil Platforms (Islamic Republic of Iran v United States of America), ICJ Reports 2003*, p 161.

[7] *Armed Activities on the Territory of the Congo (Democratic Republic of the Congo v Uganda), Judgment, ICJ Reports 2005*, p 168.

[8] *Military and Paramilitary Activities in and against Nicaragua (Nicaragua v United States of America), Merits, Judgment, ICJ Reports 1986*, p 14, para 190.

[9] 1982 *UNYB* 1320.   [10] 1991 *UNYB* 189.

including territorial and boundary disputes, peacefully. This duty was further elaborated in the *Definition of Aggression* and the *Declaration on Friendly Relations*. Nevertheless, China does not exclude the right to use force to recover the island of Taiwan on the basis that it is part of China, while other States have called for a peaceful settlement of the controversy.

Another problem with the interpretation of 'international relations' has arisen over the categorization of conflicts: is the situation an inter-State conflict to which Article 2(4) applies or is it an internal conflict governed by different rules? This issue of categorization was crucial in the Vietnam and Korean Wars during the Cold War; Western States argued that these were inter-State wars initiated when an aggressor Communist State invaded its neighbour and that the international community was able to respond in collective self-defence or collective action under Chapter VII of the UN Charter. The Communist bloc position was that Vietnam and Korea were both unitary States engaged in struggles against colonial intervention. Disagreements as to whether the conflict was a civil war or an inter-State conflict also arose with regard to the break-up of the former Yugoslavia.[11]

B. THE MEANING OF 'THREAT OR USE OF FORCE'

Developed and developing States are divided on the meaning of 'force'; the former maintain that this means only armed force, whereas developing States claim that it covers also economic coercion. However, this division is perhaps more of symbolic than of practical importance; economic coercion is now expressly prohibited in General Assembly resolutions, such as the *Declaration on Friendly Relations*. More recently, commentators have debated whether cyber-attacks can be classified as a use of force.

The pronouncements of the ICJ in the *Nicaragua* case are of central importance with regard to the interpretation of 'force'. The ICJ was called on to categorize the various actions of the USA aimed at the overthrow of the government of Nicaragua. It held that not only the laying of mines in Nicaraguan waters and attacks on Nicaraguan ports and oil installations by US forces but also support for the opposition forces—the *contras*—engaged in forcible struggle against the government could constitute the 'use of force'. The arming and training of the *contras* involved the unlawful use of force against Nicaragua. The mere supply of funds did not in itself amount to a use of force, but could constitute unlawful intervention.[12]

The prohibition of the 'threat of force' has attracted less discussion than the actual 'use of force'. The ICJ in the *Nicaragua* case and in the Advisory Opinion on the *Legality of Nuclear Weapons* was faced with questions as to the meaning of 'threat of force' but offered little by way of guidance, limiting itself to the not very surprising conclusion that a threat of force is unlawful where the actual use of the force threatened would itself be unlawful; the Court refused to find that the mere possession of nuclear weapons was an unlawful threat of force.

---

[11] See Gray, 1996. See also ICTY, Appeals Chamber, *Prosecutor v Dusko Tadić, Decision on the Defence Motion for Interlocutory Appeal on Jurisdiction (Interlocutory Appeal)*, Case No IT-94-1-AR72 (2 October 1995).

[12] *Military and Paramilitary Activities in and against Nicaragua (Nicaragua v United States of America)*, Merits, Judgment, ICJ Reports 1986, p 14, para 228. This categorization is clearly significant for the assessment of the legality of assistance to opposition forces in the civil war that started in 2012 in Syria.

C. THE USE OF FORCE 'AGAINST THE TERRITORIAL INTEGRITY AND POLITICAL INDEPENDENCE OF ANY STATE, OR IN ANY OTHER MANNER INCONSISTENT WITH THE PURPOSES OF THE UNITED NATIONS'

The most fundamental debate on the interpretation of Article 2(4) is whether it is an absolute prohibition on the use of force or whether it should be interpreted to allow the use of force for aims which are consistent with the purposes of the UN. Can there be a use of force which does not harm the territorial integrity or political independence of a State? There have been debates as to whether the use of force to rescue nationals, to promote democracy, and to further self-determination could be compatible with Article 2(4). States were divided as to whether NATO's forcible humanitarian intervention in Kosovo in 1999 was prohibited by Article 2(4).

During the Cold War some, mostly US, writers argued that Article 2(4) represents only a limited prohibition; they maintained that it should be interpreted in the context of the whole Charter and thus that the prohibition of force depends on the functioning of the Charter scheme for collective security under Chapter VII. In the Cold War the Security Council could not use its powers effectively and therefore Article 2(4) should be interpreted to allow the use of force to further the principles and purposes of the UN. Others rejected this approach, arguing that Article 2(4) should be strictly construed; the non-functioning of the UN system made it all the more important that States should not use force except in self-defence. The debate as to whether Article 2(4) is a wide or a narrow prohibition on the use of force has outlasted the Cold War.

In practice few States openly relied on a narrow interpretation of Article 2(4) to justify their use of force during the Cold War. The apparent adoption of the restrictive argument on Article 2(4) by the UK in the *Corfu Channel* case was exceptional; the UK argued that its forcible intervention in Albanian territorial waters to recover evidence (as to which State was responsible for laying naval mines that had led to the destruction of two British warships) did not violate Article 2(4) because its action did not threaten the territorial integrity or political independence of Albania.[13] The Court rejected this claim, but there was some debate as to whether this was merely a limited rejection of the UK claim on the particular facts or a total rejection of the narrow interpretation of Article 2(4). The ICJ in the *Nicaragua* case seems to have taken the latter view of the ruling.[14] In later incidents the USA and Israel also expressly took a narrow view of Article 2(4) as not prohibiting the rescue of nationals. This was argued by Israel to justify its rescue of nationals on a hijacked plane from Entebbe in Uganda (1976) and by the USA in its more extensive operation in Grenada (1983), but this was not the sole justification for the use of force and was not taken up by other States. In these cases other justifications were also offered by the USA and Israel for their use of force; they did not rely solely on the controversial narrow interpretation of Article 2(4). So express reliance on the argument that Article 2(4) should be interpreted to allow the use of force if this was consistent with the aims of the UN remained exceptional.

1. Force in pursuit of self-determination

During the era of decolonization States were divided as to whether force could be used by colonial peoples in pursuit of the right of self-determination (Wilson, 1988). Former

---

[13] *Corfu Channel, Merits, Judgment, ICJ Reports 1949*, p 4 at p 34.
[14] *Military and Paramilitary Activities in and against Nicaragua (Nicaragua v United States of America), Merits, Judgment, ICJ Reports 1986*, p 14, para 202.

colonies and developing States maintained that Article 2(4) did not prohibit such use of force; Western and former colonial powers did not accept this and voted against the General Assembly resolutions which expressly affirmed a right to use force. Those resolutions which were adopted by consensus, such as the *Definition of Aggression* and the *Friendly Relations Resolution*, were deliberately ambiguous. They spoke of the right of peoples with the right to self-determination to 'struggle' for that end; by this developing States understood armed struggle and the developed States peaceful struggle. There was agreement, however, that force should not be used against a people with the right of self-determination. Even though many groups continue to invoke self-determination and to turn to armed force in pursuit of independence, there is no support by developing States for any legal right to use force other than in pursuit of decolonization. The virtual end of decolonization therefore means that the legal debate does not have great practical significance today, except in the context of the struggle of the Palestinians for self-determination to end the illegal occupation by Israel of the West Bank and Gaza Strip. Even in this context there was little public debate of this legal issue with regard to the Gaza conflict in 2008–9.

2. Force in pursuit of democracy

The claim that pro-democratic force—the use of force to restore a democratic govern-ment—is not prohibited by Article 2(4) has been put forward by writers such as D'Amato (1990), but not by States. It is notable that when the USA invaded Panama in 1989 it specifically disavowed any legal doctrine of pro-democratic invasion, preferring to rely instead on self-defence. When the former President Noriega refused to stand down after defeat in the election the USA intervened, claiming that it was acting in self-defence of its nationals in Panama. It distinguished between its political interest in the protection of democracy and its legal justification for intervention.[15] Although the UN may have a power to authorize force to restore democratic government in exceptional cases, such as that of Haiti after its first democratically elected government was overthrown in a coup in 1991, it is not possible to extrapolate from this a right of unilateral intervention by States. It is significant that even though the 2006 *US National Security Strategy* produced during the presidency of George W Bush devoted considerable attention to the promotion of democracy, it did not support the use of force for this end.

D. HUMANITARIAN INTERVENTION AND RESPONSIBILITY TO PROTECT

The NATO action over Kosovo in 1999 led to prolonged debate as to whether Article 2(4) allowed the use of force for humanitarian intervention, and produced a fundamental split between NATO States on the one hand and China, Russia, and the Non-Aligned Movement on the other.[16] Acting in response to Yugoslavia's repression and displacement of ethnic Albanians in Kosovo, NATO conducted a 78-day air campaign starting in March 1999. Although NATO did not offer a fully elaborated legal argument for its air campaign, it seemed to put forward in justification a mixture of implied authorization by the Security Council and humanitarian arguments. Member States set out their legal arguments in the Security Council debates and in their pleadings in the *Legality of Use of Force* case brought by Yugoslavia before the International Court of Justice against NATO States.[17]

---

[15] 1989 *UNYB* 172.   [16] 1999 *UNYB* 332.

[17] *Legality of Use of Force (Yugoslavia v Belgium), Provisional Measures, Order of 2 June 1999, ICJ Reports 1999*, p 124.

The UK more than any other State has developed a doctrine of humanitarian intervention as an autonomous institution. It has argued that the interpretation of Article 2(4) has changed over time; that international law in this field has developed to meet new situations. This apparently new doctrine was first put forward with regard to US and UK action over Iraq. After Iraq invaded Kuwait in 1990 and was driven out by coalition forces in *Operation Desert Storm*, the UN Security Council established a binding cease-fire which was accepted by Iraq. However, the cease-fire regime in Resolution 687 failed to make provision for the protection of human rights in Iraq; Iraq turned on the Kurds of the north and the Shiites and Marsh Arabs of the south. In response the Security Council passed Resolution 688[18] asking Iraq to end its repression and to allow access to humanitarian agencies. This resolution was not a binding resolution passed under Chapter VII; it expressly refers to Article 2(7) UN Charter which provides that nothing in the Charter authorizes UN organs to intervene in matters which are essentially within the domestic jurisdiction of States; it did not authorize force. The USA, the UK, and, to a lesser extent, France nevertheless intervened in Iraq to protect the endangered civilians and subsequently proclaimed no-fly zones over north and south Iraq. The legal basis for this was not made clear at first, but the UK subsequently developed the doctrine of humanitarian intervention. To justify the use of force to protect the no-fly zones over north and south Iraq, the UK said that 'We believe that humanitarian intervention without the invitation of the country concerned can be justified in cases of extreme humanitarian need'. In contrast, the USA and France did not offer humanitarian intervention as the justification for their use of force in Iraq. States became polarized over the legality of the operations in the no-fly zones which continued for over ten years until *Operation Iraqi Freedom*. France withdrew its initial support; China and Russia did not accept the legality of the no-fly zones (Gray, 2002).

Those who support a doctrine of humanitarian intervention often rely on earlier, pre-Iraq, practice; they invoke as precedents India's intervention to end repression and support self-determination in Bangladesh (1971), Tanzania's intervention which overthrew the regime of Idi Amin in Uganda (1979), and Vietnam's use of force which ended the murderous rule of Pol Pot in Cambodia (1978). But in these episodes the States using force did not actually invoke a doctrine of humanitarian intervention; they preferred to rely on the better established right to self-defence. Several States said that violations of human rights could not justify the use of force. Some commentators attempt to re-write history in order to try to justify the action in Kosovo. This requires that we ignore what the States in question actually said, and therefore seems inconsistent with the approach of the ICJ in the *Nicaragua* case. The Court in considering whether a new doctrine of forcible intervention to help opposition forces to overthrow the government had emerged through State practice put great stress on the fact that neither the USA itself, nor other States, had claimed such a right.[19]

As regards Kosovo there was little express support from States for an autonomous doctrine of humanitarian intervention, other than from the UK. However, Belgium in its arguments to the ICJ did resort to this doctrine on the interpretation of Article 2(4). It said that the NATO campaign was an action to rescue a population in danger and was not directed against the territorial integrity or political independence of Yugoslavia. Other States such as Germany and France stressed the unique nature of the NATO operation and

---

[18] SC Res 688 (5 April 1991). This was adopted with ten votes in favour, three against, and with two abstentions.

[19] *Military and Paramilitary Activities in and against Nicaragua (Nicaragua v United States of America), Merits, Judgment, ICJ Reports 1986*, p 14, paras 206–9.

made clear that they did not regard it as a precedent for future humanitarian intervention. Most States arguing in support of the NATO campaign in the Security Council and before the ICJ did not rely on humanitarian intervention alone as an autonomous justification for the use of force; they seemed to rely on a combination of humanitarian intervention and implied authorization by the Security Council.

Those against the NATO bombing argued that Article 2(4) should be construed strictly. It was an absolute prohibition of the use of force and it was for the Security Council under Chapter VII to authorize the use of force; unilateral action by NATO was illegal. Yugoslavia's pleadings argued that there was no right of humanitarian intervention in international law. The practice of States after the creation of the UN did not justify any argument that there had been a change in the meaning of Article 2(4). General Assembly resolutions such as the *Definition of Aggression* and the *Declaration on Friendly Relations* excluded intervention in absolute terms. However, the attempt to secure a Security Council resolution condemning the NATO action was rejected - an indication of considerable political sympathy for NATO, if not conclusive as to the legality of its action.

Therefore, even if a legal doctrine of humanitarian intervention could be said to have emerged from the NATO action in Kosovo, its scope is far from clear (Chesterman, 2001). Is humanitarian intervention an autonomous right or does it depend on a prior determination by the Security Council under Chapter VII? Must it always be collective action and if so how many States should be involved? Can a bombing campaign amount to humanitarian action? Yugoslavia argued that, even if there is a right of humanitarian intervention, the modalities chosen were inconsistent with humanitarian aims: a high-level bombing campaign and the wide range of targets chosen put the population of the whole of Yugoslavia at risk.

There have been attempts by the UK and by scholars to develop a detailed framework for humanitarian intervention.[20] Moreover, Article 4(h) of the African Union Constitutive Act (2000) includes provision for humanitarian intervention pursuant to a decision of the African Union (AU) Assembly. But there is still no general agreement on a right of unilateral intervention. Many States in many different fora within and outside the UN after the NATO campaign have made a point of condemning the NATO action in Kosovo as illegal. The Non-Aligned Movement rejects humanitarian intervention as having no legal basis in the Charter. The doctrine therefore remains controversial. It is noteworthy that it was not used to justify the use of force against Afghanistan in *Operation Enduring Freedom* or against Iraq in *Operation Iraqi Freedom*, despite the choice of names for these operations.

In recent years attention has shifted away from humanitarian intervention to the concept of the 'responsibility to protect' (Stahn, 2007 and see Zifcak, Ch 17 in this book). Provision for this was included in the 2005 UN World Summit Outcome Document which was adopted unanimously by States. This responsibility arises in cases of genocide, ethnic cleansing or other serious violations of international humanitarian law. When a State fails to act to protect its own citizens, the international community has a responsibility to act, by force if necessary. But the action should be taken through the UN Security Council. There was no agreement on a right of unilateral intervention. The 2011 military intervention in Libya was hailed by many as a successful implementation of the 'responsibility to protect', in that it led to the overthrow of Colonel Gaddafi and the end to his regime's violent actions against the opposition, but this operation was seen by others as discrediting the concept. The African Union opposed the military intervention. The Security Council

---

[20] See, for example, (2000) 71 *BYIL* 644, and the *Report of the International Commission on Intervention and State Sovereignty, The Responsibility to Protect* (2001).

Resolution authorizing the military intervention did refer to 'responsibility to protect', but only to that of Libya rather than that of the international community. The actual legal basis for the use of force was a Security Council authorization under Chapter VII. Many States, including Russia and China, regarded the invocation of 'responsibility to protect' with regard to Libya as a pretext for regime change; accordingly they have been reluctant to support forcible intervention under the doctrine of 'responsibility to protect' in the subsequent civil war in Syria.

III. INTERVENTION, CIVIL WARS, AND INVITATION

The prohibition of the use of force in the UN Charter is directed at inter-State conflict, but apart from the many minor border incidents since the Second World War the most common use of force has been civil war, sometimes purely internal and sometimes fuelled by outside involvement. The rules against forcible intervention in civil conflict have been developed by General Assembly resolutions which elaborate on the Charter provisions on the use of force and complement the prohibitions of intervention in the constitutions of regional organizations. Thus the *Friendly Relations Declaration* (1970) makes clear that every State has the duty to refrain from organizing, instigating, assisting, or participating in acts of civil strife in another State and the duty not to foment, incite, or tolerate subversive, terrorist, or armed activities directed towards the violent overthrow of the regime of another State. There is a general consensus between States as to the principles to be applied to forcible intervention in civil conflicts, but their application in particular conflicts has caused fundamental disagreement (Doswald Beck, 1985; Roth, 1999).

The *Nicaragua* case set out the general doctrine in this area.[21] Nicaragua brought this case against the USA not only for unlawful use of force but also for unlawful intervention against the government through its support for the military and paramilitary operations of the *contra* forces. The ICJ affirmed that the principle of non-intervention involves the right of every State to conduct its affairs and to choose its own form of government without outside interference; it acknowledged that breaches of this principle were common but nevertheless found that the principle was customary international law. It held that the USA through 'recruiting, training, arming, equipping, financing, supplying and otherwise encouraging, supporting, aiding and directing military and paramilitary actions in and against Nicaragua' had violated international law.

In this case the Court distinguished between assistance to the government of a State and assistance to an opposition forcibly to overthrow the government. The former is allowed, the latter is forbidden. If forcible assistance to the opposition were allowed nothing would remain of the principle of non-intervention. The Court stressed that States in practice had not claimed such a right to help opposition forces against the government outside the context of national liberation movements seeking the right of self-determination, and that in the *Nicaragua* case the USA itself had not invoked a right to intervene but had relied on collective self-defence to justify its use of force against Nicaragua. The ICJ reaffirmed this approach in 2005 in *Armed Activities in the Territory of the Congo*.[22]

---

[21] *Military and Paramilitary Activities in and against Nicaragua (Nicaragua v United States of America), Merits, Judgment, ICJ Reports 1986*, p 14, paras 202–9.
[22] *Armed Activities on the Territory of the Congo (Democratic Republic of the Congo v Uganda), Judgment, ICJ Reports 2005*, p 168.

During the Cold War States which assisted opposition forces generally did so covertly; they also tended to challenge the legitimacy of the governments they were trying to overthrow. Thus when the USA assisted the opposition forces in Angola, Cambodia, and Afghanistan its use of force was covert and it challenged the legitimacy of the government in all these cases. No objective determination of the legitimacy of governments by the Security Council was possible in the Cold War. Since the end of the Cold War it is sometimes possible for the Security Council to determine which is the legitimate government and to distinguish between it and the opposition, for example in the context of arms embargoes. In the case of the complex conflict which broke out in the Democratic Republic of Congo (DRC) in 1998 the Security Council distinguished between those States lawfully in the DRC at the invitation of the government and those unlawfully assisting opposition forces. However, during the current conflict in Syria the Security Council has not been able to agree whether the government or the opposition forces are the legitimate representatives of the Syrian people.

As for military intervention at the request of a government, the ICJ in *Nicaragua* said simply that this was allowed. The *Definition of Aggression* acknowledges that a State may invite a foreign army into its territory. The right to use force to keep a government in power or to maintain domestic order has been taken for granted if the level of unrest falls below the threshold of civil war. France repeatedly intervened in its former colonies in Africa, ostensibly to maintain order. Similarly the USA denied military intervention in the long-lasting civil war in Colombia, but maintained that it was merely assisting the government to fight the drugs trade and terrorism. In 2011 the government of Bahrain invited troops from Saudi Arabia to suppress domestic protests. This last example illustrates that, although forcible intervention to assist a government may not violate the law on the use of force, it may be open to challenge on other grounds.

However, the legal position is less clear when the conflict amounts to a civil war. During the Cold War there was some agreement on the principle that any form of outside interference was unlawful during a civil war. However, it is clear that States manipulated the rules in pursuit of their own interests. Certain States attempted to justify their intervention by claiming that it was in response to a prior foreign intervention against the government. The USSR interventions in Czechoslovakia in 1968 and in Afghanistan in 1979 are examples of such claims. In both cases the claim that there had been an invitation was a fiction because the USSR had itself installed the government whose invitation it claimed to rely on, and in both the intervention was condemned by the General Assembly. More recently, the USA has justified its drone strikes in Yemen and Somalia as part of the war on Al Qaida, and thus as military assistance to governments in their struggle with terrorists, rather than as intervention in a civil war.

IV. SELF-DEFENCE

The main exception to the prohibition on the use of force in Article 2(4) is the right of self-defence. There are deep divisions between States and between scholars as to whether this right of self-defence is a wide or a narrow right (Corten, 2010). The controversy as to the scope of the right has intensified following the terrorist attacks of 11 September 2001. The basic UN Charter provision on self-defence is Article 51, which provides:

> Nothing in the present Charter shall impair the inherent right of individual or collective self-defence if an armed attack occurs against a Member of the United Nations, until the Security Council has taken measures necessary to maintain international peace and

security. Measures taken by Members in the exercise of this right of self-defence shall be immediately reported to the Security Council and shall not in any way affect the authority and responsibility of the Security Council under the present Charter to take at any time such action as it deems necessary in order to maintain or restore international peace and security.

As a matter of treaty interpretation, the debate centres on whether Article 51 is an exhaustive statement of the right to self-defence or whether there is a wider customary law right of self-defence going beyond the right to respond to an armed attack. Those supporting a wide right of self-defence argue, first, that the reference to 'inherent right' in Article 51 preserves a customary law right of self-defence and, second, that such a customary law right is wider than Article 51 and allows self-defence other than against an armed attack (Bowett, 1958; Arend and Beck, 1993). They argue for a right of anticipatory self-defence and of protection of nationals abroad. Those against a wide view of self-defence argue that this interpretation deprives Article 51 of any purpose; Article 51 imposes restrictions on the right of self-defence in response to armed attack and so it would be strange at the same time to preserve a wider right of self-defence unlimited by these restrictions. Also, as the right of self-defence is an exception to the prohibition on the use of force, it should be narrowly construed (Brownlie, 1963, p 251). Those arguing for a narrow right of self-defence also deny that customary law in 1945 included a wide right of self-defence which was preserved by Article 51. Given this fundamental disagreement on the proper interpretation of the UN Charter, State practice since 1945 is crucial for an understanding of the scope of the right of self-defence.

A. THE SCOPE OF SELF-DEFENCE: NECESSITY AND PROPORTIONALITY

Despite the fundamental disagreement on the scope of the right of self-defence, all are agreed that self-defence must be necessary and proportionate. This requirement of necessity and proportionality is not explicit in the UN Charter but is part of customary international law. It is generally taken as limiting self-defence to action which is necessary to recover territory or repel an attack on a State's forces and which is proportionate to this end. These customary law requirements of necessity and proportionality have been reaffirmed in the *Nicaragua* case,[23] the *Nuclear Weapons* Advisory Opinion,[24] the *Oil Platforms* case,[25] and *Armed Activities on the Territory of the Congo*.[26] The agreement between States that all self-defence should be necessary and proportionate makes it possible for them to reject many claims to self-defence on this basis without going into the more controversial doctrinal debates such as the existence of a right to anticipatory self-defence or the right to protect nationals or self-defence against terrorism.

B. THE MEANING OF 'ARMED ATTACK'

Article 51 specifies that self-defence is permissible in response to an armed attack. The definition of armed attack is left to customary international law. The most straightforward

---

[23] *Military and Paramilitary Activities in and against Nicaragua (Nicaragua v United States of America)*, *Merits, Judgment, ICJ Reports 1986*, p 14, para 194.

[24] *Legality of the Threat or Use of Nuclear Weapons, Advisory Opinion, ICJ Reports 1996*, p 266, para 141.

[25] *Oil Platforms (Islamic Republic of Iran v United States of America), ICJ Reports 2003*, p 161.

[26] *Armed Activities on the Territory of the Congo (Democratic Republic of the Congo v Uganda), Judgment, ICJ Reports 2005*, p 168.

type of armed attack is that by a regular army of one State against the territory or against the land, sea, or air forces of another. The meaning of armed attack at sea was considered in some detail in the recent *Oil Platforms* case; mine and missile attacks aimed at US-flagged military ships could constitute 'armed attacks', but attacks on US-owned ships did not amount to attacks on the State.

'Armed attack' extends beyond attacks by regular forces; it can also cover attacks by armed bands, irregulars, and mercenaries. In the *Nicaragua* case the ICJ used the *Definition of Aggression* paragraph 3(g) to help interpret the meaning of armed attack in customary international law. It held that an armed attack must be understood as including 'the sending by or on behalf of a State of armed bands, groups, irregulars or mercenaries, which carry out acts of armed force against another State of such gravity as to amount to an actual armed attack, or its substantial involvement therein.' But the ICJ did not consider that the concept of armed attack stretched as far as assistance to rebels in the form of the provision of weapons or logistical or other support.[27] The Court's conception of armed attack clearly requires a significant degree of government involvement.

However, it has been argued that the 9/11 terrorist attacks by Al Qaida on the World Trade Center and Pentagon in the USA have further expanded the notion of armed attack to cover the use of force by terrorist organizations, even in the absence of State involvement in the attack. The Security Council stopped short of an express pronouncement that the terrorist attack amounted to an 'armed attack', preferring to characterize it as a 'threat to the peace', but it did affirm the right of self-defence in the preambles to Resolutions 1368 and 1373 condemning the terrorist attacks;[28] this may amount to an implicit acceptance that the terrorist attacks on the USA were armed attacks, but it leaves unclear the exact nature of Afghanistan's involvement in the actions of Al Qaida terrorists. Similar questions arose about Hezbollah's attacks on Israel from Lebanon, Hamas' rocket attacks on Israel from Gaza and attacks by the PKK (Kurdish terrorists) on Turkey from Iraq: could these be classified as armed attacks giving a right to use force in response? What degree of State involvement is necessary to allow self-defence against Lebanon and Iraq? The law on this question remains controversial, and the ICJ deliberately avoided pronouncing on it in *Armed Activities on the Territory of the Congo*.[29]

C. THE USE OF FORCE IN PROTECTION OF NATIONALS

One controversy as to the scope of self-defence concerns the right of States to use force to protect their nationals abroad (Ronzitti, 1985). This right has been asserted by developed States such as the USA, the UK, and Israel under Article 51. It has been exercised in practice by the USA in the Dominican Republic (1965), Grenada (1983), and Panama (1989), by the UK in Suez (1956) and by Israel in Entebbe (1976). Most recently it has been invoked by Russia to justify its use of force against Georgia (2008). Developing States are more doubtful about the existence of this right. Where the host State consents or acquiesces or where there is no effective government, there is not usually a hostile response by other States if the forcible action is limited to the evacuation of nationals and not a pretext for more far-reaching intervention.

---

[27] *Military and Paramilitary Activities in and against Nicaragua (Nicaragua v United States of America), Merits, Judgment, ICJ Reports 1986*, p 14, para 195. These types of assistance could nevertheless constitute unlawful intervention.

[28] SC Res 1368 (12 September 2001); SC Res 1373 (28 September 2001).

[29] *Armed Activities on the Territory of the Congo (Democratic Republic of the Congo v Uganda), Judgment, ICJ Reports 2005*, p 168, para 147.

One of the most discussed and most controversial examples of the use of force to protect nationals abroad was by the USA in the small Caribbean island of Grenada.[30] The
USA relied on a series of justifications for sending forces into Grenada in response to
a coup which brought a socialist government to power. One of its arguments was that
US nationals were under threat and that the operation was designed to rescue them. But
there was considerable doubt as to the existence of the danger, and the use of force was
condemned by the UN General Assembly. In the Security Council the USA vetoed the
resolution condemning its intervention. One of the grounds for doubt about the legality
of the US operation, insofar as it was based on protection of nationals, was that the use of
force went beyond what was necessary and proportionate. All too often the protection of
nationals is a mere pretext to mask the real intent of overthrowing the government; this
was the case in all the episodes listed earlier, with the exception of the Entebbe intervention. Even here a majority of States did not accept the legality of the intervention, though
there was sympathy for Israel's position.[31]

When Russia invoked the protection of nationals to justify its use of force against
Georgia, western States did not oppose this doctrine as a matter of principle. Instead
they challenged Russia's motives and the proportionality of its action. In August 2008
Georgia mounted a military action to assert control over separatists in the region of South
Ossetia.[32] Russia's response was to send troops into South Ossetia to protect its nationals;
many ethnic Ossetians held Russian passports. The conflict spread to Abkhazia, another
area of separatist conflict, and Russia went on to attack military bases and transport links
throughout Georgia. Georgia was forced to withdraw its forces from South Ossetia and
Abkhazia which subsequently proclaimed their independence. Western States asserted
that Russia's intervention was unlawful because it was not limited to the protection of its
nationals, but was really designed to lead to the dismemberment of Georgia and the independence of South Ossetia and Abkhazia.

D. ANTICIPATORY OR PRE-EMPTIVE SELF-DEFENCE

Another major controversy over the scope of self-defence concerns the right of 'anticipatory' self-defence; that is, does the right of a State to self-defence arise only after an
armed attack has started under Article 51 or is there a wider right to anticipate an *imminent* attack? Is there even a right of pre-emptive self-defence where there is no imminent
attack? The controversy over the legality of anticipatory self-defence was so strong that
no provision on self-defence could be included in the UN General Assembly resolutions
such as the *Definition of Aggression* and the *Declaration on Friendly Relations*. States such
as the USA, the UK, and Israel have claimed a wide right of self-defence, but the doctrine
is so controversial that such claims have been rare in practice. Although the USA has
sometimes adopted wide Rules of Engagement which allow its own forces to use force in
response to demonstrations of 'hostile intent' by opposing forces rather than requiring
them to wait for an actual armed attack, it has tended to play down any anticipatory element in operations such as those by its naval convoys in the Gulf during the 1980–88 Iran/
Iraq War, and those by its aircraft over the no-fly zones proclaimed in Iraq to protect the
civilian population after Iraq invaded Kuwait in 1990. Thus, in the case of the shooting
down of the civilian Iran Airbus by the *USS Vincennes* in 1988, an incident which may be
taken to show the hazards of anticipatory self-defence, the USA argued that it had acted

---

[30] 1983 *UNYB* 211.   [31] 1976 *UNYB* 315.
[32] 2009 Report by Independent International Fact-Finding Mission http://www.ceiig.ch/Report.html.

in the context of an ongoing armed attack on its naval convoy in the Gulf to respond to what it (mistakenly) believed to be imminent attack by a hostile Iranian military aircraft. Iran took the case to the ICJ, but it was settled without the need for the Court to make any authoritative pronouncement on anticipatory self-defence. Similarly in the *Oil Platforms* case the USA preferred to rely on an extensive notion of armed attack rather than claim any right of anticipatory self-defence.

The express invocation of self-defence by Israel to justify its pre-emptive attack on an Iraqi nuclear reactor in 1981 is therefore unusual. Israel (itself a nuclear-weapons State) argued that the Iraqi reactor under construction was designed to produce nuclear weapons for use against Israel and therefore that it was entitled to take pre-emptive action. This attack was condemned by both the Security Council and by the General Assembly, but the resolutions do not directly address the fundamental doctrinal issue; it is left open to question whether the condemnation should be taken as a total rejection of anticipatory self-defence (as many States had argued) or just a rejection on the particular facts (as was the position of the USA).[33]

Those in favour of a right to anticipatory self-defence against an imminent attack argue that it is not realistic to expect States to wait for an attack before responding; those against argue that anticipatory self-defence involves a risk of escalation in that the State may mistake the intentions of the other or react disproportionately. Insofar as a wide conception of armed attack based on the capabilities of modern weapons is adopted, the gap between the two positions may shrink.

The ICJ in the *Nicaragua* case deliberately left the matter unresolved.[34] It did so again in *Armed Activities on the Territory of the Congo* (2005), a clear indication of the controversial nature of the doctrine.[35]

E. THE IMPACT OF THE TERRORIST ATTACKS OF 9/11 ON THE LAW OF SELF-DEFENCE

The attacks by Al Qaida on the World Trade Center and the Pentagon on 11 September 2001 brought a revolutionary challenge to the doctrine of self-defence.[36] Before 9/11 the use of force in response to terrorist attacks had been controversial; only Israel and the USA had expressly claimed such a right, and this was generally exercised in response to attacks on nationals abroad. There was no general support for such a right. In response to the 9/11 attacks on US territory, the USA began *Operation Enduring Freedom* with the aim of disrupting the use of Afghanistan as a terrorist base. It relied on self-defence as the basis for its use of force against Afghanistan; in its report to the Security Council under Article 51 the USA claimed to be acting in self-defence. This claim may seem controversial in the light of the previous doubts as to whether the right to self-defence could extend to action against past terrorist attacks, but *Operation Enduring Freedom* received massive support and the action was almost universally accepted as self-defence. NATO invoked Article 5 of the NATO Treaty for the first time; this provides that an attack on one member State is an attack on all. Other collective self-defence organizations, including the Organization

---

[33] 1981 *UNYB* 275.

[34] *Military and Paramilitary Activities in and against Nicaragua (Nicaragua v United States of America), Merits, Judgment, ICJ Reports 1986,* p 14, para 194.

[35] *Armed Activities on the Territory of the Congo (Democratic Republic of the Congo v Uganda), Judgment, ICJ Reports 2005,* p 168, para 143.

[36] See account of the facts in (2002) 96 *AJIL* 237, and editorial comments in (2001) 95 *AJIL* 833.

of American States (OAS), also took the view that the attack was an armed attack for the purposes of collective self-defence. The EU, China, Russia, Japan, and Pakistan supported this view. Many States have played a role in the military campaign. Only Iran and Iraq expressly challenged the legality of the operation. In the preambles of Resolution 1368 condemning the attacks and Resolution 1373 on measures against international terrorism the Security Council recognized the right of self-defence. This was the first time that the Security Council had implicitly recognized the right to use force in self-defence in the context of terrorist action, but the legal significance of this is not clear.

This use of force against Afghanistan raises many questions about the traditional model of self-defence. First, does the response to 9/11 widen the concept of armed attack? The drafters of Article 51 originally envisaged self-defence against an attack by a State, and those invoking the right generally took care to attribute responsibility to a State. Now some States argue that the words of Article 51 are wide enough to mean that a terrorist attack on a State's territory by a non-State actor may be an armed attack which justifies a response against the State which harboured those responsible. However, considerable uncertainty remains as to the degree of State involvement required, and as to whether force could be used in self-defence against terrorists in a State which was not complicit in the terrorist attack (Becker, 2006) The ICJ did not elaborate on the law in this controversial area in *Armed Activities on the Territory of the Congo* and the *Wall* Advisory Opinion. There are few express claims in State practice since 9/11 to support such a wide right of self-defence, but some commentators have taken an extensive view of the legal significance of 9/11 and its aftermath (Tams, 2009). The USA has argued that it may carry out targeted killing of members of Al Qaida and affiliated groups in States which are unwilling or unable to act against the terrorists, but the legal basis for such wide claims remains obscure.

Second, the right to self-defence claimed by the USA and the UK in response to the 9/11 terrorist attacks was also pre-emptive. Both the USA and the UK in their letters to the Security Council said that their military action was in response to the attack on the World Trade Center; for the USA the aim is to deter further attacks on the USA, for the UK 'to avert the continuing threat of attacks from the same source'. That is, although the initial attack had ended and thus it would be difficult to invoke self-defence against that attack, the USA and the UK clearly felt the need to avoid the appearance of punitive (and unlawful) reprisals. Many States in the past had rejected the legality of pre-emptive self-defence, but they accepted the legality of *Operation Enduring Freedom*. However, there is still controversy as to the significance of this acceptance; it is not clear that the international response should be construed as a general acceptance of anticipatory or pre-emptive use of force outside the context of terrorism or of *Operation Enduring Freedom*. Another possible restriction on this apparently very wide and, for many States, new doctrine of self-defence is that the right of self-defence against terrorism may exist only in cases where the right has been recognized by the Security Council, as here in Resolutions 1368 and 1373. Several States regarded this Security Council backing as crucial to the US claim to self-defence.

Also questions arise as to necessity and proportionality. The USA at the start of *Operation Enduring Freedom* warned that the 'Global War on Terror' could take many years. In a campaign to prevent future terrorist attacks it is difficult to identify an appropriate end to the action, but the longer it continues and the more destruction it involves the more difficult it is to argue that it is proportionate. If the use of force proves ineffective in deterring terrorist attacks, it is also difficult to argue that it is necessary. *Operation Enduring Freedom* in Afghanistan is now in its twelfth year. The UN Security Council apparently accepts its legality, but it is not entirely clear whether its legal basis is now the consent of the government of Afghanistan or an independent—and long-lasting—right of self-defence.

1. Lebanon (2006)

Questions concerning the scope of self-defence after 9/11 arose with regard to the 2006 conflict in Lebanon. The conflict began when Hezbollah launched a minor cross-border attack on Israeli forces in northern Israel from Lebanon, killing eight Israeli soldiers and abducting two.[37] In response Israel mounted a month-long land, sea, and air attack on Lebanon causing serious destruction to its infrastructure and massive displacement of its people. In the Security Council States avoided discussion of the fundamental questions whether there could be an 'armed attack' by non-State actors in the absence of Lebanon's involvement, and whether Israel had the right of self-defence against Lebanon under the UN Charter, preferring to focus on the issue of proportionality. Most States eventually condemned Israel's use of force as disproportionate. If seen as a response to the minor action by Hezbollah, Israel's action was clearly not proportionate. But Israel, the USA, and the UK took a different approach to proportionality: they argued that terrorist attacks by Hezbollah posed an existential threat to Israel and that massive forcible action to stop future attacks was proportionate to the threat posed.

Similar questions about the scope of self-defence in response to terrorist acts arose with regard to the 2008–9 Gaza conflict and Ethiopia's intervention in Somalia (2006–8). The Gaza conflict was precipitated by Hamas rocket attacks on Israel; Israel responded by three weeks of intense land, sea, and air military action, leading to 1,300 Palestinian deaths and 130 Israeli deaths, and massive destruction of property within Gaza. Was this action justified as self-defence? The fundamental issue was the status of Gaza: Israel had taken it by force from Egypt in 1967 and it remained as occupied territory until 2005. In 2005 Israel withdrew its troops, but maintained control over movement in and out of the territory. If Gaza remained occupied territory under international law in 2008, then the relevant law would be that governing occupation rather than any right of self-defence under Article 51. This is the ICJ view, as expressed in a rather obscure paragraph on self-defence in the *Wall* Advisory Opinion with regard to the occupied West Bank: Security Council Resolutions 1368 and 1373 could not apply to allow self-defence in response to terrorist attacks from occupied territory.[38] In the Security Council debates States were initially broadly sympathetic to Israel, but they preferred to avoid express discussion of the issue of whether Israel had a right of self-defence under Article 51 against attacks from Gaza, and the related question of the classification of the conflict, instead focusing on the international humanitarian law applicable during armed conflict.

F. A 'BUSH DOCTRINE' OF PRE-EMPTIVE SELF-DEFENCE?

After it had undertaken *Operation Enduring Freedom* in Afghanistan, the USA shifted its focus in the 'global war on terror' to the threat posed by the 'Axis of Evil': Iran, Iraq, and North Korea. In the light of the alleged new dangers facing it after 9/11, the USA developed a new *National Security Strategy* (2002): the USA must be prepared to stop rogue States and global terrorists from threatening to use weapons of mass destruction against it.[39] Accordingly it asserted that there was a need to re-examine the law of self-defence.

[37] Gray, 2008, p 237.
[38] *Legal Consequences of the Construction of a Wall in the Palestinian Occupied Territories, Advisory Opinion,* ICJ Reports 2004, p 136, para 139.
[39] (2002) 41 ILM 1478.

The USA had always taken the wide view that anticipatory self-defence was lawful in the case of an imminent armed attack, but now it argued that the requirement of imminence should be reconsidered. However, it did not make clear what would trigger such pre-emptive (or preventive) action. The 2006 US *National Security Strategy* repeated the commitment to pre-emptive self-defence, but did not elaborate further.

There is little sign of support for a fundamental transformation of self-defence along the lines suggested in the US *National Security Strategy* under President Bush. The UN set up a High-level Panel of Experts to respond to the new challenges to the collective security system after 9/11; in its Report of December 2004 it accepted the controversial right of anticipatory self-defence, but firmly rejected the doctrine of pre-emptive self-defence.[40] It said that there is no right to self-defence if the threat of armed attack is not imminent. If there are good arguments for preventive military action, with good evidence to support them, they should be put to the Security Council which can authorize action if it chooses to. A unilateral right of pre-emptive self-defence would be dangerously destabilizing. Similarly, the ICJ in *Armed Activities on the Territory of the Congo* (2005) said that Article 51 may justify a use of force in self-defence only within the strict confines there laid down. It does not allow the use of force by a State to protect perceived security interests beyond those parameters. Other means are available to a concerned State, including recourse to the Security Council.[41] Thus, the UK supports anticipatory self-defence but rejects a wider doctrine of pre-emptive self-defence. The position of President Obama on this issue was left deliberately unclear. The USA has not ruled out the use of force against Iran or North Korea to prevent their development of nuclear weapons, but it has not attempted to provide any legal justification for such action.

G. COLLECTIVE SELF-DEFENCE

The express provision for collective self-defence in Article 51 of the UN Charter is generally seen as an innovation, included in response to the desire of Latin American States to retain regional autonomy. The right of collective self-defence formed the basis for the NATO Treaty and the Warsaw Pact and for many regional treaties after the Second World War; these treaties provided that an attack on one was an attack on all and provided for a collective response. As mentioned earlier, NATO invoked Article 5 for the first time with regard to the 9/11 attacks. The USA took the major role in *Operation Enduring Freedom* against Afghanistan, but it received some assistance from other States acting in collective self-defence. Opinion is divided as to whether collective self-defence is a valuable safeguard for small States or a dangerous doctrine justifying intervention by distant and powerful States in remote conflicts. It was not often invoked during the Cold War and the few instances where it was invoked—such as the USA in the Vietnam War (1961–75) and in Nicaragua, and the USSR interventions in Hungary (1956), Czechoslovakia (1968), and Afghanistan (1979)—were controversial. In all these cases there was dispute as to whether there had been an armed attack or a genuine request for help from the victim State.

---

[40] Report of the Secretary-General's High-level Panel on Threats, Challenges and Change, UN Doc A/59/565. The UN Secretary-General in his response to the High-level Panel, 'In Larger Freedom' (March 2005), also accepted this previously controversial doctrine, although in more cautious terms, saying that 'imminent threats are fully covered by Article 51' (UN Doc A/59/2005). The Non-Aligned Movement reaffirmed its rejection of a wide doctrine of self-defence.

[41] *Armed Activities on the Territory of the Congo (Democratic Republic of the Congo v Uganda), Judgment,* ICJ Reports 2005, p 168.

The *Nicaragua* case played a crucial role in establishing the scope of the right of collective self-defence. The USA had attempted to justify its use of force against Nicaragua by relying on collective self-defence, but the ICJ held that the use of force by the USA did not satisfy any of the criteria for legitimate collective self-defence. There had been no armed attack by Nicaragua on Costa Rica, El Salvador, or Honduras, no declaration by any of these States that it was the victim of an armed attack, and no invitation by them to the USA to come to their aid. Finally, the mining of harbours and bombing of ports by the USA was not necessary to repel alleged attacks by Nicaragua on El Salvador, and was not proportionate. The USA had not reported its actions to the Security Council under Article 51. This decision was controversial at the time, but accurately reflects State practice on collective self-defence.

H. THE ROLE OF THE SECURITY COUNCIL

In theory the Security Council has a central role with regard to individual and collective self-defence: under Article 51 States must report their use of force in self-defence to the Security Council immediately and the right of the State to self-defence is temporary until the Security Council takes the measures necessary to maintain international peace and security. In practice the Security Council does not generally make pronouncements on the legality of claims to self-defence. Thus in the case of inter-State conflict between Iran and Iraq (1980–88) and Ethiopia and Eritrea (1998–2000) the Security Council did not initially attribute responsibility for the start of the conflict, and did not decide who had the right of self-defence. In contrast when Iraq invaded Kuwait in 1990 the Security Council did expressly uphold the right of Kuwait to self-defence.

States have taken care to report their self-defence to the Security Council, especially since the *Nicaragua* case where the Court held that the failure by the USA to report its use of force to the Security Council was an indication that the USA was not itself convinced that it was acting in self-defence. This approach was followed in *Armed Activities on the Territory of the Congo*[42] and by the Eritrea/Ethiopia Claims Commission.[43] In the past there has been some controversy as to whether the right to self-defence has been terminated because the Security Council has taken action and thus has taken 'measures necessary to maintain international peace and security'. It seems to be generally accepted that it is not enough for the Security Council simply to pass a resolution or even to impose economic measures if the aggressor is left in occupation of territory it has seized illegally. This was the argument of the UK with regard to the Falkland Islands (Islas Malvinas); it claimed the right to use force in self-defence when Argentina seized the Falklands despite the Security Council resolutions calling for a peaceful resolution. The UK argued that it retained its right to self-defence until Argentina was driven out.[44] Unless the Security Council has expressly passed a binding resolution declaring the right to be terminated, there will be room for doubt on this issue. If a State wishes to make the position clear, it should try to secure an express recognition of its right by the Security Council. Thus in the Iraq/Kuwait conflict, even when economic measures were taken by the Security Council, in the same resolution it affirmed the right of self-defence;[45] and in regard to the 9/11 attacks the Security Council expressly referred to the continuing right to self-defence.[46]

---

[42] *Armed Activities on the Territory of the Congo (Democratic Republic of the Congo v Uganda), Judgment, ICJ Reports 2005*, p 168, para 145.

[43] See Ethiopia's *Ius ad Bellum* claims 1–8, (2006) 45 ILM 430.   [44] 1982 *UNYB* 1320.

[45] SC Res 661 (16 August 1990).

[46] SC Res 1368 (12 September 2001), 1373 (14 November 2001).

V. THE USE OF FORCE UNDER CHAPTER VII OF THE UN CHARTER

The original intent behind the UN Charter was that control over the use of force would lie with the Security Council which would have a standing army at its disposal to enable it to take enforcement action against aggression in order to restore international peace and security. This ambitious plan has not been realized and the original Charter scheme has been modified through practice. Under Article 24 of the UN Charter the Security Council has the primary responsibility for the maintenance of international peace and security, but during the Cold War the veto possessed by the five permanent members of the Security Council under Article 27 generally blocked effective action by the Security Council. Chapter VII sets out the framework for its enforcement powers; under Article 2(7) these powers are not limited by the normal duty on the UN not to intervene in matters essentially within the domestic jurisdiction of States. Thus Chapter VII gives very wide powers to the Security Council. The Council in practice does not generally make express reference to specific Articles within Chapter VII; it more commonly makes a reference to Chapter VII in general terms (Sarooshi, 1999). However, since the use of force against Iraq in 2003, certain members of the Security Council have ensured that its resolutions on Iran and North Korea (concerning the proliferation of nuclear weapons) refer expressly to specific Charter Articles, in order to prevent any invocation of those resolutions to justify the use of force.

Under Article 39 the Security Council is 'to determine the existence of any threat to the peace, breach of the peace or act of aggression' and then to make recommendations or decide measures under Articles 41 and 42. The Council has been reluctant to find an act of aggression under Article 39; rare examples are resolutions condemning South Africa (under the apartheid regime) and Israel for attacks on neighbouring States. It has determined the existence of a breach of the peace only in cases of inter-State conflicts as in the 1980–88 Iran/Iraq conflict and in response to the 1990 Iraqi invasion of Kuwait.

The Security Council has consistently taken a wide view of 'threat to the peace' and has been prepared to identify such a threat as arising out of internal conflicts such as those in the DRC and Somalia, overthrow of democratic government as in Haiti, and refusal to act against terrorism in the cases of Libya, Sudan, and the Taliban regime in Afghanistan. It is not clear whether any other body such as the ICJ would have the power to challenge a finding under Article 39 by the Security Council. The Court has never made an authoritative ruling on the matter; it avoided the issue in the *Lockerbie*[47] and *Bosnia-Herzegovina Genocide* cases.[48]

Article 40 provides for provisional measures and the Security Council has invoked this as the basis for its call for cease-fires as, for example, in Resolution 598 (1987) with regard to the 1980–88 Iran/Iraq conflict. This resolution was unusual in that it made express reference to Articles 39 and 40.

---

[47] *Questions of Interpretation and Application of the 1971 Montreal Convention arising from the Aerial Incident at Lockerbie (Libyan Arab Jamahirya v United States of America)*, Preliminary Objections, Judgment, *ICJ Reports 1998*, p 115.

[48] *Application of the Convention on the Prevention and Punishment of the Crime of Genocide*, Provisional Measures, Order of 8 April 1993, *ICJ Reports 1993*, p 3, Order of 13 September, *ICJ Reports 1993*, p 325.

A. MEASURES UNDER ARTICLE 41

Article 41 allows the Security Council to decide on measures not involving the use of armed force to give effect to its decisions; these include 'complete or partial interruption of economic relations and of rail, sea, air, postal, telegraphic, radio, and other means of communication, and the severance of diplomatic relations'. Article 41 was little used in the Cold War: only in the comprehensive trade embargo on the illegal white minority government in Rhodesia (now Zimbabwe) in a series of resolutions from 1965 and in the arms embargo on South Africa in 1977. But there has been a massive increase in the use of Article 41 since then (Gray, 2008, p 266). Indeed there is now increasing concern about the effects of trade embargoes on 'innocent' populations and the Security Council has attempted to develop 'smart' sanctions, targeted on those responsible for any non-compliance with its decisions. The official position is that Article 41 measures are not punishment but should be designed to secure compliance with decisions of the Security Council. They have been imposed on States and also on non-State actors, such as the Bosnian Serbs and UNITA in Angola. Recently they have been imposed on Iran and North Korea in an attempt to halt their development of nuclear weapons; these resolutions refer expressly to Article 41 in order to prevent any argument that they could be invoked to justify the use of force.

In many civil wars the imposition of an arms embargo is the immediate response of the Security Council to calls for it to act; thus arms embargoes were imposed in response to civil war in Yugoslavia, Somalia and Rwanda, and Liberia. Also, for the first time an arms embargo was imposed on both sides in the inter-State conflict between Ethiopia and Eritrea.

B. THE USE OF FORCE UNDER CHAPTER VII OF THE UN CHARTER

In cases where Article 41 measures would not be sufficient or had proved insufficient to maintain or restore international peace and security the original Charter scheme under Articles 42–9 was that the UN would have its own standing army able to take measures involving armed force. Member States were to make agreements to put troops at the disposal of the Security Council which would 'take such action by air, sea or land forces as may be necessary to maintain or restore international peace and security' under Article 42. But in practice member States did not conclude agreements to put troops at the disposal of the UN under Article 43 and no standing army was created. Cold War divisions help to explain this failure to implement the Charter scheme, but even today States remain unwilling to hand over control of troops for enforcement action. Because of the failure of States to conclude agreements under Article 43 there was a doctrinal debate as to whether the whole Charter scheme was therefore frustrated and Article 42 was inoperative (Simma, 2012, p 1337).

However, the Security Council interpreted Chapter VII flexibly to authorize the establishment of a UN force in Korea in 1950. Although it did not make clear the exact constitutional basis for its actions, it referred to Chapter VII in general terms. When North Korea invaded South Korea in 1950 the Security Council intervened, although neither was a member State; it recommended member States to 'furnish such assistance to South Korea as may be necessary to repel the armed attack and to restore international peace and security in the area'. There was heated debate at the time as to the legal basis for this action, especially as the Security Council was able to act only because the USSR had stayed away from the relevant meeting in protest at the representation of China by the Taiwan government rather than the effective Communist government. Commentators disagreed as to whether this was collective security under Article 39, 42, or Chapter VII generally or whether it was only an authorization of collective self-defence. The debate leading to the Security Council decision sheds no light on this dilemma and it appears to have little practical significance.

No further forcible action was authorized under Chapter VII until the end of the Cold War. When Iraq invaded Kuwait in 1990 the Security Council passed Resolution 678 (1990) authorizing member States to use 'all necessary means to secure the withdrawal of Iraqi troops and to restore international peace and security in the area'.[49] It is clear from the Security Council debates that the phrase 'all necessary means' was intended to cover the use of force. The action against Iraq in *Operation Desert Storm* was seen at the time as the beginning of a new era for the Security Council, the start of a New World Order. In contrast with Korea the force did not operate under the UN flag, but it did act under the authorization of the Security Council, even if the precise constitutional basis was again unclear.

This use of Chapter VII to authorize member States to use force has been repeated many times in many different situations. It has certainly become clear that Chapter VII action is not limited to collective self-defence. The Security Council has not again authorized force against an aggressor State, but it has authorized force in internal conflicts, for example in response to non-cooperation with UN-brokered cease-fires; to secure the delivery of humanitarian aid as in Somalia and in Yugoslavia; to protect safe havens and enforce no-fly zones in Bosnia-Herzegovina; to restore democracy in Haiti; to act against Somali pirates; to support the government of Mali in recovering control of its territory from terrorists and armed groups; as well as to secure the implementation of economic measures under Article 41. A controversial recent instance of the authorization of force by the Security Council was in Libya. In Resolution 1973 (2011) the Security Council authorized member States to use 'all necessary means' to protect civilians and civilian populated areas under threat of attack. There were deep divisions between States as to whether the ensuing military operations went beyond the scope of this authority (Ulfstein and Christiansen, 2013). The Security Council has also authorized massive member State forces to maintain order and engage in peace-building after the end of conflicts in East Timor, Kosovo, Afghanistan, and Iraq.

The UN Secretary-General recognizes that the UN does not itself have the resources for enforcement action, and that it will have to continue to turn to 'coalitions of the willing' or to regional organizations, but he acknowledges that there is a danger that the UN may be sidelined. The Security Council has made greater attempts to keep some control of the member State forces since *Operation Desert Storm* when it set no time limit for the operation against Iraq. The mandates authorizing member States to use force are now usually for a fixed period and they may stress the need for impartiality; States are required to report regularly to the Security Council.

C. IMPLIED OR REVIVED AUTHORIZATION OF FORCE?

More controversial than the express authorization of member States to use force under Chapter VII has been the issue of implied or revived authorization (Lobel and Ratner, 1999). States seeking legitimacy for their use of force but unable or unwilling to obtain a Chapter VII resolution have sought to rely on implied or revived authorization. Thus,

---

[49] SC Res 678 (29 April 1990).

the USA and the UK in using force against Iraq in the decade after the cease-fire of Security Council Resolution 687 claimed that Iraq's violations of the cease-fire regime justified them in using force under Chapter VII in 1993 and 1998. The same argument was put forward by several States with regard to Kosovo. NATO's legal justification for its air campaign against the government of Yugoslavia was brief, but there were indications that it claimed implied authorization under Security Council Resolutions 1160 (1998), 1199 (1998), and 1203 (1998). Those impatient with the difficulty of securing agreement from China and Russia to the use of force even after the end of the Cold War argued that there was no need for express authorization of the use of force. It was enough that the resolutions identified a threat to international peace and security under Chapter VII, made certain demands on Yugoslavia, and determined that it had violated international agreements. This interpretation of the relevant Security Council resolutions was strongly resisted by Russia and China as a distortion of the words of the resolutions, not justified in the light of the Security Council debates, and a dangerous threat to the authority of the Security Council.

1. Operation Iraqi Freedom (2003)

These arguments arose again over *Operation Iraqi Freedom* in March 2003. Deep divisions as to the legality of the use of force against Iraq existed not only between the USA and China and Russia, but also within NATO and Europe. The USA, the UK and Australia (with the support of a 'coalition' of about forty-five other States including Spain, Poland, and others from eastern Europe) undertook *Operation Iraqi Freedom* to secure the disarmament of Iraq of weapons of mass destruction. The legal justification they offered was that they were acting on the basis of Security Council authority under a combination of three resolutions (678, 687, and 1444) adopted under Chapter VII of the Charter.[50] They claimed that military operations were necessary because of the threat posed by Iraq's alleged development of weapons of mass destruction in violation of its disarmament obligations. Other States such as Russia, China, France, and Germany argued for the continuation of UN weapons inspections; military action was not necessary.

Only the USA invoked (pre-emptive) self-defence as a possible basis for *Operation Iraqi Freedom* and it did not provide any detailed justification of this position; the UK and Australia did not rely on this doctrine. After *Operation Iraqi Freedom* drove Saddam Hussein from power in April 2003 it became apparent that Iraq did not possess weapons of mass destruction or the immediate capacity to produce them. Serious doubts emerged about the intelligence on the basis of which the use of force had been justified, and for many this provided a dramatic illustration of the dangers of pre-emptive action.

The argument as to the legality of *Operation Iraqi Freedom* turned on the interpretation of the three Security Council resolutions. Resolution 1441 was passed unanimously in November 2002 to give Iraq a 'final opportunity' to comply with its disarmament obligations imposed under the cease-fire regime.[51] The Security Council recalled its earlier resolutions and, acting under Chapter VII, decided that Iraq had been and remained in material breach of its obligations under Resolution 687 (1991), the cease-fire regime imposed by the Security Council requiring Iraq to disarm its weapons of mass destruction and to cooperate with UN weapons inspectors.[52] The UN weapons inspectors were to return to Iraq under an enhanced system of weapons inspection and Iraq was to provide a complete declaration of all aspects of its weapons programme; any omissions would

---

[50] For the UK case, see 52 *ICLQ* (2003) 811. The US position has been set out in Taft and Buchwald, 2003, p 553. For a description of the sequence of events, see Murphy, 2003, p 419.
[51] SC Res 1441 (8 November 2002).   [52] SC Res 687 (3 April 1991).

constitute a further material breach by Iraq. In the event of reports of non-compliance the Security Council would reconvene to consider the situation. Resolution 1441 clearly did not expressly authorize force against Iraq; several permanent members of the Security Council were not willing to agree to such authorization.

Following this resolution Iraq produced a lengthy declaration on the state of its weapons programme and UN weapons inspectors returned to Iraq. Iraq was at first slow to cooperate with the inspectors, but from February 2003 this improved. The USA and the UK argued that Iraq was in material breach of its obligations, but there was no such formal determination by the Security Council itself. The USA and the UK tried to secure a second resolution expressly authorizing force against Iraq but failed to convince other member States that military action was justified. They then proceeded to argue that no second resolution was necessary: Resolution 1441 had not expressly required a second resolution; its effect was to revive the authority to use force given in Resolution 678 (1991) in the event of material breach by Iraq of disarmament requirements under the cease-fire regime established by Resolution 687.

The main problems with this line of argument are, first, that it relies on the revival of Resolution 678, passed ten years earlier in response to Iraq's invasion of Kuwait. Those supporting *Operation Iraqi Freedom* argued that the authorization to use force in Resolution 678 could be revived as it had been suspended but not terminated by the cease-fire in Resolution 687. Resolution 678 did not contain any time limit and Iraq continued to pose a threat to international peace and security. Second, the 'coalition' case assumed that it was possible for them unilaterally to determine that there had been a material breach by Iraq and that the use of force was justified. States opposed to the use of force, such as Russia, China, France, and Germany, argued that such decisions were exclusively for the Security Council; this was also the view of the UN Secretary-General.

VI. UN PEACEKEEPING

A. THE INCEPTION OF PEACEKEEPING

UN peacekeeping is not expressly provided for in the UN Charter; it developed through practice during the Cold War (Higgins, 1969–81). When the UN Security Council proved unable to take action in response to breaches of the peace, threats to the peace, and acts of aggression, because its decision-making was obstructed by the divisions between the Western and Eastern blocs, peacekeeping was developed as a partial substitute. The General Assembly initially took on a (controversial) role in this area under the *Uniting for Peace Resolution* (1950)[53] which allowed it to call emergency meetings and make recommendations to States on the use of force when the Security Council was prevented from acting by the lack of unanimity of the permanent members. The *Certain Expenses* Advisory Opinion[54] considered the constitutionality of a force set up by the General Assembly: could member States be required to pay the expenses of such operations? The ICJ held that, although the Security Council had primary responsibility for the maintenance of international peace and security under Article 24, this was primary and not exclusive; it was open to the General Assembly to recommend peacekeeping but not to decide on enforcement action which was the exclusive province of the Security Council.

---

[53] GA Res 377 (V), (3 November 1950).
[54] *Certain Expenses of the United Nations, Advisory Opinion, ICJ Reports 1962*, p 151.

In practice it has been the Security Council which has subsequently exercised the main responsibility for peacekeeping. The UN Charter does not make any express provision for peacekeeping and its precise constitutional basis remains unclear, but discussion now centres on the nature rather than on the legality of the institution. There was initially a clear distinction between peacekeeping and Chapter VII enforcement action, but the peacekeeping label has come to cover a wide range of operations and the distinctions between peacekeeping and enforcement action have blurred. From 1948–88 15 peacekeeping forces were created (United Nations, 1996). The first major force was UNEF, established by the General Assembly in the Middle East from 1956–67; the principles on which this operation was based provided guidelines for future operations. UNEF was established with the consent of the host State and was terminated when Egypt withdrew its consent; it was an impartial and neutral force and used force only in self-defence. Like UNEF, most Cold War peacekeeping operations functioned between States, and most were limited operations mandated only to monitor cease-fires or borders. The five permanent members of the Security Council generally did not take part in peacekeeping forces in order to insulate peacekeeping from Cold War divisions and States with historic or geographical interests in the conflict were also excluded.

ONUC was the second major peacekeeping operation and it departed to some extent from the guidelines described. It operated within the Congo which had descended into chaos on the withdrawal of the colonial power in 1960. The original mandate of ONUC was expanded to allow the use of force beyond self-defence; the Security Council used the language of Chapter VII in authorizing force to prevent the occurrence of civil war and the secession of the province of Katanga, but made no express reference to it.

Five of the first fifteen peacekeeping forces are still in existence: three in the Middle East, one in Kashmir, and one in Cyprus; this reflects the danger that a peacekeeping force may simply freeze a situation.

B. PEACEKEEPING AFTER THE END OF THE COLD WAR

After the end of the Cold War the Security Council expanded its peacekeeping functions and there is now a continuing debate about the nature of peacekeeping. Over fifty new peacekeeping forces have been created, most within States. UN peacekeeping forces played a role in the settlement of Cold War conflicts in Namibia, Angola and Mozambique, Afghanistan, Cambodia, and Central America. These forces are sometimes called the second generation of peacekeeping; they were generally ambitious operations going beyond military and humanitarian operations to bringing about national reconciliation and re-establishing effective government. They met with mixed success and faced serious problems of non-cooperation in Angola and Cambodia.

New conflicts broke out after the Cold War in the Former Yugoslavia, the former USSR and in Africa, and more peacekeeping forces were created. The Security Council took an innovative approach in many ways: the distinction between peacekeeping and enforcement action was blurred; peacekeeping forces were expected to carry out their functions at the same time as member State enforcement forces; UN peacekeeping was combined with regional peacekeeping. A third generation of peacekeeping was conceived in 1999 when UNMIK was established in Kosovo and UNTAET in East Timor. The UN Secretary-General said that these were qualitatively different from almost any other the UN had ever undertaken; in each place the UN formed the administration responsible for fulfilling all the functions of a State (Wilde, 2008).

C. CHALLENGES TO PEACEKEEPING: YUGOSLAVIA AND SOMALIA 1991–5

The peacekeeping operations in Yugoslavia and Somalia will be considered in some detail because they posed a major challenge to the traditional principles governing peacekeeping - the principles that peacekeeping is distinct from enforcement action under Chapter VII of the Charter, and that a peacekeeping force should be impartial, use force only in self-defence, and operate with the consent of the host State. In Yugoslavia UNPROFOR was created as a peacekeeping force, first in Croatia and then in Bosnia-Herzegovina, initially without reference to Chapter VII. However, there was no effective cease-fire and no real cooperation from the parties on the ground. UNPROFOR was given an ambitious and unrealistic mandate 'to create the conditions of peace and security required for the negotiation of a settlement'. This mandate was incrementally expanded in a long series of resolutions, most of which were passed under Chapter VII. These gave UNPROFOR the power to use force to secure the delivery of humanitarian aid, to enforce no-fly zones and to protect safe havens declared to protect Bosnian Muslims in Bosnia-Herzegovina. This authority to use force brought UNPROFOR into conflict with the Bosnian Serbs. But member States were not willing to provide enough troops to enable UNPROFOR to carry out its wide mandate. Instead the UN turned to NATO air forces to take enforcement action under Chapter VII.

The UN had a similar experience in Somalia. The Security Council was slow to get involved in the civil war which broke out in 1991. It established a peacekeeping force, UNOSOM, to provide security for those delivering humanitarian aid. When this met non-cooperation on the ground it was supplemented by a US-led member State force. Both were later replaced by UNOSOM II, the first UN peacekeeping operation which was actually created under Chapter VII. But UNOSOM II was drawn into the conflict and proved unable to carry out its mandate. In both Yugoslavia and Somalia UN peacekeeping forces on the ground had to try to operate at the same time as member State forces authorized to use force under Chapter VII. This combination proved unworkable during these conflicts.

The peacekeeping forces subsequently created in Georgia, Liberia, and Tajikistan were not established under Chapter VII, and were not given powers under Chapter VII.

This looked like a return to traditional peacekeeping in response to the experience of Yugoslavia and Somalia. However, events in Rwanda led to further reappraisal of peacekeeping.

D. PEACEKEEPING IN AFRICA

The demands of the major operations in Yugoslavia and Somalia made developed States reluctant to intervene in Rwanda in 1994 when the Hutu government turned on the Tutsis and massacred over 500,000 people in three months. The relatively small UN peacekeeping force in Rwanda was not authorized or equipped to prevent the genocide. The UN was subjected to serious criticism for the failure, and there were calls for more robust peacekeeping in the protection of civilians. The Security Council has repeatedly been accused of double standards with regard to its treatment of Africa. However, seven of the fifteen current peacekeeping operations are in Africa and these involve nearly three-quarters of all UN peacekeeping personnel. Several of them are complex multi-dimensional operations with robust mandates. However, the UN still encounters difficulties in securing adequate resources for these operations. There is concern about the unwillingness of developed States to provide peacekeeping troops in difficult situations, especially in Africa (Berman and Sams, 2000). Calls for 'robust peacekeeping' meet the reluctance of developed States to contribute troops in situations where there is no peace to keep and no cooperation on the ground.

E. PEACEKEEPING AFTER THE *BRAHIMI REPORT*

In response to the experiences in Yugoslavia, Somalia, and Rwanda, the UN set up a panel to carry out the first comprehensive review of peacekeeping since its inception. The panel presented the *Brahimi Report* at the 2000 UN Millennium Summit, making proposals for major reform.[55] The most important called for an increase in resources for the UN Department of Peacekeeping to enable it properly to manage complex and demanding peacekeeping operations. The Report also stressed the need for the Security Council to provide a clear and realistic mandate for peacekeeping forces, and suggested that no resolution creating a peacekeeping force be passed until the Security Council has commitments from member States for troops. The Report also called for better cooperation between the Security Council and troop-contributing countries; this raises issues about control of the force and the balance of power between the Security Council with its primary responsibility for the maintenance of international peace and security and those States contributing troops.

But the most serious problem facing UN peacekeeping remains one of resources; if developed States are unwilling to provide troops and to allow their forces to be placed under UN command in the more complex operations which need better trained and equipped forces, the UN will be unable to take effective action. There has been a major surge in peacekeeping since 2003. This reflects the success of peacekeeping as the 'flagship of the UN', but the increased demand created by the establishment of complex, multi-dimensional forces in difficult environments has placed an enormous strain on UN resources and on the ability of member States to provide funds, troops, and equipment. The reforms which followed the *Brahimi Report* have proved insufficient to cope with these increased demands, and a further reform programme is underway. In order to cope with the increasing demands the UN is turning increasingly to regional organizations.

VII. REGIONAL ACTION UNDER CHAPTER VIII OF THE UN CHARTER

The Charter provides for UN action to be supplemented by regional action under Chapter VIII: 'regional arrangements or agencies' are to deal with such matters relating to the maintenance of international peace and security as are appropriate for regional action, provided that their actions are consistent with the purposes and principles of the UN (Article 52). Any enforcement action should be authorized by the Security Council; the Security Council may choose to utilize regional arrangements for enforcement action (Article 53). The Charter does not define 'regional arrangements or agencies' but the UN has accepted that the main regional organizations, the African Union (AU), the Organization of American States (OAS), and the Arab League come within this heading. Also certain sub-regional organizations not originally set up under Chapter VIII have taken on peacekeeping powers and have drawn up new constitutional instruments to

---

[55] (2000) 39 ILM 1432.

regulate this. These include the Economic Community of West African States (ECOWAS), the Southern African Development Community (SADC), and the Intergovernmental Authority on Development (IGAD). In its resolutions the Security Council has taken a flexible, non-formalistic approach to the issue of which organizations come within Chapter VIII.

A. A GREATER ROLE FOR REGIONAL ORGANIZATIONS

Since the end of the Cold War regional organizations have become much more active, and there has been a significant increase in cooperation between regional organizations and the UN.[56] UN and regional or sub-regional forces have combined in Georgia, Tajikistan, Liberia, Sierra Leone, Côte d'Ivoire, the DRC, and Chad/Central African Republic and have undertaken complementary roles. Regional organizations may possess the advantages of proximity, an informed understanding of the causes of conflicts and of local norms; they may be able to deploy quickly when the UN Security Council is unable or unwilling to act. Developed States have given significant financial assistance, logistical support and military training to regional and sub-regional organizations in Africa. They have encouraged the AU in particular to take an increased role in peacekeeping. The AU has developed its own legal framework and institutions for this purpose. It has deployed peacekeeping forces in Burundi, Darfur (Sudan), and Somalia. The first hybrid AU-UN operation was established in Sudan in December 2007. But the AU still faces serious resource problems and depends on outside support for its peacekeeping operations. Its forces have struggled to cope with the extremely challenging conditions in Darfur and Somalia (Omorogbe, 2011).

Since the end of the Cold War regional organizations have been authorized to use enforcement action under Chapter VII; in Yugoslavia the Security Council authorized 'member States acting nationally or through regional agencies or arrangements' to use force to implement economic embargoes imposed under Article 41. A similar resolution was passed with regard to the enforcement of economic measures against Haiti after the 1991 anti-democratic coup. Although the Security Council did not expressly refer to Article 53, or specify exactly which regional organization was envisaged, it seems that these are the first instances of resort to Article 53. The Security Council has since gone further: acting under Chapter VII it has authorized States acting through regional arrangements or agencies to use force to facilitate the delivery of humanitarian aid in Yugoslavia, to ensure compliance with the ban on flights over Bosnia-Herzegovina, and to protect the safe havens; it has also authorized the member States of ECOWAS to use force in Côte d'Ivoire and Liberia, the EU to conduct operations in the DRC, the AU to establish a Chapter VII force in Somalia and, in cooperation with ECOWAS, to send an African-led force to help the government of Mali to regain control of its territory.

B. CONTROVERSY AS TO THE INTERPRETATION OF CHAPTER VIII

During the Cold War and subsequently, the distinction between regional peacekeeping action with the consent of the host State, for which no Security Council authorization was necessary, and regional enforcement action which required such authorization under Article 53 has been problematic. When the OAS intervened against Cuba (1962)

---

[56] UN Secretary-General's Reports on UN/regional relations, UN Doc S/2006/590, S/2008/186.

and the Dominican Republic (1965) there was controversy as to whether this was legal under the UN Charter (Akehurst, 1967). The Eastern and Western blocs were divided as to whether economic measures constituted enforcement action requiring authorization; more recently it seems to have been implicitly accepted that Security Council authorization is not needed for regional economic sanctions. The other main question which arose as to the legality of the OAS actions with regard to Cuba and to the Dominican Republic was whether acquiescence or failure to condemn by the Security Council amounted to authorization of enforcement action under Article 53. Such claims seem far-fetched where it is the veto or the threat of a veto by a permanent member which has led to the failure to condemn.

During the Cold War there was sometimes suspicion that major powers were manipulating regional organizations to further their own ends. For example, there was doubt as to whether the Syrian-dominated Arab League intervention in Lebanon (1976–83) was truly impartial peacekeeping in accordance with the purposes and principles of the UN. There were also concerns about the relation between the USA and the OAS and about the sub-regional Organization of East Caribbean States (OECS) intervention in Grenada in 1983. This provoked lengthy discussion in the Security Council as to whether the action was legitimate peacekeeping or whether it amounted to unlawful interference in the domestic affairs of a State in order to overthrow an unsympathetic government.[57] There was a coup in 1983 and a pro-Cuban government seized power. The USA which was not itself a member of the OECS, led an OECS intervention and oversaw the installation of a new government. It offered a variety of legal justifications for its use of force, including an argument that the intervention was regional action under Chapter VIII at the request of the Governor-General of Grenada. Many States did not accept that the Governor-General had such power to represent the State of Grenada, but the main reason for their criticism of the invasion was that the action went beyond peacekeeping and constituted unlawful intervention. The UN General Assembly and the OAS condemned the intervention; in the Security Council the USA vetoed a resolution calling for the withdrawal of foreign troops from Grenada (Gilmore, 1984).

C. REGIONAL PEACEKEEPING AFTER THE COLD WAR

Questions about the distinction between peacekeeping and enforcement action and concerns about the impartiality of regional action continue to arise after the Cold War, in particular with regard to the CIS operations in Georgia and Tajikistan in the former USSR and also with regard to ECOWAS operations in Liberia (1990–97) and Sierra Leone (1997–2000). ECOWAS, a sub-regional organization of 15 member States, established in 1975 and originally concerned with economic matters, took a major role in attempting to end civil wars in Sierra Leone and Liberia through its Economic Community of West African States Monitoring Group (ECOMOG) force. Commentators expressed doubts as to whether there were genuinely impartial peacekeeping forces or whether the major regional power, Nigeria, was pursuing its own agenda through ECOWAS. In both conflicts ECOMOG seemed to go beyond limited peacekeeping action, but ECOWAS did not openly claim wide powers or seek authorization under Article 53 by the Security Council. Its official position was that ECOMOG used force only in self-defence or to secure implementation of a UN economic embargo. The Security Council acquiesced in the ECOMOG action; it avoided discussion of legality under the UN Charter, leading some commentators

---

[57] 1983 *UNYB* 211.

to argue that these operations marked the inception of a new wide right of regional action to restore democracy or to undertake humanitarian intervention. However, the Security Council itself was cautious and did not expressly approve any use of force going beyond self-defence or in performance of the provisions of peace agreements. It is difficult to read approval for any radical change in the doctrine of regional peacekeeping into its resolutions. But some commentators have argued for a reinterpretation of the UN Charter in the light of these developments (Franck, 2002, 162). Subsequent regional operations do not support such claims: enforcement action has been expressly authorized by the Security Council. States including China and Russia stress the need for regional action to be conducted strictly in accordance with the Charter framework.

VIII. CONCLUSION

The UN Charter provisions on the use of force by States, Article 2(4) on the prohibition of force and Article 51 on self-defence, have produced fundamental divisions between States. There is disagreement as to whether the prohibition on force should be interpreted strictly or whether it allows humanitarian intervention, as in Kosovo. There is also disagreement as to whether the right of self-defence is wide or narrow. The response to the 9/11 terrorist attacks has led to an unresolved disagreement about the law in this area. As regards collective security, the original scheme of the UN Charter for the Security Council to play a primary role in the maintenance of international peace and security through its own standing army has not been fully implemented. Instead the UN has turned to member States to use force under Security Council authority in 'coalitions of the willing'. It is extremely controversial in the light of *Operation Iraqi Freedom* whether member States may ever use force without express authority. Also, UN peacekeeping has developed through practice. UN peacekeeping forces deployed in ongoing conflicts face a tension between impartiality and effectiveness. The relationship between peacekeeping operations and Chapter VII has yet to be satisfactorily resolved.

REFERENCES

AKEHURST, M (1967), 'Enforcement Action by Regional Agencies, with Special Reference to the OAS', 41 *BYIL* 175.

AREND, A and BECK, R (1993), *International Law and the Use of Force* (London & New York: Routledge).

BECKER, T (2006), *Terrorism and the State* (Oxford: Hart Publishing).

BERMAN, E and SAMS, K (2000), *Peacekeeping in Africa: Capabilities and Culpabilities* (Geneva: United Nations Institute for Disarmament Research).

BOWETT, D (1958), *Self-Defence in International Law* (Manchester: Manchester University Press).

BROWNLIE, I (1963), *International Law and the Use of Force by States* (Oxford: Oxford University Press).

CHESTERMAN, S (2001), *Just War or Just Peace? Humanitarian Intervention and International Law* (Oxford: Oxford University Press).

CORTEN, O (2010), *The Law against War* (Oxford: Hart Publishing).

D'AMATO, A (1990), 'The Invasion of Panama was a Lawful Response to Tyranny', 84 *AJIL* 516.

DOSWALD BECK, L (1985), 'The Legal Validity of Military Intervention by Invitation of the Government', 56 *BYIL* 189.

FRANCK, T (2002), *Recourse to Force* (Cambridge: Cambridge University Press).

GILMORE, W (1984), *The Grenada Intervention* (London: Mansell).

GRAY, C (1996), 'Bosnia and Herzegovina: Civil War or Inter-State Conflict?', 67 *BYIL* 155.

—— (2002), 'From Unity to Polarisation: International Law and the Use of Force Against Iraq', 13 *EJIL* 1.

—— (2008), *International Law and the Use of Force*, 3rd edn (Oxford: Oxford University Press).

HIGGINS, R (1969–81), *United Nations Peacekeeping*, vols I–IV (Oxford: Oxford University Press).

LOBEL, J and RATNER, M (1999), 'Bypassing the Security Council: Ambiguous Authorizations to Use Force, Cease-fires and the Iraqi Inspection Regime', 93 *AJIL* 124.

MURPHY, SD (ed) (2003), 'Contemporary Practice of the United States relating to International Law', 97 *AJIL* 419.

OMOROGBE, E (2011), 'Can the African Union deliver peace and security?', 16 *Journal of Conflict and Security Law* 35.

PATIL, A (1992), *The UN Veto in World Affairs 1946–1992* (London: Mansell).

RONZITTI, N (1985), *Rescuing Nationals Abroad* (Dordrecht: Martinus Nijhoff).

ROTH, B (1999), *Governmental Illegitimacy in International Law* (Oxford: Oxford University Press).

SAROOSHI, D (1999), *The United Nations and the Development of Collective Security* (Oxford: Clarendon Press).

SIMMA, B (ed), (2012), *The Charter of the United Nations: A Commentary*, 3rd edn (Oxford: Oxford University Press).

STAHN, C (2007), 'Responsibility to Protect', 101 *AJIL* 99.

TAFT, WH and BUCHWALD, TF (2003), 'Pre-emption, Iraq and International Law', 97 *AJIL* 553.

TAMS, C (2009), 'The use of force against terrorists', 20 *EJIL* 359.

ULFSTEIN, G and CHRISTIANSEN, C (2013), 'The Legality of the NATO bombing in Libya', 62 *ICLQ* 159.

UNITED NATIONS (1996), *The Blue Helmets*, 3rd edn (New York, NY: United Nations Dept of Public Information).

WILDE, R (2008), *International Territorial Administration* (Oxford: Oxford University Press).

WILSON, H (1988), *International Law and the Use of Force by National Liberation Movements* (Oxford: Oxford University Press).

FURTHER READING

GENERAL TEXTBOOKS

BROWNLIE, I (1963), *International Law and the Use of Force by States* (Oxford: Oxford University Press).

CORTEN, O (2010), *The Law against War* (Oxford: Hart Publishing).

FRANCK, T (2002), *Recourse to Force* (Cambridge: Cambridge University Press).

GRAY, C (2008), *International Law and the Use of Force*, 3rd edn (Oxford: Oxford University Press).

WHITE, N and HENDERSON C, (eds) (2013), *Research Handbook on International Conflict and Security Law* (Cheltenham: Edward Elgar Publishing).

THE INTERPRETATION OF ARTICLE 2(4)

CHESTERMAN, S (2000), *Just War or Just Peace? Humanitarian Intervention and International Law* (Oxford: Oxford University Press).

REISMAN, M (1984), 'Coercion and Self-determination: Construing Charter Article 2(4)' and the reply by Schacter, O (1984), 'The Legality of Pro-democratic Invasion', 78 *AJIL* 642, 646.

STÜRCHLER, N (2007), *The Threat of Force in International Law* (Cambridge: Cambridge University Press).

SELF-DEFENCE

BECKER, T (2006), *Terrorism and the State* (Oxford: Hart Publishing).

LUBELL, N (2010), *Extraterritorial Use of Force against Non-state Actors* (Oxford: Oxford University Press).

O'CONNELL, M-E, 'The Ban on the Bomb - and Bombing', 78 *Syracuse Law Journal* 497.

RONZITTI, N (1985), *Rescuing Nationals Abroad* (Dordrecht: Martinus Nijhoff).

RUYS, T (2010), *Armed Attack and Article 51 of the UN Charter* (Cambridge: Cambridge University Press).

SCHACTER, O (1989), 'Self-defence and the Rule of Law', 83 *AJIL* 259.

UN ENFORCEMENT AND PEACEKEEPING

BLOKKER, N and SCHRIJVER, N (2005), *The Security Council and the Use of Force* (Leiden/Boston: Martinus Nijhoff Publishers).

GREENWOOD, C (1992), 'New World Order or Old? The Invasion of Kuwait and the Rule of Law', 55 *MLR* 153.

KONDOCH, B (ed) (2007), *International Peacekeeping* (Aldershot: Ashgate Publishing).

LOWE, AV, ROBERTS, A, WELSH, J, and ZAUM, D (eds) (2008), *The UN Security Council and War* (Oxford: Oxford University Press).

MATHESON, M (2006), *The Council Unbound* (Washington DC: US Institute of Peace Press).

SAROOSHI, D (1999), *The United Nations and the Development of Collective Security* (Oxford: Clarendon Press).

ZACKLIN, R (2010), *The UN Secretariat and the Use of Force in a Unipolar World* (Cambridge: Cambridge University Press).

WEBSITES

http://www.un.org
The United Nations website

http://www.africa-union.org
The African Union website

http://www.ecowas.int
ECOWAS website

http://www.nato.int
NATO website

PART VII

THE APPLICATION OF INTERNATIONAL LAW

22

THE LAW OF THE SEA

Malcolm D Evans

SUMMARY

Historically, the principal division in the law of the sea has been between the territorial seas, which form a part of the territory of the State but within which other States enjoy a number of restricted rights, and the high seas, which are open to use by all. This has now changed, with the recognition and development of new zones of functional and resource-oriented jurisdiction, accompanied by complex realignments of jurisdictional competences which cut across—and, in the eyes of some, threaten to undermine—the traditional principles of governance at sea. This chapter traces these developments. It also provides an introduction to the basic rules concerning the principle zones of maritime jurisdiction, as well as looking at the rules concerning the construction of baselines—which is foundational to the entire subject—and to the problem of determining boundaries where entitlements to maritime zones overlap.

I. INTRODUCTION

The law of the sea is regulated in a complex yet subtle manner, providing an interesting contrast to the rather absolutist approach to questions concerning sovereignty and jurisdiction which still hold sway in other areas of international law. Sovereignty and jurisdiction are, of course, the basic building blocks of the law of the sea, providing the basis upon which all else is founded. Over time, they have, however, been moulded and melded in an extremely sophisticated manner in order to better reflect the changing nature of the competing interests at stake in the utilization of the seas.

The earliest doctrinal debates concerned whether the seas could be made subject to the exclusive sovereignty of a single State. In the middle ages, before State-sponsored exploration of the oceans and the intensification of international trade by sea, this was, in truth, not really a question at all. It was in the fifteenth and sixteenth centuries that the question became significant, and the arguments advanced largely mirrored the prevailing interests of the sovereigns concerned. Those who argued that the seas should be 'closed' and subject to the jurisdiction of a single (usually the coastal) State did so either for reasons of security (to keep threatening forces at a distance) or for reasons of trade (to operate profitable customs regimes). Those that argued in favour of the seas being 'open' did so in order to foster and facilitate their developing long-distance overseas trading interests. The balance that finally emerged reflected both concerns: whereas States were to enjoy sovereignty over those waters proximate to their coasts, reflecting their interests in security and control, in the waters beyond, where trade and navigation issues assumed a greater significance, the principle of the freedom of the seas—famously argued for by Grotius in his work *Marem Liberum*—prevailed (Anand, 1993; O'Connell, 1982, pp 18–30).

This, then, established the basic division that has dominated the law of the sea for some 400 years; between the territorial sea which was subject to the jurisdiction of the coastal State and the high seas beyond, which were open to all. At the same time, it also reflected a belief that the seas were to be used purposively, and thus the balance struck should reflect the needs of those seeking to do so. Inevitably, then, as strategic interests have changed and as economic and technological developments have increased the ability to access and harvest the resources of the sea and seabed, new accommodations between competing interests have had to be made (see also Posner and Sykes, 2010). The challenges presented by these changes have been made more complex in recent years by the rapid expansion of the number of States, significant shifts in the political balance of power, the recognition of international community interests in the seas and the increasing awareness of the need not only to access and exploit the resources of the seas and the marine environment but also to conserve and protect them.

In the early years of the twentieth century ambitious plans were made to 'codify' much of international law, including the law of the sea. Although the overall project made little headway, one positive outcome was the 1930 'Hague Codification Conference'. Although this did not produce any finished text on the law of the sea it did provide useful experience which was extensively drawn on when, after the Second World War, the International Law Commission (ILC) decided to examine the subject. In 1956 the ILC produced sets of draft Articles which were considered at the First UN Conference on the Law of the Sea (UNCLOS I) held in Geneva in 1958. This conference produced the four 'Geneva Conventions' on the Law of the Sea[1] which in part reflected customary international law but also contained much that was 'progressive development'.

Although impressive in their scope, the Geneva Conventions left some key issues open. The most significant of these concerned the vexed question of the breadth of the territorial sea and in 1960 a second UN Conference was convened in Geneva (UNCLOS II) to address this and other related questions but it ended without agreement. One reason for this failure was the mounting pressure for a more fundamental review of the law of the sea which would take account of the growing demands for access to resources and, in the process, erode the rigidity of the territorial sea/high seas dichotomy. Admittedly, the four 1958 Conventions themselves represented a limited break with this approach. Two of those conventions reflected the traditional divisions, one dealing with the territorial sea (and contiguous zone) and another with the high seas. The other two 1958 Conventions reflected new concerns, these being the continental shelf and fisheries conservation and management. Although the fisheries convention did not gain much international support, and elements of the continental shelf convention have since been jettisoned, adopting 'general' conventions on these 'functional' issues indicated that the way forward did not lie only in fixing on new outer limits for the territorial sea and further refining the relationship between the territorial seas and high seas. Rather, it showed that the future lay in creating new zones and forms of jurisdictional competence that would co-exist alongside them. UNCLOS II had attempted to go down this path by suggesting that, rather than extend the territorial sea to 12 n. miles, States be permitted to exercise exclusive jurisdiction over fishing in a 6 n. mile belt beyond a 6 n. mile territorial sea. Moreover, this general

---

[1] These being the Convention on the Territorial Sea and Contiguous Zone (TSC); Convention on the High Seas (HSC); Convention on the Continental Shelf (CSC); and the Convention on Fisheries and Conservation of the Living Resources of the High Seas (CFC).

approach was endorsed by the International Court of Justice (ICJ) in the *North Sea*[2] and *Fisheries Jurisdiction*[3] cases, where the emergence of the continental shelf and exclusive fisheries zones was acknowledged and accepted.

The basic idea underlying the distinction between the territorial seas and high seas was that it divided those maritime spaces over which a single State exercised jurisdiction and control from those over which no single State exercised jurisdiction or control. In practice, therefore, the resources of the high seas were available for unilateral exploitation by anyone and everyone. As will be seen later, the extension of coastal State jurisdiction over resources located in the seabed and subsoil beyond the territorial sea was already having the effect of breaking down this clear distinction but the essence of the underlying approach nevertheless remained intact. In 1967, however, a fundamental challenge was made to this traditional approach when, at the prompting of Arvid Pardo, the Maltese ambassador to the UN, the UN General Assembly adopted the first of a series of resolutions[4] in which it recognized that the resources of the seabed in areas beyond national jurisdiction should be considered to be the 'Common Heritage of Mankind' and be exploited for the benefit of the international community as a whole (Schmidt, 1989, pp 18–30).

There was, then, a complex matrix of unresolved issues and emerging agendas which needed to be addressed and these were considered at the third UN Conference on the Law of the Sea (UNCLOS III) which met from 1974–82 and culminated in the adoption of the 1982 Convention on the Law of the Sea (LOSC). Negotiations at UNCLOS III were tortuous and the convention attempted to balance a myriad of competing interests in a 'package deal' that ultimately satisfied few. Although by the early 1990s the number of ratifications approached the 60 required by LOSC Article 308 for the convention to enter into force there was relatively little support from developed States, whose acceptance was critical to the success of the convention. This focused the minds of all concerned and, assisted by changes in the world political order at that time following the collapse of communism in eastern Europe, a rather euphemistically entitled 'Implementation Agreement' was agreed in July 1994 which, in fact if not in name, amended Part XI of the convention (the provisions concerning the 'Common Heritage' and seabed mining in the area beyond national jurisdiction) in order to make it acceptable to a broader range of States (Anderson, 1993; 1995; Harrison, 2011, 85–99). The LOSC entered into force on 16 November 1994 and at the time of writing there are 166 States parties (including the EU). The Implementation Agreement entered into force in July 1996 and currently has 145 States parties. However, Article 7 of the 1994 Agreement allowed for its provisional application pending its entry into force and so for those States party to both the 1982 Convention and the 1994 Agreement, the 'original' version of Part XI as set out in the 1982 Convention never became binding on them at all. Much of the 1982 Convention now reflects customary law and so is relevant to the increasingly small number of States which are not bound by it as a matter of treaty law[5]. As a result, it provides the starting point for any presentation of the contemporary law of the sea. However, parts of the convention are of a 'framework' nature and it has been supplemented by a number of other major conventions addressing certain issues in greater detail. Developments in other areas of

---

[2] *North Sea Continental Shelf, Judgment, ICJ Reports 1969*, p 3.

[3] *Fisheries Jurisdiction (United Kingdom v Iceland), Merits, Judgment, ICJ Reports 1974*, p 3.

[4] See UNGA Res 2340(XII) (18 December 1967) which established an 'Ad Hoc Committee to Study the Peaceful Uses of the Sea-Bed and the Ocean Floor beyond the Limits of National Jurisdiction' and, in particular, the 'Declaration of Principles Governing the Sea-Bed and the Ocean Floor, and the Subsoil thereof, Beyond the Limits of National Jurisdiction', UNGA Res 2749 (XXV) (17 December 1970).

[5] Including, for example, the USA and Turkey who are not States parties to the LOSC.

international law have also had an impact on the convention framework and customary law continues to play an important role by further supplementing and amplifying its provisions (Boyle, 2005; Harrison, 2011).

Since a chapter of this length cannot be comprehensive, it aims to give a flavour of the convention's approach and illustrate the manner in which competing interests are accommodated in some key areas.

II. CONSTRUCTING BASELINES

A. INTRODUCTION: THE NORMAL RULE

International law parcels the sea into various zones in which States enjoy a variety of jurisdictional competences. The general rule is that coastal States exercise the greatest degree of jurisdictional competence over those zones that lie closest to them. Logically enough, a State exercises full powers of territorial sovereignty within areas of water which are 'internal'. This obviously includes lakes and rivers but also includes harbours and other areas of water which are landward of 'baselines' from which the various zones of seawards jurisdiction are generally[6] measured.

Determining baselines is, then, very important and a number of detailed rules were set out in the 1958 TSC and largely repeated in the 1982 LOSC. Most of these rules reflect customary law. Since the further seawards a coastal State is able to 'push' its baselines the further seawards its jurisdiction will extend, the practical application of these rules often gives rise to controversy. It should also be remembered that islands, defined in LOSC Article 121(1) as 'a naturally formed area of land, surrounded by water, which is above water at high tide', have baselines which generate maritime zones, no matter how small, miniscule even, they might be. However, LOSC Article 121(3) provides the important exception that 'Rocks which cannot sustain human habitation or economic life of their own shall have no exclusive economic zone or continental shelf'. In 2012 the ICJ finally concluded that 'the legal régime of islands set out in UNCLOS Article 121 forms an indivisible régime, all of which ... has the status of customary international law',[7] thus finally ending doubts concerning the customary law status of Article 121(3). Nevertheless, the precise scope of this provision remains uncertain, as the terms 'rock' and 'economic life' are not expressly defined (Charney, 2000; Lavalle, 2004; Prescott and Schofield, 2005, pp 61–89).

Whether island or mainland territory, '... the normal baseline for measuring the breadth of the territorial sea is the low-water line along the coast as shown by the appropriate symbols on charts officially recognized by the coastal state' (LOSC Article 5). Although relatively easy to apply, this method can produce unwieldy results when a coastline is not comparatively straight and/or there are a considerable number of islands in the vicinity of a mainland coast. Therefore, a number of rules have been devised which address some exceptional situations. States do not have to adopt one method of drawing baselines but may use those methods most appropriate for each portion of their coast (LOSC Article 14).

---

[6] The continental shelf is, in part, an exception to this. See later in this chapter.

[7] *Territorial and Maritime Dispute (Nicaragua v Colombia), Judgment of 19 November 2012*, para 139. But cf Tanaka, 2012, pp 66–8 who, writing shortly before the ICJ judgment, concluded that there was insufficient consistent State practice to justify such a conclusion.

B. STRAIGHT BASELINES

In the *Anglo-Norwegian Fisheries* case[8] the UK challenged the right of Norway to claim a territorial sea drawn not from the low-water line but from a series of artificial lines linking the outermost points of the 'skaergaard' (a fringe of rocks and islands) that lay off the Norwegian coast. The Court noted that it might be inconvenient to use the low-water mark as the baseline in such geographically complicated circumstances and accepted the legitimacy of drawing 'straight baselines' under certain circumstances. The judgment was reflected in TSC Article 4, the essence of which was repeated in LOSC Article 7 (Reisman and Westerman, 1992; Kopela, 2013, Ch 2).

Straight baselines may only be drawn if a coastline is 'deeply indented and cut into' or 'if there is a fringe of islands along the coast in its immediate vicinity' (LOSC Article 7(1)). If these criteria are not met the normal rule applies. Even if straight baselines *may* be drawn, there are limitations upon *how* they are to be drawn. These include restrictions on the use of Low Tide Elevations,[9] that straight baselines 'must not depart to any appreciable extent from the general direction of the coast' and that 'the sea areas lying within the lines must be sufficiently closely linked to the land domain to be subject to the regime of internal waters' (LOSC Article 7(4)). This latter, rather impressionistic, requirement is particularly important. Waters on the landward side of a straight baseline are by definition internal waters over which the coastal State enjoys full territorial jurisdiction and control (subject to an exception to be considered later) and straight baselines must not be used to bring into the territorial domain waters which lack an intrinsic nexus with the coast. That nexus might be established by non-geographic criteria: in keeping with the *Anglo-Norwegian Fisheries* case, LOSC Article 7(5) permits local and well-established economic interests to be taken into account when establishing particular baselines, but only in those situations where the geographical threshold criteria set out in Article 7(1) are met.

C. BAYS

A further exception to the 'normal' rule concerns bays and is addressed by LOSC Article 10, which is generally considered to reflect customary law (Westerman, 1987). The motivation for departing from the normal rule here is not so much based on convenience but to avoid situations in which the territorial sea—or even fingers of high seas—penetrate the mouths of bays and intrude into areas intrinsically connected with the land domain. The problem is greatest where entrances to bays are relatively narrow but open out into broader expanses of water. The aim is to differentiate areas of water which are essentially of an 'internal' nature from those which are not and this is achieved by drawing 'closing lines' across the mouth of bays and using that 'closing line' as the baseline from which the territorial sea and other zones of jurisdiction are measured.[10]

Once again, there are two stages to this process. First, the distance between the 'natural entrance points' of a bay is measured and a semi-circle is drawn along a line of that length. The area of this semi-circle is then compared to the area of water on the landward side of the closing line. If the area of the semi-circle is less than that of the area of water, the indentation is, for the purposes of baseline construction, a bay; if the area of the semi-circle is

---

[8] *Fisheries, Judgment, ICJ Reports 1951*, p 116.

[9] A 'Low Tide Elevation' is 'a naturally formed area of land which is surrounded by and above water at low tide but submerged at high tide' (LOSC Article 13).

[10] It is important to remember that a bay closing line and a straight baseline are legally speaking two very different types of line, though both have the same general function.

greater than the area of the water on the landward side of the closing line, the indentation is not—for legal purposes—a bay. The second stage is to draw a closing line. If the distance between the natural entrance points used for the previous calculation is less than 24 nautical miles (n. miles), the closing line may be drawn between them. If that distance exceeds 24 n. miles, then a closing line of up to that length can be drawn 'within the bay in such a manner as to enclose the maximum area of water that is possible with a line of that length' (LOSC Article 10(6)). This seemingly simple provision is very complex to apply in practice, with the identification of the natural entry points being a particular problem,[11] and the bay being a 'well marked indentation' another.[12]

It may be the case that the coastline of a bay belongs to more than one State. This poses an additional difficulty since the exceptional rule in LOSC Article 10 only applies to those bays whose coasts belong to a single State. However, in the *Land, Island and Maritime Frontier Dispute* the ICJ sought to identify a concept of a 'pluri-State' bay, where the coasts belong to a number of States yet a closing line might still be drawn.[13] Whilst such an approach might be appropriate if, as in that case, there is a particular historical justification, it is difficult to see how it could be used more generally, if only because the waters behind the closing line would be 'internal' to all of the States concerned and this would simply generate a further need to differentiate between them. It seems to create more problems than it solves and is not found in State practice. In any case, LOSC Article 10(6) expressly renders the convention regime inapplicable to 'historic bays', these being indentations claimed by the coastal State as a part of its internal waters on the basis of a long-standing claim, assertion of jurisdiction, and acquiescence by others' (O'Connell, 1982, Ch 11). This offers an alternative route for States wishing to make claims in respect of indentations which cannot fulfil the criteria set out in the convention. However, such claims are difficult to substantiate and will often meet with considerable protest, as is the case with the Libyan claim to the Gulf of Sirte, a 'bay' nearly 300 n. miles in extent (Ahnish, 1993, Ch 7).

D. ARCHIPELAGOES

The 1951 *Anglo-Norwegian Fisheries* case also addresses what might be called 'coastal archipelagoes'. But what of States comprised wholly or partly of groups of islands? Should the waters be enclosed and treated as internal? What of the navigational rights of third States? At UNCLOS III the interests of archipelagic States, such as Indonesia and the Philippines, and the concerns of adjacent maritime neighbours, such as Australia, combined to produce a particular regime, set out in Part IV of the convention, applicable to 'archipelagic states'. Rather self-referentially, LOSC Article 46 defines an archipelagic State as a State 'constituted wholly by one or more archipelagoes' and other islands, where an 'archipelago' is itself further defined as a group of islands, or parts of islands, and their interconnecting waters which are so closely interconnected as to form, or be regarded as forming, an intrinsic entity, or which have been historically regarded as such. Therefore Indonesia, the Philippines, Fiji, Japan, and the UK are archipelagic States for convention purposes and so are entitled to draw archipelagic baselines, whereas island groups such as the Azores (belonging to Spain) and the Galapagos (belonging to Ecuador) are not.[14]

---

[11] See, eg *Post Office* v *Estuary Radio* [1968] 2 QB 740. See also Marston, 2002.

[12] See, eg the US Supreme Court judgment in *United States* v *Alaska* 545 US 17 (2005), pp 17–20.

[13] *Land, Island and Maritime Frontier Dispute (El Salvador/Honduras: Nicaragua) Judgment of 11 September 1992, ICJ Reports 1992*, p 351, para 395. The entire concept was roundly criticized by Judge Oda in his Dissenting Opinion, ibid, p 732, paras 1–26.

[14] For the position regarding such non-coastal dependent archipelagos, see Kopela, 2013.

However, not all archipelagic States are able to construct archipelagic baselines since such baselines must conform to strict criteria, the principal elements of which are that they must link the main islands of the group; no baseline may be more than 100 n. miles long, except that 3% of the total may be up to 125 n. miles in length; they must follow the general configuration of the island grouping; and, most importantly, fulfil the requirement that the ratio of water to land within the baselines must be not less than 1:1 and not more than 9:1 (LOSC Article 47). The result is both that those archipelagic States which primarily consist of a few large islands (such as Japan and the UK) and those which are composed of very small and widely spaced islands (such as Kiribati) are unable to draw archipelagic baselines even though they fall within the definition of an archipelagic State. It is the latter category of small and scattered island States which stood to gain most from the concept but they were unable to influence the negotiations in their favour and the details of the regime found in the convention favour the interests of the larger archipelagic States. It may be that, in time, State practice and customary law might develop in a fashion which is somewhat less rigid than the convention regime.

The waters within archipelagic baselines are 'archipelagic waters' rather than internal waters and are subject to special rules concerning, *inter alia*, fishing and navigation which will be considered later (LOSC Articles 49–53). Once again, and whatever its shortcomings, the archipelagic regime offers another example of the manner in which the convention sought to forge a new approach to the division of jurisdictional competences, and moved away from a strict approach based on the distinction between the territorial and high seas.

III. THE INTERNAL WATERS, TERRITORIAL SEA, AND CONTIGUOUS ZONE

A. INTRODUCTION

The idea that States are entitled to exercise authority over the waters beyond their land territory (and internal and archipelagic waters) is deeply entrenched in international legal thinking. Although it was once argued that the competences States enjoyed within waters off their coasts fell short of territorial sovereignty and had to be positively asserted,[15] it is now clear that this authority flows automatically from the sovereignty exercised over land territory and so all coastal States do in fact have a territorial sea.[16] Practically speaking, however, States need to make some form of pronouncement, if only to determine the extent of their jurisdiction.

The breadth of water over which a State might legitimately exercise sovereign jurisdiction has been the subject of lengthy debate down the ages, but at the dawn of the twentieth century the preponderance of known practice fixed that distance at 3 n. miles. The conflict between those who favoured broadening this zone, in order to enhance coastal State security or to increase control over navigation and resources, and those who opposed this in the name of the freedom of navigation (and of fishing on the high seas) not only underpinned the development of the various functional maritime zones which will be

---

[15] This view found reflection—somewhat unexpectedly—in *R v Keyn* (1876) 2 Ex D 63, the substance of which was subsequently reversed by the 1878 Territorial Waters Jurisdiction Act.

[16] A view expressed by Judge McNair in his Dissenting Opinion in *Fisheries, Judgment, ICJ Reports 1951*, p 116 at p 160.

considered shortly but was also responsible for the failure of UNCLOS I and II to settle the issue. By the time of UNCLOS III, however, it seemed clear that an expansion of territorial seas to 12 n. miles was inevitable and the only question was the price that its opponents could extract from its proponents. LOSC Article 3 now recognizes the right to establish a territorial sea of up to 12 n. miles, the overwhelming majority of States—some 140— have done so and this is now the position under customary international law.[17] Although described as the territorial sea, the sovereignty of the State extends to the airspace above and the seabed and subsoil beneath (LOSC Article 2(2)).

It is important that States make their position clear since possession of a territorial sea not only entails rights but also duties: in his Separate Opinion in the *Fisheries Jurisdiction* case Judge Fitzmaurice pointed out that coastal States were obliged to maintain navigational aids within their territorial sea[18] and could be held responsible for damage flowing from the failure to do so. Clearly, the scope of this obligation depends on the extent of the territorial sea.

B. JURISDICTION OF THE COASTAL STATE

Although the coastal State exercises 'sovereignty' within its territorial sea, this sovereignty is circumscribed in a number of ways which will be considered in this section. It is also helpful to consider the jurisdiction enjoyed by a State within its territorial sea alongside that which it may exercise within its internal waters and in the contiguous zone that lies beyond, since these together represent a progression from the strongest to the weakest form of jurisdictional competences over maritime spaces which are grounded upon territorial sovereignty.

1. Internal waters

Predictably, a coastal State exercises sovereignty to its fullest extent within its internal waters. No State is obliged to allow foreign vessels into its internal waters, except in cases of distress and, exceptionally, where drawing straight baselines has the result of enclosing as internal waters waters not previously considered as such, the right of innocent passage (described later) remains (LOSC Article 8(2)). Otherwise, coastal States are free to restrict or impose whatever conditions they wish upon entry into internal waters, including entry into its ports,[19] the waters of which form part of its 'internal waters'.

Once a foreign vessel has entered internal waters it is subject to the domestic legislation of that State which can, in principle, be enforced against it.[20] On entering a port, the port State (as the coastal State then becomes known) is particularly well-placed to take enforcement action against vessels, if only because it can prevent them from leaving. The expansion of 'port State jurisdiction' over vessels is a feature of contemporary law, particularly as regards vessels which have breached health and safety regulations or have been causing pollution outside of the territorial sea of the State concerned (eg LOSC Articles 218–20,

---

[17] See, for example, *Territorial and Maritime Dispute (Nicaragua v Colombia), Judgment of 19 November 2012*, para 177.

[18] *Fisheries Jurisdiction (United Kingdom v Iceland), Jurisdiction of the Court, Judgment, ICJ Reports 1973*, p 3 at p 27.

[19] Whether vessels have a right of access to a port of a third State is a matter of controversy. For a helpful summary see Klein, 2011, pp 65–7.

[20] No enforcement action may be taken against foreign warships, however, as they enjoy immunity from local jurisdiction. See LOSC Article 32 and '*ARA Libertad*' (*Argentina v Ghana), Provisional Measures, Order of 15 December 2012, ITLOS Reports 2012*, para 95.

and see Özçayir, 2001; Marten, 2013). Indeed, there is an increasing trend to encourage the use of port State jurisdiction as a means of addressing the failures of flag States to exercise jurisdiction over vessels acting in breach of international standards (see Molenaar, 2006 and, as regards, fishing, see also Section VII B.3 in this chapter). However, States generally exercise restraint in enforcing local law over incidents taking place on board foreign vessels in their ports, limiting this to matters such as the infringement of customs laws, or activities which threaten to disrupt the peace of the port. This may include offences such as murder,[21] which have an intrinsic gravity that on-board scuffles between crew members lack. Such restraint reflects the temporary nature of the vessel's presence in a port and the fact that the flag State of the vessel itself has the right to exercise jurisdiction and that it is often more appropriate for it do so. States will, however, generally exercise jurisdiction over incidents occurring whilst the vessel is in port and which also involve non-crew members, as these concern more than the 'internal economy' of the vessel, and also in situations where the captain requests intervention.

2. Territorial sea

The dominant view is that coastal State jurisdiction automatically extends to the territorial sea, with the logical corollary that the entire body of State law applies there. However, this does not mean that the coastal State has an unfettered discretion regarding the content of that legislation since international law places imposes a number of important restrictions upon what the coastal State might render unlawful activity within the territorial sea, the most important of which concerns vessels exercising the right of innocent passage, considered later. Moreover, logic does not necessarily make for practicality and the full rigours of this approach (assuming it to be doctrinally correct) are mitigated by a more restrictive approach to the enforcement of domestic law within the territorial sea, irrespective of whether a vessel is engaged in innocent passage or not.

It would be odd if States were to enforce their criminal law over vessels merely passing through their territorial seas in circumstances which would not have triggered enforcement within internal waters. Therefore, LOSC Article 27(1) exhorts States to refrain from investigating or arresting those suspected of offences committed on board a vessel in its territorial sea unless: the consequences extended to the coastal State; it was of a kind to disturb the peace of the country or the good order of the territorial sea; assistance was requested; or it was necessary for the suppression of illicit traffic in drugs (LOSC Article 27(1)(a)–(d)). If the vessel has just left the State's internal waters it need show no such restraint (LOSC Article 27(2)), but in all cases the coastal State is to have 'due regard to the interests of navigation' when deciding whether, or how, to carry out an arrest within the territorial sea. These provisions apply to the criminal jurisdiction of the State. There are further exhortations against the exercise of jurisdiction over vessels in respect of civil matters, the chief of which is that vessels should not be stopped in order to exercise civil jurisdiction over an individual or with regard to actions *in rem*, rather than in respect of the activities of the vessel itself (LOSC Article 28). Finally, and unsurprisingly, coastal States are not permitted to arrest a warship or other vessels being used for governmental purposes which belong to another State. Rather, such vessels may be 'required' to leave the territorial sea immediately (LOSC Article 30) and it is implicit in this that the requisite degree of force necessary to ensure compliance with such a request might be used.

---

[21] Eg *United States* v *Wildenhaus*, 120 US 1 (1887), concerning the assertion of jurisdiction by the local courts over a murder on board a Belgian vessel in New York harbour.

3. Contiguous zone

Traditionally, where the territorial sea ended, the high seas began and the laws of the coastal State no longer applied. However, policing maritime zones is no easy matter and, unlike land boundaries, they are simple to cross and it is therefore easy for vessels to commit offences within the territorial sea but to evade arrest by moving just a little further seawards. The answer was to permit coastal States to arrest vessels outside their territorial seas in connection with offences that either had been committed or which it was suspected were going to be committed within their territorial sea. Under LOSC Article 33 (and following a compromise first agreed upon in the 1958 TSC Article 24), the coastal State is permitted to 'prevent' and 'punish' infringements of some, but not all, of its laws (those concerned being 'customs, fiscal, immigration or sanitary laws and regulations') in a zone which might be up to 24 n. miles from the baselines (thus permitting a State with a three mile territorial sea to have a contiguous zone of up to 21 n. miles). Not all States have declared a contiguous zone, but their usefulness is such that an increasing number do so.[22]

The ability to 'punish' means that vessels that have committed such offences within the territory of the State may be arrested even though they have left the territorial seas. The ability to 'prevent' suggests that a State might stop a vessel from entering its waters when it has reason to believe that such an offence would be committed should that vessel enter. This is clearly open to abuse. Indeed, the entire concept represents a not insignificant extension of coastal State authority and there is a tendency for States to assert jurisdiction for a more ambitious range of matters than those mentioned in the convention text.

C. NAVIGATION IN THE TERRITORIAL SEA

The desire of coastal States to assert their jurisdiction in the waters off their coasts is matched by the needs of the international community to ensure that the seas remain open to navigation. Once again, there has been progressive development in both the range and the content of regimes applicable to navigation within waters over which coastal States exercise sovereignty. The principal regime concerns innocent passage through the territorial sea and the manner in which that regime has sought to balance the relevant competing interests has shifted over time. In addition, some entirely new regimes of passage have been developed that reflect other developments.

1. Innocent passage

Ships of all States enjoy a right of 'innocent passage' through the territorial seas of coastal States. For these purposes, 'passage' means that the vessel is in the process of travelling through the territorial sea and is doing so in a 'continuous and expeditious' fashion, though there are exceptions for stops which are 'incidental to ordinary navigation' or as a result of *force majeure* (LOSC Article 18). Thus a ship loitering within the territorial sea or traversing in a circuitous manner would not be engaged in 'passage' at all.

Not all passage is 'innocent'. According to the 1958 TSC Article 14(4), 'Passage is innocent so long as it is not prejudicial to the peace, good order or security of the coastal state'. It is, however, unclear who is to make that determination. In the *Corfu Channel* case[23] the

---

[22] Approaching 90 States currently claim contiguous zones for a variety of purposes (not all in compliance with the LOSC) and the overwhelming majority are of 24 n. miles.

[23] *Corfu Channel, Merits, Judgment, ICJ Reports 1949*, p 4 at pp 30–31.

ICJ adopted a fairly objective approach, suggesting that the innocent nature of passage was capable of objective assessment, that the opinion of the coastal State was not decisive and the mere fact that a violation of local law had occurred was not in itself sufficient to demonstrate prejudice to the interests of the coastal State. The difficulty that faced the Court was that it needed to allow coastal States sufficient scope to decide whether to take measures against vessels exercising the right of innocent passage but it also needed to guard against their acting in an arbitrary and capricious fashion. The approach adopted in the *Corfu Channel* case seemed to favour the interests of ships in passage over that of the coastal State. The balance struck by the 1958 TSC seemed to adopt a rather more subjective and coastal-State oriented approach. It also provided for two special cases in which the very manner of passage would be enough to result in the loss of innocence, irrespective of whether there was in fact any prejudice to the coastal State or not: these concerned infringements by foreign fishing vessels of local legislation concerning fishing in the territorial sea (TSC Article 14(5)) and the requirement that submarines were to 'navigate on the surface and show their flag' (TSC Article 14(6)). Such activities were deemed to be incompatible with 'innocent passage' altogether.

These provisions in the 1958 TSC were widely regarded as unsatisfactory, particularly given the trend towards establishing increasingly broad belts of territorial seas and they were revisited at UNCLOS III. Although LOSC Article 19(1) endorses the general principle established in TSC Article 14(1), it takes a more objective approach to the determination of innocence by setting out in Article 19(2) a considerably longer list of activities and circumstances in which innocence is deemed to be lost, irrespective of whether there is any actual prejudice or infringement of local law. Moreover, these heads are themselves rather open textured, particularly the final catch-all provision of 'any other activity not having a direct bearing on passage' (LOSC Article 19(2)(j)). At first sight this might suggest that the right of innocent passage has been limited even further by the LOSC. This has to be balanced against the argument that the list of exceptions is now exhaustive and closed, an argument forcefully put by the USA and former USSR in a joint statement in 1989. However, the wording of the convention is ambiguous on this matter, to say the least. Churchill and Lowe also point out that Article 19(2) refers to 'activities' and so the mere 'presence' of a vessel may no longer be sufficient to deprive it of innocence (Churchill and Lowe, 1999, p 85). It is clear that there is still considerable controversy surrounding this Article, but it would be consonant with the general thrust of the convention if it were to be understood as representing a modest move towards enhanced, but objectively verifiable, coastal State control over passage through the territorial sea.[24]

Even this assessment must be balanced against developments concerning the other plank of the innocent passage regime. Being engaged in innocent passage does not exempt a vessel from the need to comply with coastal State legislation, but the coastal State may only legislate for the range of issues that are set out in LOSC Article 21. These concern the safety of navigation, cables and pipelines; the conservation of living resources and prevention of infringements of fisheries laws; matters concerning the preservation of the environment and marine pollution, marine scientific research, and prevention of infringements of customs, fiscal, immigration, and sanitary laws. By way of checks and balance, however, the coastal State may not use these legislative competences in ways which hamper innocent passage by, for example, imposing onerous or discriminatory requirements (LOSC Article 24(1)). Moreover, such laws 'shall not apply to the design, construction,

---

[24] See further Rothwell and Stephens, 2010, p 217, where they also note, however, that 'there is little State practice to suggest that this provision has been abused'.

manning or equipment of foreign ships unless they are giving effect to generally accepted international rules or standards' (LOSC Article 21(2)), these being those agreed under the auspices of the International Maritime Organization (IMO). The coastal State does have the power to 'suspend temporarily' innocent passage in specified areas, but only if this is non-discriminatory, is 'essential for the protection of its security', and is duly publicized (LOSC Article 25(3)).[25]

Vessels violating such laws are liable to arrest in accordance with LOSC Article 27 even though they may be exercising the right of innocent passage through the territorial sea. It would, of course, be in breach of international law for a coastal State to enforce laws on matters other than these upon a vessel simply because it ceased to be engaged in innocent passage by reason of entering internal waters. The more exacting standards that can be applied to ships not engaged in innocent passage can only be enforced against those whose passage ceased to be innocent *whilst in the territorial sea* and in accordance with Article 27.

A final question concerns the range of vessels which are entitled to exercise innocent passage. The convention texts refer to 'ships' and in the *Passage through the Great Belt* case[26] Denmark questioned whether the regime was applicable to structures such as oil rigs. The better view is that a broad, purposive approach should be taken in unusual cases such as this, but the most controversial issue is whether warships can exercise a right of innocent passage. No agreement could be reached on this issue at UNCLOS I or III, and the matter is not dealt with directly by the TSC or the LOSC. The major maritime powers favour warships enjoying the right of innocent passage, but this is opposed by many smaller States or those in strategically sensitive locations.

There are three schools of thought: that the passage of warships requires the prior authorization of the coastal State; that such passage must be notified to the coastal State, though no express authorization need be requested or given; or that such passage is possible provided that it conforms to the general rules on innocent passage as set out in the convention. For some, this last approach is implausible since they consider the mere presence of a foreign warship within a territorial sea to be prejudicial to the coastal State's interests. However, the move towards focusing upon 'activities' rather than the presence of ships within the territorial sea in the LOSC makes this argument unpersuasive (see Klein, 2011, p 31). Moreover, the convention texts provide some support for warships enjoying innocent passage: the general rules are set out in a section headed 'Rules Applicable to all Ships'; some of the activities listed in Article 19(2) as leading to the loss of innocence can only (or largely) be undertaken by warships; and submarines, most (but not all) of which are warships, can exercise that right if surfaced and showing their flag (Churchill and Lowe, 1999, p 89; Rothwell and Stevens, 2010, pp 222–3). None of these arguments is wholly convincing and State practice is as diverse as it is predictable, with major maritime powers such as the UK and the USA (joined by the USSR in their 1989 Joint Statement)[27] arguing in favour of warships enjoying the right of innocent passage and less powerful coastal States enacting legislation requiring authorization or notification (Tanaka, 2012, pp 88–91). Despite the growing trend towards increased coastal State dominance of offshore areas, the imperatives of essential military interests would suggest that this is likely

---

[25] Notifications made to the UN Secretary-General are publicized on the UN website at http://www.un.org/depts/los.

[26] *Passage Through the Great Belt (Finland v Denmark), Provisional Measures, Order of 29 July 1991, ICJ Reports 1991*, p 12.

[27] USA-USSR Uniform Interpretation of Norms of International Law Government Innocent Passage (1989), 14 *Law of the Sea Bulletin* 12. See Schachte, 1993, pp 182–3.

to remain a matter of controversy for some time to come, though on a day-to-day basis pragmatic approaches are usually found which respect the positions of all concerned.

2. Straits

The regime of innocent passage is a concession by coastal States to accommodate the interests of navigation but, as has been seen, the coastal State still enjoys a formidable array of jurisdictional competences. Whilst this might be acceptable where there is no real need, other than convenience or desire, to enter the territorial seas, different considerations apply to narrow straits wholly comprised of territorial seas but which are also used for international navigation, such as the straits of Dover, Gibraltar, and Hormuz. In such cases, international law shifts the balance somewhat in favour of the freedom of navigation (see generally Nandan and Anderson, 1989; Jia, 1998).

In the *Corfu Channel* case the ICJ concluded that, irrespective of the position more generally, warships were entitled to exercise a right of innocent passage through straits used for international navigation and that coastal States were not entitled to 'suspend' innocent passage within such straits for any form of ship.[28] This variant on innocent passage only applied in straits which linked one part of the high seas with another and which were actually used as a route of international navigation. Importantly, the existence of a relatively convenient alternative (in this case, around the western side of the Island of Corfu) did not deprive it of this status. Arguably, this was an overly generous approach to the interests of the international community at the expense of the coastal State but it was nevertheless reflected in 1958 TSC Article 16(4), which further expanded the regime by applying it to straits linking the high seas with the territorial sea of a third State at the head of a Gulf (this being intended to facilitate access to the Israeli port of Eilat at the head of the Gulf of Aqaba). This latter gloss did not reflect customary law, and was rejected by Arab States, but it was retained in Article 45 of the LOSC which reflects the TSC approach, though now expanded to take account of the Exclusive Economic Zone (EEZ).

Under the LOSC, the *Corfu Channel* regime of 'non-suspendable innocent passage' has something of a residual flavour, now applying only to straits not covered by the new regime of transit passage, considered later. However, there is no doubting the customary law status of the *Corfu Channel* regime which provides an assured minimum guarantee of passage though international straits for all vessels, including warships.

3. Transit passage

A major problem facing UNCLOS III concerned the consequences of the breadth of the territorial sea increasing from 3 to 12 n. miles. This meant that many major strategic waterways which had previously been high seas, such as the Straits of Dover, could become entirely territorial seas and at best be subject to the regime of non-suspendable innocent passage. During the Cold War, when super-power security was thought to depend in part on relatively undetectable submarine-based nuclear missiles, the idea that submarines should surface and show their flags when prowling the oceans was an additional concern. The result was a compromise that sought to further reduce the ability of coastal States to restrict passage within their territorial seas.

The LOSC regime of transit passage applies to all straits connecting high seas or EEZs with other areas of high seas or EEZs and which are used for international navigation unless there is a corridor of high seas or EEZ running through it (LOSC Article (36)) or the strait is formed by an island which belongs to the coastal State and seawards of which

---

[28] *Corfu Channel, Merits, Judgment, ICJ Reports 1949*, p 4 at p 28.

there is an alternative route (LOSC Article 38(1)). In cases covered by this latter rule, known as the 'Messina Strait' exception (after the Straits between Italy and Sicily), the *Corfu Channel* regime of non-suspendable innocent passage continues to apply. Straits covered by particular treaty regimes, such as the Turkish Straits (the Dardanelles and the Bosphorus), are also expressly excluded from the scope of the provisions concerning transit passage (LOSC Article 35(c)).

Whereas innocent passage only applies to ships and submarines, transit passage also applies to aircraft which are accorded the right of overflight. Although not expressly stated, the regime applies to military ships and aircraft, and submarines may proceed submerged. Ships or aircraft must 'proceed without delay' and 'refrain from any threat or use of force' against the States bordering the strait (thus, for example, hurrying through the Straits of Gibraltar to conduct military activities in the eastern Mediterranean would be permissible). Although ships and aircraft must comply with generally accepted international regulations regarding safety matters (LOSC Article 39), coastal States may themselves only regulate a very circumscribed list of activities: maritime safety (including traffic separate schemes); internationally approved regulations concerning discharges of oil, oily waste, and noxious substances in the strait; with respect to fishing vessels, prevention of fishing and the stowage of fishing gear; and loading and unloading in connection with customs, fiscal, immigration, or sanitary laws (LOSC Article 42(1)). The balance struck clearly favours the freedom of navigation. The customary law status of transit passage has been challenged (de Yturriaga, 1991) and remains unclear, although State practice outside the convention framework increasingly reflects these provisions. Whilst the increasing numbers of States party to the LOSC has taken some of the heat out of this debate, it remains the case that maritime powers which are not party to the Convention, including the USA, may need to rely on the customary status of transit passage in order to be assured of passage for warships and overflight of aircraft through or over straits of key strategic significance.

4. Archipelagic sea lane passage

Drawing archipelagic baselines converts vast tracts of waters which were previously either high seas or territorial seas into 'archipelagic waters'. LOSC Article 52 provides that the right of innocent passage applies throughout such waters and, moreover, Article 53 provides for a right of 'archipelagic sea lane passage' in 'corridors' to be designated by the archipelagic State. Archipelagic sea lane passage is similar to transit passage, meaning that the jurisdiction of archipelagic States over a wide range of matters in waters within their baselines is substantially reduced.[29] As a result, the demands of international navigation have been given precedence over local control.

IV. THE HIGH SEAS

A. THE FREEDOMS OF THE SEAS

The idea that beyond the territorial seas lie the high seas which are free for use by all lies at the heart of the law of the sea. Both the 1958 HSC and the LOSC proclaim the high

---

[29] The first example of a designation was that of Indonesia. See Indonesian Government Reg No 37 on the Rights and Obligations of Foreign Ships and Aircraft Exercising the Right of Archipelagic Sea Lane Passage through Designated Archipelagic Sea Lanes, 28 June 2002 (2003) 52 *Law of the Sea Bulletin* 20.

seas to be free and open to vessels of all States and give non-exhaustive lists of freedoms. The HSC mentions navigation, fishing, overflight, and cable laying (HSC Article 2), and the LOSC adds the construction of artificial islands and marine scientific research. All are to be enjoyed with 'due regard' (in the HSC, 'reasonable regard') to the interests of others (LOSC Article 87).

It has already been seen how that space has been eroded by the expansion of the territorial seas, and some of the balances that have been struck as a consequence. Later sections will look at how the high seas have been further eroded by the creation of zones of functional jurisdiction. This section considers how freedom of navigation on the high seas has fared.

The key to regulating activities within the high seas is the concept of flag-State jurisdiction. All vessels must be registered according to the laws of a State and, in consequence, are subject to its legislative jurisdiction and, whilst on the high seas or within its own territorial sea or EEZ, to its enforcement jurisdiction. In principle, a flag State enjoys exclusive jurisdiction over its vessels, although there are exceptions. However, if a ship is stateless, or flies more than one flag so that its true State of registry is not clear, then any State can exercise jurisdiction over it.[30]

Although the content of domestic laws applicable to vessels will vary considerably, there are an increasingly large number of international conventions relating to matters such as pollution control, resource management, and health and safety at sea which seek to ensure as common an approach as possible. Beyond this lies the problem of enforcement. A State is obliged to 'effectively exercise its jurisdiction and control' over ships operating under its flag (LOSC Article 94(1)) but this is often easier said than done. Many States simply do not have the capacity to enforce their laws over vessels flying their flag, (many of which may only rarely, if ever, put into port in their State of registry), whilst others simply lack the will to do so. Moreover, States are entitled to set their own conditions for registering ships, and although a 'genuine link' must exist between the vessel and State (LOSC Article 91),[31] attempts to lend greater precision to this requirement have not been successful and the problem of vessels being registered under 'flags of convenience', which exercise little effective control over their activities, remains. It is against this background that the subtle but steady erosion of the exclusive jurisdictional competence of the flag State over its registered vessels must be assessed.

B. THE EXCEPTIONS TO FLAG-STATE JURISDICTION

1. Visit

It is axiomatic that the authorities of one State may not board a vessel flying the flag of another without the consent of the flag State. There is, however, an increasingly long and increasingly detailed list of exceptions to this general principle. These exceptions will be outlined later, but since it will not always be immediately apparent whether such action is permissible, international law recognizes an intermediary position in which the authorities of a non-flag State are entitled to board a vessel on the high seas in order to verify whether their suspicions are justified (see generally Guilfoyle, 2009; Papastavridis, 2013). These instances arise where there are reasonable grounds for suspecting that a ship is engaged in piracy, the slave trade, or unauthorized radio broadcasting (LOSC Article 110(1)(a)–(c)),

---

[30] See, eg *Molvan v Attorney General for Palestine* [1948] AC 351.
[31] But cf Tanaka, 2012, p 159 who wonders if it is really possible for a State to refuse to recognize the nationality on a vessel in the absence of a 'genuine link'.

the consequences of which are considered later. In addition, a ship might be visited to confirm that it is either stateless or, in cases of doubt, that it is in fact of the nationality of the visiting authorities, meaning that the visiting authority can assert its jurisdiction on the basis of the principles outlined in the previous section. In all of these cases a visit and any subsequent action may only be undertaken by a warship or other vessel or aircraft duly authorized and clearly marked (LOSC Articles 110(5) and 107), but the right of visit cannot be exercised in respect of a warship of another State or any other non-flag State vessel entitled to immunity.

2. Piracy

Under both customary international law and the 1958 and 1982 Conventions all States may take action on the high seas, or in any other place beyond the national jurisdiction of a State, against individuals or vessels involved in acts of piracy. Those committing acts of piracy are often said to have rendered themselves 'enemies of all mankind' and piracy is the oldest and most well-attested example of an act which attracts universal jurisdiction.[32] However, the LOSC definition of piracy is comparatively narrow, covering only 'illegal acts of violence or detention, or any act of depredation, committed for private ends by the crew or passengers of a private ship or private aircraft and directed (i) on the high seas, against another ship or aircraft, or against persons or property on board such a ship or aircraft; (ii) against a ship, aircraft, persons or property in a place outside the jurisdiction of any State' (LOSC Article 101(a)).[33]

This definition conjures up a vision of pirates roaming the seas in their own private and unregistered vessels, beyond the reach of any flag State, and preying on other vessels whose own flag State may not be in a position to react or respond. Whilst this may seem something of a caricature, reflecting historical experience (and Hollywood stereotypes), it still resonates with the current reality in a number of regions and, in particular where weak or failing States have produced the forms of legal vacuum in which piracy flourishes. The situation off the coast of Somalia has given rise to particular concern in recent times and a number of powers have stationed military vessels in the vicinity in order to deter and offer protection. In June 2008 the UN Security Council, with Somalia's consent and acting under Chapter VII of the UN Charter, adopted Resolution 1816 which called on States to cooperate in tackling piracy off the coast of Somalia and authorized them to enter Somalia's territorial seas in order to exercise enforcement jurisdiction over acts of piracy or armed robbery which had occurred either in international waters or in the territorial sea itself[34] (Guilfoyle, 2008). Later that year, in Resolution 1846, the Security Council went further and authorized States to take action against vessels reasonably suspected of involvement in piracy.[35] Shortly afterwards the Council went further again, calling on States to take all necessary measures within the territory of Somalia itself to

---

[32] See, eg *Arrest Warrant of 11 April 2000 (Democratic Republic of Congo v Belgium), Preliminary Objections and Merits, Judgment, ICJ Reports 2002*, p 3. Separate Opinion of Judges Higgins, Kooijmans, and Buergenthal, para 61; Separate Opinion of President Guillaume, para 5.

[33] It also includes voluntarily participating in operating a ship or aircraft, in the knowledge that it is being used for the purposes of piracy and inciting or intentionally facilitating piracy (LOSC Article 101(b) and (c)). In *US v Ali*, the US Court of Appeals, District of Colombia (11 June 2013) decided that, whilst the definition embraces aiding and abetting piracy, it does not extend to conspiracy to commit acts of piracy, which, it believed, fell outside the scope of piracy as defined under international law.

[34] SC Res 1816 (2 June 2008). This authorization was for a period of six months from the date of the resolution.

[35] SC Res 1846 (2 Dec 2008), extending the authorizations given in SC Res 1816 for a further 12 months. This has recently been extended for a further 12 months by SC Res 2077 (13 November 2012).

suppress piracy and armed robbery at sea[36] (Guilfoyle, 2009, pp 61–78; Treves, 2013). In response to these calls, an unprecedentedly complex web of multilateral arrangements have been entered into in order to protect shipping from attack and to apprehend, try and punish those suspected of piracy (see generally Giess and Petrig, 2011; Guilfoyle, 2013). It remains to be seen whether this unusually innovative and expansive response to piracy off Somalia offers a model which might be employed more generally or whether its relevance is limited by the very particular situation within that country.

Previous responses to the shortcomings of the definition of piracy in LOSC 110 have also left an enduring legacy, even if they have fallen short of what was required to address the problems posed by piracy off the coasts of Somalia. The *Achille Lauro* incident in the mid-1980s concerned a situation in which a group of passengers turned hijacker and seized control of an Italian cruise liner, and subsequently killed one of the other passengers. Although those responsible were clearly susceptible to, *inter alia*, Italian jurisdiction, this incident prompted the adoption of the 1988 Rome Convention on the Suppression of Unlawful Acts Against the Safety of Maritime Navigation (known as the 1988 SUA Convention). Following the pattern of numerous other international conventions, it sets out an extensive range of offences which States parties must make criminal under their domestic law and obliges them either to extradite or to submit the cases of those suspected of committing such acts to their prosecuting authorities. Although the SUA Convention does not grant States parties further jurisdictional competencies at sea, it does oblige them to extend and use their domestic law against those who imperil the freedom of navigation. Moreover, Article 17 of the SUA Convention sets out a highly developed framework for facilitating cooperation between contracting States, including procedures for flag States to authorize the boarding and searching of vessels suspected of prohibited activities by those requesting to do so. These provisions have been built upon in other contexts, as will be described later.

3. Hot pursuit

The problem of how to deal with vessels which commit offences within internal waters or the territorial sea but evade arrest by moving outside the zones of coastal State jurisdiction has already been mentioned and one response—that of the contiguous zone—has already been noted. The doctrine of 'hot pursuit' provides another means of addressing the same problem and forms another exception to the principle of exclusive flag-State jurisdiction. According to this doctrine, the rather complex details of which are set out at length in LOSC Article 111, warships or military aircraft of a coastal State which have commenced the pursuit of a vessel within their territorial sea (or within their the contiguous zone or EEZ, if the offence in question is one for which an arrest might have been made there) may continue that pursuit outside of it provided that the pursuit is continuous, although the actual ship or aircraft involved in the pursuit might change: indeed, practice suggests that ships or aircraft of several nationalities may cooperate in arresting a vessel in the exercise of a right of hot pursuit.[37]

A further variant on this is 'constructive presence'. Rather than commit an offence within the territorial sea, some vessels choose to remain just outside and dispatch smaller boats, for example, to take illegal goods ashore. Under such circumstances, the 'mother'

---

[36] See SC Res 1851 (8 December 2008).

[37] In 2003 the *Viarsa 1* was arrested following a pursuit lasting some 21 days and extending over some 3,900 km and which involved vessels from Australia, South Africa, and the UK. See Molenaar, 2004.

vessel might be chased and arrested even though it has never entered the territorial sea and the pursuit begins outside of it. The same is true should boats be sent out from the coastal State to meet the 'mother' vessel: in both cases there has been teamwork that implicates the vessel operating outside of the territorial seas with those committing offences within it.

How far can this approach be taken? In *R v Mills*, the *Poseidon*, a vessel registered in St Vincent, transferred a consignment of drugs on the high seas to a trawler sailing from Ireland to the UK. Following the arrest of the trawler in the UK, the *Poseidon* was also arrested, this being justified on the basis of 'constructive presence' (Gilmore, 1995). Taken to extremes, this suggests that any vessel which whilst at sea colludes with another vessel in the commission of an illegal act within the jurisdiction of a State is liable to arrest by that State anywhere on the high seas. Though not irreconcilable, this expansive approach sits rather uneasily with the caution expressed by the International Tribunal on the Law of the Sea (ITLOS) in *M/V Saiga (No 2)* in which stressed the need for a strict approach to be taken to the application of LOSC Article 111.[38]

4. Broadcasting

In the 1960s elements of the international community became agitated about the rise of commercial broadcasting into a country from foreign registered vessels on the high seas and over which they could not exercise any control (or extract revenues).[39] Regional State practice to address this problem in the North Sea through cooperative measures was subsequently built on, with the result that LOSC Article 109 permits the arrest and prosecution of any person engaged in 'unauthorized radio broadcasting' from ships or installations on the high seas by a range of States, including the State where the transmissions are received (Anderson, 2006, pp 340–41). A perhaps unexpected consequence of this arose in the early 1990s when a vessel called the *Goddess of Democracy* planned to broadcast messages of solidarity and support for those arrested in the pro-democracy demonstrations in Bejing. The Chinese authorities made it clear they would arrest the vessel if it did so, and the mission was aborted.

5. Slavery

The rather heavy-handed approach taken in respect of unauthorized broadcasting contrasts with the comparatively feeble manner in which other, more pressing, issues were tackled. The international prohibition of slavery is well-established in international law yet the 1982 Convention does not permit the arrest of vessels engaged in slave trading by non-flag States; it merely provides that a State 'shall take effective measures to prevent and punish the transport of slaves in ships authorized to fly its flag' (LOSC Article 99). Admittedly, that Article also provides that any slave fortunate enough to escape and take refuge on a non-flag State vessel 'shall *ipso facto* be free' and since there is a right to visit vessels suspected of being involved in slave trading (LOSC Article 110(1)(b)) this should not be difficult to manufacture. Nevertheless, it remains difficult to see why those involved in the slave trade, and their vessels, should not be susceptible to arrest under such circumstances without the express authorization of the flag State. More attention has been paid to the related practice of smuggling migrants across boarders and the 'Migrant Smuggling Protocol' to the UN Convention against Transnational Organized Crime adopted in

[38] *M/V Saiga No 2* (*St Vincent and the Grenadines v Guinea*), Case No 2, Judgment of 1 July 1999, paras 146–52. Cf also *M/V Louisa* (*St Vincent and the Grenadines v Spain*), Case No 18, Judgment, 28 May 2013, paras 86–7 for a further example of ITLOS taking a strict approach to a similar question.

[39] See generally Guilfoyle, 2009, Ch 7. The film *The Ship that Rocked* (2008) provides an entertaining account of the issues as seen at the time.

2000 follows the model of the 1988 Vienna Convention against Illicit Traffic in Narcotics (considered later) in constructing a regime to encourage and facilitate the acquisition of flag-State consent to board and undertake other 'appropriate measures' to 'prevent and suppress' migrant smuggling.[40]

6. Drugs trafficking

As with slavery, the LOSC provisions concerning drugs trafficking have also been found wanting. Article 108 is an anodyne provision which merely provides that States 'shall co-operate' in the suppression of the drugs trade by vessels on the high seas and that a State which suspects a vessel flying its flag is involved in trafficking 'may request the co-operation of other states to suppress such traffic'. This states the obvious. The 1988 Vienna Convention Against Illicit Traffic in Narcotic Drugs and Psychotropic Substances takes the matter further, developing and institutionalizing a more detailed framework for cooperation, but boarding a vessel still requires flag-State authorization and there is no right of visit under LOSC Article 110. This was vividly illustrated in *R v Charrington* where irregularities in the manner in which the UK Customs and Excise obtained the consent of the Maltese authorities to board a vessel carrying £15m of cannabis resulted in the collapse of the domestic prosecution (Gilmore, 2000). State practice has gone further and, building on the model provided by the 1988 Convention, arrangements for mutual enforcement and assistance have been concluded in a number of spheres, particularly fishing. In addition, the UK has concluded bilateral arrangements permitting US authorities to board British vessels suspected of drugs offences on the high seas within the Caribbean region and has concluded a regional treaty to facilitate more widespread cooperation.[41]

Once again, it may be that long-standing dogmas have stood in the way of devising rather more effective means of tackling a matter of major international concern.

7. Terrorism and weapons of mass destruction

The 1988 SUA Convention was drafted in the wake of a terrorist outrage akin to piracy and so it was not surprising that the response was tailored to that form. As new concerns have emerged they too have been addressed within the model that the SUA provides; that is, through the identification and definition of additional forms of unlawful conduct and the utilization of cooperative arrangements to enable flag-State consent to be more readily obtained for boarding, search and, if necessary, arrest of vessels by non-flag States. In October 2005 the International Maritime Organization adopted a Protocol to the SUA which would make it an offence under the convention to engage in an extremely broad range of activities at sea when the purpose of the activity, given its nature and context, is intended to 'intimidate a population, or to compel a government or an international organization to do or to abstain from any act', or to knowingly transport persons who have committed such unlawful acts.[42] Moreover, the Protocol would permit participating States to notify the IMO Secretary General in advance that permission for boarding and

---

[40] The Protocol entered into force in 2004 and currently has 137 States parties. See generally Guilfoyle, 2009, pp 184–226 for this and a consideration of related State practice.

[41] Agreement Concerning Co-operation in Suppressing Illicit Maritime and Air Trafficking in Narcotic Drugs and Psychotropic Substances in the Caribbean Area, 10 April 2003. See Gilmore, 2005. For a more general review of the topic see Guilfoyle, 2009, Ch 5; Papastavridis, 2013, Ch 7.

[42] These acts not only embrace the use or discharge of any explosive, radioactive material or BCN (biological, chemical, nuclear) weapon in a manner that causes or is likely to cause death or serious injury or damage but also include the transportation of explosive or radioactive materials in the knowledge that they are intended to be so used, knowingly transporting a BCN weapon and a further range of related activities including the

searching is to be presumed if no reply is given to a requesting State within four hours of a request being made. This goes a long way to creating a presumption in favour of boarding by those States with reasonable grounds for suspicion and a heavy onus on those flag States that might seek to deny such a request. Although the 2005 Protocol entered into force in 2010, it has not been widely ratified as yet.[43]

The 2005 Protocol had already been prefigured by the 'Proliferation Security Initiative' (PSI), instigated by the USA in 2003 and which provides an enhanced framework for cooperation between its now over 100 participating States when seeking to undertake an interdiction at sea. (see Byers, 2004; Guilfoyle, 2009, Ch 9; Klein, 2011, pp 193–208; Papastavridis, 2013, Ch 5). The USA has also entered into reciprocal bilateral treaties with a number of States which, like the 2005 Protocol, provide for a presumption that a request for boarding has been granted if no response if given within a limited period of time.[44] Once again, these developments are consonant with the traditional principles of high seas and flag-State jurisdiction, but point to a reality very different from that which those principles suggest for those willing to accept them through participating in the SUA Protocol, PSI or other bilateral arrangements. However, there is as yet no evidence to suggest that such broad-ranging rights and facilitative arrangements for boarding and search—even in this context—are reflective of customary international law.

C. CONCLUSION

The freedom of navigation has, then, been the subject of some whittling away, both by reason of the increasing breadth of the territorial sea, outlined in Section III, and by the erosion of exclusive flag-State jurisdiction outlined earlier. However, the modifications to the regime of innocent passage and the regime of transit passage, as well as the limited and piecemeal nature of the increased jurisdictional competence over non-flag-State vessels, all point in the direction of the continuing significance of the freedom of navigation, albeit that this is 'freedom under the law' (Anderson, 2006, p 345). This is further underscored by the remaining sections of this chapter which chart the rise of functional zones of jurisdiction and which, although representing a marked diminution in other freedoms of the high seas, left navigation relatively untouched and also ensured that the increase in the breadth of the territorial sea was kept within modest bands.

V. RESOURCE JURISDICTION

A. THE CONTINENTAL SHELF

During the opening decades of the twentieth century improvements in technology made the exploration and exploitation of seabed and subsoil resources beyond the territorial

---

transportation of any equipment, materials or software or related technology that significantly contributes to the design, manufacture or delivery of a BCN weapon with the intention that they will be used for such purposes. See 2005 Protocol, adding Article 3 *bis* to the SUA. See generally Klein, 2011, pp 170–84.

[43] The Protocol has 28 States Parties, compared to the 161 Parties to the 1988 SUA.

[44] The USA has so far concluded nine such bilateral agreements, with Antigua and Barbuda (2010), the Bahamas (2008), Belize (2005), Croatia (2005), Cyprus (2005), Liberia (2004), Malta (2007), Marshall Islands (2004), Mongolia (2007), Panama (2004), and St Vincent and the Grenadines (2010). See Klein, 2011, pp184–90. These States account for much of the registered shipping in the world. The time period for notification before the presumption in its favour takes effect in these agreements is the even shorter period of two hours.

sea—particularly oil and then natural gas—both increasingly possible and economically viable. In theory, these deposits were available to all since legally speaking they were high seas resources. However, orderly and effective development required some degree of involvement by a proximate coastal State and in the Truman Proclamation (1945), the US President declared 'the natural resources of the subsoil and seabed of the continental shelf beneath the high seas but contiguous to the coasts of the US as appertaining to the US, subject to its jurisdiction and control'.[45] Following consideration by the ILC, the 1958 CSC provided that 'The coastal state exercises over the continental shelf sovereign rights for the purpose of exploring it and exploiting its natural resources' and did so independently of express acts or declarations (Articles 2(1) and 2(3)). In the *North Sea* cases the ICJ recognized this as a statement of customary law, stressing that these rights existed '*ipso facto and ab initio*'.[46] LOSC Article 77 reiterates this approach.

Natural resources include both mineral and other non-living resources of the seabed and subsoil and well as 'sedentary species' (CSC Article 2(4); LOSC Article 77(4)). Thus pearling is clearly covered by this definition, whereas jurisdiction over wrecks is not. Whether crabs and lobsters are continental shelf resources is more controversial, although the EEZ now provides an alternative means of securing coastal State jurisdiction over such resources.

The most vexed question concerns the outer limit of continental shelf jurisdiction. The seabed off a coast may not be a 'continental shelf' in a geophysical sense at all: the coast may swiftly plunge to great depths, as it does off the western coasts of much of South America, or merely be shallow indentations into which water has flooded, as in the Gulf region of the Middle East. The continental shelf proper is merely a component of the 'continental margin' which comprises the gently sloping shelf, which gives way to a steep slope which then levels off into the continental rise that emerges from the ocean floor (sometimes rather prosaically described as the 'Abyssal Plain'). The 1958 CSC did not draw directly on any of these concepts and defined the continental shelf, for legal purposes, as comprising the seabed and subsoil adjacent to the coast but outside the territorial sea, extending to the point where the waters above were 200 metres deep, or as far seawards as it was possible to exploit (CSC Article 1). This was most unsatisfactory since it permitted States to claim ever more distant areas as technology rapidly developed. Moreover it ran into the claim advanced in the late 1960s that the deep seabed was the 'common heritage' of all mankind and not subject to single State jurisdiction. It was, then, necessary to place some limit on the seawards expansion of continental shelf jurisdiction.

In the *North Sea* cases the ICJ argued that the continental shelf represented the 'natural prolongation' of the landmass into and under the sea,[47] implying some limit to its seawards expansion. However, this still did not address the claims of States which had no 'natural prolongation' as such, but who nevertheless sought jurisdiction over offshore seabed and subsoil resources and who therefore argued that the continental shelf should be a fixed distance, measured from the baselines, irrespective of the nature of the seabed. This approach was opposed by some of the so-called 'broad shelf' States which already exercised jurisdiction on the basis of 'natural prolongation' beyond the most likely fixed limit of 200 n. miles.

This conundrum was resolved by the complex compromise found in LOSC Article 76(1), according to which the continental shelf extends (a) to the outer edge of continental margin

[45] 1 *New Directions in the Law of the Sea* 106.

[46] *North Sea Continental Shelf, Judgment, ICJ Reports 1969*, p 3, paras 19, 39, and 43.

[47] Ibid, para 18. For an extended discussion see Hutchinson, 1985.

(this being seen as the natural prolongation), or (b) to a distance of 200 n. miles from the baselines from which its territorial sea is measured, whichever is the further. LOSC Article 76(2)–(7) then set out details of how the outer edge of the continental margin is to be calculated. This is to be done with reference to the 'foot' of the continental slope, this being the point where the continental slope gives way to the continental rise. From this point, a State might either exercise jurisdiction for a further 60 n. miles seawards, or as far as a point where the depth of the 'sedimentary rock' (loose, rather than bedrock) overlying the continental rise is more than 1% of the distance of that point from the foot of the slope. These outer lines are then subject to one of two alternative limitations: they cannot be drawn more than 350 miles from the baselines of a State, or more than 100 miles from a point at which the depth of the water is 2,500 metres. This complicated formula is difficult to apply and its customary law status unclear. In the *Territorial and Maritime Boundary Dispute (Nicaragua v Colombia)*, the ICJ confirmed that Article 76(1) was customary law, but reserved its position as regards the remainder of that Article, noting that it was not necessary to decide on its customary law status for the purposes of the case.[48] As a result, it now is accepted that the continental shelf has two elements: an 'inner shelf', of 200 n. miles to which all coastal States are entitled, and an 'outer shelf', where its continental margin extends beyond that distance. However, the detailed means by which the limits of the 'outer continental shelf' are to be determined is as yet only governed by treaty, rather than by customary law—a most unsatisfactory state of affairs.[49]

Nevertheless, it is vital to determine the outer limit of each State's continental shelf since the seabed beyond forms part of the 'Area', governed by its own legal regime (considered in Section V D in this chapter). LOSC Article 76(8) therefore establishes the Commission on the Limits of the Continental Shelf, to which States parties must submit details of their claims to outer limits beyond 200 n. miles from the baseline and 67 claims have so far done so.

The role of the Commission is to examine these submissions and to make recommendations to States 'on the basis of which' the State establishes its final boundary (see generally Cook and Carlton, 2000). This is clearly opaque —for example, it is unclear what happens should the State reject the Commission's recommendations. The Commission has so far issued 18 recommendations, summaries of which are made public and which reveal the extremely complex nature of its tasks.[50] What is clear is that the entire regime reflects a careful balancing act between the interests of coastal States with varied geophysical relationships to the sea; to the economic interests of the international community as a whole and to the interests of the freedom of navigation and of the high seas, which it leaves substantially untouched.

B. THE EXCLUSIVE FISHING ZONE

As States watched the international community recognize and legitimate coastal State jurisdiction over the resources of the seabed and subsoil, it was inevitable that the argument

---

[48] *Territorial and Maritime Dispute (Nicaragua v Colombia), Judgment of 19 November 2012*, para 118. Whilst both parties had accepted that Article 76(1) reflected customary international law, Colombia had contested Nicaragua's claim that Articles 76(2)-(7) were also rules of customary international law.

[49] LOSC Article 82 make exploitation beyond 200 n. miles subject to the State making 'payments or contributions in kind' through the International Seabed Authority. It is particularly difficult to see how Article 82 could have a life outside the convention framework.

[50] This might account for why the Commission is only able to produce only some three of four Recommendations per year, meaning that at current rates there is a ten-year backlog of submissions. See Subedi, 2011. For an overview of the practice of the Commission see Llewellyn, 2007; Rothwell and Stevens, 2010, pp 111–17; and the essays in Vidas, 2010, Pt V.

would be made that resources of the water column be treated likewise. This was always going to be controversial since the seabed was, by and large, chiefly of potential economic importance, whereas high seas fishing was already of very real economic importance and excluding foreign-flagged fishing vessels from waters beyond narrow belts of territorial seas would have serious consequences for many communities and economies. However, the increased capacity of vessels to harvest fish was putting stocks at risk and so there was a tension between maximizing access to resources and promoting effective conservation. Viewed in this light, increased coastal State control appeared more beneficial than high seas freedoms and this was reflected in the developing law of fisheries. This will be considered further in Section VII but it is important to note here the emergence of the Exclusive Fishing Zone (EFZ) as an autonomous zone of resource jurisdiction.

Neither UNCLOS I nor II could agree upon the establishment of an EFZ but State practice moved steadily in the direction of recognizing the right of a coastal State to assert jurisdiction over fisheries within 12 n. miles of its baselines and in the 1974 *Fisheries Jurisdiction* case the ICJ recognized this as reflecting customary law.[51] By this time claims for zones of up to 200 n. miles were being advanced yet the Court was unwilling to go further and endorse Iceland's claim for an EFZ of up to 50 n. miles. It did, however, suggest that a State might exceptionally be entitled to preferential access to the high seas resources within such a distance under certain circumstances.[52] Such hesitations were subsequently swept away by the development of the EEZ and, although there is no mention of the EFZ as an autonomous regime within the LOSC, it is clear that customary law now recognizes EFZ claims of up to 200 n. miles.[53]

C. THE EXCLUSIVE ECONOMIC ZONE

The previous sections have already identified the reasons why during the 1960s and 1970s many coastal States wanted to have exclusive access to the resources of the seabed and the water column but were reluctant to extend the breadth of their territorial seas. In order to balance the competing interests, Latin and South American States advanced the claim that there should be a single zone of up to 200 n. miles in which the coastal State enjoyed sovereign rights over all natural living and non-living resources but within which the other freedoms of the seas, and in particular navigation, would be unaffected. Over time, this claim became refined into what is now known as the EEZ, which became recognized as reflecting customary international law during the UNCLOS III process[54] and, of course, is established as a matter of treaty law by the LOSC itself.[55]

Under the regime established by the convention, States may claim an EEZ of up to 200 n. miles (LOSC Article 57) within which the range of matters reserved for the coastal State are so extensive that the Zone is comprised of neither territorial seas nor high seas but is considered to be '*sui generis*' and subject to a distinct jurisdictional framework (LOSC Article 55). First and foremost, coastal States exercise sovereign rights within the EEZ for the purposes of 'exploring and exploiting, conserving and managing' both its living and non-living natural resources (LOSC Article 56(1)(a)). Although this may seem to be an amalgamation of the jurisdictional capacities which States already were able to enjoy on

---

[51] *Fisheries Jurisdiction (United Kingdom v Iceland), Merits, Judgment, ICJ Reports 1974*, p 3, para 53.

[52] Ibid, paras 55–60.

[53] See *Maritime Delimitation in the Area between Greenland and Jan Mayen, Judgment, ICJ Reports 1993*, p 316, accepting uncritically the Norwegian claim to an EFZ of this distance.

[54] See *Continental Shelf (Libyan Arab Jamahiriya/Malta), Judgment, ICJ Reports 1985*, p 13.

[55] For general studies of the origins and background of the EEZ see Attard, 1986; Orrego-Vicuna, 1989.

the basis of the continental shelf and the EFZ regimes, the EEZ does in fact embrace additional elements, including the harnessing of wind and wave power. The coastal State also has jurisdiction, subject to the other provisions of the convention, over the establishment and use of artificial islands and installations, marine scientific research, and the preservation of the marine environment, as well as a range of other matters (LOSC Article 56(b) and (c)).

Despite its 'sui generis' nature, the EEZ is pulled in a number of different directions. As regards jurisdiction over the resources of the seabed and subsoil, it is closely aligned with the continental shelf (LOSC Article 56(3)). Article 58 provides that three of the freedoms of the seas expressly mentioned in the convention—navigation, overflight, and laying cables and pipelines, and related activities—are to be exercised by all States within an EEZ in accordance with the general framework for the high seas, as provided for in Articles 87–116. Thus of the six high seas freedoms identified in the convention, three pass to the predominant control of the coastal State within its EEZ whilst three remain open to the international community at large. This list of freedoms is not exhaustive and in situations not specifically provided for the question of whether a matter falls within the jurisdiction of the coastal State 'should be resolved on the basis of equity and in the light of all the relevant circumstances, taking into account the respective importance of the interests involved to the parties as well as to the international community as a whole' (LOSC Article 59). The *M/V Saiga (No 2)* illustrates the type of problem that might arise. Guinea arrested a vessel in its EEZ and argued, *inter alia*, that it was entitled to do so because the vessel had been 'bunkering' (transferring oil to) a fishing vessel and thereby avoiding customs duties. The ITLOS found it unnecessary to decide this point,[56] but it is clear that had bunkering occurred within the territorial sea, and the arrest taken place within internal waters, the territorial sea, or a contiguous zone, the legitimacy of the arrest would not have been an issue at all.

The heart of the EEZ concerns jurisdiction over fisheries and this is considered in Section VII in this chapter. However, it should be noted here that coastal States enjoy broad-ranging legislative jurisdiction (LOSC Article 63(4)) and may take measures including 'boarding, inspection, arrest and judicial proceedings' which are necessary to enforce laws and regulations concerning its sovereign right to 'explore, exploit, conserve and manage' living resources of the EEZ (LOSC Article 73). This is not without difficulties. For example, the 1986 *Franco-Canadian Fisheries Arbitration*[57] took the view that a vessel engaged in processing fish at sea fell outside the range of activities over which the coastal State was entitled to exercise and enforce jurisdiction (for criticism see Churchill and Lowe, 1999, p 291). The convention also balances the potentially intrusive power of the coastal State over vessels within its EEZ against the risk of abuse by requiring that vessels or crew arrested 'shall be promptly released upon the posting of reasonable bond or other securities' and by restricting the nature of the penalties to which they might be subject (LOSC Article 73). Moreover, the International Tribunal on the Law of the Sea enjoys an automatic jurisdiction over claims concerning the prompt release of vessels arrested for contravening coastal state law relating to the exploitation of living resources of the EEZ (LOSC Articles 292 and 73) and this has generated a considerable number of the cases it has considered.[58]

---

[56] *M/V Saiga No 2 (St Vincent and the Grenadines* v *Guinea)*, Case No 2, Judgment of 1 July 1999, paras 56–9. ITLOS is currently considering the question of bunkering within the EEZ once again in the *M/V Virginia G (Panama/Guinea-Bissau)*, Case No 19, judgment in which is expected shortly.

[57] *Franco-Canadian Fisheries Arbitration* (1986) 90 *RGDIP* 713. See also the provisional measures Order by ITLOS in *The 'Arctic Sunrise'* v *Russian Federation, Provisional Measures*, Case No 22, *Order of 22 November 2013* which again illustrates the tension between the exercise of the freedom of navigation within the EEZ and the legislative and enforcement jurisdiction of the coastal state.

[58] A total of 22 cases have been submitted to the ITLOS since its inception, nine of which have concerned applications for prompt release.

D. THE DEEP SEABED

The final zone of resource jurisdiction which has been carved out of the high seas is the most dramatic in both kind and extent. The claim that the seabed beyond the limits of national jurisdiction form the 'common heritage of mankind', fuelled initially by some near fantastical estimates of the potential mineral wealth at stake, has already been noted. The difficulty lay in translating that idea into a workable regime: the developed world favoured a loosely structured international agency to oversee and regulate activities of those wishing to conduct mining whereas the developing world generally favoured creating a strong international mechanism that would itself undertake mining activity and distribute the proceeds as appropriate, taking account of the needs of developing countries and developing land-based producers. Negotiations at UNCLOS III were tortuous and produced an outcome—Part XI of the LOSC—which satisfied few and was considered completely unacceptable by the developed world in general and the USA in particular (Schmidt, 1989).

Even at the time of its adoption, it was clear that the convention text would need to be modified in some way in order to accommodate the interests of the major industrialized powers whose support would be necessary for the regime to become a practical reality. Some concessions were made in Resolutions I and II which were appended to the Final Act of the Conference. These granted certain privileges to 'pioneer investors', States and companies registered in States which had already made a significant investment in seabed mining. This, however, proved to be too little too late. The breakthrough came in the early 1990s when the likelihood of the convention's entry into force, coupled with the demise of communism and changing economic and geo-political factors, produced a climate in which it was possible to revisit the convention text, sweep away some of the more bureaucratic and arcane layers of regulation and strike a new balance between the interests of those States and those companies which were already practically engaged in activities relating to mining the deep seabed and the more general interests of the international community as a whole. Far reaching changes were made in the 1994 Implementation Agreement which paved the way for widespread ratification of the convention (Section I of this chapter; Harrison, 2011, Ch 5). Underlying this change of approach was the realization that the financial rewards were likely to be considerably less than originally thought—if, indeed, there were likely to be any at all.[59]

Under the current arrangements, resource exploration and exploitation of the seabed and subsoil beyond the limits of national jurisdiction, known as the 'Area', is administered by the International Seabed Authority (ISA) to which applicants must submit 'plans of work'. These must identify two areas of roughly equal mining potential, one of which is to be mined by the applicant whilst the other will be 'reserved' for exploitation by the international community. In the original convention scheme, exploitation of the 'reserved' site would be undertaken by the 'Enterprise', an independent commercial mining arm of the ISA but under the 1994 Agreement the 'Enterprise' was given a considerably reduced role and, at least initially, might only engage in joint ventures. If the Enterprise does not undertake the mining of a reserved site within 15 years, the original applicant may do so. Moreover, if it does seek to mine the site, the original applicant is to be offered the chance to participate in the joint venture. The reality of the situation is that the Enterprise does not

---

[59] Indeed, commercial interest was already switching away from polymetallic nodules, primarily located beyond national jurisdiction in the Area, and becoming more focused on polymetallic sulphides which are more usually found within areas of national jurisdiction within the continental shelf and EEZ, further lessening the significance of the Deep Seabed regime.

yet exist as an entity, and the ISA is currently fulfilling its functions. It will only be established should seabed mining becomes commercially feasible, and it may be that it never will be. In the meanwhile, the Authority has since 2001 entered into a number of 15-year contracts with a range of governments,[60] government entities and commercial consortia, whose activities are largely focused on exploration and research at present, in the Clarion-Clipperton Zone in the Pacific Ocean and the Central Indian Ocean Basin.

The details of the regime, and the manner in which it balances the interests of various interest groups—including consumer States, investing States, producing States, developing States, landlocked States, and others—is such as to defy easy and succinct description and may be pursued elsewhere.[61] For current purposes what is significant is the manner in which the international community—after a number of false starts—was able to agree that the resource potential of the seabed and subsoil should no longer be considered as a part of the high seas regime and that yet another 'bespoke' regime of resource jurisdiction should be created,[62] whilst preserving the integrity of the general jurisdictional framework applicable to the law of the sea.

VI. DELIMITATION OF MARITIME ZONES BETWEEN OPPOSITE OR ADJACENT STATES

It will often be impossible for States to extend their jurisdiction as far seawards as international law permits because of the claims of other States. The resulting problem of delimiting maritime zones between opposite or adjacent coastal States whose claims overlap is extremely difficult and has given rise to more cases before the ICJ than any other single subject, as well as having generated a considerable number of ad hoc arbitrations.

A. EQUIDISTANCE OR EQUITABLE PRINCIPLES?

LOSC Article 15 provides that, in the absence of agreement to the contrary, States may not extend their territorial seas beyond the median, or equidistance line, unless there are historic or other 'special' circumstances that dictate otherwise. This 'equidistance/special circumstances' rule has been accepted by the ICJ as customary international law[63] and it is clear that only in exceptional cases will the equidistance line not form the basis of the boundary

---

[60] States may also sponsor commercial applicants. See further *Responsibilities and Obligations of States Sponsoring Persons and Entities with Respect to Activities in the Area, Advisory Opinion, ITLOS Reports 2011*, nyr; (2011) 50 ILM 458 and see Evans and Okowa, 2013, pp 127–36.

[61] For details see the information available on the International Sea Bed Authority website: http://www.isa.org.jm. For a helpful overview of its early work see Nandan, 2006.

[62] The discovery of new forms of resource potential in hydrothermal vents, and the marine genetic resources associated with them, is posing new challenges to the division between the seabed/suboil and water column beyond national jurisdiction, it being unclear whether such resources are best understood as a resource of the 'Area' or of the high seas. Their interdependence is such that, in fact, they are a resource of both. See generally Leary, 2006 and the various essays in Vidas, 2010, Pt IV.

[63] *Maritime Delimitation and Territorial Questions Between Qatar and Bahrain (Qatar v Bahrain), Merits, Judgment, ICJ Reports 2001*, p 40, paras 175–6. Cf Separate Opinion of Judge Oda, paras 13–21, who challenged the Court's views of customary law. The Court reaffirmed its view in *Territorial and Maritime Dispute between Nicaragua and Honduras in the Caribbean Sea (Nicaragua v Honduras), Judgment, ICJ Report 2007*, p 659, paras 268 and 281.

between overlapping territorial seas, although there have been examples of such exceptions in recent practice.[64]

Article 6 of the 1958 CSC adopted the same approach to the delimitation of overlapping continental shelves but its application in this context has had a more chequered history (see generally Evans, 1989; Weil, 1989; Antunes, 2003; Tanaka, 2006). In the *North Sea* cases Denmark and the Netherlands argued that Article 6 represented customary law and so bound Germany, a non-State party. Applying this rule mechanically to the concave German coastline sandwiched between Denmark and Norway restricted Germany to a modest triangle of continental shelf, to the substantial benefit of its neighbours. Rather than ameliorate this outcome by arguing that the concave nature of the coast was a 'special circumstance' justifying another line, the ICJ decided that Article 6 did not reflect customary law, and that customary law required continental shelf delimitation to be conducted on the basis of equitable principles and taking account of relevant circumstances.[65]

This ushered in a period in which supporters of the more formulaic 'equidistance/special circumstances' approach vied with supporters of the relatively more flexible 'equitable principles/relevant circumstances' approach—though it is doubtful whether there was ever much to choose between them.[66] At UNCLOS III groups of States championed the approach they considered best suited their interests and, as no consensus could be found, an anodyne formula, applicable to both continental shelf and EEZ delimitation, was adopted in the dying days of the conference. Thus LOSC Articles 74(1) and 83(1) both provide that such delimitations are to be 'effected by agreement on the basis of international law, as referred to in Article 38 of the Statute of the International Court of Justice, in order to achieve an equitable solution'. This avoids mentioning equidistance, equitable principles, special or relevant circumstances—and is virtually devoid of substantive content.

Around this time the ICJ delivered a trilogy of judgments, all of which emphasized the role of equity at the expense of equidistance, though in varying degrees.[67] Perhaps these cases were too close in time to UNCLOS III to shake off the ideological hostility to equidistance. By 1993, however, the Court was prepared to declare in the *Jan Mayen* case that, 'Prima facie, a median line delimitation between opposite coasts results in general in an equitable solution'[68] (Evans, 1999) and in 2002 confirmed, in the *Cameroon v Nigeria*

---

[64] In the *Territorial and Maritime Boundary Dispute between Nicaragua and Honduras in the Caribbean* the ICJ, whilst emphasizing that equidistance remained the general rule, took the view that both the configuration and unstable nature of the relevant coastal area made it impossible to identify basepoints and construct a provisional equidistance line at all. This amounted to a 'special circumstance' justifying the use of an alternative method, the use of a line which bisected two lines drawn along the coastal fronts of the two States. See *Territorial and Maritime Dispute between Nicaragua and Honduras in the Caribbean Sea* (*Nicaragua v Honduras*), *Judgment, ICJ Report 2007*, p 659, paras 268–81. Also in that year the Annex VII Arbitration Award in the case concerning *Guyana/Suriname*, 17 September 2007, paras 323–5 concluded that historical and navigational issues were considered to amount to special circumstances justifying a departure from the use of the equidistance line for the territorial sea.

[65] *North Sea Continental Shelf, Judgment, ICJ Reports 1969*, p 3, para 101(c)(1).

[66] Thus the 1977 *Anglo-French Arbitration*, Cmnd 7438, 18 ILM 397, generally considered to lean towards the equitable principles school of thought, proceeded on the basis that although CSC Article 6 and custom were different the practical result of their application would be the same.

[67] *Continental Shelf (Tunisia/Libyan Arab Jamahiriya), Judgment, ICJ Reports 1982*, p 18; *Delimitation of the Maritime Boundary in the Gulf of Maine Area, Judgment, ICJ Reports 1984*, p 246; *Continental Shelf (Libyan Arab Jamahiriya/Malta), Judgment, ICJ Reports 1985*, p 13.

[68] *Maritime Delimitation in the Area between Greenland and Jan Mayen, Judgment, ICJ Reports 1993*, p 316, para 64, a position affirmed in the *Eritrea-Yemen Arbitration, Second Phase, Award of 17 December 1999*, para 131.

case,[69] that equidistance would provide the starting point in cases in adjacency too. Thus after 35 years of hesitation, the ICJ finally accepted what it had rejected in the *North Sea* cases, that the equidistance/special circumstances approach reflects customary international law (Evans, 2006). It has subsequently confirmed that this is the case both for the delimitation of the territorial sea[70] and for the delimitation of the continental shelf, EEZ, or when drawing a single delimitation line.[71]

In the *Black Sea* case in 2009 the Court seemed to have gone even further when it set out a three-stage approach: (a) the drawing of a provisional line, which 'will be' an equidistance line, 'unless there are compelling reasons that make this unfeasible in the particular case';[72] (b) it will then 'consider whether there are factors calling for the adjustment or shifting of the provisional equidistance line in order to achieve an equitable result';[73] finally, (c) it will 'verify that the line (a provisional equidistance line which may or may not have been adjusted by taking into account the relevant circumstances) does not, as it stands, lead to an inequitable result by reason of any marked disproportion between the ratio of the respective coastal lengths and the ratio between the relevant maritime area of each State by reference to the delimitation line'.[74] This three-stage test was subsequently endorsed by the ITLOS in the *Myanmar/Bangladesh* case,[75] its first boundary delimitation case, and by the ICJ in the *Nicaragua v Colombia* case.[76] However, whilst endorsing the approach, both the ITLOS and the ICJ applied it in such a fashion as to cast very serious doubt upon the weight to be given to equidistance in practice; ITLOS once again emphasizing the importance of the equitable solution[77] and setting equidistance aside in favour of a bisector methodology,[78] and the ICJ, whilst purporting to apply it,[79] producing an outcome which bears so little relationship to the 'provisional' equidistance line as to cast doubt on its real place within the delimitation process, other than being a point of departure. In short, it appears that 'equity' rather than 'equidistance' may be re-emerging, yet again, as the dominant approach.

B. FACTORS AFFECTING DELIMITATION

It has always been clear that even if equidistance provides the starting point, this does not mean it will be the finishing line. All formulations of the rule accept that it can be modified to take account of other factors. Although the categories of potentially relevant factors are never closed, the potential relevance of some factors—and the comparative irrelevance

---

[69] *Land and Maritime Boundary between Cameroon and Nigeria (Cameroon v Nigeria: Equatorial Guinea Intervening), Merits, Judgment, ICJ Reports 2002*, p 303, para 288. See also *Barbados/Trinidad and Tobago*, Award of 11 April 2006, paras 242–4 and 306.

[70] *Territorial and Maritime Dispute between Nicaragua and Honduras in the Caribbean Sea (Nicaragua v Honduras)*, Judgment of 8 October 2007, nyr, paras 262–98.

[71] *Guyana/Suriname*, Award of 17 September 2007, paras 376–92; *Maritime Delimitation in the Black Sea (Romania v Ukraine)*, Judgment of 2 February 2009, para 116.

[72] *Maritime Delimitation in the Black Sea (Romania v Ukraine)*, Judgment of 2 February 2009, para 116.

[73] Ibid, para 120.

[74] Ibid, para 122.

[75] *Delimitation of the Maritime Boundary in the Bay of Bengal (Bangladesh/Myanmar), Case No 16, Judgment of 14 March 2012, ITLOS Reports 2012*, nyr, para 240.

[76] *Territorial and Maritime Dispute (Nicaragua v Colombia), Judgment of 19 November 2012*, paras 190–94.

[77] *Delimitation of the Maritime Boundary in the Bay of Bengal (Bangladesh/Myanmar), Case No 16, Judgment of 14 March 2012, ITLOS Reports 2012*, nyr, para 235.

[78] Ibid, para 334.

[79] *Territorial and Maritime Dispute (Nicaragua v Colombia), Judgment of 19 November 2012*, para 199.

of others—is well attested (Crawford, 2012, pp 288–9; Tanaka, 2012, pp 198–214). Close attention is usually paid to ensuring that areas appertaining to each State are not disproportionate to the ratio between the lengths of their 'relevant coasts' adjoining the area, with a substantial difference in coastal length itself being capable of amounting to a relevant factor circumstance (though determining such coastal lengths for such purposes is clearly open to gerrymandering). Likewise, the presence of islands capable of generating claims to a continental shelf or EEZ is a complicating factor[80] and their impact upon an equidistance line can be reduced or discounted in numerous ways (Jayawardene, 1990). On the other hand, geological factors are not considered relevant where the distance between the coasts is less than 400 n. miles[81] and economic factors are generally considered irrelevant by courts and tribunals, although they probably play a significant role in negotiated boundary agreements.

It is difficult to go beyond this with certainty, and it is certainly not possible to predict how the various factors will be taken into account. Courts and tribunals increasingly refrain from indicating how—or why—the factors considered relevant combine with the chosen methodology to produce the final line. Some judgments seem to do little more than 'split the difference' between competing claims (Churchill and Lowe, 1999, p 191). However, in the *Cameroon* v *Nigeria* case the ICJ dismissed the relevance of all the various factors put forward by the parties and used an equidistance line in an unmodified fashion, despite the presence of a number of factors that might have been thought to have some claim to consideration.[82] The subsequent Arbitral Award in the *Guyana/Suriname* case and the judgment of the ICJ in the *Romania* v *Ukraine* case also dismissed the relevance of all factors put forward by the parties.[83] Predictably, perhaps, in the light of their more equity-driven approaches, the recent judgments from ITLOS and the ICJ in the *Myanmar/ Bangladesh* and *Nicaragua* v *Colombia* cases have both taken other factors into account. What does seem clear is that there is need for caution and clear reasoning, particularly when presenting claims which call for a departure from the equidistance line on grounds other than factors flowing from coastal geography (see Tanaka, 2004; Evans, 2006).[84] Overall, it seems that despite the endorsement of the three-stage test, recent decisions have introduced a greater degree of unpredictability into the delimitation process.

A further emerging complexity concerns the delimitation of the 'outer continental shelf', generated on the basis of natural prolongation over the continental margin beyond 200 n. miles, where this may overlap with an 'inner' continental shelf or EEZ of up to 200 n. miles, generated on the basis of distance.[85] In the *Nicaragua* v *Honduras* case the ICJ noted that it 'need not address' the issue of whether a claim to an 'outer' shelf beyond 200 n. miles could affect the entitlement of another State to a full 'inner' continental shelf of 200 n. miles drawn from its baselines. However, in September 2013 Nicaragua submitted an application to the International Court requesting it to delimit the boundary resulting from what it claims to be the overlap between its outer continental shelf and the inner

---

[80] This posed particular problems in the 2012 *Nicaragua* v *Colombia* case, where it was the presence of Colombian islands proximate to the coast of Nicaragua which generated the overlap of maritime zones which the Court was called on to address.

[81] *Continental Shelf (Libyan Arab Jamahiriya/Malta), Judgment, ICJ Reports 1985*, p 13, para 39.

[82] *Land and Maritime Boundary between Cameroon and Nigeria (Cameroon* v *Nigeria: Equatorial Guinea Intervening), Merits, Judgment, ICJ Reports 2002*, p 303, paras 293–306.

[83] *Maritime Delimitation in the Black Sea (Romania* v *Ukraine)*, Judgment of 2 February 2009, paras 185–218.

[84] See also *Barbados/Trinidad and Tobago*, Award of 11 April 2006, paras 233–40. But cf n 48 in this chapter.

[85] See Colson, 2003; Nelson 2009; Magnusson, 2013. For an early consideration of this as a potential problem, see Evans, 1993.

continental shelf of Colombia.[86] Assuming it has jurisdiction to hear the case, the ICJ may, then, finally have to address this fundamental issue.

VII. FISHERIES

A. THE BASIC SCHEME OF REGULATION

Given its significance, it is perhaps surprising that the LOSC does not address fisheries as a discrete topic. However, the manner in which the seas are divided for jurisdictional purposes means that one has to look at how fisheries are regulated in each particular maritime zone. The basic scheme seems simple enough; the coastal State exercises sovereignty over the territorial seas and sovereign right to explore, exploit, conserve, and manage fishing in any EEZ or EFZ that it might claim. In the high seas the freedom of fishing remains and fish stocks are open to all, but the activities of fishing vessels are subject to the jurisdiction and control of their flag State. The problems are, however, enormous. Overfishing has endangered many fish stocks and there is a pressing need to agree upon and implement effective strategies for conservation and management in the increased threat from 'Illegal, Unreported and Unregulated' (IUU) fishing.[87] At the same time, the economic and nutritional needs of communities must be borne in mind. The result is that the piecemeal approach to regulation is under increasing pressure and a more holistic approach, built around the idea of sustainable development may be in the process of emerging (see Edeson, 1999; Orrego-Vicuna, 1999). However, any system that is ultimately dependent upon flag-State enforcement will be vulnerable to abuse.

One particularly noteworthy trend is the establishment of Regional Fisheries Bodies (RFBs) and Regional Fisheries Management Organisations (RFMOs) which provide means through which States may work together in the conservation, management and development of fishing in particular areas or of particular stocks. Multilateral treaty practice is moving beyond merely encouraging States to participate in such regimes and is increasingly requiring them to do so in order to have access to them (Serdy, 2011). However, such obligations only bind States which become a party to such agreements and many major fishing States simply choose not to do so and continue to claim the right to fish these stocks as an aspect of the freedom of the high seas. An alternative response is to extend coastal State jurisdiction still further seawards but this also runs into fierce opposition. Some years ago Canada adopted a slightly different approach, by asserting its right to enforce conservation and management measures adopted by the relevant regional body (NAFO) over non-flag-State vessels fishing beyond its 200 n. mile EEZ. The subsequent arrest in 1995 of the Spanish registered *Estai* on the high seas prompted a serious incident between the EC and Canada[88] and illustrated the difficulty of pursuing the unilateral route. For the moment, then, we can merely chart the trends in this direction whilst outlining the major elements of the regimes applicable beyond the limits of the territorial seas.

---

[86] See the Application of the Republic of Nicaragua Instituting Proceedings against the Republic Of Colombia, 16 September 2013, ICJ Press Release, 2013/21 (17 September 2013).

[87] The responsibilities of States under LOSC in relation to IUU fishing is currently the subject of a request for an Advisory Opinion by ITLOS. See *Request for an Advisory opinion Submitted by the Sub-Regional Fisheries Commission (SRFC), Order of 24th May 2013, ITLOS Reports 2013, nyr.*

[88] See Davies, 1995. Spain subsequently brought a case against Canada before the ICJ which the Court was unable to consider because Canada had previously removed such disputes from the scope of its consent to the Court's jurisdiction. (See de LaFayette, 1999.)

B. MANAGING FISHERIES

1. EEZ

Some 80–90% of all fishing takes place within EEZs. The coastal State does not enjoy a completely unfettered right to exploit the fisheries resources of the EEZ under the LOSC (though this may not be the position in customary law). LOSC Article 61(1) requires the coastal State to 'determine the allowable catch' (known as the TAC) of living resources. A number of factors feed into this determination, including the need to 'ensure through proper conservation and management measures that the maintenance of the living resources…is not endangered by over-exploitation' (Article 61(2)). At the same time, these measures must themselves be designed 'to maintain or restore populations of harvested species at levels which can produce the maximum sustainable yield' (Article 61(3)). This, then, looks to conserving stocks, but Article 62(1) switches to the obligation to 'promote the objective of optimum utilization of the living resources of the EEZ' by requiring the coastal State 'to determine its capacity to harvest' them. Where the harvestable capacity falls short of the TAC, the coastal State is to give other States access to that surplus (Article 62(2)), with particular regard being given to the requirements of developing States in the area (Article 62(3)), as well as the interests of landlocked and geographically disadvantaged States (Articles 69 and 70; Vasciannie, 1990) in determining to whom access will be offered.[89] Despite these provisions, since coastal States have their hands on both levers—determining both the TAC and the harvestable capacity—their control over EEZ fisheries is hardly troubled by these provisions which have more symbolic than substantial significance. If it were otherwise, the attraction of declaring an EEZ rather than an EFZ (in which these provisions would not apply) would be significantly diminished.

The convention also provides special rules for particular categories of species, including anadromous stocks, such as salmon, which spend most of their time at sea but spawn in freshwater rivers (LOSC Article 66), catadromous stocks, such as eels, which spawn at sea but spend most of their lives in fresh water (LOSC Article 67) which again reflect the theme of reconciling the interests of the State of origin with the established interests of others, and for marine mammals (LOSC Article 65). The situation regarding 'straddling stocks' and 'highly migratory species' (LOSC Articles 63 and 64) will be considered later.

Although the coastal State in principle enjoys complete control over fishing within the EEZ, this has not prevented overfishing. Some States refuse to accept the need for conservation of fish stocks in the face of more pressing and immediate economic or political interests, whilst others are simply unable to control the fishing activities of foreign-flagged vessels within their EEZ, both licensed and illegal.

2. High seas

It is often forgotten that the freedom of fishing upon the high seas is not unfettered. The 1958 Convention on Fishing and Conservation of the Living Resources of the High Seas (CFC) had recognized the 'special interest' of the coastal State in fishing activities in areas adjacent to its territorial waters and sought to reflect that through cooperative arrangements with States engaged in high seas fishing in the interests of conservation and management (CFC Article 6). LOSC Article 116(b) now expressly subjects that freedom to the interests that coastal States have in the particular classes of species identified in LOSC

---

[89] Such access can, of course, be subject to licensing and fees and is more generally regulated by LOSC Article 64.

Articles 63–7 as well as the more general obligation to conserve the living resources of the high seas by setting total allowable catches, based on the maximum sustainable yield (LOSC Article 119). It has to be said that, to the extent that this implies unilateral determinations and self-imposed restrictions, this is little short of wishful thinking. How can the practice of a single State significantly affect the overall pattern when its self-restraint may simply make more space for others to over-exploit?

The key lies in coordinated and cooperative activities by all involved in fishing a given stock or region and LOSC Article 118 recognizes this by requiring that States 'whose nationals exploit identical living resources, or different living resources in the same area, shall enter into negotiations with a view to taking the measures necessary for the conservation of the living resources concerned. They shall, as appropriate, co-operate to establish sub-regional or regional fisheries organizations to this end'. This approach is not new, having echoes in the 1958 CFC, and, as mentioned above, a considerable number of RFBs and RFMOs have been established.[90] Some have been relatively successful, notably the Northwest Atlantic Fisheries Organization (NAFO) and the Commission for the Conservation of Antarctic Marine Resources (CCAMLR), though even these have suffered from poor records of enforcement at times. Others have been less successful, such as the 1993 Commission for the Conservation of Southern Bluefin Tuna (CCSBT), where some years ago the failure of the three States parties (Japan, Australia, and New Zealand) to agree a TAC and the introduction of an 'experimental fishing programme' by Japan prompted a case under the LOSC dispute settlement provisions (Churchill, 2000; Boyle, 2001). This gives a flavour of the difficulties which need to be overcome.

It is difficult to resist the conclusion that the problems of over-utilization of the living resources of the high seas will remain until the right to exploit them is made conditional upon participation in a unified international regulatory framework. However, the experience of creating the International Seabed Authority suggests this might also be a route to paralysis and is bound to be fraught with difficulties. Unless there is a further expansion of coastal State jurisdiction—itself no panacea since some coastal States have themselves fished their own resources to near extinction—it is difficult to see what the international community can do except continue to press the case for cooperation and coordination. This it continues to do, as illustrated by the most recent addition to the family of regulatory instruments: in November 2009 the FAO built on the trend of utilizing port State jurisdiction by adopting the Agreement on Port State Measures to Prevent, Deter and Eliminate Illegal, Unreported and Unregulated Fishing (Harrison, 2011, pp 221–4) but this is still not yet in force.[91] It remains to be seen whether moving towards a more enforcement oriented approach is more successful than reliance on restraint, cooperation and self-regulation.

3. Straddling stocks and highly migratory species

Fish do not respect man-made boundaries and many stocks 'straddle' the limits of maritime zones. Where stocks straddle boundaries the LOSC provides that those States concerned in the fisheries should, either directly or through appropriate organizations should they exist, agree upon appropriate measures of conservation and development (LOSC

---

[90] There are currently 44 Regional Fisheries Bodies, 20 of which are RFMOs. The distinguishing feature of an RFMO is that, unlike a RFB, it is able to adopt measures which are binding on its members. For a full list of regional fishing bodies, and links to their websites, see http://www.fao.org. For a helpful overview see Harrison, 2011, pp 227–33.

[91] Twenty five States or regional organizations must express their consent to be bound before the Agreement enters into force. At the time of writing only eight have done so.

Article 63). Other stocks, such as tuna, are highly mobile and travel great distances in the course of their regular life cycle, migrating through both EEZs and high seas making them particularly vulnerable to predatory exploitation as they pass. Once again, the convention's response is to call for cooperation with respect to a list of species contained in Annex I to the convention, with the objective of optimum utilization, and also calls for the establishment of appropriate regional organizations where none exist (LOSC Article 64).

These rather open-textured provisions have since been built upon by the 1995 UN Agreement on Straddling Stocks and Highly Migratory Species (SSC).[92] This, *inter alia*, obliges States parties fishing for such stocks either to become members of those fisheries management organizations that exist for the relevant region or stock, or to agree to apply the measures which such an organization establishes, and States parties to the Agreement which do not do so are debarred from having access to the stock (SSC Articles 8(3) and (4)). In other words, States parties to the Agreement may not fish for such stocks outside of the framework established by any such organization (SSC Article 17). Since most fishing undertaken on the high seas involves either straddling stocks or highly migratory species, this is an extremely significant self-denying ordinance. Moreover, where RFMOs exist, SSC Article 21 permits the authorized inspectors of any State party to board and inspect fishing vessels flying the flag of other State parties in order to ensure compliance with the conservation and management measure that the organization has established and, in cases where there are 'clear grounds' for suspecting that 'serious violations' have occurred, the vessel might be taken to the nearest appropriate port—though it should be noted that in both cases enforcement action against the vessel can only be taken by the flag State or with the flag State's consent.

Once again, it is possible to see in this how the international community is striving to address a complex problem by incremental diminutions in the freedom of the high seas in favour of communal responses, backed by equally incremental incursions into the principle of flag-State jurisdiction. However, this is entirely dependent upon States choosing to fetter themselves in this way and many remain reluctant to do so whilst others remain free to take advantage of their self-restraint.[93]

VIII. CONCLUSION

There are a great many important topics that have not been touched upon in this chapter, including, *inter alia*, marine scientific research, pollution and the marine environment, military uses of the seas, and the dispute settlement provisions of the LOSC. Although a number of these topics are touched on elsewhere in this volume, these omissions remain regrettable. However, by focusing in some detail on some foundational aspects of the division of ocean space and its principles of governance, this chapter introduces the complexities that must be grappled with and the manner in which this has been attempted. The underlying tension remains the same as ever: balancing the competing demands of access to ocean space whilst recognizing the need to preserve order and good governance. The law of the sea has undergone a remarkable transformation in the last 60 years yet more still needs to be done if that balance is to be achieved. Perhaps at the end of the day the

---

[92] See Davies and Redgwell, 1996; Orrego-Vicuna, 1999, chs 5–9; Stokke, 2001 and Harrison, 2011, pp 99–113.

[93] The SSC entered into force in December 2001, having secured 30 ratifications. At the time of writing 81 States and other entities (including the European Community) have become a party to it.

problem is the perception, uttered by the ICJ in the *North Sea* cases in the context of the delimitation of maritime boundaries, that 'the land dominates the sea'.[94] We are coming to realize that, in many ways, it is the sea that dominates the land and, as they are projected seawards, our concepts of sovereignty, rights, and jurisdiction, no matter how subtle or sophisticated their application, seem increasingly cumbersome instruments for addressing the resulting issues. But for the moment, they remain the best we have.

REFERENCES

AHNISH, FA (1993), *The International Law of Maritime Boundaries and the Practice of States in the Mediterranean Sea* (Oxford: Clarendon Press).

ANAND, RM (1983), *Origin and Development of the Law of the Sea* (The Hague: Martinus Nijhoff).

ANDERSON, DH (1993), 'Efforts to Ensure Universal Participation in the UN Convention on the Law of the Sea', 42 *ICLQ* 654.

—— (1995), 'Legal Implication of the Entry into Force of the UN Convention on the Law of the Sea', 44 *ICLQ* 313.

—— (2006), 'Freedoms of the High Seas in the Modern Law of the Sea', in Freestone, D, Barnes, R, and Ong, D (eds), *The Law of the Sea: Progress and Prospects* (Oxford: Oxford University Press), p 327.

ANTUNES, NM (2003), *Towards the Conceptualisation of Maritime Delimitation* (The Hague: Martinus Nijhoff).

ATTARD, D (1986), *The Exclusive Economic Zone* (Oxford: Clarendon Press).

BOYLE, A (2001), 'The Southern Bluefin Tuna Arbitration', 50 *ICLQ* 447.

—— (2005), 'Further Development of the Law of the Sea Convention: Mechanisms for Change', 54 *ICLQ* 563.

BYERS, M (2004), 'Policing the High Seas: the Proliferation Security Initiative', 98 *AJIL* 526.

CHARNEY, J (2000), 'Rocks that Cannot Sustain Human Habitation', 96 *AJIL* 863.

CHURCHILL, RR (2000), 'The Southern Bluefin Tuna Cases', 49 *ICLQ* 979.

—— and LOWE, AV (1999), *The Law of the Sea*, 3rd edn (Manchester: Manchester University Press).

COLSON, D (2003), 'The Delimitation of the Outer Continental Shelf between Neighbouring States', 97 *AJIL* 91.

COOK, PJ and CARLTON, C (2000), *Continental Shelf Limits* (Oxford: Oxford University Press).

CRAWFORD, J (2012), *Brownlie's Principles of Public International Law*, 8th edn (Oxford: Oxford University Press).

DAVIES, PGG (1995), 'The EC/Canadian Fisheries Dispute in the Northwest Atlantic', 44 *ICLQ* 933.

—— and REDGWELL, C (1996), 'The International Legal Regulation of Straddling Fish Stocks', 67 *BYIL* 199.

DE LAFAYETTE, L (1999), 'The Fisheries Jurisdiction Case (*Spain v Canada*)', 48 *ICLQ* 664.

DE YTURRIAGA, JA (1991), *Straights Used for International Navigation* (Dordrecht: Martinus Nijhoff).

EDESON, W (1999), 'Towards Long-term Sustainable Use: Some Recent Developments in the Legal Regime of Fisheries', in Boyle, A and Freestone, D (eds), *International Law and Sustainable Development* (Oxford: Oxford University Press), p 165.

EVANS, MD (1989), *Relevant Circumstances and Maritime Delimitation* (Oxford: Clarendon Press).

---

[94] *North Sea Continental Shelf, Judgment, ICJ Reports 1969, p 3*, para 96.

—— (1993), 'Delimitation and the Common Maritime Boundary', 64 *BYIL* 283.

—— (1999), 'Maritime Delimitation after *Denmark v Norway*. Back to the Future?', in Goodwin-Gill, GS and Talmon, S (eds), *The Reality of International Law* (Oxford: Clarendon Press), p 153.

—— (2006), 'Maritime Boundary Delimitation: Where Do We Go From Here?', in Freestone, D, Barnes, R, and Ong, D (eds), *The Law of the Sea: Progress and Prospects* (Oxford: Oxford University Press), p 137.

—— and OKOWA, PN (2013), 'Approaches to Responsibility in International Courts', in Evans, M and Koutrakos, P, *The International Responsibility of the European Union: European and International Perspectives* (Oxford: Hart Publishing), p 101.

GEISS, R and PETRIG, A (2011), *Piracy and Armed Robbery at Sea* (Oxford: Oxford University Press).

GILMORE, W (1995), 'Hot Pursuit: The Case of *R v Mills* and Others', 44 *ICLQ* 949.

—— (2000), 'Drugs Trafficking at Sea: The Case of *R v Charrington* and Others', 49 *ICLQ* 477.

—— (2005), *Agreement Concerning Co-Operation in Suppressing Illicit Maritime and Air Trafficking in Narcotic Drugs and Psychotropic Substances in the Caribbean Area, 2003* (London: TSO).

GUILFOYLE, D (2008), 'Piracy off Somalia: UN Security Council Resolution 1816 and IMO Regional Counter-Piracy Efforts', 57 *ICLQ* 690.

—— (2009), *Shipping Interdiction and the Law of the Sea* (Cambridge: Cambridge University Press).

—— (ed) (2013), *Modern Piracy: Legal Challenges and Responses* (Cheltenham: Edward Elgar).

HARRISON, J (2011), *Making the Law of the Sea* (Cambridge: Cambridge University Press).

HUTCHINSON, D (1985), 'The Seawards Limit to Continental Shelf Jurisdiction in Customary International Law', 56 *BYIL* 133.

JAYAWARDENE, H (1990), *The Regime of Islands in International Law* (Dordrecht: Martinus Nijhoff).

JIA, BB (1998), *The Regime of Straits in International Law* (Oxford: Clarendon Press).

KLEIN, N (2011), *Maritime Security and the Law of the Sea* (Oxford: Oxford University Press).

KOPELA, S (2013), *Dependent Archipelagos in International Law* (Leiden: Martinus Nijhoff Publishers).

LAVALLLE, R (2004), 'Not Quite a Sure Thing: The Maritime Areas of Rocks and Low Tide Elevations under the UN Convention on the Law of the Sea', 19 *IJMCL* 43.

LEARY, D (2006), *International Law and the Genetic Resources of the Deep Sea* (Leiden: Martinus Nijhoff).

LLEWELLYN, H (2007), 'The Commission on the Limits of the Continental Shelf: Joint Submission by France, Ireland, Spain and the United Kingdom', 56 *ICLQ* 677.

MAGNUSSON, BM (2013), 'Outer Continental Shelf Boundary Agreements', 62 *ICLQ* 345.

MARSTON, G (2002), 'Redrawing the Territorial Sea Boundary in the Firth of Clyde', 51 *ICLQ* 279.

MARTEN, D (2013), *Port State Jurisdiction and the Regulation of International Merchant Shipping* (Heidelburg: Springer).

MOLENAAR, EJ (2004), 'Multilateral Hot Pursuit and Illegal Fishing in the Southern Ocean: The Pursuits of the *Viarsa 1* and *South Tomi*', 19 *IJMCL* 19.

—— (2006), 'Port State Jurisdiction: towards Mandatory and Comprehensive Use', in Freestone, D, Barnes, R, and Ong, D (eds), *The Law of the Sea: Progress and Prospects* (Oxford: Oxford University Press), p 137.

NANDAN, SM (2006), 'Administering the Mineral Resources of the Deep Sea Bed', in Freestone, D, Barnes, R, and Ong, D (eds),

The Law of the Sea: Progress and Prospects (Oxford: Oxford University Press), p 75.

—— and ANDERSON, DH (1989), 'Straits Used for International Navigation', 90 *BYIL* 159.

NELSON, D (2009), 'The Settlement of Disputes Arising from Conflicting Outer Continental Shelf Claims, 24 *IJMCL* 409.

O'CONNELL, DP (1982), *The International Law of the Sea*, vol I (Oxford: Clarendon Press).

ORREGO-VICUNA, F (1989), *The Exclusive Economic Zone* (Cambridge: Cambridge University Press).

—— (1999), *The Changing Law of High Seas Fisheries* (Cambridge: Cambridge University Press).

ÖZÇAYIR, ZO (2001), *Port State Control* (London: LLP Professional Publishing).

PAPASTAVRIDIS, E (2013), *Interception of Vessels on the High Seas* (Oxford: Hart).

POSNER, E and SYKES, A (2010), 'The Economic Foundations of the Law of the Sea', 104 *AJIL* 569.

PRESCOTT, V and SCHOFIELD, C (2005), *The Maritime Political Boundaries of the World*, 2nd edn (Leiden: Martinus Nijhoff).

REISMAN, WM and WESTERMAN, GS (1992), *Straight Baselines in International Maritime Boundary Delimitation* (London: Macmillan).

ROTHWELL, DR and STEVENS, T (2010), *The International Law of the Sea* (Oxford: Hart Publishing).

SCHACHTE, WL (1993), 'International Straits and Navigational Freedoms', 24 *ODIL* 179.

SCHMIDT, M (1989), *Common Heritage or Common Burden?* (Oxford: Clarendon Press).

SERDY, A (2011), 'Postmodern International Fisheries Law, or We Are All Coastal States Now', 60 *ICLQ* 387.

STOKKE, OV (ed) (2001), *Governing High Seas Fisheries* (Oxford: Oxford University Press).

SUBEDI, S (2011), 'Problems and Prospects of the CLCS in Dealing with Submissions by Coastal States in Relation to Ocean Territory beyond 200 N Miles', 26 *IJMCL* 413.

TANAKA, Y (2004), 'Reflections on the Maritime Delimitation in the Cameroon/Nigeria Case', 53 *ICLQ* 369.

—— (2006), *Predictability and Flexibility in the Law of Maritime Delimitation* (Oxford: Hart Publishing).

—— (2012), *The International Law of the Sea* (Cambridge: Cambridge University Press).

TREVES, T (2013), 'Piracy and the International Law of the Sea', in Guilfoyle, D (ed), *Modern Piracy: Legal Challenges and Responses* (Cheltenham: Edward Elgar), p 117.

VASCIANNIE, SC (1990), *Land-Locked and Geographically Disadvantaged States in the Law of the Sea* (Oxford: Clarendon Press).

VIDAS, D (ed) (2010), *Law, Technology and Science for Oceans in Globalisation* (Leiden: Martinus Nijhoff).

WEIL, P (1989), *The Law of Maritime Delimitation—Reflections* (Cambridge: Grotius).

WESTERMAN, G (1987), *The Juridical Bay* (Oxford: Clarendon Press).

FURTHER READING

CHARNEY, JI and ALEXANDER, LM (eds), *Maritime Boundary Agreements*, vol I (1993), vol II (1993), vol III (1998); Charney JJ and Smith RW (eds), vol IV (2002); Colson, D (ed), vol V (2005); Colson, D and Smith, RW (eds), vol VI (2011) (The Hague: Martinus Nijhoff).

A compendium of State practice, with commentaries and an excellent series of essays relating to boundary delimitation.

CHURCHILL, RR and LOWE, AV (1999), *The Law of the Sea*, 3rd edn (Manchester: Manchester University

Press). This remains the essential *vade mecum* to the subject.

FREESTONE, D, BARNES, R, and ONG, D (2006), *The Law of the Sea: Progress and Prospects* (Oxford: Oxford University Press). An important collection of essays exploring practical and conceptual issues in considerable detail.

HARRISON, J (2011), *Making the Law of the Sea* (Cambridge: Cambridge University Press). A very helpful survey of the development of the law of the sea, focusing on the period following the conclusion of the 1982 Law of the Sea Convention.

KLEIN, N (2011), *Maritime Security and the Law of the Sea* (Oxford: Oxford University Press). An important survey of the Law of the Sea, considered from the perspective of maritime security.

NORDQUIST, MN et al, *United Nations Convention on the Law of the Sea 1982: A Commentary*, vol I (1985), vol II (1993), vol III (1995), vol IV (1990), vol V (1989), vol VI (2002), Vol VII (2011) (The Hague: Martinus Nijhoff). This is an excellent source of reference, tracing and commenting upon the evolution of each Article of 1982 Law of the Sea Convention.

O'CONNELL, DP, *The International Law of the Sea*, vol I (1982), vol II (1984) (Oxford: Clarendon Press). Although now considerably out of date, this remains a classic and magisterial point of reference.

PRESCOTT, V and SCHOFIELD, C (2005), *The Maritime Political Boundaries of the World*, 2nd edn (Leiden: Martinus Nijhoff). An excellent overview of the construction of maritime boundaries.

23

INTERNATIONAL ENVIRONMENTAL LAW

Catherine Redgwell

SUMMARY

The development of international environmental law is typically divided into three periods. The first demonstrates little genuine environmental awareness but rather views environmental benefits as incidental to largely economic concerns such as the exploitation of living natural resources. The second phase demonstrates a significant rise in the number of treaties directed to pollution abatement and to species and habitat conservation. Here an overt environmental focus is evident, yet the approach is still largely reactive and piecemeal. The final phase, which characterizes current international environmental law, demonstrates a precautionary approach to environmental problems of global magnitude such as biodiversity conservation and climate change. Concern transcends individual States, with certain global problems now considered the common concern of humankind. This chapter first defines international environmental law, its key sources and actors, and the difficulties of enforcement, before embarking on a sectoral examination of the extensive treaty law applicable in this field.

I. INTRODUCTION: WHAT IS INTERNATIONAL ENVIRONMENTAL LAW?[1]

This chapter addresses one of the more recent areas of development in international law, international environmental law. It is an area of public international law marked by the application of principles which have evolved in the environmental context, such as the precautionary and no harm principles, yet also forms part of, and draws from, the general corpus of public international law elaborated elsewhere in this text such as the sources of public international law principles of the exercise of State jurisdiction, and State responsibility. This is well illustrated by cases involving environmental issues which also involve issues of general international law, such as the extensive discussion of the law of treaties, State responsibility, and international watercourses in the *Gabčíkovo-Nagymaros* case before the ICJ.[2] International environmental law should thus be viewed as part and parcel of general public international law and not an entirely separate, self-contained discipline (Birnie, Boyle, and Redgwell, 2009; Crawford, 2012, p 353). In this sense it is analogous

---

[1] For discussion of *why* the environment is protected, see Gillespie, 1997.
[2] *Gabčíkovo-Nagymaros project (Hungary/Slovakia), Judgment, ICJ Reports 1997*, p 7.

to, say, international human rights law, the law of the sea, or international economic law, all applications of international law addressed in this volume. Institutionally it is less well-developed than these fields: there is no 'global environmental organization' with competence over environmental matter analogous to, say, the World Trade Organization (WTO), or a dispute settlement body analogous to the WTO's Dispute Settlement Body or the Law of the Sea Convention's International Tribunal for the Law of the Sea.

Moreover, notwithstanding significant growth in the body of general and particularized rules governing State conduct in respect of the environment, it remains the case that there is not yet any general customary or treaty law obligation on States to protect and preserve the environment *per se*. To be sure there is a relevant negative obligation found in customary international law—the no harm principle, or the obligation imposed on States not to allow their territory to be used in a such a manner so as to cause significant harm to the territory of other States, or to the global commons, which may be traced back to the seminal *Trail Smelter Arbitration*.[3] Positive obligations, however, remain largely sectoral in focus, the most outstanding examples being the obligation in Article 192 of the 1982 Law of the Sea Convention to protect and preserve the marine environment and the obligation in Article 2 of the 1991 Protocol on Environmental Protection to the 1959 Antarctic Treaty comprehensively to protect the Antarctic environment and dependent and related ecosystems. But as for a general obligation to protect and preserve the environment wherever situated, one looks in vain. This is partly explained by the piecemeal development of the subject, elaborated in the next section. Early international regulation of environmental activities dealt with conservation of common property resources subject to over-exploitation and customary international law first developed to restrain State actions causing transboundary harm—primarily economic harm—in the territory of another State. International environmental regulation of State behaviour penetrating *within* the State has been less rapid to develop, particularly since it encounters the twin yet related obstacles of State sovereignty and permanent sovereignty over natural resources. Nonetheless it is possible to detect the impact of international environmental law on the evolution of the principle of permanent sovereignty over natural resources, most notably in the concept of sustainable development, importing duties as well as rights in respect of natural resource management (Schrijver, 1997). Undoubtedly one of the challenges facing international environmental law in the twenty-first century is achieving a holistic and integrated approach to environmental regulation which applies within as well as between and beyond States. The 1992 Convention on Biological Diversity is one example of a treaty instrument moving in this direction.

II. DEFINING 'THE ENVIRONMENT'

'The environment' is an amorphous term that has thus far proved incapable of precise legal definition save in particular contexts. Even the Law of the Sea Convention, which comprehensively defines pollution of the marine environment, does not define the marine environment as such. A rare exception is Article 2(10) of the 1993 Council of Europe Convention on Civil Liability for Damage Resulting from Activities Dangerous for the

---

[3] (1939) 33 *AJIL* 182 and (1941) 35 *AJIL* 684; see also Principle 21 of the 1972 Declaration of the UN Conference on the Human Environment (Stockholm) and Principle 2 of the 1992 Declaration of the UN Conference on Environment and Development (Rio) reproduced in Birnie and Boyle, 1995, at pp 1 and 9 respectively.

Environment. It defines the environment to include 'natural resources both abiotic and biotic, such as the air, water, soil, fauna, and flora and the interaction between the same factors; property which forms part of the cultural heritage; and the characteristic aspects of the landscape'. This broad definition encompasses natural and cultural heritage protection (regulated by the 1972 UNESCO Convention for the Protection of the World Cultural and Natural Heritage for example); species and habitat protection (see, for example, the 1992 UN Convention on Biological Diversity); and pollution prevention (regulated, *inter alia*, by the 1972 London (Dumping) Convention and the 1979 UN ECE Convention on Long-Range Transboundary Air Pollution (LRTAP)). As will be seen shortly, this in fact encapsulates the development of international law, especially treaty law, in the field of the environment: from sectoral pollution and conservation treaties to ecosystem and holistic environmental protection, with increasing attention to issues of liability, compensation, and compliance. It demonstrates 'the broad range of issues now addressed by international environmental law, including conservation and sustainable use of natural resources and biodiversity; conservation of endangered and migratory species; prevention of deforestation and desertification; preservation of Antarctica and areas of outstanding natural heritage; protection of oceans, international watercourses, the atmosphere, climate and ozone layer from the effects of pollution; safeguarding human health and the quality of life' (Birnie, Boyle, and Redgwell, 2009).

III. THE DEVELOPMENT OF INTERNATIONAL ENVIRONMENTAL LAW

Although the origins of international environmental regulation may be traced to the nineteenth century, the modern development of the subject dates from the post-Second World War era. Indeed, the development of international environmental law shares much in common with the development of domestic environmental law which arose concomitantly with concerns about environmental degradation highlighted especially in the 1960s. A turning point was undoubtedly the UN-sponsored 1972 Stockholm Conference on the Human Environment which produced a non-binding Declaration of Principles and a Programme for Action. Subsequently not only did national departments of environmental protection proliferate, but the UN established a specialized subsidiary body of the UN General Assembly—the UN Environment Programme (UNEP), headquartered in Nairobi. Today UNEP remains the only international body exclusively concerned with environmental matters, although many other specialized bodies within the UN family concern themselves with environmental matters as part of their broader remit, such as the fisheries conservation efforts of the Food and Agriculture Organization (FAO) in Rome and the marine environmental protection activities of the International Maritime Organization (IMO) in London.

The UN General Assembly has also played a significant role in shaping international environmental law and policy notwithstanding the absence of any mention of the environment in the UN Charter. Undoubtedly dynamic interpretation of the Charter—especially of Articles 1 and 55—and the implied powers approach adopted by the ICJ in the *Reparations* case[4] would support reading environmental matters into the competence of

---

[4] *Reparations for Injuries Suffered in the Service of the United Nations, Advisory Opinion, ICJ Reports 1949*, p 174.

the UN. The establishment of UNEP following the Stockholm Conference in 1972, and of the UN Commission on Sustainable Development[5] following the 1992 Rio Conference on Environment and Development, is ample testament to the suppleness of the Charter treaty text. Today a number of significant global treaties has resulted from UN auspices, including the 1992 Conventions on Climate Change and Biological Diversity and their subsequent protocols. The UN has also played a significant role in regional developments through, for example, the regional seas programme of UNEP and the UN's economic commissions. The UN Economic Commission for Europe (ECE) has been particularly active in the environmental field and is responsible for two significant procedural treaties addressing environmental impact assessment (the 1991 Espoo Convention on Environmental Assessment in a Transboundary Context) and access to environmental information, public participation, and access to justice (the 1998 Aarhus Convention on Access to Information, Public Participation in Environmental Decision-Making, and Access to Justice in Environmental Matters) as well as for sectoral pollution regulation (the 1979 Convention on Long-Range Transboundary Air Pollution and the 1992 Conventions on the Transboundary Effects of Industrial Accidents, and on the Protection and Use of Transboundary Watercourses and International Lakes).

It is common to divide the development of international environmental law into three (Francioni, 1994) or four (Sands and Peel, 2012; Fitzmaurice, 2001) stages. The first pre-dates the 1972 Stockholm Conference and is characterized by piecemeal and reactive responses to particular problems of resource use and exploitation (eg the 1946 International Convention for the Regulation of Whaling), including shared resources (eg the 1909 Treaty Between the USA and Great Britain Respecting Boundary Waters Between the USA and Canada), and pollution (eg the 1954 International Convention for the Prevention of Pollution of the Sea by Oil). Some writers sub-divide this first stage into two, commencing the second stage with the creation of international institutions from 1945 and seeing its culmination in the 1972 Stockholm Conference on the Human Environment inaugurating on this analysis the third phase of development. It produced a Declaration[6] and an Action Programme, a template followed by the 1992 Rio Conference on Environment and Development 20 years later. In addition, the run-up to and conclusion of the Stockholm Conference stimulated a great deal of regional and global treaty-making activity, much of it directed towards protection of the marine environment. The 1972 London (Dumping) Convention dates from this period, as does the regional seas programme of UNEP which from 1976 onwards has led to the conclusion of a number of regional seas agreements including environmental protection provisions. The terrestrial environment was also the focus of attention, with the conclusion of major treaties regarding the natural and cultural heritage (the 1972 UNESCO Convention Concerning the Protection of the World Cultural and Natural Heritage), species and habitat protection (eg the 1971 Ramsar Convention on Wetlands of International Importance Especially as Waterfowl Habitat, the 1973 Convention on International Trade in Endangered Species and, in direct response to a recommendation at Stockholm, the 1979 Bonn Convention on the Conservation of Migratory Species of Wild Animals). With one or two exceptions such as the 1980 Convention on the Conservation of Antarctic Marine Living Resources with its novel ecosystem approach, this period of international legislative activity is characterized by a sectoral and fragmented approach to achieving environmental protection.

---

[5] See UN GA Res 47/191 (1992) in Birnie and Boyle, 1995, p 658. See further http://sustainabledevelopment.un.org/csd.html.

[6] For seminal analysis of the Stockholm Declaration on the Human Environment, see Sohn, 1973.

The third (or fourth) period witnesses instruments adopting a holistic approach to environmental protection and seeks to marry such protection with economic development, embraced in the concept of sustainable development. This was the theme of the 1992 Rio Conference on Environment and Development which, in addition to producing a Declaration of Principles and a programme of action for the twenty-first century (Agenda 21) saw the conclusion of two major treaties under UN auspices—the 1992 Framework Convention on Climate Change and the 1992 Convention on the Conservation of Biological Diversity. It was hoped also to adopt binding texts relating to forests and to deserts, but in the event only a soft law text on forests was also adopted (the 'Non-Binding Authoritative Statement of Principles for a Global Consensus on the Management, Conservation and Sustainable Development of all Types of Forest'). In 1994 the Convention to Combat Desertification was adopted, as was the International Tropical Timber Agreement (ITTA), (replacing a 1983 agreement and itself superseded by a new agreement in 2006). While paying greater attention to sustainable development than its predecessors, the 2006 ITTA is largely concerned with facilitating sustainable timber trade and not with forest biodiversity *per se*, which thus falls under the remit of the Biodiversity Convention. Both forests and deserts have proved resistant to international regulation largely owing to concerns about the infringement of State sovereignty. Nonetheless the general outcome of the Rio Conference, and the conclusion of the Biodiversity and Climate Change Conventions in particular, marked a new phase in international environmental regulation with the acknowledgement in each that the conservation of biological diversity or preventing further adverse changes in the earth's climate are the common concern of humankind. Proposals further to develop the institutional framework of international environmental law to reflect these common and intergenerational concerns have not yet made any significant headway. Suggestions for revamping the UN Trusteeship Council to address matters to do with the global commons have become linked with broader and more vexed questions of UN institutional reform. The 10-year follow-up to the Rio Conference, the 2002 Johannesburg World Summit on Sustainable Development, achieved neither environmental institutional reform nor resulted in significant multilateral law-making, though making a significant contribution, *inter alia*, to developments within the Southern African region.[7] The 2012 UN Conference on Sustainable Development, dubbed 'Rio+20', provided an opportunity to assess the limited progress towards achieving sustainable development since 1992,[8] and produced a political outcome document entitled 'The Future We Want'.[9] Amongst other things, the Commission on Sustainable Development, viewed as largely ineffectual, was replaced in 2013 by a High-level Political Forum (HLPF) on Sustainable Development, with a renewed emphasis on the science and policy interface. While major institutional reform as part of this process is highly unlikely, the first report of the HLPF calls for a 'UN institutional platform for sustainable development models and scenarios' as support for the production of the Global Sustainable Development Report called for in the Rio+20 outcome document.[10]

[7] See the Johannesburg Declaration on Sustainable Development and Plan of Implementation, http://www.johannesburgsummit.org.
[8] See the Report of the UN Secretary-General, *Lessons Learned from the Commission on Sustainable Development*, UN Doc A/67/757, 26 February 2013, available at http://sustainabledevelopment.un.org/csd.html.
[9] 'The Future We Want', UN Doc A/RES/66/288 available at http://sustainabledevelopment.un.org/futurewewant.html.
[10] Ibid, para 85k. See the Global Sustainable Development Report—Executive Summary: Building the Common Future We Want (New York: United Nations Department of Economic and Social Affairs, Division for Sustainable Development, 2013) available at http://sustainabledevelopment.un.org/globalsdreport.

The past decades have witnessed an evolution in law-making focus from environmental regulation incidental to the primary focus, such as economic regulation of a resource, to an holistic approach to environmental protection within and beyond State borders. These stages are not necessarily sequential, however, with evidence in the present of international rules reflecting each of these stages of evolution. This is particularly evident in the tension between permanent sovereignty over natural resources and the common concern of humankind contained in the Biodiversity Convention, and in the continuing resistance to robust international regulation of forest and desertification issues because of the perceived threat to State sovereignty. Moreover what is absent from the corpus of international rules thus developed is a comprehensive codification of the basic rules and principles applicable to international regulation of the environment analogous to the 1948 Universal Declaration of Human Rights or the 1982 Law of the Sea Convention.[11] The Stockholm and Rio Declarations were political attempts to articulate such principles, though only some of the principles contained in them are of a sufficiently norm-creating character, and enjoy the widespread and consistent State practice and buttressing *opinio juris*, for recognition as customary international law. Given the wide range of environmental issues confronting humankind, many of which require a detailed, standard-setting regulatory response, it is not surprising that the vast bulk of international environmental law is found in tailor-made treaty arrangements. Nonetheless, as discussed in Section V of this chapter certain key customary law principles have also emerged. The parallels with human rights and law of the sea are again apparent.

IV. KEY ENVIRONMENTAL ACTORS

While States remain the central actors in environmental law-making and enforcement activities, they are not the exclusive actors. The 1992 and 2012 Rio and 2002 Johannesburg summits evidence a further feature of international environmental law, which is the increased participation of non-State actors, in particular non-governmental organizations (NGOs). Witness the range of actors identified in Section 3 of the Earth's Action Plan (Agenda 21) agreed at Rio in 1992: women, youth, indigenous peoples, NGOs, local authorities, workers and trade unions, business and industry, the scientific and technological community, and farmers. Of course this is not a unique feature of the environmental field, though particularly marked within it (and in the human rights area, as Ch 26 of this book attests). The role of NGOs in particular has been significant both in shaping the treaty-negotiating process and also in stimulating subsequent developments within treaty regimes.[12] Perhaps the outstanding example is the influence of the International Council for Bird Preservation (ICBP) and the International Waterfowl and Wetlands Research Bureau (IWRB) in the conclusion and implementation of the 1971 Ramsar Convention, for which the International Union for the Conservation of Nature (IUCN), a unique union of governmental and non-governmental actors, acts as the secretariat.

NGO influence is achieved primarily through the mechanism of participation, viz as observers in international organizations, at treaty negotiations, and within treaty institutions. This may be expressly provided for in the treaty text, or in the rules of procedure or through practice. For example, the meetings of the conference of the parties to the 1992 Climate Change Convention and its subsidiary bodies provide for the participation of

---

[11] One such attempt is the *International Union for the Conservation of Nature's Draft International Covenant on Environment and Development*, 2nd edn (IUCN, 2000).

[12] See further Chinkin and Boyle, 2007.

NGO representatives to observe with limited scope for active participation (Yamin and Depledge, 2004). These reflect the diverse constituencies of the convention including business and industry NGOs (principally the major natural resource companies), environmental and local government NGOs and indigenous peoples organizations. These developments may be viewed as a wider trend towards viewing international society in terms broader than a community of States alone.[13] This is recognized in recent environmental treaties such as the Climate Change and Biodiversity Conventions, where we have seen that the global climate and biological diversity respectively are expressly recognized as the common concern of humankind. However, as yet there is limited participation of non-State actors as treaty parties. A notable exception is the European Community[14] which possesses international legal personality coupled with the requisite internal constitutional competence to participate in international treaties alongside the member States. Thus, for example, the EC is a party to the 1992 Climate Change Convention and the 1997 Kyoto Protocol which expressly provide for the participation of regional economic integration organizations.[15] Yet it is not a party to the 1973 Convention on International Trade in Endangered Species, because the treaty text does not presently make provision for non-State participation. Thus only the member States may become parties in their individual capacities. This has not prevented the EC from regulating trade in endangered species within the European area, but it does so in the exercise of internal legal competence over the matter and not in furtherance of an expressly undertaken international obligation.

In addition to participation in international environmental law-making, non-State actors may play a significant role in enforcement, whether through transnational litigation before national courts, in treaty compliance procedures (where permitted, as under the Aarhus Convention procedure) or in the indirect enforcement of environmental norms through human rights litigation. Civil liability regimes are concerned with the liability of non-State actors—shipowners under oil pollution liability; nuclear operators under the nuclear liability regimes, for example. Increasing attention is also being paid to corporate environmental accountability; however, corporations are not directly bound by environmental treaties or customary international law, and national courts have not been highly receptive to international environmental law arguments, especially in horizontal litigation.[16] Corporations may nonetheless voluntarily adhere to environmental standards (eg ISO 14000 series environmental standards) as a form of corporate self-regulation;[17] corporate social responsibility discussions also evidence an environmental dimension, illustrated by three of the ten principles of the non-binding UN Global Compact[18] and Part VI of the OECD Guidelines for Multinational Enterprises.[19]

---

[13] See, eg the Commission on Global Governance, 1995.

[14] The Treaty of Lisbon, which entered into force on 1 December 2009, now provides for the international legal personality of the EU.

[15] The European Court of Justice has held an environmental treaty to which the EC is a party to be directly effective in the member States 'so that any interested party is entitled to rely on those provisions before national courts': see *Syndicat professionnel coordination des pêcheurs de l'étang de Berre and de la région v Électricité de France (EDF)*, Case C-213/03, [2004] ECR I-7357, para 47. The provision in question was Article 6(3) of the 1980 Athens Protocol for the Protection of the Mediterranean Sea against Pollution from Land-Based Sources (now Article 6(1) of the amended Protocol, 1996).

[16] See Anderson and Galizzi, 2002.

[17] See Muchlinski, 2007.

[18] Principles 7 (precautionary principle); 8 (environmental responsibility) and 9 (environmentally friendly technologies): see http://www.unglobalcompact.org.

[19] The fifth and more recent update, on 25 March 2011, is available at: http://www.oecd.org/daf/inv/mne/oecdguidelinesformultinationalenterprises.htm.

V. SOURCES OF INTERNATIONAL ENVIRONMENTAL LAW

Since international environmental law is concerned with the application of general international law to environmental problems, it is not surprising that its sources include the traditional ones enumerated in Article 38 of the Statute of the International Court of Justice. However, two points should be highlighted in this context. The first is that treaties are by far and away the most significant source of binding rules of international environmental law. The adoption of consensus and 'package-deal' approaches to treaty negotiation have been particularly beneficial in the environmental context, permitting States to reach agreement on issues such as transboundary air pollution, climate change, and the conservation of biological diversity, even in the face of sharp differences of view about the very existence of the problems and about their solution. Sometimes environmental treaties are preceded by a non-binding instrument—for example, the UNEP Guidelines which preceded the 1989 Basel Convention and the UNEP and FAO Guidelines and Code which preceded the 1998 Rotterdam Convention on the Prior Informed Consent Procedure for Certain Hazardous Chemicals and Pesticides in International Trade. Indeed, the prevalence and importance of such 'soft law' is the other feature of international environmental law meriting closer attention later.[20]

A. TRADITIONAL SOURCES OF INTERNATIONAL ENVIRONMENTAL LAW

The vast bulk of environmental law is contained in treaty texts which are given dynamic force in part because they usually provide an institutional mechanism for their implementation (Churchill and Ulfstein, 2000). A common format is to provide for regular meetings of the Conference of the Parties (COP),[21] a number of subsidiary Committees reporting to the COP, most commonly comprising at least a Committee for Scientific and Technical Advice, and a Secretariat to provide support at and between meetings of these bodies. The dynamic force of many environmental treaties derives from the need to respond to changes in the physical environment regulated thereby and is most generally effected through the COP via a subsidiary scientific body. A significant number of environmental treaties adopt a framework approach to facilitate more rapid change than is generally the case through the normal (and time-consuming) process of treaty amendment. This approach enables the treaty to contain general principles and set forth the organizational structure of the treaty bodies (the framework), while further protocols and/or annexes embody specific standards and are generally subject to a more flexible amendment process.

An excellent example of a framework treaty is the regional 1979 ECE Convention on Long-Range Transboundary Air Pollution, now accompanied by eight protocols; the 1992 UN Framework Convention on Climate Change and the 1997 Kyoto Protocol is another good example at the global level. More flexible amendment procedures were pioneered by the International Maritime Organization with the use of the 'tacit amendment procedure' with its 1973/78 Convention for the Prevention of Pollution from Ships (MARPOL), to

---

[20] On environmental treaty-making, see Redgwell, 2000; on the interaction of treaty and soft law, see Boyle, 1999; and on compliance with non-binding norms in the environment and natural resources field, see the case studies in the edited volume by Shelton, 2000.

[21] For recent analysis of the role of the COP, including in compliance procedures, see Brunee, 2002.

which there are now six annexes. Changes to the annexes come into force for *all* contracting parties within a minimum of 16 months of adoption of the change unless objection is lodged within a certain time period (10 months) by one-third of the contracting parties or by the number of contracting parties whose combined merchant shipping fleets represent at least 50% of world gross tonnage. A more recent and further example of this framework approach is the 1992 Convention for the Protection of the Environment of the North-East Atlantic (OSPAR), where the Convention is accompanied by five annexes and three appendices, with the latter embodying matters exclusively of a technical, scientific, or administrative nature. Both appendices and annexes are more readily amended and modified than the convention text itself, thus permitting the convention more readily to grow and adapt to changing scientific and other data.[22]

Further flexibility is found in recent treaty texts that allow for differentiation in the implementation obligations for States taking on treaty commitments (French, 2000; Cullet, 2003). For example, Article 3(1) of the 1992 Climate Change Convention recognizes the common but differentiated responsibilities and respective capabilities of States in implementing the obligation to protect and preserve the climate system for the benefit of present and future generations (Rajamani, 2000). Developed country parties 'should take the lead in combating climate change and the adverse effects thereof'; indeed, under the 1997 Kyoto Protocol it is only Annex I (developed country) parties which are subject to specific targets and timetables for greenhouse gas emission reductions. As the climate regime evolves, however, there is a trend towards symmetry—obligations for 'all Parties'—with a key issue for negotiation of the post-2020 legal framework being the basis for, and extent of, differentiation in the application of the common but differentiated responsibilities principle (Rajamani, 2012). Other instruments adopt similar methods of differentiation based on the parties' capabilities. For example, a number of the substantive treaty obligations of States party to the 1992 UN Convention on Biological Diversity are qualified by the words 'in accordance with [each contracting party's] particular conditions and capabilities'.

While the vast majority of the rights and obligations of States with respect to the environment derive from voluntarily assumed treaty obligations, it would be misleading to suggest that no customary international law norms govern State conduct. State practice has given rise to a number of customary law principles, buttressed by the process of treaty and customary law interaction (see generally De Sadeleer, 2002; Thirlway, Ch 4 of this book). Of these the most significant is the 'good neighbour' or so-called 'no harm' principle, pursuant to which States have a duty to prevent, reduce, and control pollution and significant transboundary environmental harm. It has been enunciated in judicial decisions as well as soft law declarations. Thus, for example, in the *Pulp Mills* case, which involved the siting of a pulp mill on a shared watercourse, the River Uruguay, the ICJ observed that 'A State is thus obliged to use all the means at its disposal in order to avoid activities which take place in its territory, or in any area under its jurisdiction, causing significant damage to the environment of another State.'[23] Far from imposing an absolute prohibition on any transboundary harm, as the 'no harm' shorthand appears to suggest, the obligation to prevent significant transboundary harm is widely viewed as imposing an

---

[22] For further discussion of the legal implications of such flexible amendment procedures under OSPAR, see de la Fayette, 1999.

[23] *Pulp Mills on the River Uruguay (Argentina v Uruguay), Judgment, ICJ Reports 2010*, p 14, para 101. See also the ILC's 2001 Draft Articles on Prevention of Transboundary Harm from Hazardous Activities which accurately reflect the current state of international law in this regard: Article 2, (ILC Yearbook 2001, Vol II Part 2, p 152).

obligation of due diligence. The ILC Commentary to the Draft Articles on Prevention of Transboundary Harm for Hazardous Activities thus accurately reflects current international law in stating that 'the obligation of the State of origin to take preventive or minimization measures is one of due diligence'.[24]

State practice further supports the customary law obligation to consult and to notify of potential transboundary harm where there are shared resources or ultrahazardous activities being carried out, and the requirement to conduct a prior transboundary environmental impact assessment. In the *Pulp Mills* case, the ICJ found the requirement to conduct a transboundary environmental impact assessment (EIA) to be a distinct and freestanding obligation in international law where significant transboundary harm is threatened. Although the specific content of such an EIA is left to the State's discretion, international law requires that an EIA is conducted and that it bears a relation to the 'nature and magnitude of the proposed development and its likely adverse impact on the environment'.[25]

Other relevant principles of customary international law include the principle of preventive action and equitable utilization of shared resources. More controversial is the customary law status of the precautionary principle or approach (Birnie, Boyle, and Redgwell, 2009), the principle of sustainable development *per se* (Lowe, 1999) and of its buttressing principles (eg sustainable use; intergenerational equity; integration of the environment into economic and development projects; and common but differentiated responsibilities) (Paradell-Trius, 2000; French, 2005), and the polluter pays principle (Birnie, Boyle, and Redgwell, 2009). Arguments range from lack of normative content to the absence of a uniform understanding of the meaning of the principles, and widely varying consequences of their application depending on the specific context. While such principles may lack legally binding force as customary international law, their impact may nonetheless be considerable when further concretized in a treaty text (eg the precautionary principle under the 1995 Straddling Fish Stocks Agreement) or used as a 'general guideline' or aid to judicial interpretation of treaty obligations between the parties (eg the concept of sustainable development and the bilateral agreement between Hungary and Slovakia in the *Gabčíkovo-Nagymaros* case). In a wide-ranging assessment of the environmental impact of deep seabed mining activities, the Seabed Disputes Chamber of the International Tribunal for the Law of the Sea in an Advisory Opinion affirmed the obligation of sponsoring States to apply a precautionary approach, relying *inter alia* on provisions of the Nodules and Sulphides Regulations.[26] It was prepared to go further, however, in noting that 'the precautionary approach is also an integral part of the general obligation of due diligence of sponsoring States, which is applicable even outside the scope of the Regulations'.[27]

General principles of law are also of significance in the environmental context, though a distinction needs to be made between the general principles of law referred to in Article 38(1)(c) of the ICJ Statute, and general principles such as those found in the Stockholm and Rio Declarations in international environmental law. To the extent that the former embraces general principles found in national law, these are of limited utility in the international environmental context (though relied on in the seminal *Trail Smelter Arbitration*). If Article 38(1)(c) includes general principles recognized at international law, then the scope is potentially significant. These operate to influence the interpretation of (but not override) treaty provisions, the application of custom, and influence judicial decisions. The reference

---

[24] ILC Yearbook 2001, Vol II Part 2, 154, commentary to Article 3, para (7).

[25] *Pulp Mills on the River Uruguay (Argentina v Uruguay), Judgment, ICJ Reports 2010*, p 14, para 205.

[26] *Responsibilities and Obligations of States Sponsoring Persons and Entities with Respect to Activities in the Area, Advisory Opinion, ITLOS Reports 2011*, paras 121–2 and 125–7.

[27] Ibid, para 131.

to 'the concept of sustainable development' by the ICJ in the *Gabčíkovo-Nagymaros* case[28] is a well-known example of the influence an internationally recognized principle of international environmental law may wield.

Indeed, as this last example illustrates, although not a formal source of international law as such, judicial decisions provide important authoritative evidence of what the law is, with a growing number of judicial and arbitral awards of importance in the environmental field. These include judgments and advisory opinions of the ICJ[29] and ITLOS[30] and judgments of the PCA[31] and other arbitral awards[32] and the decisions of human rights courts.[33]

B. SOFT LAW

In addition to the traditional sources of international law identified earlier, a variety of non-binding instruments such as codes of conduct, guidelines, resolutions, and declarations of principles, may be resorted to by States and non-State actors alike.[34] As discussed earlier (Boyle, 1999, Ch 5), these are non-binding instruments non-compliance with which does not entail international responsibility. Soft law may be employed because its origins are not law-creating either because the body promulgating the 'law' does not have law-making authority (eg an autonomous treaty supervisory body or an NGO) or because a law-making body chooses a non-binding instrument with which to embody a statement of particular principles (eg States at the 1992 Rio Conference on Environment and Development adopting the binding 1992 Climate Change Convention and the non-binding 1992 Rio Declaration of Principles on Environment and Sustainable Development). International environmental law is a particularly fertile area for soft law norms, since it allows agreement on collective but non-binding action where, for example, the scientific evidence is inconclusive or the economic costs uncertain. It may, and not infrequently does, lead to 'hard' law, such as the UNEP Guidelines mentioned earlier, although as the discussion of the climate change regime in Section VII of this chapter illustrates, this process is not necessarily a linear one.

VI. ENFORCEMENT OF INTERNATIONAL ENVIRONMENTAL LAW

A question of over-arching importance is what happens in the event of the breach of an environmental obligation?[35] Here the traditional rules regarding State responsibility (see

---

[28] *Gabčíkovo-Nagymaros Project (Hungary/Slovakia), Judgment, ICJ Reports 1997*, p 7, para 140.

[29] See, for example, *Gabčíkovo-Nagymaros Project (Hungary/Slovakia), Judgment, ICJ Reports 1997*, p 7; *Legality of the Threat or Use of Nuclear Weapons, Advisory Opinion, ICJ Reports 1996*, p 226; *Pulp Mills on the River Uruguay (Argentina v Uruguay), Judgment, ICJ Reports 2010*, p 14.

[30] See, for example, *MOX Plant Case (Ireland v United Kingdom), Provisional Measures, Order of 3 December 2001, ITLOS Reports 2001*, p 95; *Responsibilities and Obligations of States Sponsoring Persons and Entities with Respect to Activities in the Area, Advisory Opinion, ITLOS Reports 2011*, nyr; (2011) 50 ILM 458.

[31] *MOX Plant Arbitration (Ireland v United Kingdom), Jurisdiction and Provisional Measures*, PCA, 16 June 2003; *Iron Rhine Arbitration (Belgium/Netherlands), PCA Award of 24 May 2005*, para 58.

[32] See, for example, *Trail Smelter Arbitration*, (1939) 33 AJIL 182; *Metalclad Corporation v United Mexican States* (ICSID Case No ARB(AF)/97/1), Award of 30 August 2000.

[33] See, for example, *Fadeyeva v Russia*, no 55723/00, ECHR 2005-IV.

[34] See Chinkin and Boyle, 2007, and Shelton, 2000; on the interaction of treaty and soft law, see Boyle, 1999.

[35] See the contributions to the edited volume by Francioni and Scovazzi, 1991; Wetterstein, 1997; and Wolfrum, 1999.

Crawford and Olleson, Ch 15 of this book) would apply. Yet these rules are of only limited assistance in the environmental field for a number of reasons (Redgwell, 2013). One is that responsibility rules generally operate once damage has already occurred, rather than to prevent damage from occurring in the first place. A second difficulty, illustrated particularly well by the climate change example, is that harm may be incremental and difficult to link to the specific actions or omissions of another State.[36] Problems of causation and proof will loom large. The generally non-reciprocal character of international environmental obligations will also render it difficult to meet the requirement of breach of an obligation owed to another State. Both the *Trail Smelter* Arbitration between the USA and Canada[37] and the *Gabčíkovo-Nagymaros Dam* dispute between Hungary and Slovakia[38] saw the application of traditional rules on State responsibility because of the bilateral character of the dispute and of the obligations thereunder. Had it proceeded to the merits, the ICJ case brought in 1974 against France by Australia and New Zealand regarding French atmospheric nuclear testing in the South Pacific would have likewise largely fit within this bilateral model.[39] But what of the example of a breach by a State of its obligation to conserve biological diversity, expressly acknowledged as 'the common concern of humankind'? A complainant State is required to show that the obligation is owed to it and (usually) that injury has resulted to it in order for standing requirements to be satisfied; there is no such thing (yet) under international law as an *actio popularis* whereby a State may bring an action on behalf of the international community.[40] There are glimmerings of such an approach in Articles 42 and 48 of the 2001 Articles on State Responsibility drafted by the International Law Commission, wherein the possibility exists for a State party to a multilateral treaty to complain of breach of a multilateral obligation by another State party.[41] While there has not yet been international judicial recognition of this possibility in the environmental context, in the 2012 *Obligation to Prosecute or Extradite* case (*Belgium* v *Senegal*), the ICJ explicitly recognized that the Convention against Torture imposed obligations *erga omnes partes* giving rise to a common interest in compliance and 'the entitlement of each State party to the Convention to make a claim concerning the cessation of an alleged breach by another State party.'[42]

There are several consequences of the inadequacies of traditional rules of State responsibility for the development of international environmental law. The first is a relative paucity of cases at the international level in which environmental matters have figured largely. Recourse to the dispute settlement under international environmental treaties is rare, a recent example being the recent invocation of the dispute settlement procedures of the 1982 LOSC and 1992 OSPAR Convention by Ireland against the UK in connection with radiological pollution from the MOX plant.[43] Moreover, few dispute settlement clauses in international environmental treaties provide for compulsory third party settlement of inter-State claims (Brus, 1995). Sparse examples include the Ozone Layer Convention and

---

[36] From a burgeoning literature see Verheyn, 2005; Fitzmaurice, 2010; Tomuschat, 2011; Lefebre, 2012.

[37] *Trail Smelter Arbitration* (1939) 33 AJIL 182 and (1941) 35 *AJIL* 684.

[38] *Gabčíkovo-Nagymaros Project (Hungary/Slovakia), Judgment, ICJ Reports 1997*, p 7.

[39] *Nuclear Tests (Australia v France), Interim Protection, Order of 22 June 1973, ICJ Reports 1973*, p 99; *Judgment, ICJ Report 1994*, p 253; *Nuclear Tests (New Zealand v France), Interim Protection, Order of 22 June 1973, ICJ Reports 1973*, p 135; *Judgment, ICJ Reports 1994*, p 457.

[40] *South West Africa, Second Phase, Judgment, ICJ Reports 1966*, p 6.

[41] 2001 Articles on State Responsibility, Article 48; for analysis see Peel, 2001.

[42] *Questions relating to the Obligation to Prosecute or Extradite (Belgium v Senegal), Judgment of 20 July 2012*, para 69.

[43] For discussion of the international and EU law aspects of the proceedings, see Churchill and Scott, 2004.

the Montreal Protocol, and the Framework Convention on Climate Change (FCCC) and the Kyoto Protocol. A second consequence has been pressure further to develop the rules of State responsibility, including standing. Few environmental treaties address standing; rarer still is to provide for reciprocal standing for non-State actors. An oft-cited example is the 1974 Nordic Environmental Protection Convention, Article 3 of which addresses access to justice for non-State actors; the 1998 Aarhus Convention may well stimulate further developments in this area.[44]

A third consequence is the development of alternatives to traditional dispute settlement techniques under specific treaty instruments directly to address the issue of non-compliance with treaty obligations from both a facilitative and a coercive point of view. The 1987 Montreal Protocol is pioneering in this regard, establishing the first non-compliance procedure in an environmental agreement. A handful of other treaty instruments have established implementation and compliance procedures, including the 1997 Kyoto Protocol to the 1992 Framework Convention on Climate Change, the 1989 Basel Convention on the Transboundary Movement of Hazardous Wastes and their Disposal, the 2000 Cartagena Protocol to the 1992 Convention on the Conservation of Biological Diversity, and the 1998 Aarhus Convention on Access to Information, Public Participation in Decision-Making, and Access to Justice in Environmental Matters. These generally exist alongside traditional dispute settlement clauses and are suspended in the event of the invocation of traditional dispute settlement procedures (Fitzmaurice and Redgwell, 2000). Finally, a further consequence of the inadequacies of State responsibility in the environmental field is the development of liability regimes which side-step the necessity to rely on the route of inter-State claims. As we will see, the development of specific liability instruments has been particularly marked in the field of activities with transboundary consequences (eg nuclear activities, vessel-source oil pollution, and hazardous waste movements) and in the protection of common spaces (eg liability arising from environmental emergencies in Antarctica under the 2005 Annex to the 1991 Environmental Protocol to the 1959 Antarctic Treaty, and the responsibility and liability of seabed contractors for environmental damage in the 2000 regulations on prospecting and exploring for polymetallic modules promulgated by the International Seabed Authority under the 1982 LOSC).

VII. SUBSTANTIVE INTERNATIONAL ENVIRONMENTAL LAW

From the foregoing it will already be apparent that there exists a considerable body of international rules applicable to environmental protection. The breadth of regulatory activity is enormous, ranging from liability and compensation for oil pollution damage through to licensing regimes for the transboundary movement of hazardous waste and the listing of sites important for wild birds or for the natural and cultural heritage. The purpose of this section is to provide a flavour of the breadth and depth of international law pertaining to the environment as developed through multilateral standards-setting conventions.

---

[44] For analysis of the convention see Davies, 2002; on public participation see generally Ebbesson, 1997.

A. PROTECTION OF THE MARINE ENVIRONMENT[45]

The protection of the marine environment was one of the key issues at the 1972 Stockholm Conference, and is clearly reflected in the flurry of law-making in this area which occurred in the early 1970s in particular. The negotiation of the 1982 LOSC, which commenced in 1973, likewise had an influence upon (and was influenced by) these developments. Thus Part XII of the resulting 1982 Convention—with its 46 Articles devoted to the marine environment—implicitly acknowledges existing marine environment treaties in the areas of dumping at sea[46] and vessel-source pollution in particular. Pollution of the oceans, and concerns about their limited absorption capacity, formed a key thrust of these 1970s law-making activities: both the global 1972 London (Dumping) Convention and the regional 1972 Oslo Dumping Convention date from this period, as does the 1973 Convention on the Prevention of Pollution from Ships (MARPOL 73/78). UNEP, established it will be recalled after the Stockholm Conference, undertook the establishment of regional seas programmes for which the 1976 Barcelona Convention for the Protection of the Mediterranean Sea Against Pollution, and subsequent protocols, formed the prototype for many other regional seas areas (only the Baltic, the North-east Atlantic/North Sea, Antarctic, and Arctic oceans, are regulated by regional instruments outside UNEP's programme). The Protocols to the Barcelona Convention range in subject matter from pollution caused by dumping, land-based sources, and seabed activities, to cooperation in emergencies, specially protected areas, and transboundary movement of hazardous waste. The convention was substantially revised in 1995 following the Rio Conference, the impact of which is observable in many other areas of regulatory activity where such 'second generation agreements' have been adopted.

Dumping is one area of regulatory activity where this progression is particularly marked. Initially, regional and global dumping conventions adopted the regulatory approach of listing prohibited, dangerous, and other substances, relying on nationally-implemented licensing schemes for their enforcement. Coastal States exercised the jurisdiction afforded them under international law to do so: territoriality and nationality (of the vessel). There was no presumptive ban operating in respect of dumping at sea, with the regulatory approach essentially one of 'permitted unless prohibited'. Wastes were divided into three categories: Annex I, the 'black list', contained a list of substances prohibited from dumping; Annex II, the 'grey list', those substances the dumping of which required a prior special permit; for all other substances, Annex III (the 'white list') required a prior general permit. However, with the replacement of the 1972 Oslo Convention (and 1974 Paris Convention for the Prevention of Marine Pollution from Land-Based Sources) by the 1992 Convention on the Protection of the Marine Environment of the North-east Atlantic (OSPAR) and the negotiation of the 1996 Protocol to the 1972 London Convention, this philosophy has been replaced by a 'prohibited unless permitted' approach. Dumping is not permitted unless it falls within one of the permitted exceptions to a general ban on dumping. The list is quite restrictive, including bulky matter such as dredged material and sewage sludge and (at least for the moment) offshore installations. A precautionary approach is very much in evidence here, with a significant shift in the burden of proof to the polluter to demonstrate that dumping at sea will not have significant harmful consequences for the marine environment. There has also been a noticeable shift away from an approach based on pollution

---

[45] For succinct treatment of the extensive law in this area, see Churchill and Lowe, 1999, Ch 15; Birnie, Boyle and Redgwell, 2009, Ch 7.

[46] For analysis of the relationship between the 1982 LOSC and both prior and subsequent treaties regulating ocean dumping, see Redgwell, 2006a.

prevention and control, the focus of the 1982 LOSC, to a more integrated approach to marine protection under these instruments (Sands and Peel, 2012).

Vessel-source pollution, though a relatively minor contributor to marine pollution, has nonetheless been subject to extensive international regulation following highly publicized oil spills such as the *Torrey Canyon* in 1967. MARPOL 73/78 adopts a framework approach in that six accompanying annexes embody the technical details of regulating oil discharges (Annex I), noxious liquids in bulk (Annex II), harmful packaged substances (Annex III), sewage (Annex IV), garbage (Annex V), and air pollution (Annex VI). Any State wishing to become a party to MARPOL 73/78 must also adopt Annexes I and II as a minimum. Annex I reflects a particular preoccupation with vessel-source oil pollution, focusing on limiting discharges of oil as part of routine tanker operations. It sets forth oil discharge and tanker design criteria[47] and requires coastal States to provide adequate reception facilities for oily residues. Some maritime areas have been designated as 'special areas' under MARPOL in which no discharge is permitted, including areas such as the North-west Atlantic Ocean and Mediterranean Sea areas, and the Antarctic Southern Ocean.

A key regulatory device under MARPOL is the use of standardized International Oil Pollution Prevention Certificates, the issuance of which is linked to regular surveying and inspection of vessels. This is supplemented by a requirement for tankers and other ships to carry an Oil Record Book itemizing all operations involving oil. In addition to the requirement that this record may be inspected by any other party to MARPOL, it is these documents which in certain circumstances coastal and port States are entitled to inspect under the 1982 LOSC, whether or not a party to MARPOL.[48] Coastal States' enforcement powers are also enhanced under the 1982 LOSC, including the power to investigate, inspect, and, in limited circumstances, to arrest vessels navigating in the Exclusive Economic Zone (EEZ) when a violation of applicable international rules and standards for the prevention, reduction, and control of pollution from vessels, eg MARPOL 73/78, has occurred which threatens or causes environmental damage.[49] Thus MARPOL 73/78, like the other marine pollution conventions, relies on general public international law and the Law of the Sea Convention in particular for the exercise of legislative and enforcement jurisdiction. As Chapter 22 makes clear, the LOSC constitutes a significant innovation in the development of port State enforcement jurisdiction upon which the success of MARPOL 73/78 has largely rested. Improved exercise of flag State jurisdiction has likewise had beneficial impact on the number of pollution incidents at sea.

Apart from prompting the regulation of marine pollution through routine operational discharges at sea, the oil tanker catastrophes of the 1960s and 1970s in particular led to the development of separate liability conventions, the 1969 Convention on Civil Liability for Oil Pollution Damage (CLC) and the 1971 Convention on the Establishment of an International Fund for Compensation for Oil Pollution Damage (Fund Convention). These follow a pattern found in the nuclear civil liability conventions, which is to limit and channel liability. Risk is assumed by, and liability is channelled through, the shipowner, which is strictly liable for oil pollution damage as defined under the conventions. A monetary ceiling on liability is fixed, enabling the shipowner to obtain insurance cover in the market through P & I Clubs. If this ceiling is exceeded under the CLC, then the Fund Convention may provide a further source of compensation funds for claimants. The Fund is based on

---

[47] Thus constituting the 'generally accepted international rules or standards' which coastal States may apply to third party shipping traversing the territorial sea fully in accordance with LOSC Article 21(2).

[48] Article 218 LOSC.   [49] Article 220, especially paras (3), (5), and (6).

levies from oil-importing countries, thus spreading the risk between the shipowner and the risk-creating States. The advantage for claimants in States party to the CLC/Fund regime is the ability to obtain compensation swiftly without recourse to the courts in their own or another State. Both conventions were updated by Protocols in 1992 with an increase in the compensation limits (further increased in 2000 and 2003), an extension of geographic coverage (to incidents in the EEZ) and the inclusion of pollution prevention costs in the recoverable heads of damage. In 2001, a further convention was concluded on pollution damage from bunker fuel from ships, the International Convention on Civil Liability for Bunker Oil Pollution Damage. Modelled on the CLC, it entered into force in 2008.

Further responses to catastrophic oil spills are reflected in the 1969 Convention Relating to Intervention on the High Seas in Cases of Oil Pollution Casualties—which permits the coastal State to intervene beyond its territorial sea—and the 1990 Oil Pollution Preparedness and Response Convention (OPRC) which requires, *inter alia*, the preparation of emergency response plans for oil spill incidents. These were international legislative responses to the 1967 *Torrey Canyon* and 1989 *Exxon Valdez* oil spill emergencies respectively. In recognition of the fact that the threat to the marine environment from vessel-source pollution extends beyond petroleum, in 1973 the Intervention Convention was extended to apply to hazardous substances other than oil and, in 2000, the OPRC was extended by Protocol to cover hazardous and noxious substances.[50]

Related to the pollution context, a further threat to the marine environment arises from the introduction of invasive species through ballast water (Rayfuse, 2007, pp 385–7), which is now regulated under the 2004 International Convention for the Control and Management of Ships' Ballast Water and Sediments. It uses techniques familiar from the oil pollution context, including the requirement to implement a management plan, carry a 'Ballast Water Record Book' and for port State inspection.

Despite this extensive legislative activity, significant gaps remain in marine environmental protection. In addition to the problem of declining fish stocks (see Evans, Ch 22 of this book) the two most notable gaps are the absence of robust global regulation of the largest source of marine pollution, land-based pollution, and international regulation of the marine environment in areas beyond national jurisdiction. The former is the subject of weak provision in the 1982 LOSC and addressed in protocols to four UNEP regional seas agreements, and in the 1992 Baltic Convention, but there is no present prospect of further regulation, not least because regulating this source of marine pollution most heavily intrudes on a wide range of human activities under the sovereignty of States. In contrast, marine protection in areas beyond national jurisdiction is part of the remit of the Ad Hoc Open-ended Informal Working Group to study issues relating to the conservation and sustainable use of marine biological diversity beyond areas of national jurisdiction, established by UN General Assembly resolution in 2006. The necessity for this gap-filling is occasioned by the failure of the 1982 LOSC to include the precautionary principle, marine protected areas management, or the ecosystem approach, gaps not surprising in a text reflecting the state of environmental law at the time. Amongst other things, marine genetic resources, and conservation and management tools such as area-based management and environmental impact assessment, are under discussion by the Working Group. A further implementation agreement may be the legal form used to fill this high seas 'marine biodiversity gap' (Oral, 2012).

---

[50] The 1996 International Convention on Liability and Compensation for Damage in Connection with Carriage of Hazardous and Noxious Substances by Sea (HNS), also modelled on the CLC, has not yet entered into force.

B. PROTECTION OF THE ATMOSPHERE

There are three principal areas of international regulatory activity in respect of protection of the atmosphere—transboundary air pollution, ozone depletion, and climate change. All share a transboundary or global dimension and in no case are the existing rules of customary law, including those on State responsibility, adequate to address the problem. In particular the persistence, scope, and intertemporal nature of environmental problems such as climate change necessitates global (preventative) action. A classic case for international regulation, it would seem. Yet in the case particularly of transboundary air pollution and of climate change, there was (and in the case of the latter, still is) some scepticism regarding the existence and scope of the problem. Moreover, unlike the marine context discussed earlier in A. Protection of the Marine Environment, there is no single instrument where the general 'law of the atmosphere' is codified, nor is this picture likely to change. In 2013 the International Law Commission adopted the topic of 'Protection of the atmosphere' in its programme of work but with express caveats including that: (a) this work would not interfere with political negotiations, including on climate change, ozone depletion, and long-range transboundary air pollution; and (b) the outcome of the work will be draft guidelines which do not seek to impose on existing treaty regimes legal principles not already contained therein.[51]

1. Transboundary air pollution[52]

The *Trail Smelter* Arbitration referred to in Section VI of this chapter was an early instance of an inter-State claim arising in respect of the harmful transboundary effects of air borne pollutants. Yet this case involved a single detectable source of air pollution (sulphur dioxide emissions from the smelter) causing quantified harm to health and property; today it would most likely be resolved through transnational litigation by access to national courts. What if the sources of air pollution are far more diffuse and its harmful effects upon the environment are widespread? These were the difficulties confronting States in negotiating the 1979 LRTAP Convention, added to which was the initial scepticism of some parties as to the very existence and nature of the problem. In fact it remains the only major regional agreement addressed to air pollution, a reflection both of the severity of the problem in Europe (though Canada and the USA are also parties[53]) and the difficulty in achieving international regulation of an activity impacting on sovereign energy and other choices.

The purpose of LRTAP is to prevent, reduce, and control transboundary air pollution from both new and existing sources. 'Air pollution' is defined in terms reminiscent of the marine pollution definition of the 1982 LOSC, and includes harm to living resources, ecosystems, and interference with amenities and legitimate uses of the environment. 'Long-range transboundary air pollution' is defined as adverse effects in the jurisdiction of one State resulting from emissions originating in the jurisdiction of another State yet the individual source of which cannot necessarily be distinguished. The framework character of LRTAP resulted in the absence of specific reduction targets in the treaty itself; rather, an environmental monitoring programme was first put in place pursuant to the first Protocol to LRTAP, in order to gather data to assess the extent of the problem, followed by the negotiation of further protocols to reduce emissions of specific air pollutants. In this respect

---

[51] See http://legal.un.org/ilc/texts/8_8.htm.   [52] See generally Okowa, 2000.

[53] As noted in Section III of this chapter, LRTAP is one of five environmental treaties concluded under the auspices of the UN's Economic Commission for Europe, membership of which comprises 56 States within Europe (east and west), the CIS and North America: see http://www.unece.org.

the LRTAP Convention is a good example of the interaction of monitoring and reporting obligations on the one hand and flexible treaty structures, easily adapted to changes in scientific knowledge, on the other. The framework approach of the convention has allowed a step-by-step approach by States allowing 'agreement' at the outset even where there is no consensus regarding the concrete steps to be taken to address a particular environmental problem. To date eight protocols on monitoring and on specific air pollutants with specific reduction targets and timetables[54] have been added to the initial framework convention, significantly expanding the scope of the parties' commitments. Although there are provisions on notification and consultation in cases of significant risk of transboundary pollution, LRTAP does not itself contain provisions on liability nor on compliance. But in 1994 a second sulphur protocol was adopted with a non-compliance procedure based on the experience of the 1987 Montreal Protocol to the Ozone Convention. In 1997 this procedure was subsumed within a broader Implementation Committee established, inter alia, to review compliance by parties with the reporting obligations of the convention and any non-compliance with the protocols.[55]

2. Ozone depletion[56]

It was UNEP which in 1981 launched negotiations for the conclusion of a treaty to protect the ozone layer, culminating in the adoption of the 1985 Vienna Convention for the Protection of the Ozone Layer (Yoshida, 2001). Like LRTAP, the initial treaty contained little by way of substantive obligations, focusing rather on the need to assess the causes and effects of ozone depletion and cooperation in the exchange of relevant information and technology. This 'largely empty framework' treaty was a result of the divergent interests of States: the USA, having taken steps for domestic reduction, was concerned to ensure a level playing field in respect of ozone-depleting substances regulation; developing States were concerned to ensure that any restraints on the use of such substances did not adversely affect industrial development and that if imposed, appropriate access to alternative technology would be assured; while the EC, where many producers were located, was concerned regarding the potential cost of steps to be taken and unconvinced of the scientific case for the harmful effects of the substances (Birnie, Boyle, and Redgwell, 2009).

The 1987 Montreal Protocol—like the 1997 Kyoto Protocol to the Climate Change Convention—radically altered this picture in several respects. In addition to introducing specific targets for the reduction and eventual elimination of ozone-depleting substances, subsequent adjustments or amendments of the Protocol have introduced financial (the Multilateral Fund) and technical incentives to encourage developing country adherence to the Protocol. Implementation and compliance is further secured through the establishment of a non-compliance procedure, the first mechanism of its kind but which is now found in a number of other agreements (see Section VI of this chapter). This is a form of 'soft enforcement' designed to address non-compliance by essentially self-implicating States through both facilitation (access to the Multilateral Fund, provision of technical assistance) and/or sanction (issuing of cautions and/or suspension of the Article 5 privilege of delay in implementation for which some 148 developing States are currently

---

[54] For texts see http://www.unece.org/env/lrtap.

[55] Decision 1997/2. The Implementation Committee's terms of reference were most recently updated in 2012 (Decision 2012/25). For the most recent available (Fifteenth) report by the Implementation Committee, Body on non-compliance cases considered by the Implementation Committee, see ECE/EB.AIR/2012/16, 2 October 2012, available at http://www.unece.org/env/lrtap/ic/reports.html.

[56] See, generally, Benedick, 1998; Yoshida, 2001; Anderson and Sarma, 2002 and http://www.ozone.unep.org.

eligible[57]). In fact compliance by developed States has been high, and it has been largely former Soviet and East European States which have experienced difficulties with full compliance largely owing to financial and technical constraints. Successive amendments to the Protocol have also set more stringent targets and timetables and added to the list of ozone-depleting substances such that recovery of the ozone layer, including the hole above Antarctica, is hoped for by the mid-twenty-first century. This projected recovery of the ozone layer, combined with wide participation in the Protocol, high compliance rates, and the dynamic and flexible operation of the treaty regime which has continued over time to strengthen controls over ozone-depleting substances, constitutes the Montreal Protocol as an all-too-rare success story in addressing environmental problems through international cooperation. Yet there may be factors impeding long-term success, including the emergence of new ozone-depleting substances not covered by the Protocol, and the fact that it encourages resort to substituting substances some of which (eg HFCs) are greenhouse gases covered by the Kyoto Protocol (Annex A) (Birnie, Boyle, and Redgwell, 2009).

3. Climate change[58]

It will be recalled that the 1992 UN Framework Convention on Climate Change was one of two treaties adopted at the Rio Conference. Negotiations followed upon recognition by the General Assembly that the atmosphere is 'the common concern of mankind' and the work of the Intergovernmental Panel on Climate Change (IPCC) in providing the scientific guidance necessary to regulate the emission of greenhouse gases on the international level.[59] The principal objective of the Convention is 'stabilization of greenhouse gas concentrations in the atmosphere at a level that would prevent dangerous anthropogenic interference with the climate system'. Although framework in character, the Convention contains specific commitments in Article 4 addressed to all parties and, additionally, specifically to developed country parties. All 194 parties have the obligation to produce inventories of greenhouse gas sources and sinks, to formulate national and, where appropriate, regional programmes to reduce global warming, to cooperate in preparing for adaptation to the impacts of climate change, and to promote scientific research. Since these obligations are addressed to developing as well as developed country parties, the convention qualifies these obligations by permitting parties to 'tak[e] into account their common but differentiated responsibilities and their specific national and regional development priorities'. No such qualification is made of the obligations for developed country parties and other parties (countries with economies in transition)—the 'Annex I' parties to the convention. For these States, Article 4 sets forth the obligation to develop national policies and measures to mitigate the adverse effects of climate change indicating that developed country parties are to take the lead in modifying longer-term trends in anthropogenic emissions. Detailed reports on such policies are to be provided 'with the aim of returning individually or jointly to their 1990 levels...of carbon dioxide and other greenhouse gases not controlled by the Montreal Protocol'. It is also the responsibility of developed country parties to provide new and additional financial resources to meet the agreed full costs incurred by developing country parties in complying with their convention obligations. The financial mechanism under the convention is the Global Environmental Facility (GEF), administered jointly by

---

[57] For the complete list see http://ozone.unep.org/new_site/en/parties_under_article5_para1.php.

[58] On the negotiation of the convention see Bodansky, 1993; on the protocol see Freestone and Streck, 2005, and on the climate regime see Depledge and Yamin, 2004. For current status and text see http://www.unfccc.int.

[59] The Fourth Assessment Report (AR4) was released in 2007, comprising four volumes (reports of the three working groups and a synthesis report) available at http://www.ipcc.ch. AR5 is scheduled for 2014.

the World Bank (as trustee), UNEP, and the UN Development Programme. The GEF is also the financial mechanism under the Biodiversity Convention.

Notwithstanding the obligations contained in Article 4, it was not until the negotiation of the 1997 Kyoto Protocol that developed country parties committed themselves to explicit, unambiguous targets and timetables for the reduction of the chief greenhouse gases and to the development of international mechanisms for ensuring the fulfilment of these commitments. The core obligation of the Protocol is contained in Article 3(1) which states that Annex I parties 'shall, individually or jointly, ensure that their aggregate anthropocentric carbon dioxide equivalent emissions' of specific greenhouse gases 'do not exceed their assigned amounts' and that overall emissions of such parties are reduced 'by at least 5 per cent below 1990 levels in the commitment period 2008–2012'. To ensure its effectiveness the Protocol could only enter into force when adhered to by 55 States including Annex I parties representing 55% of that group's 1990 carbon dioxide emissions. Annex I party participation was contingent on satisfactory elaboration of the three 'flexibility mechanisms' in the Protocol for achieving these targets and timetables, namely, joint implementation (projects between Annex I parties), the clean development mechanism (between Annex I and non-Annex I parties), and emissions trading. At COP 7 (2001) significant breakthrough had been achieved in realizing the details of implementation such that both Canada and Russia announced at the Johannesburg summit in 2002 that they would ratify the Protocol. The participation of both States was essential for the attainment of the entry into force threshold of the Protocol given the USA's stated determination to remain outside the Protocol. The Protocol duly entered into force on 16 February 2005,[60] leaving less than eight years remaining for Annex I parties to achieve the reductions mandated for the first commitment period (2008–12). The Protocol has a Compliance Committee, with both a facilitative branch and an enforcement branch, to facilitate, promote, and enforce compliance with the Protocol.[61]

At COP 13 in 2007 the parties agreed the 'Bali Roadmap' with the aim of reaching agreement on a post-2012 governance framework by COP15/MOP5 to be held in Copenhagen at the end of 2009.[62] Two ad hoc working groups—on long-term cooperation action under the convention, and on further commitments of the Annex I parties to the protocol—prepared draft texts for consideration at Copenhagen. In the event a controversial non-binding 'Copenhagen Accord' was concluded by representatives of major economics and regions, which is not based on the Working Group drafts, and of which the COP decision to which it is attached as an unofficial document 'took note'.[63] Unlike the Kyoto Protocol, the Accord does not contain binding targets for emissions reduction but rather relies on a 'bottom-up' approach of pledged reductions. Nonetheless, over 141 States have made pledges to date, representing 87.24% of global emissions.

The future of the climate change regime has been the subject of continuing international negotiations following Copenhagen, with meetings at Cancun (2010) and Durban (2011) continuing along the dual track of the Convention (long-term cooperative action) and the Protocol (further commitments). COP 16 in Cancun concluded agreements on each of these tracks, and took note of the mitigation targets agreed at Copenhagen. Important areas of disagreement remain, including most notably over long-term global emissions

---

[60] It presently has 192 parties including the EU (but not the USA). Canada announced its withdrawal from the Protocol in 2011, which pursuant to Article 27(1) of the Kyoto Protocol took effect from 15 December 2012.

[61] For discussion of the evolution of the mechanism and comparison with the Montreal Protocol non-compliance procedure, see Werksman, 1998; see also Fitzmaurice and Redgwell, 2000.

[62] On the legal implications of the possible outcomes, see Rajamani, 2009.

[63] See Decision 2/CP.15.

targets and the conclusion of sectoral agreements for aviation and maritime transport. At COP 17 in Durban in 2011, agreement was reached on a second commitment period, to 2020, but not on what legal form future commitments would take, with some States continuing to register opposition to the conclusion of a 'second Kyoto Protocol' (eg Japan, Russia, and Canada—in the latter case unsurprising given the announcement of its withdrawal from the Kyoto Protocol with effect from 15 December 2012). The possibility of a legally binding outcome remains on the table owing to careful drafting of the Durban outcome, the 'Durban Platform', which launched 'a process to develop a protocol, another legal instrument or an agreed outcome with legal force under the Convention' by 2015.[64] Indeed, the relationship between soft and hard law in the climate change regime has not been a simple linear trajectory but rather has meandered from hard to soft, though with a likely return to hard law in 2015 (French and Rajamani, 2013). What is clear is that some form of agreement will be concluded in 2015 and that there is political commitment, confirmed at COP 18 in Doha in 2013, to end the current Kyoto Protocol by 2020.

One consequence of evolution in the climate change regime has been an apparent shift from differential treatment in favour of developing countries toward symmetry in legal requirements placed on (all) countries, a leveling down of mitigation commitments, and an increased focus on bottom-up processes with the likelihood of national determination of mitigation targets and monitoring of their fulfilment (French and Rajamani, 2013). These developments, combined with the approach of the newest multilateral agreement to be concluded, the 2013 Minamata Convention on Mercury (see Section D of this chapter), has led some scholars to ponder whether there is a wider move in international environmental law towards symmetrical non-prescriptive obligations for all parties and greater deference to national circumstances (French and Rajamani, 2013).

C. NUCLEAR RISKS

The nuclear sector has been the subject of considerable regulatory activity at the international level.[65] Given that nuclear energy activities are ultrahazardous in character with potentially devastating transboundary implications, this degree of international regulatory activity is unsurprising. The first international agreements, at both global and regional level, were concerned with regulating liability and compensation for nuclear damage largely with a view to rendering a fledgling energy industry commercially viable. They also reflected the generally unsatisfactory nature of the general customary international law principles in respect of State responsibility discussed earlier, as well as the magnitude of the potential harm to humans and the environment.

At the regional level, the 1960 Paris Convention on Third Party Liability in the Field of Nuclear Energy and the 1963 Brussels Supplementary Convention, were adopted under the auspices of the Nuclear Energy Agency of the Organization for Economic Cooperation and Development (OECD). These are designed to elaborate and harmonize legislation relating to third party liability to ensure that compensation is paid for persons suffering nuclear damage, while at the same time ensuring that the development and use of nuclear energy remains commercially feasible. Channelling and limiting liability achieves both of these aims, with the nuclear operator initially liable, then the State of operation and, finally, all contracting parties. Financial limits for liability, which is strict, are set for each

---

[64] Establishment of an Ad Hoc Working Group on a Durban Platform for Enhanced Action 2011, available at http://unfccc.int/2860.php. For analysis see Rajamani, 2012.

[65] For succinct overview, see Ghaleigh in Birnie, Boyle, and Redgwell, 2009, Ch 6.

level. In 2004 amendments to the Paris/Brussels regime (not yet in force) were made which increase compensation levels, enhance operator liability, and enlarge their geographic scope. The definition of nuclear damage thereunder includes not only personal injury and damage to property, but also economic losses such as the cost of preventive measures and of measures to reinstate an impaired environment, which may constitute the major portion of the damage caused by a nuclear incident. However, there has not yet been a serious test of these provisions within Europe. The Chernobyl incident in 1986 did not fall under the Paris/Brussels regime since, as a non-OECD member, the Soviet Union was not a party to the convention (nor is the Russian Federation now) and the convention does not apply to incidents outside convention States. In 1988 a Joint Protocol was concluded which links this regional system with the similar global regime, the 1963 Vienna Convention on Civil Liability for Nuclear Damage, with a further 1997 Supplemental Convention (in force 2003) increasing the amount of compensation available for nuclear damage.

These global instruments have been concluded under the auspices of the International Atomic Energy Agency (IAEA), a UN body which was established in 1957 to facilitate the peaceful development of nuclear energy and adherence to non-proliferation safeguards. Following the Chernobyl accident in 1986, the IAEA concluded two further international treaties addressed to early notification (1986 Convention on Early Notification of a Nuclear Accident or Radiological Emergency) and to assistance in the event of an international nuclear incident (1986 Convention on Assistance in the Case of a Nuclear Accident or Radiological Emergency). The former embraces in treaty form the customary law obligation to notify in the event of serious transboundary harm. In more preventive vein, a further IAEA convention, the 1994 Convention on Nuclear Safety, is designed to ensure the safe operation of land-based nuclear power plants. The effectiveness of this instrument came under scrutiny following the Fukushima Daiichi nuclear plant incident in Japan in 2011 (Kus, 2011). An extraordinary meeting of the parties to the Convention was held in 2012 to consider the implications of the Fukushima incident for the Convention, which identified several key weaknesses including the non-binding peer review mechanism for national reports submitted under the Convention. Procedural changes have been instituted to strengthen peer review and transparency, which unlike treaty amendment may have immediate effect, with a working group established to consider further strengthening through amendment of the Convention.[66]

Safety and security issues form an increasingly important area of the IAEA's activities with the object, *inter alia*, of protecting humans and the environment from harmful radiation exposure. In 1997 a further Joint Convention on the Safety of Spent Fuel and Radioactive Waste Management was concluded, modelled on the 1994 Convention, to ensure high safety standards and the prevention of accidents in the disposal of nuclear waste. In many respects these recent developments of both the OECD and IAEA regimes demonstrate parallels with the regulation of oil pollution liability: preventive concern to ensure that the activity is carried out to minimize or avert pollution consequences; emergency response and notification systems; and a liability regime which increasingly acknowledges the environmental costs of prevention and of reinstatement.

Despite the extent of legislative activity at the global level and regional levels, a significant gap remains in the legal regime for disposal of radioactive waste. In addition to the recognition of the Antarctic continent as the first 'nuclear waste free zone' (Antarctic Treaty (1959) Article 5), it is widely recognized that the disposal of radioactive waste on

---

[66] For the outcome of the second extraordinary meeting of the parties to the Convention on Nuclear Safety, see http://www-ns.iaea.org/conventions/nuclear-safety.asp?s=6&l=41.

or below the seabed is prohibited by international law. This flows either from specific treaty prohibition (ie London Convention Article IV(1)(a); London Protocol Article 4(1); OSPAR Article 3, Annex II), or from the more general treaty and customary international law duty to protect the marine environment (eg LOSC Article 192), with which such disposal is regarded as inconsistent. While this leaves States with the exclusive option of land-based disposal, international law continues to play a role in the regulation of safe disposal of nuclear material, largely through the work of the IAEA. However, it is unclear whether the existing nuclear liability regime would extend to geological or subsurface disposal of high-level waste and spent nuclear waste. This is because (strict) liability is channelled through the operator of a 'nuclear installation' upon proof of nuclear damage, but the definition of 'nuclear installation' under the 1963 Vienna Convention on Civil Liability for Nuclear Damage appears to include only a nuclear reactor, a nuclear factory, or 'any facility where nuclear material is stored,' (Article I(j))—there is no explicit reference to disposal. While there is a clear technical distinction between storage, however long term, and permanent disposal,[67] the legal distinction between them is less clear: does 'storage' include 'disposal' for the purposes of the application of the liability regime? Legal certainly could be achieved, for example, were a determination made by the Steering Committee for Nuclear Energy of the OECD that a disposal facility with nuclear fuel or radioactive products or waste is an 'installation' for the purposes of the liability regime. Whether it should be so extended is another question, given that geological disposal of high-level nuclear waste and spent fuel raises issues different from even the long-term storage of nuclear waste, and may thus require a bespoke legal response (Redgwell and Rajamani, 2014).

D. OTHER HAZARDOUS SUBSTANCES AND ACTIVITIES[68]

Apart from the nuclear sector there has also been considerable regulation of other hazardous activities and substances, focusing on environmentally sound management and regulation of the transboundary movement of such substances. Four instruments are of particular importance in this area, three of which are of relatively recent origin. The 1989 Basel Convention on the Transboundary Movement of Hazardous Wastes and their Disposal[69] was the first to occupy the field, and was the international response to 'toxic traders' seeking to avoid the increasingly higher costs of hazardous waste disposal in developed countries through cheaper disposal in developing and East European countries. It has had an influence on the scope and application of two other instruments with which it is closely linked, namely, the 1998 Rotterdam Convention on Prior Informed Consent Procedure for Certain Hazardous Chemicals and Pesticides in International Trade and the 2001 Stockholm Convention on Persistent Organic Pollutants. Together these three instruments are intended to provide for the environmentally sound management of hazardous chemicals throughout their life-cycle. Indeed, pursuant to synchronized synergies decisions by each treaty body, cooperation has been enhanced through a UNEP-facilitated synergies oversight team (SOT) mandated, *inter alia*, with preparing the first trilateral extraordinary meeting of the parties to the three conventions to be held in 2010. A fourth instrument, the 2000 Cartagena Protocol to the 1992 Biodiversity Convention, is addressed

---

[67] IAEA, *The Long Term Storage of Radioactive Waste: Safety and Sustainability, A Position Paper of International Experts* (2003) 3, stressing permanence with no intention to remove.

[68] See, generally, Pallemaerts, 2003; Wirth, 2007.

[69] Regional regulation is found in the 1991 Bamako Convention on the Import into Africa and the Control of Transboundary Movement and Management of Hazardous Wastes within Africa and in Protocols to the Regional Seas Agreements discussed in Section VII A of this chapter.

to the transboundary movement of living modified organisms, on the hazardous character of which there is as yet no international consensus. Further linkages between these instruments are provided by UNEP, as indicated, which functions as the secretariat for each of the four instruments (jointly with the Food and Agriculture Organization (FAO) in the case of the Rotterdam Convention). UNEP is also responsible for the latest multilateral environmental agreement to be concluded, the 2013 Minamata Convention on Mercury, which is brought within the Basel framework through, *inter alia*, the definition of mercury as 'waste' for the purposes of the latter.

1. 1989 Basel Convention on the Transboundary Movement of Hazardous Wastes and their Disposal[70]

The Basel Convention has achieved widespread adherence with 172 parties at present, including significant developing country participation which was facilitated by the early establishment of a Trust Fund and a Technical Cooperation Fund. It is concerned both with regulating the transboundary movement of hazardous waste and ensuring sound environmental management in respect of its disposal. This is reflected in the annexes to the convention which address not only the categories of waste controlled (Annex I) or requiring special consideration (Annex II) but seeks to standardize the definition of hazardous characteristics (Annex III), regulate disposal operations (Annex IV), and ensure adequate information is provided about hazardous characteristics, etc (Annex V). There is also provision for arbitration (Annex VI) and, concluded in 1999 but not yet in force, a Protocol on Liability and Compensation for Damage (including environmental damage). The convention affirms the sovereign right of States to prohibit imports of hazardous waste and ensures the corresponding export prohibition will be respected by other States parties. Where transboundary movement does take place it must be grounded in the prior consent of the importing State (and any transit States), with both importing and exporting States obliged to ensure that waste is managed in an environmentally sound manner. Trade with non-parties is prohibited; moreover hazardous waste disposal from OECD to non-OECD countries is also now prohibited under the convention. This move to prohibition is characteristic of other pollution treaties, most notably in the case of dumping at sea under both the global 1996 London Protocol and under the regional 1992 Convention for the Protection of the Marine Environment of the Northeast Atlantic. These treaties also share with the Basel Convention (and with the Stockholm and Minamata Conventions) an increasing focus on sound environmental management seeking to eliminate waste generation at source through best environmental practices and available techniques, signalling a shift in emphasis from remediation to prevention. The Basel Convention parties are also increasingly focused on the effective implementation and enforcement of the regulatory framework established over the decade of the 1990s. The convention joins an increasing number of environmental treaties to address not only the liability of non-State actors and compensation for, *inter alia*, environmental damage (the 1999 Protocol), but also compliance by States with their convention obligations. In 2002 the Basel Convention established a compliance mechanism to facilitate early detection of implementation and compliance problems such as illegal trafficking or meeting reporting obligations, a move possible only through the establishment of concrete norms and standards against which to benchmark State compliance and the political will of the parties to achieve more effective implementation of its provisions.[71]

---

[70] For a thorough analysis see Kummer, 2000.

[71] For reports of the Compliance Committee to date, see http://www.basel.int/legalmatters/compcommitee.

2. 1998 Rotterdam Convention on Prior Informed Consent and the 2001 Stockholm Convention on Persistent Organic Pollutants[72]

The Rotterdam and Stockholm Conventions arose from Chapter 19 of Agenda 21 which highlighted the regulatory gap in respect of substances that are 'toxic, persistent and bio-accumulative and whose use cannot be controlled'. Like the Basel Convention, soft law guidance in the form of UNEP/FAO Guidelines preceded their negotiation, with both instruments fairly rapidly entering into force with relatively widespread adherence by States. The Rotterdam Convention (PIC) was applied provisionally from its conclusion in 1998 until its entry into force on 24 February 2004, and currently has 131 parties. It establishes a prior informed consent regime in respect of the importation of toxic substances, many of which are also subject to the Stockholm Convention. It does not ban outright the import/export of hazardous chemicals and pesticides but rather subjects them to a regime of the prior informed consent of the importing party before export of a banned or severely restricted chemical or severely hazardous pesticide to which the convention applies may take place between parties. These are listed in Annex III of the convention, which provides a mechanism for amending the list of substances through the Conference of the Parties. Ultimately of course the convention relies on exchange of information among parties about potentially hazardous chemicals that may be exported and imported and requires national decision-making processes to be established regarding import and compliance by exporters with these decisions. The 2001 Stockholm Convention entered into force on 17 May 2004 and presently has 168 parties. It initially addressed environmentally sound management of a so-called 'dirty dozen' of toxic substances, to which a further nine chemicals were added at COP4 in 2009. The fundamental objective is to protect human health and the environment from persistent organic pollutants (POPs), which remain intact in the environment for long periods, becoming widely distributed geographically, and accumulate in the fatty tissues of living organisms thus posing a toxic threat both to humans and to wildlife. The Stockholm Convention seeks to eliminate or reduce the release of POPs into the environment through controls over the production or use of intentionally produced POPs (ie industrial chemicals and pesticides), management and reduction of stockpiles, and minimization and elimination of unintentionally produced POPs (eg industrial by-products such as dioxins and furans). Unlike the PIC Convention, POPs explicitly relies on a precautionary approach (Article 1).

3. 2000 Cartagena Protocol on Living Modified Organisms[73]

The Cartagena Protocol on Living Modified Organisms (LMOs) to the 1992 Convention on Biological Diversity was concluded in 2000 and entered into force on 11 September 2003. It presently has 157 parties. The focus of the Protocol is upon the transboundary movement of LMOs which may have adverse effects on biological diversity and human health. 'LMO' is defined as 'any living organism that possesses a novel combination of genetic material obtained through the use of modern biotechnology'. In fact the Protocol addresses two general categories of LMO: (i) those intended for release into the environment (eg seeds for cultivation or animal breeding stock); and (ii) those intended for use in food or feed, or for processing (eg corn, cotton, and soy). The latter was of particular concern to exporters of genetically modified crops (including the USA, though not yet a party to the Protocol), and are subject to a less onerous regime (Article 11) than that

---

[72] See further http://www.pic.int and http://chm.pops.int, respectively.
[73] See further Redgwell, 2006b; McKenzie *et al*, 2003; and http://www.cbd.int/biosafety.

applicable to LMOs intended for direct release into the environment (Articles 7–10). The chief regulatory technique employed under the Protocol is the 'advanced informed agreement' (AIA) procedure, which is designed to ensure that contracting parties are provided with the information necessary to make informed decisions before agreeing to the import of LMOs into their territory. AIA marks the Protocol out from the 'prior informed consent' procedures of the 1989 Basel and 1998 Rotterdam Conventions, which are based on prior multilateral agreement on the hazardous substances to be regulated and which are set out in annexes. No such agreement exists regarding LMOs; in consequence, a marked feature of the Protocol is its overtly precautionary approach, with Article 1 making express reference to the precautionary approach contained in Principle 15 of the 1992 Rio Declaration. To facilitate information exchange and to assist with national implementation, a Biosafety Clearing-House has been established. Facilitative financing is also available through the Global Environmental Facility (the financial mechanism for the parent Convention on the Conservation of Biological Diversity (CBD) as well). A Compliance Committee, expressly contemplated under the Protocol to address problems of implementation and non-compliance, was established at the first meeting of the parties, and is still at the stage of refining its rules of procedure. It has not yet considered specific instances of non-compliance (a 2009 submission by an NGO regarding a party was held inadmissible) although it has reviewed compliance in general terms based on national reports submitted by the parties after four years' operation of the Protocol. In common with similar mechanisms in other environmental treaties, it is intended to be principally facilitative and non-adversarial in function, with more coercive measures (eg the issuing of cautions and the publication of non-compliance details in the Biosafety Clearing-House) left to the decision of the Meeting of the Parties under the Protocol.

4. The 2013 Minamata Convention on Mercury[74]

In 2009 the process of negotiating a new Convention to address mercury pollution was initiated under UNEP's auspices, with five negotiating sessions between 2010 and 2013. In October 2013 the text was formally opened for signature in Minamata, Japan, the location of serious mercury poisoning and loss of life caused by consumption of fish and shellfish contaminated by industrial wastewater from a chemical factory. The objective of this new Convention 'is to protect human health and the environment from anthropogenic emissions and releases of mercury and mercury compounds' (Article 1). It addresses the reduction of mercury emissions to the air from power plants and other point sources (Articles 8 & 9), and of the use of mercury in products and industrial processes (Articles 4 & 5), and mercury supply and trade (Article 3). In addition, it contains provisions to address the severe and growing problem of mercury use in artisanal gold mining (Article 7). Safe interim storage and sound management of mercury, and management of contaminated sites, is also emphasized. Indeed, in common with the instruments noted earlier, the Minamata Convention employs environmental tools such as best environmental practices and best available techniques (both defined in Article 2), and makes provision for capacity-building, technical assistance and technology transfer (Article 14). From the outset a financial mechanism is to be established to support effective implementation of the Convention, although notably resources may come from domestic funding as well as relying on the Global Environmental Facility Trust Fund (Article 13). Building on the experience of other instruments, the Minamata Convention establishes at the outset an

---

[74] Final text of the Convention together with the Report of the Fifth and final negotiation session is available at http://www.unep.org/hazardoussubstances/Mercury/Negotiations/INC5/INC5Report/tabid/3496/Default.aspx.

Implementation and Compliance Committee and requires review of the effectiveness of the Convention no later than six years after its entry into force.

While it is, of course, early days for the evaluation of a Convention which has only recently been adopted, two observations may be made. The first is the relative absence of overt differential treatment in the Convention, which refers to the principle of common but differentiated responsibilities in the preamble but in the main imposes obligations on all parties (or provides exceptions open to all, not just developing States). The second is the 'menu of options' approach to eg mercury emissions (Article 8(5)) and releases (Article 9(5)), with greater deference to national circumstances resulting in differential treatment for all, not just for developing States (French and Rajamani, 2013). Thus Article 8(5) uses mandatory language—'shall include' and 'shall implement', but permits a choice of measures ('one or more of the following measures') with ample scope for national differentiation ('taking into account its national circumstances, and the economic and technical feasibility and affordability of the measures').

E. CONSERVATION OF NATURE

The evolution of treaties for the protection of species and habitat reflects in many respects the evolution of international environmental law itself. Some of the earliest treaties in the environmental field were concerned with the incidental regulation of wildlife, though their primary purpose was economic, eg the 1902 Paris Convention on the Protection of Birds Useful to Agriculture and the 1911 Treaty of Washington on the Protection of Fur Seals. One of the first cases to consider (and reject) the concept of coastal State stewardship over common property resources on the adjacent high seas likewise concerned fur seals, the 1898 *Bering Fur Seals Fisheries Arbitration*.[75] There are now dozens of bilateral, regional,[76] and multilateral treaties concerned with species and habitat protection, ranging from the protection of seals, bears, whales, and turtles, to holistic environmental regulation of the Antarctic environment.[77] For present purposes it is not intended exhaustively to scrutinize the detailed legal mosaic of species and habitat regulation at the bilateral and regional levels, but rather to focus upon the 'big five' of multilateral species and habitat treaties, namely, the 1971 Ramsar Convention on Wetlands of International Importance Especially As Waterfowl Habitat (Ramsar Convention); the 1972 UNESCO Convention Concerning the Protection of the World Cultural and Natural Heritage (WHC); the 1973 Convention on International Trade in Endangered Species of Wild Fauna and Flora (CITES); the 1979 Bonn Convention on the Conservation of Migratory Species of Wild Animals (Bonn Convention); and the 1992 Convention on the Conservation of Biological Diversity (see Bowman, Davies, and Redgwell, 2010).

1. 1971 Convention on Wetlands of International Importance (Ramsar Convention)[78]

The Ramsar Convention is the only global environmental treaty addressed to a particular ecosystem, the conservation and wise use of wetlands primarily as habitat for wild

---

[75] (1893) *Moore's International Arbitrations* 755 (*Great Britain v US*).

[76] In particular the 1968 African Convention on the Conservation of Nature and Natural Resources (revised 2003, not yet in force), the 1979 Council of Europe Convention on the Conservation of European Wildlife and Natural Habitats (Berne Convention).

[77] On which see Rothwell, 1996, Ch 9; Redgwell, 1994.

[78] See http://www.ramsar.org; Ramsar Convention Secretariat, 2007, *Ramsar Handbooks for the Wise Use of Wetlands*, 3rd edn; Bowman, Davies, and Redgwell, 2010, Ch 13.

birds. The mission of the convention has broadened over time, so that today 'wise use' is interpreted to mean 'sustainable use' and the concept of wetlands now embraces fish as well as bird species and habitat. Integration of the conservation of wetland biodiversity with sustainable development, considered as synonymous with the convention's concept of 'wise use', is at the heart of the current strategic plan for the convention. There are currently 159 contracting parties to the Ramsar Convention, with 1,880 sites designated for the List of Wetlands of International Importance covering a total surface area of nearly 185 million hectares (larger than the combined surface area of France, Germany, and Switzerland).

Much has been accomplished under a convention of initially rather unpromising beginnings. It is still an extraordinarily brief instrument of only 13 articles, but these have been subject to extensive elaboration through the Guidelines issued by the Regular Meetings of the COP. The chief regulatory device of the convention is the listing of sites for protection that is then afforded such sites under national laws. Each contracting party is required to designate 'suitable wetlands' within its territory for inclusion on the List of Wetlands of International Importance, the 'flagship' of the convention. Indeed, a State is not considered a full party to the convention unless and until a site has been designated (in contrast with the World Heritage Convention, for example). So long as the proposed site fulfils one of the Criteria for Identifying Wetlands of International Importance and has been designated by the appropriate national authority it will be added to the list. Contracting parties are required to submit triennial reports on the implementation of the treaty to the contracting parties, thus providing an opportunity for review of national implementation measures.

Once designated, Ramsar sites are to be protected under national law but also acquire recognition under international law as being significant for the international community as a whole. Failure to promote the conservation of wetlands on the list and their wise use may lead to listing on the 'Montreux Record of Ramsar sites requiring priority attention', established in 1990, and which highlights threats to designated sites. The ultimate sanction is de-listing because of the irremediable loss of the values which led to Ramsar listing in the first instance. This has never occurred; nor have any sites been deleted owing to 'urgent national interests' as provided for in the convention.[79] The only instance of removal was of three sites designated before the development of the Criteria which they then failed to meet, and were replaced with other designations.

Sites requiring priority attention may not formally be added to the Record without the consent of the State concerned. There are currently 50 sites which have been added to the Montreux Record with the consent of the States concerned.[80] An additional and facilitative feature of the Ramsar Convention is the awareness that failure to conserve wetlands may result from lack of capacity. Thus, a Small Grants Fund for Wetland Conservation and Wise Use was also established in 1990 with the express purpose of facilitating compliance, along with other forms of technical assistance, and the Ramsar Advisory Mission was established as a technical assistance mechanism to provide further advice regarding the problems or threats which have caused Montreux listing to be contemplated. Site visits are an integral part of this mechanism and, as with the Montreux

---

[79] Article 2.5 provides that in the urgent national interest the boundaries of a site may be deleted or restricted. Parties have invoked the 'urgent national interest' clause to *restrict* the boundaries of a Ramsar site on three occasions only: Belgium in the 1980s, Australia in 1997 (though not ultimately implemented) and Germany in 2000. Further guidance on implementation of Article 2.5 is found in Resolution VIII.20 (2002).

[80] See http://www.ramsar.org; and Bowman, Davies, and Redgwell, 2010, Ch 13.

listing procedure itself, are conditional upon the agreement of the contracting party concerned. For sites covered by both Ramsar and the World Heritage Convention, such visits may be requested and carried out jointly. For example, Ichkeul National Park in Tunisia is on both the Ramsar Montreux Record and the WHC Heritage in Danger List owing to the impact of dam projects on the river flowing into Ichkeul.[81] Conservation efforts may be assisted by listing on the Montreux Record with consequent access to technical assistance and facilitative financing under the Convention and elsewhere: the listing of the Azraq Oasis in Jordan assisted in obtaining funding from the Global Environmental Facility and of the Austrian Donau-March-Auen in obtaining European Commission funding.

2. The World Heritage Convention[82]

The World Heritage Convention (WHC) was adopted on 16 November 1972 under UNESCO auspices, mere months after the 1972 Stockholm Conference. There are presently 186 States party to the convention. Participation by developing States in particular is enhanced through the World Heritage Fund, a trust fund constituted by compulsory and voluntary contributions made by States parties to the convention. The purpose of the WHC is the identification, protection, conservation, presentation, and transmission to future generations of the cultural and natural heritage. The WHC is thus unusual in its express linkage of nature conservation and preservation of cultural properties, seeking to achieve a balance between the two. Protection of designated natural and cultural heritage is conferred by inscription on the World Heritage List of natural and cultural sites satisfying the inscription criteria under the convention. At present there are 890 properties on the list, 689 cultural, 176 natural, and 25 mixed properties in 148 States parties. However, unlike under the Ramsar Convention, it is not necessary to have a site listed to become a full participating party to the WHC.[83] The effectiveness of the convention is thus dependent upon States parties offering up sites for designation since UNESCO has no independent listing power. Independent evaluation of proposed sites is carried out by two advisory bodies, the International Council on Monuments and Sites (ICOMOS) in respect of cultural properties and the World Conservation Union (IUCN) in respect of natural properties. The criteria for inscription on the World Heritage List are set forth in *Operational Guidelines* which are revised regularly by one of the convention bodies, the World Heritage Committee, in order to reflect changes in the concept of world heritage.

Listing applications must include details of how the site is managed and protected under national legislation. Subsequent protection is thus a task for national law, subject to the general treaty obligation already indicated to protect and preserve such heritage. The convention makes clear that *international* protection of the world cultural and natural heritage is limited to 'the establishment of a system of international cooperation and assistance designed to support States parties to the convention in their efforts to conserve and identify that heritage'. The chief regulatory tools at the disposal of the convention organs for the achievement of such international protection are monitoring entry to and departure from listed status of sites of world natural and/or cultural heritage based on the

---

[81] In fact, the Park is one of a few sites which are protected by listing under three agreements: Ramsar (1980), WHC (1979), and Biosphere Reserve (1977). Details of listings can be found on the Ramsar website: http://www.ramsar.org.

[82] For commentary on the Convention, see Francioni with Lenzerini, 2008.

[83] For a full list by country and property, see http://whc.unesco.org.

data supplied by States parties in their national inventory and implementation reports and providing international assistance, including access to the resources of the World Heritage Fund.

In addition to stipulating the criteria for listing, published in the *Operational Guidelines*, the World Heritage Committee is also responsible for establishing the 'List of World Heritage in Danger', the latter designation signalling that major operations are necessary to conserve the site and for which assistance has been requested under the convention. The ultimate consequence of a State's failure to fulfil its obligations under the convention is deletion from the World Heritage List. Unlike Ramsar, there have been two deletions from the World Heritage List: the Arabian Oryx Sanctuary in Oman (2007) and the Dresden Elbe Valley in Germany (2009). Danger listing may be perceived either as a form of 'name and shame' or 'dishonour', or as a means of highlighting for the international community difficulties in conserving heritage values and seeking assistance in addressing them. Whatever the perception, the clear expectation upon danger listing is that steps will be taken by the State party concerned to reduce and/or eliminate the danger posed to world cultural and natural heritage, often in consultation with the key stakeholders in the site and activities related thereto. At present there are thirty-one properties on the danger list.

3. 1973 Convention on International Trade in Endangered Species[84]

Unlike the other treaties considered here, the direct purpose of the 1973 Convention on International Trade in Endangered Species (CITES) is not the protection of animal and plant species or habitat *per se*. Rather, its objective is to control or prohibit trade in species or their products where those species are in danger of extinction. It addresses one of the reasons for species decline apart from loss of habitat, which is increased exploitation to which commercial trade is a contributory factor. Over 5,000 animal species 'from leeches to lions' and 25,000 plant species 'from pine trees to pitcher plants' are now covered in the 175 States presently parties to CITES.

The convention controls the import and export of endangered species and products on a global scale through a permitting system operated by designated national authorities, a procedure familiar from the discussion of the dumping conventions in Section VI A of this chapter. Three appendices are used. Appendix I forbids trade in the listed species which are in danger of extinction, subject to some exceptions which are controlled by export, re-export, and import permits as required. Appendix II permits trade subject to certain restrictions in the species listed therein which are not threatened with extinction but may become so if trade is not controlled and monitored. Here only export (or re-export) permits apply. Appendix III encompasses species covered by national regulation where a State seeks international cooperation in controlling (external) trade, in which case an export permit is required. As may be expected, much of the controversy surrounding CITES has focused on listing (and de-listing) in the Appendices, with the listing of the African elephant particularly contentious. For a short time the African elephant was on Appendix I, but the adverse socio-economic consequences for Range States led to a partial relaxation in the ban in an attempt to seek a compromise between wildlife protection and human development. Populations in Botswana, Namibia, South Africa, and Zimbabwe are presently on Appendix II, with one-off sales of existing ivory stocks permitted in 1997 and 2007 (following the establishment of baseline data on poaching and wild populations).

---

[84] See http://www.cites.org; and Bowman, Davies, and Redgwell, 2010, Ch 15.

In common with the other treaties examined here, the effectiveness of CITES is dependent on national implementation. Each party is required to establish at least one Management
Authority and Scientific Authority to implement the permitting scheme, while the CITES
Secretariat is responsible for monitoring the overall operation of the Treaty and facilitating exchange of information obtained through performance of States' monitoring and
(annual) reporting obligations. NGOs also play a significant role under CITES in monitoring trade, such as the Wildlife Trade Monitoring Unit and IUCN/WWF's TRAFFIC
(Trade Records Analysis of Flora and Fauna in Commerce). CITES' compliance review
process is based on infractions reports by the Secretariat to the COP with the effective
sanction for non-compliance being suspension of trade in specimens of CITES-listed species with the non-complying party. Presently there are 24 States subject to a recommendation to suspend trade in certain species, including four non-parties (Bahrain, Haiti, Iraq,
and Tajikistan). In practice this has served as a potent tool for ensuring proper national
implementation of CITES' obligations to enact legislation, develop work plans, control
legal/illegal trade, and/or improve the basis for government decision-making (Yeater and
Vasquez, 2001).

4. 1979 Convention on the Conservation of Migratory Species[85]

The Convention on the Conservation of Migratory Species (Bonn Convention) is not
quite a pygmy amongst the giants of the other 'big five' species and habitat treaties, but
it certainly has the lowest profile. This is in part due to its relatively slow start; however, today there are 112 parties, of whom about half are developing countries. Activity
under the convention was also hampered by the failure of many States parties to pay
their contributions and expenses, which led to the Bonn Secretariat being chroni-
cally short-staffed and underfunded. Nonetheless the Bonn Convention has achieved
some modest success in its primary objective, which is to conserve habitat and protect
migratory species threatened with extinction. The need for such regulatory action was
highlighted in the Stockholm Action Plan in 1972, offering an holistic approach to protection of both land-based and marine migratory species not readily afforded by other
international instruments. The two techniques employed under the convention are first
to impose obligations on Range States to protect migratory species through restoration
of habitat and removing obstacles to migration of species listed in Appendix I as endangered throughout all or a significant portion of their range. Taking of such species must
be prohibited under domestic law. Secondly, the convention provides for the conclusion
of conservation 'AGREEMENTS' (including Memoranda of Understanding) between
Range States for the conservation and management of migratory species listed in
Appendix II as having 'unfavourable conservation status' requiring international agreement,[86] or at least which would benefit significantly from international cooperation. The
Bonn Convention thus has a framework character, encouraging Range States to conclude regional or global AGREEMENTS in respect of Appendix II species. In practice it
is possible for dual-listing of species under the Bonn Convention and for species also to
be subject to protection under other existing international agreements (marine mammals in particular fall into this category). Thus in concluding AGREEMENTS parties to

---

[85] See, generally, http://www.cms.int and Bowman, Davies, and Redgwell, 2010, Ch 16.
[86] For an example of such international cooperation see the 1991 Agreement on the Conservation of Small
Cetaceans of the Baltic and North Seas (ASCOBANS). For a full list of the Agreements and Memoranda of
Understanding concluded within the framework of the Bonn Agreement see http://www.cms.int.

the Bonn Convention are to ensure that rights and obligations under other treaties are not affected.

5. 1992 UN Convention on Biological Diversity[87]

Notwithstanding the extent of international environmental regulation of species and habitat protection outlined earlier, a gap persisted: no global instrument regulated the interaction of species and habitat, and of ecosystems, in a holistic rather than a piecemeal manner.[88] The closest perhaps is the regional Convention on the Regulation of Antarctic Marine Living Resources which expressly adopts an ecosystem approach but this applies only to the southern ocean and, at the time of the adoption of the CBD in 1992, had yet successfully to operationalize its novel ecosystem approach. UNEP perceived this 'biodiversity gap' and initiated negotiations to conclude a Convention on Biological Diversity (CBD) in time for signature at Rio. This was duly accomplished, and the convention entered swiftly into force a mere 18 months later.[89] Today it has virtually universal support with 193 States parties (including the EC and all of its member States). This includes significant developing country participation, crucial to the effectiveness of the convention given that the most biologically rich parts of the planet are located within developing equatorial States. Participation is facilitated through funding (the GEF is the funding mechanism for the CBD) and differentiation of implementation obligations through 'according to respective capabilities' language. The convention also provides a framework for national regulation of access to biological resources ('bioprospecting') on mutually agreed terms and benefit-sharing where such resources are exploited for commercial benefit. The role of indigenous peoples' knowledge and the application of traditional intellectual property rights principles remain areas of acute controversy under the convention though without impairing developing country participation. Here it is developed States, in particular the USA, which expressed concerns regarding the intellectual property and technology transfer provisions of the convention (Articles 15 and 16) and has remained outside the convention regime.

In its role as 'biodiversity gap-filler' the CBD defines biodiversity broadly to encompass the variability among living organisms from all sources, including, *inter alia*, terrestrial, marine, and other aquatic ecosystems and the ecological complexes of which they are part. The CBD's objectives are: the conservation of biological diversity; sustainable use of its components; and fair and equitable sharing of the benefits arising out of the utilization of genetic resources, including by appropriate access to genetic resources; transfer of relevant technologies, taking into account all rights over those resources; and funding. Each is addressed in further detail in the body of the CBD. Significant reliance is placed upon national measures for implementation, in accordance with each State's particular conditions and capabilities. It is thus up to individual contracting parties to determine the manner of implementation of their obligations, subject of course to scrutiny of national implementation by the COP through the reporting requirements of the convention. Concrete obligations are few and far between in the convention, a reflection both of the resistance to targets, lists, and the identification of species and sites for protection (though some States such as France preferred to adopt the listing model of the WHC for the CBD) and of the realization that there already exist a number of conventions with concrete

---

[87] See, generally, http://www.cbd.int; Bowman, Davies, and Redgwell, 2010, Ch 17; and the CBD Handbook, 3rd edn, available at http://www.cbd.int/handbook.

[88] For contributions placing the CBD in its broader context, see Bowman and Redgwell, 1996.

[89] For discussion of the 2000 Cartagena Protocol to the CBD, see Section VII D.3 of this chapter.

obligations in respect of species and habitat such as Ramsar and the WHC. Indeed, coop-eration with other closely linked treaties regimes has been facilitated by the conclusion of memoranda of understanding between secretariats. In addition, the CBD COP and its subsidiary organs have continued to supplement the treaty text principally through seven thematic work programmes comprising: marine and coastal biodiversity; mountain bio-diversity; agricultural biodiversity; forest biodiversity; inland waters biodiversity; dry and sub-humid lands biodiversity; and island biodiversity. These are buttressed by a number of cross-cutting issues such as access to genetic resources and benefit-sharing, alien species, biodiversity and tourism, and sustainable use of biodiversity. As discussed in Section VII D 3 of this chapter, the 2000 Cartegena Protocol addresses one of the issues outstanding from Rio, namely, the impact upon biological diversity of the transboundary movement of living modified organisms.

The CBD constitutes an important milestone in its preambular recognition of the intrinsic value of biodiversity and of the conservation of biodiversity as a 'common concern of humankind'. However, it should be observed that this falls far short of any internationalization of biological resources either in their ownership or in their con-trol—common concern is thus not akin to the 'common heritage of mankind' concept applicable to the resources of the deep seabed. Indeed, there is an inherent tension in the CBD in that the preamble also reaffirms States' permanent sovereignty over their natural resources. Linkage between these concepts is found in the responsibility of States for conserving their biological diversity and for using their biological resources in a sus-tainable manner (Glowka, 1994). Permanent sovereignty is thus responsible sovereignty under the CBD, a theme which pervades many of the instruments discussed earlier in this chapter.

F. CONSERVATION OF MARINE LIVING RESOURCES

Regulation of marine living resources was one of the first areas of international environ-mental regulatory activity, stimulated by the need to regulate common property resources of significant economic value such as seals, whales, and fish stocks. Of course in the nine-teenth and early twentieth centuries, most coastal States claimed only a 3 mile territorial sea with the seas beyond regarded as high seas open to exploitation of the resources therein. The Bering Fur Sea Arbitration established that adjacent coastal States had no legal interest in the protection of living resources beyond their initial belt of territorial sea. Today of course the picture is rather different, particularly with the development of the 200 mile Exclusive Economic Zone which accords coastal States exclusive rights over the living resources of this zone (see Evans, Ch 22, Section V C of this book). International regulation of marine living resources tends to focus on areas beyond national jurisdic-tion—high seas fisheries for example—and/or fish stocks which are straddling or highly migratory, spending at least part of their life-cycle beyond coastal State zones. In 1995 the Straddling Stocks Agreement (SSA) was concluded to address this problem, supplement-ing not only the 1982 LOSC but also the myriad regional fisheries organizations (RFOs) regulating such stocks (see Ch 22, Section VII B.2–3 of this book). Of particular note in the latter context is the North Atlantic Fisheries Convention and the 1980 Convention on the Regulation of Antarctic Marine Living Resources (CCAMLR) with its ecosystem approach.

The approach of most fisheries treaties is to establish a fixed quota (a total allowable catch) for particular stocks, regulate fishing methods (eg stipulated mesh size, open and close fishing seasons, and/or a prohibition of certain methods such as drift or purse seine nets) and to require monitoring and reporting obligations to be observed. Some form of inspection system is also common, as is the establishment of a scientific body to assess catch data and generally to advise on sustainable levels of fishing activity. In the Antarctic context the determination of permissible fishing effort is related not only to an analysis of the individual stocks but also of the interaction between predator and prey, in order to set a level of catch consistent with maintenance of the marine ecosystem as a whole. Common to all these instruments, however, is the persistent problem of illegal fishing, usually by 'free riders' outside the relevant treaty and thus exercising the high seas freedom to fish. The 1995 SSA seeks to encourage participation in RFOs where established for the areas in question, though here again such provision depends on the free rider States being party to the SSA. There have also been unilateral attempts to address illegal fishing, whether by States party to an RFO (eg Canada's arrest of the Spanish trawler the *Estai* outside its 200-mile EEZ for violation of NAFO measures)[90] or by coastal States exercising control over landing rights the exercise of which are crucial in ensuring transit of fresh fish to lucrative European and other markets.[91] Particular fish stocks, such as highly migratory tuna stocks,[92] are the subject of species specific regulation as are a wide range of marine mammals such as dolphins,[93] seals,[94] and whales (which are also protected under CITES). Here we see a shift in regulatory focus, for whilst fisheries regulation continues to be primarily concerned with conserving the economic value of the resource through good fisheries management practices, there is no doubt the 1946 International Convention for the Regulation of Whaling has seen a shift in approach from regulation of the (over) exploitation of an economic resource to a moratorium on whaling based at least in part on the more diffuse anthropocentric concern to protect the species.[95]

VIII. CONCLUSION

The breadth and scope of international environmental law is of course much greater than that briefly introduced in this chapter. Regional regulation of the Antarctic has contributed much to international environmental protection of both marine living resources and the terrestrial Antarctic environment; the regulation of the non-navigable uses of international watercourses has recently been codified and rests alongside extensive regional and bilateral regulation of riparian uses, including those which may have significant environmental impact; and marine living resources, from fish to mammals, have been subject to a myriad of global, regional, and bilateral arrangements only touched on here. Fertile areas for further exploration are the intersection of international environmental law with other areas addressed in this volume, most notably human rights (including access to environmental justice and public participation in environmental decision-making) and trade, as well as the effect of armed conflict on the environment.

---

[90] For analysis see Davies, 1995; more generally on straddling stocks, Davies and Redgwell, 1996.

[91] See the Special Chamber of the ITLOS established on 20 December 2000 in the *Case Concerning the Conservation and Sustainable Exploitation of Swordfish Stocks in the South-Eastern Pacific Ocean* (*Chile/European Community*) (proceedings suspended by agreement).

[92] See the 1949 Convention for the Establishment of an Inter-American Tropical Tuna Commission.

[93] See, eg the 1991 ASCOBANS, n 86 above.

[94] Such as the 1972 Convention on the Conservation of Antarctic Seals.

[95] See Birnie, 1997; Bowman, Davies, and Redgwell, 2010, Ch 6.

With its development over the last several decades, international environmental law has been transformed from mere incidental regulation of the environmental effects of human activities, to holistic regulation of global issues of common and intertemporal concern reaching both within and beyond the State. Its maturation is reflected in present concerns regarding State compliance with international obligations, reflected in the growing number of treaty-based compliance mechanisms, and in the crucial importance of effective national implementation and enforcement. Future developments will therefore see significant emphasis upon the effective enforcement of international environmental law at the global, regional, national, and local levels, with less emphasis on the generation of new rules.

REFERENCES

ANDERSON, M and GALIZZI, P (eds) (2002), *International Environmental Law in National Courts* (London: British Institute of International and Comparative Law), Ch 1.

ANDERSON, S and SARMA, K (eds) (2002), *Protecting the Ozone Layer; The United Nations History* (London: Earthscan Publications Limited).

BENEDICK, R (1998), *Ozone Diplomacy: New Directions in Safeguarding the Planet*, enlarged edn (Cambridge, Mass.: Harvard University Press).

BIRNIE, P (1997), 'Are Twentieth Century Marine Conservation Conventions Adaptable to Twenty-First Century Goals and Principles?', 12 *IJMCL* 307 and 488.

—— and BOYLE, A (1995), *Basic Documents on International Law* (Oxford: Oxford University Press).

——, ——, and REDGWELL, C (2009), *International Law and the Environment*, 3rd edn (Oxford: Oxford University Press).

BODANSKY, D (1993), 'UN Convention on Climate Change', 18 *Yale ILJ* 451.

BOWMAN, M and REDGWELL, C (eds) (1996), *International Law and the Conservation of Biological Diversity* (The Hague: Kluwer).

——, DAVIES, P, and REDGWELL, C (2010), *Lyster's International Wildlife Law*, 2nd edn (Cambridge: Cambridge University Press).

BOYLE, A (1999), 'Some Reflections on the Relationship of Treaties and Soft Law', 48 *ICLQ* 901.

BRUNNEE, J (2002), 'COPing with Consent: Law-Making under Multilateral Environmental Agreements', 15 *Leiden JIL* 1.

BRUS, M (1995), *Third Party Dispute Settlement in an Interdependent World* (The Hague: Martinus Nijhoff).

CHINKIN, C and BOYLE, A (2007), *The Making of International Law* (Oxford: Oxford University Press).

CHURCHILL, RR and LOWE, AV (1999), *The Law of the Sea*, 3rd edn (Manchester: Manchester University Press).

—— and SCOTT, J (2004), 'The MOX Plant Litigation: The First Half-Life', 53 *ICLQ* 643.

—— and ULFSTEIN, G (2000), 'Autonomous Institutional Arrangements in Multilateral Environmental Agreements: A Little-Noticed Phenomenon in International Law', 94 *AJIL* 623.

COMMISSION ON GLOBAL GOVERNANCE (1995), *Our Global Neighbourhood* (Oxford: Oxford University Press).

CRAWFORD, J (2012), *Brownlie's Principles of Public International Law*, 8th edn, (Oxford: Oxford University Press).

CULLET, P (2003), *Differential Treatment in International Environmental Law* (Aldershot: Ashgate).

DAVIES, PGG (1995), 'The EC/Canadian Fisheries Dispute in the Northwest Atlantic', 44 *ICLQ* 933.

——— (2002), 'Public Participation, the Aarhus Convention, and the European Community', in Zillman, D, Lucas, A, and Pring, G (eds), *Human Rights in Natural Resource Development: Public Participation in the Sustainable Development of Mining and Energy Resources* (Oxford: Oxford University Press), p 155.

——— and REDGWELL, C (1996), 'The International Legal Regulation of Straddling Fish Stocks', LXVII *BYIL* 199.

DE LA FAYETTE, L (1999), 'The OSPAR Convention Comes into Force: Continuity and Progress', 14 *IJMCL* 247.

DEPLEDGE, J and YAMIN, F (2004), *The International Climate Change Regime: A Guide to Rules, Institutions and Procedures* (Cambridge: Cambridge University Press).

DE SADELEER, N (2002), *Environmental Principles: From Political Slogans to Legal Rules* (Oxford: Oxford University Press).

EBBESSON, J (1997), 'The Notion of Public Participation in International Environmental Law', 8 *YBIEL* 51.

FITZMAURICE, M (2001), 'International Environmental Protection of the Environment', 293 *Recueil des Cours* 13.

——— (2010), 'Responsibility and Climate Change', 53 *German Yearbook of International Law* 89.

——— and REDGWELL, C (2000), 'Environmental Non-Compliance Procedures and International Law', XXXI *NYIL* 35.

FRANCIONI, F (1994), 'Developments in Environmental Law from Sovereignty to Governance: The EC Environmental Policy', in Markesinis, B (ed), *The Gradual Convergence: Foreign Ideas, Foreign Influences, and English Law on the Eve of the 21st Century* (Oxford: Clarendon Press), p 205.

——— and SCOVAZZI, T (eds) (1991), *International Responsibility for Environmental Harm* (Dordrecht: Kluwer).

——— with LENZERINI, F (eds) (2008), *The 1972 World Heritage Convention*

A Commentary (Oxford: Oxford University Press).

FREESTONE, D and STRECK, C (eds) (2005), *Legal Aspects of Implementing the Kyoto Protocol* (Oxford: Oxford University Press).

FRENCH, D (2000), 'Developing States and International Environmental Law: The Importance of Differentiated Responsibilities', 49 *ICLQ* 38.

——— (2005), *International Law and Policy of Sustainable Development* (Manchester: Juris Publishing/Manchester University Press).

FRENCH, D and RAJAMANI, L (2013), 'Climate Change and International Environmental Law: Musings on a Journey to Somewhere', 25 *Journal of Environmental Law* 4.

GILLESPIE, A (1997), *International Environmental Law, Policy and Ethics* (Oxford: Oxford University Press).

GLOWKA, L et al (1994), *A Guide to the Convention on Biological Diversity*, IUCN Environmental Policy and Law Paper No 30.

IUCN (2000), *Draft International Covenant on Environment and Development*, 2nd edn (IUCN).

KUMMER, K (2000), *International Management of Hazardous Wastes* (Oxford: Clarendon Press).

KUS, S (2011), 'International Nuclear Law in the 25 Years between Chernobyl and Fukushima and Beyond', 87 *Nuclear Law Bulletin* 7.

LEFEBRE, R (2012), 'Climate Change and State Responsibility', in Rayfuse, R and Scott, SV (eds), *International Law in the Era of Climate Change* (Cheltenham: Edward Elgar).

LOWE, AV (1999), 'Sustainable Development and Unsustainable Arguments', in Boyle, AE and Freestone, D (eds), *International Law and Sustainable Development: Past Achievements and Future Challenges* (Oxford: Oxford University Press).

McKENZIE, R et al (2003), *An Explanatory Guide to the Cartagena Protocol on Biosafety* (Gland: IUCN Environmental Policy and Law Paper No 46).

MUCHLINSKI, P (2007), *Multinational Enterprises and the Law* (Oxford: Oxford University Press).

OKOWA, P (2000), *State Responsibility for Transboundary Air Pollution in International Law* (Oxford: Oxford University Press).

ORAL, N (2012), '1982 UNCLOS+30: Confronting New Complexities in the Protection of Biodiversity and Marine Living Resources in the High Seas', in *Proceedings of the 106th Annual Meeting of the American Society of International Law* (Washington: ASIL), p 403.

PALLEMAERTS, M (2003), *Toxics and Transnational Law* (Oxford: Hart Publishing).

PARADELL-TRIUS, L (2000), 'Principles of International Environmental Law: an Overview', 9:2 *RECIEL* 93.

PEEL, J (2001), 'New State Responsibility Rules and Compliance with Multilateral Environmental Obligations—Some case studies of how the new rules might apply in the international environmental context', 10:1 *RECIEL* 82.

RAJAMANI, L (2000), 'The Principle of Common but Differentiated Responsibility and the Balance of Commitments under the Climate Regime', 9 *RECIEL* 120.

—— (2009), 'Addressing the "Post-Kyoto" Stress Disorder; Reflections on the Emerging Legal Architecture of the Climate Regime', 58 *ICLQ* 803.

—— (2012), 'The Durban Platform for Enhanced Action and the Future of the Climate Regime', 61 *ICLQ* 501.

RAYFUSE, R (2007), 'Biological Resources', in Bodansky, D, Brunnee, J, and Hey, E (eds), *The Oxford Handbook of International Environmental Law* (Oxford: Oxford University Press).

REDGWELL, C (1994), 'Environmental Protection in Antarctica: the 1991 Protocol', 43 *ICLQ* 599.

—— (2000), 'Multilateral Environmental Treaty-Making', in Gowlland-Debbas, V (ed), *Multilateral Treaty-Making: The Current Status of Challenges to and Reforms Needed in the International Legislative Process* (The Hague: Martinus Nijhoff), p 89.

—— (2006a), 'From Permission to Prohibition: the 1982 LOSC and Protection of the Marine Environment', in Freestone, D, Barnes, R, and Ong, D (eds), *The Law of the Sea: Progress and Prospects* (Oxford: Oxford University Press), p 180.

—— (2006b), 'Biotechnology, Biodiversity and International Law', in Holder, J (ed), *Current Legal Problems* (Oxford: Oxford University Press), p 543.

—— (2013), 'The Wrong Trousers: State Responsibility and International Environmental Law', in Evans, M and Koutrakos, P (eds), *The International Responsibility of the European Union: European and International Perspectives* (Oxford: Hart Publishing), p 257.

—— and RAJAMANI, L (2014), 'Energy Underground: What's International Law Got To Do With It?', in Zillman, D et al (eds), *Energy Underground* (Oxford: Oxford University Press).

ROTHWELL, D (1996), *The Polar Regions and the Development of International Law* (Cambridge: Cambridge University Press).

SANDS, P and PEEL, J (2012), *Principles of International Environmental Law*, 3rd edn (Cambridge: Cambridge University Press).

SCHRIJVER, N (1997), *Sovereignty Over Natural Resources: Balancing Rights and Duties* (Cambridge: Cambridge University Press).

SHELTON, D (ed) (2000), *Commitment and Compliance: The Role of Non-Binding Norms in the International Legal System* (Oxford: Oxford University Press).

SOHN, L (1973), 'The Stockholm Declaration on the Human Environment', 14 *Harv ILJ* 423.

TOMUSCHAT, C (2011), 'Global Warming and State Responsibility' in Hestermeyer, H et al (eds), *Law of the Sea in Dialogue* (Berlin: Springer-Verlag).

VERHEYEN, R (2005), *Climate Change Damage and International Law: Prevention Duties and State Responsibility* (Netherlands: Brill Academic Publishers).

WERKSMAN, J (1998), 'Compliance and the Kyoto Protocol: Building a Backbone into a "Flexible" Regime', 9 *YBIEL* 48.

WETTERSTEIN, P (ed) (1997), *Harm to the Environment: The Right to Compensation and the Assessment of Damages* (Oxford: Clarendon Press).

WIRTH, D (2007), 'Hazardous Substances and Activities', in Bodansky, D, Brunnee, J, and Hey, E (eds) (2007), *The Oxford Handbook of International Environmental Law* (Oxford: Oxford University Press).

WOLFRUM, R (1999), 'Means of Ensuring Compliance with and Enforcement of International Environmental Law', 272 *Recueil des Cours* 9.

YAMIN, F and DEPLEDGE, J (2004), *The International Climate Change Regime: A Guide to Rules, Institutions and Procedures* (Cambridge: Cambridge University Press), Ch 3.

YEATER, M and VASQUEZ, J (2001), 'Demystifying the Relationship between CITES and the WTO', 10:3 *RECIEL* 271.

YOSHIDA, O (2001), *The International Legal Regime for the Protection of the Stratospheric Ozone Layer* (The Hague: Kluwer).

FURTHER READING

BIRNIE, P, BOYLE, A, and REDGWELL, C (2009), *International Law and The Environment*, 3rd edn (Oxford: Oxford University Press). Of the general textbooks on international environmental law, this is the best and one of the most recent.

BODANSKY, D, BRUNNEE, J, and HEY, E (eds) (2007), *The Oxford Handbook of International Environmental Law* (Oxford: Oxford University Press). This edited volume follows the pattern of this work, with chapters submitted by the leading authorities in the international environmental field. An invaluable source to supplement the standard texts and specialized edited collections.

BOWMAN, M, DAVIES P, and REDGWELL, C (2010), *Lyster's International Wildlife Law*, 2nd edn (Cambridge: Cambridge University Press). This is the much-anticipated second edition of a highly readable account of the principal treaties concerned with wildlife protection.

BOYLE, A and ANDERSON, M (eds) (1996), *Human Rights Approaches to Environmental Protection* (Oxford: Clarendon Press). A splendid overview of the intersection of human rights and the environment.

—— and FREESTONE, D (eds) (1999), *International Law and Sustainable Development: Past Achievements and Future Challenges* (Oxford: Oxford University Press). A valuable resource not only for discussion of sustainable development but for contextual analysis drawing on many topical international environmental issues.

FITZMAURICE, M (2001), 'International Protection of the Environment', 293 *Recueil des Cours* 13. These Hague Academy lectures on international environmental law provide a helpful overview of the subject with case studies of the ozone layer protection and international watercourses.

FRANCIONI, F (ed) (2001), *Environment, Human Rights and International Trade* (Oxford: Hart Publishing). This contains a number of stimulating contributions not only on the general issue but also examining the compatibility of specific environmental treaties, in particular the Cartagena Protocol, with the WTO agreements.

HURRELL, A and KINGSBURY, B (eds) (1992), *International Politics of the Environment* (Oxford: Clarendon Press). This places environmental issues in their international relations context.

MORRISONC, FL and WOLFRUM, R (eds) (2000), *International, Regional and National Environmental Law* (The Hague: Kluwer). This edited volume includes chapters on the EC and North American cooperation, and in-depth analysis of German and USA law.

SANDS, P and PEEL, J (2012), *Principles of International Environmental Law*, 3rd edn (Cambridge: Cambridge University Press). Another very useful textbook with detailed treatment of principles and of specific treaty regimes.

The principal treaty texts are compiled with useful commentary and guidance for further reading in BIRNIE, P and BOYLE, A (1995), *Basic Documents on International Law and the Environment* (Oxford: Oxford University Press) and in GALIZZI, P, and SANDS, P (2004), *Documents in International Environmental Law* (Cambridge: Cambridge University Press).

Finally, the major cases on international environmental law may be found in ROBB, C (ed), *International Environmental Law Reports* (Cambridge: Cambridge University Press), four volumes to date addressed to early decisions, trade and environment, human rights and environment, and international environmental law in national courts.

WEBSITES

Those searching for access to the web pages of the key environmental treaties will find the UNEP (http://www.unep.org) and IMO (http://www.imo.org) sites useful gateways.

24

INTERNATIONAL INVESTMENT LAW

Surya P Subedi

SUMMARY

This chapter explores what international investment law is, how it has changed over time, and the state of the law today. In order to do so, it will present the evolution of the law of foreign investment, international efforts to regulate foreign investment, the main principles of the international law of foreign investment governing international economic relations among States, regulation under bilateral investment treaties, free trade agreements and regional trade and investment agreements, and the case law developed by various international courts and tribunals, including the International Court of Justice and the International Centre for the Settlement of Investment Disputes. The aim is to provide an understanding of current and evolving principles of the law of foreign investment, and the interplay between law and politics in regulating foreign investment.

I. INTRODUCTION: WHAT IS INTERNATIONAL INVESTMENT LAW?

International investment law governs relations between foreign investors, including private and State owned companies, and investor-receiving States (known as host States), as well as between investor States and investment receiving States. The law of foreign investment is one of the oldest and most complex areas of international law. Attempts have been made in the last 65 or so years (both within and outside of the UN) to codify and develop rules of international law in a number of areas. Consequently, there is now a sizeable body of treaty law dealing with different areas of international activity. However, there is as yet no single comprehensive treaty on the law of foreign investment. While there is a comprehensive treaty, the 1982 Convention on the Law of the Sea, governing the activities of States in the seas and oceans of the world, there are a number of core international treaties in the fields of human rights and environmental protection that constitute the core body of law in the subjects concerned. However, this is not the case in international investment law. Most of the law of foreign investment is still based on customary international law, which has evolved out of diplomatic exchanges, the jurisprudence of international courts and tribunals, bilateral investment treaties, and a host of 'soft law' instruments adopted under the auspices of the UN and its specialized agencies. (see generally Dolzer and Schreur, 2012; Subedi, 2012).

Attempts were made within the UN in the 1970s and 1980s to adopt a comprehensive code of conduct for trans-national corporations. However, when in the early 1990s political and economic events overtook these efforts, the efforts were abandoned. The Organisation for Economic Cooperation and Development (OECD) tried in the late 1990s to conclude a multilateral agreement on investment (MAI), but it too resulted in failure. The World Trade Organization (WTO) then decided to include foreign investment in its agenda for the Development Round of trade negotiations through the Doha Declaration of November 2001. In July 2004 the WTO decided to set aside the project. It was too complex an area also for the WTO, since there existed among the WTO members an unwieldy number of differences of opinion as to the nature, scope and desirability of the conclusion of an international treaty on such a matter under the auspices of the WTO.

However, the absence of a global comprehensive treaty on foreign investment does not mean that there is no identifiable or generally accepted body of law regulating foreign investment. To begin with, there is a set of generally accepted rules of international law providing protection to foreign investors. Next are thousands of bilateral investment treaties (BITs) or free trade agreements (FTAs) (which include substantial and substantive provisions dealing with investment) as well as regional trade and investment treaties that regulate foreign investment, provide protection for foreign investment and include a dispute resolution mechanism. Finally, there is a burgeoning body of case law of international courts and tribunals that have fleshed out the provisions in both customary international law and treaty law.

II. EVOLUTION OF INTERNATIONAL INVESTMENT LAW

Since time immemorial people have travelled abroad to invest and to engage in business. When European traders began to sail to Asia, Africa, and Latin America to trade with the people in local communities, it was held that the local law could not be applied to the traders since they were already subject to the law of their respective home countries. This argument was based on the assumption that the businessmen carried the law of the country of their nationality with them wherever they went and were thus not subject to the local law. Foreigners coming from European countries sought special and superior treatment from the local population in much of Asia, Africa and Latin America. The implication of this attitude was that their assets could not be expropriated or nationalized through legislation enacted by the local population. Since local law was 'inferior', it could not apply to the foreigners who were subject to the 'superior' body of law of their home countries.

Thus, in the early years of the development of the law of foreign investment it was understood that no State could expropriate or nationalize foreign assets. States could not invoke national laws as a reason for avoiding their international obligations arising from the notion of an international minimum standard. Only in the next phase of development when the number of independent States grew did it come to be accepted that States could expropriate the assets of foreigners under narrowly defined conditions and against the payment of compensation.

A. NATIONAL TREATMENT V THE INTERNATIONAL MINIMUM STANDARD

When colonial territories began to gain independence, they started to challenge the concept that foreigners residing and conducting business in those countries could not be governed by the local law. Relying on the doctrine of sovereignty and sovereign equality, they asserted that every sovereign State had the right to expropriate or nationalize foreign assets provided that the foreign investor was provided with compensation. The very notion of sovereignty meant that foreigners residing within the national borders of the country were subject to the law of the land. For instance, Article 9 of the Convention on the Rights and Duties of States (one of the first international instruments to support the idea of national treatment), signed at the Seventh Pan-American Conference, provided that:

> The jurisdiction of states within the limits of national territory applies to all the inhabitants. Nationals and foreigners are under the same protection of the law and the national authorities and the foreigners may not claim rights other or more extensive than those of the nationals.[1]

The Latin American countries were the first group of States to gain independence from their colonial rulers. After independence these States began to assert that foreign investors were not entitled to any greater protection than those accorded to the nationals of the country, under the law of the land. If the host States treated foreign investors on a par with the nationals of the country, the host States were acting within the norms of international law. Consequently, the right to expropriate the assets of foreign companies with compensation was accepted as an appropriate corollary to State sovereignty. However, it was submitted that if the local law were considered not well developed, or it failed to meet the standards of justice and equity, the international minimum standard rather than national law would apply to foreign investors. The assertion was that as international law provided for the international minimum standard, all States had to conform to the international minimum standard by bringing their national laws up to this standard. Consequently, the focus was on interpreting what constituted the international minimum standard (Oppenheim, 1992, pp 931–5).

One of the advocates of applying an international minimum standard to the question of the treatment of aliens (including foreign investors) was Elihu Root. He was a leading American international lawyer who in 1910 argued that there existed a standard of justice that formed a part of international law. Any national law dealing with the treatment of aliens had to conform to this general international standard:

> If any country's system of law does not conform to that standard, although the people of the country may be content or compelled to live under it, no other country can be compelled to accept it as furnishing a satisfactory measure of treatment to its citizens.[2]

A prominent British international lawyer, Schwarzenberger, added his voice in support of this argument:

> The national standard cannot be used as a means of evading international obligations under the minimum standard of international law. Even if the standard of national treatment is laid down in a treaty, the presumption is that it has been the intention of the parties to secure

---

[1] The Convention on the Rights and Duties of States (Montevideo Convention, 1933), 165 LNTS 19. For text see (1976) 70 *AJIL* 445.

[2] Root, 1910, pp 521–2.

to their nationals in this manner additional advantages, but not to deprive them of such rights as, in any case, they would be entitled to enjoy under international customary law or the general principles of law recognised by civilised nations.[3]

Scholarly views such as these have been supported by the decisions of international courts and tribunals. For instance, in the *Barcelona Traction* case, the International Court of Justice (ICJ) stated that:

> When a state admits into its territory foreign investments of foreign nationals, whether natural or juristic persons, it is bound to extend to them the protection of the law and assumes obligations concerning the treatment to be afforded them.[4]

When it was submitted that the international minimum standard rather than national law was applicable to foreign investment, an attempt was made to define the international minimum standard in the light of the general principles of justice and equity, the practice of States on the treatment of foreign investment, and the existing rules of both conventional and customary international law of human rights. In other words, human rights principles, including the right to property, were also invoked to define what constituted the international minimum standard. Under the evolving principles of international human rights law, every individual, both physical and juridical and whether national or alien, residing within any country, was entitled to their basic human rights (including property rights) as protected by law. Consequently, when it came to defining what constituted the minimum international standard, not only the law of foreign investment, but also the law of human rights (including the property rights of the individuals, whether national or alien) had to be taken into account (Borchard, 1940, p 445).

B. THE CALVO DOCTRINE

Those who were opposed to accepting the law of the investor countries in the name of the international minimum standard were of the view that no State should be required to offer greater protection to foreign investors than that accorded to its own nationals. There had to be equality of treatment. If the State in question were not discriminating against foreign investors, it was not violating any rules of customary international law. The argument was that to accord a higher standard of treatment to foreign investors would be difficult for some countries, such as those which are newly independent, have not attained the level of economic development required or have not acquired a developed legal system.

At the forefront of the argument in favour of national treatment of foreign investors and the right of States to expropriate the assets of foreign companies was a leading nineteenth-century Latin American jurist, Carlos Calvo of Argentina, who articulated the position dependent on the doctrine of economic sovereignty of States in the following terms:

> It is certain that aliens who establish themselves in a country have the same right to protection as nationals, but they ought not to lay claim to a protection more extended. If they suffer any wrong, they ought to count on the government of the country prosecuting the delinquents, and not claim from the state to which the authors of the violence belong any pecuniary indemnity.

---

[3] Schwarzenberger, 1957, p 248.
[4] *Barcelona Traction, Light and Power Company, Limited, Second Phase, Judgment, ICJ Reports 1970*, p 3, para 33.

The rule that in more than one case it has been attempted to impose on American states is that foreigners merit more regard and privileges more marked and extended than those accorded even to the nationals of the country where they reside. The principle is intrinsically contrary to the law of equality of nations.[5]

The central element of the Calvo doctrine was to require that aliens submit disputes arising in a country to that country's courts. As deduced by Verwey and Schrijver (1984, p 23), the Calvo doctrine basically stipulates that the principle of territorial sovereignty of the State entails the principle of absolute equality before the law between nationals and foreigners, the exclusive subjection of foreigners and their property to the laws and juridical regimes of the State in which they reside or invest, and strict abstention from interference by other governments, notably the governments of the States of which the foreigners are nationals, in disputes arising over the treatment of foreigners or their property (ie abstention from diplomatic protection). In simple terms, according to the Calvo doctrine land and other natural resources belong to the State by virtue of the doctrine of sovereignty and no foreign entity can permanently own land in the host States.[6]

C. THE HULL FORMULA

After the Communist Revolution in Russia in 1917 and the agrarian revolution in Mexico at around the same time, the governments of these countries proclaimed State ownership of land. The assets of foreign companies were expropriated and nationalized without proper compensation, through invoking the sovereignty of States. The actions of the Soviet and Mexican governments were opposed by the Western States, who held the view that although sovereign States had the right to expropriate the assets of foreign companies, they could do so only under certain narrowly defined conditions stipulated in international law and especially under prompt, adequate and effective compensation.

After years of negotiations a bi-national claims commission was established in 1927 between the USA and Mexico to consider the claims of those US foreign investors whose assets (mainly land) had been expropriated by Mexico. However, since not a single claim had been adjusted or paid by 1938, the USA in that year intensified its diplomatic efforts. The US Secretary of State, Cordell Hull, began a series of diplomatic exchanges with the Mexican government; the content of these diplomatic exchanges, in which Hull articulated the US views on compensation, came to be known as the 'Hull formula' in the international law of foreign investment. Outlining the US position on the issue of expropriation and the nature of compensation under international law, Secretary Cordell Hull stated that the taking of property without compensation was not expropriation: it was confiscation. He went on to state that:

> If it were permissible for a government to take the private property of the citizens of other countries and pay for it as and when, in the judgment of that government, its economic circumstances and local legislation may perhaps permit, the safeguards which the constitutions of most countries and established international law have sought to provide would be illusory. Governments would be free to take property far beyond their ability or willingness to pay, and the owners thereof would be without recourse. We cannot question the right of a foreign government to treat its own nationals in this fashion if it so desires. This is a matter of domestic concern. But we cannot admit that a foreign government may take the property

---

[5] Translated and quoted from Calvo's work which was written in Spanish by Shea, 1995, pp 17–19.
[6] See, generally, Lipstein, 1945; Freeman, 1946.

of American nationals in disregard for the rule of compensation under international law. Nor can we admit that any government unilaterally and through its municipal legislation can, as in this instant case, nullify this universally-accepted principle of international law, based as it is on reason, equity and justice.

However, the Mexican Foreign Minister disagreed with Hull's views on international law applicable to the subject-matter. He replied by stating that there was in international law:

> [N]o rule universally accepted in theory nor carried out in practice, which makes obligatory the payment of immediate compensation nor even of deferred compensation, for expropriations of a general and impersonal character like those which Mexico has carried out for the purpose of redistribution of the land.

Rejecting the arguments advanced by the Mexican Foreign Minister and his interpretation of the status of foreign investment in international law, Secretary Hull responded in the following terms:

> The Government of the United States merely adverts to a self-evident fact when it notes that the applicable precedents and recognised authorities on international law support its declaration that, under every rule of law and equity, no government is entitled to expropriate private property, for whatever purpose, without provision for prompt, adequate and effective payment thereof. In addition, clauses appearing in the constitutions of almost all nations today, and in particular in the constitutions of the American republics, embody the principle of just compensation. These, in themselves, are declaratory of the like principles in the law of nations.[7]

In his response the Mexican Foreign Minister rejected Secretary Hull's assertion and justified the Mexican expropriations as being a move designed to achieve social justice in the country. However, just before the Second World War spread to the Western hemisphere, Mexico and the USA reached an agreement to establish a commission to determine the compensation for the US nationals affected by the Mexican agrarian expropriations that took place after 30 August 1927. A deal designed to compensate the US investors was struck between the two countries.

III. THE EFFORTS TO REGULATE FOREIGN INVESTMENT BY THE UN

The attempt to regulate foreign investment immediately after the establishment of the UN was a fundamental struggle between the defenders of the old law and the proponents of the new. The area of conflict lay between the sanctity of the existing agreements and the attempt to rewrite the law by introducing certain new principles, such as the permanent sovereignty of States over their natural resources. With the establishment of the UN, a new world order, both economic and political, was envisaged for the world. While the UN was seen primarily as a political body, the World Bank and the International Monetary Fund were established as financial and monetary institutions respectively. Part of this grand vision for a new world order was the establishment of an international organization

---

[7] See the correspondence between the US and Mexican Foreign Secretaries in (1938) 32 *AJIL* supp 181–207.

dealing with international trade. Accordingly, a UN conference on Trade and Employment was held at Havana, Cuba, between 21 November 1947 and 24 March 1948.

The draft Havana Charter submitted to the Conference contained no provision on regulating foreign investment. One of the reasons for this deliberate omission seems to have been the fear on the part of the USA that investment provisions negotiated at a multilateral conference might express the lowest common denominator of protection to which any of the participants would be willing to agree. Nevertheless, when a chapter on economic development was added to the initial draft Charter proposed by the USA, a number of provisions making reference to foreign investment were included. In the end, the Charter itself never came into effect due, *inter alia*, to the US decision to abandon it in 1950. The States participating in the Havana Conference had decided, through Chapter VII of the Charter, to establish the International Trade Organization (ITO) whose functions could have included making recommendations for and promoting bilateral and multilateral agreements on measures designed 'to assure just and equitable treatment for the enterprise, skills, capital, arts and technology brought from one member country to another.'[8] However, the ITO itself never came into existence and the Charter remained merely a document of historical interest.

A. PERMANENT SOVEREIGNTY OF STATES OVER THEIR NATURAL RESOURCES

When the colonial territories of Asia, Africa and other parts of the world gained political independence their priority was to assert economic independence. Many newly independent States had inherited a situation under which the natural resources of the country were controlled or being exploited by foreign companies under concessions or other agreements concluded by the previous colonial administration. The people of the newly independent States had their hopes of a better standard of living; the political leaders had to strive hard to realize these hopes. When looking around for means of economic development, one of the first actions these States could take was to devise a policy to utilize the natural resources of the country for the benefit of the people. However, the newly independent States relied on the doctrine of economic sovereignty to claim permanent sovereignty of States over their natural resources, since such natural resources were being exploited by foreign companies under the existing concessions and other agreements. The idea was that once the permanent sovereignty of States over their natural resources (PSNR) was acknowledged, sovereign States would be able to negotiate their way out of the old agreements and concessions.

While the well-established principle expressed in the maxim *pacta sunt servanda* (ie treaties must be respected in good faith) of the law of treaties required States to respect the sanctity of the existing agreements, an equally (if not more) powerful doctrine of international law had to be deployed to allow States to take back the control over their natural resources into their own hands. To this end, the doctrine of PSNR was claimed, relying on one of the most powerful doctrines of international law—the sovereignty of States. It was an attempt not to rewrite the law completely, but to give a new direction to the law of foreign investment on the basis of certain rules of public international law, including economic sovereignty and the right to the self-determination of States. Indeed, without achieving economic sovereignty States would not be fully sovereign. Although these States could also invoke the right to expropriate the assets of foreign companies, this right is

---

[8] Havana Charter (1948), Article 11(2)(a).

limited in scope, is technical in character, and comes with a number of conditions: it would not have allowed States to achieve full economic sovereignty *vis-à-vis* their natural resources. Rather, the idea was to strengthen and expand, *inter alia*, the right not only to expropriate the assets of foreign investment, but also other rights of States flowing from the doctrine of sovereignty through the principle of PSNR.

It was against this background that the General Assembly adopted Resolution 1803 (XVII), on 14 December 1962, on the Permanent Sovereignty of States over their Natural Resources. The resolution provides, *inter alia*, that:

1. The right of peoples and nations to permanent sovereignty over their natural wealth and resources must be exercised in the interest of their national development and of the well-being of the people of the state concerned;

2. The exploration, development and disposition of such resources, as well as the import of the foreign capital required for these purposes, should be in conformity with the rules and conditions which the peoples and nations freely consider to be necessary or desirable with regard to the authorisation, restriction or prohibition of such activities;

3. In cases where authorisation is granted, the capital imported and the earnings on that capital shall be governed by the terms thereof, by the national legislation in force, and by international law. The profits derived must be shared in the proportions freely agreed upon, in each case, between the investors and the recipient state, due care being taken to ensure that there is no impairment, for any reason, of that state's sovereignty over its natural wealth and resources;

4. Nationalisation, expropriation or requisitioning shall be based on grounds or reasons of public utility, security, or the national interest which are recognised as overriding purely individual or private interests, both domestic and foreign. In such cases the owner shall be paid appropriate compensation, in accordance with the rules in force in the state taking such measures in the exercise of its sovereignty and in accordance with international law. In any case where the question of compensation gives rise to a controversy, the national jurisdiction of the state taking such measures shall be exhausted. However, upon agreement by sovereign states and other parties concerned, settlement of dispute should be made through arbitration or international adjudication.[9]

Thus, Resolution 1803 of the General Assembly sought to strike a balance between the interests of both the hosts' and the investors' home countries by incorporating into one single instrument the issues of vital concern for both of these groups of States. For instance, when outlining principles applicable to the nationalization or expropriation of foreign investment, the Resolution conforms neither to the Hull formula nor to the Calvo doctrine, yet contains elements of both. While it seeks to limit the conditions under which nationalization or expropriation can take place, it lists enough conditions to enable a country to embark upon nationalization and expropriation when necessary. It speaks of appropriate compensation rather than of prompt, adequate and effective compensation, and of remaining in accordance with international law. Although the principle of PSNR represented an attempt to develop certain new rules in favour of the developing countries on the basis of the extant and evolving rules of international economic law, it was accepted by the international community with little opposition from any quarter. Indeed, the UN

---

[9] GA Res 1803 (XVII) (14 December 1962). For the record of its adoption see UN Doc A/C.2/SR.835.

General Assembly Resolution to this effect has been regarded as a good compromise between the developed and developing countries, stating the law acceptable to both sides. This principle has in some decisions of international courts and tribunals been regarded as reflecting customary international law. Thus in the *Texaco* v *Libya* case, for example, the arbitrator held that Resolution 1803 reflected the state of customary international law existing in this field.[10]

B. THE CONCEPT OF A NEW INTERNATIONAL ECONOMIC ORDER

When the developing countries gained a numerical majority in the UN, they sought to use the UN system to introduce a much more fundamental reform of the law governing international economic relations among States. The developing countries introduced the agenda of a new international economic order (NIEO) within the UN as they were encouraged and influenced by the oil crisis of the early 1970s and disappointed at the lack of progress in addressing the issues of economic equality and prosperity for all. One of the items on the agenda was concerned with regulating foreign investment in a manner more favourable to developing countries (Hossain, 1980). Accordingly, the UN General Assembly adopted a Declaration on the Establishment of a New International Economic Order,[11] and a Programme of Action on the implementation of the Declaration.[12]

Article 4 of the Declaration listed the principles on which the NIEO had to be founded. One included in sub-Article (e) relates to the question of PSNR and the issue of expropriation and nationalization. It recognized the 'full permanent sovereignty of every State over its natural resources and all economic activities.' It went on to add that:

> In order to safeguard these resources, each state is entitled to exercise effective control over them and their exploitation with means suitable to its own situation, including the right to nationalisation or transfer of ownership to its nationals, this right being an expression of the full permanent sovereignty of the state. No state may be subjected to economic, political or any other type of coercion to prevent the free and full exercise of this inalienable right.

As part of the drive for an NIEO, and in order to restructure the legal order for the world economy, the General Assembly adopted the Charter of Economic Rights and Duties of States on 12 December 1974.[13] The Charter of Economic Rights and Duties of States is perhaps the most comprehensive international instrument outlining the economic rights and duties of States. However, it is not a 'hard law' instrument, since it was adopted by means of a General Assembly resolution and the powers of the General Assembly are limited by the UN Charter to the making of recommendations. Moreover, it was adopted by a vote of 120 in favour, with six against and ten abstentions (see Chatterjee, 1991). Thus, although it is an instrument of limited legal significance, it was seen as an instrument of far-reaching implications by a vast majority of States who voted in favour of the resolution of the General Assembly; it has since its adoption had a measure of influence on the development of international legal order. For instance, in the *Texaco* v *Libya* case

---

[10] *Texaco Overseas Petroleum Co* v *Libyan Arab Republic*, Arbitral Award (1977), 53 ILR 389, para 87. For similar views see *Kuwait* v *American Independent Oil Co ('Aminoil' case)* (1982), 66 ILR 518; 21 *ILM* 976, paras 143, 144.

[11] GA Res 3201(S-VI) (1 May 1974).   [12] GA Res 3202 (S-VI) (1 May 1974).

[13] GA Res 3281 (XXIX) (12 December 1974).

the arbitrator was not prepared to accept that this provision of CERD reflected customary international law.[14]

C. THE UN DRAFT CODE OF CONDUCT FOR TRANS-NATIONAL CORPORATIONS

The NIEO resolutions cited earlier in B The Concept of a New International Economic Order had called for the adoption of two codes of conduct: one on the transfer of technology and another on the regulation of trans-national corporations (TNCs). One of the achievements of the NIEO bandwagon was the establishment in 1974 of the UN Commission on Trans-national Corporations (CTC) by the Economic and Social Council to consider proposals for the regulation of multinational enterprises.[15] The activities of the CTC were linked to the efforts to realize the ideals of the NIEO. Much of the debate throughout the 1970s and 1980s focused on the content of a code of conduct for TNCs and whether it should be a voluntary or a mandatory code of conduct (see Horn, 1980). When the CTC in 1988 finally formulated a draft code of conduct for TNCs it became clear that there remained so many areas of major disagreement among States that the CTC itself seemed resigned to the possibility of adopting an internationally-agreed code. Consequently, through a letter of 31 May 1990 to the President of the ECOSOC,[16] the Chairman of the reconvened special session of the CTC forwarded the Draft Code of conduct.[17] In sum, nothing much came out of this endeavour as the world moved on in the aftermath of the events of 1989–90; then, the economic and political landscape of the world was transformed by the collapse of the Soviet Union, the demise of Communism in Europe, the fall of the Berlin Wall, and the consequent and subsequent disarray in Third World solidarity.

IV. THE INVOLVEMENT OF OTHER ACTORS

As seen in the preceding paragraphs, the failings of the UN to offer a final or definitive word on foreign investment law left the door open for other actors to enter the stage. Some of the international bodies that tried to become involved are the World Bank, the OECD, the WTO and the Human Rights Council.

A. THE ROLE OF THE WORLD BANK

The World Bank has had a long-standing interest in promoting foreign investment for economic development and has associated itself with a number of initiatives in this area. Among the initiatives are: the Convention for the Settlement of Investment Disputes of 1965; the Convention Establishing the Multilateral Investment Guarantee Agency of 1985, and the 1992 Guidelines on the Treatment of Foreign Direct Investment (see Shihata, 1991).

1. The International Convention on the Settlement of Investment Disputes

Foreign investors wish to have legal certainty when making investment decisions. One of those certainties is to have a credible mechanism for the settlement of investment

---

[14] *Texaco Overseas Petroleum Co v Libyan Arab Republic*, Arbitral Award (1977), 53 ILR 389, para 88.
[15] ECOSOC Resolutions 1908 (LVII) (2 August 1974) and 1913 (LVII) (5 December 1974).
[16] UN Doc E/1990/94 (12 June 1990).   [17] UN Doc E/1988/39/Add1.

disputes. The perceived wisdom is that if foreign private investors are assured that, in the event of a dispute between them and the State in question, the dispute can be referred to an independent international tribunal, they would be encouraged to invest in that State. Foreign investors would generally be unwilling to invest in countries where the judiciary is not fully independent and the political situation is unstable. However, such investors would be encouraged to invest in such States if the State in question has agreed through an international agreement to settle any investment dispute with potential foreign investors. Accordingly, the International Convention on the Settlement of Investment Disputes between States and nationals of other States (ICSID) was concluded in 1965 (see Schreuer, 2001). Its aim was of establishing an international centre for the settlement of investment disputes and encouraging States to refer investment disputes with foreign private investors to an international arbitration tribunal. Under this Convention, the Bank is the host of the International Centre for the Settlement of Investment Disputes, which is similar in many respects to other international arbitration centres in existence. Under Article 25(1) the jurisdiction of the Centre is as follows:

> The jurisdiction of the centre shall extend to any legal dispute arising directly out of an investment, between a contracting state (or any constituent subdivision or agency of a contracting state designated to the centre by that state) and a national of another contracting state, which the parties to the dispute consent in writing to submit to the centre. When the parties have given their consent, no party may withdraw its consent unilaterally.

The provision in Article 42(1) is perhaps one of the most important ones because it stipulates the law applicable to a dispute submitted to the arbitration tribunal of the ICSID Centre:

> The Tribunal shall decide a dispute in accordance with such rules of law as may be agreed by the parties. In the absence of such agreement, the Tribunal shall apply the law of the contracting state party to the dispute (including its rules on the conflict of laws) and such rules of international law as may be applicable.

The adoption of the ICSID signalled that other positive developments relating to the law of foreign investment could also take place outside of the UN framework and away from politics.

2. The Multilateral Investment Guarantee Agency

In addition to legal certainty, potential foreign investors need some sort of guaranteed protection of their investment when they invest in developing countries. Many individual developed countries have their own respective internal systems of investment guarantee for those investing in developing countries and investment risks could also be covered through private insurance, yet it was thought desirable to have an international system of investment guarantee against non-commercial risks, such as expropriation, nationalization and other political risks.

This would be in order to promote foreign investment in general and private foreign investment in particular. Of course, protection was available to foreign investors under bilateral investment treaties, international law principles relating to the treatment of foreign investment, and diplomatic channels; however, it was considered desirable to have an additional mechanism designed to alleviate concerns related to non-commercial risks. This would promote the flow of foreign investment to developing countries. Therefore, as a measure complementary to already existing national and regional investment guarantee programmes and to private insurers of non-commercial risks, as well as supplementary to the activities of the World Bank Group, the Convention Establishing the Multilateral Investment Guarantee Agency (MIGA) was in 1985 adopted.

3. The 1992 Guidelines on the Treatment of Foreign Direct Investment

As stated earlier, the promotion of foreign investment has long been an area of interest for the World Bank. It was joined by the MIGA, whose constituent document states that it is supposed to carry out research, undertake activities to promote investment flows, and disseminate information on investment opportunities in developing member countries. Accordingly, the Development Committee, a joint committee of the World Bank and the International Monetary Fund (IMF) in 1991 requested the MIGA to prepare a 'legal framework' to promote foreign direct investment. In 1992, the Development Committee adopted a set of Guidelines on the Treatment of Foreign Direct Investment.[18] It should be noted here that neither the Bank nor the IMF nor the MIGA has the competence to adopt any legally binding instrument for the international community, nor to modify the existing rules of international law on the subject-matter. Strictly speaking, these organizations lack the capacity even to adopt 'soft law' instruments for the international community. Nevertheless, the document adopted as a result of the work carried out under the auspices of these three important financial organizations does carry certain weight and thus merits examination.

B. THE OECD GUIDELINES AND THE MULTILATERAL AGREEMENT ON INVESTMENT

The 1976 Declaration of the OECD on International Investment and Multinational Enterprises includes Guidelines for Multilateral Enterprises. As a next step in consolidating the rules governing foreign investment protection, the OECD in 1998 sought once again to conclude a multilateral agreement on investment (MAI).[19] However, the OECD attempt was abandoned when the draft MAI came under criticism from some member States and civil society for not being a balanced document that would protect the interests of both foreign investors and investor-receiving countries. After failing in its attempt to adopt a legally binding MAI, the OECD in 2000 adopted a set of revised guidelines for multinational enterprises (MNEs).[20] The OECD issued new updated Guidelines in 2011. They provide non-binding principles and standards for responsible business conduct in a global context consistent with applicable laws and internationally recognized standards. The updated Guidelines and the related Decision were adopted by the 43 adhering governments on 25 May 2011 at the OECD's 50th Anniversary Ministerial Meeting. The updated Guidelines include:

— a new human rights chapter which is consistent with the Guiding Principles on Business and Human Rights: Implementing the United Nations 'Protect, Respect and Remedy' Framework;

— a new and comprehensive approach to due diligence and responsible supply chain management representing significant progress relative to earlier approaches;

---

[18] *Legal Framework for the Treatment of Foreign Investment, Volume II: Guidelines* available at http://www-wds.worldbank.org/servlet/WDSContentServer/WDSP/IB/1999/11/10/000094946_99090805303082/Rendered/PDF/multi_page.pdf.

[19] OECD DAFEE/MAI (98)7/REV1 (22 April 1998, footnotes omitted).

[20] 40 *ILM* 237 (2000).

— important changes in many specialised chapters, such as on Employment and Industrial Relations; Combating Bribery, Bribe Solicitation and Extortion, Environment, Consumer Interests, Disclosure and Taxation;

— clearer and reinforced procedural guidance to strengthen the role of the National Contact Points (NCPs) improve their performance and foster functional equivalence; and

— a proactive implementation agenda to assist enterprises in meeting their responsibilities as new challenges arise.[21]

This was an attempt to reconcile investment protection with other competing principles of international law, including environmental protection. This was also one of the first major attempts to give some practical meaning to the UN 'Guiding Principles on Business and Human Rights: Implementing the UN "Protect, Respect and Remedy" Framework' developed by the UN Special Representative on business and human rights, Professor John Ruggie, to be discussed later in section D.

C. THE WTO AND FOREIGN INVESTMENT

After the failures of the OECD and the CTC of the UN to formulate a balanced and comprehensive set of standards on foreign investment, efforts were made by the EU at the Doha Ministerial Conference. Although efforts had been made during various GATT Rounds of Trade Negotiations to include investment onto the international trade agenda and the WTO itself had since 1997 been engaged in analysis and debate about the relationship between international trade and investment, it was only at the Doha conference that the WTO committed itself to including investment as part of its main agenda.[22] However, when the State members of the WTO met in July 2004 to agree on the work programme for the Doha Development Round, they too decided to set aside the idea of negotiating an international agreement on foreign investment under the auspices of the WTO. A decision taken by the General Council of the WTO on 31 July 2004, known as the 'July Package', stated that a number of issues, including the relationship between trade and investment, would not form part of the Work Programme of the Doha Development Round.[23]

Thus, the idea of adopting an international treaty regulating foreign investment was, once again, effectively removed from the scope of action of an inter-governmental body for the time being. Having said this, the 1994 TRIMS Agreement of the WTO does deal with certain aspects of foreign investment. It prohibits governments from requiring foreign investors to purchase inputs locally or to sell their output domestically rather than exporting it.[24]

D. THE UN HUMAN RIGHTS COUNCIL

Although the UN itself is not at present actively engaged in efforts to regulate foreign investment as such, some of its agencies, such as the UN Human Rights Council, are looking

---

[21] *Guidelines for Multinational Enterprises: 2011 edn:* available at http://dx.doi.org/10.178 7/9789264115415-en.

[22] WT/MIN(01)/DEC/W/1 (14 November 2001).

[23] WT/GC/W/535 (1) (31 July 2004).

[24] See World Trade Organization, 1999, pp 143–6 at 146.

at the interaction between business and human rights. The UN Special Representative on the Issues of Human Rights and Trans-national Corporations and Other Business Enterprises, appointed by the Secretary-General, submitted a series of reports on business and human rights. In March 2011, he submitted his final report to the UN Human Rights Council, appending a document entitled, 'Guiding Principles on Business and Human Rights: Implementing the United Nations "Protect, Respect and Remedy" Framework'[25] containing a set of 31 standards to support the implementation of the UN 'Protect, Respect and Remedy' policy framework and in June 2011 the UN Human Rights Council unanimously endorsed the Guiding Principles.[26]

The UN Special Representative identified three core principles: 'the state duty to protect against human rights abuses by third parties, including business; the corporate responsibility to respect human rights; and the need for more effective access to remedies.' He argued that the State had a duty to protect because it lies at the very core of the international human rights regime and the corporate responsibility entailed respecting human rights by companies because it is the basic expectation society has of business. Although this UN document is not legally binding, its endorsement by the Human Rights Council has established the Guiding Principles as the authoritative global reference point for business and human rights. When it endorsed the Guiding Principles, the Human Rights Council also established a Working Group composed of five independent experts on business and human rights to promote the implementation of the Guiding Principles, as well as an annual forum on business and human rights under the guidance of the Working Group.

V. GENERAL PRINCIPLES OF THE INTERNATIONAL LAW OF FOREIGN INVESTMENT

A. CUSTOMARY INTERNATIONAL LAW

On the basis of the foregoing account of the evolution of international law, it can be submitted that certain aspects of the law on regulating foreign investment are settled in international law. In addition to the Calvo doctrine and the Hull formula governing expropriation, there are a number of other principles deeply rooted in international law and practice that govern the relations among nations concerning foreign investment. Accordingly, among the settled rules of customary international law on foreign investment the following are the major principles:

1. Host States are entitled to expropriate or nationalize the assets of foreign companies, but expropriation or nationalization can take place only if the following four main conditions are met: (a) it must be for a public purpose; (b) it must be non-discriminatory; (c) it must be against fair and equitable compensation, and (d) it must be in accordance with the law.

2. The compensation must be equivalent to the fair market value of the investment expropriated, immediately before the expropriation or before the impending expropriation became public knowledge, whichever is the earlier, shall include interest

---

[25] UN Doc A/HRC/17/13 (21 March 2011).   [26] UN Doc A/HRC 17/14 (6 June 2011).

at a commercially reasonable rate until the date of payment, shall be made without unreasonable delay, be effectively realizable, and be freely transferable.

3. The affected investor has the right, in conformity with the laws of the host State that makes the expropriation, to the prompt review, by a judicial or other independent authority of that State, of its case, in order to decide if the expropriation and assessment of its investment have been adopted pursuant to the principles of international law.

4. Foreign investors and their investment enjoy the protection of the principle of non-discrimination;

5. They should be accorded the most-favoured-nation treatment (MFN);

6. Once admitted into the country foreign investors are entitled to national treatment; and

7. Foreign investors enjoy the protection accorded under the principle of fair and equitable treatment.

8. Non-discriminatory regulatory measures by a host that are designed and applied to protect legitimate public welfare objectives including the protection of health, safety and environment do not constitute expropriation or nationalization; except in rare circumstances, where those measures are so severe that they cannot be reasonably viewed as having been adopted and applied in good faith for achieving their objectives.

9. Actions and awards by judicial bodies of a host State that are designed, applied or issued in public interest including those designed to address health, safety and environmental concerns, do not constitute expropriation or nationalization.

10. Multinational companies have a duty to respect human rights in the countries where they do their business.

Ensuring non-discrimination in the conduct of international business is the underlying idea behind these principles. They are employed in international practice to secure a certain level of treatment for foreign investment in host countries. The purpose of the MFN principle is to grant foreign investors treatment comparable to the foreign investors from third countries operating in the host country, but the object of the national treatment principle is to grant treatment comparable to domestic investors operating in the host country itself. The principle of fair and equitable treatment brings in the elements of fairness and equity drawn from international law, especially the principle of international minimum standard, and practice as well as municipal law principles in the overall treatment of foreign investment in a host country. The problem with this principle is that it is difficult to define in concrete terms and is open to different interpretations. The precise meaning of the phrase 'fair and equitable treatment' has been the subject of interest and often controversy both in literature and in the case law dealing with the treatment of foreign investment.

B. THE BILATERAL INVESTMENT TREATIES

States have traditionally welcomed foreign investment for a variety of reasons. Foreign investment has been regarded as an engine of economic growth, a source of foreign currency income, a stimulator of the local economy, and a source of foreign skills, information and know-how, among other features. Foreign investment takes place in different forms, including, through committing capital resources abroad either directly or through portfolio investment, by licensing the use of technology, and managerial know-how.

Because of the form such investment takes, it requires special protection under the law of the country concerned. This is because foreigners who purchase land and other immovable property or enter into joint ventures to create a new company cannot leave the host country as and when they want. Their commitment to the host country is long-term, hence the need for long-term protection under special laws. Traditionally, such protection has been sought under international law and lately under bilateral investment treaties (BITs).

1. The Origins of Bilateral Investment Treaties

Unlike local laws on foreign investment, which can also offer adequate protection and incentives to foreign investors but are liable to change with a change of government, no State can unilaterally change international law or the provisions of BITs. Such treaties are of long duration, usually ten years, with a provision for automatic renewal unless and until the contracting parties agree otherwise. The formal safeguards and guarantees that BITs provide on non-commercial risks have acted as an incentive to potential investors and as a useful reassurance to those with existing investments in the signatory States. Therefore, when it comes to promoting foreign investment, States have sought additional safeguards and guarantees under international law; BITs are designed to set standards of protection. Any protection provided for foreign investment is always under the law of the host country; however, this law has to conform to the commitments undertaken by the State concerned either under BITs, FTAs or other principles of international law, or under all.

A bilateral investment treaty is a relatively recent phenomenon, a German development perfected over the years by the USA and the UK. Initially, BITs were seen as a challenge to international efforts by developing countries in order for them to regulate foreign investment through an international instrument adopted under the auspices of the UN. The Federal Republic of Germany was the first country to conclude BITs with certain developing countries in order to protect German investment in these countries. Outlining the utility of a BIT, a Presidential communication to Congress stated the main US objectives in the conclusion this BIT in the following words:

Investment of nationals and companies of one Party in the territory of the other Party (investments) receive the better of the treatment accorded to domestic investments in like circumstances (national treatment), or the treatment accorded to third country investments in like circumstances (most-favoured-nation (MFN) treatment), both on establishment and thereafter, subject to certain specified exceptions;

— Investments are guaranteed freedom from performance requirements, such as obligations to use local products or export goods;

— Companies which are investments may hire top managers of their choice, regardless of nationality;

— Expropriation can occur only in accordance with international law standards: in a non-discriminatory manner; for a public purpose; and upon payment of prompt, adequate, and effective compensation;

— Investment-related funds are guaranteed unrestricted transfer in a freely usable currency; and

— Nationals and companies of either Party, and their investments, have access to binding international arbitration in investment disputes with the host government, without first resorting to domestic courts.[27]

---

[27] US Treaty Doc 103-2, Focus – 32 of 48 Documents, 1991 UST LEXIS 176.

These are the main reasons why States conclude BITs with other countries and especially those in which their nationals have made foreign direct investment or are likely to invest. The BITs offer an added layer of protection to the regime of protection already in existence by virtue of customary international law or other treaties existing between the countries concerned.

2. The Content of Bilateral Investment Treaties

Most BITs follow a standard format whereby they provide a definition of investment and investors; the standards of protection of investment, which includes protection against expropriation (both direct and indirect expropriations), and nationalization; compensation in the event of expropriation; the principles of non-discrimination; most-favoured nation treatment; national treatment; fair and equitable treatment, and an international dispute resolution mechanism. More recent BITs have also started to include provisions for regulatory expropriation primarily in favour of environmental protection.

The host States have, by and large, accepted the Hull formula and agreed to the provisions favoured by the home or investor countries when it came to negotiating bilateral investment treaties, regardless of the negotiating position taken by various States on international platforms. While the debate was taking place within the UN about the codification and progressive development of the law of foreign investment, the business of regulating foreign investment through bilateral investment treaties gathered pace outside of the UN. Those developed countries who wanted to protect investment by their nationals in foreign countries also wanted to conclude BITs of *sui generis* or *lex specialis* character rather than wait for international legislation under the auspices of the UN. Most of these treaties incorporated provisions more akin to the traditional position taken by the developed countries such as the Hull formula. When new regional trading blocs such as NAFTA were created to promote the free flow of capital, goods and services among the countries of the region they, too, followed the pattern of bilateral investment treaties.

The practice of conforming to the Hull formula and offering as many incentives as possible to foreign investors through a BIT was confined to the treaties concluded not only between one developed country and another, but also between the developed and developing countries. Therefore, the law on foreign investment has been understood in many quarters to be the law as incorporated in the modern bilateral and regional investment treaties. When the international efforts to conclude an internationally acceptable treaty or a mandatory code of conduct within the UN remained unsuccessful, increasing numbers of States (including those leading developing countries which had championed the international regulation of foreign investment) also started concluding bilateral investment treaties along the pattern favoured by the developed countries. This is one reason why greater weight has been accorded to the content of such treaties in determining what the law is on foreign investment.

When the developing countries themselves started competing with each other for foreign direct investment that was flowing from developed countries into developing countries, they were in competition to offer greater incentives to foreign investors. Thus, they agreed to provisions designed to strengthen the position of foreign investors. The term 'investment' itself was defined as broadly as possible so as to accord protection to all conceivable forms of investment under the treaties, including asset-based investments (eg portfolio investment). Of course, there are some BITs that exclude portfolio investment from the definition of the term 'investment', but the general trend seems to be to include it. For instance, a bilateral investment treaty concluded between Jordan and the USA in July 1997 defines the term 'investment' as comprehensively as possible in Article I (d) in the following terms:

> '[I]nvestment' of a national or company means every kind of investment owned or controlled directly or indirectly by that national or company, and includes investment consisting or taking the form of:
>
> (a) a company;
>
> (b) shares, stock, and other forms of equity participation, and bonds, debentures, and other forms of debt interests, in a company;
>
> (c) contractual rights, such as under turnkey, construction or management contracts, production of revenue-sharing contracts, concessions, or other similar contracts;
>
> (d) tangible property, including real property; and intangible property, including rights, such as leases, mortgages, liens, and pledges;
>
> (e) intellectual property rights, including copyrights and related rights, industrial property rights, patents, rights in plant varieties, utility models, industrial designs or models, rights in semiconductor layout design, indications of origin, trade secrets, including know-how, confidential business information, trade and service marks, and trade names; and rights conferred pursuant to law, such as licenses and permits.

With regard to the treatment and protection of investment, the Jordan–USA treaty is illustrative of the practice of States. The provisions included in Article II of the treaty are typical of the trend of the 1990s:

> Treatment and protection of investment
>
> With respect to the establishment, acquisition, expansion, management, conduct, operation and sale or other disposition of covered investments, each contracting party shall accord treatment no less favourable than that it accords, in like situations, to investments in its territory of its own nationals or companies (hereinafter 'national treatment') or investments in its territory or nationals or companies of a third country (hereinafter 'most favoured nation treatment'), whichever is most favourable (hereinafter 'national and most favoured nation treatment'). Each contracting party shall ensure that its state enterprises, in the provision of their goods or services, accord national and most favoured nation treatment to covered investments...

The Jordan–USA BIT goes on to state that each contracting party 'shall at all times accord to covered investments fair and equitable treatment and full protection and security, and shall in no case accord treatment less favourable than that required by international law.' With regard to expropriation and nationalization the BIT provides the following protection:

1. Neither contracting party shall expropriate or nationalize a covered investment either directly or indirectly through measures tantamount to expropriation or nationalisation ('expropriation') except for a public purpose; in a non-discriminatory manner; upon payment of prompt, adequate and effective compensation; and in accordance with due process of law and the general principles of treatment provided for in Article II(3).

2. Compensation shall be paid without delay; be equivalent to the fair market value of the expropriated investment immediately before the expropriatory action was taken ('the date of expropriation'); and be fully realisable and freely transferable. The fair market

value shall not reflect any change in value occurring because the expropriatory action had become known before the date of expropriation.[28]

However, a bilateral investment treaty concluded in 1994 between India and the UK varies slightly from other BITs. The Indo–UK Treaty does not fully subscribe to the Hull formula in respect of every type of expropriation or nationalization. Rather, it speaks of 'fair and equitable compensation' as opposed to 'prompt, adequate and effective' compensation with regard to most forms of foreign investment and 'prompt, adequate and effective' compensation only with regard to compensation for foreign shareholders in an expropriated company. The provision concerning the nationalization and expropriation of foreign investment admits the possibility of expropriation and nationalization not simply for 'a public purpose', but for 'a public purpose related to the internal requirements for regulating economic activity'.[29]

3. Dispute Resolution

One of the main reasons why foreign investors wish to see the conclusion of a BIT is for a separate or distinct international dispute resolution mechanism for disputes arising out of the interpretation or application of the provisions of the treaty. A demand of this nature springs from a vote on the part of foreign investors of no confidence in the ability of the national judiciary to provide impartial, speedy and effective justice in the event of a dispute between a host State and a foreign investor. Indeed, the judiciary in many developing countries, especially those not fully democratic or lacking a long tradition of democracy, is not always as independent as it should be, and may be full of political cronyism, corruption, and inefficiencies.

Foreign investors who invest in such countries with weaker reputations, especially those who make longer-term investments and commit sizeable capital to such countries, seek an assurance against political risks; one of the means of providing that assurance is through a promise to remove a dispute with the host government out of the jurisdiction of that country, thus to an international court or tribunal that is generally independent and impartial and can provide effective, speedy and efficient justice. Against this background most BITs provide for an international dispute settlement mechanism. There are two kinds of disputes that can arise in relation to BITs: first, between a foreign investor and investor-receiving country also known as a host country and, second, between the contracting parties themselves. With regard to the former kinds of disputes most BITs include a provision for settlement of such disputes by international investment tribunals. For instance, one of the recent BITs concluded by India and Nepal in 2011 provides the following mechanism:

Article 9: Settlement of Disputes between an Investor and a Contracting Party

(1) Any dispute between an investor of one Contracting Party and the other Contracting Party in relation to an investment of the former under this Agreement shall, as far as possible, be settled amicably through negotiations between the parties to the dispute.

(2) Any such dispute which has not been amicably settled within a period of six months may, if both parties agree, be submitted:

   (i) for resolution, in accordance with the law of the Contracting Party which has admitted the investment to that Contracting Party's competent judicial, arbitral or administrative bodies; or

---

[28] 36 *ILM* 1498 (1997).   [29] 34 *ILM* 935 (1995).

(ii) to international conciliation under the Conciliation Rules of the United Nations
Commission on International Trade Law.

(3) Should the parties fail to agree on a dispute settlement procedure provided under
paragraph (2) of this Article or where a dispute is referred to conciliation but conciliation proceedings are terminated other than by signing of a settlement agreement, the dispute may be referred to Arbitration.[30]

This is an elaborate and flexible mechanism with a number of options for the settlement of
disputes between, on the one hand, an Indian investor and the Government of Nepal and,
on the other, a Nepalese investor and the Indian Government. The emphasis is very much
on a negotiated settlement of disputes. Only when negotiations fail to produce a mutually
satisfactory outcome will the other options, including referring the matter to an international arbitration, arise. Only when the options of negotiation and conciliation fail to produce a mutually satisfactory outcome and both of the disputing parties have failed to agree
to refer the matter to national judicial, arbitral or administrative bodies of either country
can a dispute be referred to an international arbitration. Even then it is not mandatory to
refer the matter to permanent arbitration mechanisms such as ICSID. The matter can be
referred to any permanent or *ad hoc* arbitration operating under the rules of UNCITRAL.

4. Free Trade Agreements

The newest generation of trade and investment treaties concluded by the USA with other
States are the so-called 'free trade agreements'. These are some of the most ambitious and
comprehensive bilateral treaties ever concluded in the history of international economic
relations. For instance, the massive 800-page treaty concluded with Chile in June 2003 and
the even longer 1,400-page treaty with Singapore in May 2003 contain detailed provisions
on foreign investment, spelling out many of the key terms and phrases whose definition
has dogged the debate on the law of foreign investment for so long.[31]

5. The Significance of Bilateral Investment Treaties

In the view of many international tribunals and publicists, the law on foreign investment
at this juncture seems to be the law supported, albeit not created, by the provisions of the
BITs and regional treaties such as NAFTA. Indeed, although the individual BITs could
be regarded as *lex specialis*, it is difficult to deny that the practice of States in concluding such treaties is capable of strengthening the rules of customary international law on
the subject-matter. These treaties have been regarded by international tribunals in various
cases as a source of law.

The BITs concluded since the introduction of ICSID in the mid-1960s made investor-to-
State dispute resolution possible for the first time. Under a typical BIT, an investor is entitled to take a host State to a binding, third-party arbitration, typically under the rules
of the ICSID, to settle any disputes involving the interpretation of the application of the
BIT. Should the host State refuse to participate, the BIT made provision for an appointing authority to appoint arbitrators on behalf of the host State to enable the arbitration to
proceed even without the cooperation of the host State. This constituted an innovation in
the history of dispute settlement at the international level.

Thus, the BITs allow the home or investor countries to extricate themselves from involvement in private investment disputes without diminishing the effectiveness of the remedies

---

[30] See, for text of the Agreement: http://www.unctadxi.org/templates/DocSearch.aspx?id=779.
[31] For text see http://www.ustr.gov/new/fta/chile.htm.

available to investors. This is because prior to the BIT era, investors from a country had to look to the government of their own country for assistance when their investment was expropriated or unlawfully impaired by a foreign government. Diplomatic protection was the only avenue open to such investors since there were no binding, third-party dispute settlement mechanisms available for foreign investors and host Sates could invoke sovereign immunity and the act of State doctrine before any municipal courts. The dispute acquires a political character when the State machinery decides to espouse a claim and pursue a remedy on behalf of its private investors through diplomatic channels or international arbitration or to impose economic sanctions on the alleged wrongdoer.

There is no need for government intervention and the politicization of investment disputes when an effective dispute settlement mechanism such as the ICSID is available to private foreign investors. Thus, one of the major positive contributions made by the BITs is the 'depoliticization' of investment disputes.

C. REGIONAL INVESTMENT TREATIES

In the absence of a global treaty on foreign investment, both BITs and regional treaties have sought to fill the vacuum and lead the way. This is especially the case with the North American Free Trade Agreement (NAFTA). At the time of its adoption, the provisions of this regional treaty provided far more protection to foreign investors than accorded hitherto in customary international law. The NAFTA set the trend for much greater protection of foreign investment throughout the 1990s, whether it be through the BITs, the TRIMS agreement of the WTO or other regional treaties.

The Energy Charter Treaty of 1994 includes equally greater protection for foreign investment than that accorded under customary international law. In the absence of a global treaty, bilateral investment treaties have been the main instruments regulating foreign investment. They have been used successfully by investor countries constantly to expand the level of protection accorded to foreign investors by host States. There is some evidence to suggest that BITs have increased foreign investment; they certainly have instilled a sense of security in foreign investors. These treaties have provided the assurance to foreign investors that should something go wrong within the host States due to governmental interference then they have an international legal remedy. BITs have made a significant contribution to the development of the international law of foreign investment.

D. THE CASE LAW ON THE TREATMENT OF FOREIGN INVESTMENT

The jurisprudence developed by international courts and tribunals with regard to the standard of treatment of foreign investors, with particular focus on issues concerning expropriation in its various forms, have played a crucial role in the development of the law of foreign investment. Some of the standard-setting decisions of the International Court of Justice, the Iran–USA Claims Tribunals and other *ad hoc* tribunals, such as those established under the ICSID, have had far-reaching implications for the development of international investment law. This is because, in the absence of a global comprehensive treaty on the regulation of foreign investment, the decisions of international courts and tribunals have 'fleshed out' the customary international law principles of the law of foreign investment on, *inter alia*, the definition of expropriation and nationalization, and the determination of the quantum of compensation. In doing so, they have extended the frontiers of the law especially in relation to expropriation and compensation.

Where the main principles pertaining to the area are not fully settled and the State practice and the efforts made within and outside of the UN point in conflicting directions, the decisions of international courts and tribunals on these matters have been relied upon to deduce the rules applicable not only to expropriation and compensation, but also to the meaning of the terms 'fair and equitable treatment', the 'due process of law', and 'full protection and security'.

Traditionally, international courts, claims commissions and tribunals have relied upon the international law of State responsibility regarding the treatment of aliens to provide legal remedy to foreign investors when their investments were expropriated or unlawfully impaired by a foreign government. For instance, supporting the idea behind diplomatic protection, the Permanent Court of International Justice held in the *Mavrommatis Palestine Concessions case* that:

> It is an elementary principle of international law that a state is entitled to protect its subjects, when injured by acts contrary to international law committed by another state, from whom they have been unable to obtain satisfaction through the ordinary channels.[32]

Cases such as the *Neer* claim *(US v Mexico)* support the notion that international law required States to treat aliens according to an international minimum standard. Indeed, the *Neer* claim decided by the Mexico–US General Claims Commission in 1926 has been relied upon to support the doctrine of an international minimum standard of treatment of foreign investors in international law.[33] The classic and often cited case pronouncing the standard of treatment to be accorded to foreign investors is the *Chorzów Factory* case, in which the Permanent Court of International Justice relied on the doctrine of State responsibility to provide legal remedy to Germany. After finding that Poland had violated the Geneva Convention of 1922 between Germany and Poland on Upper Silesia, the Court held that 'it is a principle of international law, and even a general conception of law, that any breach of an engagement involves an obligation to make reparation.' The Court held that:

> The essential principle contained in the actual notion of an illegal act—a principle which seems to be established by international practice and in particular by decisions of arbitral tribunals—is that reparation must, as far as possible, wipe out all the consequences of the illegal act and re-establish the situation which would, in all probability, have existed if that act had not been committed.[34]

The opinion of the court in this case has been relied upon heavily by international courts and tribunals established in later years, among which the Iran–USA Claims Tribunal is a prominent example. There is a great deal of literature on defining what constitutes a 'taking of property', commonly known as expropriation or nationalization. The meaning of these terms has also been the preoccupation of international courts and tribunals on a number of cases referred to them. Some of the more recent cases seek to cover not only direct, express or outright cases of the compulsory taking of foreign property, but also indirect 'constructive taking' or 'creeping expropriation' such as that considered by the ICJ in the *ELSI* case.[35]

Many of the decisions of international tribunals, especially those of the Iran–USA Claims Tribunal, have followed the definition of taking of property in various decisions

---

[32] *Mavrommatis Palestine Concessions, Judgment No 2, 1924, PCIJ, Ser A, No 2, p 12.*
[33] *Neer* claim *(US v Mexico)* (1926), 4 *RIAA* 60.
[34] *Factory at Chorzów, Merits, Judgment No 13, 1928, PCIJ, Ser A, No 17, at p 29.*
[35] *Elettronica Sicula SpA (ELSI), Judgment, ICJ Reports 1989, p 15, para 119.*

of the PCIJ and the ICJ. For instance, in the *Starrett Housing Corporation* v *Iran (interlocutory order)* the Tribunal held that since the Starrett company, an American company, had been deprived of the effective use, control and benefits of their property rights by the Government of Iran in the aftermath of the Islamic Revolution, this amounted to 'creeping' or 'constructive' expropriation:

> It is recognised in international law that measures taken by a state can interfere with property rights to such an extent that these rights are rendered so useless that they must be deemed to have been expropriated, even though the state does not purport to have expropriated them and the legal title to the property formally remains with the original owner.[36]

In the *Amoco International Finance Corporation* v *Iran* case, the issue involved was the nationalization of the Iranian oil industry under the Single Article Act in the aftermath of the Islamic Revolution during which *Khemco*, an Iranian company jointly owned and managed by Amoco, was also nationalized. In delivering its award the Tribunal held that:

> Expropriation, which can be defined as a compulsory transfer of property rights, may extend to any right which can be the object of a commercial transaction i.e. freely sold and bought, and thus has a monetary value. It is because Amoco's interests under the Khemco Agreement have such an economic value that the nullification of those interests by the Single Article Act can be considered as a nationalisation.[37]

Thus, the lawful taking of foreign property is expropriation which would attract compensation, but illegal expropriation or confiscation such as that which occurred in relation to *Chorzów Factory* would give rise to State responsibility and attract reparation or restitution.

The ICSID tribunals have in recent years made their own contribution to clarifying the standard of treatment and nature of compensation available to foreign investors. For instance, in the *SD Myers Inc.* v *Canada* case, an ICSID tribunal sitting under the NAFTA drew, citing the *Chorzów* pronouncements, a clear distinction between the standard of compensation for otherwise lawful expropriation, on the one hand, and on the other the measure of damages for unlawful expropriation resulting from discrimination or violation of treaty obligations.[38]

In the *Asian Agricultural Products Ltd* v *Republic of Sri Lanka* case an ICSID tribunal established Sri Lanka's State responsibility for failing to take the appropriate precautionary measures to protect the interests of Asian Agricultural Products, a British company having its business in an area where fighting was taking place between the government and rebel forces.[39]

VI. CONCLUSION

Over the centuries the law of foreign investment has evolved in response to both the economic and political realities of the world. The developing countries sought in the 1960s, 1970s, and 1980s to regulate foreign investment through an international instrument, rather than leaving the matter to international customary law. The idea was to impose certain conditions on foreign investors, including TNCs, requiring them, among other

---

[36] *Starrett Housing Corporation* v *Iran (Interlocutory Order)* 23 ILM 1090 (1984); 4 *Iran–US CTR* 122 (1983).
[37] *Amoco International Finance Corporation* v *Iran*, 15 *Iran–US CTR* 189 (1987).
[38] http://www.naftalaw.org/disputes_canada_sdmyers.htm; NAFTA Ch 11 Arbitration Tribunal, 2000–2002.
[39] *Asian Agricultural Products Ltd* v *Republic of Sri Lanka* (1991) 30 ILM 577.

duties, to use local raw material, to employ local people, and to refrain from interfering in the internal affairs of the host States.

However, in the 1990s these very developing countries became reluctant to support the notion of the regulation of foreign investment under the auspices of the WTO. When the developing countries sought to regulate foreign investment under the auspices of the UN, many developed countries resisted the attempt, perhaps fearing that such an international instrument would be more in the interests of host States than of the home States. An attempt was made through the OECD to adopt an international agreement on foreign investment; the developing countries opposed it, fearing that the instrument would be in the greater interest of home States than of the host States. This is also the reason why many developing countries were opposed to the regulation of foreign investment under the auspices of the WTO.

Thanks to globalization neither the host nor home countries are able to regulate or control the activities of foreign investors in general or the multinational enterprises (MNEs) in particular. While the people in developing nations are concerned about violations of human rights and degradation of the environment by the MNEs, those in the developed countries are concerned that MNEs are relocating or outsourcing their business operations to developing countries in order to avoid tax, to escape from environmental compliance and other regulatory regimes, to exploit cheap labour, and to pursue profit at the expense of other responsibilities. The interests of both developed and developing countries seem to be converging gradually towards the adoption of an international agreement to regulate foreign investment.

What is required is to balance the interests of both host and home countries. There is a plausible case in favour of the conclusion of a comprehensive international treaty on foreign investment. Unless there is a chance perhaps within the WTO to revive the negotiations for a treaty on foreign investment, the matter should be referred back to the UN, after which either the ECOSOC or UNCTAD should be entrusted with the task of developing and negotiating such a treaty.

REFERENCES

BORCHARD, E (1940), 'The Minimum Standard of Treatment of Aliens', 38 *Mich LR* 445.

CHATTERJEE, SK (1991), 'The Charter of Economic Rights and Duties of States: An Evaluation after 15 Years', 40 *ICLQ* 669.

DOLZER, R and SCHREUR, C (2012), *Principles of International Investment Law* (Oxford: Oxford University Press).

FREEMAN, AV (1946), 'Recent Aspects of the Calvo Doctrine and the Challenge to International Law', 40 *AJIL* 131.

HORN, N (ed) (1980), *Legal Problems of Codes of Conduct for Multinational Enterprises* (Deventer: Kluwer).

HOSSAIN, K (ed) (1980), *Legal Aspects of a New International Economic Order* (London: Frances Pinter).

LIPSTEIN, K (1945), 'The Place of the Calvo Clause in International Law', 24 *BYIL* 130.

OPPENHEIM, L, JENNINGS, SIR R and WATTS, SIR A (1992) (eds), *Oppenheim's International Law*, 9th edn, (Harlow: Longmans).

ROOT, E (1910), 'The Basis of Protection to Citizens Residing Abroad', 4 *AJIL* 517.

SCHREUER, C (2001), *The ICSID Convention: A Commentary* (Cambridge: Cambridge University Press).

SCHWARZENBERGER, G (1957), *International Law as Applied by International Courts and Tribunals*, 3rd edn, (London: Stevens and Sons).

SHIHATA, IFI (1991), *The World Bank in a Changing World: Selected Essays* (Dordrecht: Martinus Nijhoff).

Subedi, SP (2012), *International Investment Law: Reconciling Policy and Principle*, 2nd edn (Oxford: Hart Publishing).

Verwey, WD and Schrijver, NJ (1984), 'The Taking of Foreign Property under International Law: A New Legal Perspective?', XV *Netherlands Yearbook of International Law* 3.

World Trade Organization (1999), *The Legal Texts: The Results of the Uruguay Round of Multilateral Trade Negotiations* (Cambridge: Cambridge University Press).

FURTHER READING

Van Harten, G (2007), *Investment Treaty Arbitration and Public Law* (Oxford: Oxford University Press).

Higgins, R (1982), 'The Taking of Property by the State', (1982-III) 176 *Recueil des Cours* 259.

McLachlan, C, Shore, L, Weiniger, M (2007), *International Investment Arbitration: Substantive Principles* (Oxford: Oxford University Press, 2007).

Montt, S (2011), *State Liability in Investment Treaty Arbitration: Global Constitutional and Administrative Law in the BIT Generation* (Oxford: Hart Publishing).

Puvimanasinghe, S F (2007), *Foreign Investment, Human Rights and the Environment: A Perspective from South Asia on the Role of Public International Law* (The Hague: Martinus Nijhoff).

Salacuse, W (2010), *The Law of International Investment Treaties* (Oxford: Oxford University Press).

Shea, DR (1955), *The Calvo Clause: A Problem of Inter-American and International Law and Diplomacy* (Minneapolis: University of Minnesota Press).

Tudor, I (2008), *The Fair and Equitable Treatment Standard in International Foreign Investment Law* (Oxford: Oxford University Press).

UNCTAD *Most-favoured-nation Treatment* (UNCTAD series on issues in international investment agreements) (New York and Geneva: UN, 1999).

UNCTAD, *Fair and Equitable Treatment* (UNCTAD series on issues in international investment agreements) (New York and Geneva: UN, 1999).

UNCTAD, *National Treatment* (UNCTAD series on issues in international investment agreements) (New York and Geneva: UN, 1999).

WEBSITES

UNCTAD BITs Online:

http://www.unctadxi.org/templates/DocSearch___779.aspx
This website contains a search engine which enables one to find BITs online.

www.ita.law.uvic.ca
It provides access to all publicly available investment treaty awards and information and resources relating to investment treaties and investment treaty arbitration.

http://www.worldbank.org/icsid
This is the website of ICSID which was established under the Convention on the Settlement of Investment Disputes between States and Nationals of Other States. Most of the ICSID awards are available here.

25

INTERNATIONAL CRIMINAL LAW

Robert Cryer

SUMMARY

This chapter deals with international crimes in the narrow sense. These are crimes which are directly criminalized by international law. It therefore discusses the material and mental aspects of the four crimes that qualify as such crimes: genocide, crimes against humanity, war crimes, and aggression. As international criminal law directly criminalizes those offences, this chapter also covers some of the general principles of liability and defences that are of particular relevance to international crimes. Therefore it explains and critiques joint criminal enterprise, co-perpetration, command responsibility, and the defence of obedience to superior orders. The chapter then looks at the international and, briefly, the national prosecution of international crimes. It covers, in particular, the Nuremberg and Tokyo Trials, the International Criminal Tribunals for former Yugoslavia and Rwanda, and the International Criminal Court. Reference is also made, *inter alia*, to the Special Court for Sierra Leone, the Special Tribunal for Lebanon, the Iraqi High Tribunal, and purely national prosecutions such as that of Adolf Eichmann in Israel. As prosecution is not the only, or predominant, response to international crimes, the chapter concludes with a discussion, and evaluation, of alternatives and complements to prosecution, such as amnesties and truth and reconciliation commissions.

I. INTRODUCTION

There are various different ways of defining international criminal law. These include those aspects of international law involving the allocation of jurisdiction, or international cooperation in criminal matters (Schwarzenberger, 1950). However, international criminal law, for the purposes of this chapter, is the branch of public international law that deals with the direct criminal responsibility of individuals. It can be summed up in the famous statement of the Nuremberg International Military Tribunal (IMT) that '[i]ndividuals have international duties which transcend the national obligations of obedience imposed by the individual State...crimes against international law are committed by men, not by abstract entities, and only by punishing individuals who commit such crimes can the provisions of international law be enforced'.[1] For international crimes, the locus of the criminal prohibition is the international legal order (although such crimes may also be criminalized in

---

[1] Nuremberg IMT, 'Judgment and Sentence', (1947) 41 *AJIL* 172, 221, 223.

domestic legal orders). There are only four clear examples of international crimes in this sense (often called the 'core' international crimes): genocide, crimes against humanity, war crimes, and aggression.

Some suggest that there are other core international crimes, most notably terrorism and individual acts of torture (Cassese *et al*, 2013, Ch 8). Indeed, the Appeals Chamber of the Special Tribunal for Lebanon (over which Cassese presided) asserted in 2011 that international law had developed to the point that there was a customary international crime of terrorism.[2] The Special Tribunal's decision, however, is largely considered unpersuasive (Saul, 2011; *contra* Ventura, 2011). Terrorism or torture may fall under the definitions of other international crimes (in particular crimes against humanity or war crimes), and when they do so they may be prosecuted as those crimes. However, as it stands, there is insufficient acceptance by States of the idea that they exist as separate categories of customary international crimes (Simma and Paulus, 1999, p 313; Saul, 2006, Ch 4).

In addition to their overlap with core crimes, terrorism and individual acts of torture are regulated by international law. There are numerous treaties covering aspects of terrorism,[3] and individual acts of torture are dealt with by the 1984 UN Convention Against Torture.[4] However, these are examples of what are known as 'transnational crime' conventions (Boister, 2003; Boister, 2012). These do not, in themselves create direct liability international crimes, but require States to create domestic crimes.

This much can be seen from a comparison of the Torture and the Genocide Conventions. Article 4(1) of the Torture Convention provides that 'Each State Party shall ensure that all acts of torture are offences under its criminal law.' Article 1 of the Genocide Convention,[5] on the other hand, provides that 'The Contracting Parties confirm that genocide, whether committed in time of peace or in time of war, is a crime under international law which they undertake to prevent and to punish.' There was a proposal in an unofficial draft of the Torture Convention that provided: 'Torture is a crime under international law'; this did not, however, make it into the first draft by a State.[6] Therefore, what the Torture Convention does is not create a crime itself, but oblige States domestically to criminalize torture. The basis of the criminal prohibition is thus the domestic, not international, legal order. The same applies to the various counter-terrorism conventions.

It is sometimes thought that the question of whether torture is an international crime turns, at least in part, on whether the Torture Convention has achieved customary status (Cassese *et al*, 2013, p 132). However, since the Convention itself does not create a direct criminal prohibition, if the Torture Convention is customary, then all States are obliged to prohibit torture domestically, rather than accept that international law directly criminalizes torture.

Sometimes international crimes are referred to as '*jus cogens* crimes' (eg Sadat, 2007, p 231). Although there is considerable overlap between *jus cogens* norms and international crimes (genocide, for example has been authoritatively determined to be 'assuredly'

---

[2] *Interlocutory Decision on the Applicable Law: Terrorism, Conspiracy, Homicide, Perpetration, Cumulative Charging, STL-11-01/I/AC/R176bis*, Appeals Chamber, 16 February 2011.

[3] Eg Convention for the Suppression of Unlawful Seizure of Aircraft, 860 UNTS 105; International Convention for the Suppression of the Financing of Terrorism, GA Res 54/109 (9 December 1999).

[4] 1465 UNTS 85.

[5] Convention on the Prevention and Punishment of the Crime of Genocide, 78 UNTS 277.

[6] Draft Convention for the Prevention and Suppression of Torture, Submitted by the International Association of Penal Law, UN Doc E/CN.4/NGO/213, Article 1; Draft Convention Against Torture and Other Cruel, Inhuman and Degrading Treatment or Punishment (Sweden), UN Doc E/CN/4/1285.

contrary to a *jus cogens* prohibition[7]), the term '*jus cogens* crime' can be apt to mislead. An international crime is created when international law directly criminalizes something. It is not required that the rule doing so has *jus cogens* status. Indeed, international crimes arose at the very latest in the Nuremburg and Tokyo IMTs, nearly 25 years before the concept of *jus cogens* was adopted in the VCLT.[8]

Similarly, that a prohibition has reached *jus cogens* status does not mean that it is automatically an international crime. Torture is contrary to a *jus cogens* norm,[9] however, that does not, in and of itself, mean that torture is an international crime. Still, the vast majority of international criminal law finds its basis in customary international law, and thus is applicable throughout the world. There are those that question the cultural sensitivity of this (Clarke, 2009). However, there is very considerable agreement about the relevant norms,[10] even if the way in which they are implemented and enforced is sometimes the matter of more debate.

A. INTERNATIONAL AND CRIMINAL LAW

International criminal law is an amalgam of international and criminal law As such its sources are those of international law, which has its own ways of thinking, and criminal law, which also has its own approach (see, eg Robinson, 2008). An appreciation of both is necessary for a full understanding of international criminal law. Sometimes, the dual nature of international criminal law has led to critique, particularly from those in civil law, systems where the principle of non-retroactivity of criminal law prohibits reliance on unwritten law (*nullum crimen sine lege scripta*) (eg Djuro-Degan, 2005, p 67). However, the *nullum crimen sine lege principle,* at the international level, does not prohibit the use of custom (Gallant, 2008, p 354), and the International Criminal Tribunal for former Yugoslavia (ICTY), in particular, has made considerable use of customary law.[11]

II. THE CRIMES

As mentioned above, there are four undoubted international crimes, genocide, crimes against humanity, war crimes, and aggression.

A. GENOCIDE

Genocide, said by some to be the 'crime of crimes' (Schabas, 2008a), is also arguably the youngest international crime. The term itself was coined by Raphaël Lemkin in 1944 to describe the Holocaust (Lemkin, 1944) by combining the Greek 'genos' (people, or race)

---

[7] *Armed Activities on the Territory of the Congo (New Application: 2002) (Democratic Republic of the Congo v Rwanda), Jurisdiction and Admissibility, Judgment, ICJ Reports 2006,* p 6, para 64. This case was also the first time the ICJ had used the term *jus cogens.*

[8] 1155 UNTS 331, Article 53. See Shelton, Ch 6 of this book.

[9] *Questions relating to the Obligation to Prosecute or Extradite (Belgium v Senegal), Judgment of 20 July 2012,* para 99; ICTY, *Prosecutor v Furundzija,* Judgment, Case No IT–95–17/1–T, Trial Chamber II (10 December 1998), para 153.

[10] But see Kelsall 2009, Chs 3–5.

[11] See, in particular, ICTY Appeals Chamber, *Prosecutor v Tadić, Decision on the Defence Interlocutory Appeal on Jurisdiction,* Case no IT–94–1–AR72, 2 October 1995, (hereafter cited as *Tadić* Appeal'). Some go as far as to say that its jurisdiction is limited to customary crimes (Shahabuddeen, 2012, pp 61–70).

and the Latin 'cide' (to kill).This provides an insight into the focus of the crime. It focuses on threats to the existence of groups. Although the term was referred to in the Nuremberg IMT indictment, the first time the term genocide was used as a term of art in positive international law was in General Assembly Resolution 96(I) (1946). The label of genocide is an exceptionally potent one. As such, debates over whether particular atrocities amount to genocide is often politically contentious (Luban, 2006–7; Akhavan, 2012; Scheffer, 2012, Ch 2).

The definition of genocide as an international crime came in the 1948 Genocide Convention. Three years later the ICJ, in the *Reservations* Case, determined that 'the principles underlying the Convention are principles which are recognized by civilized nations as binding on States, even without any conventional obligation'.[12] As discussed in Section I of this chapter, the ICJ has also made clear that the prohibition has achieved *jus cogens* status.[13]

Article II of the Genocide Convention (which is repeated essentially verbatim in the ICTY, International Criminal Tribunal for Rwanda (ICTR) and International Criminal Court (ICC) Statutes) defines genocide as:

any of the following acts committed with intent to destroy, in whole or in part, a national, ethnical, racial or religious group, as such:

(a) Killing members of the group;

(b) Causing serious bodily or mental harm to members of the group;

(c) Deliberately inflicting on the group conditions of life calculated to bring about its physical destruction in whole or in part;

(d) Imposing measures intended to prevent births within the group;

(e) Forcibly transferring children of the group to another group.

Genocide is characterized in particular by its mental element, but it is also worth looking at the controversies that have surrounded the conduct element.

1. Conduct Element

The paradigmatic example of genocide's conduct element is killing. This has not caused too many difficulties in practice, and it is generally accepted that the killing has to be intentional. Genocide may also be committed in other ways, which are provided for in Article II. The second means of committing genocide is causing serious bodily or mental harm. The former was given a progressive (but entirely defensible) interpretation by the ICTR in the *Akayesu* case.[14] There the ICTR accepted that rape and other forms of sexual violence are covered by Article II. The ICC's Elements of Crimes (EoC) agree.[15] Deliberately inflicting conditions of life designed to destroy a group, like most of the acts of genocide, tracks Nazi policies. The EoC for the ICC provide that 'The term "conditions of life" may include, but is not necessarily restricted to, deliberate deprivation of resources indispensable for survival, such as food or medical services, or systematic expulsion from homes.'[16] It is not enough that these conditions are imposed, they must also be calculated to destroy the group, which is a mental element.

---

[12] *Reservations to the Convention on the Prevention and Punishment of the Crime of Genocide, Advisory Opinion, ICJ Reports 1951*, p 15, p 23.

[13] See above, n 4.

[14] ICTR Trial Chamber I, *Prosecutor v Akayesu*, Judgment, Case No ICTR-95-4-T, 2 September 1998 para 731 (hereafter cited as '*Akayesu*').

[15] Elements of Crimes for Article 6(b), footnote 3.   [16] Elements of Crimes for Article 6(c), footnote 4.

The inclusion of 'imposing measures intended to prevent births within the group' was also a response to Nazi policies. The EoC do not contain much elaboration of this crime; however, the ICTR has made clear that the measures may be physical or mental.[17] Finally, Article II also includes transferring children of a group to another group. For this purpose, children are those under 18 years old, and 'forcible' includes physical force and mental coercion, 'such as that caused by fear of violence, duress, detention, psychological oppression or abuse of power, against such person or persons or another person, or by taking advantage of a coercive environment'.[18] This last phrase is rather vague, and will need judicial interpretation, although to date, there have been no authoritative rulings on this point.

The final part of the external aspect of genocide is provided for in the EoC: this is that '[t]he conduct took place in the context of a manifest pattern of similar conduct directed against that group or was conduct that could itself effect such destruction'.[19] It is controversial whether this is something inherent in the concept of genocide, or a non-customary addition to the crime solely for the purposes of the ICC. The ICTY in the *Krstić* case took the view that the element was not customary.[20] However, a Pre-Trial Chamber in the ICC, while not determining the customary status of the element has applied it as it was not in 'irreconcilable contradiction' with the ICC Statute.[21] What is notable, however, is that a 'manifest pattern of similar conduct' is not the same as a genocidal policy, as the term 'conduct' was chosen carefully to avoid that implication (Oosterveld, 2001, pp 47–8), and a single, large-scale act (for example the detonation of a weapon of mass destruction) can also fulfil the element.

2. Mental Element

The factor that distinguishes genocide from 'mere' mass killing is the 'intent to destroy, in whole or in part, a national, ethnical, racial or religious group, as such.' This aspect of the definition is contested between those who would interpret the mental element broadly, to legally label more killings and the like as 'genocide' so it reflects the popular concept of genocide more closely and those who take the view that it must be kept narrow, for fear of diluting the opprobrium that attaches to conduct legally classified as genocide (Schabas, 2008a, pp 10–11).

The first question is whether 'intent' in the definition means motive, direct, or indirect intention.[22] The ICJ, ICTY, and the ICC have taken the view that although proof of motive is not required, direct intention is necessary for genocide; indirect intent is insufficient.[23] In part as a result of this, proving genocidal intent is difficult, and the ICJ only found genocidal intent in former Yugoslavia in Srebrenica.[24] These difficulties have led the Tribunals

[17] *Akayesu*, paras 507–8.   [18] Elements of Crimes for Article 6(e), element 5 and footnote 5.

[19] Eg Elements of Crimes for Article 6(a), element 4.

[20] ICTY Appeals Chamber, *Prosecutor v Krstić, Judgment*, Case No IT-98-33-A, 19 April 2004, para 224 (hereafter cited as '*Krstić* Appeal').

[21] ICC Pre Trial Chamber 1, *Prosecutor v al-Bashir*, Case No 02/05-01/09, 4 March 2009, para 132.

[22] Direct intention requires wanting something to occur, indirect intention is when a person, whilst not wanting something to occur, accepts it as a virtually certain consequence of their conduct.

[23] *Application of the Convention on the Prevention and Punishment of the Crime of Genocide (Bosnia and Hercegovina v Serbia and Montenegro), Merits Judgment, ICJ Reports 2007*, para 189 (hereafter cited as '*Bosnian Genocide*'); ICTY Appeals Chamber, *Prosecutor v Jelesić, Judgment*, Case No IT-95-10-A, 5 July 2001, para 49; *al Bashir*, para 114; ICTY Trial Chamber II, *Prosecutor v Kupreškić*, Judgment, Case No IT-95-16-T, 14 January 2000, para 636 (hereafter cited as '*Kupreškić*').

[24] *Bosnian Genocide*, paras 278–97.

into controversial waters, as some have claimed that indirect intention should suffice, and the approach of the ad hoc Tribunals in particular has often been to use modes of liability that require lower mental elements to circumvent the high thresholds they have otherwise set (Greenawalt, 1999). Either way, proof of intent often depends on circumstantial factors. The ICTR has identified, *inter alia,* the following as useful evidence:

> The overall context in which the crime occurred, the systematic targeting of the victims on account of their membership in a protected group, the fact that the perpetrator may have targeted the same group during the commission of other criminal acts, the scale and scope of the atrocities committed, the frequency of destructive and discriminatory acts, whether the perpetrator acted on the basis of the victim's membership in a protected group and the perpetration of acts which violate the very foundation of the group or considered as such by their perpetrators.[25]

The second controversy is whether the intention to destroy the group refers to physical or cultural destruction. Some support the idea of 'cultural genocide',[26] but this has been rejected as a matter of law, probably most authoritatively by the ICJ in the *Bosnian Genocide* case.[27] Still, as it said in that case, adopting the ICTY's view, 'where there is physical or biological destruction there are often simultaneous attacks on the cultural and religious property and symbols of the targeted group as well, attacks which may legitimately be considered as evidence of an intent to physically destroy the group'.[28] Equally, the means of genocide of transfer of children to other groups has links to cultural destruction.

Some of the thorniest issues relating to genocide concern the definitions of the protected groups and what those groups should be (Nersessian, 2010). Although one Trial Chamber in the ICTR argued that the Convention protects all stable and permanent groups,[29] this remains a minority view. As the ICJ has said: 'the essence of the intent is to destroy the protected group, in whole or in part, as such. It is a group which must have particular positive characteristics—national, ethnical, racial or religious...'.[30] On this basis the ICJ, more controversially, also rejected the idea that a group could be defined negatively, such as 'all non-Serbs'.[31]

The question of the existence of a group protected from genocide and its membership is also complex. In *Akayesu* the ICTR tried to define all four terms separately. This proved to be problematic, not least as on the definitions the Trial Chamber gave, there was no relevant distinction in the Rwandan context between Hutus and Tutsis. A more satisfactory approach was taken by the ICTY in the *Krstić* case, where the ICTY explained:

> The preparatory work of the convention shows that setting out such a list was designed more to describe a single phenomenon, roughly corresponding to what was recognized, before the second world war, as 'national minorities', rather than to refer to several distinct prototypes of human groups. To attempt to differentiate each of the named groups on the basis of scientifically objective criteria would thus be inconsistent with the object and purpose of the Convention.[32]

---

[25] ICTR Trial Chamber III, *Prosecutor v Ncamihigo, Judgment,* Case No ICTR-01-63-T, 12 November 2008, para 331.

[26] See the discussion in Schabas, 2008a, 207–21.   [27] *Bosnian Genocide,* para 344.

[28] Ibid.   [29] *Akayesu,* para 516   [30] *Bosnian Genocide,* para 193.

[31] Ibid. See *contra* Shahabuddeen, 2012, pp 193–5.

[32] ICTY Trial Chamber I, *Prosecutor v Krstić, Judgment,* Case No IT-98-33-T, 2 August 2001, para 556.

Part of the difficulty is that groups exist, at least partially, at the level of (often fostered) perception, rather than objective fact (Wilson, 2011, Ch 7). In addition, even against this backdrop, group membership is complex, as some people may not consider themselves belonging to a group, but others may do so, and vice versa (Schabas, 2008a, pp 124–9). Owing to this, the better view is that if such a group is considered to exist in the relevant cultural context, then the perception of the perpetrator that the victim is a member of that group suffices for them to be considered a member for the purposes of genocide.[33] The ICJ has noted this approach, but has not expressly endorsed it, as the parties agreed on point and the issue did not arise in the case.[34]

Finally, as can be seen from the language of the Genocide Convention, it suffices if the perpetrator intended to destroy a part of the group. It therefore becomes very important to define what the group is and what size a part of the group has to be. The ICTY has tended to take the view that it is all members of the group in the country. So, for example, in the *Krstić* case, the prosecution argued that the relevant group was the Bosnian Muslims of the Srebreniča area. The ICTY disagreed, saying that the relevant group was the Bosnian Muslims, and the Bosnian Muslims of the Srebreniča area were a part of the group.[35] They also determined that the part of the group must be 'substantial',[36] something the ICJ has also accepted.[37]

B. CRIMES AGAINST HUMANITY

Crimes against humanity were first defined in Article 6(c) of the London Charter, which set up the Nuremberg Tribunal, as 'murder, extermination, enslavement, deportation, and other inhumane acts committed against any civilian population, before or during the war; or persecutions on political, racial or religious grounds in execution of or in connection with any crime within the jurisdiction of the Tribunal, whether or not in violation of the domestic law of the country where perpetrated.' Since then there have also been definitions in, inter alia, the Statutes of the Tokyo IMT (Article 5(c)), ICTY (Article 5), ICTR (Article 3) and SCSL (Article 2). Unfortunately none of them are identical. This has led to calls for a comprehensive convention on crimes against humanity (Bassiouni, 1994). There are current non-governmental drafts of such a treaty (Sadat, 2011).

The most widely ratified treaty-based definition of crimes against humanity is contained in Article 7 of the ICC Statute. This reads:

1. For the purpose of this Statute, 'crime against humanity' means any of the following acts when committed as part of a widespread or systematic attack directed against any civilian population, with knowledge of the attack:

   (a) Murder;

   (b) Extermination;

   (c) Enslavement;

   (d) Deportation or forcible transfer of population;

   (e) Imprisonment or other severe deprivation of physical liberty in violation of fundamental rules of international law;

---

[33] See, eg ICTR Trial Chamber I, *Prosecutor v Semanza*, *Judgment*, Case N. ICTR-97-20-T, 15 May 2003, para 317.
[34] *Bosnian Genocide*, para 191.   [35] *Krstić* Appeal, para 12.   [36] Ibid.
[37] *Bosnian Genocide*, para 198.

(f) Torture;

(g) Rape, sexual slavery, enforced prostitution, forced pregnancy, enforced sterilization, or any other form of sexual violence of comparable gravity;

(h) Persecution against any identifiable group or collectivity on political, racial, national, ethnic, cultural, religious, gender...or other grounds that are universally recognized as impermissible under international law, in connection with any act referred to in this paragraph or any crime within the jurisdiction of the Court;

(i) Enforced disappearance of persons;

(j) The crime of apartheid;

(k) Other inhumane acts of a similar character intentionally causing great suffering, or serious injury to body or to mental or physical health.[38]

Crimes against humanity are a complex crime, and there are many definitional controversies. The crime has conduct, contextual, and mental elements.[39]

1. Conduct Element

For reasons of space, it is not possible to deal with all of the conduct elements in great detail. Article 7(2) and the EoC provide further elaboration of the varied conduct amounting to crimes against humanity. For example, Article 7(2)(c) defines enslavement as 'the exercise of any or all of the powers attaching to the right of ownership over a person and includes the exercise of such power in the course of trafficking in persons, in particular women and children.' One of the more controversial definitions was that of enforced pregnancy. Article 7(2)(f) defines that crime as 'the unlawful confinement of a woman forcibly made pregnant, with the intent of affecting the ethnic composition of any population or carrying out other grave violations of international law. This definition shall not in any way be interpreted as affecting national laws relating to pregnancy'. The additional intent requirement was included, as well as the last sentence, were added at the insistence of some States, who thought that this crime could potentially be used to condemn domestic laws limiting or prohibiting abortion (von Hebel and Robinson, 1999, p 100). The additions render the crime narrower than customary law (Cryer, 2005, p 258).

Another controversial addition to the requirements set by customary law is the condition in Article 7(1)(h) that persecutive crimes against humanity can only be prosecuted if they occur 'in connection with any act referred to in this paragraph or any crime within the jurisdiction of the Court'. This was included on the basis that some States felt that some of their family laws could be interpreted as contrary to the prohibition of gender-based persecutions.[40] It remains the case, however, that this limitation also makes the Rome Statute's definition of crimes against humanity more restrictive than customary law.[41]

2. Contextual Element

The core of crimes against humanity, the thing that renders conduct which generally amounts to a domestic crime (such as rape and murder) into an international crime, is

---

[38] Although it must be noted that this definition is not necessarily entirely reflective of customary international law on the point: Cassese, 2013, pp 123–6.

[39] The question of whether or not genocide has a contextual element is controversial, see Section II B 2 of this chapter.

[40] The definition of gender was similarly controversial (von Hebel and Robinson, 1999, p 101).

[41] *Kupreškić*, para 580.

the context in which it occurs. This context has been the subject of conflicting definitions. For example, in the Nuremberg and Tokyo IMT's definitions there was a requirement of the existence of an armed conflict.[42] This is no longer the case (if it ever was) in customary law,[43] and it does not appear in any later definitions other than that in the ICTY Statute. In that context, the limitation has been explained on the basis that the Security Council simply wished to grant the ICTY jurisdiction over a limited subset of crimes against humanity rather than make an assertion about customary law (Shahabuddeen, 2012, p 65).

The core of the customary contextual element is that the conduct occurs in the context of a widespread or systematic attack on a civilian population. As the ICTY has said ' "Widespread" refers to the large-scale nature of the attack and the number of victims, while the phrase "systematic" refers to the organized nature of the acts of violence and the improbability of their random occurrence.'[44] In Rome the question of whether the terms 'widespread' and 'systematic' ought to be included in the alternative or cumulatively (ie whether it was widespread and systematic or widespread or systematic). The latter was chosen, however, as part of the compromise, Article 7(2) defines an attack on the civilian population as being 'a course of conduct involving the multiple commission of acts referred to in paragraph 1 against any civilian population, pursuant to or in furtherance of a State or organizational policy to commit such attack'.

This definition means that if the prosecution seeks to prove a crime against humanity on the basis that it was widespread they will also have to prove a (perhaps) more limited form of the systematic element (a 'policy') while if they seek to prove the crime against humanity on the basis that the attack was systematic, they will have to prove a more limited version of the widespread requirement (Robinson, 1999, pp 450–51). The ICTY has expressly rejected the customary basis the policy requirement in the *Kunarac* case,[45] although the rather conclusionary nature of the discussion in that case has been criticized (Schabas, 2008b, pp 958–69). There are considerable disagreements about whether there ought to be such a requirement, and, if so, what level of organization an entity needs before it can be considered sufficiently organized to have such a policy (Kress, 2010; Halling, 2010; Schabas, 2010; Werle and Burghardt, 2012).

The question of what amounts to a civilian population, and who can be a victim of a crime against humanity have also proved divisive. On the former point, the ICTY has adopted the view that:

> the use of the word population does not mean that the entire population of the geographical entity in which the attack is taking place must have been subjected to that attack. It is sufficient to show that enough individuals were targeted in the course of the attack, or that they were targeted in such a way to satisfy the Chamber that the attack was in fact directed against a civilian population, rather than against a limited and randomly selected number of individuals.[46]

Furthermore, the presence of some non-civilians in a population does not render that population non-civilian so long as it is 'predominantly' so.[47] In wartime situations, who is a civilian is to be interpreted in accordance with the relevant applicable humanitarian

---

[42] London Charter, Article 6(c); Tokyo IMT Charter, Article 5(c).

[43] *Tadić* Appeal, para 141.

[44] ICTY Appeals Chamber, *Prosecutor v Kunarac, Kovać and Vuković, Judgment*, Case No IT-96-23/1-A, 12 June 2002, para 94 (hereafter cited as '*Kunarac* Appeal'). The ICC has, so far, agreed: see *al-Bashir*, para 81.

[45] Ibid, para 98.   [46] *Kunarac* Appeal, para 90.

[47] ICTY Trial Chamber II, *Prosecutor v Tadić*, Opinion and Judgment, Case No IT-94-1-T, 7 May 1997, para 638.

law.[48] It was often thought that only civilians can be the victims of crimes against humanity. However, what is required is that the attack is against the civilian population, not that all of the victims are civilians. As a result, the ICTY has held that those non-civilians who are hors de combat (such as PoWs) may also be the victims of crimes against humanity so long as the attack as a whole is directed at a civilian population.[49]

3. Mental Element

The mental element applicable to crimes against humanity is, first, that the person had the mental element required for the underlying crime (murder, etc.). Second, they had knowledge of the broader context in which their crimes are committed, in other words, that they took place in the context of a widespread or systematic attack on the civilian population, or intended it to be. There is nothing which excludes a personal motive from co-existing with this knowledge though.[50] For persecutive crimes against humanity there is an additional mental element that the perpetrator has to intend to discriminate against the victims.[51] The EoC require that the perpetrator 'targeted' the members of the relevant group, which implies the same.

C. WAR CRIMES

The law of war crimes is, in essence, the criminal phase of humanitarian law (Sivakumaran, 2012, pp 77–83). As such war crimes are parasitic upon that law (for which see Turns, Ch 27 of this book). The relationship, between them, however, is not simple or uncontested. There are three main views on this point. The first is that all violations of humanitarian law are war crimes (eg Nuremberg IMT Statute, Article 6(b)). This would almost fuse the substantive norms of humanitarian law and the law of war crimes. There are those that have argued that some norms of humanitarian law (particularly some of the highly detailed technical rules governing PoWs) are not well suited to criminal enforcement. Hence the second approach which is that all serious violations of humanitarian law amount to war crimes (Greenwood, 1996, pp 279–80). This is the view with the most support in practice, but some go further, arguing that in addition there has to be a separate rule criminalizing each rule of humanitarian law for that rule to enter the corpus of war crimes law (Abi-Saab, 2001, p 112). The ICTY has adopted this position,[52] although the reasoning in this part of *Tadić* is thin, and proof of separate customary rules criminalizing violations has not always been convincing.

As with humanitarian law more generally, the law of war crimes differs depending on whether the armed conflict is international or non-international. In international armed conflicts, there are treaty-based and customary norms that are relevant. Of the treaty-based norms, possibly the most important are grave breaches of the Geneva Conventions (see Symposium, 2009), these are explained in Article 8(2)(a) of the ICC Statute as being:

any of the following acts against persons or property protected under the provisions of the relevant Geneva Convention [essentially the wounded, sick, shipwrecked, PoWs and interned civilians and civilians in occupied territory]...:

(i) Wilful killing;

(ii) Torture or inhuman treatment, including biological experiments;

---

[48] ICTY Appeals Chamber, *Prosecutor v Blaškić*, Judgment, Case No IT-95-14-A, 29 July 2004, para 113–15.
[49] ICTY Appeals Chamber, *Prosecutor v Martić* Judgment, Case No IT-95-11-A, 8 October 2008, para 313.
[50] ICTY Appeals Chamber, *Prosecutor v Tadić*, Judgment, Case No IT-94-1-A, 15 July 1999, para 248.
[51] ICTY Trial Chamber II, *Prosecutor v Krnojelac*, Judgment, Case No IT-97-25-T, 13 March 2002, para 435.
[52] *Tadić* Appeal, para 94.

(iii) Wilfully causing great suffering, or serious injury to body or health;

(iv) Extensive destruction and appropriation of property, not justified by military necessity and carried out unlawfully and wantonly;

(v) Compelling a prisoner of war or other protected person to serve in the forces of a hostile Power;

(vi) Wilfully depriving a prisoner of war or other protected person of the rights of fair and regular trial;

(vii) Unlawful deportation or transfer or unlawful confinement;

(viii) Taking of hostages.

Outside the ICC, such acts are also subject to mandatory extradition or prosecution on the basis of universal jurisdiction (eg Geneva Convention I, Article 49). There are also grave breaches provisions in Additional Protocol I (Article 85, see Sandoz, Swiniarski, and Zimmerman, 1987, pp 899ff), although the extent to which universal jurisdiction inheres in those grave breaches depends on their customary status (which is likely, but not guaranteed: see Henkaerts and Doswald-Beck, 2005).

The Nuremberg (Article 6(b)) and Tokyo IMTs (Article 5(b)), as well as the ICTY (Article 3) were given jurisdiction over an open-ended list of war crimes, and were thus able to prosecute any applicable customary war crime. The ICC, on the other hand, has only been granted jurisdiction over (in addition to grave breaches of the Geneva Conventions (Article 8(2)(a)) a closed list of 26 customary crimes, which include those relating to a limited number of weapons offences (eg Article 8(2)(b)(xviii) (employing chemical weapons contrary to the 1925 Geneva Gas Protocol)), declaring no quarter (Article 8(2)(b)(xii), sexual offences (Article 8(2)(b)(xxii), attacking civilians (Article 8(2)(b)(i), using human shields (Article 8(2)(b)(xxiii) and launching an attach which will cause disproportionate collateral damage (Article 8(2)(b)(iv)). The definitions in, and the inclusions and exclusions from, the list of crimes in the Rome Statute were extremely controversial (Cullen, 2011, p 148).

Turning to non-international armed conflict, the ICTR (Article 4), SCSL (Article 3) and the ICC (Article 8(2)(c)) all have jurisdiction to prosecute violations of common Article 3 to the Geneva Conventions,[53] which reads (in relevant part):

the following acts are and shall remain prohibited at any time and in any place whatsoever with respect to the above-mentioned persons [persons taking no active part in hostilities]:

(a) violence to life and person, in particular murder of all kinds, mutilation, cruel treatment and torture;

(b) taking of hostages;

(c) outrages upon personal dignity, in particular humiliating and degrading treatment;

(d) the passing of sentences and the carrying out of executions without previous judgment pronounced by a regularly constituted court, affording all the judicial guarantees which are recognized as indispensable by civilized peoples.

The ICTR (Article 5) and SCSL (Article 3) also have jurisdiction over violations of Additional Protocol II, as those States were parties to that treaty before the beginning of the respective Courts' jurisdictions. The Special Court for Sierra Leone had jurisdiction over three named offences that may be committed in non-international armed conflict

---

[53] The ICTY also has jurisdiction over this, as it interpreted Article 3 of its Statute to cover all applicable humanitarian law in force during the Yugoslav wars of dissolution, *Tadić* Appeal, paras 86–93.

(Article 4—attacking civilians, attacking peacekeepers entitled to protection as civilians, and conscripting, enlisting or using child soldiers). The ICC has a closed list of 12 customary war crimes for non-international armed conflicts (Article 8(2)(e)). In addition to those included in the SCSL Statute, these include prohibitions on pillage (Article 8(2)(e)(v)), perfidy (Article 8(2)(e)(ix)) and sexual offences (Article 8(2)(e)(vi)). In 2010, the parties to the Rome Statute adopted an amendment to the Statute to harmonize its weapons prohibitions in international and non-international armed conflicts. The amendment came into force in September 2012, and currently has sixteen parties.[54] As identified *inter alia* in the *Tadić* decision, there is a body of customary war crimes law, applicable to both types of conflicts that goes beyond what has been included in the Rome Statute.

As with many of the activities that amount to crimes against humanity, many war crimes would also amount to domestic crimes, and domestic crimes also occur in times of armed conflict and occupation. As a result, for conduct to amount to a war crime, there has to be a 'nexus' to the armed conflict. The ICTY has explained the position as follows: 'what distinguishes a war crime from a purely domestic offence is that a war crime is shaped by and dependent upon the environment—the armed conflict—in which it was committed.'[55] This means that:

> The armed conflict need not have been causal to the commission of the crime, but the existence of an armed conflict must, at a minimum, have played a substantial part in the perpetrator's ability to commit it, his decision to commit it, the manner in which it was committed or the purpose for which it was committed...[56]

As such, conduct such as a brawl that occurs in an occupied territory is not a war crime simply because of the fact that it occurs in that situation.

D. AGGRESSION

Aggression was first prosecuted (as 'Crimes Against Peace') before the Nuremberg IMT. The prosecution proceeded on the basis of Article 6(a) of the Nuremberg IMT Charter, which criminalized 'planning, preparation, initiating or waging of a war of aggression, or a war in violation of international treaties, agreements or assurances, or participation in a common plan or conspiracy for any of the foregoing'. That Article (to which Article 5(a) of the Tokyo IMT's Statute essentially conforms) does not provide a definition of aggression. It is also highly doubtful that aggression was criminal prior to the war; although the Kellog-Briand pact rendered recourse to non-defensive force unlawful, it did not contain any hint of criminal responsibility for its breach (Schwarzenberger, 1947, pp 346–8). That did not stop those Tribunals (and other post-War courts) from convicting people of that offence.

Unfortunately neither the Nuremberg or Tokyo IMTs (nor the later Control Council Law 10 trials) provided a direct definition of aggression, although all made determinations of whether or not particular conflicts were aggressive or not, thus giving sufficient practice to indicate a customary definition.[57] However, the project for a permanent international criminal court stalled in the 1950s in part owing to disagreements about the definition of aggression. Even after the General Assembly created a definition of the concept (not necessarily the crime) of aggression in 1974 in Resolution 3314, this did not settle the question. None of the ICTY, ICTR, or SCSL were given jurisdiction over aggression. The matter was deeply controversial in the negotiations for the Rome Statute. As a result Article 5(1) of the

---

[54] RC/Res 5 (10 June 2010).   [55] *Kunarac* Appeal, para 58.   [56] Ibid, paras 58–9.
[57] *R* v *Jones et al* [2006] UKHL 16, para 19.

Rome Statute includes aggression as a crime in the jurisdiction of the ICC. But Article 5(2) declares that the ICC may not exercise jurisdiction over the crime of aggression unless and until a definition is included by an amendment to the Statute. In spite of the difficulties in finding agreement, the 2010 Kampala Review Conference of the Rome Statute adopted an amendment to the Statute containing a definition of aggression.

The definition is 'the planning, preparation, initiation or execution, by a person in a position effectively to exercise control over or to direct the political or military action of a State, of an act of aggression which, by its character, gravity and scale, constitutes a manifest violation of the Charter of the United Nations'.[58] This is supplemented by a set of acts of aggression drawn from Resolution 3314.

Some of the aspects of this definition, such that the perpetrator must be in a high leadership position, are relatively uncontroversial. However, others, such as what amounts to a 'manifest' violation of the UN Charter, or what 'gravity, character and scale' mean and how they interrelate are the subject of controversy (Special Issue, 2012). In part, but not only because of this, the ICC's jurisdiction over aggression is subject to a stringent regime.[59] If ratified by 30 States the amendment will enter into force. Even then, the ICC is not able to exercise jurisdiction over aggression unless and until there is a determination by the Assembly of States Party to the Rome Statute (which cannot occur before 2017) that it may do so. Even then it may do so in limited, and contested jurisdictional circumstances, probably when both the alleged victim and aggressor States have ratified the amendment. That said, once the amendment enters into force, the ICC can act irrespective of ratification of the Statute or the amendments when the Security Council passes an alleged aggression to the ICC (Article 15 *bis, 15 ter*).

III. PRINCIPLES OF LIABILITY AND DEFENCES

International law also provides for principles of liability and defences (see generally van Sliedregt, 2012). Many of them, such as aiding, abetting, duress, and self-defence will be familiar to those who have a grounding in domestic criminal law.[60] However, international law does have a number of specialized forms of liability and defences that are worthy of note, although they have been criticized on the basis that they do not have strong doctrinal foundations (Fletcher, 2012). On the liability side, these are joint criminal enterprise, co-perpetration and command responsibility. For defences, superior orders are controversial.

A. JOINT CRIMINAL ENTERPRISE

It is a characteristic of many (although not all) international crimes that they tend to be committed by groups of people, some of whom are remote from the actual scene of the commission of the actual crime. As a result, the ICTY has adopted a theory of liability claimed to exist in customary law, of joint criminal enterprise. The *actus reus* is made up of three aspects, set out authoritatively in the *Tadić* case as being:

i. A plurality of persons.

ii. The existence of a common plan, design or purpose which amounts to or involves the commission of a crime provided for in the Statute.

---

[58] RC/Res 6 (10 June 2010), (Article 8 *bis*).

[59] Thirteen parties to the Rome Statute have so far (January 2014) ratified the amendment.

[60] See ICC Statute, Articles 25 and 31.

iii. Participation of the accused in the common design involving the perpetration of one of the crimes provided for in the Statute.[61]

The *mens rea* is an intention that the group commit the crime or, more controversially,

the *intention* to participate in and further the criminal activity or the criminal purpose of a group and to contribute to the joint criminal enterprise or in any event to the commission of a crime by the group. In addition, responsibility for a crime other than the one agreed upon in the common plan arises only if, under the circumstances of the case, (i) it was *foreseeable* that such a crime might be perpetrated by one or other members of the group and (ii) the accused *willingly took that risk*.[62]

The last part, often known as 'type three' joint criminal enterprise expands liability a long way, although it is noteworthy that it still requires a subjective mental element. This, alongside the fact that the direct perpetrators of the offences do not have to be a part of the joint criminal enterprise ensures that the doctrine provides for liability of policy-makers, but also renders the doctrine, for some, to be excessively broad and vague.[63]

B. CO-PERPETRATION

It is notable that the ICC has not adopted joint criminal enterprise in the way the ICTY has. They have, instead, relied on 'co-perpetration', including 'indirect co-perpetration' (where the perpetration is done through other people). This form of liability, which is said to have its basis in Article 25(3)(a) rather than customary law,[64] has two objective aspects, and three subjective ones.

The objective aspects are the existence of an explicit or implicit agreement or common plan between the co-perpetrators and a coordinated essential contribution by the suspect for the commission of the objective elements of the crime.[65] This contribution can be made through control of a hierarchically structured organization in which interchangeable subordinates can be relied upon to carry out orders.[66]

In relation to *mens rea*, it is necessary that the defendant has the *mens rea* of the relevant offence, the co-perpetrators realize that the common plan will result in that crime,[67] and that the defendant is aware of the circumstances that allow them to jointly control the crime.[68] This is similar to, but narrower than, joint criminal enterprise. The basis of liability that has been adopted for co-perpetration, joint control of the crime, has been the subject of considerable critique,[69] not least as a number of opinions of the ICC have relied specifically on doctrinal studies from one jurisdiction (Germany).

---

[61] *Tadić* Appeal, para 227.   [62] Ibid, para 228.

[63] See, eg Ohlin, 2007, Danner and Martinez, 2005, although for a contrary view see Cassese, 2007.

[64] ICTY Appeals Chamber, *Prosecutor v Stakić*, Judgment, Case No IT-97-24-A, 22 March 2006, para. 62.

[65] ICC Pre-Trial Chamber I, *Prosecutor v Lubanga*, Decision on the Confirmation of Charges, Case No ICC-01/04-01/06, 29 January 2007, paras 343–8 (hereafter cited as '*Lubanga*, confirmation of charges').

[66] ICC Pre-Trial Chamber, *Prosecutor v Katanga and Ngudjolo*, Decision on the Confirmation of Charges, Case No ICC-01/04-01/07, 30 September 2008, paras 500–10.

[67] ICC Pre-Trial Chamber II, *Prosecutor v Bemba Gombo*, Decision on the Confirmation of Charges, 15, Case No ICC-01/05-01/08, 15 June 2009, paras 352–69 (hereafter cited as '*Bemba Gombo*').

[68] *Lubanga*, confirmation of charges, paras 349–67.

[69] *Prosecutor v Lubanga*, Judgment Pursuant to Article 74 of the Statute, Case No ICC-01/04-01/06, 14 March 2012, Separate Opinion of Judge Fulford; *Prosecutor v Ngudjolo Chui*, Judgment Pursuant to Article 74 of the Statute, Case No ICC-01/04-02/12,18 December 2012, Concurring Opinion of Judge van den Wyngaert. For support of this approach see Wirth, 2012.

C. COMMAND RESPONSIBILITY

Command responsibility is the responsibility of those who have effective control over sub-ordinates for offences committed by them, where they failed to prevent or punish them. It received its modern judicial confirmation in the *Yamashita* case in 1945.[70] The current treaty-based statement of this principle of liability comes in Article 28 of the Rome Statute, which does not entirely reflect custom. Article 28 reads:

(a) A military commander or person effectively acting as a military commander shall be crimi-nally responsible for crimes within the jurisdiction of the Court committed by forces under his or her effective command and control, or effective authority and control as the case may be, as a result of his or her failure to exercise control properly over such forces, where:

   (i) That military commander or person either knew or, owing to the circumstances at the time, should have known that the forces were committing or about to commit such crimes; and

   (ii) That military commander or person failed to take all necessary and reasonable measures within his or her power to prevent or repress their commission or to sub-mit the matter to the competent authorities for investigation and prosecution.

(b) With respect to superior and subordinate relationships not described in paragraph (a), a superior shall be criminally responsible for crimes within the jurisdiction of the Court committed by subordinates under his or her effective authority and control, as a result of his or her failure to exercise control properly over such subordinates, where:

   (i) The superior either knew, or consciously disregarded information which clearly indicated, that the subordinates were committing or about to commit such crimes;

   (ii) The crimes concerned activities that were within the effective responsibility and control of the superior; and

   (iii) The superior failed to take all necessary and reasonable measures within his or her power to prevent or repress their commission or to submit the matter to the competent authorities for investigation and prosecution.

The ICTY has elaborated the requirements of command responsibility under custom-ary law. These are a superior/subordinate relationship; the 'mental element' and a failure to take reasonable measures to prevent or punish international crimes.[71] The Rome Statute also requires that a failure of the defendant's command had a causal relationship to the commission of the crimes.

The superior/subordinate relationship is characterized, for both military and civilian superiors, as being 'effective control', although it is accepted that the manner in which such control is exercised may differ between those superiors. Effective control means 'a material ability to prevent or punish criminal conduct', alongside a formal, or informal hierarchy.[72] A legal position is unnecessary, but may be useful evidence of effective control.[73]

The mental element of command responsibility is a matter of contention. Early cases, such as *Yamashita,* took the view that it was sufficient that the defendant 'knew, or should

---

[70] *US v Yamashita* (1945) 327 US 1.

[71] ICTY Trial Chamber II, *Prosecutor v Delalić, Mučić, Delić and Landžo*, Judgment, Case No IT-96-21-T, 16 November 1998, para 344 (known as, and hereafter cited as, '*Čelebići*').

[72] ICTY Appeals Chamber, *Prosecutor v Delalić, Mučić, Delić and Landžo* Judgment, Case No IT-96-23-A, 20 February 2001, para 256 (known as, and hereafter cited as, '*Čelebići* Appeal'). See generally Mettraux, 2009.

[73] *Čelebići* Appeal, para 197.

have known'; of the offences. The ICTY, however, interpreted the standard in its Statute (Article 7(3)) that the defendant knew, or had reason to know, of the offences, as being:

> where: (1) he had actual knowledge, established through direct or circumstantial evidence, that his subordinates were committing or about to commit crimes... or (2) where he had in his possession information of a nature, which at the least, would put him on notice of the risk of such offences by indicating the need for additional investigation in order to ascertain whether such crimes were committed or were about to be committed by his subordinates.[74]

This standard is the one accepted by later cases both in the ICTY and ICTR[75] is somewhat narrower than the 'should have known' standard, and, in the view of many, customary law (eg Kolb, 2000, p 301). The ICC, with respect to military superiors, has taken the view that the 'should have known' standard in Article 28 of the Rome Statute is broader, including negligent failures to obtain information, something not covered by the ICTY's formula.[76] The Rome Statute, does for the first time, expressly distinguish military and civilian superiors. The *mens rea* for civilian superiors, that they 'knew, or consciously disregarded information that clearly indicated' that offences occurred, or were going to, is a novelty in international law, and not necessarily a welcome one.

What the precise measures that the superior has to take in relation to subordinates has been said by the ICTY to be those which:

> can be taken within the competence of a commander as evidenced by the degree of effective control he wielded over his subordinates... What constitutes such measures is not a matter of substantive law but of evidence.[77]

Relevant evidence on this point, according to the ICC, building upon ICTY jurisprudence, includes activities:

> (i) to ensure that superior's forces are adequately trained in international humanitarian law;
> (ii) to secure reports that military actions were carried out in accordance with international law; (iii) to issue orders aiming at bringing the relevant practices into accord with the rules of war; (iv) to take disciplinary measures to prevent the commission of atrocities by the troops under the Superior's command.[78]

When it comes to punishment, it is possible that the superior is unable to punish the person personally. Where this is the case it can be sufficient that the superior 'submit[s] the matter to the competent authorities for investigation and prosecution.'[79]

As mentioned earlier in this section, the ICC Statute adds a requirement that the offences occur as a result of the superior's failure to exercise control. This creates a difficult issue relating to causation (Robinson, 2012). The ICTY has consistently rejected such a requirement;[80] the Rome Statute, however, is clear on the point. The ICC, has, nonetheless, done its best to minimize this requirement, by saying that:

> There is no direct causal link that needs to be established between the superior's omission and the crime committed by his subordinates. Therefore, the Chamber considers that it is only necessary to prove that the commander's omission increased the risk of

---

[74] Ibid, paras 223 and 241.   [75] *Blaškić* Appeal, paras 58–64.   [76] *Bemba Gombo*, para 432–4.

[77] *Blaškić* Appeal, para 72.   [78] *Bemba Gombo*, para 438.

[79] Rome Statute, Articles 28(a)(ii) and 28(b)(iii).

[80] ICTY Appeals Chamber, *Prosecutor v Hadžihasanović and Kubura*, Judgment, Case No IT-01-47-A, 22 April 2008, para 39 (hereafter cited as '*Hadžihasanović Appeal*').

the commission of the crimes charged in order to hold him criminally responsible under Article 28(a) of the Statute.[81]

This requirement also relates to the nature of command responsibility. Early case-law considered it a form of liability for the underlying crimes (Meloni, 2007, pp 621–3); however, amongst the judges in the ICTY, there is an increasing view that command responsibility is a sui generis form of liability, in that 'Command responsibility imposes responsibility on a commander for failure to take corrective action in respect of a crime committed by another; it does not make the commander party to the crime committed by that other.'[82] This is deeply contested (Meloni, 2007, Shahabuddeen, 2012, pp 213–16; Robinson, 2012), but nonetheless has implications for the ambit of command responsibility, as the ICTY accepted, in particular in relation to the question of whether a commander could be responsible for failing to punish offences that occurred prior to the superior taking up post.

D. DEFENCES

Defences are sometimes a taboo amongst international criminal lawyers (Eser, 1996, p 251). However, the defences that are applicable to international crimes, such as self-defence, duress, necessity, insanity, and intoxication[83] are similar to those in most domestic systems.[84] The defence that has caused most comment in international criminal law is obedience to superior orders.[85] The first major international document dealing with superior orders was the Nuremberg IMT's Charter, Article 8 of which excluded reliance on the defence, a position that was questionably consonant with the pre-existing customary position. However, the defence was also excluded in the Tokyo IMT's Statute (Article 7). The ICTY (Article 7(4)), ICTR (Article 6(4)), and SCSL (Article 6(4)) Statutes also exclude the defence. The ICC Statute, on the other hand, permits the defence in narrow circumstances for war crimes (Article 33), which reads:

1. The fact that a crime within the jurisdiction of the Court has been committed by a person pursuant to an order of a Government or of a superior, whether military or civilian, shall not relieve that person of criminal responsibility unless:

    (a) The person was under a legal obligation to obey orders of the Government or the superior in question;

    (b) The person did not know that the order was unlawful; and

    (c) The order was not manifestly unlawful.

2. For the purposes of this article, orders to commit genocide or crimes against humanity are manifestly unlawful.

The provision is quite tightly drafted, and all three conditions (that the person was under a duty to obey orders, that they did not know it was unlawful, and it was not manifestly

---

[81] *Bemba Gombo*, paras 424–5.

[82] *Hadžihasanović* Appeal, Judge Shahabuddeen, para 33. See also ICTY Appeals Chamber, *Prosecutor v Orić*, Judgment, Case No IT-03-68-A, 3 July 2008.

[83] See ICC Statute, Article 31.

[84] One difference to UK law though is that duress is not *a priori* excluded for intentional killings (Article 31(d)), although the ICTY has, by a bare majority, taken a different view: ICTY Appeals Chamber, *Prosecutor v Erdemović*, Judgment, Case No IT-96-22-A, 7 October 1997.

[85] See, eg Dinstein, 1965.

unlawful) have to be fulfilled before the defence may be relied on. Not all issues are entirely clear, for example, like earlier formulations this provision does not clarify to whom the illegality must be manifest. The customary status of Article 33 is contested (Gaeta, 1999; Garraway, 1999).

IV. PROSECUTION OF INTERNATIONAL CRIMES

A. THE NUREMBERG AND TOKYO IMTS[86]

Prosecutorial responses to international crimes have occurred at both the national and international levels, with varying degrees of success. The first international tribunal was the Nuremberg IMT, which sat between 1945 and 1946 to prosecute high-ranking Nazis. It was set up by France, the UK, the USA, and the USSR. Pursuant to Article 6 of its Charter, the Tribunal had jurisdiction over crimes against peace (aggression), crimes against humanity, and war crimes. Articles 9 and 10 of the Charter also permitted it to make declarations of criminality against organizations, which would permit domestic prosecutions of their members for that membership. Six such organizations were prosecuted (the SS, SD, SA, High Command, Leadership Corps of the Nazi party, and the Gestapo) alongside 24 individuals. They were chosen for their representative nature of the Nazi party, the Army, Navy, and civilian supporters of the regime. The most famous of the defendants was Hermann Göring.

Three of the indicted organizations were acquitted (the SA, High Command, and Leadership Corps). Three of the defendants (Hjalmar Schacht, Hans Fritzsche, and Franz von Papen) were also acquitted. All the other defendants were convicted, although not of all charges laid against them. The judgment is a seminal document in international criminal law, and, although not without its flaws, the trial process was basically fair. There were critiques of the Nuremberg Trial, many of which focus on the crimes against peace charge, which was novel in 1945 (Schwarzenberger, 1947, 346–8), and the fact that allegations of war crimes by Allied forces were not heard. This latter claim has some validity, but this is not generally thought to entirely undermine the legitimacy of the Nuremberg Trial.

There was a lesser-known counterpart to Nuremberg in Tokyo, designed to prosecute the leaders of martial Japan. It was set up by Australia, Canada, China, India, France, the Netherlands, New Zealand, the Philippines, the UK, the USA, and the USSR, all of whom appointed one judge. Article 5 of the Tokyo IMT's Charter gave the Tribunal jurisdiction over crimes against peace, crimes against humanity, and war crimes. The indictment charged 28 Japanese leaders, both military and civilian, with crimes against peace, war crimes, and murder. These last charges were based on the prosecution's theory that killings in aggressive wars were not covered by belligerent privilege, and were therefore, simply, murder. The Tribunal considered these charges as overlapping with the crimes against peace charges, so did not pronounce on their validity.[87]

The majority judgment, which was delivered in 1948, largely followed the Nuremberg judgment on issues of law such as the criminality of crimes against peace, and the exclusion of superior orders,[88] but, also dealt with command responsibility, including of civilians.[89] It found a large-scale conspiracy on the part of the defendants (all of whom who lived through to the judgment were convicted, although not of all counts) to dominate Asia as far back as 1928,

---

[86] See, eg Taylor, 1993; Boister and Cryer, 2008.   [87] Tokyo IMT Judgment, p 48,449.
[88] Ibid, pp 48,437–48,439.   [89] Ibid, 48,443–48,447.

and various war crimes. The judgment was not unanimous though, and there were various separate and dissenting opinions. One of the judges, Judge Bernard (France) thought that the proceedings were so flawed that he could not determine the charges against the defendants.[90] Judge Jaranilla, on the other hand, was of the view that the Tribunal had been too lenient both in terms of the charges that were not pronounced upon, and the sentences imposed.[91] Judge Webb, who presided over the trial used his opinion to criticize the absence of the Emperor of Japan from the dock.[92]

Judge Röling doubted the existence of a crime against peace in international law at the time, but argued that those responsible for such offences could lawfully be interned in the interests of international security.[93] He also raised factual doubts about some of the convictions.[94] The largest, and most famous, dissent was that of the Indian justice, Judge Pal. Pal denied the existence of crimes against peace,[95] found that there was no conspiracy,[96] and that none of the war crimes found were attributable to the defendants.[97] He would have acquitted them all, and accused the prosecuting States of hypocrisy owing to their colonialism and use of the atomic bomb.[98] The critiques of the Tokyo IMT are similar to those of the Nuremberg IMT, although there has also been significant, and not unjustifiable, criticism of the running of the trial.[99]

B. THE ICTY AND ICTR[100]

There were no international proceedings after the Nuremberg and Tokyo IMTs until after the end of the Cold War. Then in 1993 the Security Council, responding to atrocities in the former Yugoslavia, created the ICTY under its powers under Chapter VII of the UN Charter, in Resolution 827 (25 May 2003).[101] The Tribunal has jurisdiction over grave breaches of the Geneva Conventions (ICTY Statute, Article 2), other war crimes (Article 3), crimes against humanity (Article 4), and genocide (Article 5) committed in former Yugoslavia since 1 January 1991. The ICTY has primacy over national courts.[102] This means that the Tribunal may require States to defer any proceedings they were contemplating or undertaking to it.[103] The Tribunal may also order any State to co-operate with the Tribunal.[104]

The early practice of the ICTY was hampered by the refusal of a number of the ex-Yugoslav States to co-operate. Of those States, only the central government in Bosnia was supportive of the ICTY. Many of those thought responsible for crimes were still in high-ranking positions in Serbia, Croatia or the *Repulika Srpska*. As a result of their refusal to hand over suspects, early cases at the court tended to be of low-ranking soldiers, which

---

[90] Dissenting Opinion of the Member from France, pp 18–23.

[91] Concurring Opinion of the Member from the Philippines, pp 7–10, 32–5.

[92] Separate Opinion of the President, pp 18–20.

[93] Opinion of the Member for the Netherlands, pp 10–53.   [94] Ibid, 178–249.

[95] Dissenting Opinion of the Member for India, Parts 1 and 2.   [96] Ibid, part 4.   [97] Ibid, part 6.

[98] Ibid, Recommendation.   [99] On such critiques, see Boister and Cryer, 2008, Ch 4.

[100] See generally Schabas, 2006.

[101] The legality of this was doubted by some (Rubin, 1994) but confirmed by the ICTY in the *Tadić* Appeal.

[102] ICTY Statute, Article 9(1).

[103] Eg *In the Matter of a Proposal for a Formal Request for Deferral to the Competence of the Tribunal Addressed to the Republic of Bosnia and Herzegovina in Respect of Radovan Karadzic, Ratko Mladic and Mico Stanisic*, IT-95-5-D, Trial Chamber (16 May 1995).

[104] ICTY Statute, Article 28.

caused criticism (Verrijn Stuart and Simons, 2009, p 53). These early cases did, however, allow the ICTY to considerably develop their processes and also international law, in particular, in the *Tadić* case.[105] By 1996 the end of the war and some political developments caused cooperation to improve, other than by Serbia. Serbia only began to co-operate with the Tribunal in any meaningful way in 2001, when they transferred ex-president Milošević to the Tribunal.

A year before that, the judges realized that their work could take 15 more years. As a result they asked the Security Council to ensure a 'completion strategy'. The Security Council responded with Resolution 1329 (5 December 2000), which allowed for the appointment of additional judges. On its side, in 2002, the ICTY adopted Rule of Procedure and Evidence 11 bis, which allowed it to refer cases back to national courts, effectively outsourcing its work. The completion strategy was followed up by Resolution 1503 (28 August 2003) and Resolution 1534 (26 March 2004), which directed the prosecutor to focus on those bearing the greatest responsibility for crimes, the judges to confirm this when reviewing indictments, and gave a timetable for the completion of investigations, trials and appeals. The timeframe for completion of the latter two aspects has had to slide. As of May 2013, the Tribunal had, of the 161 people charged, completed proceedings against 136 accused with 69 convictions and 18 acquittals. It is continuing proceedings against 25 accused (others have had their indictments withdrawn, the proceedings referred to domestic courts under Rule 11 *bis*, or died).[106] The Tribunal currently has custody over all indictees over whom it wishes to assert jurisdiction.

The ICTY itself has set out a number of its achievements.[107] These are, *inter alia,* that it has promoted accountability rather than impunity, including of leaders, established the facts of the crimes in former Yugoslavia, brought justice to victims and given them a voice, developed international law and strengthened the rule of law.[108] The Tribunal has, to some extent, fulfilled these goals, although critiques of the Tribunals that they are expensive and slow are not entirely untrue (Zacklin, 2004, pp 543–4). The ICTY is intended to finish its work in 2016, although whether it will be able to do so is a matter of conjecture. When its primary work is complete, the lasting functions of the ICTY, such as dealing with possible new facts, and parole decisions are to be passed to an entity known as the 'Residual Mechanism', set up by the Security Council, which started work in 2012.[109]

Shortly after the creation of the ICTY, the Security Council created the ICTR, to prosecute international crimes committed in Rwanda in 1994. Notably, Rwanda was, at the time a non-permanent member of the Security Council. Although it was initially supportive of the creation of the ICTR, owing to the refusal of other members to include the death penalty in the sentencing regime of the Court, it voted against the Resolution that established the Court.[110] The ICTR has jurisdiction over genocide (ICTR Statute, Article 2), crimes against humanity (Article 3) and some war crimes—violations of common Article 3 and Additional Protocol II (Article 4). It has the same powers in relation to primacy and cooperation as the ICTY. They also have a joint appeals chamber, to ensure consistency of their jurisprudence.[111]

Unlike the early practice of the ICTY, some African States were quick to co-operate with the ICTR, although Rwanda was not always amongst them. This was a problem, as most of the evidence and witnesses, and many of the suspects, were in Rwanda. The ICTR was,

[105] *Tadić* Appeal.   [106] http://www.icty.org/sections/TheCases/KeyFigures.
[107] http://www.icty.org/sid/324.   [108] Ibid.   [109] SC Res 1966 (22 December 2010).
[110] SC Res 955 (8 November 1994).   [111] ICTR Statute, Article 12(2).

initially, slow to move, there were staffing problems, and a damning report on the management and administration of the ICTR in 1997 was highly damaging.

Things appeared to improve in 1998, when the ex-Prime minister of Rwanda, Jean Kambanda, pleaded guilty to genocide, admitting that this had occurred in Rwanda. The first trial, of a Mayor, Jean-Paul Akayesu, proceeded to judgment in September 1998. 1999 proved more difficult. In protest at a decision of the Appeals Chamber in the *Barayagwiza* case to release a defendant whose human rights had been violated in pre-trial detention in Cameroon,[112] Rwanda refused to co-operate with the ICTR at all. This practically caused trials to stop. The Appeals Chamber revisited its decision in early 2000, and determined that Barayagwiza should remain in detention and sent for trial.[113] Rwanda resumed cooperation as a result. Some have suggested that this showed the extent that Rwanda was able to guide the practice of the Court (Schabas, 2000, p 565).

In 2003 the ICTR also was given a very similar completion strategy by the Security Council in the same Resolutions. As of April 2013, the Tribunal had completed its trial phase, trying 75 people, 63 of whom were convicted (although 17 of these defendants have pending appeals). The other defendants who have appeared before the Tribunal either died pre-judgment, had their indictments withdrawn or their cases were referred to domestic courts pursuant to the ICTR's Rule of Procedure and evidence *11 bis*. Although it has not tried all of the ringleaders of the genocide, it has proceeded against many of them (van den Herik, 2005, p 263).

There have been considerable criticisms of the ICTR for failing to prosecute possible offences committed by the Rwandan Patriotic Front (RPF), particularly in the aftermath of the genocide, and it has been suggested that this is because the RPF, having defeated the génocidaires in 1994, became (and remain) the government of Rwanda, and control cooperation with the ICTR. The prosecutor has argued, on the other hand that the allegations are less serious than those against Hutu defendants and because of the completion strategy, there is no time to engage in prosecution of allegations against the RPF (Peskin, 2008, Ch 8; Thalman, 2008, pp 1001–2). The ICTR is meant to finish its work in 2014. A residual mechanism similar to that set up for the ICTY is in place for the ICTR, and has taken over many of the ICTR's functions already.[114] Unlike the ICTY, the ICTR has three high-ranking fugitives not in custody. Their trials, if and when they are caught, will be before the residual mechanism.

C. THE INTERNATIONAL CRIMINAL COURT (ICC)

Probably the most important development in international criminal law, at least since Nuremberg, was the creation of the ICC.[115] The ICC's Statute was finalized in 1998 in difficult negotiations in Rome. The ICC actually came into being in 2002, when the required 60 ratifications were obtained. There are currently 122 States parties to the ICC Statute. The Court has jurisdiction over genocide, crimes against humanity, and a closed list of war crimes (ICC Statute, Articles 5–8).[116] The ICC also has jurisdiction over the crime

---

[112] ICTR Appeals Chamber, *Prosecutor v Barayagwiza*, Decision, ICTR-97-19-AR72, 19 November 1999.

[113] ICTR Appeals Chamber, *Prosecutor v Barayagwiza*, Decision (Prosecutor's Request for Review or Reconsideration) ICTR-97-19-AR72, 31 March 2000.

[114] S/RES/1966 (22 December 2010)   [115] See generally, Triffterer, 2008.

[116] Owing to concerns about the possible limiting effect of the Statute's definitions on customary law Article 10 of the Statute provides that 'Nothing in this Part shall be interpreted as limiting or prejudicing in any way existing or developing rules of international law for purposes other than this statute.'

of aggression, but it that jurisdiction is yet to be triggered by the entry into force of the relevant amendment to the Rome Statute. The Statute also contains a detailed treatment of the general principles of criminal law such as principles of liability and defences (Articles 25, 28, 30–33).

Other than for aggression, the jurisdiction of the Court is over crimes committed by nationals of States parties or on their territories (Article 12), or over any situation referred to it by the Security Council (Article 13(b)). The jurisdiction of the ICC is prospective, it began, for its States parties at that date, in 2002, when the Statute came into force (Article 11(1)). For States that were not parties then, unless they make a specific declaration that it may, the ICC can only exercise its jurisdiction in relation to the relevant offences committed after then entry into force of the Statute for them (Article 11(2)).

There are three ways for the prosecutor to initiate an investigation: the first is after the referral of the situation by a State party to the Rome Statute (Article 12(a)). Contrary to expectations, this provision has led to the practice of 'Self Referrals' where States refer the situations in their own territories to the ICC (Arsanjani and Reisman, 2005). This has happened four times (the Democratic Republic of Congo, Mali, Central African Republic, and Uganda). There is nothing in law to prevent this, but there have been suggestions that the ICC may be too close to governments who wish it to prosecute crimes by rebels, but not their own misdeeds. The next method of the ICC beginning an investigation is that the prosecutor may, with the consent of a Pre-Trial Chamber, initiate an investigation on his own motion (Article 15). This was controversial at Rome, but has been invoked, *inter alia*, by the prosecutor in relation to post-election violence in Kenya[117] and the Côte d'Ivoire.

The Security Council also has the power to refer a situation anywhere in the world to the ICC (Article 13(b)). The Security Council has, contrary to expectation done this twice, referring the situation in Darfur, Sudan, to the ICC in 2005 in Resolution 1593 (Cryer, 2006), and Libya in 2011 in Resolution 1970. The Council has, however, been very wary of taking enforcement measures in support of the ICC and its orders. The Security Council has the power under Article 16 of the ICC Statute to require the prosecutor to defer investigation or prosecution for a one-year period that can be renewed indefinitely. Its practice under this Article, in Resolutions 1422 and 1487 were heavily criticized (Jain, 2005), although these Resolutions now seem to have been relegated to the annals of history, having not been renewed for some years now.

In contrast to the ICTY and ICTR, who enjoy primacy over national courts, the ICC's jurisdiction is said to be 'complementary' to domestic jurisdictions (Article 1).[118] This means that the ICC can only exercise jurisdiction where it determines that a competent national court is 'unwilling or unable genuinely' to prosecute a case itself (Article 17). Unwillingness is elaborated upon by Article 17(3):

(a) the proceedings were or are being undertaken or the national decision was made for the purpose of shielding the person concerned from criminal responsibility for crimes within the jurisdiction of the court referred to in Article 5;

(b) there has been an unjustified delay in the proceedings which in the circumstances is inconsistent with an intent to bring the person concerned to justice;

(c) the proceedings were not or are not being conducted independently or impartially, and they were or are being conducted in a manner which, in the circumstances, is inconsistent with an intent to bring the person concerned to justice.

---

[117] *Request for Authorisation of an Investigation Pursuant to Article 15*, ICC-01/09, 26 November 2009.
[118] See generally Kleffner, 2008, Stahn and El-Zeidy, 2011.

Inability is the subject of Article 17(3), which reads: 'In order to determine inability in a particular case, the Court shall consider whether, due to a total or substantial collapse or unavailability of its national judicial system, the State is unable to obtain the accused or the necessary evidence and testimony or otherwise unable to carry out its proceedings.' The precise interpretation of these terms will be an important task for the Court. This is a process which is currently embryonic, although the Appeals Chamber has made clear that where there is inactivity by the relevant State, the case is admissible without the necessity of determining unwillingness or inability.[119] What has proved controversial is the definition of a 'case' in complementarity. Early practice of the Court has said that a 'case' encompasses both that this had both a personal and a conduct-based element. In other words, the person must be being investigated and/or prosecuted for the conduct that forms the basis of the proposed arrest warrant before a case can be declared inadmissible on the basis of Article 17.[120] This is a surprisingly stringent requirement for inadmissibility, and has been criticized as too exacting (Schabas, 2011, pp 197–8).

There are both legal and political critiques of the ICC. It is sometimes the case that the former reflect the latter. The main legal challenge, which was first raised by the US government, is the allegation that as the ICC can exercise its jurisdiction over nationals of non-State parties (where they commit international crimes on the territory of States parties) the Rome Statute violates international law (Scheffer, 1999, p 71). The most sophisticated version of this critique does not deny that States can exercise their own territorial jurisdiction over non-nationals, but that they cannot delegate that power to an international organization (Morris, 2001, pp 26–52). However, there is no existing prohibition of this in international law (Akande, 2003, pp 625–34).

Some of the early practice of the Court, in particular that the situations currently before the ICC are all in Africa, has led to criticism from some quarters, alleging that the prosecutor is acting selectively, by not confronting powerful (especially Western) countries (see generally Ambos, 2013). The Office of the Prosecutor has responded strongly, arguing that they are only applying the law, that the situations chosen are the most serious, and the critique ignores African victims.[121] Whatever the merits of those claims, the indictment of President al-Bashir of Sudan has caused some to question whether the possibility of peace is being sacrificed on the altar of justice.[122] Such claims are perhaps best addressed to the Security Council, who has the power under Article 16 to defer investigations before the ICC in the interests of peace, rather than criticizing the ICC for doing what it was designed to do, which is to investigate and prosecute international crimes.

D. 'INTERNATIONALIZED' AND NATIONAL COURTS

There are also a diverse group of courts which come under the heading of 'internationalized'.[123] Some, such as the SCSL, and the Special Tribunal for Lebanon are more akin to

---

[119] ICC Appeals Chamber, *Prosecutor v Katanga and Chui*, Judgment on the Appeal of Mr. Germain Katanga against the Oral Decision of Trial Chamber II of 12 June 2009 on the Admissibility of the Case, Case No ICC-01/04-01/07, 25 September 2009, paras 1–2.

[120] *Prosecutor v Lubanga*, Decision on the Prosecutor's Application for a Warrant of Arrest, Article 58, ICC-01-04-01/06, Pre-Trial Chamber I, 10 February 2006, paras 37–9.

[121] Deputy Prosecutor's Remarks, 'Introduction to the Rome Statute Establishing the ICC and Africa's Involvement with the ICC' 14 April 2009.

[122] See the Decision of the African Union Assembly/AU/Dec 245 (XIII) 3 July 2009.

[123] See generally, Cryer, Friman, Robinson, and Wilmshurst, 2014, Ch 9. On their promise, see Dickinson, 2003. For a more sombre analysis, see McAuliffe, 2013.

international courts than domestic courts, as their founding documents are treaties or Security Council Resolutions rather than domestic legislation. Others, such as the Iraqi High Tribunal and the Extraordinary Chambers in the Courts of Cambodia are far closer to ordinary domestic courts, as their jurisdiction is founded on domestic law—they simply have some form of international support, usually in the form of international staff. Each such court is rather different, both in the level of internationalization and jurisdiction. The SCSL, for example, was described by the Secretary-General as 'a treaty-based *sui generis* court of mixed jurisdiction and composition'.[124] It has jurisdiction over international crimes, such as crimes against humanity and some war crimes (SCSL Statute Articles 2–4) and domestic offences, such as arson (Article 5). The Special Tribunal for Lebanon, on the other hand has jurisdiction over Lebanese domestic crimes only, although it uses international law principles of liability (STL Statute, Articles 2–3). The Iraqi High Tribunal and Extraordinary Chambers prosecute domestic crimes, but which are based on implementations of international criminal law. The diversity of these courts makes generalizations about them often unhelpful.

The bulk of prosecutions of international crimes are intended to be in domestic courts. States are entitled to assert universal jurisdiction over genocide, crimes against humanity and war crimes.[125] However, in spite of a number of well-known trials, such as the *Eichmann* trial,[126] for the most part domestic courts have been slow to react to international crimes. Often political difficulties in the territorial or nationality jurisdiction impede prosecutions, and other States are unwilling to become involved, with the bulk of prosecutions being of Nazis, former-Yugoslav and Rwandan accused, where there is almost unanimous agreement on the need for prosecution (Langer, 2011). There are some signs that there is an increased willingness of domestic courts to prosecute international crimes. Part of the reason for this is a positive side-effect of the complementarity provisions of the ICC Statute, which create an incentive for domestic authorities to prosecute international crimes rather than see them prosecuted internationally.

V. NON-PROSECUTORIAL RESPONSES TO INTERNATIONAL CRIMES

Although there is an increasing swing towards prosecution of international crimes, both historically and currently there are other methods of dealing with international crimes. The lawfulness of some of them are increasingly being contested, however, at least some of them can be seen as complementary to prosecution, although others (such as amnesties) have to be seen as alternatives.

A. AMNESTIES

Amnesties are conferred by a law that blocks criminal action against people in the State in which it is passed. At the end of a conflict, the practice was frequently, at least until recently, to offer an amnesty to all of those who committed crimes. They were very controversial in the 1980s when various military regimes granted themselves amnesties, or required them

---

[124] Report by the Secretary-General on the Establishment of a Special Court for Sierra Leone, UN Doc S/2000/915 (4 October 2000), para 9.

[125] See Staker, Ch 11 of this book.

[126] *Attorney-General of the Government of Israel* v *Eichmann* (1961) 36 ILR 5.

as a condition for handing over power. The most well-known amnesty offered in the recent past was that in South Africa, following truth and reconciliation proceedings after the end of apartheid.

There are various types of amnesties,[127] which go from those granted by regimes to themselves to those which are voted upon by the population. Although the latter are usually thought more legitimate than the former, it must also be said that often there is little practical choice for the electorate.[128] A further distinction must be made between 'blanket' amnesties, which prevent legal proceedings against all persons without distinction, and those, such as the South African amnesty legislation, which required certain conduct (often full confession of crimes) and/or certain motivations for the crimes (usually political ones) before an amnesty was granted. The latter seem to obtain a greater level of support.

The legality of amnesties is hotly contested. There are those who argue that amnesties are inevitably unlawful (Orentlicher, 1991). These arguments tend to rely on either human rights concerns, or the assertion that there is an all-encompassing duty to prosecute international crimes. It is true that there are certain treaties that impose a duty to prosecute certain international crimes, such as the Geneva Conventions grave breaches regime (eg Geneva Convention 1 Article 49), the Genocide Convention (Articles IV, VI) and the Torture Convention (Article 5). However, these do not cover, for example crimes against humanity or war crimes other than grave breaches. Therefore, authors supporting the existence of this duty tend to revert to customary law. However, there is not sufficient State practice yet to assert that customary law imposes a duty to prosecute all international crimes, and certainly not on the basis of universal jurisdiction.[129]

Looking to the human rights arguments, The Inter-American Court of Human Rights and Commission have been the most strident in declaring amnesties unlawful:

> all amnesty provisions, provisions on prescription and the establishment of measures designed to eliminate responsibility are inadmissible, because they are intended to prevent the investigation and punishment of those responsible for serious human rights violations such as torture, extrajudicial, summary or arbitrary execution and forced disappearance, all of them prohibited because they violate non-derogable rights recognized by international human rights law.[130]

However, it is by no means clear that this is reflective of a more general principle of human rights law, and probably has much to do with the particular context of Latin America and the fact that the Peruvian amnesty under discussion were granted by a regime to itself in a developed State.[131] The other regional human rights courts, and the Human Rights Committee have not gone so far as the inter-American Court, and so despite the fact that the scope for lawful amnesties appears to be narrowing, it has not been completely removed.[132]

---

[127] For a detailed survey see Mallinder, 2008.   [128] Osiel, 1997, p 138.

[129] SCSL Appeals Chamber, *Prosecutor* v *Kallon and Kamara*, Decision on Challenge to Jurisdiction: Lomé Amnesty Accord, SCSL-2004-15-AR72(E) and SCSL-2004-16-AR72(E), 13 March 2004, para 82. But see Akhavan, 2010.

[130] Inter American Court of Human Rights, *Chumbipuma Aguierre et al* v *Peru (Barrios Altos Case)*, Judgment, 14 March 2001 Series C No 75, [2001] IACHR 5, para 41. See Binder, 2011.

[131] Siebert-Fohr, 2009, p109.

[132] SCSL Appeals Chamber, *Prosecutor* v *Kondewa*, Decision on Lack of Jurisdiction/Abuse of Process: Amnesty provided by the Lome Accord, SCSL-2004-14-AR72(E) 25 May 2004, para 48: but see Bell, 2008, pp 240–41.

B. TRUTH AND RECONCILIATION COMMISSIONS

A frequently used response to international crimes is a truth and reconciliation commission (TRC). These have been defined as bodies that '(1) focus on the past, rather than ongoing, events; (2) investigate a pattern of events that took place over a period of time; (3) engage directly and broadly with the affected population, gathering information on their experiences; (4) are temporary bodies, with the aim of concluding with a final report; and (5) are officially authorized by the State under review'.[133] One of the most famous of these was the South African TRC. However, there have also been TRCs in, for example Guatemala, Liberia, and Sierra Leone. In the latter case, difficulties were encountered, as there were also proceedings ongoing before the SCSL and the TRC wanted to testimony from some of those indicted before the Tribunal. This led to tensions as the Special Court was unwilling to allow this on the terms the Commission wanted.[134]

The success or otherwise of TRCs depends on various factors, including the terms of reference that they have and the personal qualities of the commissioners. A great deal depends on the quality of the information that they can obtain. This can be difficult, as perpetrators are unlikely to be willing to fully confess their activities without some promise of amnesty or immunity, and victims may be unwilling to talk about sensitive matters. Although sometimes the hearings can be cathartic affairs, this is not always the case, and some victims are not satisfied with truth without more. It has also been questioned if truth-telling does lead to reconciliation (Hayner, 2011, Ch 13) Similarly, it has been doubted if truth and reconciliation are congruent goals. Most take the view that there is a relationship though (ibid).

C. OTHER RESPONSES

One way in which some countries have dealt with large-scale criminality is by lustration, which is the compulsory removal of people from their jobs.[135] This is usually done on a mass, rather than individual, basis and as such has fallen from favour, as the innocent are punished alongside the guilty. There were elements of lustration involved in the de-Baathification of Iraq, which was, in itself, subject to criticism.

In some countries civil claims relating to international crimes are permitted. For example, there has been a series of civil suits in the USA against alleged human rights violators (including international criminals) under its Alien Tort Claims Act where their conduct occurred outside the USA. The first such case *Filártiga* v *Peña-Irala*[136] was considered groundbreaking in this regard, and has led to a large number of civil claims in US courts. However, more recent cases have put significant limitations on this line of authority,[137] in particular the extraterritorial applicability of the Act, which has been significantly curtailed.[138]

Whether these are sufficient is sometimes the subject of doubt, but in the absence of prosecutions such proceedings can find the facts and provide some measure of justice for victims, even if where they occur outside the *locus delicti* enforcing such awards can

---

[133] Hayner, 2011, pp 11–12.

[134] *Report of the Truth and Reconciliation Commission for Sierra Leone*, vo. 3b, Ch 6.

[135] See generally Teitel, 2002, Ch 5.   [136] *Filartiga* v *Peña-Irala*, 630 F2d 876 (2nd Cir 1980).

[137] Eg *Sosa* v *Alvarez-Machain* (2004) 542 US 692; although this may not have affected claims relating to allegations of international crimes.

[138] *Kiobel* v *Royal Dutch Petroleum Co*, 133 S Ct 1659 (2013).

be very difficult. Immunities can also be a problem in third States where government behaviour is at issue. In many societies where there have been international crimes, there simply are insufficient resources to satisfy claims. In some societies, it is suggested that rather than prosecution, people ought to undergo culturally appropriate traditional justice mechanisms aimed at reconciliation rather than prosecution. Local justice mechanisms are supported by many, on the basis that they 'may have greater legitimacy and capacity than devastated formal systems, and they promise local ownership, access and efficiency' (Waldorf, 2006, p 4). However, critics have said that they can also be exclusionary, in fact government, not people-led, anachronistic, not designed to deal with international crimes, and dubious on human rights grounds (Drumbl, 2005, p 549). As is very often the case, a great deal depends on the particular process and its context, making sweeping acceptances or rejections of such measures ill-advised.

REFERENCES

ABI-SAAB, G (2001), 'The Concept of War Crimes', in Yee, S and Tieya, W (eds), *International Law and the Post-Cold World: Essays in Honour of Li Haopei*, (London: Routledge), p 99.

AKANDE, D (2003), 'The Jurisdiction of the International Criminal Court Over Nationals of Non-Parties: Legal Basis and Limits', 1 *JICJ* 618.

AKHAVAN, P (2010), 'Whither National Courts? The Rome Statute's Missing Half: Towards An Express and Enforceable Obligation For the National Repression of International Crimes', 8 *JICJ* 1245.

—— (2012), *Reducing Genocide to Law: Definition, Meaning and the Ultimate Crime* (Cambridge: Cambridge University Press).

AMBOS, K (2013), 'Expanding the focus of the 'African Criminal Court', in Schabas, WA, McDermott, Y, and Hayes, N (eds), *The Ashgate Research Companion to International Criminal Law: Critical Perspectives* (Farnham: Ashgate), p 499.

ARSANJANI, M and REISMAN, R, (2005), 'The Law-in-action of the International Criminal Court', 99 *AJIL* 385.

BASSIOUNI, MC (1994), 'Crimes Against Humanity: The Need for a Specialized Convention', 31 *Columbia Journal of Transnational Law* 457.

BELL, C (2008), *On the Law of Peace: Peace Agreements and the Lex Pacificatoria* (Oxford: Oxford University Press).

BINDER, C (2011), 'The Prohibition of Amnesties by the Inter-American Court of Human Rights', 12 *German Law Journal* 1203.

BOISTER, N (2003), 'Transnational Criminal Law?', 14 *EJIL* 953.

—— (2012), *An Introduction to Transnational Criminal Law* (Oxford: Oxford University Press).

—— and CRYER, R (2008), *The Tokyo International Military Tribunal: A Reappraisal* (Oxford: Oxford University Press).

CASSESE, A (2007), 'The Proper Limits of Criminal Liability Under the Doctrine of Joint Criminal Enterprise', 5 *JICJ* 109.

—— et al (2013), *Cassese's International Criminal Law* (Oxford: Oxford University Press).

CLARKE, KM (2009), *Fictions of Justice: The International Criminal Court and the Challenge of Legal Pluralism in Sub-Saharan Africa* (Cambridge: Cambridge University Press).

CRYER, R (2005), *Prosecuting International Crimes: Selectivity and the International Criminal Law Regime* (Cambridge: Cambridge University Press).

—— (2006), 'Sudan Resolution 1593 and International Criminal Justice', 19 *Leiden Journal of International Law* 195.

——, FRIMAN, H, Robinson, D, and WILMSHURST, E (2014), *An Introduction to International Criminal Law and Procedure*, 3rd edn (Cambridge: Cambridge University Press).

CULLEN, A (2011), 'War Crimes', in Schabas, WA and Bernaz N (eds), *Routledge Handbook of International Criminal Law* (London: Routledge), p 139.

DANNER, AM and MARTINEZ, JS (2005), 'Guilty Associations: Joint Criminal Enterprise, Command Responsibility and the Development of International Criminal Law', 93 *California Law Review* 75.

DICKINSON, L (2003), 'The Promise of Hybrid Courts', 97 *AJIL* 295.

DINSTEIN, Y (1965), The Defence of 'Obedience to Superior Orders', in *International Criminal Law* (Leyden: A W Sitjhoff).

DJURO-DEGAN, V (2005), 'On the Sources of International Criminal Law', 4 *Chinese Journal of International Law* 45.

DRUMBL, M (2005), 'Collective Violence and Individual Punishment: The Criminality of Mass Atrocity', 99 *Northwestern University Law Review* 539.

ESER, A (1996), 'Defences in War Crimes Trials' in Dinstein, Y and Tabory, M (eds), *War Crimes in International Law* (Dordrecht: Martinus Nijhoff), p 251.

FLETCHER, G (2012), 'The Theory of Criminal Liability and International Criminal Law', 10 *JICJ* 1029.

GAETA, P (1999), 'The Defence of Superior Orders: The Statute of the International Criminal Court Versus Customary International Law', 10 *EJIL* 172.

GALLANT, K (2008), *The Principle of Legality in International and Comparative Law* (Cambridge: Cambridge University Press).

GARRAWAY, C (1999), 'Superior Orders and the International Criminal Court: Justice Delivered or Justice Denied?', 836 *International Review of the Red Cross* 785.

GREENAWALT, AKA (1999), 'Rethinking Genocidal Intent: The Case for a Knowledge-Based Interpretation', 99 *Columbia Law Review* 2265.

GREENWOOD, C (1996), 'International Humanitarian Law and the Tadić Case', (1996) 7 *EJIL* 265.

HALLING, M (2010), 'Push The Envelope Watch It Bend: Removing the Policy Requirement and Extending Crimes Against Humanity', 23 *Leiden Journal of International Law* 829.

HAYNER, P (2011), *Unspeakable Truths: Confronting State Terror and Atrocity*, 2nd edn (London: Routledge).

HENCKAERTS, J-M, and DOSWALD-BECK, L (2005), *Customary International Humanitarian Law* (Cambridge: Cambridge University Press).

JAIN, N (2005), 'A Separate Law for Peacekeepers; the Clash between the Security Council and the International Criminal Court', 16 *EJIL* 239.

KELSALL, T (2009), *Culture Under Cross-Examination: International Justice and the Special Court for Sierra Leone* (Cambridge: Cambridge University Press).

KLEFFNER, J (2008), *Complementarity in the Rome Statute and National Criminal Jurisdictions* (Oxford: Oxford University Press).

KOLB, R (2000), 'The Jurisprudence of the Yugoslav and Rwandan Criminal Tribunals on Their Jurisdiction and on International Crimes', 69 *BYIL* 259.

KRESS,C (2010), 'On the Outer Limits of Crimes against Humanity: The Concept of Organization within the Policy Requirement: Some Reflections on the March 2010 ICC Kenya Decision', 23 *Leiden Journal of International Law* 855.

LANGER, M (2011), 'The Diplomacy of Universal Jurisdiction: The Political Branches and the Transnational Prosecution of International Crimes', 105 *AJIL* 1.

LEMKIN, R (1944), *Axis Rule in Occupied Europe* (New York: Carnegie Endowment for International Peace).

LUBAN, D (2006–7), 'Calling Genocide by Its Rightful Name: Lemkin's Word, Darfur, and the UN Report', 7 *Chicago Journal of International Law* 303.

MALLINDER, L (2008), *Amnesty, Human Rights and Political Transitions: Bridging the Gap in International Law* (Oxford: Hart).

MCAULIFFE, P, (2013), 'Hybrid Courts in Retrospect: Of Lost Legacies and Modest Futures', in Schabas, WA, McDermott, Y, and Hayes, N (eds), *The Ashgate Research Companion to International Criminal Law: Critical Perspectives* (Farnham: Ashgate), p 453.

MELONI, C (2007), 'Command Responsibility: Mode of Liability for Subordinates or Separate Offence of the Superior?', 5 *JICJ* 619.

METTRAUX, G (2009), *The Law of Command Responsibility* (Oxford: Oxford University Press).

MORRIS, M (2001), 'High Crimes and Misconceptions: The ICC and Non-Party States', 64 *Law and Contemporary Problems* 131.

NERSESSIAN, DL (2010), *Genocide and Political Groups* (Oxford: Oxford University Press).

OHLIN, J (2007), 'Three Conceptual Problems with the Doctrine of Joint Criminal Enterprise', 5 *JICJ* 69.

OOSTERVELD, V (2001), 'Context of Genocide', in Lee, R et al (eds), *The International Criminal Court: Elements of Crimes and Rules of Procedure and Evidence* (Ardsley: Transnational), p 44.

ORENTLICHER, D (1991), 'Settling Accounts: The Duty to Prosecute Violations of a Prior Regime', 100 *Yale Law Journal* 2537.

OSIEL, M (1997), *The International Criminal Court: Elements of Crimes and Rules of Procedure and Evidence* (Ardsley: Transnational) (New Brunswick: Transaction).

PESKIN, V (2008), *International Justice in Rwanda and the Balkans: Virtual Trials and the Struggle for State Cooperation* (Cambridge: Cambridge University Press).

ROBINSON, D (2008), 'The Identity Crisis of International Criminal Law', 21 *Leiden Journal of International Law* 925.

—— (2012), 'How Command Responsibility Got So Complicated: A Culpability Contradiction, Its Obfuscation, and a Simple Solution', 12 *Melbourne Journal of International Law* 1.

ROBINSON, G (1999), *Crimes Against Humanity: the Struggle for Global Justice* (London: Penguin).

RUBIN, A (1994), 'An International Criminal Tribunal for Former Yugoslavia', 6 *Pace International Law Review* 7.

SADAT, L (2007), 'The Effect of Amnesties Before Domestic and International Tribunals, Law, Morality, Politics', in Hughes, E, Schabas, W, and Thakur, R, (eds), *Atrocities and International Accountability: Beyond Transitional Justice* (Tokyo: UN University Press).

—— (ed) (2011), *Forging a Convention on Crimes Against Humanity* (Cambridge: Cambridge University Press).

SANDOZ, Y, SWINIARSKI, C, and ZIMMERMANN, B (eds) (1987), *Commentary on the Additional Protocols of 8 June 1977* (Geneva: ICRC/Martinus Nijhoff).

SAUL, B (2006), *Defining Terrorism in International Law* (Oxford: Oxford University Press).

—— (2011), 'Legislating from a Radical Hague: The United Nations Special Tribunal for Lebanon Invents an International Crime of Transnational Terrorism', 24 *Leiden Journal of International Law* 677.

SCHABAS, W (2000), 'Prosecutor v. Barayagwiza', (2000) 94 *AJIL* 563.

—— (2006), *The UN International Criminal Tribunals: Yugoslavia, Rwanda, Sierra Leone* (Cambridge: Cambridge University Press).

—— (2008a), *Genocide In International Law: The Crime of Crimes,* 2nd edn (Cambridge: Cambridge University Press).

—— (2008b), 'The State Policy as an Element of International Crimes', 98 *Journal of Criminal Law and Criminology* 953.

—— (2010), 'Prosecuting Dr Strangelove, Goldfinger and the Joker at the International Criminal Court: Closing the Loopholes', 23 *Leiden Journal of International Law* 850.

—— (2011), *An Introduction to the International Criminal Court* 4th edn (Cambridge: Cambridge University Press).

SCHEFFER, D (1999), 'The International Criminal Court: The Challenge of Jurisdiction', 63 *ASIL Proceedings* 68.

—— (2012), *All The Lost Souls: A Personal History of the War Crimes Tribunals* (Princeton: Princeton University Press).

SCHWARZENBERGER, G (1947), 'The Judgment of Nuremberg', 21 *Tulane Law Review* 329.

—— (1950), 'The Problem of an International Criminal Law', 3 *Current Legal Problems* 263.

SHAHABUDDEEN, M (2012), *International Criminal Justice at the Yugoslav Tribunal: A Judge's Recollection* (Oxford: Oxford University Press).

SIEBERT-FOHR, A (2009), *Prosecuting Serious Human Rights Violations* (Oxford: Oxford University Press).

SIMMA, B, and PAULUS, A (1999), 'The Responsibility of Individuals for Human Rights Violations in Internal Conflicts: A Positivist View', 93 *AJIL* 302.

SIVAKUMARAN, S (2012), *The Law of Non-International Armed Conflict* (Oxford: Oxford University Press).

SPECIAL ISSUE (2012), 'After Kampala, Aggression', 10 *JICJ* 1.

STAHN C, and EL-ZEIDY M (eds) (2011), *The International Criminal Court and Complementarity* (Cambridge: Cambridge University Press).

SYMPOSIUM (2009), 7 *JICJ* 653.

TAYLOR, T (1993), *The Anatomy of the Nuremberg Trial* (London: Bloomsbury).

TEITEL, R (2002), *Transitional Justice* (New York: Oxford University Press).

THALMAN, V (2008), 'French Justice's Endeavours to Substitute for the ICTR', (2008) 6 *JICJ* 995.

TRIFFTERER, O (ed) (2008), *Commentary on the Rome Statute of the International Criminal Court* (Oxford: Hart).

VAN DEN HERIK, L (2005), *The Contribution of the Rwanda Tribunal to the Development of International Law* (The Hague: Brill).

VAN SLIEDREGT, E (2012), *Individual Criminal Responsibility in International Law* (Oxford: Oxford University Press).

VENTURA, MJ (2011), 'Terrorism According to the STL's Interlocutory Decision on the Applicable Law: A Defining Moment or a Moment of Defining?', 9 *JICJ* 1021.

VERRIJN STUART, H, and SIMONS, M (eds) (2009), *The Prosecutor and the Judge: Benjamin Ferencz and Antonio Cassese: Interviews and Writings* (Amsterdam: Amsterdam University Press).

VON HEBEL, H and ROBINSON, D (1999) 'Crimes Within the Jurisdiction of the Court', in Lee, R (ed), The International Criminal Court (The Hague: Martinus Nijhoff).

WALDORF, L (2006), 'Mass Justice for Mass Atrocity: Rethinking Local Justice as Transitional Justice', 79 *Temple Law Review* 1.

WERLE, D and BURGHARDT, B (2012), 'Do Crimes Against Humanity Require the Participation of a State or "State-Like" Organization?', 10 *JICJ* 1151.

WILSON, RA (2011), *Writing History in International Criminal Trials* (Cambridge: Cambridge University Press).

WIRTH, S (2012), 'Co-Perpetratorship in the *Lubanga* Trial Judgment', 10 *JICJ* 971.

ZACKLIN, R (2004), 'The Failings of ad hoc International Tribunals', 2 *JICJ* 541.

FURTHER READING

ALVAREZ, J (1999), 'Crimes of Hate/Crimes of State, Lessons from Rwanda', 24 *Yale Journal of International Law* 365.

AMBOS, K (2013), *A Treatise on International Criminal Law Volume I: Foundations and General Part* (Oxford: Oxford University Press).

BASSIOUNI, MC (ed) (2008), *International Criminal Law,* 3rd edn (The Hague: Martinus Nijhoff).

CASSESE, A, GAETA, P, and JONES, J, (eds) (2002), *The Rome Statute: A Commentary* (Oxford: Oxford University Press).

—— et al (eds) (2008), *The Oxford Companion to International Criminal Justice* (Oxford: Oxford University Press).

MCGOLDRICK, D, ROWE, P, and DONNELLY, E (eds) (2004), *The International Criminal Court: Legal and Policy Issues* (Oxford: Hart).

MINOW, M (1998), *Between Vengeance and Forgiveness* (Boston: Beacon Press).

OLÁSOLO, H (2009), *The Criminal Responsibility of Senior Political and Military Leaders as Principals to International Crimes* (Oxford: Hart).

RATNER, S, ABRAMS, J, and BISCHOFF, J (2009), *Accountability for Human Rights Atrocities in International Law: Beyond the Nuremberg Legacy,* 3rd edn (Oxford: Oxford University Press).

SADAT, L (2002), *The International Criminal Court and the Transformation of International Law: Justice for a New Millennium* (Ardsley: Transnational Publishers).

SCHABAS, W (2010), *The International Criminal Court: A Commentary on the Rome Statute* (Oxford: Oxford University Press).

WERLE, G (2009), *Principles of International Criminal Law* 2nd edn (Cambridge: Cambridge University Press).

ZAPPALÀ, S (2003), *Human Rights in International Criminal Proceedings* (Oxford: Oxford University Press).

26

INTERNATIONAL HUMAN RIGHTS LAW

Sir Nigel Rodley

SUMMARY

The human rights idea developed as a non-clerical counterweight to the increasing power of the emerging modern State, establishing limits to the imposition of State power over individuals. Despite nineteenth-century concern with slavery, especially the slave trade, human rights did not become a full-fledged issue of international concern until the advent of the UN Charter, which made the advancement of human rights a purpose of the UN. The Charter paved the way for the adoption of the International Bill of Human Rights which framed human rights as an issue of general international law, as well as giving treaty form to specific obligations and providing machinery for monitoring compliance with the treaties' provisions. The main categories of human rights—civil and political/economic and social—are addressed by international law. The former, classic, human rights are mainly about the freedom and autonomy of the individual within the larger society, whereas economic and social rights typically require State action to guarantee them. However, to an extent, civil and political rights require action by the State to protect people from the actions of others in society (including corporations). The bearers of human rights remain individuals and the duty to safeguard them remains with the State. Human rights are accepted, at least as a matter of law, to represent universal obligations; they are not the privilege of inhabitants of States with a 'Western' culture. Civil and political rights include both intellectual freedom (conscience, expression, association, assembly) and physical freedom (liberty and security of person, movement, prohibition of slavery). Human dignity, an underlying principle in the International Bill of Human Rights, is the main value protecting physical integrity and life. From the 1960s a substantial network of treaty-based and UN-Charter-based machinery developed to lend international protection for internationally recognized human rights.

I. INTRODUCTION[1]

The original notion of human rights referred to those rights that the individual might assert against the organized power of the State (Freeman, 2011, pp 15–36). It is a notion that grew in the West in the seventeenth and eighteenth centuries, at a time when feudalism was being replaced by mercantilism and religion had begun to lose its position as a

---

[1] The text of this introduction is borrowed from Rodley, 2013, Ch 29.

counterweight to royal power that was giving way to the emergent, industrializing State. Indeed, it was the State that claimed a monopoly of the use of physical force with a view to protecting people from each other (Weber, 1919). It was the Leviathan that would tame the dangerous, predatory jungle.[2] But it too required taming and from Locke[3] to Rousseau[4] and Thomas Paine,[5] from Magna Carta and the English Bill of Rights to the Virginia Bill of Rights[6] and the *Déclaration des droits de l'homme et du citoyen*,[7] the idea of an individual human *domaine réservé* was born and consecrated.[8] The human gift of conscience was now not only of equal worth and respect as the duty to obey the sovereign,[9] it was now, in some limited but basic respect, superior to that duty, whether the sovereign be hereditary or institutional/constitutional. The social contract, by which each individual ceded some of his or her naturally endowed autonomy to ensure the meeting of shared needs, did not require the total surrender of that autonomy. Human rights marked the boundary of the cession. The individual retained sovereignty too.

At this point we are dealing with a philosophical construct. For it to be materialized, it had to be translated into law and would sometimes assume constitutional form. It took time, but nowadays hardly a constitution exists that does not recognize human rights. The international human rights project was mainly a post-World War II development, but so was the coming into existence of a majority of the world's States (principally through the process of decolonization). As a result, many constitutional bills of rights owe much to the Universal Declaration of Human Rights, the International Covenant on Civil and Political Rights and the European Convention on Human Rights (see the next section). It is the legal, rather than the philosophical manifestation of human rights that is the focus of this chapter.

A brief section on the historical origins of international human rights law is followed by a discussion of the basis of obligation in the field. Then there is a consideration of various modes of human rights classification that have been put forward and in which 'core' economic and social rights are identified. A summary treatment of the almost-outdated political discourse as to whether human rights are truly universal or culturally specific precedes a more extensive elaboration of the major substantive principles of civil and political rights and the values underlying them. The main universal machinery for monitoring or implementing human rights, both treaty-based and UN-Charter-based, as well as regional machinery, is then reviewed.

---

[2] The Leviathan was Hobbes' image for that 'man or assembly of men' to whom each vulnerable individual member of society would surrender 'all their power and strength' for 'our peace and defence'. See Hobbes, 1651, Ch XVII.

[3] Eg Locke, 1689.

[4] Rousseau, 1762, especially Book I, Ch 4 on the limits of sovereign power (that democratically reflects the General Will).

[5] Paine, 1791.

[6] (English) Bill of Rights (1689), http://www.parliament.uk/about/living-heritage/evolutionofparliament/parliamentaryauthority/revolution/collections/billofrights/image-3/; Virginia Bill of Rights (1776), http://www.ddleague-usa.net/vbor.htm.

[7] *Déclaration des droits de l'homme et du citoyen* (1789), http://www.assemblee-nationale.fr/histoire/dudh/1789.asp.

[8] See Henkin, 1978, pp 3–13. On the history of human rights generally, see Ishay, 2008, pp 63–116.

[9] The primacy of conscience is sometimes sourced to Antigone, who had to choose between obedience to her king and her obligation to bury her brother (Weston, 1989, p 13). In fact, even though she chose the latter, Sophocles at any rate does not seem to make clear that this was the morally superior stance: Sophocles, *Antigone* (442 BCE, trans Jebb, RC, http://classics.mit.edu/Sophocles/antigone.html).

II. HISTORICAL ORIGINS OF INTERNATIONAL HUMAN RIGHTS LAW (IHRL)

It is not surprising that human rights entered the domain of international law only relatively late and slowly.

International law was and remains a system of law designed to make inter-State coexistence as smooth as possible: its function is to provide the norms and means to attenuate transnational friction. Like any legal system, its overall goal has been the avoidance and resolution of conflict, the pursuit of peace. During most of its life, international law was predicated on a notion of the sovereign independence of States that excluded any consideration of the 'internal affairs' of States, which were seen as matters of domestic jurisdiction. After all, international law was the normative expression of international relations, just as much as national law can be said to be the normative expression of any national political dispensation. According to perhaps the most influential school, international relations are about the pursuit of the national interest (the maximization of power) in economic, trade, territorial, political, military areas, with international law as a means of securing a non-violent balance of the aggregate of national interests.[10] Indeed, factoring human rights into the mix of material interests that are the traditional content of international relations would, it has been asserted, make matters of principle (human rights) merely another commodity to be traded in the market of national interests.[11]

Human rights are inherently intra-State matters and that means that in the international context they are capable of becoming additional sources of friction between States, rather than balm, thus multiplying the challenge to the international legal system. They seemed to be a cuckoo in the nest of the doves of peace, even if the hawks of war had little affinity for them either. To vary the metaphor, human rights may well have been felt by diplomats and international civil servants to be grit thrown into the oil designed to lubricate the cogs of the machinery of international discourse.

Nevertheless, as early as the nineteenth century, one human rights issue, slavery, entered the domain of international law. Starting with Britain in 1807, the major European slave-owning and slave-trading nations abandoned the practice and then worked to strangle other States' slave-trading practices.[12] By the time of the 1926 Slavery Convention, chattel slavery and its associated trade were largely historical relics,[13] but until the early twentieth century, action was focused more on the international trade in slaves than on the practice of slavery. Escaping slaves might find freedom in States that did not recognize or no longer recognized the status of slaves, but the slavery-free were not insisting that international law required that the status of slavery be abolished in those jurisdictions that retained it.

The advent of the League of Nations after the First World War brought further developments. Recognizing that the denial of national minority aspirations had been a factor leading to the war—the assassination by Serb nationalists of the Archduke Franz Ferdinand

---

[10] The realist school (*Realpolitik*) whose most influential exponent was Hans Morgenthau. See Morgenthau, 1967, Chs 1 and 6 and *passim*.

[11] See the observations of Ernst Haas concerning the (then) new Carter Administration's human-rights-focussed foreign policy: 'The United States has embarked on the most naïve and moralistic campaign since Woodrow Wilson' (Haas, 1977, p 72).

[12] Abolition of the Slave Trade Act. In 1811, the trade was made a felony in the British Empire.

[13] It has managed to be abolished three times in Mauritania, in 1905, 1981, and 2007: see Corrigan, 2007.

of Austria is generally considered the spark that set fire to the European tinder box—the League presided over the creation of a series of treaties concerned with minorities, aimed at avoiding a repetition of the problem. Of course, it was not all minorities that would be protected, only those in the Balkans and eastern Europe, so this was a limited human rights incursion into international law.[14]

Also limited was the inclusion of human rights clauses into the mandates given by the League to some colonial powers to administer the former colonies of the defeated powers, notably the Germans. This was no general project of incorporating human rights into the administration of colonies as a whole, still less one aimed at decolonization, but it must have been perceived as a signal that those subjected to colonialism deserved to have their human rights respected.[15]

The most significant post-World War I development in the field of human rights was the creation in 1919 of the International Labour Organization (ILO). Here was established an organization designed to promote and protect a certain category of rights—freedom of association—at least as regards the rights of trade unionists. This development too was a response to political events, notably the 1917 Russian Revolution, which led to the withdrawal of Russia from the global conflict of World War I. The ILO was effectively an enlightened response aimed at showing workers that their interests could be met by something less radical than communist revolution. With its imaginative tri-partite structure (States, trade union organizations and employers' organizations) and its serious machinery for addressing allegations of violations of workers' unionists' rights, particularly the Committee on Freedom of Association, it was a real example of the possibility of the international protection of human rights (Swepston, 2013, Ch 20).

A. CHARTER OF THE UN

The foundations of modern international human rights law are to be found in the Charter of the United Nations. One of the goals of the UN laid down in its Article 1 is the achievement of 'international cooperation in...promoting and encouraging respect for human rights and fundamental freedoms for all without distinction as to race, sex, language or religion'. It was far from inevitable that human rights would figure prominently, if at all, in what was to become the nearest thing to a world constitution. It took intense lobbying by what we now call civil society, especially American non-governmental organizations (NGOs). The argument that prevailed was that a paradigm-changing lesson had to be learned from the Second World War (Lauren, 2011, Chs 5 and 6). Nazi Germany's genocide of Jews and Roma and other crimes against humanity, and its territorial aggressiveness were seen as part of the same phenomenon. A ruthless, lawless regime that could commit carnage in parts of its own population and brutally repress any opposition to it was seen to be part and parcel of a project of violent deployment of force internationally. The frontier between the previous hermetically sealed realms of the inter-State and the intra-State was now seen to be porous. Once in the Charter, human rights had in one leap, become a matter of international concern and, thus, of international legal relevance.

---

[14] See *Treatment of Polish Nationals and Other Persons of Polish Origin or Speech in the Danzig Territory, Advisory Opinion, 1932, PCIJ Series A/B, No 44,* p 4.

[15] Mandates were allocated pursuant to Article 22, League of Nations Covenant; see *South West Africa, Second Phase, Judgment, ICJ Reports 1966,* p 6; *Legal Consequences for States of the Continued Presence of South Africa in Namibia (South West Africa) notwithstanding Security Council Resolution 276 (1970), Advisory Opinion, ICJ Reports 1971,* p 16.

III. THE BASIS OF OBLIGATION IN INTERNATIONAL HUMAN RIGHTS LAW

The UN Charter language of 'cooperation' for 'promoting and encouraging respect' for human rights was not exactly a demand for the immediate *observance* of human rights. However, later provisions came closer to this. Thus, Article 55 of the Charter requires that, '[w]ith a view to the creation of conditions of stability and well-being which are necessary for peaceful and friendly relations among nations,'[16] the UN 'shall promote...universal respect for and observance of, human rights for all without distinction as to race, sex, language or religion.' Here we at least had the goal of securing respect for, and observance of, human rights on a universal basis. This still fell short of imposing direct human rights obligations on States, but Article 56 did address this point: '[a]ll members pledge themselves to take joint and separate action in cooperation with the Organization for the achievement of the purposes set forth in Article 55'. So, States had to work not only jointly but each on its own to achieve promotion of respect for, and observance of, human rights.

In the early decades of the UN, there was disagreement as to whether this language should be read as an exhortation or a direct obligation (Schwelb, 1972). By 1971, the answer for the International Court of Justice (ICJ) was that the provisions involved a directly binding obligation and that South Africa had, by applying its apartheid system in South-West Africa under the mandate it was given by the League of Nations, violated these provisions.[17] It might still have been possible to interpret this decision as being restricted to the obligation to respect human rights 'without distinction as to race' and so on (Humphrey, 1979, p 36), but if so, the ICJ certainly put paid to that notion in the later Teheran Hostages case, where it affirmed:

> Wrongfully to deprive human beings of their freedom and to subject them to physical constraint in conditions of hardship is in itself manifestly incompatible with the principles of the Charter of the United Nations, as well as with the fundamental principles enunciated in the Universal Declaration of Human Rights.[18]

The reference to the Universal Declaration of Human Rights (UDHR) is important for two reasons: first, the UN Charter itself provided no elaboration of what was meant by the term 'human rights and fundamental freedoms', second, the UDHR was, as will be seen, contained in a resolution of the General Assembly and so not *per se* binding.

A. THE INTERNATIONAL BILL OF HUMAN RIGHTS

The first task of the UN Commission on Human Rights, established pursuant to Article 68 of the Charter,[19] was the drafting of an International Bill of Human Rights that would consist, first, of a declaration of human rights principles (this would become the UDHR),

---

[16] Thus echoing the lesson learned in Article 1.

[17] *South West Africa, Second Phase, Judgment, ICJ Reports 1966*, p 6, para 131: 'To establish instead, and to enforce, distinctions, exclusions, restrictions and limitations exclusively based on grounds of race, colour, descent or national or ethnic origin which constitute a denial of fundamental human rights is a flagrant violation of the purposes and principles of the Charter.'

[18] *United States Diplomatic and Consular Staff in Tehran, Judgment, ICJ Reports 1980*, p 3.

[19] The only 'Functional Commission' of ECOSOC that was specifically to be established under Article 68 was the one on human rights.

followed by obligations consecrated in treaty form. The purpose of the treaties would be both to give clear legal force and more precision to the UDHR and to provide machinery for monitoring the implementation of the substantive provisions. The latter will be returned to in section VII.

To the extent that the eventual treaties were perceived to be needed, not only for the creation of monitoring procedures but also for legal specificity, did that mean that the UDHR was devoid of force? The matter was controversial from the beginning. There were those who held that it had no legal force. Under Article 14 of the Charter, the General Assembly had only the power to make recommendations; it was not intended to be a world legislature. Moreover, by its very terms, the UDHR purported to be no more than a 'common standard of achievement for all peoples and all nations'.[20] On the other side, whatever the legal status of the UDHR as such, it contained the catalogue of human rights and fundamental freedoms that were referred to by UN Charter articles on human rights, especially Articles 1, 55, and 56. So, to the extent that these provisions contained binding obligations, it was to the UDHR that one would have to look to discover their content (de Schutter, 2012, p 39).

The arguments began to be finalized by the time of the 1968 UN International Conference on Human Rights which adopted the Proclamation of Teheran. According to paragraph 2 of that Proclamation, the UDHR 'states a common understanding of the peoples of the world concerning the inalienable and inviolable rights of members of the human family and constitutes an obligation for members of the international community'.[21] A quarter of a century later, a World Conference on Human Rights would declare: 'Human rights and fundamental freedoms are the birthright of all human beings; their protection and promotion is the first responsibility of governments'.[22] From that point on one rarely heard a challenge to the idea that States had human rights obligations other than by virtue of human rights treaties. By the time of the UN Millennium Declaration in 2000, the General Assembly was able to resolve to 'respect fully and uphold the Universal Declaration of Human Rights' and in 2005 the World Summit Conference could proclaim:

> We recommit ourselves to protect and promote human rights, the rule of law and democracy, and recognize that they are interlinked and mutually reinforcing and that they constitute together universal and indivisible core values and principles of the United Nations, and call upon all parts of the United Nations system to promote human rights and fundamental freedoms.[23]

B. GENERAL INTERNATIONAL LAW

Because of the quasi-constitutional nature of the UN Charter, it would be misleading to conceive of the human rights obligations it contains as merely themselves treaty obligations. The better approach is to understand them in the same way as the State obligations on the use of force, that is to say, as norms of general or universal international law (Charney, 1993). They are norms of customary international law, generally binding on all

---

[20] GA Res 217A III (10 December 1948), proclamatory paragraph.

[21] Proclamation of Tehran, proclaimed by the International Conference on Human Rights at Tehran, 22 April–13 May 1968, UN Doc A/CONF.32/41, para 2.

[22] Vienna Declaration and Programme of Action, adopted by World Conference on Human Rights, Vienna, 14–25 June 1993, UN Doc A/CONF.157/23, para 1.

[23] UN Millennium Declaration, General Assembly resolution 55/2 (2000), para 25; World Summit Outcome Document, GA Res 60/1 (24 October 2005), para 98.

States and often rooted in all three major sources of international law, customary international law, treaty law, and general principles of law (see Thirlway, Ch 4 of this book).

Some of the rules have firmly become rules of *jus cogens* (Bianchi, 2008). After the prohibition of genocide[24] the most evident would be the prohibition of torture that is non-derogable in universal and regional human rights treaties and has been recognized as a rule of *jus cogens* by the ICJ, a body generally cautious about attributing that status to specific rules of customary or general international law.[25] Logic would suggest that the Charter-based exclusion of (implicitly adverse) distinctions based on race, sex, language, or religion would enjoy *jus cogens* status. The prohibition of racial discrimination would certainly seem to fall into the category;[26] although there is less manifest authority for the proposition as regards discrimination on grounds of language or religion, if only because they have not received the same amount of attention. This cannot be said as regards discrimination on grounds of sex, which, like racial discrimination has been addressed in widely ratified treaties. So far, the ICJ has not been called upon to express its view.

Not too much should be made of the distinction between a norm of general international law and one of *jus cogens*. The origins of the distinction lie in that between traditional customary international law and *jus cogens*. The point about ordinary rules of international law is that they may not be binding on 'persistent objectors', or may be departed from by means of regional custom, or by treaty. It is the latter dimension that *jus cogens* addresses directly: treaties may not depart from rules of *jus cogens*.[27] In reality, the possibilities of evading or modifying rules of customary international law discussed earlier arise out of the synallagmatic nature of most of the traditional customary international law rules.[28] International human rights law is by nature non-synallagmatic; its rules are, by definition *erga omnes*.[29] It is instructive in this respect to note the great range of UN Human Rights Council 'special procedures' which have come to deal with most of the rights contained in the UDHR, in the expectation that all States are bound to respect them. In fact, as will appear later, the area of potential dispute nowadays lies not in whether States are bound to respect most if not all, of the rights contained in the UDHR, but in differences about the scope and nature of those rights. That is to say, there may be some room for interpretation of the obligation implied in the right in question.

C. TREATY LAW

The advantage of treaties as a source of international legal obligation over other sources is that there is generally no dispute as to the existence of a legal obligation. In principle, the only question to be answered is not whether there is a rule, but only whether the facts in question do or do not conform to the stated rule. After all, the State party to a treaty will

---

[24] See *Armed Activities on the Territory of the Congo (New Application: 2002) (Democratic Republic of the Congo v Rwanda), Jurisdiction and Admissibility, Judgment, ICJ Reports 2006*, p 6, para 64.

[25] *Questions relating to the Obligation to Prosecute or Extradite (Belgium v Senegal), Judgment of 20 July 2012*, para 99.

[26] Eg the Draft Articles on the Responsibility of States for Internationally Wrongful Acts, with Commentaries, Yearbook of the International Law Commission, 2001, Vol II, Part 2, Article 40, Commentary, para 4.

[27] Vienna Convention on the Law of Treaties (1969), Article 53.

[28] Ie a series of bilateral relationships.

[29] Ie opposable to the whole community of States or, in the case of treaties, States parties to the treaty. See Human Rights Committee, General Comment No 31, 'The Nature of the General Legal Obligation Imposed on States Parties to the [International] Covenant [on Civil and Political Rights]', UN Doc CCPR/C/21/Rev.1/ Add.13 (2004), para 2.

be expected to have freely undertaken its obligations as a solemn act of sovereign power. And, as with other fields of international law, treaties in the field of human rights have been widely resorted to.

The speedy adoption in 1948 of the Genocide Convention[30] was a necessary response to the holocaust of Jews and Roma. It took until 1966 for the International Bill of Human Rights to be completed, by adding to the UDHR (also 1948), the International Covenants on Economic, Social and Cultural Rights (IECSCR) and on Civil and Political Rights (ICCPR), together with the (first) Optional Protocol to the ICCPR. In fact, the process of adopting the Covenants was so protracted that a subject-specific treaty was adopted a year earlier, namely the 1965 International Convention on the Elimination of All Forms of Racial Discrimination (ICERD). Other subject-specific treaties followed and there are now nine 'core' UN human rights treaties.[31]

Meanwhile, regional treaties came into existence, sometimes preceding the UN treaties, sometimes following them. The most influential and long-standing general ones are the European and American Conventions on Human Rights and the African Charter on Human and Peoples' Rights. There are also regional subject-specific ones, such as the Inter-American Convention to Prevent and Punish Torture[32] and the African Charter on the Rights and Welfare of the Child.

IV. CATEGORIES OF RIGHTS

If the original notion of human rights connoted the limits of governmental power over the individual, and so concerned the rights of the individual against the State, there have been further claims to the title of human rights. A common set of categorizations of such claims, in addition to individual human rights as traditionally understood and commonly denominated civil and political rights (considered later in this chapter), is collective and group rights.[33]

Collective rights would be those that are needed by, or that pertain to, segments of the population, particularly the most vulnerable, and demand government action. The term 'economic and social rights' is typically used to encompass such rights, which consist essentially of expectation of the fulfilment of claims on governments (or society as

---

[30] Convention on the Prevention and Punishment of the Crime of Genocide, GA Res 260A III (9 December 1948).

[31] The core treaties are: International Convention on the Elimination of all Forms of Racial Discrimination (ICERD), 66 UNTS 195 (21 December 1965); International Covenant on Economic, Social and Cultural Rights (ICESCR), GA Res 2200 A (XXI) (16 December 1966); International Convention on Civil and Political Rights (ICCPR), GA Res 2200 A (16 December 1966); Convention on the Elimination of All Forms of Discrimination against Women (CEDAW), GA Res 34/180 (18 December 1979); Convention against Torture and Other Cruel, Inhuman or Degrading Treatment or Punishment (UNCAT), GA Res 39/46 (10 December 1984); the Convention of the Rights of the Child (CRC), GA Res 44/25 (20 November 1989); International Convention on the Protection of All Migrant Workers and Members of Their Families (CMW), GA Res 45/158 (18 December 1990); the Convention on the Rights of Persons with Disabilities (CRPD), GA Res 61/106 (13 December 2006); and the International Convention for the Protection of All Persons from Enforced Disappearance (ICED), GA Res 61/177 (20 December 2006).

[32] There is also the 1987 European Convention for the Prevention of Torture and Inhuman or Degrading Treatment or Punishment (ECPT), (CETS No 126); it is non-normative, confining itself to establishing a Committee for the Prevention of Torture (CPT) which visits places of detention in States parties.

[33] The eminent commentator Karel Vasak once described these three categories as the 'three generations of human rights' (Vasak, 1977). This catchy term did little service to clarity of thought about human rights.

a whole) to meet basic human needs, such as health, food, shelter, and education. What distinguishes them conceptually is that the centre of gravity of the idea of civil and political rights is individual freedom *from* government, while that of economic and social rights is the claim for action *by* governments. What they have in common is that those subject to governmental authority are the rights-bearers and governments are the duty-bearers.

'*Group rights*' are a wholly different species. They are said to inhere not in the individual but in populations. They seem to cover such issues as self-determination, development, a clean and healthy environment, and peace.[34] The asserted rights in question may not even be within the power of the State to respect. Rather, at least implicitly, their centre of gravity involves the claims by the State vis-à-vis the international community or even the rights of States against their own populations and the individual constituting the latter.[35] Space does not allow for an analysis of the legal existence or content of any of these asserted rights. It is evident that there is nothing in the structure of international law that would prevent such groups having rights, even if at present the amount of discussion and writing about them seems in inverse proportion to any agreed content. The point is that to call them 'human rights' is a misnomer that totally denatures a term that should be limited to denoting the rights of individual human beings in relation to the State.

However, one of them must be addressed, if only because of its juridical pedigree, before we move on, and that is the right of all peoples to self-determination—for is not the right specified as the first article of both the ICESCR and the ICCPR? At first sight that of itself would appear to lay to rest any objection to its existence as a human right. In fact, as is often the case, first sight is misleading, requiring a second look. It is evident from the structure and organization of the Covenants that the right to self-determination is apart from other rights. Each Covenant is divided into five parts. Part I has Article 1 on the right to self-determination standing alone. Part II provides general jurisdictional and obligational articles. Only Part III sets out specific human rights. Part IV deals with monitoring procedures and Part V has the Final Clauses. This structure, separating the right to self-determination from the rights-articulating part by a non-rights-articulating part compels the conclusion that the right to self-determination is contextual to other rights rather than a self-standing Covenant-protected right.[36] It is neither a civil nor political, nor economic nor social human right.

Similarly, it cannot be ignored that States have adopted a Declaration on the Right to Development that specifically refers to its subject as 'an inalienable human right'.[37] The provisions of this instrument, most of which use the hortatory 'should', are so devoid of

---

[34] For self-determination and development, see next paragraph; for environment see, eg African Charter on Human and Peoples' Rights, Article 23; for peace: ibid, Article 24 and Protocol of San Salvador to the American Convention on Human Rights, Article 11.

[35] Thus, Algeria invokes an asserted right to peace to justify avoidance of accountability and perpetuate impunity for its brutal repression in the 1990s of an Islamist revolt involving thousands of enforced disappearances. Eg Human Rights Committee, *Guezout et al v Algeria* (Communication No 1753/2008), UN Doc CCPR/C/105/D/1753/2008 (2012), para 4.6.

[36] Thus, the Human Rights Committee took account of the article in interpreting Article 25 (right to participate in government); in fact, it found that the exclusion of certain French and other foreign citizens (persons not resident for the previous ten years) from participating in a referendum on self-determination for New Caledonia did not violate Article 25 read together with Article 1: *Gillot et al v France* (Communication No 932/2000), UN Doc CCPR/C/75/D/932/2000 (2002), para 13.4. This was a case of external self-determination from colonial control, pursuant to the General Assembly Declaration on the Granting of Independence to Colonial Countries and People, GA Res 1514 (XV) (14 December 1960). It is unclear whether or how the right may apply in internal situations.

[37] GA Res 41/128 (4 December 1986), Article 1.

specificity or precision as to make their meaning, if any, elusive. The other asserted 'group rights' are even more vacuous, making them still more doubtful candidates for the title of 'rights', much less 'human rights'. What follows will therefore focus on civil and political rights, and on economic and social rights, more or less as reflected respectively in the ICCPR and the ICESCR.

A. CIVIL AND POLITICAL/ECONOMIC AND SOCIAL

According to the 1993 Vienna Declaration and Programme of Action, all human rights are 'indivisible and independent and interrelated'. This does not mean that they are indistinguishable. Certainly, the (necessarily exaggerated) paradigm indicated earlier—that civil and political equals freedom from government action, while economic and social equals demand for such action—can be misleading. For example, the 'freedom from' idea is often thought of as requiring abstention or *negative* action, while the 'demand for' idea is seen as involving *positive* action. In reality, much in the civil and political rights domain also requires positive action, for example, a decent system of administration of justice, including a humane penitentiary system, or an effective, clean law enforcement apparatus. Similarly, access to economic and social goods can sometimes be facilitated by State *inaction*, for instance, by not standing in the way of humanitarian assistance.

However, the similarities should not mask the reality of dissimilarities. The financial cost of a system of decent government capable of respecting the rule of law is surely infrastructural to the whole rights project and so, arguably, *prior* to the costs of guaranteeing any particular right. Deduct these costs from the 'price' of ensuring civil and political rights and not so much remains. And much of what does remain is in the realm of the so-called horizontal obligations of States (considered in subsection B), whereas the major costs of meeting people's needs are so central to the economic and social rights project that States have shied away from assuming the same type of legal obligation.

Thus, whereas Article 2 ICCPR pledges States 'to respect and to ensure' the rights recognized by the Covenant, the comparable Article 2 ICESCR requires them only 'to take steps, individually and through international assistance and cooperation...to the maximum of its available resources, with a view to achieving progressively the full realization of the rights recognized' by the Covenant. Even discounting the muddying of the nature of the duty-bearer (international cooperation is not within the gift of the State party in question), an obligation on a State to 'take steps', within 'available' resources to achieve rights 'progressively' cannot be equated with the peremptory notions of 'respect and ensure'.

The Committee on Economic, Social and Cultural Rights (see later) has noted that the obligation of non-discrimination is of immediate effect,[38] even though the same obligation would anyway apply to a State party to the ICCPR (Article 26). The same Committee has insisted that there is 'a minimum core obligation to ensure the satisfaction of, at the very least, minimum essential levels of each of the rights' of the Covenant.[39] So, where 'a significant number of individuals is deprived of essential foodstuffs, of essential primary health care, of basic shelter and housing, or of the most basic forms of education', the State in question 'is *prima facie* failing to discharge its obligations under the Covenant'.[40] This observation

---

[38] General Comment No. 3 (1990) (The Nature of States parties obligations (Article 2, para 1 of the Covenant)), Committee on Economic, Social and Cultural Rights, Fifth Session, Report (UN Doc ESCOR 1991, Supp 3) Annex III, para 1.

[39] Ibid, para 10; see generally, Chapman and Russell, 2002.

[40] General Comment No 3, ibid, para 10.

would have been more helpful to the individuals concerned had it not been accompanied by a further observation that acknowledges the legitimacy of the State's 'failure to meet at least its minimum care obligations' on the basis of a 'lack of available resources' provided that it has made every effort to satisfy the obligations.[41] Ten years later, the Committee, in a General Comment on the Right to Health, affirmed the following core obligations:

(a) To ensure the right of access to health facilities, goods and services on a non-discriminatory basis, especially for vulnerable or marginalized groups;

(b) To ensure access to the minimum essential food which is nutritionally adequate and safe, to ensure freedom from hunger to everyone;

(c) To ensure access to basic shelter, housing and sanitation, and an adequate supply of safe and potable water;

(d) To provide essential drugs, as from time to time defined under the WHO Action Programme on Essential Drugs;

(e) To ensure equitable distribution of all health facilities, goods and services.[42]

It also required States to 'adopt and implement a national public health strategy and plan of action'.[43] This peremptory language tracks that of Article 4 of the ICCPR, which makes certain rights in that Covenant non-derogable. There is no comparable language in the ICESCR itself.

Much attention has been given to whether or not economic and social rights are justiciable, in the sense that they are the sorts of subject-matter that are suitable for judicial, rather than policy decision by legislatures and executives. There is a certain artificiality to the discussion in so far as any polity may grant any functions to its courts. Certainly, at the international level, it will be interesting to follow the work of the Committee on Economic, Social and Cultural Rights under the 2008 Optional Protocol that grants the right of individual petition to it for violations of obligations under the Covenant. The challenge for the Committee will be to identify specific violations on the basis of such unclear obligational requirements.

B. VERTICAL AND HORIZONTAL OBLIGATIONS

A sub-species of positive obligations is in the domain of 'horizontal' obligations of States. If the paradigmatic human rights construct envisages a vertical relationship—the State *vis-à-vis* the individuals subject to the States' jurisdiction—there is nevertheless a 'horizontal' dimension, in the sense that there is also an expectation that the State will protect individuals from other individuals (or groups or legal entities). This is not the same as saying that individuals can violate the human rights of other individuals. As the Human Rights Committee has affirmed, ICCPR obligations are binding on States and 'do not, as such, have *direct* horizontal effect as a matter of international law'.[44] But, the Committee goes on to state that:

the positive obligations on States Parties to ensure Covenant rights will only be fully discharged if individuals are protected by the State, not just against violations of Covenant rights by its agents, but also against acts committed by private persons or entities that would

---

[41] Ibid, para 10.
[42] General Comment No 14 (2000) (The right to the highest attainable standard of health (Article 12 of the ICESCR)) para 43(a)–(e).
[43] Ibid, para 43(f).
[44] Human Rights Committee, General Comment No 31 (n 29), para 8 (emphasis added).

impair the enjoyment of Covenant rights in so far as they are amenable to application by private persons or entities.[45]

First, this passage recognizes that, even in the area of civil and political rights, States have positive obligations of protection. This goes beyond the provision of a clean, rule-of-law-respecting system of governance (see earlier). Thus, for example, the right to life and the prohibition of torture require the State to investigate allegations of violations of those provisions and bring perpetrators to justice (especially State officials who have inflicted or acquiesced in the harm in question).[46] Similarly, States may be in violation of their obligations to ensure such rights, as a result of 'permitting or failing to take appropriate measures or to exercise due diligence to prevent, punish, investigate or redress the harm caused by such acts by private persons or entities'.[47] The attraction of this approach is that it allows holding the State accountable when it seeks to use private persons or entities to inflict the harm (or to claim that private persons or entities are responsible for inflicting the harm); while it may not be possible to attribute direct responsibility to the State, it will remain possible to attribute indirect responsibility for failure to discharge its positive obligations.

The obligation to use 'due diligence' to protect against harms is not restricted to those areas where there may be conceded State responsibility (for acts that must otherwise have served governmental interests). The Human Rights Committee frequently reminds governments, for example, of their obligation to use due diligence to prevent domestic violence. Here the harm will rarely, if at all, have been inflicted in pursuit of a governmental interest, but that does not mean that there is no foundation of responsibility on any State to protect people from threats to life or limb at the hands of others.

Equally, these positive obligations are not open-ended to the point of losing the vertical paradigm dimension in favour of the horizontal dimension to prevent any harm inflicted by one person on another. This is what is meant by the phrase 'in so far as [the rights in question] are amenable to application by private persons or entities'. An evident example of a right that *is* so amenable is that offered by the Human Rights Committee itself: 'In fields affecting basic aspects of ordinary life, such as work or housing, individuals are to be protected from discrimination within the meaning of Article 26.'[48]

C. RIGHTS-HOLDERS AND DUTY-BEARERS

As has been seen, the only conceptually consistent and generally accepted rights-holders are individuals. States or comparable collectivities may have rights under international law, but not human rights. However, there is an extensive discourse, to the point of polemic, as to whether other entities may be human rights duty-bearers, that is, bound to respect human rights, failing which they would be considered human rights violators (Clapham, 2006; Rodley, 2013).

For instance, there is little resistance to the notion that intergovernmental organizations (IGOs) are capable of violating human rights. Conceptually, it should be self-evident

---

[45] Ibid.   [46] Ibid, para 18.   [47] Ibid, para 8.

[48] Ibid. Article 26 provides for equality under the law and non-discrimination 'on any ground such as race, colour, sex, language, religion, political or other opinion, national or social origin, property, birth or other status'.

that, if a State acting alone can commit a human rights violation, then a group of States pooling their powers and acting in the same way should be similarly capable of violating human rights. Indeed, the opposite would be subversive of the whole project: States would merely have to act collaboratively to relieve themselves of their human rights obligations. That IGOs were capable of having rights and obligations under international law has been acknowledged since the 1949 *Reparations Case*. Here the ICJ held that an IGO, the UN, must protect its own personnel and must accordingly have the power to bring a claim against States for harm done by them to such personnel.[49] As the UN has found itself increasingly involved not only in peace-keeping, but also in peace-enforcement and peace-building operations, the UN slowly came to accept that it too would have obligations of a general international humanitarian law and general international human rights law nature.[50]

The precedent of the *inter*-State organization having duties and responsibilities hardly serves to justify the claim that (other) *non*-state actors (NSAs) can and do have human rights obligations. Yet claims are made in respect of various NSAs, including armed opposition groups, organized crime gangs, transnational business enterprises and even individuals. One cannot look to human rights treaties to clarify the situation, since these only bind the States that become party to them. This drives us to look to customary or general international law for guidance. Here too we have a dearth of authority. It would be plausible to apply the criterion that human rights treaty bodies invoke to establish State responsibility: is the State in effective control?[51] *Pari passu*, we could ask the same question in respect of the other candidates for potential human rights violation status.

So, it would be consistent at least with the principles of international humanitarian law to consider armed opposition groups (typically called terrorists by the governments in question) as capable of having international human rights law obligations. If such a group has the attributes of a party to an armed conflict, which would normally involve, if not territorial control (as in international armed conflict),[52] at least similar exclusive *de facto* control of parts of a population, then it would not do violence to the international human rights law project to consider the group as being required also to respect at least those human rights for which that the level of control permits it to incur responsibility. In the absence of such status, then the acts of the group are no more than any government

[49] *Reparation for Injuries Suffered in the Service of the United Nations, Advisory Opinion, ICJ Reports 1949*, p 174 at p 183.

[50] See UN Secretary-General, Secretary-General's Bulletin: Observance by UN Forces of International Humanitarian Law, 6 August 1999, UN Doc ST/SGB/1999/13. Remarks of the UN Legal Counsel, Nicolas Michel, to the Security Council meeting on 'Strengthening International Law: rule of law and maintenance of international peace and security', UN Doc S/PV.5474 (2006), pp 3–5; UN Secretariat, 'Human Rights Due Diligence Policy on UN support to non-UN security forces (HRDDP) (July 2012), which confirms 'the Organization's Purposes and Principles in the Charter and its *obligations under international law to respect*, promote and encourage respect for *international* humanitarian, *human rights* and refugee *law*' (emphasis added).

[51] See, eg Human Rights Committee, General Comment No 31, 'The Nature of the General Legal Obligation Imposed on States Parties to the [International] Covenant [on Civil and Political Rights]', UN Doc CCPR/C/21/Rev.1/Add.13 (2004), para 10.

[52] Article 3 common to the four Geneva Conventions of 12 August 1949 does not specify the attributes of a non-state party to an armed conflict. Additional Protocol II to the Conventions, relating to the protection of victims of armed conflict refers to 'dissident armed forces or other organized armed groups which, under responsible command, exercise such control over a part of [a state's] territory as to enable them to carry out sustained and concerted military operations and to implement this Protocol', Article 2(1). Common Article 3 is not generally interpreted to require such a high threshold for an entity to be considered a party to a non-international armed conflict.

would consider them to be, namely, criminal acts, which the government would be expected to seek to repress. To dignify their perpetrators as anything more than criminal seems to serve no purpose. For international human rights law to pipe up 'me too' with the State in question will hardly serve to ameliorate the harms inflicted or offer any redress. Of course, this is without prejudice to the (limited) role of international criminal law as regards crimes against humanity. However, to the extent that the group, whose members may have committed crimes against humanity, fails to meet the criteria of a party to an armed conflict, it must still have sufficient organizational density and structure to be in a position to meet the threshold test for crimes against humanity, that is, that there be an attack against a civilian population, that the acts be committed on a widespread or systematic basis and that they be committed pursuant to an organizational policy.[53] Close as this may come to being a party to an armed conflict within the meaning of international humanitarian law (IHL), it is not clear what the 'value added' would be of calling the groups human rights violators. Certainly, there is little legal authority for the proposition.[54]

All these arguments apply *a fortiori* as regards ordinary criminal gangs and yet more so for individuals. The most cited latter manifestation would be domestic violence. According to a feminist critique, the traditional human rights paradigm relates to the public sphere and is therefore male-oriented. Apparently this fails to take account of the reality of the millions of women round the world who are kept in the private sphere and out of the public sphere. It is hard to give credence to a critique that would appear to legitimate a situation that inherently violates the rights and power of women to act autonomously and in the public sphere, on terms of equality with men. To the extent that they are denied that right and the State has not exercised due diligence to address that deprivation, this is a matter of State responsibility (see earlier) and should, of course, be vigorously addressed as such.

As to the suggestion that business enterprises, transnational or otherwise, may be considered as bodies having direct human rights responsibilities under international law, it is certainly true that these are sometimes perceived as having more power than governments, at least insofar as the availability or otherwise of their investments and business activity can have major consequences for a State's economy. However, except perhaps in the area of personnel policy or security measures, their activities pose limited *direct* challenge to human rights. Rather it is the territorial State that is most likely to be the direct violator. Indeed, few States would deny that it is *their* responsibility to protect people from harms committed by business enterprises and thus should exercise the appropriate due diligence to that end. It is certainly the case that the international legal evidence is consistent with that approach.

Thus, in 2003 the UN Sub-Commission on the Promotion and Protection of Human Rights submitted to the Commission on Human Rights (see later) a draft text entitled 'Norms on the Responsibilities of Transnational Corporations and Other Business Enterprises with regard to Human Rights'.[55] The Norms purported to vest in the corporations and enterprises 'the obligation to promote, secure the fulfilment of, respect, ensure respect of and protect human rights recognized in international...law'.[56] Even though the Norms acknowledged the 'primary responsibility' of States to ensure that the corporations

---

[53] See International Criminal Court, Elements of Crimes, UN Doc PCNICC/2000/1/Add.2 (2000), Article 7, Introduction.

[54] However, Ben Emmerson QC, the UN Human Rights Council's Special Rapporteur on the promotion and protection of human rights while countering terrorism, has rejected this approach as 'legalistic' though he cites no primary sources to sustain the refutation: UN Doc A/HRC/20/14 (2012), para 13.

[55] UN Doc E/CN.4/Sub.2/2003/12/Rev.2 (13 August 2003).   [56] Ibid, para 1.

and enterprises respect human rights,[57] the Norms' acceptance of the principle that international law would target such enterprises directly led to their being abandoned.

Eight years later, the UN Human Rights Council (successor to the Commission, see later) was able to adopt by consensus a new text of 'Guiding Principles on Business and Human Rights', drafted by Professor John Ruggie[58] and a year later the Council even established a working group to promote the Principles.[59] There is no mystery as to what led to the changed reception. The Ruggie Principles, as they are known, focus heavily on the responsibility of *States* to ensure that business enterprises respect human rights. To the (important) extent that the Principles address businesses directly, it is mainly to encourage them to respect human rights by avoiding activities with potentially adverse human rights impacts.[60] The introductory commentary to the Principles expressly eschews their creating 'new international law obligations'. Hopefully, the Principles will be a catalyst to encourage further State activity to hold their corporations, whether acting domestically or abroad, to a human rights-respecting posture and to permit civil society and shareholders to put the political spotlight on non-rights-respecting enterprises.

V. HUMAN RIGHTS: UNIVERSAL OR CULTURALLY SPECIFIC

For some decades a view was propounded that human rights was a Western notion that was being foisted on the rest of the world. For example, 'Asian values' would be invoked by some States of that region in opposition to the idea of a universal concept of human rights. While the problem still inspires academic discussion (Freeman, 2013), it has little of relevance to say from the perspective of international human rights law. As we have seen, human rights and fundamental freedoms are thoroughly grounded in the UN Charter and most States of all regions of the world have freely become parties to most of the core international human rights treaties (see earlier), including the ICCPR and the ICESCR. At some time or another, they will all vote for (or join a consensus on) resolutions taking up human rights issues in other countries.

In fact, as early as 1993, the Vienna Declaration and Program of Action was untypically direct on the issue, declaring in its first paragraph: 'The universal nature of these rights and freedoms is beyond question'.

The same document, while insisting on the duty of States to promote and protect human rights, did nevertheless signal delphically that 'the significance of national and regional particularities and various historical, cultural and religious backgrounds must be borne in mind' (para 5). This should not be seen as clawing back the general orientation of universality; rather it is indicating that, as with any international norms, the method of securing compliance with them is a matter for any State's internal legal system. It may also be a signal that there may be some limited margin for the interpretation of the content of rights (see later).

The relativist argument is also specious. It ignores the fact that one very Western construct, the modern State, is gratefully adopted by some non-Western societies however

[57] Ibid.
[58] Human Rights Council Res 17/4 (16 June 2011), para 1; the Principles are contained in Professor Ruggie's final report: UN Doc A/HRC/17/31, Annex (25 May 2011); see Principles 11–24.
[59] Human Rights Council Res17/4 (16 June 2011), para 6.   [60] Principles 11–24.

alien to their indigenous cultures. Since respect for human rights has become a feature of the modern State—a means of limiting the overweening power of the State—it is not convincing to claim a right to exercise the powers of statehood without accepting the constraints needed to ensure that the State represents, rather than subjugates, those within its jurisdiction.

Meanwhile, a robust debunking of cultural relatively approaches to human rights was given as early as 1978 by the late Senator José Diokno of the Philippines: speaking of a cultural justification for Asian authoritarianism, he pointed out that this meant that 'the Asian conception of freedom differs from that in the West; that, in short, Asians are not fit for democracy'; this he dismissed as 'racist nonsense'.[61] Indeed, insofar as States are the effective-power-holders responsible for human rights violations, it is axiomatic that it is only at the State level that human rights can be guaranteed.

What international law does not dictate is how this guarantee is to be achieved and, as with all international law rules, that is a matter for the State. For instance, in principle, monist States will permit international law obligations generally, or international human rights obligations in particular, to be directly justiciable in their courts, whereas in principle, dualist States will not allow their courts to adjudicate international law or IHRL issues, unless they have in some way, typically by legislative act, been incorporated into national law. For example, the courts of the (more or less) dualist UK could not directly apply the provisions of the European Convention of Human Rights until the Human Rights Act 1998 directly incorporated it into UK law.[62] By contrast, the courts of generally monist Netherlands had been doing just that (de Wet, 2008, Ch 5).

In reality, the two paradigms tend to be caricatural. The courts of States considering themselves dualist may well be willing at least to seek to interpret national law in a manner consistent with international law.[63] Meanwhile, monist States are rarely totally monist: they may be restricted to adjudicating treaty law rather than customary international law or they may treat a treaty provision as ordinary legislation that can be varied by subsequent legislation.[64] The courts themselves may clip their own wings by adopting doctrines such as the non-self-executing treaty, by which they decide that the particular treaty or treaty-obligation is not one that was intended to be justiciable without legislation.[65] In any event, lawyers and or judges may just be unfamiliar or uncomfortable with international (human rights) law and so avoid invoking or applying it. These are only some of the points on a continuum between the monist and dualist paradigms.

In practice, human rights treaty bodies will not typically expect the provisions of their treaties to be expressly incorporated into national law.[66] However, as the Human Rights

---

[61] Quoted in Shue, 1980, p 66.

[62] Even under the Act, the Courts cannot strike down legislation that they cannot reconcile with the ECHR; they may only issue a certificate of incompatibility that then would require the amending legislator to repair the incompatibility (s 4).

[63] An early UK (Scottish) example not involving human rights is *Mortensen v Peters* (1906) 14 *Scots Law Times* 227. It took until the 1990s before the Courts would feel comfortable with ECHR-based arguments for interpretive purposes: see Besson, 2008, p 48; the ICCPR is generally overlooked.

[64] This is US practice: *Whitney v Robertson* 124 US 190 (1888) (Supreme Court).

[65] See, for example *Foster and Eelam v Neilson*, 2 Pet 253 (1829) (US Supreme Court); also the refusal of the courts of clearly monist Senegal to try exiled Chadian President Hissène Habré in the absence of legislation implementing the universal jurisdiction clauses of the UNCAT: *Questions relating to the Obligation to Prosecute or Extradite (Belgium v Senegal), Judgment of 20 July 2012*, para 18.

[66] See, eg Human Rights Committee, General Comment No 31 (n 29), para 13. Note, however, the practice of the Committee against Torture under UNCAT, which maintains that States are obliged to incorporate

Committee has put it, 'Covenant guarantees may receive enhanced protection in those States where the court is automatically or through specific incorporation part of the domestic legal order.'[67] Whatever the level of incorporation, the judiciary may, like the other branches of government, be capable of placing a State in violation of its international human rights law obligations.[68]

VI. PRINCIPLES OF INTERNATIONAL HUMAN RIGHTS LAW

It is not in the nature of international law to articulate the conceptual premises on which its elements are based. This is also true of international human rights law, and whereas we can look to notions of national law and social contract theory for the origins of human rights thinking in the West, the international level offers no such explanatory sources. The one idea that recurs in the preambles of the UDHR and the two Covenants that constitute the International Bill of Human Rights is that of human dignity. Thus, the first preambular paragraphs of the UDHR and the Covenants, echoing similar language from the UN Charter,[69] announced that 'recognition of the inherent dignity and of the equal and inalienable rights of all members of the human family is the foundation of freedom, justice and peace in the world'. The Covenants then proclaim that 'these rights *derive* from the inherent dignity of the human person'.[70] In the UDHR, the first article continues the invocation: 'All human beings are born free and equal in dignity and rights. They are endowed with reason and conscience and should act towards one another in a spirit of brotherhood'. The notion of 'reason' perhaps resonates with that of reason that underlies natural law whether theist or non-theist in doctrine.[71] Clearly, in addition to human dignity, other deep principles are freedom, equality, justice and brotherhood. Yet others are identifiable, although not spelled out, notably fairness and impartiality (of which equality is a dimension), participation, and accountability.[72] Between them they can be considered to embrace most, if not all, internationally recognized human rights. Some rights will be more associated with one principle than another. Evidently a key value underlying the core economic and social rights is that of brotherhood, but as will be seen to be the case with civil and political rights, most could fall within more than one of these deep values.

What follows in this section is limited to civil and political rights, as the key economic and social rights have already been identified. It is also the case that virtually all the jurisprudence at the universal level at this stage concerns civil and political rights. As noted, the work of the Committee on Economic, Social and Cultural Rights under its Optional Protocol could affect the picture.

---

into domestic law the crime of torture, containing the elements of torture as defined in UNCAT Article 1: see Committee against Torture General Comment No 2 (Implementation of Article 2 by States parties), UN Doc CAT/C/GC/2 (2008), para 8.

[67] General Comment No 31, para 13.   [68] See, eg Rodley, 2008.   [69] Preambular para 2.

[70] Common preambular para 2. For an examination of the notion, see Jeremy Waldron, 'Is Dignity the Foundation of Human Rights?' (3 January 2013); available at SSRN http://ssrn.com/abstract=2196074.

[71] See Friedman, 1960, pp 58–9 (on St Thomas Aquinas) and 64–5 (on Grotius).

[72] I have here borrowed from the taxonomy I have previously used in Rodley, 2012, p 106.

A. FREEDOM

The notion of freedom has two broad connotations: *intellectual* freedom and *physical* freedom. Under the former fall most of the so-called fundamental freedoms that are the hallmark of a free civil society: freedom of opinion and expression; of thought, conscience and religion; of association; and right of peaceful assembly. It is hard to imagine a society in which all these freedoms are broadly respected that could be characterized as repressive.

There may, of course, be some limitations on such freedoms, especially where the rights of the individual and those of the group are not clearly compatible: indeed, giving the lie to the communitarian taunt that these traditional liberal freedoms connote a privileging of the individual over the legitimate needs of a society are the so-called 'claw-back' clauses that permit restrictions necessary to preserve such group values as national security, public order and the rights of others.[73] Of course, any such restrictions must be the minimum necessary to achieve the declared goal and must not be such as to render the rights nugatory. Expression invoking incitement to racial hatred may well require to be restricted,[74] but evidently there is no justification for restricting the distribution of copies of the UDHR on Human Rights Day![75]

It is also not uncommon to speak of 'balancing', in the sense of balancing the right of an individual with the group value[76] or balancing the apparent demands of one right with another.[77] This implies an element of subjectivity that would allow anyone to make what would effectively be a 'judgement call'. A better conception is that of identifying the correct *scope* of each right internally and vis-à-vis other rights. The notion is captured vividly by the famous aphorism: 'the right to swing my fist ends where the other man's nose begins'[78] It is not always possible to highlight so clearly the frontier between the rights and other recognized (group) values or between the rights themselves, but tests of necessity and proportionality that are integrated to the analytical process are a guide to the delimitation of the proper scope of the particular right in the context of the particular facts.[79]

The primordial instance of a right engaging *physical* freedom is, axiomatically, the right to liberty and security of person and its obverse, the prohibition of arbitrary detention. While not raising the same kinds of conceptual issues as the intellectual fundamental freedoms, there are areas of potential uncertainty in the notion of what is arbitrary. That a detention be provided for by law is not sufficient to dispose of the matter. For the Human Rights Committee, 'arbitrariness' connotes 'elements of inappropriateness, injustice and lack

---

[73] See ICCPR Article 19 (3) (freedom of opinion and expression); Article 18 (3) (freedom of thought, conscience and religion); Article 22 (2) (freedom of association); and Article 21, second sentence (right of peaceful assembly).

[74] Human Rights Committee General Comment No 34 (Article 19: Freedoms of Opinion and Expression), UN Doc CCPR/C/GC/34 (2011), paras 50–52.

[75] *Velichkin* v *Belarus* (Communication No 1022/2001), UN Doc CCPR/C/85/D/1022/2001 (2005).

[76] Eg *Coleman* v *Australia* (Communication No 1157/2003), UN Doc CCPR/C/87/D/1157/2003 (2006), ICCPR Article 19 being violated by 'disproportionate' reaction (fine and imprisonment) to public speaking in a shopping mall without a permit: para 7.3. Note the joint concurring opinion of Committee Members Nisuke Ando, Michael O'Flaherty, and Walter Kälin to permit the permit system allowing the authorities to 'strike a balance' between freedom of expression and 'countervailing' interests: ibid, Appendix.

[77] *Ross* v *Canada* (Communication No 736/1997), UN Doc CCPR/C/70/D/736/1997 (2000), upholding restrictions placed on a teacher in a school district with Jewish children, who publicly expressed anti-Jewish sentiments.

[78] Commonly attributed to the great nineteenth-century American jurist and judge, Oliver Wendell Holmes Jr.

[79] See General Comment No 31 (n 29), paras 33–7.

of predictability'.[80] Issues also arise in relation to 'security of person' which, for the European Court of Human Rights, is inseparable from deprivation of liberty, whereas the `Human Rights Committee considers it to cover threats, such as death threats. Such threats come close to engaging freedom of movement. This latter freedom is evidently another physical freedom right and one that raises especially difficult issues when it comes to the rights of aliens lawfully within a State's territory: it touches a raw nerve under a traditional principle under international law that permits States the sovereign right to determine which aliens may be within their territory.[81]

A final freedom right is found in the prohibition of slavery and while chattel slavery may thankfully be of merely historical interest, other 'contemporary forms of slavery' persist, such as that associated with human trafficking, and may require strenuous action by States to protect its victims.

B. FAIRNESS AND IMPARTIALITY: EQUAL TREATMENT AND NON-DISCRIMINATION

It is hard to think of anything that so offends one's sense of justice than to be treated differently from others for reasons extraneous to the issue at stake and on the basis of attributes that are, or are felt to be, beyond choice. Hence, the UN Charter's constant mention of 'without distinction as to race, sex, language or religion'. The first three criteria are evidently beyond all choice while the same may not be true in quite the same way for religion, since freedom of religion involves a right to 'adopt' a religion, evidently implying choice. Nevertheless, the inclusion of religion here was inevitable in that it was the inseparable link between race and religion that was the basis for the Jewish holocaust perpetrated by Nazi Germany. This genocide, as we have seen, was pivotal to the inclusion of human rights in the UN Charter. A further factor must have been that it is in the nature of religion or similar profoundly held beliefs as to the nature and purpose of humanity that the holder feels him or herself to be impotent simply to abandon such beliefs.

By the time of the adoption of the UDHR, other prohibited criteria of discrimination were added: 'colour, as well as political or other opinion, national or social origin, property, birth or other status'.[82] Again, most of these attributes are not a matter of individual choice, just ones that the individual was simply 'landed with'. This is also the case for property at birth, but not necessarily in later life when the acquisition or loss of property may be very much a matter of choice. As to political or other opinion, there is more personal freedom of choice, at least in respect of the decision to *express* one's political or similar opinions. The point is captured in the very freedom itself: under Article 19 ICCPR, there is a right to hold opinions without interference; it is only the expression of them that may, as noted, be restricted on certain grounds. What then of the notion of 'other status'? Assuming the *ejusdem generis* rule applies,[83] the question arises as to what amounts to 'the same kind'. The underlying idea seems to be that of attributes that are biologically or psychologically beyond choice. Thus, sexual orientation has come to be recognized as falling within the prohibited categories of discrimination.[84] In

---

[80] *Van Alphen* v *Netherlands* (Communication No 305/1988), UN Doc CCPR/C/39/D/305/1988 (1990), para 5.8.

[81] Thus, under ICCPR Article 13, such an alien is provided only with procedural, rather than normative, protections.

[82] Article 2.

[83] That is, the rule of interpretation that open clauses after a list should be understood as limiting further examples to those 'of the same kind' as those specified in the list.

[84] Nowak correctly points out that a specific decision of the Committee involving the criminalization of homosexual behaviour was found to violate Article 17(1) (private life) together with Article 2(1) (on the basis

one major respect, the ICCPR goes beyond the UN Charter and UDHR, in the sense that it has a free-standing non-discrimination article. The earlier texts required the rights protected to be enjoyed without discrimination,[85] but Article 26 of the ICCPR requires equality under the law generally and non-discrimination on the listed grounds in respect of *all* legal rights. The Human Rights Committee, as other treaty bodies, accepts that offensive discrimination may be indirect as well as direct, but that some distinctions may be made as long as they are reasonable and objective.[86]

The same principles of fairness, impartiality, and equality also underlie the protection of the rights of (members of) ethnic, linguistic, or religious minorities found in Article 27 ICCPR. It is not clear to what extent this provision goes beyond the provisions on non-discrimination, direct or indirect (Rodley, 1995).

C. HUMAN DIGNITY

While the human dignity value appears to underlie the whole corpus of international human rights law, some rights are especially associated directly with this value. Thus the UN Declarations against Torture and other Cruel, Inhuman or Degrading Treatment or Punishment, and against Enforced Disappearance both consider their subject-matter to be 'an offence to human dignity'.[87] The only international treaty on the right to life, the Second Optional Protocol to the ICCPR, aiming at the abolition of the death penalty, affirms that abolition 'contributes to the enhancement of human dignity'.[88]

Indeed, few human rights issues have received as much attention as the prohibitions of torture and ill-treatment and of enforced disappearance, which are prohibited by every general human rights treaty.[89]

Enforced disappearance, while not specifically addressed in general human rights conventions, violates many of the rights contained in those conventions, most evidently the prohibition of arbitrary arrest and detention/right to liberty and security of person and the prohibition of torture and similar ill-treatment. To at least this extent, that links the latter right directly to the human dignity value, as well as the freedom value. In addition to the just-mentioned Declaration there are now a universal and a regional convention on this abhorrent violation.[90] Even though the UN conventions define the notions of torture and enforced disappearance, there remain outstanding issues of scope, such as whether pain or suffering for 'torture' has to be more severe than for 'inhuman treatment' or whether enforced disappearance requires, beyond refusal to acknowledge the detention and/or the whereabouts of the person, an additional element involving placing the person outside the protection of law.[91]

---

of the word 'sex'). The Committee did not explain this deviation from the issue as it was litigated, namely, as an Article 26 issue in relating to 'other status'; Nowak, 2005, referring to *Toonen v Australia* (Communication No 488/1992), UN Doc CCPR/C/50/D/488/1992 (1994).

[85] And, indeed, ICCPR Article 2(1).

[86] See General Comment 18 (1989) (Non-discrimination), paras 10 and 13 respectively.

[87] GA Res 3452 (9 December 1975), Article 2 (torture); GA Res 47/133 (18 December 1992), Article 1 (enforced disappearance).

[88] GA Res 44/128 (15 December 1989), preambular para 1; see also African Charter on Human and Peoples' Rights, Article 5, and American Convention on Human Rights, Article 5.

[89] ICCPR, Article 7; ECHR, Article 3; ACHR, Article 5; ACHPR, Article 5; Arab CHR, Article 8; see generally Rodley and Pollard, 2009, Ch 2.

[90] International Convention for the Protection of All Persons from Enforced Disappearance, GA Res 61/177 (20 December 2006) and Inter-American Convention on the Forced Disappearance of Persons, OAS General Assembly, Twenty-fourth Regular Session, 9 June 1994, OAS TS A-60.

[91] See Rodley and Pollard, 2009, pp 85–124 (torture) and 332–7 (enforced disappearance).

The right to life, while non-derogable, is not absolute in the sense that not all deprivations of life will be considered arbitrary and thus violating the right. Accordingly, deployment of potentially lethal force in international armed conflict permissible under IHL would also be consistent with international human rights law. Similarly, law enforcement officials may use such force to protect life and limb if no other means are available. Once again, as with restrictions on fundamental freedoms, we see notions of necessity and proportionality at work. An especially difficult area is posed by the continuing existence of the death penalty in some national jurisdictions, despite the fact that there are one universal and three regional abolitionist protocols to treaties whose original texts expressly contemplate the death penalty as an exception to the right to life, albeit subject to certain important restrictions.[92] Meanwhile, with (so far) increasing majorities, the UN General Assembly has been urging States to adopt moratoria on the use of the death penalty.[93]

D. JUSTICE AND LEGALITY

In broad terms, the justice value connotes fairness and equality as indicated earlier. It also has the specific connotation in the sense of administration of justice: the legal justice system. If that system acts arbitrarily or without integrity, there can be no secure legal rights. The right to a fair trial or hearing—due process of law—is thus infrastructural. The relevant article of the ICCPR is Article 14, and Human Rights Committee General Comment 32 deals with it at length. One noteworthy element is the increasing scepticism as to the ability of military or special courts to deliver justice either to those who are accused of crime or those who may be the victims of crimes committed by military or security personnel.[94] Unless one has the means of knowing the content of one's legal obligations and the consequence of non-compliance, any notion of legality—and so justice—is fatally undermined. The principle of non-retroactivity of crime and punishment (*nullum crimen, nulla poena sine lege*) is found in the non-derogable Article 15 ICCPR.

E. PARTICIPATION

Intellectual fundamental freedoms represent both a condition and a means of meaningful participation in society. The right to participate in the government of one's society is evidently a direct manifestation of this value (Article 25 ICCPR). It covers a range of issues, from equality of access to the civil service to the right to choose a State's political leaders or indeed to stand for election. To the extent that competitive democratic elections have become the system of choice since the end of the Cold War, the Human Rights Committee has felt able to find the requirement that candidates for political office should belong to parties or to specific parties to be an 'unreasonable restriction on the right to participate in public affairs'.[95] Like the

---

[92] Second Optional Protocol to the ICCPR, GA Res 44/128 (15 December 1989); Protocol No 6 (1982), CETS No 114) and 13 (2013), CETS No 187) to the European Convention on Human Rights, and Protocol to the American Convention on Human Rights to Abolish the Death Penalty (1990), OAS TS 73.

[93] Most recently at the time of writing, GA Res 67/176 (20 December 2012): 111 for; 41 against; 34 abstaining (UN Doc A/67/PV.60, pp 16–17).

[94] See Human Rights Committee General Comment No 32 (2007) (Article 14: Right to equality before courts and tribunals and to a fair trial), UN Doc CCPR/C/GC/32, para 22 (civilians before military or special courts); *Kholodova v Russian Federation* (Communication No 1548/2007), UN Doc CCPR/C/106/D/1548/2007 (2012) (public officials acquitted by military tribunal for murder of a journalist).

[95] General Comment No 25 (1996), UN Doc CCPR/C/21/Rev.1/Add.7, para 17.

European Court of Human Rights, it has also found a blanket prohibition on prisoners' voting to violate the right.[96]

F. ACCOUNTABILITY

Numerous rights that respond to other values also respond to the value of accountability. Obvious examples would be the right to freedom to receive and impart information (a dimension of freedom of opinion and expression) and hold elected representatives accountable by voting for others (see the preceding paragraph). Especially important are the provisions for remedies in case of violation of rights. While the right to compensation is the standard means, it can go much further to include an obligation on the State to investigate criminal violations of human rights and bring perpetrators to justice.[97]

G. THE PRIVATE SPHERE

The right to be left undisturbed in one's home and to a private life is not a typical manifestation of the freedom value, but although precisely not in the public domain, it could be considered a form of freedom to be insulated from social intrusion.[98] It certainly connects up with freedom of expression, on the scope of which it represents a limitation. The protection of the family and childhood[99] are primary positive obligations on the State and are not easily assignable to one of the core values. They may be seen as preconditions to the full flourishing of the human personality, without which the other rights and the values on which they are based cannot be meaningfully enjoyed.

VII. INTERNATIONAL MACHINERY ON HUMAN RIGHTS

Anyone attending the principal UN political human rights organ, the Human Rights Council, would find it difficult to credit the difference between it and its predecessor, the Commission on Human Rights, in the latter's early years. Nowadays, States and NGOs routinely make oral interventions (under certain agenda items) on any human rights issue or any country. NGOs also routinely submit written information for circulation as UN documents on the same issues. It was only in the late 1970s and early 1980s that it came to be accepted that the previous pervasive silence on specific human rights cases and situations in member States could be left behind. There is now a substantial network of what are usually called Charter-based human rights procedures.

---

[96] *Yevdokimov and Rezanov v Russian Federation* (Communication No 1410/2005), UN Doc CCPR/C/101/D/1410/2005 (2011), following *Hirst v United Kingdom* (74025/01) ECHR 6 October 2005.

[97] Human Rights Committee, General Comment No 31 (n 29), paras 15 and 18.

[98] See ICCPR, Article 17.   [99] See ICCPR, Articles 23 and 24.

A. UNIVERSAL CHARTER-BASED HUMAN RIGHTS PROCEDURES

1. UN Commission on Human Rights

The Commission established by the Economic and Social Council (ECOSOC) pursuant to Article 68 of the UN Charter, understood its early role to be one of standard-setting. Very early in its existence, in 1947, it decided 'that it has no power to take any action in regard to any complaint concerning human rights', a stance confirmed by ECOSOC Resolution 75 V (1947). A confidential list of complaints, without details, was to be compiled by the UN Secretariat, with original texts of the complaints being made accessible to members. No public discussion of the complaints took place, nor, even in closed discussion, did members raise alleged human rights violations in other States.

a. Country-specific procedures

A breakthrough came two decades later in 1967, when the Commission and its Sub-Commission[100] were authorized by ECOSOC Resolution 1235 XLII to make 'a thorough study' of alleged consistent patterns of human rights violation and investigate gross human rights violations. Examples given were the human rights situation in southern Africa, that is, South Africa, Southwest Africa (now Namibia) and secessionist Southern Rhodesia. When in 1968 the Sub-Commission took this mandate seriously, forwarding material from NGOs not only on the southern African situation, but also on the independent sovereign States of Greece (after a 1967 military coup) and Haiti (languishing under the dictatorship of President-for-life Dr François (Papa Doc) Duvalier), the Commission, unwilling to let NGOs dictate its agenda, established a confidential complaints procedure reflected in ECOSOC Resolution 1503 XLVIII (27 May 1970) ('the 1503 procedure'). This was a confidential procedure, whereby the confidential list of communications[101] would be examined by a working group on communications of five members of the Sub-Commission ('working group on communications'). The working group could forward to the full Sub-Commission communications 'which appear to reveal a consistent pattern of gross and reliably attested violations of human rights'. The Sub-Commission could then send on any such situation to the Commission.

The Commission in turn established its own working group ('working group on situations'), composed of five of its members, to recommend to the Commission what action to take. Such activity, occasionally involved a 'thorough study' carried out by a special rapporteur appointed by the Commission,[102] sometimes a request to the UN Secretary-General to report to the next annual session of the Commission. Usually, the Commission would merely decide to keep the situation 'under review' from year to year. On occasion it would

---

[100] A body of up to 26 individual experts, then known as the Sub-Commission on Prevention of Discrimination and Protection of Minorities, later re-named Sub-Commission on the Promotion and Protection of Human Rights, until it was dissolved at the same time as the parent inter-governmental Commission on Human Rights.

[101] By ECOSOC Res 728F (30 July 1959), the Secretariat had been authorized to prepare a confidential list of communications (complaints) alleging human rights violations in specific countries, the list being circulated to members of the Sub-Commission and the Commission. This list became the basis for the '1503 procedure'.

[102] The term 'special rapporteur' is a portmanteau term for individual experts charged with a specific function by a UN body and expected to report to the body. Here, we are talking about experts mandated to investigate or fact-find for the body appointing them.

simply decide to drop consideration of the situation, regardless of its seriousness. It never used its power under resolution 1503 to establish an investigative committee.

However, the '1503 procedure' dictated how 'communications' from private sources, including NGOs, should be treated. It did not constrain individual members of the Commission, nor of the Sub-Commission. If they wanted to raise situations of their own motion, they could. Already a working group on southern Africa had been established in 1967. Its mandate was extended briefly to cover the territories occupied by Israel in the June 1967 war—until the General Assembly itself established a working group on that situation. Public consideration of human rights country problems at the UN only moved beyond southern Africa and the Israeli-occupied territories (IOT) in 1975 in response to international concern with a friendless military government in Chile that had brutally seized power in 1973 from a constitutionally elected government.

Slowly after this other countries were taken up in public session, with a special rapporteur[103] usually appointed to examine the situation, provided the State in question was not too influential. There are at the time of writing some 13 country mandates. Despite the appalling record of the military government of Argentina in the latter half of the 1990s, whose barbarities included thousands of enforced disappearances, there was insufficient political will to initiate a study of the situation in that country. This lamentable situation in fact led to a positive development. If the Commission could not examine the situation in Argentina, perhaps it could consider the phenomenon that most characterized that situation, that is, enforced disappearance (Kramer and Weissbrodt, 1981).

b. Thematic special procedures

The outcome was the establishment of the first of the thematic special procedures, the Working Group on Enforced or Involuntary Disappearances (1980). Its initial mandate was merely to study the phenomenon of enforced disappearances and it was created for a year. However, the Working Group's first report, in 1981, was something of an institutional earthquake. It provided a summary of all the cases it had received and transmitted to the governments impugned, as well as summaries of any replies from them. It also began the practice of making urgent appeals where people had been detained in circumstances indicating that they might be at risk of enforced disappearance. The Working Group did not draw any conclusions regarding State responsibility, considering its role to be humanitarian and non-judgmental, albeit there was nothing requiring such caution in the resolution setting it up. It also began undertaking country visits, the reports of which evidently struggled, none too successfully, to avoid judgment.

The next thematic mechanisms to be created were those of the Special Rapporteurs on extra-judicial, summary and arbitrary executions (1982) and on torture and ill-treatment (1985) (see Rodley, 1986). Their reports followed the style of those of the Working Group. There are now some 36 thematic mandates. Some (mainly in the field of civil and political rights) are more action-oriented, based on individual case work; others (mainly in the field of economic and social rights) are more study-oriented. But there is no hard and fast dividing line, as evidenced by the joint work of a number of civil and political rights mandates with that on the right to health in respect of the situation in the US Naval Station at Guantánamo Bay, Cuba. Only one, the Working Group on Arbitrary Detention, is expressly mandated to make individual case-specific conclusions. However,

---

[103] Sometimes the term 'special representative' (usually, then, to be appointed by the Secretary-General) or 'independent expert' would be used. The terminology was no guide to the function.

the other original mandates have long since abandoned any pretence of not arriving at country-specific evaluations.

2. UN Human Rights Council

The 'double-standards' implied in the politically-grounded selection of countries for public consideration by the Commission had been noted from the early days of focus on the IOT and southern Africa exclusively. The inability to address the situation in Argentina directly has already been noted. Another high-profile example was the impunity of Iraq under the bloody dictatorship of President Saddam Hussein. Even after the gas bombing of 5,000 of its own people in Halabja in 1988, it was not possible to get a majority to vote for public consideration. Indeed, Iraq even managed to get itself dropped from the confidential 1503 procedure. Two years later, after Iraq invaded Kuwait, the Commission could then appoint a special rapporteur on the human rights situation in Iraq.[104]

Yet it was not until 2004 that a High-Level Panel on Threats, Challenges and Change, established by Secretary-General Kofi Annan found that the Commission had become discredited and should eventually be replaced by another body.[105] The political selectivity matter was the key issue. One reason for this, it was suggested, was that States with poor human rights records were more inclined to stand and work hard for election to this 53-member State body[106] so as to deflect possible attention from themselves. The solution of the High-Level Panel was to have a body, either at Charter-level or, at any rate, reporting to the General Assembly, that would be universal in membership. It would thus not be a distorted cross-section of the UN membership and it would have instantly enhanced status by reporting directly to the Assembly rather than to ECOSOC. The Secretary-General, with strong support from the USA, came out in favour of a smaller body elected by the General Assembly, with a two-thirds majority vote (implicitly guaranteeing that States with poor human rights records would not be elected).[107] After an extensive negotiation General Assembly resolution 251/60 was adopted in 2006 and a 47-member Human Rights Council elected by a simple majority of the General Assembly was created; it would report direct to the Assembly, not to ECOSOC.

Even if there is no competition for regional slots, any candidate has to secure a majority of positive votes in the General Assembly rather than obtain the seat by acclamation. Moreover, no State may have more than two successive three-year terms. The Council is also required to institute a system of universal periodic review (UPR) of the human rights of all UN member States. It is easier to call special sessions to deal with urgent situations (one-third of Council members can request, not over a half as before) and, anyway, the Council meets much more frequently than the one annual six-week session of the Commission. Meanwhile, the Council inherits the system of special procedures and a 'complaints mechanism' modelled on the '1503 procedure'. Of particular significance, there is the UPR.

It is too early to attempt an authoritative evaluation; the Council is a work-in-progress. At first, it looked as though it would be retrogressive. The institution-building package that emerged after its first year was not encouraging.[108] While the use of country rapporteurs was continued, they were limited in practice to those that had already been

---

[104] And another one on occupied Kuwait. See Commission on Human Rights Res 1991/74 (6 March 1991), para 5 (Iraq) and 1991/67 (6 March 1991), para 9 (occupied Kuwait).

[105] UN Doc A/59/565 (2004).   [106] Ibid, para 283.

[107] *In Larger Freedom: Towards Development, Security and Human Rights for All*, Report of the Secretary-General, UN Doc A/59/2005, para 183.

[108] Human Rights Council Res 5/1 (18 June 2007).

taken up by the Commission; two, Belarus and Cuba were even dropped as part of the political deal to get the package.[109] By 2011, a willingness to take up new situations emerged (Côte d'Ivoire, Syria) with others following (Eritrea, 2012; Mali, 2013). Others that had been dropped earlier reappeared (Iran, 2011; Belarus, 2012), one, Sudan, as early as 2009.

The earliest special sessions were overwhelmingly focused on the IOT (and Israel's 2006 incursion into Lebanon). An apparent breakthrough on the situation in Sri Lanka proved illusory when the Council adopted an uncritical resolution proposed by Sri Lanka itself.[110] The Council retrieved itself by adopting resolutions in 2012 and 2013 expressing concern at various grave human rights violations,[111] a concern confirmed late in 2013 by the High Commissioner for Human Rights.[112] A convincing indication of real moving away from political selectivity or 'double-standards' would be if the Council were to appoint a special rapporteur on Sri Lanka's (at the time of writing) continuously deteriorating situation.[113] On the other hand, after the Sri Lanka setback, there were significant special sessions on Côte d'Ivoire (2010) Libya (2011), and Syria (two in 2011 and one in 2012).

Meanwhile, although UPR does not lead to country-specific evaluations by the Council as such,[114] it is generally thought to be playing a role that encourages States to make pledges, such as to ratify unratified human rights treaties or to issue standing invitations to special procedures to visit the country in question. Also, the very process of having to face questions and recommendations, based on the report submitted by the country and reports prepared by the Office of the High Commissioner for Human Rights (OHCHR), on the concerns of special procedures and treaty bodies (see next section) and on those expressed by 'stakeholders' (national human rights institutions and NGOs), can be at least a means of nudging the State towards improving its performance to some extent.

B. UNIVERSAL TREATY BODIES

As already indicated, the presumption in the early days of the UN was that only by treaty adherence could States' human rights behaviour be submitted to international scrutiny. What follows is a consideration of the 'system' of the nine treaty bodies (Committees) established pursuant to the 'core' human rights treaties referred to earlier.[115] There are in fact ten treaty bodies, as a second one on torture was created by an Optional Protocol

---

[109] Human Rights Council Dec 1/102 (30 June 2006); for the background, see Boyle, 2009, pp 28–44.

[110] Human Rights Council Res S-11/1 (27 May 2009).

[111] Human Rights Council, Res 19/2 (22 March 2012) and 22/1 (21 March 2013).

[112] Opening remarks by UN High Commissioner for Human Rights at a press conference during her mission to Sri Lanka, Colombo, 31 August 2013: http://www.ohchr.org/EN/NewsEvents/Pages/DisplayNews.aspx?NewsID=13673&LangID=Es.

[113] Ibid.

[114] The UPR process outcome consists of recommendations made by other States together with the response of the examined State to each recommendation; there is no corporate conclusion or recommendation made by the Council as a whole.

[115] Committee on the Elimination of Racial Discrimination (CERD), Committee on Economic, Social and Cultural Rights (CESCR) (uniquely, established by ECOSOC, the body originally provided for by ICESCR to perform the monitoring function), Human Rights Committee (HRC), Committee on the Elimination of Discrimination against Women (CEDAW Committee), the Committee against Torture (CAT), the Committee on the Rights of the Child (CRC Committee), the Committee on the Protection of All Migrant Workers and Members of Their Families (CMW Committee), the Committee on the Rights of Persons with Disabilities (CRPD Committee), and the Committee on Enforced Disappearances (CED).

to UNCAT (OPCAT), that is, the Sub-Committee on Prevention of Torture (SPT). Its functions are innovative and will be briefly touched on at the end. The first one, the Committee against Torture (CAT) established under UNCAT, has more usual functions.

The treaty bodies are composed of between 10 and 25 members, with the mean being eighteen. The members are expected to be experts and are nominated by the States parties to the respective treaty to serve in their individual capacities. They are typically elected to four-year terms and may be re-elected without limit under some treaties, while two mandates are the maximum under other (more recent) ones. The expertise required is that of the subject-matter, not necessarily law, although their job is to seek to interpret and apply a legal instrument that normally falls to be interpreted according to the law of treaties, a discipline likely to be more familiar to persons with legal training. In principle it may be easier for persons who are not government members to act in a genuinely individual capacity. Nevertheless, some treaty body members are government officials, often senior diplomats.[116] In practice, the discourse that takes place reflects far more that of individual expertise than intergovernmental negotiation.

1. Functions

a. State reports

In respect of all but the Committee on Enforced Disappearances (CED) and evidently the Committee for the Prevention of Torture and Inhuman or Degrading Treatment or Punishment (CPT), the States parties to a treaty are required to submit periodic reports to the Committees and reviewing these State reports is the one common function across the nine core treaty bodies. The periodicity of reports, when specified, is between two and five years. For the Human Rights Committee, the treaty body of the ICCPR, it is when the Committee specifies, but in practice the Committee uses a range of three to six years depending on the seriousness of the situation. The outlier CED will only receive as of right and automatically an initial report, after which it is up to the Committee to decide whether it wants further reports. This doubtless reflects the fact that most States parties will not engage in the practice of enforced disappearance and should not be required to report unnecessarily.

Several of the Committees put written questions before the hearing to the State, in the form of a 'list of issues' (LOI), requesting States to respond in writing, so that when the actual oral hearing takes place with a delegation from the State, the process of information clarification is already underway. Some have gone further and offered States wishing to ease what the latter call the 'reporting burden' the option of 'focused reporting' that is simply responding to a 'list of issues prior to reporting' (LOIPR) once the initial reports of the States has been examined.[117] After the written and oral exchange, the Committee will adopt 'concluding observations'; these are mainly a list of concerns about areas of possible non-compliance with treaty provisions and recommendations to address the concerns. Concluding observations began only in 1992.[118] Some Committees have also established

---

[116] It is a long-standing practice of most committees, now enshrined in the 'Guidelines on the Independence and Impartiality of Members of Human Rights Treaty Bodies ('the Addis Ababa Guidelines')', adopted by the Twenty-fourth annual meeting of chairs of the treaty bodies (UN Doc A/67/222 (2012) Annex), for members to refrain from participating in work on their own countries.

[117] See Rodley, 2013, pp 621, 627 (LOI) and 629–30 (LOIPR).

[118] Before that there was no agreement that the bodies could interpret their powers as including the issuance of country-specific evaluations: ibid, 628–9.

a follow-up procedure consisting of a further round of exchanges, under the guidance of a special rapporteur, on a number of the recommendations. The Committees refer to the overall process as the 'constructive dialogue'.[119]

Many States become overdue in submitting their reports, some for up to two decades. This has led some Committees to institute a procedure of considering a situation in the absence of a report, applied to the most seriously overdue. Here usually the Committee will announce its intention to initiate the procedure. As is intended, this may often result in the State in question submitting a report. If it does not, the Committee may draft a LOI and, again, the State may respond. In the absence of a response then the hearing will go ahead, the State being invited to send a delegation, which the State may well do. The least satisfactory (and rarest) outcome will be an actual hearing in the absence of any written contribution from the State or any delegation. A constant problem for the Committees is that they generally have a backlog of reports submitted but yet to be considered, while also faced with overdue reports; if the latter were to be submitted, the backlog would be even greater.

b. General comments

The Committees have developed a practice of issuing 'general comments', consisting of guidance to States on the Committees' understanding of what States' obligations under the respective treaty may be. These were developed by the Human Rights Committee in the early 1980s, during the Cold War, when there was no agreement to issue country-specific evaluation of the sort found in what are now called 'concluding observations'. These are seen as authoritative interpretations of the treaties, developed on the basis of extensive experience of reviewing periodic reports and of examining individual cases (see following section). General comments are now typically the result of protracted discussion over several sessions of the Committee in question. The practice of consulting civil society and governments during the process has also emerged over time.

c. Individual complaints

It was not by oversight that the only obligation States were willing to assume from the beginning was that of reviewing periodic reports submitted by governments. This process was in effect the lowest common denominator of what States were prepared to accept by way of international supervision of their compliance with their human rights obligations. Nevertheless, from the beginning the idea of a court that would hear individual complaints was advanced by some.[120] Yet outside the European and, later, Inter-American regions there was no political will for such a radical idea. What was, however, in the realm of the possible was an optional system of having individual complaints submitted to the Committees. This was first made available by States making declarations under Article 14 ICERD and Article 22 UNCAT or by their ratifying the (First) Optional Protocol to the ICCPR. Later other treaty bodies were given the same power to consider individual complaints, either by an optional declaration under a new treaty or by ratifying an optional protocol, usually adopted later. The Convention on the Elimination of All Forms of Discrimination Against Women (CEDAW) was the first of these with its optional protocol

---

[119] See, eg Report by Navanetham Pillay, *Strengthening the United Nations Human Rights Treaty Body System: A Report by the United Nations High Commissioner for Human Rights*, (22 June 2012) section 3.1.1 (available at http://www.ohchr.org/EN/HRBodies/HRTD/Pages/TBStrengthening.aspx).

[120] Eg Lauterpacht, 1950, Ch 3, discussing the possibility of amending Article 34 of the Statute of the International Court of Justice to permit individuals, rather than just States, to seise the Court.

and now it is or will be possible for all treaty bodies to receive individual complaints. So far, it is the Human Rights Committee that has most practice on such complaints, followed by CAT and then the CEDAW Committee and CERD.

Although the 'views' that are the outcome of the Committees' deliberations on individual complaints are not *per se* legally binding on the States in question, the (written, confidential) process by which they are adopted are modelled on judicial practice. Both parties are given full opportunity to respond to each other's pleadings and the Committees' deliberations are indistinguishable from those of a court. The views are adopted 'in a judicial spirit'.[121] The 'jurisprudence' or 'case law' emanating from the cases is in the public domain and widely resorted to by international lawyers seeking authoritative interpretation of the treaties. Some Committees have also established a follow-up procedure, whereby the good offices of a special rapporteur are used to seek compliance with the adverse findings of the Committee.

The practice has emerged, similar to that of the ICJ and the European Court of Human Rights, of seeking interim measures to discourage action by the State party that would render the process nugatory. Thus, if 'irreparable harm' appears imminent, such as the application of the death penalty or the deportation of someone to a State where they face torture or other prohibited ill-treatment, the State will be requested to refrain from taking the action, pending consideration of the case. Non-compliance with the request will be considered a violation of the instrument providing for the right of individual petition.[122]

d. Inter-State complaints

A number of treaties provide for inter-State complaints, that is, on a reciprocal basis, the consideration of complaints by one State against another. Uniquely within the UN treaty bodies system, ICERD makes such complaints an automatic possibility (Article 12). The others, like that under Article 41 ICCPR are all optional on a reciprocal basis. The procedure has not once been used and so will not further detain us here.

e. Inquiries

The drafters of UNCAT introduced a novel function for a UN human rights instrument. Provision was made for undertaking inquiries into the alleged systematic practices of torture (Article 20). The innovation was sufficiently controversial that a special provision had to be made for States to be able to opt out of the procedure by means of a reservation at the time of ratification (Article 28). Even without availing themselves of the 'opt out', States could refuse to permit the treaty body to have access to their territories when undertaking an inquiry.[123] Subsequently, other instruments came to envisage a similar power, starting with the Optional Protocol to CEDAW. The principal practice to date is that by UNCAT, followed by CEDAW. The UNCAT practice has been more limited than was expected at the time of drafting, consisting of only eight published inquiry reports.

---

[121] The language of the Human Rights Committee: General Comment No 33 (2008) (The Obligations of States Parties under the Optional Protocol to the [ICCPR]) UN Doc CCPR/C/GC/33, para 11.

[122] Ibid, para 19, following *Piandiong et al* v *The Philippines* (Communication No 869/1999), UN Doc CCPR/C/70/D/869/1999 (2000), para 5.2.

[123] UN Doc A/51/44 (1996), paras 216–18 (refusal of Egypt—no other refusal of a CAT visit is known to have occurred).

f. Other functions

Committee on Enforced Disappearances

No doubt reflecting the especial gravity of the phenomenon of enforced disappearances, the CED is empowered to refer serious situations—apparent systematic or widespread practices of enforced disappearance—to the attention of the General Assembly (Article 34). It may also request urgent action (not just requests for interim measures) in respect of a feared enforced disappearance (Article 30).

Sub-Committee for the Prevention of Torture and Other Cruel, Inhuman or Degrading Treatment or Punishment (SPT)

As indicated earlier, OPCAT establishes a wholly novel body. It has no similarity with the other treaty bodies. Modelled broadly on the functions of the Committee for the Prevention of Torture and Inhuman or Degrading Treatment or Punishment (CPT) established under the 1987 European Convention of the same name, the SPT has the right without further permission to undertake periodic missions to States parties and visit places of detention. The idea is that institutions subject to visits will be deterred from engaging in the prohibited practices. Unlike the CPT, there is no express power for it to undertake ad hoc visits, though it may be that the dearth of available resources for frequent visits will be more of an obstacle to the achievement of this deterrent function.

However, the OPCAT also provides for States parties to establish their own national preventive mechanisms (NPM), whose function would be the same as the SPT or, for that matter, the CPT. This dimension may then suggest that the principal contribution of the SPT in practice will be in its ability to support and so enhance the effectiveness of the NPMs.

2. The legal nature of treaty body outputs

In some ways, the human rights treaty drafters sought to steer clear of endowing the treaty bodies with the same power to issue binding decisions of judgments as courts would have. Nevertheless, the output of a body provided for *within* a treaty and appointed by States parties to the treaties, operating in a judicial spirit, must have the sort of juridical authority that governments could not simply dismiss as merely recommendatory. The point could not have been stated more clearly, in respect of the Human Rights Committee, by the ICJ:

> Since it was created, the Human Rights Committee has built up a considerable body of interpretative case law, in particular through its findings in response to the individual communications which may be submitted to it in respect of States parties to the first Optional Protocol, and in the form of its 'General Comments'. Although the Court is in no way obliged, in the exercise of its judicial functions, to model its own interpretation of the Covenant on that of the Committee, it believes that it should ascribe great weight to the interpretation adopted by this independent body that was established specifically to supervise the application of that treaty. The point here is to achieve the necessary clarity and the essential consistency of international law, as well as legal security, to which both the individuals with guaranteed rights and the States obliged to comply with treaty obligations are entitled.[124]

---

[124] *Ahmadou Sadio Diallo (Republic of Guinea v Democratic Republic of the Congo), Merits, Judgment, ICJ Reports 2012*, p 639, para 66.

3. Proposals for improvements to the system

The core treaty bodies are thought to represent a reporting burden on States, thus giving a reason for delays in reporting and, as noted earlier, there are backlogs that would increase with removal of the delays in reporting. There are also elements of duplication across the treaty bodies: many of the subjects of the topic-specific treaties also fall within the scope of the general treaties (the Covenants). There are also possibilities in the latter areas for contradictions in the outputs of the treaty bodies.

Various proposals have been mooted to address these issues: a single, unified treaty body,[125] a consolidated report for submission to all the bodies[126] and, most recently, a comprehensive reporting calendar.[127] There is no space here to analyse why, so far, none of these solutions has been able to overcome assorted legal or political obstacles. It remains the case that most improvements are made by the treaty bodies themselves, sometimes individually and sometimes collectively.[128] Thus, the treaty bodies have developed the LOI and LOIPR, as well as the consideration of situations in the absence of a report. It is instructive that the latest proposal from the High Commissioner for Human Rights—the comprehensive reporting calendar (or 'master calendar') is predicated on the now optional LOI and LOIPR procedures being made compulsory and operating together with the procedure of a review in the absence of a report.

At the time of writing, it seems that it will remain necessary for the treaty bodies to continue their own initiatives to increase the efficiency of their procedures. The main obstacle to their attempts in this direction is the constant limitation on their resources, aggravated by periodic financial crises.

4. The special procedures and the treaty body system

The treaty bodies were created, it will be recalled, because in the early decades of the UN it was thought that international scrutiny of States' human rights performance could only be engaged in by means of freely accepted treaty obligations. The development of the special procedures of the Human Rights Council did not impede their development.

Under the circumstances, it is surprising that there is not more overlap and even competition between the two systems. So far, there is more complementarity than competition between them. The special procedures do not engage in reviews of State periodic reports. Even the advent of UPR that could have been at odds with that core function of the treaty bodies has not turned out that way, since UPR does not lead to corporate conclusions and recommendations like those of the treaty bodies. On the contrary, treaty body concluding observations have proved a fertile source of recommendations by Council members to States undergoing UPR (Rodley, 2012, pp 328–30).

Similarly, except for the Working Group on Arbitrary Detention, special procedures do not routinely come to conclusions about specific individual allegations of human rights violations. Apart from the CED, it is left to the special procedures to undertake urgent appeals. It will be interesting to see how the CED and Working Group on

---

[125] See Report of Philip Alston, *Effective Functioning of Bodies Established Pursuant to United Nations Human Rights Instruments: Final Report on Enhancing the Long-Term Effectiveness of the United Nations Human Rights Treaty System* (27 March 1997), UN Doc E/CN.4/1997/74.

[126] *Strengthening of the United Nations: An Agenda for Further Change: Report of the Secretary-General*, UN Doc A/57/387 (9 September 2002), para 54.

[127] *Strengthening the United Nations Human Rights Treaty Body System: A Report by the United Nations High Commissioner for Human Rights*, (22 June 2012), pp 37–46.

[128] Ibid.

Enforced or Involuntary Disappearances deal with their overlapping powers to make such appeals.

One area of definite potential overlap is that of inquiries into systematic practices. However, while such inquiries, typically involving country visits, are routine for the special procedures, they have not yet attained the same standard practice for even those treaty bodies with the power to pursue such inquiries. In any event, as long as the inquiries do not take place at the same time, it is possible that they can still be complementary, with each inquiry able to build on the previous one (Rodley, 2012, p 339–40).

C. REGIONAL BODIES

If the universal system was slow to get off the ground, there was progress at the regional level, no doubt reflecting a sense of shared priorities and a preference to settle issues, as it were, *en famille*.

The first was the *European Convention on Human Rights* (ECHR). This is the only human rights instrument that establishes a court to which any individual can call to account the State exercising jurisdiction over him or her, and expect a legally binding decision on the case. This radical development emerged relatively recently. When the ECHR was adopted in 1950, there was not even an automatic right to individual petition: the Convention created a European Commission of Human Rights and a European Court of Human Rights. The Commission could consider inter-State complaints as of right. It could only deal with individual complaints in respect of States that chose to make the requisite declaration.[129] The Court's jurisdiction was also optional.

Moreover, even when States parties to the ECHR accepted the Court's jurisdiction, that did not entitle the individual directly to seise the court of a complaint. Any complaint was first considered by the Commission. Once the Commission had issued its report, it could itself refer the case to the Court if the State party concerned had accepted the court's jurisdiction.[130] Moreover, the State party concerned could also choose to refer the case to the Court,[131] in effect giving the defendant State a right of appeal not enjoyed by the individual applicant, albeit the State of nationality of the applicant, if the applicant were not a national of the accused State, could also refer the case of its national to the Court.

It was only in 1990 that Protocol 9 to the ECHR was adopted to permit individuals from States that chose to accept this Protocol to refer a case to the Court. It took Protocol 11 (1994) that had to be accepted by all States parties to the ECHR before the Commission was dissolved and all individuals from all States parties could apply directly to the Court for a remedy.[132] All members of the Council of Europe are parties to the Convention and adherence to it is now a condition of membership for new candidates to join the Council of Europe. This in turn means that 820 million citizens and others within the jurisdiction of the 47 States now have direct access to a human rights court outside their own countries' legal systems. This has resulted in the Court's having a major challenge in dealing with its docket.[133]

---

[129] Article 25.   [130] Article 48.

[131] Ibid; the State of the alleged victim's nationality could also refer the case to the Court.

[132] In force 1 November 1998.

[133] See Lord Woolf *et al*, Review of the Working Methods of the European Court of Human Rights, December 2005, 49; available at: http://www.echr.coe.int/Documents/2005_Lord_Woolf_working_methods_ENG.pdf.

The Court, as mentioned, has jurisdiction to hear inter-State complaints in respect of any State party to the ECHR (Article 33). There have been only four of these.[134] It was vested with a new power pursuant to Protocol 11 (1994) by which it could issue advisory opinions at the request of the Committee of Ministers, the body representing all member States of the Council of Europe (Article 47). Neither of the two so far requested has concerned the interpretation of substantive Convention rights.

The next regional system to come into being was the inter-American one, first, directly under the Charter of the Organization of American States (OAS) and later by virtue of the *American Convention on Human Rights* (ACHR). The latter Convention incorporated the Inter-American Commission on Human Rights that had earlier been established by the political organs of the OAS, and examined cases in respect of alleged violations of the American Declaration on the Rights and Duties of Man. There is an automatic right of individual petition by anyone in the 35 member States of the OAS.[135] In respect of the 23 States parties to the ACHR, the Commission (now a treaty body) applies the provisions of the Convention. The Commission retains its original jurisdiction over the other 12 member States, applying the Declaration.

Unlike the European system where inter-State complaints were always possible in respect of all parties to the ECHR, inter-State complaints to the Inter-American Commission are optional requiring separate acceptance, by both the State against which the complaint is made and the State making the complaint. Also, unlike in the European system, the Commission may also, *propio motu* investigate *situations* of apparent violations of human rights.

Meanwhile, paralleling the earlier practice of the ECHR, the ACHR established an Inter-American Court of Human Rights. Its jurisdiction is optional and individuals from the 18 States that have accepted the jurisdiction of the Court do not have a right to refer their case directly to the Court. Rather, the Commission must first consider the case and only then may it be referred whether by the Commission itself or the State concerned, to the Court.

The Court may also issue advisory opinions, at the request of a number of entities established by the Charter of the OAS. Individual member States, regardless of whether they are parties to the ACHR, may also request advisory opinions (Article 64) This function was an original part of the Court's work and, unlike its later arrival under the ECHR, it has been used.

Following its European and inter-American predecessors (the ECHR and ACHR), the *African Charter on Human and Peoples' Rights* (ACHPR, 1981) creates an expert body, the African Commission on Human and Peoples' Rights (ACNHPR) composed of eleven African personalities of the highest reputation.[136] The Commission mainly deals with complaints both of individual and general practices of violations of human rights, on the basis of communications submitted by individuals and NGOs, and like its UN counterparts it reviews periodic reports.

By a 1998 Protocol, the OAU established an African Court of Human and Peoples' Rights of 11 judges.[137] Twenty-six of the States parties to the Charter have ratified the Protocol. The Commission, the States parties concerned and African IGOs may refer cases

---

[134] There were others dealt with by the Commission including the landmark *Greek Case* (1969) 12 *Yearbook of the European Commission of Human Rights* 468.

[135] The population of the Americas is estimated at 953 million.   [136] Article 31.

[137] Protocol to the African Charter on Human and Peoples' Rights on the Establishment of an African Court of Human Rights, Article 12 (in force 2004). The Court will merge with the proposed African Court of Justice after 15 African Union member States have ratified the 2008 Protocol on the Statute of the African Court of Justice and Human Rights; three had done so at the time of writing.

to the Court, after they have been considered by the Commission. A major step is the possibility of NGOs or individuals bringing cases directly to the Court, by-passing the Commission, if the State concerned has accepted its jurisdiction.[138]

To date, five States have accepted this jurisdiction. The Court may also issue advisory opinions, at the request of OAU member States, the OAU or any of its organs or 'any African organization recognized by the OAU' (Article 4). This element of the jurisdiction has not to date been used.

Other regional systems have been created but have not so far sufficiently advanced to indicate the need for detailed consideration. Thus, the revised Arab Charter on Human Rights (2004), which entered into force in 2008 and established a seven-member Arab Human Rights Committee, only provides the Committee with a power to review State reports. This procedure has not to date yielded any public outcome (Rishmawi, 2013, pp 52–3). Expectations are not high for the ASEAN Intergovernmental Commission on Human Rights, composed of State representatives. A recent authoritative review of the system described the it as 'nascent rather than well-established' (Muntarbhorn, 2013).

VIII. CONCLUSION

Human rights really entered the corpus of international law only after their promotion became a purpose of the UN Charter. There had been forerunners: the abolition of slavery and, especially the slave trade, in the nineteenth century, and the protection of freedom of association for labour; the rights of minorities in the Balkans; and the rights of residents in League of Nations mandate territories after World War I.

The notion of human rights in the crucial, classical sense of being the limits of States' authority over those subject to their jurisdiction, was a product of the European Enlightenment. If the church had been a counterweight to the feudal State, human rights were the non-clerical counterweight to the emergent, industrializing modern Western State that spread all over the world with the end of the colonial period. It took the cataclysm of World War II, characterized by aggression externally and crimes against humanity (genocide, systematic and widespread gross violations of human rights) internally and externally, for the world to accept that human rights was not something that could be left in the *domaine reservé* of States.

After some early doubt about whether the UN Charter's human rights clauses were merely hortatory or peremptory, it gradually became accepted that the latter was true. The Universal Declaration of Human Rights may formally only have had the status of a resolution of the General Assembly, that is, a recommendation, but it came to be accepted as reflecting the actual content of human rights and fundamental freedoms of which the UN Charter spoke. It also took time for the Charter provisions to be accepted as containing obligations to comply with human rights. The early decades of the UN assumed that the UN could not address allegations of human rights violations other than by treaty-obligation.

The UDHR from the beginning aimed to address, not only freedom from fear (human rights as traditionally understood), but also freedom from want (requiring State action to secure economic and social needs). So-called group rights (eg to self-determination, development, a healthy environment and even peace), whatever their status may be under international law, cannot qualify as human rights, as the latter have to be seen to be the rights of the individual in relation to the State, unless the term is to be deprived of all content.

---

[138] Ibid, Articles 5 and 34(6).

There have been hypocritical and self-serving attempts to separate the modern State from its obverse side—human rights—in the name of asserted local cultural traditions. While the idea may still be heard in political discourse, international human rights law has nailed the issue: human rights are universal.

The nature and content of economic and social rights has been somewhat elusive. Authoritative statements affirm that there are identifiable core obligations: ensuring the right of non-discriminatory access to health facilities, goods and services; to minimum essential, nutritionally adequate food and freedom from hunger; to basic shelter, housing and sanitation and potable water; to essential drugs; and to ensure equitable distribution of health facilities, goods and services.

Even if, paradigmatically, economic and social rights imply (extensive) State action, while civil and political rights imply State abstention, both conceive of human rights such that the rights-holders are individuals and the duty-bearers are States (or States acting together in IGOs). The idea that corporations, bands of organized criminals or politically-motivated armed opposition groups may also be duty-bearers directly under international law (they remain subject to national law) is incompatible with the basic conception of human rights and unsupported by persuasive authority.

The standard civil and political rights reflect a number of basic values: intellectual freedom (conscience, expression, association, and assembly), physical freedom (liberty and security of person/prohibition of arbitrary arrest and detention; freedom of movement; and prohibition of slavery), fairness (equal treatment, non-discrimination and protection of rights of minority members), human dignity (personal integrity, including prohibition of torture and ill-treatment, and right to life), justice and legality (due process, no retroactive crime or punishment), participation (especially in government), accountability (right to remedy), and the legitimacy of a non-public or private sphere (respect for home and private life).

Slowly a broad network of monitoring, supervisory and complaints mechanisms developed. The first to be recognized, being juridically unchallengeable, were bodies established by treaty. Later, the main political organ of the UN dealing with human rights—formerly the Commission on Human Rights, later the Human Rights Council—created a web of country-specific and thematic 'special procedures'. Generally, their activities are complementary, with the main area of overlap between some treaty bodies and most special procedures being the power of country visits. The record of treaty bodies in this respect is too limited to suggest the existence of extensive duplication. The potential for overlap and even competition in the area of periodic review conducted by treaty bodies and the Human Rights Council has not, so far, materialized.

At the regional level, there has been more progress, both with regard to the power to examine individual complaints by expert treaty bodies and to have them adjudicated by human rights courts.

REFERENCES

BESSON, S (2008), 'The Reception Process in Ireland and the United Kingdom', in Keller H and Stone Sweet, A (eds), *A Europe of Rights: The Impact of the ECHR on National Legal Systems* (Oxford: Oxford University Press), p 31.

BIANCHI, A (2008), 'Human Rights and the Magic of *Jus Cogens*', 19 *EJIL* 491.

BOYLE, K (2009), *New Institutions for Human Rights Protection* (Oxford: Oxford University Press).

CHAPMAN, A and RUSSELL S (eds) (2002), *Core Obligations: Building a Framework for Economic, Social and Cultural Rights* (Antwerp/Oxford: Intersentia).

CHARNEY, JI (1993), 'Universal International Law', 87 *AJIL* 529.

CLAPHAM, A (2006), *Human Rights Obligations of Non-State Actors* (Oxford: Oxford University Press).

CORRIGAN, T (2007), 'Mauritania Made Slavery Illegal Last Month', South African Institute of International Affairs website: http://www.saiia.org.za/opinion-analysis/mauritania-made-slavery-illegal-last-month.

de SCHUTTER, O (2012), 'The Status of Human Rights in International Law', in Krause, C and Scheinin, M (eds), *International Protection of Human Rights. A Textbook*, 2nd edn (Turku: Åbo Akademi University Institute of Human Rights).

de WET, E (2008), 'The Reception Process in the Netherlands and Belgium', in Keller H and Stone Sweet, A (eds), *A Europe of Rights: The Impact of the ECHR on National Legal Systems* (Oxford: Oxford University Press), p 229.

FREEMAN, M (2011), *Human Rights: An Interdisciplinary Approach*, 2nd edn (Cambridge: Polity Press).

———— (2013), 'Universalism of Human Rights and Cultural Relativism', in Sheeran, S and Rodley, N (eds), *Routledge Handbook on International Human Rights Law* (London: Routledge).

FRIEDMAN, W (1960), *Legal Theory*, 4th edn (London: Stevens and Sons).

HAAS, E (1977), 'Human Rights: A New Policy by a New Administration', in *Proceedings of the Annual Meeting of the American Society of International Law, 21–23 April 1977*, 71 *AJIL* 68.

HENKIN, L (1978), *The Rights of Man Today* (London: Stevens and Sons).

HOBBES, T (1651), *Leviathan* (Oakeshott, M (ed) (1957)), (Oxford: Blackwell).

HUMPHREY, J P (1979), 'The Universal Declaration of Human Rights: Its History, Impact and Juridical Character', in Ramcharan, BJ (ed) *Human Rights: Thirty Years after the Universal Declaration* (The Hague: Martinus Nijhoff).

ISHAY, M (2008), *The History of Human Rights: From Ancient Times to the Globalization Era* (Berkeley: University of California Press).

KRAMER, D and WEISSBRODT, D (1981), 'The 1980 UN Commission on Human Rights and the Disappeared', 3 *Human Rights Quarterly* 18.

KRAUSE, C and SCHEININ, M (eds) (2009), *International Protection of Human Rights. A Textbook*, 2nd edn (Turku: Åbo Akademi University Institute of Human Rights).

LAUREN, P G (2011), *The Evolution of International Human Rights: Visions Seen*, 3rd edn (Philadelphia: University of Pennsylvania Press).

LAUTERPACHT, H (1950), *International Law and Human Rights* (London: Stevens and Sons).

LOCKE, J (1689) *A Letter Concerning Toleration* (Popple, W (ed), (1983) (Indianapolis: Hackett Publishing Corporation).

MORGENTHAU, HJ (1967), *Politics Among Nations: The Struggle for Power and Peace*, 4th edn (New York: Alfred A Knopf).

MUNTARBHORN, V (2013), 'The South-East Asia System for Human Rights Protection', in Sheeran, S and Rodley, N (eds), *Routledge Handbook on International Human Rights Law* (London: Routledge).

Nowak, M (2004), *Introduction to the International Human Rights Regime* (The Hague: Martinus Nijhoff Publishers).

OWEN, D and STRONG, T B (eds) (2004), *Max Weber, The Vocation Lectures: Science as a Vocation—Politics as a Vocation* (trans Livingstone, R) (Indianapolis: Hackett Publishing Corporation).

PAINE, T (1791), *Rights of Man*, (Philp, M (ed) (2008)) (Oxford: Oxford University Press).

RAMCHARAN, BJ (ed) (1979), *Human Rights: Thirty Years after the Universal Declaration* (The Hague: Martinus Nijhoff).

RISHMAWI, M (2013), 'The League of Arab States in the Wake of the "Arab Spring"', *Cairo Institute of Human Rights, Annual Report 2013*, 52–3; available at http://www.cihrs.org.

RODLEY, NS (1986), 'U.N. Action Procedures against "Disappearances", Summary or Arbitrary Executions, and Torture', 8 *Human Rights Quarterly* 700.

—— (1995), 'Conceptual Problems Concerning Minorities—International Legal Developments', 17 *Human Rights Quarterly* 48.

—— (2008), 'The *Singarasa* Case: *Quis Custodiet*...? A Test for the Bangalore Principles of Judicial Conduct', 41 *Israel Law Review* 500.

—— (2012), 'UN Treaty Bodies and the Human Rights Council', in Keller H and Ulfstein, G (eds), *UN Human Rights Treaty Bodies: Law and Legitimacy* (Cambridge: Cambridge University Press), p 320.

—— (2013), 'The Role and Impact of Treaty Bodies', in Shelton, D (ed), *The Oxford Handbook of International Human Rights* (Oxford: Oxford University Press), p 621.

—— (2013), 'Non-State Actors and Human Rights', in Sheeran, S and Rodley, N (eds), *Routledge Handbook on International Human Rights Law* (London: Routledge).

—— and POLLARD, M (2009), *The Treatment of Prisoners under International Law*, 3rd edn (Oxford: Oxford University Press).

ROUSSEAU, J-J (1762), *The Social Contract* (trans Cole GDH 1782) http://www.constitution.org/jjr/socon.htm.

SCHWELB, E (1972), 'The International Court of Justice and the Human Rights Clauses of the Charter', 66 *AJIL* 350–51.

SHEERAN, S and RODLEY, N (eds) (2013), *Routledge Handbook on International Human Rights Law* (London: Routledge).

SHUE, H (1980), *Basic Rights: Subsistence, Affluence and U.S. Foreign Policy*, 2nd edn (Princeton NJ: University of Princeton Press).

SWEPSTON, L (2013), 'The International Labour Organization and the International Human Rights System', in Sheeran, S and Rodley, N (eds), *Routledge Handbook on International Human Rights Law* (London: Routledge).

VASAK, K (1977), 'Human Rights: A Thirty-Year Struggle', in *UNESCO Courier* 30:11 (Paris, UNESCO, November 1977).

WEBER, M (1919), *Politics as a Vocation*, reproduced in Owen, D and Strong, TB (eds) (2004), *Max Weber, The Vocation Lectures: Science as a Vocation—Politics as a Vocation* (trans Livingstone, R) (Indianapolis: Hackett Publishing Corporation).

WESTON, B (1989), 'Human Rights', in Claude RP and Weston, B (eds), *Human Rights in the World Community* (Philadelphia: University of Pennsylvania Press), p 14.

FURTHER READING

de SCHUTTER, O (2010), *International Human Rights Law: Cases, Materials, Commentary* (Cambridge: Cambridge University Press).

DONNELLY, J (2012), *International Human Rights: Dilemmas in World Politics*, 4th edn (Boulder, Col.; Westview Press).

FREEMAN, M (2011), *Human Rights*, 2nd edn (Cambridge: Polity Press).

ISHAY, M (2008), *The History of Human Rights: from Ancient Times to the Globalisation Era* (Berkeley: University of California Press).

KÄLIN, W and KÜNZLI, J (2009), *The Law of International Human Rights Protection* (New York: Oxford University Press).

KRAUSE, C and SCHEININ, M (2012), *International Protection of Human*

Rights: A Textbook, 2nd rev edn (Turku: Abo Akademi University Institute for Human Rights).

MARKS, S and CLAPHAM, A (2005), *International Human Rights Lexicon* (Oxford: Oxford University Press).

MOECKLI, D, SHAH, S, SIVAKUMARAN, S, and Harris, D, 2nd edn (2013), *International Human Rights Law* (Oxford: Oxford University Press).

NIFOSI, I (2005), *The UN Special Procedures in the Field of Human Rights* (Antwerp/Oxford, Intersentia).

NOWAK, M (2005), *UN Covenant on Civil and Political Rights: CCPR Commentary*, 2nd edn (Kehl am Rhein: Engel).

OBERLEITNER, G (2007), *Global Human Rights Institutions* (Cambridge: Polity Press).

RODLEY, NS and POLLARD, M (2009), *The Treatment of Prisoners under International Law*, 3rd edn (Oxford: Oxford University Press).

SHEERAN, S and RODLEY, NS (2013), *The Routledge Handbook on International Human Rights Law* (London: Routledge).

SHELTON, D (2013), *The Oxford Handbook of International Human Rights Law* (Oxford: Oxford University Press).

SMITH, RKM (2011), *Textbook on International Human Rights*, 5th edn (Oxford: Oxford University Press).

WEISSBRODT, D and DE LA VEGA, C (2007), *International Human Rights Law: An Introduction* (Philadelphia: University of Pennsylvania Press).

27

THE LAW OF ARMED CONFLICT (INTERNATIONAL HUMANITARIAN LAW)

David Turns

SUMMARY

The international law of armed conflict (also known as international humanitarian law, also known as the law of war) regulates the conduct of hostilities—including the use of weaponry—and the protection of victims in situations of both international and non-international armed conflict. Rooted in customary law, often of very great antiquity, since the late nineteenth century it has become one of the most intensively codified areas of international law. The 1949 Geneva Conventions, which form the cornerstone of contemporary humanitarian law, have been ratified by every single State on the face of the planet; yet implementation and enforcement are, if anything, even more problematic in this than in other areas of public international law, which has led to a symbiotic link between international humanitarian and international criminal law. Indeed, it was the creation of international criminal tribunals to deal with the aftermath of appalling atrocities in the former Yugoslavia and Rwanda, in the early 1990s, which sparked a renewal of interest in substantive humanitarian law, leading to its reaffirmation and development. This chapter outlines the scope of application of the law, issues of personal status (combatants and civilians), the conduct of hostilities (methods and means of warfare, including choice of weapons and targeting operations), the protection of victims (sick, wounded, shipwrecked, prisoners of war, and civilians), and various ways of securing the law's implementation and enforcement.

I. INTRODUCTION

It is a fact of life that armed conflict—the resort to organized force between States or within States—is, and always has been, an integral part of the human condition. Disregarding such indicia as the duration or intensity of the fighting, the number of casualties incurred or whether hostilities are active or 'frozen', there are currently some 43 situations in the world where there is either an actual armed conflict or a degree of tension so heightened that there is a real risk of resort to force. Given this state of affairs, coupled with the increase in humanitarian activism, the so-called 'CNN effect' of constant televised reporting from conflict zones, and enhanced mechanisms for securing the international legal liability of both governments (under the doctrine of State responsibility) and individuals (under the doctrine of individual criminal responsibility), it is unsurprising that international humanitarian law (IHL) has re-emerged from the shadows of public international law during the last two decades. The well-known aphorism, 'If international law is in some ways at the vanishing point of law, the law of war is, perhaps even more conspicuously, at the vanishing point of international law' (Lauterpacht, 1952, p 382), may have been accurate enough half a century ago, but it is certainly no longer so today. Although the First Gulf War (1991) was the first modern armed conflict of which it could be said that, '[d]ecisions were impacted by legal considerations at every level, [the law] proved invaluable in the decision-making process',[1] the law of war—now more commonly referred to as IHL or, alternatively, the law of armed conflict (LOAC)[2]—is of very much greater antiquity (Green, 2008, pp 26–45).

For much of its existence, the primary purpose of the law of war was to regulate in a technical sense the conduct of hostilities between belligerents. During the Middle Ages in Europe, war was regarded as a kind of game played by princes, nobles and knights on horseback; like any game, it had to have a set of rules. The Second Lateran Council's ban on crossbows in 1139, for instance, was formulated not by reason of the pain and suffering which the weapon might cause to anyone unfortunate enough to be struck by one of its bolts, but because, by enabling a man to strike from a distance without himself being struck, it was considered a disgraceful and ignoble weapon which violated the rules of chivalry (Draper, 1965, pp 18–19).

The 'rules of the game' that constituted the laws of war at this time, however, were of little relevance to the feudal peasants who constituted the foot soldiery of European armies, nor were they believed to be of any application to wars against 'uncivilised enemies' – infidels and 'primitive peoples'. By the time of the Peace of Westphalia (1648), war had become a more public activity, in which regular armies fought on behalf of their countries, rather than as a feudal obligation to their overlords. This contributed during the eighteenth century to the growth of the concept of reciprocity: captured enemy soldiers, for example, should be well treated because there was a vested interest in having the adverse party accord the same treatment to one's own soldiers who were captured on the battlefield.

The law at this time was almost exclusively customary in nature, encompassing a wide variety of rules and practices that had been mutually observed by warring forces for many centuries. By the mid-nineteenth century and such conflicts as the Crimean (1853–5) and Franco-Austrian (1859) Wars, the exponential growth in human suffering, caused by a combination of developing military technology and inadequate provision for military medical facilities, together with increased reporting of the battlefield (the latter developed further by the advent of war photography in the American Civil War, 1861–5), led to the rise of humanitarianism as a major concern in the regulation of conflicts. This desire to provide for the protection of victims of hostilities in turn encouraged the increasing use of multilateral treaties to codify the existing rules—and develop new ones.

Today IHL is very largely codified in a series of some 58 multilateral treaties. However, the customary laws of war continue to retain considerable significance, in part because of the recognition (as long ago as 1899)[3] that treaties could not cover every eventuality

---

[1] General Colin Powell, Chairman of the US Joint Chiefs of Staff, cited in US Department of Defense, *Final Report to Congress on the Conduct of the Persian Gulf War, Appendix O* (1992) 31 ILM 615.

[2] The terms 'IHL' and 'LOAC' are synonymous and are used interchangeably throughout this chapter. The term 'law of war', while still appropriate in an historical context, has been generally abandoned in the contemporary legal discourse.

[3] In the 'Martens Clause', Preamble to The Hague Convention II with Respect to the Laws and Customs of War on Land (1899).

that might arise in an armed conflict; the International Committee of the Red Cross (ICRC) has reinforced this with the publication of a major piece of research identifying 161 'rules' of customary international humanitarian law and collating the evidence (examples of State practice and *opinio juris sive necessitatis*) on which they are based (Henckaerts and Doswald-Beck, 2005). Furthermore, the 1949 Geneva Conventions are now so widely accepted—they attained their 195th accession (by South Sudan) in 2013[4]—that they are considered to have passed in their entirety into customary international law. This enabled them to be applied in arbitration proceedings between Ethiopia and Eritrea relating to their 1998–2000 conflict: Eritrea, having attained independence only five years before the commencement of hostilities, had not at the time become a party to the Geneva Conventions. Nevertheless, it accepted their application *ex post facto* on the basis of their universal acceptance as customary law.[5]

For all their etymological similarity to each other, and notwithstanding the fact that the language of many provisions of humanitarian law relating especially to non-international armed conflicts is clearly influenced by the language of human rights,[6] it is important to emphasize that international humanitarian law and international human rights law are not the same thing at all. If humanitarian law has been characterized by the International Court of Justice (ICJ) as the *lex specialis* applicable in situations of armed conflict and mostly concerned with how belligerent States treat nationals of adverse and neutral parties, human rights law is better viewed as *a lex generalis* broadly applicable in all situations—both peace and war—and mostly concerned with how States treat their own nationals. In relation to situations of armed conflict, humanitarian law is almost invariably more detailed and comprehensive than the law of human rights.[7] That said, the application of these two bodies of law has become increasingly blurred in recent years, largely in consequence of a complaint brought to the European Court of Human Rights (ECtHR) by Serbs in relation to the bombing of the Federal Republic of Yugoslavia (FRY) by air forces of the North Atlantic Treaty Organisation (NATO) in 1999.

The applicants in that case sought to argue that the NATO States had violated the right to life of Serbs in the FRY by the conduct of their bombing campaign, specifically in relation to the destruction of the Serbian Radio and Television studios in Belgrade. In dismissing the application, the ECtHR found that FRY nationals were not 'within the jurisdiction' of the NATO States in the terms of Article 1 of the European Convention of Human Rights (ECHR) because, *inter alia*, bombing an area from 30,000 feet did not amount to having 'effective control' of that area for the purposes of applying human rights obligations.[8] An aerial bombing campaign, however, is distinguished for the purposes of ECHR application from a military occupation: thus, Turkey has been held responsible for the application of the ECHR in the 'Turkish Republic of Northern Cyprus' because it has 'effective control' over that territory.[9] A series of recent decided cases in the UK and the European Court of Human Rights has indicated that human rights law is applicable in respect of certain

---

[4] The Conventions do not apparently apply to Hong Kong, since in 1997 the UK's ratification ceased to have effect for that territory upon its reversion to Chinese sovereignty. The Beijing government has not extended its ratification of the Conventions to Hong Kong, although it did so in respect of Macau (in 1999).

[5] Ethiopia-Eritrea Claims Commission, *Partial Awards on the Claims Relating to Prisoners of War* (2003) 42 ILM 1056 and 1083.

[6] This is especially the case in respect of Additional Protocol (AP) II (1977).

[7] *Legality of the Threat or Use of Nuclear Weapons, Advisory Opinion, ICJ Reports 1996*, p 226, paras 24–5.

[8] *Banković et al v Belgium et al* (Dec) [GC], no 52207/99, paras 67–81, ECHR 2001-XII; 123 ILR 94. For detailed discussion of this and other cases concerning extraterritorial jurisdiction under the ECHR, see Byron, 2007, pp 869–78.

[9] *Loizidou v Turkey (Preliminary Objections)*, Judgment of 23 March 1995, Ser A, no 310, 20 *EHRR* 99 paras 56–64. On the applicability of human rights law in territory under belligerent occupation, see *Legal Consequences of the Construction of a Wall in the Occupied Palestinian Territory, Advisory Opinion, ICJ Reports 2004*, p 136, paras 105–13.

situations that may arise during military operations overseas, most notably where forces are in occupation of territory and have physical custody of individuals (which the House of Lords in *Al-Skeini* likened to having extraterritorial 'effective control' of a prison).[10] All this is not to say, however, that human rights law regulates *prima facie* the conduct of soldiers during active hostilities on the battlefield; indeed, it would be entirely counterintuitive to reach that conclusion. One of the most basic human rights is the right to life; yet it is precisely that right that may, with certain limitations, lawfully and violently be taken away in armed conflicts. Humanitarian law has evolved highly detailed and technical provisions to govern soldiers' and civilians' conduct in such situations, and it will continue to be the primary body of law applicable in all situations of armed conflict.

II. SCOPE OF APPLICATION OF HUMANITARIAN LAW

The international law of armed conflict applies in all armed conflicts, however they are characterized, and applies to all parties in a conflict, irrespective of the legality of the resort to force. There is no direct relationship at all between *jus ad bellum* and *jus in bello*: the application of the latter in no way depends upon the former, and the legality of a conflict as such has no bearing whatsoever on the use of IHL. It would thus be quite incorrect to suggest that, for instance, prisoners belonging to a party alleged to be acting wrongfully are not protected by IHL, or conversely that the victim of an act of aggression has the right to attack the civilian population of the aggressor.[11] The question, however, of when and how humanitarian law applies ('scope of application') is not quite as straightforward as it might initially seem. This is partly because of some uncertainties surrounding the definition of armed conflict itself, and partly because of the different types of armed conflicts that are recognized in the contemporary law.

Traditionally, application of the law of war was triggered by a declaration of war, which had the legal effect of suspending most peacetime legal relations between belligerent States. Although a declaration of war did not invariably precede the actual start of hostilities,[12] it usually followed in due course once hostilities were under way; conversely, although there did not need to be active hostilities in progress at all times after a declaration of war had been issued, the existence of such a declaration was conclusive evidence as to the existence of a formal state of war. The state of war would normally be terminated only by a peace treaty, at which point the international law of peacetime relations would resume and the law of war would no longer be operative.[13] However, as has been suggested in recent years, with some understatement:

> Developments in international law since 1945, notably the United Nations (UN) Charter, including its prohibition on the threat or use of force in international relations,

---

[10]   *Al-Skeini and others* v *United Kingdom* [2011] ECHR 1093; [2011] 53 EHRR 18; *Al-Jedda* v *United Kingdom* [2011] ECHR 1092; [2011] 53 EHRR 23; *Al-Saadoon and Mufdhi* v *United Kingdom* [2010] ECHR 285; [2010] 51 EHRR 9; see also *Secretary of State for Defence* v *R (Smith)* [2009] EWCA Civ 441; [2009] 3 WLR 1099; *Smith* v *Ministry of Defence* [2013] UKSC 41.

[11]   Some advocates of the Palestinian cause aver that, because Israel is illegally occupying Palestinian land, it is legitimate to target Israeli civilians: see, eg *The New York Times*, 5 May 2009.

[12]   Eg the Japanese surprise attacks on the Imperial Russian Far East Squadron in Port Arthur (1904) and the US Pacific Fleet in Pearl Harbor (1941).

[13]   The lack of peace treaties between Israel and its Arab neighbours (with the exception of Egypt and Jordan) could be said to imply that those countries remain in a state of war with each other, as the Armistice Agreements of 1949 did not terminate hostilities, but merely suspended them: Maoz, 2005, pp 36–44. A similar point may be made in relation to the situation between North and South Korea since the armistice agreement suspending hostilities in the Korean War in 1953.

may well have made the declaration of war redundant as a formal international legal instrument.[14]

In point of fact, there have been no formal declarations of war since the Soviet declaration of war on Japan in August 1945; the association of such declarations with the appearance of aggression has led to the procedure becoming defunct. The kind of confusion implicit in British Prime Minister Anthony Eden's statement in 1956, that the UK was not at war with Egypt during the Suez Crisis but merely in a state of armed conflict with that country,[15] is now a thing of the past in international law: the term 'armed conflict' is preferred to the term 'war',[16] as the former is a purely factual description of a situation, without connotations of right and wrong as regards the *jus ad bellum*. It is additionally often perceived to be in a State's interest to refrain from such an unequivocal declaration of hostile intent, as the *status mixtus*—simultaneously observing the law of war for some purposes and the law of peace for others—affords more room to manoeuvre, both diplomatically and politically. This may be the case especially in a 'low-intensity conflict', wherein neither side provokes the other into escalation, resulting in a conflict that is relatively limited and easily contained, from which belligerents may back away without necessarily appearing to have been defeated in a military sense (Green, 2008, pp 91-3). During Indonesia's policy of *Konfrontasi* ('Confrontation') with Malaysia from 1962 to 1966, British troops were actively engaged in armed hostilities against Indonesian forces in North Borneo, but diplomatic and commercial relations between the UK and Indonesia continued throughout the four years over which the Confrontation persisted.[17]

In any event the application of humanitarian law in no way affects the legal status of parties to a given conflict; it depends on neither the legality of the initial resort to force, nor the formal recognition of a state of war or armed conflict by the belligerents. The Geneva Conventions, for example, are expressly stated to apply to 'declared war or any other armed conflict'.[18] In 1982 during the Falklands War, the UK publicly denied that it was at war with Argentina, yet it applied the law of armed conflict in all its military operations.[19]

The difficulty lies in the fact that the law of armed conflict nowhere defines precisely what an 'armed conflict' is for the purposes of application of the law, despite the use of the phrase in the Geneva Conventions and other treaties that constitute this body of law. The ICRC indicates that, 'any difference arising between States and leading to the intervention of members of the armed forces is an armed conflict' (Pictet, 1952, vol I, p 32), but this is problematic because, in its reference to States alone, it takes no account of non-international armed conflicts; it also implies that even a very limited military operation of only a few hours' duration and not followed by any other hostilities would have

---

[14] House of Lords Select Committee on the Constitution, Fifteenth Report of Session 2005–6, *Waging war: Parliament's role and responsibility, Volume I: Report* (HL Paper 236-I, 27 July 2006), para 10.

[15] See *Hansard, HC Debs*, 1 November 1956, vol 558, cols 1639–43. Regarding legal characterization of the Korean War, see Jessup, 1954.

[16] On the official characterization of hostilities between the UK and Iraq in 2003 as 'armed conflict' but not 'war', see *Amin v Brown* [2005] EWHC 1670 (Ch).

[17] See *Hansard, HL Debs*, 14 November 1963, vol 253, cols 153–5.

[18] Geneva Conventions (GC), Common Article 2 (1949).

[19] See, eg *Hansard, HC Debs*, 26 April 1982, vol 22, col 616 (on the treatment of Argentine prisoners of war—the Prime Minister's statement that they were not prisoners of war because the UK was 'not at war' with Argentina was subsequently retracted, and all captured Argentines were treated in accordance with GCIII); ibid, 11 June 1982, vol 25, col 170W (on the repatriation of Lieutenant-Commander Alfredo Astiz of the Argentine Navy); ibid, 14 June 1982, col 611 (on the establishment by the ICRC of a neutralized zone in Port Stanley, in accordance with GCIV Article 15).

to be considered an armed conflict, a position which is not supported by State practice. Although there are court decisions on point from various national jurisdictions (including the UK),[20] these invariably have been concerned with defining 'war' in municipal law for such purposes as interpreting liability exclusion clauses in insurance contracts, rather than having anything to do with IHL. In 1995 the International Criminal Tribunal for the Former Yugoslavia (ICTY) held that:

> an armed conflict exists whenever there is a resort to armed force between States or protracted armed violence between governmental authorities and organized armed groups or between such groups within a State. International humanitarian law applies from the initiation of such armed conflicts and extends beyond the cessation of hostilities until a general conclusion of peace is reached; or, in the case of internal conflicts, a peaceful settlement is achieved. Until that moment, international humanitarian law continues to apply in the whole territory of the warring States or, in the case of internal conflicts, the whole territory under the control of a party, whether or not actual combat takes place there.[21]

The statement in *Tadić* has since come to be widely accepted as a useful formulation of the concept of an armed conflict in customary international law. At least implicit in the formulation is the requirement that hostilities be 'substantial', 'protracted' and 'large-scale'.[22] Thus, it is possible for a very brief or limited military operation to take place, yet for there to be no armed conflict between the States involved, as in the Entebbe Raid (1976), when Israel mounted a military operation to rescue hostages being detained by hijackers on Ugandan territory. Although Ugandan soldiers did resist the Israelis and there were some exchanges of fire between them, resulting in casualties on both sides and the destruction of several Ugandan Air Force fighters, it was never suggested that there was an armed conflict between Israel and Uganda.

Notwithstanding the possibility that military forces might be deployed on active operations absent a state of armed conflict, the military doctrine of many major military powers today requires that their armed forces comply with the spirit and principles of LOAC in all their operations, irrespective of whether they are formally considered to be in a state of armed conflict.[23] It is not necessary for there to be actual fighting at all times in an armed conflict for the law to be applicable. Some of the treaties that constitute LOAC also apply in situations where actual fighting may no longer be taking place: eg prisoners of war continue to benefit from protection under the law until their final release and repatriation,[24] while the law relevant to military occupation and protection of the civilian population continues to apply as long as an occupation subsists, even if other substantive military operations ceased at an earlier date.[25]

Until the mid-twentieth century, international law only recognized armed conflicts between States as being subject to its legal regulation. This was partly because of the dominant concept of State sovereignty over internal affairs and partly because of the then prevalent view that international law was concerned only with the regulation of international relations between States. Possibilities for extending the reach of international law to non-international conflicts were traditionally limited although some did exist, even before 1949 (Moir, 2002,

---

[20] Eg *Kawasaki Kisen Kabushiki Kaisha of Kobe* v *Bantham Steamship Co* [1939] KB 544.

[21] *Prosecutor* v *Dusko Tadić*, Decision on the Defence Motion for Interlocutory Appeal on Jurisdiction (Interlocutory Appeal), Case No IT–94–1–AR72 (2 October 1995) 35 ILM 35, para 70.

[22] Ibid.

[23] Eg US Department of Defense, Directive 2311.01E, 9 May 2006, *DoD Law of War Program*, para 4.1.

[24] GCIII Article 5.

[25] GCIV Article 6.

pp 4–18). In that year, Common Article 3 of the Geneva Conventions extended certain basic humanitarian rules of protection to 'armed conflicts not of an international character'; these were supplemented in 1977 by Additional Protocol II. A recent trend has also emerged whereby certain rules are extended to all types of armed conflict, irrespective of their classification (Henckaerts and Doswald-Beck, 2005).[26] This trend is particularly apparent in, though not limited to, the treaties regulating weaponry (Turns, 2006).[27] While fulfilment of the trend would have the virtue of simplifying greatly the legal standards and their consistent application in all armed conflicts, however, the distinction between international and non-international conflicts retains its traditional importance in respect of several key legal provisions. 'Grave breaches' of the Geneva Conventions, for example, exist and may be punished exclusively in the context of international armed conflicts;[28] the distinction between combatants and civilians, so crucial to targeting operations, does not exist as such in non-international armed conflicts.

Armed conflicts today, therefore, are normally classified into one of two types: international or non-international (internal). In addition, a non-international armed conflict may become 'internationalized' in certain circumstances by the participation of forces from another State (Byron, 2001). The *lex lata* essentially restricts the internationalizing effect of such interventions to cases where the foreign State is intervening on the side of *insurgents* in an internal conflict, because then the requirement of an international armed conflict, for two or more *States* to be in conflict with each other, is met. On the other hand, situations where a State intervenes in an internal conflict by providing assistance to *government* forces fighting against insurgents are said to remain non-international in nature, because the intervening State is not fighting against the host State. Thus, the UK technically considers itself to be engaged in a non-international armed conflict in Afghanistan since the Taliban were displaced as the *de facto* government of that country in December 2001.[29] The international law basis for this somewhat counterintuitive position derives exclusively from the practice of the Coalition States presently operating in Afghanistan and admittedly is supported by a strict interpretation of the wording of Common Article 2 of the Geneva Conventions, but otherwise lacks any doctrinal support in decided case law and is not unproblematic, in that the 'inviting' government may actually lack the legitimacy genuinely to invite foreign forces onto the State's territory. It also takes no account of the UN Security Council's role in 'internationalizing' a previously internal situation. Nevertheless, it does seem to represent the current received opinion.

Under the Geneva Conventions an international armed conflict is defined as 'all cases of declared war or of any other armed conflict which may arise between two or more of the High Contracting Parties',[30] while an armed conflict 'not of an international character' simply has to occur 'in the territory of one of the High Contracting Parties'.[31] The rather formalistic requirement that the conflict be between two or more 'High Contracting Parties' was a direct descendant of the stipulation, in the 1899 and 1907 Hague Conventions, that their provisions applied only 'between contracting Powers, and then only if all the belligerents are parties to the Convention'.[32] These 'all-participation clauses' had to some extent

---

[26] *Prosecutor v Dusko Tadić*, Decision on the Defence Motion for Interlocutory Appeal on Jurisdiction (Interlocutory Appeal), Case No IT–94–1–AR72 (2 October 1995), paras 97–127; cf ibid, Separate Opinion of Judge Abi-Saab.

[27] Eg UN Convention on Conventional Weapons (1981), Amended Article 1 (2001).

[28] *Prosecutor v Dusko Tadić*, Decision on the Defence Motion for Interlocutory Appeal on Jurisdiction (Interlocutory Appeal), Case No IT–94–1–AR72 (2 October 1995), paras 79–84.

[29] *GS v Secretary of State for the Home Department* [2009] UKAIT 00010. [30] Common Article 2.

[31] Common Article 3. [32] The Hague Convention (HC) IV, Article 2 (1907).

already been discredited by notable abuse by Germany and Japan during World War II, when the Germans refused to apply the 1929 Geneva Convention on the Treatment of Prisoners of War *vis-à-vis* the Soviet Union, ostensibly on the grounds that the latter was not a party to that instrument.[33] Japan, also not a party to the Geneva Convention, punctiliously sent diplomatic notifications to the governments responsible for Allied forces in the Far East, stating that it would nevertheless apply the terms of that Convention, *mutatis mutandis*—and then went on to treat captured Allied nationals with systematically casual cruelty.[34] With both the Geneva Conventions and The Hague Regulations considered as customary international law, however, the 'all-participation clauses' are considered redundant today: IHL is truly universal in its application once there is a factual situation of armed conflict.

The scope of application provisions of the two 1977 Additional Protocols, which added to the definitions of armed conflicts, have been a major reason for some States' unwillingness to sign or ratify the Protocols. Article 1(4) of Protocol I extends the Protocol's scope of application to include:

> armed conflicts in which peoples are fighting against colonial domination and alien occupation and against racist regimes in the exercise of their right to self-determination, as enshrined in the Charter of the United Nations and the Declaration on Principles of International Law concerning Friendly Relations and Co-operation among States in accordance with the Charter of the United Nations.

Article 96(3) of the Protocol further provides that an 'authority' representing a people engaged in such an armed conflict may unilaterally undertake to apply the Geneva Conventions and the Protocol by means of a declaration to that effect.

With the stroke of a pen, the Protocol thus made armed struggles that had previously been seen as internal to individual States, matters for international regulation. After 1977, acts of violence committed by non-State actors could be viewed as legitimate acts of war if the persons committing them claimed to be acting in the name of national liberation or self-determination. Naturally enough, those States that are engaged in armed struggles against such groups have opposed the imposition of international regulation for their conflicts against what they often style mere 'criminals' or 'terrorists'. In many cases this has resulted in important military powers either not becoming parties to the Protocol at all,[35] or becoming parties, but with substantial reservations that have the specific effect of negating the expanded scope of application. The Irish Republican Army (IRA), in its long armed struggle against the UK security forces in Northern Ireland during 'the Troubles', sought to claim that it was acting in pursuit of Irish self-determination, to 'liberate' Northern Ireland from 'illegal British occupation', and was thus engaged in an international armed conflict against the UK. This led the IRA to demand prisoner of war (POW) status for its captured operatives. The UK, for its part, consistently denied that there was an armed conflict of any kind in Northern Ireland[36]—and specifically denied the entitlement of captured IRA members to any special status akin to that of a POW, preferring to regulate their activity under national law and to regard them as nothing more than common criminals (Walker,

---

[33] *The Trial of German Major War Criminals*, 1946, Judgment, pp 46–8. A 1941 Soviet offer to apply the Geneva Convention *mutatis mutandis* was left unanswered by Germany.

[34] *International Military Tribunal for the Far East*, 1948, Judgment, pp 1096–106.

[35] Eg the USA, Turkey, Israel, India, Pakistan, and Indonesia. On the official US attitude to the Protocol, see President Ronald Reagan, *Message to the Senate Transmitting a Protocol to the 1949 Geneva Conventions* (1987) 26 ILM 561.

[36] See, eg *Hansard, HC Debs*, 14 December 1977, vol 941, col 237W.

1984). Concern about attempts to apply the Protocol to Northern Ireland contributed to the UK's decision to delay ratification of the Protocol: although it signed the instrument in 1977, the UK did not ratify it until 1998. Moreover, upon ratification, the UK was careful to enter the following 'statement of understanding' in respect of Articles 1(4) and 96(3):

> It is the understanding of the UK that the term 'armed conflict' of itself and in its context denotes a situation of a kind which is not constituted by the commission of ordinary crimes including acts of terrorism whether concerted or in isolation.
>
> The UK will not, in relation to any situation in which it is itself involved, consider itself bound in consequence of any declaration purporting to be made under [Article 96(3)] unless the UK shall have expressly recognised that it has been made by a body which is genuinely an authority representing a people engaged in an armed conflict of the type to which [Article 1(4)] applies.[37]

There has to date been no successful attempt to invoke Article 1(4) as the basis for applying the law of international armed conflict to any situation, although in 1989 the Palestine Liberation Organisation (PLO) notified the Swiss Government (as the depositary of the Geneva Conventions and the Additional Protocols) of its decision to adhere to those instruments. The Swiss Government declined to confirm that the PLO's decision was a valid accession to the instruments, '[d]ue to the uncertainty within the international community as to the existence or the non-existence of a State of Palestine'.[38]

If the expanded definition of international armed conflicts has proved controversial, that of non-international conflicts has been all but unworkable. Article 1 of Protocol II defines non-international armed conflicts to which it applies as:

> all armed conflicts which are not covered by Article 1 of Protocol I and which take place in the territory of a High Contracting Party between its armed forces and dissident armed forces or other organised armed groups which, under responsible command, exercise such control over a part of [the State's] territory as to enable them to carry out sustained and concerted military operations and to implement this Protocol.
>
> This Protocol shall not apply to situations of internal disturbances and tensions, such as riots, isolated and sporadic acts of violence and other acts of a similar nature, as not being armed conflicts.

Quite apart from the fact that States with internal conflicts on their territories have been unsurprisingly reluctant to submit to international legal regulation of their violent struggles against 'bandits' or 'terrorists', the main problem with the definition of non-international conflicts, which has largely sabotaged attempts to apply the Protocol in practice, is the requirement for the dissident party to be in control of territory. Illogically enough, this requirement is placed at a higher threshold than is required for national liberation movements in Additional Protocol I, which do not have to control any territory in order to have their struggle legally classified as an *international* armed conflict. The requirement that dissident movements be able to carry out 'sustained and concerted military operations' and to implement the Protocol has been a gift to States seeking to deny the Protocol's applicability to their own internal conflicts, as rebel movements are rarely in such a strong position and rarely have any incentive to apply international humanitarian law in their operations.[39] In effect, the definition of a non-international armed conflict under Protocol II has a threshold so high as to preclude the vast majority of armed rebellions from being subject to its regulation. To date fewer than half a dozen States, and even fewer insurgent

---

[37] Roberts & Guelff, 2000, p 510.   [38] Ibid, p 362.   [39] Cf Sivakumaran, 2006.

movements, have indicated any willingness to be bound by the Protocol in the conduct of their respective internal conflicts (Moir, 2002, pp 119–32). During the Sri Lankan Civil War (1983-2009), the Liberation Tigers of Tamil Eelam (LTTE) undeniably controlled substantial parts of the north-east of the country and mounted 'sustained and concerted' military operations against government forces; yet Sri Lanka is not a party to Protocol II and neither the government nor the LTTE showed any effective application of IHL.[40]

The technicalities of the definitions of international and non-international armed conflicts make it difficult for military personnel to know when to treat irregular opponents as legitimate combatants, civilians directly participating in hostilities, 'dissident armed forces' under Protocol II, a national liberation movement under Protocol I, or common criminals engaged in violence and entitled to no specific protections under IHL. This has led to an increase in the importance of governmental determinations as to the classification of armed conflicts in which regular forces are engaged and as to the applicable scope of application of IHL. Unfortunately, as the official US reaction to the events of 11 September 2001 in terms of the treatment of detainees captured in the course of the new 'Global War on Terror' showed, such determinations may do more harm than good. The US Administration of George W Bush persisted in viewing the 'War on Terror' as an international armed conflict within the LOAC paradigm, albeit one in which captured enemy combatants could be detained until the end of 'active hostilities'[41] but were not entitled to be treated as POWs under Geneva Convention III.[42] The US Supreme Court, however, took a radically different view in one of their more celebrated decisions regarding the status and treatment of detainees captured by US forces and held in Guantánamo Bay, Cuba. The plurality of the court held, obiter, that because the conflict between the USA and Al-Qaeda terrorists was neither against a High Contracting Party to the Geneva Conventions, nor in the territory of one such party, it was by default an 'armed conflict not of an international character' in the terms of Common Article 3.[43]

It is worth noting that virtually no other State agreed with the US legal approach to this situation and, indeed, the Administration of Barack Obama abandoned such contortions of logic from its first days in office in January 2009. In Israel it has been suggested that such conflicts are better viewed as being in the nature of international armed conflicts, to which the fullest possible extent of IHL should be applied, by reason of the transnational nature of such conflicts—ie the fact that they cross international borders—and the military capabilities of modern terrorist organizations.[44] In the UK, determinations about the existence and characterization of an armed conflict are made as a matter of policy, depending on the facts on the ground and the status of the parties to the conflict.[45] It follows that the UK does not accept that there is a single armed conflict between itself and Al-Qaeda; rather, there are discrete conflicts in theatres such as Iraq (until the withdrawal of British forces in 2009) and Afghanistan. IHL is applied by British forces in all such military operations.

---

[40] See UN, *Report of the Secretary-General's Panel of Experts on Accountability in Sri Lanka* (31 March 2011), http://www.un.org/News/dh/infocus/Sri_Lanka/POE_Report_Full.pdf.

[41] GCIII Article 118.

[42] GCIII Article 5 requires that if there is any doubt as to a detainee's status under LOAC, s/he shall be treated as a POW until their status is determined by a competent tribunal. Cf President Bush, *Military Order: Detention, Treatment and Trial of Certain Non-Citizens in the War Against Terrorism* (2001) 41 ILM 252; Attorney-General Alberto Gonzales, *Memorandum to the President re Application of the Geneva Convention on Prisoners of War to the Conflict with Al Qaeda and the Taliban* (2002) (reproduced in Greenberg and Datrel, 2005, p 118).

[43] *Hamdan v Rumsfeld* (2006) 548 US 557.

[44] *Public Committee against Torture in Israel* v *Government of Israel (targeted killings)* HCJ 769/02; (2006) 46 ILM 375.

[45] UK Ministry of Defence, 2004, paras 3.1–13.

The spectrum of conflict is well illustrated by the case of Iraq since 2003: after an initial phase of international armed conflict (March-April 2003) to which the fullest extent of LOAC applied, there followed a period of belligerent occupation (April 2003–June 2004) during which certain parts of IHL (notably Geneva Convention IV) continued to be applicable. After the formal end of occupation, however, the legal position became substantially less clear in that Coalition forces were operating extraterritorially against non-State actors; this resulted in the haphazard application of an ad hoc hodgepodge of rules cobbled together from the laws relating to both international and non-international armed conflicts, supplemented by a dose of human rights law and overshadowed by the significance of UN Security Council resolutions regarding the rights of foreign forces in Iraq.

Finally, it is worth noting that broadly the same rules apply in all domains of conflict: land, sea, air, and cyber. Although the bulk of the law was formulated with land warfare in mind, the centuries-old customary law of maritime warfare continues to be applicable: it was largely codified in 1907[46] and in the 1930s,[47] and has since been comprehensively restated in the International Institute of Humanitarian Law's *San Remo Manual on International Law Applicable to Armed Conflicts at Sea* (1994). Aerial warfare has been a feature of armed conflicts since 1911, but has to date not been the subject of a specific adopted treaty; although the rules on targeting in API clearly apply to air warfare, it was only in 2009 that the *Manual on International Law Applicable to Air and Missile Warfare* was produced by the Harvard Program on Humanitarian Policy and Conflict Research, containing a comprehensive restatement of the law in such operations.[48] Considerable attention has been devoted to cyber warfare recently, following the cyber operations (attributed to Russia) which were targeted at Estonia in 2007 and Georgia in 2008; this has culminated in another manual produced by an international group of experts, the *Tallinn Manual on the International Law Applicable to Cyber Warfare* (Schmitt). It should be noted that these manuals are the work of academic specialists and legal practitioners working in a personal capacity, and the extent to which they will be accepted by States as *lex lata* remains uncertain.

III. THE ACTORS IN HUMANITARIAN LAW

Once the scope of application of IHL has been determined, the crucial feature of the modern law in international armed conflicts is the distinction between combatants and civilians. The former may legitimately be targeted in military operations, while the latter—subject to certain exceptions[49]—may not. Conversely, and as a direct consequence of their status, the former are entitled to certain rights and privileges upon capture, while the latter—again, subject to certain exceptions—are not. Therefore, in the planning and execution of military operations, a distinction must always be made between combatants on the one hand, and civilians on the other. This was an easy enough task when battles were fought by organized armies on discrete (mostly rural) battlefields largely denuded of their civilian inhabitants; however, the proliferation of irregular forces in modern warfare, which also is frequently conducted in an urban environment where the civilian population remains present, has made distinction exceedingly difficult in practice.

---

[46] The Hague Conventions VI-XI and XIII.

[47] The London Procès-verbal on Submarine Warfare (1936); the Nyon Agreement (1938).

[48] See http://www.ihlresearch.org/amw/manual/.

[49] Principally, if civilians directly participate in hostilities, they lose their protected status and may legitimately be targeted 'for such time' as they do so: see ICRC, *Interpretive Guidance on the Notion of Direct Participation in Hostilities under International Humanitarian Law* (2008) 90 IRRC 991.

Historically, the laws of war did not provide a definition of the concept of a 'combatant'. Warfare was carried on by soldiers, who generally were easily distinguishable from the civilian population. This was so even before the issue of standardized uniforms to European armies began to become common practice in the late seventeenth century. Although a concept of lawful combatancy was present in the literature by the late eighteenth century (Green, 2008, pp 125–8), there was little controversy in practice before the Franco-Prussian War (1870–71). In that conflict, the swift advance of Prussian forces into French territory led to the definition of two new categories of persons whose proper combatant status was initially a matter of some legal uncertainty: *francs-tireurs* and the *levée en masse*. The latter category ('mass levy') had been recognized since its use by the French Republic in 1793[50] and referred to the spontaneous requisitioning of the civilian population of an invaded—but unoccupied—territory, without time for military organization; its members are regarded as combatants, provided they 'carry arms openly and... respect the laws and customs of war'.[51] They are entitled to POW status upon capture.[52]

The former category ('free-shooters'), on the other hand, referred to civilians who—whether in occupied territory or not—take up arms on their own initiative to fight, independently of any governmental or military control, against an invading army. In 1870, members of rifle clubs or unofficial paramilitary shooting societies in eastern France formed irregular bands that carried out ambushes and attacks on Prussian lines of communication, isolated military posts and reconnaissance patrols; nominally under the control of the French Ministry of War, they were in fact entirely outside any military discipline, wearing no uniforms and electing their own officers. Prussian practice was to treat captured *francs-tireurs* as non-combatants found illegally participating in hostilities, and to execute them as such. Their activities also often led to reprisal actions being conducted against nearby French villages. This pattern of conduct occasioned some legal controversy when it was repeated in World War II, with the Germans treating members of the French Resistance as *francs-tireurs* not entitled to any protection under the laws of war, while the Allies insisted that their degree of organization and allegiance to the French Government-in-Exile entitled them to POW status upon capture. Although one prominent subsequent war crimes trial of German generals found that captured partisans in the Balkans had been correctly subjected to the death penalty as *francs-tireurs*,[53] treaty law since has endorsed the contrary position.

As it was generally understood at the turn of the twentieth century that members of regular armies were combatants who were subject to the rights and duties of the laws of war, the main legal issue became how to define others who might be so entitled. Article 1 of the 1907 Hague Regulations accordingly provides that:

The laws, rights, and duties of war apply not only to armies, but also to militia and volunteer corps fulfilling the following conditions:

1. To be commanded by a person responsible for his subordinates;

2. To have a fixed distinctive emblem recognizable at a distance;

3. To carry arms openly; and

4. To conduct their operations in accordance with the laws and customs of war.

---

[50] French National Convention, Decree of 23 August 1793.
[51] The Hague Regulations (HR), Article 2 (1907).   [52] GCIII Article 4(A)(6).
[53] *The Hostages Trial (United States of America v Wilhelm List and Others)* [1949] VIII Law Reports of Trials of War Criminals 38.

Apart from designating those persons who can lawfully be attacked in wartime, the other principal significance of the concept of lawful combatancy is that it entitles a person, on capture, to the benefit of treatment as a POW. In 1949, Article 4 of Geneva Convention III expanded entitlement to POW status to the following principal groups:

1. members of the regular armed forces,[54] and of militias or volunteer corps forming part of the armed forces, of a party to the conflict;[55]

2. members of other militias or volunteer corps of a party to the conflict, including organized resistance movements, provided that they satisfy the requirements for lawful combatancy listed in Article 1 of The Hague Regulations;

3. authorized persons who accompany the armed forces without actually being members thereof, eg war correspondents,[56] supply contractors, members of military labour units, etc; and

4. participants in a *levée en masse*.

Military medical and religious personnel, on the other hand, are non-combatant members of the armed forces. They may if captured be retained by the Detaining Power in order to assist POWs, and benefit from the protections of the Convention, but are not formally considered POWs.[57]

This comparatively simple regime was supplemented in 1977 by the controversial provisions of Additional Protocol I, which set up a new regime with regard to lawful combatant and POW status; this inevitably is distinctly favourable to the national liberation movements whose conflicts were recognized by the Protocol as being international in nature. Article 43 of the Protocol defines the armed forces, and accordingly lawful combatants, as, 'all organized armed forces, groups and units which are under a command responsible to [a Party to the conflict] for the conduct of its subordinates, even if that Party is represented by a government or an authority not recognized by an adverse Party'. This shifts the irrelevance of recognition from the existence of a state of war, as stipulated in Common Article 2 of the 1949 Conventions, to the representation of a party to the conflict: a change very much to the benefit of non-State actors, who are seldom if ever legally recognized by the States against which they are fighting. It is not hard to see why certain States continue to object to this formulation.

Lawful combatants, as defined in Article 43, are entitled on capture to POW status,[58] subject to the following:

> In order to promote the protection of the civilian population from the effects of hostilities, combatants are obliged to distinguish themselves from the civilian population while they are engaged in an attack or in a military operation preparatory to an attack. Recognizing, however, that there are situations in armed conflicts where, owing to the nature of the hostilities an armed combatant cannot so distinguish himself, he shall retain his status as a combatant, provided that, in such situations, he carries his arms openly:
>
> (a) during each military engagement; and
>
> (b) during such time as he is visible to the adversary while he is engaged in a military deployment preceding the launching of an attack in which he is to participate.[59]

---

[54] Including paratroopers, marine commandos or other special forces, as long as they fight in their correct uniform and with the appropriate unit badges: see Parks, 2003.

[55] The criterion of belonging to a State has been used to deny POW status to captured guerrillas: *Prosecutor v Kassem* (1969) 42 ILR 470.

[56] Journalists not formally accredited as war correspondents are treated as civilians: API, Article 79 (1977).

[57] GCIII Article 33. [58] API Article 44(1). [59] Ibid, Article 44(3).

The first sentence relaxes the pre-existing standard in that it does not specify the way in which combatants must distinguish themselves from civilians (as opposed to The Hague Regulations' requirement of a 'fixed, distinctive sign'); it also requires such distinction to have effect only during 'an attack or...a military operation preparatory to an attack' (whereas The Hague Regulations contain no temporal element as regards lawful combatancy). The second sentence, however, goes even further towards accommodating guerrillas, and remains deeply controversial for several States. Its assumption that there are situations in which a combatant cannot distinguish himself is limited—the UK considers that these can only arise in occupied territory or in respect of national liberation movements (NLMs)[60]—and the interpretation favoured by some NLMs, to the effect that arms need only be carried openly immediately before opening fire (as opposed to continually while visible to the enemy and moving into an attack position), have received little support in the literature or State practice[61] and States not party to the Protocol continue to be bound only by the stricter standards from The Hague Regulations and Geneva Convention III.

Thus, there are effectively two different legal standards for the determination of lawful combatancy; the undesirability of this situation has been plainly demonstrated by the conflict in Afghanistan since 2001. US President Bush's determination that Al-Qaeda and Taliban fighters captured by US forces were 'unlawful combatants' who were not entitled to POW status, could be detained indefinitely without charge and (eventually) prosecuted for war crimes generated enormous controversy in theory and proved unworkable in practice.[62] On his second day in office, President Obama announced the intended closure of the detention facility at Guantánamo Bay, Cuba,[63] although to date it still has not been closed and the eventual fate of the remaining detainees has not been determined.

Any 'person who takes part in hostilities' without being a combatant under the terms of the Protocol shall upon capture be presumed to be a POW and therefore entitled to protection under IHL, unless and until a competent tribunal decides otherwise.[64] This provision is in essence the same as that in Article 5 of Geneva Convention III, but its scope of application is more controversial. It applies a presumption of actual POW status (as opposed to Article 5's assertion that a captive of doubtful legal status will be treated as if he were a POW until a competent tribunal determines his actual status) to all persons participating in hostilities in armed conflicts covered by the Protocol. The overall effect of Articles 43-5 is to shift the balance of presumptions and entitlements very much in favour of a captive who, prior to the Protocol, would not have had such benefits under traditional LOAC but would have been automatically subject to trial merely for illegally participating in hostilities. Now the Protocol necessitates charges of specific criminal conduct, as opposed to mere participation in hostilities, if any trial is to take place.

Although in mediaeval Europe and until the advent of mass-recruited citizen-armies in the eighteenth century the use of mercenaries was lawful and indeed widespread,[65] the post-1945

---

[60] Roberts & Guelff, 2000, p 510.   [61] For the UK position on this point, see ibid.

[62] *Military Order*. In *Rasul* v *Bush* (2004) 542 US 466 the US Supreme Court held that detainees were entitled to challenge in the US courts the legality of their detention by US forces. In *Hamdan* v *Rumsfeld* (2006) 548 US 557 the Court held that the Military Commissions established by the Bush Administration for the trial of 'unlawful combatants' did not meet the requirements of the Geneva Conventions. On 4 June 2007 the original charges in the first two substantive cases to be tried by Military Commissions, *United States* v *Hamdan* and *United States* v *Khadr*, were both dismissed for lack of jurisdiction on the grounds that the defendants' status under LOAC had not been properly determined: 1 MC 6 & 152.

[63] Executive Order 13,493 (22 January 2009), 74 Fed Reg 4901.   [64] API Article 45(1).

[65] Mercenaries are not to be confused with the foreign professional soldiers used in certain armies, eg the British Army's Brigade of Gurkhas and the French Foreign Legion. These units are regularly constituted and subject to the discipline of the armies in which they serve, and are lawful combatants.

decolonization period saw large numbers of demobilized professional soldiers from Western nations enrolling for financial gain in the armies of colonial powers in Africa who were fighting against NLMs claiming self-determination (or, as in the Congo and Nigeria, for secessionist rebellions). Condemnation of mercenarism consequently became widespread and it is not surprising that special provision for it was eventually made in Additional Protocol I, Article 47 of which removes any possibility of mercenaries being regarded as lawful combatants entitled to POW status if captured. The salient features of the definition of a mercenary are that his motivation is the desire for private gain, and that he is neither a national nor a resident of a party to an armed conflict, nor a member of the armed forces thereof. This was subsequently added to by the UN General Assembly's International Convention against the Recruitment, Use, Financing and Training of Mercenaries, which extended the Protocol's definition of a mercenary to include the purpose of 'participating in a concerted act of violence aimed at overthrowing a government or otherwise undermining the constitutional order...or...the territorial integrity of a State'.[66] The Convention offence is committed even if a person recruited as a mercenary does not actually take part in a conflict—a departure from Article 47's requirement that he take a direct part in hostilities.

These provisions have not managed to prevent or deter the repeated use of mercenaries since the early 1990s in conflicts such as those in the former Yugoslavia and Sierra Leone.[67] The issue continues to be pertinent in light of the 'privatization of war' in the first decade of the twenty-first century: since the occupation of Iraq in 2003-4, several States have increasingly outsourced many military services and types of expertise to a growing array of private contractors or 'private military security companies' (PMSCs). These are generally composed of former military personnel who undertake a range of duties from serving as bodyguards for political leaders and diplomats, through the provision of training and advice in the reorganization of State military capabilities in countries such as Nigeria and Bulgaria, to actual military missions in countries such as Colombia (where they have piloted aircraft and helicopter gunships engaged in the destruction of coca crops). Their tendency, exhibited in Iraq, to be somewhat 'trigger-happy' has attracted considerable notoriety.[68] US and British PMSCs operate under national regulation[69] but their legal position under LOAC is uncertain. The UN General Assembly has condemned them as one of 'the new modalities of mercenarism',[70] but they could also arguably be assimilated in certain circumstances to 'supply contractors' who benefit from POW status,[71] and their right to use force in self-defence is lawfully mandated under their contracts of employment. Ultimately, their status under LOAC is most likely to be that of civilians, since they are not part of the armed forces and cannot be regarded as militia; the legal issue is then whether or not their precise function in a given situation involves direct participation in hostilities.

It is a tragic reality of modern warfare, particularly in certain parts of Africa, that child soldiers form a significant part of the combatant forces. This has been notably evident in

---

[66] GA Res 44/34 (1989), Article 1(2)(a).

[67] The UN Convention on Mercenaries entered into force in 2001 but still has only 33 States Parties.

[68] In *United States v Slough et al*, five employees of the PMSC Blackwater Worldwide were charged with manslaughter in connection with the killing of 17 unarmed Iraqi civilians in Baghdad: *The New York Times*, 8 December 2008.

[69] In the USA, PMSCs are now subject to the Uniform Code of Military Justice: HR 5122, John Warner National Defense Authorization Act for Fiscal Year 2007, Section 552. In the UK, s 370 and Sch 15 to the Armed Forces Act 2006 make civilians accompanying the armed forces in certain circumstances subject to military law.

[70] GA Res 62/145 (4 March 2008).   [71] GCIII Article 4(A)(4).

such cases as the Lord's Resistance Army in Uganda and the Revolutionary United Front in Sierra Leone; in the latter country especially, many of the worst atrocities in the conflict were committed by children (Happold, 2005).[72] Article 77 of Protocol I requires States to 'take all feasible measures in order that children who have not attained the age of fifteen years do not take a direct part in hostilities and, in particular, [to] refrain from recruiting them...'. Measures for the protection of children in armed conflicts are repeatedly called for by the UN Security Council[73] and provided for in legal terms also by the 1989 UN Convention on the Rights of the Child and its 2000 Optional Protocol on the Involvement of Children in Armed Conflict, although these instruments use a higher cut-off age of eighteen years.

IV. CONDUCT OF HOSTILITIES

The 1907 Hague Regulations, together with certain provisions of 1977 Additional Protocol I, are the modern sources of the law on the conduct of hostilities—a topic often referred to as 'methods and means of warfare'—but their much older genesis lies in the interaction of the customary principles of humanity, chivalry, and military necessity. Nowhere is this truer than in the context of the law of targeting, which is dominated by what the ICJ has termed the two 'cardinal' principles of IHL: the rule of distinction, and the prohibition of the use of weapons causing unnecessary suffering or superfluous injury.[74] The law on the conduct of hostilities also determines the difference between battlefield practices that are forbidden, and those that are permitted, although it should be noted that even if a given practice is allowed under international LOAC, it may well be prohibited under the national law of the belligerents. Thus, while The Hague Regulations do not forbid such classic wartime activities as espionage or sabotage, a spy or saboteur who is captured out of uniform will be tried as such and, under the national laws of many States, may be sentenced to death.[75] Other practices, such as perfidy—'[a]cts inviting the confidence of an adversary to lead him to believe that he is entitled to, or is obliged to accord, protection under the rules of [LOAC], with intent to betray that confidence'[76]—and denial of quarter, are clearly forbidden under LOAC.

A. DISTINCTION AND PROPORTIONALITY

Given the importance which attaches to personal status in international armed conflicts, it is logical that the principle of distinction should lie at the heart of the modern LOAC, notably in relation to targeting operations; as such it forms part of customary international law, although it is codified in Article 48 of Additional Protocol I. It requires belligerents at all times to distinguish between combatants and military objectives on the one hand, and civilians and civilian objects on the other, and to attack the former only (subject to certain exceptions which will be detailed later in this section). Basically, anyone who is not a combatant is a civilian, but because in contemporary warfare the two categories are not always clearly distinguishable

---

[72] *Prosecutor v Sesay, Kallon & Gbao*, Trial Chamber Special Court for Sierra Leone, Judgement of 25 February, pp 482–519.

[73] Eg SC Res 1882 (4 August 2009).

[74] *Legality of the Threat or Use of Nuclear Weapons, Advisory Opinion, ICJ Reports 1996*, p 226, para 78.

[75] Eg *Ali v Public Prosecutor* [1969] 1 AC 430.

[76] API Article 37(1). Examples of perfidious conduct include feigning: intent to surrender, incapacitation by wounds or sickness, or non-combatant status.

from each other, the principle of distinction is moderated by a proportionality test. The law recognizes the permissibility of civilian casualties or damage to civilian objects, during an otherwise lawful attack on a military target, by the grim but functional doctrine of 'collateral damage': such casualties or damage is proportionate if it is not clearly excessive in relation to the concrete and direct military advantage anticipated from the attack.[77] In effect, the law accepts that at least *some* civilian casualties and/or *some* damage to civilian objects will be inevitable in most military operations, however carefully conducted.

In both World Wars it was considered acceptable to attack the enemy civilian population's morale as such, but such practices would be clearly illegal today: Article 51(2) of Protocol I prohibits attacks designed to spread terror among the civilian population. The key question, then, is: what constitutes a military target? Article 52(2) of the Protocol defines military objectives as, 'those objects which by their nature, location, purpose or use make an effective contribution to military action and whose total or partial destruction, capture or neutralization, in the circumstances ruling at the time, offers a definite military advantage'. Thus, while certain objects—such as an air force base—are intrinsically military in nature, others—an apartment block, for example—may be located, or used by the enemy, in such a way that they make an effective contribution to military action. On the other hand, blanket determinations of military significance for objects which are not intrinsically military but clearly have some military uses in wartime, such as roads, railways or bridges, are not allowed. The Protocol requires a presumption, in case of doubt as to whether a civilian object is actually being used to make an effective contribution to military action, that it is not in fact being so used;[78] it also requires the commander to take all feasible precautions in planning and launching an attack, to warn the civilian population of an impending attack and to cancel or suspend an attack if it becomes apparent that the object is not a military objective or that the attack cannot be executed without disproportionate collateral damage.[79] A particularly important aspect of these provisions is the heavy burden they place on the attacking commander: the law to some extent expects him to place the safety of the civilian population ahead of that of his own troops or his legitimate military objectives: despite widespread condemnation of Israeli operations in the Gaza Strip since 2000, on a number of occasions Israeli military commanders have cancelled planned airstrikes that would have eliminated senior Palestinian militant leaders, when it became apparent that Palestinian civilians were flocking to the area in question in an attempt to shield the target.[80]

With so-called 'dual-use objects', a case-by-case determination must be made as to whether a definite military advantage would be obtained by attacking that object, not tomorrow or the day after, but today. It would also be reasonable, however, to take into account longer-term military advantages and effects on the civilian population, such as the eventual strategic consequences of an attack, or impairment of the civilian population's means of survival.[81] The Protocol unhelpfully does not mention dual-use objects as such, but the principles for determining the legality of an attack on such targets are the same as those of general application. The critical issue will generally be whether the anticipated collateral damage (if any) would be proportionate to the military advantage expected. In 1999 NATO treated the Serbian Radio and Television building in Belgrade as a military

---

[77] API, Article 57(2).

[78] Certain objects may never be attacked (unless they are being abused by the enemy): eg medical facilities, personnel and transport, and cultural property.

[79] API, Article 57.   [80] *The Jerusalem Post*, 19 November 2006.

[81] API Article 56 prohibits attacks on dams, dykes and nuclear electrical generating stations if such attack is likely to release dangerous forces which would cause severe losses to the civilian population.

target, because in addition to its normal function of providing entertainment and information to the civilian population, it also in wartime served as a back-up communications
network for the Serbian armed forces. As it was located in the middle of Belgrade, the
required assessment of collateral damage had to estimate how many civilians were likely
to become casualties in the attack, and whether such casualties would be proportionate to
the military advantage which would be gained by knocking out a back-up military communications network. In the event, NATO proceeded with the attack in the middle of the
night, when the smallest possible number of civilian employees was likely to be present
in the building: in the event, 16 civilians died and broadcasting resumed from a back-up
transmitter in a secret location within 24 hours. Although it was unfortunate that 16 civilians died, NATO took the required precautions in attack and made a proper assessment of
likely collateral damage and proportionality. The circumstances disclosed no prima facie
violation of LOAC on NATO's part.[82]

It is important to emphasize that there is no mathematical formula for deciding what
would, or would not, be a proportionate level of collateral damage in any given case.
Everything depends on the circumstances ruling at the time and the operational context;
the decision whether or not to attack a given target is that of the commander, who must
base his assessment on the intelligence that is reasonably available to him, in the light of
recommendations by his military legal adviser. It is wrong, therefore, to assume that any
case of civilians being killed in a military operation ipso facto constitutes a war crime: as
long as the target was a military objective or a dual-use object and the attacking force
undertook the required precautions in attack to the best of their ability in the circumstances ruling at the time, the relevant rules of IHL have been complied with. Civilian
deaths or damage to civilian objects in these circumstances is a tragedy, to be sure; but it is
one that the law factors into its strictures.

B. WEAPONS

Article 22 of The Hague Regulations lays down a general principle that, 'The right of belligerents to adopt means of injuring the enemy is not unlimited.' From this, and from the
principle of distinction, flow two specific customary rules affecting the choice of weaponry
in armed conflicts:

1. it is forbidden to employ methods or means of warfare that may be expected to cause
   superfluous injury or unnecessary suffering;[83] and

2. it is forbidden to employ methods or means of warfare that are indiscriminate, ie cannot be directed against a specific military objective.[84]

In addition, there are specific treaty obligations not to use methods and means of warfare
that may be expected to have negative effects on the environment.

The first rule, in particular, has prompted many treaties banning specific weapons. The
Hague formula prohibits weapons 'calculated to cause' unnecessary suffering, while its
more modern counterpart in Protocol I uses the phrase, 'of a nature to cause' such injury
or suffering. The latter is the better formulation in practice, as it relies less on the intention
with which a weapon is used—any weapon can be used in such a way as to cause unnecessary suffering—and more on its intrinsic nature. This is the case with white phosphorus,

---

[82] See ICTY, *Final Report to the Prosecutor by the Committee Established to Review the NATO Bombing Campaign Against the Federal Republic of Yugoslavia* (2000) 39 ILM 1257, paras 71–9.
[83] HR Article 23(e), API Article 35(2).   [84] API Article 51(4).

which is not currently prohibited by LOAC but can certainly have very deleterious burning or asphyxiating effects if used directly against human beings; nevertheless, it is in the armoury of many States, including Russia, Israel, the USA and UK, for use against military objectives because of its obscurant or illuminating effect. Its use as an anti-personnel weapon, to flush out Iraqi insurgents in Fallujah in 2004, was therefore probably a violation of the rule.[85] It is important, however, to remember that suffering is an integral part of war, and therefore the concept of *unnecessary* suffering is inevitably both subjective and relative. The difficulties have been well expressed in the following terms:

> The law does not specify the permissible level of disablement. In contemporary military operations, while the killing of enemy combatants is still contemplated, so is wounding them to put them out of action. This may cause them permanent injury. In either case suffering is implicit. But the law does not define unnecessary suffering, and views can differ markedly. Some are horrified by the prospect of blindness, others by the blast injuries caused by mines, and many regard burn injuries as particularly serious, but it is difficult to compare one type of injury with another and say that it necessarily signifies unnecessary suffering.... [T]herefore, all that can be done, in very general terms, is to try and balance the military utility of weapons with the wounding and incidental effects that they have.[86]

The ban on indiscriminate weapons is a corollary of the rules on protection of civilians, discussed earlier in this section. It serves to prohibit such practices as area bombardment – treating an entire area as a military target, as was done by the German deployment of V1 and V2 rockets against southern England in World War II, and Iraq's use of Scud missiles against large areas of the desert in Saudi Arabia and heavily populated Israel in 1991.

In addition to these general principles, treaty provisions exist to ban or restrict the use of the following specified weapons, *inter alia*:

1. explosive bullets or projectiles under 400 grammes weight;
2. dum-dum bullets;
3. poison and poisoned weapons;
4. asphyxiating and poison gases, along with bacteriological and chemical weapons;
5. weapons causing injury by fragments in the human body undetectable by X-ray;
6. anti-personnel landmines and booby-traps;
7. incendiary weapons;
8. blinding laser weapons; and
9. cluster munitions.

The 1977 Environmental Modification Treaty also prohibits the deliberate manipulation of the environment as a method of warfare.

The one type of weapon that is conspicuous by its absence from explicit regulation in LOAC is nuclear weapons, the use of which is not forbidden by any treaty. Whether customary law prohibits the use of nuclear weapons is less obvious: their use has been condemned on many occasions by the UN General Assembly, which in 1994 requested an Advisory Opinion from the ICJ on the subject. The resulting Opinion,[87] which saw the Court split down the middle with seven votes in favour and seven against (one chair on the

---

[85] See US Defends Use of White Phosphorus Munitions in Iraq (2006) 100 AJIL 487; cf Israeli Ministry of Foreign Affairs, *The Operation in Gaza: Factual and Legal Aspects*, July 2009, paras 406–30.

[86] UK Ministry of Defence, 2004, para 6.1.2.

[87] *Legality of the Threat or Use of Nuclear Weapons, Advisory Opinion, ICJ Reports 1996*, p 226.

Court being vacant at the time the Opinion was rendered, due to the death of the previous incumbent), was widely derided as an exercise in evasiveness. The ICJ found that, while there was no specific prohibition or permissive rule in international law regarding the use of nuclear weapons, their use nevertheless would have to comply with 'the principles and rules' of IHL—in particular the rules relating to unnecessary suffering, in light of the injuries caused by radiation. In that context, the Court found that it would 'generally be contrary' to IHL to use nuclear weapons,[88] an opaque conclusion that has drawn considerable criticism. In fairness to the ICJ, it should be mentioned that its credibility would have suffered irreparable damage had it ruled conclusively either for or against legality: in the former case, non-nuclear States, which constitute a large majority in the world, would have condemned it as out of step with world opinion. But in the latter case, the nuclear weapons States would surely have simply ignored the Advisory Opinion. The UK's position, for instance, is that none of the rules of Additional Protocol I have any effect on, regulate or prohibit, the use of nuclear weapons.[89] The ICRC, in its *Customary Law Study*, declined to express any position on the matter, ostensibly because it was *sub judice* the ICJ at the time of research for the Study (Henckaerts and Doswald-Beck, 2005, p 255).

In fact, it is difficult to see how the use of such tremendously destructive weapons could ever be IHL-compliant, given also the inestimable military advantage that their use would create for the party using them. The two sides of the equation would therefore seem to cancel each other out. However, it is conceivable that a tactical nuclear weapon, deployed for instance by a submarine against an enemy surface fleet on the high seas, could be targeted against a purely military objective and be both necessary and proportionate in terms of IHL. Conversely, the use of a nuclear weapon against a civilian population would clearly be unlawful, not because of the nature of the weapon, but because of its deliberate use against a civilian object. Finally, the use of such weapons in a setting where their effects would be indiscriminate—for example, against military installations located near civilian population centres—would violate the ban on indiscriminate weapons generally, rather than any specific rule on nuclear weapons.

The first decade of the twenty first century saw the rise to prominence of unmanned aerial vehicles (UAVs, or 'drones') as a 'weapon of choice' for technologically advanced States in asymmetric conflicts; the US, in particular, uses them to carry out 'targeted killings' of 'terrorists' in such lawless territories as Yemen, Afghanistan and the Tribal Areas of Pakistan. Currently some 80 States around the world possess drone technology, and their use has widely been condemned as unlawful, usually because of the civilian casualties that they often cause and the perception that their use against named individuals amounts to 'extrajudicial execution' or prohibited assassination.[90] However, this criticism conflates paradigms of human rights and humanitarian law. It should be noted that UAVs are not inherently illegal under LOAC; indeed, they are not really even a weapon as such, merely a platform for the delivery of a weapon (ie a missile). They are attractive to commanders as they permit several important military functions (principally intelligence-gathering and the application of lethal force) to be executed with no risk to their own troops, since the UAVs are remotely piloted. However, the real issues in terms of their compliance with LOAC are: (1) whether the persons targeted are in fact combatants; and (2) whether any resulting collateral damage is actually excessive in relation to the corresponding military advantage. In the background lurks the admittedly sinister question of whether fully

---

[88] Ibid, para 105(2)(E).   [89] Roberts and Guelff, 2000, p 510.
[90] Eg UN Human Rights Council, *Report of the Special Rapporteur on extrajudicial, summary or arbitrary executions, Philip Alston – Addendum: Study on targeted killings*, UN Doc A/HRC/14/24/Add.6, 28 May 2010.

autonomous battlefield systems will be introduced—killing machines without humans 'in the loop' to apply IHL when they authorize the application of deadly force.

V. PROTECTION OF VICTIMS

For the purposes of legal protection, IHL defines three categories of person as 'victims' of armed conflicts, in the sense that they have specific rights as a consequence of their status. These categories are: the wounded and sick (including persons shipwrecked at sea), prisoners of war and civilians. Each is subject to a detailed separate regime of legal protection; in the case of the wounded and sick on land, the treaty in question is the oldest in the canon of contemporary humanitarian law.

A. THE WOUNDED AND SICK

The Geneva Convention for the Amelioration of the Condition of the Wounded in Armies in the Field (1864), which famously resulted from Henri Dunant's experiences at the Battle of Solferino (1859) and the subsequent foundation of the ICRC (1863), was the first treaty to make specific provision for the protection of soldiers who had become *hors de combat* by virtue of wounds or sickness. The foundation principles of this area of the law, as laid down in the 1864 Convention and expanded in subsequent Geneva Conventions,[91] are:

1. relief must be provided for the wounded and sick without distinction as to status, allegiance or nationality;

2. the inviolability of medical personnel, establishments and units must be respected; and

3. the distinctive protective signs must be recognized and respected.

Enemy wounded may not be attacked, but must be collected and cared for, with the same access to medical treatment as the State's own wounded.[92] The same protection from attack extends to enemy medical transports, units and hospitals, provided they do not forfeit this protection by being used to commit hostile acts; even then, they may be attacked only after due warning.[93] Medical personnel may carry weapons for their own defence and that of the wounded and sick in their care; neither they nor those in their care may be the object of reprisals. The Red Cross and its associated protective signs[94] may be used only for marking the personnel, transports, and establishments of the ICRC, military medical services and other medical bodies (eg national Red Cross societies) specifically authorized to use

---

[91] GCI (1929); GCI (1949) (wounded and sick on land); GCII (1949) (wounded, sick and shipwrecked at sea).

[92] Suggestions that wounded Taliban fighters captured in Afghanistan should not be treated in the same field hospitals as wounded British soldiers would, if implemented, have amounted to a violation of GCI Article 12 or the Conventions' Common Article 3: *The Guardian*, 23 January 2009.

[93] GCI Article 21. The same is true in respect of individual medical personnel.

[94] Since 1929 many (though not all) Islamic States have used the Red Crescent as a recognized alternative to the Red Cross—its use originated in the Russo-Turkish War (1877–8), when Ottoman medical units adopted it for protection. Persia used its own (equally recognized) traditional emblem of the Red Lion and Sun from 1922, and reserves the right to use it still, although its use was discontinued after the 1979 Islamic Revolution because of its association with the former Shah's regime. Israel's unrecognized use of the Red Shield of David eventually contributed to the adoption of Additional Protocol III (2005), which provides for a third, universal protective emblem devoid of potential religious or national symbolism: the Red Crystal.

the emblems. Misuse of any of the emblems will normally constitute a criminal offence under national law, and may additionally amount to the war crime of perfidy.

B. PRISONERS OF WAR

Since the advent of the Nation-State and regularly conscripted citizen-armies in the late seventeenth century, it has been accepted that soldiers who surrender to the enemy are under the protection of the enemy State and not at the whim of the individual enemy commander. The sole reason for detaining them was that they should not be able to rejoin the enemy's forces and thereby negate the military advantage accrued by their removal from the field, although it was common for prisoners to be 'paroled', whereby they were released on a promise not to re-enlist and resume fighting. The notion of reciprocity as a principle underpinning the law of war also provided an incentive for States to ensure that enemy soldiers taken prisoner should be well treated. Geneva Conventions II (1929) and III (1949) have since ensured that this aspect of IHL is particularly highly regulated, with many technical provisions deriving from the grant of POW status.

An essential aspect of the protection of POWs is that they are not in the hands of the individual units or commanders who have captured them, but in those of the State (the Detaining Power), which is then responsible in international law for their good treatment.[95] A POW is neither a criminal, although he may be prosecuted for crimes committed before capture,[96] nor a hostage. The Detaining State is under an absolute duty to ensure that POWs are not murdered, tortured, ill-treated[97] or otherwise abused (eg by exposure to insults and public curiosity).[98] POWs cannot be the object of reprisals and no considerations of military necessity can justify their ill-treatment; thus, it would be unlawful to use them as human shields, 'to render certain points or areas immune from military operations'.[99] Equally, although the Detaining Power has a legitimate interest in questioning POWs in order to obtain intelligence, they are obliged to provide only their name, rank, date of birth and military number, and it is illegal to coerce them to provide any other information.[100] They must be held in special camps located away from the combat zones; although the Detaining Power may transfer them to the custody of another State Party to the Convention,[101] the State that originally captured them may remain responsible for their good treatment. POWs must be released and repatriated after the cessation of

---

[95]   GCIII Articles 12–13.

[96]   Usually, though not invariably, for violations of IHL committed during the conflict in which he was captured. Cf the American trial of General Manuel Noriega for drug trafficking prior to the 1989 US invasion of Panama, *United States* v *Noriega* (1992) 808 F. Supp. 791 (S.D.Fla), and the British refusal to prosecute Astiz, captured on South Georgia during the Falklands War, for crimes committed during the 'Dirty War' in Argentina in the late 1970s: see Meyer, 1983.

[97]   During the 2003 Gulf War there were instances of Iraqi POWs being beaten by American soldiers: *The Guardian*, 6 January 2004.

[98]   In the 2003 Gulf War some Coalition POWs were shown being questioned on Iraqi television, while Western networks also carried footage of blindfolded Iraqi POWs: *The Christian Science Monitor*, 26 March 2003. See also Rogers, 2004, pp 52–3. British practice is not to broadcast such images if they enable any POW to be individually recognized. Broadcasting pictures of the captured Saddam Hussein undergoing medical and dental examination, however, were arguably justified as a factual demonstration of his capture.

[99]   GCIII Article 23. Iraq clearly violated this provision in its treatment of Coalition POWs during the 1991 Gulf War: Rowe, 1993, pp 196–7.

[100]   GCIII Article 17.

[101]   See, eg arrangements for transfer of British-captured POWs in the 1991 Gulf War to US custody, reprinted in Rowe, 1993, at pp 348–9.

active hostilities,[102] although this requirement is not interpreted as authorizing forcible repatriation of POWs who do not wish to be repatriated: after the 1991 Gulf War many Iraqi POWs chose to remain in Saudi Arabia rather than return to Iraq.

C. CIVILIANS

The definition of civilians in IHL is a negative one: a civilian is anyone who is not a combatant as defined by Geneva Convention III and, for those States that are party to it, Additional Protocol I. Much of the emphasis of contemporary IHL is on the protection of the civilian population and individual civilians: this is achieved both by safeguarding them in most circumstances from the direct effect of hostilities (as discussed earlier) and by providing for the specific protection of civilians who are in the power of a State of which they are not nationals. Unlike the sick and wounded or POWs, civilians were not previously covered by LOAC; while this was mainly because the nature of warfare prior to the early twentieth century was such that civilians were rarely subjected to direct attack and specific measures of protection were thus not thought necessary, the experience of 'total war' in the various conflicts of the 1930s and 1940s made it clear that development of the law in this direction was urgently required. The result was the entirely innovative Geneva Convention IV (1949).

The Convention protects nationals of one belligerent who find themselves in the power of another belligerent, either through being in the territory of an enemy State or in territory under belligerent occupation. It does not protect nationals of neutral States caught up in a conflict,[103] unless they are in occupied territory, in which case they benefit from the general protections accorded to all civilians in such territory. Thus, British citizens in Kuwait at the time of the Iraqi invasion in 1990 were covered by the Convention but those in Iraq itself were not, since the UK at that time was not a party to any conflict with Iraq and the UK still had diplomatic relations with that State. Only when Coalition military action started in 1991 did British citizens in Iraq come under the protection of the Convention. Civilians in the territory of an enemy State should normally be allowed to leave the State at any time during the conflict, although permission to leave may be refused if their departure would be contrary to the national interests of the State;[104] they may even be interned if absolutely necessary for security reasons,[105] although this would not authorize the mass internment of members of specific ethnic groups. If internment does occur, civilians are entitled to a standard of treatment effectively analogous to that accorded POWs. Civilians must not be subjected to reprisals or collective punishments,[106] held hostage[107] or otherwise ill-treated.

D. BELLIGERENT OCCUPATION

Similar legal standards govern the treatment of civilians in occupied territory, who additionally must not be deported to any other State (including the Occupying Power).[108] The Occupying Power also has various detailed obligations concerning maintenance of the physical welfare of the civilian population, respect for private property and the administration of law and order (Benvenisti, 1993).[109] While these provisions of the Convention were adopted as a reaction to the systematic abuse of occupied territories by the Axis Powers in World War II, they built upon legal foundations already instituted by The Hague

---

[102] GCIII Article 118.   [103] GCIV Article 4(2).   [104] Ibid, Article 35.   [105] Ibid, Article 42.
[106] Ibid, Article 33.   [107] Ibid, Article 34.   [108] Ibid, Article 49.   [109] Ibid, Articles 50–78.

Regulations (1907). The greatest contemporary controversies surrounding their implementation have been in relation to the Israeli occupation of the Palestinian Territories
(OPT) since 1967, and the Coalition occupation of Iraq (2003-4).

Although Israel denies the formal applicability of Convention IV to the West Bank on the
grounds that it was not legally recognized as 'the territory of a High Contracting Party' (ie
Jordan) prior to 1967, as required by Article 2 of the Convention, this argument has never
been accepted by the international community; in any event, Israel claims to apply the
provisions of the Convention on a *de facto* basis.[110] The principal criterion for the applicability of the law of belligerent occupation, as stated in Article 42 of The Hague Regulations,
which as customary law is binding on Israel, is that territory be 'actually placed under
the authority of the hostile army...where such authority has been established and can be
exercised'. The legal status of the territory prior to occupation is therefore irrelevant: the
test for determining the existence of an occupation is the factual one of effective control.[111]
By the same token, *de facto* annexation or other changes to the legal status of the occupied
territory—as were effected by Israel in East Jerusalem and parts of the Golan Heights in
1967, by Argentina in the Falkland Islands in 1982 and by Iraq in Kuwait in 1990—cannot
affect the *de jure* application of the law of belligerent occupation.[112] Those parts of the West
Bank that are under the jurisdiction of the Palestinian Authority since the implementation of the Oslo Accords in 1993 are technically no longer under belligerent occupation;
neither, since Israel's withdrawal in 2005, is the Gaza Strip, although uncertainty persists
in relation to the latter, in light of Israel's continuing control over its borders, coast and
airspace (Shany, 2006). Further controversy has been caused by the naval blockade which
Israel imposed on Gaza in 2009 to prevent weapons from being landed in the territory,
where they might be used by Hamas to attack targets in Israel. Although Israel was harshly
criticized for its violent enforcement of the blockade on the high seas against a Turkish and
international aid flotilla bound for the Gaza coast in 2010, a subsequent UN inquiry found
that in the *sui generis* continuing state of *de facto* international armed conflict between
Israel and Gaza, the former was entitled under international law to institute the blockade
and to enforce it, albeit not in an unreasonable and excessive manner.[113]

The comparatively brief occupation of Iraq gave rise to a different set of concerns under
IHL. Although the USA and the UK, as the leading members of the Coalition Provisional
Authority (CPA), formally accepted that they were *de jure* Occupying Powers within the
meaning of Geneva Convention IV, the situation in Iraq from April 2003 was one of debel-
latio—the total defeat and extinction of authority in the occupied territory, a situation
that had not occurred since the unconditional surrender of Germany in 1945. Occupying
Powers are under an obligation to respect, 'unless absolutely prevented', the laws previously in force in the occupied territory,[114] because belligerent occupation in no way grants
legal title to the Occupying Power and cannot affect the legal status of the territory under
general international law: thus, Iraq continued to be a sovereign State in international law,
although its powers of government were temporarily exercised by the CPA. The latter,
however, substantively changed Iraqi law on a number of matters, most notably by the

---

[110] *Legal Consequences of the Construction of a Wall in the Occupied Palestine Territory, Advisory Opinion, ICJ
Reports 2004*, p 136, paras 90–101.
[111] Cf *Armed Activities on the Territory of the Congo (Democratic Republic of the Congo v Uganda), ICJ
Reports 2005*, p 168, paras 172–8.
[112] See, on Israel, SC Res 681 (20 December 1990); on Iraq, SC Res 670 (25 September 1990).
[113] See UN, *Report of the Secretary-General's Panel of Inquiry on the 31 May 2010 Flotilla Incident*, September
2011, http://www.un.org/News/dh/infocus/middle_east/Gaza_Flotilla_Panel_Report.pdf.
[114] HR Article 43.

wholesale privatization of Iraq's previous centrally planned economy and opening it up to foreign investment, providing tax incentives for foreign corporations wishing to do business in the country and suspending all trade tariffs. The CPA also amended Iraqi criminal law by providing for the immunity of foreign contractors in Iraqi courts. The CPA's delegation to the Iraqi Governing Council of the power to create a special civilian court for the trial of officials of Saddam Hussein's regime was also problematic, as the Occupying Power may only create 'non-political military courts' for offences committed against the Occupying Power,[115] or for breaches of the laws and customs of war.[116]

The experience of occupation in Iraq also demonstrated the significance of involvement by the UN Security Council in mandating the occupation regime. The Council gave an *ex post facto* mandate to the CPA[117] which in some respects, as noted in the preceding paragraphs, went further than the traditional law of belligerent occupation would permit (Scheffer, 2003; Kaikobad, 2005; Roberts, 2006).

VI. THE LAW IN NON-INTERNATIONAL ARMED CONFLICTS

A substantial majority of the armed conflicts that have taken place since 1945 have been non-international in nature, yet none of the substantive LOAC applied to such conflicts before the adoption of Common Article 3 of the Geneva Conventions in 1949 and the concept of liability for war crimes committed in such conflicts was not enunciated until the ICTY's 1995 decision in *Tadić*. In that case, the Appeals Chamber opined that, 'What is inhumane, and consequently proscribed, in international wars, cannot but be inhumane and inadmissible in civil strife.'[118] Neither Common Article 3 nor the 1977 Additional Protocol II included any provision for individual criminal responsibility; nor did they purport to regulate methods and means of warfare, but focused exclusively on the protection of victims.

Common Article 3 has been described as 'a Convention in miniature' (Pictet, 1952, p 48) and 'a minimum yardstick' of humanitarian protection in all armed conflicts, whatever their characterization.[119] It requires that persons taking no part in hostilities, including those who have surrendered or are *hors de combat*, be treated humanely and without adverse discrimination; to that end, it prohibits 'violence to life and person', hostage-taking, humiliating and degrading treatment, and 'the passing of sentences and the carrying out of executions without previous judgment pronounced by a regularly constituted court...'. Within three decades recognition of the generality and vagueness of these provisions resulted in more detailed provision for fundamental guarantees, treatment of the wounded and sick, and protection of the civilian population in Additional Protocol II.

However, with a mere 15 substantive articles (compared to 84 in Protocol I), and no concept of grave breaches or compulsory enforcement, Protocol II is widely viewed as lacking teeth. It took a horrified Security Council's response to the Rwandan genocide to secure the Protocol's enforcement by criminal prosecutions, and even that was on a

---

[115] GCIV Article 66.   [116] Ibid, Article 70.

[117] SC Res 1483 (22 May 2003), 1511 (16 October 2003) and 1546 (8 June 2004).

[118] *Prosecutor v Dusko Tadić*, Decision on the Defence Motion for Interlocutory Appeal on Jurisdiction (Interlocutory Appeal), Case No IT–94–1–AR72 (2 October 1995), para 516.

[119] *Military and Paramilitary Activities In and Against Nicaragua (Nicaragua v United States of America), ICJ Reports 1986*, p 14, para 218.

strictly ad hoc basis.[120] The *Tadić* decision played a seminal role in expanding, and providing some detail on, the rules of customary IHL applicable in non-international armed conflicts; a charge to which the ICRC returned with its 2005 *Study on Customary International Humanitarian Law*. Although these creative approaches have not been uncontroversial, largely due to methodological concerns in the deduction of customary norms of international law (Wilmshurst and Breau, 2007), and the fact that certain States not party to the Protocols have seen the Study in particular as an attempt to import various rules contained in those instruments into customary law 'by the back door',[121] they have served the valuable function of ensuring that the question of detailed legal regulation of conduct in non-international armed conflicts does not become a dead letter.

As noted in relation to the scope of application of IHL, there is a spectrum of conflict: apart from internal disturbances and tensions—including, in the British interpretation, acts of terrorism—which are not subject to LOAC at all, the lowest level is conflict 'not of an international character', which is governed by Common Article 3. If non-State forces have sufficient control of territory to satisfy the requirements of Protocol II, non-international conflicts are governed by the Protocol in addition to Common Article 3; finally, if other States intervene the conflict may become 'internationalized', leading to the application of the Geneva Conventions in full, plus Protocol I if the States concerned are parties thereto.

VII. IMPLEMENTATION AND ENFORCEMENT

Notwithstanding chronic weaknesses in the enforcement of international law generally, there are several methods by which compliance with IHL may be secured. In roughly ascending order of impact and effectiveness, these are:

1. recourse to belligerent reprisals;
2. States' responsibility for violations committed by their armed forces;
3. States' duty to disseminate IHL and provide for its instruction to their armed forces;
4. commanders' duty to supervise conduct and repress violations;
5. States' duty to implement IHL and provide criminal sanctions for its violation in their national legal systems;
6. criminal investigation and, where appropriate, prosecution of individuals accused of violations; and
7. external scrutiny and pressure by third parties.

A. REPRISALS

Belligerent reprisals—not to be confused with armed reprisals under the *jus ad bellum*—are violations of LOAC which may be permitted in response to prior violations by the enemy, as long as they are proportionate to those prior violations and have no other object than securing the cessation of illegal activity by the adverse party (Kalshoven, 1971). Historically they were seen as a not only legitimate, but often quite effective, method of forcing an

---

[120] SC Res 955 (8 November 1994).

[121] See US Departments of State and Defense, *Letter to International Committee of the Red Cross Regarding Customary International Law Study* (2006) 46 ILM 514; also Parks, 2005.

enemy to comply with the law; however, the extent to which they have survived modern trends in both warfare and law since 1949 is doubtful. The Geneva Conventions prohibit reprisals against any persons protected by those instruments[122] and Protocol I additionally prohibits them against the civilian population and civilian objects generally.[123] Although these treaty provisions are clear, the extent to which reprisals are prohibited in customary law remains uncertain. Their last documented substantial use in an international armed conflict was during the Iran-Iraq War (1980-88), when each belligerent attacked the other's cities and claimed that they were engaged in limited reprisals to stop similar attacks by the enemy (Henckaerts and Doswald-Beck, 2005, vol I, pp 521-2). The ICRC's *Study on Customary International Humanitarian Law* asserted that reprisals are also prohibited in non-international armed conflicts, a position which is arguably difficult to maintain in the light of State practice and *opinio juris* (Wilmshurst and Breau, 2007, pp 370-72).

The essential problem with reprisals is the risk that, 'far from enforcing the law, [they] can produce an escalating spiral of atrocities completely undermining respect for the law' (Greenwood, 1989, p 36), thereby achieving precisely the opposite effect to what was intended. The British use of poison gas on the Western Front in 1915, for instance, although intended as retaliation for the German use of the weapon in the Second Battle of Ypres, simply resulted in its adoption on all fronts and by all belligerents for the duration of World War I.

Today, while many States expressly reserve the right to take belligerent reprisals, they generally do so with stringent conditions attached and subject to political approval at the highest level.[124]

B. STATE RESPONSIBILITY

As a general rule of public international law, States are legally responsible, and liable to pay compensation for, violations of LOAC committed by their armed forces. The rule is enunciated with reference to international armed conflicts in Article 3 of The Hague Convention IV (1907), and reparations have been required from defeated enemies in respect of their troops' depredations: for example, Part VIII of the Treaty of Versailles (1919), requiring Germany to pay compensation to the Allied Powers, was based upon the notion of German responsibility for the tremendous damage inflicted on Allied lives and property during World War I. In 1991, the Security Council confirmed Iraq's legal responsibility for depredations of its troops during the occupation of Kuwait and established a UN Compensation Commission to process claims and allocate compensation for losses resulting therefrom.[125] Following the conclusion of their 1998–2000 conflict in the Horn of Africa, Ethiopia and Eritrea agreed the establishment of a joint Claims Commission to arbitrate all claims for loss or damage, including violations of IHL, which had occurred in the conflict.[126]

The weakness of the State responsibility doctrine in the armed conflict context is that it does not cover responsibility for violations committed by non-State actors: it is easy to hold States to account for their armed forces' actions in asymmetric conflicts, but their irregular opponents fall outside the framework of State responsibility (unless they win the war and the new government subsequently adopts legal responsibility for their actions, as

---

[122] GCI Article 46, GCII Article 47, GCIII Article 13 and GCIV Article 33.

[123] API Articles 51(6), 52(1), 53(c), 54(4), 55(2) and 56(4).

[124] UK Ministry of Defence, 2004, paras 16.16–19.   [125] SC Res 687 (3 April 1991).

[126] See, eg *Partial Awards on Prisoners of War (Ethiopia's Claim 4)* (2003) 42 ILM 1056; *Eritrea's Claim 17*, ibid, 1083.

was done by the State of Israel in respect of the assassination of Count Folke Bernadotte by members of the Stern Gang in 1949).

C. DISSEMINATION AND SUPERVISION

In order to ensure that soldiers are aware of their rights and duties under international law, the Geneva Conventions and Protocol I impose obligations upon States parties to disseminate their provisions to their armed forces, and as widely as possible among the civilian population at large.[127] Most armed forces, therefore, have training programmes which include instruction in LOAC, both internally and by way of attendance at external (often academic) courses. Dissemination is usually undertaken by the military legal advisory services of the armed forces themselves,[128] but in the case of States that lack the relevant in-house military legal expertise, the ICRC plays a crucial and extensive role by providing seminars, training materials, consultancy and other assistance.

Arguably the most crucial aspect of ensuring compliance in the armed forces is military discipline and the role of the commander in the supervision of conduct and repression of violations. Article 43(1) of Protocol I requires that armed forces 'shall be subject to an internal disciplinary system which, *inter alia,* shall enforce compliance with the rules of international law applicable in armed conflict'. The key component in this system is the commander, who must ensure that the troops under his command comply with LOAC and must therefore himself be familiar with his rights and responsibilities. The contemporary law of command responsibility, which in modern terms is based on Article 86(2) of Protocol I, holds the commander liable in a variety of ways, if he:

1. personally himself sees or hears of illegal acts being committed;

2. receives reports of the illegal conduct of his troops through his officers (commissioned or not), staff and chain of command, yet fails to act to put a stop to their violations; or

3. is so negligent or reckless in the discharge of his command that he unaware of the conduct of his troops.[129]

Article 87 then requires commanders to prevent and suppress violations of the law and report them to the appropriate authorities; it requires, however, that commanders be 'aware' of violations.

In a famous precedent in 1946, the former Commander-in-Chief of Japanese forces in the Philippines was executed as a war criminal despite his lack of knowledge, due to a breakdown in communications and the chain of command, of atrocities committed by troops under his overall command in Manila;[130] the modern doctrine, however, requires that a commander have actual effective control—not merely nominal or titular authority—over troops and actual knowledge of, or information concerning, crimes being committed,[131] a position which arguably gives rise to a concept of the 'reasonable commander'.

---

[127] GCI Article 47, GCII Article 48, GCIII Article 127, GCIV Article 144 and API Article 83.

[128] The requirement to have such military legal advisory services is itself an obligation of API Article 82.

[129] A commander who gives an illegal order or himself commits a criminal act is of course equally liable, but not under the doctrine of command responsibility, which is concerned only with acts of omission.

[130] *Application of Yamashita* (1946) 327 US 1.

[131] *Prosecutor v Hadžihasanović & Kubura*, Judgment, Case No IT-01-47-T, Trial Chamber II, (15 March 2006).

Thus the standard of knowledge has shifted from a 'should have known' to a 'knew or had reason to know' test, a position which is undoubtedly fairer to the individual commander.

D. IMPLEMENTATION AND PROSECUTION

The most dramatic, although not the most effective, way of securing compliance with LOAC is to investigate and punish violations after they have occurred, through either international or national criminal courts. Acceptance of individual criminal responsibility for such crimes has been uncontroversial since the Nuremberg and Tokyo Trials after World War II. On the international level, the creation of the ICTY (1993) and International Criminal Tribunal for Rwanda (1994), followed by the establishment of other specialized criminal tribunals to deal with atrocities in Sierra Leone and Cambodia, among others, heralded a new age of activism in this respect. The first decade of the 21st Century saw the establishment of the world's first permanent International Criminal Court.

For centuries States have asserted the right to prosecute both captured enemy nationals for violations of the laws and customs of war and their own soldiers for similar offences charged under national military or criminal law. Violations of the laws and customs of war, generically described as war crimes, are subject to universal criminal jurisdiction in customary international law; other types of offences specifically relevant, though not limited, to armed conflicts are crimes against humanity and genocide. States will usually have recourse to international war crimes law only when prosecuting foreign nationals; violations committed by their own troops will normally be treated as offences under the ordinary national criminal or military law. Thus, Lieutenant William Calley was charged with four counts of premeditated murder in violation of Article 118 of the US Uniform Code of Military Justice for his role in the massacre of Vietnamese civilians at My Lai in 1968. In respect of war crimes, the Geneva Conventions and Protocol I place all States parties under a duty to investigate and prosecute grave breaches of those instruments, or extradite suspects to another State; they must also enact legislation implementing these offences in their national criminal law.[132] In the UK, as in many other countries, there is special legislation in force to give effect to these obligations.[133] The degree of scrupulousness with which States investigate and prosecute violations committed by their own armed forces varies considerably, but it has certainly been a significant aspect of the response to violations committed by British forces in Iraq in 2003–4.[134]

Liability for war crimes applies throughout the military hierarchy. As discussed in the previous section, commanders are responsible for the acts of their subordinates; conversely a soldier cannot plead, in defence to a war crimes charge, that he was following superior orders—in the UK as in many other States, soldiers are clearly forbidden to obey illegal orders. This represents a shift from the widely held pre-1944 position that superior orders were an absolute defence to a war crimes charge and a soldier would be liable to court-martial if he refused to obey an order,[135] and is clearly preferable in that otherwise, the vast majority of perpetrators would invariably be able to escape liability for their acts. It is equally no defence to claim that a war crime was committed for reasons of military

---

[132] GCI Article 49, GCII Article 50, GCIII Article 129, GCIV Article 146, API Articles 85, 86(1), 88, and 89.

[133] Geneva Conventions Act 1957, Geneva Conventions (Amendment) Act 1995, International Criminal Court Act 2001, Geneva Conventions and United Nations Personnel (Protocols) Act 2009.

[134] See UK Ministry of Defence, *The Aitken Report – An Investigation into Cases of Deliberate Abuse and Unlawful Killing in Iraq in 2003 and 2004*, 25 January 2008.

[135] Although this would not be the case if the order was manifestly illegal: see *The Llandovery Castle* (1921) 16 AJIL 708.

necessity: allowance for the exigencies of military necessity is already made in many LOAC treaties, so that conduct that would otherwise constitute a violation may be permitted in certain circumstances. But if the rule is an absolute one, such as the prohibition of the wilful killing of protected persons, a plea of military necessity would be rejected.[136]

Prosecutions are an imperfect tool for enforcing LOAC: the difficulties of securing reliable evidence in respect of incidents occurring in combat conditions—leading many cases to be abandoned or dismissed—cannot be underestimated. It is also true that war crimes trials are often derided as 'victor's justice', in the sense that the defeated party does not have a chance to hold its enemies to account for ill-conduct. Nevertheless, they are often the prism through which consciousness of IHL is embedded in the general public.

E. EXTERNAL SCRUTINY

The proliferation of media reporting of abuses in armed conflicts since the early 1990s has had the effect of greatly increasing the importance of external scrutiny of States' forces' conduct and pressure for investigations. Sometimes this comes from public opinion, but more frequently it is prompted by reports from non-governmental organizations like Human Rights Watch or international organizations like the UN and its specialized agencies.[137] This sort of external pressure is not mandated by the law, but it can help to generate an independent process of internal scrutiny, which in turn can contribute to increased respect for the law. The Geneva Conventions and Protocol I, however, in any event make provision for monitoring compliance with IHL by the mechanisms of the Protecting Power system and the International Humanitarian Fact-Finding Commission.

The Protecting Power system pre-dates World War II and in its current form is contained in all four 1949 Conventions.[138] It was instituted to enable a belligerent in an international armed conflict to designate another State, the Protecting Power, to represent its interests and those of its nationals *vis-à-vis* enemy belligerents in matters relating to the conflict. The Protecting Power has rights of access to POW and detention camps, may attend trials of POWs and civilians held by the enemy belligerent, and may make representations to the enemy belligerent concerning compliance with LOAC generally. In the Falklands War the UK designated Switzerland, and Argentina designated Brazil, to act as their respective Protecting Powers; but on the whole the system has been underused in contemporary conflicts, usually because one side is reluctant to agree to the other side's nominee. Neither the Iran-Iraq, nor the Second Gulf, Wars saw the appointment of any Protecting Powers. Indeed, since 1949, only four international armed conflicts have seen Protecting Powers designated by both parties (Wylie, 2006, p 13).[139]

The International Humanitarian Fact-Finding Commission, which became operational in 1992, is mandated by Article 90 of Protocol I to investigate allegations of violations of the Protocol and the Conventions, but it may only act at the invitation of a State that has recognized its competence and only against a State that has indicated the same acceptance (to date 72 of the States parties to the Protocol have done so). Its reports are confidential to the parties concerned and it has no power of enforcement.

---

[136] *The Peleus Trial* [1945] I LRTWC 1.

[137] Eg UN Human Rights Council, *Report of the United Nations Fact-Finding Mission on the Gaza Conflict*, UN Doc A/HRC/12/48, 25 September 2009; Res A/HRC/RES/S-12/1.B, 16 October 2009.

[138] GCI, GCII, GCIII Article 10; GCIV Article 11.

[139] Since the 2008 conflict between Russia and Georgia, Switzerland has acted as Protecting Power for both States.

Finally, it is pertinent to mention the invaluable role of the ICRC, which not only seeks to provide humanitarian assistance to the victims of armed conflicts, but also is an indefatigable advocate of IHL and, in particular, of the Geneva Conventions and their Additional Protocols. The ICRC operates under very strict limitations as to publicity—its reports on unrestricted inspection visits to POW and detention camps are confidential, although one on ill-treatment of Iraqi detainees held by the Coalition in 2004 was famously leaked to the public—and also depends on the consent of the parties to the conflict for their voluntary co-operation, although the latter must accept any offer by the ICRC to fulfil the humanitarian functions of a Protecting Power where none is appointed. It usually restricts itself to making private representations to the parties concerned, to urge them to comply with their obligations under IHL. Nevertheless, it does sometimes issue public reminders to all parties in a conflict to respect IHL and generally commands unrivalled respect and efficacy in improving compliance with the law in armed conflicts.

REFERENCES

BENVENISTI, E (1993), *The International Law of Occupation* (Princeton: Princeton University Press).

BYRON, C (2001), 'Armed Conflicts: International or Non-International?', 6 *JCSL* 63.

—— (2007), 'A Blurring of the Boundaries: The Application of International Humanitarian Law by Human Rights Bodies', 47 *Virginia JIL* 839.

DRAPER, GIAD (1965), 'The Interaction of Christianity and Chivalry in the Historical Development of the Law of War', 46 *Int Rev Red Cross* 3.

GREEN, LC (2008), *The Contemporary Law of Armed Conflict*, 3rd edn (Manchester: Manchester University Press).

GREENBERG, KJ and DATREL, JL (2005), *The Torture Papers* (Cambridge: Cambridge University Press).

GREENWOOD, C (1989), 'The Twilight of the Law of Belligerent Reprisals', 20 *Neth YBIL* 35.

HAPPOLD, M (2005), *Child Soldiers in International Law* (Manchester: Manchester University Press).

HENCKAERTS, J-M and DOSWALD-BECK, L (eds) (2005), *Customary International Humanitarian Law* (Cambridge: Cambridge University Press).

JESSUP, PC (1954), 'Should International Law Recognize an Intermediate Status between Peace and War?', 48 *AJIL* 98.

KAIKOBAD, KH (2005), 'Problems of Belligerent Occupation', 43 *ICLQ* 253.

KALSHOVEN, F (1971), *Belligerent Reprisals* (Leiden: Nijhoff).

LAUTERPACHT, H (1952), 'The Problem of Revision of the Law of War', 29 *BYIL* 382.

MAOZ, A (2005), 'War and Peace—an Israeli Perspective', 24 *Constitutional Forum* 35.

MEYER, MA (1983), 'Liability of Prisoners of War for Offences Committed Prior to Capture: The Astiz Affair', 32 *ICLQ* 948.

MOIR, L (2002), *The Law of Internal Armed Conflict* (Cambridge: Cambridge University Press).

PARKS, WH (2003), 'Special Forces' Wear of Non-Standard Uniforms', 4 *Chicago JIL* 493.

—— (2005), 'The ICRC Customary Law Study: a Preliminary Assessment', *ASIL Proceedings* 208.

PICTET, J (ed) (1952), *Commentary on the Geneva Convention (I) for the Amelioration of the Condition of the Wounded and Sick in Armed Forces in the Field* (Geneva: ICRC).

ROBERTS, A (2006), 'Transformative Military Occupation: Applying the Laws of War and Human Rights', 100 *AJIL* 580.

—— and GUELFF, R (2000), *Documents on the Laws of War*, 3rd edn (Oxford: Oxford University Press).

ROGERS, APV (2004), *Law on the Battlefield*, 2nd edn (Manchester: Manchester University Press).

ROWE, PJ (ed) (1993), *The Gulf War 1990–91 in International and English Law* (London: Routledge).

SCHEFFER, DJ (2003), 'Beyond Occupation Law', 97 *AJIL* 842.

SCHMITT, MN (2013), *Tallin Manual on the International Law Applicable to Cyber Warfare* (Cambridge: Cambridge University Press).

SHANY, Y (2005), 'Faraway, So Close: The Legal Status of Gaza After Israel's Disengagement', 8 *YBIHL* 369.

SIVAKUMARAN, S (2006), 'Binding Armed Opposition Groups', 55 *ICLQ* 369.

TURNS, D (2006), 'Weapons in the ICRC Study on Customary International Humanitarian Law', 11 *JCSL* 201.

UNITED KINGDOM MINISTRY OF DEFENCE (2004), *The Manual of the Law of Armed Conflict* (Oxford: Oxford University Press).

WALKER, CP (1984), 'Irish Republican Prisoners—Political Detainees, Prisoners of War or Common Criminals?', XIX *The Irish Jurist* 89.

WILMSHURST, E and BREAU, S (eds) (2007), *Perspectives on the ICRC Study on Customary International Humanitarian Law* (Cambridge: Cambridge University Press).

WYLIE, N (2006), 'Protecting Powers in a Changing World', 40 *Politorbis* 6.

FURTHER READING

The literature on this area of law has grown exponentially in the last 15 years. What follows is a necessarily selective list of suggestions for further reading in the area; all the works cited either provide insightful general commentary on international humanitarian law, or focus detailed analysis on specific topics within the area.

GENERAL

FLECK, D (ed) (2008), *The Handbook of International Humanitarian Law* (Oxford: Oxford University Press).

GREENWOOD, C (1987), 'The Concept of War in Modern International Law', 36 *ICLQ* 283.

—— (1996), 'International Humanitarian Law and the *Tadić Case*', 7 *EJIL* 265.

NEFF, S (2005), *War and the Law of Nations: A General History* (Cambridge: Cambridge University Press).

SCHMITT, MN (2007), '21st Century Conflict: Can the Law Survive?', 8 *Melb JIL* 443.

SCOPE OF APPLICATION

GREEN, LC (1951), 'The Nature of the "War" in Korea', 4 *ILQ* 462.

GREENWOOD, C (2003), 'War, Terrorism and International Law', 56 *Current Legal Problems* 505.

ROBERTS, A (2005), 'Counter-terrorism, Armed Force and the Laws of War', 44 *Survival* 7.

STEWART, JG (2003), 'Towards a Single Definition of Armed Conflict in International Humanitarian Law: A Critique of Internationalized Armed Conflict', 850 *Int Rev Red Cross* 313.

TURNS, D (2007), 'The "War on Terror" Through British and International Humanitarian Law Eyes: Comparative Perspectives on Selected Legal Issues', 10 *NY City LR* 435.

CONDUCT OF HOSTILITIES

BOOTHBY, WH (2009), *Weapons and the Law of Armed Conflict* (Oxford: Oxford University Press).

CORN, GS (2005), ' "Snipers in the Minaret—What is the Rule?" The Law of War and the Protection of Cultural Property: A Complex Equation', *The Army Lawyer* 28.

CRYER, R (2002), 'The Fine Art of Friendship: *Jus in Bello* in Afghanistan', 7 *JCSL* 37.

DINSTEIN, Y (2004), *The Conduct of Hostilities under the Law of International Armed Conflict* (Cambridge: Cambridge University Press).

GREENWOOD, C (1988), 'Belligerent Reprisals and the 1977 Protocols to the Geneva Conventions of 1949', 37 *ICLQ* 818.

SCHMITT, MN (2005), 'Precision Attack and International Humanitarian Law', 859 *Int Rev Red Cross* 445.

—— (2010), 'Military Necessity and Humanity in International Humanitarian Law: Preserving the Delicate Balance', 50 *Virginia JIL* 795

—— (2010), 'Deconstructing Direct Participation in Hostilities: The Constitutive Elements', 42 *NYU J Int'l Law & Politics* 697.

PROTECTION OF VICTIMS

DÖRMANN, K (2003), 'The Legal Situation of "Unlawful/Unprivileged Combatants" ', 850 *Int Rev Red Cross* 45.

HAMPSON, FJ (1991), 'The Geneva Conventions and the Detention of Civilians and Alleged Prisoners of War', *Public Law* 507.

ROBERTS, A (2005), 'The End of Occupation: Iraq 2004', 54 *ICLQ* 27.

IMPLEMENTATION AND ENFORCEMENT

BANTEKAS, I (1999), 'The Contemporary Law of Superior Responsibility', 93 *AJIL* 573.

GARRAWAY, C (1999), 'Superior Orders and the International Criminal Court: Justice Delivered or Justice Denied?', 836 *Int Rev Red Cross* 785.

ROGERS, APV (1990), 'War Crimes Trials under the Royal Warrant: British Practice 1945–1949', 39 *ICLQ* 780.

INDEX